# MyBCommLab®

MyBCommLab is an online assessment and preparation solution that helps you actively study and prepare material for class. Chapter-by-chapter activities, including study plans, focus on what you need to learn and to review in order to succeed.

Visit **www.mybcommlab.com** to learn more.

TWELFTH
EDITION

# Business Communication Today

## Courtland L. Bovée

PROFESSOR OF BUSINESS COMMUNICATION
C. ALLEN PAUL DISTINGUISHED CHAIR
GROSSMONT COLLEGE

## John V. Thill

CHAIRMAN AND CHIEF EXECUTIVE OFFICER
GLOBAL COMMUNICATION STRATEGIES

**PEARSON**

Boston Columbus Indianapolis New York San Francisco Upper Saddle River
Amsterdam Cape Town Dubai London Madrid Milan Munich Paris Montreal
Toronto Delhi Mexico City São Paulo Sydney Hong Kong Seoul Singapore Taipei Tokyo

| | |
|---|---|
| Editor in Chief: Stephanie Wall | Interior and Cover Designer: Laura Ierardi |
| Acquisitions Editor: Sarah McCabe | Cover Image: Igor Kovalchuk/Shutterstock; Vlad61/Shutterstock |
| Director of Editorial Services: Ashley Santora | Senior Media Editor: Denise Vaughn |
| Program Manager: Claudia Fernandes | Media Project Manager, Production: Lisa Rinaldi |
| Director of Marketing: Maggie Moylan | Full-Service Project Management: Christian Holdener, S4Carlisle |
| Senior Managing Editor: Judy Leale | Publishing Services |
| Senior Project Manager: Karalyn Holland | Composition: S4Carlisle Publishing Services |
| Procurement Specialist: Nancy Maneri | Printer/Binder: R.R. Donnelley/Willard |
| Creative Director: Blair Brown | Cover Printer: Lehigh-Phoenix Color/Hagerstown |
| Senior Art Director: Kenny Beck | Text Font: Minion Pro |

Credits and acknowledgments borrowed from other sources and reproduced, with permission, in this textbook appear on the appropriate page within the text.

Microsoft and/or its respective suppliers make no representations about the suitability of the information contained in the documents and related graphics published as part of the services for any purpose. All such documents and related graphics are provided "as is" without warranty of any kind. Microsoft and/or its respective suppliers hereby disclaim all warranties and conditions with regard to this information, including all warranties and conditions of merchantability, whether express, implied or statutory, fitness for a particular purpose, title and non-infringement. In no event shall Microsoft and/or its respective suppliers be liable for any special, indirect or consequential damages or any damages whatsoever resulting from loss of use, data or profits, whether in an action of contract, negligence or other tortious action, arising out of or in connection with the use or performance of information available from the services.

The documents and related graphics contained herein could include technical inaccuracies or typographical errors. Changes are periodically added to the information herein. Microsoft and/or its respective suppliers may make improvements and/or changes in the product(s) and/or the program(s) described herein at any time. Partial screen shots may be viewed in full within the software version specified.

Microsoft® and Windows®, and Microsoft Office® are registered trademarks of the Microsoft Corporation in the U.S.A. and other countries. This book is not sponsored or endorsed by or affiliated with the Microsoft Corporation.

This publication contains references to the products of SAP AG. SAP, R/3, SAP NetWeaver, Duet, PartnerEdge, ByDesign, SAP BusinessObjects Explorer, StreamWork, SAP HANA, and other SAP products and services mentioned herein as well as their respective logos are trademarks or registered trademarks of SAP AG in Germany and other countries.

Business Objects and the Business Objects logo, BusinessObjects, Crystal Reports, Crystal Decisions, Web Intelligence, Xcelsius, and other Business Objects products and services mentioned herein as well as their respective logos are trademarks or registered trademarks of Business Objects Software Ltd. Business Objects is an SAP company.

Sybase and Adaptive Server, iAnywhere, Sybase 365, SQL Anywhere, and other Sybase products and services mentioned herein as well as their respective logos are trademarks or registered trademarks of Sybase Inc. Sybase is an SAP company.

Crossgate, m@gic EDDY, B2B 360°, and B2B 360° Services are registered trademarks of Crossgate AG in Germany and other countries. Crossgate is an SAP company.

All other product and service names mentioned are the trademarks of their respective companies. Data contained in this document serves informational purposes only. National product specifications may vary.

SAP AG is neither the author nor the publisher of this publication and is not responsible for its content. SAP Group shall not be liable for errors or omissions with respect to the materials. The only warranties for SAP Group products and services are those that are set forth in the express warranty statements accompanying such products and services, if any. Nothing herein should be construed as constituting an additional warranty.

Many of the designations by manufacturers and sellers to distinguish their products are claimed as trademarks. Where those designations appear in this book, and the publisher was aware of a trademark claim, the designations have been printed in initial caps or all caps.

**Library of Congress Cataloging-in-Publication Data**

Bovée, Courtland L.
   Business communication today / Courtland L. Bovée, John V. Thill.—Twelfth edition.
      pages cm
   Includes bibliographical references and index.
   ISBN 978-0-13-297129-4 (alk. paper)
   1. Business communication—United States—Case studies.   2. Communication in organizations—United States—Case studies.   I. Thill, John V.   II. Title.
   HF5718.B66 2014
   658.4'5—dc23
                                                                        2013016204

10 9 8 7 6 5 4 3 2 1

ISBN 10:      0-13-297129-1
ISBN 13: 978-0-13-297129-4

# Contents in Brief

# Contents

## PART 4
# Brief Messages **257**

# 10 Writing Routine and Positive Messages **258**

# 11 Writing Negative Messages **288**

# 12 Writing Persuasive Messages **325**

# Real-Time Updates—Learn More

Real-Time Updates "Learn More" is a unique feature students will see strategically located throughout the text, connecting them with dozens of carefully selected online media items. These elements—categorized by the icons shown below representing interactive websites, online videos, infographics, PowerPoint presentations podcasts, PDF files, and articles—complement the text's coverage by providing contemporary examples and valuable insights from successful professionals. See page xvii for an illustration of how Real-Time Updates works.

**REAL-TIME UPDATES**
### LEARN MORE BY READING THIS ARTICLE

**REAL-TIME UPDATES**
### LEARN MORE BY LISTENING TO THIS PODCAST

**REAL-TIME UPDATES**
### LEARN MORE BY WATCHING THIS VIDEO

**REAL-TIME UPDATES**
### LEARN MORE BY READING THIS PDF

 **REAL-TIME UPDATES**
### LEARN MORE BY READING THIS INFOGRAPHIC

**REAL-TIME UPDATES**
### LEARN MORE BY VISITING THIS WEBSITE

**REAL-TIME UPDATES**

LEARN MORE BY WATCHING THIS PRESENTATION

**REAL-TIME UPDATES**

LEARN MORE BY VISITING THIS INTERACTIVE WEBSITE

**REAL-TIME UPDATES**

LEARN MORE BY EXPLORING THIS WEBSITE

# Major Changes and Improvements in This Edition

Bovée and Thill texts have long set the benchmark in this field for rigorous, high-value revisions that make sure instructors and students have the most comprehensive, realistic, and contemporary materials available. In keeping with that standard, the twelfth edition of *Business Communication Today* offers numerous, changes, additions, and improvements. (Please refer to the Instructor's Manual for a detailed, chapter-by-chapter list of changes and improvements.)

## CHANGES TO THE TABLE OF CONTENTS

Video has become a core business medium, and many messages that in past years would have been delivered through written media are now supported by or even replaced by video messages. And just as document design, presentation slides, web writing, and other communication tasks moved out of the specialist realm and became mainstream skill expectations, more and more employees are now expected to be able to do basic video work for training courses, product demos, video news releases, customer service, and other purposes. In addition, with companies such as Zappos encouraging video uploads from job applicants, video could become significant in employment communication as well.

In keeping with *Business Communication Today*'s goal of covering the full spectrum of contemporary business communication practices, the twelfth edition adds a unique section on producing business videos. It guides students through preproduction, production, and postproduction, with simple hands-on advice at each stage. To accommodate this addition and the growing coverage of electronic and social media, we made several important changes to the table of contents:

- Chapter 7 from the previous edition (Crafting Messages for Electronic Media) has been split into two chapters: Chapter 7 (Electronic Media) and Chapter 8 (Social Media).
- The coverage of web and wiki writing has been moved from the report chapters. Web writing is now in Chapter 7, and wiki writing is now in Chapter 8.
- Video production has been added to what was Chapter 12 in the previous edition (Designing Visual Communication), and this chapter is now Chapter 9 (Visual Media). This chapter also includes expanded coverage of infographics.
- To maintain the same 19-chapter length as the previous edition, the three-chapter part on report writing has been compressed to two chapters. Chapter 14 (Planning Reports and Proposals) is essentially the same as in the previous edition, but the separate chapters on writing and completing reports have been merged into a single, streamlined Chapter 15 (Writing and Completing Reports and Proposals).
- Even with the addition of video and other new material and figures, we rigorously edited the entire book to reduce the word count, so the twelfth edition is 32 pages shorter than the eleventh.

## SIGNIFICANT CONTENT ADDITIONS AND UPGRADES

In addition to the high-level TOC changes outlined above, the following sections within various chapters are all new, revised with new material, or streamlined for more efficient coverage:

- *Communicating as a Professional* (in Chapter 1)
- *The Art of Professionalism: Maintaining a Confident, Positive Outline* (highlight box in Chapter 1)
- *Technologies for Collaborative Writing* (in Chapter 2)

- *Business Etiquette in the Workplace* (in Chapter 2)
- *Business Etiquette in Social Settings* (in Chapter 2)
- *Business Etiquette Online* (in Chapter 2)
- *Communication Close-Up at Ernst & Young* (in Chapter 3)
- *Gender Differences* (in Chapter 3)
- *The Art of Professionalism: Being Dependable and Accountable* (highlight box in Chapter 5)
- *Communication Close-up at the U.S. Small Business Administration* (in Chapter 7)
- *Writing Email Messages (use of emoticons)* (in Chapter 7)
- *Website Content* (in Chapter 7)
- *The Art of Professionalism: Striving to Excel* (highlight box in Chapter 7)
- *Information and Media Sharing Sites* (in Chapter 8)
- *Media Curation Sites* (in Chapter 8)
- *Microblogging* (in Chapter 8)
- *Infographics* (in Chapter 9)
- *Producing Business Videos* (in Chapter 9)
- *Providing Recommendations and References* (in Chapter 10)
- *Fostering Goodwill* (in Chapter 10)
- *Offering Condolences* (in Chapter 10)
- *Continuing with a Clear Statement of the Bad News* (in Chapter 11; revised coverage of using conditionals)
- *Responding to Negative Information in a Social Media Environment* (in Chapter 11)
- *Refusing Social Networking Recommendation Requests* (in Chapter 11)
- *Giving Negative Performance Reviews* (in Chapter 11)
- *Developing Marketing and Sales Messages* (in Chapter 12; entire section compressed to allow more room for coverage of persuasive business messages)
- *Drafting Report Content* (in Chapter 15)
- *Drafting Proposal Content* (in Chapter 15)
- *Completing Reports and Proposals* (in Chapter 15)
- *Advantages and Disadvantages of Structured Slides* (in Chapter 17)
- *Advantages and Disadvantages of Free-Form Slides* (in Chapter 17)
- *Designing Effective Slides* (in Chapter 17)
- *Designing Slides Around a Key Visual* (in Chapter 17)
- *The Art of Professionalism: Being a Team Player* (highlight box in Chapter 17)
- *Finding the Ideal Opportunity in Today's Job Market* (in Chapter 18)
- *Considering Photos, Videos, Presentations, and Infographics* (in Chapter 18)
- *Planning Your Résumé* (in Chapter 18)
- *Motivating Action* (in Chapter 19, regarding application letters)
- *Follow-Up Messages* (in Chapter 19, formerly titled *Thank You Messages*)

## NEW FIGURES IN THE TWELFTH EDITION

Providing students with an array of carefully chosen and crafted examples is one of the most important functions of a business communication textbook. The twelfth edition offers nearly 80 new figures, including many annotated model documents and a number of new before/after pairs that demonstrate how to fix specific problem areas in a message. Here are the new figures in this edition:

| Chapter | Figure | Title | Before/After Pair | Annotated Model Document | Real Company |
|---|---|---|---|---|---|
| 1 | 1 | Sharing Information | | | |
| 1 | 2 | Ineffective Versus Effective Business Communication | X | X | |
| 1 | 4 | A Model of the Communication Process | | | |
| 2 | 4 | Typical Meeting Agenda | | | |
| 2 | 6 | Virtual Meetings | | | X |

| Chapter | Figure | Title | Before/After Pair | Annotated Model Document | Real Company |
|---|---|---|---|---|---|
| 3 | 3a | Intercultural Business Letter: Ineffective Original Draft | X | X | |
| 3 | 3b | Intercultural Business Letter: First Revision | X | X | |
| 3 | 3c | Intercultural Business Letter: Final Revision | X | X | |
| 3 | 3d | Intercultural Business Letter: Translated | X | | |
| 3 | 4 | Writing for Multilingual Audiences | X | X | |
| 4 | 3 | Predicting the Effects of Audience Composition | | | |
| 4 | 4 | Media Choices | | | X |
| 4 | 5 | Visual Media | | | X |
| 4 | 9 | Organizing Your Thoughts with a Clear Outline | | X | |
| 4 | 10 | Improving the Organization of a Message | X | X | |
| 4 | 11 | Storytelling as a Way to Organize Messages | | | X |
| 5 | 2 | Building Credibility | | X | X |
| 6 | 4 | Comments Attached to a PDF File | | X | |
| 6 | 5 | Designing for Readability | | X | X |
| 6 | 6 | Multimedia Tools | | | |
| 6 | 7 | A Typical Business Memo | | X | X |
| 7 | 1 | Compositional Modes for Electronic Media | | X | X |
| 7 | 4 | Information Architecture | | | X |
| 7 | 5 | Writing for the Web | | X | X |
| 8 | 2 | Business Communication on Social Networks | | | X |
| 8 | 4 | Effective Business Blogging | | X | X |
| 8 | 5 | Business Uses of Twitter | | X | X |
| 8 | 6 | Wikis | | | X |
| 9 | 11a | Data Visualization: Gephi Network Map | | | X |
| 9 | 13 | Geographic Information Displays | | | X |
| 9 | 15a | Infographics: Stylized Data Charts | | | |
| 9 | 15b | Infographics: Data Narration | | | X |
| 9 | 16 | Creating Effective Business Videos | | | |
| 9 | 17 | Framing Your Shots | | | |
| 10 | 4 | Responding to a Claim When the Customer Is at Fault | X | X | |
| 10 | 6 | Sharing Routine Information | | X | X |
| 10 | 7 | Social Media News Release | | X | X |
| 11 | 1 | Comparing the Indirect and Direct Approaches for Negative Messages | | | |

(*continued*)

| Chapter | Figure | Title | Before/<br>After Pair | Annotated<br>Model<br>Document | Real<br>Company |
|---------|--------|-------|-----------------------|-------------------------------|-----------------|
| 11 | 2 | Choosing the Direct or Indirect Approach | | | |
| 11 | 3 | Meeting Audience Needs in a Direct-Approach Message | | X | X |
| 11 | 6 | Message to Refuse a Claim | X | X | |
| 11 | 7 | Internal Message Providing Bad News About Company Operations | X | X | |
| 12 | 2 | The AIDA Model for Persuasive Messages | | | |
| 12 | 3 | Balancing Logical and Emotional Appeals | | | |
| 12 | 4 | Persuasive Argumentation | X | X | |
| 12 | 6 | Persuasive Messages in Social Media | | X | X |
| 13 | 4 | Summarizing Effectively | | | |
| 14 | 6 | Effective Informational Report | | X | X |
| 15 | 1 | Achieving the Appropriate Tone for a Report | | X | X |
| 15 | 2 | Executive Summary | | X | |
| 17 | 3 | Using a Key Visual to Organize Points on a Slide | | | |
| 17 | 5 | Writing Text for Slides | | | |
| 17 | 8 | Designing Effective Visuals: Selected Slides | | | |
| 18 | 1 | Writing the Story of You | | X | |
| 18 | 3 | Crafting Your Résumé, Scenario 1: Positioning Yourself for an Ideal Opportunity | | X | |
| 18 | 4 | Crafting Your Résumé, Scenario 2: Repositioning Yourself for Available Opportunities | | X | |
| 18 | 5 | Crafting Your Résumé, Scenario 3: Positioning Yourself for More Responsibility | | X | |
| 18 | 6 | Infographic Resume | | | X |
| 19 | 2 | Unsolicited Application Letter | X | X | |
| 19 | 3 | Job Task Simulations | | | X |
| 19 | 6 | Follow-up Message | X | X | |
| 19 | 7 | Request for a Time Extension | X | X | |

# A Unique Online Resource That Reinforces Learning and Keeps Content Fresh Throughout Your Entire Course

You no longer need to spend hours of your limited prep time searching for current examples, discussion materials, and classroom media. *Business Communication Today*'s Real-Time Updates solves the age-old problems of maintaining the currency of textbook content by providing you with a steady stream of new examples, lecture materials, and media to enliven your classes. This unique suite of web technologies, developed by the authors, automatically provides weekly content updates, including interactive websites, podcasts, PowerPoint presentations, infographics, online videos, PDF files, and articles. Simply visit the website whenever you need material—or get new items delivered to your desktop automatically via RSS newsreader.

You can access Real-Time Updates by visiting http://real-timeupdates.com/bct12.

1 Read messages from the authors and access over 175 media items available only to instructors.
(Students have access to their own messages, assignments, and media items.)

2 Click on any chapter to see the updates and media items for that chapter.

3 Scan headlines and click on any item of interest to read the article or download the media item.
Every item is personally selected by the authors to complement the text and support in-class activities.

4 Media items are categorized by type so you can quickly find podcasts, videos, infographics, PowerPoints, and more.

5 Subscribe via RSS to individual chapters to get updates automatically for the chapter you're currently teaching.

# The One Book You Count On to Cover the Full Spectrum of Contemporary Business Communication Practices

With new material on business video in this edition, *Business Communication Today* continues to lead the field in up-to-the-minute coverage of the concepts and skills students are expected to have in today's workplace. Video joins a long list of feature and coverage innovations that Bovée-Thill adopters have benefited from in recent years:

- Unique coverage of the *social communication model* that revolutionized business communication and redefined the relationship between companies and their stakeholders
- Advice on writing promotional messages in a social media environment
- The use of social networking in the job search process
- Interactive Document Makeovers that help students quickly see how to improve written messages
- A unique wiki simulator that lets students practice wiki writing in a secure, private environment
- Downloadable documents, presentations, and podcasts for student analysis
- The groundbreaking Business Communication Headline News blog and the unique Real-Time Updates content-updating service
- The Twitter-enabled *backchannel* that is defining the dynamics of business presentations
- The nine compositional modes for electronic media
- Storytelling as an organizing model for business messages
- Writing strategies for social networks
- Personal branding advice to guide students in their job search and career management efforts
- The Bovée & Thill YouTube channel
- Online instructor communities on Facebook and LinkedIn
- Webinars hosted by Court Bovée that offer instructors practical advice on teaching new media skills

## EXPERTISE INFORMED BY HANDS-ON EXPERIENCE

Beyond the research and presentation of new ideas and tools in our textbooks, we are among the most active users of social media in the entire field of business communication:

- Sponsorship of Teaching Business Communication instructors' communities (open to all) and Bovée & Thill's Inner Circle for Business Communication (for adopters only) on LinkedIn and Facebook
- Our instructor tips and techniques blog and Twitter feed
- Numerous free webinars on new communication practices and social media topics
- The Bovée & Thill channel on YouTube, with videos that offer advice on teaching the new elements of business communication
- The unique Real-Time Updates content-updating service
- The popular Business Communication Headline News service
- A variety of videos and PowerPoint presentations on SlideShare
- More than 500 infographics, videos, articles, podcasts, and PowerPoints on Pinterest.
- A visual display of trending Bovée & Thill tweets on Twylah

We also invite you to peruse Bovée & Thill's Online Magazines for Business Communication on Scoop.it:

- *Business Communication 2.0: Social Media and Electronic Communication*
- *Teaching a Modern Business Communication Course*
- *Teaching Business Communication and Workplace Issues*
- *Teaching Business Communication and Interpersonal Communication*
- *Teaching Oral Communication in a Business Communication Course*
- *Teaching Business Communication and Employment*
- *Teaching Visual Communication*

Links to all these services and resources can be found at http://blog.business-communicationnetwork.com/2012/08/28/free-resources-to-enhance-your-business-communication-course/

This deep base of experience informs every aspect of the latest edition of *Business Communication Today*. Of course, media skills are only one element of successful communication. *Business Communication Today* presents these technologies in the context of proven communication strategies and essential business writing skills.

## TARGET AUDIENCE

With its comprehensive coverage of business communication concepts and up-to-the-minute treatment of contemporary practices and technologies, *Business Communication Today* is ideal for business communication courses in any curriculum. It is particularly suited to full-spectrum communication courses that address the broad range of contemporary business media. (The authors' *Excellence in Business Communication* and *Essentials of Business Communication* are a better fit for courses that focus exclusively or primarily on business writing.) Moving beyond the basics, this text also addresses vital strategic issues such as crisis communication and the management of communication programs in a social media environment, making it a strong choice for courses that emphasize managerial communication.

Colleges and universities vary in the prerequisites established for the business communication course, but we advise at least one course in English composition. Some coursework in business studies will also give students a better perspective on communication challenges in the workplace. However, we have taken special care not to assume students have any in-depth business experience, so *Business Communication Today* works quite well for those with limited work experience or business coursework.

## FULL SUPPORT FOR AACSB LEARNING STANDARDS

The American Association of Collegiate Schools of Business (AACSB) is a not-for-profit corporation of educational institutions, corporations, and other organizations devoted to the promotion and improvement of higher education in business administration and accounting. A collegiate institution offering degrees in business administration or accounting may volunteer for AACSB accreditation review. The AACSB makes initial accreditation decisions and conducts periodic reviews to promote continuous quality improvement in management education. Pearson Education is a proud member of the AACSB and is pleased to provide advice to help you apply AACSB Learning Standards.

Curriculum quality is one of the most important criteria for AACSB accreditation. Although no specific courses are required, the AACSB expects a curriculum to include learning experiences in such areas as

- Communication skills
- Ethical reasoning
- Analytic skills
- Use of information technology
- Multicultural and diversity awareness
- Reflective thinking

Throughout *Business Communication Today*, you'll find student exercises and activities that support the achievement of these important goals.

# A Total Teaching and Learning Solution

*Business Communication Today* has helped more than 2 million students master essential skills for succeeding in the workplace. This twelfth edition continues that tradition by offering an unmatched set of tools that simplify teaching, promote active learning, and stimulate critical thinking. These components work together at four levels to provide seamless coverage of vital knowledge and skills: previewing, developing, enhancing, and reinforcing.

## PREVIEWING

Each chapter provides clear learning objectives that prepare students for the material to come and provide a framework for the chapter content. New in this edition, each learning objective aligns with a major heading in the chapter, and this structure is carried on through to the end-of-chapter and online activities, making it easier for instructors and students to gauge learning progress.

After the learning objectives, a compelling Communication Close-Up vignette featuring a successful professional role model shows students how the material they will encounter in the chapter is put to use in actual business situations.

## DEVELOPING

Chapter content develops, explains, and elaborates on concepts with a carefully organized presentation of textual and visual material. The three-step process of planning, writing, and completing is clearly explained and reinforced throughout the course. Some texts introduce a writing process model and then rarely, if ever, discuss it again, giving students few opportunities to practice it and leaving them to wonder just how important the process really is. *Business Communication Today* adapts the three-step process to every category of messages in every medium, from traditional memos and reports to email, blogs, IM, podcasts, wikis, and online videos.

## ENHANCING

Contemporary examples show students the specific elements that contribute to—or detract from—successful messages. *Business Communication Today* has an unmatched portfolio of realistic examples for students to emulate, including 95 model documents and nearly 70 exhibits that feature communication efforts from real companies. In addition, Real-Time Updates "Learn More" connects students with dozens of carefully selected online media elements that provide examples and insights from successful professionals. Finally, unique social media screencasts help students get up to speed on business use of Twitter, Facebook, and LinkedIn.

*Business Communication Today* also extends students' awareness beyond the functional aspects of communication, with thorough and well-integrated coverage of business etiquette and ethics—vital issues that some texts raise briefly and then quickly forget. In light of employer concerns about the etiquette shortcomings of today's new-hires and the continuing struggles with business ethics, we integrate ethics and etiquette throughout the book and give students numerous opportunities to ponder ethical dilemmas and practice communication etiquette.

## REINFORCING

Hundreds of realistic exercises and activities help students practice vital skills and put newfound knowledge to immediate use. Unique features include downloadable Word documents, podcasts, PowerPoint presentations for students to analyze, and the innovative Bovée and Thill wiki simulator. Interactive Document Makeovers, pioneered by Bovée and Thill, let students experience firsthand the elements that make a document successful, giving them the insights they need in order to analyze and improve their own business messages. Nearly 150 communication cases, featuring dozens of real companies, encourage students to think about contemporary business issues as they put their skills to use in a variety of media, including blogging, social networking, and podcasting.

Quick Learning Guides are a convenient review tool at the end of every chapter. Each one summarizes the chapter learning objectives, lists essential terminology from the chapter, and collects copies of the checklists in one handy place.

At every stage of the learning experience, *Business Communication Today* provides the tools instructors and students need in order to succeed.

| Features that help students build essential knowledge and skills | Previewing | Developing | Enhancing | Reinforcing |
| --- | --- | --- | --- | --- |
| Learning objectives (beginning of chapter) | • | | | |
| Communication Close-up (beginning of chapter) | • | | | |
| Concise presentations of fundamentals (within chapter) | | • | | |
| Managerial and strategic perspectives on key topics (within chapter) | | • | | |
| Three-step writing process discussion and diagrams (within chapter) | | • | | |
| Real-life examples (within chapter) | | | • | |
| Annotated model documents (within chapter) | | | • | |
| Highlight boxes (within chapter) | | | • | |
| Handbook of Grammar, Mechanics, and Usage (end of book) | | | • | |
| Learn More media resources (online) | | | • | |
| Social media screencasts (online) | | | • | |
| MyBCommLab (online) | | | • | • |
| Real-Time Updates (online) | | | • | • |
| Marginal notes for quick review (within chapter) | | | | • |
| Checklists (within chapter) | | | | • |
| Communication Challenges (end of chapter) | | | | • |
| Quick Learning Guide (end of chapter) | | | | • |
| Test Your Knowledge questions (end of chapter) | | | | • |
| Apply Your Knowledge questions (end of chapter) | | | | • |
| Practice Your Skills activities and exercises (end of chapter) | | | | • |
| Expand Your Skills web activities (end of chapter/online) | | | | • |
| Bovée and Thill wiki simulator (online) | | | | • |
| Cases (following Chapters 7, 8, 9, 10, 11, 12, 15, 17, 18, and 19) | | | | • |
| Document Makeovers (online) | | | | • |

# Unmatched Coverage of Essential Communication Technologies

The Bovée and Thill series continues to lead the field with unmatched coverage of communication technologies, reflecting the expectations and opportunities in today's workplace:

- Applicant tracking systems
- Assistive technologies
- Automated bots
- Automated reputation analysis
- Avatars
- Backchannel
- Blogs
- Cloud computing
- Clustering engines
- Community Q&A websites
- Computer animation
- Crowdsourcing
- Data visualization
- Electronic documents
- Electronic forms
- Electronic presentations
- Electronic résumé production
- Electronic whiteboards
- Email
- Email hygiene
- Emoticons
- Enterprise instant messaging
- E-portfolios
- Extranets
- Gamification
- Geographic information systems
- Graphics software
- Groupware and shared online workspaces
- Infographics
- Information architecture
- Instant messaging
- Intellectual property rights
- Interactivity
- Internet telephony (VoIP)
- Interview simulators
- Intranets
- Knowledge management systems
- Lifestreaming
- Linked and embedded documents
- Location-based social networking
- Media curation
- Microblogs
- Mobile business apps
- Multimedia documents

- Multimedia presentations
- Multimedia résumés
- Newsfeeds
- Online brainstorming systems
- Online research techniques
- Online survey tools
- Online video
- Podcasts
- PowerPoint animation
- Really Simple Syndication (RSS)
- Screencasts
- Search and metasearch engines
- Search engine optimization (SEO)
- Security and privacy concerns in electronic media

- Sentiment analysis
- Social bookmarking
- Social commerce
- Social media
- Social media résumés
- Social networking
- Syndication of social media content
- Tagging
- Templates and style sheets
- Teleconferencing and telepresence
- Text messaging
- Translation software
- User-generated content
- Video interviews

- Video production and editing
- Video résumés
- Videoconferencing
- Virtual meetings
- Virtual whiteboards
- Virtual communities
- Voice recognition and synthesis
- Web 2.0
- Web content management systems
- Web directories
- Webcasts
- Website accessibility
- Wikis
- Workforce analytics

## Course Planning Guide

Although *Business Communication Today* follows a conventional sequence of topics, it is structured so that you can address topics in whatever order best suits your needs. For instance, if you want to begin by reviewing grammar, sentence structure, and other writing fundamentals, you can ask students to read Chapter 5, "Writing Business Messages" and then the "Handbook of Grammar, Mechanics, and Usage." Conversely, if you want to begin with employment-related communication, you can start with the Prologue, "Building a Career with Your Communication Skills," followed by Chapters 18 and 19.

The following table suggests a sequence and a schedule for covering the chapters in the textbook, with time allocations based on the total number of class hours available.

| | Chapter/Section Number and Title | Hours Devoted to Each Chapter/Section | | |
| --- | --- | --- | --- | --- |
| | | 30-Hour Course | 45-Hour Course | 60-Hour Course |
| | Prologue: Building a Career with Your Communication Skills | 1 | 1 | 1 |
| 1 | Achieving Career Success Through Effective Business Communication | 1 | 1 | 1 |
| 2 | Mastering Team Skills and Interpersonal Communication | 1 | 1 | 2 |
| 3 | Communicating in a World of Diversity | 1 | 2 | 3 |
| 4 | Planning Business Messages | 2 | 3 | 4 |
| 5 | Writing Business Messages | 2 | 3 | 4 |
| 6 | Completing Business Messages | 2 | 3 | 4 |
| | Handbook of Grammar, Mechanics, and Usage | 1 | 2 | 2 |
| A | Format and Layout of Business Documents | 1 | 1 | 1 |
| 7 | Electronic Media | 1 | 2 | 3 |
| 8 | Social Media | 1 | 2 | 3 |
| 9 | Visual Media | 1 | 1 | 2 |
| 10 | Writing Routine and Positive Messages | 2 | 2 | 3 |
| 11 | Writing Negative Messages | 2 | 2 | 3 |
| 12 | Writing Persuasive Messages | 2 | 2 | 3 |
| 13 | Finding, Evaluating, and Processing Information | 1 | 2 | 3 |
| 14 | Planning Reports and Proposals | 1 | 2 | 3 |
| 15 | Writing and Completing Reports and Proposals | 1 | 2 | 3 |
| B | Documentation of Report Sources | 1 | 1 | 2 |

| Chapter/Section Number and Title | | Hours Devoted to Each Chapter/Section | | |
|---|---|---|---|---|
| | | 30-Hour Course | 45-Hour Course | 60-Hour Course |
| 16 | Developing Oral and Online Presentations | 1 | 3 | 3 |
| 17 | Enhancing Presentations with Slides and Other Visuals | 1 | 1 | 1 |
| 18 | Building Careers and Writing Résumés | 2 | 3 | 3 |
| 19 | Applying and Interviewing for Employment | 1 | 3 | 3 |

## BUSINESS COMMUNICATION HEADLINE NEWS

Stay on top of hot topics, important trends, and new technologies with Business Communication Headline News (http://businesscommunicationheadlinenews.com/), the most comprehensive business communication site on the Internet. Every weekday during the school year, we offer fresh lecture content and provide a wide range of research and teaching tools on the website, including a custom web search function that we created expressly for business communication research.

Take advantage of the newsfeeds to get late-breaking news in headlines with concise summaries. You can scan incoming items in a matter of seconds and simply click through to read the full articles that interest you. All articles and accompanying multimedia resources are categorized by topic and chapter for easy retrieval at any time.

This free service for adopters offers numerous ways to enhance lectures and student activities:

- Keep current with the latest information and trends in the field.
- Easily update your lecture notes with fresh material.
- Create visuals for your classroom presentations.
- Supplement your lectures with cutting-edge handouts.
- Gather podcasts, online video, and other new media examples to use in the classroom.
- Enhance your research projects with the newest data.
- Compare best practices from other instructors.
- Improve the quality and effectiveness of your teaching by reading about new teaching tips and techniques.

At the website, you also get free access to these powerful instructional resources:

- **Business Communication Web Search,** featuring a revolutionary approach to searching developed by the authors that lets you quickly access more than 325 search engines. The tool uses a simple and intuitive interface engineered to help business communication instructors find precisely what they want, whether it's PowerPoint files, PDF files, Microsoft Word documents, Excel files, videos, or podcasts.
- **Real-Time Updates** are newsfeeds and content updates tied directly to specific points throughout the text. Each content update is classified by the type of media featured: interactive website, article, video, podcast, PowerPoint, or PDF. Additional sections on the site include Instructor Messages and Instructor Media (both password protected), Student Messages, and Student Assignments.

You can subscribe to Business Communication Headline News and get delivery by email, MyYahoo or iGoogle homepage, RSS newsreader, mobile phone, instant messenger, MP3, Twitter, Facebook, and a host of other options.

## BOVÉE & THILL BUSINESS COMMUNICATION BLOG

The Bovée & Thill Business Communication Blog (http://blog.businesscommunication-network.com/) offers original articles that help instructors focus their teaching to help students learn more efficiently and effectively. Articles discuss a wide variety of topics, including new topics instructors should be teaching their students, resources instructors can use in their classes, solutions to common teaching challenges, and great examples and activities instructors can use in class.

### AUTHORS' EMAIL HOTLINE FOR FACULTY

Integrity, excellence, and responsiveness are our hallmarks. That means providing you with textbooks that are academically sound, creative, timely, and sensitive to instructor and student needs. As an adopter of *Business Communication Today*, you are invited to use our Email Hotline (hotline@businesscommunicationblog.com) if you ever have a question or concern related to the text or its supplements.

## Instructor's Resource Center

At www.pearsonhighered.com/educator instructors can access a variety of digital and presentation resources available with this text in downloadable format. Registration is simple and gives you immediate access to new titles and new editions. As a registered faculty member, you can download resource files and receive immediate access and instructions for installing course management content on your campus server.

If you ever need assistance, our dedicated technical support team is ready to help with the media supplements that accompany this text. Visit http://247pearsoned.custhelp .com/ for answers to frequently asked questions and toll-free user support phone numbers.

The following supplements are available to adopting instructors (for detailed descriptions, please visit www.pearsonhighered.com/educator):

- Instructor's Manual
- Test item file
- TestGen test generating software (converted for use in BlackBoard, WebCT, Angel, D2L, Moodle, Sakai, and Respondus)
- PowerPoint slides
- Image Library

## Student Resources

*Business Communication Today* supports students with a variety of supplements designed to save them time and money:

- **MyBCommLab.** Students can use www.MyBCommLab.com to test their understanding of the concepts presented in the text.
- **CourseSmart eTextbooks.** CourseSmart is an online choice for students looking to save money. As an alternative to buying the print textbook, students can purchase an electronic version of the same content and receive a significant discount off the suggested list price of the print text. With a CourseSmart eTextbook, students can search the text, make notes online, print out reading assignments that incorporate lecture notes, and bookmark important passages for later review. For more information or to purchase access to the CourseSmart eTextbook, visit www.coursesmart.com.

## About the Authors

Courtland L. Bovée and John V. Thill have been leading textbook authors for more than two decades, introducing millions of students to the fields of business and business communication. Their award-winning texts are distinguished by proven pedagogical features, extensive selections of contemporary case studies, hundreds of real-life examples, engaging writing, thorough research, and the unique integration of print and electronic resources. Each new edition reflects the authors' commitment to continuous refinement and improvement, particularly in terms of modeling the latest practices in business and the use of technology.

Professor Bovée has 22 years of teaching experience at Grossmont College in San Diego, where he has received teaching honors and was accorded that institution's C. Allen Paul Distinguished Chair. Mr. Thill is a prominent communications consultant who has worked with organizations ranging from Fortune 500 multinationals to entrepreneurial startups. He formerly held positions with Pacific Bell and Texaco.

Courtland Bovée and John Thill were recently awarded proclamations from the Governor of Massachusetts for their lifelong contributions to education and for their commitment to the summer youth baseball program that is sponsored by the Boston Red Sox.

# Acknowledgments

The twelfth edition of *Business Communication Today* reflects the professional experience of a large team of contributors and advisors. We express our thanks to the many individuals whose valuable suggestions and constructive comments influenced the success of this book.

## REVIEWERS OF PREVIOUS EDITIONS

Thank you to the following professors: Lydia E. Anderson, Fresno City College; Victoria Austin, Las Positas College; Faridah Awang, Eastern Kentucky University; Jeanette Baldridge, University of Maine at Augusta; Diana Baran, Henry Ford Community College; JoAnne Barbieri, Atlantic Cape Community College; Kristina Beckman, John Jay College; Judy Bello, Lander University; Carol Bibly, Triton College; Nancy Bizal, University of Southern Indiana; Yvonne Block, College of Lake County; Edna Boroski, Trident Technical College; Nelvia M. Brady, Trinity Christian College; Arlene Broeker, Lincoln University; David Brooks, Indiana University Southeast; Carol Brown, South Puget Sound Community College; Domenic Bruni, University of Wisconsin; Jeff Bruns, Bacone College; Gertrude L. Burge, University of Nebraska; Sharon Burton, Brookhaven College; Robert Cabral, Oxnard College; Dorothy Campbell, Brevard Community College; Linda Carr, University of West Alabama; Alvaro Carreras, Jr., Florida International University; Sharon Carson, St. Philip's College; Rick Carter, Seattle University; Dacia Charlesworth, Indiana University–Purdue University Fort Wayne; Jean Chenu, Genesee Community College; Connie Clark, Lane Community College; Alvin Clarke, Iowa State University; Jerrie Cleaver, Central Texas College; Clare Coleman, Temple University; Michael P. Collins, Northern Arizona University; M. Cotton, North Central Missouri College; Pat Cowherd, Campbellsville University; Pat Cuchens, University of Houston–Clear Lake; Walt Dabek, Post University; Cathy Daly, California State University–Sacramento; Linda Davis, Copiah–Lincoln Community College; Christine R. Day, Eastern Michigan University; Harjit Dosanjh, North Seattle Community College; Amy Drees, Defiance College; Cynthia Drexel, Western State College of Colorado; Lou Dunham, Spokane Falls Community College; Donna Everett, Morehead State University; Donna Falconer, Anoka–Ramsey Community College; Kate Ferguson Marsters, Gannon University; Darlynn Fink, Clarion University of Pennsylvania; Bobbi Fisher, University of Nebraska-Omaha; Laura Fitzwater, Community College of Philadelphia; Lynda K. Fuller, Wilmington University; Matthew Gainous, Ogeechee Technical College; Yolande Gardner, Lawson State Community College; Gina Genova, University of California–Santa Barbara; Lonny Gilbert, Central State University; Camille Girardi-Levy, Siena College; Nancy Goehring, Monterey Peninsula College; Dawn Goellner, Bethel College; Robert Goldberg, Prince George's Community College; Jeffrey Goldberg, MassBay Community College; Helen Grattan, Des Moines Area Community College; Barbara Grayson, University of Arkansas at Pine Bluff; Deborah Griffin, University of Houston–Clear Lake; Alice Griswold, Clarke College; Bonnie Grossman, College of Charleston; Lisa Gueldenzoph, North Carolina A&T State University; Wally Guyot, Fort Hays State University; Valerie Harrison, Cuyamaca College; Tim Hartge, The University of Michigan–Dearborn; Richard Heiens, University of South Carolina–Aiken; Maureece Heinert, Sinte Gleska University; Leighanne Heisel, University of Missouri–St. Louis; Gary Helfand, University of Hawaii–West Oahu; Cynthia Herrera, Orlando Culinary Academy; Kathy Hill, Sam Houston State University; Pashia Hogan, Northeast State Tech Community College;

Sarah Holmes, New England Institute of Technology; Ruth Hopkins Zajdel, Ohio University–Chillicothe; Sheila Hostetler, Orange Coast College; Michael Hricik, Westmoreland County Community College; Rebecca Hsiao, East Los Angeles College; Mary Ann Hurd, Sauk Valley Community College; Pat Hurley, Leeward Community College; Harold Hurry, Sam Houston State University; Marcia James, University of Wisconsin–Whitewater; Frank Jaster, Tulane University; Jonatan Jelen, Parsons The New School For Design; Irene Joanette Gallio, Western Nevada Community College; Edgar Dunson Johnson III, Augusta State University; Mark Johnson, Rhodes State College; Joanne Kapp, Siena College; Jeanette A. Karjala, Winona State University; Christy L. Kinnion, Lenior Community College; Deborah Kitchin, City College of San Francisco; Lisa Kirby, North Carolina Wesleyan College; Claudia Kirkpatrick, Carnegie Mellon University; Betty Kleen, Nicholls State University; Fran Kranz, Oakland University; Jana Langemach, University of Nebraska–Lincoln; Joan Lantry, Jefferson Community College; Kim Laux, Saginaw Valley State University; Kathryn J. Lee, University of Cincinnati; Anita Leffel, The University of Texas, San Antonio; Ruth Levy, Westchester Community College; Nancy Linger, Moraine Park Technical College; Jere Littlejohn, University of Mississippi; Dana Loewy, California State University–Fullerton; Jennifer Loney, Portland State University; Susan Long, Portland Community College; Sue Loomis, Maine Maritime Academy; Thomas Lowderbaugh, University of Maryland–College Park; Jayne Lowery, Jackson State Community College; Lloyd Matzner, University of Houston–Downtown; Ron McNeel, New Mexico State University at Alamogordo; Dr. Bill McPherson, Indiana University of Pennsylvania; Phyllis Mercer, Texas Woman's University; Donna Meyerholz, Trinidad State Junior College; Annie Laurie I. Meyers, Northampton Community College; Catherine "Kay" Michael, St. Edward's University; Kathleen Miller, University of Delaware; Gay Mills, Amarillo College; Julie Mullis, Wilkes Community College; Pamela Mulvey, Olney Central College; Jimidene Murphey, Clarendon College; Cindy Murphy, Southeastern Community College; Dipali Murti-Hali, California State University–Stanislaus; Shelley Myatt, University of Central Oklahoma; Cora Newcomb, Technical College of the Lowcountry; Ron Newman, Crafton Hills College; Linda Nitsch, Chadron State College; Leah Noonan, Laramie County Community College; Mabry O'Donnell, Marietta College; Diana Oltman, Central Washington University; Ranu Paik, Santa Monica College; Lauren Paisley, Genesee Community College; Patricia Palermo, Drew University; John Parrish, Tarrant County College; Diane Paul, TVI Community College; John T. Pauli, University of Alaska–Anchorage; Michael Pennell, University of Rhode Island; Sylvia Beaver Perez, Nyack College; Melinda Phillabaum, Indiana University; Ralph Phillips, Geneva College; Laura Pohopien, Cal Poly Pomona; Diane Powell, Utah Valley State College; Christine Pye, California Lutheran University; Norma Pygon, Triton College; Dave Rambow, Wayland Baptist University; Richard David Ramsey, Southeastern Louisiana University; Charles Riley, Tarrant County College–Northwest Campus; Jim Rucker, Fort Hays State University; Dr. Suzan Russell, Lehman College; Danielle Scane, Orange Coast College; Calvin Scheidt, Tidewater Community College; Nancy Schneider, University of Maine at Augusta; Brian Sheridan, Mercyhurst College; Melinda Shirey, Fresno City College; Bob Shirilla, Colorado State University; Joyce Simmons, Florida State University; Gordon J. Simpson, SUNY Cobleskill; Peggy Simpson, Dominican University; Eunice Smith, Bismarck State College; Jeff Smith, University of Southern California; Lorraine M. Smith, Fresno City College; Harvey Solganick, LeTourneau University–Dallas campus; Stephen Soucy, Santa Monica College; Linda Spargo, University of Mississippi; W. Dees Stallings, Park University; Sally Stanton, University of Wisconsin-Milwaukee; Mark Steinbach, Austin Community College; Angelique Stevens, Monroe Community College; Steven Stovall, Wilmington College; Alden Talbot, Weber State University; Michele Taylor, Ogeechee Technical College; Wilma Thomason, Mid-South Community College; Ed Thompson, Jefferson Community College; Ann E. Tippett, Monroe Community College; Lori Townsend, Niagara County Community College; Lani Uyeno, Leeward Community College; Wendy Van Hatten, Western Iowa Tech Community College; Jay Wagers, Richmond Community College; John Waltman, Eastern Michigan University; Jie Wang, University of Illinois at Chicago; Chris Ward, The University of Findlay; Dorothy Warren, Middle Tennessee State University; Glenda Waterman, Concordia University; Kellie Welch, Jefferson Community College; Bradley S. Wesner, Nova Southeastern University; Mathew

Williams, Clover Park Technical College; Beth Williams, Stark State College of Technology; Brian Wilson, College of Marin; and Sandra D. Young, Orangeburg–Calhoun Technical College.

## REVIEWERS OF DOCUMENT MAKEOVERS

We sincerely thank the following reviewers for their assistance with the Document Makeover feature: Lisa Barley, *Eastern Michigan University*; Marcia Bordman, *Gallaudet University*; Jean Bush-Bacelis, *Eastern Michigan University*; Bobbye Davis, *Southern Louisiana University*; Cynthia Drexel, *Western State College of Colorado*; Kenneth Gibbs, *Worcester State College*; Ellen Leathers, *Bradley University*; Diana McKowen, *Indiana University*; Bobbie Nicholson, *Mars Hill College*; Andrew Smith, *Holyoke Community College*; Jay Stubblefield, *North Carolina Wesleyan College*; Dawn Wallace, *Southeastern Louisiana University*.

## REVIEWERS OF MODEL DOCUMENTS

The many model documents in the text and their accompanying annotations received invaluable review from Dacia Charlesworth, *Indiana University–Purdue University Fort Wayne*; Diane Todd Bucci, *Robert Morris University*; Estelle Kochis, *Suffolk County Community College*; Sherry Robertson, *Arizona State University*; Nancy Goehring, *Monterey Peninsula College*; James Hatfield, *Florida Community College at Jacksonville*; Avon Crismore, *Indiana University*.

## PERSONAL ACKNOWLEDGMENTS

We wish to extend a heartfelt thanks to our many friends, acquaintances, and business associates who provided materials or agreed to be interviewed so that we could bring the real world into the classroom.

A very special acknowledgment goes to George Dovel, whose superb writing skills, distinguished background, and wealth of business experience assured this project of clarity and completeness. Also, recognition and thanks go to Jackie Estrada for her outstanding skills and excellent attention to details. Her creation of the "Peak Performance Grammar and Mechanics" material is especially noteworthy.

We also feel it is important to acknowledge and thank the Association for Business Communication, an organization whose meetings and publications provide a valuable forum for the exchange of ideas and for professional growth.

# Dedication

This book is dedicated to the many instructors who have used Bovée and Thill texts to help shape the careers of more than two million students. We appreciate the opportunity to assist you in your teaching efforts, and we wish you and your students success and satisfaction.

Courtland L. Bovée

John V. Thill

# Prologue

## BUILDING A CAREER WITH YOUR COMMUNICATION SKILLS

## Using This Course to Help Launch Your Career

This course will help you develop vital communication skills you'll use throughout your career—and those skills can help you launch an interesting and rewarding career, too. This brief prologue sets the stage by helping you understand today's dynamic workplace, the steps you can take to adapt to the job market, and the importance of creating an employment portfolio and building your personal brand. Take a few minutes to read it while you think about the career you hope to create for yourself.

## Understanding the Changing World of Work

There is no disguising the fact that you are entering a tough job market, but there are several reasons for at least some hope over the longer term. First, the U.S. economy will recover from the Great Recession, although it's going to take a while before the majority of employers feel confident enough to ramp up hiring significantly. Second, the large demographic bulge of baby boomers is moving into retirement, which should set off a chain reaction of openings from the tops of companies on downward. Third, political and business leaders here and abroad are keenly aware of the problem of unemployment among young adults, both as it affects people looking for work and in the loss of vitality to the economy. For example, programs aimed at helping graduates start companies right out of college, rather than enter the conventional job market, are springing up under government and philanthropic efforts.[1]

The ups and downs of the economic cycle are not the only dynamic elements that will affect your career. The nature of employment itself is changing, with a growing number of independent workers and loosely structured *virtual organizations* that engage these workers for individual projects or short-term contracts, rather than hire employees. In fact, one recent study predicted that independent workers will outnumber conventional employees in the United States by 2020.[2]

This new model of work offers some compelling advantages for workers and companies alike. Companies can lower their fixed costs, adapt more easily to economic fluctuations and competitive moves, and get access to specialized talent for specific project needs.[3] Workers can benefit from the freedom to choose the clients and projects that interest them the most, the flexibility to work as much or as little as they want, and (thanks to advances in communication technology) access to compelling work even if they live far from major employment centers such as New York City or California's Silicon Valley.[4]

On the other hand, this new approach also presents some significant challenges for all parties. These flexibilities and freedoms can create more complexity for workers and managers, diminished loyalties on both sides, uncertainty about the future, issues with skill development and training, and problems with accountability and liability.[5] Many of these issues involve communication, making solid communication skills more important than ever.

These changes could affect you even if you pursue traditional employment throughout your career. Within organizations, you're likely to work with a combination of "inside" employees and "outside" contractors, which can affect the dynamics of the workplace. And the availability of more independent workers in the talent marketplace gives employers more options and more leverage, so full-time employees may find themselves competing against freelancers, at least indirectly.

As you navigate this uncertain future, keep two vital points in mind. First, don't wait for your career to just happen: Take charge of your career and stay in charge of it. Explore all your options and have a plan—but be prepared to change course as opportunities and threats appear on the horizon. Second, don't count on employers to take care of you. The era of lifetime employment, in which an employee committed to one company for life with the understanding it would return the loyalty, is long gone. From finding opportunities to developing the skills you need to succeed, it's up to you to manage your career and look out for your own best interests.

## HOW EMPLOYERS VIEW TODAY'S JOB MARKET

From an employer's perspective, the employment process is always a question of balance. Maintaining a stable workforce can improve nearly every aspect of business performance, yet many employers want the flexibility to shrink and expand payrolls as business conditions change. Employers obviously want to attract the best talent, but the best people are more expensive and more vulnerable to offers from competitors, so there are always financial trade-offs to consider.

Employers also struggle with the ups and downs of the economy. When unemployment is low, the balance of power shifts to employees, and employers have to compete in order to attract and keep top talent. When unemployment is high, the power shifts back to employers, who can afford to be more selective and less accommodating. In other words, pay attention to the economy; at times you can be more aggressive in your demands, but at other times you need to be more accommodating.

Companies view employment as a complex business decision with lots of variables to consider. To make the most of your potential, regardless of the career path you pursue, you need to view employment in the same way.

## WHAT EMPLOYERS LOOK FOR IN JOB APPLICANTS

Given the complex forces in the contemporary workplace and the unrelenting pressure of global competition, what are employers looking for in the candidates they hire? The short answer: a lot. Like all "buyers," companies want to get as much as they can for the money they spend. The closer you can present yourself as the ideal candidate, the better your chances of getting a crack at the most exciting opportunities.

Specific expectations vary by profession and position, of course, but virtually all employers look for the following general skills and attributes:[6]

- **Communication skills.** The reason this item is listed first isn't that you're reading a business communication textbook. Communication is listed first because it is far and away the most commonly mentioned skill set when employers are asked about what they look for in employees. Improving your communication skills will help in every aspect of your professional life.
- **Interpersonal and team skills.** You will have many individual responsibilities on the job, but chances are you won't work alone very often. Learn to work with others—and help them succeed as you succeed.
- **Intercultural and international awareness and sensitivity.** Successful employers tend to be responsive to diverse workforces, markets, and communities, and they look for employees with the same outlook.
- **Data collection, analysis, and decision-making skills.** Employers want people who know how to identify information needs, find the necessary data, convert the data into useful knowledge, and make sound decisions.

- **Computer and electronic media skills.** Today's workers need to know how to use common office software and to communicate using a wide range of electronic media.
- **Time and resource management.** If you've had to juggle multiple priorities during college, consider that great training for the business world. Your ability to plan projects and manage the time and resources available to you will make a big difference on the job.
- **Flexibility and adaptability.** Stuff happens, as they say. Employees who can roll with the punches and adapt to changing business priorities and circumstances will go further (and be happier) than employees who resist change.
- **Professionalism.** Professionalism is the quality of performing at the highest possible level and conducting oneself with confidence, purpose, and pride. True professionals strive to excel, continue to hone their skills and build their knowledge, are dependable and accountable, demonstrate a sense of business etiquette, make ethical decisions, show loyalty and commitment, don't give up when things get tough, and maintain a positive outlook.

# Adapting to Today's Job Market

Adapting to the workplace is a lifelong process of seeking the best fit between what you want to do and what employers (or clients, if you work independently) are willing to pay you to do. It's important to think about what you want to do during the many thousands of hours you will spend working, what you have to offer, and how to make yourself more attractive to employers.

## WHAT DO YOU WANT TO DO?

Economic necessities and the vagaries of the marketplace will influence much of what happens in your career, of course, and you may not always have the opportunity to do the kind of work you would really like do. Even if you can't get the job you want right now, though, start your job search by examining your values and interests. Doing so will give you a better idea of where you want to be eventually, and you can use those insights to learn and grow your way toward that ideal situation. Consider these questions:

- **What would you like to do every day?** Research occupations that interest you. Find out what people really do every day. Ask friends, relatives, alumni from your school, and contacts in your social networks. Read interviews with people in various professions to get a sense of what their careers are like.
- **How would you like to work?** Consider how much independence you want on the job, how much variety you like, and whether you prefer to work with products, machines, people, ideas, figures, or some combination thereof.
- **How do your financial goals fit with your other priorities?** For instance, many high-paying jobs involve a lot of stress, sacrifices of time with family and friends, and frequent travel or relocation. If location, lifestyle, intriguing work, or other factors are more important to you, you may well have to sacrifice some level of pay to achieve them.
- **Have you established some general career goals?** For example, do you want to pursue a career specialty such as finance or manufacturing, or do you want to gain experience in multiple areas with an eye toward upper management?
- **What sort of corporate culture are you most comfortable with?** Would you be happy in a formal hierarchy with clear reporting relationships? Or do you prefer less structure? Teamwork or individualism? Do you like a competitive environment?

You might need some time in the workforce to figure out what you really want to do or to work your way into the job you really want, but it's never too early to start thinking about where you want to be. Filling out the assessment in Table 1 might help you get a clearer picture of the nature of work you would like to pursue in your career.

## TABLE 1 CAREER SELF-ASSESSMENT

| Activity or Situation | Strongly Agree | Agree | Disagree | No Preference |
|---|---|---|---|---|
| 1. I want to work independently. | | | | |
| 2. I want variety in my work. | | | | |
| 3. I want to work with people. | | | | |
| 4. I want to work with technology. | | | | |
| 5. I want physical work. | | | | |
| 6. I want mental work. | | | | |
| 7. I want to work for a large organization. | | | | |
| 8. I want to work for a nonprofit organization. | | | | |
| 9. I want to work for a small business. | | | | |
| 10. I want to work for a service business. | | | | |
| 11. I want to start or buy a business someday. | | | | |
| 12. I want regular, predictable work hours. | | | | |
| 13. I want to work in a city location. | | | | |
| 14. I want to work in a small town or suburb. | | | | |
| 15. I want to work in another country. | | | | |
| 16. I want to work outdoors. | | | | |
| 17. I want to work in a structured environment. | | | | |
| 18. I want to avoid risk as much as possible. | | | | |
| 19. I want to enjoy my work, even if that means making less money. | | | | |
| 20. I want to become a high-level corporate manager. | | | | |

## WHAT DO YOU HAVE TO OFFER?

Knowing what you want to do is one thing. Knowing what a company is willing to pay you to do is another thing entirely. You may already have a good idea of what you can offer employers. If not, some brainstorming can help you identify your skills, interests, and characteristics. Start by jotting down achievements you're proud of and experiences that were satisfying, and think carefully about what specific skills these achievements demanded of you. For example, leadership skills, speaking ability, and artistic talent may have helped you coordinate a successful class project. As you analyze your achievements, you may well begin to recognize a pattern of skills. Which of them might be valuable to potential employers?

Next, look at your educational preparation, work experience, and extracurricular activities. What do your knowledge and experience qualify you to do? What have you learned from volunteer work or class projects that could benefit you on the job? Have you held any offices, won any awards or scholarships, mastered a second language? What skills have you developed in nonbusiness situations that could transfer to a business position?

Take stock of your personal characteristics. Are you aggressive, a born leader? Or would you rather follow? Are you outgoing, articulate, great with people? Or do you prefer working alone? Make a list of what you believe are your four or five most important qualities. Ask a relative or friend to rate your traits as well.

If you're having difficulty figuring out your interests, characteristics, or capabilities, consult your college career center. Many campuses administer a variety of tests that can help you identify interests, aptitudes, and personality traits. These tests won't reveal your "perfect" job, but they'll help you focus on the types of work best suited to your personality.

## HOW CAN YOU MAKE YOURSELF MORE VALUABLE?

While you're figuring out what you want from a job and what you can offer an employer, you can take positive steps toward building your career. First, look for volunteer projects, temporary jobs, freelance work, or internships that will help expand your experience base and skill set.[7] You can look for freelance projects on Craigslist (www.craigslist.org) and numerous other websites; some of these jobs have only nominal pay, but they do provide an opportunity for you to display your skills. Also consider applying your talents to *crowdsourcing* projects, in which companies and nonprofit organizations invite the public to contribute solutions to various challenges.

These opportunities help you gain valuable experience and relevant contacts, provide you with important references and work samples for your *employment portfolio*, and help you establish your *personal brand* (see the following sections).

Second, learn more about the industry or industries in which you want to work and stay on top of new developments. Join networks of professional colleagues and friends who can help you keep up with trends and events. Many professional societies have student chapters or offer students discounted memberships. Take courses and pursue other educational or life experiences that would be difficult while working full time.

For more ideas and advice on planning your career, check out the resources listed in Table 2.

## BUILDING AN EMPLOYMENT PORTFOLIO

Employers want proof that you have the skills to succeed on the job, but even if you don't have much relevant work experience, you can use your college classes to assemble that proof. Simply create and maintain an *employment portfolio*, which is a collection of projects that demonstrate your skills and knowledge. You can create a *print portfolio* and an *e-portfolio*; both can help with your career effort. A print portfolio gives you something tangible to bring to interviews, and it lets you collect project results that might not be easy to show online, such as a handsomely bound report. An e-portfolio is a multimedia presentation of your skills and experiences.[8] Think of it as a website that contains your résumé, work samples, letters of recommendation, relevant videos or podcasts you have recorded, any blog posts or articles you have written, and other information about you and your skills. If you have set up a *lifestream* (a real-time aggregation of your content creation, online interests, and social media interactions) that is professionally focused, consider adding that to your e-portfolio. The portfolio can be burned on a CD or DVD for physical distribution, or, more commonly, it can be posted online—whether it's a personal website, your college's site (if student pages are available), a specialized portfolio hosting site such as Behance (www.behance.com), or a résumé hosting site such as VisualCV (www.visualcv.com) that offers multimedia résumés. To see a selection of student e-portfolios from colleges around the United States, go to http://real-timeupdates.com/bct12, click on Student Assignments, and then click on Prologue to locate the link to student e-portfolios.

### TABLE 2 | CAREER PLANNING RESOURCES

| Resource | URL |
| --- | --- |
| Career Rocketeer | www.careerrocketeer.com |
| The Creative Career | http://thecreativecareer.com |
| Brazen Careerist | www.brazencareerist.com |
| Daily Career Connection | http://dailycareerconnection.com |
| The Career Key | http://careerkey.blogspot.com |
| Rise Smart | www.risesmart.com/risesmart/blog |
| Women's Leadership Blog | http://bx.businessweek.com/women-in-leadership/blogs/ |
| The Career Doctor | www.careerdoctor.org/career-doctor-blog |

Throughout this course, pay close attention to the business communication cases marked Portfolio Builder (they start in Chapter 7). These items will make particularly good samples of not only your communication skills but also your ability to understand and solve business-related challenges. By combining these projects with samples from your other courses, you can create a compelling portfolio when you're ready to start interviewing. Your portfolio is also a great resource for writing your résumé because it reminds you of all the great work you've done over the years. Moreover, you can continue to refine and expand your portfolio throughout your career; many professionals use e-portfolios to advertise their services.

As you assemble your portfolio, collect anything that shows your ability to perform, whether it's in school, on the job, or in other venues. However, you *must* check with employers before including any items you created while you were an employee and check with clients before including any *work products* (anything you wrote, designed, programmed, and so on) they purchased from you. Many business documents contain confidential information companies don't want distributed to outside audiences.

For each item you add to your portfolio, write a brief description that helps other people understand the meaning and significance of the project. Include such items as these:

- **Background.** Why did you undertake this project? Was it a school project, a work assignment, or something you did on your own initiative?
- **Project objectives.** Explain the project's goals, if relevant.
- **Collaborators.** If you worked with others, be sure to mention that and discuss team dynamics if appropriate. For instance, if you led the team or worked with others long distance as a virtual team, point that out.
- **Constraints.** Sometimes the most impressive thing about a project is the time or budget constraints under which it was created. If such constraints apply to a project, consider mentioning them in a way that doesn't sound like an excuse for poor quality. If you had only one week to create a website, for example, you might say that "One of the intriguing challenges of this project was the deadline; I had only one week to design, compose, test, and publish this material."
- **Outcomes.** If the project's goals were measurable, what was the result? For example, if you wrote a letter soliciting donations for a charitable cause, how much money did you raise?
- **Learning experience.** If appropriate, describe what you learned during the course of the project.

Keep in mind that the portfolio itself is a communication project, so be sure to apply everything you'll learn in this course about effective communication and good design. Assume that potential employers will find your e-portfolio site (even if you don't tell them about it), so don't include anything that could come back to haunt you. Also, if you have anything embarrassing on Facebook, Twitter, or any other social networking site, remove it immediately.

To get started, first check with the career center at your college; many schools offer e-portfolio systems for their students. (Some schools now require e-portfolios, so you may already be building one.) You can also find plenty of advice online; search for "e-portfolio," "student portfolio," or "professional portfolio."

## BUILDING YOUR PERSONAL BRAND

Products and companies have brands that represent collections of certain attributes, such as the safety emphasis of Volvo cars, the performance emphasis of BMW, or the luxury emphasis of Cadillac. Similarly, when people who know you think about you, they have a particular set of qualities in mind based on your professionalism, your priorities, and the various skills and attributes you have developed over the years. Perhaps without even being conscious of it, you have created a **personal brand** for yourself.

As you plan the next stage of your career, start managing your personal brand deliberately. Branding specialist Mohammed Al-Taee defines personal branding succinctly as "a way of clarifying and communicating what makes you different and special."[9]

| TABLE 3 | PERSONAL BRANDING RESOURCES |
| --- | --- |
| **Resource** | **URL** |
| Personal Branding Blog | www.personalbrandingblog.com |
| Mohammed Al-Taee | http://altaeeblog.com |
| Brand Yourself | http://blog.brand-yourself.com |
| Krishna De | http://krishnade.com |
| Cube Rules | http://cuberules.com |
| Jibber Jobber | www.jibberjobber.com/blog |
| The Engaging Brand | http://theengagingbrand.typepad.com |

You can learn more about personal branding from the sources listed in Table 3, and you will have multiple opportunities to plan and refine your personal brand during this course. For example, Chapter 8 offers tips on business applications of social media, which are key to personal branding, and Chapters 18 and 19 guide you through the process of creating a résumé, building your network, and presenting yourself in interviews. To get you started, here are the basics of a successful personal branding strategy:[10]

- **Figure out the "story of you."** Simply put, where have you been in life, and where are you going? Every good story has dramatic tension that pulls readers in and makes them wonder what will happen next. Where is your story going next? Chapter 18 offers more on this personal brand-building approach.
- **Clarify your professional theme.** Volvos, BMWs, and Cadillacs can all get you from Point A to Point B in safety, comfort, and style—but each brand emphasizes some attributes more than others to create a specific image in the minds of potential buyers. Similarly, you want to be seen as something more than just an accountant, a supervisor, a salesperson. What will your theme be? Brilliant strategist? Hard-nosed, get-it-done tactician? Technical guru? Problem solver? Creative genius? Inspirational leader?
- **Reach out and connect.** Major corporations spread the word about their brands with multimillion-dollar advertising campaigns. You can promote your brand for free or close to it. The secret is networking, which you'll learn more about in Chapter 18. You build your brand by connecting with like-minded people, sharing information, demonstrating skills and knowledge, and helping others succeed.
- **Deliver on your brand's promise—every time, all the time.** When you promote a brand, you make a promise—a promise that whoever buys that brand will get the benefits you are promoting. All of this planning and communication is of no value if you fail to deliver on the promises your branding efforts make. Conversely, when you deliver quality results time after time, your talents and professionalism will speak for you.

We wish you great success in this course and in your career!

# ENDNOTES

**1.** Peter Coy, "The Youth Unemployment Bomb," *Bloomberg Businessweek*, 2 February 2011, www.businessweek.com.

**2.** Ryan Kim, "By 2020, Independent Workers Will Be the Majority," GigaOm, 8 December 2011, http://gigaom.com.

**3.** Darren Dahl, "Want a Job? Let the Bidding Begin," *Inc.*, March 2011, 93–96; Thomas W. Malone, Robert J. Laubacher, and Tammy Johns, "The Age of Hyperspecialization," *Harvard Business Review*, July–August 2011, 56–65; Jennifer Wang, "The Solution to the Innovator's Dilemma," *Entrepreneur*, August 2011, 24–32.

**4.** "LiveOps and Vision Perry Create New Work Opportunities for Rural Tennessee," LiveOps press release, 18 July 2011, www.liveops.com; Malone et al., "The Age of Hyperspecialization."

**5.** Adapted from Dahl, "Want a Job? Let the Bidding Begin"; Malone et al., "The Age of Hyperspecialization"; Wang, "The Solution to the Innovator's Dilemma"; Marjorie Derven, "Managing the Matrix in the New Normal," *T+D*, July 2010, 42–47.

**6.** Courtland L. Bovée and John V. Thill, *Business in Action*, 5th ed. (Upper Saddle River, N.J.: Pearson Prentice Hall, 2010), 18–21; Randall S. Hansen and Katharine Hansen, "What Do Employers Really Want? Top Skills and Values Employers Seek from Job-Seekers," QuintCareers.com, accessed 17 August 2010, www.quintcareers.com.

**7.** Nancy M. Somerick, "Managing a Communication Internship Program," *Bulletin of the Association for Business Communication* 56, no. 3 (1993): 10–20.

**8.** Jeffrey R. Young, "'E-Portfolios' Could Give Students a New Sense of Their Accomplishments," *The Chronicle of Higher Education*, 8 March 2002, A31.

**9.** Mohammed Al-Taee, "Personal Branding," Al-Taee blog, accessed 17 August 2010, http://altaeeblog.com.

**10.** Pete Kistler, "Seth Godin's 7-Point Guide to Bootstrap Your Personal Brand," Personal Branding blog, 28 July 2010, www.personalbrandingblog; Kyle Lacy, "10 Ways to Building Your Personal Brand Story," Personal Branding blog, 5 August 2010, www.personalbrandingblog; Al-Taee, "Personal Branding"; Scot Herrick, "30 Career Management Tips—Marketing AND Delivery Support Our Personal Brand," Cube Rules blog, 8 September 2007, http://cuberules.com; Alina Tugend, "Putting Yourself Out There on a Shelf to Buy," *New York Times*, 27 March 2009, www.nytimes.com.

No other skill can help your career in as many ways as communication. Discover what business communication is all about, why communication skills are essential to your career, and how to adapt your communication experiences in life and college to the business world. Improve your skills in such vital areas as team interaction, etiquette, listening, and nonverbal communication. Explore the advantages and the challenges of a diverse workforce, and develop the skills that every communicator needs to succeed in today's multicultural business environment.

Yuri Arcurs/Shutterstock

## LEARNING OBJECTIVES

After studying this chapter, you will be able to

**1** Explain the importance of effective communication to your career and to the companies where you will work.

**2** Explain what it means to communicate as a professional in a business context.

**3** Identify five unique challenges of business communication.

**4** Describe the communication process model and the ways social media are changing the nature of business communication.

**5** List four general guidelines for using communication technology effectively.

**6** Define ethics, explain the difference between an ethical dilemma and an ethical lapse, and list six guidelines for making ethical communication choices.

---

## MyBCommLab®

⭐ **Improve Your Grade!** Over 10 million students improved their results using the Pearson MyLabs. Visit **mybcommlab.com** for simulations, tutorials, and end-of-chapter problems.

---

### COMMUNICATION CLOSE-UP AT
### Toyota www.facebook.com/toyota

Imagine you're in the market for a new car and need to learn about the various models, options, dealers, and other factors involved in this important purchase. Fortunately, a friend has just gone through this process and can provide valuable information from a consumer's perspective.

Now imagine that you have a hundred or a thousand or ten thousand friends who have recently purchased cars. Imagine how much information you could get from so many people—and all you need to do is jump on Facebook, Epinions, or another social media website.

Consumers have been sharing information online for as long as computers have been connected, but the rapid growth of social media has merged these isolated conversations into a global phenomenon that has permanently changed the nature of business communication. The Japanese automaker Toyota is one of the millions of companies around the world using social media

Toyota's user-generated content campaign, Auto-Biography, invited owners to submit stories, photos, and videos that describe their favorite moments and memories with their Toyota vehicles.

to supplement or even replace traditional forms of customer communication.

Toyota was looking for some positive communication after concerns about sticking gas pedals led to the recall of millions of vehicles and prompted the company to halt sales of eight models while it investigated the problem. The situation was potentially serious, to be sure, but Toyota executive Bob Zeinstra said loyal Toyota owners responded with an "outpouring of support and care."

To capitalize on this goodwill, built up through years of delivering safe, dependable vehicles, Toyota invited owners to tell their stories through a Facebook campaign it called "Auto-Biography." The program featured a customized Facebook application that encouraged owners to share stories of their favorite moments with their Toyota vehicles.

Thousands of Toyota owners contributed, sharing everything from the pet names they gave their cars to how they use their cars for work or play to the way their families passed down a Toyota from one generation to the next. Many listed the number of miles they had on their cars, some up to 300,000 or more, making strong statements to support the Toyota message of reliability. Many owners also personalized their stories with photos or videos of themselves and their cars. Toyota highlighted a small number of the stories through professionally produced animated or live videos, which it then featured prominently on the Auto-Biography page and used in print and television advertising.

By inviting satisfied customers to the tell their own stories through *user-generated content* (which you'll read more about in Chapter 8), the campaign helped Toyota repair its reputation among potential car buyers and respond to negative stories in the news media. Moreover, Zeinstra says the Facebook initiative also reminded current Toyota owners "why they love their cars so much."[1]

# Understanding Why Communication Matters

Whether it's as simple as a smile or as ambitious as a Facebook campaign, **communication** is the process of transferring information and meaning between *senders* and *receivers*, using one or more written, oral, visual, or electronic media. The essence of communication is sharing—providing data, information, insights, and inspiration in an exchange that benefits both you and the people with whom you are communicating.[2] As Figure 1.1 on the next page indicates, this sharing can happen in a variety of ways, including simple and successful transfers of information, negotiations in which the sender and receiver arrive at an agreed-upon meaning, and unsuccessful attempts in which the receiver creates a different message than the one the sender intended.

You will invest a lot of time and energy in this course to develop your communication skills, so it's fair to ask whether the effort will be worthwhile. This section outlines the many ways in which good communication skills are critical for your career and for any company you join.

**1 LEARNING OBJECTIVE**
Explain the importance of effective communication to your career and to the companies where you will work.

Communication is the process of transferring information and meaning between senders and receivers.

## COMMUNICATION IS IMPORTANT TO YOUR CAREER

Improving your communication skills may be the single most important step you can take in your career. You can have the greatest ideas in the world, but they're no good to your company or your career if you can't express them clearly and persuasively. Some jobs, such as sales and customer support, are primarily about communicating. In fields such as engineering or finance, you often need to share complex ideas with executives, customers, and colleagues, and your ability to connect with people outside your field can be as important as your technical expertise. If you have the entrepreneurial urge, you will need to communicate with a wide range of audiences, from investors, bankers, and government regulators to employees, customers, and business partners.

As you take on leadership and management roles, communication becomes even more important. The higher you rise in an organization, the less time you will spend using the technical skills of your particular profession and the more time you will spend communicating. Top executives spend most of their time communicating, and businesspeople who can't communicate well don't stand much chance of reaching the top.

Employers sometimes express frustration at the poor communication skills of employees—particularly recent college graduates who haven't yet learned how to adapt their communication styles to a professional business environment. If you learn to write well, speak well,

Ambition and great ideas aren't enough; you need to be able to communicate with people in order to succeed in business.

Strong communication skills give you an advantage in the job market.

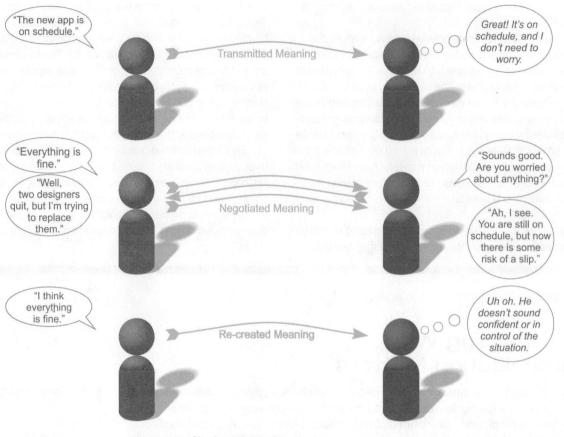

**Figure 1.1** **Sharing Information**
These three exchanges between a software project manager (left) and his boss (right) illustrate the variety of ways in which information is shared between senders and receivers. In the top exchange, the sender's meaning is transmitted intact to the receiver, who accepts what the sender says at face value. In the middle exchange, the sender and receiver negotiate the meaning by discussing the situation. The negotiated meaning is that everything is fine *so far*, but the risk of a schedule slip is now higher than it was before. In the bottom exchange, the receiver has a negative emotional reaction to the word "think" and as a result creates her own meaning—that everything probably *is not* fine, in spite of what the sender says.

listen well, and recognize the appropriate way to communicate in any situation, you'll gain a major advantage that will serve you throughout your career.[3]

This course teaches you how to send and receive information more effectively and helps you improve your communication skills through practice in an environment that provides honest, constructive criticism. You will discover how to collaborate in teams, listen effectively, master nonverbal communication, and participate in productive meetings. You'll learn about communicating across cultural boundaries. You'll learn a three-step process that will help you write effective business messages, and you'll get specific tips for crafting a variety of business messages using a wide range of media, from social networks to blogs to online presentations. Develop these skills, and you'll start your business career with a clear competitive advantage.

## COMMUNICATION IS IMPORTANT TO YOUR COMPANY

Aside from the personal benefits, communication should be important to you because it is important to your company. Effective communication helps businesses in numerous ways. It provides[4]

Effective communication yields numerous business benefits.

- Closer ties with important communities in the marketplace
- Opportunities to influence conversations, perceptions, and trends

- Increased productivity and faster problem solving
- Better financial results and higher return for investors
- Earlier warning of potential problems, from rising business costs to critical safety issues
- Stronger decision making based on timely, reliable information
- Clearer and more persuasive marketing messages
- Greater employee engagement with their work, leading to higher employee satisfaction and lower employee turnover

## WHAT MAKES BUSINESS COMMUNICATION EFFECTIVE?

Effective communication strengthens the connections between a company and all of its **stakeholders**, those groups affected in some way by the company's actions: customers, employees, shareholders, suppliers, neighbors, the community, the nation, and the world as a whole.[5] To make your communication efforts as effective as possible, focus on making them practical, factual, concise, clear, and persuasive:

- **Provide practical information.** Give recipients useful information, whether it's to help them perform a desired action or understand a new company policy.
- **Give facts rather than vague impressions.** Use concrete language, specific detail, and information that is clear, convincing, accurate, and ethical. Even when an opinion is called for, present compelling evidence to support your conclusion.
- **Present information in a concise, efficient manner.** Concise messages show respect for people's time, and they increase the chances of a positive response.
- **Clarify expectations and responsibilities.** Craft messages to generate a specific response from a specific audience. When appropriate, clearly state what you expect from audience members or what you can do for them.
- **Offer compelling, persuasive arguments and recommendations.** Show your readers precisely how they will benefit by responding the way you want them to respond to your message.

*Effective messages are practical, factual, concise, clear, and persuasive.*

Keep these five important characteristics in mind as you compare the ineffective and effective versions of the message in Figure 1.2 on the next page.

# Communicating as a Professional

You've been communicating your entire life, of course, but if you don't have a lot of work experience yet, meeting the expectations of a professional environment might require some adjustment. A good place to start is to consider what it means to be a professional. **Professionalism** is the quality of performing at a high level and conducting oneself with purpose and pride. It means doing more than putting in the hours and collecting a paycheck: True professionals go beyond minimum expectations and commit to making meaningful contributions. Professionalism can be broken down into six distinct traits: striving to excel, being dependable and accountable, being a team player, demonstrating a sense of etiquette, making ethical decisions, and maintaining a positive outlook (see Table 1.1 on page 7).

**2 LEARNING OBJECTIVE**
Explain what it means to communicate as a professional in a business context.

A key message to glean from Table 1.1 is how much these elements of professionalism depend on effective communication. For example, to be a team player, you have to be able to collaborate, resolve conflicts, and interact with a wide variety of personalities. Without strong communication skills, you won't be able to perform to your potential—and others won't recognize you as the professional you'd like to be.

Communication is an essential part of being a successful professional.

This section offers a brief look at the skills employers will expect you to have, the nature of communication in an organizational environment, and the importance of adopting an audience-centered approach.

**Subject:** social media strategy

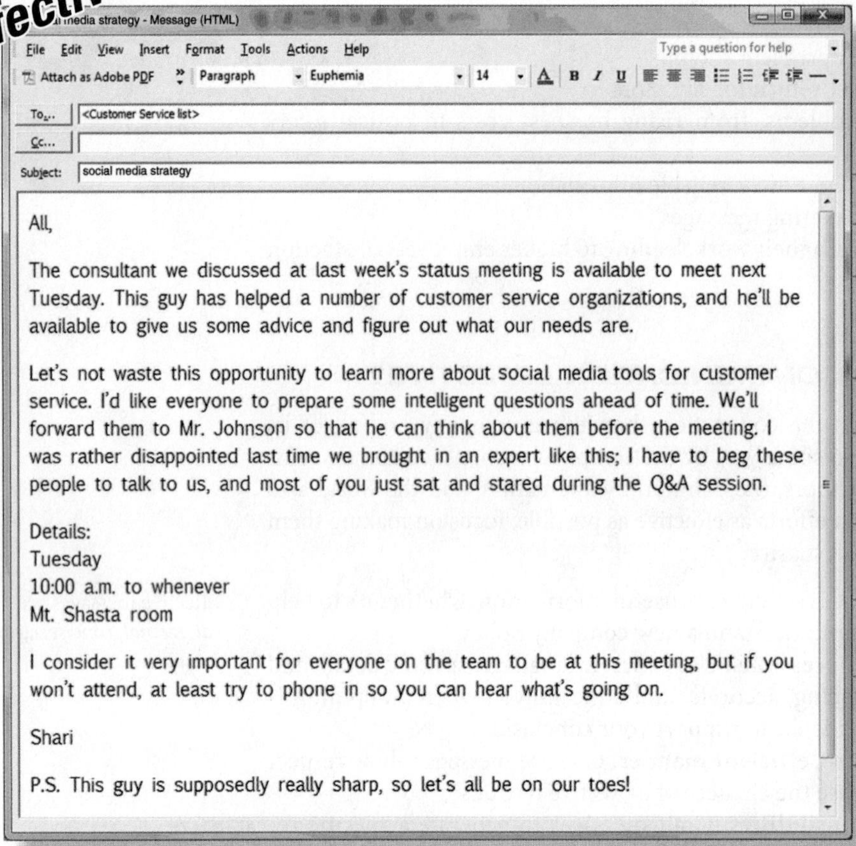

All,

The consultant we discussed at last week's status meeting is available to meet next Tuesday. This guy has helped a number of customer service organizations, and he'll be available to give us some advice and figure out what our needs are.

Let's not waste this opportunity to learn more about social media tools for customer service. I'd like everyone to prepare some intelligent questions ahead of time. We'll forward them to Mr. Johnson so that he can think about them before the meeting. I was rather disappointed last time we brought in an expert like this; I have to beg these people to talk to us, and most of you just sat and stared during the Q&A session.

Details:
Tuesday
10:00 a.m. to whenever
Mt. Shasta room

I consider it very important for everyone on the team to be at this meeting, but if you won't attend, at least try to phone in so you can hear what's going on.

Shari

P.S. This guy is supposedly really sharp, so let's all be on our toes!

- The vague subject line fails to alert people to the upcoming meeting.
- The greeting is cold and off-putting.
- The opening paragraph fails to provide necessary background information for anyone who missed the meeting.
- A negative, accusatory tone here puts readers on the defensive.
- This request for action fails to clarify who needs to do what by when.
- The meeting information includes the day, not the date, which could lead to confusion.
- The wording here assumes that people who won't attend don't want to, which might not be true.
- The lack of a closing (such as "thank you") contributes to the harsh, abrupt tone.
- The writer fails to provide alternative contact information or invite questions about the meeting.

**Subject:** social media strategy meeting, Tues. 10 a.m.–2 p.m.

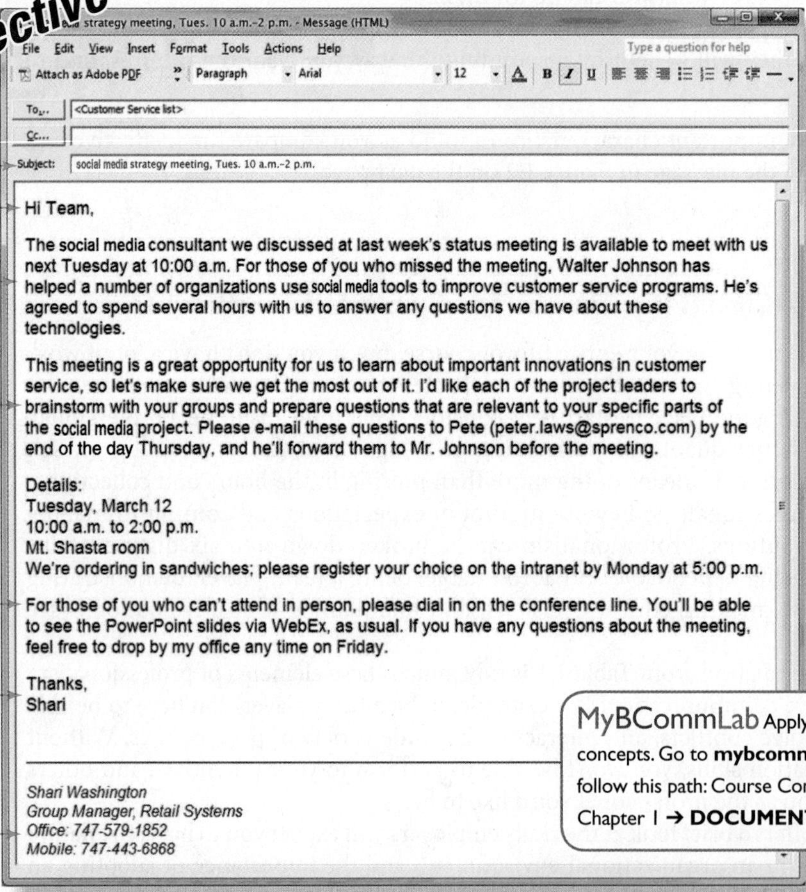

Hi Team,

The social media consultant we discussed at last week's status meeting is available to meet with us next Tuesday at 10:00 a.m. For those of you who missed the meeting, Walter Johnson has helped a number of organizations use social media tools to improve customer service programs. He's agreed to spend several hours with us to answer any questions we have about these technologies.

This meeting is a great opportunity for us to learn about important innovations in customer service, so let's make sure we get the most out of it. I'd like each of the project leaders to brainstorm with your groups and prepare questions that are relevant to your specific parts of the social media project. Please e-mail these questions to Pete (peter.laws@sprenco.com) by the end of the day Thursday, and he'll forward them to Mr. Johnson before the meeting.

Details:
Tuesday, March 12
10:00 a.m. to 2:00 p.m.
Mt. Shasta room
We're ordering in sandwiches; please register your choice on the intranet by Monday at 5:00 p.m.

For those of you who can't attend in person, please dial in on the conference line. You'll be able to see the PowerPoint slides via WebEx, as usual. If you have any questions about the meeting, feel free to drop by my office any time on Friday.

Thanks,
Shari

Shari Washington
Group Manager, Retail Systems
Office: 747-579-1852
Mobile: 747-443-6868

- An informative subject line helps people grasp key content immediately.
- The greeting is friendly without being too casual.
- The opening paragraph fills in missing information so that everyone can grasp the importance of the message.
- This paragraph emphasizes the importance of the meeting, and the request provides enough information to enable readers to respond.
- The writer offers everyone a chance to participate, without making anyone feel guilty about not being able to attend in person. (*WebEx* is an online meeting system.) The closing paragraph also invites questions ahead of time so that they don't derail the meeting.
- Like the greeting, the close has a warm and personal tone, without being too casual.
- The *email signature* provides additional information and alternative contact options.

MyBCommLab Apply Figure 1.2's key concepts. Go to **mybcommlab.com** and follow this path: Course Content → Chapter 1 → **DOCUMENT MAKEOVERS**

**Figure 1.2  Ineffective and Effective Business Communication**
At first glance, this email message looks like a reasonable attempt at communicating with the members of a project team. However, review the blue annotations to see just how many problems the message really has.
*Source:* Used by permission of Microsoft.

| TABLE 1.1 | Elements of Professionalism |
|---|---|

| Trait | What It Means |
|---|---|
| Be the best | • Pros strive to excel, to be the best they can be at everything they do.<br>• Excelling at every level is how pros build a great career. |
| Be dependable | • Pros keep their promises and meet their commitments.<br>• Pros learn from their mistakes and take responsibility for their errors. |
| Be a team player | • Pros know how to contribute to a larger cause.<br>• Team players make others around them better. |
| Be respectful | • Pros know that good business etiquette is a sign of respect for those around them.<br>• Respecting others is not only good etiquette, it's good for one's career. |
| Be ethical | • Responsible professionals strive to avoid ethical lapses.<br>• Pros weigh their options carefully when facing ethical dilemmas. |
| Be positive | • Successful people believe in what they're doing and in themselves.<br>• Pros don't complain about problems; they find them and fix them. |

## UNDERSTANDING WHAT EMPLOYERS EXPECT FROM YOU

Today's employers expect you to be competent at a wide range of communication tasks. Fortunately, the skills employers expect from you are the same skills that will help you advance in your career:[6]

- Organizing ideas and information logically and completely
- Expressing ideas and information coherently and persuasively
- Actively listening to others
- Communicating effectively with people from diverse backgrounds and experiences
- Using communication technologies effectively and efficiently
- Following accepted standards of grammar, spelling, and other aspects of high-quality writing and speaking
- Communicating in a civilized manner that reflects contemporary expectations of business etiquette, even when dealing with indifferent or hostile audiences
- Communicating ethically, even when choices aren't crystal clear
- Managing your time wisely and using resources efficiently

*Employers expect you to possess a wide range of communication skills.*

You'll have the opportunity to practice these skills throughout this course—but don't stop there. Successful professionals continue to hone communication skills throughout their careers.

---

### THE ART OF PROFESSIONALISM

## Maintaining a Confident, Positive Outlook

Spend a few minutes around successful people in any field, and chances are you'll notice how optimistic they are. They believe in what they're doing, and they believe in themselves and their ability to solve problems and overcome obstacles.

Being positive doesn't mean displaying mindless optimism or spewing happy talk all the time. It means acknowledging that things may be difficult but then buckling down and getting the job done anyway. It means no whining and no slacking off, even when the going gets tough. We live in an imperfect world, no question—jobs can be boring or difficult, customers can be unpleasant, and bosses can be unreasonable. But when you're a pro, you find a way to power through.

Your energy, positive or negative, is also contagious. Both in person and online, you'll spend as much time with your colleagues as you spend with family and friends. Personal demeanor is therefore a vital element of workplace harmony. No one expects (or wants) you to be artificially upbeat and bubbly every second of the day, but one negative personality can make an entire office miserable and unproductive. Every person in a company has a responsibility to contribute to a positive, energetic work environment.

### CAREER APPLICATIONS
1. Do you have an ethical obligation to maintain a positive outlook on the job? Why or why not?
2. How can you lift your spirits when work is dragging you down?

## COMMUNICATING IN AN ORGANIZATIONAL CONTEXT

The formal communication network mirrors the company's organizational structure.

In addition to having the proper skills, you need to learn how to apply those skills in the business environment, which can be quite different from the social and scholastic environments you are accustomed to. Every organization has a **formal communication network**, in which ideas and information flow along the lines of command (the hierarchical levels) in the company's organization structure (see Figure 1.3). Throughout the formal network, information flows in three directions. *Downward communication* flows from executives to employees, conveying executive decisions and providing information that helps employees do their jobs. *Upward communication* flows from employees to executives, providing insight into problems, trends, opportunities, grievances, and performance, thus allowing executives to solve problems and make intelligent decisions. *Horizontal communication* flows between departments to help employees share information, coordinate tasks, and solve complex problems.[7]

Every organization also has an **informal communication network**, often referred to as the *grapevine* or the *rumor mill*, which encompasses all communication that occurs outside the formal network. Some of this informal communication takes place naturally as a result of employee interaction on the job and in social settings, and some of it takes place when the formal network doesn't provide information that employees want. In fact, the inherent limitations of formal communication networks helped spur the growth of social media in the business environment.

## ADOPTING AN AUDIENCE-CENTERED APPROACH

An audience-centered approach involves understanding, respecting, and meeting the needs of your audience members.

An **audience-centered approach** involves understanding and respecting the members of your audience and making every effort to get your message across in a way that is meaningful to them. This approach is also known as adopting the **"you" attitude**, in contrast to messages that are about "me." Learn as much as possible about the biases, education, age, status, style, and personal and professional concerns of your receivers. If you're addressing people you don't know and you're unable to find out more about them, try to project yourself into their position by using common sense and imagination. This ability to relate to the needs of others is a key part of *emotional intelligence*, which is widely considered to be a vital characteristic of

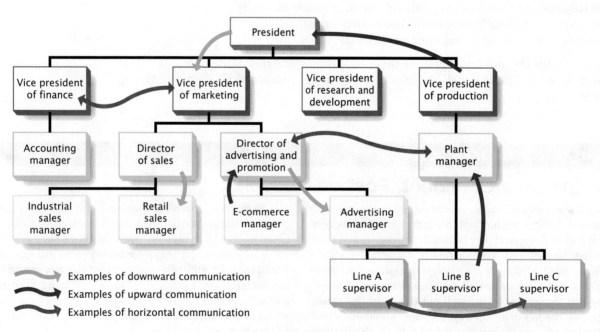

**Figure 1.3** **Formal Communication Network**
The formal communication network is defined by the relationships between the various job positions in the organization. Messages can flow *upward* (from a lower-level employee to a higher-level employee), *downward* (from a higher-level employee to a lower-level employee), and *horizontally* (across the organization, between employees at the same or similar levels).

successful managers and leaders.[8] The more you know about the people you're communicating with, the easier it will be to concentrate on their needs—which, in turn, will make it easier for them to hear your message, understand it, and respond positively.

A vital element of audience-centered communication is **etiquette**, the expected norms of behavior in any particular situation. In today's hectic, competitive world, etiquette might seem a quaint and outdated notion. However, the way you conduct yourself and interact with others can have a profound influence on your company's success and your career. When executives hire and promote you, they expect your behavior to protect the company's reputation. The more you understand such expectations, the better chance you have of avoiding career-damaging mistakes. The principles of etiquette discussed in Chapter 2 will help you communicate with an audience-centered approach in a variety of business settings.

> Etiquette, the expected norms of behavior in any particular situation, can have a profound influence on your company's success and your career.

# Understanding the Unique Challenges of Business Communication

Although you have been communicating with some success your entire life, business communication is often more complicated and demanding than the social communication you typically engage in with family, friends, and school associates. This section highlights five issues that illustrate why business communication requires a high level of skill and attention.

> **3 LEARNING OBJECTIVE**
> Identify five unique challenges of business communication.

## THE GLOBALIZATION OF BUSINESS AND THE INCREASE IN WORKFORCE DIVERSITY

Today's businesses increasingly reach across international borders to market their products, partner with other businesses, and employ workers and executives—an effort known as **globalization**. Many U.S. companies rely on exports for a significant portion of their sales, sometimes up to 50 percent or more, and managers and employees in these firms need to communicate with many other cultures. Moreover, thousands of companies from all around the world vie for a share of the massive U.S. market, so chances are you'll do business with or even work for a company based in another country at some point in your career.

> Smart employers recognize the benefits of a more diverse workforce—and the additional challenges of ensuring smooth communication between people from diverse backgrounds.

Businesses are paying more attention to **workforce diversity**—all the differences among people who work together, including differences in age, gender, sexual orientation, education, cultural background, religion, ability, and life experience. As Chapter 3 discusses, successful companies realize that a diverse workforce can yield a significant competitive advantage, but it also requires a more conscientious approach to communication.

## THE INCREASING VALUE OF BUSINESS INFORMATION

As global competition for talent, customers, and resources continues to grow, the importance of information continues to escalate as well. Companies in virtually every industry rely heavily on **knowledge workers**, employees at all levels of an organization who specialize in acquiring, processing, and communicating information. Three examples help to illustrate the value of information in today's economy:

> Information has become one of the most important resources in business today.

- **Competitive insights.** The more a company knows about its competitors and their plans, the better able it will be to adjust its own business plans.
- **Customer needs.** Information about customer needs can be analyzed and summarized in order to develop goods and services that better satisfy customer demands.
- **Regulations and guidelines.** Today's businesses must understand and follow a wide range of government regulations and guidelines covering such areas as employment, environment, taxes, and accounting.

No matter what the specific type of information, the better you are able to understand it, use it, and communicate it to others, the more competitive you and your company will be.

## THE PERVASIVENESS OF TECHNOLOGY

Business communication today is heavily dependent on a growing array of technologies.

Technology influences virtually every aspect of business communication today. To benefit from technological tools, however, you need to have at least a basic level of skills. If your level of technical expertise doesn't keep up with that of your colleagues and coworkers, the imbalance can put you at a disadvantage and complicate the communication process. Throughout this course, you'll gain insights into using numerous tools and systems more effectively.

## THE EVOLUTION OF ORGANIZATIONAL STRUCTURES AND LEADERSHIP STYLES

Organizations with tall structures may unintentionally restrict the flow of information; flatter structures can make it easier to communicate effectively.

Every firm has a particular structure that defines the relationships among units in the company, and these relationships influence the nature and quality of communication throughout the organization. *Tall structures* have many layers of management between the lowest and highest positions, and they can suffer communication breakdowns and delays as messages are passed up and down through multiple layers.[9] To overcome such problems, many businesses have adopted *flat structures* that reduce the number of layers and promote more open and direct communication. However, with fewer formal lines of control and communication in these organizations, individual employees are expected to assume more responsibility for communication.

Unconventional organization structures such as matrixes and networks present special communication challenges.

Specific types of organization structures present unique communication challenges. In a *matrix structure*, for example, employees report to two managers at the same time, such as a project manager and a department manager. The need to coordinate workloads, schedules, and other matters increases the communication burden on everyone involved. In a *network structure*, sometimes known as a *virtual organization*, a company supplements the talents of its employees with services from one or more external partners, such as a design lab, a manufacturing firm, or a sales and distribution company.

Open corporate cultures benefit from free-flowing information and employee input.

Regardless of the particular structure a company uses, communication efforts will also be influenced by the organization's **corporate culture**: the combination of values, traditions, and habits that gives a company its atmosphere and personality. Many successful companies encourage employee contributions by fostering an *open climate* that promotes candor and honesty, helping employees feel free enough to admit their mistakes, disagree with the boss, and share negative or unwelcome information.

## A HEAVY RELIANCE ON TEAMWORK

Working in a team makes you even more responsible for communicating effectively.

Both traditional and innovative company structures can rely heavily on teamwork, and you will probably find yourself on dozens of teams throughout your career. Teams are commonly used in business today, but they're not always successful—and a key reason that teams fail to meet their objectives is poor communication. Chapter 2 offers insights into the complex dynamics of team communication and identifies skills you need in order to be an effective communicator in group settings.

# Exploring the Communication Process

**4 LEARNING OBJECTIVE** Describe the communication process model and the ways social media are changing the nature of business communication.

Even with the best intentions, communication efforts can fail. Messages can get lost or simply ignored. The receiver of a message can interpret it in ways the sender never imagined. In fact, two people receiving the same information can reach different conclusions about what it means.

Viewing communication as a process helps you identify steps you can take to improve your success as a communicator.

Fortunately, by understanding communication as a process with distinct steps, you can improve the odds that your messages will reach their intended audiences and produce their intended effects. This section explores the communication process in two stages: first by following a message from one sender to one receiver in the basic communication model and then by expanding on that approach with multiple messages and participants in the social communication model.

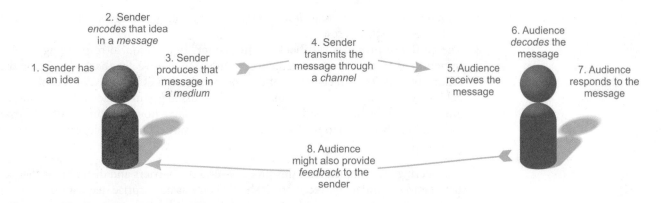

**Figure 1.4   The Basic Communication Process**
This eight-step model is a simplified view of how communication works in real life, but understanding this basic model is vital to improving your communication skills.

## THE BASIC COMMUNICATION MODEL

By viewing communication as a process (Figure 1.4), you can identify and improve the skills you need to be more successful. Many variations on this process model exist, but these eight steps provide a practical overview:

1. **The sender has an idea.** Whether a communication effort will ultimately be effective starts right here and depends on the nature of the idea and the motivation for sending it. For example, if your motivation is to offer a solution to a problem, you have a better chance of crafting a meaningful message than if your motivation is merely to complain about a problem.
2. **The sender encodes the idea as a message.** When someone puts an idea into a **message**—which you can think of as the "container" for an idea—he or she is **encoding** it, or expressing it in words or images. Much of the focus of this course is on developing the skills needed to successfully encode your ideas into effective messages.
3. **The sender produces the message in a transmittable medium.** With the appropriate message to express an idea, the sender now needs a **communication medium** to present that message to the intended audience. To update your boss on the status of a project, for instance, you might have a dozen or more media choices, from a phone call to an instant message to a slideshow presentation.
4. **The sender transmits the message through a channel.** Just as technology continues to increase the number of media options at your disposal, it continues to provide new **communication channels** you can use to transmit your messages. The distinction between medium and channel can get a bit murky, but think of the medium as the *form* a message takes (such as a Twitter update) and the channel as the system used to *deliver* the message (such as the Internet).
5. **The audience receives the message.** If the channel functions properly, the message reaches its intended audience. However, mere arrival at the destination is no guarantee that the message will be noticed or understood correctly. As "How Audiences Receive Messages" (page 13) explains, many messages are either ignored or misinterpreted as noise.
6. **The audience decodes the message.** After a message is received, the receiver needs to extract the idea from the message, a step known as **decoding**. "How Audiences Decode Messages" (page 13) takes a closer look at this complex and subtle step in the process.
7. **The audience responds to the message.** By crafting messages in ways that show the benefits of responding, senders can increase the chances that recipients will respond in positive ways. However, as "How Audiences Respond to Messages" (page 14) points out, whether a receiver responds as the sender hopes depends on the receiver

The medium is the *form* a message takes and the channel is the system used to *deliver* the message.

(a) *remembering* the message long enough to act on it, (b) being *able* to act on it, and (c) being *motivated* to respond.

8. **The audience provides feedback to the sender.** In addition to responding (or not responding) to the message, audience members may give **feedback** that helps the sender evaluate the effectiveness of the communication effort. Feedback can be verbal (using written or spoken words), nonverbal (using gestures, facial expressions, or other signals), or both. Just like the original message, however, this feedback from the receiver also needs to be decoded carefully. A smile, for example, can have many meanings.

Considering the complexity of this process—and the barriers and distractions that often stand between sender and receiver—it should come as no surprise that communication efforts often fail to achieve the sender's objective. Fortunately, the better you understand the process, the more successful you'll be.

The following sections take a closer look at two important aspects of the process: environmental barriers that can block or distort messages and the steps audiences take to receive, decode, and respond to messages.

### Barriers in the Communication Environment

Within any communication environment, messages can be disrupted by a variety of **communication barriers**. These barriers include noise and distractions, competing messages, filters, and channel breakdowns:

*A number of barriers can block or distort messages before they reach the intended audience.*

- **Noise and distractions.** External distractions range from uncomfortable meeting rooms to computer screens cluttered with instant messages and reminders popping up all over the place. Internal distractions are thoughts and emotions that prevent audiences from focusing on incoming messages. The common habit of *multitasking*, attempting more than one task at a time, is practically guaranteed to create communication distractions. Moreover, research suggests that "chronic multitasking" can reduce productivity and increase errors.[10]
- **Competing messages.** Having your audience's undivided attention is a rare luxury. In most cases, you must compete with other messages that are trying to reach your audience at the same time, which is why it is so essential to craft messages your audience will care about.
- **Filters.** Messages can be blocked or distorted by *filters*, any human or technological interventions between the sender and the receiver. Filtering can be both intentional (such as automatically filing incoming messages based on sender or content) or unintentional (such as an overly aggressive spam filter that deletes legitimate emails). As mentioned earlier, the structure and culture of an organization can also inhibit the flow of vital messages. And, in some cases, the people or companies you rely on to deliver your message can distort it or filter it to meet their own needs.
- **Channel breakdowns.** Sometimes the channel simply breaks down and fails to deliver your message at all. A colleague you were counting on to deliver a message to your boss might have forgotten to do so, or a computer server might have crashed and prevented your blog from updating.

*Minimizing barriers and distractions in the communication environment is everyone's responsibility.*

Everyone in an organization can help minimize barriers and distractions. As a communicator, try to be aware of any barriers that could prevent your messages from reaching their intended audiences. As a manager, keep an eye out for any organizational barriers that could be inhibiting the flow of information. In any situation, a small dose of common sense and courtesy goes a long way. Turn off that mobile phone before you step into a meeting. Don't talk across the tops of other people's cubicles. Be sensitive to personal differences, too; for instance, some people enjoy working with music on, but music is a huge distraction for others.[11]

Finally, take steps to insulate yourself from distractions. Don't let messages interrupt you every minute of the day. Instead, set aside time to attend to messages all at once so that you can focus the rest of the time.

## Inside the Mind of Your Audience

After a message works its way through the communication channel and reaches the intended audience, it encounters a whole new set of challenges. Understanding how audiences receive, decode, and respond to messages will help you create more effective messages.

**How Audiences Receive Messages**   For an audience member to receive a message, three events need to occur: The receiver has to *sense* the presence of a message, *select* it from all the other messages clamoring for attention, and *perceive* it as an actual message (as opposed to random, pointless noise).[12] You can appreciate the magnitude of this challenge by driving down any busy street in a commercial section of town. You'll encounter hundreds of messages—billboards, posters, store window displays, car stereos, pedestrians waving or talking on mobile phones, car horns, street signs, traffic lights, and so on. However, you'll sense, select, and perceive only a small fraction of these messages.

To actually receive a message, audience members need to sense it, select it, then perceive it as a message.

Today's business audiences are much like drivers on busy streets. They are inundated with so many messages and so much noise that they can miss or ignore many of the messages intended for them. Through this course, you will learn a variety of techniques to craft messages that get noticed. In general, follow these five principles to increase your chances of success:

- **Consider audience expectations.** Deliver messages using the media and channels that the audience expects. If colleagues expect meeting notices to be delivered by email, don't suddenly switch gears and start delivering the notices via blog postings without telling anyone. Of course, sometimes going *against* expectations can stimulate audience attention, which is why advertisers sometimes do wacky and creative things to get noticed. However, for most business communication efforts, following the expectations of your audience is the most efficient way to get your message across.
- **Ensure ease of use.** Even if audiences are actively looking for your messages, they probably won't see the messages if you make them hard to find, hard to navigate, or hard to read.
- **Emphasize familiarity.** Use words, images, and designs that are familiar to your audience. For example, most visitors to company websites expect to see information about the company on a page called "About" or "About Us."
- **Practice empathy.** Make sure your messages speak to the audience by clearly addressing *their* wants and needs—not yours. People are inclined to notice messages that relate to their individual concerns.[13]
- **Design for compatibility.** For the many messages delivered electronically these days, be sure to verify technological compatibility with your audience. For instance, if your website requires visitors to have a particular video capability in their browsers, you won't reach those audience members who don't have that software installed or updated.

To improve the odds that your messages will be successfully perceived by your audience, pay close attention to expectations, ease of use, familiarity, empathy, and technical compatibility.

**How Audiences Decode Messages**   A received message doesn't "mean" anything until the recipient decodes it and assigns meaning to it, and there is no guarantee the receiver will assign the same meaning the sender intended. Even well-crafted, well-intentioned communication efforts can fail at this stage, because assigning meaning through decoding is a highly personal process that is influenced by culture, individual experience, learning and thinking styles, hopes, fears, and even temporary moods. Moreover, audiences tend to extract the meaning they expect to get from a message, even if it's the opposite of what the sender intended.[14] In fact, rather than "extract" your meaning, it's more accurate to say that your audience members re-create their own meaning—or meanings—from the message.

Decoding is a complex process; receivers often extract different meanings from messages than the meanings senders intended.

Cultural and personal beliefs and biases influence the meaning audiences get from messages. For instance, the human brain organizes incoming sensations into a mental "map" that represents the person's individual **perception** of reality. If an incoming detail doesn't fit into that perception, a message recipient may simply distort the information to make it fit rather than rearrange his or her mental map—a phenomenon known as **selective perception**.[15] For example, an executive who has staked her reputation on a particular business strategy might distort or ignore evidence that suggests the strategy is failing.

Selective perception occurs when people ignore or distort incoming information to fit their preconceived notions of reality.

Differences in language and usage also influence received meaning. If you ask an employee to send you a report on sales figures "as soon as possible," does that mean within

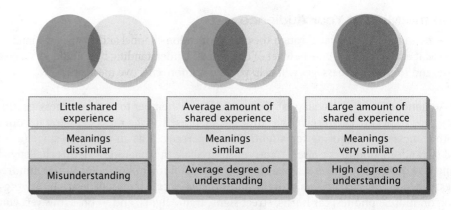

**Figure 1.5   How Shared Experience Affects Understanding**
The more two people or two groups of people share experiences—personal, professional, and cultural—the more likely it is that receivers will extract the intended meanings senders encode into the messages.

10 seconds, 10 minutes, or 10 days? By clarifying expectations and resolving potential ambiguities in your messages, you can minimize such uncertainties. In general, the more experiences you share with another person, the more likely you are to share perception and thus share meaning (see Figure 1.5).

Individual thinking styles are another important factor in message decoding. For example, someone who places a high value on objective analysis and clear logic might interpret a message differently than someone who values emotion or intuition (reaching conclusions without using rational processes).

**How Audiences Respond to Messages**   Your message has been delivered, received, and correctly decoded. Now what? Will audience members respond in the way you'd like them to? Only if three events occur.

First, the recipient has to *remember* the message long enough to act on it. Simplifying greatly, memory works in several stages: *Sensory memory* momentarily captures incoming data from the senses; then, whatever the recipient pays attention to is transferred to *short-term memory*. Information in short-term memory will quickly disappear if it isn't transferred to *long-term memory*, which can be done either actively (such as when a person memorizes a list of items) or passively (such as when a new piece of information connects with something else the recipient already has stored in long-term memory). Finally, the information needs to be *retrieved* when the recipient wants to act on it.[16] In general, people find it easier to remember and retrieve information that is important to them personally or professionally. Consequently, by communicating in ways that are sensitive to your audience's wants and needs, you greatly increase the chance that your messages will be remembered and retrieved.

Second, the recipient has to be *able* to respond as you wish. Obviously, if recipients simply cannot do what you want them to do, they will not respond according to your plan. By understanding your audience (you'll learn more about audience analysis in Chapter 4), you can work to minimize these unsuccessful outcomes.

Third, the recipient has to be *motivated* to respond. You'll encounter many situations in which your audience has the option of responding but isn't required to. For instance, a record company may or may not offer your band a contract, or your boss may or may not respond to your request for a raise. Throughout this course, you'll learn techniques for crafting messages that can help motivate readers to respond.

## THE SOCIAL COMMUNICATION MODEL

The basic model presented in Figure 1.4 illustrates how a single idea moves from one sender to one receiver. In a larger sense, it also helps represent the traditional nature of much business communication, which was primarily defined by a *publishing* or *broadcasting* mindset. Externally, a company issued carefully scripted messages to a mass audience that often had few

Audiences will likely respond to a message if they remember it, if they're able to respond, and if they're properly motivated to respond.

By explaining how audiences will benefit by responding positively to your messages, you'll increase their motivation to respond.

The social communication model is interactive, conversational, and usually open to all who wish to participate.

options for responding to those messages or initiating messages of their own. Customers and other interested parties had few ways to connect with one another to ask questions, share information, or offer support. Internally, communication tended to follow the same "we talk, you listen" model, with upper managers issuing directives to lower-level supervisors and employees.

However, in recent years, a variety of technologies have enabled and inspired a new approach to business communication. In contrast to the publishing mindset, this **social communication model** is interactive, conversational, and usually open to all who wish to participate. Audience members are no longer passive recipients of messages but active participants in a conversation. Social media have given customers and other stakeholders a voice they did not have in the past. And businesses are listening to that voice. In fact, one of the most common uses of social media among U.S. businesses is monitoring online discussions about a company and its brands.[17]

Instead of transmitting a fixed message, a sender in a social media environment initiates a conversation by sharing valuable information. This information is often revised and reshaped by the web of participants as they share it and comment on it. People can add to it or take pieces from it, depending on their needs and interests.

Just as the term Web 2.0 has been applied to the second generation of World Wide Web technologies (blogs, wikis, and other social media tools), Business Communication 2.0 is a convenient label for this approach to business communication. Figure 1.6 lists some of the deep and profound differences between traditional and social models of business communication.

The social communication model offers many advantages, but it has a number of disadvantages as well. Potential problems include information overload, fragmented attention, information security risks, distractions that hurt productivity, the need to monitor and respond to numerous conversational threads, and blurring of the line between personal and professional lives, which can make it difficult for people to disconnect from work.[18]

Of course, no company, no matter how enthusiastically it embraces the social communication model, is going to be run as a club in which everyone has a say in every business matter. Instead, a hybrid approach is emerging in which

The conversational and interactive *social communication model* is revolutionizing business communication.

The "Business Communication 2.0" approach can increase the speed of communication, lower costs improve access to expertise, and boost employee satisfaction.

For all their advantages, social media tools also present a number of communication challenges.

**REAL-TIME UPDATES**

LEARN MORE BY READING THIS INFOGRAPHIC

**See how small businesses are using social media**

Small businesses are some of the most enthusiastic adopters of new media tools. Go to http://real-timeupdates.com/bct12 and click on Learn More. If you are using MyBCommLab, you can access Real-Time Updates within each chapter or under Student Study Tools.

| **Business Communication 1.0** <br> **"We Talk, You Listen"** | **Business Communication 2.0** <br> **"Let's Have a Conversation"** |
|:---:|:---:|
| **Tendencies** | **Tendencies** |
| Publication, broadcast | Conversation |
| Lecture | Discussion |
| Intrusion | Permission |
| Unidirectional | Bidirectional, multidirectional |
| One to many | One to one, many to many |
| Control | Influence |
| Low message frequency | High message frequency |
| Few channels | Many channels |
| Information hoarding | Information sharing |
| Static | Dynamic |
| Hierarchical | Egalitarian |
| Structured | Amorphous |
| Isolated | Collaborative |
| Planned | Reactive |
| Resistive | Responsive |

**Figure 1.6   Business Communication: 1.0 Versus 2.0**
Business Communication 2.0 differs from conventional communication strategies and practices in a number of significant ways. You're probably already an accomplished user of many new-media tools, and this experience will help you on the job.

some communications (such as strategic plans and policy documents) follow the traditional approach, while others (such as project management updates and customer support messages) follow the social model.

You can learn more about business uses of social media in Chapter 8.

# Using Technology to Improve Business Communication

**5** **LEARNING OBJECTIVE**
List four general guidelines for using communication technology effectively.

Today's businesses rely heavily on technology to enhance communication. In fact, many of the technologies you might use in your personal life, from microblogs to video games, are also used in business. You will find technology discussed extensively throughout this book, with specific advice on using both common and emerging tools. The four-page photo essay "Powerful Tools for Communicating Efficiently" (see pages 18–21) provides an overview of the technologies that connect people in offices, factories, and other business settings.

However, anyone who has used advanced technology knows the benefits are not automatic. Poorly designed or inappropriately used technology can hinder communication more than help. To communicate effectively, learn to keep technology in perspective, guard against information overload and information addiction, use technological tools productively, and disengage from the computer frequently to communicate in person.

## KEEPING TECHNOLOGY IN PERSPECTIVE

Don't rely too much on technology or let it overwhelm the communication process.

Perhaps the single most important point to remember about technology is that it is simply a tool, a means by which you can accomplish certain tasks. Technology is an aid to interpersonal communication, not a replacement for it. Technology can't think for you or communicate for you, and if you lack some essential skills, technology can't fill in the gaps.

## GUARDING AGAINST INFORMATION OVERLOAD

Information overload results when people receive more information than they can effectively process.

The overuse or misuse of communication technology can lead to **information overload**, in which people receive more information than they can effectively process (see Figure 1.7). Information overload makes it difficult to discriminate between useful and useless information, lowers productivity, and amplifies employee stress both on the job and at home—even to the point of causing health and relationship problems.[19]

You often have some level of control over the number and types of messages you choose to receive. Use the filtering features of your communication systems to isolate high-priority messages that deserve your attention. Also, be wary of subscribing to too many Twitter streams and other sources. Focus on the information you truly need in order to do your job.

As a sender, you can help reduce information overload by making sure you don't send unnecessary messages. In addition, when you send messages that aren't urgent or crucial, let people know so they can prioritize. Also, most

**Figure 1.7** Message overload, whether on the street or on the screen, is a constant challenge in contemporary life. Your business messages must compete with many others clamoring for the audience's attention.

Exactostock/Superstock

communication systems let you mark messages as urgent; however, use this feature only when it is truly needed. Its overuse leads to annoyance and anxiety, not action.

*An important step in reducing information overload is to avoid sending unnecessary messages.*

## USING TECHNOLOGICAL TOOLS PRODUCTIVELY

Facebook, Twitter, YouTube, IM, and other technologies are key parts of what has been called the "information technology paradox," in which information tools can waste as much time as they save. Concerns over inappropriate use of social networking sites, for example, have led many companies to ban employees from accessing them during work hours.[20]

Inappropriate web use not only distracts employees from work responsibilities but can leave employers open to lawsuits for sexual harassment if inappropriate images are displayed in or transmitted around the company.[21] Social media have created another set of managerial challenges, given the risk that employee blogs or social networking pages can expose confidential information or damage a firm's reputation in the marketplace. With all these technologies, the best solution lies in developing clear policies that are enforced evenly for all employees.[22]

Managers need to guide their employees in productive use of information tools because the speed and simplicity of these tools is also one of their greatest weaknesses. The flood of messages from an expanding array of electronic sources can significantly affect employees' ability to focus on their work. In one study, workers exposed to a constant barrage of email, IM, and phone calls experienced an average 10-point drop in their functioning intelligence quotient (IQ).[23]

In addition to using your tools appropriately, knowing how to use them efficiently can make a big difference in your productivity. You don't have to become an expert in most cases, but you need to be familiar with the basic features and functions of the tools you are expected to use on the job. As a manager, you also need to ensure that your employees have sufficient training to productively use the tools you expect them to use.

*Communicating in today's business environment requires at least a basic level of technical competence.*

## RECONNECTING WITH PEOPLE

Even the best technologies can hinder communication if they are overused. For instance, a common complaint among employees is that managers rely too heavily on email and don't communicate face-to-face often enough.[24] Speaking with people over the phone or in person can take more time and effort and can sometimes force you to confront unpleasant situations directly, but it is often essential for solving tough problems and maintaining productive relationships.[25]

Moreover, even the best communication technologies can't show people who you really are. Remember to step out from behind the technology frequently to learn more about the people you work with—and to let them learn more about you.

*No matter how much technology is involved, communication is still about people connecting with people.*

> **REAL-TIME UPDATES**
> LEARN MORE BY READING THIS ARTICLE
> **Twelve reasons why talking can be better than texting**
> Professor Ellen Bremen offers a dozen reasons why she thinks talking promotes more effective communication than texting. Go to http://real-timeupdates.com/bct12 and click on Learn More. If you are using MyBCommLab, you can access Real-Time Updates within each chapter or under Student Study Tools.

# Committing to Ethical and Legal Communication

**Ethics** are the accepted principles of conduct that govern behavior within a society. Ethical behavior is a companywide concern, but because communication efforts are the public face of a company, they are subjected to particularly rigorous scrutiny from regulators, legislators, investors, consumer groups, environmental groups, labor organizations, and anyone else

**6 LEARNING OBJECTIVE** Define ethics, explain the difference between an ethical dilemma and an ethical lapse, and list six guidelines for making ethical communication choices.

(*continued on page 22*)

The tools of business communication evolve with every advance in digital technology. The 20 technologies highlighted on the next four pages help businesses redefine the office, collaborate and share information, connect with stakeholders, and build communities of people with shared interests and needs. For more examples of business uses of social media tools in particular, see pages 204–205 in Chapter 8.

## Web-Based Meetings

Andresr/Shutterstock

Web-based meetings allow team members from all over the world to interact in real time. Meetings can also be recorded for later playback and review. Various systems support instant messaging, video, collaborative editing tools, and more.

## Videoconferencing and Telepresence

.shock/Fotolia

Videoconferencing provides many of the benefits of in-person meetings at a fraction of the cost. Advanced systems feature *telepresence*, in which the video images of meeting participants are life-sized and extremely realistic.

### REDEFINING THE OFFICE

Thanks to advances in mobile and distributed communication, the "office" is no longer what it used to be. Technology lets today's professionals work on the move while staying in close contact with colleagues, customers, and suppliers. These technologies are also redefining the very nature of some companies, as they replace traditional hierarchies with highly adaptable, virtual networks.

## Mobile Business Apps

As the range of business software applications on smartphones and tablet computers continues to expand, almost anything that can be accomplished on a regular computer can be done on a mobile device (although not always as efficiently or with the same feature sets).

## Shared Online Workspaces

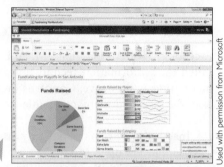

Used with permission from Microsoft

Online workspaces help teams work productively, even if they are on the move or spread out across the country. In addition to providing controlled access to shared files and other digital resources, some systems include such features as project management tools and real-time document sharing (letting two or more team members view and edit a document on screen at the same time).

## Voice Technologies

Marnie Burkhart/Alamy

*Speech recognition* (converting human speech to computer commands) and *speech synthesis* (converting computer commands to human speech) can enhance communication in many ways, including simplifying mobile computing, assisting workers who are unwilling or unable to use keyboards, and allowing "one-sided" conversations with information systems.

Antun Hirsman/Shutterstock

## Instant Messaging

Instant messaging (IM) is one of the most widely used digital communication tools in the business world, replacing many conversations and exchanges that once took place via email or phone calls. *Enterprise IM systems* are similar to consumer IM systems in many respects but have additional security and collaboration features.

## Data Visualization

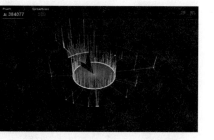

Data visualization is a powerful tool for presenting and exploring sets of data that are very large, complex, or dynamic. As more companies rely on "big data" to identify and capitalize on market opportunities, the ability to extract insights from these large data sets can be an important competitive advantage.

## COLLABORATING AND SHARING INFORMATION

The need to work with and share information quickly and easily is a constant in business. A wide variety of tools have been developed to facilitate collaboration and sharing, from general purpose systems such as instant messaging to more specialized capabilities such as data visualization.

## Interactive Websites

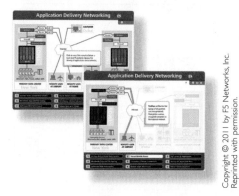

Interactivity can make online communication much more engaging and effective, such as by personalizing the presentation of information or allowing website visitors to isolate and focus on specific topics.

## Wikis

Wikis promote collaboration by simplifying the process of creating and editing online content. Anyone with access (some wikis are private; some are public) can add and modify pages as new information becomes available.

## Crowdsourcing and Collaboration Platforms

*Crowdsourcing,* inviting input from groups of people inside or outside the organization, can give companies access to a much wider range of ideas, solutions to problems, and insights into market trends.

## Applicant Tracking Systems

*Applicant tracking systems* now play a huge role in employment-related communications. At virtually all large companies and many medium and small companies, your résumé and application information will be entered into one of these systems. Recruiters use various tools to identify promising candidates and manage the interview and selection process. After hiring, some firms use *talent management systems* to track employee development through workers' entire careers at the company.

## Online Video

The combination of low-cost digital video cameras and video-sharing websites such as YouTube has spurred a revolution in business video. Product demonstrations, company overviews, promotional presentations, and training seminars are among the most popular applications of business video. *Branded channels* allow companies to present their videos as an integrated collection in a customized user interface.

## CONNECTING WITH STAKEHOLDERS

Electronic media and social media in particular have redefined the relationships businesses have with internal and external stakeholders. Any groups affected by a company's decisions now have tools to give voice to their opinions and needs, and companies have many more conversational threads that need to be monitored and managed.

## Blogging

Blogs let companies connect with customers and other audiences in a fast and informal way. Commenting features let readers participate in the conversation, too.

## Media Curation and Content Sharing

*Media curation*, selecting videos and other items of interest to followers of a website or blog, has become one of the most popular ways to connect with stakeholders. Pinterest and Scoop.it are among the leading technologies in this area.

## Podcasting

With the portability and convenience of downloadable audio and video recordings, podcasts have become a popular means of delivering everything from college lectures to marketing messages. Podcasts are also used for internal communication, replacing conference calls, newsletters, and other media.

## User-Generated Content Sites

User-generated content sites let businesses host photos, videos, software programs, technical solutions, and other valuable content for their customer communities.

## Microblogging

Microblogging services (of which Twitter is by far the best known) are a great way to share ideas, solicit feedback, monitor market trends, and announce special deals and events.

## Social Networking

Businesses use a variety of social networks as specialized channels to engage customers, find new employees, attract investors, and share ideas and challenges with peers.

## BUILDING COMMUNITIES

One of the most significant benefits of new communication technologies is the ease with which companies can foster a sense of community among customers, enthusiasts, and other groups. In some instances, the company establishes and manages the online community, while in others the community is driven by *product champions* or other enthusiasts.

## Community Q&A Sites

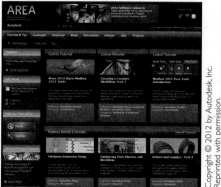

Many companies now rely heavily on communities of customers to help each other with product questions and other routine matters.

## Gaming Technologies

Encouraging people to play games, even games as simple as "checking in" at various retail locations, can build interest in a company and its brands.

affected by business activities. **Ethical communication** includes all relevant information, is true in every sense, and is not deceptive in any way. In contrast, unethical communication can distort the truth or manipulate audiences in a variety of ways:[26]

Any time you try to mislead your audience, the result is unethical communication.

- **Plagiarizing.** Plagiarism is presenting someone else's words or other creative product as your own. Note that plagiarism can be illegal if it violates a **copyright**, which is a form of legal protection for the expression of creative ideas.[27]
- **Omitting essential information.** Information is essential if your audience needs it to make an intelligent, objective decision.
- **Selective misquoting.** Distorting or hiding the true intent of someone else's words is unethical.
- **Misrepresenting numbers.** Statistics and other data can be unethically manipulated by increasing or decreasing numbers, exaggerating, altering statistics, or omitting numeric data.
- **Distorting visuals.** Images can be manipulated in unethical ways, such as altering photos in order to deceive audiences or changing the scale of graphs and charts to exaggerate or conceal differences.
- **Failing to respect privacy or information security needs.** Failing to respect the privacy of others or failing to adequately protect information entrusted to your care can also be considered unethical (and is sometimes illegal).

Transparency gives audience members access to all the information they need in order to process messages accurately.

The widespread adoption of **social media** has increased the attention given to the issue of **transparency**, which in this context refers to a sense of openness, of giving all participants in a conversation access to the information they need to accurately process the messages they are receiving. In addition to the information itself, audiences deserve to know when they are being marketed to and who is behind the messages they read or hear. For example, with *stealth marketing*, companies recruit people to promote products to friends and other contacts in exchange for free samples or other rewards, without requiring them to disclose the true nature of the communication. Critics, including the U.S. Federal Trade Commission (FTC), assert that such techniques are deceptive because they don't give their targets the opportunity to raise their instinctive defenses against the persuasive powers of marketing messages.[28]

Aside from ethical concerns, trying to fool the public is simply bad for business. As LaSalle University communication professor Michael Smith puts it, "The public backlash can be long, deep, and damaging to a company's reputation."[29]

**REAL-TIME UPDATES**

LEARN MORE BY VISITING THIS WEBSITE

**Social media disclosure guidelines that ensure transparency**

The Word of Mouth Marketing Association social media disclosure guide offers simple tips for avoiding ethical lapses. Go to http://real-timeupdates.com/bct12 and click on Learn More. If you are using MyBCommLab, you can access Real-Time Updates within each chapter or under Student Study Tools.

## DISTINGUISHING ETHICAL DILEMMAS FROM ETHICAL LAPSES

An ethical dilemma is a choice between alternatives that may all be ethical and valid.

Some ethical questions are easy to recognize and resolve, but others are not. Deciding what is ethical can be a considerable challenge in complex business situations. An **ethical dilemma** involves choosing among alternatives that aren't clear-cut. Perhaps two conflicting alternatives are both ethical and valid, or perhaps the alternatives lie somewhere in the gray area between clearly right and clearly wrong. Every company has responsibilities to multiple groups of people inside and outside the firm, and those groups often have competing interests. For instance, employees naturally want higher wages and more benefits, but investors who have risked their money in the company want management to keep costs low so that profits are strong enough to drive up the stock price. Both sides have a valid ethical position.

An ethical lapse is making a choice you know to be unethical.

In contrast, an **ethical lapse** is a clearly unethical choice. With both internal and external communication efforts, the pressure to produce results or justify decisions can make unethical communication a tempting choice. Telling a potential customer you can complete a project by a certain date when you know you can't is simply dishonest, even if you need the contract to save your career or your company. There is no ethical dilemma here.

Compare the messages in Figures 1.8 and 1.9 for examples of how business messages can be unethically manipulated.

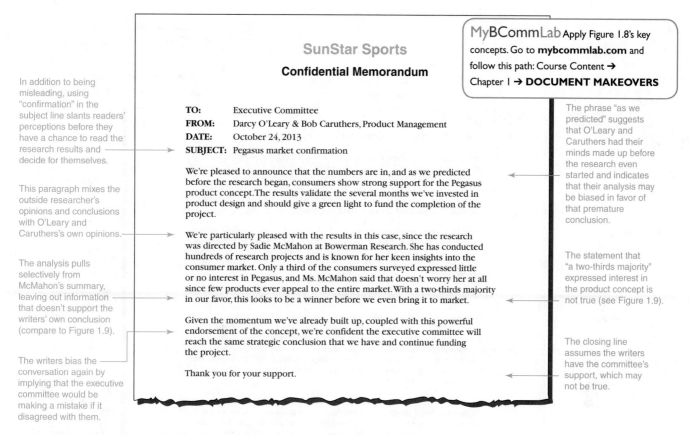

The annotations surrounding the memo read:

*In addition to being misleading, using "confirmation" in the subject line slants readers' perceptions before they have a chance to read the research results and decide for themselves.*

*This paragraph mixes the outside researcher's opinions and conclusions with O'Leary and Caruthers's own opinions.*

*The analysis pulls selectively from McMahon's summary, leaving out information that doesn't support the writers' own conclusion (compare to Figure 1.9).*

*The writers bias the conversation again by implying that the executive committee would be making a mistake if it disagreed with them.*

MyBCommLab Apply Figure 1.8's key concepts. Go to **mybcommlab.com** and follow this path: Course Content → Chapter 1 → **DOCUMENT MAKEOVERS**

*The phrase "as we predicted" suggests that O'Leary and Caruthers had their minds made up before the research even started and indicates that their analysis may be biased in favor of that premature conclusion.*

*The statement that "a two-thirds majority" expressed interest in the product concept is not true (see Figure 1.9).*

*The closing line assumes the writers have the committee's support, which may not be true.*

The memo itself reads:

**SunStar Sports**

**Confidential Memorandum**

TO:  Executive Committee
FROM:  Darcy O'Leary & Bob Caruthers, Product Management
DATE:  October 24, 2013
SUBJECT:  Pegasus market confirmation

We're pleased to announce that the numbers are in, and as we predicted before the research began, consumers show strong support for the Pegasus product concept. The results validate the several months we've invested in product design and should give a green light to fund the completion of the project.

We're particularly pleased with the results in this case, since the research was directed by Sadie McMahon at Bowerman Research. She has conducted hundreds of research projects and is known for her keen insights into the consumer market. Only a third of the consumers surveyed expressed little or no interest in Pegasus, and Ms. McMahon said that doesn't worry her at all since few products ever appeal to the entire market. With a two-thirds majority in our favor, this looks to be a winner before we even bring it to market.

Given the momentum we've already built up, coupled with this powerful endorsement of the concept, we're confident the executive committee will reach the same strategic conclusion that we have and continue funding the project.

Thank you for your support.

**Figure 1.8  Unethical Communication**
The writers of this memo clearly want the company to continue funding their pet project, even though the marketing research doesn't support such a decision. By comparing this memo with the version shown in Figure 1.9, you can see how the writers twisted the truth and omitted evidence in order to put a positive "spin" on the research.

## ENSURING ETHICAL COMMUNICATION

Ensuring ethical business communication requires three elements: ethical individuals, ethical company leadership, and the appropriate policies and structures to support employees' efforts to make ethical choices.[30] Moreover, these three elements need to work in harmony. If employees see company executives making unethical decisions and flouting company guidelines, they might conclude that the guidelines are meaningless and emulate their bosses' unethical behavior.

Employers have a responsibility to establish clear guidelines for ethical behavior, including ethical business communication. Many companies establish an explicit ethics policy by using a written **code of ethics** to help employees determine what is acceptable. A code is often part of a larger program of employee training and communication channels that allow employees to ask questions and report instances of questionable ethics. To ensure ongoing compliance with their codes of ethics, many companies also conduct **ethics audits** to monitor ethical progress and to point out any weaknesses that need to be addressed.

However, whether or not formal guidelines are in place, every employee has a responsibility to communicate in an ethical manner. In the absence of clear guidelines, ask yourself the following questions about your business communications:[31]

- Have you defined the situation fairly and accurately?
- What is your intention in communicating this message?
- What impact will this message have on the people who receive it or who might be affected by it?
- Will the message achieve the greatest possible good while doing the least possible harm?
- Will the assumptions you've made change over time? That is, will a decision that seems ethical now seem unethical in the future?
- Are you comfortable with your decision? Would you be embarrassed if it were printed in tomorrow's newspaper or spread across the Internet? Think about a person whom you admire and ask yourself what he or she would think of your decision.

*Responsible employers establish clear ethical guidelines for their employees to follow.*

*If you can't decide whether a choice is ethical, picture yourself explaining your decision to someone whose opinion you value.*

The neutral subject line doesn't try to "sell" the conclusion before readers have the opportunity to review the evidence for themselves.

The writers offer full disclosure of all the background information related to the research project.

By providing the complete text of the researcher's summary, the memo allows readers to reach their own conclusions about what she wrote.

The writers are careful to separate the researcher's observations and opinions from their own.

The close invites further discussion of the situation.

---

### SunStar Sports

### Confidential Memorandum

**TO:**       Executive Committee
**FROM:**   Darcy O'Leary & Bob Caruthers, Product Management
**DATE:**    October 24, 2013
**SUBJECT:** Market research summary for Pegasus project

The market research for the Pegasus Project concluded last week with phone interviews of 236 sporting goods buyers in 18 states. As in the past, we used Bowerman Research to conduct the interviews, under the guidance of Bowerman's survey supervisor, Sadie McMahon. Ms. McMahon has directed surveys on more than 200 consumer products, and we've learned to place a great deal of confidence in her market insights.

A complete report, including all raw data and verbatim quotes, will be available for downloading on the Engineering Department intranet by the end of next week. However, in light of the project-funding discussions going on this week, we believe the conclusions from the research warrant your immediate attention.

**Sadie McMahon's research summary**

*Consumer interest in the new product code-named Pegasus is decidedly mixed, with 34% expressing little or no interest in the product but 37% expressing moderate to strong interest. The remaining 29% expressed confusion about the basic product concept and were therefore unable to specify their level of interest. The segment expressing little or no interest is not a cause for concern in most cases; few products appeal to the entire consumer market.*

*However, the portion of the market expressing confusion about the fundamental design of the product is definitely cause for concern. We rarely see more than 10 or 15% confusion at this stage of the design process. A 29% confusion figure suggests that the product design does not fit many consumers' expectations and that it might be difficult to sell if SunStar goes ahead with production.*

**Our recommendations**

At $7.6 million, the development costs for Pegasus are too high to proceed with this much uncertainty. The business case we prepared at the beginning of the project indicated that at least 50% consumer acceptance would be needed in order to generate enough sales to produce an acceptable return on the engineering investment. We would need to convince nearly half of the "confused" segment in order to reach that threshold. We recommend that further development be put on hold until the design can be clarified and validated with another round of consumer testing.

Please contact Darcy at ext. 2354 or Bob at ext. 2360 if you have any questions or concerns.

---

MyBCommLab Apply Figure 1.9's key concepts. Go to **mybcommlab.com** and follow this path: Course Content → Chapter 1 → **DOCUMENT MAKEOVERS**

The opening emphasizes the skills of the researcher without biasing the readers regarding her conclusions.

The writers explain that more in-depth information will be available soon but emphasize the importance of reviewing this summary right now.

This quotation clearly indicates that the market expert is concerned about the project.

The recommendation states clearly and honestly that the project probably will not live up to original hopes.

**Figure 1.9   Ethical Communication**
This version of the memo presents the evidence in a more honest and ethical manner.

## ENSURING LEGAL COMMUNICATION

In addition to ethical guidelines, business communication is also bound by a wide variety of laws and regulations, including the following areas:

Business communication is governed by a wide variety of laws designed to ensure accurate, complete messages.

- **Promotional communication.** Marketing specialists need to be aware of the many laws that govern truth and accuracy in advertising. These laws address such issues as product reviews written by bloggers who receive compensation from the companies involved, false and deceptive advertising, misleading or inaccurate labels on product packages, and "bait and switch" tactics in which a store advertises a lower-priced product to lure consumers into a store but then tries to sell them a more expensive item.[32] Chapter 12 explores this area in more detail.
- **Contracts.** A **contract** is a legally binding promise between two parties in which one party makes a specified offer and the other party accepts. Contracts are fundamental to

virtually every aspect of business, from product sales to property rental to credit cards and loans to professional service agreements.[33]

- **Employment communication.** A variety of local, state, and federal laws govern communication between employers and both potential and current employees. For example, job descriptions must be written in a way that doesn't intentionally or unintentionally discriminate against women, minorities, or people with disabilities.[34]

- **Intellectual property.** In an age when instant global connectivity makes copying and retransmitting electronic files effortless, the protection of intellectual property (IP) has become a widespread concern. **Intellectual property** includes patents, copyrighted materials, trade secrets, and even Internet domain names.[35] Bloggers in particular need to be careful about IP protection, given the carefree way that some post the work of others without offering proper credit. For guidelines on this hot topic, get the free *Legal Guide for Bloggers* at www.eff.org/issues/bloggers/legal.

- **Financial reporting.** Finance and accounting professionals who work for publicly traded companies (those that sell stock to the public) must adhere to stringent reporting laws. For instance, a number of corporations have recently been targets of both government investigations and shareholder lawsuits for offering misleading descriptions of financial results and revenue forecasts.

- **Defamation.** Negative comments about another party raise the possibility of **defamation**, the intentional communication of false statements that damage character or reputation.[36] (Written defamation is called *libel*; spoken defamation is called *slander*.) Someone suing for defamation must prove (1) that the statement is false, (2) that the language is injurious to the person's reputation, and (3) that the statement has been published.

- **Transparency requirements.** Governments around the world are taking steps to help ensure that consumers and other parties know who is behind the information they receive, particularly when it appears online. The European Union, for instance, outlaws a number of online marketing tactics, including "flogs," short for "fake blogs," in which an employee or a paid agent posing as an independent consumer posts positive stories about a company's products.[37] In the United States, the FTC requires product-review bloggers to disclose any relationship—such as receiving payments or free goods—they have with the companies whose products they discuss in their blogs.[38]

If you have any doubts about the legality of a message you intend to distribute, ask for advice from your company's legal department. A small dose of caution can prevent huge legal headaches and protect your company's reputation in the marketplace.

For the latest information on ethical and legal issues in business communication, visit http://real-timeupdates.com/bct12 and click on Chapter 1.

---

**REAL-TIME UPDATES**

LEARN MORE BY WATCHING THIS PRESENTATION

**Tips for avoiding ethical problems with social media**

New media choices have created a new set of ethical dilemmas and challenges. This presentation will help you steer clear of problem areas. Go to http://real-timeupdates.com/bct12 and click on Learn More. If you are using MyBCommLab, you can access Real-Time Updates within each chapter or under Student Study Tools.

---

## COMMUNICATION CHALLENGES AT Toyota

You've recently joined the staff of Bob Zeinstra, the executive in charge of product management, advertising, and communication strategy at Toyota Motor Sales, USA. In your role as a social media specialist, you look for opportunities to help Toyota build positive relationships with all its stakeholders. Use what you've learned in this chapter to address the following challenges.

**INDIVIDUAL CHALLENGE:** Review the most recent postings on Toyota's Facebook page at www.facebook.com/toyota. In light of what you know about effective business communication and your perceptions as a consumer, how would you rate the effectiveness of the company's Facebook presence? Do any posts make you feel more positively or negatively inclined toward the

Toyota brand? Why? Summarize your analysis in a brief post on your class blog.

**TEAM CHALLENGE:** User-generated content can expose a company to a variety of legal and public relations risks. With a team assigned by your instructor, brainstorm general guidelines that Toyota could use to protect itself while still taking advantage of the potential of user-generated content. For example, should the company accept user-submitted videos that show images of risky driving behavior or stories that include critical comments about Toyota products or dealers? Summarize your recommendations in a class presentation or other format as your instructor directs.

# Quick Learning Guide

## SUMMARY OF LEARNING OBJECTIVES

**1** Explain the importance of effective communication to your career and to the companies where you will work. Effective communication is important to your career because no matter what line of work you pursue, you need to be able to share information with other people. You can have the greatest business ideas in the world, but they're no good to anyone if you can't express them clearly and persuasively. In addition to benefiting you personally, your communication skills will help your company in multiple ways, offering (1) closer ties with important communities in the marketplace; (2) opportunities to influence conversations, perceptions, and trends; (3) increased productivity and faster problem solving; (4) better financial results; (5) earlier warning of potential problems; (6) stronger decision making; (7) clearer and more persuasive marketing messages; and (8) greater employee engagement with work.

**2** Explain what it means to communicate as a professional in a business context. Communicating as a professional starts with being a professional, which embodies striving to excel, being dependable and accountable, being a team player, demonstrating a sense of etiquette, making ethical decisions, and maintaining a positive outlook.

As a professional, you will be expected to bring a wide range of communication skills, including organizing ideas and information; expressing yourself coherently and persuasively in a variety of media; building persuasive arguments; evaluating data and information critically; actively listening to others; communicating effectively with diverse audiences; using communication technologies; following accepted standards of grammar, spelling, and other aspects of high-quality writing and speaking; adapting your messages and communication styles as needed; demonstrating strong business etiquette; communicating ethically; respecting confidentiality; following applicable laws and regulations; and managing your time wisely and using resources efficiently.

Applying these skills effectively in an organizational context involves learning how to use both the *formal* and *informal* communication networks in your organization. The formal network mirrors the official hierarchy and structure of the organization; the informal network involves all the communication among members of the organization, regardless of their job positions. Adopting an *audience-centered approach* involves understanding and respecting the members of your audience and making every effort to get your message across in a way that is meaningful to them. This approach is also known as adopting the *"you" attitude* (where "you" is the recipient of the message you are sending).

**3** Identify five unique challenges of business communication. Five unique challenges are (1) the globalization of business and the increase in workforce diversity, (2) the increasing value of business information, (3) the pervasiveness of technology, (4) the evolution of organizational structures and leadership styles, and (5) a heavy reliance on teamwork.

**4** Describe the communication process model and the ways that social media are changing the nature of business communication. Communication is a complex and subtle process, and any attempt to model it will involve some simplification, but it is helpful to view the process as eight steps: (1) the sender starts with an *idea* to share; (2) the sender *encodes* the meaning of that idea as a *message*; (3) the sender produces the message in a transmittable *medium*; (4) the sender transmits the message through a *channel*; (5) the audience receives the message; (6) the audience *decodes* the message to extract its meaning; (7) the audience responds to the message; and (8) the audience provides *feedback* to sender.

Social media are transforming the practice of business communication and changing the nature of the relationships between companies and their stakeholders. Traditional business communication can be thought of as having a "publishing" mindset, in which a company produces carefully scripted messages and distributes them to an audience that has few options for responding to the company or interacting with one another. In contrast, the "Business Communication 2.0" approach uses social media tools to create an interactive and participative environment in which all parties have a chance to join the conversation. Many of the old rules and expectations, including tight control of the content and distribution of the message, no longer apply in this new environment.

**5** List four general guidelines for using communication technology effectively. First, keep technology in perspective. Make sure it supports the communication effort rather than overwhelming or disrupting it. Second, guard against information overload and information technology addiction. Third, learn how to use technological tools productively—and avoid using them in deliberately unproductive ways. Fourth, reconnect in person from time to time to ensure that communication is successful and that technology doesn't come between you and the people you need to reach.

**6** Define *ethics*, explain the difference between an ethical dilemma and an ethical lapse, and list six guidelines for making ethical communication choices. *Ethics* are the accepted principles of conduct that govern behavior within a society. Ethical communication is particularly important in business because communication is the public face of a company, which is why communication efforts are intensely scrutinized by company stakeholders. The difference between an ethical dilemma and an ethical lapse is a question of clarity. An ethical dilemma occurs when the choice is unclear because two or more alternatives seem equally right or equally wrong. In contrast, an ethical lapse occurs when a person makes a conscious choice that is clearly unethical.

To make ethical choices in any situation, ask yourself these six questions: (1) Have I defined the situation fairly and accurately? (2) What is my intention in communicating this message? (3) What impact will this message have on the people who receive it, or who might be affected by it? (4) Will the message achieve the greatest possible good while doing the least possible harm? (5) Will the assumptions I've made change over time? That is, will a decision that seems ethical now seem unethical in the future? (6) Am I truly comfortable with my decision?

## KEY TERMS

**audience-centered approach** Understanding and respecting the members of your audience and making every effort to get your message across in a way that is meaningful to them

**code of ethics** A written set of ethical guidelines that companies expect their employees to follow

**communication** The process of transferring information and meaning using one or more written, oral, visual, or electronic media

**communication barriers** Forces or events that can disrupt communication, including noise and distractions, competing messages, filters, and channel breakdowns

**communication channels** Systems used to deliver messages

**communication medium** The form in which a message is presented; the four categories of media are oral, written, visual, and electronic

**contract** A legally binding promise between two parties, in which one party makes a specified offer and the other party accepts

**copyright** A form of legal protection for the expression of creative ideas

**corporate culture** The mixture of values, traditions, and habits that give a company its atmosphere and personality

**decoding** Extracting the idea from a message

**defamation** The intentional communication of false statements that damage character or reputation

**encoding** Putting an idea into a message (words, images, or a combination of both)

**ethical communication** Communication that includes all relevant information, is true in every sense, and is not deceptive in any way

**ethical dilemma** Situation that involves making a choice when the alternatives aren't completely wrong or completely right

**ethical lapse** A clearly unethical choice

**ethics** The accepted principles of conduct that govern behavior within a society

**ethics audits** Ongoing efforts to monitor ethical progress and to point out any weaknesses that need to be addressed

**etiquette** The expected norms of behavior in any particular situation

**feedback** Information from receivers regarding the quality and effectiveness of a message

**formal communication network** Communication channels that flow along the lines of command

**globalization** Efforts by businesses to reach across international borders to market their products, partner with other businesses, and employ workers and executives

**informal communication network** All communication that takes place outside the formal network; often referred to as the grapevine or the rumor mill

**information overload** Condition in which people receive more information than they can effectively process

**intellectual property** Assets including patents, copyrighted materials, trade secrets, and even Internet domain names

**knowledge workers** Employees at all levels of an organization who specialize in acquiring, processing, and communicating information

**message** The "container" for an idea to be transmitted from a sender to a receiver

**perception** A person's awareness or view of reality; also, the process of detecting incoming messages

**professionalism** The quality of performing at a high level and conducting oneself with purpose and pride

**selective perception** The inclination to distort or ignore incoming information rather than change one's beliefs

**social communication model** An interactive, conversational approach to communication in which formerly passive audience members are empowered to participate fully

**social media** Electronic media such as social networks and blogs that transform passive audiences into active participants in the communication process by allowing them to share content, revise content, respond to content, or contribute new content

**stakeholders** Groups affected by a company's actions: customers, employees, shareholders, suppliers, neighbors, the community, and the world at large

**transparency** Giving all participants in a conversation access to the information they need to accurately process the messages they are receiving

**workforce diversity** All the differences among the people who work together, including differences in age, gender, sexual orientation, education, cultural background, religion, ability, and life experience

**"you" attitude** Communicating with an audience-centered approach; creating messages that are about "you," the receiver, rather than "me," the sender

## Test Your Knowledge

To review chapter content related to each question, refer to the indicated Learning Objective.

1. What benefits does effective communication give you and your organization? [LO-1]
2. What are the five attributes of effective business communication? [LO-1]
✪ 3. What are the six traits of professionalism? [LO-2]
✪ 4. Why should communicators take an audience-centered approach to communication? [LO-2]
5. What steps have to occur before an audience member perceives the presence of an incoming message? [LO-3]
✪ 6. What are the most common barriers in any communication environment? [LO-3]
7. How is communication affected by information overload? [LO-4]
8. What is an ethical dilemma? [LO-5]
9. What is an ethical lapse? [LO-5]

## Apply Your Knowledge

To review chapter content related to each question, refer to the indicated Learning Objective.

✪ 1. Why do you think communication is vital to the success of every business organization? Explain briefly. [LO-1]
✪ 2. How does the presence of a reader comments feature on a corporate blog reflect audience-centered communication? [LO-2]
3. Is it possible for companies to be too dependent on communication technology? Explain briefly. [LO-4]
✪ 4. Because of your excellent communication skills, your boss always asks you to write his reports for him. When you overhear the CEO complimenting him on his logical organization and clear writing style, your boss responds as if he'd written all those reports himself. What kind of ethical choice does your boss's response represent? What can you do in this situation? Briefly explain your solution and your reasoning. [LO-5]

## Practice Your Skills

### Message for Analysis: Analyzing Communication Effectiveness [LO-1]

Read the following blog posting and then (1) analyze whether the message is effective or ineffective (be sure to explain why) and (2) revise the message so that it follows this chapter's guidelines.

It has come to my attention that many of you are lying on your time cards. If you come in late, you should not put 8:00 on your card. If you take a long lunch, you should not put 1:00 on your time card. I will not stand for this type of cheating. I simply have no choice but to institute an employee monitoring system. Beginning next Monday, video cameras will be installed at all entrances to the building, and your entry and exit times will be logged each time you use electronic key cards to enter or leave.

Anyone who is late for work or late coming back from lunch more than three times will have to answer to me. I don't care

if you had to take a nap or if you girls had to shop. This is a place of business, and we do not want to be taken advantage of by slackers who are cheaters to boot.

It is too bad that a few bad apples always have to spoil things for everyone.

### Exercises

Each activity is labeled according to the primary skill or skills you will need to use. To review relevant chapter content, you can refer to the indicated Learning Objective. In some instances, supporting information will be found in another chapter, as indicated.

1. **Writing: Compositional Modes: Summaries [LO-1], Chapter 4** Write a paragraph introducing yourself to your instructor and your class. Address such areas as your background, interests, achievements, and goals. Submit your paragraph using email, blog, or social network, as indicated by your instructor.

2. **Media Skills: Microblogging [LO-1], Chapter 7** Write four effective messages of no more than 140 characters each (short enough to work as Twitter tweets, in other words) to persuade other college students to take the business communication course. Think of the first message as the "headline" of an advertisement that makes a bold promise regarding the value this course offers every aspiring business professional. The next three messages should be support points that provide evidence to back up the promise made in the first message.[39]

3. **Fundamentals: Analyzing Communication Effectiveness [LO-1]** Identify a video clip (on YouTube or another online source) that you believe represents an example of effective communication. It can be in any context, business or otherwise, but make sure it is something appropriate to discuss in class. Post a link to the video on your class blog, along with a brief written summary of why you think this example shows effective communication in action.

4. **Planning: Assessing Audience Needs [LO-2], Chapter 3** Choose a business career that sounds interesting to you and imagine that you are getting ready to apply for jobs in that field. Naturally, you want to create a compelling, audience-focused résumé that answers the key questions a hiring manager is most likely to have. Identify three personal or professional qualities you have that would be important for someone in this career field. Write a brief statement (one or two sentences) regarding each quality, describing in audience-focused terms how you can contribute to a company in this respect. Submit your statements via email or class blog.

5. **Communication Etiquette: Communicating with Sensitivity and Tact [LO-2]** Potential customers frequently visit your production facility before making purchase decisions. You and the people who report to you in the sales department have received extensive training in etiquette issues because you deal with high-profile clients so often. However, the rest of the workforce has not received such training, and you worry that someone might inadvertently say or do something that would offend one of these potential customers. In a two-paragraph email, explain to the general

manager why you think anyone who might come in contact with customers should receive basic etiquette training.

6. **Collaboration: Team Project; Planning: Assessing Audience Needs [LO-2], Chapter 2, Chapter 4** Your boss has asked your work group to research and report on corporate child-care facilities. Of course, you'll want to know who (besides your boss) will be reading your report. Working with two team members, list four or five other things you'll want to know about the situation and about your audience before starting your research. Briefly explain why each of the items on your list is important.

7. **Planning: Constructing a Persuasive Argument [LO-3], Chapter 12** You are the customer service manager for a company that sells a software package used by not-for-profit organizations to plan and manage fundraising campaigns. The powerful software is complicated enough to require a fairly extensive user's manual, and the company has always provided a printed manual to customers. Customers frequently email your department with questions about using the software and suggestions for using the software to maximize fundraising efforts. You know that many customers could benefit from the answers to those questions and the suggestions from fellow customers, but with a printed manual issued once every couple years, you don't have any way to collect and distribute this information in a timely fashion.

You've been researching wikis and believe this would be a great way to let customers participate in an ongoing conversation about using the software. In fact, you'd like to convert the printed manual to a wiki on which any registered customer could add or edit pages. Rather than spending thousands of dollars printing a manual that is difficult to expand or update, the wiki would be a "living" document that continually evolves as people ask and answer questions and offer suggestions. The rest of the management team is extremely nervous, however. "We're the experts—not the customer," one says. Another asks, "How can we ensure the quality of the information if any customer can change it?" They don't deny that customers have valuable information to add; they just don't want customers to have control of an important company document. Making up any information you need, write a brief email to your colleagues, explaining the benefits of letting customers contribute to a wiki-based user manual. (You can refer to pages 214–215 to learn more about wikis.)

8. **Planning: Constructing a Persuasive Argument [LO-3], Chapter 12** Blogging has become a popular way for employees to communicate with customers and other parties outside the company. In some cases, employee blogs have been quite beneficial for both companies and their customers by providing helpful information and "putting a human face" on other formal and imposing corporations. However, in some other cases, employees have been fired for posting information that their employers said was inappropriate. One particular area of concern is criticism of the company or individual managers. Should employees be allowed to criticize their employers in a public forum such as a blog? In a brief email message, argue for or against company policies that prohibit critical information in employee blogs.

9. **Fundamentals: Analyzing Communication Effectiveness [LO-3]** Use the eight phases of the communication process to analyze a miscommunication you've recently had with a coworker, supervisor, classmate, teacher, friend, or family member. What idea were you trying to share? How did you encode and transmit it? Did the receiver get the message? Did the receiver correctly decode the message? How do you know? Based on your analysis, identify and explain the barriers that prevented your successful communication in this instance.

10. **Technology: Using Communication Tools [LO-4]** Find a free online communication service that you have no experience using as a content creator or contributor. Services to consider include blogging (such as Blogger), microblogging (such as Twitter), community Q&A sites (such as Yahoo! Answers), and user-generated content sites (such as Flickr). Perform a basic task such as opening an account or setting up a blog. Was the task easy to perform? Were the instructions clear? Could you find help online if you needed it? Is there anything about the experience that could be improved? Summarize your conclusions in a brief email message to your instructor.

11. **Communication Ethics: Distinguishing Ethical Dilemmas and Ethical Lapses [LO-5]** Knowing that you have numerous friends throughout the company, your boss relies on you for feedback concerning employee morale and other issues affecting the staff. She recently asked you to start reporting any behavior that might violate company policies, from taking home office supplies to making personal long-distance calls. List the issues you'd like to discuss with her before you respond to her request.

12. **Communication Ethics: Distinguishing Ethical Dilemmas and Ethical Lapses [LO-5]** In less than a page, explain why you think each of the following is or is not ethical.

    a. Keeping quiet about a possible environmental hazard you've just discovered in your company's processing plant

    b. Overselling the benefits of instant messaging to your company's managers; they never seem to understand the benefits of technology, so you believe it's the only way to convince them to make the right choice

    c. Telling an associate and close friend that she needs to pay more attention to her work responsibilities, or management will fire her

    d. Recommending the purchase of equipment your department doesn't really need in order to use up your allocated funds before the end of the fiscal year so that your budget won't be cut next year—when you might have a real need for the money

13. **Communication Ethics: Providing Ethical Leadership [LO-5]** Cisco, a leading manufacturer of equipment for the Internet and corporate networks, has developed a code of ethics that it expects employees to abide by. Visit the company's website, at www.cisco.com, and find its *code of conduct*. In a brief paragraph, describe three specific examples of things you could do that would violate these provisions; then list at least three opportunities that Cisco provides its employees to report ethics violations or ask questions regarding ethical dilemmas.

## Expand Your Skills

### Critique the Professionals

Locate an example of professional communication from a reputable online source. It can reflect any aspect of business communication, from an advertisement or a press release to a company blog or website. Evaluate this communication effort in light of any aspect of this chapter that is relevant to the sample and interesting to you. For example, is the piece effective? Audience-centered? Ethical? Using whatever medium your instructor requests, write a brief analysis of the piece (no more than one page), citing specific elements from the piece and support from the chapter.

### Sharpening Your Career Skills Online

Bovée and Thill's Business Communication Web Search, at http://businesscommunicationblog.com/websearch, is a unique research tool designed specifically for business communication research. Use the Web Search function to find an online video, a podcast, or a PowerPoint presentation that explains at least one essential business communication skill. Write a brief email message to your instructor or a post for your class blog, describing the item that you found and summarizing the career skills information you learned from it.

---

## MyBCommLab

Go to **mybcommlab.com** for Auto-graded writing questions as well as the following Assisted-graded writing questions:

1-1. How does the social communication model differ from traditional business communication practices? [LO-3]

1-2. How are social networks, wikis, and other Web 2.0 technologies changing the practice of business communication? [LO-3]

1-3. Mybcommlab Only—comprehensive writing assignment for this chapter.

---

## Endnotes

1. Toyota Facebook page, accessed 20 December 2012, www.facebook.com/toyota; Lisa Lacy, "Toyota Pushes 'Auto-Biography' Facebook Campaign," ClickZ, 2 August 2010, www.clickz.com; Alan Ohnsman and Makiko Kitamura, "Is Toyota's Reputation Finished?" *Bloomberg Businessweek*, 28 January 2010, www.businessweek.com.

2. Richard L. Daft, *Management*, 6th ed. (Cincinnati: Thomson South-Western, 2003), 580.

3. Julie Connelly, "Youthful Attitudes, Sobering Realities," *New York Times*, 28 October 2003, E1, E6; Nigel Andrews and Laura D'Andrea Tyson, "The Upwardly Global MBA," *Strategy +Business* 36, 60–69; Jim McKay, "Communication Skills Found Lacking," *Pittsburgh Post-Gazette*, 28 February 2005, www.delawareonline.com.

4. Brian Solis, *Engage!* (Hoboken: John Wiley & Sons, 2010), 11–12; "Majority of Global Companies Face an Engagement Gap," Internal Comms Hub website, 23 October 2007, www.internalcommshub.com; Gary L. Neilson, Karla L. Martin, and Elizabeth Powers, "The Secrets to Successful Strategy Execution," *Harvard Business Review*, June 2008, 61–70; Nicholas Carr, "Lessons in Corporate Blogging," *BusinessWeek*, 18 July 2006, 9; Susan Meisinger, "To Keep Employees, Talk—and Listen—to Them!" *HR Magazine*, August 2006, 10.

5. Daft, *Management*, 147.

6. "CEOs to Communicators: 'Stick to Common Sense,'" Internal Comms Hub website, 23 October 2007, www.internalcommshub.com; "A Writing Competency Model for Business," BizCom101.com, 14 December 2007, www.business-writing-courses.com; Sue Dewhurst and Liam FitzPatrick, "What Should Be the Competency of Your IC Team?" white paper, 2007, http://competentcommunicators.com.

7. Philip C. Kolin, *Successful Writing at Work*, 6th ed. (Boston: Houghton Mifflin, 2001), 17–23.

8. Laura L. Myers and Mary L. Tucker, "Increasing Awareness of Emotional Intelligence in a Business Curriculum," *Business Communication Quarterly*, March 2005, 44–51.

9. Don Hellriegel, Susan E. Jackson, and John W. Slocum, Jr., *Management: A Competency-Based Approach* (Cincinnati: Thomson South-Western, 2002), 447.

10. Pete Cashmore, "10 Web Trends to Watch in 2010," CNN Tech, 3 December 2009, www.cnn.com.

11. Stephanie Armour, "Music Hath Charms for Some Workers—Others It Really Annoys," *USA Today*, 24 March 2006, B1–B2.

12. Paul Martin Lester, *Visual Communication: Images with Messages* (Belmont, Calif.: Thomson South-Western, 2006), 6–8.

13. Michael R. Solomon, *Consumer Behavior: Buying, Having, and Being*, 6th ed. (Upper Saddle River, N.J.: Pearson Prentice Hall, 2004), 65.

14. Anne Field, "What You Say, What They Hear," *Harvard Management Communication Letter*, Winter 2005, 3–5.

15. Chuck Williams, *Management*, 2nd ed. (Cincinnati: Thomson South-Western, 2002), 690.

16. Charles G. Morris and Albert A. Maisto, *Psychology: An Introduction*, 12th ed. (Upper Saddle River, N.J.: Pearson Prentice Hall, 2005), 226–239; Saundra K. Ciccarelli and Glenn E. Meyer, *Psychology* (Upper Saddle River, N.J.: Prentice Hall, 2006), 210–229; Mark H. Ashcraft, *Cognition*, 4th ed. (Upper Saddle River, N.J.: Prentice Hall, 2006), 44–54.

17. Ben Hanna, *2009 Business Social Media Benchmarking Study* (published by Business.com), 2 November 2009, 11.

18. Michael Killian, "The Communication Revolution—'Deep Impact' About to Strike," Avaya Insights blog, 4 December 2009, www.avayablog.com.

19. Tara Craig, "How to Avoid Information Overload," *Personnel Today*, 10 June 2008, 31; Jeff Davidson, "Fighting Information Overload," *Canadian Manager*, Spring 2005, 16+.

20. "The Top Ten Ways Workers Waste Time Online," 24/7 Wall St., 30 September 2010, http://247wallst.com.

21. Eric J. Sinrod, "Perspective: It's My Internet—I Can Do What I Want," News.com, 29 March 2006, www.news.com.

22. Eric J. Sinrod, "Time to Crack Down on Tech at Work?" News.com, 14 June 2006, www.news.com.

23. Jack Trout, "Beware of 'Infomania,'" *Forbes*, 11 August 2006, www.forbes.com.

24. "Many Senior Managers Communicate Badly, Survey Says," Internal Comms Hub, 6 August 2007, www.internalcommshub.com.

25. Mike Schaffner, "Step Away from the Computer," *Forbes*, 7 August 2009, www.forbes.com.

26. Philip C. Kolin, *Successful Writing at Work*, 6th ed. (Boston: Houghton Mifflin, 2001), 24–30.

27. Nancy K. Kubasek, Bartley A. Brennan, and M. Neil Browne, *The Legal Environment of Business*, 3rd ed. (Upper Saddle River, N.J.: Prentice Hall, 2003), 172.

28. Word of Mouth Marketing Association, "WOM 101," accessed 2 June 2010, http://womma.org; Nate Anderson, "FTC Says Stealth Marketing Unethical," *Ars Technica*, 13 December 2006, http://arstechnica.com; "Undercover Marketing Uncovered," CBSnews.com, 25 July 2004, www.cbsnews.com; Stephanie Dunnewind, "Teen Recruits Create Word-of-Mouth 'Buzz' to Hook Peers on Products," *Seattle Times*, 20 November 2004, www.seattletimes.com.

29. Linda Pophal, "Tweet Ethics: Trust and Transparency in a Web 2.0 World," *CW Bulletin*, September 2009.

30. Daft, *Management*, 155.

31. Based in part on Robert Kreitner, *Management*, 9th ed. (Boston: Houghton Mifflin, 2004), 163.

32. Henry R. Cheeseman, *Contemporary Business and E-Commerce Law*, 4th ed. (Upper Saddle River, N.J.: Prentice Hall, 2003), 841–843.

33. Cheeseman, *Contemporary Business and E-Commerce Law*, 201.

34. John Jude Moran, *Employment Law: New Challenges in the Business Environment*, 2nd ed. (Upper Saddle River, N.J.: Prentice Hall, 2002), 186–187; Kubasek et al., *The Legal Environment of Business*, 562.

35. Cheeseman, *Contemporary Business and E-Commerce Law*, 325.

36. Kubasek et al., *The Legal Environment of Business*, 306.

37. Robert Plummer, "Will Fake Business Blogs Crash and Burn?" BBC News, 22 May 2008, http://news.bbc.co.uk.

38. Tim Arango, "Soon, Bloggers Must Give Full Disclosure," *New York Times*, 5 October 2009, www.nytimes.com.

39. The concept of a four-tweet summary is adapted from Cliff Atkinson, *The Backchannel* (Berkeley, Calif.: New Riders, 2010), 120–121.

## LEARNING OBJECTIVES

After studying this chapter, you will be able to

**1** List the advantages and disadvantages of working in teams, describe the characteristics of effective teams, and highlight four key issues of group dynamics.

**2** Offer guidelines for collaborative communication, identify major collaboration technologies, and explain how to give constructive feedback.

**3** List the key steps needed to ensure productive team meetings.

**4** Identify the major technologies used to enhance or replace in-person meetings.

**5** Identify three major modes of listening, describe the listening process, and explain the problem of selective listening.

**6** Explain the importance of nonverbal communication and identify six major categories of nonverbal expression.

**7** Explain the importance of business etiquette and identify three key areas in which good etiquette is essential.

### MyBCommLab®

⭐ **Improve Your Grade!** Over 10 million students improved their results using the Pearson MyLabs. Visit **mybcommlab.com** for simulations, tutorials, and end-of-chapter problems.

■■■■■■■■
COMMUNICATION CLOSE-UP AT

## Rosen Law Firm

www.rosen.com

When communication tools function at their best, they can go beyond mere facilitation to transformation. Such was the case at Rosen Law Firm, based in Raleigh, North Carolina. Lee Rosen, the firm's owner and chief executive, wanted to replace an expensive, complicated, and inflexible computer system that employees relied on for everything from contact lists to appointment calendars to document storage. The solution he chose was a wiki, the same technology that enables thousands of people around the world to contribute to Wikipedia.

Once in place, the wiki not only helped cut costs by handling much of the firm's document storage and formal communication, it introduced an informal social element that is helping employees bond as a community. Many have added personal pages with information about themselves, helping employees get to know their colleagues on a more personal level.

Lee Rosen, Rosen Law Firm.

Lee Rosen's law firm uses a wiki to manage thousands of documents while boosting teamwork and collaboration.

In implementing the wiki, Rosen faced a common challenge with new communication tools: getting people to give up familiar ways of doing things and embrace change. Knowing that the value of a company wiki depends on the level of employee contribution—and that having some of the staff switch while others cling to old ways would seriously disrupt communication—he encouraged use of the new wiki with a friendly competition. For each page an employee created during the three-month competition, he or she was given one possible combination to the company safe, which contained a $1,000 cash prize. From time to

time, Rosen also forced use of the wiki by publishing important information only on the wiki.

As often happens when companies face significant changes, the move to the wiki did cause some turmoil. Two camps of employees argued over the best way to organize information and got caught up in an "edit war," repeatedly undoing each other's decisions. They eventually reached a compromise that resolved the disagreement and had lasting benefits for teamwork and interpersonal communication across the firm. According to Rosen, "It forced everybody to learn about each other's job."[1]

# Communicating Effectively in Teams

The teamwork interactions among the employees at Rosen Law Firm (profiled in the chapter-opening Communication Close-Up) represent one of the most essential elements of interpersonal communication. **Collaboration**—working together to meet complex challenges—has become a core job responsibility for roughly half the U.S. workforce.[2] No matter what career path you pursue, it's a virtual guarantee that you will be expected to collaborate in at least some of your work activities. Your communication skills will pay off handsomely in these interactions, because the productivity and quality of collaborative efforts depend heavily on the communication skills of the professionals involved.

A **team** is a unit of two or more people who share a mission and the responsibility for working to achieve a common goal.[3] **Problem-solving teams** and **task forces** assemble to resolve specific issues and then disband when their goals have been accomplished. Such teams are often *cross-functional*, pulling together people from a variety of departments who have different areas of expertise and responsibility. The diversity of opinions and experiences can lead to better decisions, but competing interests can lead to tensions that highlight the need for effective communication. **Committees** are formal teams that usually have a long life span and can become a permanent part of the organizational structure. Committees typically deal with regularly recurring tasks, such as an executive committee that meets monthly to plan strategies and review results.

**1 LEARNING OBJECTIVE**
List the advantages and disadvantages of working in teams, describe the characteristics of effective teams, and highlight four key issues of group dynamics.

Collaboration, working together to solve complex problems, is an essential skill for knowledge workers in every profession.

Team members have a shared mission and are collectively responsible for their work.

## ADVANTAGES AND DISADVANTAGES OF TEAMS

When teams are successful, they can improve productivity, creativity, employee involvement, and even job security.[4] Teams are often at the core of **participative management**, the effort to involve employees in the company's decision making. A successful team can provide a number of advantages:[5]

- **Increased information and knowledge.** By pooling the experience of several individuals, a team has access to more information.
- **Increased diversity of views.** Team members can bring a variety of perspectives to the decision-making process—as long as these diverse viewpoints are guided by a shared goal.[6]
- **Increased acceptance of a solution.** Those who participate in making a decision are more likely to support it and encourage others to accept it.
- **Higher performance levels.** Working in teams can unleash new levels of creativity and energy in workers who share a sense of purpose and mutual accountability. Effective teams can be better than top-performing individuals at solving complex problems.[7]

Effective teams can pool knowledge, take advantage of diverse viewpoints, and increase acceptance of solutions the team proposes.

**ETHICS DETECTIVE**

## Solving the Case of the Missing Team

Your entire team has been looking forward to this meeting for weeks. When the company president assembled this team to find creative solutions to the company's cash flow problems, few people thought it would succeed. However, through plenty of hard work, you and your colleagues have found new sources of investment capital. Now it's time to present your accomplishments to the board of directors. Because appearing in front of the board can be a major career boost, the team planned to present the results together, giving each person a few minutes in the limelight.

However, Jackson Mueller, the chief financial officer and leader of your team, had a surprise for you this morning. He'd received word at the last minute that the board wanted a short, concise presentation, and he said the best way to comply was with a single presenter. No one was happy about the change, but Mueller is the highest-ranking employee on the team and the only one with experience presenting to the board.

Disappointment turned to dismay as you and your teammates watched from the back of the conference room. Mueller deftly compressed your 60-minute presentation down to 20 minutes, and the board showered him with praise. However, he never introduced any of the other team members, so your potential moment in the sun passed without recognition.

### ANALYSIS

1. Did Mueller behave unethically by not introducing you and your colleagues to the board? Explain your answer.
2. Later on, you complain to a colleague that by stressing "my team" so often, Mueller actually made the presentation all about him, not the team. But one of your colleagues argues that the team's assignment was to solve the problem, not to score career points with the board, so that goal shouldn't have been such a top priority. Explain why you agree or disagree.

Although teamwork has many advantages, it also has a number of potential disadvantages. At the worst, working in teams can be a frustrating waste of time. Teams need to be aware of and work to counter the following potential disadvantages:

*Teams need to avoid the negative impact of groupthink, hidden agendas, and excessive costs.*

- **Groupthink.** Like other social structures, business teams can generate tremendous pressures to conform with accepted norms of behavior. **Groupthink** occurs when peer pressures cause individual team members to withhold contrary or unpopular opinions. The result can be decisions that are worse than the choices the team members might have made individually.
- **Hidden agendas.** Some team members may have a **hidden agenda**—a private, counterproductive motive, such as a desire to take control of the group, to undermine someone else on the team, or to pursue a business goal that runs counter to the team's mission.
- **Cost.** Aligning schedules, arranging meetings, and coordinating individual parts of a project can eat up a lot of time and money.

### CHARACTERISTICS OF EFFECTIVE TEAMS

*Effective teams have a clear sense of purpose, open and honest communication, consensus-based decision making, creativity, and effective conflict resolution.*

The most effective teams have a clear objective and shared sense of purpose, have a strong sense of trust, communicate openly and honestly, reach decisions by consensus, think creatively, and know how to resolve conflict.[8] Teams that have these attributes can focus their time and energy on their work, without being disrupted by destructive conflict (see page 36).

In contrast, teams lacking one or more of these attributes can get bogged down in conflict or waste time and resources pursuing unclear goals. Two of the most common reasons cited for unsuccessful teamwork are lack of trust and poor communication. A lack of trust can result from team members being suspicious of one another's motives or ability to contribute.[9] Communication breakdowns are most likely to occur when teams operate across cultures, countries, or time zones.[10]

### GROUP DYNAMICS

*Group dynamics are the interactions and processes that take place in a team.*

The interactions and processes that take place among the members of a team are called **group dynamics**. Productive teams tend to develop clear **norms**, informal standards of conduct that members share and that guide member behavior. Group dynamics are influenced by several factors: the roles team members assume, the current phase of team development, the team's success in resolving conflict, and the team's success in overcoming resistance.

| TABLE 2.1 | Team Roles—Functional and Dysfunctional | | |
|---|---|---|
| **Dysfunctional: Self-Oriented Roles** | **Functional: Team-Maintenance Roles** | **Functional: Task-Facilitating Roles** |
| **Controlling:** Dominating others by exhibiting superiority or authority | **Encouraging:** Drawing out other members by showing verbal and nonverbal support, praise, or agreement | **Initiating:** Getting the team started on a line of inquiry |
| **Withdrawing:** Retiring from the team either by becoming silent or by refusing to deal with a particular aspect of the team's work | **Harmonizing:** Reconciling differences among team members through mediation or by using humor to relieve tension | **Information giving or seeking:** Offering (or seeking) information relevant to questions facing the team |
| **Attention seeking:** Calling attention to oneself and demanding recognition from others | **Compromising:** Offering to yield on a point in the interest of reaching a mutually acceptable decision | **Coordinating:** Showing relationships among ideas, clarifying issues, summarizing what the team has done |
| **Diverting:** Focusing the team's discussion on topics of interest to the individual rather than on those relevant to the task | | **Procedure setting:** Suggesting decision-making procedures that will move the team toward a goal |

## Assuming Team Roles

Members of a team can play various roles, which fall into three categories (see Table 2.1). Members who assume **self-oriented roles** are motivated mainly to fulfill personal needs, so they tend to be less productive than other members. "Dream teams" composed of multiple superstars often don't perform as well as one might expect because high-performing individuals can have trouble putting the team's needs ahead of their own.[11] In addition, highly skilled and experienced people with difficult personalities might not contribute, for the simple reason that other team members may avoid interacting with them.[12] Far more likely to contribute to team goals are members who assume **team-maintenance roles** to help everyone work well together and those who assume **task-oriented roles** to help the team reach its goals.[13]

Each member of a group plays a role that affects the outcome of the group's activities.

## Allowing for Team Evolution

Teams typically evolve through a number of phases on their way to becoming productive (see Figure 2.1). A variety of models have been proposed to describe the evolution toward becoming a productive team. Here is how one commonly used model identifies the phases a problem-solving team goes through as it evolves:[14]

1. **Orientation.** Team members socialize, establish their roles, and begin to define their task or purpose. Team-building exercises and activities can help teams break down barriers and develop a sense of shared purpose.[15] For geographically dispersed virtual teams, creating a "team operating agreement" that sets expectations for online meetings, communication processes, and decision making can help overcome the disadvantages of distance.[16]
2. **Conflict.** Team members begin to discuss their positions and become more assertive in establishing their roles. Disagreements and uncertainties are natural in this phase.

Teams typically evolve through a variety of phases, such as orientation, conflict, brainstorming, emergence, and reinforcement.

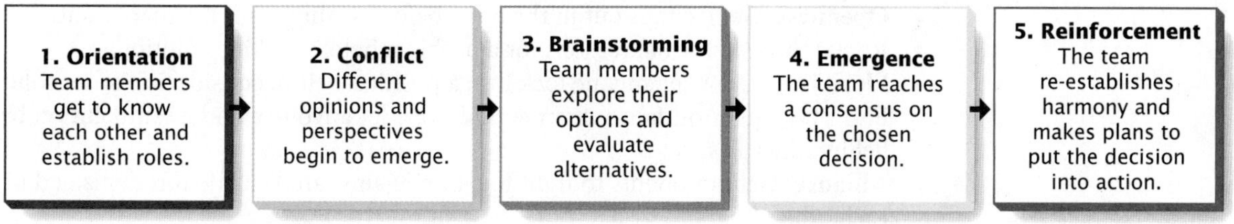

**1. Orientation** Team members get to know each other and establish roles. → **2. Conflict** Different opinions and perspectives begin to emerge. → **3. Brainstorming** Team members explore their options and evaluate alternatives. → **4. Emergence** The team reaches a consensus on the chosen decision. → **5. Reinforcement** The team re-establishes harmony and makes plans to put the decision into action.

**Figure 2.1  Phases of Group Development**
Groups generally progress through several stages on their way to becoming productive and reaching their objectives.
*Sources:* Adapted from B. Aubrey Fisher, *Small Group Decision Making: Communication and the Group Process*, 2nd ed. (New York: McGraw-Hill, 1980), 145–149; Stephen P. Robbins and David A. DeCenzo, *Fundamentals of Management*, 4th ed. (Upper Saddle River, N.J.: Prentice Hall, 2004), 334–335; Richard L. Daft, *Management*, 6th ed. (Cincinnati: Thomson South-Western, 2003), 602–603.

3. **Brainstorming.** Team members air all the options and fully discuss the pros and cons. At the end of this phase, members begin to settle on a single solution to the problem. Note that while group brainstorming remains a highly popular activity in today's companies, it may not always be the most productive way to generate new ideas. Some research indicates that having people brainstorm individually and then bring their ideas to a group meeting is more successful.[17]

4. **Emergence.** Consensus is reached when the team finds a solution that all members are willing to support (even if they have reservations).

5. **Reinforcement.** The team clarifies and summarizes the agreed-upon solution. Members receive their assignments for carrying out the group's decision, and they make arrangements for following up on those assignments.

You may also hear the process defined as *forming*, *storming*, *norming*, *performing*, and *adjourning*, the phases identified by researcher Bruce Tuckman when he proposed one of the earliest models of group development.[18] Regardless of the model you consider, these stages are a general framework for team development. Some teams may move forward and backward through several stages before they become productive, and other teams may be productive right away, even while some or all members are in a state of conflict.[19]

### Resolving Conflict

Conflict in team activities can arise for a number of reasons: competition for resources, disagreement over goals or responsibilities, poor communication, power struggles, or fundamental differences in values, attitudes, and personalities.[20] Although the term *conflict* sounds negative, conflict isn't necessarily bad. Conflict can be *constructive* if it forces important issues into the open, increases the involvement of team members, and generates creative ideas for solving a problem. Teamwork isn't necessarily about happiness and harmony; even teams that have some interpersonal friction can excel with effective leadership and team players committed to strong results. As teamwork experts Andy Boynton and Bill Fischer put it, "Virtuoso teams are not about getting polite results."[21]

In contrast, conflict is *destructive* if it diverts energy from more important issues, destroys the morale of teams or individual team members, or polarizes or divides the team.[22] Destructive conflict can lead to *win-lose* or *lose-lose* outcomes, in which one or both sides lose, to the detriment of the entire team. If you approach conflict with the idea that both sides can satisfy their goals to at least some extent (a *win-win* strategy), you can minimize losses for everyone. For a win-win strategy to work, everybody must believe that (1) it's possible to find a solution that both parties can accept, (2) cooperation is better for the organization than competition, (3) the other party can be trusted, and (4) greater power or status doesn't entitle one party to impose a solution.

The following seven measures can help team members successfully resolve conflict:

- **Proactive behavior.** Deal with minor conflict before it becomes major conflict.
- **Communication.** Get those directly involved in a conflict to participate in resolving it.
- **Openness.** Get feelings out in the open before dealing with the main issues.
- **Research.** Seek factual reasons for a problem before seeking solutions.
- **Flexibility.** Don't let anyone lock into a position before considering other solutions.
- **Fair play.** Insist on fair outcomes and don't let anyone avoid a fair solution by hiding behind the rules.
- **Alliance.** Get opponents to fight together against an "outside force" instead of against each other.

### Overcoming Resistance

One particular type of conflict that can affect team progress is resistance to change. Sometimes this resistance is clearly irrational, such as when people resist any kind of change, whether it makes sense or not. Sometimes, however, resistance is perfectly logical. A change may require

---

*Conflict in teams can be either constructive or destructive.*

*Destructive conflict can lead to win-lose or lose-lose outcomes.*

someone to relinquish authority or give up comfortable ways of doing things. If someone is resisting change, you can be persuasive with calm, reasonable communication:

- **Express understanding.** You might say, "I understand that this change might be difficult, and if I were in your position, I might be reluctant myself." Help the other person relax and talk about his or her anxiety so that you have a chance to offer reassurance.[23]
- **Bring resistance out into the open.** When people are noncommittal and silent, they may be tuning you out without even knowing why. Continuing with your argument is futile. Deal directly with the resistance, without accusing. You might say, "You seem to have reservations about this idea. Have I made some faulty assumptions?" Such questions force people to face and define their resistance.[24]
- **Evaluate others' objections fairly.** Use active listening to focus on what the other person is expressing, both the words and the feelings. Get the person to open up so that you can understand the basis for the resistance. Others' objections may raise legitimate points that you'll need to discuss, or they may reveal problems that you'll need to minimize.[25]

Hold your arguments until the other person is ready for them. Getting your point across depends as much on the other person's frame of mind as it does on your arguments. You can't assume that a strong argument will speak for itself. By becoming more audience centered, you will learn to address the other person's emotional needs first.

When you encounter resistance or hostility, try to maintain your composure and address the other person's emotional needs.

> **REAL-TIME UPDATES**
> LEARN MORE BY LISTENING TO THIS PODCAST
> **How to keep small battles from escalating into big ones**
> Use these insights to manage adversarial relationships in the workplace and keep them from getting destructive. Go to http://real-timeupdates.com/bct12 and click on Learn More. If you are using MyBCommLab, you can access Real-Time Updates within each chapter or under Student Study Tools.

# Collaborating on Communication Efforts

When a team collaborates on reports, websites, presentations, and other communication projects, the collective energy and expertise of the various members can produce results that transcend what each individual could do alone.[26] However, collaborating on team messages requires special effort and planning.

**2  LEARNING OBJECTIVE**
Offer guidelines for collaborative communication, identify major collaboration technologies, and explain how to give constructive feedback.

## GUIDELINES FOR COLLABORATIVE WRITING

In any collaborative effort, team members coming from different backgrounds may have different work habits or priorities: A technical expert may focus on accuracy and scientific standards, an editor may be more concerned about organization and coherence, and a manager may focus on schedules, cost, and corporate goals. In addition, team members differ in writing styles, work habits, and personality traits.

To collaborate effectively, everyone must be flexible and open to other opinions, focusing on team objectives rather than on individual priorities.[27] Successful writers know that most ideas can be expressed in many ways, so they avoid the "my way is best" attitude. The following guidelines will help you collaborate more successfully:[28]

- **Select collaborators carefully.** Whenever possible, choose a combination of people who together have the experience, information, and talent needed for each project.
- **Agree on project goals before you start.** Starting without a clear idea of what the team hopes to accomplish inevitably leads to frustration and wasted time.
- **Give your team time to bond before diving in.** If people haven't had the opportunity to work together before, make sure they can get to know each other before being asked to collaborate.
- **Clarify individual responsibilities.** Because members will be depending on each other, make sure individual responsibilities are clear.
- **Establish clear processes.** Make sure everyone knows how the work will be managed from start to finish.

Successful collaboration on writing projects requires a number of steps, from selecting the right partners and agreeing on project goals to establishing clear processes and avoiding writing as a group.

- **Avoid composing as a group.** The actual composition is the only part of developing team messages that does not usually benefit from group participation. Brainstorming the wording of short pieces of text, particularly headlines, slogans, and other high-visibility elements, can be an effective way to stimulate creative word choices. However, for longer projects, it is usually more efficient to plan, research, and outline together but assign the task of writing to one person or divide larger projects among multiple writers. If you divide the writing, try to have one person do a final revision pass to ensure a consistent style.
- **Make sure tools and techniques are ready and compatible across the team.** Even minor details such as different versions of software can delay projects.
- **Check to see how things are going along the way.** Don't assume that everything is working just because you don't hear anything negative.

## TECHNOLOGIES FOR COLLABORATIVE WRITING

A variety of tools are available to help writers collaborate on everything from short documents to entire websites (see Figure 2.2). The simplest tools are software features such as *commenting* (which lets colleagues write comments in a document without modifying the document text) and *change tracking* (which lets one or more writers propose changes to the text while keeping everyone's edits separate and reversible). The widely used Adobe Acrobat electronic document system (PDF files) also has group review and commenting features, including the option for live collaboration.

Writing for websites often involves the use of a **content management system**, which organizes and controls website content and can include features that help team members work together on webpages and other documents. These tools range from simple blogging systems on up to *enterprise* systems that manage web content across an entire corporation. Many systems include *workflow* features that control how pages or documents can be created, edited, and published.

In contrast to the formal controls of a content management system, a **wiki**, from the Hawaiian word for *quick*, is a website that allows anyone with access to add new material

> A wide variety of collaboration tools now exist to help professionals work on reports, presentations, and other communication efforts.

> Wiki benefits include simple operation and the ability to post new or revised material instantly without a formal review process.

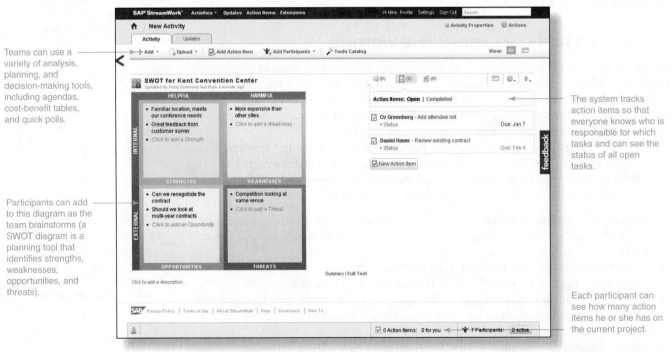

Teams can use a variety of analysis, planning, and decision-making tools, including agendas, cost-benefit tables, and quick polls.

Participants can add to this diagram as the team brainstorms (a SWOT diagram is a planning tool that identifies strengths, weaknesses, opportunities, and threats).

The system tracks action items so that everyone knows who is responsible for which tasks and can see the status of all open tasks.

Each participant can see how many action items he or she has on the current project.

**Figure 2.2 Collaboration Technologies**
Collaboration technologies such as SAP's StreamWork system help team members work together in real time, with documents, decisions, messages, and other vital project elements accessible to everyone.
*Source:* © Copyright 2011. SAP AG. All rights reserved.

Each project and program gets its own workspace, which can be shared with designated users inside or outside the company.

Within each workspace, the system organizes tasks, links, messages, project assignments, message archives, and all the other resources a team needs.

The system tracks all recent activity on a project, creating a searchable record of messages, task assignments, and other important details.

**Figure 2.3   Shared Workspaces**
Zig Marketing uses the WizeHive platform to create shared online workspaces for its employees, business partners, and clients.
*Source:* Copyright © 2011 by Wize Hive, Inc. Used by permission.

and edit existing material. Public wikis (Wikipedia is the best known of these) allow any registered user to edit pages; private wikis are accessible only with permission. A key benefit of wikis is the freedom to post new or revised material without prior approval. Chapter 8 offers guidelines for effective wiki collaboration.

Teams and other work groups can also take advantage of a set of broader technologies often referred to as *groupware* or *collaboration platforms*. These technologies let people communicate, share files, review previous message threads, work on documents simultaneously, and connect using social networking tools. These systems help companies capture and share knowledge from multiple experts, bringing greater insights to bear on tough challenges.[29] Collaboration systems often take advantage of *cloud computing*, a somewhat vague term that refers to "on-demand" capabilities delivered over the Internet, rather than through conventional on-site software.[30]

**Shared workspaces** are online "virtual offices" that give everyone on a team access to the same set of resources and information (see Figure 2.3). You may see some of these workspaces referred to as *intranets* (restricted-access websites that are open to employees only) or *extranets* (restricted sites that are available to employees and to outside parties by invitation only). Many intranets have now evolved into social networking systems that include a variety of communication and collaboration tools, from microblogging to video clip libraries. For example, the performance troupe Blue Man Group uses a *social intranet* to help its 500 employees plan, stage, and promote shows all over the world.[31]

## SOCIAL NETWORKS AND VIRTUAL COMMUNITIES

Social networking technologies are redefining teamwork and team communication by helping erase the constraints of geographic and organization boundaries. Some companies use social networks to form *virtual communities* or *communities of practice* that link employees with similar professional interests throughout the company and sometimes with customers and suppliers as well.

The huge advantage that social networking brings to these team efforts is in identifying the best people to collaborate on each problem or project, no matter where they are around the world or what their official roles are in the organization. Such communities are similar to teams in many respects, but one major difference is in the responsibility for accumulating organizational knowledge over the long term. For example, the pharmaceutical company

A *community of practice* links professionals with similar job interests; a key benefit is accumulating long-term organizational knowledge.

Internal social networks help companies assemble the best resources for a given task, regardless of where the employees are located.

**TABLE 2.2 | Giving Constructive Feedback**

| How to Be Constructive | Explanation |
|---|---|
| Think through your suggested changes carefully. | Many business documents must illustrate complex relationships between ideas and other information, so isolated and superficial edits can do more harm than good. |
| Discuss improvements rather than flaws. | Instead of saying "this is confusing," for instance, explain how the writing can be improved to make it clearer. |
| Focus on controllable behavior. | The writer may not have control over every variable that affected the quality of the message, so focus on those aspects the writer can control. |
| Be specific. | Comments such as "I don't get this" or "Make this clearer" don't give the writer much direction. |
| Keep feedback impersonal. | Focus comments on the message, not on the person who created it. |
| Verify understanding. | If in doubt, ask for confirmation from the recipient to make sure that the person understood your feedback. |
| Time your feedback carefully. | Respond in a timely fashion so that the writer will have sufficient time to implement the changes you suggest. |
| Highlight any limitations your feedback may have. | If you didn't have time to give the document a thorough edit, or if you're not an expert in some aspect of the content, let the writer know so that he or she can handle your comments appropriately. |

Pfizer has a number of permanent product safety communities that provide specialized advice on drug safety issues to researchers throughout the organization.[32]

Social networking can also help a company maintain a sense of community even as it grows beyond the size that normally permits a lot of daily interaction. At the online retailer Zappos, fostering a supportive work environment is the company's top priority. To encourage the sense of community among its expanding workforce, Zappos uses social networking tools to track employee connections and encourage workers to reach out and build relationships.[33]

### GIVING—AND RESPONDING TO—CONSTRUCTIVE FEEDBACK

> When you give writing feedback, make it constructive by focusing on how the material can be improved.

Aside from processes and tools, collaborative communication often involves giving and receiving feedback about writing efforts. **Constructive feedback**, sometimes called *constructive criticism*, focuses on the process and outcomes of communication, not on the people involved (see Table 2.2). In contrast, **destructive feedback** delivers criticism with no guidance to stimulate improvement.[34] For example, "This proposal is a confusing mess, and you failed to convince me of anything" is destructive feedback. The goal is to be more constructive: "Your proposal could be more effective with a clearer description of the manufacturing process and a well-organized explanation of why the positives outweigh the negatives." When giving feedback, avoid personal attacks and give the person clear guidelines for improvement.

> When you receive constructive feedback on your writing, keep your emotions in check and view it as an opportunity to improve.

When you receive constructive feedback, resist the understandable urge to defend your work or deny the validity of the feedback. Remaining open to criticism isn't easy when you've invested lots of time and energy in a project, but good feedback provides a valuable opportunity to learn and to improve the quality of your work.

## Making Your Meetings More Productive

> **3 LEARNING OBJECTIVE**
> List the key steps needed to ensure productive team meetings.
>
> Much of the communication you'll participate in will take place in meetings.

Much of your workplace communication will occur during in-person or online meetings, so to a large degree, your ability to contribute to the company—and to be recognized for your contributions—will depend on your meeting skills. Well-run meetings can help companies solve problems, develop ideas, and identify opportunities. Meetings can also be a great way to promote team building through the experience of social interaction.[35] As useful as meetings can be, though, they can be a waste of time if they aren't planned and managed well. You can help ensure productive meetings by preparing carefully, conducting meetings efficiently, and using meeting technologies wisely.

## PREPARING FOR MEETINGS

The first step in preparing for a meeting is to make sure the meeting is really necessary. Meetings can consume hundreds or thousands of dollars of productive time while taking people away from other work, so don't hold a meeting if some other form of communication (such as a blog post) can serve the purpose as effectively.[36] If a meeting is truly necessary, proceed with these four planning tasks:

- **Define your purpose.** Meetings can focus on exchanging information, reaching decisions, or collaborating to solve problems or identify opportunities. Whatever your purpose, define the best possible result of the meeting (such as "we carefully evaluated all three product ideas and decided which one to invest in"). Use this hoped-for result to shape the direction and content of the meeting.[37]
- **Select participants for the meeting.** The rule here is simple: Invite everyone who really needs to be involved, and don't invite anyone who doesn't. For decision-making meetings, for example, invite only those people who are in a direct position to help the meeting reach its objective. The more people you have, the longer it will take to reach consensus. Meetings with more than 10 or 12 people can become unmanageable if everyone is expected to participate in the discussion and decision making.
- **Choose the venue and the time.** Online meetings (see page 43) are often the best way and sometimes the only way to connect people in multiple locations or to reach large audiences. For in-person meetings, review the facility and the seating arrangements. Is theater-style seating suitable, or do you need a conference table or some other arrangement? Pay attention to room temperature, lighting, ventilation, acoustics, and refreshments; these details can make or break a meeting. If you have control over the timing, morning meetings are often more productive because people are generally more alert and not yet engaged with the work of the day.
- **Set the agenda.** The success of a meeting depends on the preparation of the participants. Distribute a carefully written agenda to participants, giving them enough time to prepare as needed (see Figure 2.4). A productive agenda answers three key questions: (1) What do we need to do in this meeting to accomplish our goals? (2) What issues will be of greatest importance to all participants? (3) What information must be available in order to discuss these issues?[38]

> To ensure a successful meeting, decide on your purpose ahead of time, select the right participants, choose the venue and time, and set a clear agenda.

## CONDUCTING AND CONTRIBUTING TO EFFICIENT MEETINGS

Everyone in a meeting shares the responsibility for making the meeting productive. If you're the leader, however, you have an extra degree of responsibility and accountability. The following guidelines will help leaders and participants contribute to more effective meetings:

> Everyone shares the responsibility for successful meetings.

- **Keep the discussion on track.** A good meeting draws out the best ideas and information the group has to offer. Good leaders occasionally need to guide, mediate, probe, stimulate, summarize, and redirect discussions that have gotten off track.
- **Follow agreed-upon rules.** The larger the meeting, the more formal you need to be to maintain order. Formal meetings use **parliamentary procedure**, a time-tested method for planning and running effective meetings. The best-known guide to this procedure is *Robert's Rules of Order* (www.robertsrules.com).
- **Encourage participation.** You may discover that some participants are too quiet and others are too talkative. Draw out nonparticipants by asking for their input. For the overly talkative, you can say that time is limited and others need to be heard.

**REAL-TIME UPDATES**

LEARN MORE BY LISTENING TO THIS PODCAST

### How to share your ideas in a meeting

On-site and online meetings can be a great forum for sharing your ideas—if you know how to do so successfully. Go to http://real-timeupdates.com/bct12 and click on Learn More. If you are using MyBCommLab, you can access Real-Time Updates within each chapter or under Student Study Tools.

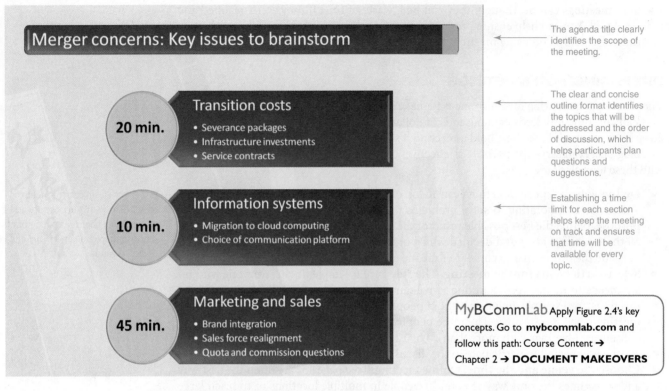

**Figure 2.4    Typical Meeting Agenda**
Agenda formats vary widely, depending on the complexity of the meeting and the presentation technologies that will be used. One good approach is to first distribute a detailed planning agenda so that presenters know what they need to prepare, then create a simpler display agenda such as this PowerPoint slide to guide the progress of the meeting. Note how the agenda includes the time limit for each topic.

- **Participate actively.** Make a point to contribute to the progress of the meeting and the smooth interaction of participants. Use your listening skills and powers of observation to size up the interpersonal dynamics of the group, then adapt your behavior to help the group achieve its goals. Speak up if you have something useful to say, but don't talk or ask questions just to demonstrate how much you know about the subject at hand.
- **Close effectively.** At the conclusion of the meeting, verify that the objectives have been met or arrange for follow-up work, if needed. Either summarize the general conclusion of the discussion or the actions to be taken. Make sure all participants have a chance to clear up any misunderstandings.

To review the tasks that contribute to productive meetings, refer to "Checklist: Improving Meeting Productivity."

For formal meetings, it's good practice to appoint one person to record the **minutes**, a summary of the important information presented and the decisions made. In smaller or informal meetings, attendees often make their own notes on their copies of the agenda. In either case, a clear record of the decisions and of the people responsible for follow-up action is essential. If your company doesn't have a specific format for minutes, follow the generic format shown in Figure 2.5.

---

**CHECKLIST ✔ Improving Meeting Productivity**

**A. Prepare carefully.**
- Make sure the meeting is necessary.
- Decide on your purpose.
- Select participants carefully.
- Choose the venue and the time.
- Establish and distribute a clear agenda.

**B. Lead effectively and participate fully.**
- Keep the meeting on track.
- Follow agreed-upon rules.
- Encourage participation.
- Participate actively.
- Close effectively.

## People Matters

The blog for HR professionals at Starfield, Inc.

**Key links**

Employee handbook

HR process metrics

Training

Recruiting

Compensation

Benefits

Regulatory guidelines

Department liaisons

---

5/15/2013

### MINUTES: Planning Committee Meeting
Human Resources Employee Programs
Wednesday, May 15, 2013

**Present:** Tabitha Brown, Peter Crantz, Kathi Kazanopolis, Agatha Myers, Julie Owens, Bob Phelps, Judith Williams

**Absent:** Joseph Kingman, Maria Lopez

Meeting called to order by Agatha Myers at 9:30 a.m.

**1. November program (speaker replacement)**

Kathi Kazanopolis offered to give a presentation about continuing education in job skills, to include detailed information about available workshops, online courses, etc.

Julie Owens volunteered to help Kathi with preparation: handouts, possible topics for small group discussions, research, etc.

**2. Future programs**

Bob Phelps contacted Edie Orlofsky, who teaches business communication courses at UCLA Extension, about the possibility of a writing skills workshop. He expects to hear from her this week.

Tax program: Still targeted for January or February. Judith Williams will try to locate a tax attorney or tax accountant as speaker.

**3. New-employee orientation**

Tabitha Brown announced that the executive team has asked the HR department to explore ways to use more computer-based training in the new-employee orientation program. Tabitha will investigate and report back next month.

08:23 Posted by Agatha Myers | Permalink | Comments (0) | E-mail this

---

**May 2013**

| S | M | T | W | T | F | S |
|---|---|---|---|---|---|---|
|   |   |   | 1 | 2 | 3 | 4 |
| 5 | 6 | 7 | 8 | 9 | 10 | 11 |
| 12 | 13 | 14 | 15 | 16 | 17 | 18 |
| 19 | 20 | 21 | 22 | 23 | 24 | 25 |
| 26 | 27 | 28 | 29 | 30 | 31 |   |

**Recent Posts**

Financial impact of employee training

Debate over pre-employment testing

Industry compensation survey

Jonathan Edwards retirement party planned for July 12

**Archives**

2013-05

2013-04

2013-03

2013-02

2013-01

2012-12

2011-11

---

The heading and subheading clearly identify the specific meeting, so there is no confusion about which meeting these minutes are for.

Listing the invited participants who did and did not attend clarifies the record in case any of the decisions made are questioned later on.

Concise summaries of each discussion serve as the official record of the meeting, in case there is confusion or disagreement about what was discussed and the details of any decisions or task assignments.

MyBCommLab Apply Figure 2.5's key concepts. Go to **mybcommlab.com** and follow this path: Course Content → Chapter 2 → **DOCUMENT MAKEOVERS**

**Figure 2.5   Typical Minutes of a Meeting**
The specific format of meeting minutes is less important than making sure you record all the key information, particularly regarding responsibilities assigned during the meeting. No matter what medium is used, key elements of meeting minutes include a list of those present and a list of those who were invited but didn't attend, followed by the times the meeting started and ended, all major decisions reached at the meeting, all assignments of tasks to meeting participants, and all subjects that were deferred to a later meeting. Minutes objectively summarize important discussions, noting the names of those who contributed major points. Outlines, subheadings, and lists help organize the minutes; additional documentation is noted in the minutes and attached.

# Using Meeting Technologies

Today's companies use a number of technologies to enhance or even replace traditional in-person meetings. Holding **virtual meetings** can dramatically reduce costs and resource usage, reduce wear and tear on employees, and give teams access to a wider pool of expertise (see Figure 2.6 on the next page). For example, by meeting customers and business partners online instead of in person, during one 18-month period Cisco Systems cut its travel-related costs by $100 million, reduced its carbon footprint by millions of tons, and improved employee productivity and satisfaction.[39]

Instant messaging (IM) and teleconferencing are the simplest forms of virtual meetings. Videoconferencing lets participants see and hear each other, demonstrate products, and transmit other visual information. *Telepresence* (see Figure 2.7 on the next page) enables realistic conferences in which participants thousands of miles apart almost seem to be in the same room.[40] The ability to convey nonverbal subtleties such as facial expressions

**4  LEARNING OBJECTIVE**
Identify the major technologies used to enhance or replace in-person meetings.

Virtual meeting technologies connect people spread around the country or around the world.

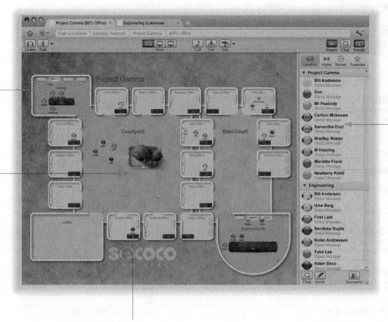

The virtual environment is made up of offices, conference rooms, and other spaces where people can interact through IM chat, voice conferencing, and document sharing.

Informal meeting spaces can also be created, such as the "courtyard" shown here.

Colleagues are available at the click of a mouse.

Employees can phone a colleague by clicking on the phone icon on his or her desk.

**Figure 2.6** **Virtual Meetings**
Virtual meeting technologies offer a variety of ways to interact online. The Team Space system from Sococo mimics the layout of an office building, allowing users to click into offices, conference rooms, and other spaces to initiate virtual meetings and presentations.
Source: Copyright © 2011 by Sococo. Used by permission.

and hand gestures makes these systems particularly good for negotiations, collaborative problem solving, and other complex discussions.[41]

The most sophisticated web-based meeting systems combine the best of real-time communication, shared workspaces, and videoconferencing with other tools, such as *virtual whiteboards*, that let teams collaborate in real time. Such systems are used for everything from spontaneous discussions among small groups to carefully planned formal events such as press conferences, training sessions, sales presentations, and *webinars* (web-based seminars).[42]

Technology continues to create intriguing opportunities for online interaction. For instance, one of the newest virtual tools is online brainstorming, in which a company can conduct "idea campaigns" to generate new ideas from people across the organization. Such brainstorming can range from small team meetings to huge events such as IBM's giant InnovationJam, in which 150,000 IBM employees, family members, and customers from more than 100 countries brainstormed online for three days. The ideas led to the creation of 10 new lines of business for the company.[43]

Conducting successful virtual meetings requires extra planning beforehand and more diligence during the meeting. Recognizing the limitations of the virtual meeting format is a

Peter Wynn Thompson/The New York Times, Redux Pictures.

**Figure 2.7** **Telepresence**
How many people are actually in this conference room in Chicago? Only the two people in the foreground are in the room; the other six are in Atlanta and London. Virtual meeting technologies such as this telepresence system connect people spread across the country or around the world.

key to using it successfully.[44] Because virtual meetings offer less visual contact and non-verbal communication than in-person meetings, leaders need to make sure everyone stays engaged and has the opportunity to contribute. Paying attention during online meetings takes greater effort as well. Participants need to stay committed to the meeting and resist the temptation to work on unrelated tasks.[45]

For the latest information on meeting technologies, visit http://real-timeupdates .com/bct12 and click on Chapter 2.

Conducting successful telephone or online meetings requires extra planning and more diligence during the meeting.

# Improving Your Listening Skills

Your long-term career prospects are closely tied to your ability to listen effectively. In fact, some 80 percent of top executives say listening is the most important skill needed to get things done in the workplace.[46] Plus, today's younger employees place a high premium on being heard, so listening is becoming even more vital for managers.[47]

Effective listening strengthens organizational relationships, alerts the organization to opportunities for innovation, and allows the organization to manage growing diversity both in the workforce and in the customers it serves.[48] Companies whose employees and managers listen effectively are able to stay informed, up to date, and out of trouble. Conversely, poor listening skills can cost companies millions of dollars per year as a result of lost opportunities, legal mistakes, and other errors. Effective listening is also vital to the process of building trust between organizations and between individuals.[49]

**5** LEARNING OBJECTIVE
Identify three major modes of listening, describe the listening process, and explain the problem of selective listening.

Listening is one of the most important skills in the workplace.

**REAL-TIME UPDATES**

LEARN MORE BY WATCHING THIS VIDEO

**Train yourself to listen more effectively**

Learn five ways that you can "retune your ears for conscious listening." Go to http://real-timeupdates.com/bct12 and click on Learn More. If you are using MyBCommLab, you can access Real-Time Updates within each chapter or under Student Study Tools.

## RECOGNIZING VARIOUS TYPES OF LISTENING

Effective listeners adapt their listening approaches to different situations. The primary goal of **content listening** is to understand and retain the information in the speaker's message. Because you're not evaluating the information at this point, it doesn't matter whether you agree or disagree, approve or disapprove—only that you understand. Try to overlook the speaker's style and any limitations in the presentation; just focus on the information.[50]

The goal of **critical listening** is to understand and evaluate the meaning of the speaker's message on several levels: the logic of the argument, the strength of the evidence, the validity of the conclusions, the implications of the message, the speaker's intentions and motives, and the omission of any important or relevant points. If you're skeptical, ask questions to explore the speaker's point of view and credibility. Be on the lookout for bias that could color the way the information is presented, and be careful to separate opinions from facts.[51]

The goal of **empathic listening** is to understand the speaker's feelings, needs, and wants so that you can appreciate his or her point of view, regardless of whether you share that perspective. By listening with empathy, you help the individual vent the emotions that prevent a calm, clear-headed approach to the subject. Avoid the temptation to jump in with advice unless the person specifically asks for it. Also, don't judge the speaker's feelings, and don't try to tell people they shouldn't feel this or that emotion. Instead, let the speaker know that you appreciate his or her feelings and understand the situation. After you establish that connection, you can help the speaker move on to search for a solution.[52]

No matter what mode they are using at any given time, effective listeners try to engage in **active listening**, making a conscious effort to turn off their own filters and biases to truly hear and understand what the other party is saying. They ask questions to verify key points and encourage the speaker through positive body language.[53]

To be a good listener, adapt the way you listen to suit the situation.

Listening actively means making the effort to turn off your internal "filters" and biases to truly hear and understand what the other person is saying.

**REAL-TIME UPDATES**

LEARN MORE BY WATCHING THIS VIDEO

**Learn why listening is a survival skill for leaders**

Amgen CEO Kevin Sharer says he was "an awful listener" as a young professional but discovered that listening is crucial for becoming a better leader. Go to http://real-timeupdates.com/bct12 and click on Learn More. If you are using MyBCommLab, you can access Real-Time Updates within each chapter or under Student Study Tools.

## UNDERSTANDING THE LISTENING PROCESS

Listening is a far more complex process than most people think—and most of us aren't very good at it. People typically listen at no better than a 25 percent efficiency rate, remember only about half of what's said during a 10-minute conversation, and forget half of that within 48 hours.[54] Furthermore, when questioned about material they've just heard, they are likely to get the facts mixed up.[55]

Why is such a seemingly simple activity so difficult? The reason is that listening is not a simple process, by any means. Listening follows the same sequence as the general communication process model described in Chapter 1 (page 11), with the added challenge that it happens in real time. To listen effectively, you need to successfully complete five steps:[56]

Listening involves five steps: receiving, decoding, remembering, evaluating, and responding.

1. **Receiving.** You start by physically hearing the message and acknowledging it. Physical reception can be blocked by noise, impaired hearing, or inattention. Some experts also include nonverbal messages as part of this stage because these factors influence the listening process as well.
2. **Decoding.** Your next step is to assign meaning to sounds, which you do according to your own values, beliefs, ideas, expectations, roles, needs, and personal history.
3. **Remembering.** Before you can act on the information, you need to store it for future processing. As you learned in Chapter 1, incoming messages must first be captured in short-term memory before being transferred to long-term memory for more permanent storage.
4. **Evaluating.** Your next step is to evaluate the message by applying critical thinking skills to separate fact from opinion and evaluate the quality of the evidence.
5. **Responding.** After you've evaluated the speaker's message, you react. If you're communicating one-on-one or in a small group, the initial response generally takes the form of verbal feedback. If you're one of many in an audience, your initial response may take the form of applause, laughter, or silence. Later on, you may act on what you have heard.

If any one of these steps breaks down, the listening process becomes less effective or may even fail entirely. As both a sender and a receiver, you can reduce the failure rate by recognizing and overcoming a variety of physical and mental barriers to effective listening.

## OVERCOMING BARRIERS TO EFFECTIVE LISTENING

Good listeners actively try to overcome barriers to successful listening.

Good listeners look for ways to overcome potential barriers throughout the listening process (see Table 2.3). You may not be able to control some factors, such as conference room acoustics or poor phone reception. However, you can control other factors, such as not interrupting speakers and not creating distractions that make it difficult for others to pay attention. And don't think you're not interrupting just because you're not talking. Such actions as texting or checking your watch can interrupt a speaker and lead to communication breakdowns.

**Selective listening** is one of the most common barriers to effective listening. If your mind wanders, you may stay tuned out until you hear a word or phrase that gets your attention again. But by that time, you're unable to recall what the speaker *actually* said; instead, you remember what you think the speaker *probably* said.[57]

Your mind can process information much faster than most speakers talk, so you need to focus to listen effectively.

One reason listeners' minds tend to wander is that people think faster than they speak. Most people speak at about 120 to 150 words per minute, but listeners can process audio information at up to 500 words per minute or more.[58] Consequently, your brain has a lot of free time whenever you're listening, and if left unsupervised, it will find a thousand other things to think about. Make the effort to focus on the speaker and use the extra time to analyze and paraphrase what you hear or to take relevant notes.

Overcoming interpretation barriers can be difficult because you may not even be aware of them. As Chapter 1 notes, selective perception leads listeners to mold messages to fit

| | |
|---|---|
| TABLE 2.3 | **What Makes an Effective Listener?** | |

| Effective Listeners | Ineffective Listeners |
|---|---|
| Listen actively. | Listen passively. |
| Take careful and complete notes, when applicable. | Take no notes or ineffective notes. |
| Make frequent eye contact with the speaker (depends on culture to some extent). | Make little or no eye contact—or inappropriate eye contact. |
| Stay focused on the speaker and the content. | Allow their minds to wander, are easily distracted, work on unrelated tasks. |
| Mentally paraphrase key points to maintain attention level and ensure comprehension. | Fail to paraphrase. |
| Adjust listening style to the situation. | Listen with the same style, regardless of the situation. |
| Give the speaker nonverbal cues (such as nodding to show agreement or raising eyebrows to show surprise or skepticism). | Fail to give the speaker nonverbal feedback. |
| Save questions or points of disagreement until an appropriate time. | Interrupt whenever they disagree or don't understand. |
| Overlook stylistic differences and focus on the speaker's message. | Are distracted by or unduly influenced by stylistic differences; are judgmental. |
| Make distinctions between main points and supporting details. | Unable to distinguish main points from details. |
| Look for opportunities to learn. | Assume they already know everything that's important to know. |

*Sources:* Adapted from Madelyn Burley-Allen, *Listening: The Forgotten Skill* (New York: Wiley, 1995), 70–71, 119–120; Judi Brownell, *Listening: Attitudes, Principles, and Skills* (Boston: Allyn & Bacon, 2002); 3, 9, 83, 89, 125; Larry Barker and Kittie Watson, *Listen Up* (New York: St. Martin's, 2000), 8, 9, 64.

their own conceptual frameworks. Listeners sometimes make up their minds before fully hearing the speaker's message, or they engage in *defensive listening*—protecting their egos by tuning out anything that doesn't confirm their beliefs or their view of themselves.

Even when your intentions are good, you can still misinterpret incoming messages if you and the speaker don't share enough language or experience. When listening to a speaker whose native language or life experience is different from yours, try to paraphrase that person's ideas. Give the speaker a chance to confirm what you think you heard or to correct any misinterpretation.

If the information you hear will be important to use later, write it down or otherwise record it. Don't rely on your memory. If you do need to memorize, you can hold information in short-term memory by repeating it silently or organizing a long list of items into several shorter lists. To store information in long-term memory, four techniques can help: (1) associate new information with something closely related (such as the restaurant in which you met a new client), (2) categorize the new information into logical groups (such as alphabetizing a list of names), (3) visualize words and ideas as pictures, and (4) create mnemonics such as acronyms or rhymes.

For a reminder of the steps you can take to overcome listening barriers, see "Checklist: Overcoming Barriers to Effective Listening."

When information is crucial, don't count on your memory—record the information mechanically or electronically.

---

**CHECKLIST** ✔ **Overcoming Barriers to Effective Listening**

- Lower barriers to physical reception whenever you can (such as avoiding interrupting speakers by asking questions or by exhibiting disruptive nonverbal behaviors).
- Avoid selective listening by focusing on the speaker and carefully analyzing what you hear.
- Keep an open mind by avoiding any prejudgment and by not listening defensively.

- Don't count on your memory; write down or record important information.
- Improve your short-term memory by repeating information or breaking it into shorter lists.
- Improve your long-term memory by using association, categorization, visualization, and mnemonics.

# Improving Your Nonverbal Communication Skills

**6** LEARNING OBJECTIVE
Explain the importance of nonverbal communication, and identify six major categories of nonverbal expression.

Nonverbal communication can supplement or even replace verbal messages (those that use words).

Nonverbal signals include facial expression, gesture and posture, vocal characteristics, personal appearance, touch, and time and space.

**Nonverbal communication** is the interpersonal process of sending and receiving information, both intentionally and unintentionally, without using written or spoken language. Nonverbal signals play a vital role in communication because they can strengthen a verbal message (when the nonverbal signals match the spoken words), weaken a verbal message (when nonverbal signals don't match the words), or replace words entirely. For example, you might tell a client that a project is coming along nicely, but your forced smile and nervous glances will send an entirely different message.

## RECOGNIZING NONVERBAL COMMUNICATION

You've been tuned in to nonverbal communication since your first contact with other human beings. Paying special attention to nonverbal signals in the workplace will enhance your ability to communicate successfully. Moreover, as you work with a diverse range of people in the global marketplace, you'll also need to grasp the different meanings of common gestures, expressions, and other signals in various cultures. Six types of signals are particularly important:

- **Facial expression.** Your face is the primary vehicle for expressing your emotions; it reveals both the type and the intensity of your feelings.[59] Your eyes are especially effective for indicating attention and interest, influencing others, regulating interaction, and establishing dominance.[60]
- **Gesture and posture.** The way you position and move your body expresses both specific and general messages, some voluntary and some involuntary. Many gestures—a wave of the hand, for example—have specific and intentional meanings. Other types of body movement are unintentional and express more general messages. Slouching, leaning forward, fidgeting, and walking briskly are all unconscious signals that can reveal whether you feel confident or nervous, friendly or hostile, assertive or passive, powerful or powerless.
- **Vocal characteristics.** Voice carries both intentional and unintentional messages. A speaker can intentionally control pitch, pace, and stress to convey a specific message. For instance, compare "*What* are you doing?" and "What are *you* doing?" Unintentional vocal characteristics can convey happiness, surprise, fear, and other emotions (for example, fear often increases the pitch and pace of your speaking voice).
- **Personal appearance.** People respond to others on the basis of their physical appearance, sometimes fairly and other times unfairly. Although an individual's body type and facial features impose some limitations on appearance, you can control grooming, clothing, accessories, piercings, tattoos, and hairstyle. To make a good impression, adopt the style of the people you want to impress. Many employers also have guidelines concerning attire, body art, and other issues, so make sure you understand and follow them.[61]
- **Touch.** Touch is an important way to convey warmth, comfort, and reassurance—as well as control. Touch is so powerful, in fact, that it is governed by cultural customs that establish who can touch whom and how in various circumstances. In the United States and Great Britain, for instance, people usually touch less frequently than people in France or Costa Rica do. Even within each culture's norms, however, individual attitudes toward touch vary widely. A manager might be comfortable using hugs to express support or congratulations, but his or her subordinates could interpret those hugs as a show of dominance or sexual interest.[62] Touch is a complex subject. The best advice: When in doubt, don't touch.
- **Time and space.** Like touch, time and space can be used to assert authority, imply intimacy, and send other nonverbal messages. For instance, some people try to demonstrate their own importance or disregard for others by making other people wait; others show respect by being on time. Similarly, taking care not to invade private space, such as standing too close when talking, is a way to show respect for others. Keep in mind that expectations regarding both time and space vary by culture.

---

**CHECKLIST** ✔ Improving Nonverbal Communication Skills

- Understand the roles that nonverbal signals play in communication, complementing verbal language by strengthening, weakening, or replacing words.
- Note that facial expressions (especially eye contact) reveal the type and intensity of a speaker's feelings.
- Watch for cues from gestures and posture.
- Listen for vocal characteristics that can signal the emotions underlying the speaker's words.

- Recognize that listeners are influenced by physical appearance.
- Be careful with physical contact; touch can convey positive attributes but can also be interpreted as dominance or sexual interest.
- Pay attention to the use of time and space.

---

## USING NONVERBAL COMMUNICATION EFFECTIVELY

Paying attention to nonverbal cues will make you a better speaker and a better listener. When you're talking, be more conscious of the nonverbal cues you could be sending. Are they effective without being manipulative? Consider a situation in which an employee has come to you to talk about a raise. This situation is stressful for the employee, so don't say you're interested in what she has to tell you and then spend your time glancing at your computer or checking your watch. Conversely, if you already know you won't be able to give her the raise, be honest in your expression of emotions. Don't overcompensate for your own stress by smiling too broadly or shaking her hand too vigorously. Both nonverbal signals would raise her hopes without justification. In either case, match your nonverbal cues to the tone of the situation.

Also consider the nonverbal signals you send when you're not talking—the clothes you wear, the way you sit, the way you walk. Are you talking like a serious business professional but dressing like you belong in a dance club or a frat house? Whether or not you think it is fair to be judged on superficial matters, the truth is that you are judged this way. Don't let careless choices or disrespectful habits undermine all the great work you're doing on the job.

When you listen, be sure to pay attention to the speaker's nonverbal cues. Do they amplify the spoken words or contradict them? Is the speaker intentionally using nonverbal signals to send you a message that he or she can't put into words? Be observant, but don't assume that you can "read someone like a book." Nonverbal signals are powerful, but they aren't infallible, particularly if you don't know a person's normal behavioral patterns.[63] For example, contrary to popular belief, avoiding eye contact and covering one's face while talking are not reliable clues that someone is lying. Even when telling the truth, most people don't make uninterrupted eye contact with the listeners, and various gestures such as touching one's face might be normal behavior for particular people.[64] Moreover, these and other behaviors may be influenced by culture (in some cultures, sustained eye contact can be interpreted as a sign of disrespect) or might just be ways of coping with stressful situations.[65]

If something doesn't feel right, ask the speaker an honest and respectful question; doing so may clear everything up, or it may uncover issues you need to explore further. See "Checklist: Improving Nonverbal Communication Skills" for a summary of key ideas regarding nonverbal skills.

> Work to make sure your nonverbal signals match the tone and content of your spoken communication.

> What signals does your personal appearance send?

# Developing Your Business Etiquette

You may have noticed a common thread running through the topics of successful teamwork, productive meetings, effective listening, and nonverbal communication: All these activities depend on mutual respect and consideration among all participants. Nobody wants to work with someone who is rude to colleagues or an embarrassment to the company. Moreover, shabby treatment of others in the workplace can be a huge drain on morale and productivity.[66] Poor etiquette can drive away customers, investors, and other critical audiences—and it can limit your career potential.

> **7 LEARNING OBJECTIVE**
> Explain the importance of business etiquette, and identify three key areas in which good etiquette is essential.

Etiquette is an essential element of every aspect of business communication.

This section addresses some key etiquette points to remember when you're in the workplace, out in public, and online. Long lists of etiquette rules can be difficult to remember, but you can get by in most every situation by remembering to be aware of your effect on others, treating everyone with respect, and keeping in mind that the impressions you leave behind can have a lasting effect on you and your company. As etiquette expert Cindy Post Senning points out, "The principles of respect, consideration, and honesty are universal and timeless."[67]

## BUSINESS ETIQUETTE IN THE WORKPLACE

Personal appearance can have considerable impact on your success in business.

Workplace etiquette includes a variety of behaviors, habits, and aspects of nonverbal communication. Although it isn't always thought of as an element of etiquette, your personal appearance in the workplace sends a strong signal to managers, colleagues, and customers. Pay attention to the style of dress where you work and adjust your style to match. Expectations for specific jobs, companies, and industries can vary widely. The financial industries tend to be more formal than high-tech firms, for instance, and sales and executive positions usually involve more formal expectations than positions in engineering or manufacturing. Observe others, and don't be afraid to ask for advice. If you're not sure, dress modestly and simply—earn a reputation for what you can do, not for what you wear. Table 2.4 offers some general guidelines on assembling a business wardrobe that's cost-effective and flexible.

Grooming is as important as attire. Pay close attention to cleanliness, and avoid using products with powerful scents, such as perfumed soaps, colognes, shampoos, and after-shave lotions (many people are bothered by these products, and some are allergic to them).

Meetings require attention to etiquette to ensure a successful outcome and productive use of everyone's time. Start by showing up on time and ready to go. While the meeting is in progress, pay attention and stay engaged. Don't carry on side conversations, and don't multitask on your phone or other device (unless it's expected that you'll be participating in a backchannel conversation—see page 471). If you intend to use your device to take notes during the meeting, let the meeting leader know that's what you're doing.[68]

---

**TABLE 2.4 | Assembling a Business Wardrobe**

| 1<br>Smooth and Finished<br>(Start with This) | 2<br>Elegant and Refined<br>(To Column 1, Add This) | 3<br>Crisp and Starched<br>(To Column 2, Add This) | 4<br>Up-to-the-Minute Trendy<br>(To Column 3, Add This) |
|---|---|---|---|
| • Choose well-tailored clothing that fits well; it doesn't have to be expensive, but it does have to fit and be appropriate for business.<br>• Keep buttons, zippers, and hemlines in good repair.<br>• Select shoes that are comfortable enough for long days but neither too casual nor too dressy for the office; keep shoes clean and in good condition.<br>• Make sure the fabrics you wear are clean, are carefully pressed, and do not wrinkle easily.<br>• Choose colors that flatter your height, weight, skin tone, and style; sales advisors in good clothing stores can help you choose. | • Choose form-fitting (but not skin-tight) clothing—not swinging or flowing fabrics, frills, or fussy trimmings.<br>• Choose muted tones and soft colors or classics, such as a dark blue suit or a basic black dress.<br>• If possible, select a few classic pieces of jewelry (such as a string of pearls or diamond cuff links) for formal occasions.<br>• Wear jackets that complement an outfit and lend an air of formality to your appearance. Avoid jackets with more than two tones; one color should dominate. | • Wear blouses or shirts that are or appear starched.<br>• Choose closed top-button shirts or button-down shirt collars, higher-neckline blouses, or long sleeves with French cuffs and cuff links.<br>• Wear creased trousers or a longer skirt hemline. | • Supplement your foundation with pieces that reflect the latest styles.<br>• Add a few pieces in bold colors but wear them sparingly to avoid a garish appearance.<br>• Embellish your look with the latest jewelry and hairstyles but keep the overall effect looking professional. |

## COMMUNICATING ACROSS CULTURES

# Whose Skin Is This, Anyway?

Generational differences abound in the workplace, but few are quite as visible as *body art*: tattoos, piercings (other than ear lobes), and hair dyes in unconventional colors. According to survey data from the Pew Research Center, people younger than 40 are much more inclined than those over 40 to display some form of body art. For example, people 26 to 40 years old are four times more likely to have tattoos than people who are 41 to 64 years old.

With such profound differences, it's no surprise that body art has become a contentious issue in many workplaces, between employees wanting to express themselves and employers wanting to maintain particular standards of professional appearance. As employment law attorney Danielle S. Urban notes, the issue gets even more complicated when religious symbolism is involved.

Who is likely to win this battle? Will the body art aficionados who continue to join the workforce and who are now rising up the managerial ranks force a change in what is considered acceptable appearance in the workplace? Or will they be forced to cover up in order to meet traditional standards?

So far, most companies appear to be relying on the judgment of their employees and managers, rather than enforcing strict guidelines. Many seem to accept that tastes and norms are changing and that body art has become a widespread form of self-expression rather than a mode of rebellion. The semiconductor giant Intel even featured photos of employee tattoos in its online technology newsletter.

Job seekers are still advised to be discreet, however, particularly with facial piercings and large, visible tattoos. The nonverbal signals you think you are sending might not be the signals a hiring manager receives.

### CAREER APPLICATIONS

1. Should companies have stricter standards of appearance for "customer-facing" employees than for employees who do not interact with customers? Why or why not?
2. Should companies allow their employees the same freedom of expression and appearance latitude as their customers exhibit? For example, if a firm's clientele tends to be heavily tattooed, should employees be allowed the same freedom? Why or why not?

*Sources:* Adapted from: "Intel Tattoos Speak Volumes," 17 March 2011, *Intel Free Press*, www.intelfreepress.com; Rita Pyrillis, "Body of Work," *Workforce Management*, November 2010, www.workforce.com; Danielle S. Urban, "What to Do About 'Body Art' at Work," *Workforce Management*, March 2010, www.workforce.com; "36%—Tattooed Gen Nexters," Pew Research Center, http://pewresearch.org.

IM and other text-based tools have taken over many exchanges that used to occur over the phone, but phone skills are still essential. Because phone calls lack the visual richness of face-to-face conversations, you have to rely on your attitude and tone of voice to convey confidence and professionalism. Table 2.5 summarizes helpful tips for placing and receiving phone calls in a confident, professional manner.

Mobile phones are a contentious point of etiquette in today's workplace. They can boost productivity if used mindfully, but they can be a productivity- and morale-draining disruption when used carelessly. Be aware that attitudes about mobile phones vary widely, and don't be surprised if you encounter policies restricting their use in offices or meeting rooms. Nearly half of U.S. companies already have such policies.[69]

> Mobile phones are a frequent source of etiquette blunders.

Like every other aspect of communication, your phone habits say a lot about how much respect you have for the people around you. Selecting obnoxious ring tones, talking loudly in open offices or public places, using your phone right next to someone else, making excessive or unnecessary personal calls during work hours, invading someone's privacy by using your camera phone without permission, taking or making calls in restrooms and other inappropriate places, texting while someone is talking to you, allowing incoming calls to interrupt meetings or discussions—all are disrespectful choices that will reflect negatively on you.[70]

## BUSINESS ETIQUETTE IN SOCIAL SETTINGS

From business lunches to industry conferences, you may be asked to represent your company in public. Make sure your appearance and actions are appropriate to the situation. Get to know the customs of other cultures when it comes to meeting new people. For example, in North America, a firm handshake is expected when two people meet, whereas a respectful bow of the head is more appropriate in Japan. If you are expected to shake hands, be aware that the passive "dead fish" handshake creates an extremely negative impression. If you are physically able, always stand when shaking someone's hand.

> You represent your company when you're out in public, so etiquette continues to be important.

| TABLE 2.5 | Quick Tips for Improving Your Phone Skills | | | |
| --- | --- | --- | --- |
| **General Tips** | **Placing Calls** | **Receiving Calls** | **Using Voice Mail** |
| Use frequent verbal responses that show you're listening ("Oh yes," "I see," "That's right"). | Be ready before you call so that you don't waste the other person's time. | Answer promptly and with a smile so that you sound friendly and positive. | When recording your own outgoing message, make it brief and professional. |
| Increase your volume just slightly to convey your confidence. | Minimize the noise level in your environment as much as possible to avoid distracting the other party. | Identify yourself and your company (some companies have specific instructions for what to say when you answer). | If you can, record temporary greetings on days when you are unavailable all day so that callers will know you're gone for the day. |
| Don't speak in a monotone; vary your pitch and inflections so people know you're interested. | Identify yourself and your organization, briefly describe why you're calling, and verify that you've called at a good time. | Establish the needs of your caller by asking, "How may I help you?" If you know the caller's name, use it. | Check your voice-mail messages regularly and return all necessary calls within 24 hours. |
| Slow down when conversing with people whose native language isn't the same as yours. | Don't take up too much time. Speak quickly and clearly, and get right to the point of the call. | If you can, answer questions promptly and efficiently; if you can't help, tell them what you can do for them. | Leave simple, clear messages with your name, number (don't assume the recipient has caller ID), purpose for calling, and times when you can be reached. |
| Stay focused on the call throughout; others can easily tell when you're not paying attention. | Close in a friendly, positive manner and double-check all vital information such as meeting times and dates. | If you must forward a call or put someone on hold, explain what you are doing first. | State your name and telephone number slowly so that the other person can easily write them down; repeat both if the other person doesn't know you. |
| | | If you forward a call to someone else, try to speak with that person first to verify that he or she is available and to introduce the caller. | Be careful what you say; most voice-mail systems allow users to forward messages to anyone else in the system. |
| | | If you take a message for someone else, be complete and accurate, including the caller's name, number, and organization. | Replay your message before leaving the system to make sure it is clear and complete. |

*Sources:* Adapted from Alan Cole, "Telephone Etiquette at Work," Work Etiquette website, 14 March 2012, www.worketiquette.co.uk; Alf Nucifora, "Voice Mail Demands Good Etiquette from Both Sides," *Puget Sound Business Journal,* 5–11 September 2003, 24; Ruth Davidhizar and Ruth Shearer, "The Effective Voice Mail Message," *Hospital Material Management Quarterly,* 45–49; "How to Get the Most Out of Voice Mail," *The CPA Journal,* February 2000, 11; Jo Ind, "Hanging on the Telephone," *Birmingham Post,* 28 July 1999, PS10; Larry Barker and Kittie Watson, *Listen Up* (New York: St. Martin's Press, 2000), 64–65; Lin Walker, *Telephone Techniques,* (New York: Amacom, 1998), 46–47; Dorothy Neal, *Telephone Techniques,* 2nd ed. (New York: Glencoe McGraw-Hill, 1998), 31; Jeannie Davis, *Beyond "Hello"* (Aurora, Colo.: Now Hear This, Inc., 2000), 2–3; "Ten Steps to Caller-Friendly Voice Mail," *Managing Office Technology,* January 1995, 25; Rhonda Finniss, "Voice Mail: Tips for a Positive Impression," *Administrative Assistant's Update,* August 2001, 5.

When introducing yourself, include a brief description of your role in the company. When introducing two other people, speak their first and last names clearly and then try to offer some information (perhaps a shared professional interest) to help the two people ease into a conversation.[71] Generally speaking, the lower-ranking person is introduced to the senior-ranking person, without regard to gender.[72]

Business is often conducted over meals, and knowing the basics of dining etiquette will make you more effective in these situations.[73] Start by choosing foods that are easy to eat. Avoid alcoholic beverages in most instances, but if drinking one is appropriate, save it for the end of the meal. Leave business documents under your chair until entrée plates have been removed; the business aspect of the meal doesn't usually begin until then.

Just as in the office, when you use your mobile phone around other people in public, you send the message that people around you aren't as important as your call and that you don't respect your caller's privacy.[74] If it's not a matter of life and death, or at least an urgent request from your boss or a customer, wait until you're back in the office.

Remember that business meals are a forum for business, period. Don't discuss politics, religion, or any other topic that's likely to stir up emotions. Don't complain about work, don't ask deeply personal questions, avoid profanity, and be careful with humor—a joke that entertains some people could easily offend others.

Virtual assistants, such as the Siri voice recognition system in Apple iPhones, raise another new etiquette dilemma. From doing simple web searches to dictating entire memos, these systems may be convenient for users, but they can create distractions and annoyances for other people.[75] As with other public behaviors, think about the effect you'll have on others before using these technologies.

## BUSINESS ETIQUETTE ONLINE

Electronic media seem to be a breeding ground for poor etiquette. Learn the basics of professional online behavior to avoid mistakes that could hurt your company or your career. Here are some guidelines to follow whenever you are representing your company while using electronic media:[76]

- **Avoid personal attacks.** The anonymous and instantaneous nature of online communication can cause even level-headed people to strike out in blog postings, social networks, and other media.
- **Stay focused on the original topic.** If you want to change the subject of an email exchange, a forum discussion, or a blog comment thread, start a new message.
- **Don't present opinions as facts, and support facts with evidence.** This guideline applies to all communication, of course, but online venues in particular seem to tempt people into presenting their beliefs and opinions as unassailable truths.
- **Follow basic expectations of spelling, punctuation, and capitalization.** Sending careless, acronym-filled messages that look like you're texting your high school buddies makes you look like an amateur.
- **Use virus protection and keep it up to date.** Sending or posting a file that contains a computer virus puts others at risk.
- **Use difficult-to-break passwords on email, Twitter, and other accounts.** If someone hacks your account, it can create spam headaches—or worse—for your contacts and followers.
- **Ask if this is a good time for an IM chat.** Don't assume that just because a person is showing as "available" on your IM system, he or she wants to chat at this moment.
- **Watch your language and keep your emotions under control.** A single indiscretion could haunt you forever.
- **Avoid multitasking while using IM and other tools.** You might think you're saving time by doing a dozen things at once, but you're probably making the other person wait while you bounce back and forth between IM and your other tasks.
- **Never assume privacy.** Assume that anything you type will be stored forever, could be forwarded to other people, and might be read by your boss or the company's security staff.
- **Don't use "Reply All" in email unless everyone can benefit from your reply.** If one or more recipients of an email message don't need the information in your reply, remove their addresses before you send.
- **Don't waste others' time with sloppy, confusing, or incomplete messages.** Doing so is disrespectful.
- **Respect boundaries of time and virtual space.** For instance, don't start using an employee's personal Facebook page for business messages unless you've discussed it beforehand, and don't assume people are available to discuss work matters around the clock, even if you do find them online in the middle of the night.
- **Be careful of online commenting mechanisms.** For example, many blogs and websites now use your Facebook login to let you comment on articles. If your Facebook profile includes your job title and company name, those could show up along with your comment.

When you represent your company online, you must adhere to a high standard of etiquette and respect for others.

Respect personal and professional boundaries when using Facebook and other social networking tools.

**REAL-TIME UPDATES**

LEARN MORE BY READING THIS ARTICLE

**Why saying "thank you" is good for you, too**

See why "thank you" and other polite expressions benefit the sender, not just the receiver. Go to http://real-timeupdates.com/bct12 and click on Learn More. If you are using MyBCommLab, you can access Real-Time Updates within each chapter or under Student Study Tools.

# Quick Learning Guide

## SUMMARY OF LEARNING OBJECTIVES

**1** List the advantages and disadvantages of working in teams, describe the characteristics of effective teams, and highlight four key issues of group dynamics. Teams can achieve a higher level of performance than individuals because of the combined intelligence and energy of the group. Motivation and creativity can flourish in team settings. Moreover, individuals tend to perform better because they achieve a sense of purpose by belonging to a group. Teams also bring more input and a greater diversity of views, which tends to result in better decisions. And because team members participate in the decision process, they are more committed to seeing the team succeed. Teams are not without disadvantages, however. Poorly managed teams can be a waste of everyone's time. For example, if members are pressured to conform, they may develop groupthink, which can lead to poor-quality decisions and ill-advised actions. Some members may let their private motives get in the way.

Four important aspects of group dynamics are assuming team roles, allowing for team evolution, resolving conflict, and overcoming resistance.

**2** Offer guidelines for collaborative communication, identify major collaboration technologies, and explain how to give constructive feedback. Key guidelines for collaborative writing include (1) selecting collaborators carefully, (2) agreeing on project goals before starting, (3) giving the team time to bond before starting the work, (4) clarifying individual responsibilities, (5) establishing clear processes, (6) avoiding composing as a group, (7) making sure tools and techniques are ready and compatible, and (8) checking to see how things are going along the way.

Major collaboration technologies include web content management systems, wikis, groupware, and shared workspaces.

To give constructive feedback, focus on the work and how it can be improved, rather than on the person and the mistakes.

**3** List the key steps needed to ensure productive team meetings. The most important step in planning a meeting is to make sure that a meeting is necessary and is the best way to accomplish the given objective. If it is, proceed by identifying the purpose of the meeting, selecting the right mix of participants to accomplish the goal, choosing the venue and time carefully, and setting a clear agenda.

Once the meeting is underway, work to keep the discussion on track, follow agreed-upon rules, encourage participation, participate actively yourself, and close the meeting effectively to make sure all decisions and action items are clearly understood.

**4** Identify the major technologies used to enhance or replace in-person meetings. Meeting enhancement and replacement technologies range from simple audio teleconferencing and IM chat sessions to videoconferences, telepresence systems, web-based meetings, and virtual worlds such as realistic-looking online conference rooms.

**5** Identify three major modes of listening, describe the listening process, and explain the problem of selective listening. *Content listening* is listening to understand and retain the information in the speaker's message. *Critical listening* is listening to understand and evaluate the meaning of the speaker's message on several levels, including the logic of the argument and the strength of the speaker's evidence. *Empathic listening* is listening to understand the speaker's feelings, needs, and wants. Regardless of the mode used, effective listeners try to engage in *active listening*, making a conscious effort to turn off their own filters and biases to truly hear and understand what the other party is saying.

The listening process involves five activities: (1) receiving (physically hearing the message), (2) decoding (assigning meaning to what you hear), (3) remembering (storing the message for future reference), (4) evaluating (thinking about the message), and (5) responding (reacting to the message, taking action, or giving feedback).

The listening process can be hampered by a variety of barriers, one of the most common of which is selective listening. When people listen selectively, they hear only parts of the speaker's message, either because they allow their minds to wander or engage in defensive listening by tuning out information that threatens their beliefs or egos.

**6** Explain the importance of nonverbal communication, and identify six major categories of nonverbal expression. *Nonverbal communication* is important because nonverbal signals can strengthen, weaken, or even replace verbal messages. The major categories of nonverbal signals are facial expression, gestures and posture, vocal characteristics, personal appearance, touch, and the use of time and space.

**7** Explain the importance of business etiquette, and identify three key areas in which good etiquette is essential. Attention to etiquette is essential to success in every form of business communication—so much so that etiquette is considered an important business skill. Poor etiquette can hinder team efforts, drain morale and productivity, drive away customers and investors, and limit your career potential. Three key areas in which good etiquette is essential are the workplace, social settings in which you represent your employer, and online interactions in which you represent your employer.

## KEY TERMS

**active listening** Making a conscious effort to turn off filters and biases to truly hear and understand what someone is saying

**collaboration** Working together to meet complex challenges

**committees** Formal teams that usually have a long life span and can become a permanent part of the organizational structure

**constructive feedback** Focuses on the process and outcomes of communication, not on the people involved

**content listening** Listening to understand and retain the speaker's message

**content management systems** Computer systems that organize and control the content for websites

**critical listening** Listening to understand and evaluate the meaning of the speaker's message

**destructive feedback** Delivers criticism with no guidance to stimulate improvement

**empathic listening** Listening to understand the speaker's feelings, needs, and wants so that you can appreciate his or her point of view

**group dynamics** The interactions and processes that take place among the members of a team

**groupthink** Situation in which peer pressure causes individual team members to withhold contrary or unpopular opinions

**hidden agenda** Private, counterproductive motives, such as a desire to take control of the group

**minutes** Written summary of the important information presented and the decisions made during a meeting

**nonverbal communication** Sending and receiving information, both intentionally and unintentionally, without using written or spoken language

**norms** Informal standards of conduct that members share and that guide member behavior

**parliamentary procedure** A time-tested method for planning and running effective meetings; the best-known guide to this procedure is *Robert's Rules of Order*

**participative management** The effort to involve employees in the company's decision making

**problem-solving teams** Teams that assemble to resolve specific issues and then disband when their goals have been accomplished

**selective listening** Listening to only part of what a speaker is saying; ignoring the parts one doesn't agree with or find interesting

**self-oriented roles** Unproductive team roles in which people are motivated mainly to fulfill personal needs

**shared workspaces** Online "virtual offices" that give everyone on a team access to the same set of resources and information

**task forces** Another form of problem-solving teams, often with members from more than one organization

**task-oriented roles** Productive team roles directed toward helping the team reach its goals

**team** A unit of two or more people who share a mission and the responsibility for working to achieve a common goal

**team-maintenance roles** Productive team roles directed toward helping everyone work well together

**virtual meetings** Meetings that take place online rather than in person

**wiki** Special type of website that allows anyone with access to add new material and edit existing material

---

**CHECKLIST** ✓
## Improving Meeting Productivity

A. **Prepare carefully.**
- Make sure the meeting is necessary.
- Decide on your purpose.
- Select participants carefully.
- Choose the venue and the time.
- Establish and distribute a clear agenda.

B. **Lead effectively and participate fully.**
- Keep the meeting on track.
- Follow agreed-upon rules.
- Encourage participation.
- Participate actively.
- Close effectively.

**CHECKLIST** ✓
## Overcoming Barriers to Effective Listening

- Lower barriers to physical reception whenever you can (such as avoiding interrupting speakers by asking questions or by exhibiting disruptive nonverbal behaviors).
- Avoid selective listening by focusing on the speaker and carefully analyzing what you hear.
- Keep an open mind by avoiding any prejudgment and by not listening defensively.
- Don't count on your memory; write down or record important information.
- Improve your short-term memory by repeating information or breaking it into shorter lists.
- Improve your long-term memory by using association, categorization, visualization, and mnemonics.

**CHECKLIST** ✓
## Improving Nonverbal Communication Skills

- Understand the roles that nonverbal signals play in communication, complementing verbal language by strengthening, weakening, or replacing words.
- Note that facial expressions (especially eye contact) reveal the type and intensity of a speaker's feelings.
- Watch for cues from gestures and posture.
- Listen for vocal characteristics that can signal the emotions underlying the speaker's words.
- Recognize that listeners are influenced by physical appearance.
- Be careful with physical contact; touch can convey positive attributes but can also be interpreted as dominance or sexual interest.
- Pay attention to the use of time and space.

## COMMUNICATION CHALLENGES AT **Rosen Law Firm**

You recently joined Rosen Law Firm and quickly became an enthusiastic user of the company's internal wiki. In your brief time being involved with the wiki, you have observed some behavior that runs counter to the spirit of collaborative writing. Study these two scenarios and decide how to respond.

**INDIVIDUAL CHALLENGE:** One particular employee keeps editing your pages on the wiki, often making changes that appear to add no value as far as you can see. She doesn't seem to be editing other employees' pages nearly so often, so you are beginning to wonder if she has a personal grudge against you. You want to address this uncomfortable situation without dragging your boss into it. First, decide how to approach your contentious colleague. Should you drop by her office unannounced, call her on the phone, send her an email message, or perhaps insert a sarcastic comment about excessive editing on one of her wiki pages? Second, whichever mode of communication you've chosen, outline the message you think you should share with her.

**TEAM CHALLENGE:** A common dilemma in every form of collaborative writing is deciding how soon to share early drafts with your colleagues in order to get their feedback and

contributions. Should you send out an unpolished rough draft for the team's input before investing a lot of time in polishing and formatting, or should you do a second or third draft to enhance readability—knowing the team might delete entire sections you've worked hard to polish? On the Rosen wiki, some contributors seem to go into "grammar attack mode" whenever a rough draft appears. They seem to ignore the message and content altogether and instead focus on punctuation, grammar, and formatting concerns. With a small team of fellow students, draft some brief guidelines for wiki contributors, conveying these three points: (1) Punctuation, grammar, and formatting are definitely important, but worrying about them too early in the writing process can hamper the free exploration of ideas and information; (2) when reviewing early drafts, wiki users need to make a conscious effort to look past the presentation and focus on the information; and (3) contributors who post rough drafts seeking input should make the pages at least minimally readable so that reviewers can focus on the content and ideas. (To learn more about editing and working with wikis, you can peek ahead to page 214 in Chapter 8.)

## Test Your Knowledge

To review chapter content related to each question, refer to the indicated Learning Objective.

1. How can organizations and employees benefit from successful teamwork? [LO-1]
2. What is groupthink, and how can it affect an organization? [LO-1]
3. How can employees and companies take advantage of social networking technologies to promote teamwork? [LO-2]
4. Why would a company use a wiki to support team collaboration rather than a content management system? [LO-2]
5. What are the advantages of virtual meetings? [LO-4]
6. What are the main activities that make up the listening process? [LO-5]
7. How does content listening differ from critical listening and empathic listening? [LO-5]
8. What are the six major categories of nonverbal communication? [LO-6]
9. Why is etiquette an important business skill? [LO-7]

## Apply Your Knowledge

To review chapter content related to each question, refer to the indicated Learning Objective.

1. You head up the interdepartmental design review team for a manufacturer of high-performance motorcycles, and

things are not going well at the moment. The design engineers and marketing strategists keep arguing about which should be a higher priority, performance or aesthetics, and the accountants say both groups are driving up the cost of the new model by adding too many new features. Everyone has valid points to make, but the team is bogging down in conflict. Explain how you could go about resolving the stalemate. [LO-1]

2. You and another manager in your company disagree about whether employees should be encouraged to create online profiles on LinkedIn and other business-oriented social networking websites. You say these connections can be valuable to employees by helping them meet their peers throughout the industry and valuable to the company by identifying potential sales leads and business partners. The other manager says that encouraging employees to become better known in the industry will only make it easier for competitors to lure them away with enticing job offers. Write a brief email message that outlines your argument. (Make up any information you need about the company and its industry.) [LO-2]

3. How can nonverbal communication help you run a meeting? How can it help you call a meeting to order, emphasize important topics, show approval, express reservations, regulate the flow of conversation, and invite a colleague to continue with a comment? [LO-3], [LO-6]

4. Why do you think people are more likely to engage in rude behaviors during online communication than during in-person communication? [LO-7]

# Practice Your Skills

### Message for Analysis: Planning Meetings [LO-3]

A project leader has made notes about covering the following items at the quarterly budget meeting. Prepare a formal agenda by putting these items into a logical order and rewriting, where necessary, to give phrases a more consistent sound.

- Budget Committee Meeting to be held on December 12, 2013, at 9:30 a.m., and we have allotted one hour for the meeting
- I will call the meeting to order.
- Real estate director's report: A closer look at cost overruns on Greentree site. (10 minutes)
- The group will review and approve the minutes from last quarter's meeting. (5 minutes)
- I will ask the finance director to report on actual versus projected quarterly revenues and expenses. (15 minutes)
- I will distribute copies of the overall divisional budget and announce the date of the next budget meeting.
- Discussion: How can we do a better job of anticipating and preventing cost overruns? (20 minutes)
- Meeting will take place in Conference Room 3, with WebEx active for remote employees.
- What additional budget issues must be considered during this quarter?

### Exercises

Each activity is labeled according to the primary skill or skills you will need to use. To review relevant chapter content, you can refer to the indicated Learning Objective. In some instances, supporting information will be found in another chapter, as indicated.

1. **Collaboration: Working in Teams [LO-1], [LO-2]** In teams assigned by your instructor, prepare a 10-minute presentation on the potential disadvantages of using social media for business communication. When the presentation is ready, discuss how effective the team was using the criteria of (1) having a clear objective and a shared sense of purpose, (2) communicating openly and honestly, (3) reaching decisions by consensus, (4) thinking creatively, and (5) knowing how to resolve conflict. Be prepared to discuss your findings with the rest of the class.

2. **Collaboration: Working in Teams [LO-1]** In teams of four or five classmates, role-play a scenario in which the team is to decide which department at your college will receive a $1 million gift from an anonymous donor. The catch: Each member of the team will advocate for a different department (decide among yourselves who represents which departments), which means that all but one member will "lose" in the final decision. Working as a team, decide which department will receive the donation and discuss the results to help everyone on the team support the decision. Be prepared to present your choice and your justification for it to the rest of the class.

3. **Negotiation and Conflict Resolution: Resolving Conflicts; Communication Ethics: Providing Ethical Leadership [LO-1], Chapter 1** During team meetings, one member constantly calls for votes or decisions before all the members have voiced their views. As the leader, you asked this member privately about his behavior. He replied that he is trying to move the team toward its goals, but you are concerned that he is really trying to take control. How can you deal with this situation without removing the member from the group?

4. **Collaboration: Collaborating on Writing Projects; Media Skills: Blogging [LO-2]** In this project, you will conduct research on your own and then merge your results with those of the rest of your team. Search Twitter for messages on the subject of workplace safety. (You can use Twitter's advanced search page at http://search.twitter.com/advanced or use the site "twitter.com" qualifier on a regular search engine.) Compile at least five general safety tips that apply to any office setting, and then meet with your team to select the five best tips from all those the team has collected. Collaborate on a blog post that lists the team's top five tips.

5. **Communication Etiquette: Etiquette in the Workplace, Participating in Meetings [LO-3], [LO-7]** In group meetings, some of your colleagues have a habit of interrupting and arguing with the speaker, taking credit for ideas that aren't theirs, and shooting down ideas they don't agree with. As the newest person in the group, you're not sure if this is accepted behavior in this company, but it concerns you both personally and professionally. Should you go with the flow and adopt their behavior or stick with your own communication style, even though you might get lost in the noise? In a two-paragraph email message or post for your class blog, explain the pros and cons of both approaches.

6. **Collaboration: Participating in Meetings [LO-3]** With a classmate, attend a local community or campus meeting where you can observe a group discussion, vote, or take other group action. During the meeting, take notes individually and, afterward, work together to answer the following questions.

    a. What is your evaluation of this meeting? In your answer, consider (1) the leader's ability to articulate the meeting's goals clearly, (2) the leader's ability to engage members in a meaningful discussion, (3) the group's dynamics, and (4) the group's listening skills.

    b. How did group members make decisions? Did they vote? Did they reach decisions by consensus? Did those with dissenting opinions get an opportunity to voice their objections?

    c. How well did the individual participants listen? How could you tell?

    d. Did any participants change their expressed views or their votes during the meeting? Why might that have happened?

    e. Did you observe any of the communication barriers discussed in Chapter 1? Identify them.

    f. Compare the notes you took during the meeting with those of your classmate. What differences do you notice? How do you account for these differences?

7. **Collaboration: Leading Meetings [LO-3], Chapter 3** Every month, each employee in your department is expected to

give a brief oral presentation on the status of his or her project. However, your department has recently hired an employee who has a severe speech impediment that prevents people from understanding most of what he has to say. As department manager, how will you resolve this dilemma? Please explain.

8. **Collaboration: Using Collaboration Technologies [LO-4]** In a team assigned by your instructor, use Zoho (www.zoho.com; free for personal use), Google Docs (https://docs.google.com/demo/), or a comparable system to collaborate on a set of directions that out-of-town visitors could use to reach a specific point on your campus, such as a stadium or dorm. The team should choose the location and the mode(s) of transportation involved. Be creative—brainstorm the best ways to guide first-time visitors to the selected location using all the media at your disposal.

9. **Interpersonal Communication: Listening Actively [LO-5]** For the next several days, take notes on your listening performance during at least a half-dozen situations in class, during social activities, and at work, if applicable. Referring to the traits of effective listeners in Table 2.3 (page 47), rate yourself using *always, frequently, occasionally,* or *never* on these positive listening habits. In a report no longer than one page, summarize your analysis and identify specific areas in which you can improve your listening skills.

10. **Interpersonal Communication: Listening to Empathize [LO-5]** Think back over conversations you have had with friends, family members, coworkers, or classmates in the past week. Select a conversation in which the other person wanted to talk about something that was troubling him or her—a bad situation at work, a scary exam on the horizon, difficulties with a professor, a health problem, financial concerns, or the like. As you replay this conversation in your mind, think about how well you did in terms of empathic listening (see page 45). For example, did you find yourself being critical when the person really just needed someone to listen? Did you let the person know, by your words or actions, that you cared about his or her dilemma, even if you were not able to help in any other way? Analyze your listening performance in a brief email message to your instructor. *Note:* Do not disclose any private information in your message; you can change the names of the people involved or the circumstances as needed to maintain privacy.

11. **Nonverbal Communication: Analyzing Nonverbal Signals [LO-6]** Select a business letter and envelope you have received at work or home. Analyze their appearance. What nonverbal messages do they send? Are these messages consistent with the content of the letter? If not, what could the sender have done to make the nonverbal communication consistent with the verbal communication? Summarize your findings in a post on your class blog or in an email message to your instructor.

12. **Nonverbal Communication: Analyzing Nonverbal Signals [LO-6]** Describe what the following body movements suggest when someone exhibits them during a conversation. How do such movements influence your interpretation of spoken words? Summarize your findings in a post on your class blog or in an email message to your instructor.

a. Shifting one's body continuously while seated
b. Twirling and playing with one's hair
c. Sitting in a sprawled position
d. Rolling one's eyes
e. Extending a weak handshake

13. **Communication Etiquette: Telephone Skills [LO-7]** Late on a Friday afternoon, you learn that the facilities department is going to move you—and your computer, your desk, and all your files—to another office first thing Monday morning. However, you have an important client meeting scheduled in your office for Monday afternoon, and you need to finalize some contract details on Monday morning. You simply can't lose access to your office at this point, and you're more than a little annoyed that your boss didn't ask you before approving the move. He has already left for the day, but you know he usually checks his voice mail over the weekend, so you decide to leave a message, asking him to cancel the move or at least call you at home as soon as possible. Using the voice-mail guidelines listed in Table 2.5 (page 52), plan your message (use an imaginary phone number as your contact number and make up any other details you need for the call). As directed by your instructor, submit either a written script of the message or a podcast recording of the actual message.

14. **Communication Etiquette: Etiquette in the Workplace [LO-7]** As the local manager of an international accounting firm, you place high priority on professional etiquette. Not only does it communicate respect to your clients, it also instills confidence in your firm by showing that you and your staff are aware of and able to meet the expectations of almost any audience. Earlier today, you took four recently hired college graduates to lunch with an important client. You've done this for years, and it's usually an upbeat experience for everyone, but today's lunch was a disaster. One of the new employees made not one, not two, but three calls on his mobile phone during lunch. Another interrupted the client several times and even got into a mild argument. The third employee kept making sarcastic jokes about politics, making everyone at the table uncomfortable. And the fourth showed up dressed like she was expecting to bale hay or work in a coal mine, not have a business lunch in a posh restaurant. You've already called the client to apologize, but now you need to coach these employees on proper business etiquette. Draft a brief memo to these employees, explaining why etiquette is so important to the company's success—and to their individual careers.

## Expand Your Skills

### Critique the Professionals

Celebrities can learn from successful businesses when it comes to managing their careers, but businesses can learn from successful celebrities, too—particularly when it comes to building communities online using social media. For instance, social media guru Dan Schawbel cites Vin Diesel, Ashton Kutcher, Lady Gaga,

Lenny Kravitz, and Michael Phelps as celebrities who have used Facebook to build their personal brands.[77] Locate three celebrities (musicians, actors, authors, or athletes) who have sizable fan bases on Facebook and analyze how they use the social network. Using whatever medium your instructor requests, write a brief analysis (no more than one page) of the lessons, positive or negative, that a business could learn from these celebrities. Be sure to cite specific elements from the Facebook pages you've chosen, and if you think any of the celebrities have made mistakes in their use of Facebook, describe those as well.

**Sharpening Your Career Skills Online**

Bovée and Thill's Business Communication Web Search, at http://businesscommunicationblog.com/websearch, is a unique research tool designed specifically for business communication research. Use the Web Search function to find an online video, a podcast, or a PowerPoint presentation that offers advice on improving your active listening skills in business situations. Write a brief email message to your instructor, describing the item you found and summarizing the career skills information you learned from it.

## MyBCommLab

Go to **mybcommlab.com** for Auto-graded writing questions as well as the following Assisted-graded writing questions:

**2-1.** As a team or department leader, what steps can you take to ensure that your meetings are successful and efficient? [LO-3]

**2-2.** Considering what you've learned about nonverbal communication, what are some of the ways in which communication might break down during an online meeting in which the participants can see video images of only the person presenting at any given time—and then only his or her head? [LO-6]

**2-3.** Mybcommlab Only—comprehensive writing assignment for this chapter.

# Endnotes

1. Rosen Law Firm website, accessed 26 December 2012, www.rosen.com; Evelyn Nussenbaum, "Boosting Teamwork with Wikis," *Fortune Small Business*, 12 February 2008, http://money.cnn.com; Doug Cornelius, "Wikis at the Rosen Law Firm," KM Space blog, 28 February 2008, http://kmspace.blogspot.com.

2. James Manyika, Kara Sprague, and Lareina Yee, "Using Technology to Improve Workforce Collaboration," What Matters (McKinsey & Company), 27 October 2009, http://whatmatters.mckinseydigital.com.

3. Courtland L. Bovée and John V. Thill, *Business in Action*, 5th ed. (Upper Saddle River, N.J.: Pearson Prentice Hall, 2011), 172.

4. "Five Case Studies on Successful Teams," *HR Focus*, April 2002, 18+.

5. Stephen R. Robbins, *Essentials of Organizational Behavior*, 6th ed. (Upper Saddle River, N.J.: Prentice Hall, 2000), 98.

6. Max Landsberg and Madeline Pfau, "Developing Diversity: Lessons from Top Teams," *Strategy + Business*, Winter 2005, 10–12.

7. "Groups Best at Complex Problems," *Industrial Engineer*, June 2006, 14.

8. Nicola A. Nelson, "Leading Teams," *Defense AT&L*, July–August 2006, 26–29; Larry Cole and Michael Cole, "Why Is the Teamwork Buzz Word Not Working?" *Communication World*, February–March 1999, 29; Patricia Buhler, "Managing in the 90s: Creating Flexibility in Today's Workplace," *Supervision*, January 1997, 241; Allison W. Amason, Allen C. Hochwarter, Wayne A. Thompson, and Kenneth R. Harrison, "Conflict: An Important Dimension in Successful Management Teams," *Organizational Dynamics*, Autumn 1995, 201.

9. Geoffrey Colvin, "Why Dream Teams Fail," *Fortune*, 12 June 2006, 87–92.

10. Vijay Govindarajan and Anil K. Gupta, "Building an Effective Global Business Team," *MIT Sloan Management Review*, Summer 2001, 631.

11. Colvin, "Why Dream Teams Fail," 87–92.

12. Tiziana Casciaro and Miguel Sousa Lobo, "Competent Jerks, Lovable Fools, and the Formation of Social Networks," *Harvard Business Review*, June 2005, 92–99.

13. Stephen P. Robbins and David A. DeCenzo, *Fundamentals of Management*, 4th ed. (Upper Saddle River, N.J.: Prentice Hall, 2004), 266–267; Jerald Greenberg and Robert A. Baron, *Behavior in Organizations*, 8th ed. (Upper Saddle River, N.J.: Prentice Hall, 2003), 279–280.

14. B. Aubrey Fisher, *Small Group Decision Making: Communication and the Group Process*, 2nd ed. (New York: McGraw-Hill, 1980), 145–149; Robbins and De Cenzo, *Fundamentals of Management*, 334–335; Richard L. Daft, *Management*, 6th ed. (Cincinnati: Thomson South-Western, 2003), 602–603.

15. Michael Laff, "Effective Team Building: More Than Just Fun at Work," *Training + Development*, August 2006, 24–35.

16. Claire Sookman, "Building Your Virtual Team," *Network World*, 21 June 2004, 91.

17. Jared Sandberg, "Brainstorming Works Best If People Scramble for Ideas on Their Own," *Wall Street Journal*, 13 June 2006, B1.

18. Mark K. Smith, "Bruce W. Tuckman—Forming, Storming, Norming, and Performing in Groups," Infed.org, accessed 5 July 2005, www.infed.org.

19. Robbins and DeCenzo, *Fundamentals of Management*, 258–259.

20. Daft, *Management*, 609–612.

21. Andy Boynton and Bill Fischer, *Virtuoso Teams: Lessons from Teams That Changed Their Worlds* (Harrow, UK: FT Prentice Hall, 2005), 10.

22. Thomas K. Capozzoli, "Conflict Resolution—A Key Ingredient in Successful Teams," *Supervision*, November 1999, 14–16.

23. Jesse S. Nirenberg, *Getting Through to People* (Paramus, N.J.: Prentice Hall, 1973), 134–142.

24. Nirenberg, *Getting Through to People,* 134–142.

25. Nirenberg, *Getting Through to People,* 134–142.

26. Jon Hanke, "Presenting as a Team," *Presentations*, January 1998, 74–82.

27. William P. Galle, Jr., Beverly H. Nelson, Donna W. Luse, and Maurice F. Villere, *Business Communication: A Technology-Based Approach* (Chicago: Irwin, 1996), 260.

28. Mary Beth Debs, "Recent Research on Collaborative Writing in Industry," *Technical Communication*, November 1991, 476–484.

29. Rob Koplowitz, "Building a Collaboration Strategy," *KM World*, November/December 2009, 14–15.

30. Eric Knorr and Galen Gruman, "What Cloud Computing Really Means," *InfoWorld*, 3 May 2012, www.infoworld.com; Lamont Wood, "Cloud Computing Poised to Transform Communication," LiveScience, 8 December 2009, www.livescience.com.

31. "How Blue Man Group Gets Creative with Its Social Intranet," Socialtext website, accessed 1 May 2012, www.socialtext.com.

32. Richard McDermott and Douglas Archibald, "Harnessing Your Staff's Informal Networks," *Harvard Business Review*, March 2010, 82–89.

33. Tony Hsieh, "Why I Sold Zappos," *Inc.*, 1 June 2010, www.inc.com.

34. Chuck Williams, *Management*, 2nd ed. (Cincinnati: Thomson South-Western, 2002), 706–707.

35. Ron Ashkenas, "Why We Secretly Love Meetings," *Harvard Business Review* blogs, 5 October 2010, http://blogs.hbr.org.

36. Douglas Kimberly, "Ten Pitfalls of Pitiful Meetings," Payroll Manager's Report, January 2010, 1, 11; "Making the Most of Meetings," *Journal of Accountancy*, March 2009, 22.

37. Cyrus Farivar, "How to Run an Effective Meeting," BNET website, accessed 12 August 2008, www.bnet.com.

38. "Better Meetings Benefit Everyone: How to Make Yours More Productive," *Working Communicator Bonus Report*, July 1998, 1.

39. Manyika, Sprague, and Yee, "Using Technology to Improve Workforce Collaboration."

40. Roger O. Crockett, "The 21st Century Meeting," *BusinessWeek*, 26 February 2007, 72–79.

41. Steve Lohr, "As Travel Costs Rise, More Meetings Go Virtual," *New York Times*, 22 July 2008, www.nytimes.com.

42. GoToMeeting website, accessed 3 May 2012, www.gotogmeeting.com; "Unlock the Full Power of the Web Conferencing," CEOworld.biz, 20 November 2007, www.ceoworld.biz.

43. IBM Jam Events website, accessed 3 May 2012, www.collaborationjam.com; "Big Blue Brainstorm," *BusinessWeek*, 7 August 2006, www.businessweek.com.

44. Nick Morgan, "How to Conduct a Virtual Meeting," *Harvard Business Review* blogs, 1 March 2011, http://blogs.hbr.org.

45. "17 Tips for More Productive Conference Calls," AccuConference, accessed 30 January 2008, www.accuconference.com.

46. Judi Brownell, *Listening*, 2nd ed. (Boston: Allyn & Bacon, 2002), 9, 10.

47. Carmine Gallo, "Why Leadership Means Listening," *BusinessWeek*, 31 January 2007, www.businessweek.com.

48. Augusta M. Simon, "Effective Listening: Barriers to Listening in a Diverse Business Environment," *Bulletin of the Association for Business Communication* 54, no. 3 (September 1991): 73–74.

49. Robyn D. Clarke, "Do You Hear What I Hear?" *Black Enterprise*, May 1998, 129.

50. Dennis M. Kratz and Abby Robinson Kratz, *Effective Listening Skills* (New York: McGraw-Hill, 1995), 45–53; J. Michael Sproule, *Communication Today* (Glenview, Ill.: Scott Foresman, 1981), 69.

51. Brownell, *Listening*, 230–231.

52. Kratz and Kratz, *Effective Listening Skills*, 78–79; Sproule, *Communication Today*, 69.

53. Bill Brooks, "The Power of Active Listening," *American Salesman*, June 2003, 12; "Active Listening," Study Guides and Strategies website, accessed 5 February 2005, www.studygs.net.

54. Bob Lamons, "Good Listeners Are Better Communicators," *Marketing News*, 11 September 1995, 13+; Phillip Morgan and H. Kent Baker, "Building a Professional Image: Improving Listening Behavior," *Supervisory Management*, November 1985, 35–36.

55. Clarke, "Do You Hear What I Hear?"; Dot Yandle, "Listening to Understand," *Pryor Report Management Newsletter Supplement* 15, no. 8 (August 1998): 13.

56. Brownell, *Listening*, 14; Kratz and Kratz, *Effective Listening Skills*, 8–9; Sherwyn P. Morreale and Courtland L. Bovée, *Excellence in Public Speaking* (Orlando, Fla.: Harcourt Brace, 1998), 72–76; Lyman K. Steil, Larry L. Barker, and Kittie W. Watson, *Effective Listening: Key to Your Success* (Reading, Mass.: Addison Wesley, 1983), 21–22.

57. Patrick J. Collins, *Say It with Power and Confidence* (Upper Saddle River, N.J.: Prentice Hall, 1997), 40–45.

58. Morreale and Bovée, *Excellence in Public Speaking*, 296.

59. Dale G. Leathers, *Successful Nonverbal Communication: Principles and Applications* (New York: Macmillan, 1986), 19.

60. Gerald H. Graham, Jeanne Unrue, and Paul Jennings, "The Impact of Nonverbal Communication in Organizations: A Survey of Perceptions," *Journal of Business Communication* 28, no. 1 (Winter 1991): 45–62.

61. Danielle S. Urban, "What to Do About 'Body Art' at Work," *Workforce Management*, March 2010, www.workforce.com.

62. Virginia P. Richmond and James C. McCroskey, *Nonverbal Behavior in Interpersonal Relations* (Boston: Allyn & Bacon, 2000), 153–157.

63. Mary Ellen Slayter, "Pamela Meyer on the Science Behind 'Liespotting,'" SmartBlog on Workforce, 14 September 2010, http://smartblogs.com.

64. Slayter, "Pamela Meyer on the Science Behind 'Liespotting.'"

65. Joe Navarro, "Body Language Myths," *Psychology Today*, 25 October 2009, www.psychologytoday.com; Richmond and McCroskey, *Nonverbal Behavior in Interpersonal Relations*, 2–3.

66. John Hollon, "No Tolerance for Jerks," *Workforce Management*, 12 February 2007, 34.

67. Linton Weeks, "Please Read This Story, Thank You," NPR, 14 March 2012, www.npr.org.

68. Janine Popick, "Business Meeting Etiquette: 8 Pet Peeves," *Inc.*, 9 April 2012, www.inc.com.

69. "Use Proper Cell Phone Etiquette at Work," Kelly Services website, accessed 11 June 2010, www.kellyservices.us.

70. J. J. McCorvey, "How to Create a Cell Phone Policy," *Inc.*, 10 February 2010, www.inc.com; "Use Proper Cell Phone Etiquette at Work."

71. Dana May Casperson, *Power Etiquette: What You Don't Know Can Kill Your Career* (New York: AMACOM, 1999), 10–14; Ellyn Spragins, "Introducing Politeness," *Fortune Small Business*, November 2001, 30.

72. Tanya Mohn, "The Social Graces as a Business Tool," *New York Times*, 10 November 2002, sec. 3, 12.

73. Casperson, *Power Etiquette*, 44–46.

74. Casperson, *Power Etiquette*, 109–110.

75. Nick Wingfield, "Oh, for the Good Old Days of Rude Cellphone Gabbers," *New York Times*, 2 December 2011, www.nytimes.com.

76. "Are You Practicing Proper Social Networking Etiquette?" *Forbes*, 9 October 2009, www.forbes.com; Pete Babb, "The Ten Commandments of Blog and Wiki Etiquette," *InfoWorld*, 28 May 2007, www.infoworld.com; Judith Kallos, "Instant Messaging Etiquette," NetM@nners blog, accessed 3 August 2008, www.netmanners.com; Michael S. Hyatt, "E-Mail Etiquette 101," From Where I Sit blog, 1 July 2007, www.michaelhyatt.com.

77. Dan Schawbel, "5 Lessons Celebrities Can Teach Us About Facebook Pages," Mashable, 15 May 2009, http://mashable.com.

# 3 | Communicating in a World of Diversity

## LEARNING OBJECTIVES

After studying this chapter, you will be able to

**1** Discuss the opportunities and challenges of intercultural communication.

**2** Define *culture*, explain how culture is learned, and define ethnocentrism and stereotyping.

**3** Explain the importance of recognizing cultural variations and list eight categories of cultural differences.

**4** List four general guidelines for adapting to any business culture.

**5** Identify seven steps you can take to improve your intercultural communication skills.

---

## MyBCommLab®

⭐ **Improve Your Grade!** Over 10 million students improved their results using the Pearson MyLabs. Visit **mybcommlab.com** for simulations, tutorials, and end-of-chapter problems.

---

## COMMUNICATION CLOSE-UP AT
### Ernst & Young www.ey.com

With 167,000 employees spread across 140 countries, the member firms of the global professional services organization Ernst & Young have deep experience with the rewards and challenges of intercultural communication. With employees and clients in virtually every corner of the world, the ability to communicate across cultures is vital to the company's success.

As you'll read in this chapter, cultural background influences almost every aspect of communication, and cultural differences

Working with colleagues and customers from diverse backgrounds and life experiences can present new communication challenges.

Huntstock, Inc/Alamy

are among the most common barriers that can get in the way of successful communication. However, those differences can also enrich communication, decision making, and other aspects of business by bringing a broader range of perspectives and experiences to the table. Guiding the communication process in ways that minimize the barriers and maximize the benefits is one of the most important tasks for every business manager.

The keys are recognizing and appreciating the diversity of today's workforces and making sure all those diverse voices have the opportunity to be heard. Karyn Twaronite, Americas Inclusiveness Officer, who oversees the Ernst & Young organization's diversity and inclusiveness strategies in its Americas Area, puts it this way: "Diversity and inclusiveness are not an appendage to our business strategy—both are central to the success of our people and our markets. All of our people bring diverse talents we can leverage, so we expect, reinforce, and reward inclusive leadership. Differences matter in our business and make us better."

Ernst & Young takes numerous steps to make sure its member firm leaders understand their diverse workforces and incorporate Ernst & Young viewpoints in both strategic planning and day-to-day business operations. Soon after she moved into her current role, for example, Twaronite went on a "listening tour" of Ernst & Young member firm offices in nearly 20 different cities, ranging from São Paulo to Mexico City, to hear what made the Ernst & Young employees feel included or excluded, how their team leaders factored into their feelings, and if they felt they could bring their "whole selves" to work.

In addition to giving employees a voice, Ernst & Young LLP in the United States also encourages collaboration and support through a variety of Professional Networks throughout the company. These include its networks for women, working parents, veterans, people with differing abilities, and LGBT, Latino, Black, Asian and many other professionals. In addition to offering employees a sense of belonging, these networks aid in mentoring, recruiting, and fostering positive relationships with various external stakeholder groups, as well as help the U.S. firm's people connect with their colleagues, clients, and communities. And in the spirit of inclusiveness, these networks are open to any employee with an interest in the needs and perspectives of a particular employee community.

Ernst & Young's proactive approach to diversity and inclusiveness pays off in multiple ways, from bottom-line profits to high levels of employee satisfaction and engagement. For example, Ernst & Young LLP was among *Fortune* magazine's "100 Best Companies to Work For" for the 15th consecutive year in 2013, and DiversityInc ranked Ernst & Young LLP sixth on The 2012 DiversityInc Top 50 Companies for Diversity list, marking the fourth consecutive year the firm appeared in the top 10. DiversityInc also frequently spotlights Ernst & Young LLP as one of the best places to work for women, people with disabilities, and LGBT employees.

As Steve Howe, the top executive in the Ernst & Young organization's Americas Area, summarizes, inclusiveness is "critical to us performing at a consistent, exceptional level all around the globe. It makes us better, more insightful; it helps us solve problems, manage risk and seize opportunities that much better."

# Understanding the Opportunities and Challenges of Communication in a Diverse World

**1 LEARNING OBJECTIVE**
Discuss the opportunities and challenges of intercultural communication.

Diversity includes all the characteristics that define people as individuals.

Ernst & Young (profiled in the chapter-opening Communication Close-Up) illustrates the opportunities and the challenges for business professionals who know how to communicate with diverse audiences. Although the concept is often framed in terms of ethnic background, a broader and more useful definition of **diversity** includes "all the characteristics and experiences that define each of us as individuals."[1] As one example, the pharmaceutical company Merck identifies 19 separate dimensions of diversity in its discussions of workforce diversity, including race, age, military experience, parental status, marital status, and thinking style.[2] As you'll learn in this chapter, these characteristics and experiences can have a profound effect on the way businesspeople communicate.

**Intercultural communication** is the process of sending and receiving messages between people whose cultural backgrounds could lead them to interpret verbal and nonverbal signs differently. Every attempt to send and receive messages is influenced by culture, so to communicate successfully, you need a basic grasp of the cultural differences you may encounter and how you should handle them. Your efforts to recognize and bridge cultural differences will open up business opportunities throughout the world and maximize the contributions of all the employees in a diverse workforce.

## THE OPPORTUNITIES IN A GLOBAL MARKETPLACE

You will communicate with people from other cultures throughout your career.

Chances are good that you'll be working across international borders sometime in your career. Thanks to communication and transportation technologies, natural boundaries and national borders are no longer the impassable barriers they once were. Local markets are opening to worldwide competition as businesses of all sizes look for new growth opportunities outside their own countries. Thousands of U.S. businesses depend on exports for significant portions of their revenues. Every year, these companies export hundreds of billions of dollars worth of materials and merchandise, along with billions more in personal and professional services. If you work in one of these companies, you may well be called on to visit or at least communicate with a wide variety of people who speak languages other than English and who live in cultures quite different from what you're used to. Of the top 10 export markets for U.S. products, only two, Canada and Great Britain, have English as an official language—and Canada also has French as an official language.[3]

Not surprisingly, effective communication is key to cross-cultural and global business. In a recent survey, nearly 90 percent of executives said their companies' profit, revenue, and market share would all improve if their international communication skills could be improved. In addition, half of these executives said communication or collaboration breakdowns had affected major international business efforts in their companies.[4] The good news here is that improving your cultural communication skills could make you a more valuable job candidate at every stage of your career.

## THE ADVANTAGES OF A DIVERSE WORKFORCE

Even if you never visit another country or transact business on a global scale, you will interact with colleagues from a variety of cultures, with a wide range of characteristics and life experiences. Over the past few decades, many innovative companies have changed the way they approach diversity, from seeing it as a legal requirement (providing equal opportunities for all) to seeing it as a strategic opportunity to connect with customers and take advantage of the broadest possible pool of talent.[5] Smart business leaders recognize the competitive advantages of a diverse workforce that offers a broader spectrum of viewpoints and ideas, helps companies understand and identify with diverse markets, and enables companies to benefit from a wider range of employee talents. "It just makes good business sense," says Gord Nixon, CEO of Royal Bank of Canada.[6] According to IBM executive Ron Glover, more-diverse teams tend to be more innovative over the long term than more-homogeneous teams (those on which team members have similar backgrounds).[7]

Diversity is simply a fact of life for all companies. The United States has been a nation of immigrants from the beginning, and that trend continues today. The western and northern Europeans who made up the bulk of immigrants during the nation's early years now share space with people from across Asia, Africa, Eastern Europe, and other parts of the world. Even the term *minority*, as it applies to nonwhite residents, makes less and less sense every year as Caucasian Americans make up less than half the population in a growing number of U.S. counties.[8]

However, you and your colleagues don't need to be recent immigrants to constitute a diverse workforce. Differences in everything from age and gender to religion and ethnic heritage to geography and military experience enrich the workplace (see Figure 3.1 on the next page). Immigration and workforce diversity both create advantages—and challenges—for business communicators throughout the world.

## THE CHALLENGES OF INTERCULTURAL COMMUNICATION

Today's increasingly diverse workforce encompasses a wide range of skills, traditions, backgrounds, experiences, outlooks, and attitudes toward work—all of which can affect communication in the workplace. Supervisors face the challenge of connecting with these diverse employees, motivating them, and fostering cooperation and harmony among them. Teams face the challenge of working together closely, and companies are challenged to coexist peacefully with business partners and with the community as a whole.

The interaction of culture and communication is so pervasive that separating the two is virtually impossible. The way you communicate is deeply influenced by the culture in which you were raised. The meaning of words, the significance of gestures, the importance of time and space, the rules of human relationships—these and many other aspects of communication are defined by culture. To a large degree, your culture influences the way you think, which naturally affects the way you communicate as both a sender and a

The diversity of today's workforce brings distinct advantages to businesses:
- A broader range of views and ideas
- A better understanding of diverse, fragmented markets
- A broader pool of talent from which to recruit

A company's cultural diversity affects how its business messages are conceived, composed, delivered, received, and interpreted.

Merck's top-line message about diversity acknowledges the strategic advantages available to companies that embrace diversity in their hiring and management practices.

Specific supporting points back up the high-level message about the company's commitment to embracing diversity in all facets of its business.

In addition to developing and supporting a diverse workforce, Merck also works closely with a diverse base of suppliers to its various business units.

This diagram lists the 19 dimensions of diversity that Merck takes into account in its management philosophy.

Significant awards and recognitions let potential employees and business partners know that Merck is serious about inclusivity.

**Figure 3.1  Diversity at Merck**
The pharmaceutical company Merck approaches employee and supplier diversity as an opportunity and a strategy imperative.
*Source:* Courtesy of Merck, Global Communications, Reputation and Branding. Copyright © 2011 by Merck, Inc. Used by permission.

receiver.[9] Intercultural communication is much more complicated than simply matching language between sender and receiver—it goes beyond mere words to beliefs, values, and emotions.

Elements of human diversity can affect communication at every stage of the communication process, from the ideas a person deems important enough to share to the habits and expectations of giving feedback. In particular, your instinct is to encode your message using the assumptions of *your* culture. However, members of your audience decode your message according to the assumptions of *their* culture. The greater the difference between cultures, the greater the chance for misunderstanding.[10]

Throughout this chapter, you'll see examples of how communication styles and habits vary from one culture to another. These examples are intended to illustrate the major themes of intercultural communication, not to give an exhaustive list of styles and habits of any particular culture. With an understanding of these major themes, you'll be prepared to explore the specifics of any culture.

Culture influences everything about communication, including
- Language
- Nonverbal signals
- Word meaning
- Time and space issues
- Rules of human relationships

# Developing Cultural Competency

**2  LEARNING OBJECTIVE**
Define *culture*, explain how culture is learned, and define ethnocentrism and stereotyping.

**Cultural competency** includes an appreciation for cultural differences that affect communication and the ability to adjust one's communication style to ensure that efforts to send and receive messages across cultural boundaries are successful. In other words, it requires a combination of attitude, knowledge, and skills.[11]

The good news is that you're already an expert in culture, at least in the culture in which you grew up. You understand how your society works, how people are expected to communicate, what common gestures and facial expressions mean, and so on. The bad news is that because you're such an expert in your own culture, your communication is largely automatic; that is, you rarely stop to think about the communication rules you're following. An important step toward successful intercultural communication is becoming more aware of these rules and of the way they influence your communication.

*Cultural competency requires a combination of attitude, knowledge, and skills.*

## UNDERSTANDING THE CONCEPT OF CULTURE

**Culture** is a shared system of symbols, beliefs, attitudes, values, expectations, and norms for behavior. Your cultural background influences the way you prioritize what is important in life, helps define your attitude toward what is appropriate in a situation, and establishes rules of behavior.[12]

*Culture is a shared system of symbols, beliefs, attitudes, values, expectations, and behavior norms.*

Actually, you belong to several cultures. In addition to the culture you share with all the people who live in your own country, you belong to other cultural groups, including an ethnic group, possibly a religious group, and perhaps a profession that has its own special language and customs. With its large population and long history of immigration, the United States is home to a vast array of cultures. As one indication of this diversity, the inhabitants of this country now speak more than 170 languages.[13] In contrast, Japan is much more homogeneous, having only a few distinct cultural groups.[14]

*You belong to several cultures, each of which affects the way you communicate.*

Members of a given culture tend to have similar assumptions about how people should think, behave, and communicate, and they all tend to act on those assumptions in much the same way. Cultures can vary in their rate of change, degree of complexity, and tolerance toward outsiders. These differences affect the level of trust and openness you can achieve when communicating with people of other cultures.

People learn culture directly and indirectly from other members of their group. As you grow up in a culture, you are taught by the group's members who you are and how best to function in that culture. Sometimes you are explicitly told which behaviors are acceptable; at other times you learn by observing which values work best in a particular group. In these ways, culture is passed on from person to person and from generation to generation.[15]

*You learn culture both directly (by being instructed) and indirectly (by observing others).*

In addition to being automatic, culture tends to be *coherent*; that is, a culture appears to be fairly logical and consistent when viewed from the inside. Certain norms within a culture may not make sense to someone outside the culture, but they probably make sense to those inside. Such coherence generally helps a culture function more smoothly internally, but it can create disharmony between cultures that don't view the world in the same way.

*Cultures tend to offer views of life that are both coherent (internally logical) and complete (able to answer all of life's big questions).*

Finally, cultures tend to be complete; that is, they provide their members with most of the answers to life's big questions. This idea of completeness dulls or even suppresses curiosity about life in other cultures. Not surprisingly, such completeness can complicate communication with other cultures.[16]

## OVERCOMING ETHNOCENTRISM AND STEREOTYPING

**Ethnocentrism** is the tendency to judge other groups according to the standards, behaviors, and customs of one's own group. Given the automatic influence of one's own culture, when people compare their culture to others, they often conclude that their own is superior.[17] An even more extreme reaction is **xenophobia**, a fear of strangers and foreigners. Clearly, businesspeople who take these views are not likely to communicate successfully across cultures.

*Ethnocentrism is the tendency to judge all other groups according to the standards, behaviors, and customs of one's own group.*

Distorted views of other cultures or groups also result from **stereotyping**, assigning a wide range of generalized attributes to an individual on the basis of membership in a particular culture or social group. For instance, assuming that an older colleague will be out of touch with the youth market or that a younger colleague can't be an inspiring leader are examples of stereotyping age groups.

*Stereotyping is assigning generalized attributes to an individual on the basis of membership in a particular group.*

Those who want to show respect for other people and to communicate effectively in business need to adopt a more positive viewpoint, in the form of **cultural pluralism**—the practice of accepting multiple cultures on their own terms. When crossing cultural boundaries, you'll be even more effective if you move beyond simple acceptance and adapt your

*Cultural pluralism is the acceptance of multiple cultures on their own terms.*

communication style to that of the new cultures you encounter—even integrating aspects of those cultures into your own.[18] A few simple habits can help:

You can avoid ethnocentrism and stereotyping by avoiding assumptions and judgments and by accepting differences.

- **Avoid assumptions.** Don't assume that others will act the same way you do, use language and symbols the same way you do, or even operate from the same values and beliefs. For instance, in a comparison of the ten most important values in three cultures, people from the United States had *no* values in common with people from Japanese or Arab cultures.[19]
- **Avoid judgments.** When people act differently, don't conclude that they are in error or that their way is invalid or inferior.
- **Acknowledge distinctions.** Don't ignore the differences between another person's culture and your own.

Unfortunately, overcoming ethnocentrism and stereotyping is not a simple task, even for people who are highly motivated to do so. Moreover, research suggests that people often have beliefs and biases that they're not even aware of—and that may even conflict with the beliefs they *think* they have. (To see whether you have some of these *implicit beliefs*, visit the Project Implicit website, at https://implicit.harvard.edu/implicit, and take some of the simple online tests.)[20]

# Recognizing Variations in a Diverse World

**3  LEARNING OBJECTIVE**
Explain the importance of recognizing cultural variations, and list eight categories of cultural differences.

You can begin to learn how people in other cultures want to be treated by recognizing and accommodating eight main types of cultural differences: contextual, legal and ethical, social, nonverbal, age, gender, religious, and ability.

## CONTEXTUAL DIFFERENCES

Cultural context is the pattern of physical cues, environmental stimuli, and implicit understanding that conveys meaning between members of the same culture.

High-context cultures rely heavily on nonverbal actions and environmental setting to convey meaning; low-context cultures rely more on explicit verbal communication.

Every attempt at communication occurs within a **cultural context**, the pattern of physical cues, environmental stimuli, and implicit understanding that convey meaning between two members of the same culture. However, cultures around the world vary widely in the role that context plays in communication.

In a **high-context culture**, people rely less on verbal communication and more on the context of nonverbal actions and environmental setting to convey meaning. For instance, a Chinese speaker expects the receiver to discover the essence of a message and uses indirectness and metaphor to provide a web of meaning.[21] The indirect style can be a source of confusion during discussions with people from low-context cultures, who are more accustomed to receiving direct answers. Also, in high-context cultures, the rules of everyday life are rarely explicit; instead, as individuals grow up, they learn how to recognize situational cues (such as gestures and tone of voice) and how to respond as expected.[22] The primary role of communication in high-context cultures is building relationships, not exchanging information.[23]

In a **low-context culture** such as the United States, people rely more on verbal communication and less on circumstances and cues to convey meaning. In such cultures, rules and expectations are usually spelled out through explicit statements such as "Please wait until I'm finished" or "You're welcome to browse."[24] The primary task of communication in low-context cultures is exchanging information.[25]

Contextual differences are apparent in the way businesspeople approach situations such as decision making, problem solving, negotiating, interaction among levels in the organizational hierarchy, and socializing outside the workplace.[26] For instance, in low-context cultures, businesspeople tend to focus on the results of the decisions they face, a reflection of the cultural emphasis on logic and progress (for example, "Will this be good for our company? For my career?"). In comparison, higher-context cultures emphasize the means or the method by which a decision will be made. Building or protecting relationships can be as important as the facts and information used in making the decisions.[27] Consequently, negotiators working on business deals in such cultures may spend most of their time together building relationships rather than hammering out contractual details.

The distinctions between high and low context are generalizations, of course, but they are important to keep in mind as guidelines. Communication tactics that work well in a high-context culture may backfire in a low-context culture, and vice versa.

## LEGAL AND ETHICAL DIFFERENCES

Cultural context influences legal and ethical behavior, which in turn can affect communication. For example, the meaning of business contracts can vary from culture to culture. While a manager from a U.S. company would tend to view a signed contract as the end of the negotiating process, with all the details resolved, his or her counterpart in many Asian cultures might view the signed contract as an agreement to do business—and only then begin to negotiate the details of the deal.[28]

As you conduct business around the world, you'll find that both legal systems and ethical standards differ from culture to culture. Making ethical choices across cultures can seem complicated, but you can keep your messages ethical by applying four basic principles:[29]

- **Actively seek mutual ground.** To allow the clearest possible exchange of information, both parties must be flexible and avoid insisting that an interaction take place strictly in terms of one culture or another.
- **Send and receive messages without judgment.** To allow information to flow freely, both parties must recognize that values vary from culture to culture, and they must trust each other.
- **Send messages that are honest.** To ensure that information is true, both parties must see things as they are—not as they would like them to be. Both parties must be fully aware of their personal and cultural biases.
- **Show respect for cultural differences.** To protect the basic human rights of both parties, each must understand and acknowledge the other's needs and preserve each other's dignity by communicating without deception.

> Honesty and respect are cornerstones of ethical communication, regardless of culture.

## SOCIAL DIFFERENCES

The nature of social behavior varies among cultures, sometimes dramatically. Some behavioral rules are formal and specifically articulated (table manners are a good example), whereas others are informal and learned over time (such as the comfortable distance to stand from a colleague during a discussion). The combination of formal and informal rules influences the overall behavior of most people in a society most of the time. In addition to the factors already discussed, social norms can vary from culture to culture in the following areas:

> Formal rules of etiquette are explicit and well defined, but informal rules are learned through observation and imitation.

- **Attitudes toward work and success.** In the United States, for instance, a widespread view is that material comfort earned by individual effort is a sign of superiority and that people who work hard are better than those who don't.
- **Roles and status.** Culture influences the roles people play, including who communicates with whom, what they communicate, and in what way. For example, in some countries women still don't play a prominent role in business, so women executives who visit these countries may find they're not taken seriously as businesspeople.[30] Culture also dictates how people show respect and signify rank. For example, people in the United States show respect by addressing top managers as "Mr. Roberts" or "Ms. Gutierrez." However, people in China are addressed according to their official titles, such as "President" or "Manager."[31]
- **Use of manners.** What is polite in one culture may be considered rude in another. For instance, asking a colleague "How was your weekend?" is a common way of making small talk in the United States, but the question sounds intrusive to people in cultures in which business and private lives are seen as separate spheres.
- **Concepts of time.** People in low-context cultures see time as a way to plan the business day efficiently, often focusing on only one task during each scheduled period and viewing time as a limited resource. However, executives from high-context cultures often see time as more flexible. Meeting a deadline is less important than building a business relationship.[32]

> Respect and rank are reflected differently from culture to culture in the way people are addressed and in their working environment.

> The rules of polite behavior vary from country to country.

> Attitudes toward time, such as strict adherence to meeting schedules, can vary throughout the world.

- **Future orientation.** Successful companies tend to have a strong *future orientation*, planning for and investing in the future, but national cultures around the world vary widely in this viewpoint. Some societies encourage a long-term outlook that emphasizes planning and investing—making sacrifices in the short term for the promise of better outcomes in the future. Others are oriented more toward the present, even to the point of viewing the future as hopelessly remote and not worth planning for.[33]

Cultures around the world exhibit varying degrees of openness toward both outsiders and people whose personal identities don't align with prevailing social norms.

- **Openness and inclusiveness.** At the national level as well as within smaller groups, cultures vary on how open they are to accepting people from other cultures and people who don't necessarily fit the prevailing norms within the culture. An unwillingness to accommodate others can range from outright exclusion to subtle pressures to conform to majority expectations.

## NONVERBAL DIFFERENCES

The meaning of nonverbal signals can vary widely from culture to culture, so you can't rely on assumptions.

As discussed in Chapter 2, nonverbal communication can be a helpful guide to determining the meaning of a message—but this situation holds true only if the sender and receiver assign the same meaning to nonverbal signals. For instance, the simplest hand gestures have different meanings in different cultures. A gesture that communicates good luck in Brazil is the equivalent of giving someone "the finger" in Colombia.[34] Don't assume that the gestures you grew up with will translate to another culture; doing so could lead to embarrassing mistakes.

When you have the opportunity to interact with people in another culture, the best advice is to study the culture in advance and then observe the way people behave in the following areas:

- **Greetings.** Do people shake hands, bow, or kiss lightly (on one side of the face or both)? Do people shake hands only when first introduced and every time they say hello or goodbye?
- **Personal space.** When people are conversing, do they stand closer together or farther away than you are accustomed to?
- **Touching.** Do people touch each other on the arm to emphasize a point or slap each other on the back to show congratulations? Or do they refrain from touching altogether?
- **Facial expressions.** Do people shake their heads to indicate "no" and nod them to indicate "yes"? This is what people are accustomed to in the United States, but it is not universal.
- **Eye contact.** Do people make frequent eye contact or avoid it? Frequent eye contact is often taken as a sign of honesty and openness in the United States, but in other cultures it can be a sign of aggressiveness or disrespect.
- **Posture.** Do people slouch and relax in the office and in public, or do they sit up and stand up straight?
- **Formality.** In general, does the culture seem more or less formal than yours?

Following the lead of people who grew up in the culture is not only a great way to learn but a good way to show respect as well.

## AGE DIFFERENCES

A culture's views on youth and aging affect how people communicate with one another.

In U.S. culture, youth is often associated with strength, energy, possibilities, and freedom, and age is sometimes associated with declining powers and the inability to keep pace. However, older workers can offer broader experience, the benefits of important business relationships nurtured over many years, and high degrees of "practical intelligence"—the ability to solve complex, poorly defined problems.[35]

In contrast, in cultures that value age and seniority, longevity earns respect and increasing power and freedom. For instance, in many Asian societies, the oldest employees hold the most powerful jobs, the most impressive titles, and the greatest degrees of freedom and decision-making authority. If a younger employee disagrees with one of these

## COMMUNICATING ACROSS CULTURES

# Us Versus Them: Generational Conflict in the Workplace

The way people view the world as adults is profoundly shaped by the social and technological trends they experienced while growing up, so it's no surprise that each generation entering the workforce has a different perspective than the generations already at work. Throw in the human tendencies to resist change and to assume that whatever way one is doing something must be the best way to do it, and you have a recipe for conflict. Moreover, generations in a workplace sometimes feel themselves competing for jobs, resources, influence, and control. The result can be tension, mistrust, and communication breakdowns.

Lumping people into generations is an imprecise science at best, but it helps to know the labels commonly applied to various age groups and to have some idea of their broad characteristics. These labels are not official, and there is no general agreement on when some generations start and end, but you will see and hear references to the following groups (approximate years of birth shown in parentheses):

- **The Radio Generation** (1925 to 1945). People in this group are beyond what was once considered the traditional retirement age of 65, but some want or need to continue working.
- **Baby Boomers** (1946 to 1964). This large segment of the workforce, which now occupies many mid- and upper-level managerial positions, got its name from the population boom in the years following World War II. The older members of this generation are now reaching retirement age, but many will continue to work beyond age 65—meaning that younger workers waiting for some of these management spots to open up might have to wait a while longer.
- **Generation X** (1965 to 1980). This relatively smaller "MTV generation" is responsible for many of the innovations that have shaped communication habits today but sometimes feels caught between the large mass of baby boomers ahead of them and the younger Generation Y employees entering the workforce. When Generation X does finally get the chance to take over starting in 2015 or 2020, it will be managing in a vastly different business landscape, one in which virtual organizations and networks of independent contractors replace much of the hierarchy inherited from the baby boomers.

- **Generation Y** (1981 to 1995). Also known as *millennials*, this youngest generation currently in the workforce is noted for its entrepreneurial instincts and technological savvy. This generation's comfort level with social media and other communication technologies is helping to change business communication practices—but is also a source of concern for managers worried about information leaks and employee productivity.
- **Generation Z** (after 1996). If you're a member of Generation Y, those footsteps you hear behind you are coming from Generation Z, also known as *Generation I* (for Internet) or the *Net Generation*. The first full generation to be born after the World Wide Web was invented will be entering the workforce soon.

These brief summaries can hardly do justice to entire generations of workers, but they give you some idea of the different generational perspectives and the potential for communication problems. As with all cultural conflicts, successful communication starts with recognizing and understanding these differences.

### CAREER APPLICATIONS

1. How would you resolve a conflict between a baby boomer manager who worries about the privacy and productivity aspects of social networking and a Generation Y employee who wants to use these tools on the job?
2. Consider the range of labels from the Radio Generation to the Net Generation. What does this tell you about the possible influence of technology on business communication habits?

*Sources:* Adapted from Anne Fisher, "When Gen X Runs the Show," *Time*, 14 May 2009, www.time.com; Deloitte, "Generation Y: Powerhouse of the Global Economy," research report, 2009, www.deloitte.com; "Generation Y," Nightly Business Report website, 30 June 2010, www.pbs.org; Sherry Posnick-Goodwin, "Meet Generation Z," *California Educator*, February 2010, www.cta.org; Ernie Stark, "Lost in a Time Warp," *People & Strategy*, Vol. 32 No. 4, 2009, 58–64; Nancy Sutton Bell and Marvin Narz, "Meeting the Challenges of Age Diversity in the Workplace," *The CPA Journal*, February 2007, www.nysscpa.org; Steff Gelston, "Gen Y, Gen X and the Baby Boomers: Workplace Generation Wars," *CIO*, 30 January 2008, www.cio.com; Heather Havenstein, "Generation Y in the Workplace: Digital Natives' Tech Needs Are Changing Companies Forever," *CIO*, 17 September 2008, www.cio.com.

senior executives, the discussion is never conducted in public. The notion of "saving face"—avoiding public embarrassment—is too strong. Instead, if a senior person seems to be in error about something, other employees will find a quiet, private way to communicate whatever information they feel is necessary.[36]

The multiple generations within a culture present another dimension of diversity. Today's workplaces can have three or even four generations working side by side. Each has been shaped by dramatically different world events, social trends, and technological advances, so it is not surprising that they often have different values, expectations, and communication habits. For instance, Generation Y workers (see "Us Versus Them: Generational Conflict in the Workplace") have a strong preference for communicating via short electronic messages, but baby boomers and Generation Xers sometimes find these brief messages abrupt and impersonal.[37]

## GENDER DIFFERENCES

Gender influences workplace communication in several important ways. First, the perception of men and women in business varies from culture to culture, and gender bias can range from overt discrimination to subtle and even unconscious beliefs.

Second, although the ratio of men and women in entry-level professional positions is roughly equal, the percentage of management roles held by men increases steadily the further one looks up the corporate ladder. This imbalance can significantly affect communication in such areas as mentoring, which is a vital development opportunity for lower and middle managers who want to move into senior positions. In one recent survey, for example, some men in executive positions expressed reluctance to mentor women, partly because they find it easier to bond with other men and partly out of concerns over developing relationships that might look inappropriate.[38]

Broadly speaking, men tend to emphasize content in their messages, while women tend to emphasize relationship maintenance.

Third, evidence suggests that men and women tend to have somewhat different communication styles. Broadly speaking, men emphasize content and outcomes in their communication efforts, whereas women place a higher premium on relationship maintenance.[39] As one example, men are more likely than women to try to negotiate a pay raise. Moreover, according to research by Linda Babcock of Carnegie Mellon University, both men and women tend to accept this disparity, viewing assertiveness as a positive quality in men but a negative quality in women. Changing these perceptions could go a long way toward improving communication and equity in the workplace.[40]

## RELIGIOUS DIFFERENCES

U.S. law requires employers to accommodate employees' religious beliefs to a reasonable degree.

As one of the most personal and influential aspects of life, religion brings potential for controversy and conflict in the workplace setting—as evidenced by a significant rise in the number of religious discrimination lawsuits in recent years.[41] Many employees believe they should be able to follow and express the tenets of their faith in the workplace. However, companies may need to accommodate employee behaviors that can conflict with each other and with the demands of operating the business. The situation is complicated, with no simple answers that apply to every situation. As more companies work to establish inclusive workplaces, you can expect to see this issue being discussed more often in the coming years.

## ABILITY DIFFERENCES

Colleagues and customers with disabilities that affect communication represent an important aspect of the diversity picture. People whose hearing, vision, cognitive ability, or physical ability to operate electronic devices is impaired can be at a significant disadvantage in today's workplace. As with other elements of diversity, success starts with respect for individuals and sensitivity to differences.

Assistive technologies help employers create more inclusive workplaces and benefit from the contribution of people with physical or cognitive impairments.

Employers can also invest in a variety of *assistive technologies* that help people with disabilities perform activities that might otherwise be difficult or impossible. These technologies include devices and systems that help workers communicate orally and visually, interact with computers and other equipment, and enjoy greater mobility in the workplace. For example, designers can emphasize *web accessibility*, taking steps to make websites more accessible to people whose vision is limited. Assistive technologies create a vital link for thousands of employees with disabilities, giving them opportunities to pursue a greater range of career paths and giving employers access to a broader base of talent.[42]

# Adapting to Other Business Cultures

4 **LEARNING OBJECTIVE**
List four general guidelines for adapting to any business culture.

Whether you're trying to work productively with members of another generation in your own office or with a business partner on the other side of the world, adapting your approach is essential to successful communication. This section offers general advice on adapting to any business culture and specific advice for professionals from other cultures on adapting to U.S. business culture.

## GUIDELINES FOR ADAPTING TO ANY BUSINESS CULTURE

You'll find a variety of specific tips in "Improving Intercultural Communication Skills," starting on the next page, but here are four general guidelines that can help all business communicators improve their cultural competency:

- **Become aware of your own biases.** Successful intercultural communication requires more than just an understanding of the other party's culture; you need to understand your own culture and the way it shapes your communication habits.[43] For instance, knowing that you value independence and individual accomplishment will help you communicate more successfully in a culture that values consensus and group harmony.
- **Ignore the "Golden Rule."** You probably heard this growing up: "Treat people the way you want to be treated." The problem with the Golden Rule is that other people don't always want to be treated the same way you want to be treated, particularly across cultural boundaries. The best approach: Treat people the way *they* want to be treated.
- **Exercise tolerance, flexibility, and respect.** As IBM's Ron Glover puts it, "To the greatest extent possible, we try to manage our people and our practices in ways that are respectful of the core principles of any given country or organization or culture."[44]
- **Practice patience and maintain a sense of humor.** Even the most committed and attuned business professionals can make mistakes in intercultural communication, so it is vital for all parties to be patient with one another. As business becomes ever more global, even people in the most tradition-bound cultures are learning to deal with outsiders more patiently and overlook occasional cultural blunders.[45] A sense of humor is a helpful asset as well, allowing people to move past awkward and embarrassing moments. When you make a mistake, simply apologize and, if appropriate, ask the other person to explain the accepted way; then move on.

An important step in understanding and adapting to other cultures is to recognize the influences that your own culture has on your communication habits.

## GUIDELINES FOR ADAPTING TO U.S. BUSINESS CULTURE

If you are a recent immigrant to the United States or grew up in a culture outside the U.S. mainstream, you can apply all the concepts and skills in this chapter to help adapt to U.S. business culture. Here are some key points to remember as you become accustomed to business communication in this country:[46]

- **Individualism.** In contrast to cultures that value group harmony and group success, U.S. culture generally expects individuals to succeed by their own efforts, and it rewards individual success. Even though teamwork is emphasized in many companies, competition between individuals is expected and even encouraged in many cases.
- **Equality.** Although the country's historical record on equality has not always been positive and some inequalities still exist, equality is considered a core American value. This principle applies to race, gender, social background, and even age. To a greater degree than people in many other cultures, Americans believe that every person should be given the opportunity to pursue whatever dreams and goals he or she has in life.
- **Privacy and personal space.** Although this appears to be changing somewhat with the popularity of social networking and other personal media, people in the United States are accustomed to a fair amount of privacy. That also applies to their "personal space" at work. For example, they expect you to knock before entering a closed office and to avoid asking questions about personal beliefs or activities until they get to know you well.
- **Time and schedules.** U.S. businesses value punctuality and the efficient use of time. For instance, meetings are expected to start and end at designated times.
- **Religion.** The United States does not have an official state religion. Many religions are practiced throughout the country, and people are expected to respect each other's beliefs.
- **Communication style.** Communication tends to be direct and focused more on content and transactions than on relationships or group harmony.

The values espoused by American culture include individualism, equality, and privacy.

As with all observations about culture, these are generalizations, of course. Any nation of more than 300 million people will exhibit a wide variety of behaviors. However, following these guidelines will help you succeed in most business communication situations.

# Improving Intercultural Communication Skills

**5** **LEARNING OBJECTIVE**
Identify seven steps you can take to improve your intercultural communication skills.

Communicating successfully between cultures requires a variety of skills (see Figure 3.2). You can improve your intercultural skills throughout your career by studying other cultures and languages, respecting preferences for communication styles, learning to write and speak clearly, listening carefully, knowing when to use interpreters and translators, and helping others adapt to your culture.

## STUDYING OTHER CULTURES

Effectively adapting your communication efforts to another culture requires not only knowledge about the culture but also the ability and motivation to change your personal habits as needed.[47]

Fortunately, you don't need to learn about the whole world all at once. Many companies appoint specialists for specific countries or regions, giving employees a chance to focus on just one culture at a time. Some firms also provide resources to help employees prepare for interaction with other cultures. On IBM's Global Workforce Diversity intranet site, for instance, employees can click on the "GoingGlobal" link to learn about customs in specific cultures.[48]

Even a small amount of research and practice will help you get through many business situations. In addition, most people

**REAL-TIME UPDATES**
LEARN MORE BY VISITING THIS INTERACTIVE WEBSITE

**Check your cultural awareness**

How much do you know about other cultures? Find out with these online quizzes. Go to http://real-timeupdates.com/bct12 and click on Learn More. If you are using MyBCommLab, you can access Real-Time Updates within each chapter or under Student Study Tools.

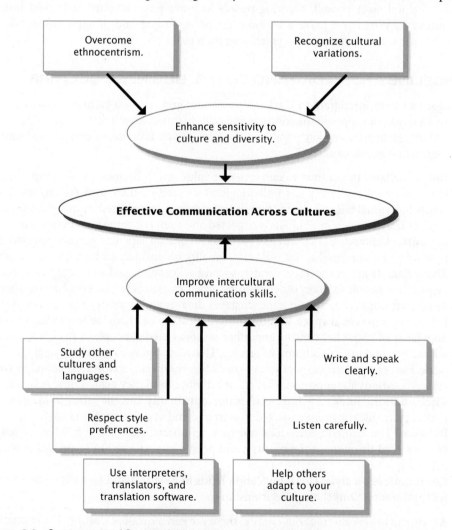

**Figure 3.2  Components of Successful Intercultural Communication**
Communicating in a diverse business environment is not always an easy task, but you can continue to improve your sensitivity and build your skills as you progress in your career.

## TABLE 3.1   Doing Business in Other Cultures

| Action | Details to Consider |
|---|---|
| Understand social customs | • How do people react to strangers? Are they friendly? Hostile? Reserved?<br>• How do people greet each other? Should you bow? Nod? Shake hands?<br>• How do you express appreciation for an invitation to lunch, dinner, or someone's home? Should you bring a gift? Send flowers? Write a thank-you note?<br>• Are any phrases, facial expressions, or hand gestures considered rude?<br>• How do you attract the attention of a waiter? Do you tip the waiter?<br>• When is it rude to refuse an invitation? How do you refuse politely?<br>• What topics may or may not be discussed in a social setting? In a business setting?<br>• How do social customs dictate interaction between men and women? Between younger people and older people? |
| Learn about clothing and food preferences | • What occasions require special attire?<br>• What colors are associated with mourning? Love? Joy?<br>• Are some types of clothing considered taboo for one gender or the other?<br>• How many times a day do people eat?<br>• How are hands or utensils used when eating?<br>• Where is the seat of honor at a table? |
| Assess political patterns | • How stable is the political situation?<br>• Does the political situation affect businesses in and out of the country?<br>• Is it appropriate to talk politics in social or business situations? |
| Understand religious and social beliefs | • To which religious groups do people belong?<br>• Which places, objects, actions, and events are sacred?<br>• Do religious beliefs affect communication between men and women or between any other groups?<br>• Is there a tolerance for minority religions?<br>• How do religious holidays affect business and government activities?<br>• Does religion require or prohibit eating specific foods? At specific times? |
| Learn about economic and business institutions | • Is the society homogeneous or heterogeneous?<br>• What languages are spoken?<br>• What are the primary resources and principal products?<br>• Are businesses generally large? Family controlled? Government controlled?<br>• What are the generally accepted working hours?<br>• How do people view scheduled appointments?<br>• Are people expected to socialize before conducting business? |
| Appraise the nature of ethics, values, and laws | • Is money or a gift expected in exchange for arranging business transactions?<br>• Do people value competitiveness or cooperation?<br>• What are the attitudes toward work? Toward money?<br>• Is politeness more important than factual honesty? |

respond positively to honest effort and good intentions, and many business associates will help you along if you show an interest in learning more about their cultures. Don't be afraid to ask questions. People will respect your concern and curiosity. You will gradually accumulate considerable knowledge, which will help you feel comfortable and be effective in a wide range of business situations.

Numerous websites (such as www.kwintessential.co.uk) and books offer advice on traveling to and working in specific cultures. Also try to sample newspapers, magazines, and even the music and movies of another country. For instance, a movie can demonstrate nonverbal customs even if you don't grasp the language. (However, be careful not to rely solely on entertainment products. If people in other countries based their opinions of U.S. culture only on the silly teen flicks and violent action movies that the United States exports around the globe, what sort of impression do you imagine they'd get?) For some of the key issues to research before doing business in another country, refer to Table 3.1.

## STUDYING OTHER LANGUAGES

As commerce continues to become more globalized and many countries become more linguistically diverse, the demand for multilingual communicators continues to grow as well. The ability to communicate in more than one language can make you a more competitive job candidate and open up a wider variety of career opportunities.

Even if your colleagues or customers in another country speak your language, it's worth the time and energy to learn common phrases in theirs. Doing so not only helps you get through

Successful intercultural communication can require the modification of personal communication habits.

Making an effort to learn about another person's culture is a sign of respect.

English is the most prevalent language in international business, but don't assume that everyone understands it or speaks it the same way.

everyday business and social situations but also demonstrates your commitment to the business relationship. After all, the other person probably spent years learning your language.

Finally, don't assume that people from two countries who speak the same language speak it the same way. The French spoken in Quebec and other parts of Canada is often noticeably different from the French spoken in France. Similarly, it's often said that the United States and the United Kingdom are two countries divided by a common language. For instance, *period* (punctuation), *elevator*, and *gasoline* in the United States are *full stop*, *lift*, and *petrol* in the United Kingdom.

## RESPECTING PREFERENCES FOR COMMUNICATION STYLE

Communication style—including the level of directness, the degree of formality, media preferences, and other factors—varies widely from culture to culture (see Figures 3.3a through 3.3d).

Language such as "cool" and "having a looking at" is too informal for external business communication, particularly for international correspondence.

The tone of this paragraph is too demanding.

"Here in the States" is too informal, and referring to the reader as "foreign" is potentially insulting.

Inflammatory language as *bad press, scandal,* and *sweatshops* will put the reader on the defensive and discourage a positive response.

The request for a response sounds too demanding, and it lacks a specific deadline.

The closing is too informal.

**Figure 3.3a  Intercultural Business Letter: Ineffective Original Draft**
This letter (from a Kentucky company that designs radio-controlled airplanes) exhibits a number of problems that would create difficulties for its intended reader (the manager of a contract manufacturing company in China). Follow the changes in Figures 3.3b, 3.3c, and 3.3d to see how the letter was adapted and then translated for its target audience.

**UpdraftRC**
4308 Preston Highway
Louisville, KY 40213
Toll Free: 1.800.FLY.RITE
Fax: (502) 555-1324
www.updraftrc.com

Zhejang Shan Tou Manufacturing Company, Ltd.
Guoliwei Industry Park
Libang Road, Longgang District
Shenzhen, Guangdong, China

Dear Mr. Li,

My company, Updraft RC, has designed a cool new line of radio-control toys that use smartphones as the controller. We are looking for a manufacturing partner, and your firm is one of the candidates we're having a look at.

This will be our first experience of partnering with an overseas manufacturer, and before we discuss specific technical details, I'd like to explore two sets of general concerns. The first set of concerns are the issues that might come into play with any manufacturing partnership, but particularly one located at quite some distance from our offices. The particular questions here are transportation costs, delays, quality control, and the risk of intellectual property theft. Can you let me know what practices and policies you have in place to minimize the downsides here?

Second, U.S. companies that work with overseas production partners face an increasing amount of scrutiny from the news media and activist groups regarding such matters as workplace safety, worker rights, and environmentally sensitive manufacturing. We can't directly control what takes place in your factories, of course, but we would have to deal with the public relations fallout if any problems are uncovered in the factories that make our products. The fact that that Nike and other major U.S. companies have spent millions and worked for years to promote positive conditions in overseas factories and still haven't been able to avoid all problems raises concerns for a small company such as ours.

Please share your company's philosophy and strategies for mitigating these two sets of concerns.

We would like to commence production in the second quarter of 2014, so a quick reply on your part would be great.

All the best,

*Henry Gatlin*

Henry Gatlin
Founder, CEO
Updraft RC

The language is still too informal in the opening paragraph.

"Overseas" avoids the negative connotations of "foreign."

Idiomatic phrases such as "come into play" and "minimize the downsides" are vulnerable to mistranslation.

The vaguely accusatory tone of this paragraph assumes that problems will occur, which is likely to offend the reader.

"Mitigating" can be replaced by a more common word.

The request now has a helpful timeline, but the phrasing is still somewhat demanding.

The closing is still too informal.

**Figure 3.3b   Intercultural Business Letter: First Revision**
This version eliminates most of the problems with overly informal phrases and potentially offensive language. However, while it would function well as a message between native speakers of English, it still has some wording and formatting issues that could create difficulties for a Chinese reader. Compare with Figure 3.3c.

Knowing what your communication partners expect can help you adapt to their particular style. Once again, watching and learning are the best ways to improve your skills. However, you can infer some generalities by learning more about the culture. For instance, U.S. workers typically prefer an open and direct communication style; they find other styles frustrating or suspect. Directness is also valued in Sweden as a sign of efficiency; but, in contrast with discussions in the United States, heated debates and confrontations are unusual. Italian, German, and French executives usually don't put colleagues at ease with praise before they criticize; doing so seems manipulative to them. However, professionals from high-context cultures, such as Japan or China, tend to be less direct.[49] Finally, in general, business correspondence in other countries is often more formal than the style used by U.S. businesspeople.

An inside address is typically not used in Chinese correspondence.

The revised opening gives the reader some helpful context and the assurance that this is a meaningful business opportunity.

The phrase "we are very willing to collaborate with you" shows respect for the reader and suggests the interest in forming a partnership.

This paragraph has been shortened to eliminate the redundant request for information.

This revised paragraph still conveys the seriousness of the writer's concerns without offending the reader.

"Minimizing" is easier for a non-native speaker to understand than "mitigating."

"Thank you" is a simple and adequately formal closing.

**Figure 3.3c  Intercultural Business Letter: Final Revision**
Here is the final English version, revised to ensure more successful translation into Chinese and to conform to standard practices in Chinese business communication (including removing the inside address).

## WRITING CLEARLY

Writing clearly is always important, of course, but it is essential when you are writing to people whose first language is not English. Follow these recommendations to make sure your message can be understood:[50]

Clarity and simplicity are essential when writing to or speaking with people who don't share your native language.

- **Choose words carefully.** Use precise words that don't have the potential to confuse with multiple meanings. For instance, the word *right* has several dozen different meanings and usages, so look for a synonym that conveys the specific meaning you intend, such as *correct, appropriate, desirable, moral, authentic,* or *privilege*.[51]
- **Be brief.** Use simple sentences and short paragraphs, breaking information into smaller chunks that are easier for readers to process.
- **Use plenty of transitions.** Help readers follow your train of thought by using transitional words and phrases. For example, tie related points together with expressions such as *in addition* and *first, second,* and *third.*

**UpdraftRC**
4308 Preston Highway
Louisville, KY 40213
Toll Free: 1.800.FLY.RITE
Fax: (502) 555-1324
www.updraftrc.com

李华先生：

　　随着智能手机的普及，越来越多的配件和周边产品正在被研发以满足市场的需求。我们的公司，Updraft RC,已经设计了一种新型的用智能手机控制的遥控玩具。我们的市场测试表明年轻客户，一个愿意尝试新产品的群体，（对我们的产品）有巨大的潜在需求。我们现在正在寻找制造伙伴，所以我们非常愿意与你们合作。

　　这是我们第一次与海外制造伙伴合作，在我们讨论具细节之前，我非常愿意让你们知道我们的两个问题。第一个问题对远距制造商合作关系来说都是一个挑战，这个挑战包括运输费用，运输延迟，质量控制和知识产权盗窃。

　　第二，与大洋对岸合作的美国公司面临着越来越高的来自新媒体和活跃组织的审查。这些审查包括工作场所安全性，劳工权益和可能对环境产生损害的制造。耐克和其他主要的美国公司已经花费了数百万美元，工作了几十年用来提升海外工厂的情况，但是他们仍然不能避免所有的问题。对于没有能力监控（海外）工厂的小公司来说，我们比较当心与制造相关的一系列问题可能影响到我们公司的形象。

　　所以请让我们知道你们公司解决这两个问题的策略和方法。

　　我们计划在 2014 年的第二个季度投入产品的生产。所以我们希望尽快得到你们公司的回应。

亨利 加特林
创始人，首席执行官
2013-5-16

**Figure 3.3d   Intercultural Business Letter: Translated Version**
Here is the translated version, formatted in accordance with Chinese business communication practice.

- **Address international correspondence properly.** Refer to Tables A.1 through A.5 in Appendix A for an explanation of different address elements and salutations commonly used in various countries.
- **Cite numbers and dates carefully.** In the United States, 12-05-14 means December 5, 2014, but in many other countries, it means May 12, 2014. Dates in Japan and China are usually expressed with the year first, followed by the month and then the day; therefore, to write December 5, 2014, in Japan, write it as 2014-12-05. Similarly, in the United States and Great Britain, 1.000 means one with three decimal places, but it means one thousand in many European countries.
- **Avoid slang, idiomatic phrases, and business jargon.** Everyday speech and writing are full of slang and **idiomatic phrases**—phrases that mean more than the sum of their literal parts. Examples from U.S. English include "Off the top of my head" and "More

bang for the buck." Your audience may have no idea what you're talking about when you use such phrases.

- **Avoid humor and other references to popular culture.** Jokes and references to popular entertainment usually rely on culture-specific information that might be completely unknown to your audience.

Although some of these differences may seem trivial, meeting the expectations of an international audience illustrates both knowledge of and respect for the other cultures (see Figure 3.4).

## SPEAKING AND LISTENING CAREFULLY

Languages vary considerably in the significance of tone, pitch, speed, and volume, which can create challenges for people trying to interpret the explicit meaning of words themselves as well as the overall nuance of a message. The English word *progress* can be a noun or a verb, depending on which syllable you emphasize. In Chinese, the meaning of the word *mà* changes depending on the speaker's tone; it can mean *mother*, *pileup*, *horse*, or *scold*. And routine Arabic speech can sound excited or angry to an English-speaking U.S. listener.[52]

Speaking clearly and getting plenty of feedback are two of the keys to successful intercultural conversations.

To ensure successful conversations between parties who speak different native languages or even regional variations of the same language, speakers and listeners alike need to make accommodations.[53] Speakers should adjust the content of their messages and the style of their delivery to accommodate the needs of their listeners and the circumstances of the conversation. For example, if you are speaking in person or over an electronic connection that includes a video component, you can use hand gestures and other nonverbal signals to clarify your spoken message. However, when you don't have a visual connection, you must take extra care to convey your meaning through words and vocal characteristics alone. Conversely, listeners need to be tolerant of accents, vocabulary choices, gestures, and other factors that might distract them from hearing the meaning of a speaker's message.

When talking with people whose native language is different from yours, remember that the processing of even everyday conversations can be difficult. For instance, speakers from the United States sometimes string together multiple words into a single, mystifying pseudoword, such as turning "Did you eat yet?" into "Jeetyet?" The French language uses a concept known as *liaison*, in which one word is intentionally joined with the next. Without a lot of practice, new French speakers have a hard time telling when one word ends and the next one begins.

To be more effective in intercultural conversations, remember these tips: (1) Speak slowly and clearly; (2) don't rephrase until it's obviously necessary (immediately rephrasing something you've just said doubles the translation workload for the listener); (3) look for and ask for feedback to make sure your message is getting through; (4) don't talk down to the other person by overenunciating words or oversimplifying sentences; and (5) at the end of the conversation, double-check to make sure you and the listener agree on what has been said and decided.

To listen more effectively in intercultural situations, accept what you hear without judgment and let people finish what they have to say.

As a listener, you'll need some practice to get a sense of vocal patterns. The key is simply to accept what you hear first, without jumping to conclusions about meaning or motivation. Let other people finish what they have to say. If you interrupt, you may miss something important. You'll also show a lack of respect. If you do not understand a comment, ask the person to repeat it. Any momentary awkwardness you might feel in asking for extra help is less important than the risk of unsuccessful communication.

## USING INTERPRETERS, TRANSLATORS, AND TRANSLATION SOFTWARE

For important business communication, use a professional interpreter (for oral communication) or translator (for written communication).

You may encounter business situations that require using an *interpreter* (for spoken communication) or a *translator* (for written communication). Interpreters and translators can be expensive, but skilled professionals provide invaluable assistance for communicating in other cultural contexts.[54] Keeping up with current language usage in a given country or culture is also critical in order to avoid embarrassing blunders. Some companies use *back-translation* to ensure accuracy. Once a translator encodes a message into another language, a different translator retranslates the same message into the original language. This back-translation is then compared with the original message to discover any errors or discrepancies.

**Ineffective**

## Assessing the Office Merger: Bad, Bad, and Not Good

APRIL 22, 2014 BY CYNTHIA MARTIN    LEAVE A COMMENT (EDIT)

When we folded the Broken Arrow office into the Tulsa headquarters last year, we anticipated some significant challenges during and after the consolidation. Closing a facility and combining two teams into one is never easy, but as I explained at the time, economic pressures—primarily the need to improve our all-important average profit per client metric—forced us to make a difficult decision.

I wish I could say that we hit this one out of the park. If one were to judge from the three most important indicators, we have not yet accomplished our goals. Our performance has actually declined in two of the three. The latest customer satisfaction survey shows a fifteen-percent increase in the number of customers who say they will consider other service providers when their current contracts expire. Employee satisfaction scores have also dropped since the offices were merged. Only seventy-two percent of employees rate their job satisfaction as "high" or "very high," compared to eighty-seven percent before the merger. The only measure of the three that has stayed steady is our average profit per client. While this might sound like good news in comparison to the other two, improving this variable was the primary reason for combining the offices in the first place.

I'll be blunt: This ain't gonna cut it, folks.

FILED UNDER: STRATEGIC PLANNING

The headline tries to be clever regarding the three factors discussed in the post, but the message is not clear.

"Folded" is an example of an English word with multiple meanings; these multiple possibilities make translation more difficult and can lead to confusion.

Complicated sentences are difficult to translate and force readers to follow multiple ideas at once.

The idiomatic phrase "hit one out of the park" might not make sense to readers who aren't familiar with baseball.

Spelling out numbers instead of using numerals creates more work for readers.

Long paragraphs are visually intimidating and more difficult to process.

Nonstandard language ("ain't") and the idiomatic phrase "cut it" will confuse some readers.

**Effective**

The clear, direct headline leaves no question about the content of the message.

Simpler sentence structures are easier to translate and create fewer chances for misunderstanding.

Breaking the long paragraph into a brief introduction and three bullet points simplifies reading and makes it easy to find the key points.

Numerals are easier to read quickly than spelled-out quantities.

Standard English and plain language decrease the potential for confusion.

## We Have Not Met Our Goals for the Office Merger

APRIL 22, 2014 BY CYNTHIA MARTIN    LEAVE A COMMENT (EDIT)

When we merged the Broken Arrow office with the Tulsa headquarters last year, we knew the move would be challenging. Closing a facility and combining two teams is never easy, but economic pressures forced us to make a difficult decision.

Unfortunately, we have not met the three goals we had for the merger: improving customer satisfaction, improving employee satisfaction, and increasing the average profit per client. In fact, our performance has actually *declined* in two of the three areas:

- The latest customer satisfaction survey shows a 15-percent increase in the number of customers who say they will consider other service providers when their current contracts expire.
- Employee satisfaction has also dropped since the offices were merged. Only 72 percent of employees rate their job satisfaction as "high" or "very high," compared to 87 percent before the merger.
- The only indicator of the three that has remained steady is our average profit per client. While this might sound like good news in comparison to the other two, improving this variable was the primary reason for combining the offices.

Clearly, we need to take a closer look at this situation to see where we went wrong and where we can make improvements.

FILED UNDER: STRATEGIC PLANNING

MyBCommLab Apply Figure 3.4's key concepts. Go to **mybcommlab.com** and follow this path: Course Content → Chapter 3 → **DOCUMENT MAKEOVERS**

**Figure 3.4 Writing for Multilingual Audiences**
In today's global and diversified work environment, chances are many of your messages will be read by people whose native language is not English. Follow the guidelines on pages 76–78 to help ensure successful communication. (Notice how following these guidelines makes the message easier for *everybody* to read, including native English speakers.)

The time and cost required for professional translation has encouraged the development of computerized translation tools. Dedicated software tools and online services such as WorldLingo (www.worldlingo.com) offer various forms of automated translation. Major search engines let you request translated versions of the websites you find. Although none of these tools can translate as well as human translators, they can be quite useful with individual words and short phrases, and they can often give you the overall gist of a message.[55]

## HELPING OTHERS ADAPT TO YOUR CULTURE

Everyone can contribute to successful intercultural communication. Whether a younger person is unaccustomed to the formalities of a large corporation or a colleague from another country is working on a team with you, look for opportunities to help people fit in and adapt their communication style. For example, if a nonnative English speaker is making mistakes that could hurt his or her credibility, you can offer advice on the appropriate words and phrases to use. Most language learners truly appreciate this sort of assistance, as long as it is offered in a respectful manner. Moreover, chances are that while you're helping, you'll learn something about the other person's culture and language, too.

You can also take steps to simplify the communication process. For instance, oral communication in a second language is usually more difficult than written forms of communication, so instead of asking a foreign colleague to provide information in a conference call, you could ask for a written response instead of or in addition to the live conversation.

For a brief summary of ideas to improve intercultural communication in the workplace, see "Checklist: Improving Intercultural Communication Skills." For additional information on communicating in a world of diversity, visit http://real-timeupdates.com/bct12 and click on Chapter 3.

**Help others adapt to your culture; it will create a more productive workplace and teach you about their cultures as well.**

## CHECKLIST ✓ Improving Intercultural Communication Skills

- Understand your own culture so that you can recognize its influences on your communication habits.
- Study other cultures so that you can appreciate cultural variations.
- Study the languages of people with whom you communicate, even if you can learn only a few basic words and phrases.
- Help nonnative speakers learn your language.
- Respect cultural preferences for communication style.
- Write clearly, using brief messages, simple language, generous transitions, and appropriate international conventions.
- Avoid slang, humor, and references to popular culture.
- Speak clearly and slowly, giving listeners time to translate your words.
- Ask for feedback to verify that communication was successful.
- Listen carefully and ask speakers to repeat anything you don't understand.
- Use interpreters and translators for important messages.

## COMMUNICATION CHALLENGES AT Ernst & Young

Karyn Twaronite is responsible for workforce diversity and inclusiveness across Ernst & Young's Americas region, but every manager throughout the company is expected to foster a climate of inclusion and support for employees of every cultural background. As a team leader in one of EY's U.S. offices, you're learning to exercise sound business judgment and use good listening skills to help resolve situations that arise within your diverse group of employees. How would you address these challenges?

**INDIVIDUAL CHALLENGE:** Fabio Silva joined your office after immigrating from Brazil three years ago. He is a brilliant financial analyst, but he resists working with other employees, even in team settings where collaboration is expected. Given the importance that you place on teamwork, how should you handle the situation? List several alternatives for addressing this dilemma, identify which one you would choose, and explain why you would choose this approach.

**TEAM CHALLENGE:** Your employees are breaking into ethnically based cliques. Members of ethnic groups eat together, socialize together, and often chat in their native languages while they work. You appreciate how these groups give their members a sense of community, but you worry that these informal communication channels are alienating nonmembers and fragmenting the flow of information. How can you encourage a stronger sense of community and teamwork across your department? Brainstorm at least three steps you can take to encourage better cross-cultural communication in your group.

# Quick Learning Guide

## MyBCommLab

Go to **mybcommlab.com** to complete the problems marked with this icon ⭐.

## SUMMARY OF LEARNING OBJECTIVES

**1 Discuss the opportunities and challenges of intercultural communication.** The global marketplace spans natural boundaries and national borders, allowing worldwide competition between businesses of all sizes. Therefore, today's businesspeople are likely to communicate across international borders with people who live in different cultures. Moreover, even domestic workforces are becoming more and more diverse, with employees having different national, religious, and ethnic backgrounds. In this environment, companies can benefit from a broad range of viewpoints and ideas, get a good understanding of diverse markets, and recruit workers from the broadest possible pool of talent. However, intercultural communication presents challenges as well, including motivating diverse employees to cooperate and to work together in teams as well as understanding enough about how culture affects language to prevent miscommunication.

**2 Define *culture*, explain how culture is learned, and define *ethnocentrism* and *stereotyping*.** Culture is a shared system of symbols, beliefs, attitudes, values, expectations, and norms for behavior. Culture is learned by listening to advice from other members of a society and by observing their behaviors. This double-edged method uses direct and indirect learning to ensure that culture is passed from person to person and from generation to generation.

Ethnocentrism is the tendency to judge other groups according to the standards, behaviors, and customs of one's own group. Stereotyping is assigning a wide range of generalized attributes to individuals on the basis of their membership in a particular culture or social group, without considering an individual's unique characteristics. To overcome ethnocentrism and stereotyping, work to avoid assumptions, avoid judgments, and acknowledge distinctions.

**3 Explain the importance of recognizing cultural variations, and list eight categories of cultural differences.** People from different cultures encode and decode messages differently, increasing the chances of misunderstanding. By recognizing and accommodating cultural differences, we avoid automatically assuming that everyone's thoughts and actions are just like ours. Begin by focusing on eight categories of differences: contextual differences (the degree to which a culture relies on verbal or nonverbal actions to convey meaning), legal and ethical differences (the degree to which laws and ethics are regarded and obeyed), social differences (how members value work and success, recognize status, define manners, and think about time), nonverbal differences (differing attitudes toward greetings, personal space, touching, facial expression, eye contact, posture, and formality), age differences (how members think about youth, seniority, and longevity), gender differences (how men and women communicate), religious differences (how beliefs affect workplace relationships), and ability differences (inclusive strategies that enable people with disabilities to more fully communicate with the rest of the workforce).

**4 List four general guidelines for adapting to any business culture.** You can adapt to any business culture by (1) becoming aware of your own cultural biases so that you can understand how these forces shape your communication habits; (2) ignoring the Golden Rule (treating people the way you want them to treat you) and instead treating them the way they want to be treated; (3) exercising tolerance, flexibility, and respect; and (4) practicing patience and maintaining a sense of humor to get you through the bumpy spots.

**5 Identify seven steps you can take to improve your intercultural communication skills.** Communicating successfully between cultures requires a variety of skills, all of which you can continue to improve throughout your career. Make your intercultural communication effective by (1) studying other cultures; (2) studying other languages; (3) respecting your audience's preferences for communication style; (4) writing as clearly as possible; (5) speaking as clearly as you can; (6) listening carefully; using interpreters, translators, and translation software when necessary; and (7) helping others adapt to your own culture.

## KEY TERMS

**cultural competency** An appreciation for cultural differences that affect communication and the ability to adjust one's communication style to ensure that efforts to send and receive messages across cultural boundaries are successful

**cultural context** The pattern of physical cues, environmental stimuli, and implicit understanding that convey meaning between two members of the same culture

**cultural pluralism** The practice of accepting multiple cultures on their own terms

**culture** A shared system of symbols, beliefs, attitudes, values, expectations, and norms for behavior

**diversity** All the characteristics and experiences that define each of us as individuals

**ethnocentrism** The tendency to judge other groups according to the standards, behaviors, and customs of one's own group

**high-context culture** Culture in which people rely less on verbal communication and more on the context of nonverbal actions and environmental setting to convey meaning

**idiomatic phrases** Phrases that mean more than the sum of their literal parts; such phrases can be difficult for nonnative speakers to understand

**intercultural communication** The process of sending and receiving messages between people whose cultural backgrounds could lead them to interpret verbal and nonverbal signs differently

**low-context culture** Culture in which people rely more on verbal communication and less on circumstances and cues to convey meaning

**stereotyping** Assigning a wide range of generalized attributes to an individual on the basis of membership in a particular culture or social group

**xenophobia** Fear of strangers and foreigners

CHECKLIST ✓

## Improving Intercultural Communication Skills

- Understand your own culture so that you can recognize its influences on your communication habits.
- Study other cultures so that you can appreciate cultural variations.
- Study the languages of people with whom you communicate, even if you can learn only a few basic words and phrases.
- Help nonnative speakers learn your language.
- Respect cultural preferences for communication style.
- Write clearly, using brief messages, simple language, generous transitions, and appropriate international conventions.
- Avoid slang, humor, and references to popular culture.
- Speak clearly and slowly, giving listeners time to translate your words.
- Ask for feedback to verify that communication was successful.
- Listen carefully and ask speakers to repeat anything you don't understand.
- Use interpreters and translators for important messages.

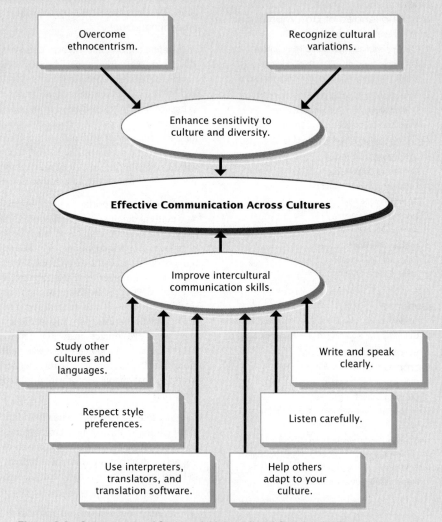

**Figure 3.2  Components of Successful Intercultural Communication**
Communicating in a diverse business environment is not always an easy task, but you can continue to improve your sensitivity and build your skills as you progress in your career.

## Test Your Knowledge

To review chapter content related to each question, refer to the indicated Learning Objective.

1. What are the potential advantages of a diverse workforce? [LO-1]
2. How do high-context cultures differ from low-context cultures? [LO-2]
3. What is ethnocentrism, and how can it be overcome in communication? [LO-2]
4. In addition to contextual differences, what other categories of cultural differences exist? [LO-3]
5. How does a sense of humor come in handy during intercultural communication? [LO-4]
6. How can the Golden Rule cause problems in intercultural communication? [LO-4]
7. What are the risks of using computerized translation when you need to read a document written in another language? [LO-5]
8. What steps can you take to help someone from another culture adapt to your culture? [LO-5]

## Apply Your Knowledge

To review chapter content related to each question, refer to the indicated Learning Objective.

1. Does a company that had no business dealings outside the United States need to concern itself with intercultural communication issues? Explain you answer. [LO-1]
2. Make a list of the top five priorities in your life (for example, fame, wealth, family, spirituality, peace of mind, individuality, artistic expression). Compare your list with the priorities that appear to be valued in the culture in which you are currently living. (You can be as broad or as narrow as you like in defining *culture* for this exercise, such as overall U.S. culture or the culture in your college or university.) Do your personal priorities align with the culture's priorities? If not, how might this disparity affect your communication with other members of the culture? [LO-2]
3. How does making an effort to avoid assumptions contribute to the practice of cultural pluralism? [LO-3]
4. Why is it important to understand your own culture when attempting to communicate with people from other cultures? [LO-4]
5. Think about the last three movies or television shows set in the United States that you've watched. In what ways would these entertainment products be helpful or unhelpful for people from other countries trying to learn about U.S. culture? [LO-5]

## Practice Your Skills

### Message for Analysis: Adapting to Cultural Differences [LO-5]

Your boss wants to send a brief email message welcoming employees recently transferred to your department from the company's Hong Kong branch. These employees, all of whom are Hong Kong natives, speak English, but your boss asks you to review his message for clarity. What would you suggest your boss change in the following email message, and why? Would you consider this message to be audience centered? Why or why not? (Hint: Do some quick research on Hong Kong to identify the style of English that people in Hong Kong are likely to speak.)

I wanted to welcome you ASAP to our little family here in the States. It's high time we shook hands in person and not just across the sea. I'm pleased as punch about getting to know you all, and I for one will do my level best to sell you on America.

### Exercises

Active links for all websites in this chapter can be found on MyBCommLab; see your User Guide for instructions on accessing the content for this chapter. Each activity is labeled according to the primary skill or skills you will need to use. To review relevant chapter content, you can refer to the indicated Learning Objective. In some instances, supporting information will be found in another chapter, as indicated.

1. **Intercultural Communication: Recognizing Cultural Variations [LO-1], [LO-3], [LO-4]** Review the definitions of the generations on page 69. Based on your year of birth, in which generation do you belong? Do you feel a part of this generation? Why or why not? If you were born outside the United States, do the generational boundaries seem accurate to you? Now consider the biases that you might have regarding other generations. For example, if you are a member of Generation Y, what do you think about the baby boomers and their willingness to embrace new ideas? Identify several of your generational biases that could create friction in the workplace. Summarize your responses to these questions in a post on your class blog or an email message to your instructor.

2. **Intercultural Communication: Adapting to Cultural Variations [LO-2]** You are a new manager at K & J Brick, a masonry products company that is now run by the two sons of the man who founded it 50 years ago. For years, the co-owners have invited the management team to a wilderness lodge for a combination of outdoor sports and annual business planning meetings. You don't want to miss the event, but you know that the outdoor activities weren't designed for someone like you, whose physical impairments prevent participation in the sporting events. Draft a short email message to the rest of the management team, suggesting changes to the annual event that will allow all managers to participate.

3. **Intercultural Communication: Recognizing Cultural Variations [LO-2]** Differences in gender, age, and physical abilities contribute to the diversity of today's workforce. Working with a classmate, role-play a conversation in which
   a. a woman is being interviewed for a job by a male personnel manager.
   b. an older person is being interviewed for a job by a younger personnel manager.
   c. an employee who is a native speaker of English is being interviewed for a job by a hiring manager who is a recent immigrant with relatively poor English skills.

How did differences between the applicant and the interviewer shape the communication? What can you do to improve communication in such situations?

4. **Intercultural Communication: Recognizing Cultural Variations [LO-3]** You represent a Canadian toy company that's negotiating to buy miniature truck wheels from a manufacturer in Osaka, Japan. In your first meeting, you explain that your company expects to control the design of the wheels as well as the materials that are used to make them. The manufacturer's representative looks down and says softly, "Perhaps that will be difficult." You press for agreement, and to emphasize your willingness to buy, you show the prepared contract you've brought with you. However, the manufacturer seems increasingly vague and uninterested. What cultural differences may be interfering with effective communication in this situation? (Canada is considered a low-context culture; Japan is high-context.) In a brief email message to your instructor or a post on your class blog, share your analysis.

5. **Intercultural Communication: Writing for Multiple-Language Audiences [LO-5]** Reading English-language content written by nonnative speakers of English can be a good reminder of the challenges of communicating in another language. The writing can be confusing or even amusing at first glance, but the key to remember here is that your writing might sound just as confusing or amusing to someone else if your roles were reversed.

Identify a company that is based in a non-English speaking country but that includes English-language text on its website. (The "Advanced" search capabilities of your favorite search engine can help you locate websites from a particular country.) Study the language on this site. Does it sound as though it was written by someone adept at English? If the first site you've found does have writing that sounds natural to a native U.S. English speaker, find another company whose website doesn't. Select a section of text, at least several sentences long, and rewrite it to sound more "American." Submit the original text and your rewritten version to your instructor.

6. **Intercultural Communication: Writing for Multiple-Language Audiences; Collaboration: Team Projects [LO-5], Chapter 2** With a team assigned by your instructor, review the Facebook pages of five companies, looking for words and phrases that might be confusing to a nonnative speaker of English. If you (or someone on the team) is a nonnative speaker, explain to the team why those word choices could be confusing. Choose three sentences, headlines, company slogans, or other pieces of text that contain potentially confusing words and rewrite them to minimize the chances of misinterpretation. As much as possible, try to retain the tone of the original—although you may find that this is impossible in some instances. Use Google Docs to compile the original selections and your revised versions, then email the documents to your instructor.

7. **Intercultural Communication: Speaking with Multiple-Language Audiences; Collaboration: Team Projects [LO-5], Chapter 2** Working with two other students, prepare a list of 10 examples of slang (in your own language) that might be misinterpreted or misunderstood during a business conversation with someone from another culture. Next to each example, suggest other words you might use to convey the same message. Do the alternatives mean *exactly* the same as the original slang or idiom? Submit your list of original words and suggested replacements, with an explanation of why each replacement is better than the original.

8. **Intercultural Communication: Studying Cultures [LO-5]** Choose a country that is unfamiliar to you. Research the culture and write a brief summary for your class blog of what a U.S. manager would need to know about concepts of personal space and rules of social behavior in order to conduct business successfully in that country.

9. **Intercultural Communication: Writing for Multiple-Language Audiences [LO-5]** Explore the powers and limitations of free online translation services such as Yahoo! Babel Fish (http://babelfish.yahoo.com) or Google Translate (http://translate.google.com). Enter a sentence from this chapter, such as "Local markets are opening to worldwide competition as businesses of all sizes look for new growth opportunities outside their own countries." First, translate the sentence from English to Spanish and click to complete the translation. Next, copy the Spanish version and paste it into the translation entry box and back-translate it from Spanish to English. Now repeat this test for German, French, Italian, or another language. Did the sentence survive the round trip? Does it still sound like normal business writing when translated back into English?

(1) What are the implications for the use of automated translation services for international correspondence? (2) Would you feel comfortable using an online tool such as this to translate an important business message? (3) How might you use this website to sharpen your intercultural communication skills? Summarize your findings in a brief report.

10. **Intercultural Communication: Speaking with Multiple-Language Audiences; Media Skills: Podcasting [LO-5], Chapter 7** Your company was one of the first to use podcasting as a business communication tool. Executives frequently record messages (such as monthly sales summaries) and post them on the company's intranet site; employees from the 14 offices in Europe, Asia, and North America then download the files to their music players or other devices and listen to the messages while riding the train to work, eating lunch at their desks, and so on. Your boss asks you to draft the opening statement for a podcast that will announce a revenue drop caused by intensive competitive pressure. She reviews your script and hands it back with a gentle explanation that it needs to be revised for international listeners. Improve the following statement in as many ways as you can:

Howdy, comrades. Shouldn't surprise anyone that we took a beating this year, given the insane pricing moves our knucklehead competitors have been making. I mean, how those clowns can keep turning a profit is beyond me, what with steel costs still going through the roof and labor costs heating up—even in countries where everybody goes to find cheap labor—and hazardous waste disposal regs adding to operating costs, too.

# Expand Your Skills

## Critique the Professionals

Find an online business document—such as a company webpage, blog post, Facebook Info tab, or LinkedIn profile—that you believe commits an intercultural communication blunder by failing to consider the needs of at least some of its target readers. For example, a website might use slang or idiomatic language that could confuse some readers, or it might use language that offends some readers. In a post on your class blog, share the text you found and explain why you think it does not succeed as effective intercultural communication. Be sure to include a link back to the original material.

## Sharpening Your Career Skills Online

Bovée and Thill's Business Communication Web Search, at http://businesscommunicationblog.com/websearch, is a unique research tool designed specifically for business communication research. Use the Web Search function to find a website, video, podcast, or PowerPoint presentation that offers advice on communicating with business contacts in another country or culture. Write a brief email message to your instructor, describing the item you found and summarizing the career skills information you learned from it.

## MyBCommLab

Go to **mybcommlab.com** for Auto-graded writing questions as well as the following Assisted-graded writing questions:

**3-1.** How have market globalization and cultural diversity contributed to the increased importance of intercultural communication? [LO-1]

**3-2.** What four principles apply to ethical intercultural communication? [LO-3]

**3-3.** Mybcommlab only—comprehensive writing assignment for this chapter.

# Endnotes

1. Michael R. Carrell, Everett E. Mann, and Tracey Honeycutt-Sigler, "Defining Workforce Diversity Programs and Practices in Organizations: A Longitudinal Study," *Labor Law Journal*, Spring 2006, 5–12.
2. "Dimensions of Diversity—Workforce," Merck website, accessed 4 January 2011, www.merck.com.
3. "Top Ten Countries with Which the U.S. Trades," U.S. Census Bureau website, accessed 29 December 2010, www.census.gov.
4. *Competing Across Borders: How Cultural and Communication Barriers Affect Business*, Economist Intelligence Unit Ltd., 2012, 4.
5. Nancy R. Lockwood, "Workplace Diversity: Leveraging the Power of Difference for Competitive Advantage," *HR Magazine*, June 2005, special section 1–10.
6. Alan Kline, "The Business Case for Diversity," *USBanker*, May 2010, 10–11.
7. Podcast interview with Ron Glover, IBM website, accessed 17 August 2008, www.ibm.com.
8. "More Than 300 Counties Now 'Majority–Minority,'" press release, U.S. Census Bureau website, 9 August 2007, www.census.gov; Robert Kreitner, *Management*, 9th ed. (Boston: Houghton Mifflin, 2004), 84.
9. Tracy Novinger, *Intercultural Communication, A Practical Guide* (Austin, Tex.: University of Texas Press, 2001), 15.
10. Larry A. Samovar and Richard E. Porter, "Basic Principles of Intercultural Communication," in *Intercultural Communication: A Reader*, 6th ed., edited by Larry A. Samovar and Richard E. Porter (Belmont, Calif.: Wadsworth, 1991), 12.
11. Arthur Chin, "Understanding Cultural Competency," *New Zealand Business*, December 2010/January 2011, 34–35; Sanjeeta R. Gupta, "Achieve Cultural Competency," *Training*, February 2009, 16–17; Diane Shannon, "Cultural Competency in Health Care Organizations: Why and How," *Physician Executive*, September–October 2010, 15–22.
12. Linda Beamer and Iris Varner, *Intercultural Communication in the Workplace*, 2nd ed. (New York: McGraw-Hill Irwin, 2001), 3.
13. "Languages of the United States," Ethnologue website, accessed 29 December 2010, www.ethnologue.com.
14. Philip R. Harris and Robert T. Moran, *Managing Cultural Differences*, 3rd ed. (Houston: Gulf, 1991), 394–397, 429–430.
15. Lillian H. Chaney and Jeanette S. Martin, *Intercultural Business Communication*, 2nd ed. (Upper Saddle River, N.J.: Prentice Hall, 2000), 6.
16. Beamer and Varner, *Intercultural Communication in the Workplace*, 4.
17. Chaney and Martin, *Intercultural Business Communication*, 2nd ed., 9.
18. Richard L. Daft, *Management*, 6th ed. (Cincinnati: Thomson South-Western, 2003), 455.
19. Lillian H. Chaney and Jeanette S. Martin, *Intercultural Business Communication*, 4th ed. (Upper Saddle River, N.J.: Pearson Prentice Hall, 2007), 53.
20. Project Implicit website, accessed 29 December 2010, http://implicit.harvard.edu/implicit.
21. Linda Beamer, "Teaching English Business Writing to Chinese-Speaking Business Students," *Bulletin of the Association for Business Communication* 57, no. 1 (1994): 12–18.
22. Edward T. Hall, "Context and Meaning," in *Intercultural Communication*, 6th ed., edited by Larry A. Samovar and Richard E. Porter (Belmont, Calif.: Wadsworth, 1991), 46–55.
23. Daft, *Management*, 459.
24. Charley H. Dodd, *Dynamics of Intercultural Communication*, 3rd ed. (Dubuque, Ia.: Brown, 1991), 69–70.
25. Daft, *Management*, 459.
26. Hannah Seligson, "For American Workers in China, a Culture Clash," *New York Times*, 23 December 2009, www.nytimes.com.
27. Beamer and Varner, *Intercultural Communication in the Workplace*, 230–233.

28. Ed Marcum, "More U.S. Businesses Abandon Outsourcing Overseas," *Seattle Times*, 28 August 2010, www.seattletimes.com.
29. Guo-Ming Chen and William J. Starosta, *Foundations of Intercultural Communication* (Boston: Allyn & Bacon, 1998), 288–289.
30. Mary A. DeVries, *Internationally Yours* (New York: Houghton Mifflin, 1994), 194.
31. Robert O. Joy, "Cultural and Procedural Differences That Influence Business Strategies and Operations in the People's Republic of China," *SAM Advanced Management Journal*, Summer 1989, 29–33.
32. Chaney and Martin, *Intercultural Business Communication*, 2nd ed., 122–123.
33. Mansour Javidan, "Forward-Thinking Cultures," *Harvard Business Review*, July–August 2007, 20.
34. Tracy Novinger, *Intercultural Communication, A Practical Guide* (Austin, Tex.: University of Texas Press, 2001), 54.
35. Peter Coy, "Old. Smart. Productive." *BusinessWeek*, 27 June 2005, www.businessweek.com; Beamer and Varner, *Intercultural Communication in the Workplace*, 107–108.
36. Beamer and Varner, *Intercultural Communication in the Workplace*, 107–108.
37. Steff Gelston, "Gen Y, Gen X and the Baby Boomers: Workplace Generation Wars," *CIO*, 30 January 2008, www.cio.com.
38. Joanna Barsh and Lareina Yee, "Changing Companies' Minds About Women," *McKinsey Quarterly*, 2011, Issue 4, 48–59.
39. John Gray, *Mars and Venus in the Workplace* (New York: HarperCollins, 2002), 10, 25–27, 61–63.
40. Jennifer Luden, "Ask for a Raise? Most Women Hesitate," NPR, 14 February 2011, www.npr.org.
41. "Religious Bias a Growing Issue," *Business Insurance*, 13 February 2012, 8; Mark D. Downey, "Keeping the Faith," *HR Magazine*, January 2008, 85–88.
42. IBM Accessibility Center, accessed 24 August 2006, www-03.ibm.com/able; AssistiveTech.net, accessed 24 August 2006, www.assistivetech.net; Business Leadership Network website, accessed 24 August 2006, www.usbln.org; National Institute on Disability

and Rehabilitation Research website, accessed 24 August 2006, www.ed.gov/about/offices/list/osers/nidrr; Rehabilitation Engineering & Assistive Technology Society of North America website, accessed 24 August 2006, www.resna.org.
43. Daphne A. Jameson, "Reconceptualizing Cultural Identity and its Role in Intercultural Business Communication," *Journal of Business Communication*, July 2007, 199–235.
44. Leslie Knudson, "Diversity on a Global Scale," *HR Management*, accessed 17 August 2008, www.hrmreport.com.
45. Craig S. Smith, "Beware of Green Hats in China and Other Cross-Cultural Faux Pas," *New York Times*, 30 April 2002, C11.
46. Sana Reynolds and Deborah Valentine, *Guide for Internationals: Culture, Communication, and ESL* (Upper Saddle River, N.J.: Pearson Prentice Hall, 2006), 3–11, 14–19, 25.
47. P. Christopher Earley and Elaine Mosakowsi, "Cultural Intelligence," *Harvard Business Review*, October 2004, 139–146.
48. Wendy A. Conklin, "An Inside Look at Two Diversity Intranet Sites: IBM and Merck," *The Diversity Factor*, Summer 2005.
49. Bob Nelson, "Motivating Workers Worldwide," *Global Workforce*, November 1998, 25–27.
50. Mona Casady and Lynn Wasson, "Written Communication Skills of International Business Persons," *Bulletin of the Association for Business Communication* 57, no. 4 (1994): 36–40.
51. Lynn Gaertner-Johnston, "Found in Translation," Business Writing blog, 25 November 2005, www.businesswritingblog.com.
52. Myron W. Lustig and Jolene Koester, *Intercultural Competence*, 4th ed. (Boston: Allyn & Bacon, 2003), 196.
53. "'Can You Spell That for Us Nonnative Speakers?' Accommodation Strategies in International Business Meetings," Pamela Rogerson-Revell, *Journal of Business Communication*, Vol 47, No 4, October 2010, 432–454.
54. James Wilfong and Toni Seger, *Taking Your Business Global* (Franklin Lakes, N.J.: Career Press, 1997), 232.
55. Sheridan Prasso, ed., "It's All Greek to These Sites," *BusinessWeek*, 22 July 2002, 18.

Every professional can learn to write more effectively while spending less time and energy in creating effective messages. Discover a proven writing process that divides the challenge of communicating into three simple steps: planning, writing, and completing messages. The process works for everything from blog posts to formal reports to your résumé. With a bit of practice, you'll be using the process to write more effectively without even thinking about it.

# Planning Business Messages

## LEARNING OBJECTIVES

After studying this chapter, you will be able to

1  Describe the three-step writing process.

2  Explain why it's important to analyze a communication situation in order to define your purpose and profile your audience before writing a message.

3  Discuss information-gathering options for simple messages and identify three attributes of quality information.

4  List the factors to consider when choosing the most appropriate medium for a message.

5  Explain why good organization is important to both you and your audience and list the tasks involved in organizing a message.

## MyBCommLab®

⭐ **Improve Your Grade!** Over 10 million students improved their results using the Pearson MyLabs. Visit **mybcommlab.com** for simulations, tutorials, and end-of-chapter problems.

## COMMUNICATION CLOSE-UP AT
## H&R Block www.hrblock.com

Many taxpayers don't think about their taxes until they absolutely have to, and then they want to think about taxes as little as possible. In this context of extreme apathy, H&R Block certainly has a challenge on its hands when it wants to communicate with taxpayers about tax preparation products and services.

H&R Block is the leading tax-preparation firm in the United States, with a range of options for virtually every class of taxpayer. Those who want to avoid the chore of doing their own taxes can hand the job over to one of the company's 90,000 tax specialists. Those taxpayers who are willing to do most or all of the work themselves can choose from a variety of digital alternatives, including both PC software and web-based solutions.

Although tax preparation is one of the least exciting consumer experiences, H&R Block has developed a reputation for creative communication efforts that make use of the latest innovations in social media. For example, for one product launch that noted media expert Shel Israel characterized as "among the most extensive business-to-consumer social media campaigns in history," the company used a variety of techniques to connect with potential customers: videos on YouTube (including a contest for user-created videos), profiles on MySpace and Facebook, Twitter microblogging, and an "H&R Block Island" in the virtual world Second Life.

The innovations aren't simply about technology, however. In the spirit of the social communication model (see Chapter 1),

The tax services giant H&R Block uses social media extensively to build relationships with clients and customers. The company's YouTube channel, for example, offers videos with tax tips and gives H&R Block employees the opportunity to answer questions from viewers.

the company emphasizes a conversational, two-way approach in which it listens as carefully as it speaks. For example, staffers follow a large number of Twitter users who have asked tax questions in the past, with the goal of maintaining an open channel of communication.

Particularly coming from a company that has a stodgy, old-school image in the minds of many people, this cutting-edge communication has surprised more than a few social media observers. Perhaps even more amazing is that H&R Block has actually generated some public interest in the field of tax preparation.[1]

# Understanding the Three-Step Writing Process

The emphasis that H&R Block (profiled in the chapter-opening Communication Close-Up) puts on connecting with customers is a lesson that applies to business messages for all stakeholders. By following the process introduced in this chapter, you can create successful messages that meet audience needs and highlight your skills as a perceptive business professional.

The three-step writing process (see Figure 4.1) helps ensure that your messages are both *effective* (meeting your audience's needs and getting your points across) and *efficient* (making the best use of your time and your audience's time):

- **Step 1: Planning business messages.** To plan any message, first *analyze the situation* by defining your purpose and developing a profile of your audience. When you're sure what you need to accomplish with your message, *gather the information* that will meet your audience's needs. Next, *select the right medium* (oral, written, visual, or electronic) to deliver your message. Then *organize the information* by defining your main idea, limiting your scope, selecting the direct or indirect approach, and outlining your content. Planning messages is the focus of this chapter.

**1** LEARNING OBJECTIVE
Describe the three-step writing process.

The three-step writing process consists of planning, writing, and completing your message.

**1 Plan** →   **2 Write** →   **3 Complete**

### Analyze the Situation
Define your purpose and develop an audience profile.

### Gather Information
Determine audience needs and obtain the information necessary to satisfy those needs.

### Select the Right Medium
Select the best medium for delivering your message.

### Organize the Information
Define your main idea, limit your scope, select a direct or an indirect approach, and outline your content.

### Adapt to Your Audience
Be sensitive to audience needs by using a "you" attitude, politeness, positive emphasis, and unbiased language. Build a strong relationship with your audience by establishing your credibility and projecting your company's preferred image. Control your style with a conversational tone, plain English, and appropriate voice.

### Compose the Message
Choose strong words that will help you create effective sentences and coherent paragraphs.

### Revise the Message
Evaluate content and review readability, edit and rewrite for conciseness and clarity.

### Produce the Message
Use effective design elements and suitable layout for a clean, professional appearance.

### Proofread the Message
Review for errors in layout, spelling, and mechanics.

### Distribute the Message
Deliver your message using the chosen medium; make sure all documents and all relevant files are distributed successfully.

**Figure 4.1  The Three-Step Writing Process**
This three-step process will help you create more effective messages in any medium. As you get more practice with the process, it will become easier and more automatic.
*Sources:* Adapted from Kevin J. Harty and John Keenan, *Writing for Business and Industry: Process and Product* (New York: Macmillan Publishing Company, 1987), 3–4; Richard Hatch, *Business Writing* (Chicago: Science Research Associates, 1983), 88–89; Richard Hatch, *Business Communication Theory and Technique* (Chicago: Science Research Associates, 1983), 74–75; Center for Humanities, *Writing as a Process: A Step-by-Step Guide* (Mount Kisco, N.Y.: Center for Humanities, 1987); Michael L. Keene, *Effective Professional Writing* (New York: D. C. Heath, 1987), 28–34.

- **Step 2: Writing business messages.** After you've planned your message, *adapt to your audience* with sensitivity, relationship skills, and an appropriate writing style. Then you're ready to *compose your message* by choosing strong words, creating effective sentences, and developing coherent paragraphs. Writing business messages is discussed in Chapter 5.
- **Step 3: Completing business messages.** After writing your first draft, *revise your message* by evaluating the content, reviewing readability, and editing and rewriting until your message comes across concisely and clearly, with correct grammar, proper punctuation, and effective format. Next, *produce your message.* Put it into the form that your audience will receive and review all design and layout decisions for an attractive, professional appearance. *Proofread* the final product to ensure high quality and then *distribute your message.* Completing business messages is discussed in Chapter 6.

Throughout this book, you'll learn how to apply these steps to a wide variety of business messages: short messages such as social network and blog posts (Chapters 7 through 12), longer reports (Chapters 14 and 15), oral presentations (Chapters 16 and 17), and the employment messages you can use to build a great career (Chapters 18 and 19).

## OPTIMIZING YOUR WRITING TIME

As a starting point, allot half your available time for planning, one-quarter for writing, and one-quarter for completing your messages—but adjust these percentages for each project.

The more you use the three-step writing process, the more intuitive and automatic it will become. You'll also get better at allotting time for each task during a writing project. Start by figuring out how much time you have to spend. Then, as a general rule, set aside roughly 50 percent of that time for planning, 25 percent for writing, and 25 percent for completing.

Reserving half your time for planning might seem excessive, but as the next section explains, careful planning usually saves time overall by focusing your writing and reducing rework. Of course, the ideal time allocation varies from project to project. Simpler and shorter messages require less planning than long reports, websites, and other complex projects. Also, the time required to produce and distribute messages can vary widely, depending on the media, the size of the audience, and other factors. However, start with the 50–25–25 split as a guideline, and use your best judgment for each project.

## PLANNING EFFECTIVELY

Trying to save time by skimping on planning usually costs you more time in the long run.

As soon as the need to create a message appears, inexperienced communicators are often tempted to dive directly into writing. However, skipping or shortchanging the planning stage often creates extra work and stress later in the process. First, thoughtful planning is necessary to make sure you provide the right information in the right format to the right people. Taking the time to understand your audience members and their needs helps you find and assemble the facts they're looking for and deliver that information in a concise and compelling way. Second, with careful planning, the writing stage is faster, easier, and a lot less stressful. Third, planning can save you from embarrassing blunders that could hurt your company or your career.

# Analyzing the Situation

**2 LEARNING OBJECTIVE** Explain why it's important to analyze a communication situation in order to define your purpose and profile your audience before writing a message.

Every communication effort takes place in a particular situation, meaning you have a specific message to send a specific audience under a specific set of circumstances. For example, describing your professional qualifications in an email message to an executive in your own company differs significantly from describing your qualifications in your LinkedIn profile. The email message is likely to be focused on one specific goal, such as explaining why you would be a good choice to head up a major project, and you have the luxury of focusing on the needs of a single, personally identifiable reader. In contrast, your social networking profile could have multiple goals, such as connecting with your peers in other companies and presenting your qualifications to potential employers, and it might be viewed by hundreds or thousands of readers, each with his or her own needs.

The underlying information for these two messages could be roughly the same, but the level of detail to include, the tone of the writing, the specific word choices—these and other choices you need to make will differ from one situation to another. Making the right choices starts with defining your purpose clearly and understanding your audience's needs.

## DEFINING YOUR PURPOSE

All business messages have a **general purpose**: to inform, to persuade, or to collaborate with the audience. This purpose helps define the overall approach you'll need to take, from gathering information to organizing your message. Within the scope of its general purpose, each message also has a **specific purpose**, which identifies what you hope to accomplish with your message and what your audience should do or think after receiving your message. For instance, is your goal simply to update your audience about some upcoming event, or do you want people to take immediate action? State your specific purpose as precisely as possible, even to the point of identifying which audience members should respond, how they should respond, and when.

After you have defined your specific purpose, take a moment for a reality check. Decide whether that purpose merits the time and effort required for you to prepare and send the message—and for your audience to spend the time required to read it, view it, or listen to it. Test your purpose by asking these four questions:

- **Will anything change as a result of your message?** Don't contribute to information overload by sending messages that won't change anything. For instance, if you don't like your company's latest advertising campaign but you're not in a position to influence it, sending a critical message to your colleagues won't change anything and won't benefit anyone.
- **Is your purpose realistic?** Recognizing whether a goal is realistic is an important part of having good business sense. For example, if you request a raise while the company is struggling, you might send the message that you're not tuned into the situation around you.
- **Is the time right?** People who are busy or distracted when they receive your message are less likely to pay attention to it. Many professions and departments have recurring cycles in their workloads, for instance, and messages sent during peak times may be ignored.
- **Is your purpose acceptable to your organization?** Your company's business objectives and policies, and even laws that apply to your particular industry, may dictate whether a particular purpose is acceptable.

When you are satisfied that you have a clear and meaningful purpose and that this is a smart time to proceed, your next step is to understand the members of your audience and their needs.

## DEVELOPING AN AUDIENCE PROFILE

Before audience members will take the time to read or listen to your messages, they have to be interested in what you're saying. They need to know the message is relevant to their needs—even if they don't necessarily want to read or see it. The more you know about your audience members, their needs, and their expectations, the more effectively you'll be able to communicate with them. Follow these steps to conduct a thorough audience analysis (see Figure 4.2 on the next page):

- **Identify your primary audience.** For some messages, certain audience members may be more important than others. Don't ignore the needs of less influential members, but make sure you address the concerns of the key decision makers.

*Your general purpose may be to inform, to persuade, or to collaborate.*

*Your specific purpose is what you hope to accomplish with your message and what your audience should do or think after receiving your message.*

Wait to send a message, or do not send it at all, if
- Nothing will change as a result of sending
- The purpose is not realistic
- The timing is not right
- The purpose is not acceptable to your organization

*If audience members have different levels of understanding of the topic, aim your message at the most influential decision makers.*

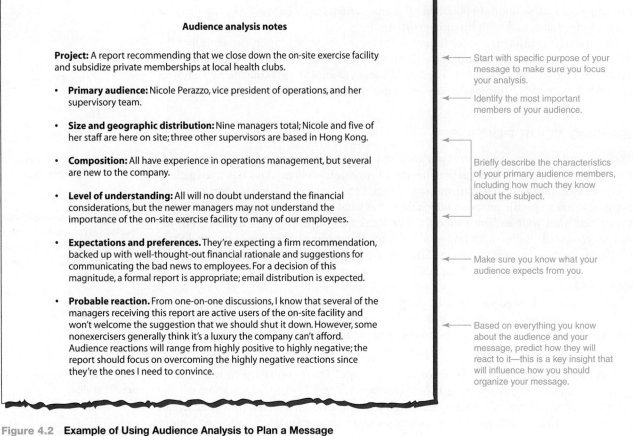

**Audience analysis notes**

**Project:** A report recommending that we close down the on-site exercise facility and subsidize private memberships at local health clubs.

- **Primary audience:** Nicole Perazzo, vice president of operations, and her supervisory team.

- **Size and geographic distribution:** Nine managers total; Nicole and five of her staff are here on site; three other supervisors are based in Hong Kong.

- **Composition:** All have experience in operations management, but several are new to the company.

- **Level of understanding:** All will no doubt understand the financial considerations, but the newer managers may not understand the importance of the on-site exercise facility to many of our employees.

- **Expectations and preferences.** They're expecting a firm recommendation, backed up with well-thought-out financial rationale and suggestions for communicating the bad news to employees. For a decision of this magnitude, a formal report is appropriate; email distribution is expected.

- **Probable reaction.** From one-on-one discussions, I know that several of the managers receiving this report are active users of the on-site facility and won't welcome the suggestion that we should shut it down. However, some nonexercisers generally think it's a luxury the company can't afford. Audience reactions will range from highly positive to highly negative; the report should focus on overcoming the highly negative reactions since they're the ones I need to convince.

*Start with specific purpose of your message to make sure you focus your analysis.*

*Identify the most important members of your audience.*

*Briefly describe the characteristics of your primary audience members, including how much they know about the subject.*

*Make sure you know what your audience expects from you.*

*Based on everything you know about the audience and your message, predict how they will react to it—this is a key insight that will influence how you should organize your message.*

**Figure 4.2   Example of Using Audience Analysis to Plan a Message**
For simple, routine messages, you usually don't need to analyze your audience in depth. However, for complex messages or messages for indifferent or hostile audiences, take the time to study their information needs and potential reactions to your message.

- **Determine audience size and geographic distribution.** A message aimed at 10,000 people spread around the globe will probably require a different approach than one aimed at a dozen people down the hall.
- **Determine audience composition.** Look for similarities and differences in culture, language, age, education, organizational rank and status, attitudes, experience, motivations, biases, beliefs, and any other factors that might affect the success of your message (see Figure 4.3).
- **Gauge audience members' level of understanding.** If audience members share your general background, they'll probably understand your material without difficulty. If not, your message will need an element of education to help people understand your message.

> To win over a skeptical audience, use a gradual approach and plenty of evidence.

- **Understand audience expectations and preferences.** For example, will members of your audience expect complete details or just a summary of the main points? In general, for internal communication, the higher up the organization your message goes, the fewer details people want to see.
- **Forecast probable audience reaction.** As you'll read later in the chapter, potential audience reaction affects message organization. If you expect a favorable response, you can state conclusions and recommendations up front and offer minimal supporting evidence. If you expect skepticism, you can introduce conclusions gradually and with more proof.

**REAL-TIME UPDATES**
LEARN MORE BY READING THIS PDF

**Dig deep into audience needs with this planning tool**

This in-depth audience analysis tool can help you analyze audiences for even the most complex communication scenarios. Go to http://real-timeupdates.com/bct12 and click on Learn More. If you are using MyBCommLab, you can access Real-Time Updates within each chapter or under Student Study Tools.

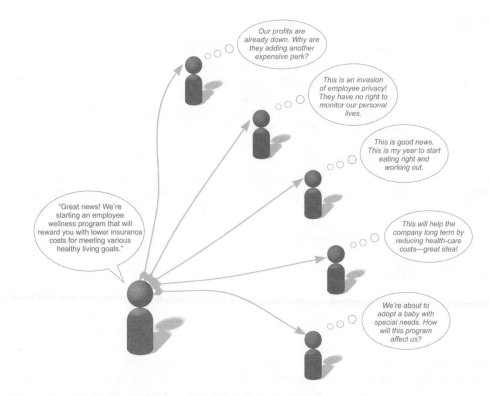

**Figure 4.3  Predicting the Effects of Audience Composition**
As just one example of why it's important to analyze the composition of your audience, the attitudes and beliefs of individual audience members can have a significant impact on the success of a message. In this scenario, for instance, a seemingly positive message about employee benefits can generate a wide range of responses from employees with different beliefs and concerns.

# Gathering Information

When you have a clear picture of your audience, your next step is to assemble the information to include in your message. For simple messages, you may already have all the information at hand, but for more complex messages, you may need to do considerable research and analysis before you're ready to begin writing. Chapter 13 explores formal techniques for finding, evaluating, and processing information, but you can often use a variety of informal techniques to gather insights and guide your research efforts:

**3 LEARNING OBJECTIVE**
Discuss information-gathering options for simple messages, and identify three attributes of quality information.

- **Consider the audience's perspective.** Put yourself in the audience's position. What are these people thinking, feeling, or planning? What information do they need in order to move forward? If you are initiating a conversation in a social media context, what information will stimulate discussion in your target communities?
- **Listen to the community.** For almost any subject related to business these days, chances are there is a community of customers, product enthusiasts, or other people who engage in online discussions. Find them and listen to what they have to say.
- **Read reports and other company documents.** Annual reports, financial statements, news releases, blogs by industry experts, marketing reports, and customer surveys are just a few of the many potential sources. Find out whether your company has a *knowledge management system*, a centralized database that collects the experiences and insights of employees throughout the organization.
- **Talk with supervisors, colleagues, or customers.** Fellow workers and customers may have information you need, or they may have good insights into the needs of your target audience.
- **Ask your audience for input.** If you're unsure what audience members need from your message, ask them, if at all possible. Admitting you don't know but want to meet their needs will impress an audience more than guessing and getting it wrong.

## UNCOVERING AUDIENCE NEEDS

If you're given a vague request, ask questions to clarify it before you plan a response.

In many situations, your audience's information needs will be obvious, or readers will be able to tell you what they need. In other situations, though, people may be unable to articulate exactly what is needed. If someone makes a vague or broad request, ask questions to narrow the focus. If your boss says, "Find out everything you can about Interscope Records," narrow the investigation by asking which aspect of the company and its business is most important. Asking a question or two often forces the person to think through the request and define more precisely what is required.

If appropriate, include additional information that might be helpful, even though the requester didn't specifically ask for it.

In addition, try to think of relevant information needs that your audience may not have expressed. Suppose you've been asked to compare two health insurance plans for your firm's employees, but your research has uncovered a third alternative that might be even better. You could then expand your report to include a brief explanation of why the third plan should be considered and compare it to the two original plans. Use judgment, however; in some situations you need to provide only what the audience expects and nothing more.

## FINDING YOUR FOCUS

You may encounter situations in which the assignment or objective is so vague that you have no idea how to get started in determining what the audience needs to know. In such cases, you can use some *discovery techniques* to help generate ideas and uncover possible avenues to research. One popular technique is **free writing**, in which you write whatever comes to mind, without stopping to make any corrections, for a set period of time. The big advantage of free writing is that you silence your "inner critic" and just express ideas as they come to you. You might end up with a rambling mess by any conventional measure, but that's not important. Within that tangle of expressions, you might also find some useful ideas and angles that hadn't occurred to you yet—perhaps the crucial idea that will jumpstart the entire project.

If you're stuck for ideas, try *free writing* or sketching ideas instead of writing them.

The best discovery option in some cases might not be writing at all, but rather *sketching*. If you're unable to come up with any words, grab a sketchpad and start drawing. While you're thinking visually, your brain might release some great ideas that were trapped behind words.

The techniques listed under "Defining Your Main Idea" on page 101 can also be helpful if you don't know where to start.

## PROVIDING REQUIRED INFORMATION

Test the completeness of your document by making sure it answers all six journalistic questions: *who, what, when, where, why,* and *how.*

After you have defined your audience's information needs, your next step is to satisfy those needs completely. One good way to test the thoroughness of your message is to use the **journalistic approach:** Check to see whether your message answers *who, what, when, where, why,* and *how.* Using this method, you can quickly tell whether a message fails to deliver. For example, consider this message requesting information from employees:

> We are exploring ways to reduce our office space leasing costs and would like your input on a proposed plan in which employees who telecommute on alternate days could share offices. Please let me know what you think of this proposal.

The message fails to tell employees everything they need to know in order to provide meaningful responses. The *what* could be improved by identifying the specific information points the writer needs from employees (such as whether individual telecommuting patterns are predictable enough to allow scheduling of shared offices). The writer also doesn't specify *when* the responses are needed or *how* the employees should respond. By failing to address such points, the request is likely to generate a variety of responses, some possibly helpful but some probably not.

### Be Sure the Information Is Accurate

Be certain that the information you provide is accurate and that the commitments you make can be kept.

The *quality* of the information you provide is every bit as important as the *quantity*. Inaccurate information in business messages can cause a host of problems, from embarrassment and lost productivity to serious safety and legal issues. You may commit the organization to promises it can't keep—and the error could harm your reputation as a reliable businessperson. Thanks to the Internet, inaccurate information may persist for years after you distribute it.

You can minimize mistakes by double-checking every piece of information you collect. If you are consulting sources outside the organization, ask yourself whether the information is current and reliable. As Chapter 13 notes, you must be particularly careful when using sources you find online. Be sure to review any mathematical or financial calculations. Check all dates and schedules and examine your own assumptions and conclusions to be certain they are valid.

## Be Sure the Information Is Ethical

By working hard to ensure the accuracy of the information you gather, you'll also avoid many ethical problems in your messages. If you do make an honest mistake, such as delivering information you initially thought to be true but later found to be false, contact the recipients of the message immediately and correct the error. No one can reasonably fault you in such circumstances, and people will respect your honesty.

Messages can also be unethical if important information is omitted (see "Ethics Detective: Solving the Case of the Missing Safety Warning"). Of course, as a business professional, you may have legal or other sound business reasons for not including every detail about every matter. Just how much detail should you include? Make sure you include enough to avoid misleading your audience. If you're unsure how much information your audience needs, offer as much as you believe best fits your definition of complete and then offer to provide more upon request.

*A clear sense of ethics should guide your decisions when determining how much detail to include in your message.*

## Be Sure the Information Is Pertinent

When gathering information for your message, remember that some points will be more important to your audience than others. Audience members will appreciate your efforts to prioritize the information they need and filter out the information they don't. Moreover, by focusing on the information that concerns your audience the most, you increase your chances of accomplishing your own communication goals.

*Audiences respond best to information that has been filtered and prioritized to meet their needs.*

If you don't know your audience or if you're communicating with a large group of people who have diverse interests, use common sense to identify points of interest. Audience

*Rely on common sense if you don't know enough about your audience to know exactly what will interest them.*

### ETHICS DETECTIVE

## Solving the Case of the Missing Safety Warning

Your company, Furniture Formations, creates a variety of home furniture products, with extensive use of fine woods. To preserve the look and feel of the wood, your craftspeople use an linseed oil–based finish that you purchase from a local wholesaler. The workers apply the finish with rags, which are thrown away after each project. After a news report about spontaneous combustion of waste rags in other furniture shops, you grow concerned enough to contact the wholesaler and ask for verification of the product's safety. The wholesaler knows you've been considering a nonflammable, water-based alternative from another source but tries to assure you with the following message:

> Seal the rags in an approved container and dispose of it according to local regulations. As you probably already know, county regulations require all commercial users of oil-based materials to dispose of leftover finishes at the county's hazardous waste facility.

You're still not satisfied. You visit the website of the oil's manufacturer and find the following cautionary statement about the product you're currently using:

> Finishes that contain linseed oil or tung oil require specific safety precautions to minimize the risk of fire. Oil-soaked rags and other materials such as steel wool must be sealed in water-filled metal containers and then disposed of in accordance with local waste management regulations. Failure to do so can lead to spontaneous combustion that results from the heat-producing chemical reaction that takes place as the finish dries. In particular, DO NOT leave wet, oil-soaked rags in a pile or discard them with other waste.

### ANALYSIS

Was the wholesaler guilty of an ethical lapse in this case? If yes, explain what you think the lapse is and why you believe it is unethical. If no, explain why you think the statement qualifies as ethical.

factors such as age, job, location, income, and education can give you clues. If you're trying to sell memberships in a health club, you might adjust your message for athletes, busy professionals, families, and people in different locations or in different income brackets. The comprehensive facilities and professional trainers would appeal to athletes, whereas the low monthly rates would appeal to college students on tight budgets.

Some messages necessarily reach audiences with a diverse mix of educational levels, subject awareness, and other variables. If possible, provide each audience segment with its own targeted information, such as by using sections in a brochure or links on a webpage.

## Selecting the Right Medium

**4** **LEARNING OBJECTIVE**
List the factors to consider when choosing the most appropriate medium for a message.

A **medium** is the form through which you choose to communicate a message. You may choose to talk face to face, post to a blog, send an email message, or create a webcast. The range of media possibilities is wide and growing wider all the time. In fact, with so many options now available, selecting the best medium for a given message is itself an important communication skill (see Figure 4.4).

Although media categories have become increasingly blurred in recent years, for the sake of discussion, you can think of media as being *oral*, *written*, *visual*, or *electronic* (which often combines several media types).

### ORAL MEDIA

Oral communication is best when you need to encourage interaction, express emotions, or monitor emotional responses.

Oral media include face-to-face conversations, interviews, speeches, and in-person presentations and meetings—whenever you talk with someone who is physically in the same place. By giving communicators the ability to see, hear, and react to each other, oral media are useful for encouraging people to ask questions, make comments, and work together to reach a consensus or decision. Face-to-face interaction is particularly helpful in complex, emotionally charged situations in which establishing or fostering a business relationship is important.[2] Experts also recommend that managers engage in frequent "walk-arounds," chatting with employees to get input, answer their questions, and interpret important business events and trends.[3]

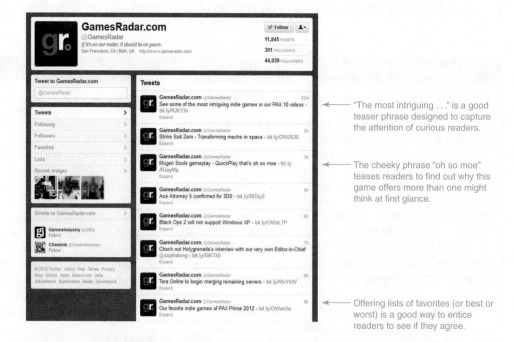

"The most intriguing . . ." is a good teaser phrase designed to capture the attention of curious readers.

The cheeky phrase "oh so moe" teases readers to find out why this game offers more than one might think at first glance.

Offering lists of favorites (or best or worst) is a good way to entice readers to see if they agree.

**Figure 4.4    Media Choices**
The online video game magazine GamesRadar.com uses Twitter as a platform for announcing new articles. This type of writing is a creative challenge, because each "teaser" (see page 178) must be compelling enough to encourage readers to click through to the website.
*Source:* Games Radar Twitter account. Copyright © 2012 by Future US, Inc. Reprinted with permission.

Of course, if you don't want a lot of questions or interaction, using oral media can be an unwise choice. However, consider your audience carefully before deciding to limit interaction by choosing a different medium. As a manager, you will encounter unpleasant situations (declining an employee's request for a raise, for example) for which sending an email message or otherwise avoiding personal contact will seem appealing to you. In many such cases, though, you owe the other party the opportunity to ask questions or express concerns. Moreover, facing the tough situations in person will earn you a reputation as an honest, caring manager.

## WRITTEN MEDIA

Written, printed messages take many forms, from traditional memos to glossy reports that rival magazines in production quality. Memos are traditionally used for the routine, day-to-day exchange of information within an organization. In many organizations, social networking, IM, email, blogs, and other electronic media have largely replaced paper memos. Letters are generally sent to recipients outside the organization. Reports and proposals are usually longer than memos and letters, although both can be created in memo or letter format. These documents come in a variety of lengths, ranging from a few pages to several hundred, and are usually fairly formal in tone. Chapters 14 and 15 discuss reports and proposals in detail.

*Written, printed messages have been replaced in many instances by electronic media, although printed messages still have a place in business today.*

## VISUAL MEDIA

The importance of visual elements in business communication continues to grow. Traditional business messages rely primarily on text, with occasional support from graphical elements such as charts, graphs, or diagrams to help illustrate points discussed in the text. However, many business communicators are discovering the power of messages in which the visual element is dominant and supported by small amounts of text. For the purposes of this discussion, you can think of *visual media* as any format in which one or more visual elements play a central role in conveying the message content (see Figure 4.5).

*In some situations, a message that is predominantly visual, with text used to support the illustration, can be more effective than a message that relies primarily on text.*

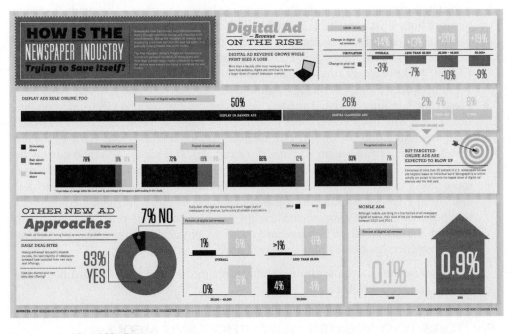

**Figure 4.5    Visual Media**
Visual media, in which a limited amount of text supports one or more dominant graphical elements, have become increasingly popular in business communication. Infographics, such as this example, try to convey facts and figures in a more visually appealing way than traditionally formatted charts or tables.
*Source:* "How the newspaper industry is trying to save itself" by GOOD and Column Five Media, originally appeared on www.GOOD.is on April 19, 2012. Copyright © 2012 by GOOD. Reprinted with permission.

Messages that combine powerful visuals with supporting text, sometimes known as *infographics*, can be effective for a number of reasons. Today's audiences are pressed for time and bombarded with messages, so anything that communicates quickly is welcome. Visuals are also effective at describing complex ideas and processes because they can reduce the work required for an audience to identify the parts and relationships that make up the whole. Also, in a multilingual business world, diagrams, symbols, and other images can lower communication barriers by requiring less language processing. Finally, visual depictions can be easier to remember than purely textual descriptions or explanations. Chapter 9 offers more information on infographics and other visual formats.

## ELECTRONIC MEDIA

In general, use electronic media to deliver messages quickly, to reach widely dispersed audiences, and to take advantage of rich multimedia formats.

The range of electronic media is broad and continues to grow even broader, from phone calls and podcasts to blogs and wikis to email and text messaging. When you want to make a powerful impression, using electronic media can increase the excitement and visual appeal with interactivity, animation, audio, and video.

The growth of electronic communication options is both a blessing and a curse for business communicators. On the one hand, you have more tools than ever before to choose from, with more ways to deliver rational and emotional content. On the other hand, the sheer range of choices can complicate your job, because you often need to choose among multiple media and you need to know how to use each medium successfully.

Today's audiences can get frustrated with the sheer number of electronic media in the workplace.

You'll learn more about using electronic and social media throughout this book (in Chapters 7 and 8, in particular), but for now, here is a quick overview of the major electronic media being used in business:

- **Electronic versions of oral media.** These media include telephone calls, teleconferencing, voice-mail messages, audio recordings such as compact discs and podcasts, *voice synthesis* (creating audio signals from computer data), *voice recognition* (converting audio signals to computer data), and even animated online characters known as avatars. *Internet telephony* services such as Skype that use VoIP (which stands for *Voice over IP*, the Internet Protocol) continue to grow in popularity.
- **Electronic versions of written media.** These options range from email and IM to blogs, websites, social networks, and wikis. These media are in a state of constant change, in terms of both what is available and who tends to use which media. For example, email has been a primary business medium for the past decade or two, but it is being replaced in many cases by IM, blogs, text messaging, and communication via social networks.[4] Chapter 7 takes a closer look at email, IM, and website content, and Chapter 8 discusses social networks, blogs, microblogs, and wikis.
- **Electronic versions of visual media.** These choices can include electronic presentations (using Microsoft PowerPoint, Google Docs, Apple Keynote, and other software), computer animation (using software such as Adobe Flash to create many of the animated sequences you see on websites, for example), and video (YouTube quickly became a major business communication channel). **Multimedia** refers to use of two or more media to craft a single message, typically some combination of audio, video, text, and visual graphics. Multimedia advances continue to create intriguing communication possibilities, such as *augmented reality*, in which computer-generated text, graphics, and sounds are superimposed onto a user's physical reality, either on a device display or directly onto the physical world itself.

For more on the latest innovations in electronic media, visit http://real-timeupdates .com/bct12 and click on Chapter 4.

## FACTORS TO CONSIDER WHEN CHOOSING MEDIA

In some situations, you have no choice of which medium to use. For instance, your department might use IM for all short internal messages and a wiki for longer status reports, and you'll be expected to use those media as well. In other situations, you'll have the opportunity to choose the medium (or media) for a particular message. Table 4.1 lists the general

## TABLE 4.1 Media Advantages and Disadvantages

| Media Type | Advantages | Disadvantages |
|---|---|---|
| Oral | • Provide opportunity for immediate feedback<br>• Promote interaction<br>• Involve rich nonverbal cues (both physical gestures and vocal inflection)<br>• Allow you to express the emotions behind the message | • Restrict participation to those physically present<br>• Unless recorded, provide no permanent, verifiable record of the communication<br>• In most cases, reduce communicator's control over the message<br>• Other than for messages that are prewritten and rehearsed, offer no opportunity to revise or edit spoken words |
| Written | • Allow you to plan and control your message<br>• Reach geographically dispersed audiences<br>• Offer a permanent, verifiable record<br>• Minimize the distortion that can result with oral and some forms of electronic messages<br>• Can be used to avoid immediate interactions<br>• Can help you control the emotional aspects of an interchange by eliminating interpersonal communication | • Offer limited opportunities for timely feedback<br>• Lack the rich nonverbal cues provided by oral media<br>• Can require more time and more resources to create and distribute, relative to oral media<br>• Elaborate documents can require special skills in preparation and production |
| Visual | • Can convey complex ideas and relationships quickly<br>• Often less intimidating than long blocks of text, particularly for nonnative readers<br>• Can reduce the burden on the audience to figure out how the pieces of a message or concept fit together | • Can require artistic skills to design<br>• Require some technical skills to create<br>• Can require more time to create than an equivalent amount of text<br>• Are more difficult to transmit and store than simple textual messages |
| Electronic | • Deliver messages quickly<br>• Reach geographically dispersed audiences<br>• Can offer the persuasive power of multimedia formats<br>• Enable audience interaction through social media features<br>• Can increase accessibility and openness within an organization and between an organization and its external stakeholders | • Are easy to overuse (sending too many messages to too many recipients)<br>• Present privacy risks and concerns (exposing confidential data; employer monitoring; accidental forwarding)<br>• Present security risks (viruses and spyware; network breaches)<br>• Create productivity concerns (frequent interruptions, lack of integration among multiple electronic media in use at the same time, and time wasted on nonbusiness uses) |

advantages and disadvantages of each medium. In addition, be sure to consider how your message is affected by these important factors:

- **Media richness.** *Richness* is a medium's ability to (1) convey a message through more than one informational cue (visual, verbal, vocal), (2) facilitate feedback, and (3) establish personal focus (see Figure 4.6). The richest medium is face-to-face communication; it's personal, provides immediate feedback (verbal and nonverbal), and conveys the emotion behind a message.[5] Multimedia presentations and multimedia webpages are also quite rich, with the ability to present images, animation, text, music, sound effects, and other elements. Many electronic media are also *interactive*, in that they enable audiences to participate in the communication process. At the other extreme are the leanest media—those that communicate in the simplest ways, provide no opportunity

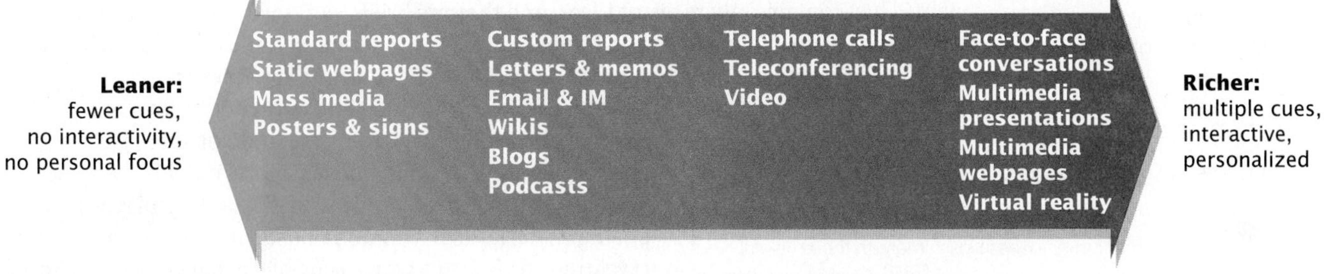

Media range from *lean* (few information cues, few feedback mechanisms, no personalization) to *rich* (many cues, simple feedback, personalization).

**Leaner:** fewer cues, no interactivity, no personal focus

| Standard reports<br>Static webpages<br>Mass media<br>Posters & signs | Custom reports<br>Letters & memos<br>Email & IM<br>Wikis<br>Blogs<br>Podcasts | Telephone calls<br>Teleconferencing<br>Video | Face-to-face conversations<br>Multimedia presentations<br>Multimedia webpages<br>Virtual reality |

**Richer:** multiple cues, interactive, personalized

**Figure 4.6** **Media Richness**
Business media vary widely in terms of *richness*, which is the number of informational cues available, their ability to incorporate feedback, and the degree to which they can be personalized.

for audience feedback, and aren't personalized. In general, use richer media to send nonroutine or complex messages, to humanize your presence throughout the organization, to share emotionally charged messages, and to gain employee commitment to company goals. Use leaner media to send routine messages or to transfer information that doesn't require significant explanation.[6]

- **Message formality.** Your media choice is a nonverbal signal that affects the style and tone of your message. For example, a printed memo or letter is likely to be perceived as a more formal gesture than an email message.
- **Media limitations.** Every medium has limitations. For instance, IM is ideal for communicating simple, straightforward messages, but it is less effective for sending complex messages.

*Some media deliver messages faster than others, but don't use instantaneous delivery to create a false sense of urgency.*

- **Urgency.** Some media establish a connection with the audience faster than others, so choose wisely if your message is urgent. However, be sure to respect audience members' time and workloads. If a message isn't urgent and doesn't require immediate feedback, choose a medium such as email that allows people to respond at their convenience.
- **Cost.** Cost is both a real financial factor and a perceived nonverbal signal. For example, depending on the context, extravagant (and expensive) video or multimedia presentations can send a nonverbal signal of sophistication and professionalism—or careless disregard for company budgets.

*When choosing the appropriate medium, don't forget to consider your audience's preferences and expectations.*

- **Audience preferences.** Be sure to consider which medium or media your audience expects or prefers.[7] For instance, businesspeople in the United States, Canada, and Germany emphasize written messages (printed or electronic), whereas in Japan professionals tend to emphasize oral messages—perhaps because Japan's high-context culture carries so much of the message in nonverbal cues and "between-the-lines" interpretation.[8]

## Organizing Your Information

**5** **LEARNING OBJECTIVE**
Explain why good organization is important to both you and your audience, and list the tasks involved in organizing a message.

Organization can make the difference between success and failure. Good organization helps your readers or listeners in three key ways. First, it helps them understand your message. In a well-organized message, you make the main point clear at the outset, present additional points to support that main idea, and satisfy all the information needs of the audience. But if your message is poorly organized, your meaning can be obscured, and your audiences may form inaccurate conclusions about what you've written or said.

*Good organization helps audience members understand your message, accept your message, and save time.*

Second, good organization helps receivers accept your message. If your writing appears confused and disorganized, people will likely conclude that the *thinking* behind the writing is also confused and disorganized. Moreover, effective messages often require a bit more than simple, clear logic. A diplomatic approach helps receivers accept your message, even if it's not exactly what they want to hear. In contrast, a poorly organized message on an emotionally charged topic can alienate the audience before you have the chance to get your point across.

Third, good organization saves your audience time. Well-organized messages are efficient. They contain only relevant ideas, and they are brief. Moreover, each piece of information is located in a logical place in the overall flow; each section builds on the one before to create a coherent whole, without forcing people to look for missing pieces.

*Good organization saves you time and energy in the writing and completing phases.*

In addition to saving time and energy for your readers, good organization saves *you* time and consumes less of your creative energy. Writing moves more quickly because you don't waste time putting ideas in the wrong places or composing material that you don't need. You spend far less time rewriting, trying to extract sensible meaning from disorganized rambling. Last but far from least, organizational skills are good for your career because they help you develop a reputation as a clear thinker who cares about your readers.

**REAL-TIME UPDATES**

LEARN MORE BY WATCHING THIS PRESENTATION

**Smart advice for brainstorming sessions**

Generate better ideas in less time with these helpful tips. Go to http://real-timeupdates.com/bct12 and click on Learn More. If you are using MyBCommLab, you can access Real-Time Updates within each chapter or under Student Study Tools.

| TABLE 4.2 | Defining Topic and Main Idea | | |
|---|---|---|---|
| **General Purpose** | **Example of Specific Purpose** | **Example of Topic** | **Example of Main Idea** |
| To inform | Teach customer service representatives how to edit and expand the technical support wiki | Technical support wiki | Careful, thorough edits and additions to the wiki help the entire department provide better customer support. |
| To persuade | Convince top managers to increase spending on research and development | Funding for research and development | Competitors spend more than we do on research and development, enabling them to create more innovative products. |
| To collaborate | Solicit ideas for a companywide incentive system that ties wages to profits | Incentive pay | Tying wages to profits motivates employees and reduces compensation costs in tough years. |

## DEFINING YOUR MAIN IDEA

The **topic** of your message is the overall subject, and your **main idea** is a specific statement about that topic (see Table 4.2). For example, if you believe that the current system of using paper forms for filing employee insurance claims is expensive and slow, you might craft a message in which the topic is employee insurance claims and the main idea is that a new web-based system would reduce costs for the company and reduce reimbursement delays for employees.

In longer documents and presentations, you often need to unify a mass of material with a main idea that encompasses all the individual points you want to make. Finding a common thread through all these points can be a challenge. Sometimes you won't even be sure what your main idea is until you sort through the information. For tough assignments like these, consider a variety of techniques to generate creative ideas:

- **Brainstorming.** Working alone or with others, generate as many ideas and questions as you can, without stopping to criticize or organize. After you capture all these pieces, look for patterns and connections to help identify the main idea and the groups of supporting ideas. For example, if your main idea concerns whether to open a new restaurant in Denver, you'll probably find a group of ideas related to financial return, another related to competition, and so on. Identifying such groups helps you see the major issues that will lead you to a conclusion you can feel confident about.
- **Journalistic approach.** The journalistic approach (see page 94) asks *who*, *what*, *when*, *where*, *why*, and *how* questions to distill major ideas from unorganized information.
- **Question-and-answer chain.** Start with a key question, from the audience's perspective, and work back toward your message. In most cases, you'll find that each answer generates new questions until you identify the information that needs to be in your message.
- **Storyteller's tour.** Some writers find it best to talk through a communication challenge before they try to write. Record yourself as you describe what you intend to write. Then listen to the playback, identify ways to tighten and clarify the message, and repeat the process until you distill the main idea down to a single concise message.
- **Mind mapping.** You can generate and organize ideas using a graphic method called *mind mapping*. Start with a main idea and then branch out to connect every other related idea that comes to mind. You can find a number of free mind-mapping tools online, including http://bubbl.us.

*The topic is the overall subject; the main idea is a specific statement about the topic.*

## LIMITING YOUR SCOPE

The **scope** of your message is the range of information you present, the overall length, and the level of detail—all of which need to correspond to your main idea. The length of some business messages has a preset limit, whether from a boss's instructions, the technology you're using, or a time frame such as individual speaker slots during a seminar. Even if you don't have a preset length, it's vital to limit yourself to the scope needed to convey your main idea—and no more (see Figure 4.7 on the next page).

*The scope of your message is the range of information you present to support your main idea.*

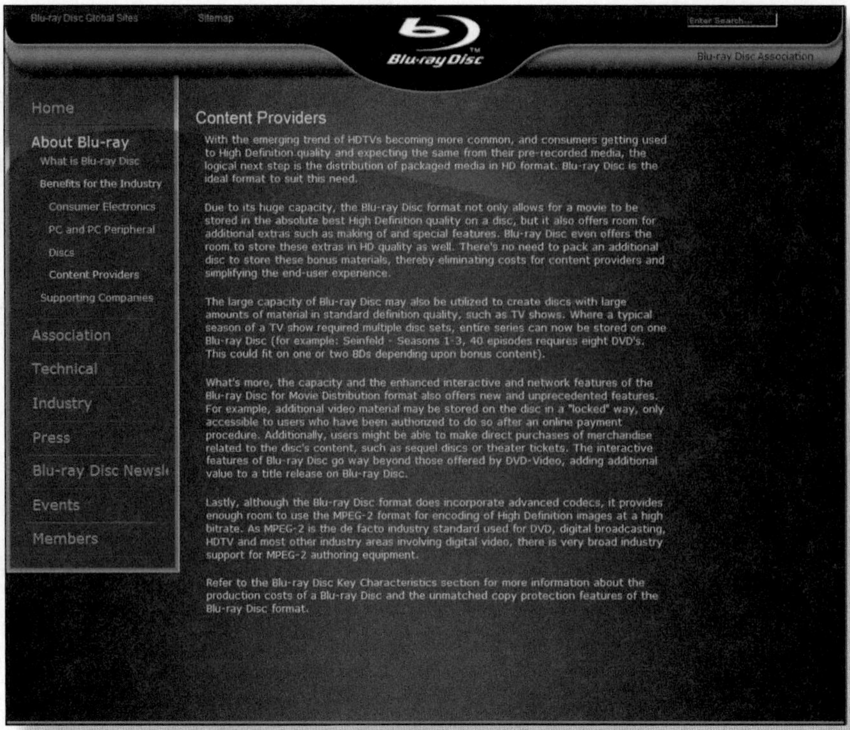

The site's navigation is designed to let individual audience segments (in this case, content providers) find messages that address their unique concerns.

The first paragraph states the main idea, that Blu-ray is the ideal format for high-definition media content.

Each of the next four paragraphs focuses on one major supporting point, with carefully chosen details to back up each supporting point—without overloading the reader with too much detail or irrelevant information.

**Figure 4.7** **Limiting the Scope of a Message**
The Blu-ray Disc Association is the industry consortium that oversees the technical standards and other matters related to Blu-ray discs used for movies, music, and data storage. In this section of its website, the association describes the benefits of the Blu-ray format, with a separate message for each of four stakeholder groups. This particular screen describes the benefits for one of those groups (*content providers*, such as movie studios). Notice how the scope of the message is limited to supporting a single main idea—the business benefits of Blu-ray for this specific audience.
*Source:* Used with permission of the Blue-ray Disc Association.

Having fewer, stronger points is a better approach than using many, weaker points.

Whatever the length of your message, limit the number of major supporting points to half a dozen or so—and if you can get your idea across with fewer points, all the better. Listing 20 or 30 supporting points might feel as though you're being thorough, but your audience is likely to view such detail as rambling and mind numbing. Instead, group your supporting points under major headings, such as finance, customers, competitors, employees, or whatever is appropriate for your subject. Look for ways to combine your supporting points so that you have a smaller number with greater impact.

The ideal length of a message depends on your topic, your audience members' familiarity with the material, their receptivity to your conclusions, and your credibility. You'll need fewer words to present routine information to a knowledgeable audience that already knows and respects you. You'll need more words to build a consensus about a complex and controversial subject, especially if the members of your audience are skeptical or hostile strangers.

## CHOOSING BETWEEN DIRECT AND INDIRECT APPROACHES

After you've defined your main idea and supporting points, you're ready to decide on the sequence you will use to present your information. You have two basic options:

- The **direct approach** starts with the main idea (such as a recommendation, a conclusion, or a request) and follows that with supporting evidence.
- The **indirect approach** starts with the evidence and builds up to the main idea.

Use the direct approach if the audience's reaction is likely to be positive and the indirect approach if it is likely to be negative.

To choose between these two alternatives, analyze your audience's likely reaction to your purpose and message (see Figure 4.8). Bear in mind, however, that Figure 4.8 presents

| | Direct Approach | Indirect Approach | |
|---|---|---|---|
| **Audience Reaction** | Eager/interested/ pleased/neutral | Displeased | Uninterested/unwilling |
| **Message Opening** | Start with the main idea, the request, or the good news. | Start with a neutral statement that acts as a transition to the reasons for the bad news. | Start with a statement or question that captures attention. |
| **Message Body** | Provide necessary details. | Give reasons to build up to the negative answer or announcement. State or imply the bad news, and make a positive suggestion. | Arouse the audience's interest in the subject. Build the audience's desire to comply. |
| **Message Close** | Close with a cordial comment, a reference to the good news, or a statement about the specific action desired. | Close cordially. | Request action. |

**Figure 4.8  Choosing Between the Direct and Indirect Approaches**
Think about the way your audience is likely to respond before choosing your approach.

only general guidelines; always consider the unique circumstances of each message and audience situation. The following sections offer more insight on choosing the best approach for routine and positive messages, negative messages, and persuasive messages.

The type of message also influences the choice of the direct or indirect approach. In the coming chapters, you'll get specific advice on choosing the best approach for a variety of communication challenges.

## OUTLINING YOUR CONTENT

After you have chosen the best approach, it's time to figure out the most logical and effective way to present your major points and supporting details. Get into the habit of creating outlines when you're preparing business messages. You'll save time, get better results, and do a better job of navigating through complicated business situations. Even if you're just jotting down three or four key points, making an outline will help you organize your thoughts for faster writing. When you're preparing a longer, more complex message, an outline is indispensable because it helps you visualize the relationships among the various parts.

You're no doubt familiar with the basic outline formats that identify each point with a number or letter and that indent certain points to show which ones are of equal status. A good outline divides a topic into at least two parts, restricts each subdivision to one category, and ensures that each subdivision is separate and distinct (see Figure 4.9 on the next page).

Another way to visualize the outline of your message is to create an organization chart similar to the charts used to show a company's management structure. Put the main idea in the highest-level box to establish the big picture. The lower-level ideas, like lower-level employees, provide the details. All the ideas should be logically organized into divisions of thought, just as a company is organized into divisions and departments.[9] Using a visual

REAL-TIME UPDATES
LEARN MORE BY WATCHING THIS PRESENTATION
**Get helpful tips on creating an outline for any project**
Learn these proven steps for creating robust, practical outlines. Go to http://real-timeupdates.com/bct12 and click on Learn More. If you are using MyBCommLab, you can access Real-Time Updates within each chapter or under Student Study Tools.

You may want to experiment with other organizational schemes in addition to traditional outlines.

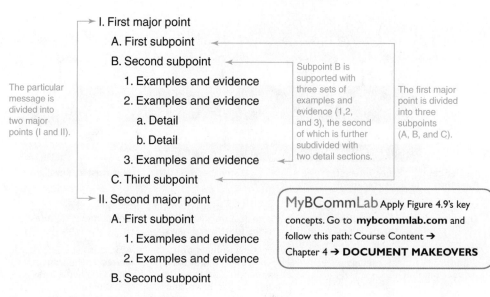

**Figure 4.9   Structuring an Outline**
No matter what outlining format you use, think through your major supporting points and the examples and evidence that can support each point.

chart instead of a traditional outline has many benefits. Charts help you (1) see the various levels of ideas and how the parts fit together, (2) develop new ideas, and (3) restructure your information flow. The mind-mapping technique used to generate ideas works in a similar way.

Whichever outlining or organizing scheme you use, start your message with the main idea, follow that with major supporting points, and then illustrate these points with evidence.

### Start with the Main Idea

*The main idea is a specific state-ment about your topic.*

The main idea helps you establish the goals and general strategy of the message, and it sum-marizes two vital considerations: (1) *what* you want your audience members to do or think and (2) *why* they should do so. Everything in your message should either support the main idea or explain its implications. As discussed earlier, the direct approach states the main idea quickly and directly, whereas the indirect approach delays the main idea until after the evi-dence is presented.

### State the Major Points

*Major supporting points clarify and explain your main idea.*

You need to support your main idea with major points that clarify and explain the main idea in concrete terms. If your purpose is to inform and the material is factual, your major points may be based on something physical or financial—something you can visualize or measure, such as activities to be performed, functional units, spatial or chronological relationships, or parts of a whole. When you're describing a process, the major points are almost inevitably steps in the process. When you're describing an object, the major points often correspond to the parts of the object. When you're giving a historical account, major points represent events in the chronological chain of events. If your purpose is to persuade or to collaborate, select major points that develop a line of reasoning or a logical argument that proves your central message and motivates your audience to act.

### Provide Examples and Evidence

*Back up your supporting points with carefully selected examples and evidence.*

After you've defined the main idea and identified major supporting points, think about exam-ples and evidence that can confirm, illuminate, or expand on your supporting points. Choose examples and evidence carefully so that these elements support your overall message with-out distracting or overwhelming your audience. One good example, particularly if it is con-veyed through a compelling story (see the next section), is usually more powerful than several

| TABLE 4.3 | Six Types of Detail | |
|---|---|---|
| **Type of Detail** | **Example** | **Comment** |
| Facts and figures | Sales are strong this month. We have two new contracts worth $5 million and a good chance of winning another worth $2.5 million. | Enhances credibility more than any other type, but can become boring if used excessively. |
| Example or illustration | We've spent four months trying to hire recent accounting graduates, but so far, only one person has joined our firm. One candidate told me that she would love to work for us, but she can get $10,000 more a year elsewhere. | Adds life to a message, but one example does not prove a point. Idea must be supported by other evidence as well. |
| Description | Upscale hamburger restaurants target burger lovers who want more than the convenience and low prices of a McDonald's burger. These places feature wine and beer, half-pound burgers, and generous side dishes (nachos, potato skins). Atmosphere is key. | Helps audience visualize the subject by creating a sensory impression. Does not prove a point but clarifies it and makes it memorable. Begins with an overview of the function, defines its purpose, lists major parts, and explains how it operates. |
| Narration (storytelling) | When Rita Longworth took over as CEO, she faced a tough choice: shut down the tablet PC division entirely or outsource manufacturing as a way to lower costs while keeping the division alive. As her first step, she convened a meeting with all the managers in the division to get their input on the two options. (Story continues from there.) | Stimulates audience interest through the use of dramatic tension. In many instances, must be supplemented with statistical data in order to prove a point convincingly. |
| Reference to authority | I discussed this idea with Jackie Loman in the Chicago plant, and she was very supportive. As you know, Jackie has been in charge of that plant for the past six years. She is confident that we can speed up the number 2 line by 150 units an hour if we add another worker. | Bolsters a case while adding variety and credibility. Works only if authority is recognized and respected by audience. |
| Visual aids | Graphs, charts, tables, infographics, data visualization | Helps audience grasp the key points about sets of data or visualize connections between ideas. |

weaker examples. Similarly, a few strong points of evidence are usually more persuasive than a large collection of minor details. Keep in mind that you can back up your major supporting points in a variety of ways, depending on the subject material and the available examples and evidence (see Table 4.3).

If your schedule permits, put your outline aside for a day or two before you begin composing your first draft. Then review it with a fresh eye, looking for opportunities to improve the flow of ideas.

Figure 4.10 on the next page illustrates several of the key themes about organizing a message: helping readers get the information they need quickly, defining and conveying the main idea, limiting the scope of the message, choosing the approach, and outlining your information.

## BUILDING READER INTEREST WITH STORYTELLING TECHNIQUES

Storytelling might seem like an odd subject for a business communication course, but narrative techniques can be an effective way to organize messages in a surprising number of business situations, from recruiting and training employees to enticing investors and customers. Storytelling is such a vital means of communicating that, in the words of management consultant Steve Tobak, "It's hard to imagine your career going anywhere if you can't tell a story."[10] Fortunately, you've been telling stories all your life, so narrative techniques already come naturally to you; now it's just a matter of adapting those techniques to business situations.

You've already been on the receiving end of thousands of business stories: Storytelling is one of the most common structures used in television commercials and other advertisements (see Figure 4.11 on page 107). People love to share stories about themselves and others, too, which makes social

**REAL-TIME UPDATES**

LEARN MORE BY VISITING THIS INTERACTIVE WEBSITE

**Mine the web to piece together stories on any topic**

Storify is a media curation site that lets you tell or follow a story by linking voices from multiple social media platforms. Go to http://real-timeupdates.com/bct12 and click on Learn More. If you are using MyBCommLab, you can access Real-Time Updates within each chapter or under Student Study Tools.

**Ineffective**

Edit  View  Insert  Format  Options  Tools  Help

From: Erik Ankerson <e.ankerson@smityardlaw.com>  - e.ankerson@smityardlaw.com

To:  bethanycourson@mailsys.com

Subject:  Incorporation

Hi Bethany,

I have to admit, my research had me longing for the simplicity of a sole proprietorship or the security of a traditional corporate job. But we have decided to move forward with this grand adventure, so onward it is!

On the question of whether we would be wiser to form a partnership or to incorporate, I came upon this tidbit, which struck me as rather unfair. One of the major disadvantages of partnership is that the general partners have unlimited liability, which means our personal assets would be vulnerable in the event the company gets sued or goes bankrupt. However, people in some professions (but not ours!) are allowed to form the limited liability partnership, which protects them from this unlimited vulnerability.

Anyway, on to the question at hand. Incorporation is clearly the better choice for us. It protects us from unlimited liability, it makes it easier to add or remove managers (since they are simply employees and not partners), and it lets us sell stock to raise capital.

Partnership does have two advantages over incorporation. First, in terms of administration and legal requirements, a partnership is easier to establish and simpler to run. Second, partnerships are subject to only a single layer of taxation on income.

These advantages are compelling, but they are outweighed by unlimited liability, the difficulty of adding or replacing partners, and the lack of any means to sell shares to the public. Corporations are more complicated to set up and run, and income is taxed twice (first on company profits and then on any dividends we might pay out to shareholders). However, these are relatively minor concerns when we consider the powerful advantages and protections that incorporation would give us.

Please let me know your thoughts,
Erik

*This vague subject line offers few clues about the topic of the message.*

*The email starts off with an irrelevant discussion, doesn't explain what research this refers to, and fails to introduce the topic of the message.*

*This paragraph introduces the topic but then shifts to an irrelevant discussion (it makes a good point about unlimited liability, but the point is buried in irrelevant material).*

*The main idea, that the pair should incorporate, is buried in the middle of the message.*

*By jumping from partnership to incorporation, back to partnership, and then back to incorporation again throughout the course of the message, the writer forces the reader to piece together the comparative evidence herself.*

**Effective**

*The subject line states the topic (incorporation vs. partnership) and the main idea (incorporation is the better choice).*

*The opening provides a context by referring to a previous conversation and then states the main idea.*

*These two paragraphs support the main idea by showing how the disadvantages of partnerships outweigh the advantages.*

*The writer continues to provide support by explaining how incorporation overcomes all three key disadvantages of partnerships.*

*The comparison is completed by identifying two disadvantages of incorporation but noting that they are outweighed by the advantages.*

View  Insert  Format  Options  Tools  Help

From: Erik Ankerson <e.ankerson@smityardlaw.com>  - e.ankerson@smityardlaw.com

To:  bethanycourson@mailsys.com

Subject:  Advantages of incorporation over partnership

Hi Bethany,

After our discussion yesterday about whether we should incorporate or form a partnership, I did some research to compare the advantages and disadvantages of the two structures. In light of our long-range plans for the business, particularly the need to raise funds for expansion, I believe the clear choice for us is incorporation.

Partnership does have two advantages over incorporation. First, in terms of administration and legal requirements, a partnership is easier to establish and simpler to run. Second, partnerships are subject to only a single layer of taxation on income.

These advantages are compelling, but they are outweighed by three disadvantages. First, the general partners in a partnership face unlimited legal liability, which means our personal assets would be vulnerable in the event of a product liability lawsuit or other calamity. Second, growth and succession issues can be tricky, such as if we decide to bring in another partner at some point or one of us wants to leave the company. Third, the inability to sell shares of stock really limits our opportunity to raise capital for expansion.

Incorporation addresses all three disadvantages of partnerships: our personal assets are not vulnerable in the event of lawsuits or company bankruptcy, adding or replacing managers is simpler because we are all employees of the corporation, and—most significantly—we can sell shares of stock to raise capital.

Yes, corporations are more complicated to set up and run, and income is taxed twice (first on company profits and then on any dividends we might pay out to shareholders). However, these are relatively minor concerns when we consider the powerful advantages and protections that incorporation would give us.

Please let me know your thoughts,
Erik

**Figure 4.10  Improving the Organization of a Message**
This writer is following up on a conversation from the previous day, in which he and the recipient discussed which of two forms of ownership, a partnership or a corporation, they should use for their new company. (*Partnership* has a specific legal meaning in this context.) That question is the topic of the message; the main idea is the recommendation that they incorporate, rather than form a partnership. Notice how the Effective version uses the direct approach to quickly get to the main idea and then supports that by comparing the advantages and disadvantages of both forms of ownership. In contrast, the Ineffective version contains irrelevant information, makes the comparison difficult to follow, and buries the main idea in the middle of the message.

Used by permission of Microsoft.

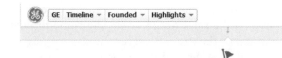

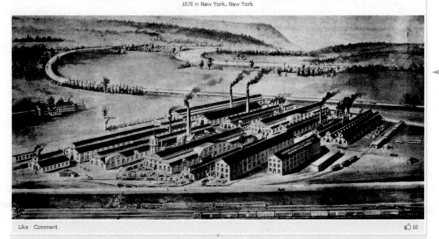

This image conveys the notion that GE has been an industrial powerhouse for nearly a century and a half.

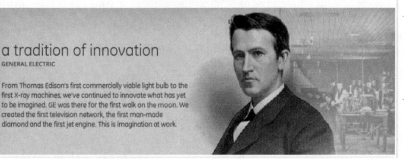

Opening the story with an image of Thomas Edison, one of the most iconic inventors in American history, reinforces the message that GE was built on "a tradition of innovation."

The accompanying text lists other key technological advances that GE pioneered or participated in.

**Figure 4.11  Storytelling as a Way to Organize Messages**
Many companies now use Facebook's timeline feature to create visual stories of their founding and early years.
*Source:* Copyright © 2012 by General Electric, Inc.

media ideal for storytelling.[11] User-generated content, such as Toyota's Auto-Biography campaign highlighted in Chapter 1, is usually all about storytelling.

Career-related stories, such as how someone sought and found the opportunity to work on projects he or she is passionate about, can entice skilled employees to consider joining a firm. Entrepreneurs use stories to help investors see how their new ideas have the potential to affect people's lives (and therefore generate lots of sales). Stories can be cautionary tales as well, dramatizing the consequences of career blunders, ethical mistakes, and strategic missteps.

A key reason storytelling can be so effective is that stories help readers and listeners imagine themselves living through the experience of the person in the story. Chip Heath of Stanford University and his brother, Dan Heath of Duke University, have spent years exploring the question of why some ideas "stick" and others disappear. One of their conclusions is that ideas conveyed through storytelling tend to thrive because stories "put knowledge into a framework that is more lifelike, more true to our day-to-day existence."[12]

In addition, stories can demonstrate cause-and-effect relationships in a compelling fashion.[13] Imagine attending a new employee orientation and listening to the trainer read off a list of ethics rules and guidelines. Now imagine the trainer telling the story of someone who sounded a lot like you in the very near future, fresh out of college and full of energy and ambition. Desperate to hit demanding sales targets, the person in the story began entering

Storytelling is an effective way to organize many business messages because it helps readers personalize the message and understand causes and consequences.

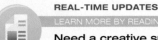

Organize stories in three parts: a beginning that introduces a sympathetic person with a dream or a challenge, a middle that shows the complications to be overcome, and an ending that resolves the situation and shows the moral or message of the story.

transactions before customers had actually agreed to purchase, hoping the sales would eventually come through and no one would be the wiser. However, the scheme was exposed during a routine audit, and the rising star was booted out of the company with an ethical stain that would haunt him for years. You may not remember all the rules and guidelines, but chances are you will remember what happened to that person who sounded a lot like you. This ability to share organizational values is one of the major benefits of using storytelling in business communication, particularly across diverse workforces.[14]

A classic story has three basic parts. The beginning of the story presents someone whom the audience can identify with in some way, and this person has a dream to pursue or a problem to solve. (Think of how movies and novels often start by introducing a likable character who immediately gets into danger, for example.) The middle of the story shows this character taking action and making decisions as he or she pursues the goal or tries to solve the problem. The storyteller's objective here is to build the audience's interest by increasing the tension: Will the "hero" overcome the obstacles in his or her path and defeat whatever adversary is keeping him or her away from her goal?[15] The end of the story answers that question and usually offers a lesson to be learned about the outcome as well.

By the way, even though these are "stories," they must not be made-up tales. Telling stories that didn't happen to people who don't exist while presenting them as real-life events is a serious breach of ethics that damages a company's credibility.[16]

Consider adding an element of storytelling whenever your main idea involves the opportunity to inspire, to persuade, to teach, or to warn readers or listeners about the potential outcomes of a particular course of action.

For fresh ideas and media materials on planning messages, visit http://real-timeupdates.com/bct12 and click on Chapter 4. For a quick refresher on message-planning tasks, see "Checklist: Planning Business Messages."

**CHECKLIST** ✓ **Planning Business Messages**

**A. Analyze the situation.**
- Determine whether the purpose of your message is to inform, persuade, or collaborate.
- Identify what you want your audience to think or do after receiving the message.
- Make sure your purpose is worthwhile and realistic.
- Make sure the time is right for your message.
- Make sure your purpose is acceptable to your organization.
- Identify the primary audience.
- Determine the size and composition of your audience.
- Estimate your audience's level of understanding and probable reaction to your message.

**B. Gather information.**
- Decide whether to use formal or informal techniques for gathering information.
- Find out what your audience needs to know.
- Provide all required information and make sure it's accurate, ethical, and pertinent.

**C. Select the best medium for your message.**
- Understand the advantages and disadvantages of oral, written, visual, and electronic media.
- Consider media richness, formality, media limitations, urgency, cost, and audience preference.

**D. Organize your information.**
- Define your main idea.
- Limit your scope.
- Choose the direct or indirect approach.
- Outline content by starting with the main idea, adding major points, and illustrating with evidence.
- Look for opportunities to use storytelling to build audience interest.

# Quick Learning Guide

## SUMMARY OF LEARNING OBJECTIVES

**1 Describe the three-step writing process.** (1) Planning consists of four tasks: analyzing the situation (defining your purpose and profiling your audience), gathering the information to meet your audience's needs, selecting the best medium for the message and the situation, and organizing the information (defining your main idea, limiting your scope, selecting an approach, and outlining your content). (2) The writing step consists of two tasks: adapting to your audience and composing the message. Adapt your message to your audience by being sensitive to audience needs, building a strong relationship with your audience, and controlling your style. Compose your message by drafting your thoughts with strong words, effective sentences, and coherent paragraphs. (3) Completing your message consists of four tasks: revising your message by evaluating content and then rewriting and editing for clarity and conciseness, producing your message by using effective design elements and suitable delivery methods, proofreading your message for mistakes in spelling and mechanics, and distributing it in a way that meets both your needs and your audience's needs.

**2 Explain why it's important to analyze a communication situation in order to define your purpose and profile your audience before writing a message.** You must know enough about your purpose to shape your message in a way that will achieve your goal. Moreover, without a clear purpose to guide you, you are bound to waste time and energy. To decide whether you should proceed with your message, answer four questions: (1) Will anything change as a result of this message? (2) Is my purpose realistic? (3) Is this the right time for this message? (4) Is the purpose acceptable to my organization? Developing an audience profile is essential as well because doing so helps you identify the information you need to include in your message and is the most effective way to structure your message.

**3 Discuss information-gathering options for simple messages, and identify three attributes of quality information.** Gathering the information that will fulfill your audience's needs is a vital step before you attempt to organize your content. For more complex documents, you may need to plan a research project to acquire all the necessary information. However, for simple messages, if you don't already have all the information you need, you can often gather it by using informal methods, such as considering the audience's perspective, reading existing reports and other company documents, talking with supervisors and others who have information and insight, and asking your audience members directly for their input. To determine whether the information you've gathered is good enough, verify that it is accurate, ethical, and pertinent to the audience's needs.

**4 List the factors to consider when choosing the most appropriate medium for a message.** The first factor to consider is media richness. Richness is determined by the medium's ability to (1) convey a message using more than one informational cue, such as sound, motion, nonverbal cues, and so on; (2) facilitate feedback; and (3) establish personal focus. Other factors to consider when selecting media include the level of formality, the specific limitations of each medium, the level of urgency, the cost of various media options, and your audience's preferences.

**5 Explain why good organization is important to both you and your audience, and list the tasks involved in organizing a message.** When you organize messages carefully, you save time and conserve creative energy because the writing process is quicker and you spend less time rewriting. Good organization also helps your audience members understand your message, it helps them accept your message, and it saves them time as well. The tasks involved in organizing your message include defining your main idea, limiting your scope to the information needed to convey and support that main idea, choosing the direct or indirect approach, and then outlining your content.

## KEY TERMS

**direct approach** Message organization that starts with the main idea (such as a recommendation, a conclusion, or a request) and follows that with your supporting evidence

**free writing** An exploratory technique in which you write whatever comes to mind, without stopping to make any corrections, for a set period of time

**general purpose** The broad intent of a message—to inform, to persuade, or to collaborate with the audience

**indirect approach** Message organization that starts with the evidence and builds your case before presenting the main idea

**journalistic approach** Verifying the completeness of a message by making sure it answers the *who, what, when, where, why,* and *how* questions

**main idea** A specific statement about the topic

**medium** The form through which you choose to communicate a message

**multimedia** Refers to the use of two or more media to deliver a message, typically some combination of audio, video, text, and visual graphics

**scope** The range of information presented in a message, its overall length, and the level of detail provided

**specific purpose** Identifies what you hope to accomplish with your message and what your audience should do or think after receiving your message

**topic** The overall subject of a message

CHECKLIST ✓

## Planning Business Messages

**A. Analyze the situation.**
- Determine whether the purpose of your message is to inform, persuade, or collaborate.
- Identify what you want your audience to think or do after receiving the message.
- Make sure your purpose is worthwhile and realistic.
- Make sure the time is right for your message.
- Make sure your purpose is acceptable to your organization.
- Identify the primary audience.
- Determine the size and composition of your audience.
- Estimate your audience's level of understanding and probable reaction to your message.

**B. Gather information.**
- Decide whether to use formal or informal techniques for gathering information.
- Find out what your audience needs to know.
- Provide all required information and make sure it's accurate, ethical, and pertinent.

**C. Select the best medium for your message.**
- Understand the advantages and disadvantages of oral, written, visual, and electronic media.
- Consider media richness, formality, media limitations, urgency, cost, and audience preference.

**D. Organize your information.**
- Define your main idea.
- Limit your scope.
- Choose the direct or indirect approach.
- Outline content by starting with the main idea, adding major points, and illustrating with evidence.
- Look for opportunities to use storytelling to build audience interest.

---

**1 Plan** → **2 Write** → **3 Complete**

### Analyze the Situation
Define your purpose and develop an audience profile.

### Gather Information
Determine audience needs and obtain the information necessary to satisfy those needs.

### Select the Right Medium
Select the best medium for delivering your message.

### Organize the Information
Define your main idea, limit your scope, select a direct or an indirect approach, and outline your content.

### Adapt to Your Audience
Be sensitive to audience needs by using a "you" attitude, politeness, positive emphasis, and unbiased language. Build a strong relationship with your audience by establishing your credibility and projecting your company's preferred image. Control your style with a conversational tone, plain English, and appropriate voice.

### Compose the Message
Choose strong words that will help you create effective sentences and coherent paragraphs.

### Revise the Message
Evaluate content and review readability, edit and rewrite for conciseness and clarity.

### Produce the Message
Use effective design elements and suitable layout for a clean, professional appearance.

### Proofread the Message
Review for errors in layout, spelling, and mechanics.

### Distribute the Message
Deliver your message using the chosen medium; make sure all documents and all relevant files are distributed successfully.

Figure 4.1 **The Three-Step Writing Process**
This three-step process will help you create more effective messages in any medium. As you get more practice with the process, it will become easier and more automatic.

## COMMUNICATION CHALLENGES AT **H&R Block**

Robert Turtledove, H&R Block's chief marketing officer, was impressed enough with your communication skills and social media experience to add you to the team that markets H&R Block's digital tax-preparation solutions. Using the insights you gained in this chapter, address these two communication challenges.

**INDIVIDUAL CHALLENGE:** Your first assignment is to write a 50-word introduction to the H&R Block At Home tax software (formerly known as TaxCut) that can be used whenever the company needs a concise summary. For example, your text will be loaded into the IM chat system so that whenever anyone asks about the software, customer service representatives can send your text with just one mouse click. Visit www.hrblock.com to learn more about the various versions of the At Home software. Use this information to write your 50-word summary and then email it to your instructor.

**TEAM CHALLENGE:** An ongoing dilemma for marketers in many industries is trying to offer targeted products and services that

meet the needs of specific market segments without creating so many versions that the range of choices overwhelms the consumer. For example, H&R Block can help taxpayers in a variety of ways: several versions of web-based tax software, several versions of downloadable software, professional preparation, and a hybrid service called Best of Both, in which the taxpayer does most of the work using the software and an H&R Block professional helps with advice and verification. Simply helping consumers understand the choices available can become a considerable communication challenge in its own right.

With your team, analyze the company's website at www.hrblock.com in terms of its ability to help a taxpayer understand the various options and choose the one that meets his or her unique needs. For example, are the services clearly distinguished from one another, and can the average taxpayer understand the distinctions being made? What improvements might you suggest? Prepare a brief summary of your analysis as a class presentation or a post on your class blog, as your instructor directs.

## Test Your Knowledge

To review chapter content related to each question, refer to the indicated Learning Objective.

1. What are the three major steps in the writing process? [LO-1]
2. What are the benefits of planning your messages carefully, particularly longer and more complex messages? [LO-1]
3. What two types of purposes do all business messages have? [LO-2]
4. What do you need to know in order to develop an audience profile? [LO-2]
5. What is the value of free writing and other discovery techniques? [LO-3]
6. What three factors determine media richness? [LO-4]
7. What are the main advantages of oral media? Of written media? Of visual media? Of electronic media? [LO-4]
8. How does the topic of a message differ from its main idea? [LO-5]
9. Why is it important to limit the scope of a message? [LO-5]
10. What three elements do you need to consider when choosing between the direct and indirect approaches? [LO-5]

## Apply Your Knowledge

To review chapter content related to each question, refer to the indicated Learning Objective.

1. Some writers argue that planning messages wastes time because they inevitably change their plans as they proceed. How would you respond to this argument? Briefly explain. [LO-1]
2. A day after sending an email to all 1,800 employees in your company regarding income tax implications of the company's retirement plan, you discover that one of the sources you relied on for your information plagiarized from other

sources. You quickly double-check all the information in your message and confirm that it is accurate. However, you are concerned about using plagiarized information, even though you did nothing wrong. Write a brief email message to your instructor, explaining how you would handle the situation. [LO-3]
3. You have been invited to speak at an annual industry conference. After preparing the outline for your presentation, you see that you've identified 14 different points to support your main idea. Should you move ahead with creating the slides for your presentation or move back and rethink your outline? Why? [LO-5]

## Practice Your Skills

**Message for Analysis: Outlining Your Content [LO-5]**

A writer is working on an insurance information brochure and is having trouble grouping the ideas logically into an outline. Using the following information, prepare the outline, paying attention to the appropriate hierarchy of ideas. If necessary, rewrite phrases to make them all consistent.

**Accident Protection Insurance Plan**

- Coverage is only pennies a day
- Benefit is $100,000 for accidental death on common carrier
- Benefit is $100 a day for hospitalization as result of motor vehicle or common carrier accident
- Benefit is $20,000 for accidental death in motor vehicle accident
- Individual coverage is only $17.85 per quarter; family coverage is just $26.85 per quarter
- No physical exam or health questions

- Convenient payment—billed quarterly
- Guaranteed acceptance for all applicants
- No individual rate increases
- Free, no-obligation examination period
- Cash paid in addition to any other insurance carried
- Covers accidental death when riding as fare-paying passenger on public transportation, including buses, trains, jets, ships, trolleys, subways, or any other common carrier
- Covers accidental death in motor vehicle accidents occurring while driving or riding in or on automobile, truck, camper, motor home, or nonmotorized bicycle

## Exercises

Each activity is labeled according to the primary skill or skills you will need to use. To review relevant chapter content, you can refer to the indicated Learning Objective. In some instances, supporting information will be found in another chapter, as indicated.

1. **Planning: Identifying Your Purpose; Media Skills: Email [LO-2]** Make a list of communication tasks you'll need to accomplish in the next week or so (for example, a homework assignment, an email message to an instructor, a job application, or a speech to a class). For each, determine a general and a specific purpose.

2. **Planning: Identifying Your Purpose [LO-2]** For each of the following communication tasks, state a specific purpose (if you have trouble, try beginning with "I want to . . .").

   a. A report to your boss, the store manager, about the outdated items in the warehouse

   b. A memo to clients about your booth at the upcoming trade show

   c. A letter to a customer who hasn't made a payment for three months

   d. A memo to employees about the department's high phone bills

   e. A phone call to a supplier, checking on an overdue parts shipment

   f. A report to future users of the computer program you have chosen to handle the company's mailing list

3. **Planning: Assessing Audience Needs [LO-2]** For each communication task that follows, write brief answers to three questions: Who is the audience? What is the audience's general attitude toward my subject? What does the audience need to know?

   a. A final-notice collection letter from an appliance manufacturer to an appliance dealer that is 3 months behind on payments, sent 10 days before initiating legal collection procedures

   b. An advertisement for digital cameras

   c. A proposal to top management, suggesting that the four sales regions in the United States be combined into just two regions

   d. Fliers to be attached to doorknobs in the neighborhood, announcing reduced rates for chimney cleaning or repairs

   e. A cover letter sent along with your résumé to a potential employer

   f. A website that describes the services offered by a consulting firm that helps accounting managers comply with government regulations

4. **Planning: Assessing Audience Needs [LO-2]** Choose a fairly simple electronic device (such as a digital music player or digital camera) that you know how to operate well. Write two sets of instructions for operating the device: one set for a reader who has never used that type of device and one set for someone who is generally familiar with that type of machine but has never operated the specific model. Briefly explain how your two audiences affect your instructions.

5. **Planning: Identifying Your Purpose [LO-2]** List five messages you have received lately, such as direct-mail promotions, letters, email messages, phone solicitations, and lectures. For each, determine the general purpose and the specific purpose; then answer the following questions: (1) Was the message well timed? (2) Did the sender choose an appropriate medium for the message? (3) Was the sender's purpose realistic?

6. **Planning: Analyzing the Situation; Media Skills: Electronic Presentations [LO-2]** Go to the PepsiCo website, at www.pepsico.com, and locate the latest annual report. Read the annual report's letter to shareholders. Who is the audience for this message? What is the general purpose of the message? What do you think this audience wants to know from the chairman of PepsiCo? Summarize your answers in a one-page report or five-slide presentation, as your instructor directs.

7. **Planning: Analyzing the Situation; Collaboration: Planning Meetings [LO-2], Chapter 2** How can the material discussed in this chapter also apply to meetings, as discussed in Chapter 2? Outline your ideas in a brief presentation or a post for your class blog.

8. **Planning: Creating an Audience Profile; Collaboration: Team Projects [LO-2], [LO-3], Chapter 2** With a team assigned by your instructor, compare the Facebook pages of three companies in the same industry. Analyze the content on all the available tabs. What can you surmise about the intended audience for each company? Which of the three does the best job of presenting the information its target audience is likely to need? Prepare a brief presentation, including slides that show samples of the Facebook content from each company.

9. **Planning: Analyzing the Situation, Selecting Media; Media Skills: Email [LO-2], [LO-4], Chapter 11** You are the head of public relations for a cruise line that operates out of Miami. You are shocked to read a letter in a local newspaper from a disgruntled passenger, complaining about the service and entertainment on a recent cruise. You need to respond to these publicized criticisms in some way. What audiences will you need to consider in your response? What medium or media should you choose? If the letter

had been published in a travel publication widely read by travel agents and cruise travelers, how might your course of action have differed? In an email message to your instructor, explain how you will respond.

10. **Planning: Assessing Audience Needs; Media Skills: Blogging; Communication Ethics: Making Ethical Choices [LO-3], Chapter 1** Your supervisor has asked you to withhold important information that you think should be included in a report you are preparing. Disobeying him could be disastrous for your working relationship and your career. Obeying him could violate your personal code of ethics. What should you do? On the basis of the discussion in Chapter 1, would you consider this situation to be an ethical dilemma or an ethical lapse? Explain your analysis in a brief email message to your instructor.

11. **Planning: Outlining Your Content [LO-5]** Using the effective version of the email message in Figure 4.10, draw an organizational chart that identifies the main idea, the major points, and the evidence provided in this message.

12. **Planning: Limiting Your Scope [LO-5]** Suppose you are preparing to recommend that top management install a new heating system that uses the cogeneration process. The following information is in your files. Eliminate topics that aren't essential and then arrange the other topics so that your report will give top managers a clear understanding of the heating system and a balanced, concise justification for installing it.

- History of the development of the cogeneration heating process
- Scientific credentials of the developers of the process
- Risks assumed in using this process
- Your plan for installing the equipment in the headquarters building
- Stories about the successful use of cogeneration technology in comparable facilities
- Specifications of the equipment that would be installed
- Plans for disposing of the old heating equipment
- Costs of installing and running the new equipment
- Advantages and disadvantages of using the new process
- Detailed 10-year cost projections
- Estimates of the time needed to phase in the new system
- Alternative systems that management might want to consider

13. **Planning: Choosing the Direct or Indirect Approach [LO-5]** Indicate whether the direct or indirect approach would be best in each of the following situations and briefly explain why. Would any of these messages be inappropriate for email? Explain.
    a. A message to the owner of an automobile dealership, complaining about poor service work
    b. A message from a recent college graduate, requesting a letter of recommendation from a former instructor
    c. A message turning down a job applicant
    d. A message announcing that because of high air-conditioning costs, the plant temperature will be held at 78°F during the summer
    e. A message from an advertising agency to a troublesome long-term client, explaining that the agency will no longer be able to work on the client's account

14. **Planning: Choosing the Direct or Indirect Approach [LO-5]** If you were trying to persuade people to take the following actions, how would you organize your argument?
    a. You want your boss to approve your plan for hiring two new people.
    b. You want to be hired for a job.
    c. You want to be granted a business loan.
    d. You want to collect a small amount of money from a regular customer whose account is slightly past due.
    e. You want to collect a large amount of money from a customer whose account is seriously past due.

15. **Planning: Using Storytelling Techniques; Communication Ethics: Providing Ethical Leadership: Media Skills: Podcasting [LO-5], Chapter 1** Research recent incidents of ethical lapses by a business professional or executive in any industry. Choose one example that has a clear story "arc" from beginning to end. Outline a cautionary tale that explains the context of the ethical lapse, the choice the person made, and the consequences of the ethical lapse. Script a podcast (aim for roughly 3 to 5 minutes) that tells the story. If your instructor directs, record your podcast and post to your class blog.

## Expand Your Skills

### Critique the Professionals

Locate an example of professional communication in any medium that you think would work equally well—or perhaps better—in another medium. Using the media selection guidelines in this chapter and your understanding of the communication process, write a brief analysis (no more than one page) of the company's media choice and explain why your choice would be at least as effective. Use whatever medium your instructor requests for your report and be sure to cite specific elements from the piece and support from the chapter.

### Sharpening Your Career Skills Online

Bovée and Thill's Business Communication Web Search, at http://businesscommunicationblog.com/websearch, is a unique research tool designed specifically for business communication research. Use the Web Search function to find a website, video, podcast, or PowerPoint presentation that offers advice on planning a report, speech, or other business message. Write a brief email message to your instructor, describing the item you found and summarizing the career skills information you learned from it.

MyBCommLab

Go to **mybcommlab.com** for Auto-graded writing questions as well as the following Assisted-graded writing questions:

**4-1.** As a member of the public relations department, which medium (or media) would you recommend using to inform the local community that your toxic-waste cleanup program has been successful? Why? [LO-4]

**4-2.** Would you use the direct or indirect approach to ask employees to work overtime to meet an important deadline? Please explain. [LO-5]

**4-3.** Mybcommlab Only—comprehensive writing assignment for this chapter.

# Endnotes

1. H&R Block website, accessed 10 January 2013, www.hrblock.com; Paula Drum, "I Got People (Online): How H&R Block Connects by Using Social Media," presentation at BlogWell conference, 22 January 2009, www.socialmedia.org; Shel Israel, "Twitterville Notebook: H&R Block's Paula Drum," Global Neighbourhoods blog, 22 December 2008, http://redcouch.typepad.com/weblog; "H&R Block's Paula Drum Talks Up Value of Online 'Presence,'" The Deal website, video interview, 6 June 2008, www.thedeal.com; Shel Israel, "SAP Global Survey: H&R Block's Paula Drum," Global Neighbourhoods blog, 4 April 2008, http://redcouch.typepad.com/weblog; "Tango in Plain English," video, accessed 27 August 2008, www.youtube.com; "H&R Block, Inc.," Hoovers, accessed 27 August 2008, www.hoovers.com; Linda Zimmer, "H&R Block Tangoes into Second Life," Business Communicators of Second Life blog, 17 March 2007, http://freshtakes.typepad.com/sl_communicators; "H&R Block Launches First Virtual Tax Experience in Second Life," press release, 27 August 2008, www.hrblock.com.

2. Carol Kinsey Gorman, "What's So Great About Face-to-Face?" *Communication World*, May–June 2011, 38–39.

3. Linda Duyle, "Get Out of Your Office," *HR Magazine*, July 2006, 99–101.

4. Caroline McCarthy, "The Future of Web Apps Will See the Death of E-Mail," Webware blog, 29 February 2008, http://news.cnet.com; Kris Maher, "The Jungle," *Wall Street Journal*, 5 October 2004, B10; Kevin Maney, "Surge in Text Messaging Makes Cell Operators :-)," *USA Today*, 28 July 2005, B1–B2.

5. Berk and Clampitt, "Finding the Right Path in the Communication Maze."

6. Samantha R. Murray and Joseph Peyrefitte, "Knowledge Type and Communication Media Choice in the Knowledge Transfer Process," *Journal of Managerial Issues*, Spring 2007, 111–133.

7. Raymond M. Olderman, *10 Minute Guide to Business Communication* (New York: Alpha Books, 1997), 19–20.

8. Mohan R. Limaye and David A. Victor, "Cross-Cultural Business Communication Research: State of the Art and Hypotheses for the 1990s," *Journal of Business Communication*, Summer 1991, 277–299.

9. Holly Weeks, "The Best Memo You'll Ever Write," *Harvard Management Communication Letter*, Spring 2005, 3–5.

10. Steve Tobak, "How to Be a Great Storyteller and Win Over Any Audience," BNET, 12 January 2011, www.bnet.com.

11. Debra Askanase, "10 Trends in Sustainable Social Media," Community Organizer 2.0 blog, 13 May 2010, www.communityorganizer20.com.

12. Chip Heath and Dan Heath, *Made to Stick: Why Some Ideas Survive and Others Die* (New York: Random House, 2008), 214.

13. Heath and Heath, *Made to Stick: Why Some Ideas Survive and Others Die*, 206, 214.

14. Randolph T. Barker and Kim Gower, "Strategic Application of Storytelling in Organizations," *Journal of Business Communication* 47, no. 3, July 2010, 295–312.

15. David Meerman Scott, "Effective Storytelling for Business," WebInkNow blog, 18 February 2013, www.webinknow.com.

16. Jennifer Aaker and Andy Smith, "7 Deadly Sins of Business Storytelling," American Express Open Forum, accessed 21 March 2011, www.openforum.com.

# 5 | Writing Business Messages

## LEARNING OBJECTIVES

After studying this chapter, you will be able to

**1** Identify the four aspects of being sensitive to audience needs when writing business messages.

**2** Explain how establishing your credibility and projecting your company's image are vital aspects of building strong relationships with your audience.

**3** Explain how to achieve a tone that is conversational but businesslike, explain the value of using plain language, and define active and passive voice.

**4** Describe how to select words that are both correct and effective.

**5** Define the four types of sentences and explain how sentence style affects emphasis within a message.

**6** Define the three key elements of a paragraph and list five ways to develop unified, coherent paragraphs.

**7** Identify the most common software features that help you craft messages more efficiently.

## COMMUNICATION CLOSE-UP AT
## Creative Commons
http://creativecommons.org

Have you ever noticed that tiny © symbol on books, DVDs, music CDs, and other media products? It means that the person or organization that created the item is granted copyright protection: the exclusive legal right to produce, distribute, and sell that creation. Anyone who wants to resell, redistribute, or adapt such works usually needs to secure permission from the current copyright holder.

However, what if you *want* people to remix the song you just recorded or use your graphic designs in whatever artistic compositions they might want to create? Or if you want to give away some of your creative works to get your name out there, without giving up all your legal rights to them? Alternatively, suppose you need a few photos or a video clip for a website? Other than for limited personal and educational use, a conventional copyright requires every person to negotiate a contract for every application or adaptation of every piece of work he or she wants to use.

The search for some middle ground between "all rights reserved" and simply giving your work away led Stanford University

Courtesy of Creative Commons.

Catherine Casserly, CEO of Creative Commons, uses a variety of communication vehicles to convince copyright owners to explore new ways of sharing and protecting their creative and intellectual works.

law professor Lawrence Lessig to cofound Creative Commons. This nonprofit organization's goal is to provide a simple, free, and legal way for musicians, artists, writers, teachers, scientists, and others to collaborate and benefit through the sharing of art and ideas. Instead of the everything-or-nothing approach of traditional copyright, Creative Commons offers a more flexible range of "some rights reserved" options.

Now led by CEO Catherine Casserly, Creative Commons continues to promote the benefits of simplifying the legal constraints on sharing and reusing intellectual property, whether for creative expression or scientific research. Millions of Creative Commons licenses have been initiated for musical works, images, short films, educational materials, novels, and more. This approach can't solve the entire dilemma of copyrights in the digital age, and not everyone agrees with the Creative Commons model, but it has created an easier way for creative people to communicate and collaborate.[1]

# Adapting to Your Audience: Being Sensitive to Audience Needs

**1 LEARNING OBJECTIVE**
Identify the four aspects of being sensitive to audience needs when writing business messages.

As they work to persuade their audiences to consider new forms of copyright protection, Catherine Casserly and her colleagues at Creative Commons (profiled in the chapter-opening Communication Close-Up) realize it takes more than just a great idea to change the way people think. Expressing ideas clearly and persuasively starts with adapting to one's audience.

Readers and listeners want to know how your messages will benefit them.

Whether consciously or not, audiences greet most incoming messages with a selfish question: "What's in this for me?" If your intended audience members think a message does not apply to them or doesn't meet their needs, they won't be inclined to pay attention to it. Follow the example set by the Creative Commons website, which addresses a diverse audience of artists, lawyers, and business professionals but fine-tunes specific messages for each group of people.

If your readers or listeners don't think you understand or care about their needs, they won't pay attention, plain and simple. You can improve your audience sensitivity by adopting the "you" attitude, maintaining good standards of etiquette, emphasizing the positive, and using bias-free language.

## USING THE "YOU" ATTITUDE

The "you" attitude is best implemented by expressing your message in terms of the audience's interests and needs.

Chapter 1 introduced the notion of audience-centered communication and the "you" attitude—speaking and writing in terms of your audience's wishes, interests, hopes, and preferences. On the simplest level, you can adopt the "you" attitude by replacing terms such as *I, me, mine, we, us,* and *ours* with *you* and *yours*:

| Instead of This | Write This |
|---|---|
| Tuesday is the only day that we can promise quick response to purchase order requests; we are swamped the rest of the week. | If you need a quick response, please submit your purchase order requests on Tuesday. |
| We offer MP3 players with 50, 75, or 100 gigabytes of storage capacity. | You can choose an MP3 player with 50, 75, or 100 gigabytes of storage. |

Messages that emphasize "I" and "we" risk sounding selfish and uninterested in the audience. Such messages feel like they are all about the sender, not the receiver.

However, the "you" attitude is more than simply using particular pronouns; it's a matter of genuine interest and concern. You can use *you* 25 times in a single page and still ignore your audience's true concerns. If you're talking to a retailer, try to think like a retailer. If you're dealing with a production supervisor, put yourself in that position. If you're writing to a dissatisfied customer, imagine how you would feel at the other end of the transaction.

Be aware that on some occasions, it's better to avoid using *you*, particularly if doing so will sound overly authoritative or accusing:

| Instead of This | Write This |
|---|---|
| You failed to deliver the customer's order on time. | The customer didn't receive the order on time. |
| You must correct all five copies by noon. | All five copies must be corrected by noon. |

Avoid using *you* and *yours* when doing so
- Makes you sound dictatorial
- Could make someone else feel unnecessarily guilty
- Is inappropriate for the culture
- Goes against your organization's style

As you practice using the "you" attitude, be sure to consider the attitudes of other cultures and the policies of your organization. In some cultures, it is improper to single out one person's achievements, because the whole team is responsible for the outcome; in that case, using the pronoun *we* or *our* (when you and your audience are part of the same team) would be more appropriate. Similarly, some companies have a tradition of avoiding references to *you* and *I* in most messages and reports.

## MAINTAINING STANDARDS OF ETIQUETTE

Good etiquette not only indicates respect for your audience but also helps foster a more successful environment for communication by minimizing negative emotional reaction:

| Instead of This | Write This |
|---|---|
| Once again, you've managed to bring down the entire website through your incompetent programming. | Let's review the last website update to explore ways to improve the process. |
| You've been sitting on our order for two weeks, and we need it now! | Our production schedules depend on timely delivery of parts and supplies, but we have not yet received the order you promised to deliver two weeks ago. Please respond today with a firm delivery commitment. |

Of course, some situations require more diplomacy than others. If you know your audience well, a less formal approach may be more appropriate. However, when you are communicating with people who outrank you or with people outside your organization, an added measure of courtesy is usually needed.

Written communication and most forms of electronic media generally require more tact than oral communication (see Figure 5.1 on the next page). When you're speaking, your words are softened by your tone of voice and facial expression. Plus, you can adjust your approach according to the feedback you get. If you inadvertently offend someone in writing or in a podcast, for example, you don't usually get the immediate feedback you would need to resolve the situation. In fact, you may never know that you offended your audience.

Although you may be tempted now and then to be brutally frank, try to express the facts in a kind and thoughtful manner.

## EMPHASIZING THE POSITIVE

During your career, you will have many occasions in which you need to communicate bad news. As you rise through the ranks of management, you will encounter situations in which unpleasant news can significantly affect the personal and financial well-being of employees, customers, and investors. However, there is a big difference between *delivering* negative news and *being* negative. When the tone of your message is negative, you put unnecessary strain on business relationships.

Never try to hide negative news, but always be on the lookout for positive points that will foster a good relationship with your audience:[2]

You can communicate negative news without being negative.

| Instead of This | Write This |
|---|---|
| It is impossible to repair your laptop today. | Your computer can be ready by Tuesday. Would you like a loaner until then? |
| We wasted $300,000 advertising in that magazine. | Our $300,000 advertising investment did not pay off. Let's analyze the experience and apply the insights to future campaigns. |

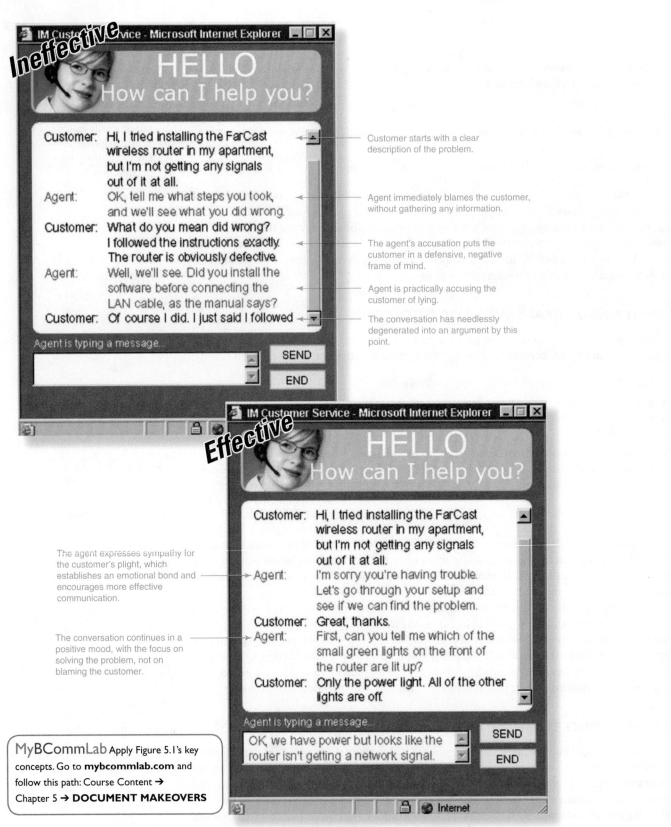

The agent expresses sympathy for the customer's plight, which establishes an emotional bond and encourages more effective communication.

The conversation continues in a positive mood, with the focus on solving the problem, not on blaming the customer.

Customer starts with a clear description of the problem.

Agent immediately blames the customer, without gathering any information.

The agent's accusation puts the customer in a defensive, negative frame of mind.

Agent is practically accusing the customer of lying.

The conversation has needlessly degenerated into an argument by this point.

MyBCommLab Apply Figure 5.1's key concepts. Go to **mybcommlab.com** and follow this path: Course Content → Chapter 5 → **DOCUMENT MAKEOVERS**

**Figure 5.1  Fostering a Positive Relationship with an Audience**
In the "ineffective" example, notice how the customer service agent's unfortunate word choices immediately derail this IM exchange. In the "effective" example, a more sensitive approach allows both people to focus on solving the problem.
*Source:* Used by permission of Microsoft.

If you find it necessary to criticize or correct, don't dwell on the other person's mistakes. Avoid referring to failures, problems, or shortcomings. Focus instead on what the audience members can do to improve the situation:

When you are offering criticism or advice, focus on what the person can do to improve.

| Instead of This | Write This |
|---|---|
| The problem with this department is a failure to control costs. | The performance of this department can be improved by tightening cost controls. |
| You failed to provide all the necessary information on the previous screen. | Please review the items marked in red on the previous screen so that we can process your order as quickly as possible. |

If you're trying to persuade audience members to buy a product, pay a bill, or perform a service for you, emphasize what's in it for them. When people recognize the benefits of doing so, they are more likely to respond positively to your appeal:

Show your audience members how they will benefit from responding to your message in the way you would like them to respond.

| Instead of This | Write This |
|---|---|
| We will notify all three credit reporting agencies if you do not pay your overdue bill within 10 days. | Paying your overdue bill within 10 days will prevent a negative entry on your credit record. |
| I am tired of seeing so many errors in the customer service blog. | Proofreading your blog postings will help you avoid embarrassing mistakes that generate more customer service complaints. |

In general, try to state your message without using words that may hurt or offend your audience. Look for appropriate opportunities to use **euphemisms**—words or phrases that express a thought in milder terms—that convey your meaning without carrying negative or unpleasant connotations. For example, one common euphemism is referring to people beyond a certain age as "senior citizens" rather than "old people." *Senior* conveys respect in a way that *old* doesn't.

Euphemisms, equivalent words or phrases that express a thought in milder terms, can ease the blow of negative news, but they must be used carefully to avoid annoying or misleading the audience.

Euphemisms can bring a tone of civility to unpleasant communication, but they must be used with great care because they are so easy—and so tempting—to misuse. Euphemisms can be annoying if they force readers to "read between the lines" to get the message, and they can be unethical if they obscure the truth. For instance, one of the toughest messages a manager ever has to write is an internal memo or email announcing layoffs. This is a difficult situation for everyone involved, and managers can be tempted to resort to euphemisms such as *streamlining, restructuring, improving efficiency, reducing layers,* or *eliminating redundancies* to avoid using the word *layoff*.[3] Doing so might ease the emotional burden on the writer and promote the illusion that the message isn't as negative as it really is. However, these euphemisms can fail the "you" attitude test, as well as the standards of ethical information, by failing to answer the question every reader in these situations has, which is simply: *Am I going to lose my job?*

If you are considering using a euphemism, ask yourself this question: Are you trying to protect the reader's feelings or your own feelings? Even if it is unpleasant, people generally respond better to an honest message delivered with integrity than they do to a sugar-coated message that obscures the truth.

## USING BIAS-FREE LANGUAGE

**Bias-free language** avoids words and phrases that unfairly and even unethically categorize or stigmatize people in ways related to gender, race, ethnicity, age, disability, or other personal characteristics. Contrary to what some may think, biased language is not simply about "labels." To a significant degree, language reflects the way we think and what we believe, and biased language may well perpetuate the underlying stereotypes and prejudices it represents.[4] Moreover, because communication is all about perception, simply *being* fair and objective isn't enough. To establish a good relationship with your audience, you must also *appear* to be fair.[5]

Biased language can perpetuate stereotypes and prejudices.

| TABLE 5.1 | Overcoming Bias in Language | |
| --- | --- | --- |
| **Examples** | **Unacceptable** | **Preferable** |
| **Gender Bias** | | |
| Using words containing *man* | Man-made | Artificial, synthetic, manufactured, constructed, human-made |
| | Mankind | Humanity, human beings, human race, people |
| | Manpower | Workers, workforce |
| | Businessman | Executive, manager, businessperson, professional |
| | Salesman | Sales representative, salesperson |
| | Foreman | Supervisor |
| Using female-gender words | Actress, stewardess | Actor, flight attendant |
| Using special designations | Woman doctor, male nurse | Doctor, nurse |
| Using *he* to refer to "everyone" | The average worker . . . he | The average worker . . . he or she OR Average workers . . . they |
| Identifying roles with gender | The typical executive spends four hours of his day in meetings. | Most executives spend four hours a day in meetings. |
| | the consumer . . . she | consumers . . . they |
| | the nurse/teacher . . . she | nurses/teachers . . . they |
| Identifying women by marital status | Mrs. Norm Lindstrom | Maria Lindstrom OR Ms. Maria Lindstrom |
| | Norm Lindstrom and Ms. Drake | Norm Lindstrom and Maria Drake OR Mr. Lindstrom and Ms. Drake |
| **Racial and Ethnic Bias** | | |
| Assigning stereotypes | Not surprisingly, Shing-Tung Yau excels in mathematics. | Shing-Tung Yau excels in mathematics. |
| Identifying people by race or ethnicity | Mario M. Cuomo, Italian-American politician and ex-governor of New York | Mario M. Cuomo, politician and ex-governor of New York |
| **Age Bias** | | |
| Including age when irrelevant | Mary Kirazy, 58, has just joined our trust department. | Mary Kirazy has just joined our trust department. |
| **Disability Bias** | | |
| Putting the disability before the person | Disabled workers face many barriers on the job. | Workers with physical disabilities face many barriers on the job. |
| | An epileptic, Tracy has no trouble doing her job. | Tracy's epilepsy has no effect on her job performance. |

Good communicators make every effort to change biased language (see Table 5.1). Bias can come in a variety of forms:

- **Gender bias.** Avoid sexist language by using the same labels for everyone, regardless of gender. Don't refer to a woman as *chairperson* and then to a man as *chairman*. Use *chair*, *chairperson*, or *chairman* consistently. (Note that it is not uncommon to use *chairman* when referring to a woman who heads a board of directors. Archer Daniels Midland's Patricia Woertz and Xerox's Ursula Burns, for example, both refer to themselves as *chairman*.[6]) Reword sentences to use *they* or to use no pronoun at all rather than refer to all individuals as *he*. Note that the preferred title for women in business is *Ms.* unless the individual asks to be addressed as *Miss* or *Mrs.* or has some other title, such as *Dr.*

- **Racial and ethnic bias.** Avoid identifying people by race or ethnic origin unless such a label is relevant to the matter at hand—and it rarely is.

- **Age bias.** Mention the age of a person only when it is relevant. Moreover, be careful of the context in which you use words that refer to age; such words carry a variety of positive and negative connotations. For example, *young* can imply energy, youthfulness, inexperience, or even immaturity, depending on how it's used.
- **Disability bias.** Physical, mental, sensory, or emotional impairments should never be mentioned in business messages unless those conditions are directly relevant to the subject. If you must refer to someone's disability, put the person first and the disability second.[7] For example, by saying "employees with physical handicaps," not "handicapped employees," you focus on the whole person, not the disability. Finally, never use outdated terminology such as *crippled* or *retarded*.

> **REAL-TIME UPDATES**
> LEARN MORE BY READING THIS PDF
>
> **Get detailed advice on using bias-free language**
>
> This in-depth guide offers practical tips for avoiding many types of cultural bias in your writing and speaking. Go to http://real-timeupdates.com/bct12 and click on Learn More. If you are using MyBCommLab, you can access Real-Time Updates within each chapter or under Student Study Tools.

# Adapting to Your Audience: Building Strong Relationships

Successful communication relies on a positive relationship between sender and receiver. Establishing your credibility and projecting your company's image are two vital steps in building and fostering positive business relationships.

**2 LEARNING OBJECTIVE**
Explain how establishing your credibility and projecting your company's image are vital aspects of building strong relationships with your audience.

## ESTABLISHING YOUR CREDIBILITY

Audience responses to your messages depend heavily on your **credibility**, a measure of your believability based on how reliable you are and how much trust you evoke in others. With audiences who don't know you and trust you already, you need to establish credibility before they'll accept your messages (see Figure 5.2 on the next page). On the other hand, when you do establish credibility, communication becomes much easier because you no longer have to spend time and energy convincing people that you are a trustworthy source of information and ideas. To build, maintain, or repair your credibility, emphasize the following characteristics:

People are more likely to react positively to your message when they have confidence in you.

- **Honesty.** Demonstrating honesty and integrity will earn you the respect of your audiences, even if they don't always agree with or welcome your messages.
- **Objectivity.** Show that you can distance yourself from emotional situations and look at all sides of an issue.
- **Awareness of audience needs.** Directly or indirectly, let your audience members know that you understand what's important to them.
- **Credentials, knowledge, and expertise.** Audiences need to know that you have whatever it takes to back up your message, whether it's education, professional certification, special training, past successes, or simply the fact that you've done your research.
- **Endorsements.** An *endorsement* is a statement on your behalf by someone who is accepted by your audience as an expert.
- **Performance.** Demonstrating impressive communication skills is not enough; people need to know they can count on you to get the job done.
- **Sincerity.** When you offer praise, don't use *hyperbole*, such as "you are the most fantastic employee I could ever imagine." Instead, point out specific qualities that warrant praise.

To enhance your credibility, emphasize such factors as honesty, objectivity, and awareness of audience needs.

> **REAL-TIME UPDATES**
> LEARN MORE BY READING THIS ARTICLE
>
> **Building credibility online**
>
> Follow these steps to build your credibility as an online voice. Go to http://real-timeupdates.com/bct12 and click on Learn More. If you are using MyBCommLab, you can access Real-Time Updates within each chapter or under Student Study Tools.

In addition, audiences need to know that you believe in yourself and your message. If you lack faith in yourself, you're likely to communicate an uncertain attitude that undermines your credibility. In contrast, if you are convinced that your message is sound, you

Photography plays an important role because clients are essentially "buying" Fraley when they buy his services. These images show him to be friendly, engaging, and confident.

The first paragraph summarizes his business background, which sends a strong message that he has the experience to back up the advice he gives.

Describing some of his career accomplishments provides persuasive support to his high-level message of being an innovator himself—not just somebody who knows how to talk about innovation.

Listing publications that have quoted him adds to his credibility as a respected expert in the field.

**Figure 5.2  Building Credibility**

Gregg Fraley is a highly regarded expert in the field of creativity and business innovation, but because his services are intangible, potential clients can't "test drive" those services before making a purchase decision. He therefore takes special care to build credibility as part of his communication efforts.

*Source:* Reprinted by permission, © Gregg Fraley Enterprises. http://www.greggfraley.com/

can state your case with authority. Look out for phrases containing words such as *hope* and *trust*, which can drain the audience's confidence in your message:

| Instead of This | Write This |
|---|---|
| We hope this recommendation will be helpful. | We're pleased to make this recommendation. |
| We trust that you'll want to extend your service contract. | By extending your service contract, you can continue to enjoy top-notch performance from your equipment. |

Finally, keep in mind that credibility can take a long time to establish—and it can be wiped out in an instant. An occasional mistake or letdown is usually forgiven, but major lapses in honesty or integrity can destroy your reputation. On the other hand, when you do establish credibility, communication becomes much easier because you no longer have to spend time and energy convincing people that you are a trustworthy source of information and ideas.

## PROJECTING YOUR COMPANY'S IMAGE

Your company's interests and reputation take precedence over your personal communication style.

When you communicate with anyone outside your organization, it is more than a conversation between two individuals. You represent your company and therefore play a vital role in helping the company build and maintain positive relationships with all its stakeholders. Most successful companies work hard to foster a specific public image, and your external communication efforts need to project that image. As part of this responsibility, the interests and preferred communication style of your company must take precedence over your own views and personal communication style.

Many organizations have specific communication guidelines that show everything from the correct use of the company name to preferred abbreviations and other grammatical details. Specifying a desired style of communication is more difficult, however. Observe more experienced colleagues, and never hesitate to ask for editorial help to make sure you're conveying the appropriate tone. For instance, with clients entrusting thousands or millions of dollars to it, an investment firm communicates in a style quite different from that of a clothing retailer. And a clothing retailer specializing in high-quality business attire communicates in a different style than a store catering to the latest trends in casual wear.

# Adapting to Your Audience: Controlling Your Style and Tone

Your communication **style** involves the choices you make to express yourself: the words you select, the manner in which you use those words in sentences, and the way you build paragraphs from individual sentences. Your style creates a certain **tone**, or overall impression, in your messages. The right tone depends on the nature of your message and your relationship with the reader.

**3   LEARNING OBJECTIVE**
Explain how to achieve a tone that is conversational but businesslike, explain the value of using plain language, and define active and passive voice.

## USING A CONVERSATIONAL TONE

The tone of your business messages can range from informal to conversational to formal (see Table 5.2). When you're communicating with your superiors or with customers, your tone may tend to be more formal and respectful.[8] However, that formal tone might sound distant and cold if used with close colleagues.

Compare the three versions of the message in Table 5.2. The first is too formal and stuffy for today's audiences, whereas the third is inappropriately casual for business. The second

Most business messages aim for a conversational style that is warm but businesslike.

| TABLE 5.2   Finding the Right Tone | |
|---|---|
| **Tone** | **Example** |
| **Stuffy:** too formal for today's audiences | Dear Ms. Navarro: |
| | Enclosed please find the information that was requested during our telephone communication of May 14. As was mentioned at that time, Midville Hospital has significantly more doctors of exceptional quality than any other health facility in the state. |
| | As you were also informed, our organization has quite an impressive network of doctors and other health-care professionals with offices located throughout the state. In the event that you should need a specialist, our professionals will be able to make an appropriate recommendation. |
| | In the event that you have questions or would like additional information, you may certainly contact me during regular business hours. |
| | Most sincerely yours, |
| | Samuel G. Berenz |
| **Conversational:** just right for most business communication | Dear Ms. Navarro: |
| | Here's the information you requested during our phone conversation on Friday. As I mentioned, Midville Hospital has the highest-rated doctors and more of them than any other hospital in the state. |
| | In addition, we have a vast network of doctors and other health professionals with offices throughout the state. If you need a specialist, they can refer you to the right one. |
| | If you would like more information, please call any time between 9:00 and 5:00, Monday through Friday. |
| | Sincerely, |
| | Samuel G. Berenz |
| **Unprofessional:** too casual for business communication | Here's the 411 you requested. IMHO, we have more and better doctors than any other hospital in the state. |
| | FYI, we also have a large group of doctors and other health professionals w/offices close to U at work/home. If U need a specialist, they'll refer U to the right one. |
| | Any? just ring or msg. |
| | L8R, |
| | S |

| TABLE 5.3 | Weeding Out Obsolete Phrases | |
|---|---|
| **Obsolete Phrase** | **Up-to-Date Replacement** |
| we are in receipt of | we received |
| kindly advise | please let me/us know |
| attached please find | enclosed is or I/we have enclosed |
| it has come to my attention | I have just learned or [someone] has just informed me |
| the undersigned | I/we |
| in due course | (specify a time or date) |
| permit me to say that | (omit; just say whatever you need to say) |
| pursuant to | (omit; just say whatever you need to say) |
| in closing, I'd like to say | (omit; just say whatever you need to say) |
| we wish to inform you that | (omit; just say whatever you need to say) |
| please be advised that | (omit; just say whatever you need to say) |

message demonstrates the **conversational tone** used in most business communication—plain language that sounds businesslike without being stuffy at one extreme or too laid-back and informal at the other extreme. You can achieve a tone that is conversational but still businesslike by following these guidelines:

- **Understand the difference between texting and writing.** The casual, acronym-laden language used in text messaging and instant messaging between friends is not considered professional business writing. Yes, texting style is an efficient way for friends to communicate—particularly taking into account the limitations of a phone keypad—but if you want to be taken seriously in business, you simply cannot write like this on the job.
- **Avoid stale and pompous language.** Most companies now shy away from such dated phrases as "attached please find" and "please be advised that." Similarly, avoid using obscure words, stale or clichéd expressions, and overly complicated sentences designed only to impress others (see Table 5.3).
- **Avoid preaching and bragging.** Readers tend to get irritated by know-it-alls who like to preach or brag. However, if you need to remind your audience of something that should be obvious, try to work in the information casually, perhaps in the middle of a paragraph, where it will sound like a secondary comment rather than a major revelation.
- **Be careful with intimacy.** Business messages should generally avoid intimacy, such as sharing personal details or adopting a casual, unprofessional tone. However, when you have a close relationship with audience members, such as among the members of a close-knit team, a more intimate tone is sometimes appropriate and even expected.
- **Be careful with humor.** Humor can easily backfire and divert attention from your message. If you don't know your audience well or you're not skilled at using humor in a business setting, don't use it at all. Avoid humor in formal messages and when you're communicating across cultural boundaries.

## USING PLAIN LANGUAGE

Audiences can understand and act on plain language without reading it over and over.

An important aspect of creating a conversational tone is using *plain language* (or *plain English* specifically when English is involved). Plain language presents information in a simple, unadorned style that allows your audience to easily grasp your meaning—language that recipients "can read, understand and act upon the first time they read it."[9] You can see how this definition supports using the "you" attitude and shows respect for your audience. In addition, plain language can make companies more productive and more profitable because people spend less time trying to figure out messages that are confusing or aren't written to meet their

The introductory sentence expresses the main idea, that the licenses are built in three layers (note that "use" would be a simpler alternative to "incorporate").

The notion of three layers is carried through the text and reinforced with the diagram.

**Three "Layers" Of Licenses**

Our public copyright licenses incorporate a unique and innovative three-layer design. Each license begins as a traditional legal tool, in the kind of language and text formats that most lawyers know and love. We call this the Legal Code layer of each license.

But since most creators, educators, and scientists are not in fact lawyers, we also make the licenses available in a format that normal people can read - the Commons Deed (also known as the "human readable" version of the license). The Commons Deed is a handy reference for licensors and licensees, summarizing and expressing some of the most important terms and conditions. Think of the Commons Deed as a user-friendly interface to the Legal Code beneath, although the Deed itself is not a license, and its contents are not part of the Legal Code itself.

The final layer of the license design recognizes that software, from search engines to office productivity to music editing, plays an enormous role in the creation, copying, discovery, and distribution of works. In order to make it easy for the Web to know when a work is available under a Creative Commons license, we provide a "machine readable" version of the license - a summary of the key freedoms and obligations written into a format that software systems, search engines, and other kinds of technology can understand. We developed a standardized way to describe licenses that software can understand called CC Rights Expression Language (CC REL) to accomplish this.

Searching for open content is an important function enabled by our approach.. You can use Google and Yahoo! to search for Creative Commons content, look for pictures at Flickr, albums at Jamendo, and general media at spinxpress. The Wikimedia Commons, which powers Wikipedia, is a core user of our licenses as well.

Taken together, these three layers of license ensure that the spectrum of rights isn't just a legal concept. It's something that the creators of works can understand, their users can understand, and even the Web itself can understand.

The paragraph on the "human readable" version explains why it exists and whom it benefits.

The purpose and function of the "machine readable" version are less obvious than in the other two versions, so this paragraph offers a more extensive explanation.

**Figure 5.3   Plain Language at Creative Commons**
Creative Commons uses this diagram and text to explain the differences among its three versions of content licenses.
*Source:* "Three 'Layers' of Licenses" from Creative Commons website. Copyright © by Creative Commons. Available under the terms of a CC-BY license. Reprinted with permission.

needs.[10] Finally, plain language helps nonnative speakers read your messages.

On the Creative Commons website, for instance, licensing terms are available in three versions: a complete "legal code" document that spells out contractual details in specific legal terms that meet the needs of legal professionals, a "human readable" version that explains the licensing terms in nontechnical language that anyone can understand, and a "machine readable" version fine-tuned for search engines and other systems (see Figure 5.3).[11]

**REAL-TIME UPDATES**
LEARN MORE BY READING THIS ARTICLE
**Take your communication skills from good to great**

These seven tips can help you transform your business writing from merely ordinary to powerful and persuasive. Go to http://real-timeupdates.com/bct12 and click on Learn More. If you are using MyBCommLab, you can access Real-Time Updates within each chapter or under Student Study Tools.

## SELECTING THE ACTIVE OR PASSIVE VOICE

Your choice of the active or passive voice affects the tone of your message. In **active voice**, the subject performs the action and the object receives the action: "Jodi sent the email message." In **passive voice**, the subject receives the action: "The email message was sent by Jodi." As you can see, the passive voice combines the helping verb *to be* with a form of the verb that is usually similar to the past tense.

Using the active voice helps make your writing more direct, livelier, and easier to read (see Table 5.4 on the following page). In contrast, the passive voice is often cumbersome, can be unnecessarily vague, and can make sentences overly long. In most cases, the active voice is your best choice.[12] Nevertheless, using the passive voice can help you demonstrate the "you" attitude in some situations:

- When you want to be diplomatic about pointing out a problem or an error of some kind (the passive version seems less like an accusation)
- When you want to point out what's being done without taking or attributing either the credit or the blame (the passive version shifts the spotlight away from the person or persons involved)
- When you want to avoid personal pronouns in order to create an objective tone (the passive version may be used in a formal report, for example)

Use passive sentences to soften bad news, to put yourself in the background, or to create an impersonal tone.

## TABLE 5.4 | Choosing Active or Passive Voice

*In general, avoid passive voice in order to make your writing lively and direct.*

| Dull and Indirect in Passive Voice | Lively and Direct in Active Voice |
|---|---|
| The new procedure was developed by the operations team. | The operations team developed the new procedure. |
| Legal problems are created by this contract. | This contract creates legal problems. |
| Reception preparations have been undertaken by our PR people for the new CEO's arrival. | Our PR people have begun planning a reception for the new CEO. |

*However, passive voice is helpful when you need to be diplomatic or want to focus attention on problems or solutions rather than on people.*

| Accusatory or Self-Congratulatory in Active Voice | More Diplomatic in Passive Voice |
|---|---|
| You lost the shipment. | The shipment was lost. |
| I recruited seven engineers last month. | Seven engineers were recruited last month. |
| We are investigating the high rate of failures on the final assembly line. | The high rate of failures on the final assembly line is being investigated. |

The second half of Table 5.4 illustrates several other situations in which the passive voice helps you focus your message on your audience.

# Composing Your Message: Choosing Powerful Words

**4 LEARNING OBJECTIVE**
Describe how to select words that are both correct and effective.

After you have decided how to adapt to your audience, you're ready to begin composing your message. As you write your first draft, let your creativity flow. Don't try to write and edit at the same time or worry about getting everything perfect. Make up words if you can't think of the right word, draw pictures, talk out loud—do whatever it takes to get the ideas out of your head and onto screen or paper. If you've scheduled carefully, you should have time to revise and refine the material later, before showing it to anyone. In fact, many writers find it helpful to establish a personal rule of never showing a first draft to anyone. By working in this "safe zone," away from the critical eyes of others, your mind will stay free to think clearly and creatively.

If you get stuck and feel unable to write, try to overcome writer's block by jogging your brain in creative ways. The introduction is often the hardest part to write, so put it aside and work on whichever parts of the document you're most comfortable with at any given moment. In most cases, you don't need to write the sections in any particular order.[13] Work on nontext elements such as graphics or your cover page. Revisit your purpose and confirm your intent in writing the message. Give yourself a mental break by switching to a different project. Sometimes all you need to do is start writing without worrying about the words you're using or how they will sound to the audience. Words will start flowing, your mind will engage, and the writing will come easier.

You may find it helpful to hone your craft by viewing your writing at three levels: strong words, effective sentences, and coherent paragraphs. Starting at the word level, successful writers pay close attention to the correct use of words.[14] If you make errors of grammar or usage, you lose credibility with your audience—even if your message is otherwise correct. Poor grammar suggests to readers that you're unprofessional, and they may choose not to trust you as a result. Moreover, poor grammar may imply that you don't respect your audience enough to get things right.

The rules of grammar and usage can be a source of worry for writers because some of them are complex and some evolve over time. Even professional editors and grammarians occasionally have questions about correct usage, and they sometimes disagree about the answers. For example, the word *data* is the plural form of *datum*, yet some experts now prefer to treat *data* as a singular noun when it's used in nonscientific material to refer to a body of facts or figures.

With practice, you'll become more skilled in making correct choices over time. If you have doubts about what is correct, you have many ways to find the answer. Check the Handbook of Grammar, Mechanics, and Usage at the end of this book, or consult the many special reference books and resources available in libraries, in bookstores, and on the Internet.

*If you're not sure of correct grammar or usage, look it up; you'll avoid embarrassing mistakes and learn at the same time.*

In addition to using words correctly, successful writers and speakers take care to use the most effective words and phrases. Selecting and using words effectively is often more challenging than using words correctly because doing so is a matter of judgment and experience. Careful writers continue to work at their craft to find words that communicate with power (see Figure 5.4).

*Effectiveness is the second consideration when choosing words.*

*In many cases, global is an absolute term and doesn't benefit from a modifier such as truly. However, economic globalization is occurring in stages, so truly here suggests the point at which globalization is nearly complete.*

*Claim is a powerful word here because it suggests a strong element of doubt.*

*The diplomatic use of passive voice keeps the focus on the issue at hand, rather than on the organizations that are involved.*

## Two Sides of the Story

Growing interest in the global acceptance of a single set of robust accounting standards comes from all participants in the capital markets. Many multinational companies and national regulators and users support it because they believe that the use of common standards in the preparation of public company financial statements will make it easier to compare the financial results of reporting entities from different countries. They believe it will help investors understand opportunities better. Large public companies with subsidiaries in multiple jurisdictions would be able to use one accounting language company-wide and present their financial statements in the same language as their competitors.

Another benefit some believe is that in a truly global economy, financial professionals including CPAs will be more mobile, and companies will more easily be able to respond to the human capital needs of their subsidiaries around the world.

Nevertheless, many people also believe that U.S. GAAP is the gold standard, and something will be lost with full acceptance of IFRS. However, recent SEC actions and global trends have increased awareness of the need to address possible adoption. According to a survey conducted in the first half of 2008 by Deloitte & Touche among chief financial officers and other financial professionals, U.S. companies have an interest in adopting IFRS and this interest is steadily growing. Thirty percent would consider adopting IFRS now, another 28 percent are unsure or do not have sufficient knowledge to decide, while 42 percent said they would not. Still, an AICPA survey conducted in Fall 2008 among its CPA members shows a significant and positive shift in the number of firms and companies that are starting to prepare for eventual adoption of IFRS. A 55 percent majority of CPAs at firms and companies nationwide said they are preparing in a variety of ways for IFRS adoption, an increase of 14 percentage points over the 41 percent who were preparing for change, according to an April 2008 AICPA survey.

Another concern is that worldwide many countries that claim to be converging to international standards may never get 100 percent compliance. Most reserve the right to carve out selectively or modify standards they do not consider in their national interest, an action that could lead to incompatibility—the very issue that IFRS seek to address.

## GAAP and IFRS, Still Differences

Great strides have been made by the FASB and the IASB to converge the content of IFRS and U.S. GAAP. The goal is that by the time the SEC allows or mandates the use of IFRS for U.S. publicly traded companies, most or all of the key differences will have been resolved.

Because of these ongoing convergence projects, the extent of the specific differences between IFRS and U.S. GAAP is shrinking. Yet significant differences do remain. For example:

- IFRS does not permit Last In First Out (LIFO) as an inventory costing method.
- IFRS uses a single-step method for impairment write-downs rather than the two-step method used in U.S. GAAP, making write-downs more likely.
- IFRS has a different probability threshold and measurement objective for contingencies.
- IFRS does not permit curing debt covenant violations after year-end.
- IFRS guidance regarding revenue recognition is less extensive than GAAP and contains relatively little industry-specific instructions.

5

*Robust goes beyond simply strong to suggest resilient and comprehensive as well.*

*Gold standard (a term borrowed from economics) refers to something against which all similar entities are compared, an unsurpassed model of excellence.*

*In the context of a survey significant means more than just important; it indicates a statistical observation that is large enough to be more than mere chance. Positive indicates the direction of the change and suggests affirmation and progress.*

*Carve out is much stronger than remove because it could suggest surgical precision if done well or perhaps violent destruction if not done with finesse. In this context, carve out is meant to express a concern about countries weakening the international financial standards by modifying them to meet their own needs.*

**Figure 5.4  Choosing Powerful Words**
Notice how careful word choices help this excerpt from a report published by the American Institute of Certified Public Accountants make a number of important points. The tone is formal, which is appropriate for a report with global, public readership. (GAAP refers to accounting standards currently used in the United States; IFRS refers to international standards.)
*Source:* Copyright © 2012 by the American Institute of Certified Public Accountants, Inc. (AICPA) Used by permission.

## UNDERSTANDING DENOTATION AND CONNOTATION

Many words have both a *denotative* (explicit, specific) meaning and a *connotative* (implicit, associative) meaning.

A word may have both a denotative and a connotative meaning. The **denotative meaning** is the literal, or dictionary, meaning. The **connotative meaning** includes all the associations and feelings evoked by the word.

The denotative meaning of *desk* is "a piece of furniture with a flat work surface and various drawers for storage." The connotative meaning of *desk* may include thoughts associated with work or study, but the word *desk* has fairly neutral connotations—neither strong nor emotional. However, some words have much stronger connotations than others and should be used with care. For example, the connotations of the word *fail* are negative and can have a dramatic emotional impact. If you say the sales department *failed* to meet its annual quota, the connotative meaning suggests that the group is inferior, incompetent, or below some standard of performance. However, the reason for not achieving 100 percent might be an inferior product, incorrect pricing, or some other factor outside the control of the sales department. In contrast, by saying the sales department achieved 85 percent of its quota, you clearly communicate that the results were less than expected without triggering all the negative emotions associated with *failure*.

## BALANCING ABSTRACT AND CONCRETE WORDS

The more abstract a word is, the more it is removed from the tangible, objective world that can be perceived with the senses.

Words vary dramatically in their degree of abstraction or concreteness. An **abstract word** expresses a concept, quality, or characteristic. Abstractions are usually broad, encompassing a category of ideas, and they are often intellectual, academic, or philosophical. *Love, honor, progress, tradition,* and *beauty* are abstractions, as are such important business concepts as *productivity, profits, quality,* and *motivation*. In contrast, a **concrete word** stands for something you can touch, see, or visualize. Most concrete terms are anchored in the tangible, material world. *Chair, table, horse, rose, kick, kiss, red, green,* and *two* are concrete words; they are direct, clear, and exact. Incidentally, technology continues to generate new words and new meanings that describe things that don't have a physical presence but are nonetheless concrete: *software, database,* and *website* are all concrete terms as well.

As you can imagine, abstractions tend to cause more trouble for writers and readers than concrete words. Abstractions tend to be "fuzzy" and can be interpreted differently, depending on the audience and the circumstances. The best way to minimize such problems is to blend abstract terms with concrete ones, the general with the specific. State the concept, then pin it down with details expressed in more concrete terms. Save the abstractions for ideas that cannot be expressed any other way. In addition, abstract words such as *small, numerous, sizable, near, soon, good,* and *fine* are imprecise, so try to replace them with terms that are more accurate. Instead of referring to a *sizable loss*, give an exact number.

## FINDING WORDS THAT COMMUNICATE WELL

By practicing your writing, learning from experienced writers and editors, and reading extensively, you'll find it easier to choose words that communicate exactly what you want to say. When you compose your business messages, think carefully to find the most powerful words for each situation and to avoid obscure words, clichés, and buzzwords that are turning into clichés (see Table 5.5):

Try to use words that are powerful and familiar.

- **Choose strong, precise words.** Choose words that express your thoughts clearly, specifically, and dynamically. If you find yourself using a lot of adjectives and adverbs, you're probably trying to compensate for weak nouns and verbs. Saying that *sales plummeted* is stronger and more efficient than saying *sales dropped dramatically* or *sales experienced a dramatic drop*.
- **Choose familiar words.** You'll communicate best with words that are familiar to both you and your readers. Efforts to improve a situation certainly can be *ameliorative*, but saying they are *helpful* is a lot more effective. Moreover, trying to use an unfamiliar word for the first time in an important document can lead to embarrassing mistakes.

Avoid clichés, be extremely careful with trendy buzzwords, and use jargon only when your audience is completely familiar with it.

- **Avoid clichés and be careful with buzzwords.** Although familiar words are generally the best choice, avoid *clichés*—terms and phrases so common that they have lost some of their power to communicate. *Buzzwords*, newly coined terms often associated with

TABLE 5.5 | **Selected Examples of Finding Powerful Words**

| Potentially Weak Words and Phrases | Stronger Alternatives (Effective Usage Depends on the Situation) |
| --- | --- |
| Increase (as a verb) | Accelerate, amplify, augment, enlarge, escalate, expand, extend, magnify, multiply, soar, swell |
| Decrease (as a verb) | Curb, cut back, depreciate, dwindle, shrink, slacken |
| Large, small | (use a specific number, such as $100 million) |
| Good | Admirable, beneficial, desirable, flawless, pleasant, sound, superior, worthy |
| Bad | Abysmal, corrupt, deficient, flawed, inadequate, inferior, poor, substandard, worthless |
| We are committed to providing . . . | We provide . . . |
| It is in our best interest to . . . | We should . . . |
| **Unfamiliar Words** | **Familiar Words** |
| Ascertain | Find out, learn |
| Consummate | Close, bring about |
| Peruse | Read, study |
| Circumvent | Avoid |
| Unequivocal | Certain |
| **Clichés and Buzzwords** | **Plain Language** |
| An uphill battle | A challenge |
| Writing on the wall | Prediction |
| Call the shots | Lead |
| Take by storm | Attack |
| Costs an arm and a leg | Expensive |
| A new ballgame | Fresh start |
| Fall through the cracks | Be overlooked |
| Think outside the box | Be creative |
| Run it up the flagpole | Find out what people think about it |
| Eat our own dog food | Use our own products |
| Mission-critical | Vital |
| Disintermediate | Get rid of |
| Green light (as a verb) | Approve |
| Architect (as a verb) | Design |
| Space (as in, "we compete in the XYZ space") | Market or industry |
| Blocking and tackling | Basic skills |
| Trying to boil the ocean | Working frantically but without focus |
| Human capital | People, employees, workforce |
| Low-hanging fruit | Tasks that are easy to complete or sales that are easy to close |
| Pushback | Resistance |

technology, business, or cultural changes, are slightly more difficult to handle than clichés, but in small doses and in the right situation, they can be useful. The careful use of a buzzword can signal that you're an insider, someone in the know.[15] However, buzzwords quickly become clichés, and using them too late in their "life cycle" can mark you as an outsider desperately trying to look like an insider. When people use clichés and overuse buzzwords, they often sound as though they don't know how to express themselves otherwise and don't invest the energy required for original writing.[16]

- **Use jargon carefully.** *Jargon*, the specialized language of a particular profession or industry, has a bad reputation, but it's not always bad. Using jargon is usually an efficient way to communicate within the specific groups that understand these terms. After all, that's how jargon develops in the first place, as people with similar interests devise ways to communicate complex ideas quickly. For instance, when a recording engineer wants to communicate that a particular piece of music is devoid of reverberation and other sound effects, it's a lot easier to simply describe the track as "dry." Of course, to people who aren't familiar with such insider terms, jargon is meaningless and intimidating—one more reason it's important to understand your audience before you start writing.

# Composing Your Message: Creating Effective Sentences

**5 LEARNING OBJECTIVE**
Define the four types of sentences, and explain how sentence style affects emphasis within a message.

Arranging your carefully chosen words in effective sentences is the next step in creating powerful messages (see Figure 5.5). Start by selecting the best type of sentence to communicate each point you want to make.

Echoing *TwitCause* at the beginning of this paragraph tells readers that this paragraph will continue on the same subject.

The transition *Additionally* signals that the topic in the previous paragraph will be expanded upon in this new paragraph.

*Following suit* functions as a transition from the previous paragraph by linking Pepsi back to the description of Home Depot.

The three sentences in this paragraph start with the broad topic (social media for charities and nonprofits) and narrow down the main idea, which is that TwitCause is a good tool for this purpose. (Note that the third sentence is really a fragment, but Hayes is selectively breaking the rules here to emphasize the suitability of TwitCause.)

*In my opinion* lets readers know she is transitioning from reporting to offering her personal thoughts on the subject at hand.

The second and third sentences in this paragraph provide an example of the observation made in the topic sentence at the beginning of the paragraph.

### TwitCause Makes Good

Olivia Hayes | February 19, 2010 | 1 Comment

Recently, using social media for charities and non-profits has been the conversation topic du jor, due in no small part to the massively successful text donation campaign for Haiti implemented by The Red Cross. Social media for non-profits and causes has been steadily evolving in both effective and creative ways because social channels are a natural way to disseminate information. Which is why TwitCause makes so much sense.

TwitCause, the brainchild of Experience Project, is a concept that builds on the idea that people are more willing to spread the word about good causes. You begin by following TwitCause on Twitter, and each Thursday they choose a new cause to tweet about. The included link sends you to a page where you can donate to the cause via PayPal, or you can choose to help by simply pressing the Retweet button and educating your followers.

Additionally, people can nominate the charities that they think should be supported by TwitCause, which then get voted on to be next up. TwitCause is hoping to get more businesses and brands involved by sponsoring matching donations, or having people tweet in order to get the brands to make donations.

In a recent guest post on Beth Kanter's blog, Julio Vasconcellos, who manages TwitCause for Experience Project, wrote that it's difficult to fundraise via individual donations. People are less likely to open up their wallets than they are to help spread a message to the people in their network.

In my opinion, it's the latter concept that is most sustainable, and recently it's looked like corporations and brands are beginning to take that stance as well. In my own recent experience with Home Depot, I had initially asked if they'd be interested in matching whatever I raised for the New Orleans rebuilding organization LowerNine.org. They generously surprised me by coming back with an offer of a $10,000 donation of gift cards from their Home Depot Foundation, arming the organization with the tools and supplies they needed most to get their work done.

You'll find Pepsi following suit with their Refresh Everything contest, while Chase Bank just wrapped up a contest where people voted on which charitable organizations they wanted to win cash. Perhaps this is the next phase in the evolution of TwitCause?

Have you had an experience with TwitCause or using Twitter as a tool for raising awareness? I'm interested to hear about it in the comments.

Rate this post: ★ ★ ★ ★ | ShareThis

**Subscribe**

**Latest Posts**
- The Two Most Important Questions in Social Media Marketing
- Writing Web Content for a Living - Notes from SXSW
- Social Media and China: It's Not What You Think: Notes from SxSW
- Taking Your Brand Mobile with an App: Notes from SxSW

**Featured Posts**
- Top 50 Branded Facebook Fan Pages of 2009
- 4 Ways Social Media Budgets will Move in 2010
- 7 Moves Facebook Has Made to Outflank Twitter in the Last 6 Months
- 2009 Social Network Analysis Report - Geographic - Demographic and Traffic Data Revealed
- 26 Social Media Marketing Examples in Detail

**Figure 5.5 Crafting Unified, Coherent Paragraphs**
Olivia Hayes, a copywriter with the social media marketing agency Ignite, demonstrates several aspects of effective writing in this blog post about the Twitter-based social contribution network TwitCause.
*Source:* Copyright © 2012 by Ignite Social Media. Used by permission.

MyBCommLab Apply Figure 5.5's key concepts. Go to **mybcommlab.com** and follow this path: Course Content → Chapter 5 → **DOCUMENT MAKEOVERS**

## CHOOSING FROM THE FOUR TYPES OF SENTENCES

Sentences come in four basic varieties: simple, compound, complex, and compound-complex. A **simple sentence** has one main *clause* (a single subject and a single predicate), although it may be expanded by nouns and pronouns that serve as objects of the action and by modifying phrases. Here's an example with the subject noun underlined once and the predicate verb underlined twice:

> Profits increased in the past year.

A **compound sentence** has two main clauses that express two or more independent but related thoughts of equal importance, usually joined by *and*, *but*, or *or*. In effect, a compound sentence is a merger of two or more simple sentences (independent clauses) that are related. For example:

> Wage rates have declined by 5 percent, and employee turnover has been high.

The independent clauses in a compound sentence are always separated by a comma or by a semicolon (in which case the conjunction—*and*, *but*, *or*—is dropped).

A **complex sentence** expresses one main thought (the independent clause) and one or more subordinate, related thoughts (dependent clauses that cannot stand alone as valid sentences). Independent and dependent clauses are usually separated by a comma. In this example, "Although you may question Gerald's conclusions" is a subordinate thought expressed in a dependent clause:

> Although you may question Gerald's conclusions, you must admit that his research is thorough.

A **compound-complex sentence** has two main clauses, at least one of which contains a subordinate clause:

> Profits have increased in the past year, and although you may question Gerald's conclusions, you must admit that his research is thorough.

When constructing sentences, choose the form that matches the relationship of the ideas you want to express. If you have two ideas of equal importance, express them as two simple sentences or as one compound sentence. However, if one of the ideas is less important than the other, place it in a dependent clause to form a complex sentence. For example, although the following compound sentence uses a conjunction to join two ideas, they aren't truly equal:

> The chemical products division is the strongest in the company, and its management techniques should be adopted by the other divisions.

By making the first thought subordinate to the second, you establish a cause-and-effect relationship and emphasize the more important idea (that the other divisions should adopt the chemical division's management techniques):

> Because the chemical products division is the strongest in the company, its management techniques should be adopted by the other divisions.

In addition to selecting the best type for each thought you want to express, using a variety of sentence types throughout a document can make your writing more interesting and

A simple sentence has one main clause.

A compound sentence has two main clauses.

A complex sentence has one main clause and one subordinate clause.

A compound-complex sentence has two main clauses and at least one dependent clause.

Writing is usually more interesting and effective if it balances all four sentence types.

effective. For example, if you use too many simple sentences in a row, you may struggle to properly express the relationships among your ideas, and your writing will sound choppy and abrupt. At the other extreme, a long series of compound, complex, or compound-complex sentences can be tiring to read.

## USING SENTENCE STYLE TO EMPHASIZE KEY THOUGHTS

In every message of any length, some ideas are more important than others. You can emphasize these key ideas through your sentence style. One obvious technique is to give important points the most space. When you want to call attention to a thought, use extra words to describe it. Consider this sentence:

You can emphasize ideas in a sentence by
- Devoting more words to them
- Putting them at the beginning or at the end of the sentence
- Making them the subject of the sentence

> The chairperson called for a vote of the shareholders.

To emphasize the importance of the chairperson, you might describe her more fully:

> Having considerable experience in corporate takeover battles, the chairperson called for a vote of the shareholders.

You can increase the emphasis even more by adding a separate, short sentence to augment the first:

> The chairperson called for a vote of the shareholders. She has considerable experience in corporate takeover battles.

You can also call attention to a thought by making it the subject of the sentence. In the following example, the emphasis is on the person:

> I can write letters much more quickly by using voice dictation.

However, by changing the subject, the voice dictation capability takes center stage:

> Using voice dictation enables me to write letters much more quickly.

Another way to emphasize an idea (in this instance, the idea of stimulating demand) is to place it either at the beginning or at the end of a sentence:

> **Less emphatic:** We are cutting the price to stimulate demand.
> **More emphatic:** To stimulate demand, we are cutting the price.

You can adjust the emphasis given to a subordinate idea by placing the dependent clause at the beginning, middle, or end of the sentence.

In complex sentences, the placement of the dependent clause hinges on the relationship between the ideas expressed. If you want to emphasize the subordinate idea, put the dependent clause at the end of the sentence (the most emphatic position) or at the beginning (the second most emphatic position). If you want to downplay the idea, put the dependent clause within the sentence:

**Most emphatic:** The electronic parts are manufactured in Mexico, which has lower wage rates than the United States.
**Emphatic:** Because wage rates are lower in Mexico than in the United States, the electronic parts are manufactured there.
**Least emphatic:** Mexico, which has lower wage rates than the United States, was selected as the production site for the electronic parts.

Techniques such as these give you a great deal of control over the way your audience interprets what you have to say.

# Composing Your Message: Crafting Unified, Coherent Paragraphs

Paragraphs organize sentences related to the same general topic. Readers expect every paragraph to be *unified*—focusing on a single topic—and *coherent*—presenting ideas in a logically connected way. By carefully arranging the elements of each paragraph, you help your readers grasp the main idea of your document and understand how the specific pieces of support material back up that idea.

**6 LEARNING OBJECTIVE**
Define the three key elements of a paragraph, and list five ways to develop unified, coherent paragraphs.

## CREATING THE ELEMENTS OF A PARAGRAPH

Paragraphs vary widely in length and form, but a typical paragraph contains three basic elements: a topic sentence, support sentences that develop the topic, and transitional words and phrases.

### Topic Sentence

An effective paragraph deals with a single topic, and the sentence that introduces that topic is called the **topic sentence**. In informal and creative writing, the topic sentence may be implied rather than stated. In business writing, the topic sentence is generally explicit and is often the first sentence in the paragraph. The topic sentence gives readers a summary of the general idea that will be covered in the rest of the paragraph. The following examples show how a topic sentence can introduce the subject and suggest the way the subject will be developed:

The medical products division has been troubled for many years by public relations problems. [In the rest of the paragraph, readers will learn the details of the problems.]

To get a refund, please supply us with the following information. [The details of the necessary information will be described in the rest of the paragraph.]

Most paragraphs consist of
- A topic sentence that reveals the subject of the paragraph
- Related sentences that support and expand the topic
- Transitions that help readers move between sentences and between paragraphs

In addition to helping your readers, topic sentences help you as a writer because they remind you of the purpose of each paragraph and thereby encourage you to stay focused. In fact, a good way to test the effectiveness of your writing is to prepare a summary version that consists of only the first sentences of all your paragraphs. If this summary communicates the essence of your message in a sensible, compelling way, you've probably done a good job of presenting your information.[17]

## Support Sentences

In most paragraphs, the topic sentence needs to be explained, justified, or extended with one or more support sentences. These related sentences must all have a bearing on the general subject and must provide enough specific details to make the topic clear:

> The medical products division has been troubled for many years by public relations problems. Since 2011 the local newspaper has published 15 articles that portray the division in a negative light. We have been accused of everything from mistreating laboratory animals to polluting the local groundwater. Our facility has been described as a health hazard. Our scientists are referred to as "Frankensteins," and our profits are considered "obscene."

The support sentences are all more specific than the topic sentence. Each one provides another piece of evidence to demonstrate the general truth of the main thought. Also, each sentence is clearly related to the general idea being developed, which gives the paragraph unity. A paragraph is well developed if it contains enough information to make the topic sentence understood and convincing, and if it doesn't contain any extraneous, unrelated sentences.

## Transitions

Transitional elements include
- Connecting words (conjunctions)
- Repeated words or phrases
- Pronouns
- Words that are frequently paired

**Transitions** connect ideas by showing how one thought is related to another. They also help alert the reader to what lies ahead so that shifts and changes don't cause confusion. In addition to helping readers understand the connections you're trying to make, transitions give your writing a smooth, even flow.

Depending on the specific need within a document, transitional elements can range in length from a single word to an entire paragraph or more. You can establish transitions in a variety of ways:

- **Use connecting words.** Use conjunctions such as *and, but, or, nevertheless, however, in addition*, and so on.
- **Echo a word or phrase from a previous paragraph or sentence.** "A system should be established for monitoring inventory levels. *This system* will provide. . . ."
- **Use a pronoun that refers to a noun used previously.** "Ms. Arthur is the leading candidate for the president's position. *She* has excellent qualifications."
- **Use words that are frequently paired.** "The machine has a *minimum* output of . . . Its *maximum* output is. . . ."

Some transitions serve as mood changers, alerting the reader to a change in mood from the previous material. Some announce a total contrast with what's gone on before, some announce a causal relationship, and some signal a change in time. Here is a list of transitions frequently used to move readers smoothly between clauses, sentences, and paragraphs:

> **Additional detail:** moreover, furthermore, in addition, besides, first, second, third, finally
> **Cause-and-effect relationship:** therefore, because, accordingly, thus, consequently, hence, as a result, so
> **Comparison:** similarly, here again, likewise, in comparison, still
> **Contrast:** yet, conversely, whereas, nevertheless, on the other hand, however, but, nonetheless
> **Condition:** although, if
> **Illustration:** for example, in particular, in this case, for instance
> **Time sequence:** formerly, after, when, meanwhile, sometimes
> **Intensification:** indeed, in fact, in any event
> **Summary:** in brief, in short, to sum up
> **Repetition:** that is, in other words, as mentioned earlier

Consider using a transition whenever it could help the reader understand your ideas and follow you from point to point. You can use transitions inside paragraphs to tie related points together and between paragraphs to ease the shift from one distinct thought to another. In longer reports, a transition that links major sections or chapters may be a complete paragraph that serves as a mini-introduction to the next section or as a summary of the ideas presented in the section just ending. Here's an example:

> Given the nature of this product, our alternatives are limited. As the previous section indicates, we can stop making it altogether, improve it, or continue with the current model. Each of these alternatives has advantages and disadvantages, which are discussed in the following section.

This paragraph makes it clear to the reader that the analysis of the problem (offered in the previous section) is now over and that the document is making a transition to an analysis of the possible solutions (to be offered in the next section).

Figure 5.5 on page 130, offers several examples of transitions and other features of effective paragraphs.

## CHOOSING THE BEST WAY TO DEVELOP EACH PARAGRAPH

You have a variety of options for developing paragraphs, each of which can convey a specific type of idea. Five of the most common approaches are illustration, comparison or contrast, cause and effect, classification, and problem and solution (see Table 5.6).

| TABLE 5.6 | Five Techniques for Developing Paragraphs | |
| --- | --- | --- |
| **Technique** | **Description** | **Example** |
| Illustration | Giving examples that demonstrate the general idea | Some of our most popular products are available through local distributors. For example, Everett & Lemmings carries our frozen soups and entrees. The J. B. Green Company carries our complete line of seasonings, as well as the frozen soups. Wilmont Foods, also a major distributor, now carries our new line of frozen desserts. |
| Comparison or contrast | Using similarities or differences to develop the topic | When the company was small, the recruiting function could be handled informally. The need for new employees was limited, and each manager could comfortably screen and hire her or his own staff. However, our successful bid on the Owens contract means that we will be doubling our labor force over the next six months. To hire that many people without disrupting our ongoing activities, we will create a separate recruiting group within the human resources department. |
| Cause and effect | Focusing on the reasons for something | The heavy-duty fabric of your Wanderer tent probably broke down for one of two reasons: (1) a sharp object punctured the fabric, and without reinforcement, the hole was enlarged by the stress of pitching the tent daily for a week or (2) the fibers gradually rotted because the tent was folded and stored while still wet. |
| Classification | Showing how a general idea is broken into specific categories | Successful candidates for our supervisor trainee program generally come from one of several groups. The largest group by far consists of recent graduates of accredited business management programs. The next largest group comes from within our own company, as we try to promote promising staff workers to positions of greater responsibility. Finally, we occasionally accept candidates with outstanding supervisory experience in related industries. |
| Problem and solution | Presenting a problem and then discussing the solution | Selling handmade toys online is a challenge because consumers are accustomed to buying heavily advertised toys from major chain stores or well-known websites such as Amazon.com. However, if we develop an appealing website, we can compete on the basis of product novelty and quality. In addition, we can provide unusual crafts at a competitive price: a rocking horse of birch, with a hand-knit tail and mane; a music box with the child's name painted on the top; and a real teepee, made by Native American artisans. |

## Being Dependable and Accountable

By any definition, a "pro" is somebody who gets the job done. Develop a reputation as somebody people can count on. This means meeting your commitments, including staying on schedule and staying within budgets. These are skills that take some time to develop as you discover how much time and money are required to accomplish various tasks and projects. With experience, you'll learn to be conservative with your commitments. You don't want to be known as someone who overpromises and underdelivers.

If you can't confidently predict how long a project will take or how much it will cost, be sure to let your client, colleagues, or supervisor know that. And if changing circumstances threaten your ability to meet a previous commitment, be sure to share that information with anyone who might be affected by your performance.

Being accountable also means owning up to your mistakes and learning from failure so that you can continue to improve. Pros don't make excuses or blame others. When they make mistakes—and everybody does—they face the situation head on, make amends, and move on.

### CAREER APPLICATIONS

1. What steps could you take to make realistic commitments on tasks and projects in which you have little or no experience?
2. Does being accountable mean you never make mistakes? Explain you answer.

---

In some instances, combining approaches in a single paragraph is an effective strategy. Notice how the example provided for "Problem and solution" in Table 5.6 also includes an element of illustration by listing some of the unique products that could be part of the proposed solution. However, when combining approaches, do so carefully so that you don't lose readers partway through the paragraph.

In addition, before settling for the first approach that comes to mind, consider the alternatives. Think through various methods before committing yourself, or even write several test paragraphs to see which method works best. By avoiding the easy habit of repeating the same old paragraph pattern time after time, you can keep your writing fresh and interesting.

# Using Technology to Compose and Shape Your Messages

**7 LEARNING OBJECTIVE**
Identify the most common software features that help you craft messages more efficiently.

Take full advantage of your software's formatting capabilities to help produce effective, professional messages in less time.

Be sure to take advantage of the tools in your word processor or online publishing systems (for websites, blogs, and other documents) to write more efficiently and effectively. The features, functions, and names vary from system to system and version to version, but you'll encounter some combination of the following capabilities:

- **Style sheets, style sets, templates, and themes.** In word processing software, blogging systems, and other tools, *style sheets*, *style sets*, *templates*, and *themes* are various ways of ensuring consistency throughout a document and from document to document. These tools also make it easy to redesign an entire document or screen simply by redefining the various styles or selecting a different design theme. Style sheets or sets are collections of formatting choices for words, paragraphs, and other elements. Rather than manually formatting every element, you simply select one of the available styles. Templates usually set overall document parameters such as page size or screen colors and provide a specific set of styles to use. Templates can be particularly handy if you create a variety of document types, such as letters, calendars, and agendas. Themes tend to address the overall look and feel of the page or screen, including color palettes and background images.
- **Boilerplate and document components.** *Boilerplate* refers to a standard block of text that is reused in multiple documents. Two common examples are company descriptions and executive biographies. Some systems offer the means to store these blocks and drop them into a document as needed, which saves time and ensures consistency. Moving beyond simple text blocks, some systems can store fully formatted document components such as cover pages, sidebars, and *pull quotes* (a piece of text copied from the main body of the document and formatted as a large, eye-catching visual element).

- **Autocorrection or autocompletion.** Some programs can automate text entry and correction using a feature called autocompletion, autocorrection, or something similar. In Microsoft Word, for example, the AutoCorrect feature lets you build a library of actions that automatically fill in longer entries based on the first few characters you type (such as entering a full description of the company after you type the word "boilerplate") or correct common typing errors (such as typing *teh* instead of *the*). Use these features carefully, though. First, they can make changes you might not want in every instance. Second, you may grow to rely on them to clean up your typing, but they won't be there to help when you're using other systems.
- **File merge and mail merge.** Most word processing software makes it easy to combine files, which is an especially handy feature when several members of a team write different sections of a report. Mail merge lets you personalize form letters by automatically inserting names and addresses from a database.
- **Endnotes, footnotes, indexes, and tables of contents.** Your computer can help you track footnotes and endnotes, renumbering them every time you add or delete references. For a report's indexes and table of contents, you can simply flag the items you want to include, and the software assembles the lists for you.

For new articles and advice on writing business messages, visit http://real-timeupdates .com/bct12 and click on Chapter 5. For a reminder of the tasks involved in writing messages, see "Checklist: Writing Business Messages."

---

### CHECKLIST ✔ Writing Business Messages

**A. Adapt to your audience.**
- Use the "you" attitude.
- Maintain good etiquette through polite communication.
- Emphasize the positive whenever possible.
- Use bias-free language.
- Establish credibility in the eyes of your audience.
- Project your company's preferred image.
- Use a conversational but still professional and respectful tone.
- Use plain language for clarity.

**B. Compose your message.**
- Choose strong words that communicate efficiently.
- Pay attention to the connotative meaning of your words.
- Balance abstract and concrete terms to convey your meaning accurately.
- Avoid clichés and trendy buzzwords.
- Use jargon only when your audience understands it and prefers it.
- Vary your sentence structure for impact and interest.
- Develop coherent, unified paragraphs.
- Use transitions generously to help your audience follow your message.

---

## COMMUNICATION CHALLENGES AT Creative Commons

To achieve their mission of popularizing a new approach to copyrighting songs, artwork, literature, and other creative works, Catherine Casserly and her staff at Creative Commons need to persuade people that the traditional approach to copyrighting doesn't meet the needs of today's digital society. This is no small challenge: Not only do they need to convince people to reconsider more than 200 years of legal precedent and habit, they also need to communicate with an extremely diverse audience—everyone from lawyers and business managers to artists, writers, musicians, and scientists. After graduating with a business degree, you've joined Creative Commons as a communication intern for a year before entering law school. Apply your knowledge of effective writing to the following scenarios.

**INDIVIDUAL CHALLENGE:** Visit the licensing section of the Creative Commons website, at http://creativecommons.org/licenses, and read the information on Attribution-NonCommercial-ShareAlike, Attribution-NonCommercial, and Attribution-NoDerivs licenses. Write a brief description that explains how these three licenses differ. Imagine that your audience is a group of music and art majors.

**TEAM CHALLENGE:** A key aspect of the communication challenge for Creative Commons is translating legal documents into language that musicians, artists, and others with no legal training can easily understand. In a small group, brainstorm ways to rewrite the following paragraph into language for a general audience:

> The above rights may be exercised in all media and formats whether now known or hereafter devised. The above rights include the right to make such modifications as are technically necessary to exercise the rights in other media and formats, but otherwise you have no rights to make adaptations.

# Quick Learning Guide

## SUMMARY OF LEARNING OBJECTIVES

**1** Identify the four aspects of being sensitive to audience needs when writing business messages. First, the "you" attitude refers to speaking and writing in terms of your audience's wishes, interests, hopes, and preferences rather than your own. Writing with this attitude is essential to effective communication because it shows your audience that you have their needs in mind, not just your own. Second, good etiquette not only indicates respect for your audience but also helps foster a more successful environment for communication by minimizing negative emotional reaction. Third, sensitive communicators understand the difference between delivering negative news and being negative. Without hiding the negative news, they look for ways to emphasize positive aspects. Fourth, being sensitive includes taking care to avoid biased language that unfairly and even unethically categorizes or stigmatizes people in ways related to gender, race, ethnicity, age, or disability.

**2** Explain how establishing your credibility and projecting your company's image are vital aspects of building strong relationships with your audience. Whether a one-time interaction or a series of exchanges over the course of many months or years, successful communication relies on a positive relationship existing between sender and receiver. Audience responses to your messages depend heavily on your credibility, a measure of your believability, based on how reliable you are and how much trust you evoke in others. When you have established credibility with an audience, communication becomes much easier because you no longer have to spend time and energy convincing people that you are a trustworthy source of information and ideas. Project your company's desired image when communicating with external audiences. You represent your company and therefore play a vital role in helping the company build and maintain positive relationships with all of its stakeholders.

**3** Explain how to achieve a tone that is conversational but businesslike, explain the value of using plain language, and define active and passive voice. To achieve a tone that is conversational but still businesslike, avoid obsolete and pompous language, avoid preaching and bragging, be careful with intimacy (sharing personal details or adopting an overly casual tone), and be careful with humor. Plain language is a way of presenting information in a simple, unadorned style so that your audience can easily grasp your meaning. By writing and speaking in plain terms, you demonstrate the "you" attitude and show respect for your audience. In the active voice, the subject performs the action and the object receives the action. In the passive voice, the subject receives the action. The passive voice combines the helping verb *to be* with a form of the verb that is usually in the past tense.

**4** Describe how to select words that are both correct and effective. To select the best words, first make sure they are correct by checking grammar and usage guides. Then choose words that have few connotations (to reduce the chance of misinterpretation) and no unintended negative connotations (to reduce the chance of offending your audience). Select words that communicate clearly, specifically, and dynamically. Choose words that are strong and familiar, avoid clichés, be extremely careful with buzzwords, and use jargon only when your audience will understand it.

**5** Define the four types of sentences, and explain how sentence style affects emphasis within a message. The four types of sentences are *simple* (one main clause), *compound* (two main clauses that express independent but related ideas of equal importance), *complex* (one main clause and one subordinate clause of lesser importance), and *compound-complex* (two main clauses, at least one of which contains a subordinate clause). Sentence style affects emphasis by playing up or playing down specific parts of a sentence. To emphasize a certain point, you can place it at the end of the sentence or make it the subject of the sentence. To deemphasize a point, put it in the middle of the sentence.

**6** Define the three key elements of a paragraph, and list five ways to develop unified, coherent paragraphs. The three key elements of a paragraph are a topic sentence that identifies the subject of the paragraph, support sentences that develop the topic and provide examples and evidence, and transitional words and phrases that help readers connect one thought to the next. Effective paragraphs are both *unified* (focused on a single idea) and *coherent* (logically organized). You can develop paragraphs through illustration (giving examples), comparison or contrast (pointing out similarities or differences), cause and effect (giving reasons), classification (discussing categories), and problem and solution (stating a problem and showing how to solve it).

**7** Identify the most common software features that help you craft messages more efficiently. Common software features that help you craft messages more efficiently include style sheets, style sets, templates, and themes; features to store and use boilerplate and document components; autocorrection or autocompletion; file merge and mail merge; and endnotes, footnotes, indexes, and tables of contents.

## KEY TERMS

**abstract word** Word that expresses a concept, quality, or characteristic; abstractions are usually broad

**active voice** Sentence structure in which the subject performs the action and the object receives the action

**bias-free language** Language that avoids words and phrases that categorize or stigmatize people in ways related to gender, race, ethnicity, age, or disability

**complex sentence** Sentence that expresses one main thought (the independent clause) and one or more subordinate, related thoughts (dependent clauses that cannot stand alone as valid sentences)

**compound sentence** Sentence with two main clauses that express two or more independent but related thoughts of equal importance, usually joined by *and*, *but*, or *or*

**compound-complex sentence** Sentence with two main clauses, at least one of which contains a subordinate clause

**concrete word** Word that represents something you can touch, see, or visualize; most concrete terms related to the tangible, material world

**connotative meaning** All the associations and feelings evoked by a word

**conversational tone** The tone used in most business communication; it uses plain language that sounds businesslike without being stuffy at one extreme or too laid-back and informal at the other extreme

**credibility** A measure of your believability, based on how reliable you are and how much trust you evoke in others

**denotative meaning** The literal, or dictionary, meaning of a word

**euphemisms** Words or phrases that express a thought in milder terms

**passive voice** Sentence structure in which the subject receives the action

**simple sentence** Sentence with one main *clause* (a single subject and a single predicate)

**style** The choices you make to express yourself: the words you select, the manner in which you use those words in sentences, and the way you build paragraphs from individual sentences

**tone** The overall impression in your messages, created by the style you use

**topic sentence** Sentence that introduces that topic of a paragraph

**transitions** Words or phrases that tie together ideas by showing how one thought is related to another

---

**CHECKLIST** ✓

## Writing Business Messages

**A. Adapt to your audience.**
- Use the "you" attitude.
- Maintain good etiquette through polite communication.
- Emphasize the positive whenever possible.
- Use bias-free language.
- Establish credibility in the eyes of your audience.
- Project your company's preferred image.
- Use a conversational but still professional and respectful tone.
- Use plain language for clarity.

**B. Compose your message.**
- Choose strong words that communicate efficiently.
- Pay attention to the connotative meaning of your words.
- Balance abstract and concrete terms to convey your meaning accurately.
- Avoid clichés and trendy buzzwords.
- Use jargon only when your audience understands it and prefers it.
- Vary your sentence structure for impact and interest.
- Develop coherent, unified paragraphs.
- Use transitions generously to help your audience follow your message.

# Test Your Knowledge

To review chapter content related to each question, refer to the indicated Learning Objective.

1. What is meant by the "you" attitude? [LO-1]
2. Why is it important to establish your credibility when communicating with an audience of strangers? [LO-2]
✪ 3. In what three situations is the passive voice appropriate? [LO-3]
4. How does an abstract word differ from a concrete word? [LO-4]
5. How does the denotative meaning of a word differ from its connotative meaning? [LO-4]
✪ 6. How can you use sentence style to emphasize key thoughts? [LO-5]
7. How can topic sentences help readers? [LO-6]
8. What functions do transitions serve? [LO-6]
9. What software functions can you use to make it easy to reuse blocks of text across multiple documents? [LO-7]

# Apply Your Knowledge

To review chapter content related to each question, refer to the indicated Learning Objective.

1. Millions of people in the United States are allergic to one or more food ingredients. Each year, thousands of these people end up in the emergency room after suffering allergic reactions, and hundreds of them die. Many of these tragic events are tied to poorly written food labels that either fail to identify dangerous allergens or use scientific terms that most consumers don't recognize.[18] Do food manufacturers have a responsibility to ensure that consumers read, understand, and follow warnings on food products? Explain your answer. [LO-1]
✪ 2. When composing business messages, how can you communicate with an authentic voice and project your company's image at the same time? [LO-2]
3. Does using plain language make you come across as less of an expert? Explain your answer. [LO-3]
✪ 4. Should you bother using transitions if the logical sequence of your message is obvious? Why or why not? [LO-6]

# Practice Your Skills

### Messages for Analysis: Creating a Businesslike Tone [LO-1], [LO-3]

Read the following email draft and then (1) analyze the strengths and weaknesses of each sentence and (2) revise the document so that it follows this chapter's guidelines. The message was written by the marketing manager of an online retailer of baby-related products in the hope of becoming a retail outlet for Inglesina strollers and high chairs. As a manufacturer of stylish, top-quality products, Inglesina (based in Italy) is extremely selective about the retail outlets through which it allows its products to be sold.

Our e-tailing site, www.BestBabyGear.com, specializes in only the very best products for parents of newborns, infants, and toddlers. We constantly scour the world looking for

products that are good enough and well-built enough and classy enough—good enough to take their place alongside the hundreds of other carefully selected products that adorn the pages of our award-winning website, www.bestbabygear.com. We aim for the fences every time we select a product to join this portfolio; we don't want to waste our time with onesey-twosey products that might sell a half dozen units per annum—no, we want every product to be a top-drawer success, selling at least one hundred units per specific model per year in order to justify our expense and hassle factor in adding it to the above mentioned portfolio. After careful consideration, we thusly concluded that your Inglesina lines meet our needs and would therefore like to add it.

## Exercises

Active links for all websites in this chapter can be found on MyBCommLab; see your User Guide for instructions on accessing the content for this chapter. Each activity is labeled according to the primary skill or skills you will need to use. To review relevant chapter content, you can refer to the indicated Learning Objective. In some instances, supporting information will be found in another chapter, as indicated.

1. **Writing: Communicating with Sensitivity and Tact [LO-1]** Substitute a better phrase for each of the following:
   a. You claim that
   b. It is not our policy to
   c. You neglected to
   d. In which you assert
   e. We are sorry you are dissatisfied
   f. You failed to enclose
   g. We request that you send us
   h. Apparently you overlooked our terms
   i. We have been very patient
   j. We are at a loss to understand

2. **Writing: Demonstrating the "You" Attitude [LO-1]** Rewrite these sentences to reflect your audience's viewpoint:
   a. Your email order cannot be processed; we request that you use the order form on our website instead.
   b. We insist that you always bring your credit card to the store.
   c. We want to get rid of all our 15-inch LCD screens to make room in our warehouse for the new 19-, 23-, and 35-inch monitors. Thus, we are offering a 25 percent discount on all sales of 15-inch models this week.
   d. I am applying for the position of bookkeeper in your office. I feel my grades prove that I am bright and capable, and I think I can do a good job for you.
   e. As requested, we are sending the refund for $25.
   f. If you cared about doing a good job, you would've made the extra effort required to learn how to use the machinery properly.
   g. Your strategy presentation this morning absolutely blew me away; there's no way we can fail with all the brilliant ideas you've pulled together—I'm so glad you're running the company now!

h. Regarding your email message from September 28 regarding the slow payment of your invoice, it's important for you to realize that we've just undergone a massive upgrade of our accounts payable system and payments have been delayed for everybody, not just you.

i. I know I'm late with the asset valuation report, but I haven't been feeling well and I just haven't had the energy needed to work through the numbers yet.

j. With all the online news sources available today, I can't believe you didn't know that MyTravel and Thomas Cook were in merger talks—I mean, you don't even have to get up from your computer to learn this!

3. **Writing: Emphasizing the Positive [LO-1]** Revise these sentences to be positive rather than negative:

   a. To avoid damage to your credit rating, please remit payment within 10 days.

   b. We don't offer refunds on returned merchandise that is soiled.

   c. Because we are temporarily out of Baby Cry dolls, we won't be able to ship your order for 10 days.

   d. You failed to specify the color of the blouse that you ordered.

   e. You should have realized that waterbeds will freeze in unheated houses during winter. Therefore, our guarantee does not cover the valve damage, and you must pay the $9.50 valve-replacement fee (plus postage).

4. **Writing: Using Unbiased Language [LO-1]** Rewrite each of the following to eliminate bias:

   a. For an Indian, Maggie certainly is outgoing.

   b. He needs a wheelchair, but he doesn't let his handicap affect his job performance.

   c. A pilot must have the ability to stay calm under pressure, and then he must be trained to cope with any problem that arises.

   d. Candidate Renata Parsons, married and the mother of a teenager, will attend the debate.

   e. Senior citizen Sam Nugent is still an active salesman.

5. **Writing: Establishing Your Credibility; Microblogging Skills [LO-2], Chapter 7** Search LinkedIn for the profile of an expert in any industry or profession. Now imagine that you are going to introduce this person as a speaker at a convention. You will make an in-person introduction at the time of the speech, but you decide to introduce him or her the day before on Twitter. Write four tweets: one that introduces the expert and three that cover three key supporting points that will enhance the speaker's credibility in the minds of potential listeners. Make up any information you need to complete this assignment, then email the text of your proposed tweets to your instructor.

6. **Writing: Using Plain Language; Communication Ethics: Making Ethical Choices, [LO-3], Chapter 1** Your company has been a major employer in the local community for years, but shifts in the global marketplace have forced some changes in the company's long-term direction. In fact, the company plans to reduce local staffing by as much as 50 percent over the next 5 to 10 years, starting with a small layoff next month.

The size and timing of future layoffs have not been decided, although there is little doubt that more layoffs will happen at some point. In the first draft of a letter aimed at community leaders, you write that "this first layoff is part of a continuing series of staff reductions anticipated over the next several years." However, your boss is concerned about the vagueness and negative tone of the language and asks you to rewrite that sentence to read "this layoff is part of the company's ongoing efforts to continually align its resources with global market conditions." Do you think this suggested wording is ethical, given the company's economic influence in the community? Explain your answer in an email message to your instructor.

7. **Writing: Using Plain Language; Media Skills: Blogging [LO-3]** Download the Securities and Exchange Commission's (SEC's) *A Plain English Handbook*, from www.sec.gov/pdf/handbook.pdf. In one or two sentences, summarize what the SEC means by the phrase *plain English*. Now scan the SEC's introduction to mutual funds at www.sec.gov/investor/pubs/inwsmf.htm. Does this information follow the SEC's plain English guidelines? Cite several examples that support your assessment. Post your analysis on your class blog.

8. **Writing: Creating Effective Sentences: Media Skills: Social Networking [LO-4], Chapter 7** If you are interested in business, chances are you've had an idea or two for starting a company. If you haven't yet, go ahead and dream up an idea now. Make it something you are passionate about, something you could really throw yourself into. Now write a four-sentence summary that could appear on the Info tab on a Facebook profile. Make sure the first sentence is a solid topic sentence, and make sure the next three sentences offer relevant evidence and examples. Feel free to make up any details you need. Email your summary to your instructor or post it on your class blog.

9. **Writing: Choosing Powerful Words [LO-4]** Write a concrete phrase for each of these vague phrases:

   a. Sometime this spring

   b. A substantial savings

   c. A large number attended

   d. Increased efficiency

   e. Expanded the work area

   f. Flatten the website structure

10. **Writing: Choosing Powerful Words [LO-4]** List terms that are stronger than the following:

   a. Ran after

   b. Seasonal ups and downs

   c. Bright

   d. Suddenly rises

   e. Moves forward

11. **Writing: Choosing Powerful Words [LO-4]** As you rewrite these sentences, replace the clichés and buzzwords with plain language (for any terms you don't recognize, you can find definitions online):

   a. Being a jack-of-all-trades, Dave worked well in his new general manager job.

   b. Moving Leslie into the accounting department, where she was literally a fish out of water, was like putting a square peg into a round hole, if you get my drift.

c. My only takeaway from the offsite was that Laird threw his entire department under the bus for missing the deadline.

d. I'd love to help with that project, but I'm bandwidth-constrained.

e. The board green-lighted our initiative to repurpose our consumer products for the commercial space.

12. **Writing: Choosing Powerful Words [LO-4]** Suggest short, simple words to replace each of the following:

   a. Inaugurate

   b. Terminate

   c. Utilize

   d. Anticipate

   e. Assistance

   f. Endeavor

   g. Ascertain

   h. Procure

   i. Consummate

   j. Advise

   k. Alteration

   l. Forwarded

   m. Fabricate

   n. Nevertheless

   o. Substantial

13. **Writing: Choosing Powerful Words [LO-4]** Write up-to-date, less-stuffy versions of these phrases; write *none* if you think there is no appropriate substitute or "delete" if the phrase should simply be deleted:

   a. As per your instructions

   b. Attached herewith

   c. In lieu of

   d. In reply I wish to state

   e. Please be advised that

14. **Writing: Choosing Powerful Words; Communication Ethics: Making Ethical Choices [LO-4], Chapter 1** Under what circumstances would you consider the use of terms that are high in connotative meaning to be ethical? When would you consider it to be unethical? Explain your reasoning.

15. **Writing: Creating Effective Sentences [LO-5]** Rewrite each sentence so that it is active rather than passive:

   a. The raw data are entered into the customer relationship management system by the sales representative each Friday.

   b. High profits are publicized by management.

   c. The policies announced in the directive were implemented by the staff.

   d. Our computers are serviced by the Santee Company.

   e. The employees were represented by Janet Hogan.

16. **Writing: Crafting Unified, Coherent Paragraphs; Media Skills: Email [LO-6], Chapter 7** Suppose that end-of-term frustrations have produced this email message to Professor Anne Brewer from a student who believes he should have received a B in his accounting class. If this message were re-cast into three or four clear sentences, the teacher might be more receptive to the student's argument. Rewrite the message to show how you would improve it:

I think that I was unfairly awarded a C in your accounting class this term, and I am asking you to change the grade to a B. It was a difficult term. I don't get any money from home, and I have to work mornings at the Pancake House (as a cook), so I had to rush to make your class, and those two times that I missed class were because they wouldn't let me off work because of special events at the Pancake House (unlike some other students who just take off when they choose). On the midterm examination, I originally got a 75 percent, but you said in class that there were two different ways to answer the third question and that you would change the grades of students who used the "optimal cost" method and had been counted off 6 points for doing this. I don't think that you took this into account, because I got 80 percent on the final, which is clearly a B. Anyway, whatever you decide, I just want to tell you that I really enjoyed this class, and I thank you for making accounting so interesting.

17. **Writing: Crafting Unified, Coherent Paragraphs [LO-6]** In the following paragraph, identify the topic sentence and the related sentences (those that support the idea of the topic sentence):

Find My Friends is a great way to share locations with friends and family. Those who share their locations with you appear on a map so you can quickly see where they are and what they're up to. And with iOS 6, you can get location-based alerts—like when your kids leave school or arrive home. Find My Friends can also notify others about your location, so you can stay connected or keep track of the ones you love.[19]

Now add a topic sentence to this paragraph:

Our analysis of the customer experience should start before golfers even drive through the front gate here at Glencoe Meadows; it should start when they phone in or log onto our website to reserve tee times. When they do arrive, the first few stages in the process are also vital: the condition of the grounds leading up to the club house, the reception they receive when they drop off their clubs, and the ease of parking. From that point, how well are we doing with check-in at the pro shop, openings at the driving range, and timely scheduling at the first tee? Then there's everything associated with playing the course itself and returning to the club house at the end of the round.

18. **Writing: Crafting Unified, Coherent Paragraphs; Collaboration: Evaluating the Work of Others [LO-6], Chapter 6** Working with four other students, divide the following five topics among yourselves and each write one paragraph on your selected topic. Be sure each student uses a different technique when writing his or her paragraph: One student should use the illustration technique, one the comparison or contrast technique, one a discussion of cause and effect, one the classification technique, and one a discussion of problem and solution. Then exchange paragraphs within the team and pick out the main idea and general purpose of the paragraph one of your teammates wrote. Was everyone able to correctly identify the main idea and purpose? If not, suggest how the paragraph could be rewritten for clarity.

   a. Types of digital cameras (or dogs or automobiles) available for sale

b. Advantages and disadvantages of eating at fast-food restaurants

c. Finding that first full-time job

d. Good qualities of my car (or house, or apartment, or neighborhood)

e. How to make a dessert (or barbecue a steak or make coffee)

19. **Writing: Using Transitions [LO-6]** Add transitional elements to the following sentences to improve the flow of ideas. (*Note:* You may need to eliminate or add some words to smooth out your sentences.)

a. Steve Case saw infinite possibilities in online business. Steve Case was determined to turn his vision into reality. The techies scoffed at his strategy of building a simple Internet service for ordinary people. Case doggedly pursued his dream. He analyzed other online services. He assessed the needs of his customers. He responded to their desires for an easier way to access information over the Internet. In 1992, Steve Case named his company America Online (AOL). Critics predicted the company's demise. By the end of the century, AOL was a profitable powerhouse. An ill-fated merger with Time Warner was a financial disaster and led to Case's ouster from the company.

b. Facing some of the toughest competitors in the world, Harley-Davidson had to make some changes. The company introduced new products. Harley's management team set out to rebuild the company's production process. New products were coming to market and the company was turning a profit. Harley's quality standards were not on par with those of its foreign competitors. Harley's costs were still among the highest in the industry. Harley made a U-turn and restructured the company's organizational structure. Harley's efforts have paid off.

c. Whether you're indulging in a doughnut in New York or California, Krispy Kreme wants you to enjoy the same delicious taste with every bite. The company maintains consistent product quality by carefully controlling every step of the production process. Krispy Kreme tests all raw ingredients against established quality standards. Every delivery of wheat flour is sampled and measured for its moisture content and protein levels. Krispy Kreme blends the ingredients. Krispy Kreme tests the doughnut mix for quality. Krispy Kreme delivers the mix to its stores. Financial critics are not as kind to

the company as food critics have been. Allegations of improper financial reporting have left the company's future in doubt.

20. **Writing: Using Technology to Compose Messages; Designing for Readability [LO-7], Chapter 6** Team up with another student and choose some form of document or presentation software that allows you to create templates or another form of "master design." (Microsoft Word, Microsoft PowerPoint, Google Docs, or their equivalents are good choices for this assignment.) Your task is to design a report template for a company that you either know about firsthand or whose general communication style you are able to analyze from its website and other materials. You can start your template from scratch or adapt an existing template, but if you adapt another template, make sure the final design is largely your own. Chapter 6 offers information on document design.

## Expand Your Skills

**Critique the Professionals**

Locate an example of professional communication from a reputable online source. Choose a paragraph that has at least three sentences. Evaluate the effectiveness of this paragraph at three levels, starting with the paragraph structure. Is the paragraph unified and cohesive? Does it have a clear topic sentence and sufficient support to clarify and expand on that topic? Second, evaluate each sentence. Are the sentences easy to read and easy to understand? Did the writer vary the types and lengths of sentences to produce a smooth flow and rhythm? Is the most important idea presented prominently in each sentence? Third, evaluate at least six word choices. Did the writer use these words correctly and effectively? Using whatever medium your instructor requests, write a brief analysis of the piece (no more than one page), citing specific elements from the piece and support from the chapter.

**Sharpening Your Career Skills Online**

Bovée and Thill's Business Communication Web Search, at http://businesscommunicationblog.com/websearch is a unique research tool designed specifically for business communication research. Use the Web Search function to find a website, video, PDF document, or PowerPoint presentation that offers advice on writing effective sentences. Write a brief email message to your instructor, describing the item that you found and summarizing the career skills information you learned from it.

## MyBCommLab

Go to **mybcommlab.com** for Auto-graded writing questions as well as the following Assisted-graded writing questions:

**5-1.** How does using bias-free language help communicators establish a good relationship with their audiences? [LO-1]

**5-2.** What steps can you take to make abstract concepts such as *opportunity* feel more concrete in your messages? [LO-4]

**5-3.** Mybcommlab Only—comprehensive writing assignment for this chapter.

# Endnotes

1. Creative Commons website, accessed 18 January 2013, www .creativecommons.org; Kenji Hall, "Online Sharing with Creative Commons," *BusinessWeek*, 15 August 2008, www.businessweek.com; Ariana Eunjung Cha, "Creative Commons Is Rewriting Rules of Copyright," *Washington Post*, 15 March 2005, www.washingtonpost .com; Steven Levy, "Lawrence Lessig's Supreme Showdown," *Wired*, October 2002, www.wired.com; "Happy Birthday: We'll Sue," Snopes .com, accessed 3 August 2005, www.snopes.com.

2. Annette N. Shelby and N. Lamar Reinsch, Jr., "Positive Emphasis and You Attitude: An Empirical Study," *Journal of Business Communication* 32, no. 4 (1995): 303–322.

3. Quinn Warnick, "A Close Textual Analysis of Corporate Layoff Memos," *Business Communication Quarterly* 73, no. 3 (September 2010): 322–326.

4. Sherryl Kleinman, "Why Sexist Language Matters," *Qualitative Sociology* 25, no. 2 (Summer 2002): 299–304.

5. Judy E. Pickens, "Terms of Equality: A Guide to Bias-Free Language," *Personnel Journal*, August 1985, 24.

6. Xerox website, accessed 17 May 2012, www.xerox.com; ADM website, accessed 17 May 2012, www.adm.com.

7. Lisa Taylor, "Communicating About People with Disabilities: Does the Language We Use Make a Difference?" *Bulletin of the Association for Business Communication* 53, no. 3 (September 1990): 65–67.

8. Susan Benjamin, *Words at Work* (Reading, Mass.: Addison Wesley, 1997), 136–137.

9. Plain English Campaign website, accessed 28 June 2010, www .plainenglish.co.uk.

10. Plain Language website; Irene Etzkorn, "Amazingly Simple Stuff," presentation 7 November 2008, www.slideshare.net.

11. Creative Commons website, accessed 16 January 2011, www .creativecommons.org.

12. Susan Jaderstrom and Joanne Miller, "Active Writing," *Office Pro*, November/December 2003, 29.

13. Mary Munter, *Guide to Managerial Communication*, 7th ed. (Upper Saddle River, N.J.: Pearson Prentice Hall, 2006), 41.

14. Portions of this section are adapted from Courtland L. Bovée, *Techniques of Writing Business Letters, Memos, and Reports* (Sherman Oaks, Calif.: Banner Books International, 1978), 13–90.

15. Catherine Quinn, "Lose the Office Jargon; It May Sunset Your Career," *The Age* (Australia), 1 September 2007, www.theage.com.au.

16. Robert Hartwell Fiske, *The Dimwit's Dictionary* (Oak Park, Ill.: Marion Street Press, 2002), 16–20.

17. Beverly Ballaro and Christina Bielaszka-DuVernay, "Building a Bridge over the River Boredom," *Harvard Management Communication Letter*, Winter 2005, 3–5.

18. Food Allergy Initiative website, accessed 5 September 2008, www.foodallergyinitiative.org; Diana Keough, "Snacks That Can Kill; Schools Take Steps to Protect Kids Who Have Severe Allergies to Nuts," *Plain Dealer*, 15 July 2003, E1; "Dawdling over Food Labels," *New York Times*, 2 June 2003, A16; Sheila McNulty, "A Matter of Life and Death," *Financial Times*, 10 September 2003, 14.

19. Apple website, accessed 7 March 2013, www.apple.com.

## LEARNING OBJECTIVES

After studying this chapter, you will be able to

**1** Discuss the value of careful revision and describe the tasks involved in evaluating your first drafts and the work of other writers.

**2** List four techniques you can use to improve the readability of your messages.

**3** Describe eight steps you can take to improve the clarity of your writing and give four tips on making your writing more concise.

**4** List four principles of effective design and explain the role of major design elements in document readability.

**5** Explain the importance of proofreading and give eight tips for successful proofreading.

**6** Discuss the most important issues to consider when distributing your messages.

---

## MyBCommLab®

⭐ **Improve Your Grade!** Over 10 million students improved their results using the Pearson MyLabs. Visit **mybcommlab.com** for simulations, tutorials, and end-of-chapter problems.

---

COMMUNICATION CLOSE-UP AT

# Jefferson Rabb
# Web Design www.jeffersonrabb.com

As a composer, game designer, photographer, programmer, and website developer, Jefferson Rabb epitomizes the "multi" in multimedia. For all the technical and creative skills he brings, however, Rabb's work never loses sight of audiences and their desire to be informed and entertained when they visit a website.

Rabb's career history includes stints at MTV.com and Sephora.com, but most of his current work as an independent designer involves projects in the publishing industry. The best-selling authors he has helped bring to the web include Dan Brown, Gary Shteyngart, Jhumpa Lahiri, Laura Hillenbrand, and Anita Shreve.

For every project, Rabb starts his design work with an in-depth analysis of the audience. The questions he asks about site visitors include their familiarity with the author's work, the range of their reading interests, and their general demographics. He

Kathy deWitt/Alamy

Authors such as Monica Ali still rely on personal contact with readers to promote books, but websites—particularly interactive, multimedia websites—have become an increasingly important element in book promotion.

also wants to know whether a site needs to serve book reviewers, bookstore buyers, and other industry professionals in addition to readers.

With some insight into who the target visitors are, Rabb puts himself in their place and imagines the knowledge and experiences they hope to gain during their visits. These needs can vary from biographical information about the author to multimedia exhibits (such as video interviews and photographs depicting locations mentioned in a book) to complex games that extend a novel's storylines. Rabb makes a point to find compelling visual connections between a book and a website, too, such as basing the design of the site for Shteyngart's *Super Sad True Love Story* on the portable communication device featured in the story. Completing the multimedia experience, he often composes music to create a specific mood that reflects the themes of a book.[1]

Your business communication efforts may not always be as elaborate as Rabb's, but you can always apply his strategy of combining methodical analysis with creative design and implementation. This chapter addresses the third step in the three-step writing process, completing your messages—which includes the important tasks of revising, producing, proofreading, and distributing your messages.

# Revising Your Message: Evaluating the First Draft

**1** **LEARNING OBJECTIVE**
Discuss the value of careful revision and describe the tasks involved in evaluating your first drafts and the work of other writers.

Successful communicators like Jefferson Rabb (profiled in the chapter-opening Communication Close-Up) recognize that the first draft is rarely as tight, clear, and compelling as it needs to be. Careful revision can mean the difference between a rambling, unfocused message and a lively, direct message that gets results. The third step of the three-step writing process involves four key tasks: revising your message to achieve optimum quality and then producing, proofreading, and distributing it.

The time required for revision can vary from just a moment or two for a simple message to many hours or even days for a complex report or multimedia document.

The revision task can vary somewhat, depending on the medium and the nature of your message. For informal messages to internal audiences, particularly when using instant messaging, text messaging, email, or blogging, the revision process is often as simple as quickly looking over your message to correct any mistakes before sending or posting it. However, don't fall into the common trap of thinking that you don't need to worry about grammar, spelling, clarity, and other fundamentals of good writing when you use such media. These qualities can be *especially* important in electronic media, particularly if these messages are the only contact your audience has with you. Audiences are likely to equate the quality of your writing with the quality of your thinking. Poor-quality messages create an impression of poor-quality thinking and can cause confusion, frustration, and costly delays.

In any medium, readers tend to equate the quality of your writing with the quality of your thinking.

For longer documents, try to put aside your draft for a day or two before you begin the revision process.

With more complex messages, try to put your draft aside for a day or two before you begin the revision process so that you can approach the material with a fresh eye. Then start with the "big picture," making sure that the document accomplishes your overall goals before moving to finer points, such as readability, clarity, and conciseness. Compare the letters in Figures 6.1 and 6.2 on the next two pages for an example of how careful revision improves a customer letter.

## EVALUATING YOUR CONTENT, ORGANIZATION, STYLE, AND TONE

When you begin the revision process, focus your attention on content, organization, style, and tone. To evaluate the content of your message, answer these questions:

- Is the information accurate?
- Is the information relevant to the audience?
- Is there enough information to satisfy the readers' needs?
- Is there a good balance between general information (giving readers enough background information to appreciate the message) and specific information (giving readers the details they need to understand the message)?

Delauny Music
56 Commerce Circle • Davenport, IA 52806
(563) 555-4001 • delaunymusic.net

June 21, 2012

← ————————— Need 7 blank lines here

Ms. Claudia Banks
122 River Heights Drive
Bettendorf, IA 52722

Dear Ms. Banks:

On behalf of everyone at Delauny Music, it is my pleasure to thank you for your recent purchase of a Yamaha CG1 grand piano. The Cg1 carries more than a century of Yamaha's heritage in design and production of world-class musical instruments and ~~you can bet it~~ will give you many years of playing and listening pleasure. Our commitment to your satisfaction doesn't stop with your purchase, however. ~~Much to the contrary, it continues for as long as you own your piano, which we hope, of course, is for as long as you live.~~ As a vital first step, please remember to call us ~~your local Yamaha dealer,~~ sometime within three to eight months after your piano was delivered to take advantage of the ~~free~~ Yamaha Servicebond℠ Assurance Program. This free service program includes a thorough evaluation and ~~adjusting~~ *adjustment* of the instrument after you've had some time to play your piano and your piano has had time to adapt to its environment.

In addition to this ~~vital~~ *important* service appointment, a regular program of tuning is ~~absolutely~~ essential to ensure ~~its~~ *your piano's* impeccable performance. Our piano specialists recommend four tunings during the first year and two tunings every year thereafter ~~that.~~ As your local Yamaha *dealer,* we are ideally positioned to provide you with optimum service for both regular tuning and any maintenance or repair needs you may have ~~over the years.~~

~~All of us at Delauny Music~~ *We* thank you for your recent purchase ~~and~~ wish you ~~many~~ many years of satisfaction with your new Yamaha CG1 grand piano.

*Sincerely,*
~~Respectfully yours in beautiful music,~~

Madeline Delauny
Owner

tjr

**The two circled sentences say essentially the same thing, so this edit combines them into one sentence.**

**Changing *adjusting* to *adjustment* makes it parallel with *evaluation*.**

**Replacing *its* with *your piano's* avoids any confusion about which noun that *it* is supposed to replace.**

**The simple complimentary close replaces a close that was stylistically over the top.**

**The phrase *you can bet* is too informal for this message.**

**The sentence beginning with "Much to the contrary . . ." is awkward and unnecessary.**

**This edit inserts a missing word (*dealer*).**

**This group of edits removes unnecessary words in several places.**

---

### Common Proofreading Symbols (see page 593 for more)

|  |  |
| --- | --- |
| ~~strikethrough~~ | Delete text |
| ℓ | Delete individual character or a circled block of text |
| ∧ | Insert text (text to insert is written above) |
| ⊙ | Insert period |
| ⋏ | Insert comma |
| ⌐ | Start new line |
| ¶ | Start new paragraph |
| ≡ | Capitalize |

---

**Figure 6.1  Improving a Customer Letter Through Careful Revision**
Careful revision makes this draft shorter, clearer, and more focused. These *proofreading symbols* (see Appendix C) are still widely used when printed documents are edited and revised. However, in many instances you'll use the electronic markup features in your word processor or other software, as shown later in this chapter, on page 157.

Delauny Music
56 Commerce Circle • Davenport, IA 52806
(563) 555-4001 • delaunymusic.net

June 21, 2012

Ms. Claudia Banks
122 River Heights Drive
Bettendorf, IA 52722

Dear Ms. Banks:

Thank you for your recent purchase. We wish you many years of satisfaction with your new Yamaha CG1 grand piano. The CG1 carries more than a century of Yamaha's heritage in design and production of world-class musical instruments and will give you many years of playing and listening pleasure.

Our commitment to your satisfaction doesn't stop with your purchase, however. As a vital first step, please remember to call us sometime within three to eight months after your piano was delivered to take advantage of the Yamaha Servicebond$^{SM}$ Assurance Program. This free service program includes a thorough evaluation and adjustment of the instrument after you've had some time to play your piano and your piano has had time to adapt to its environment.

In addition to this important service appointment, a regular program of tuning is essential to ensure your piano's impeccable performance. Our piano specialists recommend four tunings during the first year and two tunings every year thereafter. As your local Yamaha dealer, we are ideally positioned to provide you with optimum service for both regular tuning and any maintenance or repair needs you may have.

Sincerely,

*Madeline Delauny*

Madeline Delauny
Owner

tjr

*The letter is now properly formatted.*

*The content is now organized in three coherent paragraphs, each with a distinct message.*

*The tone is friendly and engaging without being flowery.*

**Figure 6.2   Revised Customer Letter**
This revised letter provides the requested information more clearly, in a more organized fashion, with a friendlier style, and with precise mechanics.

When you are satisfied with the content of your message, you can review its organization. Answer another set of questions:

- Are all the points covered in the most logical order?
- Do the most important ideas receive the most space, and are they placed in the most prominent positions?
- Would the message be more convincing if it were arranged in a different sequence?
- Are any points repeated unnecessarily?
- Are details grouped together logically, or are some still scattered through the document?

Next, consider whether you have achieved the right tone for your audience. Is your writing formal enough to meet the audience's expectations without being too formal or academic? Is it too casual for a serious subject?

Spend a few extra moments on the beginning and end of your message; these sections usually have the greatest impact on the audience. Be sure that the opening is relevant,

The beginning and end of a message usually have the greatest impact on your readers, so make sure they are clear, concise, and compelling.

interesting, and geared to the reader's probable reaction. In longer messages, ensure that the first few paragraphs establish the subject, purpose, and organization of the material. Review the conclusion to be sure that it summarizes the main idea and leaves the audience with a positive impression.

## EVALUATING, EDITING, AND REVISING THE WORK OF OTHERS

At many points in your career, you will be asked to evaluate, edit, or revise the work of others. Whether you're suggesting improvements or actually making the improvements yourself (as you might on a wiki site, for example), you can make a contribution by using all the skills you are learning in Chapters 4 through 6.

Before you dive into someone else's work, recognize the dual responsibility that doing so entails. First, unless you've been specifically asked to rewrite something in your own style or to change the emphasis of the message, remember that your job is to help the other writer succeed at his or her task, not to impose your writing style or pursue your own agenda. In other words, make sure your input focuses on making the piece more effective, not on making it more like something you would've written. Second, make sure you understand the writer's intent before you begin suggesting or making changes. If you try to edit or revise without knowing what the writer hoped to accomplish, you run the risk of making the piece less effective, not more. With those thoughts in mind, answer the following questions as you evaluate someone else's writing:

*Before you evaluate and revise someone else's writing, make sure you understand the writer's intent with the message.*

- What is the purpose of this document or message?
- Who is the target audience?
- What information does the audience need?
- Does the document provide this information in a well-organized way?
- Does the writing demonstrate the "you" attitude toward the audience?
- Is the tone of the writing appropriate for the audience?
- Can the readability be improved?
- Is the writing clear? If not, how can it be improved?
- Is the writing as concise as it could be?
- Does the design support the intended message?

You can read more about using these skills in the context of wiki writing in Chapter 8.

# Revising to Improve Readability

After confirming the content, organization, style, and tone of your message, make a second pass to improve *readability*. Most professionals are inundated with more reading material than they can ever hope to consume, and they'll appreciate your efforts to make your documents easier to read. You'll benefit from this effort, too: If you earn a reputation for creating well-crafted documents that respect the audience's time, people will pay more attention to your work.

**2  LEARNING OBJECTIVE**
List four techniques you can use to improve the readability of your messages.

You may be familiar with one of the many indexes that have been developed over the years in an attempt to measure readability. For example, the Flesch-Kincaid Grade Level score computes reading difficulty relative to grade-level achievement, with, for instance, a score of 10 suggesting that a document can be read and understood by the average 10th grader. Most business documents score in the 8–11 range. Technical documents often score in the 12–14 range. A similar scoring system, the Flesch Reading Ease score, ranks documents on a 100-point scale; the higher the score, the easier the document is to read. If these measurements aren't built into your word processing software, you can find a number of calculators for various indexes at websites such as www.editcentral.com.

Readability indexes offer a useful reference point, but they are limited by what they are able to measure: word length, number of syllables, sentence length, and paragraph length. They can't measure any of the other factors that affect readability, such as document design, the "you" attitude, clear sentence structure, smooth transitions, and proper word usage. Compare these two paragraphs:

> Readability indexes offer a useful reference point, but they are all limited by what they are able to measure: word length, number of syllables, sentence length, and paragraph length. They can't measure any of the other factors that affect readability, from "you" orientation to writing clarity to document design.
>
> Readability indexes can help. But they don't measure everything. They don't measure whether your writing clarity is good. They don't measure whether your document design is good or not. Reading indexes are based on word length, syllables, sentences, and paragraphs.

Readability formulas can't measure everything that affects readability, so don't rely on them as a test of true readability.

The second paragraph scores much better on both grade level and reading ease, but it is choppy, unsophisticated, and poorly organized. As a general rule, then, don't assume that a piece of text is readable if it scores well on a readability index—or that it is difficult to read if it doesn't score well.

Beyond using shorter words and simpler sentences, you can improve the readability of a message by making the document interesting and easy to skim. Most business audiences—particularly influential senior managers—tend to skim documents, looking for key ideas, conclusions, and recommendations. If they determine that a document contains valuable information or requires a response, they will read it more carefully when time permits. Four techniques will make your message easier to read and easier to skim: varying sentence length, using shorter paragraphs, using lists and bullets instead of narrative, and adding effective headings and subheadings.

Use effective headings, bullet lists, and other features to help your readers skim through documents quickly to find the major ideas, conclusions, and recommendations.

## VARYING YOUR SENTENCE LENGTH

To keep readers' interest, use a variety of long, medium, and short sentences.

Varying the length of your sentences is a creative way to make your messages interesting and readable. By choosing words and sentence structure with care, you can create a rhythm that emphasizes important points, enlivens your writing style, and makes information more appealing to your reader. For example, a short sentence that highlights a conclusion at the end of a substantial paragraph of evidence makes your key message stand out. Try for a mixture of sentences that are short (up to 15 words or so), medium (15–25 words), and long (more than 25 words).

Each sentence length has its advantages. Short sentences can be processed quickly and are easier for nonnative speakers and translators to interpret. Medium-length sentences are useful for showing the relationships among ideas. Long sentences are often the best for conveying complex ideas, listing multiple related points, or summarizing or previewing information.

Of course, each sentence length also has disadvantages. Too many short sentences in a row can make your writing choppy. Medium sentences can lack the punch of short sentences and the informative power of longer sentences. Long sentences can be difficult to understand because they contain more information and usually have a more complicated structure. Because readers can absorb only a few words per glance, longer sentences are also more difficult to skim. By choosing the best sentence length for each communication need and remembering to mix sentence lengths for variety, you'll get your points across while keeping your messages lively and interesting.

## KEEPING YOUR PARAGRAPHS SHORT

Long paragraphs are visually intimidating and can be difficult to read.

Large blocks of text can be visually daunting, particularly on screen, so the optimum paragraph length is short to medium in most cases. Unless you break up your thoughts somehow, you'll end up with lengthy paragraphs that are guaranteed to intimidate even the most dedicated reader. Short paragraphs, generally 100 words or fewer (this paragraph has 84 words), are easier to read than long ones, and they make your writing look inviting. You can also emphasize ideas by isolating them in short, forceful paragraphs.

However, don't go overboard with short paragraphs. In particular, be careful to use one-sentence paragraphs only occasionally and only for emphasis. Also, if you need to divide a subject into several pieces to keep paragraphs short, be sure to help your readers keep the ideas connected by guiding them with plenty of transitional elements.

## USING LISTS TO CLARIFY AND EMPHASIZE

An effective alternative to using conventional sentences is to set off important ideas in a list— a series of words, names, or other items. Lists can show the sequence of your ideas, heighten their impact visually, and increase the likelihood that a reader will find key points. In addition, lists help simplify complex subjects, highlight main points, break up a page or screen visually, ease the skimming process for busy readers, and give readers a breather. Compare these two treatments of the same information:

*Lists are effective tools for highlighting and simplifying material.*

**Narrative**

Owning your own business has many potential advantages. One is the opportunity to pursue your own personal passion. Another advantage is the satisfaction of working for yourself. As a sole proprietor, you also have the advantage of privacy because you do not have to reveal your financial information or plans to anyone.

**List**

Owning your own business has three advantages:

- Opportunity to pursue personal passion
- Satisfaction of working for yourself
- Financial privacy

You can separate list items with numbers, letters, or bullets (a general term for any kind of graphical element that precedes each item). Bullets are generally preferred over numbers, unless the list is in some logical sequence or ranking or you need to refer to specific list items elsewhere in the document. For example, the following three steps need to be performed in the order indicated, and the numbers make that clear:

1. Find out how many employees would like on-site day-care facilities.
2. Determine how much space the day-care center would require.
3. Estimate the cost of converting a conference room for the on-site facility.

Lists are easier to locate and read if the entire numbered or bulleted section is set off by a blank line before and after, as the preceding examples demonstrate. Furthermore, make sure to introduce lists clearly so that people know what they're about to read. One way to introduce lists is to make them a part of the introductory sentence:

The board of directors met to discuss the revised annual budget. To keep expenses in line with declining sales, the directors voted to

- Cut everyone's salary by 10 percent
- Close the employee cafeteria
- Reduce travel expenses

Another way to introduce a list is to precede it with a complete introductory sentence, followed by a colon:

The decline in company profit is attributable to four factors:

- Slower holiday sales
- Increased transportation and fuel costs
- Higher employee wages
- Slower inventory turnover

| TABLE 6.1 | Achieving Parallelism |
| --- | --- |
| **Method** | **Example** |
| Parallel words | The letter was approved by Clausen, Whittaker, Merlin, and Carlucci. |
| Parallel phrases | We are gaining market share in supermarkets, in department stores, and in specialty stores. |
| Parallel clauses | I'd like to discuss the issue after Vicki gives her presentation but before Marvin shows his slides. |
| Parallel sentences | In 2012 we exported 30 percent of our production. In 2013 we exported 50 percent. |

Regardless of the format you choose, the items in a list should be parallel; that is, they should all use the same grammatical pattern. For example, if one list item begins with a verb, every item should begin with a verb. If one item is a noun phrase, every one should be a noun phrase:

**Nonparallel List Items**
**(a mix of verb and noun phrases)**

- Improve our bottom line
- Identification of new foreign markets for our products
- Global market strategies
- Issues regarding pricing and packaging size

**Parallel List Items**
**(all verb phrases)**

- Improving our bottom line
- Identifying new foreign markets for our products
- Developing our global market strategies
- Resolving pricing and packaging issues

Parallel forms are easier to read and skim. You can create parallelism by repeating the pattern in words, phrases, clauses, or entire sentences (see Table 6.1).

## ADDING HEADINGS AND SUBHEADINGS

Use headings and subheadings to show the organization of your material, draw the reader's attention to key points, and show connections between ideas.

A **heading** is a brief title that tells readers about the content of the section that follows. **Subheadings** are subordinate to headings, indicating subsections with a major section. Headings and subheadings serve these important functions:

- **Organization.** Headings show your reader at a glance how the document is organized. They act as labels to group related paragraphs and organize lengthy material into shorter sections.
- **Attention.** Informative, inviting, and in some cases intriguing headings grab the reader's attention, make the text easier to read, and help the reader find the parts he or she needs to read—or skip.
- **Connection.** Using headings and subheadings together helps readers see the relationship between main ideas and subordinate ones so that they can understand your message more easily. Moreover, headings and subheadings visually indicate shifts from one idea to the next.

Informative headings are generally more helpful than descriptive ones.

Headings and subheadings fall into two categories. **Descriptive headings**, such as "Cost Considerations," identify a topic but do little more. **Informative headings**, such as "Redesigning Material Flow to Cut Production Costs," guide readers to think in a certain way about the topic. They are also helpful in guiding your work as a writer, especially if cast as questions you plan to address in your document. Well-written informative headings are self-contained, which means readers can read just the headings and subheadings and understand them without reading the rest of the document. For example, "Introduction" conveys little information, whereas the heading "Staffing Shortages Cost the Company $150,000 Last Year" provides a key piece of information and captures the reader's attention. Whatever types of headings you choose, keep them brief and use parallel construction throughout the document.

# Editing for Clarity and Conciseness

**3** LEARNING OBJECTIVE
Describe eight steps you can take to improve the clarity of your writing and give four tips on making your writing more concise.

After you've reviewed and revised your message for readability, your next step is to make sure your message is as clear and as concise as possible.

## EDITING FOR CLARITY

Make sure every sentence conveys the message you intend and that readers can extract that meaning without needing to read it more than once. To ensure clarity, look closely at your paragraph organization, sentence structure, and word choices. Can readers make sense of the related sentences in a paragraph? Is the meaning of each sentence easy to grasp? Is each word clear and unambiguous (meaning it doesn't have any risk of being interpreted in more than one way)?

Clarity is essential to getting your message across accurately and efficiently.

See Table 6.2 for examples of the following tips:

- **Break up overly long sentences.** If you find yourself stuck in a long sentence, you're probably trying to make the sentence do more than it can reasonably do, such as expressing

## TABLE 6.2 | Revising for Clarity

| Issues to Review | Ineffective | Effective |
|---|---|---|
| **Overly Long Sentences** | | |
| Taking compound sentences too far | The magazine will be published January 1, and I'd better meet the deadline if I want my article included because we want the article to appear before the trade show. | The magazine will be published January 1. I'd better meet the deadline because we want the article to appear before the trade show. |
| **Hedging Sentences** | | |
| Over-qualifying sentences | I believe that Mr. Johnson's employment record seems to show that he may be capable of handling the position. | Mr. Johnson's employment record shows that he is capable of handling the position. |
| **Unparallel Sentences** | | |
| Using dissimilar construction for similar ideas | Mr. Simms had been drenched with rain, bombarded with telephone calls, and his boss shouted at him. | Mr. Sims had been drenched with rain, bombarded with telephone calls, and shouted at by his boss. |
| | To waste time and missing deadlines are bad habits. | Wasting time and missing deadlines are bad habits. |
| **Dangling Modifiers** | | |
| Placing modifiers close to the wrong nouns and verbs | Walking to the office, a red sports car passed her. [suggests that the car was walking to the office] | A red sports car passed her while she was walking to the office. |
| | Reduced by 25 percent, Europe had its lowest semiconductor output in a decade. [suggests that Europe shrank by 25 percent] | Europe reduced semiconductor output by 25 percent, its lowest output in a decade. |
| **Long Noun Sequences** | | |
| Stringing too many nouns together | The window sash installation company will give us an estimate on Friday. | The company that installs window sashes will give us an estimate on Friday. |
| **Camouflaged Verbs** | | |
| Changing verbs into nouns | The manager undertook implementation of the rules. Verification of the shipments occurs weekly. reach a conclusion about give consideration to | The manager implemented the rules. We verify shipment weekly. conclude consider |
| **Sentence Structure** | | |
| Separating subject and predicate | A 10% decline in market share, which resulted from quality problems and an aggressive sales campaign by Armitage, the market leader in the Northeast, was the major problem in 2010. | The major problem in 2010 was a 10% loss of market share, which resulted from quality problems and an aggressive sales campaign by Armitage, the market leader in the Northeast. |
| Separating adjectives, adverbs, or prepositional phrases from the words they modify | Our antique desk lends an air of strength and substance with thick legs and large drawers. | With its thick legs and large drawers, our antique desk lends an air of strength and substance. |
| **Awkward References** | | |
| | The Law Office and the Accounting Office distribute computer supplies for legal secretaries and beginning accountants, respectively. | The Law Office distributes computer supplies for legal secretaries; the Accounting Office distributes those for beginning accountants. |

two dissimilar thoughts or peppering the reader with too many pieces of supporting evidence at once. (Did you notice how difficult this long sentence was to read?)

*Hedging*, or qualifying your statements, is sometimes necessary, but doing it too often undermines your credibility.

- **Rewrite hedging sentences.** *Hedging* means pulling back from making a confident, definitive statement about a topic. Granted, sometimes you have to write *may* or *seems* to avoid stating a judgment or prediction as a fact. However, when you hedge too often or without good reason, you come across as being unsure of what you're saying.
- **Impose parallelism.** When you have two or more similar ideas to express, make them parallel by using the same grammatical construction. Parallelism shows that the ideas are related, of similar importance, and on the same level of generality.
- **Correct dangling modifiers.** Sometimes a modifier is not just an adjective or an adverb but an entire phrase modifying a noun or a verb. Be careful not to leave this type of modifier *dangling*, with no connection to the subject of the sentence.
- **Reword long noun sequences.** When multiple nouns are strung together as modifiers, the resulting sentence can be hard to read. See if a single well-chosen word will do the job. If the nouns are all necessary, consider moving one or more to a modifying phrase, as shown in Table 6.2.

Camouflaged verbs are verbs that have been changed into nouns; they often increase the length of a sentence without adding any value.

- **Replace camouflaged verbs.** Watch for words that end in *-ion, -tion, -ing, -ment, -ant, -ent, -ence, -ance,* and *-ency.* These endings often change verbs into nouns and adjectives, requiring you to add a verb to get your point across.

Keep the subject and predicate as close together as possible, and keep modifiers close to the words they modify.

- **Clarify sentence structure.** Keep the subject and predicate of a sentence as close together as possible. When the subject and predicate are far apart, readers may need to read the sentence twice to figure out who did what. Similarly, adjectives, adverbs, and prepositional phrases usually make the most sense when they're placed as close as possible to the words they modify.

### COMMUNICATION MISCUES

## Missing the Message with Prescription Medications

Few messages in life are as important as the instructions for prescription medications. Yet, according to the American Academy of Pediatrics, nearly half of all parents fail to correctly follow the information contained on the labels of medications prescribed for their children. Errors also abound among elderly patients, who often need to take multiple medications every day. Blaming the parents and patients for these errors may be tempting, but evidence suggests that the labels themselves are responsible for many mistakes.

Experts cite such communication problems as confusing terminology, information overload, and poor prioritization—emphasizing nonessential information such as the name of the pharmacy at the expense of truly critical information, such as the correct dosage, drug interaction warnings, or even the name of the medication itself. The situation can get even worse in households where two or more people have prescriptions, creating the possibility of patients accidentally taking the wrong medication. Moreover, the information now included with many medications is split among the label on the bottle, the box the bottle comes in, and a government-mandated printed insert. Ironically, those inserts are meant to clarify important information for the patient, but many patients toss them aside rather than read what can be several pages of dense, tiny type and unfamiliar terminology.

Fortunately, some improvements are taking place. After her grandmother accidentally took some of her grandfather's

pills, graphic designer Deborah Adler decided that a major change was needed. Overhauling the round pill bottle that has been in use and unchanged for 60 years, Adler and industrial designer Klaus Rosburg crafted a new design that features a large, flat labeling surface that wraps over the top of the bottle. The label makes vital information—particularly the name of the drug, the patient's name, and dosage instructions—easy to find and easy to read. Color-coded bands can be attached as well to help various members of a household identify the right bottles. Adler's design, named ClearRx, is now in use at Target pharmacies nationwide.

### CAREER APPLICATIONS

1. Why is information prioritization so important with medicine labels?
2. Aside from medications, what other situations have you encountered in your life in which confusing labels, signs, instructions, or other messages created health or safety hazards? Choose one of these situations and write a brief description of the poor communication and your advice on how it could have been improved.

*Sources:* Adapted from "ClearRx," Target website, accessed 22 January 2013, www.target.com; "Medications—The Importance of Reading the Label," American Academy of Pediatrics, accessed 9 September 2008, www.medem.com; Sarah Bernard, "The Perfect Prescription," *New York Magazine*, 18 April 2005, accessed 30 September 2006, www.newyorkmetro.com.

- **Clarify awkward references.** If you want readers to refer to a specific point in a document, avoid vague references such as *the above-mentioned, as mentioned above, the aforementioned, the former, the latter,* and *respectively.* Use a specific pointer such as "as described in the second paragraph on page 22."

## EDITING FOR CONCISENESS

Efforts to improve clarity often reduce overall word count, so at this point you've probably eliminated most of the excess verbiage in your document. The next step is to examine the text with the specific goal of reducing the number of words you use. Readers appreciate conciseness and are more likely to read your documents if you have a reputation for efficient writing. See Table 6.3 on the next page for examples of the following tips:

- **Delete unnecessary words and phrases.** To test whether a word or phrase is essential, try the sentence without it. If the meaning doesn't change, leave it out.
- **Shorten long words and phrases.** Short words and phrases are generally more vivid and easier to read than long ones. Also, by using infinitives (the "to" form of a verb) in place of some phrases, you can often shorten sentences while making them clearer.
- **Eliminate redundancies.** In some word combinations, the words say the same thing. For instance, "visible to the eye" is redundant because *visible* is enough without further clarification; "to the eye" adds nothing.
- **Recast "It is/There are" starters.** If you start a sentence with an indefinite pronoun such as *it* or *there,* odds are the sentence could be shorter and more active. For instance, "We believe . . ." is a stronger opening than "It is believed that . . ." because it is shorter and because it identifies who is doing the believing.

As you rewrite, concentrate on how each word contributes to an effective sentence and on how each sentence helps build a coherent paragraph. For a reminder of the tasks involved in revision, see "Checklist: Revising Business Messages."

## USING TECHNOLOGY TO REVISE YOUR MESSAGE

When it's time to revise and polish your message, software features can help you add, delete, and move text, using functions such as *cut and paste* (taking a block of text out of one section of a document and pasting it in somewhere else) and *search and replace* (finding words or phrases and changing them if you need to). Be careful using the "Replace All" option; it can result in unintended errors. For example, finding *power* and replacing all occurrences with *strength* will also change the word *powerful* to *strengthful,* which isn't a word.

> Improving clarity often makes messages shorter, but you can make them shorter still by using some specific revision techniques.

> Early drafts often have words and phrases that don't add anything and can easily be cut out.

---

**CHECKLIST** ✔ Revising Business Messages

**A. Evaluate content, organization, style, and tone.**
- Make sure the information is accurate, relevant, and sufficient.
- Check that all necessary points appear in logical order.
- Verify that you present enough support to make the main idea convincing and compelling.
- Be sure the beginning and ending of the message are effective.
- Make sure you've achieved the right tone for the audience and the situation.

**B. Review for readability.**
- Consider using a readability index but be sure to interpret the answer carefully.
- Use a mix of short, medium, and long sentences.
- Keep paragraphs short.

- Use bulleted and numbered lists to emphasize key points.
- Make the document easy to skim with headings and subheadings.

**C. Edit for clarity.**
- Break up overly long sentences and rewrite hedging sentences.
- Impose parallelism to simplify reading.
- Correct dangling modifiers.
- Reword long noun sequences and replace camouflaged verbs.
- Clarify sentence structure and awkward references.

**D. Edit for conciseness.**
- Delete unnecessary words and phrases.
- Shorten long words and phrases.
- Eliminate redundancies.
- Rewrite sentences that start with "It is" or "There are."

TABLE 6.3 | **Revising for Conciseness**

| Issues to Review | Ineffective | Effective |
|---|---|---|
| **Unnecessary Words and Phrases** | | |
| Using wordy phrases | for the sum of | for |
| | in the event that | if |
| | prior to the start of | before |
| | in the near future | soon |
| | at this point in time | now |
| | due to the fact that | because |
| | in view of the fact that | because |
| | until such time as | when |
| | with reference to | about |
| Using too many relative pronouns | Cars that are sold after January will not have a six-month warranty. | Cars sold after January will not have a six-month warranty. |
| | Employees who are driving to work should park in the underground garage. | Employees driving to work should park in the underground garage.<br>OR<br>Employees should park in the underground garage. |
| Using too few relative pronouns | The project manager told the engineers last week the specifications were changed. | The project manager told the engineers last week that the specifications were changed. |
| | | The project manager told the engineers that last week the specifications were changed. |
| **Long Words and Phrases** | | |
| Using overly long words | During the preceding year, the company accelerated productive operations. | Last year the company sped up operations. |
| | The action was predicated on the assumption that the company was operating at a financial deficit. | The action was based on the belief that the company was losing money. |
| Using wordy phrases rather than infinitives | If you want success as a writer, you must work hard. | To succeed as a writer, you must work hard. |
| | He went to the library for the purpose of studying. | He went to the library to study. |
| | The employer increased salaries so that she could improve morale. | The employer increased salaries to improve morale. |
| **Redundancies** | | |
| Repeating meanings | absolutely complete | complete |
| | basic fundamentals | fundamentals |
| | follows after | follows |
| | free and clear | free |
| | refer back | refer |
| | repeat again | repeat |
| | collect together | collect |
| | future plans | plans |
| | return back | return |
| | important essentials | essentials |
| | end result | result |
| | actual truth | truth |
| | final outcome | outcome |
| | uniquely unusual | unique |
| | surrounded on all sides | surrounded |
| Using double modifiers | modern, up-to-date equipment | modern equipment |
| ***It Is/There Are* Starters** | It would be appreciated if you would sign the lease today. | Please sign the lease today. |
| Starting sentences with *It* or *There* | There are five employees in this division who were late to work today. | Five employees in this division were late to work today. |

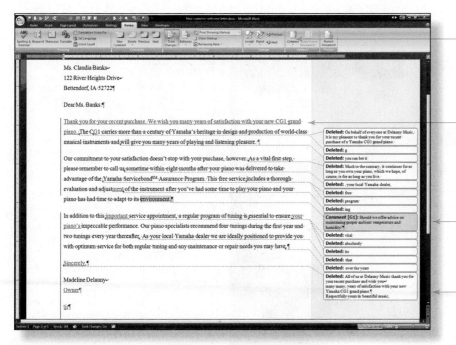

A writer who has received suggested changes from a reviewer can easily accept or reject each change.

Each addition or deletion is highlighted in turn so that the writer can consider whether to accept or reject it.

Reviewers can also leave comments, which don't affect the text (the writer simply deletes the comments after reading them).

Various programs have different options for displaying suggested changes from reviewers; in this example, insertions are underlined in the text, and deletions are displayed in bubbles off to the side.

**Figure 6.3   Revision Marks in Microsoft Word**
Microsoft Word, the most commonly used word processor in business offices, offers handy tools for reviewing draft documents. In this example, text to be added is shown in red, and text to be deleted is shown in balloons in the right margin. The writer can then choose to accept or reject each suggested change.
*Source:* Used with permission from Microsoft, Inc.

To assist with revision, software features such as *revision marks* or *change tracking* (see Figure 6.3) and *commenting* (see Figure 6.4 on the next page) show proposed editing changes electronically and provide a history of a document's revisions. Using revision marks and commenting features is a great way to keep track of editing changes made by multiple reviewers, too.

In addition to the many revision tools, four software functions can help bring out the best in your documents. First, a *spell checker* compares your document with an electronic dictionary, highlights unrecognized words, and suggests correct spellings. Spell checkers are wonderful for finding typos, but they are no substitute for good spelling skills and careful work. For example, if you use *their* when you mean to use *there*, your spell checker won't notice because *their* is spelled correctly (although a grammar checker might catch it; see below).

Second, a computer *thesaurus* (either within your software or on a website such as www.merriam-webster.com or http://thesaurus.com) offers alternatives to a particular word. The best uses of a thesaurus are to find fresh, interesting words when you've been using the same word too many times and to find words that most accurately and precisely convey your intended meaning. Don't use a thesaurus simply to find impressive-sounding words, however, and don't assume that all the alternatives suggested are correct for each situation.

Third, a *grammar checker* tries to do for your grammar what a spell checker does for your spelling. Because the program doesn't have a clue about what you're trying to say, it can't tell whether you've said it clearly or completely. However, grammar checkers can highlight items you should consider changing, such as passive voice, long sentences, and words that tend to be misused (such as *their* versus *there*).

Fourth, a *style checker* can monitor your word and sentence choices and suggest alternatives that might produce more effective writing. For instance, the style-checking options in Microsoft Word range from basic issues, such as spelling out numbers and using contractions, to more subjective matters, such as sentence structure and the use of technical terminology.

Revision marks and commenting features are great ways to track the revision process when multiple reviewers are involved.

Spell checkers, grammar checkers, and computerized thesauruses can all help with the revision process, but they can't take the place of good writing and editing skills.

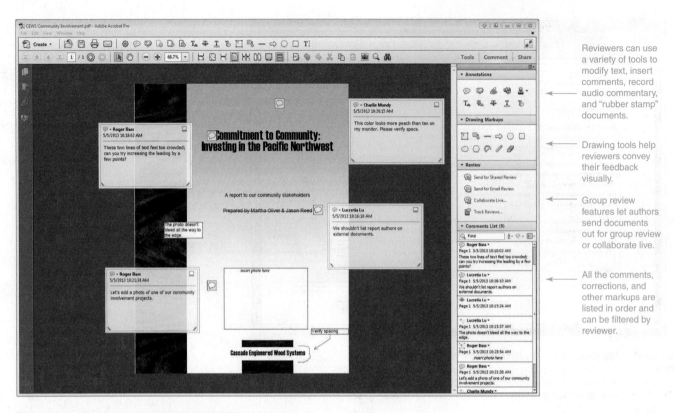

**Figure 6.4   Comments Attached to a PDF File**
Adobe Acrobat lets reviewers attach comments to any document in PDF format, even if it was originally
created using software the reviewers don't have.
*Source:* Adobe product screenshot reprinted with permission from Adobe Systems Incorporated.

By all means, use any software tools that you find helpful when revising your documents. Just remember that it's unwise to rely on them to do all your revision work, and you're responsible for the final product.

# Producing Your Message

**4** **LEARNING OBJECTIVE**
List four principles of effective design and explain the role of major design elements in document readability.

Production quality affects readability and audience perceptions of you and your message.

Document design sends strong nonverbal signals—make sure the signals you send are positive and appropriate.

Now it's time to put your hard work on display. The *production quality* of your message—the total effect of page or screen design, graphical elements, typography, and so on—plays an important role in the effectiveness of your message. A polished, inviting design not only makes your material easier to read but also conveys a sense of professionalism and importance.[2]

## DESIGNING FOR READABILITY

Design affects readability in two important ways. First, if used carefully, design elements can improve the effectiveness of your message. In contrast, poor design decisions, such as using distracting background images behind text, pointless animations, or tiny typefaces, act as barriers to communication. Second, the visual design sends a nonverbal message to your readers, influencing their perceptions of the communication before they read a single word.

Effective design helps you establish the tone of your document and helps guide your readers through your message (see Figure 6.5). To achieve an effective design, pay careful attention to the following design elements:

Aim for consistent design within each message and from message to message.

- **Consistency.** Throughout each message, be consistent in your use of margins, typeface, type size, and space. Also be consistent when using recurring design elements, such as vertical lines, columns, and borders. In many cases, you'll want to be consistent from

The layout is *statically balanced*, with equal visual weight on either side of the vertical centerline.

The picture of the anvil (a device used by blacksmiths to shape pieces of iron) plays off the company name and provides visual interest without overwhelming the page.

These three concise labels are the "subheadings" of the website, directing readers to each of the major sections of content.

These introductory paragraphs offer succinct summaries of the three content areas. The centered paragraphs promote the look of calm balance, and in these small sections the centered text is easy to read.

When a reader clicks on any of the three sections above, this area presents the next level of detail.

Readers can "drill down" through layers of information without getting overwhelmed by large amounts of text or distracting visual elements.

IRON IRON

HANDSOME DESIGN AND DEVELOPMENT

ABOUT | SERVICES | CONTACT

Iron to Iron loves the Web, we love what it has to offer and we recognize the value within it. Our goals reflect process, professionalism, and quality of work. We strive to make the Web a better place through handsome design & development.

We live on the Web. Our entire process is dedicated to focusing on quality, efficiency, and partnering with clients throughout a continued relationship. We recognize the gravity of doing things right and take pride in our work from start to finish.

We're thankful that our craft involves working with people. That partnership is something we aim to cultivate, as we recognize the value in meeting other experts in so many different fields. We'd honestly love to hear from you.

**WEB DESIGN & DEVELOPMENT**

Web design deserves significant thought and devotion. Your presence wasn't established overnight, it took careful thought and planning; your Web presence should be treated the same way. Each design is custom tailored to fulfill a specific set of goals in an effort to solve a significant problem. In turn, quality development brings a design to life, ensuring the experience is withheld. We value it all.

With more than a decade of experience behind us, we acknowledge the benefits of a small, specialized team as a method of affording the highest degree of focus. That's why we established Iron to Iron, to facilitate the importance we believe the Web deserves.

TOUCH BASE | VIEW OUR WORK ➡

**KEVIN RICHARDSON**
CO-OWNER, PRINCIPAL DESIGN

Email: kevin@irontoiron.com
Twitter: @encrgothers
Personal Site: encourageothers.com

**JONATHAN CHRISTOPHER**
CO-OWNER, PRINCIPAL DEVELOPMENT

Email: jonathan@irontoiron.com
Twitter: @jchristopher
Personal Site: mondaybynoon.com

**Figure 6.5 Designing for Readability**
The website of the web development firm Iron to Iron is a model of elegant design that promotes easy reading.
*Source:* Copyright © 2013 by Iron to Iron, LLC. Used by permission.

MyBCommLab Apply Figure 6.5's key concepts. Go to **mybcommlab.com** and follow this path: Course Content ➔ Chapter 6 ➔ **DOCUMENT MAKEOVERS**

message to message as well; that way, audiences who receive multiple messages from you recognize your documents and know what to expect.

- **Balance.** Balance is an important but subjective issue. One document may have a formal, rigid design in which the various elements are placed in a grid pattern, whereas another may have a less formal design in which elements flow more freely across the page—and both could be in balance. Like the tone of your language, visual balance can be too formal, just right, or too informal for a given message.

- **Restraint.** Strive for simplicity in design. Don't clutter your message with too many design elements, too many typeface treatments, too many colors, or too many decorative touches. Let "simpler" and "fewer" be your guiding concepts.

- **Detail.** Pay attention to details that affect your design and thus your message. For instance, extremely wide columns of text can be difficult to read; in many cases a better solution is to split the text into two narrower columns.

Simple designs are usually more effective than more complex designs.

Even without special training in graphic design, you can make your printed and electronic messages more effective by understanding the use of white space, margins and line justification, typefaces, and type styles.

## White Space

White space separates elements in a document and helps guide the reader's eye.

Any space that doesn't contain text or artwork, both in print and online, is considered **white space**. (Note that "white space" isn't necessarily white; it is simply blank.) These unused areas provide visual contrast and important resting points for your readers. White space includes the open area surrounding headings, margins, paragraph indents, space around images, vertical space between columns, and horizontal space between paragraphs or lines of text. To increase the chance that readers will read your messages, be generous with white space; it makes pages and screens feel less intimidating and easier to read.[3]

## Margins and Justification

Margins define the space around text and between text columns. In addition to their width, the look and feel of margins is influenced by the way you arrange lines of text, which can be set (1) *justified* (which means they are *flush*, or aligned vertically, on both the left and the right), (2) flush left with a *ragged-right* margin, (3) flush right with a *ragged-left* margin, or (4) centered. This paragraph is justified, whereas the paragraphs in Figure 6.2 on page 148 are flush left with a ragged-right margin.

Magazines, newspapers, and books often use justified type because it can accommodate more text in a given space. However, justified type needs to be used with care. First, it creates a denser look because the uniform line lengths decrease the amount of white space along the right margin. Second, it produces a more formal and less personalized look. Third, unless it is used with some skill and attention, justified type can be more difficult to read because it can produce large gaps between words and excessive hyphenation at the ends of lines. The publishing specialists who create magazines, newspapers, and books have the time and skill needed to carefully adjust character and word spacing to eliminate these problems. (In some cases, sentences are even rewritten in order to improve the appearance of the printed page.) Because most business communicators don't have that time or skill, it's best to avoid justified type in routine business documents.

Most business documents use a flush-left margin and a ragged-right margin.

In contrast to justified type, flush-left, ragged-right type creates a more open appearance on the page, producing a less formal and more contemporary look. Spacing between words is consistent, and only long words that fall at the ends of lines are hyphenated.

Centered type is rarely used for text paragraphs but is commonly used for headings and subheadings. Flush-right, ragged-left type is rarely used in business documents.

## Typefaces

**Typeface** refers to the physical design of letters, numbers, and other text characters. (*Font* and *typeface* are often used interchangeably, although strictly speaking, a font is a set of characters in a given typeface.) Typeface influences the tone of your message, making it look authoritative or friendly, businesslike or casual, classic or modern, and so on (see Table 6.4). Be sure to choose fonts that are appropriate for your message; many of the fonts on your computer are not appropriate for business use.

**Serif typefaces** have small crosslines (called serifs) at the ends of each letter stroke. Serif typefaces such as Times New Roman are commonly used for regular paragraph text (as in this book), but they can look busy and cluttered when set in large sizes for headings.

The classic style of document design uses a sans serif typeface for headings and a serif typeface for regular paragraph text; however, many contemporary documents now use all sans serif.

**Sans serif typefaces** have no serifs (*sans* is French for "without"). The visual simplicity of sans serif typefaces such as Helvetica and Arial makes them ideal for the larger sizes used in headlines. Sans serif faces can be difficult to read in long blocks of text, however, unless they are formatted with generous amounts of *leading* (pronounced *ledding*), or spacing between lines.

The classic style of document design uses a sans serif typeface for headings and a serif typeface for regular paragraph text. However, many contemporary documents and websites

| TABLE 6.4 | Typeface Personalities: Serious to Casual to Playful | |
| --- | --- | --- |
| Serif Typefaces (Best for Text) | Sans Serif Typefaces (Best for Headlines; Some Work Well for Text) | Specialty Typefaces (For Decorative Purposes Only) |
| Bookman Old Style | Arial | Bauhaus |
| Century Schoolbook | Calibri | Spring LP |
| Courier | **Eras Bold** | Old English |
| Garamond | Franklin Gothic Book | Brush Script |
| Georgia | Gill Sans | **MANITO** |
| Times New Roman | Verdana | **STENCIL** |

now use a sans serif face for both. Whichever combination you use, make sure that the result is reader-friendly and that it conveys the right personality for the situation.

For most documents, generally avoid using more than two typefaces, although if you want to make captions or another special text element stand out, you can use a third face for that.[4] Using too many typefaces clutters a document and can produce an amateurish look.

## Type Styles

**Type style** refers to any modification that lends contrast or emphasis to type, including boldface, italic, underlining, color, and other highlighting and decorative styles. Using boldface type for subheads breaks up long expanses of text. You can also boldface individual words or phrases to draw more attention to them. For example, the key terms in each chapter in this book are set in bold. Italic type also creates emphasis, although not as pronounced as boldface. Italic type has specific uses as well, such as highlighting quotations and indicating foreign words, irony, humor, book and movie titles, and unconventional usage.

As a general rule, avoid using any style in a way that slows your audience's progress through the message. For instance, underlining or using all-uppercase letters can interfere with a reader's ability to recognize the shapes of words, and shadowed or outlined type can seriously hinder legibility. Also, avoid overusing any type style. For example, putting too many words in boldface dilutes the impact of the special treatment by creating too many focal points in the paragraph.

Type size is an important consideration as well. For most printed business messages, use a size of 10 to 12 points for regular text and 12 to 18 points for headings and subheadings (1 point is approximately 1/72 inch). Resist the temptation to reduce type size too much in order to squeeze in extra text or to enlarge it to fill up space. Type that is too small is hard to read, whereas extra-large type looks unprofessional. Be particularly careful with small type online. Small type that looks fine on a medium-resolution screen can be hard to read on both low-resolution screens (because these displays can make letters look jagged or fuzzy) and high-resolution screens (because these monitors reduce the apparent size of the type even further).

*Avoid using any type style in ways that might interfere with reading.*

## DESIGNING MULTIMEDIA DOCUMENTS

A **multimedia document** contains a combination of text, graphics, photographs, audio, animation, video, and interactivity (such as hyperlinks that access webpages or software programs). Most electronic media now support multiple media formats, so you have a variety of options for creating multimedia documents. For example, you can add photos to a

The window at the left shows all the storied audio and video elements available for use.

The window at the right preview the video or screencast, frame by frame.

All the audio and video elements are arranged in sequence on this timeline, making it easy to add, delete, or move individual pieces.

**Figure 6.6  Multimedia Tools**
Desktop software tools such as the Camtasia screencasting program let business communicators assemble a variety of multimedia documents and presentations.
*Source:* Copyright © 2012 by TechSmith Corporation. Reprinted with permission.

word processor file, audio commentary to a PDF, video clips to a blog posting, and animation to webpages (see Figure 6.6).

As rich media, multimedia documents can convey large amounts of information quickly, engage people in multiple ways, express emotions, and allow recipients to personalize the communication process to their own needs. However, these documents are more difficult to create than documents that contain only text and static images. To design and create multimedia documents, you need to consider the following factors:

- **Creative and technical skills.** Depending on what you need to accomplish, creating and integrating multimedia elements can require some creative and technical skills. Fortunately, many basic tasks, such as adding photographs or video clips to a webpage, have gotten much easier in recent years. And even if you don't have the advantage of formal training in design, by studying successful examples, you can start to get a feel for what works and what doesn't.

- **Tools.** The hardware and software tools needed to create and integrate media elements are now widely available and generally affordable. For example, with simpler and less expensive consumer versions of professional photo and video editing software, you can often perform all the tasks you need for basic multimedia.

- **Time and cost.** The time and cost of creating multimedia documents has dropped dramatically in recent years. However, you still need to consider these elements—and exercise good judgment when deciding whether to include multimedia and how much to include. Make sure the time and money you plan to spend will be paid back in communication effectiveness.

- **Content.** To include various media elements in a document, you obviously need to create or acquire them. If you have the skills, time, and tools, you might be able to create graphics or other media elements. If not, you'll need to find these items and secure the right to use them. Millions of graphics, photos, video clips, and other elements are available online,

Multimedia documents can be powerful communication vehicles, but they require more time, tools, and skills to create.

Make sure you have the legal right to use any media elements that you include in your documents.

but you need to make sure you can legally use each item. One good option is to search Creative Commons (www.creativecommons.org) for multimedia elements available for use at no charge but with various restrictions (such as giving the creator credit).

- **Message structure.** Multimedia documents often lack a rigid linear structure from beginning to end, which means you need to plan for readers to take multiple, individualized paths through the material. In other words, a conventional outline is often inadequate. Chapter 7 discusses the challenge of *information architecture*, the structure and navigational flow of websites and other multimedia documents.
- **Compatibility.** Some multimedia elements require specific software to be installed on the recipient's viewing device. Another challenge is the variety of screen sizes and resolutions, from huge, high-resolution computer monitors to older, low-resolution monitors to small mobile phone displays. Make sure you understand the demands your message will place on the audience.

## USING TECHNOLOGY TO PRODUCE YOUR MESSAGE

Production tools vary widely, depending on the software and systems you're using. Some IM and email systems offer limited formatting and production capabilities, whereas some word processors now offer capabilities that rival those of professional publishing software for many day-to-day business needs. *Desktop publishing* software such as Adobe InDesign goes beyond word processing, offering more advanced and precise layout capabilities that meet the technical demands of publication-quality printing. (Such programs are used mainly by design professionals.) For online content, web publishing and blogging systems make it easy to post great-looking content quickly without worrying too much about design or production.

No matter what system you're using, become familiar with the basic formatting capabilities. A few hours of exploration on your own or an introductory training course can help you dramatically improve the production quality of your documents. Depending on the types of messages you're creating, you'll benefit from being proficient with the following features:

> Learning to use the basic features of your communication tools will help you produce better messages in less time.

- **Templates, themes, and stylesheets.** As Chapter 5 notes, you can save a tremendous amount of time by using templates, themes, and stylesheets. Many companies provide these tools to their employees to ensure a consistent look and feel for all print and online documents.
- **Page setup.** Use page setup to control margins, orientation (*portrait* is vertical; *landscape* is horizontal), and the location of *headers* (text and graphics that repeat at the top of every page) and *footers* (similar to headers but at the bottom of the page).
- **Column formatting.** Most business documents use a single column of text per page, but multiple columns can be an attractive format for documents such as newsletters. Columns are also handy for formatting long lists.
- **Paragraph formatting.** Take advantage of paragraph formatting controls to enhance the look of your documents. For instance, you can offset quotations by increasing margin width around a single paragraph, subtly compress line spacing to fit a document on a single page, or use *hanging indents* to offset the first line of a paragraph.
- **Numbered and bulleted lists.** Let your software do the busywork of formatting numbered and bulleted lists. It can also automatically renumber lists when you add or remove items.
- **Tables.** Tables are great for displaying any information that lends itself to rows and columns, including calendars, numeric data, comparisons, and multicolumn bulleted lists. Use paragraph and font formatting thoughtfully within tables for the best look.
- **Pictures, text boxes, and objects.** Print and online publishing software lets you insert a wide variety of pictures (using industry-standard formats such as .jpg, .gif, and .png). *Text boxes* are small blocks of text that stand apart from the main text and can be placed anywhere on the page; they are great for captions, callouts, margin notes, and so on. *Objects* can be anything from a spreadsheet to a sound clip to an engineering drawing. Similarly, blogging systems, wikis, and other web development tools let you insert a variety of pictures, audio and video clips, and other multimedia elements.

By improving the appearance of your documents with these tools, you'll improve your readers' impressions of you and your messages, too.

# FORMATTING FORMAL LETTERS AND MEMOS

Business letters typically have the following elements:
- Preprinted letterhead
- Date
- Inside address
- Salutation
- Complimentary close
- Signature block

Formal business letters usually follow certain design conventions, as the letter in Figure 6.2 illustrates. Most business letters are printed on *letterhead stationery*, which includes the company's name, address, and other contact information. The first element to appear after the letterhead is the date, followed by the inside address, which identifies the person receiving the letter. Next is the salutation, usually in the form of *Dear Mr.* or *Ms. Last Name*. The message comes next, followed by the complimentary close, usually *Sincerely* or *Cordially*. And last comes the signature block: space for the signature, followed by the sender's printed name and title. Your company will probably have a standard format to follow for letters, possibly along with a template in Microsoft Word or whatever word processor is standard in the organization. For in-depth information on letter formats, see Appendix A, "Format and Layout of Business Documents."

Memos are usually identified by a title such as *Memo* or *Memorandum*.

Like letters, business memos usually follow a preset design (see Figure 6.7). Memos have largely been replaced by electronic media in many companies, but if they are still in use at the firm you join, the company may have a standard format or template for you to

Standard company memo stationery includes a title indicating that this is a memo.

These four headings are commonly used in memos.

Memos typically do not include an opening salutation.

Memos typically do not include a complimentary close or a signature block.

## Carnival
### FUN FOR ALL. ALL FOR FUN.
### INTERNAL MEMORANDUM

MyBCommLab Apply Figure 6.7's key concepts. Go to **mybcommlab.com** and follow this path: Course Content → Chapter 6 → **DOCUMENT MAKEOVERS**

**DATE:** March 18, 2013
**TO:** Carnival's PR Department
**FROM:** Vance Gulliksen, Senior PR Manager
**SUBJECT:** News to Use for 2013–14

Following are some bullet points highlighting upcoming itinerary deployments and other news involving the Carnival fleet for the coming year. Please note that this information will be posted on our Website, provided to journalists on as-needed basis and included in all press kits:

**U.S. Debut of New Carnival Breeze**—The 3,690-passenger Carnival Breeze launched year-round six- and eight-day Caribbean cruises from Miami in November, becoming the largest Carnival ship ever based in South Florida. In addition to many popular features that debuted on Carnival Magic—including the Caribbean-inspired RedFrog Pub, Cucina del Capitano family-style Italian restaurant, and SportSquare outdoor recreation area—Carnival Breeze introduced the Thrill Theater, with interactive special effects that make viewers feel as if they are part of the movie, and new culinary choices such as Bonsai Sushi, the line's first full-service sushi restaurant, and a complimentary open-air outdoor dining venue called Fat Jimmy's C-Side BBQ.

**Carnival Destiny Becomes Carnival Sunshine After $155 Million Refit**—Representing Carnival's most ambitious transformation project ever, Carnival Destiny will undergo a $155 million makeover incorporating all of the "Fun Ship 2.0" dining, bar and entertainment features, as well as adding 182 new cabins and new choices such as Havana Bar, ShakeSpot, JavaBlue Café, Pizzeria del Capitano, a three-level Serenity adults-only retreat, a full-service Asian restaurant called Jiji Asian Kitchen and a racing-themed water park. The redesign will be so extensive that the ship will be renamed Carnival Sunshine following an extensive dry dock, which takes place this spring. Carnival Sunshine will sail the Mediterranean before repositioning to New Orleans for year-round Caribbean cruises this fall.

**25<sup>th</sup> 'Fun Ship' Set to Debut in 2016**—Carnival Cruise Lines' parent company, Carnival Corporation & plc, has reached an agreement with Italian shipbuilder Fincantieri for the construction of a new 135,000-ton vessel that will be the largest in the "Fun Ship" fleet. Representing a new class of vessel for the line, the 4,000-passenger ship is scheduled for delivery in 2016. The as-yet-unnamed ship will incorporate many of the dining, bar and entertainment innovations that are part of the line's "Fun Ship" 2.0 enhancement initiative along with several new options unique to this vessel.

**Continued Rollout of $500 Million Fun Ship 2.0 Enhancement Program**—The rollout of Carnival's $500 million "Fun Ship 2.0" enhancement program continues with the renovation of Carnival Conquest and Carnival Glory late last year. The line's most ambitious program to date, Fun Ship 2.0 is transforming the line's on-board experience through branded spaces and celebrity partnerships. The initiative includes partnerships with George Lopez, who serves as the line's creative director for comedy to enhance the fleetwide Punchliner Comedy Clubs, and Food Network personality Guy Fieri, who developed a new free burger venue called Guy's Burger Joint, as well as top brands such as EASPORTS Bar and Hasbro. New food and beverage concepts such as the poolside RedFrog Rum Bar, BlueIguana Tequila Bar and BlueIguana Cantina and the "cocktail pharmacy" Alchemy Bar, along with entertainment choices and Playlist Productions and a partnership with celebrity song master DJ IRIE, are also included.

Please let me know if you have any questions or require additional information. Thanks.

**Figure 6.7** **A Typical Business Memo**
This document shows the elements usually included in a formal business memo.
*Source:* "News to Use for 2011," by Vance Gulliksen, Senior PR Manager, Carnival Internal Memorandum, March 18, 2013. Copyright © 2013 by Carnival Cruise Lines. Used by permission.

use. Most memos begin with a title such as *Memo, Memorandum,* or *Interoffice Correspondence.* Following that are usually four headings: *Date, To, From,* and *Subject.* (*Re:,* short for *Regarding,* is sometimes used instead of *Subject.*) Memos usually don't use a salutation, complimentary close, or signature, although signing your initials next to your name on the *From* line is standard practice in most companies. Bear in mind that memos are often distributed without sealed envelopes, so they are less private than most other message formats.

# Proofreading Your Message

Proofreading is the quality inspection stage for your documents, your last chance to make sure that your document is ready to carry your message—and your reputation—to the intended audience. Even a small mistake can doom your efforts, so take proofreading seriously.

**5** **LEARNING OBJECTIVE**
Explain the importance of proofreading, and give eight tips for successful proofreading.

Look for two types of problems: (1) undetected mistakes from the writing, design, and layout stages and (2) mistakes that crept in during production. For the first category, you can review format and layout guidelines in Appendix A on page 569 and brush up on writing basics with the Handbook of Grammar, Mechanics, and Usage on page 594. The second category can include anything from computer glitches such as missing fonts to broken web links to problems with the ink used in printing. Be particularly vigilant with complex documents and complex production processes that involve multiple colleagues and multiple computers. Strange things can happen as files move from computer to computer, especially when lots of fonts and multimedia elements are involved.

**REAL-TIME UPDATES**
LEARN MORE BY WATCHING THIS PRESENTATION

**Practical advice for thorough proofreading**

Identify and correct common problems in business writing with this handy guide. Go to http://real-timeupdates.com/bct12 and click on Learn More. If you are using MyBCommLab, you can access Real-Time Updates within each chapter or under Student Study Tools.

Resist the temptation to treat proofreading as a casual scan up and down the page or screen. Instead, approach it as a methodical procedure in which you look for specific problems that may occur. Use these techniques from professional proofreaders to help ensure high-quality output:

A methodical approach to proofreading will help you find the problems that need to be fixed.

- **Make multiple passes.** Go through the document several times, focusing on a different aspect each time. For instance, look for content errors the first time and layout errors the second time.
- **Use perceptual tricks.** You've probably experienced the frustration of reading over something a dozen times and still missing an obvious error. This happens because your brain has developed a wonderful skill of subconsciously supplying missing pieces and correcting mistakes when it knows what is *supposed* to be on the page. To keep your brain from tricking you, you need to trick it by changing the way you process the visual information. Try (1) reading each page backward, from the bottom to the top, (2) placing your finger under each word and reading it silently, (3) making a slit in a sheet of paper that reveals only one line of type at a time, and (4) reading the document aloud and pronouncing each word carefully.
- **Double-check high-priority items.** Double-check the spelling of names and the accuracy of dates, addresses, and any number that could cause grief if incorrect (such as telling a potential employer that you'd be happy to work for $5,000 a year when you meant to say $50,000).
- **Give yourself some distance.** If possible, don't proofread immediately after finishing a document; let your mind wander off to new topics and then come back fresh later on.
- **Be vigilant.** Avoid reading large amounts of material in one sitting and try not to proofread when you're tired.
- **Stay focused.** Concentrate on what you're doing. Try to block out distractions and focus as completely as possible on your proofreading task.
- **Review complex electronic documents on paper.** Some people have trouble proofreading webpages, online reports, and other electronic documents on-screen. If you have trouble, try to print the materials so you can review them on paper.
- **Take your time.** Quick proofreading is not careful proofreading.

The amount of time you need to spend on proofing depends on the length and complexity of the document and the situation. A typo in an email message to your team may not be a big deal, but a typo in a financial report, a contract, or a medical file certainly could be serious. As with every other task in the writing process, practice helps—you become more familiar with what errors to look for and more skilled in identifying those errors. See "Checklist: Proofing Business Messages" for a handy list of items to review during proofing.

# Distributing Your Message

**6 LEARNING OBJECTIVE**
Discuss the most important issues to consider when distributing your messages.

With the production finished, you're ready to distribute your message. As with every other aspect of business communication, your options for distribution multiply with every advance in technology. In some cases, the choice is obvious: Just click the Send button in your email program or the Publish button on your blog. In other cases, such as when you have a 100-page report with full-color graphics or a massive multimedia file, you need to plan the distribution carefully so that your message is received by everyone who needs it. When choosing a means to distribute messages, consider the following factors:

- **Cost.** Cost isn't a concern for most messages, but for lengthy reports or multimedia productions, it may well be. Printing, binding, and delivering reports can be expensive, so weigh the cost versus the benefits. Be sure to consider the nonverbal message you send regarding cost as well. Overnight delivery of a printed report could look responsive in one situation but wasteful in another, for example.

Make sure your delivery method is convenient for your audience members.

- **Convenience.** How much work is involved for you and your audience? For instance, if you use a file-compression utility to shrink the size of email attachments, make sure your recipients have the means to expand the files on arrival. For extremely large files, consider recordable media such as DVDs or one of the many free or low-cost file-hosting sites now available.

- **Time.** How soon does the message need to reach the audience? Don't waste money on overnight delivery if the recipient won't read the report for a week. And speaking of time, don't mark any messages, printed or electronic, as "urgent" if they aren't truly urgent.

- **Security and privacy.** The convenience offered by electronic communication needs to be weighed against security and privacy concerns. For the most sensitive messages, your company will probably restrict both the people who can receive the messages and the means you can use to distribute them. In addition, most computer users are wary of opening attachments these days. Instead of sending word processor files, you can use Adobe Acrobat or an equivalent product to convert your documents to PDF files (which are more immune to viruses).

Chapters 7 and 8 offer more advice on distributing podcasts, blogs, and other messages in electronic formats. For news on the latest news on revision, proofreading, and other topics related to this chapter, visit http://real-timeupdates.com/bct12 and click on Chapter 6.

---

**CHECKLIST ✓ Proofing Business Messages**

**A. Look for writing errors.**
- Typographical mistakes
- Misspelled words
- Grammatical errors
- Punctuation mistakes

**B. Look for missing elements.**
- Missing text sections
- Missing exhibits (drawings, tables, photographs, charts, graphs, online images, and so on)
- Missing source notes, copyright notices, or other reference items

**C. Look for design, formatting, and programming mistakes.**
- Incorrect or inconsistent font selections
- Problems with column sizing, spacing, and alignment
- Incorrect margins
- Incorrect special characters
- Clumsy line and page breaks
- Problems with page numbers
- Problems with page headers and footers
- Lack of adherence to company standards
- Inactive or incorrect links
- Missing files

# Quick Learning Guide

## SUMMARY OF LEARNING OBJECTIVES

**1** **Discuss the value of careful revision, and describe the tasks involved in evaluating your first drafts and the work of other writers.** Revision is a vital step in producing effective business messages; even if the first draft conveys the necessary information, chances are it can be made tighter, clearer, and more compelling—making it more successful for you. Careful revision also helps you locate and correct errors that can reduce the effectiveness of messages and damage your reputation as a communicator.

When evaluating your first drafts, check the *content* (is the content accurate, relevant, complete, and well balanced between general and specific information?), the *organization* (are your points grouped and sequenced logically, with focus on the most important ideas?), and the *tone* (is the tone appropriate for the audience and the specific situation?).

**2** **List four techniques you can use to improve the readability of your messages.** Four techniques that help improve readability are varying sentence length, keeping paragraphs short, using lists, and adding headings and subheadings. Varying sentence length helps keep your writing fresh and dynamic while giving you a chance to emphasize the most important points. Paragraphs, on the other hand, are usually best kept short to make it easier for readers to consume your information in manageable chunks. Lists are effective devices for delineating sets of items, steps in a procedure, or other collections of related information. Headings and subheadings organize your message, call attention to important information, and help readers make connections between related pieces of information.

**3** **Describe eight steps you can take to improve the clarity of your writing, and give four tips on making your writing more concise.** To clarify your writing, (1) break up overly long sentences, (2) rewrite hedging sentences, (3) impose parallelism, (4) correct dangling modifiers, (5) reword long noun sequences, (6) replace camouflaged verbs, (7) clarify sentence structure, and (8) clarify awkward references. To make messages more concise, (1) delete unnecessary words and phrases, (2) shorten overly long words and phrases, (3) eliminate redundancies, and (4) recast sentences that begin with "It is" and "There are."

**4** **List four principles of effective design, and explain the role of major design elements in document readability.** Four important principles of effective design are *consistency* (using design elements in a consistent and predictable way throughout a document), *balance* (creating a balanced effect on page or screen, whether that balance is dynamic and informal or symmetrical and formal), *restraint* (striving for visual simplicity to avoid drawing attention away from your ideas), and *detail* (making sure that details are handled correctly so that errors or design misjudgments don't detract from your message).

The major design elements for textual messages include white space, margins, typefaces, and type styles. White space provides contrast and gives readers a resting point. Margins define the space around the text and contribute to the amount of white space. Margins can affect both readability and the overall visual appeal of your messages. Typefaces influence the tone of the message and should be chosen carefully for each use to ensure maximum readability. Type styles such as boldface, italics, and underlining provide contrast or emphasis.

**5** **Explain the importance of proofreading, and give eight tips for successful proofreading.** Proofreading is essential because it is your final opportunity to verify the quality of your communication efforts and to make sure that no errors in writing, design, or production will undo all the hard work you've put in. Proofreading should be more than just a quick glance through the document. Use the techniques the pros use to make sure your documents are top quality: (1) Make multiple passes, looking for specific types of problems each time; (2) use perceptual tricks such as reading aloud or reading backward to prevent your brain from fooling you by filling in pieces or correcting errors; (3) double-check high-priority items such as names, dates, addresses, and financial data; (4) give yourself some distance by putting the document aside for a few hours or even a few days if possible; (5) stay vigilant by proofing only small sections at a time and not proofing when you are tired; (6) stay focused on your work; (7) review complex electronic documents on paper if possible; and (8) take your time.

**6** **Discuss the most important issues to consider when distributing your messages.** Consider cost, convenience, time, security, and privacy when choosing the method to distribute your messages. Cost isn't a major issue for most messages, although production, printing, and distribution of lengthy or complex reports can be a concern. In general, balance the cost with the importance and urgency of the message. Make sure the distribution method is convenient for your audience. For example, attaching a document to an email message might be easy for you, but that might not be the best approach for a given audience. As with cost, balance the time factor with your needs and the needs of your audience. Finally, consider security and privacy issues before distributing documents that contain sensitive or confidential information. Your company may have restrictions on the type of information that can be distributed through various media and channels.

## KEY TERMS

**descriptive headings** Headings that simply identify a topic

**heading** A brief title that tells readers about the content of the section that follows

**informative headings** Headings that guide readers to think in a certain way about the topic

**multimedia document** Electronic document that contains a combination of text, graphics, photographs, audio, animation, video, and interactivity

**sans serif typefaces** Typefaces whose letters lack serifs: example

**serif typefaces** Typefaces with small crosslines (called serifs) at the ends of letter strokes: example

**subheadings** Titles that are subordinate to headings, indicating subsections with a major section

**type style** Any modification that lends contrast or emphasis to type, including boldface, italic, underlining, color, and other highlighting and decorative styles

**typeface** The physical design of letters, numbers, and other text characters (*font* and *typeface* are often used interchangeably, although strictly speaking, a font is a set of characters in a given typeface)

**white space** Space (of any color) in a document or screen that doesn't contain any text or artwork

---

**CHECKLIST** ✓
## Revising Business Messages

**A. Evaluate content, organization, style, and tone.**
- Make sure the information is accurate, relevant, and sufficient.
- Check that all necessary points appear in logical order.
- Verify that you present enough support to make the main idea convincing and compelling.
- Be sure the beginning and ending of the message are effective.
- Make sure you've achieved the right tone for the audience and the situation.

**B. Review for readability.**
- Consider using a readability index but be sure to interpret the answer carefully.
- Use a mix of short, medium, and long sentences.
- Keep paragraphs short.
- Use bulleted and numbered lists to emphasize key points.
- Make the document easy to skim with headings and subheadings.

**C. Edit for clarity.**
- Break up overly long sentences and rewrite hedging sentences.
- Impose parallelism to simplify reading.
- Correct dangling modifiers.
- Reword long noun sequences and replace camouflaged verbs.
- Clarify sentence structure and awkward references.

**D. Edit for conciseness.**
- Delete unnecessary words and phrases.
- Shorten long words and phrases.
- Eliminate redundancies.
- Rewrite sentences that start with "It is" or "There are."

---

**CHECKLIST** ✓
## Proofing Business Messages

**A. Look for writing errors.**
- Typographical mistakes
- Misspelled words
- Grammatical errors
- Punctuation mistakes

**B. Look for missing elements.**
- Missing text sections
- Missing exhibits (drawings, tables, photographs, charts, graphs, online images, and so on)
- Missing source notes, copyright notices, or other reference items

**C. Look for design, formatting, and programming mistakes.**
- Incorrect or inconsistent font selections
- Problems with column sizing, spacing, and alignment
- Incorrect margins
- Incorrect special characters
- Clumsy line and page breaks
- Problems with page numbers
- Problems with page headers and footers
- Lack of adherence to company standards
- Inactive or incorrect links
- Missing files

■■■■■■■■  ■  ■  ■
| COMMUNICATION CHALLENGES AT **Jefferson Rabb Web Design**

Jefferson Rabb's web business is doing so well that he has hired you to help with a variety of writing and design tasks. Use what you've learned in this chapter about revising messages and designing for readability.

**INDIVIDUAL CHALLENGE:** The writer Alexander McCall Smith, one of Rabb's clients, is so prolific that summarizing his career is a challenge—and being a best-selling novelist is only one aspect of his varied life's work. Review his biography at www.randomhouse.com/features/mccallsmith (click "About the Author"), which currently runs about 650 words. Rewrite the

bio so that it will fit on a book referral website that limits author bios to 200 words.

**TEAM CHALLENGE:** With a team of classmates assigned by your instructor, visit three of the book websites on which Rabb has worked. You can find links from his website at www.jeffersonrabb.com. Evaluate and compare the sites' readability based on the advice given in the chapter regarding white space, margins, typefaces, and type styles. Prepare a class presentation of your analysis.

## Test Your Knowledge

To review chapter content related to each question, refer to the indicated Learning Objective.

1. What are the three main tasks involved in revising a business message? [LO-1]
✪ 2. What are your two primary responsibilities when editing or revising the work of another writer? [LO-1]
3. What are the relative advantages of short, medium, and long sentences? [LO-2]
4. What functions do headings serve? [LO-2]
5. What are some ways you can make a document more concise? [LO-3]
6. What are hedging sentences, and why should they be avoided unless truly necessary? [LO-4]
7. How do readers benefit from white space? [LO-4]
✪ 8. Why is proofreading an important part of the writing process? [LO-5]
9. What perceptual tricks can you use to improve your chances of spotting errors during proofreading? [LO-5]
✪10. What factors should you consider when choosing a distribution method for your messages (other than for systems where you don't have a choice)? [LO-6]

## Apply Your Knowledge

To review chapter content related to each question, refer to the indicated Learning Objective.

1. How does Target's decision to adopt the ClearRx medicine labeling and packaging system (see "Missing the Message with Prescription Medication" on page 154) fit the definition of ethical communication from Chapter 1? [LO-3]
2. Why should you limit the number of typefaces and type styles in most business documents? [LO-4]
✪ 3. How can you demonstrate good business sense in the choices you make regarding message distribution? [LO-6]

## Practice Your Skills

### Message for Analysis 6.A: Revising to Improve Readability [LO-2]

Analyze the strengths and weaknesses of this message, then revise it so that it follows the guidelines in Chapters 4 through 6:

As an organization, the North American Personal Motorsports Marketing Association has committed ourselves to helping our members—a diverse group comprising of dealers of motorcycles, all-terrain vehicles, Snowmobiles, and personal watercraft—achieve their business objectives. Consequently, our organization, which usually goes under the initials NAPMMA, has the following aims, goals, and objectives. Firstly, we endeavor to aid or assist our members in reaching their business objectives. Second, NAPMMA communicates ("lobbying" in slang terms) with local, state, and national governmental agencies and leaders on issues of importance to our members. And lastly, we educate the motorsports public, that being current motorsports vehicle owners, and prospective owners of said vehicles, on the safe and enjoyable operation of they're vehicles.

### Message for Analysis 6.B: Designing for Readability [LO-4]

To access this message, visit http://real-timeupdates.com/bct12, click on Student Assignments, select Chapter 6, and then select Message 6.B. Download and open the Microsoft Word document. Using the various page, paragraph, and font formatting options available in your word processor, modify the formatting of the document so that its visual tone matches the tone of the message.

### Message for Analysis 6.C: Evaluating the Work of Another Writer [LO-1]

To access this message, visit http://real-timeupdates.com/bct12, click on Student Assignments, select Chapter 6, and then select Message 6.C. Download and open the Microsoft Word document. Using your knowledge of effective writing and the tips on page 149 for evaluating the work of other writers, evaluate this message. After you set Microsoft Word to track changes, make any necessary corrections. Insert comments, as needed, to explain your changes to the author.

### Exercises

Active links for all websites in this chapter can be found on MyBCommLab; see your User Guide for instructions on accessing the content for this chapter. Each activity is labeled according to the primary skill or skills you will need to use. To review relevant chapter content, you can refer to the indicated Learning

Objective. In some instances, supporting information will be found in another chapter, as indicated.

1. **Evaluating the Work of Other Writers [LO-1]** Find a blog post (at least three paragraphs long) on any business-related topic. Evaluate it using the 10 questions on page 149. Email your analysis to your instructor, along with a permalink (a permanent link to this specific post, rather than to the blog overall) to the blog post.

2. **Revising for Readability (Sentence and Paragraph Length) [LO-2]** Rewrite the following paragraph to vary the length of the sentences and to shorten the paragraph so it looks more inviting to readers:

Although major league baseball remains popular, more people are attending minor league baseball games because they can spend less on admission, snacks, and parking and still enjoy the excitement of America's pastime. Connecticut, for example, has three AA minor league teams, including the New Haven Ravens, who are affiliated with the St. Louis Cardinals; the Norwich Navigators, who are affiliated with the New York Yankees; and the New Britain Rock Cats, who are affiliated with the Minnesota Twins. These teams play in relatively small stadiums, so fans are close enough to see and hear everything, from the swing of the bat connecting with the ball to the thud of the ball landing in the outfielder's glove. Best of all, the cost of a family outing to see rising stars play in a local minor league game is just a fraction of what the family would spend to attend a major league game in a much larger, more crowded stadium.

3. **Revising for Readability (Using Lists) [LO-2]** Rewrite the following paragraph using a parallel bulleted list and one introductory sentence:

Our forensic accounting services provide the insights needed to resolve disputes, recover losses, and manage risk intelligently. One of our areas of practice is insurance claims accounting and preparation services, designed to help you maximize recovery of insured value. Another practice area is dispute advisory, in which we can assist with discovery, expert witness testimony, and economic analysis. A third practice: construction consulting. This service helps our clients understand why large-scale construction projects fail to meet schedule or budget requirements. Fourth, we offer general investigative and forensic accounting services, including fraud detection and proof of loss analysis.[5]

4. **Revising for Readability (Sentence Length) [LO-2]** Break the following sentences into shorter ones by adding more periods and revise as needed for smooth flow:

   a. The next time you write something, check your average sentence length in a 100-word passage, and if your sentences average more than 16 to 20 words, see whether you can break up some of the sentences.

   b. Don't do what the village blacksmith did when he instructed his apprentice as follows: "When I take the shoe out of the fire, I'll lay it on the anvil, and when I nod my head, you hit it with the hammer." The apprentice did just as he was told, and now he's the village blacksmith.

   c. Unfortunately, no gadget will produce excellent writing, but using a yardstick like the Fog Index gives us some guideposts to follow for making writing easier to read because its two factors remind us to use short sentences and simple words.

   d. Know the flexibility of the written word and its power to convey an idea, and know how to make your words behave so that your readers will understand.

   e. Words mean different things to different people, and a word such as *block* may mean city block, butcher block, engine block, auction block, or several other things.

5. **Editing for Conciseness (Unnecessary Words) [LO-3]** Cross out unnecessary words in the following phrases:

   a. Consensus of opinion
   b. New innovations
   c. Long period of time
   d. At a price of $50
   e. Still remains

6. **Editing for Conciseness (Long Words) [LO-3]** Revise the following sentences, using shorter, simpler words:

   a. The antiquated calculator is ineffectual for solving sophisticated problems.
   b. It is imperative that the pay increments be terminated before an inordinate deficit is accumulated.
   c. There was unanimity among the executives that Ms. Jackson's idiosyncrasies were cause for a mandatory meeting with the company's personnel director.
   d. The impending liquidation of the company's assets was cause for jubilation among the company's competitors.
   e. The expectations of the president for a stock dividend were accentuated by the preponderance of evidence that the company was in good financial condition.

7. **Editing for Conciseness (Lengthy Phrases) [LO-3]** Use infinitives as substitutes for the overly long phrases in these sentences:

   a. For living, I require money.
   b. They did not find sufficient evidence for believing in the future.
   c. Bringing about the destruction of a dream is tragic.

8. **Editing for Conciseness (Lengthy Phrases) [LO-3]** Rephrase the following in fewer words:

   a. In the near future
   b. In the event that
   c. In order that
   d. For the purpose of
   e. With regard to
   f. It may be that
   g. In very few cases
   h. With reference to
   i. At the present time
   j. There is no doubt that

9. **Editing for Conciseness (Lengthy Phrases) [LO-3]** Revise to condense these sentences to as few words as possible:

   a. We are of the conviction that writing is important.
   b. In all probability, we're likely to have a price increase.

c. Our goals include making a determination about that in the near future.

d. When all is said and done at the conclusion of this experiment, I'd like to summarize the final windup.

e. After a trial period of three weeks, during which time she worked for a total of 15 full working days, we found her work was sufficiently satisfactory so that we offered her full-time work.

10. **Editing for Conciseness (Unnecessary Modifiers) [LO-3]** Remove all the unnecessary modifiers from these sentences:

a. Tremendously high pay increases were given to the extraordinarily skilled and extremely conscientious employees.

b. The union's proposals were highly inflationary, extremely demanding, and exceptionally bold.

11. **Editing for Clarity (Hedging) [LO-3]** Rewrite these sentences so that they no longer contain any hedging:

a. It would appear that someone apparently entered illegally.

b. It may be possible that sometime in the near future the situation is likely to improve.

c. Your report seems to suggest that we might be losing money.

d. I believe Nancy apparently has somewhat greater influence over employees in the e-marketing department.

e. It seems as if this letter of resignation means you might be leaving us.

12. **Editing for Clarity (Indefinite Starters) [LO-3]** Rewrite these sentences to eliminate the indefinite starters:

a. There are several examples here to show that Elaine can't hold a position very long.

b. It would be greatly appreciated if every employee would make a generous contribution to Mildred Cook's retirement party.

c. It has been learned in Washington today from generally reliable sources that an important announcement will be made shortly by the White House.

d. There is a rule that states that we cannot work overtime without permission.

e. It would be great if you could work late for the next three Saturdays.

13. **Editing for Clarity (Parallelism) [LO-3]** Revise these sentences to present the ideas in parallel form:

a. Mr. Hill is expected to lecture three days a week, to counsel two days a week, and must write for publication in his spare time.

b. She knows not only accounting, but she also reads Latin.

c. Both applicants had families, college degrees, and were in their thirties, with considerable accounting experience but few social connections.

d. This book was exciting, well written, and held my interest.

e. Don is both a hard worker and he knows bookkeeping.

14. **Editing for Clarity (Awkward References) [LO-3]** Revise the following sentences to delete the awkward references:

a. The vice president in charge of sales and the production manager are responsible for the keys to 34A and 35A, respectively.

b. The keys to 34A and 35A are in executive hands, with the former belonging to the vice president in charge of sales and the latter belonging to the production manager.

c. The keys to 34A and 35A have been given to the production manager, with the aforementioned keys being gold embossed.

d. A laser printer and an inkjet printer were delivered to John and Megan, respectively.

e. The walnut desk is more expensive than the oak desk, the former costing $300 more than the latter.

15. **Editing for Clarity (Dangling Modifiers) [LO-3]** Rewrite these sentences to clarify the dangling modifiers:

a. Full of trash and ripped-up newspapers, we left Dallas on a plane that apparently hadn't been cleaned in days.

b. Lying on the shelf, Ruby found the operations manual.

c. With leaking plumbing and outdated wiring, I don't think we should buy that property.

d. Being cluttered and filthy, Sandy took the whole afternoon to clean up her desk.

e. After proofreading every word, the letter was ready to be signed.

16. **Editing for Clarity (Noun Sequences) [LO-3]** Rewrite the following sentences to eliminate the long strings of nouns:

a. The focus of the meeting was a discussion of the bank interest rate deregulation issue.

b. Following the government task force report recommendations, we are revising our job applicant evaluation procedures.

c. The production department quality assurance program components include employee training, supplier cooperation, and computerized detection equipment.

d. The supermarket warehouse inventory reduction plan will be implemented next month.

e. The State University business school graduate placement program is one of the best in the country.

17. **Editing for Clarity (Sentence Structure) [LO-3]** Rearrange the following sentences to bring the subjects closer to their verbs:

a. Trudy, when she first saw the bull pawing the ground, ran.

b. It was Terri who, according to Ted, who is probably the worst gossip in the office (Tom excepted), mailed the wrong order.

c. William Oberstreet, in his book *Investment Capital Reconsidered*, writes of the mistakes that bankers through the decades have made.

d. Judy Schimmel, after passing up several sensible investment opportunities, despite the warnings of her friends and family, invested her inheritance in a jojoba plantation.

e. The president of U-Stor-It, which was on the brink of bankruptcy after the warehouse fire, the worst tragedy in the history of the company, prepared a press announcement.

18. **Editing for Clarity (Camouflaged Verbs) [LO-3]** Rewrite each sentence so that the verbs are no longer camouflaged:

a. Adaptation to the new rules was performed easily by the employees.

b. The assessor will make a determination of the tax due.

c. Verification of the identity of the employees must be made daily.

d. The board of directors made a recommendation that Mr. Ronson be assigned to a new division.

e. The auditing procedure on the books was performed by the vice president.

19. **Completing: Designing for Readability; Media Skills: Blogging [LO-4], Chapter 8** Compare the home pages of Bloomberg (www.bloomberg.com) and MarketWatch (www.marketwatch.com), two websites that cover financial markets. What are your first impressions of these two sites? How do their overall designs compare in terms of information delivery and overall user experience? Choose three pieces of information that a visitor to these sites would be likely to look for, such as a current stock price, news from international markets, and commentary from market experts. Which site makes it easier to find this information? Why? Present your analysis in a post for your class blog.

20. **Communication Ethics: Making Ethical Choices; Media Skills: Blogging [LO-3], Chapter 8** The time and energy required for careful revision can often benefit you or your company directly, such as by increasing the probability that website visitors will buy your products. But what about situations in which the quality of your writing and revision work really doesn't stand to benefit you directly? For instance, assume that you are putting a notice on your website, informing the local community about some upcoming construction to your manufacturing plant. The work will disrupt traffic for nearly a year and generate a significant amount of noise and air pollution, but knowing the specific dates and times of various construction activities will allow people to adjust their commutes and other activities to minimize the negative impact on their daily lives. However, your company does not sell products in the local area, so the people affected by all this are not potential customers. Moreover, providing accurate information to the surrounding community and updating it as the project progresses will take time away from your other job responsibilities. Do you have an ethical obligation to keep the local community informed with accurate, up-to-date information? Why or why not?

21. **Proofreading [LO-5]** Proofread the following email message and revise it to correct any problems you find:

Our final company orrientation of the year will be held on Dec. 20. In preparation for this sesssion, please order 20 copies of the Policy handbook, the confindentiality agreenemt, the employee benefits Manual, please let me know if you anticipate any delays in obtaining these materials.

## Expand Your Skills

### Critique the Professionals

Identify a company website that in your opinion violates one or more of the principles of good design discussed on pages 158–161. Using whatever medium your instructor requests, write a brief analysis of the site (no more than one page), citing specific elements from the piece and support from the chapter.

### Sharpening Your Career Skills Online

Bovée and Thill's Business Communication Web Search, at http://businesscommunicationblog.com/websearch, is a unique research tool designed specifically for business communication research. Use the Web Search function to find a website, video, PDF document, or PowerPoint presentation that offers advice on effective proofreading. Write a brief email message to your instructor, describing the item you found and summarizing the career skills information you learned from it.

## MyBCommLab

Go to mybcommlab.com for Auto-graded writing questions as well as the following Assisted-graded writing questions:

6-1. Why is it helpful to put your first draft aside for a while before you begin the editing process? [LO-1]

6-2. Why is it important to spend extra time reviewing and polishing the beginning and end of a message? [LO-1]

6-3. Mybcommlab Only—comprehensive writing assignment for this chapter.

## Endnotes

1. Jefferson Rabb website, accessed 21 January 2013, www.jeffersonrabb.com; Joshua Bodwell, "Artful Author Web Sites," Poets & Writers, January/February 2011, 79–84; *Super Sad True Love Story* website, accessed 22 January 2011, http://supersadtruelovestory.com; *Beat the Reaper* website, accessed 22 January 2011, www.beatthereaper.com.
2. Deborah Gunn, "Looking Good on Paper," *Office Pro*, March 2004, 10–11.
3. Jacci Howard Bear, "Desktop Publishing Rules of Page Layout," About.com, accessed 22 August 2005, www.about.com.
4. Jacci Howard Bear, "Desktop Publishing Rules for How Many Fonts to Use," About.com, accessed 22 August 2005, www.about.com.
5. The writing sample in this exercise was adapted from material on the Marsh Risk Consulting website, accessed 2 October 2006, www.marshriskconsulting.com.

# Electronic, Social, and Visual Media

Choosing the best medium for every business message and using it effectively are essential communication skills. Fortunately, you probably have a fair amount of experience with various electronic, social, and visual media. The three chapters in this part will help you adapt that experience to the unique demands of business communication.

Goodluz/Shutterstock

# 7 | Electronic Media

## LEARNING OBJECTIVES

After studying this chapter, you will be able to

**1** Identify the major electronic media available for business messages and list nine compositional modes used in electronic media.

**2** Describe the evolving role of email in business communication and explain how to adapt the three-step writing process to email messages.

**3** Describe the business benefits of instant messaging (IM) and identify guidelines for effective IM in the workplace.

**4** Explain why organizing website content is so challenging and explain the concept of information architecture.

**5** Explain how to adapt the three-step writing process to podcasting.

**MyBCommLab®**

⭐ **Improve Your Grade!** Over 10 million students improved their results using the Pearson MyLabs. Visit **mybcommlab.com** for simulations, tutorials, and end-of-chapter problems.

**COMMUNICATION CLOSE-UP AT**
**the U.S. Small Business Administration** www.sba.gov

Imagine that you need to provide information to all these audiences:

- People who are considering starting a business and would like more information about it; they may be looking for articles, online training courses, or in-person counseling
- Small business owners who are struggling with everything from personnel management to financing
- Homeowners and small business owners seeking financial assistance in the wake of natural disasters
- Business owners who want to learn more about negotiating contracts to sell goods and services to the federal government
- Whistleblowers looking to report fraud, waste, or abuse
- Companies looking for advice on exporting their products
- Financial institutions wanting to know more about lending money to small businesses through various government-backed programs
- Journalists and other stakeholders who want information about your organization

Taken individually, these writing projects wouldn't be terribly difficult to organize, because each one is fairly narrow and has a clearly defined audience. However, the catch in this case is that all these audiences and more are coming to the same website.

The website of the U.S. Small Business Administration serves the information needs of a diverse range of visitors. Carefully devised information architecture helps ensure that every visitor can find what he or she is looking for.
*Source:* U.S. Small Business Administration website.

174

If you were in charge of organizing the content and navigational linkages on this site, your challenge would be to make sure every user can find the information he or she is looking for in the fastest, most logical way.

Such is the task facing the U.S. Small Business Administration (SBA), whose website has well over 700 individual pages on dozens of topics. It's a challenge shared by all organizations with massive websites—those of multinational corporations can run to many thousands of individual pages.

In addition to the sheer amount of content on these large sites, some information is "evergreen," meaning it stays current for months or years after publication, whereas other information is dynamic and might change every day. Moreover, the information on large sites can't always be split cleanly into parallel categories. In addition, some site visitors know exactly what they're looking for, but others may have only a vague idea of what they need. Finally, levels of computer experience, education, and comfort with written English can vary widely across the target audience.

Designing a satisfying web experience in the face of these challenges starts with the *information architecture*, a plan that shows the organization of a website's content and the navigational linkages that let individual users map their own path through the site. Unlike letters, reports, email messages, and other *linear* media, the web is a *nonlinear* medium in which readers can jump from location to location—forward, backward, and

sideways. This flexibility can be tremendously helpful if readers can easily choose their paths to get the specific information they need, but it can also irritate readers if the navigation is confusing or needlessly complicated. Knowing the needs of each audience segment is crucial to designing navigational paths that are as short and logical as possible.

The SBA website's architecture is built around six high-level divisions. Three of these are parallel categories of information that reflect the various challenges and opportunities a business owners is likely to face: "Starting & Managing," which offers advice on launching and managing a small business; "Loans & Grants," which offers guidance on applying for financial support; and "Contracting," which advises business owners on selling to the U.S. government. Visitors can start with these general categories and drill down to find specific topics. The other three categories are the "Learning Center," which provides access to training videos and other resources; "Local Assistance," which connects visitors to a variety of resources available through local SBA offices around the country; and "SBA Direct," which lets visitors filter the information they see according to personal preferences.

By structuring the site content by these information and activity categories, the SBA website does an effective job of making a vast collection of information accessible to a wide range of audience members. You can see two examples from the website in Figure 7.1 (page 177) and Figure 7.4 (page 185).[1]

# Electronic Media for Business Communication

The website challenges faced by the Small Business Administration (profiled in the chapter-opening Communication Close-Up) highlight one of the most important considerations in using electronic media. In addition to providing quality content, you need to use your chosen medium wisely to maximize its potential and minimize its drawbacks.

**1** **LEARNING OBJECTIVE**
Identify the major electronic media available for business messages and list nine compositional modes used in electronic media.

## ELECTRONIC AND SOCIAL MEDIA OPTIONS

The considerable range of electronic media available for business messages continues to grow as communication technologies evolve:

- **Email.** Conventional email has long been a vital medium for business communication, although it is being replaced in many instances by other tools that provide better support for instant communication and real-time collaboration.
- **Instant messaging (IM).** IM usage now rivals email in many companies. IM offers even greater speed than email, as well as simple operation and fewer problems with unwanted messages or security and privacy problems.
- **Text messaging.** Phone-based text messaging has a number of applications in business communication, including order and status updates, marketing and sales messages, electronic coupons, and customer service.[2]
- **Web content.** Websites are one of the most important electronic media types, from small business sites with a few pages up to large corporate sites with hundreds or thousands of pages.
- **Podcasting.** You may be familiar with podcasts as the online equivalent of recorded radio or video broadcasts. Businesses are now using podcasts to replace or supplement

Business communicators use the full range of electronic media options from conventional email and IM to newer social networking tools.

some conference calls, newsletters, training courses, and other communication activities.

- **Social networks.** Social networks have evolved into a major business communication technology, from well-known public networks to the private, internal networks that many companies now use.
- **Information and media sharing sites.** In addition to social networks, a variety of systems have been designed specifically for sharing content, including user-generated content sites, media curation sites, and community Q&A sites.
- **Wikis.** The collaborative nature of wikis—websites that can be expanded and edited by teams, user communities, or the public at large—make them a natural for aggregating "crowd knowledge."
- **Blogging and microblogging.** The ability to update content quickly and easily makes blogs and microblogs (such as Twitter) a natural medium when communicators want to get messages out in a hurry.
- **Online video.** Now that YouTube and similar websites have made online video available to hundreds of millions of web users, video has been transformed from a fairly specialized tool to a mainstream business communication medium. More than half of the world's largest companies now have their own *branded channels* on YouTube, for example.[3]

The first five of these—email, IM, text messaging, web content, and podcasting—are covered in this chapter. The various social media, from social networks to microblogs, are addressed in Chapter 8. Online video is covered in Chapter 9 along with other visual media.

Note that the lines between these media often get blurry as systems expand their capabilities or people use them in new ways. For example, Facebook Messages integrates IM, text messages, and email capabilities, in addition to being a social networking system.[4] Moreover, the mobile variants of all these technologies add another layer of challenges and opportunities for business communicators. For example, the ability to scan coded labels such as barcodes or the similar *Quick Response (QR) codes* attached to printed materials, products, or store windows (or the ability to pick up radio signals from new *near-field communication* tags) gives smartphone users a way to get more information—from the companies themselves and from other consumers providing reviews on social websites.

Most of your business communication is likely to be via electronic means, but don't overlook the benefits of printed messages. (For more on formatting printed letters and memos, see Chapter 6 and Appendix A.) Here are several situations in which you should consider using a printed message rather than electronic alternatives:

- **When you want to make a formal impression.** For special messages, such as sending congratulations or condolences, the formality of printed documents usually makes them a much better choice than electronic messages.
- **When you are legally required to provide information in printed form.** Business contracts and government regulations sometimes require that information be provided on paper.
- **When you want to stand out from the flood of electronic messages.** If your audience's computers are overflowing with Twitter updates, email, and IM, sometimes a printed message can stand out enough to get noticed.
- **When you need a permanent, unchangeable, or secure record.** Letters and memos are reliable. Once printed, they can't be erased with a single keystroke or surreptitiously modified the way some electronic messages can be. Printed documents are also more difficult to copy and forward.

Even with the widespread use of electronic media, printed memos and letters still play an important role in business communication.

## COMPOSITIONAL MODES FOR ELECTRONIC MEDIA

As you practice using electronic media in this course, it's best to focus on the fundamentals of planning, writing, and completing messages, rather than on the specific details of any one medium or system.[5] Fortunately, the basic communication skills required usually transfer from one system to another. You can succeed with written communication in virtually all electronic media by using one of nine *compositional modes* (see Figure 7.1):

Note how this navigation component makes it easy to move up and down the hierarchy of the site outline.

These short teasers provide enough information for visitors to decide whether the information is of interest.

**Figure 7.1  Compositional Modes for Electronic Media**
When writing for electronic media, you will use to up nine compositional modes, such as the *teasers* shown in the middle column of this website.
*Source:* U.S. Small Business Administration website.

- **Conversations.** IM is a great example of a written medium that mimics spoken conversation. And just as you wouldn't read a report to someone sitting in your office, don't use conversational modes to exchange large volumes of information or to communicate with more than a few people at once.

- **Comments and critiques.** One of the most powerful aspects of social media is the opportunity for interested parties to express opinions and provide feedback, whether by leaving comments on a blog post or reviewing products on an e-commerce site. Sharing helpful tips and insightful commentary is also a great way to build your personal brand. To be an effective commenter, focus on short chunks of information that a broad spectrum of other site visitors will find helpful. Rants, insults, jokes, and blatant self-promotion are usually of little benefit to others.

- **Orientations.** The ability to help people find their way through an unfamiliar system or subject is a valuable writing skill and a talent that readers greatly appreciate. Unlike summaries (see next item), orientations don't give away the key points in the collection of information but rather tell readers where to find those points. Writing effective orientations can be a delicate balancing act because you need to know the material well enough to guide others through it while being able to step back and view it from the inexperienced perspective of a "newbie."

- **Summaries.** At the beginning of an article or webpage, a summary functions as a miniature version of the document, giving readers all the key points while skipping over

Communicating successfully with electronic media requires a wide range of writing approaches.

details. In some instances, this is all a reader needs or is willing to read. In other instances, the up-front summary helps a reader decide whether to invest the time needed to read the full document. At the end of an article or webpage, a summary functions as a review, reminding readers of the key points they've just read.

- **Reference material.** One of the greatest benefits of the Internet is the access it can provide to vast quantities of reference materials—numerical or textual information that people typically don't read in a linear way but rather search through to find particular data points, trends, or other details. One of the challenges of writing reference material is that you can't always know how readers will want to access it. Making the information accessible via search engines is an important step. However, readers don't always know which search terms will yield the best results, so consider an orientation and organize the material in logical ways with clear headings that promote skimming.

- **Narratives.** The storytelling techniques covered in Chapter 4 can be effective in a wide variety of situations. Narratives work best when they have an intriguing beginning that ignites readers' curiosity, a middle section that moves quickly through the challenges that an individual or company faced, and an inspiring or instructive ending that gives readers information they can apply in their own lives and jobs.

- **Teasers.** Teasers intentionally withhold key pieces of information as a way to pull readers or listeners into a story or other document. Teasers are widely used in marketing and sales messages, such as a bit of copy on the outside of an envelope that promises important information on the inside. In electronic media, the space limitations and URL linking capabilities of Twitter and other microblogging systems make them a natural tool for the teaser approach. Although they can certainly be effective, teasers need to be used with respect for readers' time and information needs. Be sure that the *payoff*, the information a teaser links to, is valuable and legitimate. You'll quickly lose credibility if readers think they are being tricked into clicking through to information they don't really want.

- **Status updates and announcements.** If you use social media frequently, much of your writing will involve status updates and announcements. However, don't post trivial information that only you are likely to find interesting. Post only those updates that readers will find useful, and include only the information they need.

- **Tutorials.** Given the community nature of social media, the purpose of many messages is to share how-to advice. Becoming known as a reliable expert is a great way to build customer loyalty for your company while enhancing your own personal value.

As you approach a new communication task using electronic media, ask yourself what kind of information audience members are likely to need and then choose the appropriate compositional mode. Of course, many of these modes are also used in written media, but over time you may find yourself using all of them in various electronic and social media contexts.

*With Twitter and other super-short messaging systems, the ability to write a compelling* teaser *is an important skill.*

# Email

**2 LEARNING OBJECTIVE**
Describe the evolving role of email in business communication, and explain how to adapt the three-step writing process to email messages.

Email has been a primary medium for many companies for several decades, and in the beginning it offered a huge advantage in speed and efficiency over the media it frequently replaced (printed and faxed messages). Over the years, email began to be used for many communication tasks simply because it was the only widely available electronic medium for written messages and millions of users were comfortable with it. However, newer tools, such as instant messaging, blogs, microblogs, social networks, and shared workspaces, are taking over specific tasks for which they are better suited.[6] For example, email is not usually the best choice for conversational communication (IM is better for this) or project management discussions and updates (blogs, wikis, and various purpose-built systems are often better for this).

*Overuse is one of the major complaints about email.*

In addition to the widespread availability of better alternatives for many communication purposes, the indiscriminate use of email has lowered its appeal in the eyes of many professionals. In a sense, email is too easy to use—it's too easy to send low-value messages to multiple recipients and to trigger long message chains that become impossible to follow as people chime in along the way. In fact, frustration with email is so high in

some companies that managers are making changes to reduce or even eliminate its use for internal communication.
The global public relations firm Weber Shandwick recently
moved its 3,000 employees from email to a custom system
described as "equal parts Facebook, work group collaboration software, and employee bulletin board."[7]

However, email still has compelling advantages that
will keep it in steady use in many companies. First, email
is universal. Anybody with an email address can reach anybody else with an email address, no matter which systems
the senders and receivers are on. Second, email is still the
best medium for many private, short- to medium-length messages, particularly when
the exchange is limited to two people. Unlike with microblogs or IM, for instance, mid-
size messages are easy to compose and easy to read on email. Third, email's noninstanta-
neous nature is an advantage when used properly. Email lets senders compose substantial
messages in private and on their own schedule, and it lets recipients read those messages
at their leisure.

**REAL-TIME UPDATES**

LEARN MORE BY WATCHING THIS VIDEO

**Find out why email starts fights—
and how to avoid them**

See why the lean medium of email can lead to
misunderstanding when used when it shouldn't be. Go to http://
real-timeupdates.com/bct12 and click on Learn More. If you are
using MyBCommLab, you can access Real-Time Updates within
each chapter or under Student Study Tools.

*In spite of its shortcomings, email
remains a major business communication medium.*

## PLANNING EMAIL MESSAGES

The solution to email overload starts in the planning step, by making sure every message has
a valid, business-related purpose. Also, be aware that many companies now have formal email
policies that specify how employees can use email, including restrictions against using company email service for personal messages, sending confidential information, or sending material that might be deemed objectionable. In addition, many employers now monitor email,
either automatically with software programmed to look for sensitive content or manually via
security staff actually reading selected email messages. Regardless of formal policies, though,
every email user has a responsibility to avoid actions that could cause trouble, from downloading virus-infected software to sending inappropriate photographs. *Email hygiene* refers to
all the efforts that companies are making to keep email clean and safe—from spam blocking
and virus protection to content filtering.[8]

Even with fairly short messages, spend a moment or two on the message planning tasks
described in Chapter 4: analyzing the situation, gathering necessary information for your
readers, and organizing your message. You'll save time in the long run because you will craft
a more effective message on the first attempt. Your readers will get the information they
need and won't have to generate follow-up messages asking for clarification or additional
information.

*Cut down on message overload
by making sure every email message you send has a valid business
purpose.*

## WRITING EMAIL MESSAGES

Business email is a more formal medium than you are probably accustomed to with email
for personal communication (see Figure 7.2 on the next page). The expectations of writing
quality for business email are higher than for personal email, and the consequences of bad
writing or poor judgment can be much more serious. For example, email messages and other
electronic documents have the same legal weight as printed documents, and they are often
used as evidence in lawsuits and criminal investigations.[9]

The email subject line might seem like a small detail, but it is actually one of the most
important parts of an email message because it helps recipients decide which messages to
read and when to read them. To capture your audience's attention, make your subject lines
informative and compelling. Go beyond simply describing or classifying your message; use
the opportunity to build interest with keywords, quotations, directions, or questions.[10] For
example, "July sales results" accurately describes the content of the message, but "July sales
results: good news and bad news" is more intriguing. Readers will want to know why some
news is good and some is bad.

In addition, many email programs display the first few words or lines of incoming
messages, even before the recipient opens them. As noted by social media public relations
expert Steve Rubel, you can "tweetify" the opening lines of your email messages to make

*Business email messages are more
formal than the email messages
you send to family and friends.*

*The subject line is often the most
important part of an email message because it can determine
whether the message gets read.*

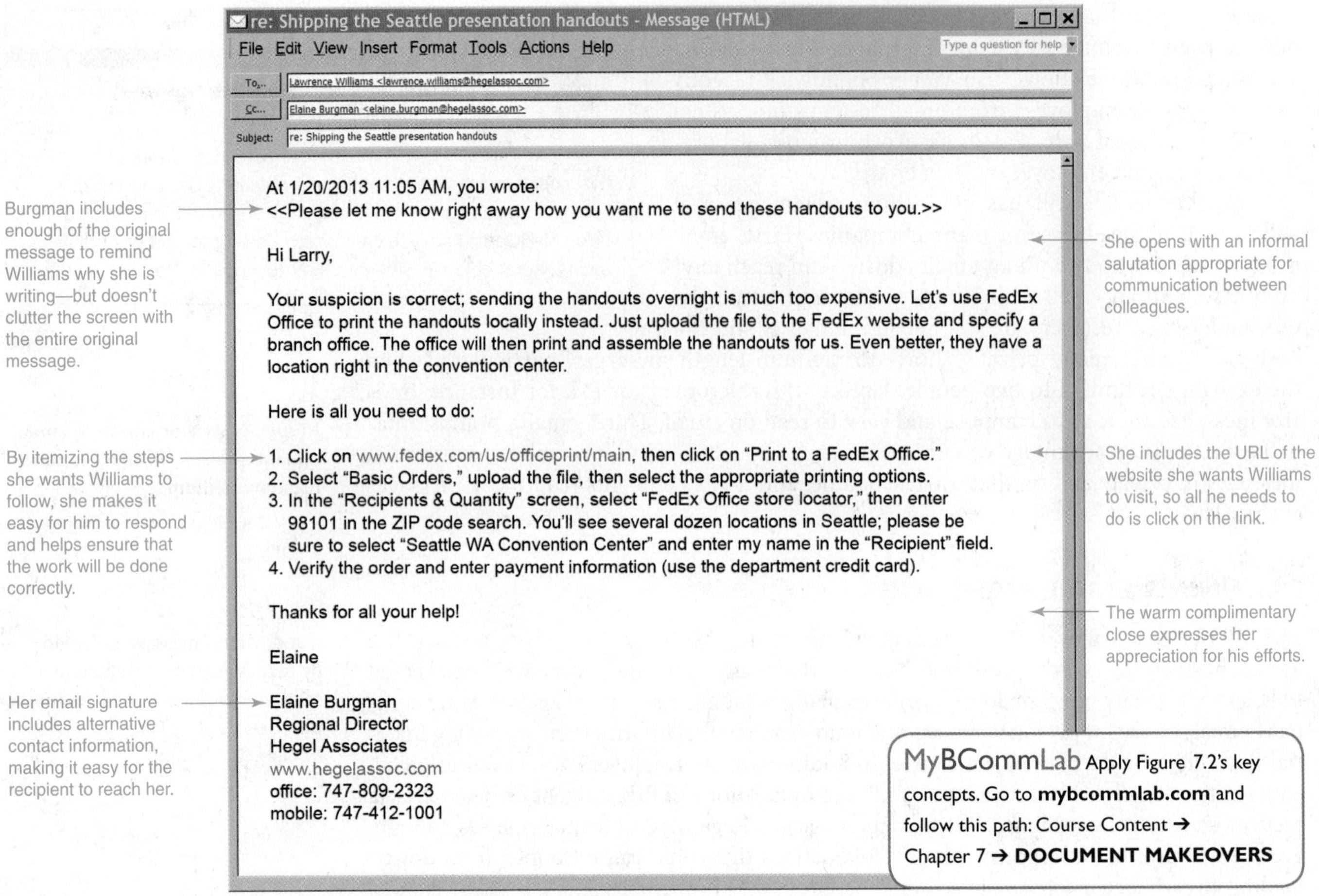

Burgman includes enough of the original message to remind Williams why she is writing—but doesn't clutter the screen with the entire original message.

By itemizing the steps she wants Williams to follow, she makes it easy for him to respond and helps ensure that the work will be done correctly.

Her email signature includes alternative contact information, making it easy for the recipient to reach her.

She opens with an informal salutation appropriate for communication between colleagues.

She includes the URL of the website she wants Williams to visit, so all he needs to do is click on the link.

The warm complimentary close expresses her appreciation for his efforts.

**Figure 7.2   Email for Business Communication**
In this response to an email query from a colleague, Elaine Burgman takes advantage of her email system's features to create an efficient and effective message.
*Source:* Used with permission from Microsoft.

them stand out. In other words, choose the first few words carefully to grab your reader's attention.[11] Think of the first sentence as an extension of your subject line.

As a lean medium, email can present challenges when you need to express emotional nuances, whether positive or negative. For years, users of email (as well as IM and text messaging) have used a variety of *emoticons* to express emotions in casual communication. For example, to express sympathy as a way to take some of the sting out of negative news, one might use a "frowny face," either the :( character string or a graphical emoticon such as ☹ or one of the colorful and sometimes animated characters available in some systems.

Over the years, the use of emoticons was widely regarded as unprofessional and therefore advised against in business communication. Recently, though, an increasing number of professionals seem to be using them, particularly for communication with close colleagues, even as other professionals continue to view them as evidence of lazy or immature writing.[12] In the face of these conflicting perspectives, the best advice is to use caution. Avoid emoticons for all types of external communication and for formal internal communication, and avoid those bright yellow graphical emoticons (and particularly animated emoticons) in all business communication.

Attitudes about emoticons in business communication are changing; you'll have to use your best judgment in every case.

## COMPLETING EMAIL MESSAGES

Particularly for important messages, taking a few moments to revise and proofread might save you hours of headaches and damage control. The more important the message, the more carefully you need to proof. Also, favor simplicity when it comes to producing your email messages. A clean, easily readable font, in black on a white background, is sufficient for nearly all email messages. Take advantage of your email system's ability to include an **email signature**, a small file that automatically includes such items as your full name, title, company, and contact information at the end of your messages.

When you're ready to distribute your message, pause to verify what you're doing before you click "Send." Make sure you've included everyone necessary—and no one else. Don't click "Reply All" when you mean to click only "Reply." The difference could be embarrassing or even career threatening. Don't include people in the cc (courtesy copy or "carbon copy," historically) or bcc (blind courtesy copy) fields unless you know how these features work. (Everyone who receives the message can see who is on the cc line but not who is on the bcc line.) Also, don't set the message priority to "high" or "urgent" unless your message is truly urgent. And if you intend to include an attachment, be sure that it is indeed attached.

To review the tips and techniques for successful email, see Table 7.1 and "Checklist: Creating Effective Email Messages" or click on Chapter 7 at http://real-timeupdates .com/bct12.

> Think twice before hitting "Send." A simple mistake in your content or distribution can cause major headaches.

### TABLE 7.1 | Tips for Effective Email Messages

| Tip | Why It's Important |
|---|---|
| When you request information or action, make it clear what you're asking for, why it's important, and how soon you need it; don't make your reader write back for details. | People will be tempted to ignore your messages if they're not clear about what you want or how soon you want it. |
| When responding to a request, either paraphrase the request or include enough of the original message to remind the reader what you're replying to. | Some businesspeople get hundreds of email messages a day and may need reminding what your specific response is about. |
| If possible, avoid sending long, complex messages via email. | Long messages are easier to read as attached reports or web content. |
| Adjust the level of formality to the message and the audience. | Overly formal messages to colleagues can be perceived as stuffy and distant; overly informal messages to customers or top executives can be perceived as disrespectful. |
| Activate a signature file, which automatically pastes your contact information into every message you create. | A signature saves you the trouble of retyping vital information and ensures that recipients know how to reach you through other means. |
| Don't let unread messages pile up in your in-basket. | You'll miss important information and create the impression that you're ignoring other people. |
| Never type in all caps. | ALL CAPS ARE INTERPRETED AS SCREAMING. |
| Don't overformat your messages with background colors, multicolored type, unusual fonts, and so on. | Such messages can be difficult and annoying to read on screen. |
| Remember that messages can be forwarded anywhere and saved forever. | Don't let a moment of anger or poor judgment haunt you for the rest of your career. |
| Use the "return receipt requested" feature only for the most critical messages. | This feature triggers a message back to you whenever someone receives or opens your message; many consider this an invasion of privacy. |
| Make sure your computer has up-to-date virus protection. | One of the worst breaches of "netiquette" is infecting other computers because you haven't bothered to protect your own system. |
| Pay attention to grammar, spelling, and capitalization. | Some people don't think email needs formal rules, but careless messages make you look unprofessional and can annoy readers. |
| Use acronyms sparingly. | Shorthand such as IMHO (in my humble opinion) and LOL (laughing out loud) can be useful in informal correspondence with colleagues, but avoid using them in more formal messages. |

---

**CHECKLIST** ✔ Creating Effective Email Messages

**A. Planning email messages**
- Make sure every email message you send is necessary.
- Don't cc or bcc anyone who doesn't really need to see the message.
- Follow company email policy; understand the restrictions your company places on email usage.
- Practice good email hygiene by not opening suspicious messages, keeping virus protection up to date, and following other company guidelines.
- Follow the chain of command.

**B. Writing email messages**
- Remember that business email is more formal than personal email.
- Recognize that email messages carry the same legal weight as other business documents.
- Pay attention to the quality of your writing and use correct grammar, spelling, and punctuation.

- Make your subject lines informative by clearly identifying the purpose of your message.
- Make your subject lines compelling by wording them in a way that intrigues your audiences.
- Use the first few words of the email body to catch the reader's attention.

**C. Completing email messages**
- Revise and proofread carefully to avoid embarrassing mistakes.
- Keep the layout of your messages simple and clean.
- Use an email signature file to give recipients your contact information.
- Double-check your recipient list before sending.
- Don't mark messages as "urgent" unless they truly are urgent.

---

# Instant Messaging and Text Messaging

**3 LEARNING OBJECTIVE**
Describe the business benefits of instant messaging (IM) and identify guidelines for effective IM in the workplace.

Computer-based **instant messaging (IM)**, in which users' messages appear on each other's screens instantly, is used extensively for internal and external communication. IM is available in stand-alone systems and as a function embedded in online meeting systems, collaboration systems, social networks, and other platforms. For conversational exchanges, it's hard to top the advantages of IM, and the technology is replacing both email and voice mail in many situations.[13] Business-grade IM systems, often referred to as *enterprise IM*, offer a range of capabilities, including basic chat, *presence awareness* (the ability to quickly see which people are at their desks and available to IM), remote display of documents, video capabilities, remote control of other computers, automated newsfeeds from blogs and websites, and automated *bot* (derived from the word *robot*) capabilities in which a computer can carry on simple conversations.[14]

Phone-based **text messaging** has a number of applications in business as well, including marketing (alerting customers about new sale prices, for example), customer service (such as airline flight status, package tracking, and appointment reminders), security (for example, authenticating mobile banking transactions), crisis management (such as updating all employees working at a disaster scene), and process monitoring (alerting computer technicians to system failures, for example).[15] As it becomes more tightly integrated with other communication media, text messaging is likely to find even more widespread use in business communication. For example, texting is now integrated into systems such as Facebook Messages and Gmail, and branded "StarStar numbers" can deliver web-based content such as videos, software apps, and electronic coupons to mobile phones.[16]

The advice offered in this section applies primarily to IM but is relevant to text messaging as well.

## UNDERSTANDING THE BENEFITS AND RISKS OF IM

IM offers many benefits:
- Rapid response
- Low cost
- Ability to mimic conversation
- Wide availability

The benefits of IM include rapid response to urgent messages, lower cost than phone calls, ability to mimic conversation more closely than email, and availability on a wide range of devices and systems.[17] In addition, because it more closely resembles one-on-one conversation, IM doesn't get misused as a one-to-many broadcast method as often as email does.[18]

The potential drawbacks of IM include security problems (computer viruses, network infiltration, and the possibility that sensitive messages might be intercepted by outsiders), the need for *user authentication* (making sure that online correspondents are really who they appear to be), the challenge of logging messages for later review and archiving (a legal requirement in some industries), incompatibility between competing IM systems, and *spim* (unsolicited commercial messages, similar to email spam). And as with email, IM is a lean medium with little opportunity to convey nonverbal signals, which increases the chances of message misinterpretation.[19]

## ADAPTING THE THREE-STEP PROCESS FOR SUCCESSFUL IM

Although instant messages are often conceived, written, and sent within a matter of seconds, the principles of the three-step process still apply:

- **Planning instant messages.** View every IM exchange as a conversation; while you may not deliberately plan every individual statement you make or question you pose, take a moment to plan the overall exchange. If you're requesting something, think through exactly what you need and the most effective way to ask for it. If someone is asking you for something, consider his or her needs and your ability to meet them before you respond. And although you rarely need to organize instant messages in the sense of creating an outline, try to deliver information in a coherent, complete way that minimizes the number of individual messages required.

  Although you don't plan individual instant messages in the usual way, view important IM exchanges as conversations with specific goals in mind.

- **Writing instant messages.** As with email, the appropriate writing style for business IM is more formal than the style you may be accustomed to with personal IM or text messaging. You should generally avoid IM acronyms (such as *FWIW* for "for what it's worth" or *HTH* for "hope that helps") except when communicating with close colleagues. In the IM exchange in Figure 7.3, notice how the participants communicate

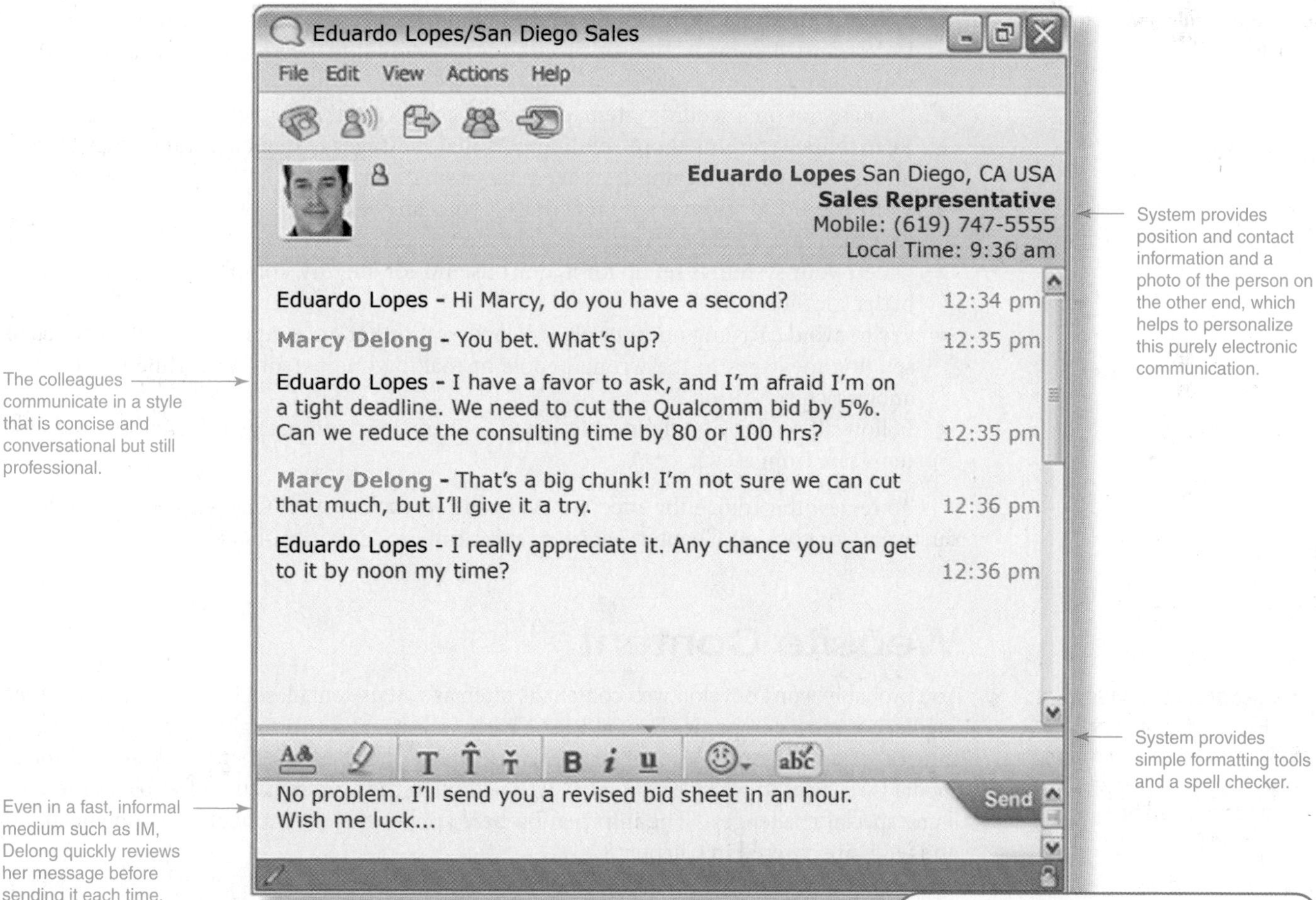

The colleagues communicate in a style that is concise and conversational but still professional.

System provides position and contact information and a photo of the person on the other end, which helps to personalize this purely electronic communication.

System provides simple formatting tools and a spell checker.

Even in a fast, informal medium such as IM, Delong quickly reviews her message before sending it each time.

**Figure 7.3   Instant Messaging for Business Communication**
Instant messaging is widely used in business, but you should not use the same informal style of communication you probably use for IM with your friends and family.

MyBCommLab Apply Figure 7.3's key concepts. Go to **mybcommlab.com** and follow this path: Course Content → Chapter 7 → **DOCUMENT MAKEOVERS**

---

**CHECKLIST** ✔ Using IM Productively

- Pay attention to security and privacy issues and be sure to follow all company guidelines.
- Treat IM as a professional communication medium, not an informal, personal tool; avoid using IM slang with all but close colleagues.

- Maintain good etiquette, even during simple exchanges.
- Protect your own productivity by making yourself unavailable when you need to focus.
- In most instances, don't use IM for confidential messages, complex messages, or personal messages.

---

quickly and rather informally but still maintain good etiquette and a professional tone. This style is even more important if you or your staff use IM to communicate with customers and other outside audiences.

- **Completing instant messages.** One of the biggest attractions of IM is that the completing step is so easy. You don't have to produce the message in the usual sense, and distribution is as simple as hitting "Enter" or clicking a "Send" button. However, don't skip over the revising and proofreading tasks. Quickly scan each message before you send it, to make sure you don't have any missing or misspelled words and that your message is clear and complete.

Regardless of the system you're using, you can make IM more efficient and effective by following these tips:[20]

> Understand the guidelines for successful business IM before you begin to use it.

- Be courteous in your use of IM; if you don't need an answer instantly, you can avoid interrupting someone by sending an email or other type of message instead.
- Unless an IM conversation or meeting is scheduled, make yourself unavailable when you need to focus on other work.
- If you're not on a secure system, don't send confidential information.
- Be extremely careful about sending personal messages—they have a tendency to pop up on other people's computers at embarrassing moments.
- Don't use IM for impromptu meetings if you can't verify that everyone concerned will be available.
- Unless your system is set up for it, don't use IM for lengthy, complex messages; email is better for those.
- Try to avoid carrying on multiple IM conversations at once, to minimize the chance of sending messages to the wrong people or making one person wait while you tend to another conversation.
- Follow all security guidelines designed to keep your company's information and systems safe from attack.

To review the advice for effective IM in the workplace, see "Checklist: Using IM Productively" or click on Chapter 7 at http://real-timeupdates.com/bct12.

# Website Content

> **4 LEARNING OBJECTIVE**
> Explain why organizing website content is so challenging, and explain the concept of information architecture.

You probably won't develop web content as often as you use email, social networks, and other media, but most companies have at least a basic website, and you might be involved in planning or expanding on it. Most of what you're learning about using other electronic and social media is relevant to website content as well, although the unique nature of websites presents some special challenges. (The information here applies to conventional web content. Blogs and wikis are covered in Chapter 8.)

## ORGANIZING WEBSITE CONTENT

As the SBA vignette at the beginning of the chapter suggests, the versatility of websites can be both a blessing and a curse. It's a blessing because a single web presence can serve multiple purposes for multiple audiences. For example, a company website can have sections for potential employees, investors, future customers, current customers, business partners, news reporters, and members of the local community. Anyone who wants to learn more about the company can visit the website and find what he or she needs.

That versatility can also be curse, however, because it makes websites more difficult to plan and organize than virtually any other type of communication. Each of the target audiences has unique information needs and often little interest in the other material that might be on the site. Visitors also enter the site at different points. Some will type in the top-level URL (such as www.apple.com or www.dell.com), some will link through to lower-level pages from other websites (a product review in a blog, for example), and many will land on specific pages after using a search engine.

The versatility of websites can make them a challenge to organize, because different visitors want different types of information.

Because the web is a multidimensional medium, readers move around in any order they please; there often is no beginning, middle, or end. When organizing a website, you need to anticipate the various paths your readers will want to follow and make sure you provide the right hyperlinks in the right places to help readers explore successfully. Professional website designers often use the term **information architecture** to describe the content structure, labeling, and navigational flow of all the parts of a website (see Figure 7.4).

Thinking through the information architecture of a website is essential to creating a rewarding experience for all visitors.

Clicking on "Starting & Managing" at the top of the screen opens this page, which serves an annotated table of contents for this section.

Each subtopic contains a number of articles on that subject. Notice how quickly you can assess the content of the site using these short, descriptive headlines.

**Figure 7.4   Information Architecture**
The "Starting & Managing" link name at the left of the top navigation bar on the SBA website is the equivalent of a first-level heading in a report. Clicking on it expands down to two second-level subheadings, "Starting a Business" and "Managing a Business." Identifying the paths site visitors might want to take is a critical step in designing the information architecture of a website.
*Source:* U.S. Small Business Administration website.

In a sense, the information architecture is a three-dimensional outline of the site, showing (1) the vertical hierarchy of pages from the homepage down to the lower level, (2) the horizontal division of pages across the various sections of the site, and (3) the links that tie all these pages together, both internally (between various pages on the site) and externally (between your site and other websites). On simpler sites with few content categories, the information architecture is fairly straightforward. However, on large corporate or organizational websites (such as your college or university's website), the architecture can be extremely complex, and it is the information architect's job to make each visitor's experience as simple as possible.

To organize a site effectively, follow these tips:[21]

Start developing the information architecture by brainstorming how all your potential visitors will want to use the site.

- Brainstorm all the likely usage scenarios—who will visit the site, where will they be coming from, what will they be looking for, and what terms will they use to identify the information they need.
- Identify all the likely entry points to the site and the target information for each visitor segment.
- Create a map or other visual tool that shows all the pathways between entry points and target information, then organize the content and links in the simplest, most direct way possible.
- Make sure visitors can always find their way back to the top level of the site, even if a search engine link plunked them onto a page deep within the site.
- Give visitors options for finding what they want. Some will want to search by key terms, for example, whereas others will prefer to follow clearly defined paths that drill down into more specific information (such as Products -> Consumer Products -> Tools -> Handheld Power Tools, for example).
- Be consistent with labels and link behaviors, and use commonly accepted terminology. For example, web visitors now expect information about a company to be on a page titled "About Us."

**REAL-TIME UPDATES**
LEARN MORE BY VISITING THIS WEBSITE
**Intrigued by the challenge of designing effective websites?**

The Information Architecture Institute can help you learn more about the IA profession. Go to http://realtimeupdates.com/bct12 and click on Learn More. If you are using MyBCommLab, you can access Real-Time Updates within each chapter or under Student Study Tools.

Think of your website as an information-delivery machine that visitors must learn how to operate in order to use efficiently. By making your machine as easy to use as possible, you'll help visitors find what they want quickly and encourage them to come back for more.

## DRAFTING WEBSITE CONTENT

Everything you know about effective writing applies to web content, but keep these extra points in mind as well:

- Take special care to build trust with your intended audiences because careful readers can be skeptical of online content. Make sure your content is accurate, current, complete, and authoritative.

With the inverted pyramid style, you summarize the key points at the beginning of a webpage, then move on to provide details.

- Wherever you can, use the *inverted pyramid* style, in which you cover the most important information briefly at first and then gradually reveal successive layers of detail—letting readers choose to see those additional layers if they want to.
- Help readers absorb information by breaking it into small, self-contained, easily readable chunks that are linked together logically. Many readers don't have the patience to read lengthy pages online.
- Present your information in a concise, skimmable format. Effective websites use a variety of means to help readers skim pages quickly, including lists, careful use of color and boldface, informative headings, and helpful summaries that give readers a choice of learning more if they want to (see Figure 7.5).
- Use direct and concise link names that serve for both site navigation and content skimming. Above all else, clearly identify where a link will take readers. Don't use cute

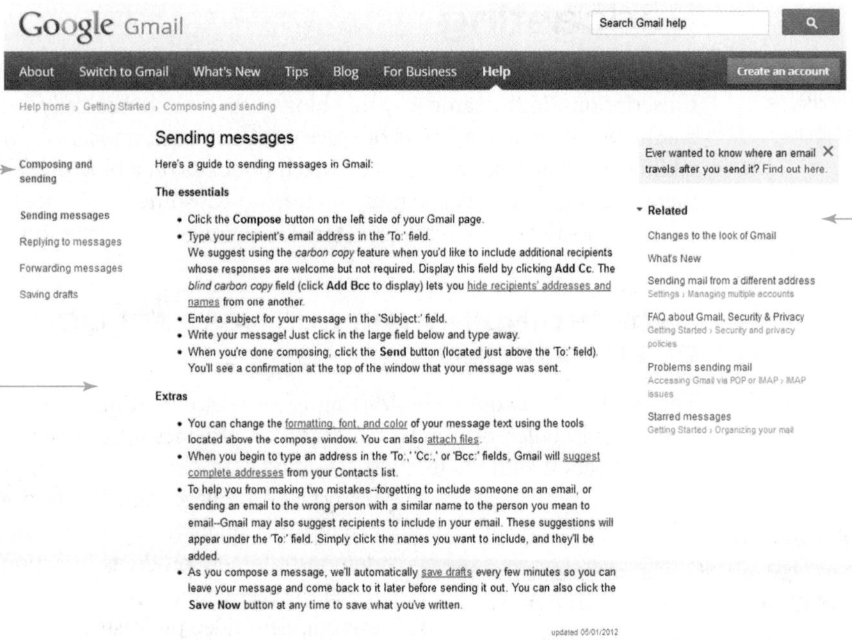


The left-hand navigation choices offer access to major topics related to composing and sending email messages; these are the topics that all readers are likely to be interested in.

The information is divided into "essentials" and "extras," allowing readers to get the most important information in a matter of seconds.

The choices on the right side of the screen are supplemental topics that may be of interest to some readers.

**Figure 7.5 Writing for the Web**
This page from the Google Help feature for Gmail demonstrates several important points about effective web writing.
*Source:* Google, 2012.

wordplay that obscures the content, and don't force readers to click through in order to figure out where they're going.

- As much as possible, adapt your content for a global audience. Translating content is expensive, however, so some companies compromise by *localizing* the homepage while keeping the deeper, more detailed content in its original language.

THE ART OF PROFESSIONALISM

## Striving to Excel

Pros are good at what they do, and they never stop improving. No matter what your job might be at any given time—even if it is far from where you aspire to be—strive to perform at the highest possible level. Not only do you have an ethical obligation to give your employer and your customers your best effort, but excelling at each level in your career is the best way to keep climbing up to new positions of responsibility. Plus, being good at what you do delivers a sense of satisfaction that is hard to beat.

In many jobs and in many industries, performing at a high level requires a commitment to continuous learning and improvement. The nature of the work often changes as markets and technologies evolve, and expectations of quality tend to increase over time as well. View this constant change as a positive thing, as a way to avoid stagnation and boredom.

Striving to excel can be a challenge when there is a mismatch between the job's requirements and your skills and knowledge. If you are underqualified for a job, you need to identify your weaknesses quickly and come up with a plan to address them. A supportive manager will help you identify these areas and encourage improvement through training or mentoring. Don't wait for a boss to tell you your work is subpar, however. If you know you're floundering, don't wait until you've failed to get help.

If you are overqualified for a job, it's easy to slip into a rut and eventually underperform simply because you aren't being challenged. However, current and future bosses aren't going to judge you on how well you performed relative to your needs and expectations; they're going to judge you on how well you performed relative to the job's requirements. Work with your boss to find ways to make your job more challenging if possible, or start looking for a better job if necessary, but be sure to maintain your level of performance until you can bring your responsibilities and talents into closer alignment.

### CAREER APPLICATIONS

1. Should you ever try to sell yourself into a job for which you are not yet 100 percent qualified? Explain your answer.
2. Do you agree that you have an ethical obligation to excel at your job? Why or why not?

# Podcasting

**5** **LEARNING OBJECTIVE**
Explain how to adapt the three-step writing process to podcasting.

**Podcasting** is the process of recording audio or video files and distributing them online via RSS subscriptions, in the same way that blog posts are automatically fed to subscribers. Podcasting combines the media richness of voice or visual communication with the convenience of portability. Audiences can listen to or watch podcasts on a blog or website, or they can download them to phones or portable music players to consume on the go. Particularly with audio podcasts, the hands-off, eyes-off aspect makes them great for listening while driving or exercising.

## UNDERSTANDING THE BUSINESS APPLICATIONS OF PODCASTING

Podcasting can be used to deliver a wide range of audio and video messages.

The most obvious use of podcasting is to replace existing audio and video messages, such as one-way teleconferences in which a speaker provides information without expecting to engage in conversation with the listeners. Training is another good use of podcasting; you may have already taken a college course via podcasts. Marketing departments can replace expensive printed brochures with video podcasts that demonstrate new products in action. Sales representatives who travel to meet with potential customers can listen to audio podcasts or view video podcasts to get the latest information on their companies' products. Human resources departments can offer video tours of their companies to entice new recruits. Podcasts are also an increasingly common feature on blogs, letting audiences listen to or watch recordings of their favorite bloggers. Some services can even transcribe blogs into podcasts and vice versa.[22]

> **REAL-TIME UPDATES**
> LEARN MORE BY WATCHING THIS VIDEO
> **Essential ideas for business podcasters**
> Veteran podcaster Cliff Ravenscraft explains how podcasting can help businesses connect with their customers. Go to http://real-timeupdates.com/bct12 and click on Learn More. If you are using MyBCommLab, you can access Real-Time Updates within each chapter or under Student Study Tools.

## ADAPTING THE THREE-STEP PROCESS FOR SUCCESSFUL PODCASTING

The three-step process adapts quite well to podcasting.

Although it might not seem obvious at first, the three-step writing process adapts quite nicely to podcasting. First, focus the planning step on analyzing the situation, gathering the information you'll need, and organizing your material. One vital planning step depends on whether you intend to create podcasts for limited use and distribution (such as a weekly audio update to your virtual team) or a **podcasting channel** with regular recordings on a consistent theme, designed for a wider public audience. If you intend to create a podcasting channel, be sure to think through the range of topics you want to address over time to verify that you have a sustainable purpose.[23] If you bounce from one theme to another, you risk losing your audience.[24] Maintaining a consistent schedule is also important; listeners will stop paying attention if they can't count on regular updates.[25]

Steering devices such as transitions, previews, and reviews are vital in podcasts.

As you organize the content for a podcast, pay close attention to previews, transitions, and reviews. These steering devices are especially vital in audio recordings because audio lacks the headings and other elements that audiences rely on in print media. Moreover, scanning back and forth to find specific parts of an audio or video message is much more difficult than with textual messages, so you need to do everything possible to make sure your audience successfully receives and interprets your message on the first try.

Plan your podcast content carefully; editing is more difficult with podcasts than with textual messages.

One of the attractions of podcasting is the conversational, person-to-person feel of the recordings, so unless you need to capture exact wording, speaking from an outline and notes rather than a prepared script is often the best choice. However, no one wants to listen to rambling podcasts that take several minutes to get to the topic or struggle to make a point, so don't try to make up your content on the fly. Effective podcasts, like effective stories, have a clear beginning, middle, and end.

The completing step is where podcasting differs most dramatically from written communication, for the obvious reason that you are recording and distributing audio or video files. Particularly for more formal podcasts, start by revising your script or thinking through your speaking notes before you begin to record. The closer you can get to recording your podcasts in one take, the more productive you'll be.

Figure 7.6 illustrates the basic process of recording and distributing podcasts, but the process can vary depending on such factors as the desired production quality and whether

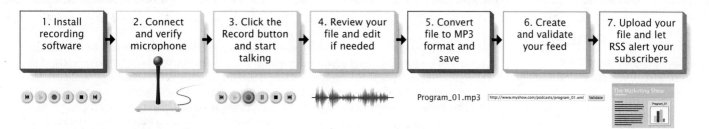

**Figure 7.6 The Podcasting Process**
Creating a podcast requires a few easy steps, and basic podcasts can be created using free or low-cost hardware and software.

you plan to record in a studio setting or on the go (using a mobile phone or digital recorder to capture your voice).

Most personal computers, smartphones, and other devices now have basic audio recording capability, including built-in microphones, and free editing software is available online (at http://audacity.sourceforge.net, for example). If you need higher production quality or greater flexibility, you'll need additional pieces of hardware and software, such as an audio processor (to filter out extraneous noise and otherwise improve the audio signal), a mixer (to combine multiple audio or video signals), a better microphone, more sophisticated recording and editing software, and perhaps some physical changes in your recording location to improve the acoustics.

Podcasts can be distributed in several ways, including through media stores such as iTunes, by dedicated podcast hosting services, or on a blog with content that supports the podcast channel. If you distribute your podcast on a blog, you can provide additional information and use the commenting feature of the blog to encourage feedback from your audience.[26]

For a quick review of the key points of business podcasting, see "Checklist: Planning and Producing Business Podcasts." For news on the latest developments in podcasting, visit http://real-timeupdates.com/bct12 and click on Chapter 7.

> For basic podcasts, your computer and perhaps even your smartphone might have the hardware you already need, and you can download free recording software.

## CHECKLIST ✓ Planning and Producing Business Podcasts

- Consider podcasting whenever you have the opportunity to replace existing audio or video messages.
- If you plan a podcast channel with a regular stream of new content, make sure you've identified a theme or purpose that is rich enough to sustain your effort.
- Pay close attention to previews, transitions, and reviews to help prevent your audience from getting lost.

- Decide whether you want to improvise or speak from a written script.
- If you improvise, do enough planning and organization to avoid floundering and rambling in search of a point.
- Remember that editing is much more difficult to do with audio or video than with textual media, and plan your content and recording carefully.

## COMMUNICATION CHALLENGES AT **SBA**

You've become intrigued by the challenge of information architecture and recently joined the SBA's web team. Apply what you've learned in this chapter to these two challenges.

**INDIVIDUAL CHALLENGE:** A friend of yours is an experienced manager in a major U.S. corporation who has been bitten by the entrepreneurial bug. Rather than starting a business from the ground up, however, she would like to buy an existing business. She wants to know if SBA-backed loans can be used for this purpose. Find the answer to this question on the SBA website (www.sba.gov). How long did it take you? Did you consider this a satisfying web experience? Did you use the search box or "drill down" through the content structure? Summarize your experience in an email message to your instructor.

**TEAM CHALLENGE:** In teams assigned by your instructor, visit your college or university's website and find the following information:

- The current academic calendar
- A description of the business communication course you are currently taking
- A map of the main campus
- Information about ordering tickets to school sporting events (if applicable)
- A biography of the school president

For each task, record how long it took to find the information and how many screens you had to click through to reach the target. Based on these data, how would you assess the organization and navigation of your school's website? How could the experience be improved for students, parents, and other website audiences? Summarize your findings in a brief presentation.

# Quick Learning Guide

## SUMMARY OF LEARNING OBJECTIVES

**1** **Identify the major electronic media available for business messages and list nine compositional modes used in electronic media.** Major electronic media for business messages include email, instant messaging (IM), text messaging, web content, podcasting, social networks, information and media sharing sites, wikis, blogging and microblogging, and online video. The nine compositional modes used in electronic communication are conversations, comments and critiques, orientations, summaries, reference materials, narratives, teasers, status updates and announcements, and tutorials.

**2** **Describe the evolving role of email in business communication, and explain how to adapt the three-step writing process to email messages.** As the earliest widely available electronic written medium, email was applied to a broad range of communication tasks—some it was well suited for and some it wasn't. Over time, newer media such as instant messaging, blogs, and social networks have been taking over some of these tasks, but email remains a vital medium that is optimum for many private, short- to medium-length messages.

The three-step process adapts easily to email communication. One of the most important planning decisions in crafting email is making sure every message has a valuable purpose. Any key planning decision is to follow the chain of command in your organization in most instances; emailing over your boss's head is a good way to stir up resentment. When writing email messages, bear in mind that the expectations of writing quality and formality are higher in business email. Also, pay close attention to the wording of an email message's subject line; it often determines whether and when recipients open and read the message. Effective subject lines are both informative (concisely identifying what the message is about) and compelling (giving readers a reason to read the message). Completing email messages is straightforward. Proof and revise messages (particularly important ones), stick with a clean design, make use of the email signature feature, and make sure you distribute the message to the right people.

**3** **Describe the business benefits of instant messaging (IM), and identify guidelines for effective IM in the workplace.** The benefits of IM include its capability for rapid response to urgent messages, lower cost than phone calls and email, ability to mimic conversation more closely than email, and availability on a wide range of devices.

As with email, business IM needs to be treated as a professional medium to ensure safe and effective communication. Be courteous in your use of IM to avoid interrupting others unnecessarily. Make yourself unavailable when you need to focus on other work, refrain from sending confidential information if you're not on a secure system, refrain from sending personal messages at work, avoid using IM for lengthy and complex messages, avoid carrying on multiple IM conversations at once, avoid IM slang with anyone other than close colleagues, and follow security guidelines.

**4** **Explain why organizing website content is so challenging, and explain the concept of information architecture.** The primary challenge in organization website content is the medium's extreme versatility. This versatility can be a blessing because a single web presence can serve multiple purposes for multiple audiences, but it also creates the challenge of providing an efficient and successful experience for all these unique visitors. The key to organizing a website is careful consideration of its information architecture, a map of the content structure, labeling, and navigational links and pathways in a website.

**5** **Explain how to adapt the three-step writing process to podcasting.** Although you'll be recording audio or video when creating podcasts, rather than writing messages, using the three-step process is an effective way to develop podcasts. Focus the planning step on analyzing the situation, gathering the information you'll need, and organizing your material. If you plan to create a series of podcasts on a given theme (the equivalent of starting a radio or TV show), make sure you've identified a range of topics extensive enough to keep your podcasts going over time. As you organize and begin to think about the words or images you'll use as content, pay close attention to previews, transitions, and reviews so that audiences don't get lost while listening or watching. Before you record, think through what you plan to say or shoot so that you don't ramble while trying to make your key points. Finally, consider the necessary level of production quality; good-quality podcasts usually require some specialized hardware and software.

## KEY TERMS

**email signature** A small file that automatically includes such items as your full name, title, company, and contact information at the end of your messages

**information architecture** Plan or map of the content structure, labeling, and navigational flow of all the parts of a website

**instant messaging (IM)** Communication system in which users' messages appear on each other's screens instantly, without the need to be opened individually, as with email

**podcasting** The process of recording audio or video files and distributing them online

**podcasting channel** Series of regular recordings on a consistent theme

**text messaging** Phone-based messaging capability

---

CHECKLIST ✓
## Creating Effective Email Messages

**A. Planning email messages**
- Make sure every email message you send is necessary.
- Don't cc or bcc anyone who doesn't really need to see the message.
- Follow company email policy; understand the restrictions your company places on email usage.
- Practice good email hygiene by not opening suspicious messages, keeping virus protection up to date, and following other company guidelines.
- Follow the chain of command.

**B. Writing email messages**
- Remember that business email is more formal than personal email.
- Recognize that email messages carry the same legal weight as other business documents.
- Pay attention to the quality of your writing and use correct grammar, spelling, and punctuation.
- Make your subject lines informative by clearly identifying the purpose of your message.
- Make your subject lines compelling by wording them in a way that intrigues your audiences.
- Use the first few words of the email body to catch the reader's attention.

**C. Completing email messages**
- Revise and proofread carefully to avoid embarrassing mistakes.
- Keep the layout of your messages simple and clean.
- Use an email signature file to give recipients your contact information.
- Double-check your recipient list before sending.
- Don't mark messages as "urgent" unless they truly are urgent.

---

CHECKLIST ✓
## Using IM Productively

- Pay attention to security and privacy issues and be sure to follow all company guidelines.
- Treat IM as a professional communication medium, not an informal, personal tool; avoid using IM slang with all but close colleagues.
- Maintain good etiquette, even during simple exchanges.
- Protect your own productivity by making yourself unavailable when you need to focus.
- In most instances, don't use IM for confidential messages, complex messages, or personal messages.

---

CHECKLIST ✓
## Planning and Producing Business Podcasts

- Consider podcasting whenever you have the opportunity to replace existing audio or video messages.
- If you plan a podcast channel with a regular stream of new content, make sure you've identified a theme or purpose that is rich enough to sustain your effort.
- Pay close attention to previews, transitions, and reviews to help prevent your audience from getting lost.
- Decide whether you want to improvise or speak from a written script.
- If you improvise, do enough planning and organization to avoid floundering and rambling in search of a point.
- Remember that editing is much more difficult to do with audio or video than with textual media, and plan your content and recording carefully.

# Test Your Knowledge

1. What are the situations in which a printed memo or letter might be preferable to an electronic message? [LO-1]
2. How do the compositional modes of orientations, summaries, and teasers differ? [LO-1]
3. Why are subject lines important in email messages? [LO-2]
4. What are the benefits of using IM in business communication? [LO-3]
5. Should you ever plan an IM exchange? Explain your answer. [LO-3]
6. What is information architecture? [LO-3]
7. Why is it important to have a long-term, sustainable purpose in mind before you launch a podcast channel? [LO-5]
8. Is it wise to speak "off the cuff," with no notes or outline, when recording business podcasts? Why or why not? [LO-5]

# Apply Your Knowledge

To review chapter content related to each question, refer to the indicated Learning Objective.

1. If you wanted to get your employees' attention about the need to reduce costs without starting up the rumor mill about the possibility of layoffs, would it be wise to send out an email with the subject line "To save everyone's job, we must reduce costs now"? Explain your answer. [LO-2]
2. Should you ever use emoticons in business email messages? Explain your answer. [LO-2]
3. Communication on a major project is suffering because several team members are in the habit of writing cryptic or careless instant messages that often force recipients to engage in several rounds of follow-up messaging to figure out what the sender had in mind. As project leader, you've spoken with these team members about the need to write clearer messages, but they respond that careful planning and writing defeats the whole purpose of *instant* messaging. How should you handle the situation? [LO-3]
4. Your company's webmaster has become a big fan of tagging, the practice of identifying web content with category labels to make it easy to later retrieve all the content on a particular topic. She thinks tags are so powerful, in fact, that there is no longer any need to organize a website in any conventional, structured way. By using tag filtering, she claims, people can find whatever they need. In an email message, explain to her why information architecture is still necessary. [LO-2], [LO-4]
5. Imagine that you've been on the job for two or three decades, and you've amassed a deep store of leadership wisdom during the years. You'd like to share your wisdom with your 800 employees in a biweekly podcast. How should you go about planning this podcast series to make sure your employees will listen regularly? [LO-5]

# Practice Your Skills

**Message 7.A: Media Skills: IM, Creating a Businesslike Tone [LO-3]**

Review this IM exchange and explain how the customer service agent could have handled the situation more effectively.

| | |
|---|---|
| Agent: | Thanks for contacting Home Exercise Equipment. What's up? |
| Customer: | I'm having trouble assembling my home gym. |
| Agent: | I hear that a lot! LOL |
| Customer: | So is it me or the gym? |
| Agent: | Well, let's see \<g\>. Where are you stuck? |
| Customer: | The crossbar that connects the vertical pillars doesn't fit. |
| Agent: | What do you mean doesn't fit? |
| Customer: | It doesn't fit. It's not long enough to reach across the pillars. |
| Agent: | Maybe you assembled the pillars in the wrong place. Or maybe we sent the wrong crossbar. |
| Customer: | How do I tell? |
| Agent: | The parts aren't labeled so could be tough. Do you have a measuring tape? Tell me how long your crossbar is. |

**Message 7.B: Media Skills: Podcasting, Planning: Outlining Your Content [LO-5]**

To access this message, visit http://real-timeupdates.com/ebc10, click on Student Assignments and select Chapter 7, Message 7.B to listen to this podcast. Identify at least three ways in which the podcast could be improved, and draft a brief email message that you could send to the podcaster, giving your suggestions for improvement.

## Exercises

Each activity is labeled according to the primary skill or skills you will need to use. To review relevant chapter content, you can refer to the indicated Learning Objective. In some instances, supporting information will be found in another chapter, as indicated.

1. **Collaboration: Working in Teams; Planning: Selecting Media [LO-1] Chapter 2** For each of these message needs, choose a medium that you think would work effectively and explain your choice. (More than one medium could work in some cases; just be able to support your particular choice.)
   a. A technical support service for people trying to use their digital music players
   b. A message of condolence to the family of an employee who passed away recently
   c. A message from the CEO of a small company to the employees of the firm, explaining that she is leaving the company to join a competitor
   d. A series of observations on the state of the industry, intended mostly for professionals within the industry
   e. A series of messages, questions, and answers surrounding the work of a team on a confidential company project
2. **Media Skills: Writing Email Subject Lines [LO-2]** Using your imagination to make up whatever details you need, revise the following email subject lines to make them more informative:
   a. New budget figures
   b. Marketing brochure—your opinion
   c. Production schedule
3. **Media Skills: Email [LO-2]** The following email message contains numerous errors related to what you've learned

about planning and writing business messages. Using the information it contains, write a more effective version.

TO: Felicia August <fb_august@evertrust.com>
SUBJECT: Those are the breaks, folks

Some of you may not like the rules about break times; however, we determined that keeping track of employees while they took breaks at times they determined rather than regular breaks at prescribed times was not working as well as we would have liked it to work. The new rules are not going to be an option. If you do not follow the new rules, you could be docked from your pay for hours when you turned up missing, since your direct supervisor will not be able to tell whether you were on a "break" or not and will assume that you have walked away from your job. We cannot be responsible for any errors that result from your inattentiveness to the new rules. I have already heard complaints from some of you and I hope this memo will end this issue once and for all. The decision has already been made.

Starting Monday, January 1, you will all be required to take a regular 15-minute break in the morning and again in the afternoon, and a regular thirty-minute lunch at the times specified by your supervisor, NOT when you think you need a break or when you "get around to it."

There will be no exceptions to this new rule!

Felicia August
Manager
Billing and Accounting

4. **Media Skills: IM, Creating a Businesslike Tone [LO-3]** Your firm, which makes professional paint sprayers, uses IM extensively for internal communication and frequently for external communication with customers and suppliers. Several customers have recently forwarded copies of messages they've received from your staff, asking if you know how casually some employees are treating this important medium. You decide to revise parts of several messages to show your staff a more appropriate writing style. Rewrite these sentences, making up any information you need, to convey a more businesslike style and tone. (Look up the acronyms online if you need to.)

   a. IMHO, our quad turbo sprayer is best model 4U.

   b. No prob; happy2help!

   c. FWIW, I use the L400 myself & it rocks

   d. Most cust see 20–30% reduct in fumes w/this sprayer— of course, YMMV.

5. **Media Skills: Web Writing, Planning: Outlining Your Content [LO-4]** Find the website of a small company or nonprofit organization; make sure it is a fairly small and simple website. Identify all the individual pages on the site, then as best you can, "reverse engineer" the site's information architecture, identifying all the linkages between the individual pages. Draw a map of the architecture, showing how the various pages are linked together. (Hint: If the website has a "Site map" link, click on that to see a hierarchical list of all the pages contained within with site.)

6. **Media Skills: Podcasting, Planning: Outlining Your Content [LO-5]** You began recording a weekly podcast to share information with your large and far-flung staff. After a month, you ask for feedback from several of your subordinates, and you're disappointed to learn that some people stopped listening to the podcast after the first couple weeks. Someone eventually admits that many staffers feel the recordings are too long and rambling, and the information they contain isn't valuable enough to justify the time it takes to listen. You aren't pleased, but you want to improve. An assistant transcribes the introduction to last week's podcast so you can review it. You immediately see two problems. Revise the introduction based on what you've learned in this chapter.

So there I am, having lunch with Selma Gill, who just joined and took over the Northeast sales region from Jackson Stroud. In walks our beloved CEO with Selma's old boss at Uni-Plex; turns out they were finalizing a deal to co-brand our products and theirs and to set up a joint distribution program in all four domestic regions. Pretty funny, huh? Selma left Uni-Plex because she wanted to sell our products instead, and now she's back selling her old stuff, too. Anyway, try to chat with her when you can; she knows the biz inside and out and probably can offer insight into just about any sales challenge you might be running up against. We'll post more info on the co-brand deal next week; should be a boost for all of us. Other than those two news items, the other big news this week is the change in commission reporting. I'll go into the details in a minute, but when you log onto the intranet, you'll now see your sales results split out by product line and industry sector. Hope this helps you see where you're doing well and where you might beef things up a bit. Oh yeah, I almost forgot the most important bit. Speaking of our beloved CEO, Thomas is going to be our guest of honor, so to speak, at the quarterly sales meeting next week and wants an update on how petroleum prices are affecting customer behavior. Each district manager should be ready with a brief report. After I go through the commission reporting scheme, I'll outline what you need to prepare.

## Expand Your Skills

### Critique the Professionals

Check out the Twitter accounts of several companies that sell products or services you use or might use in the future. Find three teaser messages that attempt to persuade you to click through to another website. In a brief summary on your class blog or in an email message to your instructor, compare the effectiveness of the three teasers. Which was most effective, and which was least effective? Why? Were the payoffs for all three teasers satisfactory and in line with what you expected to see?

### Sharpening Your Career Skills Online

Bovée and Thill's Business Communication Web Search, at http://businesscommunicationblog.com/websearch, is a unique research tool designed specifically for business communication research. Use the Web Search function to find a website, video, PDF document, podcast, or PowerPoint presentation that offers advice on writing effective email messages. Write a brief email message to your instructor, describing the item that you found and summarizing the career skills information you learned from it.

# Cases

## EMAIL SKILLS

**1. Media Skills: Email; Career Management: Personal Branding [LO-2], Prologue**   You've been laboring all summer at an internship, learning how business is conducted. You've done work nobody else wanted to do, but that's okay. Even the smallest tasks can make a good impression on your future résumé.

This morning, your supervisor asks you to write a description of the job you've been doing. "Include everything, even the filing," she suggests, "and address it to me in an email message." She says a future boss might assign such a task prior to a performance review. "You can practice describing your work without exaggeration—or too much modesty," she says, smiling.

**Your task:**   Using good techniques for short messages and relying on your real-life work experience, write an email that will impress your supervisor. Make up any details you need.

## EMAIL SKILLS   /   PORTFOLIO BUILDER

**2. Media Skills: Email; Message Strategies: Marketing and Sales Messages [LO-2], Chapter 12**   One-quarter of all motor vehicle accidents that involve children under age 12 are side-impact crashes—and these crashes result in higher rates of injuries and fatalities than those with front or rear impacts.[27]

**Your task:**   You work in the consumer information department at Britax, a leading manufacturer of car seats. Your manager has asked you to prepare an email message that can be sent out whenever parents request information about side-impact crashes and the safety features of Britax seats. Start by researching side-impact crashes at www.britaxusa.com (click on "Safety Center" and then "Side Impact Protection Revealed"). Write a three-paragraph message that explains the seriousness of side-impact crashes, describes how injuries and fatalities can be minimized in these crashes, and describes how Britax's car seats are designed to help protect children in side-impact crashes.

## EMAIL SKILLS

**3. Media Skills: Email; Message Strategies: Negative Messages [LO-2], Chapter 11**   Many companies operate on the principle that the customer is always right, even when the customer *isn't* right. They take any steps necessary to ensure happy customers, lots of repeat sales, and a positive reputation among potential buyers. Overall, this is a smart and successful approach to business. However, most companies eventually encounter a nightmare customer who drains so much time, energy, and profits that the only sensible option is to refuse the customer's business. For example, the nightmare customer might be someone who constantly berates you and your employees, repeatedly makes outlandish demands for refunds and discounts, or simply requires so much help that you not only lose money on this person but also no longer have enough time to help your other customers. "Firing" a customer is an unpleasant step that should be taken only in the most extreme cases and only after other remedies have been attempted (such as talking with the customer about the problem), but it is sometimes necessary for the well-being of your employees and your company.

**Your task:**   If you are currently working or have held a job in the recent past, imagine that you've encountered just such a customer. If you don't have job experience to call on, imagine that you work in a retail location somewhere around campus or in your neighborhood. Identify the type of behavior this imaginary customer exhibits and the reasons the behavior can no longer be accepted. Write a brief email message to the customer to explain that you will no longer be able to accommodate him or her as a customer. Calmly explain why you have had to reach this difficult decision. Maintain a professional tone and keep your emotions in check.

## EMAIL SKILLS   /   TEAM SKILLS

**4. Media Skills: Email; Collaboration: Team Projects [LO-2], Chapter 2**   For the first time in history (aside from special situations such as major wars), more than half—51 percent—of all U.S. adult women now live without a spouse. (In other words, they live alone, with roommates, or as part of an unmarried couple.) Twenty-five percent have never married, and 26 percent are divorced, widowed, or married but living apart from their spouses. In the 1950s and into the 1960s, only 40 percent of women lived without a spouse, but every decade since, the percentage has increased. In your work as a consumer trend specialist for Seymour Powell (www.seymourpowell.com), a product design firm based in London that specializes in the home, personal, leisure, and transportation sectors, it's your business to recognize and respond to demographic shifts such as this.

**Your task:**   With a small team of classmates, brainstorm possible product opportunities that respond to this trend. In an email message to be sent to the management team at Seymour Powell, list your ideas for new or modified products that might sell well in a society in which more than half of all adult women live without a spouse. For each idea, provide a one-sentence explanation of why you think the product has potential.[28]

## IM SKILLS

**5. Media Skills: IM; Compositional Modes: Tutorials [LO-1], [LO-3]**   High-definition television can be a joy to watch—but, oh, what a pain to buy. The field is littered with competing technologies and arcane terminology that is meaningless to most consumers. Moreover, it's nearly impossible to define one technical term without invoking two or three others, leaving consumers swimming in an alphanumeric soup of confusion. The manufacturers themselves can't even agree on which of the *18* different digital TV formats truly qualify as "high definition." As a sales support manager for Crutchfield (www.crutchfield.com), a leading online retailer of audio and video systems, you understand the frustration buyers feel; your staff is deluged daily by their questions.

**Your task:**   To help your staff respond quickly to consumers who ask questions via Crutchfield's online IM chat service, you are developing a set of "canned" responses to common questions.

When a consumer asks one of these questions, a sales advisor can simply click on the ready-made answer. Start by writing concise, consumer-friendly definitions of the following terms: *resolution*, *HDTV*, *1080p*, and *HDMI*. Explore the Learning Center on the Crutchfield website to learn more about these terms. Answers.com and CNET.com are two other handy sources.[29]

## IM SKILLS

**6. Media Skills: IM; Collaboration: Working in Teams [LO-3]** Instant messaging is frequently used in customer support situations where a customer needs help selecting, using, or troubleshooting a problem. In this activity, two two-person teams will use IM to simulate problem solving by helping classmates discuss important academic or life decisions. One team will be the "clients," who are struggling with the decisions, and the other will be the "advisors," who coach them toward solutions.

**Your task:** First choose a free IM/chat system such as Google Talk, Facebook chat, or any other system on which you can communicate privately in real time. Now choose two decision-making scenarios from your school or personal lives, such as deciding on a major, choosing whether to work during the upcoming summer or attend class, figuring out where to live next year, or any other decision you're willing to have the group discuss and then later to discuss in front of the whole class. Choose decisions that are complicated enough to support an IM conversation lasting at least five minutes.

Decide which team will be the advisors and which will be the clients, and move the teams to separate locations (make sure you have Internet access). In each team, one person will be the communicator first, and the other will be the observer, monitoring how well the IM conversation progresses and making note of any confusion, inefficiencies, or other issues.

When you're set up in your separate locations, begin the IM exchange with the communicator from the client team asking the advisor for help with a decision. The advisor should ask probing questions to find out what the client really wants to gain from the decision and help him or her work through the various alternatives. Discuss the decision scenario for at least five minutes. The observers should take notes but should not be involved in the IM exchange in any way.

After working through one of the decision scenarios, swap roles inside each team so that the observer becomes the communicator and vice versa. Now work through the second decision scenario.

Meet as a full team after the role playing and compare notes about how well each conversation went, how well the technology supported the communicators' needs, and what you might do differently in a business context to ensure smooth communication and customer satisfaction. Be prepared to discuss your observations and conclusions with the rest of the class.

## WEB WRITING SKILLS / TEAM SKILLS

**7. Message Strategies: Online Content; Collaboration: Team Projects [LO-4], Chapter 2** If you're like many other college students, your first year was more than you expected: more difficult, more fun, more frustrating, more expensive, more exhausting, more rewarding—more of everything, positive and negative. Oh, the things you know now that you didn't know then!

**Your task:** With several other students, identify five or six things you wish you would've realized or understood better before you started your first year of college. These can relate to your school life (such as "I didn't realize how much work I would have for my classes" or "I should've asked for help as sooner") and your personal and social life ("I wish I would've been more open to meeting people"). Use these items as the foundation of a brief informational report that you could post on a blog that is read by high school students and their families. Your goal with this report is to help the next generation of students make a successful and rewarding transition to college.

## WEB WRITING SKILLS

**8. Message Strategies: Online Content [LO-4]** As you probably experienced, trying to keep all the different schools straight in one's mind while researching and applying for colleges can be rather difficult. Applicants and their families would no doubt appreciate a handy summary of your college or university's key points as they relate to the selection and application process.

**Your task:** Adapt content from your college or university's website to create a one-page "Quick Facts" sheet about your school. Choose the information you think prospective students and their families would find most useful. (Note that adapting existing content would be acceptable in a real-life scenario like this, because you would be reusing content on behalf of the content owner. Doing so would definitely *not* be acceptable if you were using the content for yourself or for someone other than the original owner.)

## PODCASTING SKILLS

**9. Media Skills: Podcasting; Career Management: Personal Branding [LO-5], Prologue** While writing the many letters and email messages that are part of the job search process, you find yourself wishing that you could just talk to some of these companies so your personality could shine through. Well, you've just gotten that opportunity. One of the companies that you've applied to has emailed you back, asking you to submit a two-minute podcast, introducing yourself and explaining why you would be a good person to hire.

**Your task:** Identify a company that you'd like to work for after graduation and select a job that would be a good match for your skills and interests. Write a script for a two-minute podcast (roughly 250 words). Introduce yourself and the position you're applying for, describe your background, and explain why you think you're a good candidate for the job. Make up any details you need. If your instructor asks you to do so, record the podcast and submit the file.

**10. Drafting Online Content [LO-4]** Write an effectively worded link for each of the following content sections on a website (make up any information you need):

a. A page that summarizes the company's most recent quarterly financial results
b. A page that lists the phone numbers and email addresses for key contacts within the company
c. A page containing a news release announcing that the company is being investigated by the Securities and Exchange Commission (SEC) for possible accounting irregularities
d. A page that announces the launch of a major new product

## PODCASTING SKILLS / PORTFOLIO BUILDER

**11. Media Skills: Podcasting; Message Strategies: Marketing and Sales Messages [LO-5], Chapter 12**   With any purchase decision, from a restaurant meal to a college education, recommendations from satisfied customers are often the strongest promotional messages.

**Your task:**   Write a script for a one- to two-minute podcast (roughly 150 to 250 words), explaining why your college or university is a good place to get an education. Your audience is high school juniors and seniors. You can choose to craft a general message, something that would be useful to all prospective students, or you can focus on a specific academic discipline, the athletic program, or some other important aspect of your college experience. Either way, make sure your introductory comments make it clear whether you are offering a general recommendation or a specific recommendation. If your instructor asks you to do so, record the podcast and submit the file electronically.

---

## MyBCommLab

Go to **mybcommlab.com** for Auto-graded writing questions as well as the following Assisted-graded writing questions:

**7-1.**   What advantages does email maintain over other electronic media? [LO-2]

**7-2.**   How can you use the inverted pyramid style of writing to craft effective website content? [LO-4]

**7-3.**   Mybcommlab Only—comprehensive writing assignment for this chapter.

# Endnotes

1. U.S. Small Business Administration website, accessed 26 January 2013, www.sba.org; "Information Architecture," Usability First, accessed 30 January 2013, www.usabilityfirst.com.

2. "Ten Ways to Use Texting for Business," *Inc.*, accessed 21 July 2010, www.inc.com; Kate Maddox, "Warrillow Finds 39% of Small-Business Owners Use Text Messaging," BtoB, 1 August 2008, www.btobonline.com; Dave Carpenter, "Companies Discover Marketing Power of Text Messaging," *Seattle Times*, 25 September 2006, www.seattletimes.com.

3. "Burson-Marsteller Fortune Global 10 Social Media Study," The Burson-Marsteller Blog, 23 February 2010, www.burson-marsteller.com.

4. "The New Messages," Facebook.com, accessed 30 January 2011, www.facebook.com.

5. Richard Edelman, "Teaching Social Media: What Skills Do Communicators Need?" in *Engaging the New Influencers; Third Annual Social Media Academic Summit* (white paper), accessed 7 June 2010, www.newmediaacademicsummit.com.

6. Reid Goldborough, "More Trends for 2009: What to Expect with Personal Technology," *Public Relations Tactics*, February 2009, 9.

7. Michelle V. Rafter, "If Tim Fry Has His Way, He'll Eradicate Email for Good," *Workforce Management*, 24 April 2012, www.workforce.com.

8. Matt Cain, "Managing Email Hygiene," ZD Net Tech Update, 5 February 2004, www.techupdate.zdnet.com.

9. Hilary Potkewitz and Rachel Brown, "Spread of Email Has Altered Communication Habits at Work," *Los Angeles Business Journal*, 18 April 2005, www.findarticles.com; Nancy Flynn, *Instant Messaging Rules* (New York: AMACOM, 2004), 47–54.

10. Mary Munter, Priscilla S. Rogers, and Jone Rymer, "Business Email: Guidelines for Users," *Business Communication Quarterly*, March 2003, 26+; Renee B. Horowitz and Marian G. Barchilon, "Stylistic Guidelines for Email," *IEEE Transactions on Professional Communication* 37, no. 4 (December 1994): 207–212.

11. Steve Rubel, "Tip: Tweetify the Lead of Your Emails," The Steve Rubel Stream blog, 20 July 2010, www.steverubel.com.

12. Judith Newman, "If You're Happy and You Know It, Must I Know, Too?" *New York Times*, 21 October 2011, www.nytimes.com.

13. Michal Lev-Ram, "IBM: Instant Messaging Has Replaced Voicemail," CNNMoney, 31 May 2011, http://tech.fortune.cnn.com; Robert J. Holland, "Connected—More or Less," Richmond.com, 8 August 2006, www.richmond.com.

14. Vayusphere website, accessed 22 January 2006, www.vayusphere.com; Christa C. Ayer, "Presence Awareness: Instant Messaging's Killer App," *Mobile Business Advisor*, 1 July 2004, www.highbeam.com; Jefferson Graham, "Instant Messaging Programs Are No Longer Just for Messages," *USA Today*, 20 October 2003, 5D; Todd R. Weiss, "Microsoft Targets Corporate Instant Messaging Customers," *Computerworld*, 18 November 2002, 12; "Banks Adopt Instant Messaging to Create a Global Business Network," *Computer Weekly*, 25 April 2002, 40; Michael D. Osterman, "Instant Messaging in the Enterprise," *Business Communications Review*, January 2003, 59–62; John Pallato, "Instant Messaging Unites Work Groups and Inspires Collaboration," *Internet World*, December 2002, 14+.

15. Paul Mah, "Using Text Messaging in Business," Mobile Enterprise blog, 4 February 2008, http://blogs.techrepublic.com.com/wireless; Paul Kedrosky, "Why We Don't Get the (Text) Message," *Business 2.0*, 2 October 2006, www.business2.com; Carpenter, "Companies Discover Marketing Power of Text Messaging."

16. "About StarStar," Zoove website, accessed 6 June 2012, www.zoove.com.

17. Mark Gibbs, "Racing to Instant Messaging," *NetworkWorld*, 17 February 2003, 74.

18. "Email Is So Five Minutes Ago," *BusinessWeek*, 28 November 2005, www.businessweek.com.

**19.** Martin Zwilling, "Texting is Killing Real Business Communication," Business Insider, 13 January 2012, www.businessinsider.com.

**20.** Leo Babauta, "17 Tips to Be Productive with Instant Messaging," Web Worker Daily, 14 November 2007, http://webworkerdaily .com; Pallato, "Instant Messaging Unites Work Groups and Inspires Collaboration."

**21.** Based in part on "Information Architecture"; Shel Holtz, *Writing for the Wired World* (San Francisco: International Association of Business Communicators, 1999), 28–29.

**22.** "Turn Your Feed into a Podcast," Lifehacker blog, 12 January 2006, www.lifehacker.com.

**23.** "Set Up Your Podcast for Success," Feed For All website, accessed 4 October 2006, www.feedforall.com.

**24.** "Set Up Your Podcast for Success," Feed For All website, accessed 4 October 2006, www.feedforall.com.

**25.** Nathan Hangen, "4 Steps to Podcasting Success," Social Media Examiner, 14 February 2011, www.socialmediaexaminer.com.

**26.** Shel Holtz, "Ten Guidelines for B2B Podcasts," Webpronews.com, 12 October 2005, www.webpronews.com.

**27.** Adapted from "Side Impact Protection Explained," Britax website, accessed 18 September 2008, www.britaxusa.com.

**28.** Adapted from Seymour Powell website, accessed 16 January 2007, www.seymourpowell.com; Sam Roberts, "51% of Women Now Living Without a Spouse," *New York Times*, 16 January 2007, www.nytimes.com.

**29.** Adapted from Crutchfield website, accessed 3 February 2011, www.crutchfield.com.

# 8 Social Media

## LEARNING OBJECTIVES

After studying this chapter, you will be able to

**1** Identify seven key points for using social media in business communication.

**2** Describe the business communication applications of social networks.

**3** Explain how information and media sharing sites are used in business communication.

**4** Describe the role of blogging in business communication today and explain how to adapt the three-step writing process to blogging.

**5** Describe the business uses of Twitter and other micro-blogging systems.

**6** Offer guidelines for becoming a valuable wiki contributor.

## MyBCommLab®

⭐ **Improve Your Grade!** Over 10 million students improved their results using the Pearson MyLabs. Visit **mybcommlab.com** for simulations, tutorials, and end-of-chapter problems.

---

## COMMUNICATION CLOSE-UP AT
## Southwest Airlines

www.blogsouthwest.com

Southwest Airlines's blog is usually a love fest—or a "luv" fest, to use one of the company's favorite words. In fact, the blog's official name is Nuts About Southwest. A typical post might highlight the community service efforts of a group of employees or congratulate a team of Southwest mechanics for winning gold at the Aviation Maintenance Olympics. Devoted customers post enthusiastic comments on nearly every article, and many seem to have bonded in virtual friendship with the 30 Southwest employees who take turns writing the blog.

Bill Owen probably didn't expect a bubbly reception to a rather workaday post titled "Why can't I make reservations further in advance?" in which he calmly explained why the company usually didn't let customers make reservations as far into the future as other airlines do. But he probably wasn't expecting the response he *did* get, either. In his words, "Talk about sticking your head in a hornet's nest!" Instead of the usual dozen or so

Southwest Airlines's multimedia, multi-author blog, Nuts About Southwest, features a variety of entertaining writers from around the company.
*Source:* Courtesy Southwest Airlines Co.

happy responses to a typical post, he received several hundred responses—many of which expressed disappointment, unhappiness, and downright anger. Customers described one scenario after another in which they had a real need to book travel further in advance than Southwest allowed, and many complained that the policy was forcing them to fly other airlines. Some Southwest employees chimed in, too, expressing their frustration with not being able to meet customer needs at times.

After bravely and patiently addressing specific customer responses over a period of several months, Owen responded with a new post titled "I blogged. You flamed. We changed." In this message, he explained that the company had listened and was changing its scheduling policies to better accommodate customer needs.

In fact, feedback from blog readers is so important that Southwest considers the blog a "customer service laboratory" that helps the company learn how to better serve its customers.[1]

# Writing Strategies for Social Media

Bill Owen from Southwest Airlines (profiled in the chapter-opening Communication Close-Up) might've used any number of media to convey the company's message about reservation policies. However, the choice of a blog post is significant because it represents a fundamental change in business communication and the relationships between companies and their stakeholders, a change enabled by the rapid growth of social media (see Figure 8.1 on the next page).

No matter what media or compositional mode you are using for a particular message, writing for social media requires a different approach than traditional media. Social media have changed the relationship between sender and receiver, so the nature of the messages needs to change as well. Whether you're writing a blog or posting a product demonstration video to YouTube, consider these tips for creating successful content for social media:[2]

- **Remember that it's a conversation, not a lecture or a sales pitch.** One of the great appeals of social media is the feeling of conversation, of people talking *with* one another instead of one person talking *at* everyone else. For all its technological sophistication, in an important sense social media provide a new spin on the age-old practice of *word-of-mouth* communication. As more and more people gain a voice in the marketplace, companies that try to maintain the old "we talk, you listen" mindset are likely to be ignored in the social media landscape.
- **Write informally but not carelessly.** Write as a human being, not as a cog in a faceless corporate machine. At the same time, don't get sloppy; no one wants to slog through misspelled words and half-baked sentences to find the message.
- **Create concise, specific, and informative headlines.** Avoid the temptation to engage in clever wordplay with headlines. This advice applies to all forms of business communication, of course, but it is essential for social media. Readers don't want to spend time and energy figuring out what your witty headlines mean. Search engines won't know what they mean, either, so fewer people will find your content.
- **Get involved and stay involved.** Social media understandably make some businesspeople nervous because they don't permit a high level of control over messages. However, don't hide from criticism. Take the opportunity to correct misinformation or explain how mistakes will be fixed.
- **If you need to promote something, do so indirectly.** Just as you wouldn't hit people with a company sales pitch during an informal social gathering, refrain from blatant promotional efforts in social media.
- **Be transparent and honest.** Honesty is always essential, of course, but a particular issue that has tripped up a few companies in recent years is hiding behind an online blogging persona—either a fictitious character whose writing is actually done by a corporate marketing specialist or a real person who fails to disclose an affiliation with a corporate sponsor.
- **Think before you post!** Because of careless messages, individuals and companies have been sued for Twitter updates, employees have been fired for Facebook wall postings, vital company secrets have been leaked, and business and personal relationships have been strained. Unless you are sending messages through a private channel, assume that every message will be read by people far beyond your original audience.

**1  LEARNING OBJECTIVE**
Identify seven key points for using social media in business communication.

Readers of social media expect to have a more engaged relationship with writers, so creating content for social media requires a new approach to writing.

Readers—and search engines—don't like spending time trying to figure out clever puns and other wordplay; make your headlines clear and direct.

A momentary lapse of concentration while using social media can cause tremendous career or company damage.

**REAL-TIME UPDATES**
LEARN MORE BY READING THIS INFOGRAPHIC

**Create compelling content when you're out of ideas**

These 22 thought stimulators can get your creative juices flowing. Go to http://real-timeupdates.com/bct12 and click on Learn More. If you are using MyBCommLab, you can access Real-Time Updates within each chapter or under Student Study Tools.

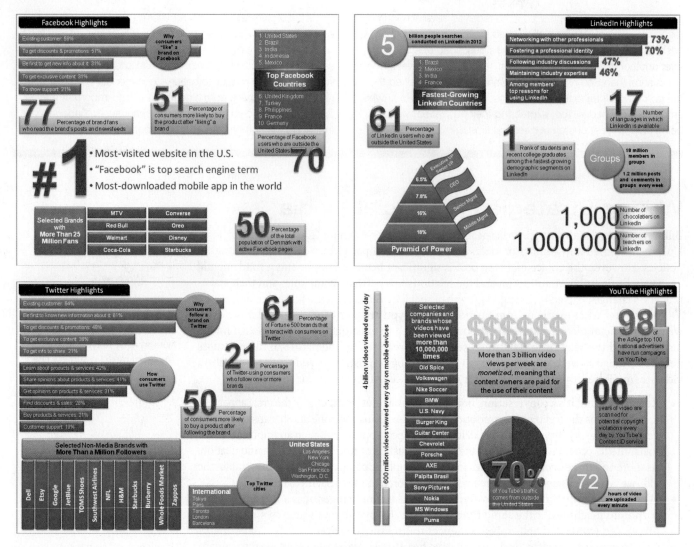

**Figure 8.1** **The Rise and Reach of Social Media**
This infographic shows the rapid rise and wide reach of four major social media platforms: Facebook, Twitter, LinkedIn, and YouTube.
*Sources:* Based on: "10 Facts about Consumer Behavior on Facebook," Social Media Quickstarter, 2012; "10 Facts about Consumer Behavior on Twitter," Social Media Quickstarter, 2012; 2012 CEO, SOCIAL MEDIA & LEADERSHIP SURVEY, Brandfog, 2012; "About Us," LinkedIn, 2013; "The Business Impact of Twitter: It's Come a Long Way" by Josh Mendelohn, from Constant Contact website, October 20, 2011; Fan Page List, 2013; "The Global LinkedIn Audience" LinkedIn, 2013; "Statistics," YouTube, 2013; "These Are the Most Engaging Brands on Facebook" by Samantha Murphy, from Mashable, May 15 2012.

# Social Networks

**2** **LEARNING OBJECTIVE**
Describe the business communication applications of social networks.

**Social networks**, online services that help people and organizations form connections and share information, have become a major force in both internal and external business communication in recent years. In addition to Facebook, a variety of public and private social networks are used by businesses and professionals. These can be grouped into three categories:

Business communicators make use of a wide range of specialized and private social networks, in addition to public networks such as Facebook and Google+.

- **Public, general-purpose networks.** Facebook is the largest of these, although Google+ is gaining membership and is attracting many companies and brands. Additionally, regionally focused networks have significant user bases in some countries, such as China's Renren and Kaixin001.[3]

- **Public, specialized networks.** Whereas Facebook and Google+ serve a wide variety of personal and professional needs, other networks focus on a particular function or a particular audience. The most widely known is LinkedIn, with its emphasis on career- and sales-related networking. Other networks address the needs of entrepreneurs, small business owners, specific professions, product enthusiasts, and other narrower audiences.

- **Private networks.** Some companies have built private social networks for internal use. For example, the defense contractor Lockheed Martin created its Unity network, complete with a variety of social media applications, to meet the expectations of younger employees accustomed to social media and to capture the expert knowledge of older employees nearing retirement.[4]

Regardless of the purpose and audience, social networks are most beneficial when all participants give and receive information, advice, support, and introductions—just as in off-line social interaction. The following two sections describe how social networks are used in business communication and offer advice on using these platforms successfully.

## BUSINESS COMMUNICATION USES OF SOCIAL NETWORKS

With their ability to reach virtually unlimited numbers of people through a variety of electronic formats, social networks are a great fit for many business communication needs. Here are some of the key applications of social networks for internal and external business communication:

- **Integrating company workforces.** Just as public networks can bring friends and family together, internal social networks can help companies grow closer, including helping new employees navigate their way through the organization, finding experts, mentors, and other important contacts; encouraging workforces to "jell" after reorganizations or mergers; and overcoming structural barriers in communication channels, bypassing the formal communication system to deliver information where it is needed in a timely fashion.

- **Fostering collaboration.** Networks can play a major role in collaboration by identifying the best people, both inside the company and in other companies, to collaborate on projects; finding pockets of knowledge and expertise within the organization; giving meeting or seminar participants a way to meet before an event takes place and to maintain relationships after events; accelerating the development of teams by helping team members get to know one another and identify individual areas of expertise; and sharing information throughout the organization. The information technology company EMC estimates that its internal social network has cut costs by more than $40 million by helping employees use company resources more effectively and reducing the need to hire outside contractors.[5]

- **Building communities.** Social networks are a natural tool for bringing together *communities of practice*, people who engage in similar work, and *communities of interest*, people who share enthusiasm for a particular product or activity. Large and geographically dispersed companies can benefit greatly from communities of practice that connect experts who may work in different divisions or different countries. Communities of interest that form around a specific product are sometimes called **brand communities**, and nurturing these communities can be a vital business communication task. A majority of consumers now trust their peers more than any other source of product information, so formal and informal brand communities are becoming an essential information source in consumer buying decisions.[6] Increasingly, these community-building efforts include some aspect of *gamification*, which is the addition of game-playing aspects, such as Foursquare's "check-in" competitions or Bunchball's Nitro competitions for sales teams.[7] Foursquare is also an example of *location-based social networking*, which links the virtual world of online social networking with the physical world of retail stores and other locations. As mobile web use in general continues to grow, location-based networking promises to become an important business

Community building, both within companies and with customers and other external parties, is an important function of social networking.

communication medium because mobile consumers are a significant economic force—through the purchases they make directly and through their ability to influence other consumers.[8]

*Socializing* a brand is becoming an increasingly important element of marketing and public relations strategies.

- **Socializing brands and companies.** According to one recent survey of company executives, *socialization* now accounts for more than half of a company or brand's global reputation.[9] **Brand socialization** is a measure of how effectively a company engages with its various online stakeholders in a mutually beneficial exchange of information. Social networks and related tools such as Twitter are the primary means of socializing companies and brands (see Figure 8.2). To be successful, the communication on these platforms must be of value to all parties, not just the company. For example, comparing posts from General Motors, Toyota, and Ford suggests that brand socialization plays a significant role in the widely varying degrees of engagement these three companies have on Facebook. Many of Ford's posts focus on its history (including classic Ford cars and the company's efforts to supply the military in past wars) and its involvement

This post features a story with historical interest to the running community.

This post offers information to help runners select the optimum shoe from the new "minimalist" style of footwear.

**Figure 8.2   Business Communication on Social Networks**
The shoe company New Balance uses Facebook to connect with the serious runners who make up its customer base.
*Source:* Copyright © 2012 by New Balance. Reprinted with permission.

in auto racing, topics of likely interest to car enthusiasts. Toyota's posts tend to feature current community-related news and events, such as results from company-sponsored contests (including a video competition for college students). GM's Facebook posts highlight community involvement as well, but tend to emphasize such company-focused items as monthly sales results, new products, and executive profiles. The fact that Toyota has three times as many Facebook fans as General Motors while Ford has four times as many (as of early 2013) is probably not a coincidence.[10]

- **Understanding target markets.** With hundreds of millions of people expressing themselves via social media, you can be sure that smart companies are listening. When asked about the value of having 33 million Facebook fans, Coca-Cola CEO Muhtar Kent replied, "The value is you can talk with them. They tell you things that are important for your business and brands."[11] In addition, a number of tools now exist to gather market intelligence from social media more or less automatically. For example, *sentiment analysis* is an intriguing research technique in which companies track social networks and other media with automated language-analysis software that tries to take the pulse of public opinion and identify influential opinion makers.[12]

  > Social networks are vital tools for distributing information as well as gathering information about the business environment.

- **Recruiting employees and business partners.** Companies use social networks to find potential employees, short-term contractors, subject-matter experts, product and service suppliers, and business partners. A key advantage here is that these introductions are made via trusted connections in a professional network. On LinkedIn, for example, members can recommend each other based on current or past business relationships, which helps remove the uncertainty of initiating business relationships with strangers.

- **Connecting with sales prospects.** Salespeople on networks such as LinkedIn can use their network connections to identify potential buyers and then to ask for introductions through those shared connections. Sales networking can reduce *cold calling*, telephoning potential customers out of the blue—a practice that few people on either end of the conversation find pleasant.

- **Supporting customers.** Customer service is another one of the fundamental areas of business communication that have been revolutionized by social media. *Social customer service* involves using social networks and other social media tools to give customers a more convenient way to get help from the company and to help each other.

- **Extending the organization.** Social networking is also fueling the growth of *networked organizations*, sometimes known as *virtual organizations*, where companies supplement the talents of their employees with services from one or more external partners, such as a design lab, a manufacturing firm, or a sales and distribution company.

**REAL-TIME UPDATES**

LEARN MORE BY READING THIS ARTICLE

**Stay on top of new terminology in social media**

The new-media field spins out new buzzwords and technical terms at a rapid pace; this glossary will help you stay on top of things. Go to http://real-timeupdates.com/bct12 and click on Learn More. If you are using MyBCommLab, you can access Real-Time Updates within each chapter or under Student Study Tools.

## STRATEGIES FOR BUSINESS COMMUNICATION ON SOCIAL NETWORKS

Social networks offer lots of business communication potential, but with those opportunities comes a certain degree of complexity. Moreover, the norms and practices of business social networking continue to evolve. Follow these guidelines to make the most of social networks for both personal branding and company communication:[13]

- **Choose the best compositional mode for each message, purpose, and network.** As you visit various social networks, take some time to observe the variety of message types you see in different parts of each website. For example, the informal status update mode works well for Facebook posts but would be less effective for company overviews and mission statements.

  > Choose the best composition mode (see Chapter 7) for every message type you post on social networks.

- **Offer valuable content to members of your online communities.** People don't join social networks to be sales targets, of course. They join looking for connections and information. *Content marketing* is the practice of providing free information that is

*(continued on page 206)*

Companies in virtually every industry use social media and continue to experiment with new ways to connect with customers and other stakeholders. From offering helpful tips on using products to helping customers meet each other, these companies show the enormous range of possibilities that new media continue to bring to business communication.[14]

## General-Purpose Social Networks

**Most everyone is familiar** with Facebook and Google+, and thousands of companies are active on these popular social networks. In addition, a number of social networks exist just for businesses and business professionals, including LinkedIn, the largest of the business networks. Kelly Financial Resources, part of the Kelly Services staffing company, maintains a profile on LinkedIn, as do several hundred of its employees.

*Source:* Screenshot courtesy of Kelly Services company LinkedIn page. Copyright © 2013 by Kelly Services, Inc. Used by permission.

## Specialized Social Networks

**A number of companies now** host their own social networking sites, where product enthusiasts interact by sharing personal stories, offering advice, and commenting on products and company news—all brief-message functions that replace more traditional media options. For example, Specialized, a major bicycle manufacturer based in Morgan Hill, California, hosts the Specialized Riders Club (www.specializedriders.com), where customers can interact with each other and the professional riders the company sponsors. Similarly, the Segway Social network connects owners of these unique personal vehicles, including helping teams organize for Segway polo matches and other events.

*Source:* Copyright © 2012 by Segway, Inc. All rights reserved. Used by permission.

## User-Generated Content

**Many companies now encourage** user-generated content as a way to engage their stakeholders and provide additional value through shared expertise. The online shoe and apparel retailer Zappos, for example, invites customers to create and upload videos that communicate their experiences with Zappos and its products.

*Source:* Copyright © 2013 by Zappos IP, Inc. Used by permission.

## Value-Added Content via Blogging

**One of the best ways** to become a valued member of a network is to provide content that is useful to others in the network. The Quizzle personal finance blog offers a steady stream of articles and advice that help people manage their finances.

*Source:* Copyright © 2013 by Quizzle. Used by permission.

## Value-Added Content via Online Video

**Lie-Nielsen Toolworks of Warren,** Maine, uses its YouTube channel to offer valuable information on choosing and using premium woodworking tools. By offering sought-after information for both current and potential customers free of charge, these videos help Lie-Nielsen foster relationships with the worldwide woodworking community and solidify its position as one of the leaders in this market. Animal Planet, Best Western, and Taco Bell are among the many other companies that make effective use of branded channels on YouTube.

*Source:* Copyright © 2013 by Lie-Nielson Toolworks, Inc. Used by permission.

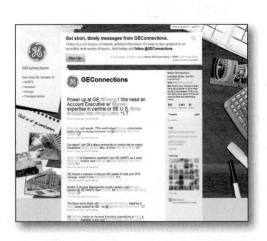

## Employee Recruiting

**General Electric (GE)** is one of many companies that now use Twitter to recruit new employees. GE uses its Twitter recruiting account (@GEConnections) to post job openings, talk about working at GE, and provide application advice to job seekers.

*Source:* Copyright © 2012 by General Electric. Used by permission.

valuable to community members but that also helps a company build closer ties with current and potential customers.[15]

- **Join existing conversations.** Search for online conversations that are already taking place. Answer questions, solve problems, and respond to rumors and misinformation.

- **Anchor your online presence in your hub.** Although it's important to join those conversations and be visible where your stakeholders are active, it's equally important to anchor your presence at your own central *hub*—a web presence you own and control. This can be a combination of a conventional website, a blog, and a company-sponsored online community, for example.[16] Use the hub to connect the various pieces of your online "self" (as an individual or a company) to make it easier for people to find and follow you. For example, you can link to your blog from your LinkedIn profile or automatically post your blog entries into the Notes tab on your Facebook page.

- **Facilitate community building.** Make it easy for customers and other audiences to connect with the company and with each other. For example, you can use the group feature on Facebook, LinkedIn, and other social networks to create and foster special-interest groups within your networks. Groups are a great way to connect people who are interested in specific topics, such as owners of a particular product.

Product promotion can be done on social networks, but it needs to be done in a low-key, indirect way.

- **Restrict conventional promotional efforts to the right time and right place.** Persuasive communication efforts are still valid for specific communication tasks, such as regular advertising and the product information pages on a website, but efforts to inject blatant "salespeak" into social networking conversations will usually be rejected by the audience.

- **Maintain a consistent personality.** Each social network is a unique environment with particular norms of communication.[17] For example, as a strictly business-oriented network, LinkedIn has a more formal "vibe" than Facebook and Google+, which cater to both consumers and businesses. However, while adapting to the expectations of each network, be sure to maintain a consistent personality across all the networks in which you are active.[18] The computer giant HP, for instance, uses the same (fairly formal-sounding) company overview on LinkedIn and Facebook, while posting Wall updates on Facebook that are "chattier" and more in keeping with the tone expected by Facebook visitors.[19]

See "Writing Promotional Messages for Social Media" in Chapter 12 (pages 340–341) for more tips on writing messages for social networks and other social media.

## Information and Media Sharing Sites

**3** LEARNING OBJECTIVE
Explain how information and media sharing sites are used in business communication.

Social networks allow members to share information and media items as part of the networking experience, but a variety of systems have been designed specifically for sharing content. The field is diverse and still evolving, but the possibilities can be divided into user-generated content sites, media curation sites, and community Q&A sites.

### USER-GENERATED CONTENT SITES

YouTube and other user-generated content sites are now important business communication channels.

YouTube, Flickr, Yelp, and other **user-generated content (UGC) sites,** in which users rather than website owners contribute most or all of the content, have become serious business tools. On YouTube, for example, companies post everything from product demonstrations and TV commercials to company profiles and technical support explanations.

Moreover, the business communication value of sites such as YouTube goes beyond the mere ability to deliver content. The social aspects of these sites, including the ability to vote for, comment on, and share material, encourage enthusiasts to spread the word about the companies and products they endorse.[20]

As with other social media, the keys to effective user-generated content are making it valuable and making it easy. First, provide content that people want to see and share with colleagues. A video clip that explains how to use a product more effectively will be more popular than a clip that talks about how amazing the company behind the product is. Also, keep videos short, generally no longer than three to five minutes, if possible.[21]

Second, make material easy to find, consume, and share. For example, a *branded channel* on YouTube lets a company organize all its videos in one place, making it easy for visitors to browse the selection or subscribe to get automatic updates of future videos. Sharing features let fans share videos through email or their accounts on Twitter, Facebook, and other platforms.

As one example of the way these sites are changing business communication, Yelp (www.yelp.com) has become a major influence on consumer behavior at a local level by aggregating millions of reviews of stores, restaurants, and other businesses in large cities across the United States.[22] With the voice of the crowd affecting consumer behavior, businesses need to (a) focus on performing at a high level so that customers reward them with positive reviews and (b) get involved on Yelp (the site encourages business owners to tell potential customers about themselves as well). These efforts could pay off much more handsomely than advertising and other conventional communication efforts.

> The "voice of the crowd," enabled through social media sites, can dramatically influence the way businesses are managed.

## MEDIA CURATION SITES

Newsfeeds from blogs and other online publishers can be a great way to stay on top of developments in any field. However, anyone who has signed up for more than a few RSS feeds has probably experienced the "firehose effect" of getting so many feeds so quickly that it becomes impossible to stay on top of them. Moreover, when a highly active publisher feeds every new article, from the essential to the trivial, the reader is left to sort it all out every day.

An intriguing alternative to newsfeeds is **media curation**, in which someone with expertise or interest in a particular field collects and republishes material on a particular topic. The authors' Business Communication Headline News (http://bchn.businesscommunicationnetwork.com), for instance, was one of the earliest examples of media curation in the field of business communication.

> Media curation is the process of collecting and presenting information on a particular topic in a way that makes it convenient for target readers.

New curation tools, including Pinterest (http://pinterest.com) and Scoop.it (www.scoop.it/), make it easy to assemble attractive online magazines or portfolios on specific topics. Although it raises important issues regarding content ownership and message control,[23] curation has the potential to bring the power of community and shared expertise to a lot of different fields; ultimately, it could reshape audience behavior and therefore the practice of business communication.

> **REAL-TIME UPDATES**
> LEARN MORE BY READING THIS ARTICLE
>
> **Putting Pinterest to work in business communication**
>
> Pinterest has been one of the fastest-growing communication platforms in recent years. See how businesses large and small are putting it to work. Go to http://real-timeupdates.com/bct12 and click on Learn More. If you are using MyBCommLab, you can access Real-Time Updates within each chapter or under Student Study Tools.

## COMMUNITY Q&A SITES

**Community Q&A sites**, on which visitors answer questions posted by other visitors, are a contemporary twist on the early ethos of computer networking, which was people helping each other. (Groups of like-minded people connected online long before the World Wide Web was even created.) Community Q&A sites include dedicated customer support communities such as those hosted on Get Satisfaction (profiled in Chapter 10), public sites such as Quora (www.quora.com) and Yahoo! Answers (http://answers.yahoo.com), and member-only sites such as LinkedIn Answers (www.linkedin.com/answers).

Responding to questions on Q&A sites can be a great way to build your personal brand, to demonstrate your company's commitment to customer service, and to counter misinformation about your company and its products (see Figure 8.3 on the next page). Keep in mind that when you respond to an individual query on a community Q&A site, you are also "responding in advance" to every person in the future who comes to the site with the same question. In other words, you are writing a type of reference material in addition to corresponding with the original questioner, so keep the long timeframe and wider audience in mind.

> Community Q&A sites offer great opportunities for building your personal brand.

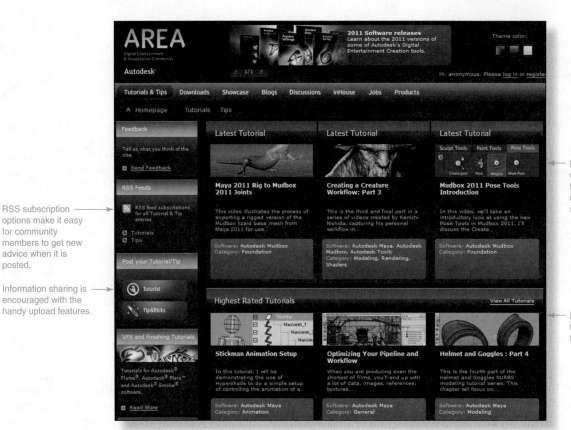

RSS subscription options make it easy for community members to get new advice when it is posted.

Information sharing is encouraged with the handy upload features.

Experienced users can upload in-depth video tutorials to give other members of the community step-by-step guidance.

Members can rate tutorials to help the community find the most helpful videos.

**Figure 8.3    Community Participation Sites**
The software company Autodesk hosts this community participation website for customers who work in the fields of digital entertainment and visualization. Users share quick tips, advice, and in-depth tutorials about using Autodesk software in video games, animations, product designs, and other creative projects.
*Source:* Copyright © 2012 by Autodesk, Inc. Used by permission.

# Blogging

Writing in a personal, authentic voice is key to attracting and keeping blog readers.

**Blogs,** online journals that are easier to personalize and update than conventional websites, are now a major force in business communication. Millions of business-oriented blogs are now in operation, and blogs have become an important source of information for consumers and professionals alike.[24] Good business bloggers pay close attention to several important elements:

- **Communicating with personal style and an authentic voice.** Traditional business messages designed for large audiences tend to be carefully scripted and written in a "corporate voice" that is impersonal and objective. In contrast, successful business blogs such as Southwest Airlines's are written by individuals and exhibit their personal style. Audiences relate to this fresh approach and often build closer emotional bonds with the blogger's organization as a result.
- **Delivering new information quickly.** Blogging tools let you post new material as soon as you create or find it. This feature not only allows you to respond quickly when needed—such as during a corporate crisis—but also lets your audiences know that active communication is taking place. Blogs that don't offer a continuous stream of new and interesting content are quickly ignored in today's online environment.
- **Choosing topics of peak interest to audiences.** Successful blogs cover topics that readers care about, and they emphasize useful information while downplaying product promotion.[25] These topics don't need to be earthshaking or cutting edge—they just need to be things that matter to target readers.

- **Encouraging audiences to join the conversation.** Not all blogs invite comments, but many bloggers consider comments to be an essential feature. These comments can be a valuable source of news, information, and insights. In addition, the relatively informal nature of blogging seems to make it easier for company representatives to let their guards down and converse with their audiences. Of course, not all comments are helpful or appropriate, which is why many bloggers *moderate* comments, previewing them before allowing them to be displayed.

> Most business blogs invite readers to leave comments as a way to encourage participation among stakeholders.

## UNDERSTANDING THE BUSINESS APPLICATIONS OF BLOGGING

Blogs are a potential solution whenever you have a continuing stream of information to share with an online audience—and particularly when you want the audience to have the opportunity to respond. Here are some of the many ways businesses are using blogs (see Figure 8.4 on the next page):[26]

- **Anchoring the social media presence.** As noted on page 206, the multiple threads of any social media program should be anchored in a central hub that the company or individual owns and control. Blogs make an ideal social media hub.
- **Project management and team communication.** Using blogs is a good way to keep project teams up to date, particularly when team members are geographically dispersed.
- **Internal company news.** Companies can use blogs to keep employees informed about general business matters, from facility news to benefit updates. By reducing the need for grapevines to spring up, blogs can enhance communication across all levels of a company.
- **Customer support.** Customer support blogs answer questions, offer tips and advice, and inform customers about new products. Also, many companies monitor the *blogosphere* (and *Twittersphere*), looking for complaints and responding with offers to help dissatisfied customers.[27]

> The business applications of blogs include a wide range of internal and external communication tasks.

---

### COMMUNICATION MISCUES

## Help! I'm Drowning in Social Media!

Anyone who has sampled today's social media offerings has probably experienced this situation: You find a few fascinating blogs, a few interesting people to follow on Twitter, a couple of podcast channels with helpful business tips, and then *wham*—within a few hours of signing up, your computer is overflowing with updates. Even if every new item is useful (which is unlikely), you receive so many that you can't stay ahead of the incoming flood. Between Twitter, newsfeeds, email, instant messaging, and social networks—not to mention a desk phone and a mobile phone—today's business professionals could easily spend their entire days just trying to keep up with incoming messages and never get any work done.

To keep social media from turning into a source of stress and information anxiety, consider these tips:

- **Understand what information you really need in order to excel in your current projects and along your intended career path.** Unfortunately, taking this advice is even trickier than it sounds because you can't always know what you need to know, so you can't always predict which sources will be helpful. However, don't gather information simply because it is interesting or entertaining; collect information that is useful or at least potentially useful.

- **Face the fact that you cannot possibly handle every update from every potentially interesting and helpful source.** You have to set priorities and make tough choices to protect yourself from information overload.
- **Add new information sources slowly.** Give yourself a chance to adjust to the flow and judge the usefulness of each new source.
- **Prune your sources vigorously and frequently.** Bloggers run out of things to say; your needs and interests change; higher-priority sources appear.
- **Remember that information is an enabler, a means to an end.** Collecting vast amounts of information won't get you a sweet promotion with a big raise. *Using* information creatively and intelligently will.

### CAREER APPLICATIONS

1. How can you determine whether a social media source is worth paying attention to?
2. Should you allow any information source to interrupt your work flow during the day (even just to signal that a new message is available)? Why or why not?

**xerox** Xerox Blogs

Blogs Home > Real Business at Xerox

## Golden State, Golden Future

Print This Post
**Submitted by: guest blogger**
Apr 4, 2012 in: Services

By Will Saunders, group president, Xerox Government Healthcare Solutions

Xerox has a great legacy in California. For starters, it's home to one of our great sources of innovation, invention and inspiration. For four decades, the Palo Alto Research Center, (PARC) –a Xerox company – has been pioneering new technologies for Xerox and the world.

We also have many long-term relationships with the state and local California governments to help them simplify operations—from managing everything from IT operations in the city of Riverside to Los Angeles' parking strategy.

One of our biggest projects in the state is managing the transaction and information processing system for its Medicaid program, Medi-Cal. Our work with Medi-Cal, which serves 7.5 million people, helps the state improve access to health care and better manage payment to health care providers.

We've been responsible for the system's operations since October 2011, and in that time have processed more than 90 million claims totaling $7.5 billion.

California's Medicaid processing system (known in the industry as an MMIS) is considered to be one of the biggest and most complex systems of its kind in the country, so the transfer of the system to Xerox from the previous vendor is a significant milestone. We have a team of smart, dedicated and hard-working people who made it all possible.

But our work is far from over. Now that the MMIS is under Xerox control, we're identifying efficiencies and finding ways for stakeholders throughout the system to benefit, including providing a more predictable payment process for doctors, nurses and other medical professionals.

The next major step is when we transition the state to Health Enterprise, a MMIS platform that will give the California flexibility to better serve and support providers and beneficiaries, to precisely and quickly pay claims, and to help prevent fraud and abuse within the program.

That change is a tremendous opportunity to transform the operations of California's biggest program, serving its most vulnerable citizens, and another chapter of Xerox's California success story.

**Post a comment**

| -- required field
Name:
Email:
(not displayed publicly)
URL:
Comments:

You may use HTML tags for style

submit

**Search this blog**

**About this blog**

Real life business is unpredictable. Ideas come from everywhere. Roadblocks come up. Opportunities open up -- more often than not when you're least expecting them. Our role at Xerox is to simplify the way work gets done in workplaces from small businesses to large global enterprises. We help our customers operate more effectively so that they can focus more on what matters most: their real business.

To learn about our blog contributors, click here

**RSS Feed**

**e-mail Subscription**

Your email:
Enter email address...

Subscribe    Unsubscribe

**Blogroll**

> Adam Dewitz's Print CEO
> Autotopia
> Bits Blog – NYTimes
> Celebrating the American Entrepreneurial Spirit
> Chris Brogan
> Dallas News Technology
> Forbes CMO Network Reach and Relevance
> Fortune Tech
> GreenMonk
> Inc. Blog
> Influential Marketing Blog
> Information Week's Healthcare IT blog
> Noel Ward's Real World Digital
> Quick Printing Industry Discussions
> ReadWriteWeb
> Richard Romano's Going Green
> The Business Insider
> The Healthcare blog
> The Huffington Post
> The Verge
> Treehugger
> Wired Epicenter
> Wired Science
> Xerox blogs

**Categories**

> Corporate
> FocusFriday
> General
> Global Citizenship

Convenient action buttons for printing and social sharing are located directly below the post title.

The clean text layout features ragged-right paragraphs and generous leading to accommodate the sans serif typeface.

The comment box makes it easy for readers to respond to and participate in a conversation about the post topic.

A search box in a prominent location helps readers who are looking for other topics on the Xerox blog.

"About this blog" gives new visitors an immediate idea of how this blog might be of interest to them, without forcing them to read multiple posts to see what the blog is about.

RSS and email subscription options let readers sign up for automated delivery of future posts.

The "Unsubscribe" option is placed in a prominent location as well, minimizing the work for subscribers who have changed their minds.

The blogroll offers links to other blogs that might be of interest to readers who find this blog helpful.

The categories listing (which continues below) is a quick way for readers to find all the posts on a particular topic.

**MyBCommLab** Apply Figure 8.4's key concepts. Go to **mybcommlab.com** and follow this path: Course Content → Chapter 8 → **DOCUMENT MAKEOVERS**

**Figure 8.4  Effective Business Blogging**
This Xerox blog, featuring a post by company executive Will Saunders, illustrates the features that make an effective, reader-friendly company blog.
*Source:* Copyright © 2012 by Xerox Corporation. Reprinted with permission.

- **Public relations and media relations.** Many company employees and executives now share company news with both the general public and journalists via their blogs.
- **Recruiting.** Using a blog is a great way to let potential employees know more about your company, the people who work there, and the nature of the company culture. In the other direction, employers often find and evaluate the blogs and microblogs of prospective employees, making blogging is a great way to build a name for yourself within your industry or profession.
- **Policy and issue discussions.** Executive blogs in particular provide a public forum for discussing legislation, regulations, and other broad issues of interest to an organization.

- **Crisis communication.** Using blogs is an efficient way to provide up-to-the-minute information during emergencies, correct misinformation, or respond to rumors.
- **Market research.** Blogs can be a clever mechanism for soliciting feedback from customers and experts in the marketplace. In addition to using their own blogs for research, today's companies need to monitor blogs that are likely to discuss them, their executives, and their products. Negative product reviews, rumors, and other information can spread across the globe in a matter of hours, and managers need to know what the online community is saying—whether it's positive or negative. *Reputation analysts* such as Evolve24 (www.evolve24.com) have developed ways to automatically monitor blogs and other online sources to see what people are saying about their corporate clients and evaluate risks and opportunities in the global online conversation.[28]
- **Brainstorming.** Online brainstorming via blogs offers a way for people to toss around ideas and build on each others' contributions.
- **Employee engagement.** Blogs can enhance communication across all levels of a company. For example, as part of a program to align its corporate culture with changes in the global beverage market, Coca-Cola solicited feedback via blog comments from more than 20,000 employees.[29]
- **Customer education.** Blogs are a great way to help current and potential customers understand and use your products and services. This can improve sales and support productivity as well, by reducing the need for one-on-one communication.
- **Word-of-mouth marketing.** Bloggers and microbloggers often make a point of providing links to other blogs and websites that interest them, giving marketers a great opportunity to have their messages spread by enthusiasts. Word-of-mouth marketing is often called *viral marketing* in reference to the transmission of messages in much the same way that biological viruses are transmitted from person to person. However, viral marketing is not really an accurate metaphor. As author Brian Solis puts it, "There is no such thing as viral marketing."[30] Real viruses spread from host to host on their own, whereas word-of-mouth marketing spreads *voluntarily* from person to person. The distinction is critical, because you need to give people a good reason—good content, in other words—to pass along your message.
- **Influencing traditional media news coverage.** According to social media consultant Tamar Weinberg, "The more prolific bloggers who provide valuable and consistent content are often considered experts in their subject matter" and are often called upon when journalists need insights into various topics.[31]
- **Community building.** Blogging is a great way to connect people with similar interests, and popular bloggers often attract a community of readers who connect with one another through the commenting function.

The possibilities of blogs are almost unlimited, so be on the lookout for new ways to use them to foster positive relationships with colleagues, customers, and other important audiences.

## ADAPTING THE THREE-STEP PROCESS FOR SUCCESSFUL BLOGGING

The three-step writing process is easy to adapt to blogging. The planning step is particularly important if you're considering starting a blog, because you're planning an entire communication channel, not just a single message. Pay close attention to your audience, your purpose, and your scope:

- **Audience.** Except with team blogs and other efforts that have an obvious and well-defined audience, defining the target audience for a blog can be challenging. You want an audience large enough to justify the time you'll be investing but narrow enough that you can provide a clear focus. For instance, if you work for a firm that develops computer games, would you focus your blog on "hardcore" players, the types who spend thousands of dollars on super-fast PCs optimized for video games, or would you broaden the reach to include all video gamers? The decision often comes down to business strategy.

Before you launch a blog, make sure you have a clear understanding of your target audience, the purpose of your blog, and the scope of subjects you plan to cover.

- **Purpose.** A business blog needs to have a business-related purpose that is important to your company and to your chosen audience. Moreover, the purpose has to "have legs"—that is, it needs to be something that can drive the blog's content for months or years—rather than focus on a single event or an issue of only temporary interest. For instance, if you're a technical expert, you might create a blog to give the audience tips and techniques for using your company's products more effectively—a never-ending subject that's important to both you and your audience. This would be the general purpose of your blog; each posting would have a specific purpose within the context of that general purpose. Finally, if you are not writing an official company blog but rather blogging as an individual employee, make sure you understand your employer's blogging guidelines. IBM, for example, gives its employees 12 specific social computing guidelines, such as identifying their role as IBM employees if they are discussing matters related to the company and respecting intellectual property laws.[32]

- **Scope.** Defining the scope of your blog can be a bit tricky. You want to cover a subject area that is broad enough to offer discussion possibilities for months or years but narrow enough to have an identifiable focus. With a clear purpose in mind, you'll have a better idea of how wide or narrow your subject can be.

After you begin writing your blog, careful planning needs to continue with each message. Unless you're posting to a restricted-access blog, such as an internal blog on a company intranet, you can never be sure who might see your posts. Other bloggers might link to them months or years later.

Write blog postings in a comfortable—but not careless—style.

Use a comfortable, personal writing style. Blog audiences don't want to hear from your company; they want to hear from *you*. Bear in mind, though, that comfortable does not mean careless. Sloppy writing damages your credibility. Successful blog content also needs to be interesting, valuable to readers, and as brief as possible.[33] In addition, although audiences expect you to be knowledgeable in the subject area your blog covers, you don't need to know everything about a topic. If you don't have all the information yourself, provide links to other blogs and websites that supply relevant information. In fact, media curation (see page 207) is one of the most valuable aspects of blogging.

As with email subject lines, compelling headlines for blog posts are an essential tool to draw in readers. A headline needs to grab the reader's attention in a split second by promising something useful, surprising, challenging, or otherwise different from what the reader already knows. Headlines should be as short as possible and suggest that the information in the post will be easy to read and use. "List" headlines that cut right to the heart of something readers care about, such as "10 Reasons You Didn't Get That Promotion" or "Seven Ways to Save Money with Your Smartphone," are particularly popular among bloggers.

Completing messages for your blog is usually quite easy. Evaluate the content and readability of your message, proofread to correct any errors, and post using your blogging system's tools. Be sure to include one or more *newsfeed options* (often called RSS newsfeeds) so that your audience can automatically receive headlines and summaries of new blog posts. Whatever blogging system you are using can provide guidance on setting up newsfeeds.

Finally, make your material easier to find by **tagging** it with descriptive words. Your readers can then click on these "content labels" to find additional posts on those topics. Tags are usually displayed with each post, and they can also be groups in a *tag cloud* display, which shows all the tags in use on your blog.

"Checklist: Blogging for Business" summarizes some of the key points to remember when creating and writing a business blog.

# Microblogging

A **microblog** is a variation on blogging in which messages are sharply restricted to specific character counts. Twitter (http://twitter.com) is the best known of these systems, but many others exist. Some companies have private microblogging systems for internal use only; these systems are sometimes referred to as *enterprise microblogging* or *internal micromessaging*.[34]

---

CHECKLIST ✔ Blogging for Business

- Consider creating a blog or microblog account whenever you have a continuing stream of information to share with an online audience.
- Identify an audience that is broad enough to justify the effort but narrow enough to have common interests.
- Identify a purpose that is comprehensive enough to provide ideas for a continuing stream of posts.
- Consider the scope of your blog carefully; make it broad enough to attract an audience but narrow enough to keep you focused.

- Communicate with a personal style and an authentic voice but don't write carelessly.
- Deliver new information quickly.
- Choose topics of peak interest to your audience.
- Encourage audiences to join the conversation.
- Consider using Twitter or other microblog updates to alert readers to new posts on your regular blog.

---

Many of the concepts of regular blogging apply to microblogging as well, although the severe length limitations call for a different approach to composition. Microblog messages often involve short summaries or teasers that provide links to more information. In addition, microblogs tend to have a stronger social aspect that makes it easier for writers and readers to forward messages and for communities to form around individual writers.[35] Note that every public tweet from every Twitter user is being archived by the Library of Congress.[36] If you plan a career in the public eye, tweet with care, because you are creating a public record.

Like regular blogging, microblogging quickly caught on with business users and is now a mainstream business medium. Microblogs are used for virtually all of the blog applications mentioned on pages 209–211. In addition, microblogs are frequently used for providing company updates, offering coupons and notice of sales, presenting tips on product usage, sharing relevant and interesting information from experts, announcing headlines of new blog posts (see Figure 8.5), and serving as the *backchannel* in meetings and presentations (see page 471).

The business communication uses of microblogging extend well beyond the publication of brief updates.

MyBCommLab Apply Figure 8.5's key concepts. Go to **mybcommlab.com** and follow this path: Course Content → Chapter 8 → **DOCUMENT MAKEOVERS**

← Links to an article in a respected business magazine

← Links to a seminar invitation on Deloitte's website

← Links to an article and information about the firm's consulting services in this market

← Links to a video on YouTube

← Links to a video on Deloitte's website

← Links to an article and information about the firm's consulting services in this market

← Links to a report on Deloitte's website

← Links to a conference invitation on Deloitte's website

**Figure 8.5   Business Uses of Twitter**
The global accounting and consulting firm Deloitte uses Twitter to announce and promote a variety of topics and resources. Rather than relying on the 140-character tweets to convey the entire message, the company's tweets instead serve as teasers, encouraging readers to click through for more detailed information.
*Source:* Copyright © 2012 Deloitte Global Services Limited. Reprinted with permission.

By following top names in your field, you can customize Twitter as your own real-time news source.[37] Customer service is becoming a popular use for Twitter as well, thanks to its ease and speed and the option to switch between public tweets and private direct messages as the situation warrants.[38] The social networking aspect of Twitter and other microblogs also makes them good for *crowdsourcing* research questions, asking one's followers for input or advice.[39] Finally, the ease of *retweeting,* the practice of forwarding messages from other Twitter users, is the microblogging equivalent of sharing other content from other bloggers via media curation.

In addition to its usefulness as a standalone system, Twitter is integrated with other social media systems and a variety of publishing and reading tools and services. Many of these make use of the informal Twitter feature known as the *hashtag* (the # symbol followed by a word or phrase), which makes it easy for people to label and search for topics of interest and to monitor ongoing Twitter conversations about particular topics.

Although microblogs are designed to encourage spontaneous communication, when you're using the medium for business communication, don't just tweet out whatever pops into your head. Make sure messages are part of your overall communication strategy. Twitter followers consider tweets that are entertaining, surprising, informative, or engaging (such as asking followers for advice) as the most valuable. In contrast, the least-valuable tweets tend to be complaints, conversations between the Twitter account owner and a specific follower, and relatively pointless messages such as saying "good morning."[40]

> Don't let the speed and simplicity of microblogging lull you into making careless mistakes; every message should support your business communication objectives.

## Wikis

**6 LEARNING OBJECTIVE**
Offer guidelines for becoming a valuable wiki contributor.

As Chapter 2 points out, using wikis is a great way for teams and other groups to collaborate on writing projects, from brief articles to long reports and reference works (see Figure 8.6). The benefits of wikis are compelling, but they do require a unique approach to writing.

**Figure 8.6   Wikis**
A wiki is an ideal solution when a company wants to encourage participation in collaborative writing.
*Source:* Copyright © 2012 by The Motley Fool. Reprinted with permission.

## UNDERSTANDING THE WIKI PHILOSOPHY

To be a valuable wiki contributor, keep these points in mind:[41]

- Let go of traditional expectations of authorship, including individual recognition and control.
- Encourage all team members to improve each other's work.
- Use page templates and other formatting options to make sure your content matches the rest of the wiki.
- Many wikis provide both editing and commenting capabilities, and participants should use the appropriate tool for each. In other words, don't insert comments or questions into the main content; use the "talk page" or other commenting feature if you want to discuss the content.
- Take advantage of the *sandbox*, if available; this is a "safe," nonpublished section of the wiki where team members can practice editing and writing.

Wikis often have guideline pages to help new contributors integrate their work into the group's ongoing effort. Be sure to read and understand these guidelines, and don't be afraid to ask for help.

> Being an effective wiki collaborator requires a different writing mindset.

## ADAPTING THE THREE-STEP PROCESS FOR SUCCESSFUL WIKI WRITING

You can easily adapt the three-step writing process for wikis, depending on whether you are creating a new wiki, adding new material to an existing wiki, or revising existing material on a wiki.

If you are creating a new wiki, think through your long-term purpose carefully, just as you would with a new blog or podcast channel. Doing so will help you craft appropriate guidelines, editorial oversight, and security policies. For instance, the PlayStation development team at Sony uses a wiki to keep top managers up to date on new products, and because this information is highly confidential, access to the wiki is tightly controlled.[42]

If you are adding a page or an article to an existing wiki, figure out how this new material fits in with the existing organization. Find out whether any similar material already exists; it might be better to expand an existing article or add a subpage than to create a new item. Also, learn the wiki's preferred style for handling incomplete articles. For example, on the wiki that contains the user documentation for the popular WordPress blogging software, contributors are discouraged from adding new pages until the content is "fairly complete and accurate."[43]

> Make sure you understand how a new wiki page will fit in with the existing content.

If you are revising or updating an existing wiki article, use the checklist on page 149 in Chapter 6 to evaluate the content before you make changes. If you don't agree with published content and plan to revise it, you can use the wiki's discussion facility to share your concerns with other contributors. The wiki environment should encourage discussions and even robust disagreements, as long as everyone remains civil and respectful.

For the latest advice on using social media in business, visit http://real-timeupdates .com/bct12 and click on Chapter 8.

---

## COMMUNICATION CHALLENGES AT Southwest Airlines

You recently joined the corporate communications group at Southwest Airlines, and one of your responsibilities is overseeing the Nuts About Southwest blog. Apply what you know about blogging to solve these two challenges.

**INDIVIDUAL CHALLENGE:** You've received a number of adamant messages saying that Nuts About Southwest won't be a "real" blog until anyone is allowed to write any sort of comment without being "censored" by a blog moderator. However, you know that every blog is vulnerable to rude, inappropriate, and irrelevant comments, and you don't want Nuts About Southwest to turn into a free-for-all shouting match. Write a brief statement to be included in the blog's User's Guide, explaining the company's reasons for continuing to moderate comments.

**TEAM CHALLENGE:** With a team of fellow students, compare the blogging and Twitter activity of three airlines that compete with Southwest. Which does the best job of engaging customers, and which does the worst? Prepare a brief presentation of your analysis.

# Quick Learning Guide

## SUMMARY OF LEARNING OBJECTIVES

**1** Identify seven key points for using social media in business communication. Seven key points for using social media are (1) remember that it's a conversation, not a lecture or a sales pitch; (2) write informally but not carelessly; (3) create concise, specific, and informative headlines that don't force readers to solve clever wordplay puzzles; (4) get involved and stay involved with conversations that concern your company; (5) promote your company and products indirectly; (6) be transparent and honest; and (7) think before you post to avoid problems caused by careless messages.

**2** Describe the business communication applications of social networks. Businesses now use a variety of social networks, including well-known public networks such as Facebook and business-oriented networks such as LinkedIn, as well as a variety of specialized networks, single-company networks for customers, and internal employee-only networks. The business communication applications of social networks are important and diverse; major uses include collaborating, gathering market intelligence, recruiting employees, connecting with business partners, marketing, and fostering brand communities.

**3** Explain how information and media sharing sites are used in business communication. User-generated content sites such as YouTube allow companies to host media items (such as videos) that customers and other stakeholders can view, comment on, and share. Media curation sites allow professionals and consumers someone with expertise or interest in a particular field to collect and republish material on a particular topic. Community Q&A sites give individuals the opportunity to build their personal brands by providing expertise, and they give companies the chance to address customer complaints and correct misinformation.

**4** Describe the role of blogging in business communication today, and explain how to adapt the three-step writing process to blogging. Blogs are used in numerous ways in business today, such as for project management and team communication, company news, customer support, public relations and media relations, employee recruiting, policy and issue discussions, crisis communication, market research, brainstorming, employee engagement, viral marketing, influencing traditional media news coverage, and community building.

The three-step process adapts readily to blogging. In planning, pay particular care to defining your audience, identifying the overall purpose of your blog and specific purposes of each post, and establishing a scope that is narrow enough to be focused but broad enough to afford a steady supply of topics. In writing, be sure to write in a personal, authentic style, without slipping into overly familiar or careless writing. Completing involves the usual tasks of proofing and revising, along with the particular tasks needed to distribute your posts via newsfeeds.

**5** Describe the business use of Twitter and microblogging systems. Microblogs such as Twitter are used for many of the same purposes as conventional blogging, along with electronic coupons, sale announcements, one-on-one customer service queries, and customized news channels created by following experts of interest. Microblogs can also serve as the backchannel during meetings and presentations.

**6** Offer guidelines for becoming a valuable wiki contributor. To become a valuable wiki contributor, let go of traditional expectations of authorship, including individual recognition and control; don't be afraid to edit and improve existing content; use page templates and other formatting options to make sure your content is formatted in the same style as the rest of the wiki; keep edits and comments separate by using the "talk page" to discuss content, rather than inserting comments directly into the text; take advantage of the sandbox to learn how use the wiki's writing and editing tools; and understand and follow the wiki's contributor guidelines.

## KEY TERMS

**blog** An easily updatable online journal; short for *weblog*

**brand communities** Groups of people united by their interest in and ownership or use of particular products

**brand socialization** A measure of how effectively a company engages with its various online stakeholders in a mutually beneficial exchange of information

**community Q&A sites** Websites on which visitors answer questions posted by other visitors or by representatives of companies

**media curation** The practice of collecting, filtering, and republishing material on a particular topic

**microblog** A variation on blogging in which messages are restricted to specific character counts; Twitter is the best-known example

**social networks** Online services that enable individual and organizational members to form connections and share information

**tagging** Attaching descriptive terms to blog posts and other articles to facilitate searching

**user-generated content (UGC) sites** Websites on which users rather than website owners contribute most or all of the content

---

CHECKLIST ✓

## Blogging for Business

- Consider creating a blog or microblog account whenever you have a continuing stream of information to share with an online audience.
- Identify an audience that is broad enough to justify the effort but narrow enough to have common interests.
- Identify a purpose that is comprehensive enough to provide ideas for a continuing stream of posts.
- Consider the scope of your blog carefully; make it broad enough to attract an audience but narrow enough to keep you focused.
- Communicate with a personal style and an authentic voice but don't write carelessly.
- Deliver new information quickly.
- Choose topics of peak interest to your audience.
- Encourage audiences to join the conversation.
- Consider using Twitter or other microblog updates to alert readers to new posts on your regular blog.

# Test Your Knowledge

To review chapter content related to each question, refer to the indicated Learning Objective.

1. What is a community of practice? [LO-2]
2. What does it mean to anchor your social media presence in a hub? [LO-2]
3. What is media curation? [LO-3]
4. How can blogs help with so-called viral marketing efforts? [LO-4]
✪ 5. Why is it important to have a long-term, sustainable purpose in mind before you launch a blog channel? [LO-4]
6. How can Twitter be used to crowdsource research? [LO-5]
✪ 7. How does the use of hashtags on Twitter help people find information of interest? [LO-5]
8. Why is it important to abandon traditional notions of ownership when writing on a wiki? [LO-6]

# Apply Your Knowledge

To review chapter content related to each question, refer to the indicated Learning Objective.

1. Can your company stay in control of its messages if it stays off social media? Why or why not?
✪ 2. Is leveraging your connections on social networks for business purposes ethical? Why or why not? [LO-2]
✪ 3. If one of the benefits of blogging and microblogging is the personal, intimate style of writing, is it a good idea to limit your creativity by adhering to conventional rules of grammar, spelling, and mechanics? Why or why not? [LO-4]
4. In your work as a video game designer, you know that eager players search the web for any scrap of information they can find about upcoming releases. In fact, to build interest, your company's public relations department carefully doles out small bits of information in the months before a new title hits the market. However, you and others in the company are also concerned about competitors getting their hands on all this "prerelease" information. If they learn too much too soon, they can use the information to improve their own products more quickly. You and several other designers and programmers maintain blogs that give players insights into game design techniques and that occasionally share tips and tricks. You have thousands of readers, and you believe that your blog helps build customer loyalty. The company president wants to ban blogging entirely so that bloggers don't accidentally share too much prerelease information about upcoming games. Would this be a wise move? Why or why not? [LO-4]
✪ 5. What are some ways the president of a hiking equipment company can use Twitter to engage potential customers without being overtly promotional?

# Practice Your Skills

**Message for Analysis 8.A: Media Skills:**
**Blogging, Creating a Businesslike Tone [LO-5]**

Revise this blog post based on what you've learned in this chapter.

[headline]

We're DOOMED!!!!!

[post]

I was at the Sikorsky plant in Stratford yesterday, just checking to see how things were going with the assembly line retrofit we did for them last year. I think I saw the future, and it ain't pretty. They were demo'ing a prototype robot from Motoman that absolutely blows our stuff out of the water. They wouldn't let me really see it, but based on the 10-second glimpse I got, it's smaller, faster, and more maneuverable than any of our units. And when I asked about the price, the guy just grinned. And it wasn't the sort of grin designed to make me feel good.

I've been saying for years that we need to pay more attention to size, speed, and maneuverability instead of just relying on our historical strengths of accuracy and payload capacity, and you'd have to be blind not to agree that this experience proves me right. If we can't at least show a design for a better unit within two or three months, Motoman is going to lock up the market and leave us utterly in the dust.

Believe me, being able to say "I told you so" right now is not nearly as satisfying as you might think!!

**Message 8.B: Revising Web Content**
**with a "You" Attitude [LO-6]**

To access this wiki exercise, visit http://real-timeupdates.com/bct12, click on Student Assignments, and select Chapter 8, Message 8.B. Follow the instructions for evaluating the existing content and revising it to make it more reader oriented.

**Message 8.C: Improving the Effectiveness**
**of a Wiki Article [LO-6]**

To access this wiki exercise, go to http://real-timeupdates.com/bct12, click on Student Assignments, and select Chapter 8, Message 8.C. Follow the instructions for evaluating the existing content and revising it to make it clear and concise.

**Exercises**

Each activity is labeled according to the primary skill or skills you will need to use. To review relevant chapter content, you can refer to the indicated Learning Objective. In some instances, supporting information will be found in another chapter, as indicated.

1. **Media Skills: Social Networking [LO-2]** Pick a company in any industry that interests you. Imagine you are doing strategic planning for this firm, and identify one of your company's key competitors. (Hint: You can use the free listings on www.hoovers.com to find several top competitors for most medium and large companies in the United States; click on the Competition tab.) Now search through social media sources to find three strategically relevant pieces of information about this competitor, such as the hiring of a new executive, the launch of a major new product, or a significant problem of some kind. In a post on your class blog, identify the information you found and the sources you used. (If you can't find useful information, pick another firm or try another industry.)

2. **Media Skills: Blogging, Creating a Businesslike Tone [LO-4]** The members of the project team of which you are the leader have enthusiastically embraced blogging as a communication medium. Unfortunately, as emotions heat up during the project, some of the blog posts are getting too casual, too personal, and even sloppy. Because your boss and other managers around the company also read this project blog, you don't want the team to look unprofessional. Revise the following blog post so that it communicates in a more businesslike manner while retaining the informal, conversational tone of a blog. (Be sure to correct any spelling and punctuation mistakes you find as well.)

Well, to the profound surprise of absolutely nobody, we are not going to be able meet the June 1 commitment to ship 100 operating tables to Southeast Surgical Supply. (For those of you who have been living in a cave the past six month, we have been fighting to get our hands on enough high-grade chromium steel to meet our production schedule.) Sure enough, we got news, this morning that we will only get enough for 30 tables. Yes, we look like fools for not being able to follow through on promises we made to the customer, but no, this didn't have to happpen. Six month's ago, purchasing warned us about shrinking supplies and suggested we advance-buy as much as we would need for the next 12 months, or so. We naturally tried to followed their advice, but just as naturally were shot down by the bean counters at corporate who trotted out the policy about never buying more than three months worth of materials in advance. Of course, it'll be us—not the bean counters who'll take the flak when everybody starts asking why revenues are down next quarter and why Southeast is talking to our friends at Crighton Manuf!!! Maybe, some day this company will get its head out of the sand and realize that we need to have some financial flexibility in order to compete.

3. **Media Skills: Blogging [LO-4]** Find a current political issue that could have a direct effect on business, such as immigration law, Internet sales tax, product safety, or international trade policy. Identify a company that is affected by this issue, and assume you are the president or CEO and want to speak out on the issue. Write a three-paragraph blog post that summarizes the issue, explains how it could affect your company, and urges a particular action from political leaders.

4. **Media Skills: Microblogging [LO-5]** Busy knitters can go through a lot of yarn in a hurry, so most keep a sharp eye out for sales. You're on the marketing staff of Knitting-Warehouse, and you like to keep your loyal shoppers up to date with the latest deals. Visit the Knitting-Warehouse website at www.knitting-warehouse.com, select any on-sale product that catches your eye, and write a 120-character Twitter update that describes the product and the sale. (Unless you are working on a private Twitter account that is accessible only by your instructor and your classmates, don't actually send this Twitter update. Email it to your instructor instead.)

5. **Media Skills: Microblogging [LO-5]** Choose a product you purchased recently or something you're considering purchasing. Compose a three-tweet sequence that (1) introduces the product, (2) lists two or three important benefits, and (3) identifies which groups of consumers can benefit from it. Email your tweets to your instructor rather than posting them on Twitter.

## Expand Your Skills

### Critique the Professionals

Compare a dozen recent Twitter updates from two companies in the same industry. Viewing them from the perspective of a potential customer, which company does a better job of engaging your attention and building your interest in its products? Using whatever medium your instructor requests, write a brief analysis of the two companies' Twitter activity and explain why one is using the social network more effectively than the other.

### Sharpening Your Career Skills Online

Bovée and Thill's Business Communication Web Search, at http://businesscommunicationblog.com/websearch, is a unique research tool designed specifically for business communication research. Use the Web Search function to find a website, video, PDF document, podcast, or PowerPoint presentation that offers advice on using social media in business. Write a brief email message to your instructor, describing the item that you found and summarizing the career skills information you learned from it.

# Cases

## SOCIAL NETWORKING SKILLS

**1. Media Skills: Social Networking; Media Skills: Microblogging [LO-2] [LO-5]** Foursquare (http://foursquare.com/) is one of the leading providers of location-based social networking services. Millions of people use Foursquare for social engagement and friendly competition, and many business owners are starting to recognize the marketing potential of having people who are on the move in local areas, broadcasting their locations and sharing information about stores, restaurants, clubs, and other merchants.

**Your task:** Review the information on Foursquare's Merchant Platform at http://foursquare.com/business/venues. Now write four brief messages, no more than 140 characters long (including spaces).

The first should summarize the benefits to stores, restaurants, and other "brick and mortar" businesses of participating in Foursquare, and the next three messages should convey three compelling points that support that overall benefit statement. If your class is set up with private Twitter accounts, use your private account to send your messages. Otherwise, email your four messages to your instructor or post them on your class blog, as your instructor directs.

## SOCIAL NETWORKING SKILLS

**2. Media Skills: Social Networking; Online Etiquette [LO-2], Chapter 2** Employees who take pride in their work are a practically priceless resource for any business. However, pride can sometimes manifest itself in negative ways when employees come under criticism—and public criticism is a fact of life in social media. Imagine that your company has recently experienced a rash of product quality problems, and these problems have generated some unpleasant and occasionally unfair criticism on a variety of social media sites. Someone even set up a Facebook page specifically to give customers a place to vent their frustrations.

You and your public relations team jumped into action, responding to complaints with offers to provide replacement products and help customers who have been affected by the quality problems. Everything seemed to be going as well as could be expected, when you were checking a few industry blogs one evening and discovered that a couple of engineers in your company's product design lab have been responding to complaints on their own. They identified themselves as company employees and defended their product design, blaming the company's production department and even criticizing several customers for lacking the skills needed to use such a sophisticated product. Within a matter of minutes, you see their harsh comments being retweeted and reposted on multiple sites, only fueling the fire of negative feedback against your firm. Needless to say, you are horrified.

**Your task:** You manage to reach the engineers by private message and tell them to stop posting messages, but you realize you have a serious training issue on your hands. Write a post for the internal company blog that advises employees on how to respond appropriately when they are representing the company online. Use your imagination to make up any details you need.

## SOCIAL NETWORKING SKILLS / PRESENTATION SKILLS

**3. Media Skills: Social Networking; Media Skills: Presentations [LO-2], Chapters 16–17** Daniel Gordon, the fourth-generation jeweler who is CEO of Samuel Gordon Jewelers in Oklahoma City, has turbocharged the century-old company with social media. During some of the roughest economic times in memory, the company's revenues and foot traffic have grown steadily while its advertising costs have dropped by 90 percent. Gordon is an active social media user, using a variety of media tools to educate jewelry buyers, let customers know about new products, and guide customers through the process of selecting wedding rings and other significant jewelry purchases.

**Your task:** With a team of classmates, study the company's website (www.samuelgordons.com/) and its social media presence (you can find various social media links on the website). You can read more about the company's social media strategy by visiting http://real-timeupdates.com/ebc10, clicking on Student Assignments and selecting Chapter 8, Case 3. Now identify a business near your college that could benefit from a similar social media strategy. Devise a social media strategy that could help this company expand its customer base and forge stronger links with the local community. Prepare a brief class presentation that describes the business and explains your proposed strategy. (Your instructor may ask you to undertake this as a service project, in which you meet with the company owner and present your proposed social media strategy.)

## SOCIAL NETWORKING SKILLS

**4. Media Skills: Social Networking [LO-2]** Social media can be a great way to, well, socialize during your college years, but employers are increasingly checking up on the online activities of potential hires to avoid bringing in employees who may reflect poorly on the company.

**Your task:** Team up with another student and review each other's public presence on Facebook, Twitter, Flickr, blogs, and any other website that an employer might check during the interview and recruiting process. Identify any photos, videos, messages, or other material that could raise a red flag when an employee is evaluating a job candidate. Write your teammate an email message that lists any risky material.

## INFORMATION SHARING SKILLS

**5. Media Skills: Community Q&A; Career Management: Personal Branding [LO-3], Prologue** Community Q&A sites offer a great opportunity to get your name out there as a subject-matter expert.

**Your task:** Browse the questions posted at LinkedIn Answers (www.linkedin.com/answers) and find a question that you can answer using information you already have or information you could gather through research. Write an appropriate answer and email it to your instructor or post it on your class blog, together with the question. Keep in mind that answers posted on community Q&A sites such as this could be read by future employers, colleagues, and customers.

## BLOGGING SKILLS

**6. Media Skills: Blogging; Compositional Modes: Tutorials [LO-4]** Studying abroad for a semester or a year can be a rewarding experience in many ways—improving your language skills, experiencing another culture, making contacts in the international business arena, and building your self-confidence.

**Your task:** Write a post for your class blog that describes your college's study abroad program and summarizes the steps involved in applying for international study. If your school doesn't offer study-abroad opportunities, base your post on the program offered at another institution in your state.

## BLOGGING SKILLS / PORTFOLIO BUILDER

**7. Media Skills: Blogging [LO-4]** Chevrolet recently introduced the Volt, a gas/electric hybrid that might finally give drivers a viable alternative to the wildly popular Toyota Prius.

**Your task:** Working with a team assigned by your instructor, write a post for GM's dealer-only blog that describes the new Volt and the benefits it offers car owners. Include at least one photo and one link to the Volt section of GM's website. You can learn more about the Volt at Chevy's website, www.chevrolet.com.

## BLOGGING SKILLS

**8. Media Skills: Blogging [LO-4]**  Comic-Con International is an annual convention that highlights a wide variety of pop culture and entertainment media, from comic books and collectibles to video games and movies. From its early start as a comic book convention that attracted several hundred fans and publishing industry insiders, Comic-Con has become a major international event with more than 135,000 attendees.

**Your task:** Several readers of your pop culture blog have been asking for your recommendation about visiting Comic-Con in San Diego next summer. Write a two- or three-paragraph posting for your blog that explains what Comic-Con is and what attendees can expect to experience at the convention. Be sure to address your posting to fans, not industry insiders. You can learn more at www.comic-con.org.[44]

## BLOGGING SKILLS

**9. Media Skills: Blogging [LO-4]**   You work for PreVisor, one of many companies that offer employee screening and testing services. PreVisors's offerings include a variety of online products and consulting services, all designed to help employers find and develop the best possible employees.

To help explain the value of its products and services, PreVisor publishes a variety of customer *case studies* on its website. Each case study describes the staffing challenges a particular company faces, the solution PreVisor was able to provide, and the results the company experienced after using PreVisor products or services.

**Your task:** Select one of the customer case studies on the PreVisor website (www.previsor.com/results/clients). Write a post that could appear on PreVisor's blog, summarizing the challenges, solutions, and results in no more than 100 words. Include a link to the complete case study on the PreVisor website.

## BLOGGING SKILLS

**10. Media Skills: Blogging [LO-4]**  The fact that 97 percent of American youth ages 12 to 17 play video games is not much of a surprise, but more than a few nongaming adults might be surprised to learn that game playing might not be quite the social and civic catastrophe it is sometimes made out to be. A recent study by the Pew Internet & American Life Project puts a least a few cracks in the stereotyped image of gamers being loners who live out violent fantasies while learning few if any skills that could make them positive members of society.[45]

**Your task:** Imagine that you're on the public relations staff at the Entertainment Software Association (ESA), an industry group that represents the interests of video game companies. You'd like to share the results of the Pew survey with parents to help ease their concerns. Visit http://real-timeupdates.com/bct12, click on Student Assignments and then Chapter 8, Case 10. Download this PDF file, which is a summary of the Pew results. Find at least three positive aspects of video game playing and write a brief message that could be posted on an ESA public affairs blog.

## MICROBLOGGING SKILLS

**11. Media Skills: Microblogging [LO-5]**   Consumers looking for beauty, health, and lifestyle magazines have an almost endless array of choices, but even in this crowded field, Logan Olson found her own niche. Olson, who was born with congenital heart disease, suffered a heart attack at age 16 that left her in a coma and caused serious brain damage. The active and outgoing teen had to relearn everything from sitting up to feeding herself. As she recovered, she looked for help and advice in conquering such daily challenges as finding fashionable clothes that were easier to put on and makeup that was easier to apply. Mainstream beauty magazines didn't seem to offer any information for young women with disabilities, so she started her own magazine. Oprah Winfrey has *Oprah*, and Logan Olson has *Logan*. The magazine not only gives young women tips on buying and using a variety of products but lets women with disabilities know there are others like them, facing and meeting the same challenges.

**Your task:** Write a 120-character message suggesting a gift subscription to *Logan* magazine as a nice birthday gift for any young woman who might benefit from the magazine. Assume that your readers are not familiar with *Logan*. (Limiting your message to 120 characters allows room for a 20-character URL, which you don't need to include in your message.) You can learn more about *Logan* at www.loganmagazine.com or on Facebook (search for Logan Magazine).[46] If your class is set up with private Twitter accounts, use your private account to send your message. Otherwise, email it to your instructor.

## MICROBLOGGING SKILLS

**12. Media Skills: Microblogging; Compositional Modes: Teasers [LO-5]**   Twitter updates are a great way to alert people to helpful articles, videos, and other online resources.

**Your task:** Find an online resource (it can be a website quiz, a YouTube video, a PowerPoint presentation, a newspaper article, or anything else appropriate) that offers some great tips to help college students prepare for job interviews. Write a teaser of no more than 120 characters that hints at the benefits other students can get from this resource. If your class is set up with private Twitter accounts, use your private account to send your message. Otherwise, email it to your instructor. Be sure to include the URL; if you're using Twitter account, the system should shorten it to 20 characters to keep you within the 140-character limit.

## MICROBLOGGING SKILLS

**13. Media Skills: Microblogging; Compositional Modes: Updates and Announcements [LO-5]**  JetBlue is known for its innovations in customer service and customer communication, including its pioneering use of the Twitter microblogging system. Nearly two million JetBlue fans and customers follow the company on Twitter to get updates on flight status during weather disruptions, facility upgrades, and other news.[47]

**Your task:**   Write a message of no more than 120 characters that announces the limited-time availability of flights and travel packages—flights plus hotel rooms, for example—at JetBlue's store on eBay. (Limiting your message to 120 characters allows room for a 20-character URL, which you don't need to include in your message.) The key selling point is that travelers may be able to purchase flights they want at steep discounts. If your class is set up with private Twitter accounts, use your private account to send your message. Otherwise, email it to your instructor.

## WIKI SKILLS

**14. Media Skills: Wiki Writing; Evaluating the Work of Other Writers [LO-6]**   Evaluating existing content is a vital step in making improvements to a wiki.

**Your task:**   Find an article on Wikipedia that needs to be updated, corrected, or otherwise improved. You can use an article that has been flagged by Wikipedia editors or find an article on a subject you are familiar with, such as the profile of a favorite musical artist. To keep the project at a manageable size, feel free to select a portion of a longer article (roughly 500 to 1,000 words). Using the guidelines on page 147 for evaluating the work of other writers, evaluate the quality of the article and identify the steps you would take to improve it. Revise the piece and post your version on your class blog or email it to your instructor. Include a brief summary of the changes you made and your reasons for making them. (Don't edit the Wikipedia entry as part of this assignment.)

---

## MyBCommLab

Go to **mybcommlab.com** for Auto-graded writing questions as well as the following Assisted-graded writing questions:

**8-1.**   Why is it important to avoid clever wordplay in social media headlines? [LO-1]

**8-2.**   Why does a personal style of writing help blogs build stronger relationships with audiences? [LO-4]

**8-3.**   Mybcommlab Only—comprehensive writing assignment for this chapter.

# Endnotes

**1.** Southwest Airlines, Nuts About Southwest blog, accessed 4 February 2013, www.blogsouthwest.com; Bill Owens, "Why Can't I Make Reservations Further in Advance?" Nuts About Southwest Blog, 24 January 2007, www.blogsouthwest.com; Bill Owens, "I Blogged. You Flamed. We Changed." Nuts About Southwest blog, 18 April 2007, www.blogsouthwest.com; "Southwest Airlines Is Nuts About Blogging," Southwest Airlines Press release, 27 April 2007, www.prnewswire.com.

**2.** Catherine Toole, "My 7 Deadly Sins of Writing for Social Media—Am I Right?" Econsultancy blog, 19 June 2007, www.econsultancy.com; Muhammad Saleem, "How to Write a Social Media Press Release," Copyblogger, accessed 16 September 2008, www.copyblogger.com; Melanie McBride, "5 Tips for (Better) Social Media Writing," Melanie McBride Online, 11 June 2008, accessed 16 September 2008, http://melaniemcbride.net.

**3.** Jon Russell, "Why 'Going Global' Makes No Sense for China's Social Networks—for Now," The Next Web, 14 May 2012, http://thenextweb.com.

**4.** Todd Henneman, "At Lockheed Martin, Social Networking Fills Key Workforce Needs While Improving Efficiency and Lowering Costs," Workforce Management, March 2010, www.workforce.com.

**5.** H. James Wilson, P.J. Guinan, Salvatore Parise, and Bruce D. Weinberg, "What's Your Social Media Strategy?" Harvard Business Review, July–August 2011, 23–25.

**6.** Patrick Hanlon and Josh Hawkins, "Expand Your Brand Community Online," Advertising Age, 7 January 2008, 14–15.

**7.** Christopher Swan, "Gamification: A New Way to Shape Behavior," Communication World, May–June 2012, 13–14.

**8.** Samantha Murphy, "Why Mobile Commerce Is on the Rise," Mashable, 7 March 2012, http://mashable.com.

**9.** Todd Wasserman, "What Drives Brand Sociability?" Mashable, 12 October 2011.

**10.** Toyota Facebook page, accessed 1 February 2013, www.facebook.com/toyota; General Motors Facebook page, accessed 1 February 2013, www.facebook.com/generalmotors; Ford Facebook page, accessed 1 February 2013, www.facebook.com/ford; B.L. Ochman, "Doing It Wrong: 11 Boring Things GM Posted on Facebook," Ad Age, 18 May 2012.

**11.** "Shaking Things Up at Coca-Cola," Harvard Business Review, October 2011, 94–99.

**12.** Alex Wright, "Mining the Web for Feelings, Not Facts," New York Times, 23 August 2009, www.nytimes.com.

**13.** Christian Pieter Hoffmann, "Holding Sway," Communication World, November–December 2011, 26–29; Josh Bernoff, "Social Strategy for Exciting (and Not So Exciting) Brands," Marketing News, 15 May 2009, 18; Larry Weber, Marketing to the Social Web (Hoboken, N.J.: Wiley, 2007), 12–14; David Meerman Scott, The New Rules of Marketing and PR (Hoboken, N.J.: Wiley, 2007), 62; Paul Gillin, The New Influencers (Sanger, Calif.: Quill Driver Books, 2007), 34–35; Jeremy Wright, Blog Marketing: The Revolutionary Way to Increase Sales, Build Your Brand, and Get Exceptional Results (New York: McGraw-Hill, 2006), 263–365.

**14.** Content for two-page feature adapted from GE Connections Twitter page, accessed 5 February 2013, https://twitter.com/GEConnections; Specialized Bicycle Components website, accessed 5 February 2013, www.specialized.com; Specialized Riders Club website, accessed 5 February 2013, www.specializedriders.com; Steven Outing, "Enabling the Social Company," white paper, September 2007, www.enthusiastgroup.com; Zappos website, accessed 5 February 2013, www.zappos.com; Lie-Nielsen Toolworks YouTube Channel, accessed 5 February 2013, www.youtube.com/user/LieNielsenToolworks.

15. Sonia Simone, "What's the Difference Between Content Marketing and Copywriting?" Copyblogger, accessed 4 June 2012, www.copyblogger.com.

16. Matt Rhodes, "Build Your Own Community or Go Where People Are? Do Both," FreshNetworks blog, 12 May 2009, www.freshnetworks.com.

17. Brian Solis, *Engage!* (Hoboken, N.J.: Wiley, 2010), 13.

18. Zachary Sniderman, "5 Ways to Clean Up Your Social Media Identity," 7 July 2010, Mashable, http://mashable.com.

19. HP company profiles on LinkedIn and Facebook, accessed 6 June 2012, www.facebook.com/hp and www.linkedin.com.

20. Vanessa Pappas, "5 Ways to Build a Loyal Audience on YouTube," Mashable, 15 June 2010, www.mashable.com.

21. Tamar Weinberg, *The New Community Rules: Marketing on the Social Web* (Sebastapol, Calif.: O'Reilly Media, 2009), 288.

22. "About Us," Yelp, accessed 6 June 2012, www.yelp.com; Lisa Barone, "Keynote Conversation with Yelp Chief Operating Officer Geoff Donaker," 5 October 2010, http://outspokenmedia.com.

23. Rohit Bhargava, "How Curation Could Save the Internet (and Your Brand)," *Communication World*, January–February 2012, 20–23.

24. "State of the Blogosphere 2011," Technorati, 4 November 2011, http://technorati.com.

25. Amy Porterfield, "10 Top Business Blogs and Why They Are Successful," Social Media Examiner, 25 January 2011, www.socialmediaexaminer.com.

26. Debbie Weil, "Why Your Blog Is the Hub of Social Media Marketing," Social Media Insights Blog, 12 January 2010, http://debbieweil.com; Ross Dawson, "A List of Business Applications for Blogging in the Enterprise," Trends in the Living Network blog, 7 July 2009, http://rossdawsonblog.com; Fredrik Wackå, "Six Types of Blogs—A Classification," CorporateBlogging.Info website, 10 August 2004, www.corporateblogging.info; Stephen Baker, "The Inside Story on Company Blogs," *BusinessWeek,* 14 February 2006, www.businessweek.com; Jeremy Wright, *Blog Marketing* (New York: McGraw-Hill, 2006), 45–56; Paul Chaney, "Blogs: Beyond the Hype!" 26 May 2005, http://radiantmarketinggroup.com.

27. Solis, *Engage!*, 314.

28. Evolve24 website, accessed 1 February 2013, www.evolve24.com.

29. Dianne Culhane, "Blog Logs a Culture Change," *Communication World*, January–February 2008, 40–41.

30. Solis, *Engage!*, 86.

31. Weinberg, *The New Community Rules: Marketing on the Social Web*, 89.

32. "IBM Social Computing Guidelines," IBM website, accessed 5 June 2012, www.ibm.com.

33. Joel Falconer, "Six Rules for Writing Great Web Content," Blog News Watch, 9 November 2007, accessed 14 February 2008, www.blognewswatch.com.

34. Dion Hinchcliffe, "Twitter on Your Intranet: 17 Microblogging Tools for Business," ZDNet, 1 June 2009, www.zdnet.com.

35. Hinchcliffe, "Twitter on Your Intranet: 17 Microblogging Tools for Business."

36. "The Library of Congress Is Archiving Your Tweets," NPR, 19 July 2010, www.npr.org.

37. B.L. Ochman, "Why Twitter Is a Better Brand Platform Than Facebook," Ad Age, 1 June 2012, *Ad Age*, http://adage.com.

38. Leon Widrich, "4 Ways to Use Twitter for Customer Service and Support," Social Media Examiner, 12 April 2012, www.socialmediaexaminer.com.

39. Paul André, Michael Bernstein, and Kurt Luther, "What Makes a Great Tweet," *Harvard Business Review*, May 2012, 36–37.

40. André et al., "What Makes a Great Tweet."

41. "Codex: Guidelines," WordPress website, accessed 16 February 2008, http://wordpress.org; Michael Shanks, "Wiki Guidelines," Traumwerk website, accessed 18 August 2006, http://metamedia.stanford.edu/projects/traumwerk/home; Joe Moxley, M.C. Morgan, Matt Barton, and Donna Hanak, "For Teachers New to Wikis," Writing Wiki, accessed 18 August 2006, http://writingwiki.org; "Wiki Guidelines," Psi, accessed 18 August 2006, http://psi-im.org.

42. Rachael King, "No Rest for the Wiki," *BusinessWeek*, 12 March 2007, www.businessweek.com.

43. "Codex: Guidelines," WordPress website, accessed 14 February 2008, http://wordpress.org.

44. Adapted from Comic-Con website, accessed 19 July 2010, www.comic-con.org; Tom Spurgeon, "Welcome to Nerd Vegas: A Guide to Visiting and Enjoying Comic-Con International in San Diego, 2006!" The Comics Reporter.com, 11 July 2006, www.comicsreporter.com; Rebecca Winters Keegan, "Boys Who Like Toys," *Time*, 19 April 2007, www.time.com.

45. Adapted from "Major New Study Shatters Stereotypes About Teens and Video Games," MacArthur Foundation, 16 September 2008, www.macfound.org.

46. Adapted from *Logan* website, accessed 3 February 2011, www.loganmagazine.com.

47. JetBlue Twitter page, accessed 3 February 2011, http://twitter.com/JetBlue; "JetBlue Lands on eBay," JetBlue website, accessed 18 September 2008, http://jetblue.com/ebay.

# 9 | Visual Media

## LEARNING OBJECTIVES

After studying this chapter, you will be able to

**1** Explain the power of business images, discuss six principles of graphic design that help ensure effective visuals, and explain how to avoid ethical lapses when using visuals.

**2** Explain how to choose which points in your message to illustrate.

**3** Describe the most common options for presenting data in a visual format.

**4** Describe the most common options for presenting information, concepts, and ideas.

**5** Explain how to integrate visuals with text and list three criteria to review in order to verify the quality of your visuals.

**6** Identify the most important considerations in the preproduction, production, and postproduction stages of producing basic business videos.

## MyBCommLab®

⭐ **Improve Your Grade!** Over 10 million students improved their results using the Pearson MyLabs. Visit **mybcommlab.com** for simulations, tutorials, and end-of-chapter problems.

COMMUNICATION CLOSE-UP AT

## XPLANE

www.xplane.com

As its name suggests, XPLANE is in the business of simplicity. The Portland, Oregon-based design consultancy specializes in distilling complex business situations down to their simplest elements to make sure clients can understand the essential elements of a problem or opportunity, devise appropriate solutions, and communicate those results to diverse audiences. Its unique approach combines collaboration, visual thinking, and people-centered design to develop solutions that clarify complexity and inspire action.

According to CEO Aric Wood,[1] "We found that using visual thinking in the collaboration process achieves dramatically more effective and lasting results. Additionally, creating the visual communication tools to drive understanding and learning, clients are able to literally 'see' the difference." XPLANE works within ambiguous and complex situations, combining collaborative consulting with multidisciplinary design methodologies and equipping clients with the tools to deliver tangible results and lasting change.

As part of its multidisciplinary approach, XPLANE applies visual thinking to some of the most difficult problems businesses face, including streamlining mergers and acquisitions, launching new ventures, educating investors, ensuring collaboration with

Courtesy of Aric Wood / Xplane

XPLANE's Aric Wood emphasizes the power of visual communication in the company's work to help businesses improve every aspect of their operations.

external business partners, and training employees on complicated business processes.

The company emphasizes "communication isn't a message sent. It's a message received." Clients are clearly receiving the message: XPLANE has successfully partnered with 16 of the world's 20 largest brands, and nearly half the Fortune 500 largest public corporations in the United States. American Express, Autodesk, The Economist, Gates Foundation, Intel, Microsoft, Nike, Unicef, and the U.S. Marines are among the many clients that have benefited from a new way of looking at their problems and opportunities.

# Understanding Visual Communication

Project teams from XPLANE (profiled in the chapter-opening Communication Close-Up) look for new ways to connect and explore business ideas through creative visuals, often helping clients see important concepts and relationships that aren't obvious using text alone. Visual communication in all its forms has become an important skill for today's business professionals and managers. This chapter is designed to help you appreciate the power of images and the visual evolution of business communication. It then explains how to identify which points in your messages to illustrate, how to select the best visual for each of those points, how to create effective visuals in any medium, from memos to reports to webpages to electronic presentations, and how to produce basic business videos.

**1** LEARNING OBJECTIVE
Explain the power of business images, discuss six principles of graphic design that help ensure effective visuals, and explain how to avoid ethical lapses when using visuals.

## THE POWER OF IMAGES

Well-designed visual elements can enhance the communication power of textual messages and, in some instances, even replace them. Visuals can often convey some message points (such as spatial relationships, correlations, procedures, and emotions) more effectively and more efficiently than words. Generally speaking, in a given amount of time, effective images can convey much more information than text.[2] In the numbers-oriented world of work, people rely heavily on trend lines, distribution curves, and other visual presentations of numeric quantities. Visuals attract and hold people's attention, helping your audience understand and remember your message. Busy readers often jump to visuals to try to get the gist of a message, and attractive visuals can draw readers more deeply into your reports and presentations. Using pictures is also an effective way to communicate with the diverse audiences that are common in today's business environment.

In addition to their direct information value, visuals often convey connotative meaning as well. As you read in Chapter 5, many words and phrases carry connotative meanings, which are all the mental images, emotions, and other impressions that the word or phrase evokes in audience members. A significant part of the power—and risk—of visual elements derives from their connotative meanings. Even something as simple as a watermark symbol embedded in letterhead stationery can boost reader confidence in the message printed on the paper.[3] Many colors, shapes, and other design elements have **visual symbolism**, and their symbolic, connotative meaning can evolve over time and mean different things in different cultures (see Figure 9.1 on the next page). Being aware of these symbolic meanings and using them to your advantage are important aspects of being an effective business communicator.

Because they have so much power to communicate, visuals must be carefully planned, competently created, and seamlessly integrated with text. An awkward sentence or grammatical error deep within a report might not be noticed by the majority of readers, but a poorly chosen or clumsily implemented visual will be noticed by most—and can confuse or alienate audiences and damage your credibility. You don't need to be a professional designer to use visuals effectively, but you do need to be aware of some basic design principles if you want to avoid making high-visibility mistakes. This chapter gives you enough background to begin creating your own business visuals, and with some practice you'll be able to craft effective visuals for nearly any communication project you might encounter.

Like words, visuals often carry connotative or symbolic meanings.

## THE VISUAL EVOLUTION IN BUSINESS COMMUNICATION

Several technological and social factors are contributing to the increasing use and importance of visuals in business communication. The process of creating and working with visual

Thanks to advances in technology and changing audience expectations, business communication is becoming more visual.

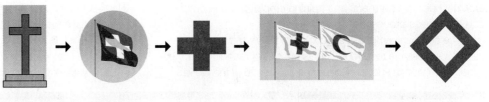

**Figure 9.1** **Visual Symbolism**
A red cross (with equal-length arms) on a white background is the well-known symbol of the Red Cross relief organization. It is also used to indicate the medical branches of many nations' military services. The red cross symbol is based on the flag of Switzerland (where the first Red Cross organization was formed), which over the course of hundreds of years developed from battle flags that originally used the Christian cross symbol. Although the Red Cross emblem is not based directly on the Christian symbol, the organization uses a red crescent in countries where Islam is the dominant religion and is known as the Red Crescent. To avoid any association with religious symbols, the International Federation of Red Cross and Red Crescent Societies (the global umbrella organization for all national Red Cross and Red Crescent organizations) recently adopted the Red Crystal as its new symbol.

elements used to be the domain of experts with complex and expensive tools. However, digital technology has changed this situation dramatically. Digital cameras and smartphones that can produce high-quality images and video are inexpensive, and the software needed to create diagrams, process photos, edit video, and prepare other visual elements continues to get both easier and more powerful all the time. Design and production tasks that used to take days can now be completed in hours or even minutes. As technologies such as wireless networking advance, business communicators will continue to reach wider audiences in less time, using equipment that costs less and requires fewer skills.[4]

While technology has been putting visual design and production into the hands of everyday business communicators in recent years, audience skills and expectations have been evolving as well. Two changes in particular could affect your communication efforts in the coming years. First, U.S. government research indicates that only half of the adult population in the United States now has the literacy skills considered necessary for success in today's workplace.[5] In other words, depending on the nature of your work, you could find yourself communicating with audiences whose skills could prevent them from successfully reading your documents. Visuals could play a vital role in communicating your messages to audiences with lower reading skills. Second, as technology has multiplied the ways in which communicators can create visuals and as people grow up and live in a more visual, media-saturated environment, audiences are likely to expect messages to be more visual.

> Visual literacy is the ability to create and interpret visuals successfully.

As a result of these changes in both the tools and the communication environment, **visual literacy**, the ability to create effective images and to correctly interpret such images, has become a key business skill.[6] Whether you are using visuals to reach an audience with limited reading skills or to magnify the impact of your written messages, knowing how to help your audience see what you see will enable you to become a more effective communicator.

## VISUAL DESIGN PRINCIPLES

> Creating effective visuals requires basic knowledge of the principles of good design.

Just as creating effective sentences and paragraphs requires working knowledge of the principles of good writing, creating effective visuals requires some knowledge of the principles of good design. Even though few businesspeople have the opportunity to formally study the "language" of line, mass, space, size, color, pattern, and texture, anyone can learn enough of the basic concepts to craft effective basic visuals.

When you encounter visuals that you find appealing or unappealing, effective or ineffective, stop and ask yourself what caused your response. Did a particular design grab you and practically force you to pay attention, or did you pass right by with hardly a notice? Did one chart reveal its information quickly and easily, while another made you spend time decoding its confusing message? Did one photo appeal to you at an emotional level and therefore draw you into a document, whereas another was off-putting and caused you to lose interest in the document? By thinking about your own reactions to visual designs, you can become a more effective designer yourself.

As you consider your reactions to various designs and create designs of your own, you'll begin to see how six fundamental principles help distinguish ineffective and effective designs:

- **Consistency.** Audiences view a series of visuals as a whole and assume that design elements will be consistent from one page to the next. Think of consistency as *visual parallelism*, in the same way that textual parallelism helps audiences understand and compare a series of ideas.[7] You can achieve visual parallelism in a variety of ways, including through consistent use of color, shape, size, texture, position, scale, or typeface.

- **Contrast.** To emphasize differences, depict items in contrasting colors, shapes, or sizes. For example, to highlight the difference between two quantities in a chart, don't use two shades of blue; instead, use blue for one and yellow or some other dramatically contrasting color for the other.

- **Balance.** Balance can be either *formal*, in which the elements in the images are arranged symmetrically around a central point or axis, or *informal*, in which elements are not distributed evenly, but stronger and weaker elements are arranged in a way that achieves an overall effect of balance. A common approach to informal balance is weighing one visually dominant element against several smaller or weaker elements.[8] Generally speaking, formal balance is more calming and serious, whereas informal balance tends to feel more dynamic and engaging.

- **Emphasis.** Audiences usually assume that the dominant element in a design is the most important, so make sure that the visually dominant element really does represent the most important information. You can do so through color, position, size, or placement, for example. Conversely, be sure to visually downplay less important items. For instance, avoid using strong colors for minor support points, and deemphasize background features such as the grid lines on a chart.

- **Convention.** Visual communication is guided by a variety of generally accepted rules or conventions, just as written communication is guided by an array of spelling, grammar, punctuation, and usage conventions. These conventions dictate virtually every aspect of design.[9] Moreover, many conventions are so ingrained that people don't even realize they are following these rules. For example, if English is your native language, you assume that ideas progress across the page from left to right because that's the direction in which English text is written. However, if you are a native Arabic or Hebrew speaker, you might automatically assume that flow on a page or screen is from right to left because that is the direction in which those languages are written. Similarly, Japanese audiences are used to reading publications from back to front, right to left. Flouting conventions often causes breakdowns in communication, but in some cases, it can be done to great effect.[10] For instance, flipping an organization chart upside down to put the customers at the top, with frontline employees directly beneath them and on down to the chief executive at the bottom, can be an effective way to emphasize that customers come first and that the managers are responsible for supporting employees in their efforts to satisfy customers.

- **Simplicity.** As a general rule, simple is better when it comes to visuals for business communication. Remember that you're conveying information, not expressing your creative flair. Limit the number of colors and design elements you use, and take care to avoid *chartjunk*, a term coined by visual communication specialist Edward R. Tufte for decorative elements that clutter documents and potentially confuse readers without adding any relevant information.[11] Computers make it far too easy to add chartjunk, from clip art illustrations to three-dimensional charts that display only two dimensions of data.

*Nearly every aspect of visual design is governed by conventions that set audience expectations.*

## THE ETHICS OF VISUAL COMMUNICATION

Power always comes with responsibility—and the potential power of visuals places an ethical burden on every business communicator. Ethical problems, both intentional and unintentional, can range from photos that play on racial or gender stereotypes, to images that imply cause-and-effect relationships that may not exist, to graphs that distort data (see Figure 9.2).

*Remember that the power to communicate with visuals comes with the responsibility to communicate ethically.*

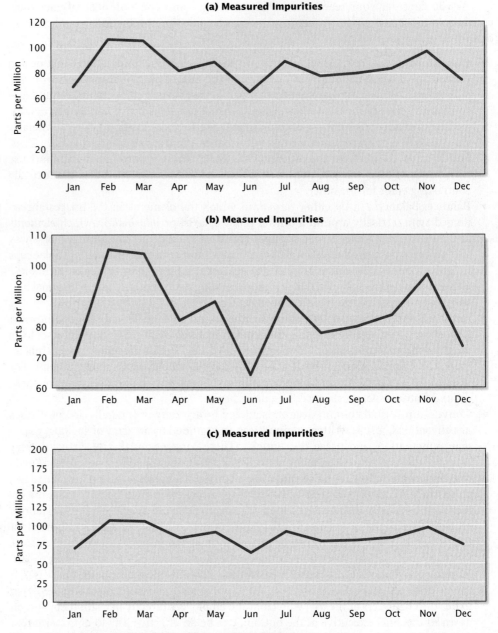

**Figure 9.2** **Influencing Perception Through Visual Design**
Figure 9.2a shows impurities measured over the course of a 12-month period; the vertical scale is set from 0 to 120, sufficient to cover the range of variations in the data. However, what if you wanted to make the variations from month to month look more severe? Less severe? Figure 9.2b, with the scale "zoomed in" to a narrow range of 60 to 110, makes the variations look much more dramatic. The result could be a stronger emotional impact on the reader, creating the impression that these impurities are out of control. In contrast, Figure 9.2c expands the scale from 0 to 200, which minimizes the appearance of the variations in the data. This graph is visually "calmer," creating the opposite impression, that there's really nothing to worry about. The data shown in all three graphs are identical, but the graphs send three different messages to the reader. Are any of the graphs unethical? That depends on the communicator's intent and whether it inhibits the audience's ability to make informed decisions.

Altering the scale of items in a visual is just one of many ways to emphasize or de-emphasize certain aspects of information. For example, to increase the perceived size of a product, an advertiser might show a close-up of it being held by someone with smaller-than-average hands. Conversely, a large hand would make the product seem smaller.

You can work to avoid ethical lapses in your visuals by following these guidelines:[12]

- **Consider all possible interpretations—and misinterpretations.** Try to view your visuals from your audience members' perspective; will their biases, beliefs, or backgrounds lead them to different conclusions than you've intended? For instance, assume that you want to show how easy your product is to use, and the photograph you've chosen just happens to show an older person operating the product. Will anyone conclude that what you really mean to say is that your product is so simple that "even an old person can use it"?

- **Provide context.** Even when they are completely accurate, visuals can show only a partial view of reality. Part of your responsibility as a communicator is to provide not only accurate visuals but enough background information to help audiences interpret the visual correctly.

- **Don't hide or minimize negative information that runs counter to your argument.** Obscuring information prevents your audiences from making fully informed decisions regarding your content.

- **Don't exaggerate information that supports your argument.** Similarly, you have a responsibility not to oversell information in support of your argument. You should also resist the temptation to alter or enhance photographs and other images in order to support your arguments.

- **Don't oversimplify complex situations.** By their very nature, visuals tend to present simplified views of reality. This is usually a benefit and one of the key reasons for using visuals. However, take care not to mislead an audience by hiding complications that are important to the audience's understanding of the situation.

- **Don't imply cause-and-effect relationships without providing proof that they exist.** For example, if you create a line chart that shows how increasing sales seem to track increasing advertising expenditures, you can claim a correlation but not necessarily a cause–effect relationship between the two. You can claim a causal relationship (meaning that the increase in advertising spending caused the increase in sales) only if you can isolate advertising spending as the *only* factor that can account for the increase in sales.

- **Avoid emotional manipulation or other forms of coercion.** For instance, a photograph of an unhappy child being treated as a social outcast because he or she doesn't own the trendiest new toys could be considered an unethical way to persuade parents to buy those products for their children.

- **Be careful with the way you aggregate data.** Preparing charts, graphs, and tables that present data often involves decisions about *aggregating*, or grouping, data. Such decisions can have a profound effect on the message your audience receives (see "Ethics Detective: Solving the Case of the Hidden Numbers"). For example, if you aggregate daily production levels to show only a single data point for each week, you might be obscuring important variations that happen from day to day.

*You can take many steps to emphasize or deemphasize specific elements in your visuals, but make sure you don't inadvertently commit an ethical lapse while doing so.*

*Visuals can't always speak for themselves; give your audience enough context to interpret your visuals correctly.*

*The ways in which you aggregate data for display can affect the messages and meanings that your audience extracts from your visuals.*

## Identifying Points to Illustrate

To help identify which parts of your message can benefit from visuals, step back and consider the flow of your message from the audience's point of view. Which parts of the message are likely to seem complex, open to misinterpretation, or even just a little bit dull? Are there any connections between ideas that might not be obvious if they are addressed only in text? Is there a lot of numeric data or other discrete factual content that would be difficult to read if presented in paragraph form? Is there a chance that the main idea won't "jump off the page" if it's covered only in text?

If you answer yes to any of these questions, you probably need one or more visuals. When you're deciding which points to present visually, think of the five Cs:

- **Clear.** The human mind is extremely adept at processing visual information, whether it's something as simple as the shape of a stop sign or as complicated as the floor plan for a new factory. If you're having difficultly conveying an idea in words, consider whether a visual element will do the job instead.

**2** **LEARNING OBJECTIVE** Explain how to choose which points in your message to illustrate.

*Effective visuals are clear, complete, concise, connected, and compelling.*

## Solving the Case of the Hidden Numbers

You've been assigned to present the results of an industrywide study of the effects of insecticide. Your audience consists of the department heads in your company, whose experience and educational backgrounds vary widely, from chemical engineering to insurance to law. You're convinced you need to keep your report as simple and as jargon-free as possible.

You're not a scientific expert on insecticides, but your supervisor has introduced you to a scientist who works for a trade association that represents chemical producers, including your firm. The scientist is familiar with the study you'll be reporting on, and she has experience in communicating technical subjects to diverse audiences. You jumped at the chance to have such a knowledgeable person review your presentation for technical accuracy, but you're uncomfortable with some of

her feedback. In particular, you question her advice to replace the following line chart, which shows the number of insecticide poisonings and deaths by age.

The scientist suggests that this chart is too busy and too difficult for nonspecialists to understand. As an alternative, she provides a bar chart that selects four specific ages from the entire range. She says this chart communicates the same basic idea as the line chart but is much easier to read.

### ANALYSIS

You agree with the scientist that the line chart is visually busy and takes more effort to process, but something bothers you about the bar chart. Does it present the insecticide situation accurately and honestly? Why or why not?

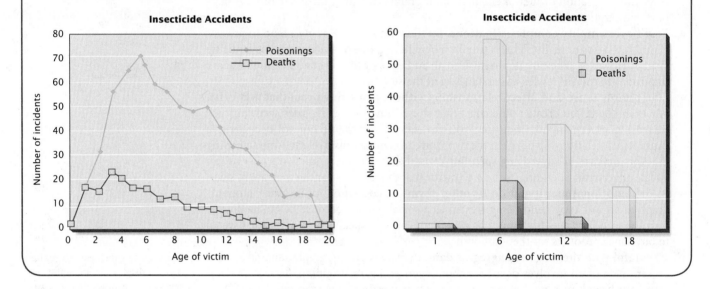

- **Complete.** Visuals, particularly tables, often serve to provide the supporting details for a main idea or recommendation. A table or another visual can provide these details without getting in the way of your main message.
- **Concise.** You've probably heard the expression "A picture is worth a thousand words." If a particular section of your message seems to require extensive description or explanation, see whether there's a way to convey this information visually. With a picture working in conjunction with text, you may be able to reduce your word count considerably.
- **Connected.** A key purpose of many business messages is showing connections of some sort—similarities or differences, correlations, cause-and-effect relationships, and so on. Whenever you want readers to see such a connection, determine whether a chart, a diagram, or another illustration might help.
- **Compelling.** Will one or more illustrations make your message more persuasive, more interesting, more likely to get read? You rarely want to insert visuals simply for decorative purposes, of course, but even if a particular point can be expressed equally well via text or visuals, consider adding the visual to make your report or presentation more compelling.

| TABLE 9.1 | When to Use Visuals |
|---|---|
| **Purpose** | **Application** |
| To clarify | Support text descriptions of "graphic" topics: quantitative or numeric information, explanations of trends, descriptions. |
| To simplify | Divide complicated descriptions into components that can be depicted with conceptual models, flowcharts, organization charts, or diagrams. |
| To emphasize | Call attention to particularly important points by illustrating them with line, bar, and pie charts. |
| To summarize | Review major points in the narrative by providing a chart or table that sums up the data. |
| To reinforce | Present information in visual form to supplement descriptions in text. |
| To attract | Make material seem more interesting by decorating the cover or title page and by breaking up the text with visual aids. |
| To impress | Build confidence by using visual forms to convey authenticity and precision. |
| To unify | Depict the relationships among various elements of a whole. |

As you identify which points in your document would benefit from a visual, make sure that each visual you decide on has a clear purpose (see Table 9.1).

## Selecting Visuals for Presenting Data

**3 LEARNING OBJECTIVE** Describe the most common options for presenting data in a visual format.

After you have identified which points would benefit most from visual presentation, your next decision is choosing which type of visual to use for each message point. As you can see in Figure 9.3 on the next page, you have many choices for business graphics, which can be roughly divided into those for presenting data and those for presenting information, concepts, and ideas.

You have many types of visuals to choose from, and each is best suited to particular communication tasks.

For some content, the decision is usually obvious. For example, to present a large set of numeric values or detailed textual information, a table is the obvious choice in most cases. However, if you're presenting data broken down geographically, a color-coded map might be more effective, to show overall patterns rather than individual data points. Also, certain visuals are used more commonly for certain applications, as you'll see in the following sections.

Business professionals have a tremendous number of choices for presenting data, from general-purpose line, bar, and pie charts to specialized charts for product portfolios, financial analysis, and other professional functions. The visuals most commonly used to present data include tables; line and surface charts; bar charts, pictograms, and Gantt charts; scatter and bubble diagrams; and pie charts. (Note that most people use the terms *chart* and *graph* interchangeably.)

### TABLES

When you need to present detailed, specific information, choose a **table**, a systematic arrangement of data in columns and rows. Tables are ideal when your audience needs information that would be either difficult or tedious to handle in the main text.

Printed tables can display extensive amounts of data, but tables for online display and electronic presentations need to be simpler.

Most tables contain the standard parts illustrated in Figure 9.4 on page 233. Every table includes vertical columns and horizontal rows, with useful headings along the top and side. For printed documents, you can adjust font size and column and row spacing to fit a considerable amount of information on the page and still maintain readability. For online documents, you'll need to reduce the number of columns and rows to make sure your tables are easily readable online. Tables for electronic presentations usually need

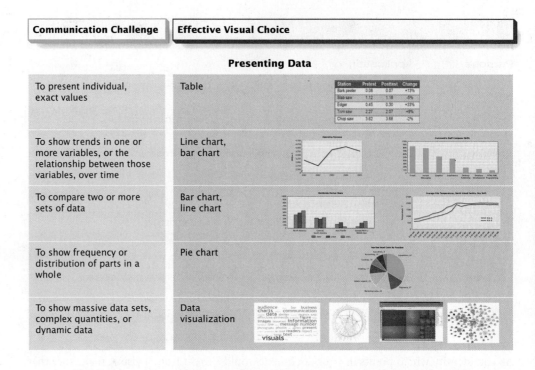

**Figure 9.3** **Selecting the Best Visual**
For each point you want to illustrate, make sure you choose the most effective type of visual.

to be the simplest of all because you can't expect audiences to read detailed information from the screen.

Although complex information may require formal tables that are set apart from the text, you can present some data more simply within the text. You make the table, in essence, a part of the paragraph, typed in tabular format. Such text tables are usually introduced with a sentence that leads directly into the tabulated information. Here's an example:[13]

Here is how five leading full-service restaurant chains compare in terms of number of locations and annual revenue:

| | **OSI Restaurant Partners** | **Dine Equity** | **Carlson** | **Brinker** | **Darden** |
|---|---|---|---|---|---|
| Major Chain(s) | Outback Steakhouse, Carrabba's | Applebee's, IHOP | Friday's, Pick Up Stix | Chili's, Maggiano's | Red Lobster, Olive Garden |
| Locations | 1,470 | 3,300 | 990 | 1,550 | 1,800 |
| Revenue ($ Million) | $3,600 | $1,414 | N/A | $2,859 | 7,113 |

*Source:* Hoover's Online, accessed 25 February 2013, www.hoovers.com; "America's Largest Private Companies," Forbes, accessed 25 February 2013, www.forbes.com; company financial reports accessed on Google Finance, accessed 25 February 2013, www.google.com/finance.

When you prepare tables, follow these guidelines to make your tables easy to read:

- Use common, understandable units and clearly identify the units you're using, whether dollars, percentages, price per ton, or some other units.
- Express all items in a column in the same unit and round off for simplicity whenever doing so won't eliminate essential details.
- Label column headings clearly, and use a subheading if necessary.
- Separate columns or rows with lines or extra space to make the table easy to follow; in complex tables, consider highlighting every other row or column in a pale, contrasting color.
- Provide totals or averages of columns or rows when relevant.
- Document the source of the data, using the same format as a text footnote (see Appendix B).

Tables can contain numerals, words, symbols, or other facts and figures. Word tables are particularly appropriate for presenting survey findings or for comparing various items against a specific standard.

## LINE AND SURFACE CHARTS

A **line chart** illustrates trends over time or plots the relationship of two or more variables. In line charts showing trends, the vertical, or *y*, axis shows the amount, and the horizontal, or *x*, axis shows the time or other quantity against which the amount is being measured. Both axes

Line charts are commonly used to show trends over time or the relationship between two or more variables.

| | Multicolumn Heading | | | Single-Column Heading |
|---|---|---|---|---|
| | Column Subheading | Column Subheading | Column Subheading | |
| Row Heading | xxx* | xxx | xxx | xxx |
| Row Heading | xxx | xxx | xxx | xxx |
| *Row Subheading* | xxx | xxx | xxx | xxx |
| *Row Subheading* | xxx | xxx | xxx | xxx |
| Row Heading | xxx | xxx | xxx | xxx |
| Row Heading | xxx | xxx | xxx | xxx |
| TOTALS | xxx | xxx | xxx | xxx |

**Figure 9.4   Parts of a Table**
Here are the standard parts of a table. No matter which design you choose, make sure the layout is clear and that individual rows and columns are easy to follow.

MyBCommLab Apply Figure 9.4's key concepts. Go to **mybcommlab.com** and follow this path: Course Content → Chapter 9 → **DOCUMENT MAKEOVERS**

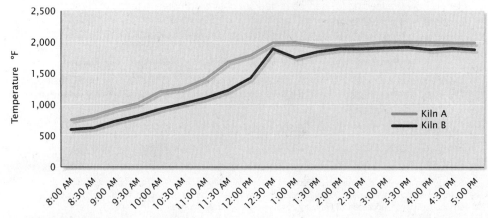

**Figure 9.5** **Line Chart**
This line chart compares the temperatures measured inside two cement kilns from 8:00 A.M. to 5:00 P.M.

often start at zero in the lower-left corner, but you can exercise a fair amount of flexibility with both axes in order to present your data as clearly as possible. For instance, to show both positive and negative values (such as profit and loss), you can have the *y* axis span from a negative value up to a positive value, with zero somewhere in between. Of course, you should always avoid distorting the data in ways that could mislead your audience, as noted in the section "The Ethics of Visual Communication," on page 227–229.

If you need to compare two or more sets of data, you can plot them on the same chart for instant visual comparison (see Figure 9.5). Two or three lines on a single chart are usually easy to read, but beyond that, things can get confusing, particularly if the lines cross.

By their very nature, line charts often raise the question "What happens next?" For instance, if you present sales data for the past 12 months, your audience may well ask what you think will happen in the next 12 months. Predicting the future is always risky, but you can use your spreadsheet's forecasting tools to extend a line into the future, using a statistical technique known as *regression analysis*. Check your spreadsheet's Help function for more information on using its *linear regression*, *trend line*, or *forecasting* functions. However, when using these tools, be aware that all they can do is extract patterns from past data and extend them into the future. They don't have any awareness of the "real-life" factors that shaped the past data and that will shape the future data.

A **surface chart**, also called an **area chart**, is a form of line chart with a cumulative effect; all the lines add up to the top line, which represents the total (see Figure 9.6). This

Spreadsheet forecasting functions can help predict future values based on past values shown in a line chart.

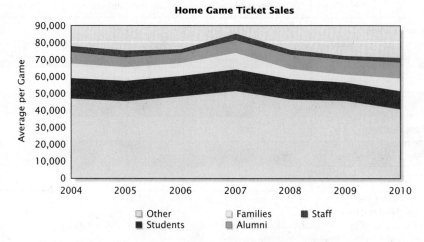

**Figure 9.6** **Surface Chart**
Surface, or area, charts can show a combination of trends over time and the individual contributions of the components of a whole.

presentation helps you illustrate changes in the composition of something over time. One common use is to show how sales of individual products contribute to the company's overall revenue.[14] When preparing a surface chart, put the most important segment on the bottom and build up from there.

## BAR CHARTS, PICTOGRAMS, AND GANTT CHARTS

A **bar chart** portrays numbers by the height or length of its rectangular bars, making a series of numbers easy to read or understand. (Vertical bar charts are sometimes called *column charts*.) Bar charts are particularly valuable when you want to

- Compare the sizes of several items at one time
- Show changes in one item over time
- Indicate the composition of several items over time
- Show the relative sizes of components of a whole

As the charts in Figure 9.7 show, the bar chart is a versatile tool that can serve many purposes. *Grouped* bar charts compare more than one set of data, using a different color or pattern for each set. *Deviation* bar charts identify positive and negative values, or winners and losers. *Segmented* bar charts, also known as *stacked* bar charts, show how individual components contribute to a total number, using a different color or pattern for each component. *Combination* bar and line charts compare quantities that require different intervals. *Paired* bar charts show the correlations between two items.

Figure 9.7 also suggests how creative you can be with bar charts. You might align the bars either vertically or horizontally, or you might use bar charts to show both positive and

You can create bar charts in a wide variety of formats; choose the form that best illustrates the data and relationships in your message.

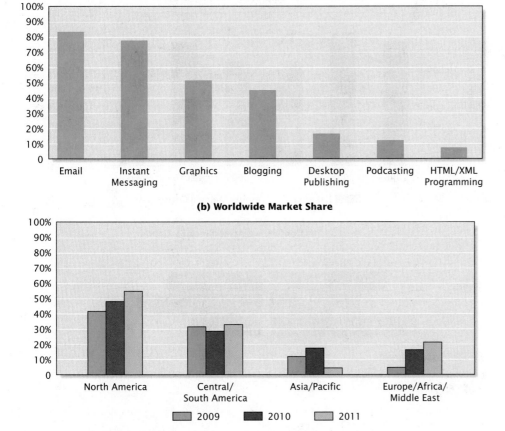

**Figure 9.7   The Versatile Bar Chart**
Here are six of the dozens of variations possible with bar charts: *singular* (9.8a), *grouped* (9.8b), *deviation* (9.8c), *segmented* (9.8d), *combination* (9.8e), and *paired* (9.8f).

*(continued)*

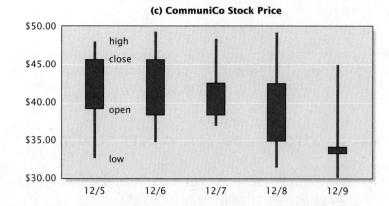

**(c) CommuniCo Stock Price**

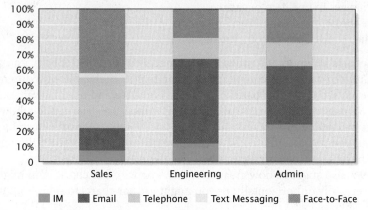

**(d) CommuniCo Preferred Communication Media**

IM   Email   Telephone   Text Messaging   Face-to-Face

**(e) CommuniCo Employee Training Costs**

Headcount   Training Costs

**(f) Conference Attendance by Gender**

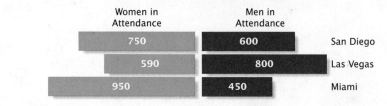

Figure 9.7   *(continued)*

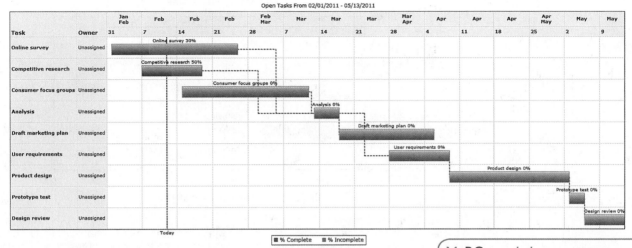

**Figure 9.8   Gantt Chart**
A Gantt chart is a specialized bar chart that uses bars to show durations of tasks and lines to show dependencies between tasks, such as when one task cannot be started before another one is completed.

negative quantities. No matter what you do, however, be sure to space the bars evenly and place them in a logical order, such as chronological or alphabetical.

You can also convert the bars of a bar chart into lines of symbols, so that the number or length of the symbols indicates the relative value of each item. A chart that portrays data as symbols instead of words or numbers is known as a **pictogram**. The chief value of pictograms is their novelty and ability to convey a more literal, visual message, but they can be more difficult to read if not designed with care, and they can present a less professional tone than a straightforward bar chart.

Closely related to the bar chart is the **time line chart**, which shows how much time is needed to complete each task in a given project. When you want to track progress toward completing a project, you can use a type of time line chart known as a **Gantt chart** (see Figure 9.8).

## SCATTER AND BUBBLE DIAGRAMS

If you need to compare several entities (companies, markets, employees, and so on) on two variables, such as revenue and profit margin, use a **scatter diagram**, also known as an **XY diagram**. This diagram is similar to a line chart in the sense that one variable is plotted along the $x$ (horizontal) axis and another along the $y$ (vertical) axis. However, in a scatter diagram, individual points are plotted, not continuous lines. The **bubble diagram** expands to three variables, with the size of the bubble representing the third variable (see Figure 9.9 on the next page).

Scatter diagrams compare entities against two variables; bubble diagrams compare them against three.

## PIE CHARTS

A **pie chart** is a commonly used tool for showing how the parts of a whole are distributed. Although pie charts are popular and can quickly highlight the dominant parts of a whole, they are often not as effective as bar charts or tables. For example, comparing percentages accurately is often difficult with a pie chart but can be fairly easy with a bar chart (see Figure 9.10 on the next page). Making pie charts easier to read with accuracy can require labeling each slice with data values, in which case a table might serve the purpose more effectively.[15]

Pie charts are used frequently in business reports, but in many instances they are not as helpful to readers as bar charts and other types of visuals would be.

## DATA VISUALIZATION

Conventional charts and graphs are limited in several ways: Most types can show only a limited number of data points before becoming too cluttered to interpret, they often can't show

Unlike conventional charts, data visualization tools are more about uncovering broad meaning and finding hidden connections.

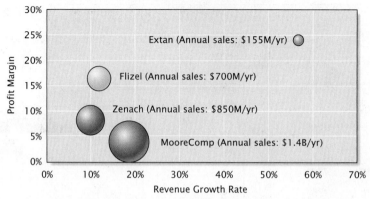

**Competitor Financial Health**

Figure 9.9 **Bubble Diagram**
A bubble diagram shows three variables: distance along the *x* and *y* axes, plus the diameter of each bubble. In this case, the rate of revenue growth is plotted on the *x* axis, profit margin is plotted on the *y* axis, and the size of the bubbles represents annual revenues. For instance, MooreComp has the greatest revenues but the lowest profit margin, although it is growing faster than two of its three competitors.

complex relationships among data points, and they can represent only numeric data. As computer technologies continue to generate massive amounts of data that can be combined and connected in endless ways, a diverse class of display capabilities known as **data visualization** work to overcome all these drawbacks. Unlike charts and graphs, data visualization is less about clarifying individual data points and more about extracting broad meaning from giant masses of data or putting the data in context.[16]

In addition to displaying large data sets and linkages within data sets, other kinds of visualization tools combine data with textual information to communicate complex or dynamic data much faster than conventional presentations can. For example, a *tag cloud* shows the relative frequency of terms, or tags (user-applied content labels), in an article, a blog, a website, survey data, or another collection of text.[17] Figure 9.11 shows a few of the many data visualization tools now available.

**REAL-TIME UPDATES**

LEARN MORE BY EXPLORING THIS WEBSITE

**Data Visualization and Infographics Gateway: A comprehensive collection for business communicators**

This unique web resource offers links to a vast array of data visualization and infographic techniques and examples. Go to http://real-timeupdates.com/bct12 and click on Learn More. If you are using MyBCommLab, you can access Real-Time Updates within each chapter or under Student Study Tools.

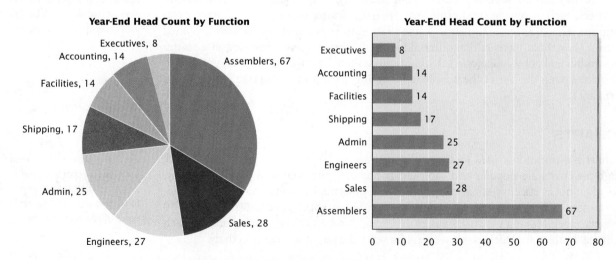

Figure 9.10 **Pie Charts Versus Bar Charts**
Pie charts are used frequently, but they aren't necessarily the best choice for many data presentations. This pie chart does make it easy to see that assemblers are the largest employee category, but other comparisons of slice sizes (such as Sales, Engineers, and Admin) are not as easy to make and require a numerical rather than a visual comparison. In contrast, the bar chart gives a quick visual comparison of every data point.

(a) Website Linkage Map. This interactive network diagram shows the most active links to and from Apple's homepage (www.apple.com). *Website linkage map by TouchGraph.com*

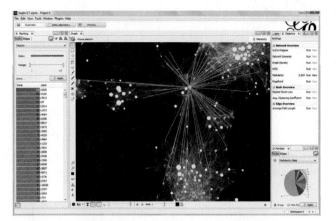

(b) Gephi. This visualization tool highlights the strongest connections in a complex network diagram.

audience *avoid* bar business charts *color* communication *create* **data** design *detailed* diagram easy effective elements *example* figure *help* images *important* information *instance* line *maps* message number photographs photos *pie* points present *product professional* re read readers report *sales* shows *size sure* tables text *textual* used usually *value* *video* **visuals** *ways*

(c) Tag Cloud. This interactive "word chart" shows the relative frequency of the 50 most-used words in this chapter on visual communication (other than common words such as *and, or,* and *the*).

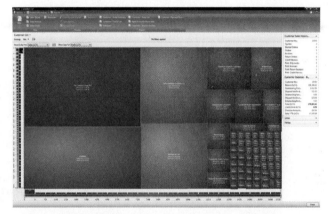

(d) Interactive Data Display. This interactive display conveys two company performance variables at once (sales and profits) for a large data set by using the size and color of the individual blocks.

**Figure 9.11   Data Visualization**
The range of data visualization displays is virtually endless; here are a few of the many different ways to display complex sets of data.
*Sources:* (a) Copyright © 2011 by TouchGraph, LLC.; (b) Copyright © 2013 by the Gephi Consortium. Used by permission.; (c) Copyright © 2013 by TagCrowd.com. Used by permission of Daniel Steinbock, Ph.D.; (d) Used with permission from Microsoft®. Microsoft Dynamics NAV 2009 can be accessed at www.microsoft.com/presspass/gallery.

# Selecting Visuals for Presenting Information, Concepts, and Ideas

In addition to facts and figures, you'll need to present other types of information, from spatial relationships to abstract ideas. In these situations, professionals often look for visual solutions to complement or even replace textual information. The most common types of visuals for these applications include flowcharts and organization charts; maps; drawings, diagrams, infographics, and photographs; and animation and video.

**4** LEARNING OBJECTIVE
Describe the most common options for presenting information, concepts, and ideas.

## FLOWCHARTS AND ORGANIZATION CHARTS

If you need to show physical or conceptual relationships rather than numeric ones, you might want to use a flowchart or an organization chart. A **flowchart** (see Figure 9.12 on the next page) illustrates a sequence of events from start to finish. It is particularly helpful when illustrating processes and procedures in which there are decision points, loops, and other complexities. For general business purposes, you don't need to be too concerned about the specific shapes, although do keep them consistent. However, be aware that there is a formal flowchart "language" in which each shape has a specific meaning (diamonds are decision

Use flowcharts to show a series of steps in a process or other sequential relationships.

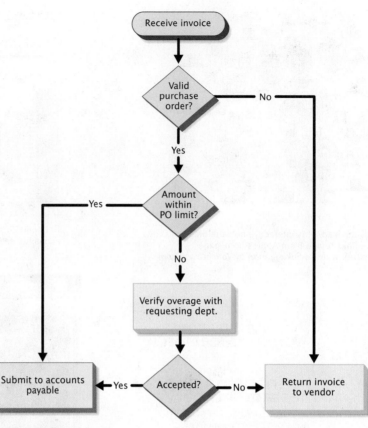

**Figure 9.12 Flowchart**
Flowcharts show sequences of events and are most valuable when the process or procedure has a number of decision points and variable paths.

points, rectangles are process steps, and so on). If you're communicating with computer programmers and others who are accustomed to formal flowcharting, make sure you use the correct symbols, to avoid confusion. Graphics programs that have flowchart symbols usually label their functions, making it easy to use the right ones.

As the name implies, an **organization chart** illustrates the positions, units, or functions of an organization and the way they interrelate (refer to Figure 1.3 on page 8 for an example). These charts aren't limited to organizational structures, of course; as you saw in Chapter 4, they can also be used to outline messages.

Use organization charts to depict the interrelationships among the parts of a whole.

## MAPS

Maps can show location, distance, points of interest (such as competitive retail outlets), and geographic distribution of data, such as sales by region or population by state. In addition to presenting facts and figures, maps are useful for showing market territories, distribution routes, and facilities locations.

Use maps for such tasks as representing statistics by geographic area or showing spatial relationships.

When combined with databases and aerial or satellite photography in *geographic information systems (GIS)*, maps become extremely powerful visual reporting tools (see Figure 9.13). As one example, retailing specialists can explore the demographic and psychographic makeup of neighborhoods within various driving distances from a particular store location. Using such information, managers can plan everything from new building sites to delivery routes to marketing campaigns.

## DRAWINGS, DIAGRAMS, AND PHOTOGRAPHS

Use drawings and diagrams to show how something works or how it is made or used; drawings are sometimes better than photographs because they let you focus on the most important details.

The opportunities to use drawings, diagrams, and photographs are virtually endless. Simple drawings can show the network of suppliers in an industry, the flow of funds through a company, or the process for completing the payroll each week. More complex diagrams, including

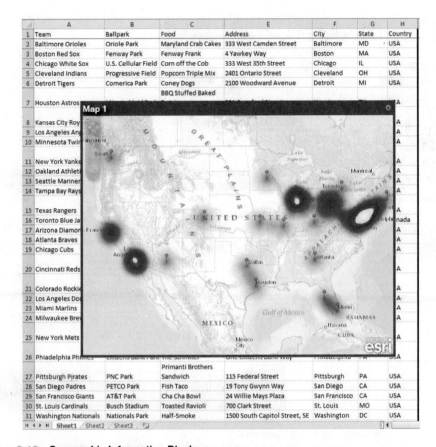

| | A | B | C | E | F | G | H |
|---|---|---|---|---|---|---|---|
| 1 | Team | Ballpark | Food | Address | City | State | Country |
| 2 | Baltimore Orioles | Oriole Park | Maryland Crab Cakes | 333 West Camden Street | Baltimore | MD | USA |
| 3 | Boston Red Sox | Fenway Park | Fenway Frank | 4 Yawkey Way | Boston | MA | USA |
| 4 | Chicago White Sox | U.S. Cellular Field | Corn off the Cob | 333 West 35th Street | Chicago | IL | USA |
| 5 | Cleveland Indians | Progressive Field | Popcorn Triple Mix | 2401 Ontario Street | Cleveland | OH | USA |
| 6 | Detroit Tigers | Comerica Park | Coney Dogs | 2100 Woodward Avenue | Detroit | MI | USA |
| 7 | Houston Astros | | BBQ Stuffed Baked | | | | |
| 8 | Kansas City Roy | | | | | | A |
| 9 | Los Angeles An | | | | | | A |
| 10 | Minnesota Twin | | | | | | A |
| 11 | New York Yanke | | | | | | A |
| 12 | Oakland Athleti | | | | | | A |
| 13 | Seattle Mariner | | | | | | A |
| 14 | Tampa Bay Rays | | | | | | A |
| 15 | Texas Rangers | | | | | | A |
| 16 | Toronto Blue Ja | | | | | | A |
| 17 | Arizona Diamon | | | | | | A |
| 18 | Atlanta Braves | | | | | | A |
| 19 | Chicago Cubs | | | | | | A |
| 20 | Cincinnati Reds | | | | | | A |
| 21 | Colorado Rockie | | | | | | A |
| 22 | Los Angeles Do | | | | | | A |
| 23 | Miami Marlins | | | | | | A |
| 24 | Milwaukee Bre | | | | | | A |
| 25 | New York Mets | | | | | | A |
| 26 | Philadelphia Phillies | Citizens Bank Park | The Schmitter | One Citizens Bank Way | Philadelphia | PA | USA |
| 27 | Pittsburgh Pirates | PNC Park | Primanti Brothers Sandwich | 115 Federal Street | Pittsburgh | PA | USA |
| 28 | San Diego Padres | PETCO Park | Fish Taco | 19 Tony Gwynn Way | San Diego | CA | USA |
| 29 | San Francisco Giants | AT&T Park | Cha Cha Bowl | 24 Willie Mays Plaza | San Francisco | CA | USA |
| 30 | St. Louis Cardinals | Busch Stadium | Toasted Ravioli | 700 Clark Street | St. Louis | MO | USA |
| 31 | Washington Nationals | Nationals Park | Half-Smoke | 1500 South Capitol Street, SE | Washington | DC | USA |

Sheet1  Sheet2  Sheet3

**Figure 9.13   Geographic Information Displays**
Businesses use geographic information systems (GIS) in a variety of ways. By overlaying maps and aerial or satellite imagery with descriptive data, companies can use these displays for such purposes as planning sales campaigns, optimizing transportation routing, and selecting retail or production sites.
*Source:* Copyright © 2013 Esri, DigitalGlobe, GeoEye, i-cubed, USDA, USGS, AEX, Getmapping, Aerogrid, IGN, IGP, swisstopo, and the GIS User Community. All rights reserved.

interactive online diagrams (see Figure 9.14 on the next page), can convey technical topics such as the operation of a machine or repair procedures.

Word processors and presentation software now offer fairly advanced drawing capabilities, but for more precise and professional illustrations, you may need a specialized package such as Adobe Illustrator or Trimble SketchUp. Moving a level beyond those programs, *computer-aided design* (CAD) systems such as Autodesk's AutoCAD can produce extremely detailed architectural and engineering drawings.

Photographs offer both functional and decorative value, and nothing can top a photograph when you need to show exact appearances. Because audiences expect photographs to show literal visual truths, you must take care when using image-processing tools such as Adobe Photoshop.

To use photographs successfully, consider these guidelines:

> Use photographs for visual appeal and to show exact appearances.

- **Consider whether a diagram would be more effective than a photograph.** Photographs are often unmatched in their ability to communicate spatial relationships, sizes, shapes, and other physical parameters, but sometimes they communicate too much information. For example, to show how to adjust a specific part of a complicated machine, a photo can be confusing because it shows all the parts within the camera's view. A simplified diagram is often more effective because it allows you to emphasize the specific parts that are relevant to the problem at hand.

- **Learn how to use basic image-processing functions.** For most business reports, websites, and presentations, you won't need to worry about more advanced image-processing functions and special effects. However, you need to know such basic operations such as the difference between resizing (changing the size of an image without removing any parts of it) and cropping (cutting away parts of the image).

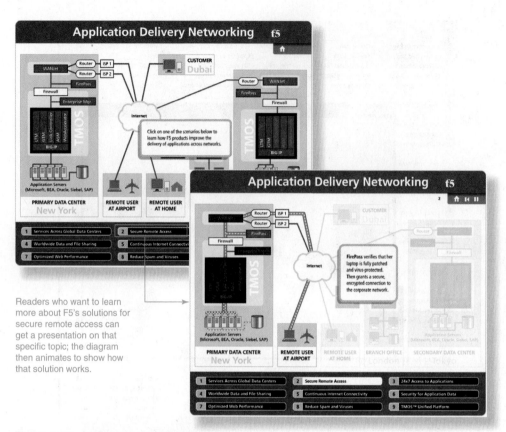

Readers who want to learn more about F5's solutions for secure remote access can get a presentation on that specific topic; the diagram then animates to show how that solution works.

**Figure 9.14** **Interactive, Animated Diagram**
Clearly drawn diagrams help audiences grasp complex ideas quickly. Extending this capability with interactivity and animation, as F5 Networks did with this networking visual, can make a diagram even more audience-focused by letting website visitors choose the information most relevant to their individual needs.
*Source:* Reproduced by permission of F5 Networks, Inc. © 2011 F5 Networks, Inc. All Rights Reserved.

Make sure you have the right to use photographs you find online.

- **Make sure the photographs have communication value.** Except for covers, title slides, and other special uses, it's usually best to avoid including photographs simply for decorative value.
- **Be aware of copyrights and model permissions.** Just as with textual information you find online, you can't simply insert online photographs into your documents. Unless they are specifically offered for free, you have to assume that someone owns the photos and is entitled to payment or at least a photo credit. In addition, professional photographers are careful to have any person who poses in photos sign a model release form, which gives the photographer permission to use the person's image.

## INFOGRAPHICS

Infographics can offer stylized versions of basic charts and graphs or more engaging narratives that tell a story or illustrate a process.

**Infographics** are a special class of diagrams that can convey both data as well as concepts or ideas. In addition, they contain enough visual and textual information to function as independent, standalone documents. Broadly speaking, there are two types of infographics, those that are stylized collections of charts or graphs and those that have a structured narrative. The first types, represented by Figure 9.15a, don't necessarily convey any more information than basic charts and graphs in a conventional report would, but their communication value lies in their ability to catch the audience's attention and the ease with which they can be distributed online. The second types, represented by Figure 9.15b, go beyond this to take full advantage of the visual medium to tell stories or show interconnected processes. These infographics can be powerful communication tools, even to the point of replacing conventional reports.

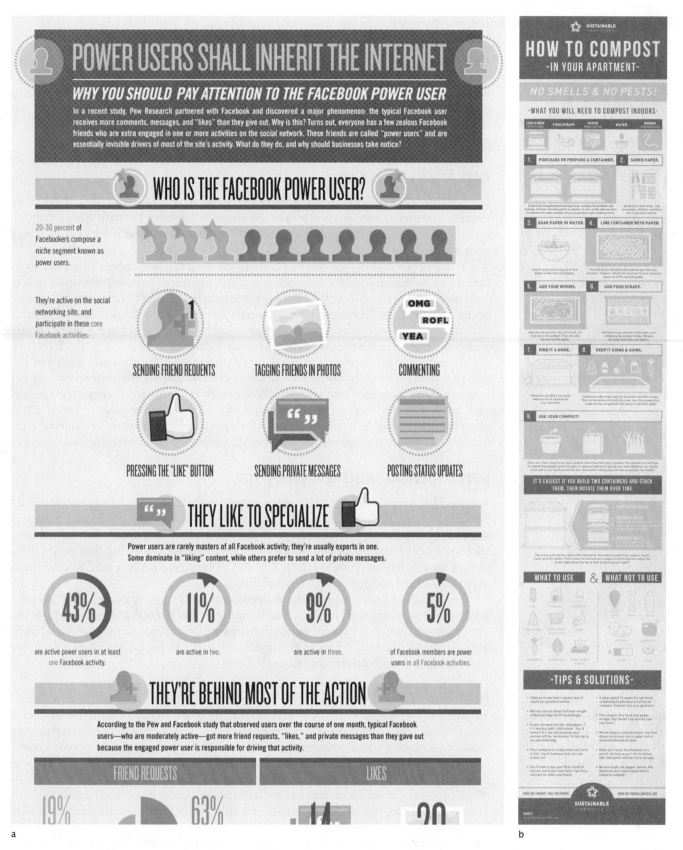

**Figure 9.15  Infographics**
Roughly speaking, infographics can be divided into simple presentations of data (Figure 9.15a) and visual narratives (Figure 9.15b) that use the full power of the medium to tell stories or illustrate processes.
*Source:* "Power Users Shall Inherit the Internet." Copyright © 2012 Demandforce, Inc. in partnership with Column Five Media. Reprinted with permission.

# Producing and Integrating Visuals

**5** **LEARNING OBJECTIVE**
Explain how to integrate visuals with text and list three criteria to review in order to verify the quality of your visuals.

Now that you understand the communication power of visuals and have chosen the best visuals to illustrate key points in your report, website, or presentation, it's time to get creative. This section offers advice on creating visuals, integrating them with your text, and verifying the quality of your visual elements.

## CREATING VISUALS

Computer software offers a variety of graphical tools but doesn't automatically give you the design sensibility that is needed for effective visuals.

Computers make it easy to create visuals, but they also make it easy to create ineffective, distracting, and even downright ugly visuals. However, by following the basic design principles discussed on pages 226–227, you can create all the basic visuals you need—visuals that are both attractive and effective.

Learning how to use your computer tools will help you save enormous amounts of time and produce better results.

Whether you're using the charting functions offered in a spreadsheet or the design features of a specialized graphics program, take a few minutes to familiarize yourself with the software's quirks and capabilities. For important visuals, try to have a professional designer set up a template for the various types of visuals you and your colleagues need to create. In addition to helping ensure an effective design, using templates saves you the time of making numerous design decisions every time you create a chart or graphic.

A visual's level of sophistication should match the communication situation.

No matter which tools you're using, take care to match the style and quality of your visuals with the subject matter and the situation at hand. The style of your visuals communicates a subtle message about your relationship with the audience. A simple sketch might be fine for a working meeting but inappropriate for a formal presentation or report. On the other hand, elaborate, full-color visuals may be viewed as extravagant for an informal report but may be entirely appropriate for a message to top management or influential outsiders.

## INTEGRATING VISUALS WITH TEXT

For maximum effectiveness and minimum disruption for the reader, visual elements need to be carefully integrated with the text of your message. In some instances, visual elements are somewhat independent from the text, as in the *sidebars* that occasionally accompany magazine articles. Such images are related to the content of the main story, but they aren't referred to by a specific title or figure number. This sort of treatment is often used in promotional materials such as brochures and advertisements.

For reports and most other business documents, however, visuals are tightly integrated with the text so that readers can move back and forth between text and visuals with as little disruption as possible. Successful integration involves four decisions: maintaining a balance between visuals and text, referring to visuals in the text, placing the visuals in a document, and writing titles and other descriptions.

### Maintaining a Balance Between Illustrations and Words

Maintain a balance between text and visuals and place your visuals so that they help emphasize your key points.

Strong visuals enhance the descriptive and persuasive power of your writing, but putting too many visuals into a report can distract your readers. If you're constantly referring to tables, drawings, and other visual elements, the effort to switch back and forth from words to visuals can make it difficult for readers to maintain focus on the thread of your message. The space occupied by visuals can also disrupt the flow of text on the page or screen.

Make sure your visuals match the needs, expectations, and interpretation skills of your audience.

As always, take into account your readers' specific needs. If you're addressing an audience with multiple language backgrounds or widely varying reading skills, you can shift the balance toward more visual elements to help get around any language barriers. The professional experience, education, and training of your audience should influence your approach as well. For instance, detailed statistical plots and mathematical formulas are everyday reading material for quality-control engineers but not for most salespeople or top executives.

### Referencing Visuals

To tie visuals to text, introduce them in the text and place them near the points they illustrate.

Unless a visual element clearly stands on its own, it should be clearly referred to by number in the text of your report. Some report writers refer to all visuals as "exhibits" and number them consecutively throughout the report; many others number tables and figures separately (everything that isn't a table is regarded as a figure). In a long report with numbered sections, illustrations may have a double number (separated by a period or a hyphen) representing the section number and the individual illustration number within that section. Whatever scheme you use, make sure it's clear, consistent, and easy to follow.

Help your readers understand the significance of visuals by referring to them before readers encounter them in the document or on the screen. The following examples show how you can make this connection in the text:

> Figure 1 summarizes the financial history of the motorcycle division over the past five years, with sales broken into four categories.
>
> Total sales were steady over this period, but the mix of sales by category changed dramatically (see Figure 2).
>
> The underlying reason for the remarkable growth in our sales of youth golf apparel is suggested by Table 4, which shows the growing interest in junior golf around the world.

When describing the data shown in your visuals, be sure to emphasize the main point you are trying to make. Don't make the mistake of simply repeating the data to be shown. Paragraphs that do are guaranteed to put the reader to sleep:

> Among those who replied to the survey, 17.4 percent earn less than $8 per hour; 26.4 percent earn $8 to $12; 25.7 percent, $13 to $20; 18.0 percent, $20 to $30; 9.6 percent, $30 to $49; and 2.9 percent, $50 and over.

The visual will (or at least should) provide all these details; there is no need to repeat them in the text. Instead, use round numbers that sum up the message:

> As Table 4.2 shows, more than two-thirds of the respondents earn less than $20 per hour.

*Help your readers understand why each visual is important.*

## Placing Visuals

Try to position your visuals so that your audience won't have to flip back and forth (in printed documents) or scroll (on-screen) between the visuals and the text. Ideally, it's best to place each visual within, beside, or immediately after the paragraph it illustrates so that readers can consult the explanation and the visual at the same time. This scheme works well both in print and online. If at all possible, avoid bunching visuals at the end of a section or the end of a document; doing so asks a lot of the reader. (Bunching is unavoidable in some cases, such as when multiple visuals accompany a single section of text—as in this chapter, for instance.) Word-processing, desktop-publishing, and web-design programs let you place graphical elements virtually anywhere you wish, so take advantage of this flexibility.

*Place each visual as close as possible to its in-text reference to help readers understand the illustration's relevance and to minimize the effort of reading.*

## Writing Titles, Captions, and Legends

Titles, captions, and legends help connect your visual and textual messages and ensure a seamless reading experience. A **title** identifies the content and purpose of the visual, along with whatever label and number you're using to refer to the visual. A **descriptive title** simply identifies the topic of the illustration, whereas an **informative title** calls attention to the conclusion that ought to be drawn from the data. Here's an example of the difference:

*A descriptive title simply identifies the topic of an illustration; an informative title helps the reader understand the conclusion to be drawn from the illustration.*

**Descriptive Title**

Relationship Between Petroleum Demand and Refinery Capacity in the United States

**Informative Title**

Refinery Capacity Declines as Petroleum Demand Continues to Grow

An informative title saves readers the work of interpreting the visual to extract the main idea from it. Regardless of whether your titles and legends are informative or descriptive, phrase them consistently throughout a document.

A **caption** usually offers additional discussion of the visual's content and can be up to several sentences long, if appropriate. Captions can also alert readers that additional discussion is available in the accompanying text. A **legend** helps readers "decode" the visual by explaining what various colors, symbols, or other design choices mean (several of the figures in this chapter use legends, for example). Legends aren't necessary for simple graphs, such as a line chart or bar chart with only one series of data, but they are invaluable with more complex graphics.

## VERIFYING THE QUALITY OF YOUR VISUALS

Visuals have a particularly strong impact on your readers and on their perceptions of you and your work, so verifying the quality of your visuals is an essential step. Ask yourself three questions about every visual element:

Review each visual to make sure it doesn't intentionally or unintentionally distort the meaning of the underlying information.

- **Is the visual accurate?** Be sure to check for mistakes such as typographical errors, inconsistent color treatment, confusing or undocumented symbols, and misaligned elements. Also verify that information in visuals and text matches. For data presentations, particularly if you're producing charts with a spreadsheet, verify any formulas used to generate the numbers and make sure you've selected the right numbers for each chart. For flowcharts, organization charts, diagrams, photos, and other visuals, make sure that each visual delivers your message accurately and that you have inserted the correct image files.
- **Is the visual properly documented?** As with the textual elements in your reports and presentations, visuals based on other people's research, information, and ideas require full citation. (Even if the graphical design is entirely yours, any underlying information taken from other sources needs to be documented.) Also, try to anticipate any questions or concerns your audience may have and address them with additional information, as needed. For instance, if you're presenting the results of survey research, many readers will want to know who participated in the survey, how many people responded, and when the questions were asked. You could answer these questions with a note in the caption along the lines of "652 accountants, surveyed the week of January 17." Similarly, if you found a visual in a secondary source, list that source on or near the graphic to help readers assess the information. Alternatively, you can list sources in an appendix.
- **Is the visual honest?** As a final precaution, step back and verify that your visuals communicate truthful messages. Make sure they don't hide information the audience needs, imply conclusions that your information doesn't support, or play on audience emotions in manipulative or coercive ways.

For a review of the important points to remember when creating visuals, see "Checklist: Creating Effective Visuals." For more information on visual communication, including design principles, ethical matters, and the latest tools for creating and displaying visuals, visit http://real-timeupdates.com/bct12 and click on Chapter 9.

# Producing Business Videos

6  LEARNING OBJECTIVE
Identify the most important considerations in the preproduction, production, and postproduction stages of producing basic business videos.

From tutorials and product demonstrations to seminars and speeches, online video is now an essential business communication medium. For videos that require the highest production quality, companies usually hire specialists with the necessary skills and equipment. However, for most routine needs, any business communicator with modest equipment and a few basic skills can create effective video.

The three-step process adapts easily to video; professionals refer to the three steps as *preproduction*, *production*, and *postproduction* (see Figure 9.16). You can refer to one of the many books available on basic video production techniques for more detail, but here are

## CHECKLIST ✔ Creating Effective Visuals

- Emphasize visual consistency to connect parts of a whole and minimize audience confusion.
- Avoid arbitrary changes of color, texture, typeface, position, or scale.
- Highlight contrasting points through color, position, and other design choices.
- Decide whether you want to achieve formal or informal balance.
- Emphasize dominant elements and deemphasize less important pieces in a design.
- Understand and follow (at least most of the time) the visual conventions your audience expects.
- Strive for simplicity and clarity; don't clutter your visuals with meaningless decoration.
- Follow the guidelines for avoiding ethical lapses.

- Carefully consider your message, the nature of your information, and your audience to choose which points to illustrate.
- Select the proper types of graphics for the information at hand and for the objective of the message.
- Be sure the visual contributes to overall understanding of the subject.
- Understand how to use your software tools to maximize effectiveness and efficiency.
- Integrate visuals and text by maintaining a balance between illustrations and words, clearly referring to visuals within the text, and placing visuals carefully.
- Use titles, captions, and legends to help readers understand the meaning and importance of your visuals.
- Verify the quality of your visuals by checking for accuracy, proper documentation, and honesty.

the key points to consider in all three steps. (A note on terminology: digital videography has inherited a number of terms from film that don't make strict technical sense but are in common use anyway, including *footage* to indicate any amount of recorded video and *filming* to indicate video recording.)

The process of creating is divided into preproduction, production, and postproduction.

### 1 Preproduction →

- Verify your purpose and scope.
- Think about the composition of the scenes you want to film.
- Decide where you'll place your camera or cameras.
- Plan lighting.
- Make arrangements for sound recording.
- Writing a shot list or full script as appropriate.
- Identify B-roll material that will enhance the final video.

### 2 Production →

- Frame each shot carefully.
- Keep the camera still while filming unless the situation demands that you move it.
- Take B-roll footage.
- Remember not to use the special effects in your camera so that you can export clean footage.

### 3 Postproduction

1. Transfer your video footage to your computer and load it into the editing software.
2. Evaluate your material, identifying the shots you want to keep and those you can delete.
3. Move sections of video around as needed to tell a coherent and compelling story.
4. Weave in B-roll images and clips.
5. Add transitions between video segments.
6. Synchronize the main audio track with the video and record narration.
7. Add an *intro* and an *outro*.
8. Add text titles and other features as needed.
9. Create a distributable file.

**Figure 9.16   Creating Effective Business Videos**
By following a methodical process in the preproduction, production, and postproduction stages, any business communicator with even basic equipment can create effective videos.

## STEP 1: PREPRODUCTION

When you're recording speeches, seminars, and other events, planning is crucial because you have only one opportunity to get the footage you need. And even when you have the flexibility to retake footage, thoughtful planning will save time and money and lead to better-looking results. For any video, be sure to think through the following seven elements:

- **Purpose and scope.** With every communication effort, of course, it's essential to identify the purpose of your message and define the scope of what you will address before you start. This is doubly important with video, however, because it is a linear medium that forces people to watch it in a predefined sequence. Most viewers won't sit through rambling or repetitive videos, so figure out what your point is and determine the briefest possible way to make it.

- **Scene composition.** Visualize what the camera is going to see. If you're demonstrating a new product, for example, do you want people to see it in a realistic setting, or would it be better to use a "clean stage" so that nothing else will compete for the viewer's attention? For "talking head" videos, in which someone talks directly into the camera, an uncluttered background is preferred unless the setting is relevant. However, you don't need to resort to a bare white wall behind the subject; this can make the video feel more like an interrogation. A tastefully decorated office will look uncluttered without feeling stark or cold. Think carefully about the overall environment as well. Trying to conduct an interview outside or at a busy tradeshow, for example, can bring all kinds of noise and visual distractions into the equation.

- **Camera placement.** As you visualize the scene or scenes you plan to shoot, think about where to place your camera. Wide, medium, and close-up positions each have their own strengths and weaknesses, depending on what you're trying to convey. For example, showing a wide shot of a crowd's reaction can emphasize the emotional impact of a speech, but a wide shot looking at the speaker from a distance will have less impact because viewers won't able to see the emotions on the speaker's face. As a technical point, position the camera as close as you can for the shot you're trying to achieve, rather than using the camera's zoom capability. Using zoom makes the recording more vulnerable to shaking and makes it more difficult for you (or the camera's autofocus function) to keep the picture in focus.[18] If you need to zoom because you can't get the camera close enough, be sure to use *optical zoom* only, not *digital zoom*, which lowers the picture quality.

- **Lighting.** Good lighting is essential for a quality production, which is why professionals sometimes spend hours lighting a single shot. Lighting can be a complicated subject, but for most business videos, the simplest solution is to get a strong but soft light directed from behind the camera toward the subject (person, place, or thing) being filmed. This ensures that the subject is well lit and the camera's exposure settings aren't overwhelmed by extraneous light coming from the background. Professionals use large "softboxes," reflectors, and other special equipment to direct light onto their subjects, but you can often take advantage of windows and natural daylight.[19] If you have artificial lighting that is too harsh, you can soften the light by filtering it through parchment paper.[20] When filming people, be particularly careful about strong overhead lights, which can create unflattering shadows. And when shooting outside, look for locations in full shade if possible to avoid the deep shadows created by direct sunlight.[21]

- **Sound.** Your camera or smartphone probably has a microphone to record sound along with video, but in most cases you should use an external microphone instead. The reason is that the camera's microphone will pick up too much noise because it is too far away from the person or persons who are speaking, and these *omnidirectional* microphones pick up sound from every angle.[22] In most cases, the best solution is to pin a small *lavaliere* microphone on each speaker's lapel. Note that you can also record one or more audio sources separately (if you have speakers in different locations, for instance) and mix them together in postproduction.

- **Shot list.** Director and professional videographer Steve Stockman advises to always think of a video in terms of discrete shots, rather than as one endless recording.[23] You can imagine shots as the equivalent of subsections or even the paragraphs in a report,

Just as painters compose a scene, with a video camera you compose a scene by making decisions about what to show and where to place your camera.

Invest the time and, if necessary, the money to get good lighting; it is essential to quality video production.

The shot list serves as your outline and checklist while you're filming.

each one leading smoothly to the next. Preparing a shot list ahead of time helps you identify all the footage you need to capture, and it serves as a check-off list when you're shooting. And going beyond a shot list, whenever you're creating a video specifically (as opposed to recording a training session or some other event), consider writing a script that describes every scene and visual and contains speaking notes or even fully written dialog. Some people are adept at improvising, and this is often fine for informal tutorials and other purposes. However, for important videos, a script is advised. The script is also an important planning and communication tool, helping you make sure all the pieces and people are ready when it's time to shoot.[24]

- **B-roll material.** The "B-roll" is another legacy term from film. It refers to a collection of secondary shots that can later be edited in to add visual interest, smooth over transitions, or otherwise improve the flow of the finished product.[25] For example, an interview with your company's CEO will look fairly static after a few minutes, but you can later cut in footage or images of your company's products, website, customers, manufacturing facilities, or other related scenes or images. Videographer Jefferson Graham makes it a point to show an image or clip of anything mentioned by a narrator or interview subject.[26] During postproduction, you can weave together your primary footage with B-roll video clips and still images, using the audio to maintain continuity from start to finish. Audiences will still get full spoken message, only with a more interesting visual presentation.

> B-roll is film terminology for extra scenes and images that can enhance your final production.

In addition to these planning considerations, be sure to identify and prepare all the equipment the shoot will require, from camera(s) to lights to props. If you plan to use a smartphone as your video camera, check out some of the apps that give you more control than the phone's built-in software provides.

## STEP 2: PRODUCTION

With all your preproduction done, you're ready to shoot your video. These four tips will help you collect great footage:

- **Frame each shot carefully.** *Framing* refers to the decisions you make regarding what the camera sees and doesn't see when you aim it (see Figure 9.17). For example, if you're filming someone demonstrating a product, you'll have to decide where the camera should

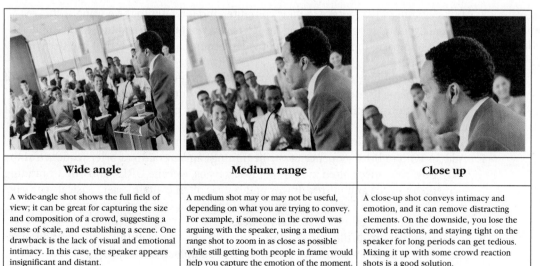

| **Wide angle** | **Medium range** | **Close up** |
|---|---|---|
| A wide-angle shot shows the full field of view; it can be great for capturing the size and composition of a crowd, suggesting a sense of scale, and establishing a scene. One drawback is the lack of visual and emotional intimacy. In this case, the speaker appears insignificant and distant. | A medium shot may or may not be useful, depending on what you are trying to convey. For example, if someone in the crowd was arguing with the speaker, using a medium range shot to zoom in as close as possible while still getting both people in frame would help you capture the emotion of the moment. | A close-up shot conveys intimacy and emotion, and it can remove distracting elements. On the downside, you lose the crowd reactions, and staying tight on the speaker for long periods can get tedious. Mixing it up with some crowd reaction shots is a good solution. |

Anatoly Tiplyashin / Shutterstock

**Figure 9.17  Framing Your Shots**
Decisions about how you frame your shots can have a dramatic effect on information delivery and emotional impact. Remember that your viewers can see everything the camera sees, but only what the camera sees.

be aimed for each of your planned shots. If the presenter is talking at one point without using the product, you might frame the shot to emphasize the speaker's face. Then when the presenter interacts with the product, you might frame the shot to emphasize his or her hands. Just remember the obvious but sometimes overlooked point that the viewer sees everything the camera sees—but only what the camera sees. The question of balance (see page 227) is important as well. Keeping a speaker's face in the center of the screen can look dull and rigid after a while, so experiment with positioning him or her just off-center to create a more dynamically balanced scene. Also, search for interesting angles for the shots you have planned.[27] In addition to filming the subject head on, for example, you might get some footage of him or her from the side or from high or low perspectives.

- **Keep the camera still.** If the camera moves around—intentionally or unintentionally—during a shot, the resulting footage puts a greater demand on your viewers. Shaky video from a handheld camera is uncomfortable to watch, so whenever possible, use a tripod or other stabilizing arrangement. And moving the camera intentionally forces viewers to process additional visual information that may or may not be relevant.[28] Moving during a shot also changes the background and lighting because the camera is looking at the scene differently. Sometimes you don't have any choice and have to follow a moving subject, but don't move the camera while filming unless you really have to.
- **Take B-roll footage.** In addition to the B-roll shots you planned in preproduction, keep an eye out for other interesting scenes and images that might enhance the finished video. It's better to shoot lots of footage you don't use than to regret not capturing something when you had the chance.
- **Don't use the special effects in your camera.** Many video cameras can add special effects such as pixilation or "old-timey" sepia tones, but using these features in the camera usually alters the video permanently. Instead, export "clean" footage to your editing software and add any effects in postproduction, where you can easily undo anything you try.[29]

Resist the temptation to move around with your camera while filming unless it is absolutely necessary.

## STEP 3: POSTPRODUCTION

Postproduction (often referred to simply as "post") is where interesting, high-quality videos come to life, as you use editing software to weave your main footage and B-roll footage into a seamless show and enhance it with music, titles, and other elements. Postproduction also lets you cut out clumsy bits of footage, record narration, potentially replace sections of dialog, and make other fixes. With even low-cost video editing software, you can produce surprisingly sophisticated videos.

Here is a general overview of the postproduction process:[30]

Postproduction involves the use of video editing software to place all your video and audio elements in the desired sequence.

1. Transfer your video footage to your computer and load it into the editing software.
2. Evaluate your material, identifying the shots you want to keep and those you can delete.
3. Use cut and paste to move sections of video around as needed to put the story in the desired order.
4. Weave in B-roll images and clips. Your company might also have a standard library of media elements to use in videos, including logos or introductory sequences.
5. Add transitions (such as a blend or quick fade to black) between video segments, if desired.
6. Synchronize the main audio track with the video and record narration as needed.
7. Add an *intro* (a brief sequence at the beginning) and an *outro* (a brief sequence at the end). Business videos often include company logos, website URLs, and other branding elements in intros and outros. Intros and outros often contain brief musical segments as well as a way to transition into and out of the spoken portion of the video.
8. Add text titles and other features as needed.
9. Create a distributable file. Video editors give you a variety of output options at different file sizes and screen resolutions, and some let you upload directly to YouTube.

As more and more companies rely on video for internal and external communication, learning some basic video skills will make you a more effective and more valuable communicator. For more on planning and producing business video, visit http://real-timeupdates .com/bct12 and click on Chapter 9.

# Quick Learning Guide

## SUMMARY OF LEARNING OBJECTIVES

**1** **Explain the power of business images, discuss six principles of graphic design that help ensure effective visuals, and explain how to avoid ethical lapses when using visuals.** Well-designed visual elements can enhance the communication power of textual messages and, in some instances, even replace textual messages. Visuals can often convey some message points (such as spatial relationships, correlations, procedures, and emotions) more effectively and more efficiently than words. In the numbers-oriented world of work, readers rely heavily on trend lines, distribution curves, and other visual presentations of numeric quantities. Visuals attract and hold people's attention, helping your audience understand and remember your message. Visuals are also an effective way to communicate with diverse audiences.

When preparing visuals, (1) use elements of design consistently so you don't confuse your audience; (2) use color and other elements to show contrast effectively; (3) strive for a visual balance, either formal or informal, that creates a feel that is appropriate for your overall message; (4) use design choices to draw attention to key elements and to visually downplay less important items; (5) understand and follow design conventions that your audience expects (even if the expectation is subconscious), although you can consider unconventional design choices if they promise to convey your message more effectively; and (6) strive for simplicity in all your visuals, making design decisions that enhance the reception and understanding of information rather than obscure or confuse it.

Communicators are responsible for avoiding both intentional and unintentional ethical lapses when using visual elements. They can work to avoid these lapses by (1) considering all possible interpretations—and misinterpretations—of their messages and avoiding design choices that could lead to unwanted interpretations; (2) providing sufficient context, whether visual or verbal, for audiences to understand the meaning and significance of visuals; (3) not hiding or minimizing negative information that runs counter to their arguments; (4) not exaggerating information that supports their arguments; (5) not oversimplifying complex situations by hiding complications that are relevant to the audience's understanding; (6) not implying cause-and-effect relationships without providing proof that they exist; (7) avoiding emotional manipulation or other forms of coercion; and (8) being careful with the way they aggregate data.

**2** **Explain how to choose which points in your message to illustrate.** To decide which points to illustrate, first step back and consider the overall flow of your message from the audience's point of view. Identify elements of the message that might be complex, vulnerable to misinterpretation, or even dull. Look for connections between ideas that should be highlighted or extensive collections of data and other discrete factual content that might be difficult to read in textual format.

**3** **Describe the most common options for presenting data in a visual format.** The visuals most commonly used to present data include tables, line and surface charts, bar charts, pictograms, Gantt charts, scatter and bubble diagrams, and pie charts. You will probably use line, bar, and pie charts most often in your business communication efforts. Moving beyond basic display formats, designers continue to invent new data visualization tools to present large or complex sets of data.

**4** **Describe the most common options for presenting information, concepts, and ideas.** Among the most commonly used visual formats in business communication are flowcharts (which depict a sequence of events in a process), organization charts (which show the relationships among people or elements in an organization), various types of maps (including data-driven map displays made possible by geographic information systems), drawings (which are often used instead of photographs because they can focus attention on specific parts of an object), diagrams (used to convey designs, interrelated ideas, and other complex entities), infographics (hybrid elements that contain enough textual and visual information to function as standalone documents), photographs (used when realism or emotional impact is important), computer animation (which can range from simple motions in presentation software such as Microsoft PowerPoint to richly complex short "films"), and video (used for everything from résumé supplements to product demonstrations).

**5** **Explain how to integrate visuals with text, and list three criteria to review in order to verify the quality of your visuals.** To integrate visuals with text, strive for a balance between text and visuals, refer to visuals clearly, place visuals to maximize the smooth flow of reading, and write helpful titles, captions, and legends. To verify the quality of your visuals, make sure every visual is accurate (there are no mistakes or missing information), properly documented (the creator of any underlying data used in the visual has been given complete credit), and honest (the visual honestly reveals the real meaning of the underlying data or information).

**6** Identify the most important considerations in the preproduction, production, and post-production stages of producing basic business videos. The key tasks in the preproduction stage are verifying your purpose and scope, thinking about the composition of the scenes you want to film, deciding where you'll place your camera or cameras, planning lighting, making arrangements for sound recording, writing a shot list or full script as appropriate, and identifying B-roll material that will enhance the final video.

During the production stage, be sure to frame each shot carefully, keep the camera still while filming unless the situation demands that you move it, take B-roll footage, and remember not to use the special effects in your camera so that you can export clean footage.

The postproduction stage generally consists of nine steps: (1) transfer your video footage to your computer and load it into the editing software; (2) evaluate your material, identifying the shots you want to keep and those you can delete; (3) move sections of video around as needed; (4) weave in B-roll images and clips; (5) add transitions between video segments, if desired; (6) synchronize the main audio track with the video and record narration as needed; (7) add an *intro* and an *outro*; (8) add text titles and other features as needed; and (9) create a distributable file.

## KEY TERMS

**area chart** Another name for a surface chart

**bar chart** Chart that portrays quantities by the height or length of its rectangular bars

**bubble diagram** Chart that expands the scatter diagram idea to three variables, with the size of the bubble representing the third variable

**caption** Brief commentary or explanation that accompanies a visual

**data visualization** A diverse class of displays that can show enormous sets of data in a single visual or show text and other complex information visually

**descriptive title** Title that simply identifies the topic of an illustration

**flowchart** Process diagram that illustrates a sequence of events from start to finish

**Gantt chart** The best known type of time line chart

**infographics** Diagrams that contain enough visual and textual information to function as independent, standalone documents

**informative title** Title that highlights the conclusion to be drawn from the data

**legend** A "key" that helps readers decode a visual by explaining what various colors, symbols, or other design choices mean

**line chart** Chart that illustrates trends over time or plots the relationship of two or more variables

**organization chart** Diagram that illustrates the positions, units, or functions of an organization and their relationships

**pictogram** Chart that portrays data as symbols instead of words or numbers

**pie chart** Circular chart that shows how the parts of a whole are distributed

**scatter diagram** Chart that plots discrete data points, with one variable along the $x$ (horizontal) axis and another along the $y$ (vertical) axis

**surface chart** Form of line chart with a cumulative effect; all the lines add up to the top line, which represents the total

**table** A systematic arrangement of data in columns and rows

**time line chart** Chart that shows how much time is needed to complete each task in a project

**title** Identifies the content and purpose of a visual

**visual literacy** The ability to create effective images and to correctly interpret such images

**visual symbolism** The connotative (as opposed to the denotative, or literal) meaning of visuals

**XY diagram** Another name for a scatter diagram

## CHECKLIST ✓
## Creating Effective Visuals

- Emphasize visual consistency to connect parts of a whole and minimize audience confusion.
- Avoid arbitrary changes of color, texture, typeface, position, or scale.
- Highlight contrasting points through color, position, and other design choices.
- Decide whether you want to achieve formal or informal balance.
- Emphasize dominant elements and deemphasize less important pieces in a design.
- Understand and follow (at least most of the time) the visual conventions your audience expects.
- Strive for simplicity and clarity; don't clutter your visuals with meaningless decoration.
- Follow the guidelines for avoiding ethical lapses.

- Carefully consider your message, the nature of your information, and your audience to choose which points to illustrate.
- Select the proper types of graphics for the information at hand and for the objective of the message.
- Be sure the visual contributes to overall understanding of the subject.
- Understand how to use your software tools to maximize effectiveness and efficiency.
- Integrate visuals and text by maintaining a balance between illustrations and words, clearly referring to visuals within the text, and placing visuals carefully.
- Use titles, captions, and legends to help readers understand the meaning and importance of your visuals.
- Verify the quality of your visuals by checking for accuracy, proper documentation, and honesty.

## COMMUNICATION CHALLENGES AT **XPLANE**

Your passion for tackling complex problems led you to a position in XPLANE's Portland, Oregon, home office after graduation. Using the principles of visual communication you learned in this chapter, tackle the following challenges.

**INDIVIDUAL CHALLENGE:** Using a flowchart as the foundation, create a visual guide to planning a fun weekend. In addition to labeling the individual shapes, feel free to add as many additional notes and other graphic elements as you need, but make sure your guide is clear and easy to use. If possible, create the piece electronically or scan it and create a file that you can submit to your instructor.

**TEAM CHALLENGE:** As part of a team of three or four students, create a visual guide to getting into college that could help high schoolers plan and manage their way through this complicated process. Start by listing all the steps required to research colleges, take necessary tests, apply for financial aid, and so on. Then choose a visual metaphor you can use to organize your information—a ladder, a road map, a treasure map, whatever works for you. Use this image as the foundation of your visual guide and then add labels and blocks of text to complete your work. If possible, create the piece electronically or scan it and create a file you can submit to your instructor.

## Test Your Knowledge

To review chapter content related to each question, refer to the indicated Learning Objective.

1. Why is simplicity important in business visuals? [LO-1]
2. What type of data visual would you use to illustrate trends over time? [LO-3]
3. When would you use a bubble diagram instead of a scatter diagram? [LO-3]
4. For what purposes are Gantt charts used? [LO-3]
5. What is the purpose of adding titles, captions, and legends to visuals in reports? [LO-5]
6. How do you check a visual for quality? [LO-5]
7. Why do experts recommend against using the built-in microphones in video cameras? [LO-6]
8. How does B-roll footage help enhance the appeal of business videos? [LO-6]

## Apply Your Knowledge

To review chapter content related to each question, refer to the indicated Learning Objective.

1. What similarities do you see between visuals and nonverbal communication? Explain your answer. [LO-1]
2. After studying the designs of corporate websites, Penn State University professor S. Shyam Sundar discovered quite an interesting phenomenon: The more interactive and engaging a website is, the more likely visitors are to "buy into whatever is being advocated" on the site. In other words, if two websites have identical content, the site with greater interactivity and more "bells and whistles" would be more persuasive.[31] Is it ethical to increase the persuasive power of a website simply by making it more interactive? Why or why not? [LO-1]
3. You're writing a report for the director of human resources on implementing team-based management throughout your company. You want to emphasize that since the new approaches were implemented six months ago, absenteeism and turnover have been sharply reduced in all but two

departments. How do you visually present your data in the most favorable light while maintaining honest communication? Explain. [LO-1]
4. In addition to telling readers why an illustration is important, why else should you refer to it in the text of your document? [LO-5]
5. Imagine that you are going to film your instructor's next lecture, and you have the luxury of using three cameras. Where would you position them and why? (If you are taking an online course with no classroom, describe a generic classroom setting.)

## Practice Your Skills

**Messages for Analysis**

**Message 9.A: Presenting Data (Bar Charts) [LO-1], [LO-3]**

Examine the bar chart in Figure 9.18 and point out any problems or errors you notice.

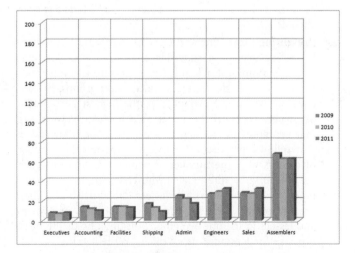

**Figure 9.18   Bar Chart for Analysis**

## Message 9.B: Presenting Data (Line Charts) [LO-1], [LO-3]

Examine the line chart in Figure 9.19 and point out any problems or errors you notice.

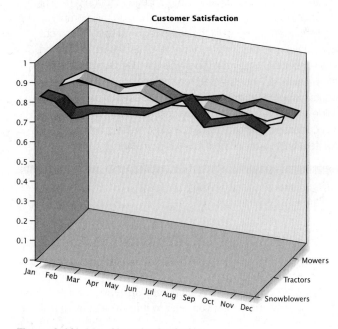

**Customer Satisfaction**

Figure 9.19 **Line Chart for Analysis**

## Exercises

1. **Applying Visual Design Principles [LO-1]** From online sources, find three visual presentations of data, information, or concepts. Which of the three presents its data or information most clearly? What design choices promote this level of clarity? What improvements would you make to the other visuals to make them clearer?

2. **Communication Ethics [LO-1]** Using a spreadsheet, create a bar chart or line chart, using data you find online or in a business publication. Alter the horizontal and vertical scales in several ways to produce different displays of the original data. How do the alterations distort the information? How might a reader detect whether a chart's scale has been altered?

3. **Presenting Data (Bar and Pie Charts) [LO-3]** As a market researcher for a statewide chain of car dealerships, you're examining car and truck ownership and lease patterns among single drivers in various age groups. By discovering which age groups have the highest percentages of owners, you will be better able to target advertising that promotes the leasing option. Using the information that follows, prepare a bar chart comparing the number of owners with the number of people who lease in each age category. Be sure to label your chart and include combined totals for owners and lessees ("total drivers"). Then prepare a pie chart showing the proportion of owners and lessees in the one age group you think holds the most promise for leasing a new vehicle. Write a sentence that prepares your company's management for the information shown in the pie chart.

| Age Group | Number of Owners (in Thousands) | Number of Lessees (in Thousands) |
|---|---|---|
| 18–24 | 1,830 | 795 |
| 25–29 | 1,812 | 1,483 |
| 30–34 | 1,683 | 1,413 |
| 35–44 | 1,303 | 1,932 |
| 45–54 | 1,211 | 1,894 |
| 55–64 | 1,784 | 1,435 |
| 65–74 | 3,200 | 1,142 |
| 75+ | 3,431 | 854 |

4. **Presenting Data (Bar Charts) [LO-3]** Team up with a classmate to design charts based on a comparison of the total tax burden of the U.S. taxpayer with that of people in other nations (see the data following this paragraph). One teammate should sketch a horizontal or vertical bar chart, and the other should sketch a pictogram from the estimates that follow. Then exchange charts and analyze how well each conveys the situation of the U.S. taxpayer. Would the bar chart look best with vertical or horizontal bars? Why? What scale is best? How does the symbol used in the pictogram enhance or obscure the meaning or impact of the data? What suggestions can each student make for improving the other's visual aid?

Estimates show that Swedish taxpayers spend 51 percent of their incomes on taxes, British taxpayers spend 48 percent, French taxpayers spend 37 percent, Japanese taxpayers spend 28 percent, and U.S. taxpayers spend 27 percent.

5. **Presenting Data (Line Charts) [LO-3]** Here are last year's sales figures for the appliance and electronics megastore

### STORE SALES (IN $ THOUSANDS)

| Month | Home Electronics | Computers | Appliances |
|---|---|---|---|
| January | $68 | $39 | $36 |
| February | 72 | 34 | 34 |
| March | 75 | 41 | 30 |
| April | 54 | 41 | 28 |
| May | 56 | 42 | 44 |
| June | 49 | 33 | 48 |
| July | 54 | 31 | 43 |
| August | 66 | 58 | 39 |
| September | 62 | 58 | 36 |
| October | 66 | 44 | 33 |
| November | 83 | 48 | 29 |
| December | 91 | 62 | 24 |

where you work. Construct a line chart that will help you explain to the store's general manager seasonal variations in each department.

6. **Presenting Data (Line Charts) [LO-3]** Using rough approximations of the data, re-create the line chart in Figure 9.6 on page 234 as a bar chart. Which of these two formats does the better job of conveying the information?

7. **Presenting Data (Data Visualization) [LO-3]** Explore several of the data visualization tools available through the Bovée & Thill Data Visualization Gateway. (Go to http://real-timeupdates.com/bct12 and click on "Learn More.") Select one that has the potential to help business managers make decisions. Write a post for your class blog, explaining how this tool could assist with decision making. Be sure to include a link to the site where you found it.

8. **Presenting Information, Concepts, and Ideas (Photographs) [LO-4]** As directed by your instructor, team up with other students, making sure that at least one of you has a digital camera or camera phone capable of downloading images to your word-processing software. Find a busy location on campus or in the surrounding neighborhood, someplace with lots of signs, storefronts, pedestrians, and traffic. Scout out two different photo opportunities, one that maximizes the visual impression of crowding and clutter, and one that minimizes this impression. For the first, assume that you are someone who advocates reducing the crowding and clutter, so you want to show how bad it is. For the second, assume you are a real estate agent or someone else who is motivated to show people that even though the location offers lots of shopping, entertainment, and other attractions, it's actually a rather calm and quiet neighborhood. Insert the two images in a word-processing document and write a caption for each that emphasizes the two opposite messages just described. Finally, write a brief paragraph, discussing the ethical implications of what you've just done. Have you distorted reality or just presented it in ways that work to your advantage? Have you prevented audiences from gaining the information they would need to make informed decisions?

9. **Selecting the Right Type of Visual [LO-3], [LO-4]** You're preparing the annual report for FretCo Guitar Corporation. For each of the following types of information, select the right chart or visual to illustrate the text. Explain your choices.
   a. Data on annual sales for the past 20 years
   b. Comparison of FretCo sales, product by product (electric guitars, bass guitars, amplifiers, acoustic guitars), for this year and last year
   c. Explanation of how a FretCo acoustic guitar is manufactured
   d. Explanation of how the FretCo Guitar Corporation markets its guitars
   e. Data on sales of FretCo products in each of 12 countries
   f. Comparison of FretCo sales figures with sales figures for three competing guitar makers over the past 10 years

10. **Presenting Information, Concepts, and Ideas (Maps) [LO-4]** You work for C & S Holdings, a company that operates coin-activated, self-service car washes. Research shows that the farther customers live from a car wash, the less likely they are to visit. You know that 50 percent of customers at each of your car washes live within a 4-mile radius of the location, 65 percent live within 6 miles, 80 percent live within 8 miles, and 90 percent live within 10 miles. C & S's owner wants to open two new car washes in your city and has asked you to prepare a report, recommending locations. Using a map of your city, choose two possible locations for car washes and create a visual depicting the customer base surrounding each location.

11. **Presenting Information, Concepts, and Ideas (Organization Charts) [LO-4]** Create an organization chart for your college or university. Start with the school's website to learn the various offices and departments.

12. **Selecting the Right Type of Visual [LO-3], [LO-4]** With a team of two or three other students, brainstorm and then sketch at least three types of charts you can use to compare the populations of all 50 states in the United States. You can use any of the graphic ideas presented in this chapter, as well as any ideas or examples you find from other sources.

13. **Planning Business Videos [LO-6]** Assume you are producing a video interview of your college or university's president. The purpose of the video is the encourage high school students to consider applying to your school. The interview will take place in the president's office, but you want to add some B-roll footage to make the video more visually appealing. Identify six scenes around campus that you could film for this purpose.

## Expand Your Skills

### Critique the Professionals

Find a business video on YouTube or another online source. This can be a product demonstration, a tutorial, a company profile, or most any other type of video other than an overt promotional video such as a TV commercial. Analyze its effectiveness in terms of lighting, sound, narration, camera placement, and the use of B-roll elements. How would you assess its overall effectiveness as a business message? Summarize your conclusions in a post on your class blog or an email to your instructor. Be sure to include a link to the video.

### Sharpening Your Career Skills Online

Bovée and Thill's Business Communication Web Search, at http://businesscommunicationblog.com/websearch, is a unique research tool designed specifically for business communication research. Use the Web Search function to find a website, video, PDF document, podcast, or PowerPoint presentation that offers advice on creating effective visuals for documents and presentations. Write a brief email message to your instructor, describing the item that you found and summarizing the career skills information you learned from it.

## MyBCommLab

Go to **mybcommlab.com** for Auto-graded writing questions as well as the following Assisted-graded writing questions:

**9-1.** Why might you use a simplified line drawing instead of a full-color digital photograph in a particular application? [LO-4]

**9-2.** In what important ways do infographics differ from other business visuals? [LO-4]

**9-3.** Mybcommlab Only—comprehensive writing assignment for this chapter.

## Endnotes

1. Aric Wood, personal communication, 12 April 2013. XPLANE website, accessed 12 February 2013, www.xplane.com; Matthew Kish, "XPLANE Returns Home," *Portland Business Journal*, 5 October 2012, www.bizjournals.com; "Small & Global," CNN, 23 June 2008, www.cnn.com; "Visionary Leaders," *Portland Monthly*, October 2007, 82–88.
2. Alexis Gerard and Bob Goldstein, *Going Visual* (Hoboken, N.J.: Wiley, 2005), 18.
3. Charles Kostelnick and Michael Hassett, *Shaping Information: The Rhetoric of Visual Conventions* (Carbondale, Ill.: Southern Illinois University Press, 2003), 177.
4. Gerard and Goldstein, *Going Visual*, 25–27.
5. "Fact Sheet Overview," *2003 National Assessment of Adult Literacy*, National Institute for Literacy, accessed 22 November 2006, www.nifl.gov.
6. Gerard and Goldstein, *Going Visual*, 103–106.
7. Edward R. Tufte, *Visual Explanations: Images and Quantities, Evidence and Narrative* (Cheshire, Conn.: Graphics Press, 1997), 82.
8. Joshua David McClurg-Genevese, "The Principles of Design," *Digital Web Magazine*, 13 June 2005, www.digital-web.com.
9. Kostelnick and Hassett, *Shaping Information: The Rhetoric of Visual Conventions*, 17.
10. Kostelnick and Hassett, *Shaping Information: The Rhetoric of Visual Conventions*, 216.
11. Edward R. Tufte, *The Visual Display of Quantitative Information* (Cheshire, Conn.: Graphic Press, 1983), 113.
12. Based in part on Tufte, *Visual Explanations: Images and Quantities, Evidence and Narrative*, 29–37, 53; Paul Martin Lester, *Visual Communication: Images with Messages*, 4th ed. (Belmont, Calif.: Thomson Wadsworth, 2006), 95–105, 194–196.
13. Data from Hoover's Online, accessed 3 December 2008, www.hoovers.com.
14. Robert L. Harris, *Information Graphics: A Comprehensive Illustrated Reference* (New York: Oxford University Press, 1999), 14.
15. Stephen Few, "Save the Pies for Dessert," *Visual Business Intelligence Newsletter*, August 2007, www.perceptualedge.com.
16. Maria Popova, "Data Visualization: Stories for the Information Age," *BusinessWeek*, 12 August 2009, www.businessweek.com.
17. "Data Visualization: Modern Approaches," Smashing Magazine website, 2 August 2007, www.smashingmagazine.com; "7 Things You Should Know About Data Visualization," Educause Learning Initiative, accessed 15 March 2008, www.educause.edu; TagCrowd website, accessed 15 March 2008, www.tagcrowd.com.
18. Steve Stockman, *How to Shoot Video That Doesn't Suck* (New York: Workman Publishing, 2011), Kindle edition.
19. Jefferson Graham, *Video Nation: A DIY Guide to Planning, Shooting, and Sharing Great Video from USA Today's Talking Tech Host* (Berkeley, Calif.: Peachpit Press, 2013), Kindle edition.
20. Graham, *Video Nation*.
21. Graham, *Video Nation*.
22. Graham, *Video Nation*.
23. Stockman, *How to Shoot Video That Doesn't Suck*.
24. Stockman, *How to Shoot Video That Doesn't Suck*.
25. Graham, *Video Nation*.
26. Graham, *Video Nation*.
27. Graham, *Video Nation*.
28. Stockman, *How to Shoot Video That Doesn't Suck*.
29. Stockman, *How to Shoot Video That Doesn't Suck*.
30. Adapted in part from Stockman, *How to Shoot Video That Doesn't Suck*; Graham, *Video Nation*.
31. "Interactive Web Sites Draw Minds, Shape Public Perception," *ScienceDaily*, 27 May 2008, www.sciencedaily.com.

# Brief Messages

Most of your communication on the job will be through brief messages, from Twitter updates and blog posts to formal letters that might run to several pages. Learning how to write these messages quickly and effectively is key to maintaining productive working relationships with colleagues and customers. In these chapters you'll find specific techniques for crafting routine, positive, negative, and persuasive messages—techniques that will help you in everything from getting a raise to calming an angry customer to promoting your next great idea.

Matt Antonino/Shutterstock

# 10 | Writing Routine and Positive Messages

## LEARNING OBJECTIVES

After studying this chapter, you will be able to

**1** Outline an effective strategy for writing routine business requests.

**2** Describe three common types of routine requests.

**3** Outline an effective strategy for writing routine replies and positive messages.

**4** Describe six common types of routine replies and positive messages.

## COMMUNICATION CLOSE-UP AT
## Get Satisfaction
http://getsatisfaction.com

For about as long as online communication has been possible, frustrated customers have been going online to complain about faulty products, confusing instructions, and poor service. When social media tools appeared, giving even nontechnical consumers a ready voice, the stream of "I need help!" messages turned into a full-time flood. On product review and shopping websites, enthusiast blogs, and various "complaint sites," consumers can vent their frustrations and ask for help when they feel they aren't getting satisfaction from the companies they do business with.

These various websites can occasionally provide answers, but they suffer from four fundamental drawbacks. First, they are randomly scattered all over the Web, so many consumers are never quite sure where to look for help. Second, the right experts from the right companies often aren't involved, meaning that customers often have to rely on each other—which sometimes works but sometimes doesn't. Third, even companies that make a valiant effort to keep their customers satisfied know that everyone can benefit if customers can share ideas, learn from one another, and participate in ongoing conversation. Fourth, companies often find that multiple customers have the same routine questions, but communicating with every customer individually can be time-consuming and expensive.

The San Francisco–based company Get Satisfaction is working to address all these issues with social networking technologies designed specifically for community-based customer

Wendy Lea, CEO of Get Satisfaction, leads the company's efforts to revolutionize customer care through social media.

support. Consumers can post questions or complaints and request notification whenever a response is posted. If someone else has already posted the same complaint, all a visitor need do is ask to be notified when the issue is resolved, saving time for the people asking and answering questions. Consumers can also suggest ideas for new products and services or improvements to existing offerings.

On the other side of the relationship, employees from companies that sell products and services can register as official representatives to answer questions, solve problems, and solicit feedback. As both knowledgeable consumers and company representatives provide answers and solutions, the responses voted most useful rise to the top, ensuring that visitors always get the most helpful information available. Companies that use Get Satisfaction's services can deploy customer service capabilities in a variety of ways, including via Facebook, Twitter, and their own company blogs, to try to capture as many customer service conversations as possible.

The idea certainly seems to be catching on, with 70,000 companies now using Get Satisfaction's "social helpdesk" approach to help millions of customers get satisfaction from the products and services they buy.[1]

# Strategy for Routine Requests

Get Satisfaction (profiled in the chapter-opening Communication Close-Up) knows that much of the vital communication between a company and its customers is about routine matters, from product operation hints and technical support to refunds and order glitches. These messages fall into two groups: routine requests, in which you ask for information or action from another party, and a variety of routine and positive messages. Chapter 11 covers messages in which you convey negative information, and Chapter 12 addresses persuasive messages.

Making requests is a routine part of business. In most cases, your audience will be prepared to comply, as long as you're not being unreasonable or asking people to do something they would expect you to do yourself. By applying a clear strategy and tailoring your approach to each situation, you'll be able to generate effective requests quickly.

Like all other business messages, a routine request has three parts: an opening, a body, and a close. Using the direct approach, open with your main idea, which is a clear statement of your request. Use the body to give details and justify your request. Finally, close by requesting specific action.

**1** LEARNING OBJECTIVE
Outline an effective strategy for writing routine business requests.

For routine requests and positive messages
- State the request or main idea
- Give necessary details
- Close with a cordial request for specific action

## STATING YOUR REQUEST UP FRONT

With routine requests, you can make your request at the beginning of the message. Of course, getting right to the point should not be interpreted as license to be abrupt or tactless:

- **Pay attention to tone.** Even though you expect a favorable response, the tone of your initial request is important. Instead of demanding action ("Send me the latest personnel cost data"), soften your request with words such as *please* and *I would appreciate*.
- **Assume that your audience will comply.** An impatient demand for rapid service isn't necessary. You can generally assume that your readers will comply with your request when they clearly understand the reason for it.
- **Be specific.** State precisely what you want. For example, if you request the latest market data from your research department, be sure to say whether you want a 1-page summary or 100 pages of raw data.

Take care that your direct approach doesn't come across as abrupt or tactless.

## EXPLAINING AND JUSTIFYING YOUR REQUEST

Use the body of your message to explain your request. Make the explanation a smooth and logical outgrowth of your opening remarks. If possible, point out how complying with the request could benefit the reader. For instance, if you would like some assistance interpreting complex quality-control data, you might point out how a better understanding of quality issues would improve customer satisfaction and ultimately lead to higher profits for the entire company.

Whether you're writing a formal letter or a simple instant message, you can use the body of your request to list a series of questions. These questions help organize your

CHECKLIST ✔ Writing Routine Requests

**A. State your request up front.**
- Write in a polite, undemanding, personal tone.
- Use the direct approach because your audience will probably respond favorably to your request.
- Be specific and precise in your request.

**B. Explain and justify your request.**
- Justify the request or explain its importance.
- Explain any potential benefits of responding.

- Ask the most important questions first.
- Break complex requests into individual questions that are limited to only one topic each.

**C. Request specific action in a courteous close.**
- Make it easy to comply by including appropriate contact information.
- Express your gratitude.
- Clearly state any important deadlines for the request.

message and help your audience identify the information you need. Just keep in mind a few basics:

If you have multiple requests or questions, start with the most important one.

- **Ask the most important questions first.** If cost is your main concern, for example, you might begin with a question such as "How much will it cost to have our new website created by an outside firm?" Then you may want to ask more specific but related questions, such as whether discounts are available for paying early.
- **Ask only relevant questions.** To help expedite the response to your request, ask only questions that are central to your main request. Doing so will generate an answer sooner and make better use of the other person's time.
- **Deal with only one topic per question.** If you have an unusual or complex request, break it down into specific, individual questions so that the reader can address each one separately. Don't put the burden of untangling a complicated request on your reader. This consideration shows respect for your audience's time and will probably get you a more accurate answer in less time.

## REQUESTING SPECIFIC ACTION IN A COURTEOUS CLOSE

Close request messages with
- A request for some specific action
- Information about how you can be reached
- An expression of appreciation

Close your message with three important elements: (1) a specific request that includes any relevant deadlines, (2) information about how you can be reached (if it isn't obvious), and (3) an expression of appreciation or goodwill. When you ask readers to perform a specific action, ask for a response by a specific date or time, if appropriate (for example, "Please send the figures by May 5 so that I can return first-quarter results to you before the May 20 conference."). Plus, by including your phone number, email address, office hours, and other contact information, you help readers respond easily.

Conclude your message by sincerely expressing your goodwill and appreciation. However, don't thank the reader "in advance" for cooperating; many people find that presumptuous. And if the reader's reply warrants a word of thanks, send it after you've received the reply. To review, see "Checklist: Writing Routine Requests."

# Common Examples of Routine Requests

2 LEARNING OBJECTIVE
Describe three common types of routine requests.

The most common types of routine messages are asking for information or action, asking for recommendations, and making claims and requesting adjustments.

## ASKING FOR INFORMATION AND ACTION

Most simple requests can be handled with three message points:

- What you want to know or what you want the reader to do
- Why you're making the request
- Why it may be in your reader's interest to help you

If your reader is able to do what you want, such a straightforward request will get the job done quickly. Use the direct approach by opening with a clear statement of your reason for writing. In the body, provide whatever explanation is needed to justify your request. Then close with a specific description of what you expect and include a deadline, if appropriate (see Figure 10.1).

### Analyze the Situation
Verify that the purpose is to request information from company managers.

### Gather Information
Gather accurate, complete information about local competitive threats.

### Select the Right Medium
Choose email for this internal message, which also allows the attachment of a Word document to collect the information.

### Organize the Information
Clarify that the main idea is collecting information that will lead to a better competitive strategy, which will in turn help the various district managers.

### Adapt to Your Audience
Show sensitivity to audience needs with a "you" attitude, politeness, positive emphasis, and bias-free language. The writer already has credibility, as manager of the department.

### Compose the Message
Maintain a style that is conversational but still businesslike, using plain English and appropriate voice.

### Revise the Message
Evaluate content and review readability; avoid unnecessary details.

### Produce the Message
Simple email format is all the design this message needs.

### Proofread the Message
Review for errors in layout, spelling, and mechanics.

### Distribute the Message
Deliver the message via the company's email system.

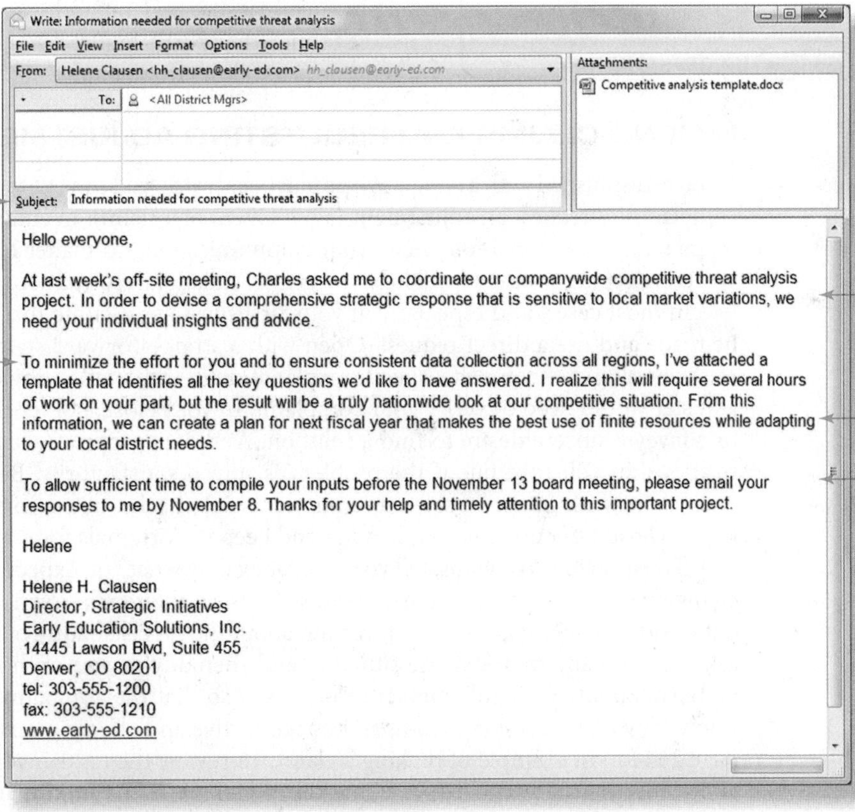

---

The informative subject line alerts the audience to an important request.

She acknowledges that responding to the request will require some work but emphasizes that the result will benefit everyone.

**Write: Information needed for competitive threat analysis**

File  Edit  View  Insert  Format  Options  Tools  Help

From: Helene Clausen <hh_clausen@early-ed.com> *hh_clausen@early-ed.com*

To: <All District Mgrs>

Subject: Information needed for competitive threat analysis

Attachments:
Competitive analysis template.docx

Hello everyone,

At last week's off-site meeting, Charles asked me to coordinate our companywide competitive threat analysis project. In order to devise a comprehensive strategic response that is sensitive to local market variations, we need your individual insights and advice.

To minimize the effort for you and to ensure consistent data collection across all regions, I've attached a template that identifies all the key questions we'd like to have answered. I realize this will require several hours of work on your part, but the result will be a truly nationwide look at our competitive situation. From this information, we can create a plan for next fiscal year that makes the best use of finite resources while adapting to your local district needs.

To allow sufficient time to compile your inputs before the November 13 board meeting, please email your responses to me by November 8. Thanks for your help and timely attention to this important project.

Helene

Helene H. Clausen
Director, Strategic Initiatives
Early Education Solutions, Inc.
14445 Lawson Blvd, Suite 455
Denver, CO 80201
tel: 303-555-1200
fax: 303-555-1210
www.early-ed.com

The opening explains the context of the message, then gets to the point of the request.

The body explains the benefit of responding to the request.

The close provides a clear deadline, then concludes in a courteous manner.

**Figure 10.1  Routine Message Requesting Action**
In this email request to district managers across the country, Helene Clausen asks them to fill out an attached information collection form. Although the request is not unusual and responding to it is part of the managers' responsibility, Clausen asks for their help in a courteous manner and points out the benefits of responding.
*Source:* Used with permission from Microsoft.

If the reader might benefit by responding positively to your request, be sure to point that out.

In some situations, readers might be unwilling to respond unless they understand how the request benefits them, so be sure to include this information in your explanation.

## ASKING FOR RECOMMENDATIONS

The need to inquire about people arises often in business. For example, before extending credit or awarding contracts, jobs, promotions, or scholarships, companies often ask applicants to supply references. Companies ask applicants to list people who can vouch for their ability, skills, integrity, character, and fitness for the job. Before you volunteer someone's name as a reference, ask permission. Some people don't want you to use their names, perhaps because they don't know enough about you to feel comfortable writing a letter or because they or their employers have a policy of not providing recommendations.

Always ask for permission before using someone as a reference.

Refresh the memory of any potential reference you haven't been in touch with for a while.

Because requests for recommendations and references are routine, you can organize your inquiry using the direct approach. Open your message by clearly stating why the recommendation is required (if it's not for a job, be sure to explain its purpose) and that you would like your reader to write the letter. If you haven't had contact with the person for some time, use the opening to trigger the reader's memory of the relationship you had, the dates of association, and any special events or accomplishments that might bring a clear and favorable picture of you to mind.

**REAL-TIME UPDATES**

LEARN MORE BY READING THIS PDF

**The right way to ask for recommendations on LinkedIn**

Follow LinkedIn's etiquette guide for students and recent graduates to increase your response rate and to maintain positive networking connections. Go to http://real-timeupdates .com/bct12 and click on Learn More. If you are using MyBCommLab, you can access Real-Time Updates within each chapter or under Student Study Tools.

Close your message with an expression of appreciation and the full name and address of the person to whom the letter should be sent. When asking for an immediate recommendation, you should also mention the deadline. Always be sure to enclose a stamped, preaddressed envelope as a convenience to the other party. Figure 10.2 provides an example of a request that follows these guidelines.

## MAKING CLAIMS AND REQUESTING ADJUSTMENTS

When writing a claim or requesting an adjustment
- Explain the problem and give details
- Provide backup information
- Request specific action

If you're dissatisfied with a company's product or service, you can opt to make a **claim** (a formal complaint) or request an **adjustment** (a settlement of a claim). In either case, it's important to maintain a professional tone in all your communication, no matter how angry or frustrated you are. Keeping your cool will help you get the situation resolved sooner.

In most cases, and especially in your first message, assume that a fair adjustment will be made and use a direct request. Open with a straightforward statement of the problem. In the body, give a complete, specific explanation of the details; provide any information an adjuster would need to verify your complaint. In your close, politely request specific action or convey a sincere desire to find a solution. And, if appropriate, suggest that the business relationship will continue if the problem is solved satisfactorily. Be prepared to back up your claim with invoices, sales receipts, canceled checks, dated correspondence, and any other relevant documents. Send copies and keep the originals for your files.

Be prepared to document any claims you make with a company. Send copies and keep the original documents.

If the remedy is obvious, tell your reader exactly what you expect to be done, such as exchanging incorrectly shipped merchandise for the right item or issuing a refund if the item is out of stock. However, if you're uncertain about the precise nature of the trouble, you could ask the company to assess the situation and then advise you on how the situation could be fixed. Supply your full contact information so that the company can discuss the situation with you, if necessary. Compare the ineffective and effective versions in Figure 10.3 on page 264 for an example of making a claim. To review the tasks involved in making claims and requesting adjustments, see "Checklist: Making Claims and Requesting Adjustments."

## CHECKLIST ✔ Making Claims and Requesting Adjustments

- Maintain a professional tone, even if you're extremely frustrated.
- Open with a straightforward statement of the problem.
- Provide specific details in the body.
- Present facts honestly and clearly.

- Politely summarize the desired action in the closing.
- Clearly state what you expect as a fair settlement or ask the reader to propose a fair adjustment.
- Explain the benefits of complying with the request, such as your continued patronage.

**Analyze the Situation**
Verify that the purpose is to request a recommendation letter from a college professor.

**Gather Information**
Gather information on classes and dates to help the reader recall you and to clarify the position you seek.

**Select the Right Medium**
The letter format gives this message an appropriate level of formality, although many professors prefer to be contacted by an email.

**Organize the Information**
Messages like this are common and expected, so a direct approach is fine.

**Adapt to Your Audience**
Show sensitivity to audience needs with a "you" attitude, politeness, positive emphasis, and bias-free language.

**Compose the Message**
Style is respectful and businesslike, while still using plain English and appropriate voice.

**Revise the Message**
Evaluate content and review readability; avoid unnecessary details.

**Produce the Message**
Simple letter format is all the design this message needs.

**Proofread the Message**
Review for errors in layout, spelling, and mechanics.

**Distribute the Message**
Deliver the message via postal mail or email if you have the professor's email address.

---

1181 Ashport Drive
Tate Springs, TN 38101
March 14, 2014

Professor Lyndon Kenton
School of Business
University of Tennessee, Knoxville
Knoxville, TN 37916

Dear Professor Kenton:

I recently interviewed with Strategic Investments and have been called for a second interview for their Analyst Training Program (ATP). They have requested at least one recommendation from a professor, and I immediately thought of you. May I have a letter of recommendation from you?

*[The opening states the purpose of the letter and makes the request, assuming the reader will want to comply with the request.]*

As you may recall, I took BUS 485, Financial Analysis, from you in the fall of 2011. I enjoyed the class and finished the term with an "A." Professor Kenton, your comments on assertiveness and cold-calling impressed me beyond the scope of the actual course material. In fact, taking your course helped me decide on a future as a financial analyst.

*[Tucker includes information near the opening to refresh her professor's memory.]*

My enclosed résumé includes all my relevant work experience and volunteer activities. I would also like to add that I've handled the financial planning for our family since my father passed away several years ago. Although I initially learned by trial and error, I have increasingly applied my business training in deciding what stocks or bonds to trade. This, I believe, has given me a practical edge over others who may be applying for the same job.

*[The body refers to the enclosed résumé and mentions experience that could set the applicant apart from other candidates—information the professor could use in writing the recommendation.]*

If possible, Ms. Blackmon in Human Resources needs to receive your letter by March 30. For your convenience, I've enclosed a preaddressed, stamped envelope.

*[She provides a deadline for response and includes information about the person who is expecting the recommendation.]*

I appreciate your time and effort in writing this letter of recommendation for me. It will be great to put my education to work, and I'll keep you informed of my progress. Thank you for your consideration in this matter.

*[The close mentions the preaddressed, stamped envelope to encourage a timely response.]*

Sincerely,

*Joanne Tucker*

Joanne Tucker

Enclosure

**Figure 10.2   Effective Request for a Recommendation**
This writer uses a direct approach when asking for a recommendation from a former professor. Note how she takes care to refresh the professor's memory because she took the class a year and a half ago. She also indicates the date by which the letter is needed and points to the enclosure of a stamped, preaddressed envelope.

MyBCommLab Apply Figure 10.3's key concepts. Go to **mybcommlab.com** and follow this path: Course Content → Chapter 10 → **DOCUMENT MAKEOVERS**

The opening has an emotional tone and burdens the reader with too many details too quickly.

The body continues with the emotional tone and includes unhelpful statements that will only put the reader on the defensive.

The close includes irrelevant information and fails to make a clear request.

Covington provides details in the body so the reader can understand why she believes that a problem exists.

She offers a helpful suggestion for resolving the problem.

The opening clearly and calmly states the problem.

The body presents details clearly, concisely, and completely.

The close requests specific action and provides contact information to make responding easy.

**Figure 10.3  Ineffective and Effective Versions of a Claim**
Note the difference in both tone and information content in these two versions. The poor version is emotional and unprofessional, whereas the improved version communicates calmly and clearly.
*Source:* Used with permission from Microsoft.

# Strategy for Routine and Positive Messages

Just as you'll make numerous requests for information and action throughout your career, you'll also respond to similar requests from other people. When you are responding positively to a request, sending routine announcements, or sending a positive or goodwill message, you have several goals: to communicate the information or the good news, answer all questions, provide all required details, and leave your reader with a good impression of you and your firm.

Readers receiving routine replies and positive messages will generally be interested in what you have to say, so use the direct approach. Place your main idea (the positive reply or the good news) in the opening. Use the body to explain all the relevant details, and close cordially, perhaps highlighting a benefit to your reader.

**3** **LEARNING OBJECTIVE**
Outline an effective strategy for writing routine replies and positive messages.

Use the direct approach for routine replies and positive messages.

## STARTING WITH THE MAIN IDEA

By opening routine and positive messages with the main idea or good news, you're preparing your audience for the details that follow. Make your opening clear and concise. Although the following introductory statements make the same point, one is cluttered with unnecessary information that buries the purpose, whereas the other is brief and to the point:

With the direct approach, open with a clear and concise expression of the main idea or good news.

**Instead of This**

I am pleased to inform you that after careful consideration of a diverse and talented pool of applicants, each of whom did a thorough job of analyzing Trask Horton Pharmaceuticals's training needs, we have selected your bid.

**Write This**

Trask Horton Pharmaceuticals has accepted your bid to provide public speaking and presentation training to the sales staff.

The best way to write a clear opening is to have a clear idea of what you want to say. Ask yourself, "What is the single most important message I have for the audience?"

## PROVIDING NECESSARY DETAILS AND EXPLANATION

Use the body to explain your point completely so that your audience won't be confused or doubtful about your meaning. As you provide the details, maintain the supportive tone established in the opening. This tone is easy to continue when your message is entirely positive, as in this example:

Your educational background and internship have impressed us, and we believe you would be a valuable addition to Green Valley Properties. As discussed during your interview, your salary will be $4,300 per month, plus benefits. Please plan to meet with our benefits manager, Paula Sanchez, at 8 A.M. on Monday, March 21. She will assist you with all the paperwork necessary to tailor our benefit package to your family situation. She will also arrange various orientation activities to help you acclimate to our company.

However, if your routine message is mixed and must convey mildly disappointing information, put the negative portion of your message into as favorable a context as possible:

Try to embed any negative information in a positive context.

**Instead of This**

No, we no longer carry the Sportsgirl line of sweaters.

**Write This**

The new Olympic line has replaced the Sportsgirl sweaters that you asked about. Olympic features a wider range of colors and sizes and more contemporary styling.

CHECKLIST ✔ Writing Routine Replies and Positive Messages

A. **Start with the main idea.**
- Be clear and concise.
- Identify the single most important message before you start writing.

B. **Provide necessary details and explanation.**
- Explain your point completely to eliminate any confusion or lingering doubts.
- Maintain a supportive tone throughout.

- Embed negative statements in positive contexts or balance them with positive alternatives.
- Talk favorably about the choices the customer has made.

C. **End with a courteous close.**
- Let your readers know you have their personal well-being in mind.
- If further action is required, tell readers how to proceed and encourage them to act promptly.

In this example, the more complete description is less negative and emphasizes how the recipient can benefit from the change. Be careful, though: You can use negative information in this type of message *only* if you're reasonably sure the audience will respond positively. Otherwise, use the indirect approach (discussed in Chapter 11).

If you are communicating with a customer, you might also want to use the body of your message to assure the person of the wisdom of his or her purchase selection (without being condescending or self-congratulatory). Using such favorable comments, often known as *resale*, is a good way to build customer relationships. These comments are commonly included in acknowledgments of orders and other routine announcements to customers, and they are most effective when they are relatively short and specific:

> The KitchenAid mixer you ordered is our best-selling model. It should meet your cooking needs for many years.

### ENDING WITH A COURTEOUS CLOSE

In the close, make sure audience members understand what to do next and how that action will benefit them (if applicable).

The close of routine replies and positive messages is usually short and simple, because you're leaving things on a neutral or positive note and not usually asking for the reader to do anything. Often, a simple thank you is all you need. However, if follow-up action is required or expected, use the close to identify who will do what and when that action will take place. For a quick reminder of the steps involved in writing routine replies and positive messages, see the checklist above.

## Common Examples of Routine and Positive Messages

**4 LEARNING OBJECTIVE**
Describe six common types of routine replies and positive messages.

Most routine and positive messages fall into six main categories: answers to requests for information and action, grants of claims and requests for adjustment, recommendations, routine information, good-news announcements, and goodwill messages.

### ANSWERING REQUESTS FOR INFORMATION AND ACTION

Every professional answers requests for information and action from time to time. If the response is a simple yes or some other straightforward information, the direct approach is appropriate. A prompt, gracious, and thorough response will positively influence how people think about you and the organization you represent.

When you're answering requests and a potential sale is involved, you have three main goals: (1) to respond to the inquiry and answer all questions, (2) to leave your reader with a good impression of you and your firm, and (3) to encourage the future sale. The following message meets all three objectives:

> Here is the brochure "Entertainment Unlimited" that you requested. This booklet describes the vast array of entertainment options available to you with an Ocean Satellite Device (OSD).

On page 12 you'll find a list of the 338 channels that the OSD brings into your home. You'll have access to movie, sports, and music channels; 24-hour news channels; local channels; and all the major television networks. OSD gives you a clearer picture and more precise sound than those old-fashioned dishes that took up most of your yard—and OSD uses only a small dish that mounts easily on your roof.

More music, more cartoons, more experts, more news, and more sports are available to you with OSD than with any other cable or satellite connection in this region. It's all there, right at your fingertips.

Just call us at 1-800-786-4331, and an OSD representative will come to your home to answer your questions. You'll love the programming and the low monthly cost. Call today!

## GRANTING CLAIMS AND REQUESTS FOR ADJUSTMENT

Even the best-run companies make mistakes, from shipping the wrong order to billing a customer's credit card inaccurately. In other cases, a customer or a third party might be responsible for a mistake, such as misusing a product or damaging a product in shipment. Each of these events represents a turning point in your relationship with your customer. If you handle the situation well, your customer is likely to be even more loyal than before because you've proven that you're serious about customer satisfaction. However, if a customer believes that you mishandled a complaint, you'll make the situation even worse. Dissatisfied customers often take their business elsewhere without notice and tell numerous friends and colleagues about the negative experience. A transaction that might be worth only a few dollars by itself could cost you many times that amount in lost business. In other words, every mistake is an opportunity to improve a relationship.

Your response to a customer complaint depends on your company's policies for resolving such issues and your assessment of whether the company, the customer, or some third party is at fault.

> **REAL-TIME UPDATES**
>
> LEARN MORE BY READING THIS INFOGRAPHIC
>
> **See why the social approach is revolutionizing routine customer communication**
>
> More and more companies rely on the social web to influence customers before the sale and support them after; these statistics explain why social help is becoming so pervasive. Go to http://real-timeupdates.com/bct12 and click on Learn More. If you are using MyBCommLab, you can access Real-Time Updates within each chapter or under Student Study Tools.

### Responding to a Claim When Your Company Is at Fault

Before you respond after your company has made a mistake, make sure you know your company's policies, which might dictate specific legal and financial steps to be taken. For serious problems that go beyond routine errors, your company should have a *crisis management plan* that outlines communication steps both inside and outside the organization (see Chapter 11).

Most routine responses should take your company's specific policies into account and do the following:

- Acknowledge receipt of the customer's claim or complaint.
- Sympathize with the customer's inconvenience or frustration.
- Take (or assign) personal responsibility for setting matters straight.
- Explain precisely how you have resolved, or plan to resolve, the situation.
- Take steps to repair the relationship.
- Follow up to verify that your response was correct.

In addition to taking these positive steps, maintain a professional demeanor. Don't blame anyone in your organization by name; don't make exaggerated, insincere apologies; don't imply that the customer is at fault; and don't promise more than you can deliver. See how this message acknowledges the problem, describes the action being taken, and works to rebuild the customer relationship:

Maintain a sincere, professional tone when responding to a complaint.

Your email message concerning your recent Klondike order has been forwarded to our director of order fulfillment. Your complete satisfaction is our goal, and a customer service representative will contact you within 24 hours to assist with the issues raised in your letter.

In the meantime, please accept the enclosed $5 gift certificate as a token of our appreciation for your business. Whether you're skiing or driving a snowmobile, Klondike Gear offers you the best protection from wind, snow, and cold—and Klondike has been taking care of customers' outdoor needs for over 27 years.

Thank you for taking the time to write to us. Your input helps us better serve you and all our customers.

### Responding to a Claim When the Customer Is at Fault

Communication about a claim is a delicate matter when the customer is clearly at fault. If you refuse the claim, you may lose your customer—as well as many of the customer's friends and colleagues, who will hear only one side of the dispute. You must weigh the cost of making the adjustment against the cost of losing future business from one or more customers. Some companies have strict guidelines for responding to such claims, whereas others give individual employees and managers some leeway in making case-by-case decisions.

*When granting a claim when the customer is at fault, try to discourage future mistakes without insulting the customer.*

If you choose to grant a claim, you can simply open with the good news, being sure to specify exactly what you're agreeing to do. The body of the message is tricky because you want to discourage such claims in the future by steering the customer in the right direction. For example, customers sometimes misuse products or fail to follow the terms of service agreements, such as forgetting to cancel hotel reservations at least 24 hours in advance and thereby incurring the cost of one night's stay. Even if you do grant a particular claim, you don't want to imply that you will grant similar claims in the future. The challenge is to diplomatically remind the customer of proper usage or procedures without being condescending ("Perhaps you failed to read the instructions carefully") or preachy ("You should know that wool shrinks in hot water"). Close in a courteous manner that expresses your appreciation for the customer's business (see Figure 10.4).

### Responding to a Claim When a Third Party Is at Fault

Some claims are the result of a mistake by a third party, such as a credit card processing company or a delivery service. Your company may not have made the mistake, but the customer could ask you to resolve the matter anyway.

*When a third party is at fault, your response depends on your company's agreements with that organization.*

No general scheme applies to every case involving a third party, so evaluate the situation carefully and know your company's policies before responding. For instance, an online retailer and the companies that manufacture its merchandise might have an agreement specifying that the manufacturers automatically handle all complaints about product quality. Regardless of who eventually resolves the problem, if customers contact you, you need to respond with messages that explain how the problem will be solved. Pointing fingers is both unproductive and unprofessional. Customers care about only one issue: resolving the situation. See "Checklist: Granting Claims and Adjustment Requests" to review the tasks involved in these kinds of business messages.

---

**CHECKLIST** ✔ Granting Claims and Adjustment Requests

**A. Responding when your company is at fault.**
- Be aware of your company's policies in such cases before you respond.
- For serious situations, refer to the company's crisis management plan.
- Start by acknowledging receipt of the claim or complaint.
- Take or assign personal responsibility for resolving the situation.
- Sympathize with the customer's frustration.
- Explain how you have resolved the situation (or plan to).
- Take steps to repair the customer relationship.
- Verify your response with the customer and keep the lines of communication open.

**B. Responding when the customer is at fault.**
- Weigh the cost of complying with or refusing the request.
- If you choose to comply, open with the good news.
- Use the body of the message to respectfully educate the customer about steps needed to avoid a similar outcome in the future.
- Close with an appreciation for the customer's business.

**C. Responding when a third party is at fault.**
- Evaluate the situation and review your company's policies before responding.
- Avoid placing blame; focus on the solution.
- Regardless of who is responsible for resolving the situation, let the customer know what will happen to resolve the problem.

**Ineffective**

Write: re: Warranty repair?

File   Edit   View   Insert   Format   Tools   Help

Send   Attach   Security   Save

Candace Parker <candacep@skatesalive.biz>   candacep@skatesalive.biz

To:   steveC955@verizonmail.net

Subject:   re: Warranty repair?

Valued customer:

We received your request for warranty repair, even though your warranty has expired. The instruction manual for your skates clearly states that the Fastrax model is intended for use on roadways and tracks that are relatively free of sand. Considering the amount of sand build-up that you describe, and the fact that you live in Florida with all those beach areas, it seems safe to conclude that you used your skates on sandy paths. The wheel bearings in our skates are precision mechanisms that must be protected from sand and dirt.

However, we have chosen to grant your request in the interest of positive customer relations. We will be sending you a complete wheel assembly replacement free of charge. We hope you appreciate this gesture on our part!

By the way, you should know that we have other models that would probably work better for you. In fact, we have a model designed specifically to repel sand and dirt from the sensitive wheel bearings. I advise you to check this one out. Also, as covered in the instruction manual, you need to remove and clean the wheel assemblies once a month and have them checked by your dealer every six months. With the right choice of skates and proper care, you can avoid mistakes like this in the future.

Sincerely,
Candace Parker
Customer Service Representative
Skates Alive!
www.skatesalive.biz
1.800.747.9999

- The salutation is cold and impersonal.
- The tone is immediately accusatory, and the opening paragraph goes on to insult the customer for not following instructions.
- The second paragraph finally delivers the good news but does so in a self-congratulatory way that is likely to destroy whatever goodwill the gesture builds.
- The concluding paragraph continues with the high-handed tone and ends on a negative note.

**Effective**

Write: re: Warranty repair?

File   Edit   View   Insert   Options   Tools   Help

Send   Attach   Security   Save

From:   Candace Parker <candacep@skatesalive.biz>   candacep@skatesalive.biz

To:   steveC955@verizonmail.net

Subject:   re: Warranty repair?

Dear Mr. Cox:

Thank you for contacting us about your in-line skates. Even though your six-month warranty has expired, Skates Alive! is sending you a complete wheel assembly replacement free of charge.

The Fastrax (model NL 562) you purchased is our best-selling and most-reliable skate. However, wheel jams may occur when fine particles of sand block the smooth rotating action of the wheels. As noted in the instruction manual, these skates perform best when used on roadways and tracks that are relatively free of sand. We suggest that you remove and clean the wheel assemblies once a month and have them checked by your dealer every six months.

Given your Florida location, you may want to consider our more advanced Glisto (model NL 988) when you decide to purchase your next pair of skates. The Glisto design protects the wheel assemblies from sand and dirt and should give you years of carefree skating.

We love hearing from our skaters, so keep in touch. All of us at Skates Alive! wish you good times and miles of healthy skating.

Sincerely,
Candace Parker
Customer Service Representative
Skates Alive!
www.skatesalive.biz
1.800.747.9999

- The writer opens by thanking the customer and then delivers the good news.
- The second paragraph explains the cause of the problem and gently suggests that the customer could have prevented it, but does so without insulting or accusing.
- The third paragraph offers a specific suggestion for the customer's next purchase and does so in a positive way.
- The salutation is personal and respectful.
- The closing ends the message on an upbeat, forward-looking note.

**Figure 10.4   Responding to a Claim When the Buyer Is at Fault**
Responding to a claim when the buyer is at fault is a positive gesture, so the content and tone of the message need to reflect that. After all, there's no point in fostering a positive relationship through actions but then undermining that through negative communication. Notice how the poor version sounds like a crabby parent who gives in to a child's demand but sends a mixed message by being highly critical anyway. The improved version is much more subtle, letting the customer know how to take care of his skates, without blaming or insulting him.
*Source:* Used with permission from Microsoft.

## PROVIDING RECOMMENDATIONS AND REFERENCES

People who need endorsements from employers or colleagues (when applying for a job, for example) often request letters of recommendation. These messages used to be a fairly routine matter, but employment recommendations and references have raised some complex legal issues in recent years (see "Can You Get Sued for Writing—or Not Writing—a Recommendation Letter?"). Employees have sued employers and individual managers for providing negative information or refusing to provide letters of recommendation, and employers have sued

Recommendation letters are vulnerable to legal complications, so consult with your company's legal department before writing one.

**Point1 Promotions**

105 E. Madison
Ann Arbor, MI 48103
tel: 800-747-9786
email: info@point1promo.net
www.point1promo.net

November 14, 2013

Ms. Clarice Gailey
Director of Operations
McNally and Associates, Inc.
8688 Southgate Ave.
Augusta, GA 30906

Dear Ms. Gailey:

I am pleased to recommend Talvin Biswas for the marketing position at McNally and Associates. Mr. Biswas has worked with Point1 Promotions as an intern for the past two summers while working toward his degree in marketing and advertising. His duties included customer correspondence, web content updates, and direct-mail campaign planning.

As his supervisor, in addition to knowing his work here, I also know that Mr. Biswas has served as secretary for the International Business Association at the University of Michigan. He tutored other international students in the university's writing center. His fluency in three languages (English, French, and Hindi) and thorough knowledge of other cultures will make him an immediate contributor to your international operations.

Mr. Biswas is a thoughtful and carful professional who will not hesitate to contribute ideas when invited to do so. In addition, because Mr. Biswas learns quickly, he will learn your company's routine with ease.

Mr. Biswas will make an excellent addition to your staff at McNally and Associates. If I can provide any additional information, please call me at the number above. If you prefer to communicate by email, my address is angela_leclerc@point1promo.net.

Sincerely,

*Angela LeClerc*

Angela LeClerc
Vice President, Marketing

LeClerc specifies the duration and nature of the relationship in the body to give credibility to her evaluation.

The opening clearly states the candidate's full name and the specific purpose of the letter.

The body continues with specific examples to support the writer's positive evaluation.

The close summarizes the writer's recommendation and invites further communication.

MyBCommLab Apply Figure 10.5's key concepts. Go to **mybcommlab.com** and follow this path: Course Content → Chapter 10 → **DOCUMENT MAKEOVERS**

**Figure 10.5**  **Effective Recommendation Letter**
This letter clearly states the nature of the writer's relationship to the candidate and provides specific examples to support the writer's endorsements.

other employers for failing to disclose negative information about job candidates. Before you write a letter of recommendation for a former employee or provide information in response to another employer's background check, make sure you understand your company's policies. Your company may refuse to provide anything more than dates of employment and other basic details, for example.[2]

If you decide to write a letter of recommendation or respond to a request for information about a job candidate, your goal is to convince readers that the person being recommended has the characteristics necessary for the job, assignment, or other objective the person is seeking. A successful recommendation letter contains a number of relevant details (see Figure 10.5):

- The candidate's full name
- The position or other objective the candidate is seeking
- The nature of your relationship with the candidate
- Facts and evidence relevant to the candidate and the opportunity
- A comparison of this candidate's potential with that of peers, if available (for example, "Ms. Jonasson consistently ranked in the top 10 percent of her class")
- Your overall evaluation of the candidate's suitability for the opportunity

# Can You Get Sued for Writing—or Not Writing—a Recommendation Letter?

Recommendation letters are classified as routine messages, but with all the legal troubles they can cause employers these days, they've become anything but routine. Over the years, employees have won lawsuits that charged former employers with defamation related to job recommendations. In addition to defamation charges—which can be successfully defended if the "defamatory" statements are proven to be true—employers have been sued by ex-employees who believed that negative letters were written expressly for purposes of revenge. And as if that weren't enough, employers have even sued each other over recommendation letters when the recipient of a letter believed the writer failed to disclose important negative information.

No wonder many companies now refuse to divulge anything more than job titles and dates of employment. But even that doesn't always solve the problem: Ex-employees have been known to sue in retaliation when their employers refused to write on their behalf. As you can imagine, this refusal to write recommendations creates worries for hiring companies. If they can't get any real background information on job candidates, they risk hiring employees who lack the necessary skills or who are disruptive or even dangerous in the workplace.

For companies that let managers write recommendations, what sort of information should or should not be included? Even though the majority of states now have laws protecting companies against recommendation-related lawsuits when the employer acts in good faith, individual cases vary so much that no specific guidelines can ever apply to all cases. However, answering the following questions before drafting a recommendation letter will help you avoid trouble:

- Does the party receiving this personal information have a legitimate right to it?

- Does all the information I've presented relate directly to the job or benefit being sought?
- Have I put the candidate's case as strongly and as honestly as I can?
- Have I avoided overstating the candidate's abilities or otherwise misleading the reader?
- Have I based all my statements on firsthand knowledge and provable facts?
- Have I been consistent in the type of information I provide for every former employee?

No matter what the circumstances, experts also advise that you always consult your human resources or legal department for advice.

## CAREER APPLICATIONS

1. A former employee was often late for work but was an excellent and fast worker who got along well with everyone. Do you think it's important to mention the tardiness to potential employers? If so, how would you handle it?
2. Step outside yourself for a moment and write a letter of recommendation about you from a former employer's perspective. Make sure your letter embodies honesty, integrity, and prudence.

*Sources:* Adapted from "Giving References for Former Employees," Nolo, accessed 30 January 2013, www.nolo.com; "How to Write Reference Letters," National Association of Colleges and Employers website, accessed 5 July 2010, www.naceweb.org; Diane Cadrain, "HR Professionals Stymied by Vanishing Job References," *HR Magazine*, November 2004, 31–40; "Five (or More) Ways You Can Be Sued for Writing (or Not Writing) Recommendation Letters," *Fair Employment Practice Guidelines*, July 2006, 1, 3–4.

---

Keep in mind that every time you write a recommendation, you're putting your own reputation on the line. If the person's shortcomings are so pronounced that you don't think he or she is a good fit for the job, the only choice is to not write the letter at all. Unless your relationship with the person warrants an explanation, simply suggest that someone else might be in a better position to provide a recommendation.

> Remember that you're putting your own reputation on the line when you write a recommendation letter.

## SHARING ROUTINE INFORMATION

Many messages involve sharing routine information, such as project updates and order status notifications (see Figure 10.6 on the next page). Use the opening of these routine messages to state the purpose and briefly mention the nature of the information you are providing. Give the necessary details in the body, and end your message with a courteous close.

Most routine communications are neutral. That is, they stimulate neither a positive nor a negative response from readers. For example, when you send departmental meeting announcements and reminder notices, you'll generally receive a neutral response from your readers (unless the purpose of the meeting is unwelcome). Simply present the factual information in the body of the message and don't worry too much about the reader's attitude toward the information.

**REAL-TIME UPDATES**

LEARN MORE BY VISITING THIS WEBSITE

**Get expert tips on writing (or requesting) a letter of recommendation**

Find helpful advice on employment recommendations, academic recommendations, and character references. Go to http://real-timeupdates.com/bct12 and click on Learn More. If you are using MyBCommLab, you can access Real-Time Updates within each chapter or under Student Study Tools.

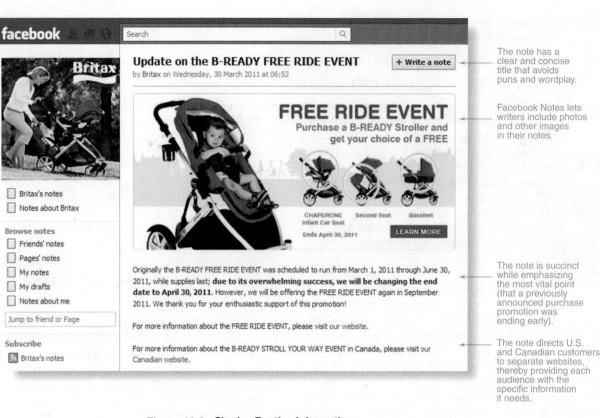

**Figure 10.6 Sharing Routine Information**
Many companies use the Notes tab on their Facebook pages to share routine informational messages with their customers and other parties.
*Source:* Copyright © 2011 by the Reynolds Communications Group.

When sharing routine information
- State the purpose at the beginning and briefly mention the nature of the information you are providing
- Provide the necessary details
- End with a courteous close

Some routine informative messages may require additional care. For instance, policy statements or procedural changes may be good news for a company, perhaps by saving money. However, it may not be obvious to employees that such savings may make additional employee resources available or even lead to pay raises. In instances in which the reader may not initially view the information positively, use the body of the message to highlight the potential benefits from the reader's perspective. (For situations in which negative news will have a profound effect on the recipients, consider the indirect techniques discussed in Chapter 11.)

## ANNOUNCING GOOD NEWS

To develop and maintain good relationships, smart companies recognize that it's good business to spread the word about positive developments. Such developments can include opening new facilities, hiring a new executive, introducing new products or services, or sponsoring community events. Because good news is always welcome, use the direct approach.

A news release, or press release is a message (usually routine, but not always) designed to share information with the news media, although many are now written with customers and other stakeholders in mind as well.

Good-news announcements are often communicated in a **news release**, also known as a *press release*, a specialized document used to share relevant information with the news media. (News releases are also used to announce negative news, such as plant closings.) In most companies, news releases are usually prepared or at least supervised by specially trained writers in the public relations department. The content follows the customary pattern for a positive message: good news followed by details and a positive close. However, traditional news releases have a critical difference: You're not writing directly to the ultimate audience (such as the readers of a newspaper); you're trying to interest an editor or a reporter in a story, and that person will then write the material that is eventually read by the larger audience. To write a successful news release, keep the following points in mind:[3]

- Above all else, make sure your information is newsworthy and relevant to the specific publications or websites to which you are sending it.
- Focus on one subject; don't try to pack a single news release with multiple, unrelated news items.

- Put your most important idea first. Don't force editors to hunt for the news.
- Be brief: Break up long sentences and keep paragraphs short.
- Eliminate clutter, such as redundancy and extraneous facts.
- Be as specific as possible.
- Minimize self-congratulatory adjectives and adverbs; if the content of your message is newsworthy, the media professionals will be interested in the news on its own merits.
- Follow established industry conventions for style, punctuation, and format.

Until recently, news releases were crafted in a way to provide information to reporters, who would then write their own articles if the subject matter was interesting to their readers. Thanks to the Internet and social media, however, the nature of the news release is changing. Many companies now view it as a general-purpose tool for communicating directly with customers and other audiences, creating *direct-to-consumer news releases.* As media expert David Meerman Scott puts it, "Millions of people read press releases directly, unfiltered by the media. You need to be speaking directly to them."[4]

The newest twist on news releases is the *social media release*, which has several advantages over the traditional release (see Figure 10.7). First, the social media release emphasizes bullet-point content over narrative paragraphs so that bloggers, editors, and others can assemble their own stories, rather than having to rewrite the material in a traditional release. Second, as an electronic-only document (a specialized webpage, essentially), the

*The social media release includes share-ready content that is easy to reuse in blog posts, tweets, and other social media formats.*

Additional information is available through these other tabs.

The high-level message is condensed to a single Twitter-friendly "sound bite."

Social media and email buttons make it easy for anyone to share this page.

A variety of product photos are available for download and social sharing.

An embedded clip provides a video version of the news release.

The full-text version of the news release message is available for reading and easy sharing.

The full narrative on the left is "bulletized" here on the right, which helps bloggers and others create their own story. Each bullet also has a Twitter button, which lets readers send the bullet point as an individual tweet.

Related links take readers to the company's main website or the specific product webpage.

**Figure 10.7   Social Media News Release**
The social media release is a news release designed to enable quick and easy sharing via social networks and other media. This particular format was created by the social media agency PitchEngine and emphasizes Twitter-friendly content.
*Source:* Copyright © 2012 by Noodles and Company. Reprinted with permission.

social media release offers the ability to include videos and other multimedia elements. Third, social sharing buttons make it easy for people to help publicize the content.[5]

## FOSTERING GOODWILL

Goodwill is the positive feeling that encourages people to maintain a business relationship.

All business messages should be written with an eye toward fostering positive relationships with audiences, but some messages are written specifically to build goodwill. You can use these messages to enhance your relationships with customers, colleagues, and other businesspeople by sending friendly, even unexpected, notes with no direct business purpose. Whether you're thanking an employee for a job well done or congratulating a colleague for a personal or professional achievement, the small effort to send a goodwill message can have a positive and lasting effect on the people around you.

Many routine messages can be adapted to foster goodwill, either by sharing helpful information or providing an element of entertainment.

In addition to creating messages for a specific goodwill reason, you can craft almost any routine message in a way to build goodwill. Two ways to do so are by providing information your readers might find helpful and by using the content and tone of your message to provide an element of entertainment. For example, if you send monthly billing statements to customers, you can include tips on how to save money by using your products in a more efficient manner.

Using routine messages to entertain customers can be a good way to build goodwill, but it must be done effectively and only when appropriate.

Using routine messages to entertain customers can be an effective goodwill builder if it is done well and doesn't detract from the primary purpose of the message. One of the best-known examples is the shipping notification email message that online music retailer CDBaby sends its customers. Company founder Derek Sivers says the original routine message ("Your order has shipped today. Please let us know if it doesn't arrive. Thank you for your business.") didn't fit his mission to "make people smile." Sivers replaced that short, serious message with a comically over-the-top message that starts with "Your CD has been gently taken from our CD Baby shelves with sterilized contamination-free gloves and placed onto a satin pillow" and continues with such lines as "Our packing specialist from Japan lit a candle and a hush fell over the crowd as he put your CD into the best gold-lined box that money can buy." The message was a hit with customers, who forwarded it to friends and posted it online, which led to thousands of new customers for the young company.[6]

Obviously, attempts to entertain customers must be appropriate for the situation. A funny message is great for a music retailer, but it would not be appropriate for a bank, a hospital, or any other firm that deals with more serious matters.

### Sending Congratulations

Taking note of significant events in someone's personal life helps foster the business relationship.

One prime opportunity for sending goodwill messages is to congratulate individuals or companies for significant business achievements (see Figure 10.8). Other reasons for sending congratulations include highlights in people's personal lives, such as weddings, births, graduations, and success in nonbusiness competitions. You may congratulate business acquaintances on their own achievements or on the accomplishments of a spouse or child. You may also take note of personal events, even if you don't know the reader well. If you're already friendly with the reader, a more personal tone is appropriate.

### Sending Messages of Appreciation

An effective message of appreciation documents a person's contributions.

An important leadership quality is the ability to recognize the contributions of employees, colleagues, suppliers, and other associates. Your praise does more than just make the person feel good; it encourages further excellence. Moreover, a message of appreciation may become an important part of someone's personnel file. So when you write a message of appreciation, try to specifically mention the person or people you want to praise. The brief message that follows expresses gratitude and reveals the happy result:

Thank you and everyone on your team for the heroic efforts you took to bring our servers back up after last Friday's flood. We were able to restore business right on schedule first thing Monday morning. You went far beyond the level of contractual service in restoring our data center within 16 hours. I would especially like to highlight the contribution of networking specialist Julienne Marks, who worked for 12 straight hours to reconnect our Internet service. If I can serve as a reference in your future sales activities, please do not hesitate to ask.

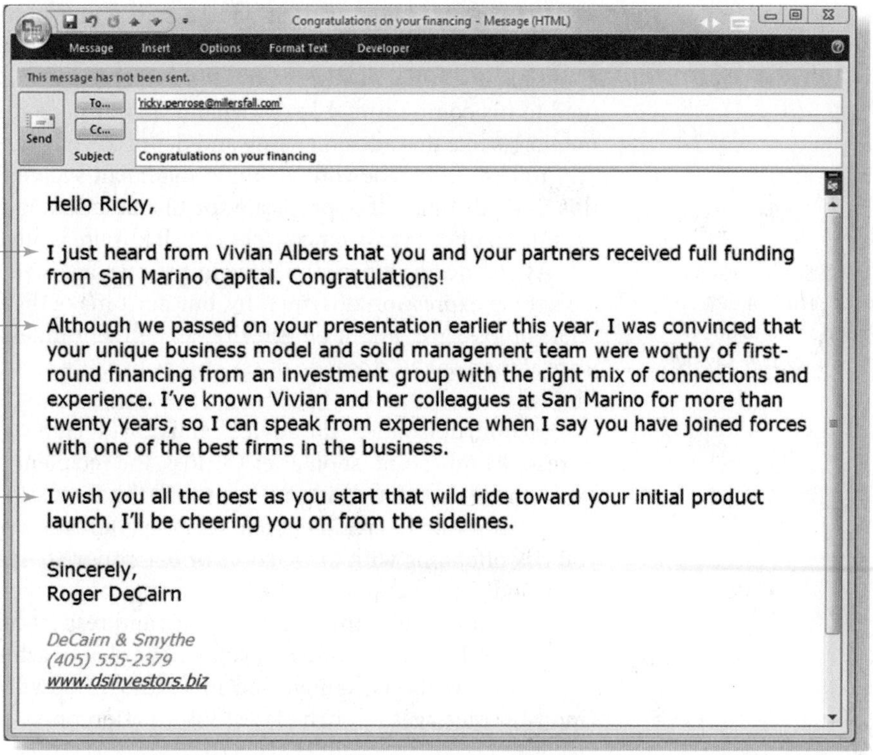
Congratulations on your financing - Message (HTML)

Message Insert Options Format Text Developer

This message has not been sent.

To... 'ricky.penrose@millersfall.com'

Cc...

Subject: Congratulations on your financing

Hello Ricky,

I just heard from Vivian Albers that you and your partners received full funding from San Marino Capital. Congratulations!

Although we passed on your presentation earlier this year, I was convinced that your unique business model and solid management team were worthy of first-round financing from an investment group with the right mix of connections and experience. I've known Vivian and her colleagues at San Marino for more than twenty years, so I can speak from experience when I say you have joined forces with one of the best firms in the business.

I wish you all the best as you start that wild ride toward your initial product launch. I'll be cheering you on from the sidelines.

Sincerely,
Roger DeCairn

*DeCairn & Smythe*
*(405) 555-2379*
*www.dsinvestors.biz*

The opening offers a positive and sincere expression of congratulations.
The body reminds the recipient of their previous meeting and offers specific points about the recipient's worthiness in a way that compliments without exaggerating.
The close maintains the upbeat tone and keeps the focus on the recipient.

**Figure 10.8 Goodwill Messages**
Goodwill messages serve a variety of business functions. In this email message, investor Roger DeCairn congratulates an entrepreneur who had previously sought start-up capital from his firm but later secured funding from another firm. The message may ultimately benefit DeCairn and his company by building goodwill, but it doesn't serve an immediate business purpose.

Hearing a sincere thank you can do wonders for morale.[7] Moreover, in today's electronic media environment, a handwritten thank-you note can be a particularly welcome acknowledgment.[8]

> **REAL-TIME UPDATES**
> LEARN MORE BY READING THIS ARTICLE
>
> **Simple rules for writing effective thank-you notes**
>
> These tips are easy to adapt to any business or social occasions in which you need to express appreciation. Go to http://real-timeupdates.com/bct12 and click on Learn More. If you are using MyBCommLab, you can access Real-Time Updates within each chapter or under Student Study Tools.

## Offering Condolences

**Condolence letters** are brief personal messages written to comfort someone after the death of a loved one. You may have occasion to offer condolences to employees or other business associates (when the person has lost a family member) or to the family of an employee or business associate (when that person has died).

These messages can feel intimidating to write, but they don't need to be. Follow these three principles: short, simple, and sincere. You don't need to produce a work of literary art; the fact that you are writing sends a message that is as meaningful as anything you can say.

The primary purpose of condolence messages is to let the audience know that you and the organization you represent care about the person's loss.

Timing and media choice are important considerations with condolence letters. The sooner your message is received, the more comforting it will be, so don't delay. And unless circumstances absolutely leave you no choice, do not use electronic media. A brief, handwritten note on quality stationery is the way to go.

Open a condolence message with a simple expression of sympathy, such as "I am deeply sorry to hear of your loss" or "I am sorry for your loss." How you continue from there depends on the circumstances and your relationships with the deceased and the person to whom you are writing. For example, if you are writing to the husband of a colleague who recently died and you have never met him, you might continue with "Having worked with Janice for more than a decade, I know what a kind and caring person she was." Such a statement accomplishes two goals: explaining why you in particular are writing and letting the recipient know that his loved one was appreciated in the workplace.

Conversely, if you are writing to a colleague who recently lost a loved one, you might continue with "After meeting Warren at last year's company picnic and hearing your stories about his involvement with your son's soccer league and the many other ways he contributed to his community, I know what a special person he was." Sharing brief and positive memories like this adds meaning and depth to your expression of sympathy.

You can conclude with a simple statement such as "My thoughts are with you during this difficult time." If appropriate for the situation and your relationship, you might also include an offer of assistance. "Please call if there is anything I do for you."

As you decide what to include in the message, keep two points in mind. First, make it a personal expression of sympathy, but don't make the whole message about you and your sense of loss. You might be grieving as well, but unless you, the deceased, and the reader were all personally close, don't say things like "I was so devastated to hear the news about Mollie."

Second, don't offer "life advice," and don't include trite sayings that you may have heard or read. At this point, soon after the loss, the recipient doesn't want your advice, only your sympathy. Also, don't bring religion into the discussion unless you have a close personal relationship with the recipient and religion is already a part of your relationship. Otherwise, you risk offending with unwelcome or inappropriate sentiments.

Condolence letters are the most personal business messages you may ever have to write, so they require the utmost in care and respect for your reader. By keeping the messages simple, short, and sincere, you will be able to achieve the right tone.

To review the tasks involved in writing goodwill messages, see "Checklist: Sending Goodwill Messages." For the latest information on writing routine and positive messages, visit http://real-timeupdates.com/bct12.

*Keep your condolence message focused on the recipient, not on your own emotions, and don't offer "life advice" or trite sayings.*

## CHECKLIST ✔ Sending Goodwill Messages

- Be sincere and honest.
- Don't exaggerate or use vague, grandiose language; support positive statements with specific evidence.
- Use congratulatory messages to build goodwill with clients and colleagues.
- Send messages of appreciation to emphasize how much you value the work of others.
- When sending condolence messages, open with a brief statement of sympathy, then adapt your message based on the circumstances and your relationship with the recipient.

# Quick Learning Guide

## SUMMARY OF LEARNING OBJECTIVES

**1** Outline an effective strategy for writing routine business requests. When writing a routine request, open by stating your specific request. Use the body to justify your request and explain its importance. Close routine requests by asking for specific action (including a deadline, if appropriate) and expressing goodwill. A courteous close contains three important elements: (1) a specific request, (2) information about how you can be reached (if it isn't obvious), and (3) an expression of appreciation or goodwill.

**2** Describe three common types of routine requests. The most common types of routine messages are asking for information or action, asking for recommendations, and making claims and requesting adjustments. Requests for information or action should explain what you want to know or what you want readers to do, why you're making the request, and why it may be in your readers' interest to help you (if applicable). Requests for recommendations should open by stating what it is you are requesting and asking the recipient to write the message in question. The body should list all the information the recipient would need to write the recommendation (refer to an attached résumé, if applicable). The close should contain an expression of appreciation and a deadline, if applicable. To make a claim (a formal complaint about a product or service) or request an adjustment (a settlement of a claim), open with a straightforward statement of the problem, use the body to give a complete explanation of the situation, and close with a polite request to resolve the situation.

**3** Outline an effective strategy for writing routine replies and positive messages. The direct approach works well for routine replies and positive messages because recipients will generally be interested in what you have to say. Place your main idea (the positive reply or the good news) in the opening. Use the body to explain all the relevant details, and close cordially, perhaps highlighting a benefit to your reader.

**4** Describe six common types of routine replies and positive messages. Most routine and positive messages fall into six categories: answers to requests for information and action, grants of claims and requests for adjustment, recommendations, informative messages, good-news announcements, and goodwill messages. Providing answers to requests for information or action is a simple task, often assisted with form responses that can be customized as needed. Granting claims and requests for adjustments is more complicated, and the right response depends on whether the company, the customer, or a third party was at fault. Recommendations also require a careful approach to avoid legal complications; some companies prohibit managers from writing recommendation letters or providing anything beyond basic employment history. Informative messages are often simple and straightforward, but some require extra care if the information affects recipients in a significant way. Good-news announcements are often handled by news releases, which used to be sent exclusively to members of the news media but are now usually made available to the public as well. Finally, goodwill messages, meant to foster positive business relationships, include congratulations, thank-you messages, and messages of condolence. To make goodwill messages effective, make them honest, sincere, and factual.

**adjustment** The settlement of a claim

**claim** A formal complaint made in response to dissatisfaction over a product or service

**condolence letters** Brief personal messages written to comfort someone after the death of a loved one

**news release** Also known as a *press release*, a specialized document traditionally used to share relevant information with the local or national news media; today, many companies issue news releases directly to the public as well

---

CHECKLIST ✓
## Writing Routine Requests

**A. State your request up front.**
- Write in a polite, undemanding, personal tone.
- Use the direct approach because your audience will probably respond favorably to your request.
- Be specific and precise in your request.

**B. Explain and justify your request.**
- Justify the request or explain its importance.
- Explain any potential benefits of responding.
- Ask the most important questions first.
- Break complex requests into individual questions that are limited to only one topic each.

**C. Request specific action in a courteous close.**
- Make it easy to comply by including appropriate contact information.
- Express your gratitude.
- Clearly state any important deadlines for the request.

CHECKLIST ✓
## Making Claims and Requesting Adjustments

- Maintain a professional tone, even if you're extremely frustrated.
- Open with a straightforward statement of the problem.
- Provide specific details in the body.
- Present facts honestly and clearly.
- Politely summarize the desired action in the closing.
- Clearly state what you expect as a fair settlement or ask the reader to propose a fair adjustment.
- Explain the benefits of complying with the request, such as your continued patronage.

---

CHECKLIST ✓
## Writing Routine Replies and Positive Messages

**A. Start with the main idea.**
- Be clear and concise.
- Identify the single most important message before you start writing.

**B. Provide necessary details and explanation.**
- Explain your point completely to eliminate any confusion or lingering doubts.
- Maintain a supportive tone throughout.
- Embed negative statements in positive contexts or balance them with positive alternatives.
- Talk favorably about the choices the customer has made.

**C. End with a courteous close.**
- Let your readers know you have their personal well-being in mind.
- If further action is required, tell readers how to proceed and encourage them to act promptly.

CHECKLIST ✓
## Sending Goodwill Messages

- Be sincere and honest.
- Don't exaggerate or use vague, grandiose language; support positive statements with specific evidence.
- Use congratulatory messages to build goodwill with clients and colleagues.
- Send messages of appreciation to emphasize how much you value the work of others.
- When sending condolence messages, open with a brief statement of sympathy, then adapt your message based on the circumstances and your relationship with the recipient.

---

CHECKLIST ✓
## Granting Claims and Adjustment Requests

**A. Responding when your company is at fault.**
- Be aware of your company's policies in such cases before you respond.
- For serious situations, refer to the company's crisis management plan.
- Start by acknowledging receipt of the claim or complaint.
- Take or assign personal responsibility for resolving the situation.
- Sympathize with the customer's frustration.
- Explain how you have resolved the situation (or plan to).
- Take steps to repair the customer relationship.
- Verify your response with the customer and keep the lines of communication open.

**B. Responding when the customer is at fault.**
- Weigh the cost of complying with or refusing the request.
- If you choose to comply, open with the good news.
- Use the body of the message to respectfully educate the customer about steps needed to avoid a similar outcome in the future.
- Close with an appreciation for the customer's business.

**C. Responding when a third party is at fault.**
- Evaluate the situation and review your company's policies before responding.
- Avoid placing blame; focus on the solution.
- Regardless of who is responsible for resolving the situation, let the customer know what will happen to resolve the problem.

## COMMUNICATION CHALLENGES AT **Get Satisfaction**

After reading the many helpful responses you, as a representative of your company, posted on the Get Satisfaction website, Thor Muller invited you to join the Get Satisfaction team as a customer service specialist; your job is to communicate with the companies that use Get Satisfaction's online services. Take what you've learned in this chapter and put it to good use as you address the following challenges. (Search for a few companies or product names on http://getsatisfaction.com to get a feel for how the system works.)

**INDIVIDUAL CHALLENGE:** When people are frustrated with a problem and are trying to discuss it via a lean medium such as online postings, emotions can sometimes boil over. You've been monitoring a conversation between a representative for one of the companies that uses Get Satisfaction and one of its customers. Over the past couple of days, their online conversation has turned into an ugly argument, with accusations of incompetence and even dishonesty flying back and forth. Although the situation doesn't involve Get Satisfaction directly, you think it reflects poorly on your company—and it certainly isn't doing anybody any good to let this "flame war" keep raging. Write a brief post (which you can email to your instructor) that acknowledges the frustration both sides are obviously feeling and offer to act as an intermediary to help get the problem resolved. Make up any information you need in order to complete the message.

**TEAM CHALLENGE:** Get Satisfaction has just made available an upgrade to its website software in *beta release* form (a free version of software that companies encourage people to use as a way to see if anything needs to be changed or fixed before the official product is released). However, the company hasn't yet announced how much the new upgrade is going to cost when it is officially released, so not surprisingly, more than a few interested customers have written questions about the anticipated price. Small-business owners in particular want to know if a less-expensive version (perhaps with fewer features) will be available to small companies. When you asked your boss for

help in answering this question, he suggested that you send the following response:

> To be as open and transparent about our pricing thinking as possible, I have to be up front: We can't speak to exact pricing yet, because we're still working on those details. We didn't want that to hold up release/use/testing of these new features, which is why we're releasing them on a "try first" beta basis right now, with the caveat that pricing will be a factor in the future for those companies who choose to continue using them.
>
> What we can say is that we are *very* committed to two things:
>
> 1) Making sure that it's a pricing structure that does in fact work both for small companies and large ones, and that if there is a tiered structure, that it scales according to a reliable set of figures/metrics that reflect those size differences.
>
> 2) Always offering a free version that has a minimum level of utility for those companies that can't for whatever reason pay.
>
> We're pretty excited about the new tools and the new functionality and want to see them spread as far and as wide as possible, so that's a significant consideration as we look to our pricing plan as well. But, you know, we've got to pay the bills somehow.
>
> Further updates as events warrant.[9]

This answer provides as much information as the company can release right now, but you think it can be more concise. (It is currently about 200 words.) In teams, as designated by your instructor, have each team member independently revise this message to make it no longer than 100 words. After everyone on the team has written a new draft, have each person share his or her version with the rest of the team. As a team, decide which version is best and then email it to your instructor.

# Test Your Knowledge

To review chapter content related to each question, refer to the indicated Learning Objective.

1. What information should be included in a routine request? [LO-1]
2. Where in a routine message should you state your actual request? [LO-1]
3. What information should you include in a request for a recommendation? [LO-2]
4. How does a claim differ from an adjustment? [LO-2]
5. What is resale information? [LO-3]
6. How does the question of fault affect what you say in a message granting a claim? [LO-4]
7. What is the appropriate strategy for responding to a request for a recommendation about a job candidate whose performance was poor? [LO-4]

8. How can you avoid sounding insincere when writing a goodwill message? [LO-4]
9. What are three principles to follow for writing condolence messages? [LO-4]

# Apply Your Knowledge

To review chapter content related to each question, refer to the indicated Learning Objective.

1. You have a complaint against one of your suppliers, but you have no documentation to back it up. Should you request an adjustment anyway? Why or why not? [LO-2]
2. The latest issue of a local business newspaper names 10 area executives who have exhibited excellent leadership skills in the past year. You are currently searching for a job, and a friend suggests that you write each executive a congratulatory

letter and mention in passing that you are looking for new career opportunities and would appreciate the opportunity for an interview. Is this a smart strategy? Why or why not? [LO-4]

✪ 3. You've been asked to write a letter of recommendation for an employee who worked for you some years ago. You recall that the employee did an admirable job, but you can't remember any specific information at this point. Should you write the letter anyway? Explain. [LO-4]

✪ 4. Your company's error cost an important business customer a new client; you know it, and your customer knows it. Do you apologize, or do you refer to the incident in a positive light without admitting any responsibility? Briefly explain. [LO-4]

## Practice Your Skills

### Messages for Analysis

Read the following messages and then (1) analyze the strengths and weaknesses of each sentence and (2) revise each document so that it follows this chapter's guidelines.

#### Message 10.A: Message Strategies: Routine Requests [LO-2]

I'm fed up with the mistakes that our current accounting firm makes. I run a small construction company, and I don't have time to double-check every bookkeeping entry and call the accountants a dozen times when they won't return my messages. Please explain how your firm would do a better job than my current accountants. You have a good reputation among homebuilders, but before I consider hiring you to take over my accounting, I need to know that you care about quality work and good customer service.

#### Message 10.B: Message Strategies: Requesting an Adjustment [LO-2]

At a local business-supply store, I recently purchased your Negotiator Pro for my computer. I bought the CD because I saw your ad for it in Macworld magazine, and it looked as if it might be an effective tool for use in my corporate seminar on negotiation.

Unfortunately, when I inserted it in my office computer, it wouldn't work. I returned it to the store, but because I had already opened it, they refused to exchange it for a CD that would work or give me a refund. They told me to contact you and that you might be able to send me a version that would work with my computer.

You can send the information to me at the letterhead address. If you cannot send me the correct disc, please refund my $79.95. Thanks in advance for any help you can give me in this matter.

#### Message 10.C: Message Strategies: Responding to Claims and Requests for Adjustments [LO-4]

We read your letter, requesting your deposit refund. We couldn't figure out why you hadn't received it, so we talked to our maintenance engineer, as you suggested. He said you had left one of the doors off the hinges in your apartment in order to get a large sofa through the door. He also confirmed that you had paid him $5.00 to replace the door since you had to turn in the U-Haul trailer and were in a big hurry.

This entire situation really was caused by a lack of communication between our housekeeping inspector and the maintenance engineer. All we knew was that the door was off the hinges when it was inspected by Sally Tarnley. You know that our policy states that if anything is wrong with the apartment, we keep the deposit. We had no way of knowing that George just hadn't gotten around to replacing the door.

But we have good news. We approved the deposit refund, which will be mailed to you from our home office in Teaneck, New Jersey. I'm not sure how long that will take, however. If you don't receive the check by the end of next month, give me a call.

Next time, it's really a good idea to stay with your apartment until it's inspected, as stipulated in your lease agreement. That way, you'll be sure to receive your refund when you expect it. Hope you have a good summer.

#### Message 10.D: Message Strategies: Providing Recommendations [LO-4]

Your letter to Kunitake Ando, president of Sony, was forwarded to me because I am the human resources director. In my job as head of HR, I have access to performance reviews for all of the Sony employees in the United States. This means, of course, that I would be the person best qualified to answer your request for information on Nick Oshinski.

In your letter of the 15th, you asked about Nick Oshinski's employment record with us because he has applied to work for your company. Mr. Oshinski was employed with us from January 5, 1998, until March 1, 2008. During that time, Mr. Oshinski received ratings ranging from 2.5 up to 9.6, with 10 being the top score. As you can see, he must have done better reporting to some managers than to others. In addition, he took all vacation days, which is a bit unusual. Although I did not know Mr. Oshinski personally, I know that our best workers seldom use all the vacation time they earn. I do not know if that applies in this case.

In summary, Nick Oshinski performed his tasks well depending on who managed him.

### Exercises

Each activity is labeled according to the primary skill or skills you will need to use. To review relevant chapter content, you can refer to the indicated Learning Objective. In some instances, supporting information will be found in another chapter, as indicated.

1. **Message Strategies: Routine Requests; Revising for Conciseness [LO-1], Chapter 6** Critique the following closing paragraphs. How would you rewrite each to be concise, courteous, and specific?

   a. I need your response sometime soon so I can order the parts in time for your service appointment. Otherwise, your air-conditioning system may not be in tip-top condition for the start of the summer season.

   b. Thank you in advance for sending me as much information as you can about your products. I look forward to receiving your package in the very near future.

    c. To schedule an appointment with one of our knowledgeable mortgage specialists in your area, you can always call our hotline at 1-800-555-8765. This is also the number to call if you have more questions about mortgage rates, closing procedures, or any other aspect of the mortgage process. Remember, we're here to make the home-buying experience as painless as possible.

2. **Message Strategies: Routine Responses; Media Skills: Email [LO-3], Chapter 7** Revise the following short email messages so they are more direct and concise; develop a subject line for each revised message.

    a. I'm contacting you about your recent email request for technical support on your cable Internet service. Part of the problem we have in tech support is trying to figure out exactly what each customer's specific problem is so that we can troubleshoot quickly and get you back in business as quickly as possible. You may have noticed that in the online support request form, there are a number of fields to enter your type of computer, operating system, memory, and so on. While you did tell us you were experiencing slow download speeds during certain times of the day, you didn't tell us which times specifically, nor did you complete all the fields telling us about your computer. Please return to our support website and resubmit your request, being sure to provide all the necessary information; then we'll be able to help you.

    b. Thank you for contacting us about the difficulty you had collecting your luggage at Denver International Airport. We are very sorry for the inconvenience this has caused you. As you know, traveling can create problems of this sort regardless of how careful the airline personnel might be. To receive compensation, please send us a detailed list of the items that you lost and complete the following questionnaire. You can email it back to us.

    c. Sorry it took us so long to get back to you. We were flooded with résumés. Anyway, your résumé made the final 10, and after meeting three hours yesterday, we've decided we'd like to meet with you. What is your schedule like for next week? Can you come in for an interview on June 15 at 3:00 p.m.? Please get back to us by the end of this workweek and let us know if you will be able to attend. As you can imagine, this is our busy season.

    d. We're letting you know that because we use over a ton of paper a year and because so much of that paper goes into the wastebasket to become so much more environmental waste, starting Monday, we're placing white plastic bins outside the elevators on every floor to recycle that paper and in the process, minimize pollution.

3. **Message Strategies: Routine and Positive Messages; Revising for Conciseness [LO-3], Chapter 6** Rewrite the following sentences so that they are direct and concise. If necessary, break your answer into two sentences.

    a. We wanted to invite you to our special 40% off by-invitation-only sale; the sale is taking place on November 9.

    b. We wanted to let you know that we are giving a tote bag and a voucher for five iTunes downloads with every $50 donation you make to our radio station.

    c. The director planned to go to the meeting that will be held on Monday at a little before 11 a.m.

    d. In today's meeting, we were happy to have the opportunity to welcome Paul Eccelson, who reviewed the shopping cart function on our website and offered some great advice; if you have any questions about these new forms, feel free to call him at his office.

4. **Message Strategies: Responding to Claims and Requests for Adjustments [LO-4]** Your company markets a line of automotive accessories for people who like to "tune" their cars for maximum performance. A customer has just written a furious email, claiming that a supercharger he purchased from your website didn't deliver the extra engine power he expected. Your company has a standard refund process to handle situations such as this, and you have the information you need to inform the customer about that. You also have information that could help the customer find a more compatible supercharger from one of your competitors, but the customer's email message is so abusive that you don't feel obligated to help. Is this an appropriate response? Why or why not?

5. **Message Strategies: Writing Positive Messages; Media Skills: Microblogging [LO-4], Chapter 8** Locate an online announcement for a new product you find interesting or useful. Read enough about the product to be able to describe it to someone else in your own words and then writer four Twitter tweets: one to introduce the product to your followers and three follow-on tweets that describe three particularly compelling features or benefits of the product.

6. **Message Strategies: Writing Goodwill Messages [LO-4]** Identify someone in your life who has recently accomplished a significant achievement, such as graduating from high school or college, completing a major project, or winning an important professional award. Write a brief congratulatory message using the guidelines presented in the chapter.

## Expand Your Skills

### Critique the Professionals

Locate an online example of a news release in which a company announces good news, such as a new product, a notable executive hire, an expansion, strong financial results, or an industry award. Analyze the release using the bullet list on pages 272–273 as a guide. In what ways did the writer excel? What aspects of the release could be improved? Using whatever medium your instructor requests, write a brief analysis of the piece (no more than one page), citing specific elements from the piece and support from the chapter.

### Sharpening Your Career Skills Online

Bovée and Thill's Business Communication Web Search, at http://businesscommunicationblog.com/websearch, is a unique research tool designed specifically for business communication research. Use the Web Search function to find a website, video, PDF document, podcast, or PowerPoint presentation that offers advice on writing goodwill messages such as thank-you notes or congratulatory letters. Write a brief email message to your instructor, describing the item that you found and summarizing the career skills information you learned from it.

## Cases

## Routine Requests

**1. Message Strategies: Requesting Information [LO-2]** You are writing a book about the advantages and potential pitfalls of using online collaboration systems for virtual team projects. You would like to include several dozen real-life examples from people in a variety of industries. Fortunately, you publish a highly respected blog on the subject, with several thousand regular readers.

**Your task:** Write a post for your blog that asks readers to submit brief descriptions of their experiences using collaboration tools for team projects. Ask them to email stories of how well a specific system or approach worked for them. Explain that they will receive an autographed copy of the book as thanks and that they will need to sign a release form if their stories are used. In addition, emphasize that you would like to use real names—of people, companies, and software—but you can keep the anecdotes anonymous if readers require. To stay on schedule, you need to have these stories by May 20.

**2. Message Strategies: Requesting a Recommendation [LO-2]** One of your colleagues, Katina Vander, was recently promoted to department manager and now serves on the company's strategic planning committee. At its monthly meeting next week, the committee will choose an employee to lead an important market research project that will help define the company's product portfolio for the next five years.

You worked side by side with Vander for five years, so she knows your abilities well and has complimented your business insights on many occasions. You know that because she has only recently been promoted to manager, she needs to build credibility among her peers and will therefore be cautious about making such an important recommendation. On the other hand, making a stellar recommendation for such an important project would show that she has a good eye for talent—an essential leadership trait.

**Your task:** Write an email message to Vander, telling her that you are definitely interested in leading the project and asking her to put in a good word for you with the committee. Mention four attributes that you believe would serve you well in the role: a dozen years of experience in the industry, an engineering degree that helps you understand the technologies involved in product design, a consistent record of excellent or exceptional ratings in annual employee evaluations, and the three years you spent working in the company's customer support group, which gave you a firsthand look at customer satisfaction and quality issues. Make up any additional details you need to write the message.

**3. Message Strategies: Routine Requests; Media Skills: Microblogging [LO-2], Chapter 8** A growing number of companies now monitor Twitter to pick up on messages from frustrated customers. Given the public visibility of such complaints, smart companies are eager to jump to the customer's aid.

**Your task:** Identify a real customer support situation in your own life in which you need information or some form of resolution from a company. This could be anything from a broken product that you're having trouble getting repaired to an erroneous charge on a credit card. If you can't identify a situation in your life, "borrow" a situation from a friend, a student in another class, or a family member that you can try to resolve on Twitter.

This will be a "live" exercise that consumes a company's time and resources, so make sure you have a real problem to solve. Also, your messages will be available for everyone to see, so be sure to communicate in a calm, respectful manner, and do not disclose any confidential or personal information in your tweets. (If your problem requires sharing such information, the company should ask you to switch to direct messaging for privacy.)

First, search Twitter to see if the company has an account. If the company is on Twitter, its account should show up in the "People results for . . ." listing. Make sure you choose the most appropriate account; many companies have more than one Twitter account. When you've located the right account, follow it from your Twitter account.

Next, send a Tweet that includes the company's account name and describes your problem clearly and as completely as possible within the character limit. Double-check the spelling of the account name, the company name, and any product name you use. Then be sure to monitor your Twitter account closely to watch for a message from the company, then send a follow-up response in a timely fashion. Work with the customer support person who contacts you to resolve the problem. Along the way, keep a copy of all the messages you send and receive.

As your instructor directs, write a summary or prepare a presentation of your experience and your analysis of the effectiveness of Twitter as a customer service tool.

**4. Message Strategies: Requesting a Recommendation [LO-2]** After five years of work in the human resources department at Cell Genesys (a company that is developing cancer treatment drugs), you were laid off in a round of cost-cutting moves that rippled through the biotech industry in recent years. The good news is that you found stable employment in the grocery distribution industry. The bad news is that in the three years since you left Cell Genesys, you have truly missed working in the exciting biotechnology field and having the opportunity to be a part of something as important as helping people recover from life-threatening diseases. You know careers in biotech are uncertain, but you have a few dollars in the bank now, and you're willing to ride that rollercoaster again.

**Your task:** Draft an email to Calvin Morris, your old boss at Cell Genesys, reminding him of the time you worked together and asking him to write a letter of recommendation for you.[10]

## IM SKILLS

**5. Message Strategies: Requesting Information [LO-2]**  Many companies now provide presales and postsales customer support through some form of instant messaging or online chat function. As a consumer looking for information, you'll get better service if you can frame your requests clearly and succinctly.

**Your task:**  Imagine that you need to replace your old laptop computer, but you're not sure whether to go with another laptop or switch to a tablet or perhaps one of the new tablet/laptop hybrids. Think through the various ways you will use this new device, from researching and note-taking during class to watching movies and interacting with friends on social media. Now imagine you're in a chat session with a sales representative from a computer company, and this person has asked how he or she can help you. Draft a message (no more than 100 words) that summarizes your computing and media requirements and asks the representative to recommend the right type of device for you.

## TEXT MESSAGING SKILLS

**6. Message Strategies: Requesting Information [LO-2]**  The vast Consumer Electronics Show (CES) is the premier promotional event in the industry. More than 130,000 industry insiders from all over the world come to see the exciting new products on display from nearly 1,500 companies—everything from video game gadgets to Internet-enabled refrigerators with built-in computer screens. You've just stumbled on a video game controller that has a built-in webcam to allow networked gamers to see and hear each other while they play. Your company also makes game controllers, and you're worried that your customers will flock to this new controller-cam. You need to know how much buzz is circulating around the show: Have people seen it? What are they saying about it? Are they excited about it?

**Your task:**  Compose a text message to your colleagues at the show, alerting them to the new controller-cam and asking them to listen for any buzz it might be generating among the attendees at the Las Vegas Convention Center and the several surrounding hotels where the show takes place. Here's the catch: Your text-messaging service limits messages to 160 characters, including spaces and punctuation, so your message can't be any longer than this.[11]

## EMAIL SKILLS

**7. Message Strategies: Requesting an Adjustment [LO-2]**  Love at first listen is the only way to describe the way you felt when you discovered SongThrong.com. You enjoy dozens of styles of music, from Afrobeat and Tropicalia to mainstream pop and the occasional blast of industrial metal, and SongThrong.com has them all for only $9.99 a month. You can explore every genre imaginable, listening to as many tracks as you like for a fixed monthly fee. The service sounded too good to be true—and sadly, it was. The service was so unreliable that you began keeping note of when it was unavailable. Last month, it was down for all or part of 12 days—well over a third of the month. As much as you like it, you've had enough.

**Your task:**  Write an email to support@songthrong.com, requesting a full refund. To get the $9.99 monthly rate, you prepaid for an entire year ($119.88), and you've been a subscriber for two months now. You know the service has been out for at least part of the time on 12 separate days last month, and while you didn't track outages during the first month, you believe it was about the same number of days.

## LETTER WRITING SKILLS

**8. Message Strategies: Requesting an Adjustment [LO-2]**  As a consumer, you've probably bought something that didn't work right or paid for a service that did not turn out the way you expected. Maybe it was a pair of jeans with a rip in a seam that you didn't find until you got home or a watch that broke a week after you bought it. Or maybe your family hired a lawn service to do some yardwork and no one from the company showed up on the day promised, and when the gardeners finally appeared, they did not do what they'd been hired for but instead did other things that wound up damaging valuable plants.

**Your task:**  Choose an incident from your own experience and write a claim letter, asking for a refund, repair, replacement, or other adjustment. You'll need to include all the details of the transaction, plus your contact address and phone number. If you can't think of such an experience, make up details for an imaginary situation. If your experience is real, you might want to mail the letter. The reply you receive will provide a good test of your claim-writing skills.

## EMAIL SKILLS

**9. Message Strategies: Requesting Action [LO-2]**  You head up the corporate marketing department for a nationwide chain of clothing stores. The company has decided to launch a new store-within-a-store concept, in which a small section of each store will showcase "business casual" clothing. To ensure a successful launch of this new strategy, you want to get input from the best retailing minds in the company. You also know it's important to get regional insights from around the country, because a merchandising strategy that works in one area might not succeed in another.

**Your task:**  Write an email message to all 87 store managers, asking them to each nominate one person to serve on an advisory team (managers can nominate themselves if they are local market experts). Explain that you want to find people with at least five years of retailing experience, a good understanding of the local business climate, and thorough knowledge of the local retail competition. In addition, the best candidates will be good team players who are comfortable collaborating long distance, using virtual meeting technologies. Also, explain that while you are asking each of the 87 stores to nominate someone, the team will be limited to no more than eight people. You've met many of the store managers, but not all of them, so be sure to introduce yourself at the beginning of the message.

# Routine Messages

## EMAIL SKILLS

**10. Message Strategies: Granting Claims [LO-4]**  Your company sells flower arrangements and gift baskets. Holidays are always a rush, and the overworked staff makes the occasional mistake. Last week, somebody made a big one. As a furious email message from a customer named Anders Ellison explains, he ordered a Valentine's Day bouquet for his wife, but the company sent a bereavement arrangement instead.

**Your task:** Respond to Ellison's email message, apologizing for the error, promising to refund all costs that Ellison incurred, informing him that the correct arrangement will arrive tomorrow (and he won't be charged anything for it), and offering Ellison his choice of any floral arrangement or gift basket for free on his wife's birthday.

## EMAIL SKILLS

**11. Message Strategies: Granting Claims [LO-4]** Like many of the staff at Razer (www.razerzone.com), you are an avid game player. You can therefore sympathize with a customer who got so excited during a hotly contested game that he slammed his Razer Anansi keyboard against his chair in celebration. Razer products are built for serious action, but no keyboard can withstand a blow like that. However, in the interest of building goodwill among the online gaming community, your manager has approved a free replacement. This sort of damage is rare enough that the company isn't worried about unleashing a flood of similar requests.

**Your task:** Respond to Louis Hapsberg's email request for a replacement, in which he admitted to inflicting some abuse on this keyboard. Explain, tongue in cheek, that the company is "rewarding" him with a free keyboard in honor of his massive gaming win, but gently remind him that even the most robust electronic equipment needs to be used with care.

## BLOGGING SKILLS

**12. Message Strategies: Providing Routine Information; Compositional Modes: Tutorials [LO-4]** Austin, Texas, advertising agency GSD&M Idea City brainstorms new advertising ideas using a process it calls *dynamic collaboration*. A handpicked team of insiders and outsiders is briefed on the project and given a key question or two to answer. The team members then sit down at computers and anonymously submit as many responses as they can within five minutes. The project moderators then pore over these responses, looking for any sparks that can ignite new ways of understanding and reaching out to consumers.

**Your task:** For these brainstorming sessions, GSD&M recruits an eclectic mix of participants from inside and outside the agency—figures as diverse as economists and professional video gamers. To make sure everyone understands the brainstorming guidelines, prepare a message to be posted on the project blog. In your own words, convey the following four points as clearly and succinctly as you can:

- **Be yourself.** We want input from as many perspectives as possible, which is why we recruit such a diverse array of participants. Don't try to get into what you believe is the mindset of an advertising specialist; we want you to approach the given challenge using whatever analytical and creative skills you normally employ in your daily work.
- **Create, don't edit.** Don't edit, refine, or self-censor while you're typing during the initial five-minute session. We don't care if your ideas are formatted beautifully, phrased poetically, or even spelled correctly. Just crank 'em out as quickly as you can.
- **It's about the ideas, not the participants.** Just so you know up front, all ideas are collected anonymously. We can't tell who submitted the brilliant ideas, the boring ideas, or the already-tried-that ideas. So while you won't get personal credit, you can also be crazy and fearless. Go for it!

- **The winning ideas will be subjected to the toughest of tests.** Just in case you're worried about submitting ideas that could be risky, expensive, or difficult to implement—don't fret. As we narrow down the possibilities, the few that remain will be judged, poked, prodded, and assessed from every angle. In other words, let us worry about containing the fire; you come up with the sparks.[12]

## PODCASTING SKILLS / PORTFOLIO BUILDER

**13. Message Strategies: Providing Routine Information; Media Skills: Podcasting [LO-4]** As a training specialist in Winnebago Industry's human resources department, you're always on the lookout for new ways to help employees learn vital job skills. While watching a production worker page through a training manual while learning how to assemble a new recreational vehicle, you get what seems to be a great idea: Record the assembly instructions as audio files that workers can listen to while performing the necessary steps. With audio instructions, they wouldn't need to keep shifting their eyes between the product and the manual—and constantly losing their place. They could focus on the product and listen for each instruction. Plus, the new system wouldn't cost much at all; any computer can record the audio files, and you'd simply make them available on an intranet site for download into smartphones, tablets, and digital music players.

**Your task:** You immediately run your new idea past your boss, who has heard about podcasting but doesn't think it has any place in business. He asks you to prove the viability of the idea by recording a demonstration. Choose a process you engage in yourself—anything from replacing the strings on a guitar to sewing a quilt to changing the oil in a car—and write a brief (one page or less) description of the process that could be recorded as an audio file. Think carefully about the limitations of the audio format as a replacement for printed text (for instance, do you need to tell people to pause the audio while they perform a time-consuming task?). If directed by your instructor, record your instructions as a podcast.

## BLOGGING SKILLS / PORTFOLIO BUILDER

**14. Message Strategies: Providing Routine Information [LO-4]** You are normally an easygoing manager who gives your employees a lot of leeway in using their own personal communication styles. However, the weekly staff meeting this morning pushed you over the edge. People were interrupting one another, asking questions that had already been answered, sending text messages during presentations, and exhibiting just about every other poor listening habit imaginable.

**Your task:** Review the advice in Chapter 2 on good listening skills and then write a post for the internal company blog. Emphasize the importance of effective listening and list at least five steps your employees can take to become better listeners.

# Routine Replies

## EMAIL SKILLS

**15. Message Strategies: Routine Responses [LO-4]** As administrative assistant to Walmart's director of marketing, you have just received a request from the company's webmaster to analyze Walmart's website from a consumer's point of view.

**Your task:** Visit www.walmart.com and browse through the site, considering the language, layout, graphics, and overall ease of use. In particular, look for aspects of the site that might be confusing or frustrating—annoyances that could prompt shoppers to abandon their quests and head to a competitor such as Target or Amazon. Summarize your findings and recommendations in an email message that could be sent to the webmaster.

## EMAIL SKILLS

**16. Message Strategies: Routine Responses [LO-4]** As the owner of Paradise Sportswear in Hawaii, Robert Hedin found himself in a battle against the Earth itself when red dirt started seeping into his warehouse and ruining his inventory. Fortunately, a friend suggested that he turn his troubles into opportunities, and he came up with Red Dirt Shirts, all made with dye created from the troublesome local dirt. Hedin's Red Dirt Sportswear designs turned out to be so popular that he added a new line, Lava Blues, made with real Hawaiian lava rock.

"You can make 500 shirts with a bucket of dirt," says Hedin with a grin as he shows you around the operation on your first day.

Recently, Hedin decided to finally give in to all the requests he's received from retail outlets on the mainland. Buyers kept coming to the islands on vacation, discovering Hedin's "natural" sportswear in local stores, and begging him to set up a deal. For a long time, his answer was no; he simply couldn't handle the extra work.

But now Hedin's hired you as a sales representative to help him slowly expand distribution on the mainland, starting with one store: Surf's Up, far away from ocean surf in Chicago, Illinois. He figures that with less competition than he'd find on either coast, his island-influenced sportswear will be a big hit in Chicago, especially in the dead of winter.

**Your task:** Write a positive response to the email received from Surf's Up buyer Ronald Draeger, who says he fell in love with the Paradise clothing concept while on a surfing trip to Maui. Let him know he'll have a temporary, four-month exclusive and that you'll be sending a credit application and other materials by snail mail.[13]

## MICROBLOGGING SKILLS

**17. Message Strategies: Routine Announcements [LO-4]** As a way to give back to the communities in which it does business, your company supports the efforts of the United Way, a global organization that works to improve lives through education, income stability, and healthy living choices.[14] Each year, your company runs a fundraising campaign in which employees are encouraged to donate money to their local United Way agencies, and it also grants employees up to three paid days off to volunteer their time for the United Way. This year, you are in charge of the company's campaign.

**Your task:** Compose a four-message sequence to be posted on the company's internal microblogging system (a private version of Twitter, essentially). The messages are limited to 200 characters, including spaces and punctuation. The first message will announce the company's annual United Way volunteering and fundraising campaign (make up any details you need), and the other three messages will explain the United Way's efforts in the areas of education, income stability, and healthy living. Visit www.unitedway.org/our-work to learn more about these three areas.

## EMAIL SKILLS

**18. Message Strategies: Providing Recommendations [LO-4]** You enjoy your duties as manager of the women's sportswear department at Clovine's—a chain of moderate to upscale department stores in south Florida. You especially enjoy being able to recommend someone for a promotion. Today, you received an email message from Rachel Cohen, head buyer for women's apparel. She is looking for a smart, aggressive employee to become assistant buyer for the women's sportswear division. Clovine's likes to promote from within, and Rachel is asking all managers and supervisors for likely candidates. You have just the person she's looking for.

Jennifer Ramirez is a salesclerk in the designer sportswear boutique of your main store in Miami, and she has caught your attention. She's quick, friendly, and good at sizing up a customer's preferences. Moreover, at recent department meetings, she has shared some insightful observations about fashion trends in south Florida.

**Your task:** Write an email reply to Rachel Cohen, head buyer, women's sportswear, recommending Jennifer Ramirez and evaluating her qualifications for the promotion. Rachel can check with the human resources department about Jennifer's educational and employment history; you're mainly interested in conveying your positive impression of Jennifer's potential for advancement.

## LETTER WRITING SKILLS  /  TEAM SKILLS

**19. Message Strategies: Providing Recommendations [LO-4]** As a project manager at Orbitz, one of the largest online travel services in the world, you've seen plenty of college interns in action. However, few have impressed you as much as Maxine "Max" Chenault. For one thing, she learned how to navigate the company's content management system virtually overnight and always used it properly, whereas other interns sometimes left things in a hopeless mess. She asked lots of intelligent questions about the business. You've been teaching her blogging and website design principles, and she's picked them up rapidly. Moreover, she is always on time, professional, and eager to assist. Also, she didn't mind doing mundane tasks.

On the downside, Chenault is a popular student. Early on, you often found her busy on the phone planning her many social activities when you needed her help. However, after you had a brief talk with her, this problem vanished.

You'll be sorry to see Chenault leave when she returns to school in the fall, but you're pleased to respond when she asks you for a letter of recommendation. She's not sure where she'll apply for work after graduation or what career path she'll choose, so she asks you to keep the letter fairly general.

**Your task:** Working with a team of your classmates, discuss what should and should not be in the letter. Prepare an outline based on your discussion and then draft the letter.

## SOCIAL NETWORKING SKILLS

**20. Message Strategies: Writing Routine Informative Messages; Composition Modes: Summarizing [LO-4]** As energy costs trend ever upward and more people become attuned to the environmental and geopolitical complexities of petroleum-based energy, interest in solar, wind, and other alternative energy sources continues to grow. In locations with high *insolation*, a measure of cumulative sunlight, solar panels can be cost-effective solutions over the long term. However, the upfront costs are still daunting for most homeowners. To help lower the entry barrier, the Foster City, California–based firm SolarCity now leases solar panels to homeowners for monthly payments that are less than their current electricity bills.[15]

**Your task:** Visit www.solarcity.com, click on "Residential," and then click "SolarLease" to read about the leasing program. Next, study SolarCity's presence on Facebook (www.facebook.com/solarcity) to get a feel for how the company presents itself in a social networking environment. Now assume that you have been assigned the task of writing a brief summary of the SolarLease program that will appear on the Notes tab of SolarCity's Facebook page. In your own language and in no more than 200 words, write an introduction to the SolarLease program and email it to your instructor.

# Positive Messages

## WEB WRITING SKILLS

**21. Message Strategies: Good News Messages [LO-4]** Amateur and professional golfers in search of lower scores want to find clubs that are optimized for their individual swings. This process of *club fitting* has gone decidedly high tech in recent years, with fitters using Doppler radar, motion-capture video, and other tools to evaluate golfers' swing and ball flight characteristics. Hot Stix Golf (www.hotstixgolf.com) is a leader in this industry, having fitted more than 200 professionals and thousands of amateurs.[16]

**Your task:** Imagine that you are the communications director at the Indian Wells Golf Resort (www.indianwellsgolfresort.com) in Indian Wells, California. Your operation has just signed a deal with Hot Stix to open a fitting center on site. Write a three-paragraph article that could be posted on the resort website. The first paragraph should announce the news that the Hot Stix center will open in six months, the second should summarize the benefits of club fitting, and the third should offer a brief overview of the services that will be available at the Indian Wells Hot Stix Center. Information on club fitting can be found on the Hot Stix website; make up any additional information you need to complete the article.

## BLOGGING SKILLS / PORTFOLIO BUILDER

**22. Message Strategies: Good-News Messages [LO-4]** Most people have heard of the Emmy, Grammy, Oscar, and Tony awards for television, music, movies, and theater performances, but fewer know what the Webby award is all about. Sponsored by the International Academy of Digital Arts and Sciences, the Webbys shine a spotlight on the best in website design, interactive media, and online film and video.[17]

**Your task:** Visit www.webbyawards.com, click on Winners, and choose one of the companies listed a winner in the Websites or Interactive Advertising categories. Now imagine you are the chief online strategist for this company, and you've just been informed your company won a Webby. Winning this award is a nice validation of the work your team has put in during the last year, and you want to share their success with the entire company. Write a brief post for the internal company blog, describing what the Webby awards are, explaining why they are a significant measure of accomplishment in the online industry, and congratulating the employees in your department who contributed to the successful web effort.

## BLOGGING SKILLS / PORTFOLIO BUILDER

**23. Message Strategies: Good-News Messages [LO-4]** In both print and online communication, it's hard to escape the impact of Adobe Systems, the company behind Acrobat, Photoshop, Flash, InDesign, and other programs used to create and share textual and visual content. Even as its impact on the communication professions continues to increase, though, Adobe works to decrease its impact on the natural environment. The company invests in a variety of techniques and technologies to reduce its energy usage, and Adobe was the first company ever to receive the Platinum Certification from the U.S. Green Building Council.

**Your task:** Write a one- or two-paragraph post for an internal blog at Adobe, letting employees know how well the company is doing in its efforts to reduce energy usage and thanking employees for the energy-saving ideas they've submitted and the individual efforts they've made to reduce, reuse, and recycle. You can learn more about the company's efforts and accomplishments at http://www.adobe.com/corporate-responsibility/environment.html.[18]

## SOCIAL NETWORKING SKILLS

**24. Message Strategies: Goodwill Messages [LO-4]** As the largest employer in Loganville, your construction company provides jobs, purchasing activity, and tax receipts that make up a vital part of the city's economy. In your role as CEO, however, you realize that the relationship between your company and the community is mutually beneficial, and the company could not survive without the efforts of its employees, the business opportunities offered by a growing marketplace, and the physical and legal infrastructure that the government provides.

The company's dependence on the community was demonstrated in a moving and immediate way last weekend, when a powerful storm pushed the Logan River past flood stage and threatened to inundate your company's office and warehouse facilities. More than 200 volunteers worked alongside your employees through the night to fill and stack sandbags to protect your buildings, and the city council authorized the deployment of heavy equipment and additional staff to help in the emergency effort. As you watched the water rise nearly 10 feet high behind the makeshift dike, you realized that the community came together to save your company.

**Your task:** Write a post for your company's Facebook page, thanking the citizens and government officials of Loganville for their help in protecting the company's facilities during the storm. Use your creativity to make up any details you need to write a 100- to 200-word message.

## LETTER WRITING SKILLS

**25. Message Strategies: Goodwill Messages [LO-4]** Shari Willison worked as a geologist in your civil engineer firm for 20 years before succumbing to leukemia. With only a few dozen employees, the company has always been a tight-knit group, and you feel like you've lost a good friend in addition to a valued employee.

**Your task:** Write a letter of condolence to Willison's husband, Arthur, and the couple's teenaged children, Jordan and Amy. You have known all three socially through a variety of company holiday parties and events over the years. Make up any details you need.

# MyBCommLab

Go to **mybcommlab.com** for Auto-graded writing questions as well as the following Assisted-graded writing questions:

**10-1.** Should you use the direct or indirect approach for most routine messages? Why? [LO-1]

**10-2.** Why is it good practice to explain why replying to a request could benefit the reader? [LO-1]

**10-3.** Mybcommlab Only—comprehensive writing assignment for this chapter.

# Endnotes

1. Get Satisfaction website, accessed 30 January 2013, http://getsatisfaction.com; Dan Fost, "On the Internet, Everyone Can Hear You Complain," *New York Times*, 25 February 2008, www.nytimes.com; Ray Wang, "Executive Profiles: Disruptive Tech Leaders In Social Business—Wendy Lea, Get Satisfaction," *Forbes*, 8 June 2011, www.forbes.com.

2. "How to Write Reference Letters," National Association of Colleges and Employers website, accessed 5 July 2010, www.naceweb.org; "Five (or More) Ways You Can Be Sued for Writing (or Not Writing) Reference Letters," *Fair Employment Practices Guidelines*, July 2006, 1, 3.

3. Fraser P. Seitel, *The Practice of Public Relations*, 9th ed. (Upper Saddle River, N.J.: Prentice Hall, 2004), 402–411; *Techniques for Communicators* (Chicago: Lawrence Ragan Communication, 1995), 34, 36.

4. David Meerman Scott, *The New Rules of Marketing and PR* (Hoboken, N.J.: Wiley, 2007), 62.

5. Shel Holz, "Next-Generation Press Releases," CW Bulletin, September 2009, www.iabc.com; Steph Gray, "Baby Steps in Social Media News Releases," Helpful Technology blog, 15 May 2009, http://blog.helpfultechnology.com.

6. Derek Sivers, "The Most Successful Email I Ever Wrote," Business Insider, 6 June 2012, www.businessinsider.com.

7. Pat Cataldo, "Op-Ed: Saying 'Thank You' Can Open More Doors Than You Think," Penn State University Smeal College of Business website, accessed 19 February 2008, www.smeal.psu.edu.

8. Jackie Huba, "Five Must-Haves for Thank-You Notes," Church of the Customer Blog, 16 November 2007, www.churchofthecustomer.com.

9. Adapted from an answer on Get Satisfaction website, 26 September 2008, http://getsatisfaction.com.

10. Adapted from Tom Abate, "Need to Preserve Cash Generates Wave of Layoffs in Biotech Industry," *San Francisco Chronicle*, 10 February 2003, www.sfgate.com.

11. Adapted from CES website, accessed 18 July 2005, www.cesweb.org.

12. Adapted from GSD&M Idea City website, accessed 7 July 2010, www.ideacity.com; Burt Helm, "Wal-Mart, Please Don't Leave Me," *BusinessWeek*, 9 October 2006, 84–89.

13. "Entrepreneurs Across America," *Entrepreneur Magazine*, accessed 12 June 1997, www.entrepreneur.com.

14. United Way website, accessed 30 January 2013, www.unitedway.org.

15. Adapted from SolarCity website, accessed 7 July 2010, www.solarcity.com.

16. Adapted from Hot Stix Golf website, accessed 8 February 2011, www.hotstixgolf.com.

17. The Webby Awards website, accessed 30 January 2013, www.webbyawards.com.

18. Adapted from Adobe website, accessed 8 February 2011, www.adobe.com; Jeff Nachtigal, "It's Easy and Cheap Being Green," *Fortune*, 16 October 2006, 53; "Adobe Wins Platinum Certification Awarded by U.S. Green Building Council," press release, 3 July 2006, www.adobe.com.

## LEARNING OBJECTIVES

After studying this chapter, you will be able to

**1** Apply the three-step writing process to negative messages.

**2** Explain how to use the direct approach effectively when conveying negative news.

**3** Explain how to use the indirect approach effectively when conveying negative news.

**4** Explain the importance of maintaining high standards of ethics and etiquette when delivering negative messages.

**5** Describe successful strategies for sending negative messages on routine business matters.

**6** List the important points to consider when conveying negative organizational news.

**7** Describe successful strategies for sending negative employment-related messages.

### COMMUNICATION CLOSE-UP AT
## Chargify http://chargify.com

If you've ever purchased anything online using a credit or debit card, you've used some form of an automated billing system. From a consumer's point of view, in which all you do is fill in a form and a charge eventually shows up on your monthly statement, billing looks fairly simple. However, many tasks need to be accomplished behind the scenes to make billing work, and they need to be done accurately, quickly, and securely. Many e-commerce companies therefore turn to specialists such as Boston-based Chargify to handle this vital business function.

Chargify charges its e-commerce clients flat monthly fees based on the number of customers *they* have. This tiered pricing plan keeps costs low for e-commerce startups that still have few revenue-generating customers. Up until late 2010, the lowest

D. Hurst / Alamy

Chargify, which offers online billing services to other companies, caused a ruckus among its own customer base when it raised prices without giving any advance notice.

tier in Chargify's pricing plan had an extremely attractive price point—it was free.

The idea behind the free tier was to attract e-commerce companies still in their startup phase; as they grew, they would advance into the higher tiers and become paying clients. However, Chargify discovered that many companies in the free tier grew very slowly, if at all, and Chargify wound up supporting a lot of users that weren't bringing in revenue.

To generate enough money to support the dependable, sustainable company that its clients needed, Chargify cofounder David Hauser realized he needed to raise prices, and that included charging lowest-tier clients for the first time. The company announced its new pricing structure in October 2010—and immediately came under attack from many of its clients for the price increases, for the lack of any advance notice, and for Chargify's refusal to "grandfather" existing customers under their original pricing plans. Some called the company "greedy" or "stupid," and a few went so far as to accuse it of bait-and-switch tactics. As bloggers and commentators across the Internet piled on, the technology news site TechCrunch summed up with the situation with an article that began, "It's been a rough day for Chargify . . ."

After spending two long days responding to criticisms on Twitter, industry blogs, and other venues, Hauser wrote an unusually frank blog post titled "How to Break the Trust of Your Customers in Just One Day: Lessons Learned from a Major Mistake." He said the company made "a massive mistake" in the way it handled the changes to its pricing model. By failing to alert customers well in advance of the change, he continued, Chargify "broke a trust that we had developed with our customers over a long period of time, and will take much to repair. We should have communicated our need and desire to remove free plans and provided more information about how this would happen, and over a period of time leading up to the change."

The kinds of services Chargify provides take money to deliver, and the price increases were necessary, but everyone involved agrees that the situation was not handled well. Hauser and his team will continue to learn new lessons as they expand Chargify, but you can bet they won't initiate any new price increases without giving their customers plenty of warning.[1]

# Using the Three-Step Writing Process for Negative Messages

David Hauser and the rest of the executive team at Chargify (profiled in the chapter-opening Communication Close-Up) are experienced and successful entrepreneurs, but even they discovered how tricky it can be to share unexpected and unwelcome news with audiences that have a lot riding on the information. Communicating negative information is a fact of life for all business professionals, whether it's saying no to a request, sharing unpleasant or unwelcome information, or issuing a public apology. With the techniques you'll learn in this chapter, however, you can communicate unwelcome news successfully while minimizing unnecessary stress for everyone involved.

Depending on the situation, you can have as many as five distinct goals when communicating negative information: (1) to convey the bad news, (2) to gain acceptance for the bad news, (3) to maintain as much goodwill as possible with your audience, (4) to maintain a good image for your organization, and (5) if appropriate, to reduce or eliminate the need for future correspondence on the matter. Five goals are clearly a lot to accomplish in one message, so careful planning and execution are particularly critical with negative messages.

## STEP 1: PLANNING A NEGATIVE MESSAGE

When planning negative messages, you can't avoid the fact that your audience does not want to hear what you have to say. To minimize the damage to business relationships and to encourage the acceptance of your message, analyze the situation carefully so you can better understand the context in which the recipient will process your message.

Be sure to consider your purpose thoroughly—whether it's straightforward (such as rejecting a job applicant) or more complicated (such as drafting a negative performance review, in which you not only give the employee feedback on past performance but also help the person develop a plan to improve future performance). With a clear purpose and your audience's needs in mind, identify and gather the information your audience requires in order to understand and accept your message. Negative messages can be intensely personal to the recipient, and in many cases recipients have a right to expect a thorough explanation of your answer.

**1 LEARNING OBJECTIVE**
Apply the three-step writing process to negative messages.

Negative messages can have as many as five goals:
- Give the bad news
- Ensure acceptance of the bad news
- Maintain reader's goodwill
- Maintain organization's good image
- Minimize or eliminate future correspondence on the matter, as appropriate

Analysis, investigation, and adaptation help you avoid alienating your readers.

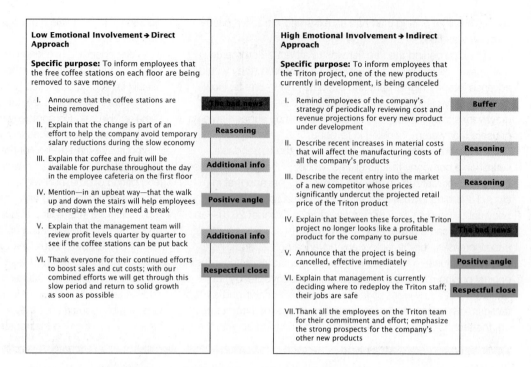

**Figure 11.1** **Comparing the Direct and Indirect Approaches for Negative Messages**
The direct and indirect approaches differ in two important ways: the position of the bad news within the sequence of message points and the use of a *buffer* in the indirect approach. ("Using the Indirect Approach for Negative Messages" on page 294 explains the use of a buffer.) Both these messages deal with changes made in response to negative financial developments, but the second example represents a much higher emotional impact for readers, so the indirect approach is called for in that case. Figure 11.2 explains how to choose the right approach for each situation.

When preparing negative messages, choose the medium with care.

Selecting the right medium is also important. For instance, bad news for employees should be delivered in person whenever possible. This helps guards their privacy, demonstrates respect, and gives them an opportunity to ask questions. Doing so isn't always possible or feasible, though, so you will have times when you need to share important negative information through written or electronic media.

Defining your main idea in a negative message is often more complicated than simply saying no. For instance, if you need to respond to a hardworking employee who requested a raise, your message might go beyond saying no to explaining how she can improve her performance by working smarter, not just harder.

Appropriate organization helps readers accept your negative news.

Finally, the organization of a negative message requires particular care. One of the most critical planning decisions is choosing whether to use the direct or indirect approach (see Figure 11.1). A negative message using the direct approach opens with the bad news, proceeds to the reasons for the situation or the decision, and ends with a positive statement aimed at maintaining a good relationship with the audience. In contrast, the indirect approach opens with the reasons behind the bad news before presenting the bad news itself.

To help decide which approach to take in any situation you encounter, ask yourself the following questions:

You need to consider a variety of factors when choosing between direct and indirect approaches for negative messages.

- **Do you need to get the reader's attention immediately?** If the situation is an emergency, or if someone has ignored repeated messages, the direct approach can help you get attention quickly.
- **Does the recipient prefer a direct style of communication?** Some recipients prefer the direct approach no matter what, so if you know this, go with direct.
- **How important is this news to the reader?** For minor or routine scenarios, the direct approach is nearly always best. However, if the reader has an emotional investment in

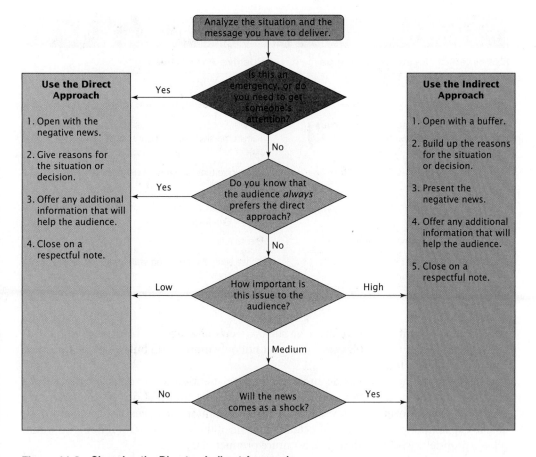

**Figure 11.2 Choosing the Direct or Indirect Approach**
Following this decision tree will help you decide whether the direct or indirect approach is better in a given situation. Of course, use your best judgment as well. Your relationship with the audience could affect your choice of approaches, for example.

the situation or the consequences to the reader are considerable, the indirect approach is often better, particularly if the bad news is unexpected

- **Will the bad news come as a shock?** The direct approach is fine for many business situations in which people understand the possibility of receiving bad news. However, if the bad news might come as a shock to readers, use the indirect approach to help them prepare for it.

Figure 11.2 offers a convenient decision tree to help you decide which approach to use.

## STEP 2: WRITING A NEGATIVE MESSAGE

When you are adapting a negative message to your audience, pay close attention to effectiveness and diplomacy. After all, your audience does not want to hear bad news or might disagree strongly with you, so messages perceived as being unclear or unkind will amplify the audience's stress. "Continuing with a Clear Statement of the Bad News" on page 296 offers advice on conveying unpleasant news with care and tact. Cultural expectations also play a role, from the organizational culture within a company to the regional variations around the world.

The disappointing nature of negative messages requires that you maintain your audience focus and be as sensitive as possible to audience needs. For example, internal audiences often have different expectations regarding negative messages than external audiences do. In some cases, the two groups can interpret the news in different or even opposite ways. Employees will react negatively to news of an impending layoff, for instance, but company shareholders might welcome the news as evidence that management is trying to control

Compared to external audiences, internal audiences often expect more detail in negative messages.

| TABLE 11.1 | Choosing Positive Words | |
|---|---|
| **Examples of Negative Phrasings** | **Positive Alternatives** |
| Your request *doesn't make any sense*. | Please clarify your request. |
| The *damage won't be fixed* for a week. | The item will be repaired next week. |
| Although it wasn't *our fault*, there will be an *unavoidable delay* in your order. | We will process your order as soon as we receive an aluminum shipment from our supplier, which we expect to happen within 10 days. |
| You are clearly *dissatisfied*. | I recognize that the product did not live up to your expectations. |
| I was *shocked* to learn that you're *unhappy*. | Thank you for sharing your concerns about your shopping experience. |
| *Unfortunately*, we haven't received it. | The item hasn't arrived yet. |
| The enclosed statement is *wrong*. | Please verify the enclosed statement and provide a correct copy. |

costs. In addition, if a negative message such as news of a layoff is being sent to internal and external audiences, employees will expect not only more detail but also to be informed before the public is told.

You may need to adjust the content of negative messages for various external audiences.

Negative messages to outside audiences require attention to the diverse nature of the audience and the concern for confidentiality of internal information. A single message might have a half-dozen audiences, all with differing opinions and agendas. You may not be able to explain things to the level of detail that some of these people want if doing so would release proprietary information such as future product plans.

If your credibility hasn't already been established with the audience, lay out your qualifications for making the decision in question. Recipients of negative messages who don't think you are credible are more likely to challenge your decision or reject your message. And, as always, projecting and protecting your company's image are prime concerns; if you're not careful, a negative answer could spin out of control into negative feelings about your company.

When you use language that conveys respect and avoids an accusing or demeaning tone, you protect your audience's pride. This kind of communication etiquette is always important, but it demands special care with negative messages. Moreover, you can ease the sense of disappointment by using positive words rather than negative, counterproductive ones (see Table 11.1).

### STEP 3: COMPLETING A NEGATIVE MESSAGE

The need for careful attention to detail continues as you complete your message. Revise your content to make sure everything is clear, complete, and concise—bearing in mind that even small flaws are likely to be magnified in readers' minds as they react to the negative news. Produce clean, professional documents and proofread carefully to eliminate mistakes. Finally, be sure to deliver messages promptly; withholding or delaying bad news can be unethical, even illegal. See Figure 11.3 for a message that conveys negative information clearly and concisely.

# Using the Direct Approach for Negative Messages

**2 LEARNING OBJECTIVE**
Explain how to use the direct approach effectively when conveying negative news.

A negative message using the direct approach opens with the bad news, proceeds to the reasons for the situation or the decision, and ends with a positive statement aimed at maintaining a good relationship with the audience. Depending on the circumstances, the message may also offer alternatives or a plan of action to fix the situation under discussion. Stating the bad

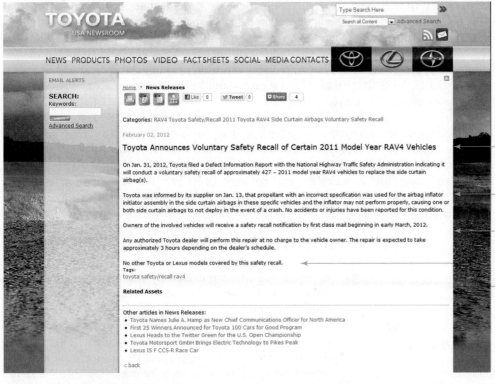

**Figure 11.3   Meeting Audience Needs in a Direct-Approach Message**
Toyota uses the direct approach in this message regarding a voluntary safety recalling involving a small number of vehicles. The message opens with the announcement and then continues with a concise explanation of the situation and information about what the company is going to do next and what the affected customers need to do next. The close assures readers that no other Toyota products are involved. *Source:* Image courtesy of Toyota Motor Sales, U.S.A., Inc. Used by permission.

news at the beginning can have two advantages: It makes a shorter message possible, and it allows the audience to reach the main idea of the message in less time.

## OPENING WITH A CLEAR STATEMENT OF THE BAD NEWS

No matter what the news is, come right out and say it, but maintain a calm, professional tone that keeps the focus on the news and not on individual failures or other personal factors. Also, if necessary, explain or remind the reader why you're writing.

## PROVIDING REASONS AND ADDITIONAL INFORMATION

In most cases, you follow the direct opening with an explanation of why the news is negative. The extent of your explanation depends on the nature of the news and your relationship with the reader. For example, if you want to preserve a long-standing relationship with an important customer, a detailed explanation could well be worth the extra effort such a message would require.

However, you will encounter some situations in which explaining negative news is neither appropriate nor helpful, such as when the reasons are confidential, excessively complicated, or irrelevant to the reader. To maintain a cordial working relationship with the reader, you might want to explain why you can't provide the information.

Should you apologize when delivering bad news? The answer isn't quite as simple as one might think, partly because the notion of *apology* is hard to pin down. To some people, it simply means an expression of sympathy that something negative has happened to another person. At the other extreme, it means admitting fault and taking responsibility for specific compensations or corrections to atone for the mistake.

Some experts have advised that a company should never apologize, even when it knows it has made a mistake, as the apology might be taken as a confession of guilt that could

Use the direct approach when your negative answer or information will have minimal personal impact.

The amount of detail you should provide depends on your relationship with the audience.

Apologies can have legal ramifications, but refusing to apologize out of fear of admitting guilt can damage a company's relationships with its stakeholders.

be used against the company in a lawsuit. However, several states have laws that specifi- cally prevent expressions of sympathy from being used as evidence of legal liability. In fact, judges, juries, and plaintiffs tend to be more forgiving of companies that express sympathy for wronged parties; moreover, an apology can help repair a company's reputation. Re- cently, some prosecutors have begun pressing executives to publicly admit guilt and apolo- gize as part of the settlement of criminal cases—unlike the common tactic of paying fines but refusing to admit any wrongdoing.[2]

The best general advice in the event of a serious mistake or accident is to immediately and sincerely express sympathy and offer help if appropriate, without admitting guilt; then seek the advice of your company's lawyers before elaborating. As one survey concluded, "The risks of making an apology are low, and the potential reward is high."[3]

If you do apologize, make it a real apology. Don't say "I'm sorry if anyone was of- fended" by what you did—this statement implies that you're not sorry at all and that it's the other party's fault for being offended.[4] For example, when Sony's PlayStation Network was breached and disabled by hackers, CEO Howard Stringer included the following statement in a post on the company's blog: "As a company we—and I—apologize for the incon- venience and concern caused by this attack."[5] Note that he did not say "*if* anyone was inconvenienced" or "*if* the attack caused any concern."

Note that you can also express sympathy with someone's plight without suggesting that you are to blame. For example, if a customer damaged a product through misuse and suf- fered a financial loss as a result of not being able to use the product, you can say something along the lines of "I'm sorry to hear of your difficulties." This demonstrates sensitivity without accepting blame.

## CLOSING ON A RESPECTFUL NOTE

After you've explained the negative news, close the message in a manner that respects the im- pact the negative news is likely to have on the recipient. If appropriate, consider offering your readers an alternative solution if you can and if doing so is a good use of your time. Look for opportunities to include positive statements, but avoid creating false hopes or writing in a way that seems to suggest that something negative didn't just happen to the recipient. Ending on a false positive can leave readers feeling "disrespected, disregarded, or deceived."[6]

In many situations, an important aspect of a respectful close is describing the actions being taken to avoid similar mistakes in the future. Offering such explanations can under- line the sincerity of an apology because doing so signals that the person or organization is serious about not repeating the error.

# Using the Indirect Approach for Negative Messages

**3 LEARNING OBJECTIVE** Explain how to use the indirect approach effectively when conveying negative news.

Use the indirect approach when some preparation will help your audience accept your bad news.

The indirect approach helps prepare readers for the bad news by presenting the reasons for it first. However, the indirect approach is *not* meant to obscure bad news, delay it, or limit your responsibility. Rather, the purpose of this approach is to ease the blow and help readers accept the situation. When done poorly, the indirect approach can be disrespectful and even unethical. But when done well, it is a good example of audience-oriented communication crafted with attention to ethics and etiquette. Showing consideration for the feelings of others is never dishonest.

## OPENING WITH A BUFFER

A well-written buffer establishes common ground with the reader.

Messages using the indirect approach open with a **buffer**: a neutral, noncontroversial state- ment that establishes common ground with the reader (refer to Figure 11.1). A good buffer can express your appreciation for being considered (if you're responding to a request), assure the reader of your attention to the request, or indicate your understanding of the reader's needs. A good buffer also needs to be relevant and sincere.

In contrast, a poorly written buffer might trivialize the reader's concerns, divert attention from the problem with insincere flattery or irrelevant material, or mislead the reader into thinking your message actually contains good news.

*Poorly written buffers mislead or insult the reader.*

Consider these possible responses to a manager of the order-fulfillment department who requested some temporary staffing help from your department (a request you won't be able to fulfill):

Our department shares your goal of processing orders quickly and efficiently. ◄──── *Establishes common ground with the reader and validates the concerns that prompted the original request—without promising a positive answer*

As a result of the last downsizing, every department in the company is running shorthanded. ◄──── *Establishes common ground, but in a negative way that downplays the recipient's concerns*

You folks are doing a great job over there, and I'd love to be able to help out. ◄──── *Potentially misleads the reader into concluding that you will comply with the request*

Those new state labor regulations are driving me crazy over here; how about in your department? ◄──── *Trivializes the reader's concerns by opening with an irrelevant issue*

Only the first of these buffers can be considered effective; the other three are likely to damage your relationship with the other manager—and lower his or her opinion of you. Table 11.2 shows several types of effective buffers you could use to tactfully open a negative message.

Given the damage that a poorly composed buffer can do, consider every buffer carefully before you send it. Is it respectful? Is it relevant? Does it avoid any chance of misleading the reader? Does it provide a smooth transition to the reasons that follow? If you can answer yes to every question, you can proceed confidently to the next section of your message. However, if any nagging doubts suggest that your buffer sounds insincere or misleading, it probably is, in which case you'll need to rewrite it.

**TABLE 11.2 Types of Buffers**

| Buffer Type | Strategy | Example |
| --- | --- | --- |
| Agreement | Find a point on which you and the reader share similar views. | We both know how hard it is to make a profit in this industry. |
| Appreciation | Express sincere thanks for receiving something. | Your check for $127.17 arrived yesterday. Thank you. |
| Cooperation | Convey your willingness to help in any way you realistically can. | Employee Services is here to assist all associates with their health insurance, retirement planning, and continuing education needs. |
| Fairness | Assure the reader that you've closely examined and carefully considered the problem, or mention an appropriate action that has already been taken. | For the past week, we have had our bandwidth monitoring tools running around the clock to track your actual upload and download speeds. |
| Good news | Start with the part of your message that is favorable. | We have credited your account in the amount of $14.95 to cover the cost of return shipping. |
| Praise | Find an attribute or an achievement to compliment. | The Stratford Group clearly has an impressive record of accomplishment in helping clients resolve financial reporting problems. |
| Resale | Favorably discuss the product or company related to the subject of the letter. | With their heavy-duty, full-suspension hardware and fine veneers, the desks and file cabinets in our Montclair line have long been popular with value-conscious professionals. |
| Understanding | Demonstrate that you understand the reader's goals and needs. | So that you can more easily find the printer with the features you need, we are enclosing a brochure that describes all the Epson printers currently available. |

## PROVIDING REASONS AND ADDITIONAL INFORMATION

An effective buffer serves as a transition to the next part of your message, in which you build up the explanations and information that will culminate in your negative news. An ideal explanation section leads readers to your conclusion before you come right out and say it. In other words, the reader has followed your line of reasoning and is ready for the answer. By giving your reasons effectively, you help maintain focus on the issues at hand and defuse the emotions that always accompany significantly bad news. In the blog post that announced Chargify's new pricing model (see page 288), for example, CEO Lance Walley explained how the company's costs had risen as it worked to improve the reliability and security of its services.[7]

*Phrase your reasons to signal the negative news ahead.*

As you lay out your reasons, guide your reader's response by starting with the most positive points first and moving forward to increasingly negative ones. Be concise, but provide enough detail for the audience to understand your reasons. You need to convince your audience that your decision is justified, fair, and logical. If appropriate, you can use the explanation section to suggest how the negative news might in fact benefit your reader in some way—but only if that is true and only if you can do so without offending your audience.

*Don't hide behind "company policy" when you deliver bad news; present logical answers instead.*

Avoid hiding behind company policy to cushion your bad news. If you say, "Company policy forbids our hiring anyone who does not have two years' supervisory experience," you imply that you won't consider anyone on his or her individual merits. Skilled and sympathetic communicators explain company policy (without referring to it as "policy") so that the audience can try to meet the requirements at a later time. Consider this response to an employee:

*Shows the reader that the decision is based on a methodical analysis of the company's needs and not on some arbitrary guideline*

*Establishes the criteria behind the decision and lets the reader know what to expect*

> Because these management positions are quite challenging, the human resources department has researched the qualifications needed to succeed in them. The findings show that the two most important qualifications are a bachelor's degree in business administration and two years' supervisory experience.

This paragraph does a good job of stating reasons for the refusal:

*Well-written reasons are*
- *Detailed*
- *Tactful*
- *Individualized*
- *Unapologetic if no one is at fault*
- *Positive*

- It provides enough detail to logically support the refusal.
- It implies that the applicant is better off avoiding a program in which he or she might fail.
- It shows that the company's policy is based on experience and careful analysis.
- It doesn't offer an apology for the decision because no one is at fault.
- It avoids negative personal expressions (such as "You do not meet our requirements").

Even valid, well-thought-out reasons won't convince every reader in every situation. However, if you've done a good job of laying out your reasoning, you've done everything you can to prepare the reader for the main idea, which is the negative news itself.

## CONTINUING WITH A CLEAR STATEMENT OF THE BAD NEWS

After you've thoughtfully and logically established your reasons and readers are prepared to receive the bad news, you can use three techniques to convey the negative information as clearly and as kindly as possible. First, deemphasize the bad news:

*To handle bad news carefully*
- *Deemphasize the bad news visually and grammatically*
- *Use a conditional statement, if appropriate*
- *Tell what you did do, not what you didn't do*

- Minimize the space or time devoted to the bad news—without trivializing it or withholding any important information.
- Subordinate bad news in a complex or compound sentence ("My department is already shorthanded, so I'll need all my staff for at least the next two months"). This construction presents the bad news in the middle of the sentence, the point of least emphasis.
- Embed bad news in the middle of a paragraph or use parenthetical expressions ("Our profits, which are down, are only part of the picture").

*Don't disguise bad news when you emphasize the positive.*

However, keep in mind that it's possible to abuse deemphasis. For instance, if the primary point of your message is that profits are down, it would be inappropriate to marginalize that news by burying it in the middle of a sentence. State the negative news clearly and then make a smooth transition to any positive news that might balance the story.

Second, if appropriate, use a conditional (*if* or *when*) statement to imply that the audience could have received, or might someday receive, a favorable answer ("When you have more managerial experience, you are welcome to reapply"). Such a statement could motivate applicants to improve their qualifications. However, you must avoid any suggestion that you might reverse the decision you've just made and refrain from any phrasing that could give a rejected applicant false hope.

Third, emphasize what you can do or have done rather than what you cannot do. Say "We sell exclusively through retailers, and the one nearest you that carries our merchandise is . . ." rather than "We are unable to serve you, so please call your nearest dealer." Also, by implying the bad news, you may not need to actually state it, thereby making the bad news less personal ("Our development budget for next year is fully committed to our existing slate of projects"). By focusing on the facts and implying the bad news, you make the impact less personal.

When implying bad news, however, be sure your audience will be able to grasp the entire message—including the bad news. Withholding negative information or overemphasizing positive information is unethical and unfair to your reader. If an implied message might lead to uncertainty, state your decision in direct terms. Just be sure to avoid overly blunt statements that are likely to cause pain and anger:

| Instead of This | Write This |
|---|---|
| I *must refuse* your request. | I will be out of town on the day you need me. |
| We *must deny* your application. | The position has been filled. |
| I *am unable* to grant your request. | Contact us again when you have established . . . |
| We *cannot afford to* continue the program. | The program will conclude on May 1. |
| *Much as I would like to* attend . . . | Our budget meeting ends too late for me to attend. |
| We *must turn down* your extension request. | Please send in your payment by June 14. |

## CLOSING ON A RESPECTFUL NOTE

As with the direct approach, the close in the indirect approach offers an opportunity to emphasize your respect for your audience, even though you've just delivered unpleasant news. Express best wishes without ending on a falsely upbeat note. If you can find a positive angle that's meaningful to your audience, by all means consider adding it to your conclusion. However, don't try to pretend that the negative news didn't happen or that it won't affect the reader. Suggest alternative solutions if such information is available and doing so is a good use of your time. If you've asked readers to decide between alternatives or to take some action, make sure that they know what to do, when to do it, and how to do it. Whatever type of conclusion you use, follow these guidelines:

A positive close
- Builds goodwill
- Offers a suggestion for action
- Provides a look toward the future

- **Avoid an uncertain conclusion.** If the situation or decision is final, avoid statements such as "I trust our decision is satisfactory," which imply that the matter is open to discussion or negotiation.
- **Manage future correspondence.** Encourage additional communication *only* if you're willing to discuss the situation further. (If you're not, avoid statements such as "If you have further questions, please write.")
- **Express optimism, if appropriate.** If the situation might improve in the future, share that with your readers if it's relevant. However, don't suggest the possibility of a positive change if you don't have insight that it might happen.
- **Be sincere.** Steer clear of clichés that are insincere in view of the bad news. (If you can't help, don't say, "If we can be of any help, please contact us.")

Keep in mind that the close is the last thing audience members have to remember you by. Even though they're disappointed, leave them with the impression that they were treated with respect.

# Maintaining High Standards of Ethics and Etiquette

**4** LEARNING OBJECTIVE
Explain the importance of maintaining high standards of ethics and etiquette when delivering negative messages.

All business messages demand attention to ethics and etiquette, of course, but these considerations take on special importance when you are delivering bad news—for several reasons. First, a variety of laws and regulations dictate the content and delivery of many business messages with potentially negative content, such as the release of financial information by a public company. Second, negative messages can have a significant negative impact on the lives of those receiving them. Even if the news is conveyed legally and conscientiously, good ethical practice demands that these situations be approached with care and sensitivity. Third, emotions often run high when negative messages are involved, for both the sender and the receiver. Senders need to manage their own emotions and consider the emotional state of their audiences.

For example, in a message announcing or discussing workforce cutbacks, you have the emotional needs of several stakeholder groups to consider. The employees who lost their jobs are likely to experience fear about their futures and possibly a sense of betrayal. The employees who kept their jobs are likely to feel anxiety about the long-term security of their jobs, the ability of company management to turn things around, and the level of care and respect the company has for its employees. These "survivors" may also feel guilty about keeping their jobs while some colleagues lost theirs. Outside the company, investors, suppliers, and segments of the community affected by the layoffs (such as retailers and homebuilders) will have varying degrees of financial interest in the outcome of the decision. Writing such messages requires careful attention to all these needs, while balancing respect for the departing employees with a positive outlook on the future.

The challenge of sending—and receiving—negative messages can tempt one to delay, downplay, or distort the bad news (see "Ethics Detective: Solving the Case of the Deceptive Soft Sell").[8] However, doing so may be unethical and even illegal. In recent years, numerous companies have been sued by shareholders, consumers, employees, and government regulators for allegedly withholding or delaying negative information in such areas as company finances, environmental hazards, and product safety. In many of these cases, the problem was slow, incomplete, or inaccurate communication between the company and external stakeholders. In others, problems stemmed from a reluctance to send or receive negative news within the organization.

Sharing bad news effectively requires commitment from everyone in the organization.

Effectively sharing bad news within an organization requires commitment from everyone involved. Employees must commit to sending negative messages when necessary and to doing so in a timely fashion, even when that is unpleasant or difficult. Conversely, managers must commit to maintaining open communication channels, truly listening when employees have negative information to share, and not punishing employees who deliver bad news.

Employees who observe unethical or illegal behavior within their companies and are unable to resolve the problems through normal channels may have no choice but to resort to **whistleblowing**, expressing their concerns internally through company ethics hotlines—or externally through social media or the news media if they perceive no other options. The decision to "blow the whistle" on one's own employer is rarely easy or without consequences; more than 80 percent of whistleblowers in one survey said they were punished in some way for coming forward with their concerns.[9] Although whistleblowing is sometimes characterized as "ratting on" colleagues or managers, it has an essential function. According to international business expert Alex MacBeath, "Whistleblowing can be an invaluable way to alert management to poor business practice within the workplace. Often whistleblowing can be the only way that information about issues such as rule breaking, criminal activity, cover-ups, and fraud can be brought to management's attention before serious damage is suffered."[10] Recognizing the value of this feedback, many companies have formal reporting mechanisms that give employees a way to voice ethical and legal concerns to management. Various government bodies have also instituted protections for whistleblowers, partly in recognition of the role that workers play in food safety and other vital areas.[11]

Negative situations can put your sense of self-control and business etiquette to the test.

Finally, recognize that some negative news scenarios will test your self-control and tempt you to respond with a personal attack. Customer service employees often undergo training specifically to help them keep their own emotions on an even keel when they are

**ETHICS DETECTIVE**

# Solving the Case of the Deceptive Soft Sell

You and your colleagues are nervous. Sales have been declining for months, and you see evidence of budget tightening all over the place—the fruit and pastries have disappeared from the coffee stations, accountants are going over expense reports with magnifying glasses, and managers are slow to replace people who leave the company. Instant messages fly around the office; everyone wants to know if anyone has heard anything about layoffs.

The job market in your area is weak, and you know you might have to sell your house—in one of the weakest housing markets in memory—and move your family out of state to find another position in your field. If your job is eliminated, you're ready to cope with the loss, but you need as much time as possible. You breathe a sigh of relief when the following item from the CEO appears on the company's internal blog:

> With news of workforce adjustments elsewhere in our industry, we realize many of you are concerned about

the possibility here. I'd like to reassure all of you that we remain confident in the company's fundamental business strategy, and the executive team is examining all facets of company operations to ensure our continued financial strength.

The message calms your fears. Should it?

## ANALYSIS

A month later, the CEO announces a layoff of 20 percent of the company's workforce—nearly 700 people. You're shocked by the news because you felt reassured by the blog posting from last month. In light of what happened, you retrieve a copy of the newsletter and reread the CEO's message. Does it seem ethical now? Why or why not? If you had been in charge of writing this newsletter item and your hands were tied because you couldn't come out and announce the layoffs yet, how would you have rewritten the message?

on the receiving end of anger or criticism from upset customers.[12] However, keep in mind that negative messages can have a lasting impact on the people who receive them and the people who send them. As a communicator, you have a responsibility to minimize the negative impact of your negative messages through careful planning and sensitive, objective writing. As much as possible, focus on the actions or conditions that led to the negative news, not on personal shortcomings or character issues. Develop a reputation as a professional who can handle the toughest situations with dignity.

For a reminder of successful strategies for creating negative messages, see "Checklist: Creating Negative Messages."

## CHECKLIST ✔ Creating Negative Messages

A. **Choose the better approach.**
- Consider using the direct approach when the audience is aware of the possibility of negative news, when the reader is not emotionally involved in the message, when you know that the reader would prefer the bad news first, when you know that firmness is necessary, and when you want to discourage a response.
- Consider using the indirect approach when the news is likely to come as a shock or surprise, when your audience has a high emotional investment in the outcome, and when you want to maintain a good relationship with the audience.

B. **For the indirect approach, open with an effective buffer.**
- Establish common ground with the audience.
- Validate the request, if you are responding to a request.
- Don't trivialize the reader's concerns.
- Don't mislead the reader into thinking the coming news might be positive.

C. **Provide reasons and additional information.**
- Explain why the news is negative.
- Adjust the amount of detail to fit the situation and the audience.

- Avoid explanations when the reasons are confidential, excessively complicated, or irrelevant to the reader.
- If appropriate, state how you plan to correct or respond to the negative news.
- Seek the advice of company lawyers if you're unsure what to say.

D. **Clearly state the bad news.**
- State the bad news as positively as possible, using tactful wording.
- To help protect readers' feelings, deemphasize the bad news by minimizing the space devoted to it, subordinating it, or embedding it.
- If your response might change in the future if circumstances change, explain the conditions to the reader.
- Emphasize what you can do or have done rather than what you can't or won't do.

E. **Close on a respectful note.**
- Express best wishes without being falsely positive.
- Suggest actions readers might take, if appropriate, and provide them with necessary information.
- Encourage further communication only if you're willing to discuss the situation further.

# Sending Negative Messages on Routine Business Matters

**5 LEARNING OBJECTIVE** Describe successful strategies for sending negative messages on routine business matters.

Professionals and companies receive a wide variety of requests and cannot respond positively to every single one. In addition, mistakes and unforeseen circumstances can lead to delays and other minor problems that occur in the course of business. Occasionally, companies must send negative messages to suppliers and other parties. Whatever the purpose, crafting routine negative responses and messages quickly and graciously is an important skill for every businessperson.

## MAKING NEGATIVE ANNOUNCEMENTS ON ROUTINE BUSINESS MATTERS

On occasion managers need to make unexpected announcements of a negative nature. For example, a company might decide to consolidate its materials purchasing with fewer suppliers and thereby need to tell several firms it will no longer be buying from them. Internally, management may need to announce the elimination of an employee benefit or other changes that employees will view negatively.

Negative announcements on routine business matters should usually be handled with the indirect approach because the news is unexpected.

Although such announcements happen in the normal course of business, they are generally unexpected. Accordingly, except in the case of minor changes, the indirect approach is usually the better choice. Follow the steps outlined for indirect messages: Open with a buffer that establishes some mutual ground between you and the reader, advance your reasoning, announce the change, and close with as much positive information and sentiment as appropriate under the circumstances.

## REJECTING SUGGESTIONS AND PROPOSALS

Managers receive a variety of suggestions and proposals, both solicited and unsolicited, from internal and external sources. For an unsolicited proposal from an external source, you may not even need to respond if you don't already have a working relationship with the sender. However, if you need to reject a proposal you solicited, you owe the sender an explanation, and because the news will be unexpected, the indirect approach is better. In general, the closer your working relationship, the more thoughtful and complete you need to be in your response. For example, if you are rejecting a proposal from an employee, explain your reasons fully and carefully so that the employee can understand why the proposal was not accepted and so that you don't damage an important working relationship.

## REFUSING ROUTINE REQUESTS

When turning down an invitation or a request for a favor, consider your relationship with the reader.

When you are unable to meet a request, your primary communication challenge is to give a clear negative response without generating negative feelings or damaging either your personal reputation or the company's. As simple as such messages may appear to be, they can test your skills as a communicator because you often need to deliver negative information while maintaining a positive relationship with the other party.

The direct approach works best for most routine negative responses. It not only helps your audience get your answer quickly and move on to other possibilities but also helps you save time, because messages with the direct approach are often easier to write than those with the indirect approach.

The indirect approach works best when the stakes are high for you or for the receiver, when you or your company has an established relationship with the person making the request, or when you're forced to decline a request that you might have accepted in the past (see Figure 11.4).

Consider the following points as you develop your routine negative messages:

If you aren't in a position to offer additional information or assistance, don't imply that you are.

- Manage your time carefully; focus on the most important relationships and requests.
- If the matter is closed, don't imply that it's still open by using phrases such as "Let me think about it and get back to you" as a way to delay saying no.
- Offer alternative ideas if you can, particularly if the relationship is important.
- Don't imply that other assistance or information might be available if it isn't.

| **1** Plan → | **2** Write → | **3** Complete |
|---|---|---|

**Analyze the Situation**

Verify that the purpose is to decline a request and offer alternatives; audience is likely to be surprised by the refusal.

**Gather Information**

Determine audience needs and obtain the necessary information.

**Select the Right Medium**

For formal messages, printed letters on company letterhead are best.

**Organize the Information**

The main idea is to refuse the request so limit your scope to that; select the indirect approach based on the audience and the situation.

**Adapt to Your Audience**

Adjust the level of formality based on your degree of familiarity with the audience; maintain a positive relationship by using the "you" attitude, politeness, positive emphasis, and bias-free language.

**Compose the Message**

Use a conversational but professional style and keep the message brief, clear, and as helpful as possible.

**Revise the Message**

Evaluate content and review readability to make sure the negative information won't be misinterpreted; make sure your tone stays positive without being artificial.

**Produce the Message**

Maintain a clean, professional appearance on company letterhead.

**Proofread the Message**

Review for errors in layout, spelling, and mechanics.

**Distribute the Message**

Deliver your message using the chosen medium.

---

InfoTech

927 Dawson Valley Road, Tulsa, Oklahoma 74151
Voice: (918) 669-4428    Fax: (918) 669-4429
www.infotech.com

March 6, 2013

Dr. Sandra Wofford, President
Whittier Community College
333 Whittier Avenue
Tulsa, OK 74150

Dear Dr. Wofford:

*The buffer eases the recipient into the message by demonstrating respect and recapping the request.* →

Infotech has been happy to support Whittier Community College in many ways over the years, and we appreciate the opportunities you and your organization provide to so many deserving students. Thank you for considering our grounds for your graduation ceremony on June 3.

We would certainly like to accommodate Whittier as we have in years past, but our companywide sales meetings will be held this year during the weeks of May 29 and June 5. With more than 200 sales representatives and their families from around the world joining us, activities will be taking place throughout our facility.

← *She provides a meaningful reason for the negative response, without apologizing (because the company is not at fault).*

*Kwan suggests an alternative, showing that she cares about the college and has given the matter some thought.* →

My assistant, Robert Seagers, suggests you contact the Municipal Botanical Gardens as a possible graduation site. He recommends calling Jerry Kane, director of public relations.

We remain firm in our commitment to you, President Wofford, and to the fine students you represent. Through our internship program, academic research grants, and other initiatives, we will continue to be a strong corporate partner to Whittier College and will support your efforts as you move forward.

← *Her close emphasizes the importance of the relationship and the company's continuing commitment.*

Sincerely,

*May Yee Kwan*

May Yee Kwan
Public Relations Director

lc

---

**Figure 11.4    Effective Letter Declining a Routine Request**

In declining a request to use her company's facilities, May Yee Kwan took note of the fact that her company has a long-standing relationship with the college and wants to maintain that positive relationship. Because the news is unexpected based on past experience, she chose an indirect approach to build up to her announcement.

## HANDLING BAD NEWS ABOUT TRANSACTIONS

Bad news about transactions is always unwelcome and usually unexpected. When you send such messages, you have three goals: (1) modify the customer's expectations, (2) explain how you plan to resolve the situation, and (3) repair whatever damage might have been done to the business relationship.

Some negative messages regarding transactions carry significant financial and legal ramifications.

The specific content and tone of each message can vary widely, depending on the nature of the transaction and your relationship with the customer. Telling an individual consumer that his new sweater will be arriving a week later than you promised is much simpler than telling Toyota that 30,000 transmission parts will be a week late, especially if you know the company will be forced to idle a multimillion-dollar production facility as a result.

Your approach to bad news about business transactions depends on what you've done previously to set the customer's expectations.

If you haven't done anything specific to set the customer's expectations—such as promising delivery within 24 hours—the message simply needs to inform the customer of the situation, with little or no emphasis on apologies (see Figure 11.5).

If you've failed to meet expectations that you set for the customer, you should include an element of apology.

If you did set the customer's expectations and now find that you can't meet them, your task is more complicated. In addition to resetting those expectations and explaining how you'll resolve the problem, you should include an apology as part of your message. The scope of the apology depends on the magnitude of the mistake. For the customer who ordered the sweater, a simple apology followed by a clear statement of when the sweater will arrive would probably be sufficient. For larger business-to-business transactions, the

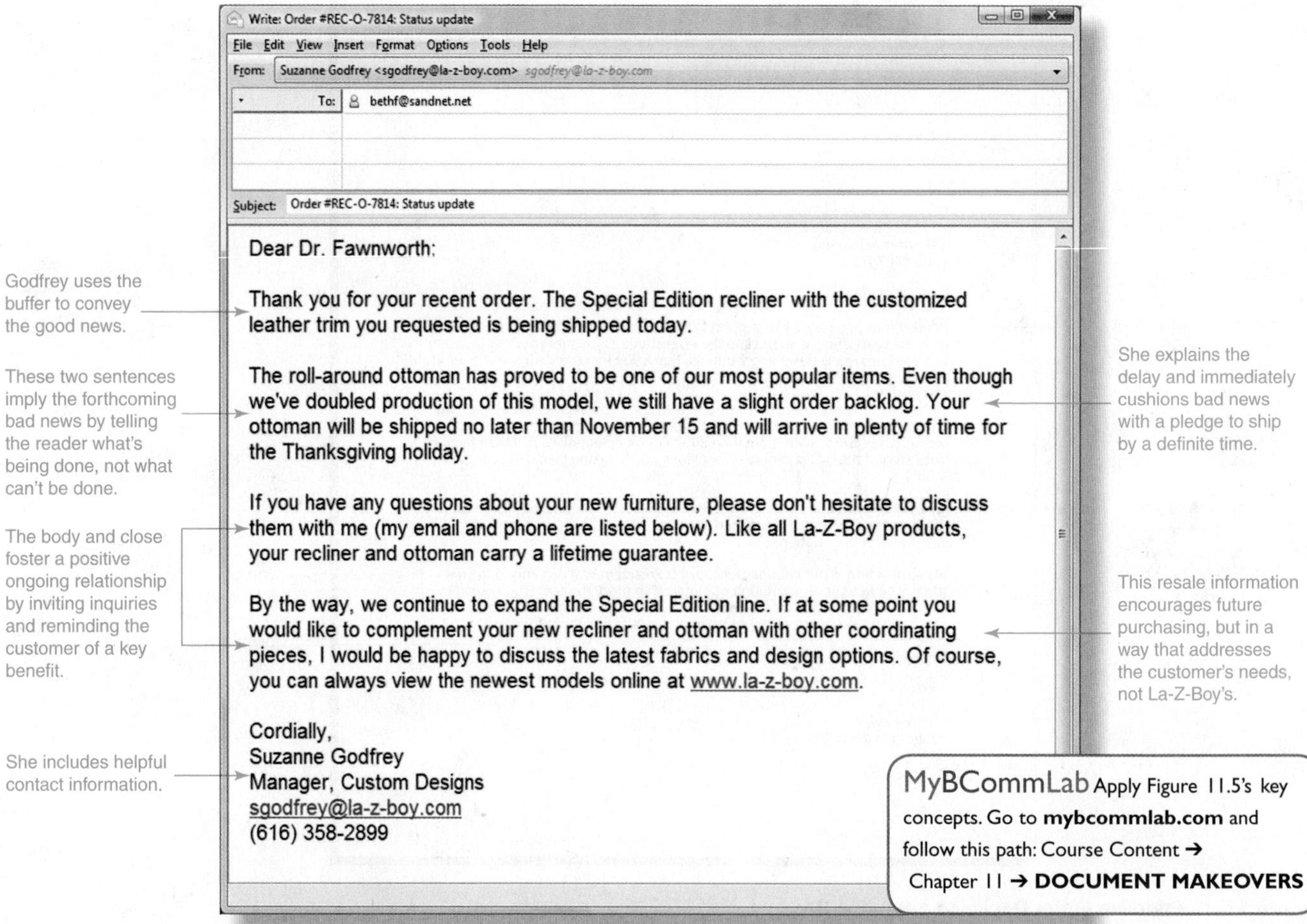

Godfrey uses the buffer to convey the good news.

These two sentences imply the forthcoming bad news by telling the reader what's being done, not what can't be done.

The body and close foster a positive ongoing relationship by inviting inquiries and reminding the customer of a key benefit.

She includes helpful contact information.

She explains the delay and immediately cushions bad news with a pledge to ship by a definite time.

This resale information encourages future purchasing, but in a way that addresses the customer's needs, not La-Z-Boy's.

---

**Write: Order #REC-O-7814: Status update**

File   Edit   View   Insert   Format   Options   Tools   Help

From:   Suzanne Godfrey <sgodfrey@la-z-boy.com>   *sgodfrey@la-z-boy.com*

To:   bethf@sandnet.net

Subject:   Order #REC-O-7814: Status update

Dear Dr. Fawnworth:

Thank you for your recent order. The Special Edition recliner with the customized leather trim you requested is being shipped today.

The roll-around ottoman has proved to be one of our most popular items. Even though we've doubled production of this model, we still have a slight order backlog. Your ottoman will be shipped no later than November 15 and will arrive in plenty of time for the Thanksgiving holiday.

If you have any questions about your new furniture, please don't hesitate to discuss them with me (my email and phone are listed below). Like all La-Z-Boy products, your recliner and ottoman carry a lifetime guarantee.

By the way, we continue to expand the Special Edition line. If at some point you would like to complement your new recliner and ottoman with other coordinating pieces, I would be happy to discuss the latest fabrics and design options. Of course, you can always view the newest models online at www.la-z-boy.com.

Cordially,
Suzanne Godfrey
Manager, Custom Designs
sgodfrey@la-z-boy.com
(616) 358-2899

MyBCommLab Apply Figure 11.5's key concepts. Go to **mybcommlab.com** and follow this path: Course Content → Chapter 11 → **DOCUMENT MAKEOVERS**

**Figure 11.5   Effective Negative Message Regarding a Transaction**
This message, which is a combination of good and bad news, uses the indirect approach—with the good news serving as a buffer for the bad news. In this case, the customer wasn't promised delivery by a certain date, so the writer simply informs the customer when to expect the rest of the order. The writer also takes steps to repair the relationship and encourage future business with her firm.
*Source:* Used with Permission from Microsoft.

## CHECKLIST ✔ Handling Bad News About Transactions

- Reset the customer's expectations regarding the transaction.
- Explain what happened and why, if appropriate.
- Explain how you will resolve the situation.

- Repair any damage done to the business relationship, perhaps offering future discounts, free merchandise, or other considerations.
- Offer a professional, businesslike expression of apology if your organization made a mistake.

customer may want an explanation of what went wrong to determine whether you'll be able to perform as you promise in the future.

To help repair the damage to the relationship and encourage repeat business, many companies offer discounts on future purchases, free merchandise, or other considerations. Even modest efforts can go a long way toward rebuilding a customer's confidence in your company. However, you don't always have a choice. Business-to-business purchasing contracts often include performance clauses that legally entitle the customer to discounts or other restitution in the event of late delivery. To review the concepts covered in this section, see "Checklist: Handling Bad News About Transactions."

## REFUSING CLAIMS AND REQUESTS FOR ADJUSTMENT

Customers who make a claim or request an adjustment tend to be emotionally involved, so the indirect approach is usually the better choice when you are denying such a request. Your delicate task as a writer is to avoid accepting responsibility for the unfortunate situation and yet avoid blaming or accusing the customer. To steer clear of these pitfalls, pay special attention to the tone of your letter. Demonstrate that you understand and have considered the complaint carefully, and then rationally explain why you are refusing the request. Close on a respectful and action-oriented note (see Figure 11.6 on the next page). And be sure to respond quickly. With so many instantaneous media choices at their disposal, some angry consumers will take their complaints public if they don't hear back from you within a few days or even a few hours.[13]

If you deal with enough customers over a long enough period, chances are you'll get a request that is particularly outrageous. You might even be positive that the person is not telling the truth. However, you need to control your emotions and approach the situation as calmly as possible to avoid saying or writing anything that the recipient might interpret as defamation (see page 25 in Chapter 1). To avoid being accused of defamation, follow these guidelines:

- Avoid any kind of abusive language or terms that could be considered defamatory.
- Provide accurate information and stick to the facts.
- Never let anger or malice motivate your messages.
- Consult your company's legal advisers whenever you think a message might have legal consequences.
- Communicate honestly and make sure you believe what you're saying is true.
- Emphasize a desire for a good relationship in the future.

Keep in mind that nothing positive can come out of antagonizing a customer, even one who has verbally abused you or your colleagues. Reject the claim or request for adjustment in a professional manner and move on to the next challenge. For a brief review of the tasks involved when refusing claims, see "Checklist: Refusing Claims."

*Use the indirect approach in most cases of refusing a claim.*

*When refusing a claim*
- *Demonstrate your understanding of the complaint*
- *Explain your refusal*
- *Suggest alternative action*

*You can help avoid committing defamation by not responding emotionally or abusively.*

## CHECKLIST ✔ Refusing Claims

- Use the indirect approach because the reader is expecting or hoping for a positive response.
- Indicate your full understanding of the nature of the complaint.
- Explain why you are refusing the request, without hiding behind company policy.
- Provide an accurate, factual account of the transaction.

- Emphasize ways things should have been handled rather than dwell on the reader's negligence.
- Avoid any appearance of defamation.
- Avoid expressing personal opinions.
- End with a positive, friendly, helpful close.
- Make any suggested action easy for readers to comply with.

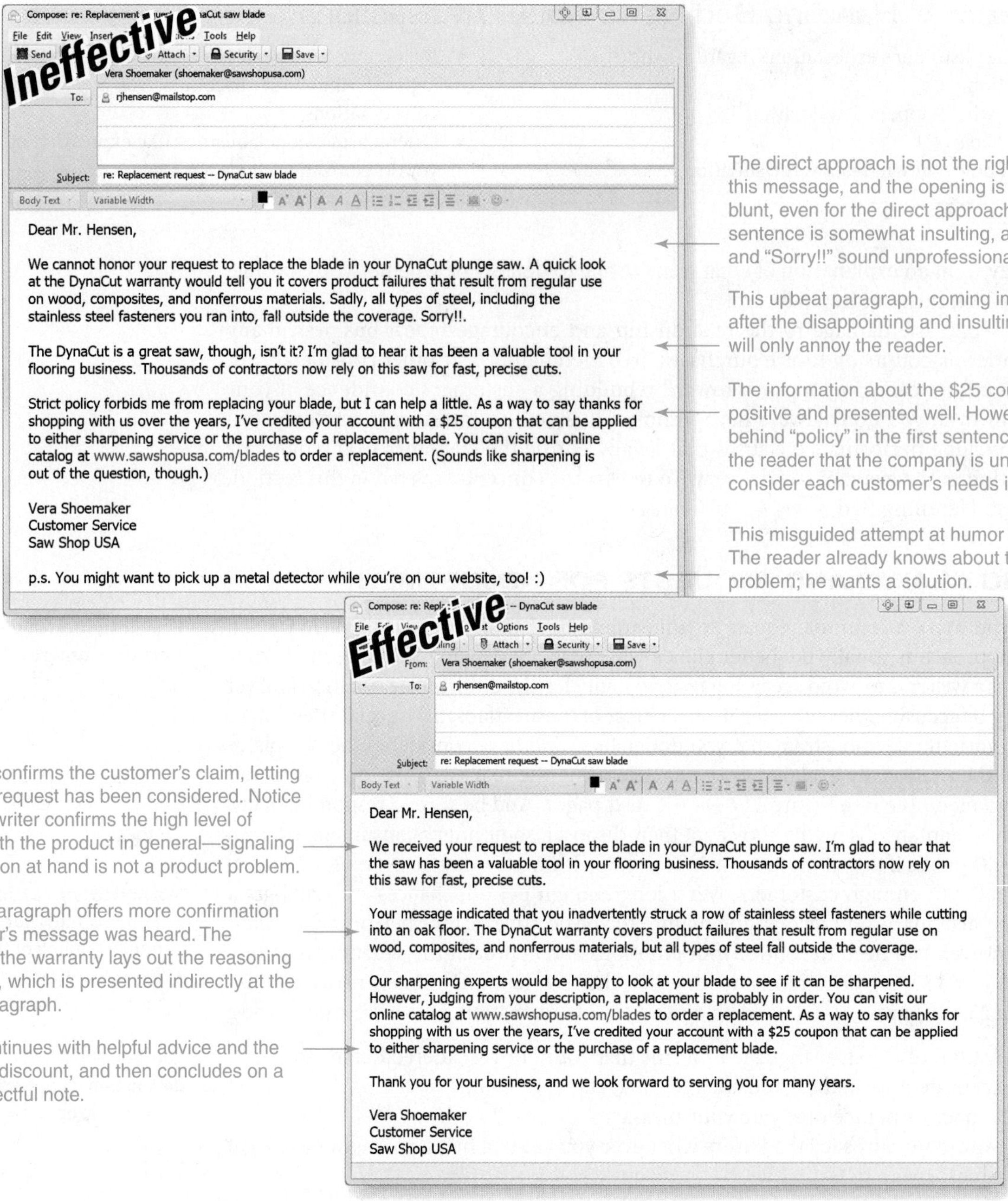

Ineffective

Compose: re: Replacement request -- DynaCut saw blade

From: Vera Shoemaker (shoemaker@sawshopusa.com)

To: rjhensen@mailstop.com

Subject: re: Replacement request -- DynaCut saw blade

Dear Mr. Hensen,

We cannot honor your request to replace the blade in your DynaCut plunge saw. A quick look at the DynaCut warranty would tell you it covers product failures that result from regular use on wood, composites, and nonferrous materials. Sadly, all types of steel, including the stainless steel fasteners you ran into, fall outside the coverage. Sorry!!.

The DynaCut is a great saw, though, isn't it? I'm glad to hear it has been a valuable tool in your flooring business. Thousands of contractors now rely on this saw for fast, precise cuts.

Strict policy forbids me from replacing your blade, but I can help a little. As a way to say thanks for shopping with us over the years, I've credited your account with a $25 coupon that can be applied to either sharpening service or the purchase of a replacement blade. You can visit our online catalog at www.sawshopusa.com/blades to order a replacement. (Sounds like sharpening is out of the question, though.)

Vera Shoemaker
Customer Service
Saw Shop USA

p.s. You might want to pick up a metal detector while you're on our website, too! :)

The direct approach is not the right choice for this message, and the opening is way too blunt, even for the direct approach. The second sentence is somewhat insulting, and "Sadly" and "Sorry!!" sound unprofessional.

This upbeat paragraph, coming immediately after the disappointing and insulting opening, will only annoy the reader.

The information about the $25 coupon is positive and presented well. However, hiding behind "policy" in the first sentence only tells the reader that the company is unwilling to consider each customer's needs individually.

This misguided attempt at humor is insulting. The reader already knows about the problem; he wants a solution.

Effective

Compose: re: Replacement request -- DynaCut saw blade

From: Vera Shoemaker (shoemaker@sawshopusa.com)

To: rjhensen@mailstop.com

Subject: re: Replacement request -- DynaCut saw blade

Dear Mr. Hensen,

We received your request to replace the blade in your DynaCut plunge saw. I'm glad to hear that the saw has been a valuable tool in your flooring business. Thousands of contractors now rely on this saw for fast, precise cuts.

Your message indicated that you inadvertently struck a row of stainless steel fasteners while cutting into an oak floor. The DynaCut warranty covers product failures that result from regular use on wood, composites, and nonferrous materials, but all types of steel fall outside the coverage.

Our sharpening experts would be happy to look at your blade to see if it can be sharpened. However, judging from your description, a replacement is probably in order. You can visit our online catalog at www.sawshopusa.com/blades to order a replacement. As a way to say thanks for shopping with us over the years, I've credited your account with a $25 coupon that can be applied to either sharpening service or the purchase of a replacement blade.

Thank you for your business, and we look forward to serving you for many years.

Vera Shoemaker
Customer Service
Saw Shop USA

The opening confirms the customer's claim, letting him know his request has been considered. Notice also how the writer confirms the high level of satisfaction with the product in general—signaling that the situation at hand is not a product problem.

The second paragraph offers more confirmation that the reader's message was heard. The description of the warranty lays out the reasoning for the refusal, which is presented indirectly at the end of the paragraph.

The writer continues with helpful advice and the offer of a $25 discount, and then concludes on a positive, respectful note.

**Figure 11.6 Message to Refuse a Claim**
Vera Shoemaker diplomatically refuses this customer's request for a new saw blade. Without blaming the customer (even though the customer clearly made a mistake), she points out that the saw blade is not intended to cut steel, so the warranty doesn't cover a replacement in this instance.
*Source:* Used with permission from Microsoft.

# Sending Negative Organizational News

**6 LEARNING OBJECTIVE**
List the important points to consider when conveying negative organizational news.

The messages described in the previous section deal with internal matters or individual interactions with external parties. From time to time, managers must also share negative information with the public at large, and sometimes respond to negative information as well. Most of these scenarios have unique challenges that must be addressed on a case-by-case basis, but the general advice offered here applies to all of them. One key difference among all these messages is whether you have time to plan the announcement. The following section addresses negative messages you do have time to plan for, and the section after that, "Communicating in a Crisis," offers advice on communication during emergencies.

## COMMUNICATING UNDER NORMAL CIRCUMSTANCES

Businesses must at times send a range of negative messages regarding their ongoing operations. As you plan such messages, take extra care to consider all your audiences and their unique needs. Keep in mind that a significant negative event such as a plant closing can affect hundreds or thousands of people in multiple stakeholder groups. Employees need to find new jobs, get training in new skills, or perhaps get emergency financial help. School districts may have to adjust budgets and staffing levels if many of your employees plan to move in search of new jobs. Your customers need to find new suppliers. Your suppliers may need to find other customers of their own. Government agencies may need to react to everything from a decrease in tax revenues to an influx of people seeking unemployment benefits.

*Negative organizational messages to external audiences can require extensive planning.*

When making negative announcements, follow these guidelines:

- **Match your approach to the situation.** A modest price increase won't shock most customers, so the direct approach is fine. However, canceling a product that people count on is another matter, so building up to the news via the indirect approach might be better.
- **Consider the unique needs of each group.** As the plant closing example illustrates, various people have different information needs.
- **Give each audience enough time to react as needed.** One of the key mistakes Chargify made (see page 288) in announcing its new pricing model was failing to let customers know ahead of time that monthly prices would be increasing.

*Give people as much time as possible to react to negative organizational news.*

- **Give yourself enough time to plan and manage a response.** Chances are you're going to be hit with complaints, questions, or product returns after you make your announcement, so make sure you're ready with answers and additional follow-up information.
- **Look for positive angles, but don't exude false optimism.** If eliminating a seldom-used employee benefit means the company can invest more in advertising, by all means promote that positive angle. On the other hand, laying off 10,000 people does not give them "an opportunity to explore new horizons." It's a traumatic event that can affect employees, their families, and their communities for years. The best you may be able to do is to thank people for their past support and wish them well in the future.
- **Seek expert advice if you're not sure.** Many significant negative announcements have important technical, financial, or legal elements that require the expertise of lawyers, accountants, or other specialists.

*Ask for legal help and other assistance if you're not sure how to handle a significant negative announcement.*

Negative situations will test your skills as a communicator and leader. Inspirational leaders try to seize such opportunities as a chance to reshape or reinvigorate the organization, and they offer encouragement to those around them (see Figure 11.7 on the next page).

## RESPONDING TO NEGATIVE INFORMATION IN A SOCIAL MEDIA ENVIRONMENT

For all the benefits they bring to business, social media and other communication technologies have created a major new challenge: responding to online rumors, false information, and attacks on a company's reputation. Consumers and other stakeholders can now communicate through blogs, Twitter, YouTube, social networking sites, advocacy sites such as http://makingchangeatwalmart.org, general complaint and feedback websites such as www.yelp.com and www.epinions.com, sites that target specific companies, community Q&A sites such as Get Satisfaction, and numerous e-commerce shopping sites that encourage product reviews.

Customers who believe they have been treated unfairly like these sites and tools because they can use the public exposure as leverage. Many companies appreciate the feedback, too, and some actively seek out complaints to improve their products and operations. However, false rumors and both fair

**REAL-TIME UPDATES**

LEARN MORE BY WATCHING THIS VIDEO

**Positive ways to engage when you pick up negative social commentary**

Aetna's Lauren Vargas talks about the challenges of moving a large corporation in a heavily regulated industry (health insurance) into social media, including the best ways to respond to negative comments online. Go to http://real-timeupdates.com/bct12 and click on Learn More. If you are using MyBCommLab, you can access Real-Time Updates within each chapter or under Student Study Tools.

## Pulling the plug on Triton

📅 JUNE 6, 2012 BY OSCAR HUERTA  💬 LEAVE A COMMENT

Many of you probably don't follow the costs of materials on the world market, but let me tell you, it's been brutal for those of us who do. We're seeing some major increases in the cost of high-grade steel, ceramics, and semiconductor-grade silicon. We can accommodate moderate increases in these costs by raising our list prices, but there's only so far we can raise prices before sales start to drop.

Of course, we periodically revisit our sales forecasts for products in development, to make sure our revenue projections are valid as well. Sad to say, Triton looks like it will get hammered when it hits the market. AMG Magnetics recently introduced a product that will compete directly with Triton, and it has both higher performance and a lower price.

This won't come as a surprise to anyone who has been looking at the numbers: we had to pull the plug on Triton. It just won't fly under these new circumstances.

Now, I don't want to hear any gossip about the Triton team failing or not being up to the task or whatever. Sue Wentworth and her crew have been putting in long hours for months, and it was tough for me at the other top managers to deliver this news.

Disruptions like this always start the rumor mill going about job security, so I'm happy to report that there is no need to worry. We have plenty of other projects that could use some extra help, and other project managers are already lobbying to get their hands on the Triton staffers.

By the way, these reviews are something the management team does every quarter to make sure we focus our time and investment on new products with the greatest potential for strong sales and profit levels, the management team reviews the costing analysis and sales projections for every R&D project once a quarter. Sometimes circumstances change after we launch a project, and the financial assumptions we made at that point might no longer be valid.

**Ineffective**

- The writer attempts the indirect approach in the body of the message but gives away the bad news in the headline of the blog post.

- This opening makes it more about the writer than the readers or the company in general.

- Saying that Triton "will get hammered when it hits the market" is too blunt for such a sensitive message.

- He started the post by saying most people don't look at the numbers, so this news will come as a surprise. Also, "pull the plug" and "It just won't fly" feel too flippant for such an important message.

- These statements about gossip and the rumor mill are uncalled for and introduce additional layers of negativity that serve no purpose.

- This information would make a good buffer (see the Improved example), but it makes a poor close because it doesn't leave the reader with anything to feel good about.

---

The post title preserves the indirect approach by not giving away the bad news.

The opening serves as an effective buffer because it explains the process that was used to reach the decision. This will put the audience in a rational frame of mind, rather than an emotional one.

This paragraph introduces the first of the two reasons that led to the decision, and it does so in a calm but authoritative way.

This paragraph introduces the second reason and narrows the focus from all products to just the Triton project. At this point, all readers should be prepared for the bad news.

He delivers the bad news will keeping the focus on the project and its financial parameters. He also immediately shifts into a positive stance, talking about the talented staff and other opportunities.

This paragraph immediately puts to rest any worries other readers will have about their jobs.

The close is respectful and demonstrates sensitivity toward the people most affected by the decision.

## Triton project: important update

**Effective**

📅 JUNE 6, 2012 BY OSCAR HUERTA  💬 LEAVE A COMMENT

As part of the ongoing effort to make sure we focus our time and investment on new products with the greatest potential for strong sales and profit levels, the management team reviews the costing analysis and sales projections for every R&D project once a quarter. Conducting these reviews every quarter gives us time to respond in the event that current circumstances no longer align with the financial assumptions we made when a particular project was launched.

On the cost side of the equation, we're seeing some major increases in the cost of high-grade steel, ceramics, and semiconductor-grade silicon. We can accommodate moderate increases in these costs by raising our list prices, but there's only so far we can raise prices before sales start to drop.

Regarding sales projections, our forecasts still look solid for every new product, except for the Triton project. AMG Magnetics recently introduced a product that will compete directly with Triton, and it has both higher performance and a lower price. Accordingly, we have had to reduce Triton's sales forecasts by 35 percent.

Unfortunately, the increase in material costs and the decrease in projected sales volume put Triton in an impossible position. We believe the company has better opportunities for investing our development capital and the time and energy of our talented engineering staff. Accordingly, we have decided to cancel Triton, effectively immediately.

Please rest assured that this will not affect staffing levels. We have plenty of other projects that can use some extra help, and other project managers are already lobbying to get the Triton staffers on their teams.

Please join me in thanking Sue Wentworth and everyone on the Triton team for the months of dedication and creativity they devoted to this project. I know they are disappointed in this outcome but recognize the necessity of focusing on our brightest prospects.

**Figure 11.7  Internal Message Providing Bad News About Company Operations**

The cancelation of a major development project before completion can be a traumatic event for a company's employees. People who worked on the project are likely to feel that all their time and energy were wasted and worry that their jobs are in jeopardy. Employees who didn't work on the project might worry about the company's financial health and the stability of their own jobs. Such messages are therefore prime candidates for the indirect approach. Note how much more effectively the revised version manages the reader's emotions from beginning to end.

and unfair criticisms can spread around the world in a matter of minutes. Responding to rumors and countering negative information requires an ongoing effort and case-by-case decisions about which messages require a response. Follow these four steps:[14]

- **Engage early, engage often.** Perhaps the most important step in responding to negative information has to be done *before* the negative information appears, and that is to engage with communities of stakeholders as a long-term strategy. Companies that have active, mutually beneficial relationships with customers and other interested parties are less likely to be attacked unfairly online and more likely to survive such attacks if they do occur. In contrast, companies that ignore constituents or jump into "spin doctoring" mode when a negative situation occurs don't have the same credibility as companies that have done the long, hard work of fostering relationships within their physical and online communities.

- **Monitor the conversation.** If people are interested in what your company does, chances are they are blogging, tweeting, podcasting, posting videos, writing on Facebook walls, and otherwise sharing their opinions. Use the available technologies to listen to what people are saying.

- **Evaluate negative messages.** When you encounter negative messages, resist the urge to fire back immediately. Instead, evaluate the source, the tone, and the content of the message and then choose a response that fits the situation. For example, the Public Affairs Agency of the U.S. Air Force groups senders of negative messages into four categories: "trolls" (those whose only intent is to stir up conflict), "ragers" (those who are just ranting or telling jokes), "the misguided" (those who are spreading incorrect information), and "unhappy customers" (those who have had a negative experience with the Air Force).

- **Respond appropriately.** After you have assessed a negative message, make the appropriate response based on an overall public relations plan. The Air Force, for instance, doesn't respond to trolls or ragers, responds to misguided messages with correct information, and responds to unhappy customers with efforts to rectify the situation and reach a reasonable solution. In addition to replying promptly, make sure your response won't make the situation even worse. For example, taking legal action against critics, even if technically justified, can rally people to their defense and create a public relations nightmare. In some instances, the best response can be to contact a critic privately (through direct messaging on Twitter, for example) to attempt a resolution away from the public forum.

Whatever you do, keep in mind that positive reputations are an important asset and need to be diligently guarded and defended. Everybody has a voice now, and some of those voices don't care to play by the rules of ethical communication.

## COMMUNICATING IN A CRISIS

Some of the most critical instances of business communication occur during crises, which can include industrial accidents, crimes or scandals involving company employees, on-site hostage situations, terrorist attacks, information theft, product tampering incidents, and financial calamities. During a crisis, customers, employees, local communities, and others will demand information. In addition, rumors can spread unpredictably and uncontrollably. You can also expect the news media to descend quickly, asking questions of anyone they can find.

The key to successful communication efforts during a crisis is having a **crisis management plan**. In addition to defining operational procedures to deal with the crisis, this plan outlines communication tasks and responsibilities, which can include everything from media contacts to news release templates (see Table 11.3 on the next page). The plan

Responding effectively to rumors and negative information in social media requires continual engagement with stakeholders and careful decision making about which messages should get a response.

**REAL-TIME UPDATES**
LEARN MORE BY READING THIS INFOGRAPHIC

**Decide how to respond to online reputation attacks**

This flowchart embodies the rumor-response process used by the U.S. Air Force. Go to http://real-timeupdates.com/bct12 and click on Learn More. If you are using MyBCommLab, you can access Real-Time Updates within each chapter or under Student Study Tools.

**REAL-TIME UPDATES**
LEARN MORE BY WATCHING THIS VIDEO

**Crisis communication and social media**

Professor Timothy Coombs discusses the role of social media in crisis communication. Go to http://real-timeupdates.com/bct12 and click on Learn More. If you are using MyBCommLab, you can access Real-Time Updates within each chapter or under Student Study Tools.

Anticipation and planning are key to successful communication in a crisis.

## TABLE 11.3 | How to Communicate in a Crisis

### WHEN A CRISIS HITS

| Do | Don't |
|---|---|
| Prepare for trouble ahead of time by identifying potential problems, appointing and training a response team, and preparing and testing a crisis management plan. | Blame anyone for anything. |
| | Speculate in public. |
| Get top management involved immediately. | Refuse to answer questions. |
| Set up a news center for company representatives and the media that is equipped with phones, computers, and other electronic tools for preparing news releases and online updates. At the news center, take the following steps: | Release information that will violate anyone's right to privacy. |
| | Use the crisis to pitch products or services. |
| | Play favorites with media representatives. |

- Issue frequent news updates, and have trained personnel available to respond to questions around the clock.
- Provide complete information packets to the media as soon as possible.
- Prevent conflicting statements and provide continuity by appointing a single person trained in advance to speak for the company.
- Tell receptionists and other employees to direct all phone calls to the designated spokesperson in the news center.
- Provide updates when new information is available via blog postings, Twitter updates, text messaging, Facebook, and other appropriate media.

Tell the whole story—openly, completely, and honestly. If you are at fault, apologize.

Demonstrate the company's concern by your statements and your actions.

should clearly specify which people are authorized to speak for the company, provide contact information for all key executives, and include a list of the news outlets and social media tools that will be used to disseminate information.

Although you can't predict catastrophes, you can prepare for them. Analysis of corporate crises over the past several decades reveals that companies that respond quickly with the information people need tend to fare much better in the long run than those that go into hiding or release inconsistent or incorrect information.[15]

# Sending Negative Employment Messages

**7** LEARNING OBJECTIVE
Describe successful strategies for sending negative employment-related messages.

As a manager, you will find yourself in a variety of situations in which you have to convey bad news to individual employees or potential employees. Recipients often have an emotional stake in your message, so taking the indirect approach is usually advised. In addition, use great care in choosing media for these messages. For instance, email and other written forms let you control the message and avoid personal confrontation, but one-on-one conversations are often viewed as more sensitive and give both sides the opportunity to ask and answer questions.

## REFUSING REQUESTS FOR EMPLOYEE REFERENCES AND RECOMMENDATION LETTERS

Managers may get requests for recommendation letters from other employers and from past employees. When sending refusals to prospective employers who have requested information about past employees, your message can be brief and direct:

Implies that company policy prohibits the release of any more information but does provide what information is available

Ends on a positive note

> Our human resources department has authorized me to confirm that Yolanda Johnson worked for Tandy, Inc., for three years, from June 2007 to July 2009. Best of luck as you interview applicants.

This message doesn't need to say, "We cannot comply with your request." It simply gives the reader all the information that is allowable.

Refusing an applicant's direct request for a recommendation letter is another matter. Any refusal to cooperate may seem to be a personal slight and a threat to the applicant's future. Diplomacy and preparation help readers accept your refusal:

> Thank you for letting me know about your job opportunity with Coca-Cola. Your internship there and the MBA you've worked so hard to earn should place you in an excellent position to land the marketing job.
>
> Although we do not send out formal recommendations here at PepsiCo, I can certainly send Coca-Cola a confirmation of your employment dates. And if you haven't considered this already, be sure to ask several of your professors to write evaluations of your marketing skills. Best of luck to you in your career.

*Uses the indirect approach since the other party is probably expecting a positive response*

*Announces that the writer cannot comply with the request, without explicitly blaming it on "policy"*

*Offers to fulfill as much of the request as possible and offers an alternative*

*Ends on a positive note*

This message tactfully avoids hurting the reader's feelings because it makes positive comments about the reader's recent activities, implies the refusal, suggests an alternative, and uses a polite close.

## REFUSING SOCIAL NETWORKING RECOMMENDATION REQUESTS

One of the greatest values offered by business social networks is the opportunity for members to make introductions and recommendations. However, the situation with recommendations in a social networking environment is more complicated than with a traditional recommendation letter because the recommendations you make become part of your online profile. With a traditional letter, only a few hiring managers might read your recommendations, but on a network such as LinkedIn, other network members (or even the general public, in some instances) can see whom you've recommended and what you've written about these people. Much more so than with traditional letters, then, the recommendations you make in a social network become part of your brand.[16] Moreover, networks make it easy to find people and request recommendations, so chances are you will get more requests than you would have otherwise—and sometimes from people you don't know well.

Fortunately, social networks give you a bit more flexibility when responding to these requests. You can simply ignore or delete the request—some people make it personal policy to ignore requests from networkers they don't know. Of course, if you do know someone, ignoring a request could create an uncomfortable situation, so you will need to decide each case based on your relationship with the person. Another option is to refrain from making recommendations at all, and just letting people know this policy when they ask. Whatever you decide, remember that it is your choice.[17]

If you choose to make recommendations and want to respond to a request, you can write as much or as little information about the person as you are comfortable sharing. Unlike an offline recommendation, you don't need to write a complete letter. You can write a briefer statement, even just a single sentence that focuses on one positive aspect.[18] This flexibility allows you to respond positively in those situations in which you have mixed feelings about a person's overall abilities.

*Social networks have created new challenges in recommendation requests, but they also offer more flexibility in responding to these requests.*

## REJECTING JOB APPLICATIONS

Application rejection messages are routine communications, but saying no is never easy, and recipients are emotionally invested in the decision. Moreover, companies must be aware of the possibility of employment discrimination lawsuits, which have been on the rise in recent years.[19] Of course, having fair and nondiscriminatory hiring practices is essential, but rejections must also be written in a way that doesn't inadvertently suggest any hint of discrimination. Expert opinions differ on the level of information to include in a rejection message, but the safest strategy is to avoid sharing any explanations for the

*Poorly written rejection letters tarnish your company's reputation and can even invite legal troubles.*

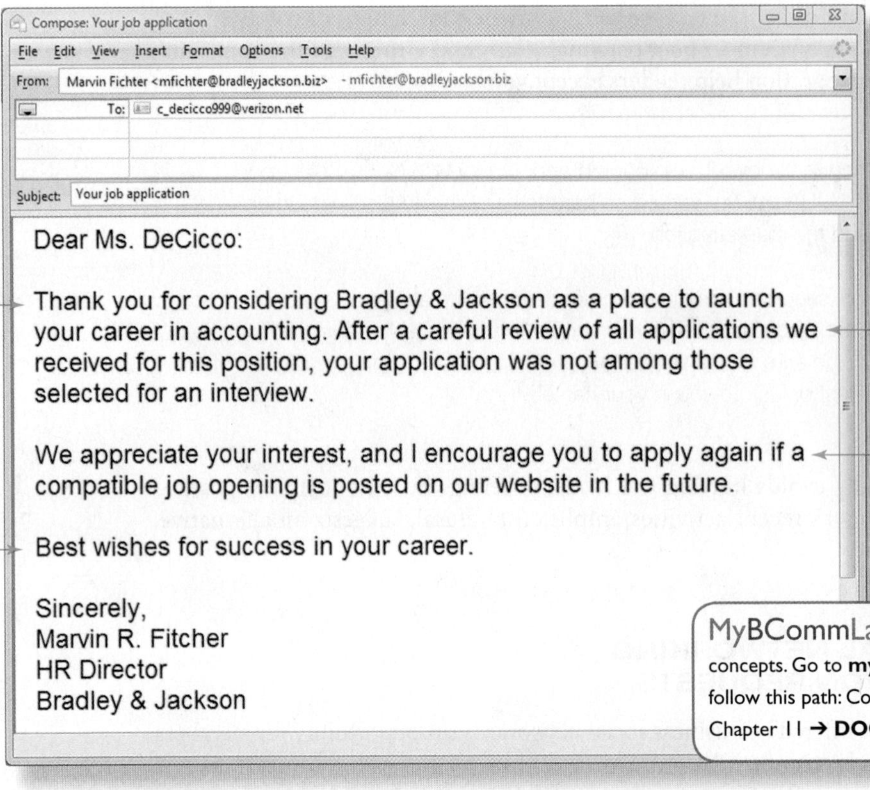

Fitcher opens with a simple expression of appreciation for being considered, which acts as a mini-buffer for the bad news to come.

He closes on a positive note without apologizing or implying that the matter is open for discussion.

The opening conveys the bad news quickly, using the passive voice to depersonalize the decision.

He invites her to reapply for any positions that may appear in the future, while avoiding any promise of reviewing her current application again.

**Compose: Your job application**

File   Edit   View   Insert   Format   Options   Tools   Help

From:   Marvin Fichter <mfichter@bradleyjackson.biz>   - mfichter@bradleyjackson.biz

To:   c_decicco999@verizon.net

Subject:   Your job application

Dear Ms. DeCicco:

Thank you for considering Bradley & Jackson as a place to launch your career in accounting. After a careful review of all applications we received for this position, your application was not among those selected for an interview.

We appreciate your interest, and I encourage you to apply again if a compatible job opening is posted on our website in the future.

Best wishes for success in your career.

Sincerely,
Marvin R. Fitcher
HR Director
Bradley & Jackson

MyBCommLab Apply Figure 11.8's key concepts. Go to **mybcommlab.com** and follow this path: Course Content → Chapter 11 → **DOCUMENT MAKEOVERS**

**Figure 11.8   Effective Message Rejecting a Job Applicant**
This message rejecting a job applicant takes care to avoid making or implying any promises about future opportunities, beyond inviting the person to apply for positions that may appear in the future. Note that this would not be appropriate if the company did not believe the applicant was a good fit for the company in general.
*Source:* Used with permission from Microsoft.

company's decision and to avoid making or implying any promises of future consideration (see Figure 11.8):[20]

- **Personalize the email message or letter by using the recipient's name.** For example, mail merge makes it easy to insert each recipient's name into a form letter.
- **Open with a courteous expression of appreciation for having applied.** In a sense, this is like the buffer in an indirect message because it gives you an opportunity to begin the conversation without immediately and bluntly telling the reader that his or her application has been rejected.
- **Convey the negative news politely and concisely.** The passive voice is helpful in this situation because it shifts focus away from the people involved and thereby depersonalizes the response. For example, "Your application was not among those selected for an interview" is less blunt than the active phrase "We have rejected your application."
- **Avoid explaining why an applicant was rejected or why other applicants were chosen instead.** Although it was once more common to offer such explanations, and some experts still advocate this approach, the simplest strategy from a legal standpoint is to avoid offering reasons for the decision. Avoiding explanations lowers the possibility that an applicant will perceive discrimination in the hiring decision or be tempted to challenge the reasons given.
- **Don't state or imply that the application will be reviewed at a later date.** Saying that "we will keep your résumé on file for future consideration" can create false hopes for the recipient and leave the company vulnerable to legal complaints if a future hiring decision is made without actually reviewing this candidate's application again. If the candidate might be a good fit for another position in the company in the future, you can suggest he or she reapply if a new job opening is posted.
- **Close with positive wishes for the applicant's career success.** A brief statement such as "We wish you success in your career" is sufficient.

Naturally, you should adjust your tactics to the circumstances. A simple and direct message is fine when someone has only submitted a job application, but rejecting a candidate who has made it at least partway through the interview process requires greater care. Personal contact has already been established through the interview process, so a phone call may be more appropriate.

## GIVING NEGATIVE PERFORMANCE REVIEWS

**Performance reviews** are designed to clarify job requirements, give employees feedback on their performance relative to those requirements, and establish a personal plan of action to ensure continued performance in the future. Performance reviews also help companies set organizational standards and communicate organizational values.[21] In addition, they document evidence of performance in the event that disciplinary action is needed or an employee later disputes management decisions regarding pay or promotions.[22]

The worst possible outcome in an annual review is a negative surprise, such as when an employee has been working toward different goals than the manager expects or has been unknowingly underperforming throughout the year but didn't receive any feedback or improvement coaching along the way.[23] To avoid negative surprises, managers should provide regular feedback and coaching as needed throughout the year if employee performance falls below expectations. In fact, some companies have gone so far as to abandon the traditional performance review altogether. The online retailer Zappos, for example, has replaced annual performance reviews with frequent status reports that give employees feedback on routine job tasks and an annual assessment of how well each employee embodies the company's core values.[24]

Regardless of the specific approach a company takes, writing an effective performance review requires careful, objective assessment and a clear statement of how well an employee has done relative to agreed-upon goals. If you need to write a review that includes negative information, keep the following points in mind:[25]

- **Document performance problems.** As you provide feedback throughout the year, keep a written record of performance issues. You will need this information in order to write an effective appraisal and to support any decisions that need to be made about pay, promotions, or termination.
- **Evaluate all employees consistently.** Consistency is not only fair but also helps protect the company from claims of discriminatory practices.
- **Write in a calm, objective voice.** The employee is not likely to welcome your negative assessment, but you can manage the emotions of the situation by maintaining professional reserve in your writing.
- **Focus on opportunities for improvement.** As you document performance problems, identify specific steps the employee can take to correct them. This information can serve as the foundation for an improvement plan for the coming year.
- **Keep job descriptions up to date.** Performance evaluations should be based on the criteria listed in an employee's job description. However, if a job evolves over time in response to changes in the business, the employees' current activities may no longer match an outdated job description.

## TERMINATING EMPLOYMENT

If an employee's performance cannot be brought up to company standards or if factors such as declining sales cause a reduction in the workforce, a company often has no choice but to terminate employment. As with other negative employment messages, termination is fraught with emotions and legal ramifications, so careful planning, complete documentation, and sensitive writing are essential.

Termination messages should always be written with input from the company's legal staff, but here are general writing guidelines to bear in mind:[26]

- Clearly present the reasons for this difficult action, whether it is the employee's performance or a business decision unrelated to performance.
- Make sure the reasons are presented in a way that cannot be construed as unfair or discriminatory.

An important goal of any performance evaluation is to give the employee a plan of action for improving his or her performance.

By giving employees clear goals and regular feedback, you can help avoid unpleasant surprises in a performance review.

Negative evaluations should provide careful documentation of performance concerns.

Carefully word a termination message to avoid creating undue ill will and grounds for legal action.

- Follow company policy, contractual requirements, and applicable laws to the letter.
- Avoid personal attacks or insults of any kind.
- Ask another manager to review the letter before issuing it. An objective reviewer who isn't directly involved might spot troublesome wording or faulty reasoning.
- Deliver the termination letter in person if at all possible. Arrange a meeting that will ensure privacy and freedom from interruptions.

Any unplanned termination is clearly a negative outcome for both employer and employee, but careful attention to content and tone in the termination message can help the employee move on gracefully and minimize the misunderstandings and anger that can lead to expensive lawsuits. To review the tasks involved in this type of message, see "Checklist: Writing Negative Employment Messages." For the latest information on writing negative messages, visit http://real-timeupdates.com/bct12 and click on Chapter 11.

---

**CHECKLIST ✔ Writing Negative Employment Messages**

**A. Refusing requests for employee references and recommendations**
- Don't feel obligated to write a recommendation letter if you don't feel comfortable doing so.
- Take a diplomatic approach to minimize hurt feelings.
- Compliment the reader's accomplishments.
- Suggest alternatives, if available.
- Use the options available to you on social networks, such as ignoring a request from someone you don't know or writing a recommendation on a single positive attribute.

**B. Rejecting job applicants**
- If possible, respond to all applications, even if you use only a form message to acknowledge receipt.
- If you use the direct approach, take care to avoid being blunt or cold.
- If you use the indirect approach, don't mislead the reader in your buffer or delay the bad news for more than a sentence or two.
- Avoid explaining why the applicant was rejected.
- Suggest alternatives if possible.

**C. Giving negative performance reviews**
- Document performance problems throughout the year.
- Evaluate all employees consistently.
- Keep job descriptions up to date as employee responsibilities change.
- Maintain an objective and unbiased tone.
- Use nonjudgmental language.
- Focus on problem resolution.
- Make sure negative feedback is documented and shared with the employee.
- Don't avoid confrontations by withholding negative feedback.
- Ask the employee for a commitment to improve.

**D. Terminating employment**
- State your reasons accurately and make sure they are objectively verifiable.
- Avoid statements that might expose your company to a wrongful termination lawsuit.
- Consult company lawyers to clarify all terms of the separation.
- Deliver the letter in person if at all possible.
- End the relationship on terms as positive as possible.

---

## COMMUNICATION CHALLENGES AT Chargify

Your combined loves of business and web technologies found a perfect home at Chargify, where you were recently hired as a software development manager, overseeing a talented team of designers and developers in the company's Needham, Massachusetts, headquarters. Use what you've learned in this chapter to address the following challenges.

**INDIVIDUAL CHALLENGE:** Another manager stopped by this morning with a request to borrow two of your best programmers for a three-week emergency. Under normal conditions, you wouldn't hesitate to help, but your team has its own scheduling challenges to deal with. Plus, this isn't the first time this manager has run into trouble, and you suspect that poor project management is the reason. In one or two sentences, diplomatically state your refusal to help while suggesting that your colleague's management skills need to be improved.

**TEAM CHALLENGE:** You've found it easy to say yes to recommendation letter requests from former employees who were top performers, and you've learned to say no to those people who didn't perform so well. The requests you struggle with are from employees in the middle—people who didn't really excel but didn't really cause any trouble either. You've just received a request from a computer systems specialist who falls smack in the middle of the middle. Unfortunately, he's applying for a job at a firm that you know places high demands on its employees and generally hires the best of the best. He's a great person, and you'd love to help, but in your heart you know that if by some chance he does get the job, he probably won't last. Plus, you don't want to get a reputation in the industry for recommending weak candidates. With your team, brainstorm a sensitive but effective buffer that will help you set the stage for the negative news.

# Quick Learning Guide

## SUMMARY OF LEARNING OBJECTIVES

**1** Apply the three-step writing process to negative messages. Because the way you convey negative information can be as damaging as the fact that you're conveying it, planning negative messages carefully is crucial. Make sure your purpose is specific, necessary, and appropriate for the medium you've chosen. Find out how your audience prefers to receive bad news. Collect all the facts necessary to support your negative decision, and adapt your tone to the situation as well as to your audience. Negative messages may be organized according to the direct or the indirect approach, and your choice depends on audience preference as well as on the situation. In addition, carefully choose positive words to construct diplomatic sentences. Finally, revision, design, and proofreading are necessary to ensure that you are saying exactly what you want to say in the best possible way and that careless errors don't aggravate an already emotional situation.

**2** Explain how to use the direct approach effectively when conveying negative news. The direct approach to negative messages puts the bad news up front, follows with the reasons (and perhaps offers an alternative), and closes with a respectful statement that is as positive as possible under the circumstances. Use the direct approach when you know your audience prefers receiving bad news up front or if the bad news will cause readers relatively little pain or disappointment. Otherwise, use the indirect approach. Even though it is direct, however, don't use the direct approach as a license to be rude or overly blunt.

**3** Explain how to use the indirect approach effectively when conveying negative news. The indirect approach for negative messages begins with a buffer (a neutral or positive statement to establish common ground with the reader), explains the reasons leading up to the decision or news, clearly states the negative news without unduly emphasizing it, and closes with a respectful statement. When using the indirect approach, you need to be careful to avoid obscuring the bad news or misleading your audience into thinking you're actually delivering good news. The key to avoiding both problems is remembering that the purpose of the indirect approach is to cushion the blow, not to avoid delivering it. When using a buffer, you must be sure it is neither deceptive nor insincere. To write an effective buffer, look for opportunities to express your appreciation for being considered, to assure your reader of your attention to the request, or to indicate your understanding of the reader's needs.

**4** Explain the importance of maintaining high standards of ethics and etiquette when delivering negative messages. Ethics and etiquette are important in every message, of course, but they take on particular significance with negative messages for three reasons. First, in many cases, the communicator needs to adhere to a variety of laws and regulations when delivering negative messages. Second, good ethical practice demands care and sensitivity in the content and delivery of negative messages, as these messages can have a profoundly negative effect on the people who receive them. Third, communicators need to manage their own emotions when crafting and distributing negative messages while at the same time considering the emotional needs of their audiences.

**5** Describe successful strategies for sending negative messages on routine business matters. When making negative announcements on routine business matters, the indirect approach is usually preferred, although the direct approach can work for minor issues. When rejecting suggestions and proposals, tailor the approach to the situation. An unsolicited proposal from an external source doesn't need as much of your attention as a solicited proposal from an internal source, for example. For refusing routine requests, the direct approach is usually sufficient, except when the matter at hand is significant, you or your company have an established relationship with the person making the request, or you're forced to decline a request that you might have said yes to in the past.

When conveying bad news about transactions, you need to modify the customer's expectations, explain how you plan to resolve the situation, and repair whatever damage might have been done to the business relationship. Whether you should apologize depends in part on the magnitude of the situation and whether you previously established specific expectations about the transaction.

When refusing a claim or a request for adjustment, the indirect approach is usually preferred because the other party is emotionally involved and expects you to respond positively. Demonstrate that you understand and have considered the complaint carefully and then rationally and calmly explain why you are refusing the request.

**6** List the important points to consider when conveying negative organizational news. Public communications about various organization matters fall into two categories: those you can plan for (and therefore have more time to prepare messages) and crises that hit without warning. The first category includes a variety of announcements, from relatively minor matters such as price increases to major matters such as layoffs and bankruptcy proceedings. For these messages, be sure to match your approach to the situation, consider the unique needs of each audience group, give each audience enough time to react as needed, give yourself enough time to plan and manage a response, look for positive angles but don't exude false optimism, and seek expert advice on legal, financial, or technical matters if you're not sure how to proceed.

The second category of negative organizational news involves communication during times of crisis. Preparation is key for successful crisis management. Although you can't anticipate the nature and circumstances of every possible crisis, you can prepare by deciding such issues as who is in charge of communications, where the press and the public can get information, and what will be said in likely emergency scenarios. A good crisis communication plan includes such items as email and phone lists for important media contacts, website templates for various emergency scenarios, and after-hours contact information for key personnel in the company.

To respond successfully to rumors and negative information in a social media environment, first be sure you are engaged with important stakeholders *before* negative situations appear. Second, monitor the conversations taking place about your company and its products. Third, when you see negative messages, evaluate them before responding. Fourth, after evaluating negative messages, take the appropriate response based on an overall public relations plan. Some messages are better ignored, whereas others should be addressed immediately with corrective information.

**7** Describe successful strategies for sending negative employment-related messages. The indirect approach is usually the better choice for negative employment messages because the recipient is always emotionally involved, and the decisions are usually significant. When refusing requests from other employers for performance-related information about past employees, your message can be brief and direct. Simply provide whatever information your company allows to be shared in these situations. Refusing a recommendation request directly from a former employee feels much more personal for the recipient, however, so the indirect approach is better. Responding to requests on social networks is somewhat easier because you have the option of recommending just one particular aspect of a person's overall skill set, even if you can't make an unqualified, overall endorsement.

Messages rejecting job applicants raise a number of emotional and legal issues and therefore must be approached with great care. Experts vary in their advice about how much information to include in these messages. However, the safest strategy is a brief message that opens with an expression of appreciation for being considered (which functions like a buffer in an indirect message), continues with a statement to the effect that the applicant was not chosen for the position applied for, and closes courteously without providing reasons for the rejection or making promises about future consideration.

Negative performance reviews should take care to document the performance problems, be sure that all employees are being evaluated consistently, be written in a calm and objective voice, and focus on opportunities for improvement. Moreover, they must be written with reference to accurate, current job descriptions that provide the basis for measuring employee performance.

Termination messages are the most challenging employment messages of all. They should clearly present the reasons for the decision, present the reasons in a way that cannot be construed as unfair or discriminatory, follow company policy and any relevant legal guidelines, and avoid personal attacks or insults of any kind. Asking a manager not directly involved in the situation to review your message can help you avoid troublesome wording or faulty reasoning. Finally, try to deliver the written message in person if possible.

## KEY TERMS

**buffer** A neutral, noncontroversial statement that establishes common ground with the reader in an indirect negative message

**crisis management plan** Plan that defines operational procedures to deal with a crisis, including communication tasks and responsibilities

**performance review** Employee evaluation procedure giving feedback on performance and guidance for future efforts

**whistleblowing** Efforts by employees to report concerns about unethical or illegal behavior

# Test Your Knowledge

To review chapter content related to each question, refer to the indicated Learning Objective.

✪ 1. Why is it particularly important to select your medium carefully and adapt your tone to your audience's needs and preferences when writing a negative message? [LO-1]

✪ 2. Under what circumstances should you avoid offering explanations in negative indirect messages? [LO-2]

3. What is the sequence of presentation in a negative message that is organized using the indirect approach? [LO-3]

4. What is a buffer, and what steps must you take to ensure that buffers you write are ethical? [LO-3]

5. What is whistleblowing? [LO-4]

6. What steps can you take to minimize chances of being accused of defamation when refusing a claim or request for adjustment? [LO-5]

7. What is a crisis management plan? [LO-6]

8. What are the five guidelines for giving negative performance reviews? [LO-7]

# Apply Your Knowledge

To review chapter content related to each question, refer to the indicated Learning Objective.

1. Would you choose the direct or indirect approach to announce that a popular employee benefit is being eliminated for cost reasons? Why? [LO-1]

2. Is intentionally deemphasizing bad news the same as distorting graphs and charts to deemphasize unfavorable data? Why or why not? [LO-3]

✪ 3. Why is it important to be engaged with stakeholders before trying to use social media during a crisis or other negative scenario? [LO-6]

✪ 4. If your social media monitoring efforts pick up a tweet that accuses your customer service staff of lying and claims to have evidence to back it up, how would you respond? [LO-6]

5. How would you respond to a LinkedIn network connection who asks for a recommendation when you barely remember working with this person and don't remember whether she was good at her job? [LO-7]

# Practice Your Skills

### Messages for Analysis

Read the following messages and then (1) analyze the strengths and weaknesses of each sentence and (2) revise each message so that it follows this chapter's guidelines.

### Message 11.A: Sending Negative Organizational News [LO-6]

From: M. Juhasz, Travel & Meeting Services
To: [mailing list]
Subject: Travel

Dear Traveling Executives:

We need you to start using some of the budget suggestions we are going to issue as a separate memorandum.

These include using videoconference equipment and web conferencing instead of traveling to meetings, staying in cheaper hotels, arranging flights for cheaper times, and flying from less-convenient but also less-expensive suburban airports.

The company needs to cut travel expenses by fifty percent, just as we've cut costs in all departments of Black & Decker. This means you'll no longer be able to stay in fancy hotels and make last-minute, costly changes to your travel plans.

You'll also be expected to avoid hotel surcharges for phone calls and Internet access. If the hotel you want to stay in doesn't offer free wireless, go somewhere else. And never, NEVER return a rental car with an empty tank! That causes the rental agency to charge us a premium price for the gas they sell when they fill it up upon your return.

You'll be expected to make these changes in your travel habits immediately.

Sincerely,
M. Juhasz
Travel & Meeting Services

### Message 11.B: Refusing Requests for Claims and Adjustments [LO-5]

I am responding to your letter of about six weeks ago asking for an adjustment on your wireless hub, model WM39Z. We test all our products before they leave the factory; therefore, it could not have been our fault that your hub didn't work.

If you or someone in your office dropped the unit, it might have caused the damage. Or the damage could have been caused by the shipper if he dropped it. If so, you should file a claim with the shipper. At any rate, it wasn't our fault. The parts are already covered by warranty. However, we will provide labor for the repairs for $50, which is less than our cost, since you are a valued customer.

We will have a booth at the upcoming trade show there and hope to see you or someone from your office. We have many new models of hubs, routers, and other computer gear that we're sure you'll want to see. I've enclosed our latest catalog. Hope to see you there.

### Message 11.C: Rejecting Job Applications [LO-7]

I regret to inform you that you were not selected for our summer intern program at Equifax. We had over a thousand résumés and cover letters to go through and simply could not get to them all. We have been asked to notify everyone that we have already selected students for the 25 positions based on those who applied early and were qualified.

We're sure you will be able to find a suitable position for summer work in your field and wish you the best of luck. We deeply regret any inconvenience associated with our reply.

### Exercises

Each activity is labeled according to the primary skill or skills you will need to use. To review relevant chapter content, you can refer to the indicated Learning Objective. In some instances, supporting information will be found in another chapter, as indicated.

1. **Planning: Choosing the Direct or Indirect Approach [LO-1]** Select which approach you would use (direct or indirect) for the following negative messages.

   a. An email message to your boss, informing her that one of your key clients is taking its business to a different accounting firm

   b. An email message to a customer, informing her that one of the books she ordered over the Internet is temporarily out of stock

   c. An instant message to a customer, explaining that the DVD recorder he ordered for his new computer is on back order and that, as a consequence, the shipping of the entire order will be delayed

   d. A blog post to all employees, notifying them that the company parking lot will be repaved during the first week of June and that the company will provide a shuttle service from a remote parking lot during that period

   e. A letter from a travel agent to a customer, stating that the airline will not refund her money for the flight she missed but that her tickets are valid for one year

   f. A form letter from a U.S. airline to a customer, explaining that the company cannot extend the expiration date of the customer's frequent flyer miles even though the customer was living overseas for the past three years and unable to use the miles during that time

   g. A letter from an insurance company to a policyholder, denying a claim for reimbursement for a special medical procedure that is not covered under the terms of the customer's policy

   h. A letter from an electronics store, stating that the customer will not be reimbursed for a malfunctioning mobile phone that is still under warranty (because the terms of the warranty do not cover damages to phones that were accidentally dropped from a moving car)

   i. An announcement to the repairs department, listing parts that are on back order and will be three weeks late

2. **Message Strategies: Refusing Routine Requests [LO-4]** As a customer service supervisor for a telephone company, you're in charge of responding to customers' requests for refunds. You've just received an email from a customer who unwittingly ran up a $500 bill for long-distance calls after mistakenly configuring his laptop computer to dial an Internet access number that wasn't a local call. The customer says it wasn't his fault because he didn't realize he was dialing a long-distance number. However, you've dealt with this situation before; you know that the customer's Internet service provider warns its customers to choose a local access number because customers are responsible for all long-distance charges. Draft a short buffer (one or two sentences) for your email reply, sympathizing with the customer's plight but preparing him for the bad news (that company policy specifically prohibits refunds in such cases).

3. **Etiquette: Communicating with Sensitivity and Tact; Collaboration: Team Projects [LO-4]** Working alone, revise the following statements to deemphasize the bad news. Then team up with a classmate and read each other's revisions. Did you both use the same approach in every case?

Which approach seems to be most effective for each of the revised statements?

   a. The airline can't refund your money. The "Conditions" section on the back of your ticket states that there are no refunds for missed flights. Sometimes the airline makes exceptions, but only when life and death are involved. Of course, your ticket is still valid and can be used on a flight to the same destination.

   b. I'm sorry to tell you, we can't supply the custom decorations you requested. We called every supplier, and none of them can do what you want on such short notice. You can, however, get a standard decorative package on the same theme in time. I found a supplier that stocks these. Of course, it won't have quite the flair you originally requested.

   c. We can't refund your money for the malfunctioning MP3 player. You shouldn't have immersed the unit in water while swimming; the users' manual clearly states that the unit is not designed to be used in adverse environments.

4. **Communication Ethics [LO-4]** The insurance company where you work is planning to raise all premiums for health-care coverage. Your boss has asked you to read a draft of her letter to customers announcing the new, higher rates. The first two paragraphs discuss some exciting medical advances and the expanded coverage offered by your company. Only in the final paragraph do customers learn that they will have to pay more for coverage starting next year. What are the ethical implications of this draft? What changes would you suggest?

5. **Sending Negative Organizational News [LO-6]** Public companies occasionally need to issue news releases to announce or explain downturns in sales, profits, demand, or other business factors. Search the web to locate a company that has issued a press release that recently reported lower earnings or other bad news and access the news release on the firm's website. Alternatively, find the type of press release you're seeking by reviewing press releases at www.prnewswire.com or www.businesswire.com. How does the headline relate to the main message of the release? Is the release organized according to the direct or the indirect approach? What does the company do to present the bad news in a favorable light—and does this effort seem sincere and ethical to you?

## Expand Your Skills

### Critique the Professionals

Locate an example online of a negative-news message from any company. Possible examples include announcements of product recalls, poor financial results, layoffs, and fines or other legal troubles. Analyze the approach the company took; was it the most effective strategy possible? Did the company apologize, if doing so would have been appropriate under the circumstances, and does the apology seem sincere? Does the tone of the message match the seriousness of the situation? Does the message end on a positive note, as appropriate? Using whatever medium your instructor requests, write a brief analysis of the message (no more than one page), citing specific elements from the piece and support from the chapter.

### Sharpening Your Career Skills Online

Bovée and Thill's Business Communication Web Search, at http://businesscommunicationblog.com/websearch, is a unique research tool designed specifically for business communication research. Use the Web Search function to find a website, video, PDF document, podcast, or PowerPoint presentation that offers advice on writing messages that convey negative information. Write a brief email message to your instructor, describing the item you found and summarizing the career skills information you learned from it.

# Cases

## Negative Messages on Routine Business Matters

##### EMAIL SKILLS  /  IM SKILLS

**1. Message Strategies: Refusing Claims and Requests for Adjustment: Media Skills: Instant Messaging [LO-4], Chapter 7**
Your company has learned that selling instructional videos presents a difficult business dilemma. For its first five years of operation, the company had a generous return policy in which customers could return any DVD after 10 days, even if it had been opened. However, as return rates began to climb, management began to suspect that some customers were abusing the policy by watching DVDs long enough to learn whatever they wanted to learn and then returning them and asking for refunds. The company disliked penalizing the majority of its customer base by changing the policy, but returns cost money, and the company's profits were taking a bigger and bigger hit every year. Starting last year, the company now accepts returns only if the product packaging has not been opened.

**Your task:** Team up with two other students. One of you will play the role of a customer who purchased the "Kickboxing Fundamentals" DVD two weeks ago. One of you will play the role of a service agent who assists customers with orders and returns.

Using Facebook's chat function or any other free IM service, role-play an exchange in which the customer initiates the conversation and asks for a refund, saying that the program doesn't meet his or her needs. The reason offered is that the techniques shown in the video are quite basic, and he or she is already past that skill level.

Early in the exchange, the service agent needs to ask whether the DVD package has been unsealed. The customer replies that it has, after which the agent will respond that the company can accept only unopened DVDs for refund or exchange. The customer can continue to argue that there is no way to truly evaluate a DVD without watching the entire program, because every person might have a different understanding of what "fundamentals" means. However, the company's policy is firm.

Make up whatever details you need to complete the exchange, keeping in mind the following points:

- The video title and the product description on the website clearly indicate that this kickboxing program is intended for beginners.
- The website clearly states that DVDs can be returned only if they are unopened.
- In addition, the online shopping cart requires customers to check a box to indicate that they have read the return policy.
- The agent might suggest to the customer that he or she could offer it for sale on Craigslist, sell to a store that buys used movies, or donate it to a library.

The third member of the team should sit beside either the customer or the agent and evaluate the IM exchange, without participating. If possible, capture the IM stream for offline analysis. The evaluator will then give both participants written feedback on the content and tone of their messages, offering suggestions for improvement. Be prepared to discuss the experience and the analysis with your class.

##### EMAIL SKILLS

**2. Message Strategies: Rejecting Suggestions and Proposals [LO-5]** Walter Joss is one of the best employees in your department, a smart and hard worker with a keen mind for business. His upbeat attitude has helped the entire department get through some rough times recently, and on a personal level, his wise counsel helped you grow into a leadership role when you were promoted to marketing manager several years ago.

You generally welcome Joss's input on the department's operations, and you have implemented several of his ideas to improve the company's marketing efforts. However, the proposal he emailed you yesterday was not his best work, to put it mildly. He proposed that the company dump the advertising agency it has used for a decade and replace it with some new agency you've never heard of. The only reasons he offered were that the agency "had become unresponsive" and that a "smaller agency could meet our needs better." He failed to address any of the other criteria that are used to select advertising agencies, such as costs, creative skills, technical abilities, geographic reach, research capabilities, and media experience.

This is the first you've heard any criticism of the agency, and in fact, their work was helped your company increase sales every year.

**Your task:** Draft an email message to Joss, rejecting his proposal. (Note that in a real-life setting, you would want to discuss this with Joss in person, rather than through email, but use email for the purposes of this exercise.)

##### EMAIL SKILLS

**3. Message Strategies: Making Routine Negative Announcements [LO-5]** You've been proud of many things your gardening tool company has accomplished as it grew from just you working in your basement shop to a nationally known company that employs more than 200 people. However, nothing made you prouder than the company's Helping Our Hometown Grow program, in which employees volunteer on company time to help residents in your city start their own vegetable gardens, using tools donated by the company. Nearly 50 employees participated directly, helping some 500 families supplement their grocery budgets with home-grown produce. Virtually everyone in the company contributed, though, because employees who didn't volunteer to help in the gardens pitched in to cover the work responsibilities of the volunteers.

Sadly, 10 years after you launched the program, you have reached the inescapable conclusion that the company can no longer afford to keep the program going. With consumers around the country still struggling with the aftereffects of a deep recession, sales have been dropping for the past three years—even as lower cost competitors step up their presence in the market. To save the program, you would have to lay off several employees, but your employees come first.

**Your task:** Write an email to the entire company, announcing the cancellation of the program.

## TELEPHONE SKILLS

**4. Message Strategies: Making Routine Negative Announcements [LO-5]** Vail Products of Toledo, Ohio, manufactured a line of beds for use in hospitals and other institutions that have a need to protect patients who might otherwise fall out of bed and injure themselves (including patients with cognitive impairments or patterns of spasms or seizures). These "enclosed bed systems" use a netted canopy to keep patients in bed rather than the traditional method of using physical restraints such as straps or tranquilizing drugs. The intent is humane, but the design is flawed: At least 30 patients have become trapped in the various parts of the mattress and canopy structure, and 8 of them have suffocated.

Working with the U.S. Food and Drug Administration (FDA), Vail issued a recall on the beds, as manufacturers often do in the case of unsafe products. However, the recall is not really a recall. Vail will not be replacing or modifying the beds, nor will it accept returns. Instead, the company is urging institutions to move patients to other beds, if possible. Vail has also sent out revised manuals and warning labels to be placed on the beds. The company also announced that it is ceasing production of enclosed beds.

**Your task:** A flurry of phone calls from concerned patients, family members, and institutional staff is overwhelming the support staff. As a writer in Vail's corporate communications office, you've been asked to draft a short script to be recorded on the company's phone system. When people call the main number, they'll hear "Press 1 for information regarding the recall of Model 500, Model 1000, and Model 2000 enclosed beds." After they press 1, they'll hear the message you're about to write, explaining that although the action is classified as a recall, Vail will not be accepting returned beds, nor will it replace any of the affected beds. The message should also assure customers that Vail has already sent revised operating manuals and warning labels to every registered owner of the beds in question. The phone system has

limited memory, and you've been directed to keep the message to 75 words or less.[27]

## EMAIL SKILLS / PORTFOLIO BUILDER

**5. Message Strategies: Rejecting Suggestions and Proposals; Communication Ethics: Making Ethical Choices [LO-5]** A not-so-secret secret is getting more attention than you'd really like after an article in a major business magazine gave the world an inside look at how much money you and other electronics retailers make from extended warranties (sometimes called service contracts). The article explained that typically half of the warranty price goes to the salesperson as a commission and that only 20 percent of the total amount customers pay for warranties eventually goes to product repair.

You also know why extended warranties are such a profitable business. Many electronics products follow a predictable pattern of failure: a high failure rate early in their lives, then a "midlife" period during which failures go way down, and concluding with an "old age" period when failure rates ramp back up again (engineers refer to the phenomenon as the *bathtub curve* because it looks like a bathtub from the side—high at both ends and low in the middle). The early failures are usually covered by manufacturers' warranties, and the extended warranties you sell are designed to cover that middle part of the life span. In other words, many extended warranties cover the period of time during which consumers are *least* likely to need them and offer no coverage when consumers need them *most*. (Consumers can actually benefit from extended warranties in a few product categories, including laptop computers and plasma televisions. Of course, the more sense the warranty makes for the consumer, the less financial sense it makes for your company.)[28]

**Your task:** Worried that consumers will stop buying so many extended warranties, your boss has directed you to put together a sales training program that will help cashiers sell the extended warranties even more aggressively. The more you ponder this challenge, though, the more you're convinced that your company should change its strategy so it doesn't rely on profits from these warranties so much. In addition to offering questionable value to the consumer, the warranties risk creating a consumer backlash that could lead to lower sales of all your products. You would prefer to voice your concerns to your boss in person, but both of you are traveling on hectic schedules for the next week. You'll have to write an email instead. Draft a brief message, explaining why you think the sales training specifically and the warranties in general are both bad ideas.

## MICROBLOGGING SKILLS

**6. Message Strategies: Making Routine Negative Announcements [LO-5]** JetBlue was one of the first companies to incorporate the Twitter microblogging service into its customer communications, and thousands of fliers and fans now follow the airline's Twittering staff members. Messages include announcements about fare sales (such as limited-time auctions on eBay or special on-site sales at shopping malls), celebrations of company milestones (such as the opening of the carrier's new terminal at New York's JFK airport), schedule updates, and even personalized responses to people who Twitter with questions or complaints about the company.[29]

**Your task:** Write a Tweet alerting JetBlue customers to the possibility that Hurricane Isaac might disrupt flight schedules from August 13 through August 15. Tell them that decisions about delays and cancellations will be made on a city-by-city basis and will be announced on Twitter and the company's website. The URL will take 20 characters, so you have 120 characters (including spaces) for your message.

## BLOGGING SKILLS / PORTFOLIO BUILDER

### 7. Message Strategies: Making Routine Negative Announcements [LO-5]
Marketing specialists usually celebrate when target audiences forward their messages to friends and family—essentially acting as unpaid advertising and sales representatives. In fact, the practice of viral marketing is based on this hope. For one Starbucks regional office, however, viral marketing started to make the company just a bit sick. The office sent employees in the Southeast an email coupon for a free iced drink and invited them to share the coupon with family and friends. To the surprise of virtually no one who understands the nature of online life, the email coupon multiplied rapidly, to the point that Starbucks stores all around the country were quickly overwhelmed with requests for free drinks. The company decided to immediately terminate the free offer, a month ahead of the expiration date on the coupon.[30]

**Your task:** Write a one-paragraph message that can be posted on the Starbucks website and at individual stores, apologizing for the mix-up and explaining that the offer is no longer valid.

## EMAIL SKILLS

### 8. Message Strategies: Rejecting Suggestions and Proposals [LO-5]
Lee Valley Tools (www.leevalley.com) sells high-quality woodworking tools across Canada through its retail stores and around the world through its website and catalogs. While weekend hobbyists can pick up a mass-produced hand plane (a tool for smoothing wood) for $20 or $30 at the local hardware store, serious woodworkers pay five or ten times that much for one of Lee Valley's precision Veritas planes. For the price, they get top-quality materials, precision manufacturing, and innovative designs that help them do better work in less time.

Lee Valley sells its own Veritas brand tools as well as 5,000 tools made by other manufacturers. One of those companies has just emailed you to ask if Lee Valley would like to carry a new line of midrange hand planes that would cost more than the mass-market, hardware-store models but less than Lee Valley's own Veritas models. Your job is to filter requests such as this, rejecting those that don't meet Lee Valley's criteria and forwarding those that do to the product selection committee for further analysis. After one quick read of this incoming email message, you realize there is no need to send this idea to the committee. While these planes are certainly of decent quality, they achieve their lower cost through lower-quality steel that won't hold an edge as long and through thinner irons (the element that holds the cutting edge) that will be more prone to vibrate during use and thus produce a rougher finish. These planes have a market, to be sure, but they're not a good fit for Lee Valley's top-of-the-line product portfolio. Moreover, the planes don't offer any innovations in terms of ease of use or any other product attribute.[31]

**Your task:** Reply to this email message, explaining that the planes appear to be decent tools, but they don't fit Lee Valley's strategy of offering only the best and most innovative tools. Support your decision with the three criteria described above. Choose the direct or indirect approach carefully, taking into consideration your company's relationship with this other company.

## EMAIL SKILLS

### 9. Message Strategies: Refusing Claims and Requests for Adjustment [LO-5]
Your company markets a line of rugged smartphone cases designed to protect the sensitive devices from drops, spills, and other common accidents. Your guarantee states that you will reimburse customers for the cost of a new phone if the case fails to protect it from any of the following: (1) a drop of no more than 6 feet onto any surface, (2) spills of any beverage or common household chemical, (3) being crushed by any object of up to 100 pounds, or (4) being chewed on by dogs, cats, or other common household pets.

Jack Simmons, a rancher from Wyoming, emailed your customer support staff, requesting a reimbursement after he dropped his iPhone in his hog barn and a 900-pound boar crushed it in a single bite.

**Your task:** Write an email response to the customer, denying his request for a new phone.

## LETTER WRITING SKILLS / PORTFOLIO BUILDER

### 10. Message Strategies: Negative Announcements on Routine Matters [LO-5]
You're a marketing manager for Stanton, one of the premier suppliers of DJ equipment (turntables, amplifiers, speakers, mixers, and related accessories). Your company's latest creation, the FinalScratch system, has been flying off retailers' shelves. Both professional and amateur DJs love the way FinalScratch gives them the feel of working with vinyl records by letting them control digital music files from any analog turntable or CD player while giving them access to the endless possibilities of digital music technology. (For more information about the product, go to www.stantondj.com.) Sales are strong everywhere except in Music99 stores, a retail chain in the Mid-Atlantic region. You suspect the cause: The owners of this chain refused to let their salespeople attend the free product training you offered when FinalScratch was introduced, claiming their people were smart enough to train themselves.

To explore the situation, you head out from Stanton headquarters in Hollywood, Florida, on an undercover shopping mission. After visiting a few Music99 locations, you're appalled by what you see. The salespeople in these stores clearly don't understand the FinalScratch concept, so they either give potential customers bad information about it or steer them to products from your competitors. No wonder sales are so bad at this chain.

**Your task:** You're tempted to pull your products out of this chain immediately, but you know how difficult and expensive it is to recruit new retailers in this market. However, this situation can't go on; you're losing thousands of dollars of potential business every week. Write a letter to Jackson Fletcher, the CEO of Music99 (14014 Preston Pike, Dover, DE 19901), expressing your disappointment in what you observed and explaining that the Music99 sales staff will need to agree to attend product training or else your company's management team will consider terminating the business relationship. You've met Mr. Fletcher in person once and talked to him on the phone several times, and you know him well enough to know that he will not be pleased by this ultimatum. Music99 does a good job selling other Stanton products—and he'll probably be furious to learn that you were "spying" on his sales staff.[32]

## PODCASTING SKILLS

**11. Message Strategies: Negative Announcements on Routine Matters [LO-5]** An employee concierge seemed like a great idea when you added it as an employee benefit last year. The concierge handles a wide variety of personal chores for employees, everything from dropping off dry cleaning to ordering event tickets to sending flowers. Employees love the service, and you know that the time they save can be devoted to work or family activities. Unfortunately, profits are way down, and concierge usage is up—up so far that you'll need to add a second concierge to keep up with the demand. As painful as it will be for everyone, you decide that the company needs to stop offering the service.

**Your task:** Script a brief podcast, announcing the decision and explaining why it is necessary. Make up any details you need. If your instructor asks you to do so, record your podcast and submit the file.

## EMAIL SKILLS / PORTFOLIO BUILDER

**12. Message Strategies: Negative Announcements on Routine Matters [LO-5]** You can certainly sympathize with employees when they complain about having their email and instant messages monitored, but you're implementing a company policy that all employees agree to abide by when they join the company. Your firm, Webcor Builders of San Mateo, California, is one of the estimated 60 percent of U.S. companies with such monitoring systems in place. More and more companies use these systems (which typically operate by scanning messages for keywords that suggest confidential, illegal, or otherwise inappropriate content) in an attempt to avoid instances of sexual harassment and other problems.

As the chief information officer, the manager in charge of computer systems in the company, you're often the target when employees complain about being monitored. Consequently, you know you're really going to hear it when employees learn that the monitoring program will be expanded to personal blogs as well.

**Your task:** Write an email message to be distributed to the entire workforce, explaining that the automated monitoring program is about to be expanded to include employees' personal blogs. Explain that, while you sympathize with employee concerns regarding privacy and freedom of speech, it is the management team's responsibility to protect the company's intellectual property and the value of the company name. Therefore, employees' personal blogs will be added to the monitoring system to ensure that employees don't intentionally or accidentally expose company secrets or criticize management in a way that could harm the company.[33]

## LETTER WRITING SKILLS

**13. Message Strategies: Negative Announcements on Routine Matters [LO-5]** Your company, PolicyPlan Insurance Services, is a 120-employee insurance claims processor based in Milwaukee. PolicyPlan has engaged Midwest Sparkleen for interior and exterior cleaning for the past five years. Midwest Sparkleen did exemplary work for the first four years, but after a change of ownership last year, the level of service has plummeted. Offices are no longer cleaned thoroughly, you've had to call the company at least six times to remind them to take care of spills and other messes they're supposed to address routinely, and they've left toxic cleaning chemicals in a public hallway on several occasions. You have spoken with the owner about your concerns twice in the past three months, but his assurances that service would improve have not resulted in any noticeable improvements. When the evening cleaning crew forgot to lock the lobby door last Thursday—leaving your entire facility vulnerable to theft from midnight until 8 a.m. Friday morning—you decided it was time for a change.

**Your task:** Write a letter to Jason Allred, owner of Midwest Sparkleen, 4000 South Howell Avenue, Milwaukee, WI, 53207, telling him that PolicyPlan will not be renewing its annual cleaning contract with Midwest Sparkleen when the current contract expires at the end of this month. Cite the examples identified above, and keep the tone of your letter professional.

## BLOGGING SKILLS / PORTFOLIO BUILDER

**14. Message Strategies: Negative Announcements on Routine Matters [LO-5]** Like many other companies these days, the accounting firm Ernst & Young is fighting a brain drain, as experienced executives and professionals leave midcareer to pursue charitable interests, devote more time to family matters, or pursue a variety of other dreams or obligations. The problem is particularly acute among women, because on average they step off the career track more often than men do. As general manager of the largest division in the company, you've been tapped to draft a set of guidelines to make it easier for employees who've taken some time off to move back into the company.

However, as soon as word gets out about what you're planning, several of your top performers, people who've never left the company for personal time off—or "taken the off-ramp," in current buzzword speak—march into your office to complain. They fear that encouraging the "off-rampers" to return isn't fair to the employees who've remained loyal to the firm, as they put it. One goes as far as to say that anyone who leaves the company doesn't deserve to be asked back. Two others claim that the additional experience and skills they've gained as they continued to work should guarantee them higher pay and more responsibilities than employees who took time off for themselves.

**Your task:** As unhappy as these several employees are, the program needs to be implemented if Ernst & Young hopes to bring "off-rampers" back into the company—thereby making sure they don't go to work for competitors instead. However, you also can't afford to antagonize the existing workforce; if the people who've already complained are any indication, you have a sizable morale problem on your hands. You decide that your first step is to clearly explain why the program is necessary, including how it will benefit everyone in the company by making Ernst & Young more competitive. Write a short posting for the company's internal blog, explaining that, despite the objections some employees have raised, the firm is going ahead with the program as planned. Balance this news (which some employees will obviously view as negative) with positive reassurances that all current employees will be treated fairly in terms of both compensation and promotion opportunities. Close with a call for continued communication on this issue, inviting people to meet with you in person or to post their thoughts on the blog.[34]

# Negative Organizational News

## MICROBLOGGING SKILLS

**15. Message Strategies: Responding to Rumors [LO-6]**  Sheila Elliot, a well-known actress, appeared on a national talk show last night and claimed that your company's Smoothstone cookware was responsible for her toddler's learning disability. Elliot claimed that the nonstick surfaces of Smoothstone pots and pans contains a dangerous chemical that affected her child's cognitive development. There's just one problem with her story—well, three problems, actually: (1) your company's cookware line is called Moonstone, not Smoothstone; (2) Moonstone does not contain and never has contained the chemical Elliot mentioned, and (3) the product she is really thinking of was called Smoothfire, which was made by another company and was pulled off the market five years ago.

Thousands of worried parents aren't waiting for the fact checkers, however. They took to the blogosphere and Twitter-sphere with a vengeance overnight, warning people to throw away anything made by your company (Tatum Housewares). Several television stations have already picked up the Twitter chatter and repeated the rumor. Retailers are already calling your sales staff to cancel orders.

**Your task:**  Write a three-message sequence to be posted on your company's Twitter account, correcting the rumor and conveying the three points outlined above. Each message will include a URL linking to your company's website, so restrict each message to 120 characters, including spaces.

## BLOGGING SKILLS

**16. Message Strategies: Negative Organizational Announcements [LO-6]**  XtremityPlus is known for its outlandish extreme-sports products, and the Looney Launch is no exception. Fulfilling the dream of every childhood daredevil, the Looney Launch is an aluminum and fiberglass contraption that quickly unfolds to create the ultimate bicycle jump. The product has been selling as fast as you can make it, even though it comes plastered with warning labels proclaiming that its use is inherently dangerous.

As XtremityPlus's CEO, you were nervous about introducing this product, and your fears were just confirmed: You've been notified of the first lawsuit by a parent whose child broke several bones after crash-landing off a Looney Launch.

**Your task:**  Write a post for your internal blog, explaining that the Looney Launch is being removed from the market immediately. Tell your employees to expect some negative reactions from enthusiastic customers and retailers, but explain that (a) the company can't afford the risk of additional lawsuits; and (b) even for XtremityPlus, the Looney Launch pushes the envelope a bit too far. The product is simply too dangerous to sell in good conscience.

## BLOGGING SKILLS

**17. Message Strategies: Negative Organizational Announcements [LO-6]**  As the U.S. economy continued to sag after receiving multiple blows from the housing and financial sectors, plant closures were a common tragedy across many industries. Shaw Industries, the world's largest manufacturer of carpeting, was among those suppliers to the housing industry that suffered as fewer houses were built or remodeled.

**Your task:**  Write a brief message for Shaw's corporate blog, covering the following points:

- With more than $5 billion in annual sales, Shaw Industries is the world's number one carpet manufacturer.
- Shaw's Milledgeville, Georgia, plant makes yarn used in the manufacture of carpeting.
- The continuing struggles in the new-housing market and the inability of many current homeowners to afford remodeling projects have lowered demand for carpet. With less demand for carpet, the Milledgeville plant can no longer operate at a profit.
- Shaw is forced to close the Milledgeville plant and lay off all 150 employees at the plant.
- The plant will close in three to four weeks from the current date.
- As openings become available in other Shaw facilities, the company hopes to be able to place some of the workers in those jobs.
- Georgia Labor Commissioner Michael Thurmond promised to help the affected employees. "The layoff at Shaw Industries in Milledgeville will create a difficult situation for the workers and their families, and I want them to know they're not alone in dealing with this problem. Our staff will work closely with the laid-off workers, company officials, and local elected officials in determining how to best assist the affected employees."
- Assistance to be provided by the State of Georgia includes career counseling, unemployment benefits, and job retraining.[35]

## EMAIL SKILLS

**18. Message Strategies: Negative Organizational Announcements [LO-6]**  People who live for an adrenaline rush can find a way to go fast from Canada's Bombardier Recreational Products. Bombardier is one of the world's top makers of snowmobiles, personal watercraft, engines for motorboats, and all-terrain vehicles (ATVs)—all designed for fast fun.

Because it sends customers hurtling across snow, water, or land at high speeds, Bombardier takes safety quite seriously. However, problems do arise from time to time, requiring a rapid response with clear communication to the company's customer base. Bombardier recently became aware of a potentially hazardous situation with the "race-ready" version of its Can-Am DS 90 X ATVs. This model is equipped with a safety device called a tether engine shutoff switch, in which a cord is connected to a special switch that turns off the engine in the event of an emergency. On the affected units, pulling the cord might not shut off the motor, which is particularly dangerous if the rider falls off—the ATV will continue on its own until the engine speed returns to idle.

**Your task:**  Write an email message that will be sent to registered owners of 2008 and 2009 DS 90 X ATVs that include the potentially faulty switch. Analyze the situation carefully as you choose the direct or indirect approach for your message. Explain that the tether engine shutoff switch may not deactivate the engine when it is pulled in an emergency situation. To prevent riders from relying on a safety feature that might not work properly, Bombardier, in cooperation with transportation safety authorities in the United States and Canada, is voluntarily recalling these models to have the tether switch removed. Emphasize the serious nature of the situation by explaining that if the rider is ejected and the engine shutoff switch does not work properly, the ATV will run away on its own, potentially resulting in significant injuries or deaths. Owners should stop riding their vehicles immediately and make an appointment with an authorized dealer to have the switch removed. The service will be performed at no charge, and customers will receive a $50 credit voucher for future purchases of Bombardier accessories. Include the following contact information: www.can-am.brp.com and 1-888-638-5397.[36]

## BLOGGING SKILLS / PORTFOLIO BUILDER

### 19. Message Strategies: Communicating in a Crisis [LO-6]
One of your company's worst nightmares has just come true. EQ Industrial Services (EQIS), based in Wayne, Michigan, operates a number of facilities around the country that dispose of, recycle, and transport hazardous chemical wastes. Last night, explosions and fires broke out at the company's Apex, North Carolina, facility, forcing the evacuation of 17,000 local residents.

**Your task:** It's now Friday, the day after the fire. Write a brief post for the company's blog, covering the following points:

- A fire broke out at the Apex facility at approximately 10 P.M. Thursday.
- No one was in the facility at the time.
- Because of the diverse nature of the materials stored at the plant, the cause of the fire is not yet known.
- Rumors that the facility stores extremely dangerous chlorine gas and that the fire was spreading to other nearby businesses are not true.
- Special industrial firefighters hired by EQIS have already brought the fire under control.
- Residents in the immediate area were evacuated as a precaution, and they should be able to return to their homes tomorrow, pending permission from local authorities.
- Several dozen residents were admitted to local hospitals with complaints of breathing problems, but most have been released already; about a dozen emergency responders were treated as well.
- At this point (Friday afternoon), tests conducted by the North Carolina State Department of Environment and Natural Resources "had not detected anything out of the ordinary in the air."

Conclude by thanking the local police and fire departments for their assistance and directing readers to EQIS's toll-free hot line for more information.[37]

## BLOGGING SKILLS

### 20. Message Strategies: Responding to Rumors and Public Criticism [LO-6]
Spreading *FUD*—fear, uncertainty, and doubt—about other companies is one of the less-honorable ways of dealing with competition in the business world. For example,

someone can start a "whisper campaign" in the marketplace, raising fears that a particular company is struggling financially. Customers who don't want to risk future instability in their supply chains might then shift their purchasing away from the company, based on nothing more than the false rumor.

**Your task:** Find the website of any company that seems interesting. Imagine you are the CEO and the company is the subject of an online rumor about impending bankruptcy. Explore the website to get a basic feel for what the company does. Making up any information you need, write a post for the company's blog, explaining that the bankruptcy rumors are false and that the company is on solid financial ground and plans to keep serving the industry for many years to come. (Be sure to review page 307 for tips.)

## SOCIAL NETWORKING SKILLS

### 21. Message Strategies: Responding to Rumors and Public Criticism [LO-6]
The consumer reviews on Yelp (www.yelp .com) can be a promotional boon to any local business—provided the reviews are positive, of course. Negative reviews, fair or not, can affect a company's reputation and drive away potential customers. Fortunately for business owners, sites like Yelp give them the means to respond to reviews, whether they want to apologize for poor service, offer some form of compensation, or correct misinformation in a review.

**Your task:** Search Yelp for a negative review (one or two stars) on any business in any city. Find a review that has some substance to it, not just a simple, angry rant. Now imagine you are the owner of that business, and write a reply that could be posted via the "Add Owner Comment" feature. Use information you can find on Yelp about the company and fill in any details by using your imagination. Remember that your comment will be visible to everyone who visits Yelp. (Be sure to review page 307 for tips.)

# Negative Employment Messages

## SOCIAL NETWORKING SKILLS / EMAIL SKILLS

### 22. Message Strategies: Refusing Requests for Recommendations [LO-7]
You're delighted to get a message from an old friend and colleague, Heather Lang. You're delighted right up to the moment you read her request that you write a recommendation about her web design and programming skills for your LinkedIn profile. You would do just about anything for Lang—anything except recommend her web design skills. She is a master programmer whose technical wizardry saved more client projects than you can count, but when it comes to artistic design, Lang simply doesn't have "it." From gaudy color schemes to unreadable type treatment to confusing layouts, her design sense is as weak as her technical acumen is strong.

**Your task:** First, write a brief email to Lang, explaining that you would be most comfortable highlighting her technical skills because that is where you believe her true strengths lie. Second, write a two-sentence recommendation that you could include in your LinkedIn profile, recommending Lang's technical skills. Make up or research any details you need.

## TELEPHONE SKILLS

**23. Message Strategies: Terminating Employment [LO-7]** As the human resources manager at Alion Science and Technology, a military research firm in McLean, Virginia, you were thrilled when one of the nation's top computer visualization specialists accepted your job offer. Claus Gunnstein's skills would have made a major contribution to Alion's work in designing flight simulators and other systems. Unfortunately, the day after he accepted the offer, Alion received news that a major Pentagon contract had been canceled. In addition to letting several dozen current employees know that the company will be forced to lay them off, you need to tell Gunnstein that Alion has no choice but to rescind the job offer.

**Your task:** Outline the points you'll need to make in a telephone call to Gunnstein. Pay special attention to your opening and closing statements. (You'll review your plans for the phone call with Alion's legal staff to make sure everything you say follows employment law guidelines; for now, just focus on the way you'll present the negative news to Gunnstein. Feel free to make up any details you need.)[38]

## EMAIL SKILLS

**24. Message Strategies: Refusing Requests for Recommendations [LO-7]** Tom Weiss worked in the office at Opal Pools and Patios for four months under your supervision (you're office manager). On the basis of what he told you he could do, you started him off as a file clerk. However, his organizational skills proved inadequate for the job, so you transferred him to logging in accounts receivable, where he performed almost adequately. Then he assured you that his "real strength" was customer relations, so you moved him to the complaint department. After he spent three weeks making angry customers even angrier, you were convinced that no place in your office was appropriate for his talents. Five weeks ago, you encouraged him to resign before being formally fired.

Today's email brings a request from Weiss, asking you to write a letter recommending him for a sales position with a florist shop. You can't assess Weiss's sales abilities, but you do know him to be an incompetent file clerk, a careless bookkeeper, and an insensitive customer service representative. Someone else is more likely to deserve the sales job, so you decide that you have done enough favors for Tom Weiss for one lifetime and plan to refuse his request.

**Your task:** Write an email reply to Weiss, indicating that you have chosen not to write a letter of recommendation for him.

## MEMO WRITING SKILLS / PORTFOLIO BUILDER

**25. Message Strategies: Negative Performance Reviews [LO-7]** Elaine Bridgewater, the former professional golfer you hired to oversee your golf equipment company's relationship with retailers, knows the business inside and out. As a former touring pro, she has unmatched credibility. She also has seemingly boundless energy, solid technical knowledge, and an engaging personal style. Unfortunately, she hasn't been quite as attentive as she needs to be when it comes to communicating with retailers. You've been getting complaints about voicemail messages gone unanswered for days, confusing emails that require two or three rounds of clarification, and reports that are haphazardly thrown together. As valuable as Bridgewater's other skills are, she's going to cost the company sales if this goes on much longer. The retail channel is vital to your company's survival, and she's the employee most involved in this channel.

**Your task:** Draft a brief (one page maximum) informal performance appraisal and improvement plan for Bridgewater. Be sure to compliment her on the areas in which she excels but don't shy away from highlighting the areas in which she needs to improve, too: punctual response to customer messages; clear writing; and careful revision, production, and proofreading. Use what you've learned in this course so far to supply any additional advice about the importance of these skills.

## MyBCommLab

Go to **mybcommlab.com** for Auto-graded writing questions as well as the following Assisted-graded writing questions:

11-1. What are the five main goals in delivering bad news? [LO-1]

11-2. What are three techniques for deemphasizing negative news? [LO-3]

11-3. Mybcommlab Only—comprehensive writing assignment for this chapter.

# Endnotes

**1.** Chargify website, accessed 31 January 2013, http://chargify.com; David Hauser, "How to Break the Trust of Your Customers in Just One Day: Lessons Learned from a Major Mistake," David Hauser blog, 13 October 2010, http://davidhauser.com; Jason Kincaid, "Subscription Billing System Chargify Missteps as It Switches from Freemium to Premium," TechCrunch, 11 October 2010, http://techcrunch.com; Lance Walley, "Chargify News: New Pricing, Features & More,"

11 October 2010, http://chargify.com; "Chargify New Pricing" comment thread, Hacker News, http://news.ycombinator.com.

**2.** Ian McDonald, "Marsh Can Do $600 Million, but Apologize?" *Wall Street Journal,* 14 January 2005, C1, C3; Adrienne Carter and Amy Borrus, "What if Companies Fessed Up?" *BusinessWeek,* 24 January 2005, 59–60; Patrick J. Kiger, "The Art of the Apology," *Workforce Management,* October 2004, 57–62.

3. Ameeta Patel and Lamar Reinsch, "Companies Can Apologize: Corporate Apologies and Legal Liability," *Business Communication Quarterly,* March 2003, www.elibrary.com.

4. John Guiniven, "Sorry! An Apology as a Strategic PR Tool," *Public Relations Tactics,* December 2007, 6.

5. Howard Stringer, "A Letter from Howard Stringer," PlayStation Blog, 5 May 2011, http://blog.us.playstation.com.

6. Quinn Warnick, "A Close Textual Analysis of Corporate Lay-off Memos," *Business Communication Quarterly,* September 2010, 322–326.

7. Walley, "Chargify News: New Pricing, Features & More."

8. "Advice from the Pros on the Best Way to Deliver Bad News," Report on *Customer Relationship Management,* 1 February 2003, www.elibrary.com.

9. Ben Levisohn, "Getting More Workers to Whistle," *BusinessWeek,* 28 January 2008, 18.

10. "Less Than Half of Privately Held Businesses Support Whistleblowing," Grant Thornton website, accessed 13 October 2008, www.internationalbusinessreport.com.

11. Steve Karnowski, "New Food Safety Law Protects Whistleblowers," *Bloomberg Businessweek,* 11 February 2011, www.businessweek.com.

12. Sue Shellenbarger, "How to Keep Your Cool in Angry Times," *Wall Street Journal,* 22 September 2010, http://online.wsj.com.

13. Christopher Elliott, "7 Ways Smart Companies Tell Customers 'No,'" CBS Money Watch, 7 June 2011, www.cbsnews.com.

14. Micah Solomon, "Mean Tweets: Managing Customer Complaints," CNBC, 22 February 2012, www.cnbc.com; "When Fans Attack: How to Defend a Brand's Reputation Online," Crenshaw Communications blog, 20 May 2010, http://crenshawcomm.com; Leslie Gaines-Ross, "Reputation Warfare," *Harvard Business Review,* December 2010, 70–76; David Meerman Scott, "The US Air Force: Armed with Social Media," WebInkNow blog, 15 December 2008, www.webinknow.com; Matt Rhodes, "How to React If Somebody Writes About Your Brand Online," FreshNetworks blog, 9 January 2009, www.freshnetworks.com; Matt Rhodes, "Social Media as a Crisis Management Tool," Social Media Today blog, 21 December 2009, www.socialmediatoday.com.

15. Courtland L. Bovée, John V. Thill, George P. Dovel, and Marian Burk Wood, *Advertising Excellence* (New York: McGraw-Hill, 1995), 508–509; John Holusha, "Exxon's Public-Relations Problem," *New York Times,* 12 April 1989, D1.

16. Omowale Casselle, "Really, You Want ME to Write YOU a LinkedIn Recommendation," RecruitingBlogs, 22 April 2010, www.recruitingblogs.com.

17. "LinkedIn Profiles to Career Introductions: When You Can't Recommend Your Friend," *Seattle Post-Intelligencer* Personal Finance blog, 16 November 2010, http://blog.seattlepi.com.

18. Neal Schaffer, "How Should I Deal with a LinkedIn Recommendation Request I Don't Want to Give?" Social Web School, 20 January 2010, http://humancapitalleague.com.

19. Dawn Wolf, "Job Applicant Rejection Letter Dos and Donts—Writing an Appropriate 'Dear John' Letter to an Unsuccessful Applicant," 31 May 2009, Employment Blawg.com, www.employmentblawg.com.

20. Wolf, "Job Applicant Rejection Letter Dos and Donts"; "Prohibited Employment Policies/Practices," U.S. Equal Employment Opportunity Commission, accessed 14 July 2010, www.eeoc.gov; Susan M. Heathfield, "Candidate Rejection Letter," About.com, accessed 14 July 2010, http://humanresources.about.com; "Rejection Letters Under Scrutiny: 7 Do's & Don'ts," *Business Management Daily,* 1 April 2009, www.businessmanagementdaily.com.

21. Judi Brownell, "The Performance Appraisal Interviews: A Multi-purpose Communication Assignment," *Bulletin of the Association for Business Communication* 57, no. 2 (1994): 11–21.

22. Susan Friedfel, "Protecting Yourself in the Performance Review Process," *Workforce Management,* April 2009, www.workforce.com.

23. Kelly Spors, "Why Performance Reviews Don't Work—And What You Can Do About It," Independent Street blog, *Wall Street Journal,* 21 October 2008, http://blogs.wsj.com.

24. Rita Pyrillis, "Is Your Performance Review Underperforming?" *Workforce Management,* May 2011, 20–22, 24–25.

25. Friedfel, "Protecting Yourself in the Performance Review Process."

26. E. Michelle Bohreer and Todd J. Zucker, "Five Mistakes Managers Make When Terminating Employees," *Texas Lawyer,* 2 May 2006, www.law.com; Deborah Muller, "The Right Things to Do to Avoid Wrongful Termination Claims," *Workforce Management,* October 2008, www.workforce.com; Maria Greco Danaher, "Termination: Telling an Employee," *Workforce Management,* accessed 14 July 2010, www.workforce.com.

27. Adapted from "FDA Notifies Public That Vail Products, Inc., Issues Nationwide Recall of Enclosed Bed Systems," FDA press release, 30 June 2005, www.fda.gov.

28. Adapted from "Bathtub Curve," *Engineering Statistics Handbook,* National Institute of Standards and Technology website, accessed 16 April 2005, www.nist.gov; Robert Berner, "The Warranty Windfall," *BusinessWeek,* 20 December 2004, 84–86; Larry Armstrong, "When Service Contracts Make Sense," *BusinessWeek,* 20 December 2004, 86.

29. Adapted from Twitter/JetBlue website, accessed 29 October 2008, http://twitter.com/JetBlue.

30. "Viral Effect of Email Promotion," Alka Dwivedi blog, accessed 19 October 2006, www.alkadwivedi.net; Teresa Valdez Klein, "Starbucks Makes a Viral Marketing Misstep," Blog Business Summit website, accessed 19 October 2006, www.blogbusinesssummit.com.

31. Adapted from Lee Valley website, accessed 29 October 2008, www.leevalley.com.

32. Adapted from Stanton website, accessed 18 August 2005, www.stantondj.com.

33. Adapted from Pui-Wing Tam, Erin White, Nick Wingfield, and Kris Maher, "Snooping Email by Software Is Now a Workplace Norm," *Wall Street Journal,* 9 March 2005, B1+.

34. Adapted from Sylvia Ann Hewlett and Carolyn Buck Luce, "Off-ramps and On-ramps," *Harvard Business Review,* March 2005, 43–54.

35. Adapted from Rodney Manley, "Milledgeville Plant to Close; 150 to Lose Jobs," Macon.com, 28 January 2009, www.macon.com; Jamie Jones, "Shaw Plant Closing in Milledgeville," *The Daily Citizen* (Dalton, Georgia), 29 January 2009, www.northwestgeorgia.com.

36. Adapted from "Recall Safety Notice," Bombardier Recreational Products website, 10 September 2008, www.brp.com; Bombardier Recreational Products website, accessed 30 October 2008, www.brp.com.

37. Adapted from Environmental Quality Company press releases, accessed 27 October 2006, www.eqonline.com; "N.C. Residents to Return After Fire," Science Daily, 6 October 2006, www.sciencedaily.com; "Hazardous Waste Plant Fire in N.C. Forces 17,000 to Evacuate," FOXNews.com, 6 October 2006, www.foxnews.com.

38. Adapted from Alion website, accessed 19 August 2005, www.alionscience.com.

# Writing Persuasive Messages

## LEARNING OBJECTIVES

After studying this chapter, you will be able to

**1** Apply the three-step writing process to persuasive messages.

**2** Describe an effective strategy for developing persuasive business messages and identify the three most common categories of persuasive business messages.

**3** Describe an effective strategy for developing marketing and sales messages and explain how to modify your approach when writing promotional messages for social media.

**4** Identify steps you can take to avoid ethical lapses in marketing and sales messages.

## MyBCommLab®

⭐ **Improve Your Grade!** Over 10 million students improved their results using the Pearson MyLabs. Visit **mybcommlab.com** for simulations, tutorials, and end-of-chapter problems.

CafeMom uses social media to replicate the in-person experience of parents sharing information, advice, and emotional support.

■■■■■■■■■■
**COMMUNICATION CLOSE-UP AT**
## CafeMom www.cafemom.com

Few roles in life require more information and insight than parenting. From prenatal care to early childhood development to education to socialization issues, parents are in continuous learning mode as their children grow. Parents also need to learn about themselves as they grow in their roles, from balancing work and home life to nurturing their own relationships. At the same time, parenting can be one of the most isolating experiences for people, often making it difficult for them to acquire the information and support they need to succeed as parents.

Two lifelong friends, actor and activist Andrew Shue and entrepreneur Michael Sanchez, pondered this age-old challenge and saw the web as a solution. The pair cofounded CafeMom, an online community and information resource that helps mothers find answers, insights, and each other.

Information resources and social networks abound on the web, and like any other web start-up, CafeMom faced the challenge of standing apart from the crowd and growing its membership large enough to create a viable business. One of the keys to its success is clear, audience-focused messages that make a compelling case for joining CafeMom. Using straightforward statements such as "Moms connecting about pregnancy, babies, home, health, and more," the company communicates the features of its various online services and the benefits of joining.

The persuasive communication effort certainly seems to have been successful: CafeMom is now the largest social networking community for mothers and continues to expand as more mothers join in search of helpful insights and friendly support from their peers.[1]

# Using the Three-Step Writing Process for Persuasive Messages

**1 LEARNING OBJECTIVE**
Apply the three-step writing process to persuasive messages.

Professionals such as Michael Sanchez, CEO of CafeMom (profiled in the chapter-opening Communication Close-Up), understand that successful businesses rely on persuasive messages in both internal and external communication. Whether you're trying to convince your boss to open a new office in Europe or encourage potential customers to try your products, you need to call on your abilities of **persuasion**—the attempt to change an audience's attitudes, beliefs, or actions.[2] Because persuasive messages ask audiences to give something of value (money in exchange for a product, for example) or take substantial action (such as changing a corporate policy), they are more challenging to write than routine messages. Successful professionals understand that persuasion is not about trickery or getting people to act against their own best interests; it's about letting audiences know they have choices and presenting your offering in the best possible light.[3]

Persuasion is the attempt to change someone's attitudes, beliefs, or actions.

## STEP 1: PLANNING PERSUASIVE MESSAGES

Having a great idea or a great product is not enough; you need to be able to convince others of its merits.

In today's information-saturated business environment, having a great idea or a great product is no longer enough. Every day, untold numbers of good ideas go unnoticed and good products go unsold simply because the messages meant to promote them aren't compelling enough to be heard above the competitive noise. Creating successful persuasive messages in these challenging situations demands careful attention to all four tasks in the planning step, starting with an insightful analysis of your purpose and your audience.

### Analyzing the Situation

Clarifying your purpose is an essential step with persuasive messages.

In defining your purpose, make sure you're clear about what you really hope to achieve. Suppose you want to persuade company executives to support a particular research project. But what does "support" mean? Do you want them to pat you on the back and wish you well? Or do you want them to give you a staff of five researchers and a $1 million annual budget?

The best persuasive messages are closely connected to your audience's desires and interests (see Figure 12.1).[4] Consider these important questions: Who is my audience? What

The main idea of "choose TD Ameritrade" is echoed from the webpage tab, through the introductory text, and down to the specific details.

The headline and introductory paragraph address universal concerns among investors.

These six supporting points—each of which reflects a key audience need—back up the top-level message of "A better way to invest."

An endorsement from a well-known source boosts the credibility of the company's promotional message.

Each of the six supporting points is presented at three levels of detail: (1) the short message of the button labels at the far left, (2) a short paragraph with a headline that echoes audience needs, and (3) additional pages (accessed via the link) with full details.

**Figure 12.1  Appealing to Audience Needs**
On this expertly written and designed webpage, TD Ameritrade echoes the concerns that individual investors are likely to have when selecting a stockbroker. Notice how well the writing moves the reader from the high-level message to six individual supporting points—each of which is a major audience need—and then on to more detailed information. The clean, focused design is equally effective and works in close harmony with the text. The layout guides the reader's eye from the upper left corner, downward to the six key support points, and then across to the right for additional layers of detail.
*Source:* Image Courtesy TD Ameritrade IP Company, Inc.

are my audience members' needs? What do I want them to do? How might they resist? Are there alternative positions I need to examine? What does the decision maker consider to be the most important issue? How might the organization's culture influence my strategy?

To understand and categorize audience needs, you can refer to specific information, such as **demographics** (the age, gender, occupation, income, education, and other quantifiable characteristics of the people you're trying to persuade) and **psychographics** (personality, attitudes, lifestyle, and other psychological characteristics). When analyzing your audiences, take into account their cultural expectations and practices so that you don't undermine your persuasive message by using an inappropriate appeal or by organizing your message in a way that seems unfamiliar or uncomfortable to your readers.

Demographics include characteristics such as age, gender, occupation, income, and education.

Psychographics include characteristics such as personality, attitudes, and lifestyle.

If you aim to change someone's attitudes, beliefs, or actions through a persuasive message, it is vital to understand his or her **motivation**—the combination of forces that drive people to satisfy their needs. Table 12.1 lists some of the needs that psychologists have

## TABLE 12.1  Human Needs That Influence Motivation

| Need | Implications for Communication |
|---|---|
| **Basic physiological requirements:** The needs for food, water, sleep, oxygen, etc. | Everyone has these needs, but the degree of attention an individual gives to them often depends on whether the needs are being met; for instance, an advertisement for sleeping pills will have greater appeal to someone suffering from insomnia than to someone who has no problem sleeping. |
| **Safety and security:** The needs for protection from bodily harm, for assurance that loved ones are safe, and for financial security, protection of personal identity, career security, and other assurances | These needs influence both consumer and business decisions in a wide variety of ways; for instance, advertisements for life insurance often encourage parents to think about the financial security of their children and other loved ones. |
| **Affiliation and belonging:** The needs for companionship, acceptance, love, and popularity | The need to feel loved, accepted, or popular drives a great deal of human behavior, from the desire to be attractive to potential mates to wearing the clothing style that a particular social group is likely to approve. |
| **Power and control:** The need to feel in control of situations or to exert authority over others | You can see many examples appealing to this need in advertisements: *Take control of your life*, *your finances*, *your future*, *your career*, and so on. Many people who lack power want to know how to get it, and people who have power often want others to know they have it. |
| **Achievement:** The need to feel a sense of accomplishment— or to be admired by others for accomplishments | This need can involve both *knowing* (when people experience a feeling of accomplishment) and *showing* (when people are able to show others that they've achieved success); advertising for luxury consumer products frequently appeals to this need. |
| **Adventure and distraction:** The need for excitement or relief from daily routine | People vary widely in their need for adventure; some crave excitement—even danger—while others value calmness and predictability. Some needs for adventure and distraction are met *virtually*, such as through horror movies, thriller novels, and violent video games. |
| **Knowledge, exploration, and understanding:** The need to keep learning | For some people, learning is usually a means to an end, a way to fulfill some other need; for others, acquiring new knowledge is the goal. |
| **Aesthetic appreciation:** The desire to experience beauty, order, and symmetry | Although this need may seem "noncommercial" at first glance, advertisers appeal to it frequently, from the pleasing shape of a package to the quality of the gemstones in a piece of jewelry. |
| **Self-actualization:** The need to "be all that one can be," to reach one's full potential as a human being | Psychologists Kurt Goldstein and Abraham Maslow popularized self-actualization as the desire to make the most of one's potential, and Maslow identified it as one of the higher-level needs in his classic hierarchy; even if people met most or all of their other needs, they would still feel the need to self-actualize. An often-quoted example of appealing to this need is the U.S. Army's one-time advertising slogan "Be all you can be." |
| **Helping others:** The need to believe that one is making a difference in the lives of other people | This need is the central motivation in fundraising messages and other appeals to charity. |

*Sources:* Adapted from Courtland L. Bovée and John V. Thill, *Business in Action*, 6th ed. (Upper Saddle River, N.J.: Prentice Hall, 2013), 219–232; Saundra K. Ciccarelli and Glenn E. Meyer, *Psychology* (Upper Saddle River, N.J.: Prentice Hall, 2006), 336–346; Abraham H. Maslow, "A Theory of Human Motivation," *Psychological Review* 50 (1943): 370–396.

identified or suggested as being important in influencing human motivation. Obviously, the more closely a persuasive message aligns with a recipient's existing motivation, the more effective the message is likely to be. For example, if you try to persuade consumers to purchase a product on the basis of its fashion appeal, that message will connect with consumers who are motivated by a desire to be in style but probably won't connect with consumers driven by functional or financial concerns.

## Gathering Information

Once your situation analysis is complete, you need to gather the information necessary to create a compelling persuasive message. You'll learn more about the types of information to include in persuasive business messages and marketing and sales messages later in this chapter. Chapter 13 presents advice on how to find the information you need.

## Selecting the Right Medium

Persuasive messages can be found in virtually every communication medium, from instant messages and podcasts to radio advertisements and skywriting. In fact, advertising agencies employ media specialists whose job is to analyze the media options available and select the most cost-effective combination for each client and each advertising campaign.

In some situations, various members of your audience might prefer different media for the same message. Some consumers like to do all their car shopping in person, whereas others do most of their car-shopping research online. Some people don't mind promotional emails for products they're interested in; others resent every piece of commercial email they receive. If you can't be sure you can reach most or all of your audience through a single medium, you need to use two or more, such as following up an email campaign with printed letters.

Social media provide some exciting options for persuasive messages, particularly marketing and sales messages. However, as "Writing Promotional Messages for Social Media" on page 340 explains, messages in these media require a unique approach.

Another important area of development is combining personal attention with technological reach and efficiency. For example, a customer support agent can carry on multiple instant messaging conversations at once, responding to one customer while other customers are typing messages. Even perceptions of human interaction created by animated *avatars* such as IKEA's "Anna" (www.ikea.com) can create a more sociable experience for shoppers, which can make websites more effective as a persuasive medium.[5]

*Persuasive messages are often unexpected and sometimes even unwelcome, so choose your medium carefully to maximize the chance of getting through to your audience.*

## ORGANIZING YOUR INFORMATION

The most effective main ideas for persuasive messages have one thing in common: They are about the receiver, not the sender. For instance, if you're trying to convince others to join you in a business venture, explain how it will help them, not how it will help you.

Limiting your scope is vital. If you seem to be wrestling with more than one main idea, you haven't zeroed in on the heart of the matter. If you try to craft a persuasive message without focusing on the one central problem or opportunity your audience truly cares about, you're unlikely to persuade successfully.[6]

Because the nature of persuasion is to convince people to change their attitudes, beliefs, or actions, most persuasive messages use the indirect approach. That means you'll want to explain your reasons and build interest before asking for a decision or for action—or perhaps even before revealing your purpose. In contrast, when you have a close relationship with your audience and the message is welcome or at least neutral, the direct approach can be effective.

*Most persuasive messages use the indirect approach.*

For persuasive business messages, the choice between the direct and indirect approaches is also influenced by the extent of your authority, expertise, or power in an organization. For instance, if you are a highly regarded technical expert with years of experience, you might use the direct approach in a message to top executives. In contrast, if you aren't well known and therefore need to rely more on the strength of your message than the power of your reputation, the indirect approach will probably be more successful.

*The choice of approach is influenced by your position (or authority within the organization) relative to your audience's.*

## STEP 2: WRITING PERSUASIVE MESSAGES

Encourage a positive response to your persuasive messages by (1) using positive and polite language, (2) understanding and respecting cultural differences, (3) being sensitive to organizational cultures, and (4) taking steps to establish your credibility.

Positive language usually happens naturally with persuasive messages because you're promoting an idea or product you believe in. However, take care not to inadvertently insult your readers by implying that they've made poor choices in the past and that you're here to save them from their misguided ways.

Be sure to understand cultural expectations as well. For example, a message that seems forthright and direct in a low-context culture might seem brash and intrusive in a high-context culture.

Just as social culture affects the success of a persuasive message, so too does the culture within an organization. For instance, some organizations handle disagreement and conflict indirectly, behind the scenes, whereas others accept and even encourage open discussion and sharing of differing viewpoints.

Finally, when you are trying to persuade a skeptical or hostile audience, credibility is essential. You must convince people that you know what you're talking about and that you're not trying to mislead them (see "Ethics Detective: Solving the Case of the Incredible Credibility"). Use these techniques:

- Use simple language to avoid suspicions of fantastic claims and emotional manipulation.
- Provide objective evidence for the claims and promises you make.
- Identify your sources, especially if your audience already respects those sources.
- Establish common ground by emphasizing beliefs, attitudes, and background experiences you have in common with the audience.
- Be objective and present fair and logical arguments.
- Display your willingness to keep your audience's best interests at heart.
- Persuade with logic, evidence, and compelling narratives, rather than trying to coerce with high-pressure, "hard sell" tactics.
- Whenever possible, try to build your credibility before you present a major proposal or ask for a major decision. That way, audiences don't have to evaluate both you and your message at the same time.[7]

**REAL-TIME UPDATES**

LEARN MORE BY WATCHING THIS VIDEO

**Persuasion skills for every business professional**

Persuasion is an essential business skill, no matter what career path you follow. This video offers great tips for understanding, practicing, and applying persuasive skills. Go to http://real-timeupdates.com/bct12 and click on Learn More. If you are using MyBCommLab, you can access Real-Time Updates within each chapter or under Student Study Tools.

*Positive language is an essential feature of persuasive messages.*

*Organizational culture can influence persuasion as much as social culture.*

*Audiences often respond unfavorably to over-the-top language, so keep your writing simple and straightforward.*

---

**ETHICS DETECTIVE**

## Solving the Case of the Incredible Credibility

As the director of human resources in your company, you're desperate for some help. You want to keep the costs of employee benefits under control while making sure you provide employees with a fair benefits package. However, you don't have time to research all the options for health insurance, wellness programs, retirement plans, family counseling, educational benefits, and everything else, so you decide to hire a consultant. You receive the following message from a consultant interested in working with you:

> I am considered the country's foremost authority on employee health insurance programs. My clients offer universally positive feedback on the programs I've designed for them. They also love how much time I save them—hundreds and hundreds of hours. I am

absolutely confident that I can thoroughly analyze your needs and create a portfolio that realizes every degree of savings possible. I invite you to experience the same level of service that has generated such comments as "Best advice ever!" and "Saved us an unbelievable amount of money."

You'd love to get results like that, but the message almost sounds too good to be true. Is it?

**ANALYSIS**

The consultant's message contains at least a dozen instances in which this writer's credibility might be questioned. Identify as many as you can, and explain how you would bolster reader confidence by providing additional or different information.

## STEP 3: COMPLETING PERSUASIVE MESSAGES

The pros know from experience that details can make or break a persuasive message, so they're careful not to skimp on this part of the writing process. For instance, advertisers may have a dozen or more people review a message before it's released to the public.

When you evaluate your content, try to judge your argument objectively and try not to overestimate your credibility. If possible, ask an experienced colleague who knows your audience well to review your draft. Make sure your design elements complement, rather than detract from, your persuasive argument. In addition, meticulous proofreading will help you identify any mechanical or spelling errors that would weaken your persuasive potential. Finally, make sure your distribution methods fit your audience's expectations and preferences.

With the three-step model in mind, you're ready to begin composing persuasive messages, starting with *persuasive business messages* (those that try to convince audiences to approve new projects, enter into business partnerships, and so on), followed by *marketing and sales messages* (those that try to convince audiences to consider and then purchase products and services).

# Developing Persuasive Business Messages

Your success as a businessperson is closely tied to your ability to encourage others to accept new ideas, change old habits, or act on your recommendations. Unless your career takes you into marketing and sales, most of your persuasive messages will consist of *persuasive business messages*, which are those designed to elicit a preferred response in a nonsales situation.

## STRATEGIES FOR PERSUASIVE BUSINESS MESSAGES

Even if you have the power to compel others to do what you want them to do, persuading them is more effective than forcing them. People who are forced into accepting a decision or plan are less motivated to support it and more likely to react negatively than if they're persuaded.[8] Within the context of the three-step process, effective persuasion involves four essential strategies: framing your arguments, balancing emotional and logical appeals, reinforcing your position, and anticipating objections. (Note that all these concepts in this section apply as well to marketing and sales messages, covered later in the chapter.)

### Framing Your Arguments

As noted earlier, most persuasive messages use the indirect approach. Experts in persuasive communication have developed a number of indirect models for such messages. One of the best known is the **AIDA model**, which organizes messages into four phases (see Figure 12.2):

- **Attention.** Your first objective is to engage your readers or listeners in a way that encourages them to want to hear about your main idea. Write a brief and compelling sentence, without making extravagant claims or irrelevant points. Look for some common ground on which to build your case. And while you want to be positive and confident, make sure you don't start out with a *hard sell*—a pushy, aggressive opening. Doing so often puts audiences on guard and on the defensive.
- **Interest.** Emphasize the relevance of your message to your audience. Continuing the theme you started with, paint a more detailed picture of the problem you propose to solve with the solution you're offering (whether it's a new idea, a new process, a new product, or whatever).
- **Desire.** Help audience members embrace your idea by explaining how the change will benefit them, either personally or professionally. Reduce resistance by identifying and answering in advance any questions the audience might have. If your idea is complex,

Careless production undermines your credibility, so revise and proofread with care.

**2** **LEARNING OBJECTIVE**
Describe an effective strategy for developing persuasive business messages and identify the three most common categories of persuasive business messages.

The AIDA model is a useful approach for many persuasive messages:
- Attention
- Interest
- Desire
- Action

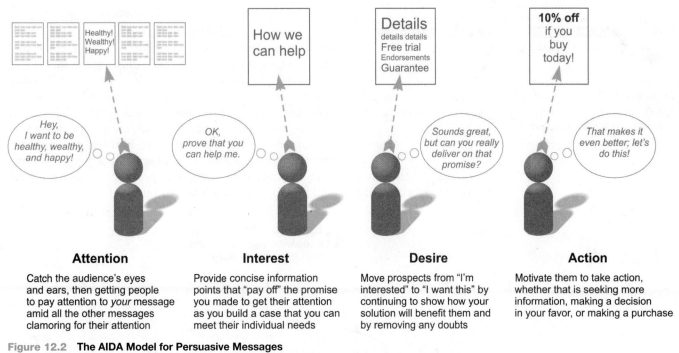

**Attention**

Catch the audience's eyes and ears, then getting people to pay attention to *your* message amid all the other messages clamoring for their attention

**Interest**

Provide concise information points that "pay off" the promise you made to get their attention as you build a case that you can meet their individual needs

**Desire**

Move prospects from "I'm interested" to "I want this" by continuing to show how your solution will benefit them and by removing any doubts

**Action**

Motivate them to take action, whether that is seeking more information, making a decision in your favor, or making a purchase

**Figure 12.2   The AIDA Model for Persuasive Messages**
With the AIDA model, you craft one or more messages to move recipients through four stages of attention, interest, desire, and action. The model works well for both persuasive business messages (such as persuading your manager to fund a new project) and marketing and sales messages.

you might need to explain how you would implement it. Back up your claims in order to increase audience willingness to take the action you suggest in the next section.

- **Action.** Suggest the action you want readers to take and phrase it in a way that emphasizes the benefits to them or to the organization they represent. Make the action as easy as possible to take, including offering to assist, if appropriate. Be sure to provide all the information the audience needs to take the action, including deadlines and contact details.

The AIDA model is tailor-made for using the indirect approach, allowing you to save your main idea for the action phase. However, you can also use AIDA for the direct approach, in which case you use your main idea as an attention-getter, build interest with your argument, create desire with your evidence, and reemphasize your main idea in the action phase with the specific action you want your audience to take.

When your AIDA message uses the indirect approach and is delivered by memo or email, keep in mind that your subject line usually catches your reader's eye first. Your challenge is to make it interesting and relevant enough to capture reader attention without revealing your main idea. If you put your request in the subject line, you might get a quick no before you've had a chance to present your arguments:

*The AIDA model is ideal for the indirect approach.*

| Instead of This | Write This |
|---|---|
| Request for development budget to add automated IM response system | Reducing the cost of customer support inquiries |

With either the direct or indirect approach, AIDA and similar models do have limitations. First, AIDA is a unidirectional method that essentially talks *at* audiences, not *with* them. Second, AIDA is built around a single event, such as asking an audience for a decision, rather than on building a mutually beneficial, long-term relationship.[9] AIDA is still a valuable tool for the right purposes, but as you'll read later in the chapter, a conversational approach is more compatible with today's social media.

*The AIDA approach does have limitations:*
- *It essentially talks* at *audiences, not* with *them*
- *It focuses on one-time events, not long-term relationships*

## Balancing Emotional and Logical Appeals

Imagine you're sitting at a control panel with one knob labeled "logic" and another labeled "emotion." As you prepare your persuasive message, you carefully adjust each knob, tuning the message for maximum impact (see Figure 12.3). Too little emotion, and your audience might not care enough to respond. Too much emotion, and your audience might think you are ignoring tough business questions or even being irrational.

Generally speaking, persuasive business messages rely more heavily on logical than on emotional appeals because the main idea is usually to save money, increase quality, or improve some other practical, measurable aspect of business. To find the optimum balance, consider four factors: (1) the

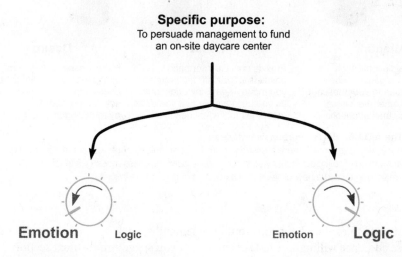

**Specific purpose:**
To persuade management to fund an on-site daycare center

**Emotion** Logic

**Proposal to improve employee satisfaction and work/life balance**

Being separated during the day is stressful for both parents and children.

Many parents are now working more hours and second jobs to make ends meet, so the situation is getting worse.

The extra travel time every morning and evening to put children in daycare adds to the stress and cost of coming to work.

When parents need to leave work to pick up sick children from daycare or stay home with them, this often creates an unfair burden on other employees to pick up the slack.

Knowing that the company cares about them and their children would boost employee morale.

Therefore, the company should provide an on-site daycare facility with a separate infirmary where sick children could stay during the day.

Emotion **Logic**

**Proposal to boost productivity and reduce absenteeism**

Analysis of employee time records shows that employees with children under the age of 10 take unscheduled days off three times more often than employees without young children.

Daycare issues are cited as the number one reason for these unscheduled days off.

In the 98 exit interviews conducted last year, 24 departing employees mentioned the need to balance family and work commitments as the primary reason for leaving.

In the last six months, HR has logged 14 complaints from employees who say they have to take on extra work when colleagues leave the office to pick up sick children from daycare.

Research shows that on-site daycare can improve productivity by as much as 20 percent—among parents and nonparents alike.

Therefore, the company should provide an on-site daycare facility with a separate infirmary where sick children could stay during the day.

**Figure 12.3   Balancing Logical and Emotional Appeals**
Whenever you plan a persuasive message, imagine you have a knob that turns from *emotion* at one extreme to *logic* at the other, letting you adjust the relative proportions of each type of appeal. Compare these two outlines for a proposal that asks management to fund an on-site daycare center. The version on the left relies heavily on emotional appeals, whereas the version on the right uses logical appeals (inductive reasoning, specifically). Through your choice of words, images, and supporting details, you can adjust the emotional–logical ratio in every message.

actions you hope to motivate, (2) your readers' expectations, (3) the degree of resistance you need to overcome, and (4) your position in the formal and informal power structure of the organization.[10]

**Emotional Appeals** As its name implies, an **emotional appeal** calls on audience feelings and sympathies rather than on facts, figures, and rational arguments. For instance, you can make use of the emotion surrounding certain words. The word *freedom* evokes strong feelings, as do words such as *success, prestige, compassion, security,* and *comfort.* Such words can help put your audience members in a positive frame of mind and help them accept your message. However, emotional appeals in business messages aren't usually effective by themselves because the audience wants proof that you can solve a business problem. Even if your audience members reach a conclusion based primarily on emotions, they'll look to you to provide logical support as well.

Emotional appeals attempt to connect with the reader's feelings or sympathies.

**Logical Appeals** A **logical appeal** calls on reasoning and evidence. The basic approach with a logical appeal is to make a claim based on a rational argument, supported by solid evidence. When appealing to your audience's logic, you might use three types of reasoning:

Logical appeals are based on the reader's notions of reason; these appeals can use analogy, induction, or deduction.

- **Analogy.** With analogy, you reason from specific evidence to specific evidence, in effect "borrowing" from something familiar to explain something unfamiliar. For instance, to convince management to add chat room capability to the company's groupware system, you could explain that it is like a neighborhood community center, only online.
- **Induction.** With inductive reasoning, you work from specific evidence to a general conclusion. To convince your team to change to a new manufacturing process, for example, you could point out that every company that has adopted it has increased profits, so it must be a smart idea.
- **Deduction.** With deductive reasoning, you work from a generalization to a specific conclusion. To persuade your boss to hire additional customer support staff, you might point to industry surveys that show how crucial customer satisfaction is to corporate profits.

Every method of reasoning is vulnerable to misuse, both intentional and unintentional, so verify your rational arguments carefully. For example, in the case of the manufacturing process, are there any other factors that affect the integrity of your reasoning? What if that process works well only for small companies with few products, and your firm is a multinational behemoth with 10,000 products? To guard against faulty logic, follow these guidelines:[11]

Using logical appeals carries with it the ethical responsibility to avoid faulty logic.

- **Avoid hasty generalizations.** Make sure you have plenty of evidence before drawing conclusions.
- **Avoid circular reasoning.** *Circular reasoning* is a logical fallacy in which you try to support your claim by restating it in different words. The statement "We know temporary workers cannot handle this task because temps are unqualified for it" doesn't prove anything because the claim and the supporting evidence are essentially identical. It doesn't prove *why* the temps are unqualified.
- **Avoid attacking an opponent.** If your persuasive appeal involves countering a competitive appeal made by someone else, make sure you attack the argument your opponent is making, not his or her character or qualifications.
- **Avoid oversimplifying a complex issue.** Make sure you present all the factors and don't reduce a wide range of choices to a simple "either/or" scenario if that isn't the case.
- **Avoid mistaken assumptions of cause and effect.** If you can't isolate the impact of a specific factor, you can't assume it's the cause of whatever effect you're discussing. The weather improves in spring, and people start playing baseball in spring. Does good weather cause baseball? No. There is a *correlation* between the two—meaning the data associated with them tend to rise and fall at the same time, but there is no *causation*—no proof that one causes the other. The complexity of many business situations makes cause and effect a particular challenge. You lowered prices, and sales went up. Were lower prices the cause of the increased sales? Perhaps, but the increase in sales might have been caused by a better advertising campaign, a competitor's delivery problems, or some other factor.
- **Avoid faulty analogies.** Be sure that the two objects or situations being compared are similar enough for the analogy to hold. For instance, explaining that an Internet

firewall is like a prison wall is a poor analogy, because a firewall keeps things out, whereas a prison wall keeps things in.

- **Avoid illogical support.** Make sure the connection between your claim and your support is truly logical and not based on a leap of faith, a missing premise, or irrelevant evidence.

### Reinforcing Your Position

After you've worked out the basic elements of your argument, step back and look for ways to bolster the strength of your position. Are all your claims supported by believable evidence? Would a quotation from a recognized expert help make your case?

*Choose your words carefully to trigger the desired responses.*

Next, examine your language. Can you find more powerful words to convey your message? For example, if your company is in serious financial trouble, talking about *fighting for survival* is a more powerful emotional appeal than talking about *ensuring continued operations*. As with any other powerful tool, though, use vivid language and abstractions carefully and honestly.

In addition to examining individual word choices, consider using metaphors and other figures of speech. If you want to describe a quality-control system as being designed to detect every possible product flaw, you might call it a "spider web" to imply that it catches everything that comes its way. Similarly, anecdotes (brief stories) can help your audience grasp the meaning and importance of your arguments. Instead of just listing the number of times the old laptop computers in your department have failed, you could describe how you lost a sale when your computer broke down during a critical sales presentation.

Beyond specific words and phrases, look for other factors that can reinforce your position. When you're asking for something, your audience members will find it easier to grant your request if they stand to benefit from it as well.

### Anticipating Objections

*Even powerful persuasive messages can encounter audience resistance.*

Even the most compelling ideas and proposals can be expected to encounter some initial resistance. The best way to deal with audience resistance is to anticipate as many objections as you can and address them in your message before your audience can even bring them up. For instance, if you know that your proposal to switch to lower-cost materials will raise concerns about product quality, address this issue head-on in your message. If you wait until people raise the concern after reading your message, they may gravitate toward another firm before you have a chance to address their concerns. By bringing up such potential problems right away, you also demonstrate a broad appreciation of the issue and imply confidence in your message.[12] This anticipation is particularly important in written messages, when you don't have the opportunity to detect and respond to objections on the spot.

*If you expect strong resistance, present all sides of an issue.*

To uncover potential audience objections, try to poke holes in your own theories and ideas before your audience does. Then find solutions to the problems you've uncovered. If possible, ask your audience members for their thoughts on the subject before you put together your argument; people are more likely to support solutions they help create.

Keep two things in mind when anticipating objections. First, you don't always have to explicitly discuss a potential objection. You could simply mention that the lower-cost materials have been tested and approved by the quality-control department. Second, if you expect a hostile audience, one biased against your plan from the beginning, present all sides of the story. As you cover each option, explain the pros and cons. You'll gain additional credibility if you present these options before presenting your recommendation or decision.[13]

## AVOIDING COMMON MISTAKES IN PERSUASIVE COMMUNICATION

When you believe in a concept or project you are promoting, it's easy to get caught up in your own confidence and enthusiasm and thereby fail to see things from the audience's perspective. When putting together persuasive arguments, avoid these common mistakes (see Figure 12.4):[14]

*Don't let confidence or enthusiasm lead you to some common mistakes in persuasive communication.*

- **Using a hard sell.** Don't push. No one likes being pressured into making a decision, and communicators who take this approach can come across as being more concerned with

It's time to call the Fast Track program what it truly is—a disaster. Everyone was excited last year when we announced the plan to speed up our development efforts and introduce at least one new product every month. We envisioned rapidly expanding market share and strong revenue growth in all our product lines. What we got instead is a nightmare that is getting worse with every launch.

As a company, we clearly underestimated the resources it would take to market, sell, and support so many new products. We can't hire and train fast enough, and our teams in every department are overwhelmed. Forced to jump from one new product to the next, with no time to focus, the sales and technical specialists can't develop the expertise needed to help buyers before the sale or support them after the sale. As a result, too many customers either buy the wrong product or buy the right product but then can't get knowledgeable help when they need it. We're losing credibility in the market, we're starting to lose sales, and it won't be long before we start losing employees who are fed up with the insanity.

To make matters even worse, some of the recent products were clearly rushed to market before they were ready, with hardware quality problems and buggy software. Returns and warranty costs are skyrocketing.

New products are the lifeblood of the company, to be sure, but there is no point in introducing products that only create enormous support headaches and cost more to support than they generate in profits. We need to put the Fast Track initiative on hold immediately so the entire company can regroup. The R&D lab can devote its time to fixing problems in the recent products, and the rest of us can catch our collective breath and figure out how to meet our sales and support goals with the current product portfolio and our current staffing levels.

The company has clearly staked a lot on this program, so opening by calling it a disaster will only put the reader on the defensive.

Word choices such as *nightmare* and *insanity* give the message an emotional, almost hysterical, tone that detracts from the serious message.

The writer mingles an observation that may be subjective (declining credibility), a hard data point (declining sales), and a prediction (possibility of employee defections).

The claim that recent products were "clearly rushed to market" is unnecessarily inflammatory (because it blames another department) and distracts the reader from the more immediate problems of poor quality.

The first sentence of the last paragraph is insulting to anyone with basic business sense—particularly the president of a company.

This neutral summary of events serves as an effective buffer for the indirect approach and provides a subtle reminder of the original goals of the program.

This paragraph contains the same information as the poor version, but does so in a calmer way that is less likely to trigger the reader's defense mechanisms and thereby keeps the focus on the facts.

Notice how the writer separates a personal hunch (about the possibility of losing employees) from an observation about the market and a measured data point.

The information about the quality problems is introduced without directing blame.

With the evidence assembled, the writer introduces the main idea of putting the program on hold. The recommendation is a judgment call and a suggestion to a superior, so the hedging clause *I believe* is appropriate.

Everyone was excited last year when we launched the Fast Track program to speed up our development efforts and introduce at least one new product every month. We envisioned rapidly expanding market share and strong revenue growth in all our product lines.

While the R&D lab has met its goal of monthly releases, as a company, we clearly underestimated the resources it would take to market, sell, and support so many new products. We can't hire and train fast enough, and our teams in every department are overwhelmed. The sales and technical specialists haven't had time to develop the expertise needed to help buyers before the sale or support them after the sale. As a result, too many customers either buy the wrong product or buy the right product but then can't get knowledgeable help when they need it.

We're losing credibility in the market, and we're starting to lose sales. If the situation continues, I fear we will being losing employees, too.

In addition, some of the recent products are generating multiple reports of hardware quality problems and buggy software. Returns and warranty costs are climbing at an unprecedented rate.

With costs rising faster than revenues and our people getting overwhelmed, I believe it is time to put the Fast Track initiative on hold until the company can regroup. The hiatus would give R&D time to address the quality problems and give the marketing, sales, and tech support team the chance to re-assess our goals with the current product portfolio and our current staffing levels.

**Figure 12.4  Persuasive Argumentation**

Imagine you're the marketing manager in a company that decided to speed up its new product launches but did too much too fast and wound up creating chaos. You decide enough is enough and write a memo to the company president advocating that the new program be shut down until the company can regroup—a suggestion you know will meet with resistance. Notice how the ineffective version doesn't quite use the direct approach but comes out swinging, so to speak, and is overly emotional throughout. The effective version builds to its recommendation indirectly, using the same information but in a calm, logical way. Because it sticks to the facts, it is also shorter.

---

**CHECKLIST** ✓ Developing Persuasive Messages

**A. Get your reader's attention.**
- Open with an audience benefit, a stimulating question, a problem, or an unexpected statement.
- Establish common ground by mentioning a point on which you and your audience agree.
- Show that you understand the audience's concerns.

**B. Build your reader's interest.**
- Expand and support your opening claim or promise.
- Emphasize the relevance of your message to your audience.

**C. Increase your reader's desire.**
- Make audience members want to change by explaining how the change will benefit them.
- Back up your claims with relevant evidence.

**D. Motivate your reader to take action.**
- Suggest the action you want readers to take.
- Stress the positive results of the action.
- Make the desired action clear and easy.

**E. Balance emotional and logical appeals.**
- Use emotional appeals to help the audience accept your message.
- Use logical appeals when presenting facts and evidence for complex ideas or recommendations.
- Avoid faulty logic.

**F. Reinforce your position.**
- Provide additional evidence of the benefits of your proposal and your own credibility in offering it.
- Use abstractions, metaphors, and other figures of speech to bring facts and figures to life.

**G. Anticipate objections.**
- Anticipate and answer potential objections.
- Present the pros and cons of all options if you anticipate a hostile reaction.

---

meeting their own goals than with satisfying the needs of their audiences. In contrast, a "soft sell" is more like a comfortable conversation that uses calm, rational persuasion.

- **Resisting compromise.** Successful persuasion is often a process of give-and-take, particularly in the case of persuasive business messages, where you don't always get everything you asked for in terms of budgets, investments, and other commitments.
- **Relying solely on great arguments.** Great arguments are important, but connecting with your audience on the right emotional level and communicating through vivid language are just as vital. Sometimes a well-crafted story can be even more compelling than dry logic.
- **Assuming that persuasion is a one-shot effort.** Persuasion is often a process, not a one-time event. In many cases, you need to move your audience members along one small step at a time rather than try to convince them to say "yes" in one huge step.

To review the steps involved in developing persuasive messages, refer to "Checklist: Developing Persuasive Messages."

## COMMON EXAMPLES OF PERSUASIVE BUSINESS MESSAGES

Throughout your career, you'll have numerous opportunities to write persuasive messages within your organization, such as reports suggesting more efficient operating procedures or memos requesting money for new equipment. Similarly, you may produce a variety of persuasive messages for people outside the organization, such as websites shaping public opinions or letters requesting adjustments that go beyond a supplier's contractual obligations. In addition, some of the routine requests you studied in Chapter 10 can become persuasive messages if you want a nonroutine result or believe that you haven't received fair treatment. Most of these messages can be divided into persuasive requests for action, persuasive presentations of ideas, and persuasive claims and requests for adjustment.

### Persuasive Requests for Action

Most persuasive business messages involve a request for action.

The bulk of your persuasive business messages will involve requests for action. In some cases, your request will be anticipated, so the direct approach is fine. In others, you'll need to introduce your intention indirectly, and the AIDA model or a similar approach is ideal for this purpose (see Figure 12.5).

| **1** Plan → | **2** Write → | **3** Complete |
|---|---|---|

**Analyze the Situation**
Verify that the purpose is to solve an ongoing problem, so the audience will be receptive.

**Gather Information**
Determine audience needs and obtain the necessary information on recycling problem areas.

**Select the Right Medium**
Verify that an email message is appropriate for this communication.

**Organize the Information**
Limit the scope to the main idea, which is to propose a recycling solution; use the indirect approach to lay out the extent of the problem.

**Adapt to Your Audience**
Adjust the level of formality based on the degree of familiarity with the audience; maintain a positive relationship by using the "you" attitude, politeness, positive emphasis, and bias-free language.

**Compose the Message**
Use a conversational but professional style and keep the message brief, clear, and as helpful as possible.

**Revise the Message**
Evaluate content and review readability to make sure the information is clear and complete without being overwhelming.

**Produce the Message**
Emphasize a clean, professional appearance.

**Proofread the Message**
Review for errors in layout, spelling, and mechanics.

**Distribute the Message**
Verify that the right file is attached and then deliver the message.

---

Cost Cutting in Plastics - Message (HTML)

To...: eleanor.tran@hmservices.com
Cc...:
Subject: Cost Cutting in Plastics
Attach...: Plastics cost analysis.PDF (96 KB)

Eleanor:

**[A]** In spite of our recent switch to purchasing plastic product containers in bulk, our costs for these containers are still extremely high. In my January 5 memo, I included all the figures showing that we purchase five tons of plastic product containers each year, and the price of polyethylene terephthalate (PET) rises and falls as petroleum costs fluctuate.

*The opening catches the reader's attention with a blunt statement of a major problem.*

**[I]** In January I suggested we purchase plastic containers in bulk during winter months, when petroleum prices tend to be lower. Because you approved that suggestion, we should realize a 10 percent savings this year. However, our costs are still out of line, around $2 million a year.

In addition to the cost in dollars of these plastic containers is the cost in image. We have recently been receiving an increasing number of consumer letters complaining about our lack of a recycling program for PET plastic containers, both on the airplanes and in the airport restaurants.

*The second paragraph builds interest in a potential solution to the problem by emphasizing how bad the problem is and highlighting an associated problem.*

**[D]** After conducting some preliminary research, I have come up with the following ideas:

- Provide recycling containers at all Host Marriott airport restaurants
- Offer financial incentives for the airlines to collect and separate PET containers
- Set up a specially designated dumpster at each airport for recycling plastics
- Contract with A-Batt Waste Management for collection

*The concisely presented list Increases the recipient's desire or willingness to take action by outlining a solution.*

**[A]** I've attached a detailed report of the costs involved. As you can see, our net savings the first year should run about $500,000. I've also spoken to Ted Macy in marketing. If we adopt the recycling plan, he wants to build a PR campaign around it. The PET recycling plan will help build our public image while improving our bottom line. If you agree, let's meet with Ted next week to get things started. Please call me at ext. 2356 if you have any questions.

*The close motivates the reader one last time with a specific cost-savings figure, then requests a specific action.*

**Figure 12.5   Persuasive Message Using the AIDA Model**
Randy Thumwolt uses the AIDA model in a persuasive message about a program that would try to reduce Host Marriott's annual plastics costs and curtail consumer complaints about the company's recycling record. Note how Thumwolt "sells the problem" before attempting to sell the solution. Few people are interested in hearing about solutions to problems they don't know about or don't believe exist. His interest section introduces an additional, unforeseen problem with plastic product containers.

MyBCommLab Apply Figure 12.5's key concepts. Go to **mybcommlab.com** and follow this path: Course Content → Chapter 12 → **DOCUMENT MAKEOVERS**

Open with an attention-getting device and show readers you understand their concerns. Use the interest and desire sections of your message to demonstrate that you have good reason for making such a request and to cover what you know about the situation: the facts and figures, the benefits of helping, and any history or experience that will enhance your appeal. Your goals are (1) to gain credibility (for yourself and your request) and (2) to make your readers believe that helping you will indeed help solve a significant problem. Close with a request for some specific action, and make that course of action as easy to follow as possible to maximize the chances of a positive response.

### Persuasive Presentations of Ideas

Sometimes the objective of persuasive messages is simply to encourage people to consider a new idea.

You may encounter situations in which you simply want to change attitudes or beliefs about a particular topic, without asking the audience to decide or do anything—at least not yet. The goal of your first message might be nothing more than convincing your audience to reexamine long-held opinions or admit the possibility of new ways of thinking.

For instance, the World Wide Web Consortium (a global association that defines many of the guidelines and technologies behind the World Wide Web) has launched a campaign called the Web Accessibility Initiative. Although the consortium's ultimate goal is making websites more accessible to people who have disabilities or age-related limitations, a key interim goal is simply making website developers more aware of the need. As part of this effort, the consortium has developed a variety of presentations and documents that highlight the problems many web visitors face.[15]

### Persuasive Claims and Requests for Adjustments

Most claims and requests for adjustment are routine messages and use the direct approach discussed in Chapter 11. However, consumers and professionals sometimes encounter situations in which they believe they haven't received a fair deal by following normal procedures. These situations require a more persuasive message.

The key ingredients of a good persuasive claim are a complete and specific review of the facts and a confident and positive tone. Keep in mind that you have the right to be satisfied with every transaction. Begin persuasive claims by outlining the problem and continue by reviewing what has been done about it so far, if anything. The recipient might be juggling numerous claims and other demands on his or her attention, so be clear, calm, and complete when presenting your case. Be specific about how you would like to see the situation resolved.

Next, give your reader a good reason for granting your claim. Show how the individual or organization is responsible for the problem, and appeal to your reader's sense of fair play, goodwill, or moral responsibility. Explain how you feel about the problem, but don't get carried away and don't make threats. People generally respond most favorably to requests that are calm and reasonable. Close on a respectful note that reflects how a successful resolution of the situation will repair or maintain a mutually beneficial working relationship.

# Developing Marketing and Sales Messages

**3  LEARNING OBJECTIVE**
Describe an effective strategy for developing marketing and sales messages and explain how to modify your approach when writing promotional messages for social media.

Marketing and sales messages use the same basic techniques as other persuasive messages, with the added emphasis of encouraging someone to participate in a commercial transaction. Although the terms *marketing message* and *sales message* are often used interchangeably, there is an important difference: **Marketing messages** usher potential buyers through the purchasing process without asking them to make an immediate decision. **Sales messages** take over at that point, encouraging potential buyers to make a purchase decision then and there. Marketing messages focus on such tasks as introducing new brands to the public and encouraging customers to visit websites for more information, whereas sales messages make an explicit request for people to buy a specific product or service. (The text of marketing and sales messages is usually referred to as "copy," by the way.)

Marketing and sales messages use many of the same techniques as persuasive business messages.

Most marketing and sales messages, particularly in larger companies, are created and delivered by professionals with specific training in marketing, advertising, sales, or public relations. However, you may be called on to review the work of these specialists or even to write such messages in smaller companies, and having a good understanding of how these messages work will help you be a more effective manager.

## PLANNING MARKETING AND SALES MESSAGES

Everything you've learned about planning messages applies in general to marketing and sales messages, but the planning steps for these messages have some particular aspects to consider as well:

- **Assessing audience needs.** As with every other business message, successful marketing and sales messages start with an understanding of audience needs. Depending on the product and the market, these needs can range from a few functional considerations (such as the size, weight, and finish of office paper) to a complicated mix of emotional and logical issues (all the factors that play into buying a house, for example).

Understanding the purchase decision from the buyer's perspective is a vital step in framing an effective marketing or sales message.

- **Analyzing your competition.** Marketing and sales messages nearly always compete with messages from other companies trying to reach the same audience. When Nike plans a marketing campaign to introduce a new shoe model to current customers, the company knows its audience has also been exposed to messages from Adidas, New Balance, Reebok, and numerous other shoe companies. Finding a unique message in crowded markets can be quite a challenge.

Marketing and sales messages have to compete for the audience's attention.

- **Determining key selling points and benefits.** With some insight into audience needs and the alternatives offered by your competitors, your next step is to decide which features and benefits to highlight. **Selling points** are the most attractive features of a product, whereas **benefits** are the particular advantages purchasers can realize from those features. In other words, selling points focus on what the product does. Benefits focus on what the user experiences or gains. Benefits can be practical, emotional, or a combination of the two. For example, the feature of a thin, flexible sole in a running shoe offers the practical benefit of a more natural feel while running. In contrast, the visual design features of the shoe offer no practical benefits but can offer the emotional benefit of wearing something stylish or unusual.

Selling points focus on the product; benefits focus on the user.

- **Anticipating purchase objections.** Marketing and sales messages usually encounter objections, and, as with persuasive business messages, the best way to handle them is to identify these objections up front and address as many as you can. They can range from high price or low quality to a lack of compatibility with existing products or a perceived risk involved with the product. By identifying potential objections up front, you can craft your promotional messages in ways that address those concerns. If price is a likely objection, for instance, you can look for ways to increase the perceived value of the purchase and decrease the perception of high cost. When promoting a home gym, you might say that it costs less than a year's worth of health club dues. Of course, any attempts to minimize perceptions of price or other potential negatives must be done ethically.

Anticipating objections is crucial to effective marketing and sales messages.

## WRITING CONVENTIONAL MARKETING AND SALES MESSAGES

Conventional marketing and sales messages are often prepared using the AIDA model or some variation of it. (See the next section on crafting messages for social media.) Here are the key points of using the AIDA model for these messages:

- **Getting the reader's attention.** By looking and listening during any given day, you'll notice the many ways advertisers try to get your attention. For example, a headline might offer an exciting product benefit, a piece of interesting news, an appeal to people's emotions or sense of financial value, or a unique solution to a common problem. Of course, words aren't the only attention-getting devices. Depending on the medium, marketers can use evocative images, music, animation, or video. "Cutting through the clutter" to get the audience's attention is one of the biggest challenges with marketing and sales messages.

*To build interest, expand on and support the promises in your attention-getting opening.*

- **Building interest.** After catching the reader's or viewer's attention, your next step is to build interest in the product, company, or idea you are promoting. A common technique is to "pay off" the promise made in the headline by explaining how you can deliver those benefits. For example, if the headline offers a way to "Get Fit for $2 a Day," the first paragraph could explain that the home gyms your company sells start at less than $700, which works out to less than $2 a day over the course of a year.

*Add details and audience benefits to increase desire for the product or service.*

- **Increasing desire.** Now that you've given the audience some initial information to start building their interest, the next step is to boost their desire for the product by expanding on your explanation of how it will benefit them. Think carefully about the sequence of support points and use plenty of subheadings, hyperlinks, video demonstrations, and other devices to help people quickly find the information they need. By keeping the focus on potential customers and their practical and emotional needs, you can layer on information that helps convince people that your product really is the best solution for them. You can also use a variety of techniques to address potential objections and minimize doubts, including testimonials from satisfied users, articles written by industry experts, competitive comparisons, offers of product samples or free demonstrations, independent test results, and money-back guarantees.

*After you've generated sufficient interest and desire, you're ready to persuade readers to take the preferred action.*

- **Motivating action.** The final step in the AIDA model is persuading the audience to take action, such as encouraging people to pick up the phone to place an order or visit an online app store to download your software. The keys to a successful *call to action* are making it easy and as risk-free as possible. If the process is confusing or time-consuming, you'll lose potential customers.

If you analyze the advertisements you encounter in any medium, you'll see variations on these techniques used again and again.

**REAL-TIME UPDATES**
LEARN MORE BY READING THIS INFOGRAPHIC

**The color of persuasion**

See the powerful influence of color in marketing and sales messages. Go to http://real-timeupdates.com/bct12 and click on Learn More. If you are using MyBCommLab, you can access Real-Time Updates within each chapter or under Student Study Tools.

## WRITING PROMOTIONAL MESSAGES FOR SOCIAL MEDIA

The AIDA model and similar approaches have been successful with marketing and sales messages for decades, but in the social media landscape, consumers are more apt to look for product information from other consumers, not the companies marketing those products. Consequently, your emphasis should shift to encouraging and participating in online conversations. Follow these guidelines:[16]

*In a social media environment, persuasive efforts require a more conversational, interactive approach.*

- **Facilitate community building.** Give customers and other audiences an opportunity to connect with you and one another, such as on your Facebook page or through members-only online forums.
- **Listen at least as much as you talk.** Listening is just as essential for online conversations as it is for in-person conversations.
- **Initiate and respond to conversations within the community.** Through content on your website, blog postings, social network profiles and messages, newsletters, and other tools, make sure you provide the information customers need in order to evaluate your products and services. Use **conversation marketing**, rather than traditional promotion, to initiate and facilitate conversations in your networked community of customers, journalists, bloggers, and other interested parties.
- **Provide information people want.** Whether it's industry-insider news, in-depth technical guides to using your products, or brief answers to questions posted on community Q&A sites, fill the information gaps about your company and its products (see Figure 12.6).
- **Identify and support your champions.** In marketing, *champions* are enthusiastic fans of your company and its products. Champions are so enthusiastic they help spread your message (through their blogs, for instance), defend you against detractors, and help other customers use your products.

The text of the post keeps the focus on the story. The phrase "on our network" is a subtle reminder that AddThis is the company behind the data, but the writer avoids any overt promotion.

The small "Powered by AddThis" label in the upper right corner of the chart is another reminder, but it doesn't intrude. Blog visitors can enjoy the story without feeling they are being sold to; the element of persuasion is effective but subdued.

MyBCommLab Apply Figure 12.6's key concepts. Go to **mybcommlab.com** and follow this path: Course Content → Chapter 12 → **DOCUMENT MAKEOVERS**

**Figure 12.6   Persuasive Messages in Social Media**

AddThis provides tools that let Internet users share items of interest across social media. The company can also track this activity to see which topics are generating the most interest at any point in time. The post on the AddThis blog, about sharing activity during the 2012 Summer Olympics, is a good example of using social media to share interesting information without promoting products or services explicitly. However, website owners who are potential customers of AddThis will recognize that the company's technology was behind the results discussed in the post.
*Source:* Copyright © 2012 by AddThis. www.addthis.com. Reprinted with permission.

- **Be real.** Trying to tack social media onto a consumer-hostile business is likely to fail as soon as stakeholders see through the superficial attempt to "be social." In contrast, social media audiences respond positively to companies that are open and conversational about themselves, their products, and subjects of shared interest.
- **Integrate conventional marketing and sales strategies at the right time and in the right places.** AIDA and similar approaches are still valid for specific communication tasks, such as conventional advertising and the product promotion pages on your website.

# Maintaining High Standards of Ethics, Legal Compliance, and Etiquette

The word *persuasion* has negative connotations for some people, especially in a marketing or sales context. However, effective businesspeople view persuasion as a positive force, aligning their own interests with what is best for their audiences. They influence audience members by providing information and aiding understanding, which allows audiences the freedom to choose.[17] To maintain the highest standards of business ethics, always demonstrate the "you" attitude by showing honest concern for your audience's needs and interests.

As marketing and selling grow increasingly complex, so do the legal ramifications of marketing and sales messages. In the United States, the Federal Trade Commission

**4** LEARNING OBJECTIVE
Identify steps you can take to avoid ethical lapses in marketing and sales messages.

Marketing and sales messages are covered by a wide range of laws and regulations.

(www.ftc.gov) has the authority to impose penalties (ranging from cease-and-desist orders to multimillion-dollar fines) on advertisers who violate federal standards for truthful advertising. Other federal agencies have authority over advertising in specific industries, such as transportation and financial services. Individual states have additional laws that may apply. The legal aspects of promotional communication can be quite complex, varying from state to state and from country to country, and most companies require marketing and salespeople to get clearance from company lawyers before sending messages.

Moreover, communicators must stay on top of changing regulations, such as the latest laws governing unsolicited bulk email ("spam"), disclosure requirements for bloggers who review products, privacy, and data security. For example, two ethical concerns that could produce new legislation are *behavioral targeting*, which tracks the online behavior of website visitors and serves up ads based on what they appear to be interested in, and *remarketing*, in which behaviorally targeted ads follow users even as they move on to other websites.[18]

For all marketing and sales efforts, pay close attention to the following legal considerations:[19]

Marketers have a responsibility to stay up to date on laws and regulations that restrict promotional messages.

- **Marketing and sales messages must be truthful and nondeceptive.** The FTC considers messages to be deceptive if they include statements that are likely to mislead reasonable customers and the statements are an important part of the purchasing decision. Failing to include important information is also considered deceptive. The FTC also looks at *implied claims*—claims you don't explicitly make but that can be inferred from what you do or don't say.
- **You must back up your claims with evidence.** According to the FTC, offering a money-back guarantee or providing letters from satisfied customers is not enough; you must still be able to support claims for your product with objective evidence such as a survey or scientific study. If you claim that your food product lowers cholesterol, you must have scientific evidence to support that claim.
- **"Bait and switch" advertising is illegal.** Trying to attract buyers by advertising a product that you don't intend to sell—and then trying to sell them another (and usually more expensive) product—is illegal.
- **Marketing messages and websites aimed at children are subject to special rules.** For example, online marketers must obtain consent from parents before collecting personal information about children under age 13.
- **Marketing and sales messages are considered binding contracts in many states.** If you imply or make an offer and then can't fulfill your end of the bargain, you can be sued for breach of contract.
- **In most cases, you can't use a person's name, photograph, or other identity without permission.** Doing so is considered an invasion of privacy. You can use images of people considered to be public figures as long as you don't unfairly imply that they endorse your message.

Meeting your ethical and legal obligations will go a long way toward maintaining good communication etiquette. However, you may still face etiquette decisions within ethical and legal boundaries. For instance, you can produce a marketing campaign that complies with all applicable laws and yet is offensive or insulting to your audience. Taking an audience-centered approach, in which you show respect for your readers and their values, should help you avoid any such etiquette missteps.

Technology also gives communicators new ways to demonstrate sensitivity to user needs. One example is automated RSS newsfeeds from blogs, alerting customers to information in which they've expressed an interest. *Opt-in* email newsletters are another technology that shows the "you" attitude at work. Unlike the unwelcome spam messages that litter email inboxes these days, opt-in messages are sent only to those people who have specifically requested information.

For the latest information on writing persuasive messages, visit http://real-timeupdates .com/bct12 and click on Chapter 12.

# Quick Learning Guide

## SUMMARY OF LEARNING OBJECTIVES

**1** Apply the three-step writing process to persuasive messages. To plan persuasive messages, carefully clarify your purpose to make sure you focus on a single goal. Understand audience needs, which can involve research to identify relevant demographic and psychographic variables and to assess audience motivations. Persuasive messages usually ask people to give up time, money, or other resources, so gathering the right information to convince readers of the benefits of responding is essential. Media choices need to be considered carefully, particularly with marketing and sales messages in a social media landscape. For organizing persuasive messages, you will usually want to choose the indirect approach in order to establish awareness and interest before asking the audience to take action.

When writing persuasive messages, use positive and polite language, understand and respect cultural differences, be sensitive to organizational cultures when writing persuasive business messages, and take steps to establish your credibility. Seven common ways to establish credibility in persuasive messages are using simple language, supporting your claims, identifying your sources, establishing common ground, being objective, displaying good intentions, and avoiding the hard sell.

The steps for completing persuasive messages are the same as for other types of messages, but accuracy and completeness are especially important because they send signals about your credibility—a crucial element in persuasive messages.

**2** Describe an effective strategy for developing persuasive business messages, and identify the three most common categories of persuasive business messages. Within the context of the three-step process, effective persuasion involves four essential strategies: framing your arguments, balancing emotional and logical appeals, reinforcing your position, and anticipating objections. One of the most commonly used methods for framing a persuasive argument is the AIDA model, in which you open your message by getting the audience's attention; build interest with facts, details, and additional benefits; increase desire by providing more evidence and answering possible objections; and motivate a specific action.

Persuasive business messages combine emotional appeals (which call on feelings and sympathies) and logical appeals (which call on reason, using analogy, induction, or deduction). To reinforce your position, look for ways to add convincing evidence, quotations from experts, or other support material.

By identifying potential objections and addressing them as you craft your message, you can help prevent audience members from gravitating toward negative answers before you have the opportunity to ask them for a positive response. You can often resolve these issues before the audience has a chance to go on the defensive.

The most common types of these messages are (1) persuasive requests for action, in which you ask the recipient to make a decision or engage in some activity; (2) persuasive presentations of ideas, in which you aren't necessarily looking for a decision or action but rather would like the audience to consider a different way of looking at a particular topic; and (3) persuasive claims and requests for adjustments, in which you believe that you have not received fair treatment under an organization's standard policies and would like the recipient to give your case fresh consideration.

**3** Describe an effective strategy for developing marketing and sales messages, and explain how to modify your approach when writing promotional messages for social media. Marketing and sales messages use the same basic techniques as other persuasive messages, with the added emphasis of encouraging someone to participate in a commercial transaction. Marketing messages do this indirectly, whereas sales messages do it directly. The basic strategy for creating these messages includes assessing audience needs; analyzing your competition; determining key selling points and benefits; anticipating purchase objections; applying the AIDA model; adapting your writing to social media, if appropriate; and maintaining high standards of ethical and legal compliance.

To use social media for promotional communication, start by engaging audiences with efforts to build networked communities of potential buyers and other interested parties. Listen to conversations taking place about your company and its products. Initiate and respond to conversations within these communities, being sure to use an objective, conversational style. Provide the information interested parties want. Identify and support the enthusiastic product champions who want to help spread your message. Be authentic and transparent in all your communication. Speak directly to customers so you don't have to rely on the news media. Finally, continue to use the AIDA model or similar approaches, but only at specific times and places.

**4** Identify steps you can take to avoid ethical lapses in marketing and sales messages. Effective and ethical persuasive communicators focus on aligning their interests with the interests of their audiences. They help audiences understand how their proposals will provide benefits to the audience, using language that is persuasive without being manipulative. They choose words that are less likely to be misinterpreted and take care not to distort the truth. Throughout, they maintain a "you" attitude with honest concern for the audience's needs and interests. By following applicable laws and regulations, marketers can avoid many ethical problems.

## KEY TERMS

**AIDA model** Message sequence that involves attention, interest, desire, and action

**benefits** The particular advantages that readers will realize from a product's selling points

**conversation marketing** Approach in which companies initiate and facilitate conversations in a networked community of customers, journalists, bloggers, and other interested parties

**demographics** Quantifiable characteristics of a population, including age, gender, occupation, income, and education

**emotional appeal** Persuasive approach that calls on audience feelings and sympathies rather than facts, figures, and rational arguments

**logical appeal** Persuasive approach that calls on reasoning and evidence

**marketing messages** Promotional messages that usher potential buyers through the purchasing process without asking them to make an immediate decision

**motivation** The combination of forces that drive people to satisfy their needs

**persuasion** The attempt to change an audience's attitudes, beliefs, or actions

**psychographics** Psychological characteristics of an audience, including personality, attitudes, and lifestyle

**sales messages** In contrast to marketing messages, sales messages encourage potential buyers to make a purchase decision then and there

**selling points** The most attractive features of a product or service

## CHECKLIST ✓
### Developing Persuasive Messages

A. **Get your reader's attention.**
- Open with an audience benefit, a stimulating question, a problem, or an unexpected statement.
- Establish common ground by mentioning a point on which you and your audience agree.
- Show that you understand the audience's concerns.

B. **Build your reader's interest.**
- Expand and support your opening claim or promise.
- Emphasize the relevance of your message to your audience.

C. **Increase your reader's desire.**
- Make audience members want to change by explaining how the change will benefit them.
- Back up your claims with relevant evidence.

D. **Motivate your reader to take action.**
- Suggest the action you want readers to take.

- Stress the positive results of the action.
- Make the desired action clear and easy.

E. **Balance emotional and logical appeals.**
- Use emotional appeals to help the audience accept your message.
- Use logical appeals when presenting facts and evidence for complex ideas or recommendations.
- Avoid faulty logic.

F. **Reinforce your position.**
- Provide additional evidence of the benefits of your proposal and your own credibility in offering it.
- Use abstractions, metaphors, and other figures of speech to bring facts and figures to life.

G. **Anticipate objections.**
- Anticipate and answer potential objections.
- Present the pros and cons of all options if you anticipate a hostile reaction.

## COMMUNICATION CHALLENGES AT **CafeMom**

You're the vice president of member services at CafeMom, reporting to CEO Michael Sanchez. In addition to developing new online services, a key part of your job responsibility is crafting messages that describe the new services and persuade members to try them. Use what you've learned in this chapter and in your own experiences as a consumer (and as a parent, if applicable) to address these challenges.

**INDIVIDUAL CHALLENGE:** You asked one of your staffers to write a benefit statement to communicate the advantages of the Groups section of the CafeMom website, which lets members find and join any of the thousands of existing groups or create new groups focused on just about any topic imaginable. She emails the following sentence: "We've worked hard to define and create a powerful online group capability; you can search far and wide on the web, but you won't find anything as great as what we've created." Write an email message in response, explaining why it's important to make marketing messages about the customer, not about the company. Include a revised version that illustrates this vital aspect of the "you" attitude. You can learn more about the Groups feature at the CafeMom website, www.cafemom.com/groups.

**TEAM CHALLENGE:** A common challenge in marketing communication is distilling a long list of features to a single compelling message that can serve as the product's "headline." With your team, review this list of features and benefits:

- The experiences of thousands of moms are now aggregated in a single place online.
- Connect with moms like you; search for moms by personal and family challenges, interests, age of kids, or location.
- Get and give support; find support and swap advice with other moms on a wide range of topics that matter most to you.
- Post questions online and get input from mothers who've been there before.
- Joining CafeMom is absolutely free.
- Setting up your own personal profile is fast and easy.
- Join groups who share your likes and concerns.
- Write as much or as little as you want to share in your personal profile.
- You have complete control over the privacy of your information.

Brainstorm three one-sentence possibilities that could serve as the headline for a webpage promoting CafeMom and then choose the most compelling of the three options. Don't assume that every feature or benefit in the list needs to be incorporated in your high-level message.

## Test Your Knowledge

To review chapter content related to each question, refer to the indicated Learning Objective.

1. What are four of the many ways you can build credibility with an audience when planning a persuasive message? [LO-1]
✪ 2. What is the AIDA model, and what are its limitations? [LO-2]
✪ 3. How do emotional appeals differ from logical appeals? [LO-2]
4. What three types of reasoning can you use in logical appeals? [LO-2]
5. What is conversation marketing? [LO-3]
6. What do marketing and sales messages differ? [LO-3]
✪ 7. What is likely to happen if you don't anticipate audience objections when crafting your messages? [LO-2], [LO-3]
8. How do benefits differ from features? [LO-3]
9. How does ethical behavior contribute to positive etiquette in persuasive messages? [LO-4]

## Apply Your Knowledge

To review chapter content related to each question, refer to the indicated Learning Objective.

1. Why is it essential to understand your readers' likely motivations before writing a persuasive message? [LO-1]
2. Why is it important to present all sides of an argument when writing a persuasive message to a potentially hostile audience? [LO-2]

✪ 3. Are emotional appeals ethical? Why or why not? [LO-2]
✪ 4. What is likely to happen if a promotional message starts immediately with a call to action? Why? [LO-3]

## Practice Your Skills

### Messages for Analysis

For Message 12.A and Message 12.B, read the following documents and then (1) analyze the strengths and weaknesses of each sentence and (2) revise each document so that it follows this chapter's guidelines.

### Message 12.A: Message Strategies: Persuasive Claims and Requests for Adjustment [LO-2]

Dear TechStar Computing:

I'm writing to you because of my disappointment with my new multimedia PC display. The display part works all right, but the audio volume is set too high and the volume knob doesn't turn it down. It's driving us crazy. The volume knob doesn't seem to be connected to anything but simply spins around. I can't believe you would put out a product like this without testing it first.

I depend on my computer to run my small business and want to know what you are going to do about it. This reminds me of every time I buy electronic equipment from what seems like any company. Something is always wrong. I thought quality was supposed to be important, but I guess not.

Anyway, I need this fixed right away. Please tell me what you want me to do.

### Message 12.B: Message Strategies: Sales Messages [LO-3]

We know how awful dining hall food can be, and that's why we've developed the "Mealaweek Club." Once a week, we'll deliver food to your dormitory or apartment. Our meals taste great. We have pizza, buffalo wings, hamburgers and curly fries, veggie roll-ups, and more!

When you sign up for just six months, we will ask what day you want your delivery. We'll ask you to fill out your selection of meals. And the rest is up to us. At "Mealaweek," we deliver! And payment is easy. We accept MasterCard and Visa or a personal check. It will save money especially when compared with eating out.

Just fill out the enclosed card and indicate your method of payment. As soon as we approve your credit or check, we'll begin delivery. Tell all your friends about Mealaweek. We're the best idea since sliced bread!

### Message 12.C: Media Skills: Podcasting [LO-2]

To access this message, visit http://real-timeupdates.com/bct11, click on Student Assignments, and select Chapter 12, Message 12.C. Listen to this podcast. Identify at least three ways in which the podcast could be more persuasive and draft a brief email message you could send to the podcaster with your suggestions for improvement.

### Exercises

Active links for all websites in this chapter can be found on MyBcommLab; see your User Guide for instructions on accessing the content for this chapter. Each activity is labeled according to the primary skill or skills you will need to use. To review relevant chapter content, you can refer to the indicated Learning Objective. In some instances, supporting information will be found in another chapter, as indicated.

1. **Choosing a Message Strategy: [LO-1], Chapters 10–11** Now that you've explored routine, positive, negative, and persuasive messages, review the following message scenarios and identify which of the four message strategies would be most appropriate for the situation. Offer a brief justification for your choices. (Depending on the particular circumstances, a scenario might lend itself to more than one type of message; just be sure to offer compelling reasons for your choices.)

   a. An unsolicited message to your department manager, explaining why you believe the company's experiment with self-managed work teams has not been successful

   b. An unsolicited message to your department manager, explaining why you believe the company's experiment with self-managed work teams has not been successful and suggesting that one of the more experienced

   employees (such as yourself) should be promoted to supervisor

   c. A message to a long-time industrial customer, explaining that a glitch in your accounting system resulted in the customer being overcharged on its last five orders, apologizing for the problem, and assuring the customer that you will refund the overcharged amount immediately

   d. A news release announcing that your company plans to invite back 50 employees who were laid off earlier in the year

2. **Message Strategies: Persuasive Business Messages; Collaboration: Team Projects [LO-2]** With another student, analyze the persuasive email message to Eleanor Tran at Host Marriott (Figure 12.5) by answering the following questions:

   a. What techniques are used to capture the reader's attention?

   b. Does the writer use the direct or indirect organizational approach? Why?

   c. Is the subject line effective? Why or why not?

   d. Does the writer use an emotional or a logical appeal? Why?

   e. What reader benefits are included?

   f. How does the writer establish credibility?

   g. What tools does the writer use to reinforce his position?

3. **Message Strategies: Persuasive Business Messages, Marketing and Sales Messages: Media Skills: Email [LO-2], [LO-3]** Compose effective subject lines for the following persuasive email messages:

   a. A recommendation was sent by email to your branch manager to install wireless networking throughout the facility. Your primary reason is that management has encouraged more teamwork, but teams often congregate in meeting rooms, the cafeteria, and other places that lack network access—without which they can't do much of the work they are expected to do.

   b. A message to area residents, soliciting customers for your new business, "Meals à la Car," a carryout dining service that delivers from most of the local restaurants. All local restaurant menus are on the Internet. Mom and Dad can dine on egg rolls and chow mein while the kids munch on pepperoni pizza.

   c. An email message to the company president, asking that employees be allowed to carry over their unused vacation days to the following year. Apparently, many employees canceled their fourth-quarter vacation plans to work on the installation of a new company computer system. Under their current contract, vacation days not used by December 31 can't be carried over to the following year.

4. **Communication Ethics: Making Ethical Choices [LO-2], [LO-4]** Your boss has asked you to post a message on the company's internal blog, urging everyone in your department to donate money to the company's favorite charity,

an organization that operates a summer camp for children with physical challenges. You wind up writing a lengthy posting, packed with facts and heartwarming anecdotes about the camp and the children's experiences. When you must work that hard to persuade your audience to take an action such as donating money to a charity, aren't you being manipulative and unethical? Explain.

5. **Message Strategies: Marketing and Sales Messages (Customer Benefits) [LO-3]** Determine whether the following sentences focus on features or benefits; rewrite as necessary to focus all the sentences on benefits.

   a. All-Cook skillets are coated with a durable, patented nonstick surface.

   b. You can call anyone and talk as long as you like on Saturdays and Sundays with our new FamilyTalk wireless plan.

   c. With 8-millisecond response time, the Samsung LN-S4095D 40-inch LCD TV delivers fast video action that is smooth and crisp.[20]

6. **Message Strategies: Marketing and Sales Messages [LO-3]** The daily mail often brings a selection of sales messages. Find a direct-mail package from your mailbox that includes a sales letter. Then answer the following questions to help analyze and learn from the approach used by the communication professionals who prepare these glossy sales messages. Your instructor might also ask you to share the package and your observations in a class discussion.

   a. Who is the intended audience?

   b. What are some of the demographic and psychographic characteristics of the intended audience?

   c. What is the purpose of the direct-mail package? Has it been designed to solicit a phone-call response, make a mail-order sale, obtain a charitable contribution, or do something else?

   d. What technique was used to encourage you to open the envelope?

   e. Did the letter writer follow the AIDA model or something similar? If not, explain the letter's organization.

   f. What emotional appeals and logical arguments does the letter use?

   g. What selling points and consumer benefits does the letter offer?

   h. Did the letter and the rest of the package provide convincing support for the claims made in the letter? If not, what is lacking?

7. **Message Strategies: Marketing and Sales Messages [LO-3]** Have you ever wondered why certain websites and blogs appear at the top of the list when you use an online search engine? Or why a site you might expect to find doesn't show up at all? Such questions are at the heart of one of the most important activities in online communication: *search engine optimization* (SEO). (SEO applies to the *natural* or *organic* search results, not the sponsored, paid results you see above, beside, or below the main search results listing.)

SEO is a complex topic that factors in dozens of variables, but even without becoming an expert in SEO, every website owner can work toward improving rankings by focusing on three important areas. First, offer fresh, high-quality, audience-oriented content. Content that doesn't appeal to people won't appeal to search engines, either. Second, use relevant keywords judiciously, particularly in important areas such as the page title that displays at the top of the browser screen. Third, encourage links to your site from other high-quality sites with relevant content. These links from other sites are crucial because they tell the search engines that other people find your content interesting and useful. Not surprisingly, given the importance of links from other sites, the content sharing encouraged by social media has had a huge impact on SEO in recent years.[21]

Locate a website for any company that sells products to consumers and write a new title for the site's homepage (the title that appears at the top of a web browser). Make the title short enough to read quickly while still summarizing what the company offers. Be sure to use one or more keywords that online shoppers would likely use when searching for the types of products the company sells. Next, identify three high-quality websites that would be good ones to link to the site you chose. For instance, if you chose a website that sells automotive parts and supplies, one of the three linking sites could be a popular blog that deals with automotive repair. Or if the site you chose sells golf equipment, you might find a sports website that covers the professional golf tours or one that provides information about golf courses around the world.

# Expand Your Skills

### Critique the Professionals

Visit the Facebook pages of six companies in several industries. How do the companies make use of their timeline? Do any of the companies use timeline posts to promote their products? Compare the material on the Info tabs. Which company has the most compelling information here? How about the use of custom tabs; which company does the best job of using this Facebook feature? Using whatever medium your instructor requests, write a brief analysis of the message (no more than one page), citing specific elements from the piece and support from the chapter.

### Sharpening Your Career Skills Online

Bovée and Thill's Business Communication Web Search, at http://businesscommunicationblog.com/websearch, is a unique research tool designed specifically for business communication research. Use the Web Search function to find a website, video, PDF document, podcast, or PowerPoint presentation that offers advice on writing persuasive messages (either persuasive business messages or marketing and sales messages). Write a brief email message to your instructor, describing the item you found and summarizing the career skills information you learned from it.

# Cases

## Persuasive Business Messages

### MICROBLOGGING SKILLS

**1. Message Strategies: Persuasive Business Messages [LO-2]** You've been trying for months to convince your boss, company CEO Will Florence, to start using Twitter. You've told him that top executives in numerous industries now use Twitter as a way to connect with customers and other stakeholders without going through the filters and barriers of formal corporate communications, but he doesn't see the value.

**Your task:** You come up with the brilliant plan to demonstrate Twitter's usefulness using Twitter itself. First, find three executives from three companies who are on Twitter (choose any companies and executives you find interesting). Second, study their tweets to get a feel for the type of information they share. Third, if you don't already have a Twitter account set up for this class, set one up for the purposes of this exercise (you can deactivate later). Fourth, write four tweets to demonstrate the value of executive microblogging: one that summarizes the value of having a company CEO use Twitter and three support tweets, each one summarizing how your three real-life executive role models use Twitter.

### BLOGGING SKILLS / TEAM SKILLS

**2. Message Strategies: Persuasive Business Messages [LO-2]** As a strong advocate for the use of social media in business, you are pleased by how quickly people in your company have taken up blogging, wiki writing, and other new-media activities. You are considerably less excited by the style and quality of what you see in the writing of your colleagues. Many seem to have interpreted "authentic and conversational" to mean "anything goes." Several of the Twitter users in the company seem to have abandoned any pretense of grammar and spelling. A few managers have dragged internal disagreements about company strategy out into public view, arguing with each other through comments on various industry-related forums. Product demonstration videos have been posted to the company's YouTube channel virtually unedited, making the whole firm look unpolished and unprofessional. The company CEO has written some blog posts that bash competitors with coarse and even crude language.

You pushed long and hard for greater use of these tools, so you feel a sense of responsibility for this situation. In addition, you are viewed by many in the company as the resident expert on social media, so you have some "expertise authority" on this issue. On the other hand, you are only a first-level manager, with three levels of managers above you, so while you have some "position authority" as well, you can hardly dictate best practices to the managers above you.

**Your task:** Working with two other students, write a post for the company's internal blog (which is not viewable outside the company), outlining your concerns about these communication practices. Use the examples mentioned above, and make up any additional details you need. Emphasize that while social media communication is often less formal and more flexible than traditional business communication, it shouldn't be unprofessional. You are thinking of proposing a social media training program for everyone in the company, but for this message you just want to bring attention to the problem.

### LETTER WRITING SKILLS

**3. Message Strategies: Persuasive Business Messages [LO-2]** The coffee shop across the street from your tiny apartment is your haven away from home—great beverages, healthy snacks, free wireless, and an atmosphere that is convivial but not so lively that you can't focus on your homework. It lacks only one thing: some way to print out your homework and other files when you need hard copies. Your college's libraries and computer labs provide printers, but you live three miles from campus, and it's a long walk or an inconvenient bus ride.

**Your task:** Write a letter to the owner of the coffee shop, encouraging her to set up a printing service to complement the free wireless access. Propose that the service run at break-even prices, just enough to pay for paper, ink cartridges, and the cost of the printer itself. The benefit to the shop would be enticing patrons to spend more time—and therefore more of their coffee and tea money—in the shop. You might also mention that you had to take the bus to campus to print this letter, so you bought your afternoon latté somewhere else.

### EMAIL SKILLS / PORTFOLIO BUILDER

**4. Message Strategies: Persuasive Business Messages [LO-2]** As someone who came of age in the "post email" world of blogs, wikis, social networks, and other Web 2.0 technologies, you were rather disappointed to find your new employer solidly stuck in the age of email. You use email, of course, but it is only one of the tools in your communication toolbox. From your college years, you have hands-on experience with a wide range of social media tools, having used them to collaborate on school projects, to become involved in your local community, to learn more about various industries and professions, and to research potential employers during your job search. (In fact, without social media, you might never have heard about your current employer in the first place.) Moreover, your use of social media on the job has already paid several important dividends, including finding potential sales contacts at several large companies, connecting with peers in other companies to share ideas for working more efficiently, and learning about some upcoming legislative matters in your state that could profoundly hamper your company's current way of doing business.

You hoped that by setting an example through your own use of social media at work, your new colleagues and company management would quickly adopt these tools as well. However, just the opposite has happened. Waiting in your email in-box this morning was a message from the CEO, announcing that the company is now cutting off access to social networking websites and banning the use of any social media at work. The message says using company time and company computers for socializing is highly inappropriate and might be considered grounds for dismissal in the future if the problem gets out of hand.

**Your task:** You are stunned by the message. You fight the urge to fire off a hotly worded reply to straighten out the CEO's misperceptions. Instead, you wisely decide to send a message to your immediate superior first, explaining why you believe the new policy should be reversed. Using your boss's favorite medium (email, of course!), write a persuasive message, explaining why Facebook, Twitter, and other social networking technologies are valid—and valuable—business tools. Bolster your argument with examples from other companies and advice from communication experts.

## EMAIL SKILLS

**5. Message Strategies: Persuasive Claims and Requests for Adjustment [LO-2]** It's hard to go through life without becoming annoyed at the way some things work. You have undoubtedly been dissatisfied with a product you've bought, a service you've received, or an action of some elected official or government agency.

**Your task:** Write a three- to five-paragraph persuasive email message request, expressing your dissatisfaction in a particular case. Specify the action you want the reader to take.

## IM SKILLS

**6. Message Strategies: Requests for Action [LO-2]** At IBM, you're one of the coordinators for the annual Employee Charitable Contributions Campaign. Since 1978, the company has helped employees contribute to more than 2,000 health and human service agencies. These groups may offer child care; treat substance abuse; provide health services; or fight illiteracy, homelessness, and hunger. Some offer disaster relief or care for the elderly. All deserve support. They're carefully screened by IBM, one of the largest corporate contributors of cash, equipment, and people to nonprofit organizations and educational institutions in the United States and around the world. As your literature states, the program "has engaged our employees more fully in the important mission of corporate citizenship."

During the winter holidays, you target agencies that cater to the needs of displaced families, women, and children. It's not difficult to raise enthusiasm. The prospect of helping children enjoy the holidays—children who otherwise might have nothing—usually awakens the spirit of your most distracted workers. But some of them wait until the last minute and then forget.

They have until December 16 to come forth with cash contributions. To make it in time for holiday deliveries, they can also bring in toys, food, and blankets through Tuesday, December 20. They shouldn't have any trouble finding the collection bins; they're everywhere, marked with bright red banners. But some will want to call you with questions or (you hope) to make credit card contributions: 800-658-3899, ext. 3342.

**Your task:** It's December 14. Write a 75- to 100-word instant message, encouraging last-minute holiday gifts.[22]

## EMAIL SKILLS

**7. Message Strategies: Requests for Action [LO-2]** Managing a new-product launch can be an aggravating experience as you try to coordinate a wide variety of activities and processes while barreling toward a deadline that is often defined more by external factors than a realistic assessment of whether you can actually meet it. You depend on lots of other people to meet their deadlines, and if they fail, you fail. The pressure is enough to push anybody over the edge. Unfortunately, that happened to you last week. After a barrage of bad news from suppliers and the members of the team you lead, you lost your cool in a checkpoint meeting. Shouting at people and accusing them of slacking off was embarrassing enough, but the situation got a hundred times worse this morning when your boss suggested you needed some low-pressure work for a while and removed you as the leader of the launch team.

**Your task:** Write an email message to your boss, Sunil, requesting to be reinstated as the project team leader. Make up any information you need.

## EMAIL SKILLS

**8. Message Strategies: Requests for Action [LO-2]** You appreciate how important phones are to your company's operations, but the amount of conversational chatter in your work area has gotten so bad that it's hard to concentrate on your work. You desperately need at least a few quiet hours every day to engage in the analytical thinking your job requires.

**Your task:** Write an email message to the division vice president, Jeri Ross, asking her to designate one of the conference rooms as a quiet-zone work room. It would have WiFi so that employees can stay connected to the corporate network, but it would not have any phone service, either landline or mobile. (Mobile reception is already weak in the conference rooms, but you will propose to equip the room with a mobile signal jammer to ensure that no calls can be made or received.) In addition, conversation of any kind would be strictly forbidden. Make up any details you need.

## MEMO WRITING SKILLS

**9. Message Strategies: Requests for Action [LO-2]** This morning as you drove to your job as food services manager at the Pechanga Casino Entertainment Center in Temecula, California, you were concerned to hear on the radio that the local Red Cross chapter put out a call for blood because national supplies have fallen dangerously low. During highly publicized disasters, people are emotional and eager to help out by donating blood. But in calmer times, only 5 percent of eligible donors think of giving blood. You're one of those few.

Not many people realize that donated blood lasts only 72 hours. Consequently, the mainstay of emergency blood supplies must be replenished in an ongoing effort. No one is more skilled, dedicated, or efficient in handling blood than the American Red Cross, which is responsible for half the nation's supply of blood and blood products.

Donated blood helps victims of accidents and disease, as well as surgery patients. Just yesterday you were reading about a girl named Melissa, who was diagnosed with multiple congenital heart defects and underwent her first open-heart surgery at one week old. Now five, she's used well over 50 units of donated blood, and she wouldn't be alive without them. In a thank-you letter, her mother lauded the many strangers who had "given a piece of themselves" to save her precious daughter—and countless others. You also learned that a donor's pint of blood can benefit up to four other people.

Today, you're going to do more than just roll up your own sleeve. You know the local Red Cross chapter takes its blood donation equipment to corporations, restaurants, beauty salons—any place willing to host public blood drives. What if you could convince the board of directors to support a blood drive at the casino? The slot machines and gaming tables are usually full, hundreds of employees are on hand, and people who've never visited before might come down to donate blood. The positive publicity will boost Pechanga's community image, too. With materials from the Red Cross, you're confident you can organize Pechanga's hosting effort and handle the promotion. (Last year, you headed the casino's successful Toys for Tots drive.)

To give blood, one must be healthy, be at least 17 years old (with no upper age limit), and weigh at least 110 pounds. Donors can give every 56 days. You'll be urging Pechanga donors to eat well, drink water, and be thoroughly rested before donating.[23]

**Your task:** Write a memo persuading the Pechanga board of directors to host a public Red Cross blood drive. You can learn more about what's involved in hosting a blood drive at www .redcrossblood.org (click on "Hosting a Blood Drive"). Ask the board to provide water, orange juice, and snacks for donors. You'll organize food service workers to handle the distribution, but you'll need the board's approval to let your team volunteer during work hours. Use a combination of logical and emotional appeals.

## EMAIL SKILLS / PORTFOLIO BUILDER

**10. Message Strategies: Requests for Action [LO-2]** Your new company, WorldConnect Language Services, started well and is going strong. However, to expand beyond your Memphis, Tennessee, home market, you need a one-time infusion of cash to open branch offices in other cities around the Southeast. At the Entrepreneur's Lunch Forum you attended yesterday, you learned about several *angels*, as they are called in the investment community—private individuals who invest money in small companies in exchange for a share of ownership. One such angel, Melinda Sparks, told the audience she is looking for investment opportunities outside of high technology, where angels often invest their money. She also indicated that she looks for entrepreneurs who know their industries and markets well, who are passionate about the value they bring to the marketplace, who are committed to growing their businesses, and who have a solid plan for how they will spend an investor's money. Fortunately, you meet all of her criteria.

**Your task:** Draft an email message to Sparks, introducing yourself and your business and asking for a meeting at which you can present your business plan in more detail. Explain that your Memphis office was booked to capacity within two months of opening, thanks to the growing number of international business professionals looking for translators and interpreters. You've researched the entire Southeast region and identified at least 10 other cities that could support a language services office such as yours. Making up whatever other information you need, draft a four-paragraph message following the AIDA model, ending with a request for a meeting within the next four weeks.

## BLOGGING SKILLS / PORTFOLIO BUILDER

**11. Message Strategies: Persuasive Presentation of Ideas [LO-2]** Like most other companies today, your firm makes extensive use of the web for internal and external communication.

However, after reading about the Web Accessibility Initiative (WAI), you've become concerned that your company's various websites haven't been designed to accommodate people with disabilities or age-related limitations. Fortunately, as one of the company's top managers, you have a perfect forum for letting everyone in the company know how important accessible web design is: Your internal blog is read by the vast majority of employees and managers throughout the company.

**Your task:** Visit the WAI website, at www.w3.org/WAI, and read the two articles "Introduction to Web Accessibility" (look in the "Introducing Accessibility" section) and "Developing a Web Accessibility Business Case for Your Organization" (in the "Managing Accessibility" section). Using the information you learn in these articles, write a post for your blog that emphasizes how important it is for your company's websites to be made more accessible. You don't have direct authority over the company's web developers, so it would be inappropriate for you to request them to take any specific action. Your goal is simply to raise awareness and encourage everyone to consider the needs of the company's online audiences. Don't worry about the technical aspects of web accessibility; focus instead on the benefits of improving accessibility.[24]

## EMAIL SKILLS

**12. Message Strategies: Persuasive Claims and Requests for Adjustment [LO-2]** You thought it was strange that no one called you on your new mobile phone, even though you had given your family members, friends, and boss your new number. Two weeks after getting the new phone and agreeing to a $49 monthly fee, you called the service provider, InstantCall, just to see if everything was working. Sure enough, the technician discovered that your incoming calls were being routed to an inactive number. You're glad she found the problem, but then it took the company nearly two more weeks to fix it. When you called to complain about paying for service you didn't receive, the customer service agent suggests you send an email to Judy Hinkley at the company's regional business office to request an adjustment.

**Your task:** Decide how much of an adjustment you think you deserve under the circumstances and then send an email message to Hinkley to request the adjustment to your account. Write a summary of events in chronological order, supplying exact dates for maximum effectiveness. Make up any information you need, such as problems that the malfunctioning service caused at home or at work.

## LETTER WRITING SKILLS

**13. Message Strategies: Requests for Information [LO-2]** As a motivated, ambitious employee, you naturally care about your performance on the job—and about making sure your performance is being fairly judged and rewarded. Unfortunately, the company has gone through a period of turmoil over the past several years, and you have reported to seven managers during the past five years. One year, your annual performance review was done by someone who had been your boss for only three weeks and knew almost nothing about you or your work. Last year, your boss was fired the day after he wrote your review, and you can't help but wonder whether you got a fair review from someone in that situation. Overall, you are worried that your career progression and wage increases have been hampered by inconsistent and ill-informed performance reviews.

The company allows employees to keep copies of their reviews, but you haven't been diligent about doing so. You would like to get copies of your last five reviews, but you heard from a colleague that the human resources department will not release copies of past reviews without approval from the managers who wrote them. In your case, however, three of the managers who reviewed you are no longer with the company, and you do not want your current boss to know you are concerned about your reviews.

**Your task:** Write an email message to the director of human resources, Leon Sandes, requesting copies of your performance reviews over the past five years. Use the information included above and make up any additional details you need.

# Marketing and Sales Messages: Conventional Media

### LETTER WRITING SKILLS / PORTFOLIO BUILDER

**14. Message Strategies: Marketing and Sales Messages [LO-3]**  Like all other states, Kentucky works hard to attract businesses that are considering expanding into the state or relocating entirely from another state. The Kentucky Cabinet for Economic Development is responsible for reaching out to these companies and overseeing the many incentive programs the state offers to new and established businesses.

**Your task:** As the communication director of the Kentucky Cabinet for Economic Development, you play the lead role in reaching out to companies that want to expand or relocate to Kentucky. Visit www.thinkkentucky.com and download the *Kentucky Facts* brochure (look under the "Why Kentucky" link). Identify the major benefits the state uses to promote Kentucky as a great place to locate a business. Summarize these reasons in a one-page form letter that will be sent to business executives throughout the country. Be sure to introduce yourself and your purpose in the letter, and close with a compelling call to action (have them reach you by telephone at 800-626-2930 or by email at econdev@ky.gov). As you plan your letter, try to imagine yourself as the CEO of a company and consider what a complex choice it would be to move to another state.[25]

### LETTER WRITING SKILLS / PORTFOLIO BUILDER

**15. Message Strategies: Marketing and Sales Messages [LO-3]**  Water polo is an active sport that provides great opportunities for exercise and for learning the collaborative skills involved in teamwork. You can learn more at www.usawaterpolo.org.

**Your task:** Write a one-page letter to parents of 10- to 14-year-old boys and girls, promoting the health and socialization benefits of water polo and encouraging them to introduce their children to the sport through a local club. Tell them they can learn more about the sport and find a club in their area by visiting the USA Water Polo website.

### WEB WRITING SKILLS

**16. Message Strategies: Marketing and Sales Messages [LO-3]**  Convincing people to give their music a try is one of the toughest challenges new bands and performers face.

**Your task:** Imagine you've taken on the job of promoting an amazing new band or performer you just discovered. Choose someone you've heard live or online and write 100 to 200 words of webpage copy describing the music in a way that will convince people to listen to a few online samples.

### EMAIL SKILLS

**17. Message Strategies: Marketing and Sales Messages [LO-3]**  The oud (rhymes with "mood") is a popular musical instrument in many cultures from northern Africa to southwest Asia, enjoying the same status in these countries as the guitar enjoys in Europe and the Americas. The oud, which dates back to the seventh century, was also the ancestor of the European-style lute that had its heyday during the Renaissance.

Many guitar players are familiar with the lute, but probably fewer with the oud. As the marketing director for Your World Instruments (www.yourworldinstruments.com), you'd like to encourage guitar players to consider the oud. Some might want to just explore another musical heritage. Others might want to expand their sonic palettes, so to speak, giving their music a broader range of sounds.

**Your task:** Write a brief email message that encourages guitar players to try something new. Or something old, more precisely. The people to whom you will be writing have heard from the company before, many are past customers, and all have opted-in to the email list. The call to action is encouraging these musicians to click through to the website to watch videos of expert oud players and to learn more about these storied instruments.[26]

### WEB WRITING SKILLS / TEAM SKILLS / PORTFOLIO BUILDER

**18. Message Strategies: Marketing and Sales Messages [LO-3]**  You never intended to become an inventor, but you saw a way to make something work more easily, so you set to work. You developed a model, found a way to mass-produce it, and set up a small manufacturing studio in your home. You know that other people are going to benefit from your invention. Now all you need to do is reach that market.

**Your task:** Team up with other students assigned by your instructor and imagine a useful product that you might have invented—perhaps something related to a hobby or sporting activity. List the features and benefits of your imaginary product, and describe how it helps customers. Then write the copy for a webpage that would introduce and promote this product, using what you've learned in this chapter and making up details as you need them. As your instructor indicates, submit the copy as a word processor file or as a webpage using basic HTML formatting.

### PODCASTING SKILLS

**19. Message Strategies: Marketing and Sales Messages [LO-3]**  Your new podcast channel, School2Biz, offers advice to business students making the transition from college to career. You provide information on everything from preparing résumés to interviewing to finding a place in the business world and building a successful career. As you expand your audience, you'd eventually like to turn School2Biz into a profitable operation (perhaps by selling advertising time during your podcasts). For now, you're simply offering free advice.

**Your task:** You've chosen Podcast Bunker (www.podcastbunker.com) as the first website on which to promote School2Biz. This site lets podcasters promote their feeds with brief text listings, such as this description of Toolmonger Tool Talk: "Chuck and Sean from the web's first tool blog, Toolmonger.com, keep you up-to-date on the newest hand and power tools, and answer your home improvement, automotive, and tool-related questions."

As your instructor directs, either write a 50-word description of your new podcast that can be posted on Podcast Bunker or record a 30-second podcast describing the new service. Make up any information you need to describe School2Biz. Be sure to mention who you are and why the information you present is worth listening to.[27]

## LETTER WRITING SKILLS / PORTFOLIO BUILDER

**20. Message Strategies: Marketing and Sales Messages [LO-3]** Kelly Services is a large staffing company based in Troy, Michigan. Client firms turn to Kelly to strategically balance their workloads and workforces during peaks and valleys of demand, to handle special projects, and to evaluate employees prior to making a full-time hiring decision. Facing the economic pressures of global competition, many companies now rely on a dynamic combination of permanent employees and temporary contractors hired through service providers such as Kelly. In addition to these staffing services, Kelly offers project services (managing both short- and long-term projects) and outsourcing and consulting services (taking over entire business functions).

**Your task:** Write a one-page sales letter that would be sent to human resources executives at large U.S.-based corporations describing Kelly's three groups of business services. For current information, visit the Kelly website at www.kellyservices.com and look in the "Business Services" section.[28]

## WEB WRITING SKILLS / PORTFOLIO BUILDER

**21. Message Strategies: Marketing and Sales Messages [LO-3]** After a shaky start as the technology matured and advertisers tried to figure out this new medium, online advertising has finally become a significant force in both consumer and business marketing. Companies in a wide variety of industries are shifting some of the ad budgets from traditional media such as TV and magazines to the increasing selection of advertising possibilities online—and more than a few companies now advertise almost exclusively online. That's fine for companies that sell advertising time and space online, but your job involves selling advertising in print magazines that are worried about losing market share to online publishers.

Online advertising has two major advantages that you can't really compete with: interactivity and the ability to precisely target individual audience members. On the other hand, you have several advantages going for you, including the ability to produce high-color photography, the physical presence of print (such as when a magazine sits on a table in a doctor's waiting room), portability, guaranteed circulation numbers, and close reader relationships that go back years or decades.

**Your task:** You work as an advertising sales specialist for the Time Inc. division of Time Warner, which publishes more than 100 magazines around the world. Write a brief persuasive message about the benefits of magazine advertising; the statement will be posted on the individual websites of Time Inc.'s numerous magazines, so you can't narrow in on any single publication. Also, Time Inc. coordinates its print publications with an extensive online presence (including thousands of paid online ads), so you can't bash online advertising, either.[29]

# Marketing and Sales Messages: Social Media

## BLOGGING SKILLS

**22. Message Strategies: Marketing and Sales Messages; Media Skills: Blogging [LO-3], Chapter 8** Other than possibly wrinkling their noses at that faint smell that wafts out of the plastic bags when they bring clothes home from the dry cleaner, many consumers probably don't pay much attention to the process that goes on behind the scenes at their neighborhood cleaner. However, traditional dry cleaning is a chemically intense process—so much so that these facilities require special environmental permits and monitoring by government agencies.

At Kansas City's Hangers Cleaners, the process is different—much different. The company's innovative machines use safe liquid carbon dioxide ($CO_2$) and specially developed detergents to clean clothes. The process requires no heat (making it easier on clothes) and has no need for the toxic, combustible perchloroethylene used in conventional dry cleaning (making it safer for employees and the environment). Customers can tell the difference, too. As one put it, "Since I started using Hangers, my clothes are softer, cleaner and they don't have that chemical smell."

**Your task:** Because many consumers aren't familiar with traditional dry cleaning, they don't immediately grasp why Hangers's method is better for clothes, employees, and the environment. Write a post for the company blog, explaining why Hangers is different. Limit yourself to 400 words. You can learn more about the company and its unique process at www.hangerskc.com.[30]

## SOCIAL NETWORKING SKILLS

**23. Message Strategies: Marketing and Sales Messages; Media Skills: Social Networking [LO-3], Chapter 8** Curves is a fitness center franchise that caters to women who may not feel at home in traditional gyms. With its customer-focused and research-based approach, Curves has become a significant force in the fitness industry and one of the most successful franchise operations in history.[31]

**Your task:** Read the Overview and History sections at www.curves.com/about-curves. Imagine that you are adapting this material for the Info tab on the company's Facebook page. Write a "Company Overview" (95–100 words) and "Mission" statement (45–50 words).

## SOCIAL NETWORKING SKILLS / TEAMWORK SKILLS

**24. Message Strategies: Marketing and Sales Messages; Media Skills: Social Networking [LO-3], Chapter 8** You chose your college or university based on certain expectations, and you've been enrolled long enough now to have some idea about whether those expectations have been met. In other words, you are something of an expert about the "consumer benefits" your school can offer prospective students.

**Your task:** In a team of four students, interview six other students who are not taking this business communication course. Try to get a broad sample of demographics and psychographics, including students in a variety of majors and programs. Ask these students (1) why they chose this college or university and (2) whether the experience has met their expectations so far. To ensure the privacy of your respondents, do not record their names with their answers. Each member of the team should then answer these same two questions, so that you have responses from a total of ten students.

After compiling the responses (you might use Google Docs or a similar collaboration tool so that everyone on the team has easy access to the information), analyze them as a team to look for any recurring "benefit themes." Is it the quality of the education? Research opportunities? Location? The camaraderie of school sporting events? The chance to meet and study with fascinating students from a variety of backgrounds? Identify two or three strong benefits that your college or university can promise—and deliver—to prospective students.

Now nominate one member of the team to draft a short marketing message that could be posted on the Notes tab of your school's Facebook page. The message should include a catchy title that makes it clear the message is a student's perspective on why this is a great place to get a college education. When the draft is ready, the other members of the team should review it individually. Finally, meet as a team to complete the message.

## MICROBLOGGING SKILLS

**25. Message Strategies: Marketing and Sales Messages; Media Skills: Microblogging [LO-3], Chapter 8** Effective microblogging messages emphasize clarity and conciseness—and so do effective sales messages.

**Your task:** Find the website of any product that can be ordered online (any product you find interesting and that is appropriate to use for a class assignment). Adapt the information on the website, using your own words, and write four tweets to promote the product. The first should get your audience's attention (with an intriguing benefit claim, for example), the second should build audience interest by providing some support for the claim you made in the first message, the third should increase readers' desire to have the product by layering on one or two more buyer benefits, and the fourth should motivate readers to take action to place an order. Your first three tweets can be up to 140 characters, but the fourth should be limited to 120 to accommodate a URL (you don't need to include the URL in your message, however).

If your class is set up with private Twitter accounts, use your private account to send your messages. Otherwise, email your four messages to your instructor or post them on your class blog, as your instructor directs.

---

# MyBCommLab

Go to **mybcommlab.com** for Auto-graded writing questions as well as the following Assisted-graded writing questions:

**12-1.** What role do demographics and psychographics play in audience analysis during the planning of a persuasive message? [LO-1]

**12-2.** Why do the AIDA model and similar approaches need to be modified when writing persuasive messages in social media? [LO-3]

**12-3.** Mybcommlab Only—comprehensive writing assignment for this chapter.

# Endnotes

1. CafeMom website, accessed 4 February 2013, www.cafemom.com; "ClubMom Introduces the MomNetwork—The Web's First Social Network for Moms," press release, 8 May 2006, www.hcp.com; "Laura Fortner Named Senior Vice President, Business Development at ClubMom," press release, 20 September 2006, http://newyork .dbusinessnews.com.

2. Jay A. Conger, "The Necessary Art of Persuasion," *Harvard Business Review*, May–June 1998, 84–95; Jeanette W. Gilsdorf, "Write Me Your Best Case for . . .," *Bulletin of the Association for Business Communication* 54, no. 1 (March 1991): 7–12.

3. "Vital Skill for Today's Managers: Persuading, Not Ordering, Others," *Soundview Executive Book Summaries*, September 1998, 1.

4. Mary Cross, "Aristotle and Business Writing: Why We Need to Teach Persuasion," *Bulletin of the Association for Business Communication* 54, no. 1 (March 1991): 3–6.

5. IKEA website, accessed 4 February 2013, www.ikea.com; Liz C. Wang, Julie Baker, Judy A. Wagner, and Kirk Wakefield, "Can a Retail Web Site Be Social?" *Journal of Marketing* 71, no. 3 (July 2007), 143–157.

6. Stephen Bayley and Roger Mavity, "How to Pitch," *Management Today*, March 2007, 48–53.

7. Robert B. Cialdini, "Harnessing the Science of Persuasion," *BusinessWeek*, 4 December 2007, www.businessweek.com.

8. Wesley Clark, "The Potency of Persuasion," *Fortune*, 12 November 2007, 48; W. H. Weiss, "Using Persuasion Successfully," *Supervision*, October 2006, 13–16.

9. Tom Chandler, "The Copywriter's Best Friend," *The Copywriter Underground blog*, 20 December 2006, http://copywriterunderground.com.

10. Raymond M. Olderman, *10-Minute Guide to Business Communication* (New York: Macmillan Spectrum/Alpha Books, 1997), 57–61.

11. John D. Ramage and John C. Bean, *Writing Arguments: A Rhetoric with Readings*, 3rd ed. (Boston: Allyn & Bacon, 1995), 430–442.

12. Philip Vassallo, "Persuading Powerfully: Tips for Writing Persuasive Documents," *Et Cetera*, Spring 2002, 65–71.

13. Dianna Booher, *Communicate with Confidence* (New York: McGraw-Hill, 1994), 102.

14. Conger, "The Necessary Art of Persuasion."

15. "Social Factors in Developing a Web Accessibility Business Case for Your Organization," W3C website, accessed 4 February 2013, www.w3.org.

16. Tamar Weinberg, *The New Community Rules: Marketing on the Social Web* (Sebastapol, Calif.: O'Reilly Media, 2009), 22; 23–24; 187–191; Larry Weber, *Marketing to the Social Web* (Hoboken, N.J.: Wiley, 2007), 12–14; David Meerman Scott, *The New Rules of Marketing and PR* (Hoboken, N.J.: Wiley, 2007), 62; Paul Gillin, *The New Influencers* (Sanger, Calif.: Quill Driver Books, 2007), 34–35; Jeremy Wright, *Blog Marketing: The Revolutionary Way to Increase Sales, Build Your Brand, and Get Exceptional Results* (New York: McGraw-Hill, 2006), 263–365.

17. Gilsdorf, "Write Me Your Best Case for. . . ."

18. Miguel Helft and Tanzina Vega, "Retargeting Ads Follow Surfers to Other Sites," *New York Times*, 29 August 2010, www.nytimes.com.

19. "How to Comply with the Children's Online Privacy Protection Rule," U.S. Federal Trade Commission website, accessed 17 July 2010, www.ftc.gov; "Frequently Asked Advertising Questions: A Guide for Small Business," U.S. Federal Trade Commission website, accessed 17 July 2010, www.ftc.gov.

20. Adapted from Samsung website, accessed 22 October 2006, www.samsung.com.

21. Adapted from "Webmaster Guidelines," Google, accessed 5 February 2013, www.google.com; Brian Clark, "How to Create Compelling Content That Ranks Well in Search Engines," Copyblogger, May 2010, www.copyblogger.com; P.J. Fusco, "How Web 2.0 Affects SEO Strategy," ClickZ, 23 May 2007, www.clickz.com.

22. Adapted from IBM website, accessed 15 January 2004, www.ibm.com; "DAS Faces an Assured Future with IBM," IBM website, accessed 16 January 2004, www.ibm.com; "Sametime," IBM website, accessed 16 January 2004, www.ibm.com.

23. Adapted from American National Red Cross website, accessed 5 February 2013, www.redcrossblood.org; American Red Cross San Diego Chapter website, accessed 19 July 2010, www.sdarc.org.

24. Adapted from Web Accessibility Initiative, World Wide Web Consortium website, accessed 7 November 2008, www.w3.org.

25. Kentucky Cabinet for Economic Development website, accessed 19 July 2010, www.thinkkentucky.com.

26. Adapted from Your World Instruments website, accessed 21 February 2011, www.yourworldinstruments.com; "Ud," *Encyclopedia Britannica,* accessed 21 February 2011, www.brittanica.com.

27. Adapted from Podcast Bunker website, accessed 19 July 2010, www.podcastbunker.com.

28. Adapted from Kelly Services website, accessed 19 July 2010, www.kellyservices.com.

29. Adapted from Time Inc. website, accessed 19 July 2010, www.timewarner.com.

30. Adapted from Hangers Cleaners (Kansas City) website, accessed 4 February 2013, www.hangerskc.com; Charles Fishman, "The Greener Cleaners," Fast Company website, accessed 11 July 2000, http://fastcompany.com; Micell Technologies website, accessed 1 September 2000, www.micell.com; Cool Clean Technologies, Inc., website, accessed 9 January 2004, www.coolclean.com.

31. Adapted from Curves website, accessed 19 July 2010, www.curves.com.

# Reports and Proposals

Reports and proposals are the "major leagues" of business communication. These are the tools you use to analyze complex problems, educate audiences, address opportunities in the marketplace, win contracts, and even launch new companies through compelling business plans. Adapt what you've learned so far to the particular challenges of long-format messages, including some special touches that can make formal reports stand out from the crowd.

koh sze kiat/Shutterstock

## LEARNING OBJECTIVES

After studying this chapter, you will be able to

1 Describe an effective process for conducting business research.

2 Define secondary research and explain how to evaluate, locate, and document information sources.

3 Define primary research and outline the steps involved in conducting surveys and interviews.

4 Describe the major tasks involved in processing research results.

5 Explain how to summarize research results and present conclusions and recommendations.

### MyBCommLab®

⭐ **Improve Your Grade!** Over 10 million students improved their results using the Pearson MyLabs. Visit **mybcommlab.com** for simulations, tutorials, and end-of-chapter problems.

### COMMUNICATION CLOSE-UP AT
### Tesco www.tesco.com

Most consumers enjoy the benefits of stiff price competition among their local grocery stores, but the competition is anything but enjoyable for grocery retailers. In the United States, the average grocery store's after-tax profit margin hovers around 1 percent. With so little room for error, grocers need to stay on top of consumer behavior to make sure they offer the right mix of products at the right prices.

Tesco, the leading grocery retailer in the United Kingdom, is not only surviving but thriving in this tough industry. Under the leadership of Richard Brasher, the company's top marketing executive in the United Kingdom, Tesco devotes considerable effort to acquiring and processing information about its customers, information that is used in a variety of documents to drive both strategic and tactical decisions.

For example, when demographic research indicated a growing number of immigrants from Poland to the UK, the store reached out to Polish-speaking consumers to learn more about their wants and needs. After a successful experiment in a few stores, Tesco expanded its Polish foods selection to roughly a hundred other stores. In another instance, the marketing team couldn't figure out why flowers and wine had become such hot sellers during a particular week at the beginning of summer that didn't coincide with any regular holidays. Analysis of sales data revealed that families were buying these items as gifts for their children's teachers at the end of the school year, so the company responded by making sure these items were stocked in plentiful supply during that week.

British retail giant Tesco relies on extensive audience research to plan and craft its consumer messages.

Research has helped the company in numerous ways, but its recent attempt to expand into the U.S. market demonstrates that simply conducting market research doesn't automatically eliminate the risks involved in major business decisions. After studying the market for two decades, Tesco opened nearly 200 Fresh & Easy Neighborhood Markets in California, Nevada, and Arizona. Within a few years, however, the company announced that the investment was not paying off as expected and it was putting the Fresh & Easy chain up for sale and leaving the U.S. market.

The company's timing had been unfortunate. It launched relatively upscale stores just as the U.S. economy was tanking and consumers began tightening their belts. But larger economic issues were not the only problem. According to retail experts, one key reason for Tesco's stumble was that, after conducting years of in-depth study on the market and U.S consumer habits, the company "then ignored much of that research, deciding to set up the stores it wanted, rather than listening to its potential customers." Gathering information, in other words, is only half the job. That information has to be put to good use, too.[1]

# Planning Your Research

Whether you're planning a simple report or an entire business plan, make sure your reporting, analysis, and recommendations are supported with solid research. Figure 13.1 outlines a five-step research process that will help you gather and use information efficiently; you'll learn more about these steps in the following sections.

With so much information now online, it's tempting just to punch some keywords into a search engine and then grab the first few results that show up. However, effective and efficient research requires a more thoughtful approach. Your favorite search engine might not be able to reach the webpages that have the information you need, the information might not be online at all, it might be online but not under the search terms you've used, or the it might not even exist in any form.

To maximize your chances of finding useful information and to minimize the time you spend looking for it, follow these planning steps: Familiarize yourself with the subject so that you can frame insightful questions, identify the most critical gaps in your information, and then prioritize your research needs. However, before launching any research project, be sure to take a moment or two to consider the ethics and etiquette of your approach.

**1** LEARNING OBJECTIVE
Describe an effective process for conducting business research.

Audiences expect you to support your business messages with solid research.

Researching without a plan wastes time and usually produces unsatisfactory results.

## MAINTAINING ETHICS AND ETIQUETTE IN YOUR RESEARCH

Your research tactics affect the people you gather data and information from, the people who read your results, and the people who are affected by the way you present those results. To avoid ethical lapses, keep the following points in mind:

- **Don't force a specific outcome by skewing your research.** Approach your research with an open mind and a willingness to accept whatever you find, even if it's not what you expect or want to see.
- **Respect the privacy of your research participants.** Privacy is a contentious issue today. Businesses believe they have a right to protect their confidential information from

Take precautions to avoid ethical lapses in your research.

Privacy is a contentious issue in the research field today.

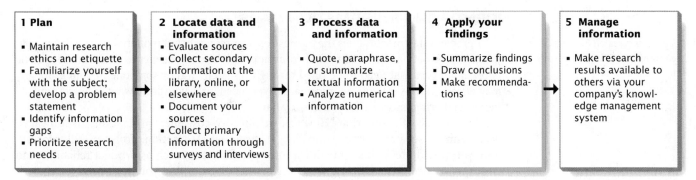

**Figure 13.1  The Research Process**
By following a methodical research process, you can save time and money while uncovering better information.

competitors, and consumers believe they have a right to protect their personal information from businesses.

- **Document sources and give appropriate credit.** Whether you are using published documents, personal interviews, or company records, citing your sources not only is fair to the people who created and provided the information but also helps your audience members confirm your information or explore it in more detail, if they so choose.

- **Respect the intellectual property and digital rights of your sources.** For example, your research might turn up a great new way to sell services online, but that doesn't mean you're free to implement that process. It might be protected by one of the many patents that have been granted in recent years for business process models.

- **Don't extract more from your sources than they actually provide.** In other words, don't succumb to the temptation to put words in a source's mouth. For instance, if an industry expert says that a sales increase is possible, don't quote him or her as saying that a sales increase is probable.

- **Don't misrepresent who you are or what you intend to do with the research results.** One classic example of ethical lapses in this area is known as *sagging*, short for *selling under the guise of research*. For example, a firm might appear to be conducting a survey when it is in fact using the questions to identify hot sales leads. Another unethical variation on sagging is following up a real survey with sales calls, using information that respondents shared in the belief that they were only participating in a survey.[2]

Research etiquette deserves careful attention, too. For example, respect the time of anyone who agrees to be interviewed or to be a research participant, and maintain courtesy throughout the interview or research process. For more information on research ethics and etiquette, review the *Code of Standards and Ethics for Survey Research* published by the Council of America Survey Research Organizations (www.casro.org).

**REAL-TIME UPDATES**
LEARN MORE BY VISITING THIS WEBSITE
**Get clear answers to murky copyright questions**

Find out what is covered by copyright, what isn't, and how to secure a copyright for your own work. Go to http://real-timeupdates.com/bct12 and click on Learn More. If you are using MyBCommLab, you can access Real-Time Updates within each chapter or under Student Study Tools.

## FAMILIARIZING YOURSELF WITH THE SUBJECT

Give yourself some unstructured time at the beginning of the project to explore the general subject area, perhaps by reading industry publications and blogs, visiting competitors' websites, and interviewing experts within your organization. Scan the tables of contents and indexes of books on the subject. Some of the newest online search tools can be quite helpful in this regard; see "Innovations in Research Technology" on page 365.

When you have a basic grasp of the subject area, develop a **problem statement** that defines the problem or purpose of your research—the decision you need to make or the conclusion you need to reach at the end of the process. You may find it easier to phrase the problem as a question, such as "How can we improve customer satisfaction?" or "Does Apple's new TV system pose a competitive threat to us?"

## IDENTIFYING INFORMATION GAPS

Your problem statement frames the purpose of your research, but it often doesn't tell you what specific information you need to find. Your next task is to dig deeper to discover the specific *information gaps* that need to be filled through research. You or someone in your company may already have some of the information you need, and you don't want to waste time or money gathering information you already have.

For instance, the question "How can we improve customer satisfaction?" is too vague because many separate factors contribute to customer satisfaction. To get useful information, you would break this topic down into specific issues, such as product reliability and customer service skills. Digging further, you may discover that you don't need to research product reliability because the company already tracks data on product repairs. However, if no one has ever measured the employees' customer service skills, you would identify that as a definite information gap.

## PRIORITIZING RESEARCH NEEDS

Prioritizing your research needs is important because you won't have the time or money to answer every question you might have. Moreover, if you'll be using interviewers or surveys, you'll need to limit the number of questions you ask so that you don't consume more time than people are willing to give. One simple way to prioritize is to divide your questions into "need to know" and "nice to know" and then toss out all the "nice to know" questions. If you start with a technique such as information gap analysis, you will get a clear idea of the information you truly need to collect.

You usually won't have enough time or money to answer every question that comes to mind, so setting priorities is a must.

# Conducting Secondary Research

With a clear plan and careful prioritization, you're ready to conduct research—and the first step is to see whether anyone else has already done some or all of the research you need. Consulting research that was done previously for another purpose is considered **secondary research**. The sources for such information include print and online periodicals, online databases, books, and other research reports. (Some companies specialize in reports on particular industries, companies, technologies, market regions, and other subjects.)

Don't let the name *secondary* fool you, though. You want to start with secondary research because it can save you considerable time and money, although you may have to pay to see someone else's results. In contrast, **primary research** (see page 366) is new research done specifically for the current project.

**2 LEARNING OBJECTIVE**
Define secondary research and explain how to evaluate, locate, and document information sources.

Primary research contains information that you gather specifically for a new research project; secondary research contains information that others have gathered for other purposes.

Start your research by conducting secondary research first.

## EVALUATING SOURCES

No matter where you're searching, it is your responsibility to separate quality information from unreliable or misleading junk, so you don't taint your results or damage your reputation. Social media have complicated this challenge by making many new sources of information available. On the positive side, independent sources communicating through blogs, wikis, Twitter, user-generated content sites, and podcasting channels can provide valuable and unique insights, often from experts whose voices might never be heard otherwise. On the negative side, these nontraditional information sources often lack the editorial boards and fact checkers commonly used in traditional publishing. You cannot assume that the information you find in blogs and other sources is accurate, objective, and current. Answer the following questions about each piece of material:

Evaluate your sources carefully to avoid embarrassing and potentially damaging mistakes.

> **REAL-TIME UPDATES**
> LEARN MORE BY WATCHING THIS VIDEO
> **Quick tips for evaluating the research quality of a website**
> This short video from the Monterey Public Library will help you determine how much trust to put in websites you use for research. Go to http://real-timeupdates.com/bct12 and click on Learn More. If you are using MyBCommLab, you can access Real-Time Updates within each chapter or under Student Study Tools.

- **Does the source have a reputation for honesty and reliability?** Naturally, you'll feel more comfortable using information from an established source that has a reputation for accuracy. But don't let your guard down completely; even the finest reporters and editors can make mistakes. For sources that are new or relatively unknown, your safest bet is to corroborate anything you learn with information from several other sources.
- **Is the source potentially biased?** The individual or organization providing the information might have a particular bias or point of view regarding the information and its context. Such bias is neither inherently bad nor unethical, but you need to be aware of it so that you can interpret the information you find.
- **What is the purpose of the material?** Was the material designed to inform others of new research, advance a position, or stimulate discussion? Was it designed to promote or sell a product? Be sure to distinguish among advertising, advocating, and informing.
- **Is the author credible?** Find out whether the person or the publisher is well known in the field. Is the author someone with hands-on experience in the subject area or merely an observer with an opinion?
- **Where did the source get *its* information?** Many sources of secondary information get their material from other secondary sources, removing you even further from the original data.

Let your readers know if you were unable to verify critical pieces of information obtained in your research.

- **Can you verify the material independently?** Verification can uncover biases or mistakes—which is particularly important when the information goes beyond simple facts to include projections, interpretations, and estimates. If you can't verify critical information, let your audience know that.
- **Is the material current?** Make sure you are using the most current information available by checking the publication or posting date.
- **Is the material complete?** Have you accessed the entire document or only a selection from it? If it's a selection, which parts were excluded? Do you need more detail?
- **Are all claims supported with evidence?** Are opinions presented as facts? Does the writer make broad claims, such as "most people believe . . ." without citing any surveys to prove his or her point?
- **Do the source's claims stand up to logical scrutiny?** Finally, step back and ask whether the information makes sense. If that little voice in your head says that something sounds suspicious, listen!

You probably won't have time to conduct a thorough background check on all your sources, so focus your efforts on the most important or most suspicious pieces of information.

## LOCATING SOURCES

Even if you intend to eventually conduct primary research, start with a review of any available secondary research. Inside the company, you might be able to find a variety of documents prepared for other projects that offer helpful information. Be sure to ask whether your company has a *knowledge management system* or some other repository for research results. (See "Managing Information" on page 374 for more on this topic.) Outside the company, you can choose from a wide range of print and online resources, some of which are included in Table 13.1.[3] (Of course, the list in this table represents a tiny fraction of the secondary resources available.) For instance, if you want to know more about a specific company, one of the first things you'll need to find out is whether the company is public (sells shares of stock to the general public) or private. Public corporations, which are required to submit extensive financial reports to government agencies, usually have more information available than private companies.

### Finding Information at the Library

Public, corporate, and university libraries offer an enormous array of business books, electronic databases, newspapers, periodicals, directories, almanacs, and government publications. Some of these printed sources provide information that is not available online, and some of the online sources provide information that is available by subscription. Don't assume that you can find everything you need through your own online research.

Libraries offer information and resources you can't find anywhere else—including research librarians who can show you how to plan and conduct effective searches.

Libraries are also where you'll find one of your most important resources: librarians. Reference librarians are skilled in research strategies and can often help you find obscure information you can't find on your own. They can also direct you to many sources of business information. Also, many library websites now have a business portal, with links to helpful resources and advice on finding information.

Whether you're trying to locate information in printed materials or in databases, each type of resource serves a special function:

- **Newspapers and periodicals.** Libraries offer access to a wide variety of popular magazines, general business magazines, *trade journals* (which provide information about specific professions and industries), and *academic journals* (which provide research-oriented articles from researchers and educators). Check the library's website or ask a librarian to see which periodicals are available in print or electronic formats.
- **Business books.** Although generally less timely than newspapers, periodicals, and online sources, business books provide in-depth coverage of a variety of business topics. Many libraries now offer online access to their card catalogs so you can see if they have specific titles in their collections.
- **Directories.** Thousands of directories are published in print and electronic formats in the United States, and many include membership information for all kinds of professions, industries, and special-interest groups.

TABLE 13.1 | Important Resources for Business Research

## COMPANY, INDUSTRY, AND PRODUCT RESOURCES (URLs are provided for online resources)

**AnnualReports.com** (www.annualreports.com). Free access to annual reports from thousands of public companies.

**Brands and Their Companies/Companies and Their Brands.** Contains data on several hundred thousand consumer products, manufacturers, importers, marketers, and distributors. Also available as an online database; ask at your library.

**CNN/Money** (http://money.cnn.com). News, analysis, and financial resources covering companies, industries, and world markets.

**D&B Directories.** A variety of directories, including America's Corporate Families (ownership connections among companies), Business Rankings (25,000 leading companies), Directory of Service Companies (more than 50,000 companies in the service sector), and Industrial Guide (more than 120,000 manufacturing companies).

**Hoover's Handbook of American Business.** Profiles of hundreds of influential public and private corporations.

**Hoover's Online** (www.hoovers.com). Database of millions of companies worldwide, including in-depth coverage of thousands of leading companies around the world. Basic information available free; in-depth information requires a subscription.

**Manufacturing & Distribution USA.** Data on thousands of companies in the manufacturing, wholesaling, and retailing sectors.

**NAICS Codes** (www.census.gov/eos/www/naics). North American Industry Classification System.

**Reference USA.** Concise information on millions of U.S. companies; subscription database.

**SEC filings** (www.sec.gov/edgar.shtml). SEC filings, including 10Ks, 10Qs, annual reports, and prospectuses for U.S. public firms.

**Standard & Poor's Net Advantage.** Comprehensive range of directories and databases focusing on publicly traded companies and their industries and markets.

**ThomasNet** (www.thomasnet.com). Information on thousands of U.S. manufacturers, indexed by company name and product.

## RESEARCH DIRECTORIES AND INDEXES

**Books in Print.** Database indexes millions of books, audio books, and video titles from around the world. Available in print and professional online versions.

**Directories in Print.** Information on thousands of business and industrial directories.

**Encyclopedia of Associations.** Index of thousands of associations, listed by broad subject category, specific subject, association, and location. Available as an online database as well.

**Reader's Guide to Periodical Literature.** Classic index of general-interest magazines, categorized by subject and author; also available in electronic format, including a version with the full text of thousands of articles.

## TRADEMARKS AND PATENTS

**Official Gazette of the United States Patent and Trademark Office** (www.uspto.gov). Weekly publication (one for trademarks and one for patents) providing official record of newly assigned trademarks and patents, product descriptions, and product names.

**United States Patent and Trademark Office** (www.uspto.gov). Trademark and patent information records.

## STATISTICS AND OTHER BUSINESS DATA

**Bureau of Economic Analysis** (www.bea.gov). Large collection of economic and government data.

**Europa—The European Union Online** (http://europa.eu/index_en.htm). A portal that provides up-to-date coverage of current affairs, legislation, policies, and EU statistics.

**FedStats** (www.fedstats.gov). Access to a full range of statistics and information from more than 70 U.S. government agencies.

**Key Business Ratios (Dun & Bradstreet).** Industry, financial, and performance ratios.

**Information Please Almanac.** Compilation of broad-range statistical data, with strong focus on labor force.

**Annual Statement Studies.** Industry, financial, and performance ratios published by the Risk Management Association.

**Statistical Abstract of the United States** (www.census.gov). Annual compendium of U.S. economic, social, political, and industrial statistics.

**The World Almanac and Book of Facts.** Facts on economic, social, educational, and political events for major countries.

**U.S. Bureau of Labor Statistics** (www.bls.gov). Extensive national and regional information on labor and business, including employment, industry growth, productivity, the Consumer Price Index (CPI), and the overall U.S. economy.

**U.S. Census Bureau** (www.census.gov). Demographic data and analysis on consumers and businesses based on census results.

## COMMERCIAL DATABASES (Require subscriptions; check with your school library)

**ABI/INFORM Trade & Industry.** Access to more than 750 periodicals and newsletters that focus on specific trades or industries.

**Business Source Premier (Ebsco).** Access to a variety of databases on a wide range of disciplines from leading information providers.

**ProQuest Dialog.** Hundreds of databases that include areas such as business and finance, news and media, medicine, pharmaceuticals, references, social sciences, government and regulation, science and technology, and more.

**ProQuest.** Thousands of periodicals and newspapers with extensive archives.

**HighBeam Research.** Thousands of full-text newspaper, magazine, and newswire sources, plus maps and photographs.

**Gale Business & Company Resource Center.** A comprehensive research tool designed for undergraduate and graduate students, job searchers, and investors; offers a wide variety of information on companies and industries.

**LexisNexis.** Several thousand databases covering legal, corporate, government, and academic subjects.

- **Almanacs and statistical resources.** Almanacs are handy guides to factual and statistical information about countries, politics, the labor force, and so on. One of the most extensive, the *Statistical Abstract of the United States*, published annually by the U.S. Department of Commerce, contains statistics about occupations, government, population, health, business, crime, and the environment (also available online at www .census.gov).

- **Government publications.** Information on laws, court decisions, tax questions, regulatory issues, and other governmental concerns is often available in collections of government documents. A librarian can direct you to the information you want.

- **Electronic databases.** Databases offer vast collections of searchable information, often in specific areas, such as business, law, science, technology, and education. Some of these are available only by institutional subscription, so the library may be your only way to gain access to them. Some libraries offer remote online access to some or all databases; for others, you need to visit in person.

Local, state, and federal government agencies publish a huge array of information that is helpful to business researchers.

Online research tools can be used to search for existing information and to monitor for new information.

## Finding Information Online

The Internet can be a tremendous source of business information, provided that you know how to approach a search, where to look, and how to use the tools available. Roughly speaking, the tools fall into two categories: those you can use to actively *search* for existing information and those you can use to *monitor* selected sources for new information. (Some tools can perform both functions.)

To be a successful online researcher, you need to expand your toolkit beyond the popular search engines.

**Online Search Tools**  The most familiar search tools are general-purpose **search engines**, such as Google and Bing, which scan millions of websites to identify individual webpages that contain a specific word or phrase and then attempt to rank the results from most useful to least useful. Search engines have the advantage of scanning millions or billions of individual webpages, and the best engines use powerful ranking algorithms to present the pages that are probably the most relevant to your search request. Table 13.2 lists some of the most popular search engines, directories, metacrawlers, and specialized search tools available today.

Today's search engines are powerful tools, but they still have important limitations.

For all their ease and power, conventional search engines have three primary shortcomings: (1) no human editors are involved to evaluate the quality or ranking of the search results; (2) various engines use different search techniques, so they often find different material; and (3) search engines can't reach all the content on some websites (this part of the Internet is sometimes called the *hidden Internet* or the *deep Internet*).

Web directories benefit from having human editors evaluate and select websites.

A variety of tools are available to overcome the three main weaknesses of general-purpose search engines, and you should consider using one or more of them in your business research. First, **web directories** such as the Open Directory Project (www.dmoz.org) and Internet Public Library (www.ipl.org) use human editors to categorize and evaluate websites. A variety of other directories focus on specific media types, such as blogs or podcasts.

Metacrawlers can save you time by employing multiple search engines at once.

Second, **metasearch engines** (such as Bovée and Thill's Web Search, at http://web-search.businesscommunicationnetwork.com) help overcome the differences among search engines by formatting your search request for multiple search engines, making it easy to find a broader range of results. With a few clicks, you can compare results from multiple search engines to make sure you are getting a broad view of the material.

Online databases give you access to some of the most important resources that search engines usually can't reach: millions of newspaper, magazine, and journal articles.

Third, **online databases** help address the challenge of the hidden Internet by offering access to newspapers, magazines, journals, electronic copies of books, and other resources often not available with standard search engines. Some of these databases offer free access to the public, but others require a subscription (check with your library). Also, a variety of specialized search engines now exist to reach various parts of the hidden Internet.

## TABLE 13.2 | The Broad Spectrum of Online Search Tools

### Search Engines

| | | | |
|---|---|---|---|
| AltaVista | www.altavista.com | Google Book search | http://books.google.com |
| AOL Search | http://search.aol.com | Google Scholar search | http://scholar.google.com |
| Ask.com | www.ask.com | Microsoft Academic Research | http://academic.research.microsoft.com |
| Bing | www.bing.com | | |
| Biznar | www.biznar.com | Yahoo! Search | http://search.yahoo.com |
| Google | www.google.com | | |

### Metacrawlers, Clustering Engines, Answer Engines, and Hybrid Sites

| | | | |
|---|---|---|---|
| Answers.com | www.answers.com | Mamma | www.mamma.com |
| Bovée & Thill Web Search | http://websearch.businesscommunicationnetwork.com | MetaCrawler | www.metacrawler.com |
| | | Questia (requires subscription) | www.questia.com |
| | | Search.com | www.search.com |
| Dogpile | www.dogpile.com | WebCrawlers | www.webcrawler.com |
| ixquick | www.ixquick.com | | |
| iZito | www.izito.com | ZapMeta | www.zapmeta.com |
| KartOO | www.kartoo.com/ | Wolfram Alpha | www.wolframalpha.com |

### Web Directories, Online Libraries, and Online Card Catalogs

| | | | |
|---|---|---|---|
| About | www.about.com | Library Spot | www.libraryspot.com |
| CEOExpress | http://ceoexpress.com | Open Directory Project | www.dmoz.com |
| Digital Librarian | www.digital-librarian.com/business.html | Refdesk | www.refdesk.com |
| | | USA.gov (U.S. government portal) | www.usa.gov |
| Internet Public Library | www.ipl.org | | |
| Library of Congress | www.loc.gov/rr/business | WorldCat | www.worldcat.org |

### News Search Engines and Social Tagging Sites

| | | | |
|---|---|---|---|
| Delicious | http://delicious.com | Reddit | www.reddit.com |
| Google News | http://news.google.com | WorldNews | www.wn.com |
| NewsNow | www.newsnow.co.uk | Yahoo! News | http://news.yahoo.com |

### Blog, Video, and Podcast Search Engines and Directories

| | | | |
|---|---|---|---|
| American Rhetoric (speeches) | www.americanrhetoric.com | Google Video search | www.google.com/videohp |
| Bing videos | www.bing.com/videos | Podcast Alley | www.podcastalley.com |
| blinkx | www.blinkx.com | Technorati | http://technorati.com |
| Bloglines | www.bloglines.com | Yahoo! Video search | http://video.search.yahoo.com |
| GetAPodcast | www.getapodcast.com/ | YouTube | www.youtube.com |
| Google Blog search | www.google.com/blogsearch | | |

**Online Monitoring Tools**   One of the most powerful aspects of online research is the ability to automatically monitor selected sources for new information so that you can get new information without doing manual searches repeatedly. The possibilities include subscribing to newsfeeds from blogs and websites, following people on Twitter and other microblogs, setting up alerts on search engines and online databases, and using specialized monitors such as TweetBeep (http://tweetbeep.com) and TweetDeck (www.tweetdeck.com) to track tweets that mention specific companies or other terms.

To stay up to date on a research topic, subscribe to RSS feeds, search engine alerts, or Twitter updates from knowledgeable individuals.

Exercise some care when setting up monitoring tools, however, because it's easy to get overwhelmed by the flood of information. Remember that you can always go back and search your information sources if you need to gather additional information.

## Search Tips

Make sure you know how each search engine, directory, database, or metasearch engine works.

Search engines, metacrawlers, and databases offer a variety of ways to find information. Unfortunately, no two of them work in exactly the same way, and you have to learn how to use each one most effectively. This learning may take a few extra minutes at the beginning of your research, but it could save you hours of lost time later on—and save you from embarrassing oversights.

The most basic form of searching is a *keyword search*, in which the engine or database attempts to find items that include all the words you enter. A *Boolean search* expands on this capability by using search operators that let you define a query with greater precision. Common operators include AND (the search must include both words before and after the AND), OR (the search can include either or both words), and NOT (the search ignores items with whatever word comes after NOT). For example:

- *corporate AND profits* finds webpages or database entries that contain both *corporate* and *profits*.
- *corporate OR profits* finds items that contain either *corporate* or *profits* but not necessarily both.
- *corporate NOT profits* finds items that contain *corporate* but excludes all those that contain the word *profits*.

Boolean searches can also include operators that let you find a particular word in close proximity to other words or use *wildcards* to find similar spellings (such as *profit*, *profits*, and *profitability*).

As a simpler alternative to Boolean searches, some search engines and databases offer *natural language searches*, which let you ask questions in normal, everyday English. (Natural language is what humans speak, as opposed to the languages computers speak.) For example, "Which video game companies are the most profitable?" is a natural language query. Be aware that some search tools let you choose keyword, Boolean, or natural language searches, so make sure you know which method you're using.

Several search tools offer *forms-based searches* that help you create powerful queries without needing to learn any special techniques. As the name implies, you simply fill out an online form that typically lets you specify parameters such as date ranges, words to include or exclude, language, Internet domain name, and even file and media types. To access these forms, click on "advanced search" or a similar option.

To make the best use of any search engine or database, keep the following points in mind:

Search engine results can create the illusion that the Internet is a complete, well-organized warehouse of reliable information. However, it is neither complete nor organized, and not all the information is reliable.

- **Think before you search.** The neatly organized results you get from a search engine can create the illusion that the Internet is an orderly warehouse of all the information in the universe, but the reality is far different. The Internet is an incomplete, unorganized hodge-podge of millions of independent websites with information that ranges in value from priceless to worse-than-worthless. After you have identified what you need to know, spend a few moments thinking about where that information might be found, how it might be structured, and what terms various websites might use to describe it.
- **Read the instructions.** You can usually find a Help or Support page that explains both basic and advanced functions, with advice on how to use a particular tool most effectively.
- **Pay attention to the details.** Details can make all the difference in a search. For example, if you use multiple words in your search phrase, Bing advises you to put the most important words first because word order affects search results.[4]
- **Review the search and display options carefully.** When searching in databases, for instance, pay close attention to whether you are searching in the title, author, subject, or document field and whether the search is limited to particular types of documents (such as

full-text documents only). Each choice will return different results. And when the results are displayed, verify the presentation order; results might be sorted by date or by relevance.

- **Try variations of terms.** If you can't find what you're looking for, try abbreviations (*CEO, CPA*), synonyms (*man, male*), related terms (*child, adolescent, youth*), different spellings (*dialog, dialogue*), singular and plural forms (*woman, women*), nouns and adjectives (*manager, management, managerial*), and open and compound forms (*online, on line, on-line*). Some search engines search for such synonyms automatically.
- **Adjust the scope of your search, if needed.** If a search yields little or no information, broaden your search by specifying fewer terms. Conversely, if you're inundated with too many hits, use more terms to narrow your search. For example, *Apple* yields many more hits than *Apple iPod*, which yields many more than *Apple iPod nano*.
- **Look beyond the first few pages of results.** Don't assume that the highest-ranking results are the best sources for you. For example, materials that haven't been optimized for search engines won't rank as highly (meaning they won't show up in the first few pages of results), but they may be far better for your purposes.

### Innovations in Research Technology

Search technologies continue to evolve rapidly, so look for new ways to find the information you need. Some tools search or monitor specific media or channels in better ways, whereas others approach searches in new ways. For instance, Yolink (www.yolink.com) finds webpages like a regular search engine does but also searches through documents and webpages that are linked to those first-level results.[5]

Other powerful search tools include *desktop search engines* that search all the files on your personal computer, *enterprise search engines* that search all the computers on a company's network, *research and content managers* such as the free Zotero browser extension (www.zotero.com), and *social tagging* or *bookmarking sites* such as Reddit (www.reddit.com), and media curation sites such as Pinterest (http://pinterest.com) and Scoop.it (www.scoop.it).

For more on the latest developments in online research tools, visit http://real-timeupdates.com/bct12 and click on Chapter 13.

Take advantage of the latest research technologies, including desktop and enterprise search engines, research and content managers, social bookmaking sites, newsfeeds, and new types of search engines.

## DOCUMENTING YOUR SOURCES

Documenting the sources you use in your writing serves three important functions: It properly and ethically credits the person who created the original material, it shows your audience that you have sufficient support for your message, and it helps your readers explore your topic in more detail, if desired. Your results might be used by people long after you conducted the research, and these people won't always have the opportunity to query you in person for more information.

Be sure to take advantage of source documentation tools whenever you can, to help ensure that you accurately track all your sources. Most word-processing programs can automatically track and number endnotes for you, and you can use the "table of authorities" feature to create a bibliography of all the sources you've used. A wide variety of *citation management* or *reference management* tools are available with popular web browsers.

You may document your sources through footnotes, endnotes, or some similar system (see Appendix B, "Documentation of Report Sources"). Whatever method you choose, documentation is necessary for books, articles, tables, charts, diagrams, song lyrics, scripted dialogue, letters, speeches, and anything else you take from someone else, including ideas and information that you've re-expressed through paraphrasing or summarizing.

However, you do not have to cite a source for general knowledge or for specialized knowledge that's generally known among your readers. For example, almost everyone knows that Nike is a large sporting goods company and that computers are pervasive in business today. You can say so on your own authority, even if you've read an article in which the author says the same thing.

Chapter 1 notes that copyright law covers the expression of creative ideas, and copyrights can apply to a wide range of materials, including reports and other documents, web content, movies, musical compositions, lectures, computer programs, and even choreographed dance routines. Copyright protection is initiated the moment the expression is put into fixed form. Copyright law does not protect such elements as titles, names, short

Proper documentation of the sources you use is an ethical responsibility—and an important resource for your readers.

Copyright protections may prevent you from using some materials without obtaining permission from the copyright holder.

phrases, slogans, familiar symbols, or lists of ingredients or contents. It also doesn't protect ideas, procedures, methods, systems, processes, concepts, principles, discoveries, or devices, although it does cover their description, explanation, or illustration.[6] (Note that many of the entities that aren't covered under copyright law are covered under other legal protections, such as patents for devices and processes and trademarks for slogans.)

Merely crediting the source is not always enough. According to the *fair use doctrine*, you can use other people's work only as long as you don't unfairly prevent them from benefiting as a result. For example, if you reproduce someone else's copyrighted questionnaire in a report you're writing, even if you properly identify the source, you may be preventing the author from selling a copy of that questionnaire to your readers.

If you want to use copyrighted information in a report, contact the copyright holder (usually the author or publisher) for permission to reprint it. You'll often be asked to pay a fee. For more information on copyrights, visit www.copyright.gov or www.creativecommons.org.

# Conducting Primary Research

**3** **LEARNING OBJECTIVE**
Define primary research and outline the steps involved in conducting surveys and interviews.

Conducting surveys and interviews are the most common primary research techniques.

If secondary research can't provide the information and insights you need, your next choice is to gather the information yourself with primary research. The two most common primary research methods for business writing are surveys and interviews, the focus of this section. Other primary techniques include *observations* and *experiments*, such as Tesco's test-marketing study with Polish foods (see the chapter-opening vignette page 356).

## GATHERING INFORMATION WITH SURVEYS

Surveys can provide invaluable insights on a wide variety of business topics, but they are useful only when they're reliable and valid. A survey is *reliable* if it produces identical results when repeated. A survey is *valid* if it measures what it's intended to measure. To conduct a survey that generates reliable and valid results, you need to choose research participants carefully and develop an effective set of questions. (A good research handbook can guide you through the process of selecting a sufficient number of representative participants. For important surveys on strategically important topics with lots at stake, you're usually better off hiring a research specialist who knows how to avoid errors during planning, execution, and analysis.)

For a survey to produce valid results, it must be based on a representative sample of the population of interest.

When selecting people to participate in a survey, the most critical task is getting a *representative sample* of the population in question. For instance, if you want to know how U.S. consumers feel about something, you can't just survey a few hundred people in a shopping mall. Different types of consumers shop at different times of the day and different days of the week, and many consumers rarely, if ever, shop at malls. A survey that doesn't represent the overall population will suffer from *sampling bias*.

Online surveys are relatively quick and inexpensive, but they require the same care in planning and analysis as offline surveys.

Online surveys (see Figure 13.2) offer a number of advantages, including speed, cost, and the ability to adapt the question set along the way based on a respondent's answers. However, they are vulnerable to the same bias because they capture only the opinions of people who visit the sites and who want to participate, which might not be a representative sample of the population. A good handbook on survey research will help you select the right people for your survey, including selecting enough people to have a statistically valid survey.[7]

To develop an effective survey questionnaire, start with the information gaps you identified earlier and then break these points into specific questions, choosing an appropriate type of question for each point. (Figure 13.3 on page 368 shows various types of survey questions.) The following guidelines will help you produce results that are both valid and reliable:[8]

Provide clear instructions in questionnaires to prevent incorrect or ambiguous answers.

- Provide clear instructions to make sure people can answer every question correctly.
- Don't ask for information that people can't be expected to remember, such as how many times they went grocery shopping in the past year.
- Keep the questionnaire short and easy to answer; don't expect people to give you more than 10 or 15 minutes of their time.
- Whenever possible, formulate questions that provide answers that are easy to analyze. Numbers and facts are easier to summarize than opinions, for instance.
- Avoid *leading questions* that could bias your survey. If you ask, "Do you prefer that we stay open in the evenings for customer convenience?" you'll no doubt get a "yes." Instead, ask, "What time of day do you normally do your shopping?"

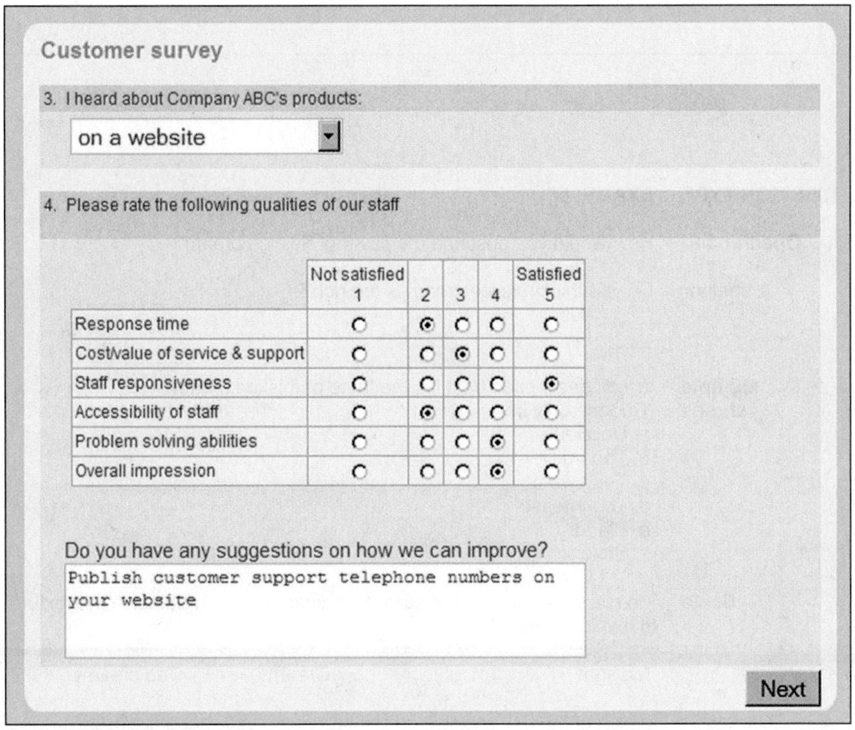

**Figure 13.2 Online Survey Tools**
Online survey systems such as this one, offered by Object Planet, make it easy to create, administer, and analyze surveys. As with all surveys, though, it's important to select a representative sample of the target population.

---

## The Art of the Question

Poorly worded questions can produce unintended and unforeseen results. For example, assume that you receive regular surveys from the human resources department in your company, dealing with such issues as productivity, employee satisfaction, and employee benefits. This month's survey contains the following questions:

1. How would you rate the food in the company cafeteria? (Choose one.)

    _____ Fantastic
    _____ Nutritious
    _____ Delicious
    _____ Filling
    _____ A good value for the money

2. What is your opinion of the improved insurance sign-up process we instituted last month?

3. If the dental benefits plan were modified relative to the current plan, wherein employees are expected to pay a $20 copayment at the time of each visit, with benefits subject to the normal companywide 80 percent co-insurance standard, provided the co-insurance ratio did not drop, would you continue to participate in the plan if copayment were increased to $50 but counterbalanced by a reduction in your monthly payroll deduction amount?

    _____ Yes
    _____ No

4. Division supervisors continue to report problems with employees reporting for work late. Do the employees in your department tend to report for work

    _____ Always on time
    _____ Mostly on time
    _____ Usually on time
    _____ Occasionally late
    _____ Frequently late

5. How many times did you personally report for work late last year?

6. Do you ever feel poorly trained or insufficiently motivated in your job?

    _____ Yes
    _____ No

### CAREER APPLICATIONS

1. Which of these questions might result in unusable information? Why?

2. How would you help the human resources manager rewrite the questions to improve the quality of information they generate?

| QUESTION TYPE | EXAMPLE |
|---|---|
| **Open-ended** | How would you describe the flavor of this ice cream? |
| **Either-or** | Do you think this ice cream is too rich?<br>_____ Yes<br>_____ No |
| **Multiple choice** | Which description best fits the taste of this ice cream?<br>(Choose only one.)<br>a. Delicious<br>b. Too fruity<br>c. Too sweet<br>d. Too intense<br>e. Bland<br>f. Stale |
| **Scale** | Please mark an X on the scale to indicate how you perceive the texture of this ice cream.<br><br>Too light     Light     Creamy     Too creamy |
| **Checklist** | Which of the following ice cream brands do you recognize?<br>(Check all that apply.)<br>_____ Ben & Jerry's<br>_____ Breyers<br>_____ Carvel<br>_____ Dreyer's<br>_____ Häagen-Dazs |
| **Ranking** | Rank these flavors in order of your preference, from 1 (most preferred) to 5 (least preferred):<br>_____ Vanilla<br>_____ Cherry<br>_____ Strawberry<br>_____ Chocolate<br>_____ Coconut |
| **Short-answer** | In the past 2 weeks, how many times did you buy ice cream in a grocery store? _____<br><br>In the past 2 weeks, how many times did you buy ice cream in an ice cream shop? _____ |

MyBCommLab Apply Figure 13.3's key concepts. Go to **mybcommlab.com** and follow this path: Course Content → Chapter 13 → **DOCUMENT MAKEOVERS**

**Figure 13.3 Types of Survey Questions**
For each question you have in your survey, choose the type of question that will elicit the most useful answers.

- Avoid ambiguous descriptors such as "often" or "frequently." Such terms mean different things to different people.
- Avoid compound questions such as "Do you read books and magazines?" People who read one but not the other won't know whether to answer yes or no.
- Make the survey *adaptive*. With an online survey, you can program the software to branch automatically based on audience inputs. Not only does this sort of real-time adaptation deliver better answers, but it reduces frustration for survey respondents as well.[9]

Be sure to test your survey before using it.

Before you conduct a survey, test it on a sample group first to identify questions that might be confusing or ambiguous (see "Communication Miscues: The Art of the Question").

## GATHERING INFORMATION WITH INTERVIEWS

Getting in-depth information straight from an expert or an individual concerned about an issue can be a great method for collecting primary information. Interviews can dig deeper than the "hands-off" approach of surveys, and skilled interviewers can also watch for nonverbal signals that provide additional insights. Interviews can take a variety of formats, from email exchanges to group discussions. For example, Tesco invites thousands of customers to visit its stores every year for meetings known as Customer Question Time, when it asks customers how the company can serve them better.[10]

Be aware that the answers you receive in an interview are influenced by the types of questions you ask, by the way you ask them, and by each subject's cultural and language background. Potentially significant factors include the person's race, gender, age, educational level, and social status.[11]

Ask **open-ended questions** (such as "Why do you believe that South America represents a better opportunity than Europe for this product line?") to solicit opinions, insights, and information. Ask **closed questions** to elicit a specific answer, such as yes or no. However, don't use too many closed questions in an interview, or the experience will feel more like a simple survey and won't take full advantage of the interactive interview setting.

Think carefully about the sequence of your questions and the subject's potential answers so you can arrange questions in an order that helps uncover layers of information. Also, consider providing the person with a list of questions at least a day or two before the interview, especially if you'd like to quote your subject in writing or if your questions might require your subject to conduct research or think extensively about the answers. If you want to record the interview, ask the person ahead of time and respect his or her wishes. During the interview, be alert to new topics you might not have considered while planning the interview, and pursue them if they will shed light on your research questions.

As soon as possible after the interview, take a few moments to write down your thoughts, go over your notes, and organize your material. Look for important themes, helpful facts or statistics, and direct quotes. If you recorded the interview, *transcribe* it (take down word for word what the person said) or take notes from the recording just as you would while listening to someone in person.

Face-to-face interviews give you the opportunity to gauge reactions to your questions and observe the nonverbal signals that accompany the answers, but interviews don't necessarily have to take place in person. For example, email interviews give subjects a chance to think through their responses thoroughly rather than rush to fit the time constraints of a face-to-face interview.[12] Also, email interviews might be the only way you will be able to access some experts.

In addition to individual interviews, business researchers can also use a form of group interview known as the **focus group**. In this format, a moderator guides a group through a series of discussion questions while the rest of the research team members observe through a one-way mirror. The key advantage of focus groups is the opportunity to learn from group dynamics as the various participants bounce ideas and questions off each other. Allowing a group to discuss topics and problems in this manner can uncover much richer information than can a series of individual interviews.[13]

As a reminder of the tasks involved in interviews, see "Checklist: Conducting Effective Information Interviews."

*Interviews are easy to conduct but require careful planning to produce useful results.*

*Choose question types that will generate the specific kinds of information you need.*

*Face-to-face interviews give you the opportunity to gauge nonverbal responses.*

---

**CHECKLIST** ✔ Conducting Effective Information Interviews

- Learn about the person you will be interviewing.
- Formulate your main idea to ensure effective focus.
- Choose the length, style, and organization of the interview.
- Select question types to elicit the specific information you want.
- Design each question carefully to collect useful answers.

- Limit the number of questions you ask.
- During the interview, be alert to new topics that you might want to probe.
- Consider recording the interview if the subject permits.
- Review your notes as soon as the interview ends.

# Processing Data and Information

**4** **LEARNING OBJECTIVE**
Describe the major tasks involved in processing research results.

After you've collected all the necessary secondary and primary information, the next step is to transform it into the specific content you need. For simple projects, you may be able to insert your material directly into your report, presentation, or other application. However, when you have gathered a significant amount of information or raw data, you need to process the material before you can use it. This step can involve quoting, paraphrasing, or summarizing textual material; analyzing numeric data; drawing conclusions; and making recommendations.

After you have collected your research results, the next step is to convert them into usable information.

## QUOTING, PARAPHRASING, AND SUMMARIZING

You can use textual information from secondary sources in three ways. *Quoting* a source means you reproduce the material exactly as you found it (giving full credit to the source, of course). Use direct quotations when the original language will enhance your argument or when rewording the passage would reduce its impact. However, be careful with direct quotes: Using too many creates a choppy patchwork of varying styles and gives the impression that all you've done is piece together the work of other people. When quoting sources, set off shorter passages with quotation marks and set off longer passages (generally, five lines or more) as separate, indented paragraphs.

Quoting a source means reproducing the content exactly and indicating who created the information originally.

You can often maximize the impact of secondary material in your own writing by *paraphrasing* it—restating it in your own words and with your own sentence structures.[14] Paraphrasing helps you maintain consistent tone, present information using vocabulary more familiar to your audience, and avoid the choppy feel of too many quotations. Of course, you still need to credit the originator of the information, through a footnote, endnote, or in-text citation.

Paraphrasing is expressing someone else's ideas in your own words.

To paraphrase effectively, follow these tips:[15]

- Read and reread the original passage until you fully understand its meaning.
- Restate the central ideas of the original passage using your own words.
- Check your version against the source to verify that you have not altered the meaning.
- Use quotation marks to identify any unique terms or phrases you have borrowed exactly from the source.
- Record the source accurately so that you can give proper credit if you use this material in your report.

Summarizing is similar to paraphrasing but distills the content into fewer words.

*Summarizing* is similar to paraphrasing but presents the gist of the material in fewer words than the original. An effective summary identifies the main ideas and major support points from your source material but leaves out minor details, examples, and other information that is less critical to your audience. Like quotations and paraphrases, summaries also require complete documentation of sources.

Of course, all three approaches require careful attention to ethics. When quoting directly, take care not to distort the original intent of the material by quoting selectively or out of context. If an interview subject said, "This market could grow dramatically next year if we invest heavily in new products," using only "this market could grow dramatically next year" in a report would be unethical.

When paraphrasing and summarizing, preserve the intended message of the original while expressing the ideas in your own words and sentences. Remember that the goal is to help your audience relate to material that supports your message. Double-check your writing to make sure you didn't subconsciously skew the other writer's message to fit your own needs (see "Ethics Detective: Solving the Case of the Imaginary Good News").

## ANALYZING NUMERIC DATA

Research often produces numeric data—everything from sales figures to population statistics to survey answers. By themselves, these numbers might not provide the insights you or your audience require. Are sales going up or going down? Are the age groups that represent your target markets growing or shrinking? What percentage of employees surveyed are so dissatisfied that they're ready to look for new jobs? These are the insights managers need in order to make good business decisions.

## ETHICS DETECTIVE

# Solving the Case of the Imaginary Good News

To deal with a growing problem of employee turnover, your company recently hired a research firm to survey employees to find out why more of them have been leaving than in past years. You and a colleague were assigned to work with the consultants and present their findings to upper management. Neither one of you welcomed the assignment because you suspect you'll have to present information that is critical of the management team.

As you feared, the researchers deliver a mixture of news that is mostly negative:

- Seventy-eight percent of employees believe management cares more about profits than people.
- Fifty-five percent aren't sure what's expected of them anymore.
- Forty percent believe wages at the company have not kept up with the industry average.
- Thirty-eight percent think management has done a good job of responding to competitive advances.
- Fifty-two percent expect to finish their careers at the company.
- Eighty percent believe the economy is too slow to support a productive job search.

While you're poring over the report, trying to figure out how you'll present the information tomorrow, an instant message from the CEO pops up on your partner's computer, asking for a quick summary of the results. Your partner types the following and then asks you to review it before she sends it:

> As you'd expect in a no-holds-barred investigation like this, the researchers did uncover some areas for improvements. The good news: Only 20 percent of the workforce is even considering other options, and we could reasonably expect that only a fraction of that group will leave anytime soon.

### ANALYSIS

You read your partner's summary twice, but something doesn't feel quite right. Does it present an accurate summary of the research? Why or why not? What's likely to happen when you present the complete research results to the CEO after first sending this IM?

## Gaining Insights

Even without advanced statistical techniques, you can use simple arithmetic to extract powerful insights from sets of research data. Three common and useful measures are shown in Table 13.3. The **mean** (which is what most people refer to when they use the term *average*) is the sum of all the items in the group divided by the number of items in that group. The **median** is the "middle of the road," or the midpoint of a series (with an equal number of items above and below). The **mode** is the number that occurs more often than any other in a sample. It's the best answer to a question such as "What is the usual amount?" Each of these three measures can give you different insights into a set of data.

Next, look at the data to spot **trends**—definite patterns taking place over time, including growth, decline, and cyclical trends that vary between growth and decline. By examining data over a period of time, you can detect patterns and relationships that help you answer important questions.

Mean, median, and mode provide insight into sets of data.

Trends identify patterns that tend to repeat over time.

| TABLE 13.3 | Three Types of Data Measures: Mean, Median, and Mode | |
|---|---|---|
| Wilson | $ 3,000 | |
| Green | 5,000 | |
| Carrick | 6,000 | |
| Cho | 7,000 | ← Mean |
| Keeble | 7,500 | ← Median |
| Lopes | 8,500 | |
| O'Toole | 8,500 | ← Mode |
| Mannix | 8,500 | |
| Caruso | 9,000 | |
| Total | $63,000 | |

*Causation* shows cause-and-effect relationships; *correlation* indicates simultaneous changes in two variables that may not necessarily be causally related.

Statistical measures and trends identify *what* is happening. To help you understand *why* those things are happening, look at **causation** (the cause-and-effect linkage between two factors, where one of them causes the other to happen) and **correlation** (the simultaneous change in two variables you're measuring, such as customer satisfaction dropping when product reliability drops). Bear in mind that causation can be easy to assume but difficult to prove. The drop in customer satisfaction might have been caused by a new accounting system that fouled up customer invoices. To prove causation, you need to be able to isolate the suspected cause as the *only* potential source of the change in the measured effect. However, eliminating all but one possible cause isn't always feasible, so you often have to apply careful judgment to correlations. Researchers frequently explore the relationships between subsets of data using a technique called *cross-tabulation*. For instance, if you're trying to figure out why total sales rose or fell, you might look separately at sales data by age, gender, location, and product type.

## Guarding Against Mistakes and Misinterpretations

Watch out for errors that might have crept in during collection and processing of data.

Numbers are easy to manipulate with spreadsheets and other computer tools, so be sure to guard against computational errors and misinterpretation of results. Double-check all calculations, and document the operation of any spreadsheets you plan to share with colleagues. Common spreadsheet mistakes to watch for include errors in math formulas, references to unintended cells in the spreadsheet (resulting in the inclusion of data you don't want or the exclusion of data you do want), and failures to verify the specific operation of the spreadsheet's built-in math functions.

In addition to watching for computer errors, step back and look at your entire set of data before proceeding with any analysis. Do the numbers make sense, based on what you know about the subject? Are any data points suspicious? If the production numbers you've been measuring have never varied more than 10 percent month to month and then suddenly jumped 50 percent last month, is that new number real or an erroneous measurement?

Even when your data points are accurate and your analysis is technically correct, it's still possible to misinterpret or misrepresent the results. Many analysis errors require statistical expertise to identify and fix, but even without advanced skills, you can take these precautions:

- **Avoid faulty comparisons.** Make sure you compare "apples to apples" and not "apples to oranges," as the saying goes.
- **Don't push research results beyond their limits.** The temptation to extract insights and assurances that aren't really there can be quite strong, particularly in situations of great uncertainty. For instance, if you're about to recommend that your company invest millions of dollars in developing a new product, based on your consumer research, you're likely to "see" every possible justification in the data. If possible, have a trusted colleague review your data to see whether he or she extracts the same conclusions.
- **Steer clear of misleading presentations.** Even valid data can be presented in invalid ways (such as with distorted graphs), and it's your responsibility to make sure the visual presentation of your data is accurate.

# Applying Your Findings

**5 LEARNING OBJECTIVE**
Explain how to summarize research results and present conclusions and recommendations.

After all your planning, research, and processing, you're finally ready to apply your findings. This step can involve summarizing your results, drawing conclusions based on your results, and making recommendations.

## SUMMARIZING YOUR RESEARCH

A summary is an unbiased presentation of information regarding a particular topic, without attempts to draw conclusions or make recommendations.

A research summary is an unbiased condensation of the information uncovered in your research. ("Summary" in this context means a summary of your entire research project, not just a summary of secondary source material.) Summaries should not include opinions, conclusions, or recommendations. Summarizing is not always a simple task, and your readers will

## Original: 116 words

Our facilities costs spiraled out of control last year. The 23 percent jump was far ahead of every other cost category in the company and many times higher than the 4 percent average rise for commercial real estate in the Portland metropolitan area. The rise can be attributed to many factors, but the major factors include repairs (mostly electrical and structural problems at the downtown office), energy (most of our offices are heated by electricity, the price of which has been increasing much faster than for oil or gas), and last but not least, the loss of two sublease tenants whose rent payments made a substantial dent in our cost profile for the past five years.

## Analyze the text to find main idea, major supporting points, and details

*Main idea* → Our facilities costs spiraled out of control last year. The 23 percent jump was far ahead of every other cost category in the company and many times higher than the 4 percent average rise for commercial real estate in the Portland metropolitan area.

*Major support points* → The rise can be attributed to many factors, but the major factors include repairs (mostly electrical and structural problems at the downtown office),

*Details* → energy (most of our offices are heated by electricity, the price of which has been increasing much faster than for oil or gas), and last but not least, the loss of two sublease tenants whose rent payments made a substantial dent in our cost profile for the past five years.

## 45-word summary

Our facilities costs jumped 23 percent last year, far ahead of every other cost category in the company and many times higher than the 4 percent local average. The major factors contributing to the increase are repairs, energy, and the loss of two sublease tenants.

## 22-word summary

Our facilities costs jumped 23 percent last year, due mainly to rising repair and energy costs and the loss of sublease income.

**Figure 13.4   Summarizing Effectively**
To summarize a section of text, first analyze it to find the main idea, the major support points, and the less-important details. Then assemble the appropriate pieces with additional words and phrases as needed to ensure a smooth flow.

MyBCommLab Apply Figure 13.4's key concepts. Go to **mybcommlab.com** and follow this path: Course Content ➔ Chapter 13 ➔ **DOCUMENT MAKEOVERS**

judge your ability to separate significant issues from less-significant details. Identify the main idea and the key support points; separate them from details, examples, and other supporting evidence (see Figure 13.4). Focus your efforts on your audience, highlighting the information that is most important to the person who assigned the project or to those who will be reading the report.

However, focusing on the audience doesn't mean conveying only the information your audience wants to hear. A good summary might contain nothing but bad news, if that's what your research uncovered. Even if the summary isn't pleasant, effective managers always appreciate and respect honest, complete, and perceptive information from their employees.

## DRAWING CONCLUSIONS

A **conclusion** is a logical interpretation of the facts and other information in a report. Reaching valid conclusions based on the evidence at hand is one of the most important skills you can develop in your business career. For a conclusion to be sound, it must meet two criteria. First, it must be based strictly on the information in your report. You shouldn't introduce any new information in your conclusion. (If something is that important, it belongs in the body of the report.) Also, you can't ignore any of the information you've presented, even if it doesn't support your conclusion. Second, the conclusion must be logical, meaning it must follow accepted patterns of inductive or deductive reasoning. Conclusions that are based on unproven premises, appeal to emotion, make hasty generalizations, or contain any other logical fallacies are not valid.

Remember that your personal values or the organization's values may also influence your conclusions; just be sure that you're aware of how these biases can affect your judgment. If a bias affects your conclusion, you should explain it to your audience. Also, don't expect all team members to examine the evidence and arrive at the same conclusion. One of the reasons for bringing additional people into a decision is to gain their unique perspectives and experiences.

Even though conclusions need to be logical, they may not automatically or obviously flow from the evidence. Many business decisions require assumptions, judgment calls, and creative thinking—in fact, the ability to see patterns and possibilities that others can't see is one of the hallmarks of innovative business leaders.

A conclusion is a logical interpretation of research results.

## MAKING RECOMMENDATIONS

A recommendation is a suggested course of action.

Whereas a conclusion interprets information, a **recommendation** suggests what to do about the information. The following example illustrates the difference between a conclusion and a recommendation:

| Conclusion | Recommendation |
|---|---|
| On the basis of its track record and current price, I believe that this company is an attractive buy. | I recommend that we offer to buy the company at a 10 percent premium over the current market value of its stock. |

To be credible, recommendations must be based on logical analysis and sound conclusions. They must also be practical and acceptable to your readers, the people who have to make your recommendations work. Finally, when making a recommendation, be certain you have adequately described the steps that come next. Don't leave your readers wondering what they need to do in order to act on your recommendation.

## MANAGING INFORMATION

Knowledge management systems, often supplemented now by social media tools, help organizations share research results and other valuable information and insights.

Conducting your research well does more than provide strong support for your own writing projects. Your individual research projects are also an important contribution to your organization's collective knowledge base. To organize information and make it readily available to everyone in the company, many firms use some form of **knowledge management (KM)**, a set of technologies, policies, and procedures that let colleagues capture and share information throughout an organization. In recent years, social media tools have been enhancing the flexibility and capability of KM systems, making it easier for more people to contribute to and benefit from shared knowledge and transforming knowledge into more of a living entity that is part of an ongoing conversation.[16]

# Quick Learning Guide

## SUMMARY OF LEARNING OBJECTIVES

**1** Describe an effective process for conducting business research. Begin the research process with careful planning to make sure you familiarize yourself with the subject area, identify the most important information gaps you face, and prioritize the questions you need to ask to fill those gaps. Then locate the required data and information, using primary and secondary research as needed. Process the results of your research, analyzing both textual and numeric information to extract averages, trends, and other insights. Apply your findings by summarizing information for someone else's benefit, drawing conclusions based on what you've learned, or developing recommendations. Finally, manage information effectively so that you and others can retrieve it later and reuse it in other projects.

**2** Define *secondary research*, and explain how to evaluate, locate, and document information sources. Secondary research involves collecting information that was originally gathered for another research project or another effort. Secondary research is generally done before primary research, to save time and money in the event someone else has already gathered the information needed.

Information should come from a credible source that has a reputation for being honest and reliable; the source should also be unbiased. The purpose of the material should be known, and the author should be credible. The information should include references to sources (if obtained elsewhere), and it should be independently verifiable. The material should be current, complete, and supported with evidence. Finally, the information should seem logical.

The tasks involved in locating secondary sources of data and information can vary widely depending on the project, but much of your efforts will involve finding information in a corporate, public, or university library or finding information online. Libraries offer an enormous array of business books, electronic databases, newspapers, periodicals, directories, almanacs, and government publications. Some of these printed sources provide information that is not available online, and some of the online sources provide information that is available by subscription. Librarians can be a huge help when you need advice on structuring an investigation or finding specific sources.

Finding information online is often more complicated than simply plugging a few terms into a search engine. General-purpose search engines are sophisticated tools, but even when they are used wisely, they are not able to find everything on the Internet. Moreover, with no human reviewers to evaluate the quality or ranking of the search results, you can't always be sure of the quality of what you find. Human-powered search engines, web directories, metacrawlers, and online databases all complement the capabilities of general-purpose search engines. Use online monitoring tools to be alerted to new materials on topics of interest.

To make the best use of any search engine or database, think about your information needs carefully before you start searching, read and understand the instructions for using each online research tool, pay attention to the details because even minor aspects of searching can influence results dramatically, review search and display options carefully to optimize results, try variations on your search terms if you can't find what you're looking for, and try narrower or broader searches to adjust the scope of what you're looking for.

**3** Define *primary research,* and outline the steps involved in conducting surveys and interviews. Primary research is research that is being conducted for the first time, and the two most common methods are surveys and interviews. Conducting a survey involves selecting a representative set of respondents from the population you are studying, developing a questionnaire using carefully written and sequenced questions, and administering the actual survey to collect information. Conducting an interview starts with learning about the person(s) you plan to interview and then formulating your main idea to make sure your interview will stay focused. Choose the length, style, and organization of the interview and then select question types to elicit the sort of information you want, with each question designed to collect useful answers. Limit your questions to the most important queries. Record the interview, if the person allows, and review your notes as soon as the interview ends.

**4** Describe the major tasks involved in processing research results. In most cases, you need to process your research results in some fashion before applying them in reports and presentations. The three basic ways to process verbal information are *quoting* (using someone else's words directly, with appropriate attribution), *paraphrasing* (restating someone else's words in your own language), and *summarizing* (creating a shorter version of an original piece of writing). Processing numeric data can involve a variety of statistical analysis techniques. Three basic computations are the *mean* (what people mean when they say "average"), the *median* (the midpoint in a series, indicating an equal number of lesser and greater values), and the *mode* (the most frequently occurring value in a series). Processing results can also involve looking for trends and distinguishing causal relationships from correlations and mere coincidences.

**5** Explain how to summarize research results and present conclusions and recommendations. Research results can be applied in several ways, depending on the purpose of the report or presentation. A *summary* is an unbiased condensation of the information uncovered in your research. It filters out details and presents only the most important ideas. A *conclusion* is your analysis of what the findings mean (an interpretation of the facts). A *recommendation* is your opinion (based on reason and logic) about the course of action that should be taken.

## KEY TERMS

**causation** Cause-and-effect linkage between two factors, where one of them causes the other to happen

**closed questions** Questions with a fixed range of possible answers

**conclusion** A logical interpretation of the facts and other information in a report

**correlation** The simultaneous change in two variables

**focus group** A form of group research interview

**knowledge management (KM)** Set of technologies, policies, and procedures that let colleagues capture and share information throughout an organization

**mean** Equal to the sum of all the items in the group divided by the number of items in that group; what people refer to when they use the term *average*

**median** The midpoint of a series, with an equal number of items above and below

**metasearch engines** Search tools that format search requests for multiple search engines simultaneously

**mode** The number that occurs more often than any other in a sample

**online databases** Online compilations of newspapers, magazines, journals, and other information sources

**open-ended questions** Questions without simple, predetermined answers; used to solicit opinions, insights, and information

**primary research** New research done specifically for the current project

**problem statement** Defines the problem or purpose of your research

**recommendation** A suggested course of action

**search engines** Online search tools that identify individual webpages that contain specific words or phrases you've asked for

**secondary research** Research done previously for another purpose

**trends** Repeatable patterns taking place over time

**web directories** Online lists of websites selected by human editors

## CHECKLIST ✓
## Conducting Effective Information Interviews

- Learn about the person you will be interviewing.
- Formulate your main idea to ensure effective focus.
- Choose the length, style, and organization of the interview.

- Select question types to elicit the specific information you want.
- Design each question carefully to collect useful answers.
- Limit the number of questions you ask.

- During the interview, be alert to new topics you might want to probe.
- Consider recording the interview if the subject permits.
- Review your notes as soon as the interview ends.

| 1 Plan | 2 Locate data and information | 3 Process data and information | 4 Apply your findings | 5 Manage information |
|--------|------------------------------|------------------------------|----------------------|---------------------|
| • Maintain research ethics and etiquette<br>• Familiarize yourself with the subject; develop a problem statement<br>• Identify information gaps<br>• Prioritize research needs | • Evaluate sources<br>• Collect secondary information at the library, online, or elsewhere<br>• Document your sources<br>• Collect primary information through surveys and interviews | • Quote, paraphrase, or summarize textual information<br>• Analyze numerical information | • Summarize findings<br>• Draw conclusions<br>• Make recommendations | • Make research results available to others via your company's knowledge management system |

**Figure 13.1  The Research Process**
By following a methodical research process, you can save time and money while uncovering better information.

■■■■■■■■
■

## COMMUNICATION CHALLENGES AT **Tesco**

As a market development manager working for Richard Brasher, Tesco's top marketing executive in the United Kingdom, you are responsible for a variety of research, planning, and customer communication projects. Using what you've learned in this chapter about effective research methods, craft solutions to these two challenges.

**INDIVIDUAL CHALLENGE:** Tesco has created several online stores (see **www.tesco.com**) and would like to expand the number of consumers who order goods and services online. What information would you need in order to devise a plan to attract more online shoppers?

**TEAM CHALLENGE:** Shoppers often make numerous purchase decisions in the store rather than arrive with a preset list of specific brands to purchase. Brasher would like more information on why consumers choose one brand over another while standing in front of an array of products on the shelf. Is it the brand name? Something about the packaging? The price? Other factors? With your team, brainstorm ways to collect this information from at least 500 shoppers. Be sure to consider the practical considerations of data collection as well as privacy concerns. Summarize your plan in a short report for your instructor.

## Test Your Knowledge

To review chapter content related to each question, refer to the indicated Learning Objective.

1. What are the five steps in the research process? [LO-1]
2. What is the purpose of identifying information gaps before starting research? [LO-1]
✪ 3. Should you conduct secondary research first or primary research? Why? [LO-2]
4. What is the *hidden Internet*? [LO-2]
5. What does it mean to make a survey adaptive? [LO-3]
6. What is paraphrasing, and what is its purpose? [LO-4]
7. What is the difference between the mean, median, and mode? [LO-4]
8. What are the characteristics of a sound conclusion? [LO-5]
9. How does a conclusion differ from a recommendation? [LO-5]

## Apply Your Knowledge

To review chapter content related to each question, refer to the indicated Learning Objective.

1. Companies occasionally make mistakes that expose confidential information, such as when employees lose laptop computers containing sensitive data files or webmasters forget to protect confidential webpages from search engine indexes. If you conducted a search that turned up competitive information on webpages that were clearly intended to be private, what would you do? Explain your answer. [LO-1]
✪ 2. Why must you be careful when citing information from online sources? [LO-2]
✪ 3. One of your employees submitted a report, comparing the market opportunities for two product ideas your company might develop. The report concludes that because the first idea yielded 340,000 hits in a Google search whereas the second idea yielded only 128,000 Google hits, the first idea clearly has more sales potential. Is this a valid conclusion? Why or why not? [LO-4]

✪ 4. While analyzing last year's sales data, you notice that sales were 10 to 15 percent higher than average during August, September, and November. The marketing department invested heavily in a search engine advertising campaign from August through December. Can you conclude that the advertising campaign caused the increase in sales? Why or why not? [LO-5]

## Practice Your Skills

**Message for Analysis: Primary Research: Conducting Interviews [LO-4]**

The following set of interview questions was prepared for a manager of Whirlpool Corporation. The goal of the interview was to learn some basic information about Whirlpool's meeting practices. Read the questions and then (1) critique them, as a whole, indicating what is effective or ineffective about this series of questions, and (2) select five questions and revise them to make them more effective.

1. What is your position in the company?
2. To whom do you report?
3. Do you attend or run many meetings?
4. Do your meetings start on time? Run late?
5. Do you distribute or receive a meeting agenda several days in advance of the meeting?
6. Do you like your job?
7. Do you travel a lot for your job?
8. Has your company cut back on travel expenditures? If so, how and why?
9. Does your company use videoconferencing or online meetings as an alternative to travel?
10. Does your company own its own videoconferencing equipment?
11. Are virtual meetings more or less effective than face-to-face meetings?

12. How long have you worked for Whirlpool?

13. Is Sears your largest retail customer?

14. How often does your management team meet with the managers of Sears?

15. Does your company produce only household appliances?

16. How do you keep your meetings on track?

17. Does someone prepare written minutes of meetings? Are the minutes distributed to meeting members?

## Exercises

Each activity is labeled according to the primary skill or skills you will need to use. To review relevant chapter content, you can refer to the indicated Learning Objective. In some instances, supporting information will be found in another chapter, as indicated.

1. **Planning Your Research; Collaboration: Team Projects [LO-1]** In a team assigned by your instructor, decide how you would structure a research project to answer the following questions. Identify any shortcomings in the approaches you have chosen.

   a. Has the litter problem on campus been reduced since the cafeteria began offering fewer take-out choices this year than in past years?

   b. Has the school attracted more transfer students since it waived the formal application process and allowed students at other colleges simply to send their transcripts and a one-page letter of application?

   c. Have the number of traffic accidents at the school's main entrance been reduced since a traffic light was installed?

   d. Has student satisfaction with the campus bookstore improved now that students can order their books online and pick them up at several convenient campus locations?

2. **Planning a Research Project [LO-1]** You and your business partners are considering buying several franchises in the fast-food business. You are all experienced managers or entrepreneurs, but none of you has experience in franchising. Visit www.amazon.com and search for books on this subject. Explore some of the books that you find by reading reviews and using the "search inside" feature.

   a. Use the information you find to develop a list of subquestions to help you narrow your focus.

   b. Write down the names of three books you might purchase to further aid your research.

   c. Summarize how a search like this can assist you with your research efforts and identify any risks of using this technique.

3. **Planning a Research Project [LO-1]** Analyze any recent school or work assignment that required you to conduct research. How did you approach your investigation? Did you rely mostly on sources of primary information or mostly on sources of secondary information? Now that you have studied this chapter, can you identify two ways to improve the research techniques you used during that assignment? Briefly explain.

4. **Conducting Secondary Research (Company and Industry Data) [LO-2]** Using online or printed sources, find the following information. Be sure to properly cite your sources, using the formats discussed in Appendix B.

   a. Contact information for the American Management Association

   b. Median weekly earnings of men and women by occupation

   c. Current market share for Perrier water

   d. Performance ratios for office supply retailers

   e. Annual stock performance for Hewlett-Packard

   f. Number of franchise outlets in the United States

   g. Composition of the U.S. workforce by profession

5. **Conducting Secondary Research (Finding Sources) [LO-2]** Businesspeople have to know where to look for secondary information when they conduct research. Identify five periodicals or online resources in each the following professions:

   a. Marketing and advertising

   b. Insurance

   c. Telecommunications

   d. Accounting

6. **Conducting Secondary Research (Documenting Sources) [LO-2]** Select five business articles from sources such as journals, books, newspapers, or websites. Develop a resource list, using Appendix B as a guideline.

7. **Conducting Secondary Research (Evaluating Sources) [LO-2]** Break into small groups and surf the Internet to find websites that provide business information such as company or industry news, trends, analysis, facts, or performance data. Using the criteria discussed under "Evaluating Sources" on page 359, evaluate the credibility of the information presented at these websites.

8. **Conducting Secondary Research (Online Monitoring); Media Skills: Microblogging [LO-2], Chapter 8** Select a business topic that interests you and configure a Twitter monitoring tool such as TweetBeep (http://tweetbeep.com) or TweetDeck (www.tweetdeck.com) to track tweets on this topic. After you've found at least a dozen tweets, identify three that provide potentially useful information and describe them in a brief email message to your instructor.

9. **Conducting Secondary Research (Company Data) [LO-2]** Select any publicly traded company and find the following information:

   a. Names of the company's current officers

   b. List of the company's products or services (summarized by product lines or divisions, if the company offers many products and services)

   c. Current issues in the company's industry

   d. Outlook for the company's industry as a whole

10. **Conducting Secondary Research (Industry Issues) [LO-2]** You'd like to know if it's a good idea to buy banner advertisements on other websites to drive more traffic to your company's website. You're worried about the expense and difficulty of running an experiment to test banner effectiveness, so you decide to look for some secondary data. Identify three secondary sources that might offer helpful data on this question.

11. **Conducting Primary Research (Surveys) [LO-3]** You work for a movie studio that is producing a young director's first motion picture, the story of a group of unknown musicians finding work and making a reputation in a competitive industry. Unfortunately, some of your friends leave the first complete screening, saying that the 182-minute movie is simply too long. Others said they couldn't imagine any sequences to cut out. Your boss wants to test the movie on a regular audience and ask viewers to complete a questionnaire that will help the director decide whether edits are needed and, if so, where. Design a questionnaire you can use to solicit valid answers for a report to the director about how to handle the audience members' reactions to the movie.

12. **Conducting Primary Research (Interviews) [LO-3]** Plan an informational interview with a professional working in your chosen field of study. Plan the structure of the interview and create a set of interview questions. Conduct the interview. Using the information you gathered, write a memo to another student, describing the tasks, advantages, and disadvantages of jobs in this field of study. (Assume that your reader is a person who also plans to pursue a career in this field of study.)

13. **Conducting Primary Research (Interviews) [LO-3]** You're conducting an information interview with a manager in another division of your company. Partway through the interview, the manager shows clear signs of impatience. How should you respond? What might you do differently to prevent this from happening in the future? Explain your answers.

14. **Processing Data and Information [LO-4]** Select an article from a business periodical such as *Bloomberg Businessweek*, *Fortune*, or *Forbes*. Read the article and highlight its key points. Summarize the article in fewer than 100 words, paraphrasing the key points.

15. **Processing Data and Information [LO-4]** Your boss has asked you to analyze and report on your division's sales for the first nine months of this year. Using the following data from company invoices, calculate the mean for each quarter and all averages for the year to date. Then identify and discuss the quarterly sales trends.

## Expand Your Skills

### Critique the Professionals

Find a recent example of a significant business blunder, such as a new product that failed in the marketplace. Based on what you can learn about the episode, how might better research have helped the company in question avoid the blunder? Using whatever medium your instructor requests, write a brief conclusion of your analysis.

### Sharpening Your Career Skills Online

Bovée and Thill's Business Communication Web Search, at http://businesscommunicationblog.com/websearch, is a unique research tool designed specifically for business communication research. Use the Web Search function to find a website, video, PDF document, podcast, or PowerPoint presentation that offers advice on using online search tools in business research. Write a brief email message to your instructor, describing the item you found and summarizing the career skills information you learned from it.

---

## MyBCommLab

Go to **mybcommlab.com** for Auto-graded writing questions as well as the following Assisted-graded writing questions:

**13-1.** How can online monitoring tools help you with research? [LO-2]

**13-2.** Why is it important to plan your research effort? [LO-1]

**13-3.** Mybcommlab Only—comprehensive writing assignment for this chapter.

---

## Endnotes

1. Tiffany Hsu, "Fresh & Easy Fail: Tesco Exits U.S. After Profit Tanks 96%," *Los Angeles Times*, 17 April 2013, http://articles.latimes.com; Fresh & Easy website, accessed 16 May 2013, www.freshandeasy.com; Tesco website, accessed 16 May 2013, www.tesco.com; "Fresh, But Not So Easy: Tesco Joins a Long List of British Failure in America," *The Guardian*, 9 December 2012, www.guardian.co.uk; "Competition and Profit," Food Marketing Institute website, accessed 5 November 2006, www.fmi.org; John E. Forsyth, Nicolo Galante, and Todd Guild, "Capitalizing on Customer Insights," *McKinsey Quarterly* 3 (2006): 42–53; "Company Spotlight: Tesco PLC," *MarketWatch: Global Round-Up*, July 2006, 76–81; James Quilter, "Tesco Hands Senior Role to Brand Planning Chief," *Marketing*, 2 August 2006, 4; Don Longo, "The British Are Coming," *Progressive Grocer*, 15 April 2006, 66–75.

2. Annie Pettit, "Mugging, Sugging and Now Rugging: I Take a Hard Stance on Privacy," LoveStats blog, 29 January 2010, http://lovestats.wordpress.com.

3. Information for this section originally adapted in part from "Finding Industry Information," accessed 3 November 1998, www.pitt.edu/~buslibry/industries.htm; Thomas P. Bergman, Stephen M. Garrison, and Gregory M. Scott, *The Business Student Writer's Manual and Guide to the Internet* (Upper Saddle River, N.J.: Prentice Hall, 1998), 67–80; Ernest L. Maier, Anthony J. Faria, Peter Kaatrude, and Elizabeth Wood, *The Business Library and How to Use It* (Detroit: Omnigraphics, 1996), 53–76; Sherwyn P. Morreale and Courtland L. Bovée, *Excellence in Public Speaking* (Fort Worth: Harcourt Brace College Publishers, 1998), 166–171.

4. "Search Effectively," Bing, accessed 23 February 2011, www.bing .com.

5. Christina Warren, "Yolink Helps Web Researchers Search Behind Links," Mashable, 24 July 2010, http://mashable.com.

6. "Copyright Office Basics," U.S. Copyright Office website, accessed 2 November 2006, www.copyright.gov.

7. A.B. Blankenship and George Edward Breen, *State of the Art Marketing Research* (Chicago: NTC Business Books, 1993), 136.

8. Naresh K. Malhotra, *Basic Marketing Research* (Upper Saddle River, N.J.: Prentice Hall, 2002), 314–317; "How to Design and Conduct a Study," *Credit Union Magazine,* October 1983, 36–46.

9. Product features page, SurveyMonkey.com, accessed 29 October 2006, www.surveymonkey.com.

10. Tesco website, accessed 9 February 2013, www.tesco.com.

11. Morreale and Bovée, *Excellence in Public Speaking,* 177.

12. Morreale and Bovée, *Excellence in Public Speaking,* 182.

13. A.B. Blankenship and George Edward Breen, *State of the Art Marketing Research* (Lincolnwood, Ill.: NTC Business Books, 1992), 225.

14. Lynn Quitman Troyka, *Simon & Schuster Handbook for Writers,* 6th ed. (Upper Saddle River, N.J.: Prentice Hall, 2002), 481.

15. "How to Paraphrase Effectively: 6 Steps to Follow," Researchpaper .com, accessed 26 October 1998, www.researchpaper.com.

16. Jonathan Reichental, "Knowledge Management in the Age of Social Media," O'Reilly Radar, 16 March 2011, http://radar.oreilly.com; Venkatesh Rao, "Social Media vs. Knowledge Management: A Generational War," *Social Computing,* 17 November 2008, www.socialcomputingmagazine .com; Jeff Kelly, "KM vs. Social Media: Beware the Warmongers," 17 November 2008, www.socialcomputingmagazine.com.

# Planning Reports and Proposals

## LEARNING OBJECTIVES

After studying this chapter, you will be able to

**1** Adapt the three-step writing process to reports and proposals.

**2** List the options for organizing informational reports and identify the key parts of a business plan.

**3** Discuss three major ways to organize analytical reports.

**4** Explain how to choose an organizational strategy when writing a proposal.

### MyBCommLab®

⭐ **Improve Your Grade!** Over 10 million students improved their results using the Pearson MyLabs. Visit **mybcommlab.com** for simulations, tutorials, and end-of-chapter problems.

## COMMUNICATION CLOSE-UP AT
### MyCityWay http://mycityway.com

Any experienced entrepreneur will tell you there's a big difference between having a great idea for a business and actually building a successful business. Many things have to go right, from creating a compelling product or service to finding the right employees to getting enough money to launch, expand, and sustain operations.

For Archana Patchirajan, Sonpreet Bhatia, and Puneet Mehta, the adventure started with the NYC BigApps competition. This contest is sponsored by the city of New York to encourage entrepreneurs to create better ways for people to use the NYC Data Mine, a huge trove of data created by all the government departments and agencies in the city.

The three partners jumped on the opportunity with NYC Way, a mobile application that helps people "navigate and explore" the city, whether they are residents looking for apartment deals or visitors looking for a great restaurant. One key aspect of the BigApps competition is that entrepreneurs must put their apps online for people to try out. By the time the contest ended, 100,000 people were using NYC Way.

Patchirajan, Bhatia, and Mehta clearly had a hit product on their hands. The next challenge was to turn it into a thriving business. As with most startups, that meant getting money to expand operations. The competition garnered the new firm,

MyCityWay's effective use of a business plan helped secure financing that allowed the company to expand far beyond its initial New York City market.

*Courtesy of Sonpreet Bhatia, Archana Patchirajan, and Puneet Mehta, mycityway.com.*

MyCityWay, priceless publicity and a small amount of seed funding that let the team set up offices and begin hiring.

Momentum continued to build as they enhanced the product and several hundred thousand more people began using it. After a successful launch in the New York City market, the next step was to conquer the world. That would require a significant infusion of capital, and to attract that, the three founders knew they needed a formal *business plan* to show potential investors why MyCityWay would be a smart place to invest their money.

With their Wall Street backgrounds, Patchirajan, Bhatia, and Mehta understood the fundamentals of business finance, which gave them a good foundation for their plan. They also got smart advice on what today's investors are looking for: short, compelling documents that strike a balance between providing enough information to be persuasive and providing so much information

that potential investors balk at reading it. With so many plans crossing their desks day after day, most venture capitalists and other investors don't have the time to slog through 50 or 60 pages of details to judge whether a company might be worth pursuing as an investment candidate. They want to be captivated in a matter of seconds and persuaded to learn more in a matter of minutes.

MyCityWay clearly found the right balance with its plan, as a second round of funding brought in $1 million in capital and then luxury carmaker BMW invested $5 million as part of its "BMW i" program, which promotes the development of innovative automotive materials and technologies. The company now has apps for more than 70 cities around the world and is well on its way to becoming a global player in the field of mobile information.[1]

# Applying the Three-Step Writing Process to Reports and Proposals

**1 LEARNING OBJECTIVE**
Adapt the three-step writing process to reports and proposals.

Whether they are printed documents or online resources, **reports** are written accounts that objectively communicate information about some aspect of a business (see Figure 14.1). **Informational reports** offer data, facts, feedback, and other types of information, without analysis or recommendations. **Analytical reports** offer both information and analysis and can also include recommendations. **Proposals** are a special category of reports that combine information delivery and persuasive communication.

The nature of these reports can vary widely, depending on the circumstances. Some of the reports you write will be voluntary, launched at your own initiative and following whatever structure you find most effective. Other reports will be in response to a manager's or customer's request, and you may or may not receive guidance regarding the organization and content. You'll also write reports that follow strict, specific guidelines for content and layout.

The purpose and content of business reports varies widely; in some cases you'll follow strict guidelines, but in others the organization and format will be up to you.

Many of your reports will be written for internal audiences, but you're also likely to write reports for a wide range of outside readers.

Your audience will sometimes be internal, which gives you more freedom to discuss sensitive information. At other times, your audience might include customers, investors, community members, or news media, any of which can create additional demands as you present company information to such external groups.

Finally, your reports will vary widely in length and complexity. You may write one-page memo- or letter-format reports that are simple and straightforward. Or you may write reports that cover complicated subjects, running into hundreds or even thousands of pages and involving multiple writers.

No matter what the circumstances, preparing reports requires all the skills and knowledge that you've gained throughout this course and will continue to gain on the job. View every business report as an opportunity to demonstrate your understanding of business challenges and your ability to contribute to your organization's success.

By adapting the three-step writing process (see Figure 14.2 on page 384), you can reduce the time required to write effective reports and still produce documents that make lasting and positive impressions on your audiences. The concepts are the same as those you explored in Chapters 4 through 6 and applied to shorter messages in Chapters 10 through 12. However, the emphasis on specific tasks can vary considerably. For instance, planning can take days or weeks for a complex report or proposal.

## ANALYZING THE SITUATION

The complexity of most reports and the magnitude of the work involved heighten the need to analyze the situation carefully. With an email or another short message, you can change

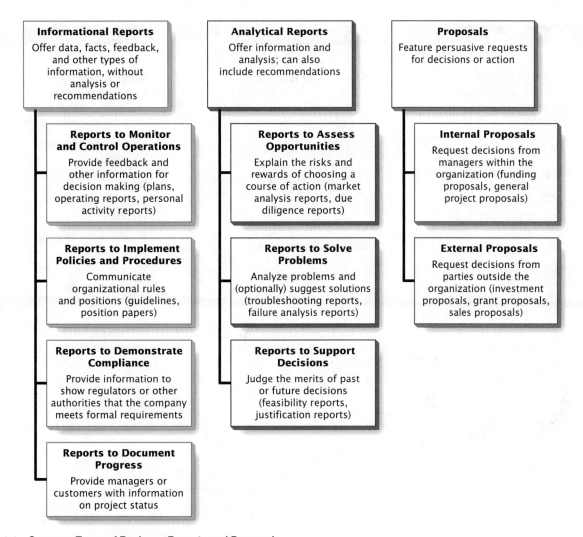

**Figure 14.1   Common Types of Business Reports and Proposals**
You will have the opportunity to read and write many types of reports in your career; here are some of the most common.

direction halfway through the first draft and perhaps lose only a few minutes of work. In contrast, if you change direction halfway through a major report, you could lose days of work. To minimize that chance, pay special attention to your statement of purpose. In addition, for anything beyond the simplest reports, take the time to prepare a work plan before you start writing.

Given the length and complexity of many reports, it's crucial to define your purpose clearly so you don't waste time with avoidable rework.

## Defining Your Purpose

Informational reports often address a predetermined need and must meet specific audience expectations. For example, you may be asked to write reports that verify your company's compliance with government regulations, that summarize sales, or that monitor a process—all of which have audiences who expect certain information in a certain format. With other informational reports, you will need to uncover audience needs before you can define the optimum purpose.

In some cases, you'll be told the purpose of the report; in others, it's up to you to identify the purpose.

Analytical reports and proposals are almost always written in response to a perceived problem or a perceived opportunity. A clear statement of this problem or opportunity helps frame the communication challenge by identifying *what* you're going to write about, but it's insufficient to guide your writing efforts. To plan effectively, address the problem or opportunity with a clear **statement of purpose** that defines *why* you are preparing the report (see Table 14.1).

| 1 Plan → | 2 Write → | 3 Complete |
|---|---|---|
| **Analyze the Situation**<br>Clarify the problem or opportunity at hand, define your purpose, develop an audience profile, and develop a work plan.<br><br>**Gather Information**<br>Determine audience needs and obtain the information necessary to satisfy those needs; conduct a research project, if necessary.<br><br>**Select the Right Medium**<br>Choose the best medium for delivering your message; consider delivery through multiple media.<br><br>**Organize the Information**<br>Define your main idea, limit your scope, select the direct or indirect approach, and outline your content using an appropriate structure for an informational report, an analytical report, or a proposal. | **Adapt to Your Audience**<br>Be sensitive to audience needs with a "you" attitude, politeness, positive emphasis, and bias-free language. Build a strong relationship with your audience by establishing your credibility and projecting your company's image. Control your style with a tone and voice appropriate to the situation.<br><br>**Compose the Message**<br>Choose strong words that will help you create effective sentences and coherent paragraphs throughout the introduction, body, and close of your report or proposal. | **Revise the Message**<br>Evaluate content and review readability, then edit and rewrite for conciseness and clarity.<br><br>**Produce the Message**<br>Use effective design elements and suitable layout for a clean, professional appearance; seamlessly combine text and graphical elements.<br><br>**Proofread the Message**<br>Review for errors in layout, spelling, and mechanics.<br><br>**Distribute the Message**<br>Deliver your report using the chosen medium; make sure all documents and all relevant files are distributed successfully. |

**Figure 14.2** **Three-Step Writing Process for Reports and Proposals**
The three-step writing process becomes even more valuable with reports and proposals. By guiding your work at each step, the process helps you make the most of the time and energy you invest.

The most useful way to phrase your purpose statement is to begin with an infinitive phrase (*to* plus a verb). Using an infinitive phrase encourages you to take control and decide where you're going before you begin. When you choose an infinitive phrase (such as

**TABLE 14.1 | Problem Statements versus Purpose Statements**

| Problem Statement | Statement of Purpose |
|---|---|
| Our company's market share is steadily declining. | To explore new ways of promoting and selling our products and to recommend the approaches most likely to stabilize our market share |
| Our current computer network lacks sufficient bandwidth and cannot be upgraded to meet our future needs. | To analyze various networking options and to recommend the system that will best meet our company's current and future needs |
| We need $2 million to launch our new product. | To convince investors that our new business would be a sound investment so that we can obtain desired financing |
| Our current operations are too decentralized and expensive. | To justify the closing of the Newark plant and the transfer of East Coast operations to a single Midwest location in order to save the company money |

*to inform*, *to confirm*, *to analyze*, *to persuade*, or *to recommend*), you pin down your general goal in preparing the report. Consider these examples for informational reports:

- To update clients on the progress of the research project (progress report)
- To develop goals and objectives for the coming year (strategic plan)
- To identify customers and explain how the company will serve them (marketing plan)
- To submit monthly sales statistics to management (operating report)
- To summarize what occurred at the annual sales conference (personal activity report)
- To explain building access procedures (policy implementation report)
- To submit required information to the Securities and Exchange Commission (compliance report)

The statement of purpose for an analytical report often needs to be more comprehensive than a statement for an informational report. For example, a report suggesting ways to reduce employee travel and entertainment (T&E) costs might have the following as a statement of purpose:

. . . to analyze the T&E budget, evaluate the impact of recent changes in airfares and hotel costs, and suggest ways to tighten management's control over T&E expenses.

If the writer had been assigned an informational report instead, she might have stated her purpose differently:

To summarize the company's spending on travel and entertainment

You can see from these two examples how much influence the purpose statement has on the scope of your report. Because she was assigned an analytical report rather than an informational report, the writer had to go beyond merely collecting data; she had to draw conclusions and make recommendations. (You can see the full report based on this statement of purpose in Chapter 15.)

Proposals must also be guided by a clear and specific statement of purpose to help you focus on crafting a persuasive message. Here are several examples:

- To secure funding in next year's capital budget for a new conveyor system in the warehouse (funding proposal)
- To get management approval to reorganize the North American salesforce (general project proposal)
- To secure $2 million in venture capital funding to complete design and production of the new line of titanium mountain bikes (investment proposal as part of a business plan)
- To convince CommuniCo to purchase a trial subscription to our latest database offering (sales proposal)

## Preparing Your Work Plan

You're already accustomed to some schedule pressure with school reports. This is good practice for your business career, in which you'll be expected to produce quality reports quickly and efficiently. Carefully thinking out a work plan is the best way to make sure you produce good work on schedule. By identifying all the tasks that must be performed, you ensure that nothing is overlooked (see Figure 14.3 on the next page).

If you are preparing a work plan for yourself, it can be relatively informal: a simple list of the steps you plan to take and an estimate of their sequence and timing. However, for more complicated projects, particularly those that involve multiple team members, you'll

A detailed work plan saves time and often produces more effective reports.

The problem statement clearly and succinctly defines the problem the writers intend to address.

This section explains how the researchers will find the data and information they need.

This paragraph identifies exactly what will be covered by the research and addressed in the final report.

The preliminary outline has enough detail to guide the research and set reader expectations.

The assignments and schedule section clearly lists responsibilities and due dates.

STATEMENT OF THE PROBLEM
The rapid growth of our company over the past five years has reduced the sense of community among our staff. People no longer feel like part of an intimate organization that values teamwork.

PURPOSE AND SCOPE OF WORK
The purpose of this study is to determine whether social networking technology such as Facebook and Socialtext would help rebuild a sense of community within the workforce and whether encouraging the use of such tools in the workplace will have any negative consequences.
The study will attempt to assess the impact of social networks in other companies in terms of community-building, morale, project communication, and overall productivity.

SOURCES AND METHODS OF DATA COLLECTION
Data collection will start with secondary research, including a review of recently published articles and studies on the use of social networking in business and a review of product information published by technology vendors. Primary research will focus on an employee and management survey to uncover attitudes about social networking tools. We will also collect anecdotal evidence from bloggers and others with experience using networks in the workplace.

PRELIMINARY OUTLINE
The preliminary outline for this study is as follows:
I. What experiences have other companies had with social networks in the workplace?
    A. Do social networks have a demonstrable business benefit?
    B. How do employees benefit from using these tools?
    C. Has network security and information confidentiality been an issue?
II. Is social networking an appropriate solution for our community-building needs?
    A. Is social networking better than other tools and methods for community building?
    B. Are employees already using social networking tools on the job?
    C. Will a company-endorsed system distract employees from essential duties?
    D. Will a company system add to managerial workloads in any way?
III. If we move ahead, should we use a "business-class" network such as Socialtext or a consumer tool such as Facebook?
    A. How do the initial and ongoing costs compare?
    B. Do the additional capabilities of a business-class network justify the higher costs?
IV. How should we implement a social network?
    A. Should we let it grow "organically," with employees choosing their own tools and groups?
    B. Should we make a variety of tools available and let employees improvise on their own?
    C. Should we designate one system as the official company social network and make it a permanent, supported element of the information technology infrastructure?
V. How can we evaluate the success of a new social network?
    A. What are the criteria of success or failure?
    B. What is the best way to measure these criteria?

TASK ASSIGNMENTS AND SCHEDULE
Each phase of this study will be completed by the following dates:

| | |
|---|---|
| Secondary research: Hank Waters | September 15, 2013 |
| Employee and management survey: Julienne Cho | September 22, 2013 |
| Analysis and synthesis of research: Hank Waters/Julienne Cho | October 6, 2013 |
| Comparison of business and consumer solutions: Julienne Cho | October 13, 2013 |
| Comparison of implementation strategies: Hank Waters | October 13, 2013 |
| Final report: Hank Waters | October 20, 2013 |

MyBCommLab Apply Figure 14.3's key concepts. Go to **mybcommlab.com** and follow this path: Course Content → Chapter 14 → **DOCUMENT MAKEOVERS**

**Figure 14.3  Work Plan for a Report**
A formal work plan such as this is a vital tool for planning and managing complex writing projects. The preliminary outline here helps guide the research; the report writers may well modify the outline when they begin writing the report.

want to prepare a formal, detailed work plan that can guide the performance of many tasks over a span of time. For consultants and others whose work output is a formal report, the work plan can also become the basis for a contract if the proposal is accepted. A formal work plan might include the following elements (especially the first two):

- **Statement of the problem or opportunity.** The problem statement clarifies the challenge you face, helps you (and anyone working with you) stay focused on the core issues, and helps everyone avoid the distractions that are likely to arise along the way.

- **Statement of the purpose and scope of your investigation.** The purpose statement describes what you plan to accomplish and therefore also defines the boundaries of your work. Delineating which subjects you will cover and which you won't is especially important for complex investigations.
- **Discussion of tasks to be accomplished.** For simple reports, the list of tasks to be accomplished will be short and probably obvious. However, longer reports and complex investigations require an exhaustive list so that you can reserve time with customers, with executives, or for outside services, such as market researchers or print shops.
- **Description of any additional products or activities that will result from your investigation.** In many cases, the only outcome of your efforts will be the report itself. In other cases, you'll need to produce something or perform some task in addition to completing the report. Make such expectations clear at the outset.
- **Review of project assignments, schedules, and resource requirements.** Indicate who will be responsible for what, when tasks will be completed, and how much the investigation will cost. If more than one person will be involved, you may also want to include a brief section on coordinating report writing and production, such as whether you'll use a wiki to develop the report content. If constraints on time, money, personnel, or data are likely to affect the quality of the report, identify these limitations up front.
- **Plans for following up after delivering the report.** Follow-up can be as simple as making sure people received the information they need or as complex as conducting additional research to evaluate the results of proposals included in your report. Even informal follow-up can help you improve your future reports and communicate that you care about your work's effectiveness and its impact on the organization.
- **Working outline.** Some work plans include a tentative outline of the report, as does the plan in Figure 14.3.

## GATHERING INFORMATION

The amount of information needed in many reports and proposals requires careful planning—and may even require a separate research project just to get the data and information you need. As Chapter 13 emphasizes, you should prioritize your information needs before you start and focus on the most important questions. Whenever possible, try to reuse or adapt existing information to save time.

Some reports require formal research projects in order to gather all the necessary information.

## SELECTING THE BEST MEDIUM

In addition to the general media selection criteria discussed in Chapter 4, consider several points for reports and proposals. First, for many reports and proposals, audiences have specific media requirements, and you might not have a choice. For instance, executives in many corporations now expect to review many reports via their in-house intranets, sometimes in conjunction with an *executive dashboard*, a customized online presentation of highly summarized business information. Second, consider how your audience members want to provide feedback on your report or proposal. Do they prefer to write comments on a printed document or edit a wiki article? Third, will people need to search through your document electronically or update it in the future? Fourth, bear in mind that your choice of medium sends a message. For instance, a routine sales report dressed up in expensive multimedia will look like a waste of valuable company resources.

In some situations, you may be required to use a specific medium for your reports.

## ORGANIZING YOUR INFORMATION

The length and complexity of most reports and proposals require extra emphasis on clear, reader-oriented organization. Your readers might have the patience to struggle through a short, disorganized email message but not through a poorly organized 200-page report. As Chapter 4 discusses, when an audience is likely to be receptive or at least open-minded, use the direct approach: Lead with a summary of your key findings, conclusions, recommendations, or proposal, whichever is relevant. This "up-front" arrangement is by far the most

Most business reports use the direct approach.

popular and convenient for business reports. It saves time and makes the rest of the report easier to follow. For those who have questions or want more information, later parts of the report provide complete findings and supporting details. The direct approach also produces a more forceful report. You sound sure of yourself when you state your conclusions confidently at the outset.

Use the indirect approach when you need to build support for your main idea or you want to avoid coming across as arrogant.

At times, however, confidence may be misconstrued as arrogance. If you're a junior member of a status-conscious organization, or if your audience is skeptical or hostile, consider the indirect approach: Introduce your complete findings and discuss all supporting details before presenting your conclusions and recommendations. The indirect approach gives you a chance to prove your points and gradually overcome your audience's reservations. By deferring the conclusions and recommendations to the end of your report, you imply that you've weighed the evidence objectively. You also imply that you're subordinating your judgment to that of the audience, whose members are capable of drawing their own conclusions when they have access to all the facts.

Although the indirect approach has advantages, some readers will always be in a hurry to get to the answer and will immediately flip to the recommendations anyway, thus defeating your purpose. Therefore, consider length before choosing the direct or indirect approach. In general, the longer the message, the less effective an indirect approach is likely to be.

Long reports sometimes combine direct and indirect approaches, building support for interim conclusions or recommendations along the way.

Because both direct and indirect approaches have merit, businesspeople often combine them. They reveal their conclusions and recommendations as they go along rather than put them either first or last. Figure 14.4 presents the introductions from two reports that follow the same general outline. In the direct version, a series of statements summarizes the conclusion reached in relation to each main topic in the outline. In the indirect version, the same topics are introduced in the same order but without drawing any conclusions about them. Instead, the conclusions appear within the body of the report.

Regardless of the format, length, or order of your report, think carefully about how your ideas will be subdivided and developed. Take care to choose the most logical argument structure—one that suits your topic and goals and that makes sense to your audience.

As you outline your content, use informative ("talking") headings rather than simple descriptive ("topical") headings (see Table 14.2). With a question or summary form, informative headings force you to really think through the content rather than simply identify the general topic area. Using informative headings also facilitates collaborative writing by reducing ambiguity about what each person needs to write.

For a quick review of adapting the three-step process to long reports, refer to "Checklist: Adapting the Three-Step Process to Reports and Proposals" on page 390. The following sections provide specific advice on how to plan informational reports, analytical reports, and proposals.

---

**TABLE 14.2 | Types of Outline Headings**

| DESCRIPTIVE (TOPICAL) OUTLINE | INFORMATIVE (TALKING) OUTLINE | |
|---|---|---|
| | Question Form | Summary Form |
| 1. Industry Characteristics | 1. What is the nature of the industry? | 1. Flour milling is a mature industry. |
|    a. Annual sales |    a. What are the annual sales? |    a. Market is large. |
|    b. Profitability |    b. Is the industry profitable? |    b. Profit margins are narrow. |
|    c. Growth rate |    c. What is the pattern of growth? |    c. Growth is modest. |
|      i. Sales |      i. Sales growth? |      i. Sales growth averages less than 3 percent a year. |
|      ii. Profit |      ii. Profit growth? |      ii. Profits are flat. |

DIRECT APPROACH

Since the company's founding 25 years ago, we have provided regular repair service for all our electric appliances. This service has been an important selling point as well as a source of pride for our employees. However, rising labor costs have made it impossible to maintain profitability while offering competitive service rates. Last year, we lost $500,000 on our repair business.

Because of your concern over these losses, you asked me to study whether we should discontinue our repair service. After analyzing the situation in depth, I have concluded that the repair service is an expensive, impractical tradition, and I recommend that the service be discontinued.

By withdrawing from the electric appliance repair business, we can substantially improve our financial performance without damaging our reputation with customers. This conclusion is based on three basic points that are covered in the following pages:

• It is highly unlikely that we will ever be able to make a profit in the repair business.

• We can refer customers to a variety of qualified repair firms without significantly reducing customer satisfaction.

• Closing down the service operation will create few internal problems.

Summarizes the situation

Immediately introduces one of the report's major conclusions

Reminds the audience why the report was prepared

Presents the report's key recommendation, that the repair service should be discontinued

Emphasizes the benefits of acting on the recommendation and addresses any fears about possible negative consequences

Lists three important conclusions that led to the recommendation to end the service (notice how the indirect approach that follows presents these same three points as questions to be considered)

Summarizes the situation

Reminds the audience why the report was prepared

Indicates that conclusions and recommendations will be presented later in the report

Introduces the three points that will eventually lead to the conclusions and ultimately to the recommendation

INDIRECT APPROACH

Since the company's founding 25 years ago, we have provided regular repair service for all our electric appliances. This service has been an important selling point as well as a source of pride for our employees. However, rising labor costs have made it impossible to maintain profitability while offering competitive service rates.

Because of your concern over these losses, you have asked me to study whether we should discontinue our repair service. I have analyzed the situation in depth, and the following pages present my findings and recommendations for your review. The analysis addressed three basic questions:

• What is the extent of our losses, and what can we do to turn the business around?

• Would withdrawal hurt our sales of electrical appliances?

• What would be the internal repercussions of closing down the repair business?

MyBCommLab Apply Figure 14.4's key concepts. Go to **mybcommlab.com** and follow this path: Course Content → Chapter 14 → **DOCUMENT MAKEOVERS**

**Figure 14.4    Direct Approach versus Indirect Approach in an Introduction**
In the direct version of this introduction, the writer quickly presents the report's recommendation, followed by the conclusions that led to that recommendation. In the indirect version, the same topics are introduced in the same order but no conclusions are drawn about them (the conclusions and the ultimate recommendation appear later, in the body of the report).

CHECKLIST ✓ Adapting the Three-Step Process to Reports and Proposals

**A. Analyze the situation.**
- Clearly define your purpose before you start writing.
- If you need to accomplish several goals in the report, identify them all in advance.
- Prepare a work plan to guide your efforts.

**B. Gather information.**
- Determine whether you need to launch a separate research project to collect the necessary information.
- Reuse or adapt existing material whenever possible.

**C. Select the best medium.**
- Base your decision on audience expectations or requirements.

- Consider the need for commenting, revising, distributing, and storing.
- Remember that the medium you choose also sends a message.

**D. Organize your information.**
- Use the direct approach if your audience is receptive.
- Use the indirect approach if your audience is skeptical.
- Use the indirect approach when you don't want to risk coming across as arrogant.
- Combine approaches if doing so will help build support for your primary message.

# Planning Informational Reports

**2 LEARNING OBJECTIVE**
List the options for organizing informational reports, and identify the key parts of a business plan.

Informational reports are used to monitor and control operations, to implement policies and procedures, to demonstrate compliance, and to document progress.

Informational reports provide the information that employees, managers, and others need in order to make decisions and take action. Although dozens of particular formats exist, they can be grouped into four general categories:

- **Reports to monitor and control operations.** Just as doctors rely on medical reports to see how well the various systems in a patient's body are functioning, business managers rely on a wide range of reports to see how well the various systems in their companies are functioning. *Plans* establish expectations and guidelines to direct future action (see "Creating Successful Business Plans" on the next page). *Operating reports* provide feedback on a wide variety of an organization's functions, including sales, inventories, expenses, shipments, and other aspects of company operations. *Personal activity reports* provide information regarding an individual's experiences during sales calls, industry conferences, market research trips, and other activities.
- **Reports to implement policies and procedures.** *Policy reports* range from brief descriptions of business procedures to manuals that run dozens or hundreds of pages. *Position papers*, sometimes called *white papers* or *backgrounders*, outline an organization's official position on issues that affect the company's success.
- **Reports to demonstrate compliance.** Even the smallest businesses are required to show that they are in compliance with government regulations of one sort or another. Some compliance reports, such as quarterly and annual tax reports, affect all businesses. Others concern particular industries, companies using hazardous materials, specific professional functions, or other special factors. Compliance reports are usually created in specific formats that must be followed exactly.

Progress reports range from simple, informal updates to comprehensive status reports.

- **Reports to document progress.** Progress reports range from simple updates to comprehensive reports that include such elements as measured progress toward goals, comparisons of budgeted versus actual expenses, and lists of ongoing concerns and risks.

## ORGANIZATIONAL STRATEGIES FOR INFORMATIONAL REPORTS

Most informational reports use a **topical organization**, arranging the material by topic in one of the following ways:

A topical organization is built around the content itself, using such arrangements as comparison, importance, sequence, chronology, geography, or category.

- **Comparison.** Showing similarities and differences (or advantages and disadvantages) between two or more entities
- **Importance.** Building up from the least important item to the most important (or from most important to the least, if you don't think your audience will read the entire report)
- **Sequence.** Organizing the steps or stages in a process or procedure
- **Chronology.** Organizing a chain of events in order from oldest to newest or vice versa

- **Geography.** Organizing by region, city, state, country, or other geographic unit
- **Category.** Grouping by topical category, such as sales, profit, cost, or investment

Whichever pattern you choose, use it consistently so that readers can easily follow your discussion from start to finish. Of course, certain reports (such as compliance or monitor-and-control reports) must follow a prescribed flow.

## CREATING SUCCESSFUL BUSINESS PLANS

A **business plan** such as the one written by the founders of MyCityWay is a comprehensive document that describes a company's mission, structure, objectives, and operations. Roughly speaking, business plans can be written during three separate phases of a company's life: (1) before the company is launched, when the founders are defining their vision of what the company will be; (2) when the company is seeking funding, in which case the business plan takes on a persuasive tone to convince outsiders that investing in the firm would be a profitable decision; and (3) after the company is up and running and the business plan serves as a monitor-and-control mechanism to make sure operations are staying on track.

At any stage, a comprehensive business plan forces you to think about personnel, marketing, facilities, suppliers, distribution, and a host of other issues vital to a company's success. (For an alternative view on the value of business plans and how much time you should spend writing them, watch the video in the Real-Time Updates "Learn More" on this page.) The specific elements to include in a business plan can vary based on the situation; here are the sections typically included in a plan written to attract outside investors:[2]

> **REAL-TIME UPDATES**
> LEARN MORE BY VISITING THIS WEBSITE
> **Step-by-step advice for developing a successful business plan**
> Take advantage of the Small Business Administration's comprehensive guide to preparing a business plan. Go to http://real-timeupdates.com/bct12 and click on Learn More. If you are using MyBCommLab, you can access Real-Time Updates within each chapter or under Student Study Tools.

- **Summary.** In one or two paragraphs, summarize your business concept, particularly the *business model*, which defines how the company will generate revenue and produce a profit. The summary must be compelling, catching the investor's attention and giving him or her reasons to keep reading. Describe your product or service and its market potential. Highlight some things about your company and its leaders that will distinguish your firm from the competition. Summarize your financial projections and indicate how much money you will need from investors or lenders and where it will be spent.
- **Mission and objectives.** Explain the purpose of your business and what you hope to accomplish.
- **Company and industry.** Give full background information on the origins and structure of your venture and the characteristics of the industry in which you plan to compete.
- **Products or services.** Concisely describe your products or services, focusing on their unique attributes and their appeal to customers.
- **Market and competition.** Provide data that will persuade investors that you understand your target market and can achieve your sales goals. Be sure to identify the strengths and weaknesses of your competitors.
- **Management.** Summarize the background and qualifications of the key management personnel in your company. Include résumés in an appendix.
- **Marketing strategy.** Provide projections of sales volume and market share; outline a strategy for identifying and reaching potential customers, setting prices, providing customer support, and physically delivering your products or services. Whenever possible, include evidence of customer acceptance, such as advance product orders.
- **Design and development plans.** If your product requires design or development, describe the nature and extent of what needs to be done, including costs and possible problems. For new or unusual products, you may want to explain how the product will be manufactured.
- **Operations plan.** Provide information on facilities, equipment, and personnel requirements.
- **Overall schedule.** Forecast important milestones in the company's growth and development, including when you need to be fully staffed and when your products will be ready for the market.

Formal business plans, particularly those used to solicit outside investment, must meet a specific set of reader expectations.

- **Critical risks and problems.** Identify significant negative factors and discuss them honestly.
- **Financial projections and requirements.** Include a detailed budget of start-up and operating costs, as well as projections for income, expenses, and cash flow for the first few years of business. Identify the company's financing needs and potential sources, if appropriate.

- **Exit strategy.** Explain how investors will be able to profit from their investment, such as through a public stock offering, sale of the company, or a buyback of the investors' interest.

Creating a complete business plan requires a considerable amount of work. However, by thinking your way through all these issues, you'll enjoy a smoother launch and a greater chance of success in your new adventure. For more insider advice on writing business plans, see Chapter 15's Communication Close-Up on page 409.

**REAL-TIME UPDATES**

LEARN MORE BY VISITING THIS WEBSITE

**Crafting your "wow" statement**

Bill Reichert of Garage Technology Ventures offers advice on capturing an investor's attention in just a matter of seconds. Go to http://real-timeupdates.com/bct12 and click on Learn More. If you are using MyBCommLab, you can access Real-Time Updates within each chapter or under Student Study Tools.

## EFFECTIVE INFORMATIONAL REPORTS: AN EXAMPLE

Effective informational reports are clearly and logically organized, with audience-centered content and generous use of previews and summaries. They are complete, without being unnecessarily long or detailed. One of the tasks your audience expects you to accomplish is to sort out the details and separate major points from minor points. In other words, readers expect you to take the time and effort needed to make the best use of their time (see Figure 14.5). In addition, effective reports are honest and objective but not unduly harsh whenever negative information must be conveyed.

# Planning Analytical Reports

**3 LEARNING OBJECTIVE**
Discuss three major ways to organize analytical reports.

Analytical reports are used to assess opportunities, to solve problems, and to support decisions.

The purpose of analytical reports is to analyze, to understand, or to explain a problem or an opportunity and figure out how it affects the company and how the company should respond. In many cases, you'll also be expected to make a recommendation based on your analysis. As you saw in Figure 14.1, analytical reports fall into three basic categories:

- **Reports to assess opportunities.** Every business opportunity carries some degree of risk and also requires a variety of decisions and actions in order to capitalize on the opportunity. For instance, *market analysis reports* are used to judge the likelihood of success for new products or sales initiatives by identifying potential opportunities as well as competitive threats and other risks. *Due diligence reports* examine the financial aspects of a proposed decision, such as acquiring another company.
- **Reports to solve problems.** Managers often assign *troubleshooting reports* when they need to understand why something isn't working properly and what can be done to fix the situation. A variation, the *failure analysis report*, studies events that happened in the past, with the hope of learning how to avoid similar failures in the future.
- **Reports to support decisions.** *Feasibility reports* are called for when managers need to explore the ramifications of a decision they're about to make (such as replacing an advertising agency or switching materials used in a manufacturing process). *Justification reports* justify a decision that has already been made.

Writing analytical reports presents a greater challenge than writing informational reports, for three reasons. First, you're doing more than simply delivering information; you're also analyzing a problem or an opportunity and presenting your conclusions. The best writing in the world can't compensate for flawed analysis. Second, when your analysis is complete, you need to present your thinking in a credible manner. Third, analytical reports often convince other people to make significant financial and personnel decisions, so your reports carry the added responsibility of the consequences of these decisions.

issue backgrounder

# FOCUS

## The Paint and Coatings Industry:
## A Key Player in the Green Building Movement

The report title establishes the ACA's position, that it plays an important role in the green building movement.

Green building standards and certification systems have evolved from little-known, voluntary programs 10 years ago to a range of standards and codes that are fundamentally changing the residential and commercial building market in the United States. Green building standards aim to produce more energy efficient buildings and reduce the environmental footprint of building construction by providing guidelines and criteria for the construction industry in the areas of building design, site location and planning, energy efficiency, construction materials and resources, water efficiency, and indoor environmental quality.

In the United States, green building has proliferated in the new construction market, growing six-fold from 2005 to 2010,[1] and it is now estimated that over 60 percent of new commercial construction projects are striving to achieve Leadership in Energy and Environmental Design (LEED) certification.[2] Local, city, and state governments are also seizing upon the trend, adopting mandatory green building codes, such as the International Green Construction Code (IgCC) in individual jurisdictions, or even the California Green Building Standards Code, which applies across the entire state of California.

Topic sentences establish the tone and direction of each paragraph.

The American Coatings Association (ACA) supports the underlying goals of the green building movement and engages in the process to develop these rating systems and codes. ACA recognizes the industry's role in green building as providing sustainable products that contribute to energy efficiency, materials and resources, and indoor air quality goals. Paint, coatings, adhesives, and sealants play an essential part in sustainability and green building by protecting and preserving critical elements of a building's structure; providing air and vapor barriers that are crucial for the building envelope and energy efficiency; replacing traditional roofing with cool roof coatings; and increasing the longevity of interior and exterior building finishes, ultimately reducing the need for virgin materials.

ACA's membership has a vested interest in the development of these green building standards and codes,

since they provide a range of products that contribute to green building objectives and goals, and meet environmental requirements for architectural paint, coatings, adhesives, and sealants. More and more, the adoption of green building rating systems and codes is eclipsing the role of governmental agencies and, as green building codes become mandatory, they are even outpacing federal and state regulations pertaining to architectural coatings. ACA represents the industry's position by engaging in the development process of these standards, asserting the need for technically and economically feasible requirements for our building products, while supporting efforts to reduce the negative impact on the environment and improve the health of building occupants. →

[1] McGraw Hill Construction, Outlook 2011: Industry Forecast and Trends.
[2] McGraw Hill Construction, Outlook 2012: Executive Conference. Webcast, December 8, 2011.

○ The Green Building Movement

○ Key Issues for Paint & Coatings

○ In Sum

inside

This modified table of contents offers an overview of what can be found inside this four-page report.

September 2012 • Vol. 20 • No. 3

## Figure 14.5   Effective Informational Report (Excerpt)
This Issue Backgrounder from the American Coatings Association (ACA), an organization that represents the paint and coatings industry, conveys ACA's position on pending legislation and other matters of interest to the industry.
*Source:* Copyright © 2012 by American Coatings Association. Reprinted with permission.

In some situations, the problem or opportunity you address in an analytical report may be defined by the person who authorizes the report. In other cases, you will have to define it yourself. Be careful not to confuse a simple topic (quarterly profits) with a problem (the decline in profits over the past six quarters). Moreover, if you're the only person who thinks a particular issue is a problem, your readers won't be interested in your solution unless your report first convinces them that a problem exists. As with marketing and sales messages, sometimes you need to "sell the problem" before you can sell the solution.

To help define the problem that your analytical report will address, answer these questions:

- What needs to be determined?
- Why is this issue important?
- Who is involved in the situation?

Clarify the problem in an analytical report by determining what you need to analyze, why the issue is important, who is involved, where the trouble is located, and how and when it started.

- Where is the trouble located?
- How did the situation originate?
- When did it start?

Not all these questions apply in every situation, but asking them helps you define the problem being addressed and limit the scope of your discussion.

*Use problem factoring to divide a complex problem into more manageable pieces.*

Another effective way to tackle a complex problem is to divide it into a series of logical, connected questions, a process sometimes called **problem factoring**. You probably subconsciously approach most problems this way. When your car won't start, what do you do? You use the available evidence to organize your investigation, to start a search for cause-and-effect relationships. For example, if the engine doesn't turn over at all, you might suspect a dead battery. If the engine does turn over but won't fire, you can conclude that the battery is okay, but perhaps you're out of gas. When you speculate on the cause of a problem, you're forming a **hypothesis**, a potential explanation that needs to be tested. By subdividing a problem and forming hypotheses based on available evidence, you can tackle even the most complex situations. With a clear picture of the problem or opportunity in mind, you're ready to consider the best structure for your report.

Whenever you are preparing an analytical report, make sure you are clear in your own mind about whether you are advocating one particular line of thought or objectively exploring all the available options.[3] Even if advocating one position is appropriate in the circumstances, your readers will expect you to have considered the other options so that you can help them understand why your answer is preferred.

## ORGANIZATIONAL STRATEGIES FOR ANALYTICAL REPORTS

*Before you choose an approach, determine whether your audience is receptive or skeptical.*

When you expect your audience to agree with you, use the direct approach to focus attention on conclusions and recommendations. When you expect your audience to disagree with you or to be hostile, use the indirect approach to focus attention on the rationale behind your conclusions and recommendations.

The three most common structural approaches for analytical reports are focusing on conclusions (a direct format), focusing on recommendations (another direct format), and focusing on logical arguments (an indirect format). See Table 14.3.

### Focusing on Conclusions

*Focusing on conclusions is often the best approach when you're addressing a receptive audience.*

When writing for audiences that are likely to accept your conclusions—either because they've asked you to perform an analysis or they trust your judgment—consider using a direct approach that focuses immediately on your conclusions. This structure communicates the main idea quickly, but it presents some risks. Even if audiences trust your judgment, they may have questions about your data or the methods you used. Moreover, starting with a conclusion

**TABLE 14.3 | Common Ways to Structure Analytical Reports**

| Element | Focus on Conclusions or Recommendations | FOCUS ON LOGICAL ARGUMENT | |
|---|---|---|---|
| | | **Use 2 + 2 = 4 Model** | **Use Yardstick Model** |
| **Reader mindset** | Are likely to accept | Hostile or skeptical | Hostile or skeptical |
| **Approach** | Direct | Indirect | Indirect |
| **Writer credibility** | High | Low | Low |
| **Advantages** | Readers quickly grasp conclusions or recommendations | Works well when you need to show readers how you built toward an answer by following clear, logical steps | Works well when you have a list of criteria (standards) that must be considered in a decision; alternatives are all measured against same criteria |
| **Drawbacks** | Structure can make topic seem too simple | Can make report longer | Readers must agree on criteria; can be lengthy because of the need to address each criteria for every alternative |

**MEASURING QUALITY IMPROVEMENTS**

I.   Introduction

II.  Conclusion: Outsourcing employee training has reduced costs and improved quality

III. Cost reductions

  A. Exceeded 15 percent cost-reduction goal with 22 percent savings in first year

  B. Achieved actual reduction of 22 percent

  C. Reassigned three staffers who used to work on training full-time

  D. Reduced management time needed to oversee training

  E. Sold the computers that used to be reserved for training

IV.  Quality improvements

  A. Employees say they are more confident in 7 out of 10 key skill areas

  B. Measurable mistakes have dropped by 12 percent

V.   Areas needing improvement

  A. Three skill areas still need improvement

  B. Two trainers received approval ratings below 80 percent

  C. Outside trainers aren't always aware of internal company issues

  D. We have lost some flexibility for scheduling courses

VI.  Summary

*In keeping with the direct approach, the report will open with the conclusion that the program is a success.*

*These two sections will support the conclusion with evidence from two key areas.*

*This section will complete the story by highlighting areas that still need improvement.*

**Figure 14.6  Preliminary Outline of a Research Report Focusing on Conclusions**
Cynthia Zolonka works on the human resources staff of a bank in Houston, Texas. Her company decided to have an outside firm handle its employee training, and a year after the outsourcing arrangement was established, Zolonka was asked to evaluate the results. Her analysis shows that the outsourcing experiment was a success, and she opens with that conclusion but supports it with clear evidence. Readers who accept the conclusion can stop reading, and those who desire more information can continue.

may create the impression that you have oversimplified the situation. You're generally better off taking this direct approach in a report only when your credibility is high—when your readers trust you and are willing to accept your conclusions (see Figure 14.6).

## Focusing on Recommendations

A slightly different approach is useful when your readers want to know what they ought to do in a given situation (as opposed to what they ought to conclude). You'll often be asked to solve a problem or assess an opportunity rather than just study it. The actions you want your readers to take become the main subdivisions of your report.

> When readers want to know what you think they should do, organize your report to focus on recommendations.

When structuring a report around recommendations, use the direct approach as you would for a report that focuses on conclusions. Then unfold your recommendations using a series of five steps:

1. Establish or verify the need for action in the introduction by briefly describing the problem or opportunity.
2. Introduce the benefit that can be achieved, without providing any details.
3. List the steps (recommendations) required to achieve the benefit, using action verbs for emphasis.
4. Explain each step more fully, giving details on procedures, costs, and benefits.
5. Summarize your recommendations.

If your recommendation carries any risks, be sure to clearly address them. Doing so not only makes your report more ethical but also offers you some protection in the event that your recommendation is implemented but doesn't work out as you had hoped. In short, make sure your readers know the potential disadvantages as well as the potential benefits.

> Whenever a recommendation carries some element of risk, you owe it to your audience to make this clear.

## Focusing on Logical Arguments

Two common logical patterns for arguments are the 2 + 2 = 4 approach (adding everything up) and the yardstick approach (comparing solutions against criteria).

When readers are likely to be skeptical or hostile to the conclusion or recommendation you plan to make, use an indirect approach. If you guide people along a logical path toward the answer, they are more likely to accept it when they encounter it. The two most common logical approaches are known as the *2 + 2 = 4 approach* and the *yardstick approach.*

**The 2 + 2 = 4 Approach**  The **2 + 2 = 4 approach** is so named because it convinces readers of your point of view by demonstrating that everything adds up. The main points in your outline are the main reasons behind your conclusions and recommendations. You support each reason with the evidence you collected during your analysis.

Start by considering using the 2 + 2 = 4 approach; it's familiar and easy to develop.

Because of its natural feel and versatility, the 2 + 2 = 4 approach is generally the most persuasive and efficient way to develop an analytical report for skeptical readers. When organizing your own reports, try this structure first. You'll find that many business situations lend themselves nicely to this pattern of logical argumentation.

The yardstick approach compares a solution or several solutions to a set of predetermined standards.

**The Yardstick Approach**  The **yardstick approach** is useful when you need to use a number of criteria to evaluate one or more possible solutions. These criteria become the "yardstick" by which you measure the various alternatives. With this approach, you begin by discussing the problem or opportunity and then list the criteria that will guide the decision. The body of the report then evaluates the alternatives against those criteria. The main points of the outline are either the criteria themselves or the alternatives (see Figure 14.7).

The yardstick approach is particularly useful for proposals when the audience has provided a list of criteria the solution must meet. Say that your company has been asked to bid on a contract to design and install a factory-floor distribution system for a large corporation. The client has listed the requirements (criteria) for the system, and you've developed a preliminary design to meet them. In the body of your proposal, you could use the client's list of requirements as the main headings and under each one explain how your preliminary design meets the requirement.

The yardstick approach has two potential drawbacks. First, your audience members need to agree with the criteria you're using in your analysis. If they don't, they won't agree with the results of the evaluation. If you have any doubt about their agreement, build consensus before you start your report, if possible, or take extra care to explain why the criteria you're using are the best ones in this particular case.

Second, the yardstick approach can get tedious when you have many options to consider or many criteria to compare them against. One way to minimize repetition is to compare the options in tables and then highlight the most unusual or important aspects of each alternative in the text so that you get the best of both worlds. This approach allows you to compare all the alternatives against the same yardstick while calling attention to the most significant differences among them.

## EFFECTIVE ANALYTICAL REPORTS: AN EXAMPLE

As national sales manager of a New Hampshire sporting goods company, Binh Phan was concerned about his company's ability to sell to its largest customers. His boss, the vice president of marketing, shared these concerns and asked Phan to analyze the situation and recommend a solution. As Phan says, "We sell to retail chains across the country. Large nationwide chains of superstores have been revolutionizing the industry, but we haven't had as much success with these big customers as we've had with smaller companies that operate strictly on a local or regional basis. With more and more of the industry in the hands of the large chains, we knew we had to fix the situation."

Phan's troubleshooting report appears in Figure 14.8 on pages 398–399. The main idea is that the company should establish separate sales teams for these major accounts rather than continue to service them through the company's four regional divisions. However, Phan knew his plan would be controversial because it requires a big change in the company's organization and in the way sales reps are paid. His thinking had to be clear and easy to follow, so he used the 2 + 2 = 4 approach to focus on his reasons.

Main Idea: We should move into the commercial irrigation equipment market but not into the residential market.

These five criteria (standards or rules) that will be used in the evaluation make up the "yardstick" in the yardstick approach.

She will evaluate the two alternatives by judging them according to the five criteria.

I. Introduction
II. Criteria for entering new markets
   A. Size and growth
   B. Profit potential
   C. Ability to compete
   D. Distribution costs and opportunities
   E. Fit with current capabilities
III. Irrigation equipment trends
   A. Water shortages leading to demand for more efficient irrigation
   B. Labor costs encouraging automation
   C. More homeowners attempting do-it-yourself projects
IV. Comparison of new market opportunities
   A. Commercial landscapers and building owners
      1. Size and growth
      2. Profit potential
      3. Ability to compete
      4. Distribution costs and opportunities
      5. Fit with current capabilities
   B. Residential landscapers and homeowners
      1. Size and growth
      2. Profit potential
      3. Ability to compete
      4. Distribution costs and opportunities
      5. Fit with current capabilities
V. Recommendations
   A. Enter the commercial segment
      1. Select a test market
      2. Learn from the test and refine our approach
      3. Roll out product marketing nationwide
   B. Do not attempt to enter the residential market at this point

Here she will give readers important background information about current trends in the marketplace.

She will recommend in favor of one alternative and against the other, based on how each fared in the "yardstick" measurement.

**Figure 14.7   Outline of an Analytical Report Using the Yardstick Approach**
This outline was prepared by J. C. Hartley, a market analyst for a large Sacramento company that makes irrigation equipment for farms and ranches. "We've been so successful in the agricultural market that we're starting to run out of customers to sell to," says Hartley. "To keep the company growing, we needed to find another market. Two obvious choices to consider were commercial buildings and residences," so she structured her report to compare these two opportunities.

# Planning Proposals

Proposals are written for both internal and external audiences. Internal proposals request decisions from managers within the organization, such as proposals to buy new equipment or launch new research projects. Examples of external proposals include *grant proposals*, which request funds from government agencies and other sponsoring organizations, and *sales proposals*, which suggest individualized solutions for potential customers and request purchase decisions.

The most significant factor in planning any proposal is whether the intended recipient has asked you to submit a proposal. *Solicited proposals* are generally prepared at the request of external parties that require a product or a service, but they may also be requested by such internal sources as management or the board of directors. When organizations require complex products, services, or systems, they often prepare a formal invitation to bid on the contract, called a **request for proposals (RFP)**, which includes instructions that specify exactly the type of work to be performed or products to be delivered, along with budgets, deadlines, and other requirements.

To attract a large pool of qualified bidders, organizations send RFPs to firms with good performance records in the field, print them in trade publications, and post them on the web. Federal government RFPs, for instance, can be found through FedBizOpps, at www.cbd-net.com.

To write a proposal in response to an RFP, you begin by reviewing the requirements. Next, you define the scope of the deliverables, determine the methods and procedures to be used, and

**4  LEARNING OBJECTIVE**
Explain how to choose an organizational strategy when writing a proposal.

Buyers often solicit proposals by publishing a request for proposals (RFP).

---

**MEMO**

TO:        Robert Mendoza, Vice President of Marketing
FROM:      Binh Phan, National Sales Manager     *BP*
DATE:      September 12, 2013
SUBJECT:   Major accounts sales problems

As you requested on August 20, this report outlines the results of my investigation into the recent slowdown in sales to major accounts and the accompanying rise in sales- and service-related complaints from some of our largest customers.

Over the last four quarters, major account sales dropped 12%, whereas overall sales were up 7%. During the same time, we've all noticed an increase in both formal and informal complaints from larger customers, regarding how confusing and complicated it has become to do business with us.

My investigation started with in-depth discussions with the four regional sales managers, first as a group and then individually. The tension I felt in the initial meeting eventually bubbled to the surface during my meetings with each manager. Staff members in each region are convinced that other regions are booking orders they don't deserve, with one region doing all the legwork only to see another region get the sale, the commission, and the quota credit.

I followed up these formal discussions by talking informally and exchanging email with several sales representatives from each region. Virtually everyone who is involved with our major national accounts has a story to share. No one is happy with the situation, and I sense that some reps are walking away from major customers because the process is so frustrating.

The decline in sales to our major national customers and the increase in their complaints stem from two problems: (1) sales force organization and (2) commission policy.

**ORGANIZATIONAL PROBLEMS**

When we divided the national sales force into four geographical regions last year, the idea was to focus our sales efforts and clarify responsibilities for each prospective and current customer. The regional managers have gotten to know their market territories very well, and sales have increased beyond even our most optimistic projections.

However, while solving one problem, we have created another. In the past 12 to 18 months, several regional customers have grown to national status, and a few retailers have taken on (or expressed interest in) our products. As a result, a significant portion of both current sales and future opportunities lies with these large national accounts.

I uncovered more than a dozen cases in which sales representatives from two or more regions found themselves competing with each other by pursuing the same customers from different locations. Moreover, the complaints from our major accounts about overlapping or nonexistent account coverage are a direct result of the regional organization. In some cases, customers aren't sure which of our representatives they're supposed to call with problems and orders. In other cases, no one has been in contact with them for several months.

*(continued)*

**Figure 14.8   Analytical Report Using the 2 + 2 = 4 Approach**
To make his logical argument both clear and compelling, Binh Phan used the 2 + 2 = 4 approach.

---

estimate time requirements, personnel requirements, and costs. Then you put it all in writing—exactly as specified in the RFP, following the precise format it requires and responding meticulously to every point it raises.[4] RFPs can seem surprisingly picky, even to the point of specifying the paper size for the proposal and the number of copies to send, but you must follow every detail.

*Unsolicited proposals* are created by organizations attempting to obtain business or funding without a specific invitation from a potential client. Such proposals may also be initiated by employees or managers who want to convince company insiders to adopt a program, a policy, or an idea. In other words, with an unsolicited proposal, the writer makes the first move. Even so, an unsolicited proposal should not come as a surprise to the recipient but rather should be the summation of a conversation that has been ongoing with the recipient.[5] This approach helps ensure acceptance, and it gives you an opportunity to explore the recipient's needs and craft your proposal around them.

Unsolicited proposals differ from solicited proposals in another important respect: Your audience may not be aware of the problem you are addressing, so your proposal

**Unsolicited proposals require additional persuasive elements because the audience isn't expecting the proposal and might not even be conscious of the problem you propose to solve.**

2

Phan brings the first problem to life by complementing the general description with a specific example.

For example, having retail outlets across the lower tier of the country, AmeriSport received pitches from reps out of our West, South, and East regions. Because our regional offices have a lot of negotiating freedom, the three were offering different prices. But all AmeriSport buying decisions were made at the Tampa headquarters, so all we did was confuse the customer. The irony of the current organization is that we're often giving our weakest selling and support efforts to the largest customers in the country.

**COMMISSION PROBLEMS**

Commission problems are the second "2" in Phan's 2 + 2 = 4 approach.

In discussing the second problem, he simplifies the reader's task by maintaining a parallel structure: a general description followed by a specific example.

The regional organization problems are compounded by the way we assign commissions and quota credit. Salespeople in one region can invest a lot of time in pursuing a sale, only to have the customer place the order in another region. So some sales rep in the second region ends up with the commission on a sale that was partly or even entirely earned by someone in the first region. Therefore, sales reps sometimes don't pursue leads in their regions, thinking that a rep in another region will get the commission.

For example, Athletic Express, with outlets in 35 states spread across all four regions, finally got so frustrated with us that the company president called our headquarters. Athletic Express has been trying to place a large order for tennis and golf accessories, but none of our local reps seem interested in paying attention. I spoke with the rep responsible for Nashville, where the company is headquartered, and asked her why she wasn't working the account more actively. Her explanation was that last time she got involved with Athletic Express, the order was actually placed from their L.A. regional office, and she didn't get any commission after more than two weeks of selling time.

**RECOMMENDATIONS**

Phan concludes the 2 + 2 = 4 approach: organizational problems + commission problems = the need for a new sales structure.

Our sales organization should reflect the nature of our customer base. To accomplish that goal, we need a group of reps who are free to pursue accounts across regional borders—and who are compensated fairly for their work. The most sensible answer is to establish a national account group. Any customers whose operations place them in more than one region would automatically be assigned to the national group.

He explains how his recommendation (a new organizational structure) will solve both problems.

In addition to solving the problem of competing sales efforts, the new structure will also largely eliminate the commission-splitting problem because regional reps will no longer invest time in prospects assigned to the national accounts team. However, we will need to find a fair way to compensate regional reps who are losing long-term customers to the national team. Some of these reps have invested years in developing customer relationships that will continue to yield sales well into the future, and everyone I talked to agrees that reps in these cases should receive some sort of compensation. Such a "transition commission" would also motivate the regional reps to help ensure a smooth transition from one sales group to the other. The exact nature of this compensation would need to be worked out with the various sales managers.

He acknowledges that the recommended solution does create a temporary compensation problem but expresses confidence that a solution to that can be worked out.

3

**SUMMARY**

The summary concisely restates both the problem and the recommended solution.

The regional sales organization is effective at the regional and local levels but not at the national level. We should establish a national accounts group to handle sales that cross regional boundaries. Then we'll have one set of reps who are focused on the local and regional levels and another set who are pursuing national accounts.

To compensate regional reps who lose accounts to the national team, we will need to devise some sort of payment to reward them for the years of work invested in such accounts. This can be discussed with the sales managers once the new structure is in place.

**Figure 14.8 Analytical Report Using the 2 + 2 = 4 Approach *(continued)***

must first convince readers that a problem or an opportunity exists before convincing them that you can address it. Thus, unsolicited proposals generally spend considerable time explaining why readers should take action and convincing them of the benefits of doing so.

Every proposal competes for something: money, time, attention, and so on.

With virtually any proposal, keep in mind that you are always competing for something—money, time, management attention, and so on. Even if yours is the only proposal on the table, you are still competing with all the other choices your audience members could make with their time, money, and attention.

Proposals can be significant writing projects, particularly when you are responding to a complex RFP. Fortunately, a variety of software products are available to lighten the load considerably. Basic features include the ability to automatically personalize the proposal, ensure proper structure, and organize storage of all your boilerplate material (identical sections of text used in every proposal, such as a description of your company). At a more advanced level, semi-automated proposal writing systems can scan RFPs to identify questions and requirements and fill in potential answers from a centralized knowledge base that contains input from all the relevant experts in your company.[6]

## ORGANIZATIONAL STRATEGIES FOR PROPOSALS

Your choice of structure for proposals depends on whether the proposal is solicited and, if so, whether you expect readers to be receptive to your specific recommendation. In general, your audience is likely to be more receptive with solicited proposals because the problem and the solution have already been identified. Submit your proposal for the solution specified in the RFP and structure the proposal using the direct approach to focus on your recommendation. As soon as possible within the constraints of the RFP requirements, identify why your solution is unique and deserves close consideration.[7]

The indirect approach following AIDA or a similar model is often the best way to build your case in an unsolicited proposal.

Depending on the circumstances and your relationship with the recipient, the indirect approach is often better for unsolicited proposals. When writing unsolicited proposals, you must first convince the audience that a problem exists and establish your credibility if you are unknown to the reader. At the same time, you need to give the reader a compelling reason to keep reading a document that he or she didn't request. Follow the AIDA model or a similar approach to grab the reader's attention quickly. For an external proposal, for instance, you might start off with an attention-getter such as "In working with other

---

**ETHICS DETECTIVE**

## Solving the Case of the Overblown Proposal

As the manager in charge of your company's New Ventures Group, you've read your share of proposals—hundreds, maybe thousands, of them. You've developed a sixth sense about these documents, an ability to separate cautious optimism from self-doubt and distinguish justified enthusiasm from insupportable hype.

Your company invests in promising smaller firms that could grow into beneficial business partners or even future acquisitions. In a typical scenario, a small company invents a new product but needs additional funding to manufacture and market it, so the owners approach you with funding proposals. Because you make the first major decision in this investment process, your choices and recommendations to the board of directors are crucial.

Moreover, the risks are considerable: If one of your recommendations doesn't pan out, the company could lose all the money it invested (often millions), and that's only the start. Failures consume your team's precious time and energy and can even put the company at risk for shareholder lawsuits and other serious headaches. In other words, mistakes in your line of work are costly.

The proposal in front of you today is intriguing. A small company in Oklahoma has designed a product called the Wireless Shopping List, and you think the idea might appeal to upscale homeowners. Small touchscreens are placed around the house, wherever occupants are likely to think of things they need to buy on the next shopping trip: on the refrigerator door, in the media room, in the nursery, in the garage, in the gardening shed. The system collects all these inputs, and on command it prints out a shopping list or downloads it to a smartphone. It's a clever idea, but one paragraph in the proposal bothers you:

> Everybody in our test market audience was absolutely stunned when we demonstrated the simulated system. They couldn't believe something like this was even possible. It was so handy and so convenient— everyone said it would change their lives forever. We haven't even specified the price yet, but every single person in the room wanted to place an order, on the spot.

### ANALYSIS

This proposal potentially oversells the idea in at least three ways. Identify them and explain how they could lead you to decline the investment opportunity.

companies in your industry, our productivity specialists were able to lower their operating costs by as much as 15 percent." Then, to convince the reader that you can back up that claim, present your solution in a logical fashion, with solid evidence, leading up to a request for a decision (see "Ethics Detective: Solving the Case of the Overblown Proposal").

## EFFECTIVE PROPOSALS: AN EXAMPLE

A good proposal explains why a project or course of action is needed, what it will involve, how much it will cost, and how the recipient will benefit. You can see all these elements in Shandel Cohen's internal proposal for an automatic mail-response system (see Figure 14.9).

A subject line with a compelling promise catches the reader's attention.

"The Solution" explains the proposed solution in enough detail to make it convincing, without burdening the reader with excessive detail.

"The Problem" describes the current situation and explains why it should be fixed.

Listing a number of compelling benefits as subheadings builds reader interest in the proposed solution.

---

**MEMO**

**TO:**       Jamie Engle
**FROM:**     Shandel Cohen
**DATE:**     July 8, 2013
**SUBJECT:**  Saving $145k/year with an automated email response system

**THE PROBLEM:**
**Expensive and Slow Response to Customer Information Requests**

Our new product line has been very well received, and orders have surpassed our projections. This very success, however, has created a shortage of printed brochures, as well as considerable overtime for people in the customer response center. As we introduce upgrades and new options, our printed materials quickly become outdated. If we continue to rely on printed materials for customer information, we have two choices: Distribute existing materials (even though they are incomplete or inaccurate) or discard existing materials and print new ones.

**THE SOLUTION:**
**Automated Email Response System**

With minor additions and modifications to our current email system, we can set up an automated system to respond to customer requests for information. This system can save us time and money and can keep our distributed information current.

Automated email response systems have been tested and proven effective. Many companies already use this method to respond to customer information requests, so we won't have to worry about relying on untested technology. Using the system is easy, too: Customers simply send a blank email message to a specific address, and the system responds by sending an electronic copy of the requested brochure.

**Benefit #1 : Always-Current Information**

Rather than discard and print new materials, we would only need to keep the electronic files up to date on the server. We could be able to provide customers and our field sales organization with up-to-date, correct information as soon as the upgrades or options are available.

**Benefit #2: Instantaneous Delivery**

Almost immediately after requesting information, customers would have that information in hand. Electronic delivery would be especially advantageous for our international customers. Regular mail to remote locations sometimes takes weeks to arrive, by which time the information may already be out of date. Both customers and field salespeople will appreciate the automatic mail-response system.

**Benefit #3: Minimized Waste**

With our current method of printing every marketing piece in large quantities, we discard thousands of pages of obsolete catalogs, data sheets, and other materials every year. By maintaining and distributing the information electronically, we would eliminate this waste. We would also free up a considerable amount of expensive floor space and shelving that is required for storing printed materials.

---

*(continued)*

**Figure 14.9  Internal Proposal**
Shandel Cohen's internal proposal seeks management's approval to install an automatic mail-response system. Because the company manufactures computers, she knows that her boss won't object to a computer-based solution. Also, because profits are always a concern, her report emphasizes the financial benefits of her proposal.

2

She acknowledges one potential shortcoming with the new approach but provides a convincing solution to that as well.

Of course, some of our customers may still prefer to receive printed materials, or they may not have access to electronic mail. For these customers, we could simply print copies of the files when we receive such requests. The new Xerox DocuColor printer just installed in the Central Services building would be ideal for printing high-quality materials in small quantities.

### Benefit #4: Lower Overtime Costs

In addition to saving both paper and space, we would also realize considerable savings in wages. Because of the increased interest in our new products, we must continue to work overtime or hire new people to meet the demand. An automatic mail response system would eliminate this need, allowing us to deal with fluctuating interest without a fluctuating workforce.

### Cost Analysis

The necessary equipment and software costs approximately $15,000. System maintenance and upgrades are estimated at $5,000 per year. However, those costs are offset many times over by the predicted annual savings:

A detailed breakdown of cost savings provides credible support for the $145k/year claim made in the subject line.

| | |
|---|---|
| Printing | $100,000 |
| Storage | 25,000 |
| Postage | 5,000 |
| Wages | 20,000 |
| **Total** | **$150,000** |

Based on these figures, the system would save $130,000 the first year and $145,000 every year after that.

### CONCLUSION

Her conclusion summarizes the benefits and invites further discussion.

An automated email response system would yield considerable benefits in both customer satisfaction and operating costs. If you approve, we can have it installed and running in 6 weeks. Please give me a call if you have any questions.

**Figure 14.9    Internal Proposal (*continued*)**

Cohen manages the customer-response section of the marketing department at a personal computer manufacturer located in the Midwest. Her section sends out product information requested by customers and the field salesforce. Cohen has observed that the demand for information increases when a new product is released and diminishes as a product matures. This fluctuating demand causes drastic changes in her section's workload.

"Either we have more work than we can possibly handle," says Cohen, "or we don't have enough to keep us busy. But I don't want to get into a hiring-and-firing cycle." Cohen is also concerned about the amount of printed material that's discarded when products are upgraded or replaced. Her report describes the problem, her proposed solutions, the benefits to the company, and the projected costs, giving her audience all the information needed to make a decision.

# Quick Learning Guide

## MyBCommLab

Go to **mybcommlab.com** to complete the problems marked with this icon ⭐.

## SUMMARY OF LEARNING OBJECTIVES

**1 Adapt the three-step writing process to reports and proposals.** The comprehensive nature of the three-step process is ideal for the work involved in most reports and proposals. Use all the advice you learned in Chapters 4 through 6, with added emphasis on a few specific points for longer documents: (1) Identify your purpose clearly to avoid rework, (2) prepare a work plan to guide the research and writing tasks, (3) determine whether a separate research project might be needed to gather the necessary information, (4) choose the appropriate medium (or media, in some cases) for your audience, and (5) organize your information by selecting the best approach for an informational or analytical report.

**2 List the options for organizing informational reports, and identify the parts of a business plan.** Informational reports focus on the delivery of facts, figures, and other types of information. Most informational reports use a topical organization, arranging material by comparison, importance, sequence, chronology, geography, or category.

Formal business plans—those that are shown to outside audiences such as investors and bankers—typically contain the following elements: a summary of the business concept, the company's mission and objectives, background on the company and the industry in which it competes, descriptions of its products and services, an analysis of target markets and key competitors, a discussion of the management team, a summary of the marketing strategy, design and development plans, an operations plan, a schedule with major milestones, an analysis of critical risks and problems, financial projections and requirements, and a description of the proposed exit strategy.

**3 Discuss three major ways to organize analytical reports.** The three most common ways to organize analytical reports are by focusing on conclusions, focusing on recommendations, and focusing on logical arguments. The first two are direct approaches; the third is an indirect approach.

**4 Explain how to choose an organizational strategy when writing a proposal.** The most significant factor in planning a proposal is whether the proposal is solicited or unsolicited. Solicited proposals are obviously expected and welcomed by the recipient, but they often must follow a specific organization, particularly when they are submitted in response to a request for proposals (RFP). For unsolicited proposals, the writer has flexibility in choosing the most effective organization, format, and content. However, because unsolicited proposals are unexpected, the writer often needs to explain why the solution offered in the proposal is even necessary for the reader to consider. Because of this, the indirect approach is usually preferred for unsolicited proposals.

## KEY TERMS

**analytical reports** Reports that offer both information and analysis; they can also include recommendations

**business plan** A comprehensive document that describes a company's mission, structure, objectives, and operations

**hypothesis** A potential explanation that needs to be tested

**informational reports** Reports that offer data, facts, feedback, and other types of information, without analysis or recommendations

**problem factoring** Dividing a problem into a series of logical, connected questions

**proposals** Reports that combine information delivery and persuasive communication

**reports** Written accounts that objectively communicate information about some aspect of a business

**request for proposals (RFP)** A formal invitation to bid on a contract

**statement of purpose** Planning statement that defines why you are preparing the report

**topical organization** Arranging material according to comparisons, importance, sequence, chronology, spatial orientation, geography, or category

**yardstick approach** Logical argumentation approach that uses a number of criteria to evaluate one or more possible solutions

**2 + 2 = 4 approach** Logical argumentation approach that convinces readers of your point of view by demonstrating how everything "adds up"

## Adapting the Three-Step Process to Reports and Proposals

**A. Analyze the situation.**
- Clearly define your purpose before you start writing.
- If you need to accomplish several goals in the report, identify them all in advance.
- Prepare a work plan to guide your efforts.

**B. Gather information.**
- Determine whether you need to launch a separate research project to collect the necessary information.
- Reuse or adapt existing material whenever possible.

**C. Select the right medium.**
- Base your decision on audience expectations or requirements.
- Consider the need for commenting, revising, distributing, and storing.
- Remember that the medium you choose also sends a message.

**D. Organize your information.**
- Use the direct approach if your audience is receptive.
- Use the indirect approach if your audience is skeptical.
- Use the indirect approach when you don't want to risk coming across as arrogant.
- Combine approaches if doing so will help build support for your primary message.

## COMMUNICATION CHALLENGES AT **MyCityWay**

You work as Archana Patchirajan's executive assistant in MyCityWay's New York headquarters, where you help her with a variety of communication projects. Use your knowledge of report and proposal writing to address the following challenges.

**INDIVIDUAL CHALLENGE:** MyCityWay works with a wide variety of local businesses that use the software for brand-building campaigns, coupons, and mobile commerce. Recently, several of these companies have called to ask about MyCityWay's relationship with BMW. Most people recognize the BMW name, but relatively few understand the new "BMW i" program. Patchirajan thinks it would be helpful to have a brief overview ready to provide business partners who have questions.

Review the information at www.bmw-i.com and draft the outline of an informational report that summarizes the "BMW i" program.

**TEAM CHALLENGE:** Many companies offer a downloadable one-page "fact sheet" that summarizes the concept of the business, its product lines, unique technologies, target markets, biographies of key executives, and other information of potential interest to various stakeholders. In a team with two or three other students, review the fact sheets (sometimes called a "company overview" or something similar) offered on the websites of three companies in any industry, and then collaborate on a one-page fact sheet for MyCityWay.

## Test Your Knowledge

To review chapter content related to each question, refer to the indicated Learning Objective.

1. What is the major difference between informational and analytical reports? [LO-1]
2. What does a statement of purpose convey? [LO-1]
✪ 3. What should you include in the work plan for a complex report or proposal? [LO-1]
4. How are reports for monitoring and controlling operations used? [LO-2]
5. What are the three major ways to organize an analytical report? [LO-3]
✪ 6. How does a feasibility report differ from a justification report? [LO-3]
7. What is problem factoring? [LO-3]
8. What is an RFP, and how does it relate to proposal writing? [LO-4]

## Apply Your Knowledge

To review chapter content related to each question, refer to the indicated Learning Objective.

1. Would "Look into employee morale problems" be an effective problem statement for a report? Why or why not? [LO-1]
✪ 2. Which of the topical organization plans listed on pages 390–391 would you use to organize an analytical report on a recent power outage in your manufacturing facility? Why? [LO-2]
3. If you want to make a specific recommendation in your report, should you include information that might support a different recommendation? Explain your answer. [LO-3]
✪ 4. Assume you are assigned the task of evaluating two firms to provide security for your company's office and factory facilities. First, you write a report recommending one of the two firms. After a thorough analysis, however, you conclude that neither firm is capable of providing quality service at

an acceptable cost. How should you structure your report? [LO-3]
✪ 5. In what ways are unsolicited proposals more challenging to write than solicited proposals? [LO-4]

## Practice Your Skills

**Message for Analysis:**
**Comparing Two Report Formats [LO-1]**

The Securities and Exchange Commission (SEC) requires all public companies to file a comprehensive annual report (form 10-K) electronically. Many companies post links to these reports on their websites, along with links to other company reports. Visit the website of HP, at www.hp.com, and find the company's most recent 10-K and Fiscal Year in Review reports. Compare the style and format of the two reports. For which audience(s) is the Year in Review targeted? Who besides the SEC might be interested in the 10-K? Which report do you find easier to read? More interesting? More detailed?

### Exercises

Each activity is labeled according to the primary skill or skills you will need to use. To review relevant chapter content, you can refer to the indicated Learning Objective. In some instances, supporting information will be found in another chapter, as indicated.

1. **Planning: Analyzing the Situation [LO-1]** Sales at The Style Shop, a clothing store for men, have declined for the third month in a row. Your boss is not sure whether this decline is due to the weak economy or some other unknown reason. She has asked you to investigate the situation and to submit a report to her, highlighting some possible reasons for the decline. Develop a statement of purpose for your report.

2. **Planning: Preparing the Work Plan [LO-1]** South by Southwest (SXSW) is a family of conferences and festivals in Austin, Texas, that showcase some of the world's most

creative talents in music, interactive media, and film. In addition to being a major entertainment venue for a week every March, SXSW is also an increasingly important *trade show*, an opportunity for companies to present products and services to potential customers and business partners. You work for a company that makes music training equipment such as an electronic keyboard with an integrated computer screen that guides learners through every step of learning to play a keyboard. Your manager has asked you to look into whether the company should rent an exhibition booth at SXSW next year. Prepare a work plan for an analytical report that will assess the promotional opportunities at SXSW and make a recommendation on exhibiting. Include the statement of purpose, a problem statement for any research you will conduct, a description of what will result from your investigation, the sources and methods of data collection, and a preliminary outline. Visit the SXSW website, at http://sxsw.com, for more information.[8]

3. **Planning: Organizing Reports [LO-1]** For each of the following scenarios, determine whether the direct or indirect approach would be advisable, and explain why.

   a. The monthly financial report prepared by the accounting department for upper management

   b. An accountant fresh out of college who wants to propose a new way to present those monthly financial results to upper management

   c. An unsolicited proposal to provide payroll processing services

   d. An analytical report, requested by the CEO, explaining why the company has been losing money in the eastern sales region for the past two years

   e. An unsolicited proposal to the board of directors, outlining why it makes strategic sense for your company to expand into international markets; the board rejected a similar—but poorly presented—idea last year

4. **Planning: Organizing Reports [LO-1]** Look through recent issues (print or online) of *Bloomberg Businessweek*, *Fortune*, or other business publications for an article that describes how an executive's conclusions about his or her company's current situation or future opportunities led to changes in policy, plans, or products. Construct an outline of the material, first using a direct approach and then using an indirect approach. Which approach do you think the executive would use when reporting these conclusions to stockholders? When reporting to other senior managers? Explain your answers.

5. **Planning: Organizing Reports (Informational Reports) [LO-1]** Assume that your college president has received many student complaints about campus parking problems. You are appointed the chair of a student committee organized to investigate the problems and recommend solutions. The president gives you a file labeled "Parking: Complaints from Students," and you jot down the essence of the complaints as you inspect the contents. Your notes look like this:

   • Inadequate student spaces at critical hours

   • Poor night lighting near the computer center

   • Inadequate attempts to keep resident neighbors from occupying spaces

   • Dim marking lines

   • Motorcycles taking up full spaces

   • Discourteous security officers

   • Spaces (often empty) reserved for college officials

   • Relatively high parking fees

   • Full fees charged to night students even though they use the lots only during low-demand periods

   • Vandalism to cars and a sense of personal danger

   • Inadequate total space

   • Resident harassment of students parking on the street in front of neighboring houses

   Prepare an outline for an informational report to be submitted to committee members. Use a topical organization that categorizes this information.

6. **Planning: Organizing Reports (Analytical Reports) [LO-1]** Three years ago, your company (a carpet manufacturer) modernized its Georgia plant in anticipation of increasing demand for carpets. Because of the depressed housing market, the increase in demand for new carpets has been slow to materialize. As a result, the company has excess capacity at both its Georgia and California plants. On the basis of your research, you have recommended that the company close the California plant. The company president, J. P. Lawrence, has asked you to prepare a justification report to support your recommendation. Here are the facts you gathered by interviewing the respective plant managers:

   **Operational Statistics**

   • Georgia plant: This plant has newer equipment, has higher productivity, employs 100 nonunion production workers, and ships $12 million in carpets a year. Hourly base wage is $16.

   • California plant: California plant employs 80 union production workers and ships $8 million in carpets a year. Hourly base wage is $20.

   **Financial Implications**

   • Savings by closing California plant: (1) Increase productivity by 17 percent; (2) reduce labor costs by 20 percent (total labor savings would be $1 million per year; see assumptions); (3) annual local tax savings of $120,000 (Georgia has a more favorable tax climate).

   • Sale of Pomona, California, land: Purchased in 1952 for $200,000. Current market value $2.5 million. Net profit (after capital gains tax) over $1 million.

   • Sale of plant and equipment: Fully depreciated. Any proceeds a windfall.

   • Costs of closing California plant: One-time deductible charge of $250,000 (relocation costs of $100,000 and severance payments totaling $150,000).

   **Assumptions**

   • Transfer five workers from California to Georgia.

   • Hire 45 new workers in Georgia.

   • Lay off 75 workers in California.

   • Georgia plant would require a total of 150 workers to produce the combined volume of both plants.

   a. Which approach (focus on conclusions, recommendations, or logical arguments) will you use to structure your report to the president? Why?

b. Suppose this report were to be circulated to plant managers and supervisors instead. What changes, if any, might you make in your approach?

c. List some conclusions you might draw from the preceding information to use in your report.

d. Using the structure you selected for your report to the president, draft a final report outline with first- and second-level informative headings.

7. **Planning Reports and Proposals [LO-2], [LO-3], [LO-4]** Using the information presented in this chapter, identify the report type represented by each of the following examples. In addition, write a brief paragraph about each, explaining who the audience is likely to be, what type of data would be used, and whether conclusions and recommendations would be appropriate.

a. A statistical study of the pattern of violent crime in a large city during the past five years

b. A report prepared by a seed company, demonstrating the benefits of its seed corn for farmers

c. A report prepared by an independent testing agency, evaluating various types of nonprescription cold remedies

d. A trip report submitted at the end of a week by a traveling salesperson

e. A report indicating how 45 acres of undeveloped land could be converted into an industrial park

f. An annual report to be sent to the shareholders of a large corporation

g. A report from a U.S. National Park wildlife officer to Washington, D.C., headquarters showing the status of the California condor (an endangered species)

h. A report outlining the risks of closing a chain of retail stores and moving the entire business online

8. **Planning Proposals [LO-4]** Follow the step-by-step hints and examples for writing a funding proposal at www.learnerassociates.com/proposal. Review the writing hints and the entire sample proposal online. What details did the author decide to include in appendixes? Why was this material placed in the appendixes and not the main body of the report? According to the author's tips, when is the best time to prepare a project overview?

9. **Planning Informational Reports [LO-2]** You're the vice president of operations for a Florida fast-food chain. In the aftermath of a major hurricane, you're drafting a report on the emergency procedures to be followed by personnel in each restaurant when storm warnings are in effect. Answer who, what, when, where, why, and how, and then prepare a one-page outline of your report. Make up any details you need.

10. **Planning Proposals [LO-4]** You're getting ready to launch a new lawn-care business that offers mowing, fertilizing, weeding, and other services. The lawn surrounding a nearby shopping center looks as if it could use better care, so you target that business for your first unsolicited proposal. To help prepare this proposal, write your answers to these questions:

a. What questions will you need to answer before you can write a proposal to solve the reader's problem? Be as specific as possible.

b. What customer benefits will you include in your proposal?

c. Will you use a letter or memo format for your proposal? Explain your answer.

11. **Planning Proposals; Collaboration: Team Projects [LO-4], Chapter 2** Break into small groups and identify an operational problem occurring at your campus, involving one of the following: registration, university housing, food services, parking, or library services. Develop a workable solution to that problem. Finally, develop a list of pertinent facts that your team will need to gather to convince the reader that the problem exists and that your solution will work.

## Expand Your Skills

### Critique the Professionals

Download any of the free reports and other offered on the American Coatings Association website at www.paint.org/publications.html. Identify the target audience(s) and purpose of the report you've chosen. Using whatever medium your instructor requests, write a brief analysis of the report, describing what works well and what doesn't work well.

### Sharpening Your Career Skills Online

Bovée and Thill's Business Communication Web Search, at http://businesscommunicationblog.com/websearch, is a unique research tool designed specifically for business communication research. Use the Web Search function to find a website, video, PDF document, or PowerPoint presentation that offers advice on writing effective business proposals. Write a brief email message to your instructor, describing the item you found and summarizing the career skills information you learned from it.

## MyBCommLab

Go to **mybcommlab.com** for Auto-graded writing questions as well as the following Assisted-graded writing questions:

14-1. What elements should be included in a formal business plan? [LO-2]

14-2. What are the seven major ways to organize an informational report? [LO-2]

14-3. Mybcommlab Only—comprehensive writing assignment for this chapter.

# Endnotes

**1.** Adapted from MyCityWay website, accessed 6 February 2013, http://mycityway.com; BMW i website, accessed 6 February 2013, www.bmw-i.com; Adam Bluestein and Amy Barrett, "How Business-Plan Competitions Reward Innovation," *Inc.*, 1 July 2010, www.inc .com; Nick Saint, "Mayor Bloomberg Announces First Investment by NYC-Sponsored Venture Fund: MyCityWay," SAI Business Insider, 25 May 2010, www.businessinsider.com; Heidi Brown, "How to Write a Winning Business Plan," *Forbes*, 18 June 2010, www.forbes.com; NYC DataMine website, accessed 5 March 2011, www.nyc.gov.

**2.** Brown, "How to Write a Winning Business Plan"; Michael Gerber, "The Business Plan That Always Works," *Her Business*, May/June 2004, 23–25; J. Tol Broome, Jr., "How to Write a Business Plan," *Nation's Business*, February 1993, 29–30; Albert Richards, "The Ernst & Young Business Plan Guide," *R & D Management*, April 1995, 253; David Lanchner, "How Chitchat Became a Valuable Business Plan," *Global Finance*, February 1995, 54–56; Marguerita Ashby-Berger, "My Business Plan—And What Really Happened," *Small Business Forum*, Winter 1994–1995, 24–35; Stanley R. Rich and David E. Gumpert, *Business Plans That Win $$$* (New York: Harper & Row, 1985).

**3.** David A. Garvin and Michael A. Roberto, "What You Don't Know About Making Decisions," Harvard Business School Working Knowledge, 15 October 2001, http://hbswk.hbs.edu.

**4.** Iris Varner, *Contemporary Business Report Writing*, 2nd ed. (Chicago: Dryden Press, 1991), 170.

**5.** Curt Kampmeier, "How to Write a Proposal That's Accepted Every Time," *Consulting to Management*, September 2000, 62.

**6.** Qvidian website, accessed 28 February 2011, www.qvidian.com; Dan MacDougall, "Orchestrating Your Proposal," *Canadian Consulting Engineer*, March–April 2003, 51–56.

**7.** "Why What You Learned in School About Writing Was Wrong," CapturePlanning.com, accessed 9 December 2008, www .captureplanning.com.

**8.** Adapted from SXSW website, accessed 2 March 2011, http://sxsw .com; Catherine Holahan and Spencer E. Ante, "SXSW: Where Tech Mingles with Music," *Business Week*, 7 March 2008, www.businessweek .com.

## LEARNING OBJECTIVES

After studying this chapter, you will be able to

**1** Explain how to adapt to your audiences when writing reports and proposals.

**2** Name five characteristics of effective report content and list the topics commonly covered in the introduction, body, and close of formal reports.

**3** List six strategies to strengthen a proposal argument and list the topics commonly covered in the introduction, body, and close of proposals.

**4** Summarize the four tasks involved in completing business reports and proposals.

**5** Identify the elements to include in a request for proposal (RFP).

### MyBCommLab®

⭐ **Improve Your Grade!** Over 10 million students improved their results using the Pearson MyLabs. Visit **mybcommlab.com** for simulations, tutorials, and end-of-chapter problems.

## Garage Technology Ventures www.garage.com

The "garage" is a well-known metaphor in entrepreneurial circles that dates back at least to the founding of the giant technology company Hewlett-Packard, which was literally started in a garage in the late 1930s by Bill Hewlett and Dave Packard. More than the physical space of a workshop, the garage suggests a mindset, with inspired visionaries working on shoestring budgets in humble surroundings but pouring their hearts and minds into business ideas that can change the world—or at least make a lot of money.

Noted entrepreneur, author, speaker, and investor Guy Kawasaki and his colleagues carry on this tradition with a venture capital firm called, appropriately enough, Garage Technology Ventures. Garage is based in the heart of Silicon Valley: Palo Alto, California (which also happens to be the current and ancestral home of Hewlett-Packard).

Venture capitalists (VCs) invest in young companies, primarily in high-technology fields, and help them through the early growth stages with an eye toward recouping their investments when the company gets big enough to go public or is sold to another company. The personal finance website Motley Fool and the online music service Pandora are among the many firms in which Garage has invested in recent years.

Amy E. Price / Getty Images

Guy Kawasaki, one of the founders of the venture capital firm Garage Technology Ventures, advises entrepreneurs to craft concise, compelling summaries of their businesses before pitching their ideas to investors.

In the Silicon Valley VC culture, the process of presenting a new company to potential investors usually involves a short presentation, "the pitch," that is supported by the *executive summary* from a business plan. The entire plan might become part of the conversation later, but in the early stages the executive summary has to carry the load by itself.

After listening to thousands of pitches and reading thousands of business plans, the Garage team has a clear idea of what it takes for entrepreneurs to get the attention—and money—of a VC. Garage advises entrepreneurs to keep their executive summaries under 20 pages and to include nine particular elements, starting with "the grab," a compelling one- or two-sentence statement that gets an investor's attention. Following that are the customer problems the entrepreneurs aim to solve, the solution they propose, and the business opportunity that this offering represents. The next three items describe the new company's competitive advantages, its

business model (how it will generate revenue), and the key personnel involved in the new venture—including why these are the right people to drive the new company forward. The final two elements are directly about money: "the promise," which is how much investors can expect to earn from their stake in the company, followed by "the ask," which is how much money the new company wants.

This is a lot of information to pack into a relatively short document, but doing so is essential. If investors don't understand the business model or don't think the startup team has honed in on a real market opportunity, they won't keep listening. Fortunately, entrepreneurs can tap into the expertise of those who have gone before them and use this advice to craft powerful business plans that get noticed. The Garage team is waiting with enthusiastic encouragement, too. As the company puts it, "We are on your side. So please help us get to know you better by telling your story clearly and concisely."[1]

# Writing Reports and Proposals: Adapting to Your Audience

**1** LEARNING OBJECTIVE
Explain how to adapt to your audiences when writing reports and proposals.

Guy Kawasaki (profiled in the chapter-opening Communication Close-Up) and all other successful report writers will tell you that reports and proposals are most effective when they are adapted to the needs and interests of their intended audiences. To ensure your own success with reports, be sensitive to audience needs, build strong relationships with your audience, and control your style and tone.

## BEING SENSITIVE TO YOUR AUDIENCE'S NEEDS

The "you" attitude is especially important with long or complex reports because they demand a lot from readers.

Chapter 5 discusses four aspects of audience sensitivity, and all four apply to reports and proposals: adopting the "you" attitude, maintaining a strong sense of etiquette, emphasizing the positive, and using bias-free language. Reports and proposals that are highly technical, complex, or lengthy can put heavy demands on readers, so the "you" attitude takes on special importance with these messages.

In addition, various audience members can have widely different information needs. For instance, if you're reporting on the results of a customer satisfaction survey, the service manager might want every detail, whereas the president might want only a top-level summary. With previews, summaries, appendixes, and other elements, you can meet the needs of a diverse audience—provided that you plan for these elements in advance.

Help your audiences navigate through your reports by providing clear directions to key pieces of content.

Today's readers often lack the time or the inclination to plow through long reports page by page or screen by screen. They typically want to browse quickly, find a section of interest, dive in for details, browse for another section, and so on. If you want readers to understand and accept your message, help them navigate your document by using headings and links, smooth transitions, and previews and reviews.

**REAL-TIME UPDATES**
LEARN MORE BY WATCHING THIS PRESENTATION
**Need clarification about plagiarism?**
Get helpful tips for avoiding plagiarism when researching and writing reports. Go to http://real-timeupdates .com/bct12 and click on Learn More. If you are using MyBCommLab, you can access Real-Time Updates within each chapter or under Student Study Tools.

### Headings

As you learned in Chapter 6, headings are brief titles that cue readers about the content of sections that follow. They improve a document's readability and are especially useful for identifying the framework of a report. They also visually indicate shifts from one idea to the next and, when used in a combination of levels, help readers see the relationship between subordinate and main ideas. In addition, busy readers can quickly understand the gist of a document simply by scanning the headings. In online reports, headings serve all these functions, plus they can be used to provide links to other sections and other websites.

Many companies specify a format for headings, either through style guides or document templates. If yours does, use that recommended format. If you are creating your own scheme, make sure the hierarchy of headings and subheadings is clear. If you have three levels of headings in a report, for example, you might use 20-point bold type for the first level headings, 16 points for the second level, and 12 points for the third level:

# First level

## Second level

### Third level

Another option is to put the first level headings in all capital letters or to emphasize them using color. The sample report on pages 425–439 does both of these, for instance.

## Transitions

Transitions (see Chapter 5) help readers move from one section of a report to the next and from key point to key point within sections. Transitions can be words, sentences, or complete paragraphs. Here's an example:

*Transitions connect ideas by helping readers move from one thought to the next.*

> . . . As you can see, our profits have decreased by 12 percent over the past eight months.
>
> To counteract this decline in profits, we can explore alternatives. First, we can raise our selling prices. Second, we can work to reduce our manufacturing costs. Third, we can introduce new products that will support higher profit margins. However, each of these alternatives has both advantages and disadvantages.

The phrase *As you can see* alerts readers to the fact that they are reading a summary of the information just presented. The phrase *this decline in profits* refers to the previous paragraph, to let readers know that the text will be saying something else about that topic. The words *first, second,* and *third* help readers stay on track as the three alternatives are introduced, and the word *however* alerts readers to the fact that evaluating the three alternatives requires some additional discussion. Effective transitions such as these can help readers summarize and remember what they've learned so far while giving them a mental framework to process new information.

## Previews and Reviews

*Preview sections* introduce important topics by helping readers get ready for new information; they are particularly helpful when the information is complex, unexpected, or unfamiliar. Think of a preview as an opportunity for readers to arrange their mental file folders before you start giving them information to put in those folders.

*Previews help readers prepare for upcoming information, and reviews help them verify and clarify what they've just read.*

*Review sections* come after a body of material and summarize the information just covered. They help readers absorb details while keeping track of the big picture. Long reports and those dealing with complex subjects can often benefit from multiple review sections, one at the end of every major subject block, as well as a more comprehensive review at the very end of a document.

Previews and reviews can be written in sentence format, in bulleted lists, or using a combination of the two. Both are effective, but bullets can increase your document's readability by adding white space to the document design. Consider the following preview, shown using both formats:

| Sentence Format | Bulleted List |
|---|---|
| The next section discusses the advantages of online advertising. Among them are currency, global reach, affordability, and interactivity. | As the next section shows, online advertising has four advantages:<br>• Currency<br>• Global reach<br>• Affordability<br>• Interactivity |

For more on writing effective bullets and lists, see "Using Lists to Clarify and Emphasize" on page 151 in Chapter 6.

## BUILDING STRONG RELATIONSHIPS WITH YOUR AUDIENCE

Your reports may continue to be read for months or years after you write them—and reach audiences you never envisioned.

Building relationships with your readers starts with planning how to adapt your style and language to meet their needs and expectations. Bear in mind that some reports— particularly those that can be transmitted online—can take on lives of their own, reaching a wider audience than you ever imagined and being read years after you write them. Consequently, choose your content and language with care. Also, because many companies have specific guidelines for communicating with public audiences, make sure you're aware of these preferences before you start writing.

As discussed in Chapter 5, establishing your credibility is vital to successful communication. To gain your audience's trust, research all sides of your topic and document your findings with credible sources. Also, be aware that setting audience expectations too high can lead to problems with your credibility if you can't deliver everything people expect you to, so take particular care with the introductory sections of important reports.

## CONTROLLING YOUR STYLE AND TONE

Adjust the level of formality to match the situation and your audience's expectations.

If you know your readers reasonably well and your report is likely to meet with their approval, you can adopt a fairly informal tone—provided that doing so is acceptable in the situation and in your company's culture. To make your tone less formal, refer to readers as *you*, and refer to yourself as *I* (or *we*, if there are multiple report authors).

A more formal tone is usually appropriate for longer reports, especially those that deal with controversial or complex information. You'll also want to use a more formal tone when your report will be sent to other parts of the organization or to outsiders, such as customers, suppliers, or members of the community (see Figure 15.1).

If the situation calls for a more formal tone, use the impersonal journalism style, eliminating all references to *you* and *I* (including *we*, *us*, and *our*). When you use an impersonal style, you impose a controlled distance between you and your readers. Your tone is not only objective but also businesslike and unemotional. Be careful to avoid jokes, and minimize the use of similes, metaphors, and overly colorful language.

However, when crafting a more formal tone, take care not to go overboard, or you'll end up sounding stiff or dull. In addition, don't inadvertently slip into the passive voice. You can avoid this potential weakness by making the report content itself the actor in a sentence. For example, to convert "I think we should buy TramCo" to a more formal tone, you could write "The financial analysis clearly shows that buying TramCo is the best alternative."

**REAL-TIME UPDATES**

LEARN MORE BY WATCHING THIS PRESENTATION

**The ten worst mistakes to make in a business plan**

Entrepreneur Tim Berry tells you what to watch out for. Go to http://real-timeupdates.com/bct12 and click on Learn More. If you are using MyBCommLab, you can access Real-Time Updates within each chapter or under Student Study Tools.

Long and somewhat rigorous sentences help give the report its formal tone. For a more consumer-oriented publication, this writing could certainly be simplified.

Eating and physical activity patterns that are focused on consuming fewer calories, making informed food choices, and being physically active can help people attain and maintain a healthy weight, reduce their risk of chronic disease, and promote overall health. The *Dietary Guidelines for Americans, 2010* exemplifies these strategies through recommendations that accommodate the food preferences, cultural traditions, and customs of the many and diverse groups who live in the United States.

By law (Public Law 101-445, Title III, 7 U.S.C. 5301 et seq.), *Dietary Guidelines for Americans* is reviewed, updated if necessary, and published every 5 years. The U.S. Department of Agriculture (USDA) and the U.S. Department of Health and Human Services (HHS) jointly create each edition. *Dietary Guidelines for Americans, 2010* is based on the *Report of the Dietary Guidelines Advisory Committee on the Dietary Guidelines for Americans, 2010* and consideration of Federal agency and public comments.

Dietary Guidelines recommendations traditionally have been intended for healthy Americans ages 2 years and older. However, *Dietary Guidelines for Americans, 2010* is being released at a time of rising concern about the health of the American population. Poor diet and physical inactivity are the most important factors contributing to an epidemic of overweight and obesity affecting men, women, and children in all segments of our society. Even in the absence of overweight, poor diet and physical inactivity are associated with major causes of morbidity and mortality in the United States. Therefore, the *Dietary Guidelines for Americans, 2010* is intended for Americans ages 2 years and older, including those at increased risk of chronic disease.

*Dietary Guidelines for Americans, 2010* also recognizes that in recent years nearly 15 percent of American households have been unable to acquire adequate food to meet their needs.[1] This dietary guidance can help them maximize the nutritional content of

A less-formal report might've said something along the lines of "Poor diet and physical inactivity are killing U.S. citizens" instead of the more formal (and more precise) "are associated with major causes of morbidity and mortality."

This paragraph mentions the troubling statistic that 15 percent of U.S. households can't afford to meet basic nutritional requirements, but because the report is presenting dietary recommendations and not public policy statements about economics or other issues, the tone is objective and dispassionate.

1. Nord M, Coleman-Jensen A, Andrews M, Carlson S. Household food security in the United States, 2009. Washington (DC): U.S. Department of Agriculture, Economic Research Service. 2010 Nov. Economic Research Report No. ERR-108. Available from http://www.ers.usda.gov/publications/err108.

viii    DIETARY GUIDELINES FOR AMERICANS, 2010

**Figure 15.1  Achieving the Appropriate Tone for a Report**    *(continued)*

This report excerpt (part of the executive summary of the *Dietary Guidelines for Americans* published by the U.S. Department of Agriculture and the U.S. Department of Health and Human Services) uses a number of techniques to create a formal tone. This is a formal policy document whose intended readers are educators, government regulators, and others charged with using the information to help inform consumers. If the document had been written with consumers in mind, you can imagine how the tone might have been lighter and less formal.

*Source:* Dietary Guidelines for Americans 2010 published by the U.S. Department of Agriculture and the U.S. Department of Health and Human Services.

their meals. Many other Americans consume less than optimal intake of certain nutrients even though they have adequate resources for a healthy diet. This dietary guidance and nutrition information can help them choose a healthy, nutritionally adequate diet.

The intent of the Dietary Guidelines is to summarize and synthesize knowledge about individual nutrients and food components into an interrelated set of recommendations for healthy eating that can be adopted by the public. Taken together, the Dietary Guidelines recommendations encompass two overarching concepts:

• **Maintain calorie balance over time to achieve and sustain a healthy weight.** People who are most successful at achieving and maintaining a healthy weight do so through continued attention to consuming only enough calories from foods and beverages to meet their needs and by being physically active. To curb the obesity epidemic and improve their health, many Americans must decrease the calories they consume and increase the calories they expend through physical activity.

• **Focus on consuming nutrient-dense foods and beverages.** Americans currently consume too much sodium and too many calories from solid fats, added sugars, and refined grains.[2] These replace nutrient-dense foods and beverages and make it difficult for people to achieve recommended nutrient intake while controlling calorie and sodium intake. A healthy eating pattern limits intake of sodium, solid fats, added sugars, and refined grains and emphasizes nutrient-dense foods and beverages—vegetables, fruits, whole grains, fat-free or low-fat milk and milk products,[3] seafood, lean meats and poultry, eggs, beans and peas, and nuts and seeds.

A basic premise of the Dietary Guidelines is that nutrient needs should be met primarily through consuming foods. In certain cases, fortified foods and dietary supplements may be useful in providing one or more nutrients that otherwise might be consumed in less than recommended amounts. Two eating patterns that embody the Dietary Guidelines are the USDA Food Patterns and their vegetarian adaptations and the DASH (Dietary Approaches to Stop Hypertension) Eating Plan.

A healthy eating pattern needs not only to promote health and help to decrease the risk of chronic diseases, but it also should prevent foodborne illness. Four basic food safety principles (Clean, Separate, Cook, and Chill) work together to reduce the risk of foodborne illnesses. In addition, some foods (such as milks, cheeses, and juices that have not been pasteurized, and undercooked animal foods) pose high risk for foodborne illness and should be avoided.

The information in the *Dietary Guidelines for Americans* is used in developing educational materials and aiding policymakers in designing and carrying out nutrition-related programs, including Federal food, nutrition education, and information programs. In addition, the *Dietary Guidelines for Americans* has the potential to offer authoritative statements as provided for in the Food and Drug Administration Modernization Act (FDAMA).

The following are the *Dietary Guidelines for Americans, 2010* Key Recommendations, listed by the chapter in which they are discussed in detail. These Key Recommendations are the most important in terms of their implications for improving public health.[4] To get the full benefit, individuals should carry out the Dietary Guidelines recommendations in their entirety as part of an overall healthy eating pattern.

*This is an example of a sentence that is precise and uses language appropriate for the purpose of this report. In contrast, a document aimed primarily at consumers might've said "We've converted the latest nutritional insights into recommendations for healthy eating."*

*In a less-formal report, the authors might've written "One of our basic premises is that nutrient needs should be met primarily through consuming foods" or even "You should meet your nutrient needs by eating food, not by taking supplements." However, to maintain a formal tone, they avoid both first- and second-person usage.*

2. Added sugars: Caloric sweeteners that are added to foods during processing, preparation, or consumed separately. Solid fats: Fats with a high content of saturated and/or *trans* fatty acids, which are usually solid at room temperature. Refined grains: Grains and grain products missing the bran, germ, and/or endosperm; any grain product that is not a whole grain.
3. Milk and milk products also can be referred to as dairy products.
4. Information on the type and strength of evidence supporting the Dietary Guidelines recommendations can be found at http://www.nutritionevidencelibrary.gov.

DIETARY GUIDELINES FOR AMERICANS, 2010          ix

**Figure 15.1** **Achieving the Appropriate Tone for a Report** *(continued)*

# Drafting Report Content

**2** **LEARNING OBJECTIVE**
Name five characteristics of effective report content and list the topics commonly covered in the introduction, body, and close of formal reports.

With a clear picture of how you need to adapt to your audience, you're ready to begin composing your first draft. Before you put those first words down on paper, though, review your outline one last time. Verify that the organization you've chosen makes sense, given everything you've learned about your topic so far. Also, review the wording of the headings and subheadings to make sure they establish the right tone. For a hard-hitting, direct tone, use informative phrasing ("Quality Problems Result in Nearly 500 Customer Defections Every Year"). For an objective, indirect tone, use descriptive phrasing ("Effects of Product Quality on Customer Retention").

Writing lengthy reports and proposals can be a huge task, so be sure to take advantage of technological tools to help throughout the process. In addition to the tools described under "Using Technology to Compose and Shape Your Messages" on page 136, look for opportunities to use *linked and embedded documents* to incorporate graphics, spreadsheets, databases, and other elements produced in other software programs. For instance, in Microsoft Office, you can choose to either *link* to another file (which ensures that changes in that file are reflected in your file) or *embed* another file (which doesn't include this automatic updating feature).

Like other written business communications, reports and proposals have three main sections: an introduction (or *opening*), a body, and a close. The content and length of each section vary with the type and purpose of the document, the document's organizational structure, the length and depth of the material, the document's degree of formality, and your relationship with your audience.

At a minimum, an effective *introduction* accomplishes these four tasks:

- It helps the reader understand the context of the report by tying it to a problem or an assignment.
- It introduces the subject matter and indicates why it is important.
- It previews the main idea (if you're using the direct approach).
- It establishes the tone and the writer's relationship with the audience.

> The introduction needs to put the report in context for the reader, introduce the subject, preview main ideas, and establish the tone of the document.

The *body* presents, analyzes, and interprets the information gathered during your investigation and supports your recommendations or conclusions. The length and content of the body can vary widely based on the subject matter.

> The body of your report presents, analyzes, and interprets the information you gathered during your investigation.

The *close* has three important functions:

- It summarizes your key points.
- It emphasizes the benefits to the reader if the document suggests a change or some other course of action.
- It brings all the action items together in one place.

> Your close is often the last opportunity to get your message across, so make it clear and compelling.

Research shows that the final section of a report or proposal leaves a strong lasting impression. The close gives you one last chance to make sure that your report says what you intended.[2] In fact, readers who are in a hurry might skip the body of the report and read only the summary, so make sure it carries a strong, clear message.

> The close might be the only part of your report some readers have time for, so make sure it conveys the full weight of your message.

Your credibility and prospects for the future are on the line with every business report you write, so make sure your content is

- **Accurate.** Information presented in a report must be factually correct. When writing reports, be sure to double-check your facts and references in addition to checking for typos. If an audience ever gets the inkling that your information is shaky, they'll start to view all your work with a skeptical eye.
- **Complete.** To help audiences make informed decisions, include all the information necessary for readers to understand the situation, problem, or proposal. Support all key assertions, using an appropriate combination of illustrations, explanations, and facts.[3] Tell your readers what they need to know—no more, no less—and present the information in a way that is geared to their needs. In a recent Tellabs annual report, for example, George Stenitzer and his team provided a concise and easily understandable overview of the company's complex and technical product line. Rather than burying the audience under technical details, the product overview clearly identifies how the company's products deliver the benefits that Internet users want and how the products offer business advantages to Tellabs's customers. The subject matter is presented in a way that any investor interested in the company's stock can comprehend.[4]
- **Balanced.** It's important to present all sides of the issue fairly and equitably and to include all the essential information, even if some of it doesn't support your line of reasoning. Omitting relevant information or facts can bias your report.
- **Clear and logical.** Save your readers time by making sure your sentences are uncluttered, contain well-chosen words,

> Effective report content is accurate, complete, balanced, clear, logical, and properly documented.

**REAL-TIME UPDATES**

LEARN MORE BY VISITING THIS WEBSITE

**Get practical advice on developing research reports**

The Online Writing Lab offers advice on developing all the sections of a typical research report. Go to http://real-timeupdates .com/bct12 and click on Learn More. If you are using MyBCommLab, you can access Real-Time Updates within each chapter or under Student Study Tools.

and proceed logically. To help your readers move from one point to the next, make your transitions clear and logical. For a successful report, identify the ideas that belong together and organize them in a way that's easy to understand.[5]

- **Documented properly.** If you use primary and secondary sources for your report or proposal, be sure to properly document and give credit to your sources, as Chapter 13 explains.

# Drafting Proposal Content

**3   LEARNING OBJECTIVE**
List six strategies to strengthen a proposal argument and list the topics commonly covered in the introduction, body, and close of proposals.

The AIDA model you learned in Chapter 12 works well for proposals, although you may need to adapt it if you're responding to an RFP.

If you're writing an unsolicited proposal, you have some latitude in the scope and organization of content. However, the scope and organization of a solicited proposal are usually governed by the request for proposals. Most RFPs spell out precisely what you should cover and in what order. This uniformity lets the recipient evaluate competing proposals in a systematic way.

The general purpose of any proposal is to persuade readers to do something, such as purchase goods or services, fund a project, or implement a program. Thus, your writing approach for a proposal is similar to that used for persuasive sales messages (see Chapter 12). Your proposal must sell your audience on your ideas, product, service, methods, and company. As with any other persuasive message, you can use the AIDA model to gain attention, build interest, create desire, and motivate action (of course, you may need to adapt it if you're responding to an RFP or working within some other constraints). Here are some additional strategies to strengthen your persuasive argument:[6]

- **Demonstrate your knowledge.** Everything you write should show the reader that you have the knowledge and experience to solve the problem or address the opportunity outlined in your proposal.
- **Provide concrete information and examples.** Avoid vague, unsupported generalizations such as "We are losing money on this program." Instead, provide quantifiable details such as the amount of money being lost, how, why, and so on. Explain how much money your proposed solution will save. Spell out your plan and give details on how the job will be done.
- **Research the competition.** Find out what alternatives your audience might choose over your proposal so that you can emphasize why your solution is the optimum choice. In some cases, potential customers face a "buy or build" decision, in which they must choose between buying a solution from an external party and building it themselves. In these cases, you are effectively competing against your target customers.

Business proposals need to provide more than just attractive ideas—readers look for evidence of practical, achievable solutions.

- **Prove that your proposal is workable.** Your proposal must be appropriate and feasible for your audience. It should be consistent with your audience's capabilities. For instance, your proposal would be pointless if it recommended a plan of action that requires three times the number of available employees or twice the available budget.
- **Adopt the "you" attitude.** Relate your product, service, or personnel to the reader's exact needs, either as stated in the RFP for a solicited proposal or as discovered through your own investigation for an unsolicited proposal.
- **Package your proposal attractively.** Make sure your proposal is letter perfect, inviting, and readable. Readers will prejudge the quality of your products or services by the proposal you submit. Errors, omissions, and inconsistencies will work against you—and may even cost you important career and business opportunities.

Proposals in various industries often have their own special challenges as well. For instance, management consultants have to convince every potential client that they have the skills and knowledge to solve the client's problem—without giving away the answer for free in the proposal. In other industries, such as transportation services, bidders may be asked to compute hundreds or thousands of individual pricing scenarios. Hands-on experience goes a long way when you're deciding what to include and exclude in a report; whenever possible, get advice from a senior colleague who's been through it before.

Consider using proposal-writing software if you and your company need to submit proposals as a routine part of doing business. These programs can automatically personalize proposals, ensure proper structure (making sure you don't forget any sections, for instance), organize storage of all your boilerplate text, integrate contact information from sales databases, scan RFPs to identify questions (and even assign them to content experts), and fill in preliminary answers to common questions from a centralized knowledge base.[7]

As with reports, approach proposals by identifying the pieces to include in the introduction, body, and close. For solicited proposals, always follow the instructions in the RFP, but here are some guidelines for unsolicited proposals. The introduction presents and summarizes the problem you want to solve or the opportunity you want to pursue, along with your proposed solution. The introduction orients readers to the remainder of the report. If your proposal is solicited, its introduction should refer to the RFP so that readers know which RFP you're responding to. If your proposal is unsolicited, your introduction should mention any factors that led you to submit your proposal, such as prior conversations with members of the recipient organization's staff.

The proposal's body gives complete details on the proposed solution and specifies what the anticipated results will be. Because a proposal is by definition a persuasive message, your audience expects you to promote your offering in a confident, professional manner. Even when you're expressing an idea you believe in passionately, be sure to maintain an objective tone so that you don't risk overselling your message.

> Readers understand that a proposal is a persuasive message, so they're willing to accommodate a promotional style—as long as it is professional and focused on their needs.

The close of a proposal generally summarizes the key points, emphasizes the benefits readers will realize from your solution, summarizes the merits of your approach, restates why you and your firm are the ones to perform the service or provide the products in question, and asks for a decision from readers. The close is your last opportunity to persuade readers to accept your proposal. In both formal and informal proposals, make this section relatively brief, assertive (but not brash or abrupt), and confident.

See Table 15.1 on the next page for a summary of the content to include in reports and proposals. You can use this table as a handy reference whenever you need to write a report in school or on the job.

# Completing Reports and Proposals

As with shorter messages (Chapter 5), when you have finished your first draft, you need to perform four tasks to complete your document: revise, produce, proofread, and distribute. The revision process is essentially the same for reports as for other business messages, although it may take considerably longer, depending on the length and complexity of your documents. Evaluate your organization, style, and tone, making sure your content is clear, logical, and reader oriented. Then work to improve the report's readability by varying sentence length, keeping paragraphs short, using lists and bullets, and adding headings and subheadings. Remember that even minor mistakes can affect your credibility.

> **4  LEARNING OBJECTIVE**
> Summarize the four tasks involved in completing business reports and proposals.

> The revision process for long reports can take considerable time, so be sure to plan ahead.

Tight, efficient writing that is easy to skim is always a plus, but it's especially important for impatient online audiences.[8] Review online content carefully; strip out all information that doesn't meet audience needs and condense everything else as much as possible. Audiences will gladly return to sites that deliver quality information quickly—and they'll avoid sites that don't.

> Tight, efficient writing is especially important with online content.

After assembling your report or proposal in its final form, review it thoroughly one last time, looking for inconsistencies, errors, and missing components. Don't forget to proof your visuals thoroughly and make sure they are positioned correctly. For online reports, make sure all links work as expected and all necessary files are active and available. If you need specific tips on proofreading documents, look back at Chapter 5.

## PRODUCING FORMAL REPORTS AND PROPOSALS

Formal reports and proposals can include a variety of features beyond the text and visuals (see Table 15.2 on page 419). Most of these elements provide additional information; a few are more decorative and add a degree of formality.

> The number and variety of parts you include in a report depend on the type of report, audience requirements, organizational expectations, and report length.

One of the most important elements to consider is an introductory feature that helps time-pressed readers get a sense of what's in the document or even get all the key points without reading the document. A **synopsis**—sometimes called an **abstract**—is a brief overview (one page or less) of a report's most important points. The phrasing of a synopsis can be *informative* (presenting the main points in the order in which they appear in the text) if you're using the direct approach or *descriptive* (simply describing what the report is about, without "giving away the ending") if you're using the indirect approach. As an alternative to a synopsis or an abstract, a longer report may include an **executive summary**—a fully

> A synopsis is a brief overview of a report's key points; an executive summary is a fully developed "mini" version of the report.

## TABLE 15.1 | Content Elements to Consider for Reports and Proposals

| Reports | Proposals |
|---|---|
| **Introduction:** Establish the context, identify the subject, preview main ideas (if using the direct approach), establish tone and reader relationship. | **Introduction:** Identify the problem you intend to solve or the opportunity you want to pursue. |
| • **Authorization.** Reiterate who authorized the report, if applicable.<br>• **Problem/purpose.** Explain the reason for the report's existence and what the report will achieve.<br>• **Scope.** Describe what will and won't be covered in the report.<br>• **Background.** Review historical conditions or factors that led up to the report.<br>• **Sources and methods.** Discuss the primary and secondary sources consulted and methods used.<br>• **Definitions.** List terms and their definitions, including any terms that might be misinterpreted. Terms may also be defined in the body, explanatory notes, or glossary.<br>• **Limitations.** Discuss factors beyond your control that affect report quality (but do not use this as an excuse for poor research or a poorly written report).<br>• **Report organization.** Identify the topics to be covered and in what order. | • **Background or statement of the problem.** Briefly review the situation at hand, establish a need for action, and explain how things could be better. In unsolicited proposals, convince readers that a problem or an opportunity exists.<br>• **Solution.** Briefly describe the change you propose, highlighting your key selling points and their benefits to show how your proposal will solve the reader's problem.<br>• **Scope.** State the boundaries of the proposal—what you will and will not do.<br>• **Report organization.** Orient the reader to the remainder of the proposal and call attention to the major divisions of thought. |
| **Body:** Present relevant information and support your recommendations or conclusions. | **Body:** Give complete details on the proposed solution and describe anticipated results. |
| • **Explanations.** Give complete details of the problem, project, or idea.<br>• **Facts, statistical evidence, and trends.** Lay out the results of studies or investigations.<br>• **Analysis of action.** Discuss potential courses of action.<br>• **Pros and cons.** Explain advantages, disadvantages, costs, and benefits of a particular course of action.<br>• **Procedures.** Outline steps for a process.<br>• **Methods and approaches.** Discuss how you've studied a problem (or gathered evidence) and arrived at your solution (or collected your data).<br>• **Criteria.** Describe the benchmarks for evaluating options and alternatives.<br>• **Conclusions and recommendations.** Discuss what you believe the evidence reveals and what you propose should be done about it.<br>• **Support.** Give the reasons behind your conclusions or recommendations. | • **Facts and evidence to support your conclusions.** Give complete details of the proposed solution and anticipated results.<br>• **Proposed approach.** Describe your concept, product, or service. Stress reader benefits and emphasize any advantages you have over your competitors.<br>• **Work plan.** Describe how you'll accomplish what must be done (unless you're providing a standard, off-the-shelf item). Explain the steps you'll take, their timing, the methods or resources you'll use, and the person(s) responsible. State when work will begin, how it will be divided into stages, when you'll finish, and whether follow-up will be needed.<br>• **Statement of qualifications.** Describe your organization's experience, personnel, and facilities—relating it all to readers' needs. Include a list of client references.<br>• **Costs.** Prove that your costs are realistic—break them down so that readers can see the costs of labor, materials, transportation, travel, training, and other categories. |
| **Close:** Summarize key points, emphasize benefits of any recommendations, list action items; label as "Summary" or "Conclusions and Recommendations." | **Close:** Summarize key points, emphasize the benefits and advantages of your proposed solution, ask for a decision from the reader. |
| • **For direct approach.** Summarize key points (except in short reports), listing them in the order in which they appear in the body. Briefly restate your conclusions or recommendations, if appropriate.<br>• **For indirect approach.** If you haven't done so at the end of the body, present your conclusions or recommendations.<br>• **For motivating action.** Spell out exactly what should happen next and provide a schedule with specific task assignments. | • **Review of argument.** Briefly summarize the key points.<br>• **Review of reader benefits.** Briefly summarize how your proposal will help the reader.<br>• **Review of the merits of your approach.** Briefly summarize why your approach will be more effective than alternatives.<br>• **Restatement of qualifications.** For external proposals, briefly reemphasize why you and your firm should do the work.<br>• **Request.** Ask for a decision from the reader. |

developed "mini" version of the report, for readers who lack the time or motivation to read the entire document (see Figure 15.2 on page 420).

Following the body of the report, possible supplemental parts (those coming after the main text of the report or proposal) include one or more appendixes, a bibliography, and an index. In general, place supporting materials here that could be of interest to some or all of your readers but that aren't crucial to the main thrust of your message.

For an illustration of how the various parts fit together in a report, see "Report Writer's Notebook: Analyzing a Formal Report," starting on page 425.

In contrast to formal reports, synopses and executive summaries are less common in proposals. In an unsolicited proposal, the letter of transmittal should catch the reader's

**TABLE 15.2 | Production Elements to Consider for Formal Reports and Proposals**

| Reports | Proposals |
|---|---|
| **Prefatory elements** (before the introduction) | **Prefatory elements** (before the introduction) |
| • **Cover.** Include a concise title that gives readers the information they need to grasp the purpose and scope of the report. For a formal printed report, choose heavy, high-quality **cover stock**. | • **Cover, title fly, title page.** Same uses as with reports; be sure to follow any instructions in the RFP, if relevant. |
| • **Title fly.** Some formal reports open with a plain sheet of paper that has only the title of the report on it, although this is certainly not necessary. | • **Copy of or reference to the RFP.** Instead of having a letter of authorization, a solicited proposal should follow the instructions in the RFP. Some will instruct you to include the entire RFP in your proposal; others may want you to simply identify it by a name and tracking number. |
| • **Title page.** Typically includes the report title, name(s) and title(s) of the writer(s), and date of submission; this information can be put on the cover instead. | • **Synopsis or executive summary.** These components are less common in formal proposals than in reports. In an unsolicited proposal, your letter of transmittal will catch the reader's interest. In a solicited proposal, the introduction will provide an adequate preview of the contents. |
| • **Letter of authorization.** If you received written authorization to prepare the report, you may want to include that letter or memo in your report. | • **Letter of transmittal.** If the proposal is solicited, treat the transmittal letter as a positive message, highlighting those aspects of your proposal that may give you a competitive advantage. If the proposal is unsolicited, the transmittal letter should follow the advice for persuasive messages (see Chapter 9)—the letter must persuade the reader that you have something worthwhile to offer that justifies reading the proposal. |
| • **Letter of transmittal.** "Cover letter" that introduces the report and can include scope, methods, limitations, highlights of the report; offers to provide follow-on information or assistance; and acknowledges help received while preparing the report. | |
| • **Table of contents.** List all section headings and major subheadings to show the location and hierarchy of the information in the report. | |
| • **List of illustrations.** Consider including if the illustrations are particularly important, and you want to call attention to them. | |
| • **Synopsis or executive summary.** See discussion on page 417. | |
| **Supplementary elements** (after the close) | **Supplementary elements** (after the close) |
| • **Appendixes.** Additional information related to the report but not included in the main text because it is too lengthy or lacks direct relevance. List appendixes in your table of contents and refer to them as appropriate in the text. | • **Appendixes.** Same uses as with reports; be sure to follow any instructions in the RFP, if relevant. |
| • **Bibliography.** List the secondary sources you consulted; see Appendix B. | • **Résumés of key players.** For external proposals, résumés can convince readers that you have the talent to achieve the proposal's objectives. |
| • **Index.** List names, places, and subjects mentioned in the report, along with the pages on which they occur. | |

interest. In a solicited proposal, the introduction provides an adequate preview of the contents. Moreover, proposals often take the indirect approach, which means they build up to the call to action at the end of the report, and summarizing this information at the beginning could undermine the carefully structured persuasive build-up (see Figure 15.3 on page 421).

## DISTRIBUTING REPORTS AND PROPOSALS

For physical distribution of important printed reports or proposals, consider spending the extra money for a professional courier or package delivery service. Doing so can help you stand out in a crowd, and it lets you verify receipt. Alternatively, if you've prepared the document for a single person or small group in your office or the local area, delivering it in person will give you the chance to personally "introduce" the report and remind readers why they're receiving it.

For electronic distribution, unless your audience specifically requests a word processor file, provide documents as portable document format (PDF) files. Using Adobe Acrobat or similar products, you can quickly convert reports and proposals to PDF files that are easy to share electronically. PDFs are generally considered safer than word processor files, but keep in mind that they can also be used to transmit computer viruses.[9] For information on protecting yourself and your readers when using PDF files, visit www.adobe.com/security.

Many businesses use the Adobe portable document format (PDF) to distribute reports electronically.

If your company or client expects you to distribute your reports via a web-based content management system, a shared workspace, or some other online location, double-check that you've uploaded the correct file(s) to the correct location. Verify the on-screen display of your reports after you've posted them, making sure graphics, charts, links, and other elements are in place and operational.

The title identifies the report and labels the section as an executive summary.

The opening paragraph offers historical perspective on the Model Ports program.

The next paragraph discusses the survey that was conducted to assess travelers' experiences under the program.

Starting here, the major points uncovered in the research are listed, along with quick-read tables and charts.

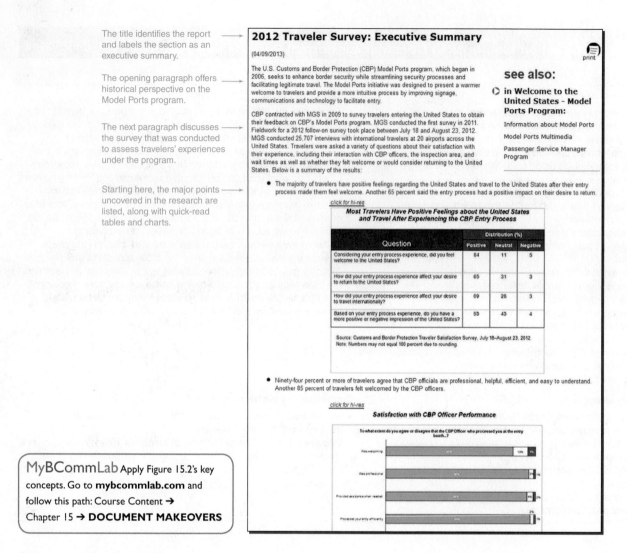

## 2012 Traveler Survey: Executive Summary

(04/09/2013)

The U.S. Customs and Border Protection (CBP) Model Ports program, which began in 2006, seeks to enhance border security while streamlining security processes and facilitating legitimate travel. The Model Ports initiative was designed to present a warmer welcome to travelers and provide a more intuitive process by improving signage, communications and technology to facilitate entry.

CBP contracted with MGS in 2009 to survey travelers entering the United States to obtain their feedback on CBP's Model Ports program. MGS conducted the first survey in 2011. Fieldwork for a 2012 follow-on survey took place between July 18 and August 23, 2012. MGS conducted 25,707 interviews with international travelers at 20 airports across the United States. Travelers were asked a variety of questions about their satisfaction with their experience, including their interaction with CBP officers, the inspection area, and wait times as well as whether they felt welcome or would consider returning to the United States. Below is a summary of the results:

**see also:**

○ in Welcome to the United States - Model Ports Program:

Information about Model Ports

Model Ports Multimedia

Passenger Service Manager Program

- The majority of travelers have positive feelings regarding the United States and travel to the United States after their entry process made them feel welcome. Another 65 percent said the entry process had a positive impact on their desire to return.

*click for hi-res*

**Most Travelers Have Positive Feelings about the United States and Travel After Experiencing the CBP Entry Process**

| Question | Distribution (%) | | |
|---|---|---|---|
| | Positive | Neutral | Negative |
| Considering your entry process experience, did you feel welcome to the United States? | 84 | 11 | 5 |
| How did your entry process experience affect your desire to return to the United States? | 65 | 31 | 3 |
| How did your entry process experience affect your desire to travel internationally? | 69 | 28 | 3 |
| Based on your entry process experience, do you have a more positive or negative impression of the United States? | 53 | 43 | 4 |

Source: Customs and Border Protection Traveler Satisfaction Survey, July 18–August 23, 2012.
Note: Numbers may not equal 100 percent due to rounding.

- Ninety-four percent or more of travelers agree that CBP officials are professional, helpful, efficient, and easy to understand. Another 85 percent of travelers felt welcomed by the CBP officers.

*click for hi-res*

**Satisfaction with CBP Officer Performance**

To what extent do you agree or disagree that the CBP Officer who processed you at the entry booth..?

**Figure 15.2  Executive Summary**
This executive summary lists the major points uncovered in a survey of travelers entering the United States. With brief bullet points and simple tables and charts, the summary lets a reader get all the report highlights in a matter of minutes.

## CHECKLIST ✔ Producing Formal Reports and Proposals

**A. Prefatory parts**
- Use your company's standard report covers, if available.
- Include a concise, descriptive title on the cover.
- Include a title fly only if you want an extra-formal touch.
- On the title page, list (1) report title; (2) name, title, and address of the group or person who authorized the report; (3) name, title, and address of the group or person who prepared the report; and (4) date of submission.
- Include a copy of the letter of authorization, if appropriate.
- If responding to an RFP, follow its instructions for including a copy or referring to the RFP by name or tracking number.
- Include a letter of transmittal that introduces the report.
- Provide a table of contents in outline form, with headings worded exactly as they appear in the body of the report.

- Include a list of illustrations if the report contains a large number of them.
- Include a synopsis (brief summary of the report) or an executive summary (a condensed, "mini" version of the report) for longer reports.

**B. Text of the report**
- Draft an introduction that prepares the reader for the content that follows.
- Provide information that supports your conclusions, recommendations, or proposals in the body of the report.
- Don't overload the body with unnecessary detail.
- Close with a summary of your main idea.

**C. Supplementary parts**
- Use appendixes to provide supplementary information or supporting evidence.
- List in a bibliography any secondary sources you used.
- Provide an index if your report contains a large number of terms or ideas and is likely to be consulted over time.

O'Donnell
&
Associates, Inc.

1793 East Westerfield Road, Arlington Heights, Illinois 60005
(847) 398-1148  Fax: (847) 398-1149  Email: dod@ix.netcom.com

MyBCommLab Apply Figure 15.3's key
concepts. Go to **mybcommlab.com** and
follow this path: Course Content →
Chapter 15 → **DOCUMENT MAKEOVERS**

July 30, 2013

Ms. Joyce Colton, P.E.
AGI Builders, Inc.
1280 Spring Lake Drive
Belvidere, Illinois, 61008

Subject: Proposal No. F-0087 for AGI Builders, Elgin Manufacturing Campus

Dear Ms. Colton:

*The opening paragraph serves as an introduction.*

O'Donnell & Associates is pleased to submit the following proposal to provide
construction testing services for the mass grading operations and utility work at the Elgin
Manufacturing Campus, 126th St., Elgin, Illinois. Our company has been providing
construction-testing services in the Chicago area since 1972 and has performed numerous
large-scale geotechnical investigations across Illinois, including more than 100 at O'Hare
International Airport, Midway Airport, Meig's Field, and other airports.

*The introduction grabs the reader's attention by highlighting company qualifications.*

**Background**

*Headings divide the proposal into logical segments for easy reading.*

It is our understanding that the work consists of two projects: (1) the mass grading
operations will require approximately six months, and (2) the utility work will require
approximately three months. The two operations are scheduled as follows:

Mass Grading Operation          September 2013–February 2014
Utility Work                    March 2014–May 2014

*The project background section acknowledges the two projects and their required timeline.*

**Proposed Approach and Work Plan**

*The work plan describes the scope of the project and outlines specific tests the company will perform.*

O'Donnell & Associates will perform observation and testing services during both the
mass grading operations and the excavation and backfilling of the underground utilities.
Specifically, we will perform field density tests on the compacted material as required by
the job specifications using a nuclear moisture/density gauge. We will also conduct
appropriate laboratory tests such as ASTM D-1557 Modified Proctors. We will prepare
detailed reports summarizing the results of our field and laboratory testing. Fill materials
to be placed at the site may consist of natural granular materials (sand), processed
materials (crushed stone, crushed concrete, slag), or clay soils. O'Donnell & Associates will
provide qualified personnel to perform the necessary testing.

*(continued)*

**Figure 15.3   External Solicited Proposal**
This proposal was submitted by Dixon O'Donnell, vice president of O'Donnell & Associates, a
geotechnical engineering firm that conducts a variety of environmental testing services. The company
is bidding on the mass grading and utility work specified by AGI Builders. As you review this document,
pay close attention to the specific items addressed in the proposal's introduction, body, and closing.

For a reminder of the tasks involved in producing formal reports and proposals, see
"Checklist: Producing Formal Reports and Proposals," and for more information, visit
http://real-timeupdates.com/bct12 and click on Chapter 15.

# Writing Requests for Proposals

At some point in your career, you might be the one receiving proposals, and learning how
to request effective proposals will simplify the process considerably. Various organizations
handle RFPs in different ways. When writing an RFP, remember that it is more than just a
request; it's an informational report that provides potential bidders with the information they

**5 LEARNING OBJECTIVE**
Identify the elements to
include in a request for proposal
(RFP).

*The work plan also explains who will be responsible for the various tasks.*

Kevin Patel will be the lead field technician responsible for the project. A copy of Mr. Patel's résumé is included with this proposal for your review. Kevin will coordinate field activities with your job site superintendent and make sure that appropriate personnel are assigned to the job site. Overall project management will be the responsibility of Joseph Proesel. Project engineering services will be performed under the direction of Dixon O'Donnell, P.E. All field personnel assigned to the site will be familiar with and abide by the Project Site Health and Safety Plan prepared by Carlson Environmental, Inc., dated April 2013.

*The project leader's résumé is attached to the proposal, providing additional detail without cluttering up the body of the proposal.*

### Qualifications

*The qualifications section grabs attention by mentioning compelling qualifications.*

O'Donnell & Associates has been providing quality professional services since 1972 in the areas of

- Geotechnical engineering
- Materials testing and inspection
- Pavement evaluation
- Environmental services
- Engineering and technical support (CADD) services

The company provides Phase I and Phase II environmental site assessments, preparation of LUST site closure reports, installation of groundwater monitoring wells, and testing of soil/groundwater samples for environmental contaminants. Geotechnical services include all phases of soil mechanics and foundation engineering, including foundation and lateral load analysis, slope stability analysis, site preparation recommendations, seepage analysis, pavement design, and settlement analysis.

O'Donnell & Associates materials testing laboratory is certified by AASHTO Accreditation Program for the testing of Soils, Aggregate, Hot Mix Asphalt and Portland Cement Concrete. A copy of our laboratory certification is included with this proposal. In addition to in-house training, field and laboratory technicians participate in a variety of certification programs, including those sponsored by the American Concrete Institute (ACI) and Illinois Department of Transportation (IDOT).

*Describing certifications (approvals by recognized industry associations or government agencies) helps build the company's credibility.*

### Costs

On the basis of our understanding of the scope of the work, we estimate the total cost of the two projects to be $100,260.00, as follows:

*(continued)*

**Figure 15.3** **External Solicited Proposal (continued)**

*When writing an RFP, be sure to give potential respondents all the information they need to craft a meaningful response to your request.*

need to craft effective proposals. Writing an RFP demands careful consideration because it starts a process that leads to a proposal, a contract, and eventually the delivery of a product or the performance of a service. In other words, mistakes at the RFP stage can ripple throughout the process and create costly headaches for everyone involved.

An RFP's specific content will vary widely from industry to industry, but all RFPs should include some combination of the following elements:[10]

- **Company background.** Give potential bidders some background information on your organization, your business priorities, and other information they might need in order to respond in an informed manner.
- **Project description.** Put your requirements in context; are you seeking bids for routine supplies or services, or do you need a major computer system?
- **Requirements.** The requirements section should spell out everything you expect from potential vendors; don't leave anything to unstated assumptions. Will potential vendors provide key equipment, or will you? Will you expect vendors to work under confidentiality restrictions, such as a nondisclosure agreement? Who will pay if costs run higher

Ms. Joyce Colton, AGI Builders　　　　　Page 3　　　　　July 30, 2013

### Cost Estimates

| Cost Estimate: Mass Grading | Units | Rate ($) | Total Cost ($) |
|---|---|---|---|
| *Field Inspection* | | | |
| Labor | 1,320 hours | $38.50 | $ 50,820.00 |
| Nuclear Moisture Density Meter | 132 days | 35.00 | 4,620.00 |
| Vehicle Expense | 132 days | 45.00 | 5,940.00 |
| *Laboratory Testing* | | | |
| Proctor Density Tests (ASTM D-1557) | 4 tests | 130.00 | 520.00 |
| *Engineering/Project Management* | | | |
| Principal Engineer | 16 hours | 110.00 | 1,760.00 |
| Project Manager | 20 hours | 80.00 | 1,600.00 |
| Administrative Assistant | 12 hours | 50.00 | 600.00 |
| Subtotal | | | $ 65,860.00 |

| Cost Estimate: Utility Work | Units | Rate ($) | Total Cost ($) |
|---|---|---|---|
| *Field Inspection* | | | |
| Labor | 660 hours | $ 38.50 | $ 25,410.00 |
| Nuclear Moisture Density Meter | 66 days | 5.00 | 2,310.00 |
| Vehicle Expense | 66 days | 45.00 | 2,970.00 |
| *Laboratory Testing* | | | |
| Proctor Density Tests (ASTM D-1557) | 2 tests | 130.00 | 260.00 |
| *Engineering/Project Management* | | | |
| Principal Engineer | 10 hours | 110.00 | 1,100.00 |
| Project Manager | 20 hours | 80.00 | 1,600.00 |
| Administrative Assistant | 15 hours | 50.00 | 750.00 |
| Subtotal | | | $ 34,400.00 |

| **Total Project Costs** | | | **$100,260.00** |
|---|---|---|---|

This estimate assumes full-time inspection services. However, our services may also be performed on an as-requested basis, and actual charges will reflect time associated with the project. We have attached our standard fee schedule for your review. Overtime rates are for hours in excess of 8.0 hours per day, before 7:00 a.m., after 5:00 p.m., and on holidays and weekends.

A clear and complete itemization of estimated costs builds confidence in dependability of the project's financial projections.

To give the client some budgetary flexibility, the proposal offers an alternative to the fixed-fee approach—which may lower any resistance to accepting the bid.

*(continued)*

**Figure 15.3　External Solicited Proposal *(continued)***

than expected? Will you require ongoing service or support? Providing this information can be a lot of work, but again, overlooking anything at this point is likely to create considerable problems once the project gets rolling.

- **Decision criteria.** Let bidders know how you'll be making the decision. Is quality more important than cost? Will you consider only certain types of vendors or only those that use certain processes or technologies? Will you entertain bids from companies that have never worked in your particular industry? The answers to such questions not only help bidders determine whether they're right for your project but also help them craft proposals that meet your needs.

- **Proposal requirements.** Explain exactly what you expect to see in the proposal itself—which sections, what media, how many copies, and so on.

- **Submission and contact information.** A well-written RFP answers most potential questions, and it also tells people when, where, and how to respond. In addition, effective RFPs always give bidders the name of a contact within the organization who can answer detailed questions.

Ms. Joyce Colton, AGI Builders          Page 4          July 30, 2013

**Authorization**

With a staff of over 30 personnel, including registered professional engineers, resident engineers, geologists, construction inspectors, laboratory technicians, and drillers, we are confident that O'Donnell & Associates is capable of providing the services required for a project of this magnitude.

If you would like our firm to provide the services as outlined in this proposal, please sign this letter and return it to us along with a certified check in the amount of $10,000 (our retainer) by August 14, 2013. Please call me if you have any questions regarding the terms of this proposal or our approach.

Sincerely,

*Dixon O'Donnell*

Dixon O'Donnell
Vice President

Enclosures

Accepted for AGI BUILDERS, INC.

By_____     Date _____

*The brief close emphasizes the bidder's qualifications and asks for a decision.*

*The call to action clarifies the steps needed to put the project in motion.*

*The customer's signature will make the proposal a binding contract.*

Figure 15.3   **External Solicited Proposal** *(continued)*

A smart approach to managing RFPs can minimize the work involved for everyone and maximize the effectiveness of the RFP. First, identify your decision criteria and then brainstorm the information you need to measure against those criteria. Don't ask bidders to submit information about every aspect of their operations if such details aren't relevant to your decision. Making such unreasonable demands is unfair to bidders, will unnecessarily complicate your review process, and will discourage some potentially attractive bidders from responding.

Second, to get quality responses that match your unique business needs, give bidders plenty of time to respond. Successful companies are usually busy responding to other RFPs and working on other projects; you can't expect them to drop everything to focus solely on your RFP.

Third, if your company generates numerous RFPs, tracking proposals can become a full-time job. Consider establishing an online system for tracking responses automatically.[11]

# Analyzing a Formal Report

The report presented in the following pages was prepared by Linda Moreno, manager of the cost accounting department at Electrovision, a high-tech company based in Los Gatos, California. Electrovision's main product is optical character recognition equipment, which is used by the U.S. Postal Service for sorting mail. Moreno's job is to help analyze the company's costs. She has this to say about the background of the report:

> For the past three or four years, Electrovision has been on a roll. Our A-12 optical character reader was a real breakthrough, and the post office grabbed up as many as we could make. Our sales and profits kept climbing, and morale was fantastic. Everybody seemed to think that the good times would last forever. Unfortunately, everybody was wrong. When the Postal Service announced that it was postponing all new equipment purchases because of cuts in its budget, we woke up to the fact that we are essentially a one-product company with one customer. At that point, management started scrambling around looking for ways to cut costs until we could diversify our business a bit.
>
> The vice president of operations, Dennis McWilliams, asked me to help identify cost-cutting opportunities in travel and entertainment. On the basis of his personal observations, he felt that Electrovision was overly generous in its travel policies and that we might be able to save a significant amount by controlling these costs more carefully. My investigation confirmed his suspicion.
>
> I was reasonably confident that my report would be well received. I've worked with Dennis for several years and know what he likes: plenty of facts, clearly stated conclusions, and specific recommendations for what should be done next. I also knew that my report would be passed on to other Electrovision executives, so I wanted to create a good impression. I wanted the report to be accurate and thorough, visually appealing, readable, and appropriate in tone.

Masterfile

When writing the analytical report that follows, Moreno based the organization on conclusions and recommendations presented in direct order. The first two sections of the report correspond to Moreno's two main conclusions: that Electrovision's travel and entertainment costs are too high and that cuts are essential. The third section presents recommendations for achieving better control over travel and entertainment expenses. As you review the report, analyze both the mechanical aspects and the way Moreno presents her ideas. Be prepared to discuss the way the various components convey and reinforce the main message.

**Reducing Electrovision's Travel and Entertainment Costs**

Large, bold type distinguishes the title from the other elements on the cover.

Prepared for
Dennis McWilliams,
Vice President of Operations
Electrovision, Inc.

The name of the recipient, if applicable, typically comes after the title.

Generous use of white space between elements gives the cover an open feel.

Prepared by
Linda Moreno, Manager
Cost Accounting Services
Electrovision, Inc.

February 15, 2013

Dating the report gives it a feeling of currency when it is submitted and conversely, as time passes, signals to future readers that the material might be out of date at that point.

The "how-to" tone of Moreno's title is appropriate for an action-oriented report that emphasizes recommendations. A more neutral title, such as "An Analysis of Electrovision's Travel and Entertainment Costs," would be more suitable for an informational report.

**MEMORANDUM**

**TO:** Dennis McWilliams, Vice President of Operations
**FROM:** Linda Moreno, Manager of Cost Accounting Services  *LM*
**DATE:** February 15, 2013
**SUBJECT:** Reducing Electrovision's Travel and Entertainment Costs

Here is the report you requested January 28 on Electrovision's travel and entertainment costs.

Your suspicions were right. We are spending far too much on business travel. Our unwritten policy has been "anything goes," leaving us with no real control over T&E expenses. Although this hands-off approach may have been understandable when Electrovision's profits were high, we can no longer afford the luxury of going first class.

The solutions to the problem seem rather clear. We need to have someone with centralized responsibility for travel and entertainment costs, a clear statement of policy, an effective control system, and a business-oriented travel service that can optimize our travel arrangements. We should also investigate alternatives to travel, such as videoconferencing. Perhaps more important, we need to change our attitude. Instead of viewing travel funds as a bottomless supply of money, all traveling employees need to act as if they were paying the bills themselves.

Getting people to economize is not going to be easy. In the course of researching this issue, I've found that our employees are deeply attached to their generous travel privileges. I think some would almost prefer a cut in pay to a loss in travel status. We'll need a lot of top management involvement to sell people on the need for moderation. One thing is clear: People will be very bitter if we create a two-class system in which top executives get special privileges while the rest of the employees make the sacrifices.

I'm grateful to Mary Lehman and Connie McIllvain for their considerable help in rounding up and sorting through five years' worth of expense reports.

Thanks for giving me the opportunity to work on this assignment. It's been a real education. If you have any questions about the report, please give me a call.

In this report, Moreno decided to write a brief memo of transmittal and include a separate executive summary. Short reports (fewer than 10 pages) often combine the synopsis or executive summary with the memo or letter of transmittal.

## CONTENTS

## LIST OF ILLUSTRATIONS

The table of contents doesn't include any elements that appear before the "Contents" page.

The headings are worded exactly as they appear in the text.

The table lists only the page number on which a section begins, not the entire range of numbers.

Moreno lists the figures because they are all significant, and the list is fairly short.

This and other prefatory pages are numbered with Roman numerals.

Moreno included only first- and second-level headings in her table of contents, even though the report contains third-level headings. She prefers a shorter table of contents that focuses attention on the main divisions of thought. She used informative titles, which are appropriate for a report to a receptive audience.

## EXECUTIVE SUMMARY

This report analyzes Electrovision's travel and entertainment (T&E) costs and presents recommendations for reducing those costs.

### Travel and Entertainment Costs Are Too High

Travel and entertainment is a large and growing expense category for Electrovision. The company spends over $16 million per year on business travel, and these costs have been increasing by 12 percent annually. Company employees make roughly 3,390 trips each year at an average cost per trip of $4,720. Airfares are the biggest expense, followed by hotels, meals, and rental cars.

The nature of Electrovision's business does require extensive travel, but the company's costs are excessive: Our employees spend more than twice the national average on travel and entertainment. Although the location of the company's facilities may partly explain this discrepancy, the main reason for our high costs is a management style that gives employees little incentive to economize.

### Cuts Are Essential

Electrovision management now recognizes the need to gain more control over this element of costs. The company is currently entering a period of declining profits, prompting management to look for every opportunity to reduce spending. At the same time, rising airfares and hotel rates are making T&E expenses more significant.

### Electrovision Can Save $6 Million per Year

Fortunately, Electrovision has a number of excellent opportunities for reducing T&E costs. Savings of up to $6 million per year should be achievable, judging by the experience of other companies. A sensible travel-management program can save companies as much as 35 percent a year (Gilligan 39–40), and we should be able to save even more, since we purchase many more business-class tickets than the average. Four steps will help us cut costs:

1. Hire a director of travel and entertainment to assume overall responsibility for T&E spending, policies, and technologies, including the hiring and management of a national travel agency.
2. Educate employees on the need for cost containment, both in avoiding unnecessary travel and reducing costs when travel is necessary.
3. Negotiate preferential rates with travel providers.
4. Implement technological alternatives to travel, such as virtual meetings.

As necessary as these changes are, they will likely hurt morale, at least in the short term. Management will need to make a determined effort to explain the rationale for reduced spending. By exercising moderation in their own travel arrangements, Electrovision executives can set a good example and help other employees accept the changes. On the plus side, using travel alternatives such as web conferencing will reduce the travel burden on many employees and help them balance their business and personal lives.

iv

Moreno decided to include an executive summary because her report is aimed at a mixed audience, some of whom are interested in the details of her report and others who just want the "big picture." The executive summary is aimed at the second group, giving them enough information to make a decision without burdening them with the task of reading the entire report.

Her writing style matches the serious nature of the content without sounding distant or stiff. Moreno chose the formal approach because several members of her audience are considerably higher up in the organization, and she did not want to sound too familiar. In addition, her company prefers the impersonal style for formal reports.

# REDUCING ELECTROVISION'S TRAVEL AND ENTERTAINMENT COSTS

## INTRODUCTION

Electrovision has always encouraged a significant amount of business travel. To compensate employees for the stress and inconvenience of frequent trips, management has authorized generous travel and entertainment (T&E) allowances. This philosophy has been good for morale, but last year Electrovision spent $16 million on travel and entertainment—$7 million more than it spent on research and development.

This year's T&E costs will affect profits even more, due to increases in airline fares and hotel rates. Also, the company anticipates that profits will be relatively weak for a variety of other reasons. Therefore, Dennis McWilliams, Vice President of Operations, has asked the accounting department to explore ways to reduce the T&E budget.

The purpose of this report is to analyze T&E expenses, evaluate the effect of recent hotel and airfare increases, and suggest ways to tighten control over T&E costs. The report outlines several steps that could reduce Electrovision's expenses, but the precise financial impact of these measures is difficult to project. The estimates presented here provide a "best guess" view of what Electrovision can expect to save.

In preparing this report, the accounting department analyzed internal expense reports for the past five years to determine how much Electrovision spends on travel and entertainment. These figures were then compared with average statistics compiled by Dow Jones (publisher of the *Wall Street Journal*) and presented as the Dow Jones Travel Index. We also analyzed trends and suggestions published in a variety of business journal articles to see how other companies are coping with the high cost of business travel.

## THE HIGH COST OF TRAVEL AND ENTERTAINMENT

Although many companies view travel and entertainment as an incidental cost of doing business, the dollars add up. At Electrovision the bill for airfares, hotels, rental cars, meals, and entertainment totaled $16 million last year. Our T&E budget has increased by 12 percent per year for the past five years. Compared to the average U.S. business traveler, Electrovision's expenditures are high, largely because of management's generous policy on travel benefits.

In her brief introduction, Moreno counts on topic sentences and transitions to indicate that she is discussing the purpose, scope, and limitations of the study.

### $16 Million per Year Spent on Travel and Entertainment

Electrovision's annual budget for travel and entertainment is only 8 percent of sales. Because this is a relatively small expense category compared with such things as salaries and commissions, it is tempting to dismiss T&E costs as insignificant. However, T&E is Electrovision's third-largest controllable expense, directly behind salaries and information systems.

Last year Electrovision personnel made about 3,390 trips at an average cost per trip of $4,720. The typical trip involved a round-trip flight of 3,000 miles, meals, and hotel accommodations for two or three days, and a rental car. Roughly 80 percent of trips were made by 20 percent of the staff—top management and sales personnel traveled most, averaging 18 trips per year.

Figure 1 illustrates how the T&E budget is spent. The largest categories are airfares and lodging, which together account for $7 out of $10 that employees spend on travel and entertainment. This spending breakdown has been relatively steady for the past five years and is consistent with the distribution of expenses experienced by other companies.

**Figure 1**
Airfares and Lodging Account for Over
Two-Thirds of Electrovision's T&E Budget

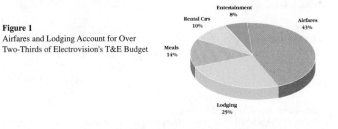

Although the composition of the T&E budget has been consistent, its size has not. As mentioned earlier, these expenditures have increased by about 12 percent per year for the past five years, roughly twice the rate of the company's sales growth (see Figure 2). This rate of growth makes T&E Electrovision's fastest-growing expense item.

**Figure 2**
T&E Expenses Continue to Increase as a
Percentage of Sales

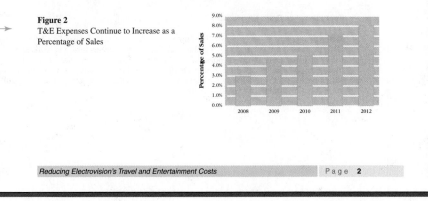

---

The visual is placed as close as possible to the point it illustrates.

Each visual has a title that clearly indicates what it's about; titles are consistently placed to the left of each visual.

Moreno opens the first main section of the body with a topic sentence that introduces an important fact about the subject of the section. Then she orients the reader to the three major points developed in the section.

**Electrovision's Travel Expenses Exceed National Averages**

Much of our travel budget is justified. Two major factors contribute to Electrovision's
high T&E budget:

*   With our headquarters on the West Coast and our major customer on the East Coast, we
    naturally spend a lot of money on cross-country flights.

*   A great deal of travel takes place between our headquarters here on the West Coast
    and the manufacturing operations in Detroit, Boston, and Dallas. Corporate managers and
    division personnel make frequent trips to coordinate these disparate operations.

However, even though a good portion of Electrovision's travel budget is justifiable, the
company spends considerably more on T&E than the average business traveler (see Figure 3).

**Figure 3**
Electrovision Employees Spend Over
Twice as Much as the Average
Business Traveler

Source: *Wall Street Journal* and
company records

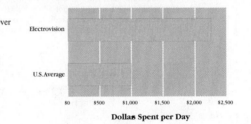

Electrovision

U.S. Average

$0    $500    $1,000    $1,500    $2,000    $2,500

**Dollars Spent per Day**

The Dow Jones Travel Index calculates the average cost per day of business travel in the
United States, based on average airfare, hotel rates, and rental car rates. The average
fluctuates weekly as travel companies change their rates, but it has been running at about
$1,000 per day for the last year or so. In contrast, Electrovision's average daily expense over
the past year has been $2,250—a hefty 125 percent higher than average. This figure is based
on the average trip cost of $4,720 listed earlier and an average trip length of 2.1 days.

**Spending Has Been Encouraged**

Although a variety of factors may contribute to this differential, Electrovision's relatively high
T&E costs are at least partially attributable to the company's philosophy and management
style. Since many employees do not enjoy business travel, management has tried to make the
trips more pleasant by authorizing business-class airfare, luxury hotel accommodations, and
full-size rental cars. The sales staff is encouraged to entertain clients at top restaurants and to
invite them to cultural and sporting events.

A bulleted list makes it easy for readers to identify and distinguish related points.

The cost of these privileges is easy to overlook, given the weakness of Electrovision's system for keeping track of T&E expenses:

- The monthly financial records do not contain a separate category for travel and entertainment; the information is buried under Cost of Goods Sold and under Selling, General, and Administrative Expenses.

- Each department head is given authority to approve any expense report, regardless of how large it may be.

- Receipts are not required for expenditures of less than $100.

- Individuals are allowed to make their own travel arrangements.

- No one is charged with the responsibility for controlling the company's total spending on travel and entertainment.

## GROWING IMPACT ON THE BOTTOM LINE

Informative headings focus reader attention on the main points. Such headings are appropriate when a report uses the direct order and is intended for a receptive audience. However, descriptive headings are more effective when a report uses the indirect order and readers are less receptive.

During the past three years, the company's healthy profits have resulted in relatively little pressure to push for tighter controls over all aspects of the business. However, as we all know, the situation is changing. We're projecting flat to declining profits for the next two years, a situation that has prompted all of us to search for ways to cut costs. At the same time, rising airfares and hotel rates have increased the impact of T&E expenses on the company's financial results.

### Lower Profits Underscore the Need for Change

The next two years promise to be difficult for Electrovision. After several years of steady increases in spending, the Postal Service is tightening procurement policies for automated mail-handling equipment. Funding for the A-12 optical character reader has been canceled. As a consequence, the marketing department expects sales to drop by 15 percent. Although Electrovision is negotiating several other promising R&D contracts, the marketing department does not foresee any major procurements for the next two to three years.

At the same time, Electrovision is facing cost increases on several fronts. As we have known for several months, the new production facility now under construction in Salt Lake City, Utah, is behind schedule and over budget. Labor contracts in Boston and Dallas will expire within the next six months, and plant managers there anticipate that significant salary and benefits concessions may be necessary to avoid strikes.

Moreover, marketing and advertising costs are expected to increase as we attempt to strengthen these activities to better cope with competitive pressures. Given the expected decline in revenues and increase in costs, the Executive Committee's prediction that profits will fall by 12 percent in the coming fiscal year does not seem overly pessimistic.

Moreno designed her report to include plenty of white space so even those pages that lack visuals are still attractive and easy to read.

### Airfares and Hotel Rates Are Rising

Business travelers have grown accustomed to frequent fare wars and discounting in the travel industry in recent years. Excess capacity and aggressive price competition, particularly in the airline business, made travel a relative bargain.

Moreno supports her argument with objective facts and sound reasoning.

However, that situation has changed as weaker competitors have been forced out and the remaining players have grown stronger and smarter. Airlines and hotels are better at managing inventory and keeping occupancy rates high, which translates into higher costs for Electrovision. Last year saw some of the steepest rate hikes in years. Business airfares (tickets most likely to be purchased by business travelers) jumped more than 40 percent in many markets. The trend is expected to continue, with rates increasing another 5 to 10 percent overall (Phillips 331; "Travel Costs Under Pressure" 30; Dahl B6).

Given the fact that air and hotel costs account for almost 70 percent of our T&E budget, the trend toward higher prices in these two categories will have serious consequences, unless management takes action to control these costs.

### METHODS FOR REDUCING T&E COSTS

The recommendations are realistic, noting both the benefits and the risks of taking action.

By implementing a number of reforms, management can expect to reduce Electrovision's T&E budget by as much as 40 percent. This estimate is based on the general assessment made by American Express (Gilligan 39) and on the fact that we have an opportunity to significantly reduce air travel costs by eliminating business-class travel. However, these measures are likely to be unpopular with employees. To gain acceptance for such changes, management will need to sell employees on the need for moderation in T&E allowances.

### Four Ways to Trim Expenses

By researching what other companies are doing to curb T&E expenses, the accounting department has identified four prominent opportunities that should enable Electrovision to save about $6 million annually in travel-related costs.

#### *Institute Tighter Spending Controls*

A single individual should be appointed director of travel and entertainment to spearhead the effort to gain control of the T&E budget. More than a third of all U.S. companies now employ travel managers ("Businesses Use Savvy Managers" 4). The director should be familiar with the travel industry and should be well versed in both accounting and information technology. The director should also report to the vice president of operations. The director's first priorities should be to establish a written T&E policy and a cost-control system.

Electrovision currently has no written policy on travel and entertainment, a step that is widely recommended by air travel experts (Smith D4). Creating a policy would clarify management's position and serve as a vehicle for communicating the need for moderation.

Moreno creates a forceful tone by using action verbs in the third-level subheadings of this section. This approach is appropriate to the nature of the study and the attitude of the audience. However, in a status-conscious organization, the imperative verbs might sound a bit too presumptuous coming from a junior member of the staff.

At a minimum, the policy should include the following:

- All travel and entertainment should be strictly related to business and should be approved in advance.

- Except under special circumstances to be approved on a case-by-case basis, employees should travel by coach and stay in mid-range business hotels.

- The T&E policy should apply equally to employees at all levels.

In addition to making key points easy to find, bulleted lists help break up the text to relieve the reader's eye.

To implement the new policy, Electrovision will need to create a system for controlling T&E expenses. Each department should prepare an annual T&E budget as part of its operating plan. These budgets should be presented in detail so that management can evaluate how T&E dollars will be spent and can recommend appropriate cuts. To help management monitor performance relative to these budgets, the director of travel should prepare monthly financial statements showing actual T&E expenditures by department.

The director of travel should also be responsible for retaining a business-oriented travel service that will schedule all employee business trips and look for the best travel deals, particularly in airfares. In addition to centralizing Electrovision's reservation and ticketing activities, the agency will negotiate reduced group rates with hotels and rental car firms. The agency selected should have offices nationwide so that all Electrovision facilities can channel their reservations through the same company. This is particularly important in light of the dizzying array of often wildly different airfares available between some cities. It's not uncommon to find dozens of fares along commonly traveled routes (Rowe 30). In addition, the director can help coordinate travel across the company to secure group discounts whenever possible (Barker 31; Miller B6).

Moreno lists the steps needed to implement her recommendations.

### Reduce Unnecessary Travel and Entertainment

One of the easiest ways to reduce expenses is to reduce the amount of traveling and entertaining that occurs. An analysis of last year's expenditures suggests that as much as 30 percent of Electrovision's travel and entertainment is discretionary. The professional staff spent $2.8 million attending seminars and conferences last year. Although these gatherings are undoubtedly beneficial, the company could save money by sending fewer representatives to each function and perhaps by eliminating some of the less valuable seminars.

Similarly, Electrovision could economize on trips between headquarters and divisions by reducing the frequency of such visits and by sending fewer people on each trip. Although there is often no substitute for face-to-face meetings, management could try to resolve more internal issues through telephone, electronic, and written communication.

Electrovision can also reduce spending by urging employees to economize. Instead of flying business class, employees can fly coach class or take advantage of discount fares. Rather than ordering a $50 bottle of wine, employees can select a less expensive bottle or dispense with

Moreno takes care not to overstep the boundaries of her analysis. For instance, she doesn't analyze the value of the seminars that employees attend every year, so she avoids any absolute statements about reducing travel to seminars.

alcohol entirely. People can book rooms at moderately priced hotels and drive smaller rental cars.

### Obtain Lowest Rates from Travel Providers

Apart from urging employees to economize, Electrovision can also save money by searching for the lowest available airfares, hotel rates, and rental car fees. Currently, few employees have the time or knowledge to seek out travel bargains. When they need to travel, they make the most convenient and comfortable arrangements. A professional travel service will be able to obtain lower rates from travel providers.

Judging by the experience of other companies, Electrovision may be able to trim as much as 30 to 40 percent from the travel budget simply by looking for bargains in airfares and negotiating group rates with hotels and rental car companies. Electrovision should be able to achieve these economies by analyzing its travel patterns, identifying frequently visited locations, and selecting a few hotels that are willing to reduce rates in exchange for guaranteed business. At the same time, the company should be able to save up to 40 percent on rental car charges by negotiating a corporate rate.

The possibilities for economizing are promising; however, making the best travel arrangements often requires trade-offs such as the following:

- The best fares might not always be the lowest. Indirect flights are usually cheaper, but they take longer and may end up costing more in lost work time.

- The cheapest tickets often require booking 14 or even 30 days in advance, which is often impossible for us.

- Discount tickets are usually nonrefundable, which is a serious drawback when a trip needs to be canceled at the last minute.

### Replace Travel with Technological Alternatives

Online meeting systems such as WebEx and GoTo Meeting offer a compelling alternative to many instances of business travel. With webcam video, application/screen sharing, and collaboration tools such as virtual whiteboards, they have made great strides toward replicating the in-person meeting experience.

As effective as they can be, though, they shouldn't automatically replace every in-person meeting. When establishing a business relationship, for example, meeting face to face is an important part of building trust and getting past the uncertainties of working with a new partner. Part of the new travel director's job would be to draft guidelines for choosing travel or on-line meeting options.

By pointing out possible difficulties and showing that she has considered all angles, Moreno builds reader confidence in her judgment.

Note how Moreno makes the transition from section to section. The first sentence under the second heading on this page refers to the subject of the previous paragraph and signals a shift in thought.

### The Impact of Reforms

By implementing tighter controls, reducing unnecessary expenses, negotiating more favorable rates, and exploring alternatives to travel, Electrovision should be able to reduce its T&E budget significantly. As Table 1 illustrates, the combined savings should be in the neighborhood of $6 million, although the precise figures are somewhat difficult to project.

**Table 1**
Electrovision Can Trim Travel and Entertainment Costs
by an Estimated $6 Million per Year

| SOURCE OF SAVINGS | ESTIMATED SAVINGS |
|---|---|
| Switching from business-class to coach airfare | $2,300,000 |
| Negotiating preferred hotel rates | 940,000 |
| Negotiating preferred rental car rates | 460,000 |
| Systematically searching for lower airfares | 375,000 |
| Reducing interdivisional travel | 675,000 |
| Reducing seminar and conference attendance | 1,250,000 |
| **TOTAL POTENTIAL SAVINGS** | **$6,000,000** |

To achieve the economies outlined in the table, Electrovision will incur expenses for hiring a director of travel and for implementing a T&E cost-control system. These costs are projected at $115,000: $105,000 per year in salary and benefits for the new employee and a one-time expense of $10,000 for the cost-control system. The cost of retaining a full-service travel agency is negligible, even with the service fees that many are now passing along from airlines and other service providers.

The measures required to achieve these savings are likely to be unpopular with employees. Electrovision personnel are accustomed to generous T&E allowances, and they are likely to resent having these privileges curtailed. To alleviate their disappointment

- Management should make a determined effort to explain why the changes are necessary.

- The director of corporate communication should be asked to develop a multifaceted campaign that will communicate the importance of curtailing T&E costs.

- Management should set a positive example by adhering strictly to the new policies.

- The limitations should apply equally to employees at all levels in the organization.

An informative title in the table is consistent with the way headings are handled throughout this report, and it is appropriate for a report to a receptive audience.

The in-text reference to the table highlights the key point the reader should get from the table.

Including financial estimates helps management envision the impact of the suggestions, even though the estimated savings are difficult to project accurately.

Note how Moreno calls attention in the first paragraph to items in the following table, without repeating the information in the table.

## CONCLUSIONS AND RECOMMENDATIONS

Electrovision is currently spending $16 million per year on travel and entertainment. Although much of this spending is justified, the company's costs are high relative to competitors' costs, mainly because Electrovision has been generous with its travel benefits.

Electrovision's liberal approach to travel and entertainment was understandable during years of high profitability; however, the company is facing the prospect of declining profits for the next several years. Management is therefore motivated to cut costs in all areas of the business. Reducing T&E spending is particularly important because the bottom-line impact of these costs will increase as airline fares increase.

Electrovision should be able to reduce T&E costs by as much as 40 percent by taking four important steps:

1. *Institute tighter spending controls.* Management should hire a director of travel and entertainment who will assume overall responsibility for T&E activities. Within the next six months, this director should develop a written travel policy, institute a T&E budget and a cost-control system, and retain a professional, business-oriented travel agency that will optimize arrangements with travel providers.

2. *Reduce unnecessary travel and entertainment.* Electrovision should encourage employees to economize on T&E spending. Management can accomplish this by authorizing fewer trips and by urging employees to be more conservative in their spending.

3. *Obtain lowest rates from travel providers.* Electrovision should also focus on obtaining the best rates on airline tickets, hotel rooms, and rental cars. By channeling all arrangements through a professional travel agency, the company can optimize its choices and gain clout in negotiating preferred rates.

4. *Replace some travel with technological alternatives.* Online meeting systems should be adequate for most of our tactical meetings with established clients and for most internal communication as well.

Because these measures may be unpopular with employees, management should make a concerted effort to explain the importance of reducing travel costs. The director of corporate communication should be given responsibility for developing a plan to communicate the need for employee cooperation.

### WORKS CITED

Barker, Julie. "How to Rein in Group Travel Costs." *Successful Meetings* Feb. 2013: 31. Print.

"Businesses Use Savvy Managers to Keep Travel Costs Down." *Christian Science Monitor* 17 July 2012: 4. Print.

Dahl, Jonathan. "2000: The Year Travel Costs Took Off." *Wall Street Journal* 29 Dec. 2007: B6. Print.

Gilligan, Edward P. "Trimming Your T&E Is Easier Than You Think." *Managing Office Technology* Nov. 2011: 39–40. Print.

Miller, Lisa. "Attention, Airline Ticket Shoppers." *Wall Street Journal* 7 July 2012: B6. Print.

Phillips, Edward H. "Airlines Post Record Traffic." *Aviation Week & Space Technology* 8 Jan. 2013: 331. Print.

"Product Overview: Cisco WebEx Meeting Center," *Webex.com*. 2011. WebEx, n.d. 2 February 2012. Web.

Rowe, Irene Vlitos. "Global Solution for Cutting Travel Costs." *European Business* 12 Oct. 2011: 30. Print.

Smith, Carol. "Rising, Erratic Airfares Make Company Policy Vital." *Los Angeles Times* 2 Nov. 2012: D4. Print.

Solheim, Shelley. "Web Conferencing Made Easy." *eWeek* 22 Aug. 2012: 26. Web.

"Travel Costs Under Pressure." *Purchasing* 15 Feb. 2012: 30. Print.

MLA style lists references alphabetically by the author's last name, and when the author is unknown, by the title of the reference. (See Appendix B for additional details on preparing reference lists.)

Moreno's list of references follows the style recommended in the *MLA Style Manual*. The box below shows how these sources would be cited following APA style.

### REFERENCES

Barker, J. (2013, February). How to rein in group travel costs. *Successful Meetings,* p. 31.

Businesses use savvy managers to keep travel costs down. (2012, July 17). *Christian Science Monitor,* p. 4.

Dahl, J. (2007, December 29). 2000: The year travel costs took off. *Wall Street Journal,* B6.

Gilligan, E. (2011, November). Trimming your T&E is easier than you think. *Managing Office Technology,* pp. 39–40.

Miller, L. (2012, July 7). Attention, airline ticket shoppers. *Wall Street Journal,* B6.

Phillips, E. (2013, January 8). Airlines post record traffic. *Aviation Week & Space Technology,* p. 331.

Rowe, I. (2011, October 12). Global solution for cutting travel costs. *European,* p. 30.

Smith, C. (2012, November 2). Rising, erratic airfares make company policy vital. *Los Angeles Times,* D4.

Solheim, S. (2012, August 22). Web conferencing made easy. *eWeek,* p. 26.

Travel costs under pressure. (2012, February 15). *Purchasing,* p. 30.

WebEx.com. (2012). *Product Overview: Cisco WebEx Meeting Center.* Retrieved from http://www.webex.com/product-overview/index.html

# Quick Reference Guide

## MyBCommLab

Go to **mybcommlab.com** to complete the problems marked with this icon ⭐.

## SUMMARY OF LEARNING OBJECTIVES

**1** **Explain how to adapt to your audiences when writing reports and proposals.** Adapt to your audience by demonstrating sensitivity to their needs (adopting the "you" attitude, maintaining a strong sense of etiquette, emphasizing the positive, and using bias-free language), building a strong relationship with your audience (making sure your writing reflects the desired image of your organization and building your credibility), and controlling your style and tone to achieve the appropriate degree of formality, given the nature of the material and your relationship with the audience.

Effective reports help readers navigate the document by using three elements: (1) headings (and links for online reports), which set off important ideas and provide the reader with clues as to the report's framework and shifts in discussion; (2) transitions, which tie together ideas and keep readers moving along; and (3) previews and reviews, which prepare readers for new information and summarize previously discussed information.

**2** **Name five characteristics of effective report content, and list the topics commonly covered in the introduction, body, and close of formal reports.** Effective report content is accurate if it is factually correct and error free. It is complete if it includes all necessary information and supports all key assertions. It is balanced if it presents all sides of an argument. It is clear and logical if it is well written and organized logically. It is properly documented if credit is given to all primary and secondary sources of information used.

The introduction highlights the person(s) who authorized the report, the purpose and scope of a report, necessary background material, the sources or methods used to gather information, important definitions, any limitations, and the order in which the various topics are covered. The body can discuss such details as problems, opportunities, facts, evidence, trends, results of studies or investigations, analysis of potential courses of action and their advantages and disadvantages, process procedures and steps, methods and approaches, evaluation criteria for options, conclusions, recommendations, and supporting reasons. The close summarizes key points, restates conclusions and recommendations, if appropriate, and lists action items.

**3** **List six strategies to strengthen a proposal argument, and list the topics commonly covered in the introduction, body, and close of formal reports.** To strengthen your argument, you should demonstrate your knowledge, provide concrete examples, research the competition, prove that your proposal is workable, adopt a "you" attitude, and make your proposal attractive and error free.

The most common elements in the introduction of a proposal are background information or a statement of the problem or opportunity, an overview of the proposed solution, a delineation of the scope of the proposal, and a description of how the proposal is organized. The body can contain a full description of the proposed solution, a work plan with schedules and other key implementation information, a statement of the firm's qualifications, and breakdown of project costs. The close usually contains a summary of key points, a brief reminder of the benefits readers will realize from the solution and the merits of proposed approach, a quick summary of qualifications, and a call to action in terms of a request for a decision.

**4** **Summarize the four tasks involved in completing business reports and proposals.** The four completion tasks of revising, producing, proofreading, and distributing all need to be accomplished with care, given the size and complexity of many reports. The production stage for a formal report or proposal can involve creating a number of elements not found in most other business documents. Possible prefatory parts (those coming before the main text of the report or proposal) include a cover, a title fly, a title page, a letter of authorization, a letter of transmittal, a table of contents, a list of illustrations, and a synopsis (a brief overview of the report) or an executive summary (a miniature version of the report). Possible supplemental parts (those coming after the main text of the report or proposal) include one or more appendixes, a bibliography, and an index.

**5** **Identify the elements to include in a request for proposals (RFP).** The content of RFPs varies widely from industry to industry and project to project, but most include background on the company, a description of the project, solution requirements, the criteria that will be used to make selection decisions, expectations for submitted proposals, and any relevant submission and contact information.

## KEY TERMS

**abstract** Name usually given to a synopsis that accompanies long technical, professional, or academic reports

**appendix** Supplementary section that contains materials related to the report but not included in the text because they are too long or perhaps not relevant to everyone in the audience

**bibliography** A list of the secondary sources consulted in the preparation of a report

**executive summary** A complete but summarized version of the report; may contain headings, well-developed transitions, and even visual elements

**index** An alphabetical list of names and subjects mentioned in a report, along with the pages on which they occur

**letter of authorization** Written authorization to prepare a report

**letter of transmittal** A specialized form of cover letter that introduces a report to the audience

**synopsis** A brief overview (one page or less) of a report's most important points, designed to give readers a quick preview of the contents

**title fly** A single sheet of paper with only the title of the report on it

**title page** Page that includes the report title; the name, title, and address of the person or organization that authorized the report (if anyone); the name, title, and address of the person or organization that prepared the report; and the date on which the report was submitted

---

CHECKLIST ✓

## Producing Formal Reports and Proposals

**A. Prefatory parts**
- Use your company's standard report covers, if available.
- Include a concise, descriptive title on the cover.
- Include a title fly only if you want an extra-formal touch.
- On the title page, list (1) report title; (2) name, title, and address of the group or person who authorized the report; (3) name, title, and address of the group or person who prepared the report; and (4) date of submission.
- Include a copy of the letter of authorization, if appropriate.
- If responding to an RFP, follow its instructions for including a copy or referring to the RFP by name or tracking number.
- Include a letter of transmittal that introduces the report.
- Provide a table of contents in outline form, with headings worded exactly as they appear in the body of the report.
- Include a list of illustrations if the report contains a large number of them.
- Include a synopsis (brief summary of the report) or an executive summary (a condensed, "mini" version of the report) for longer reports.

**B. Text of the report**
- Draft an introduction that prepares the reader for the content that follows.
- Provide information that supports your conclusions, recommendations, or proposals in the body of the report.
- Don't overload the body with unnecessary detail.
- Close with a summary of your main idea.

**C. Supplementary parts**
- Use appendixes to provide supplementary information or supporting evidence.
- List in a bibliography any secondary sources you used.
- Provide an index if your report contains a large number of terms or ideas and is likely to be consulted over time.

## COMMUNICATION CHALLENGES AT Garage Technology Ventures

You recently joined Guy Kawasaki and the rest of the team at Garage Technology Ventures in Palo Alto. Among your responsibilities is screening executive summaries of business plans submitted by start-up companies seeking financing. Review the criteria discussed in the chapter-opening vignette on page 409 to address the following challenges.

**INDIVIDUAL CHALLENGE:** You've just received an intriguing executive summary from a start-up company whose technology reduces the cost of providing Internet service by nearly 30 percent, an amount that would spark interest from just about every Internet service provider in the world. The financial projections in the executive summary are realistic—and quite positive. Even if this investment panned out only half as well as the numbers suggest, it would bring in a sizable amount of cash when the company eventually goes public. The technological solution is sound, too; you used to work as a network engineer, and these people know what they're doing. There is just one problem: the submission is entirely anonymous. The document describes, in vague terms, four experienced technical and business specialists but without giving their names or their specific work experiences. A note attached to the plan apologizes for the secrecy but says the four principals in the new firm can't reveal themselves until they get

financing and can therefore leave their current jobs. Do you reject the submission or pass it on to Kawasaki and the other managing directors for their consideration? Explain your answer.

**TEAM CHALLENGE:** Review these "grabs" presented in three executive summaries. Discuss their strengths and weaknesses and decide which one of the three you would forward to Kawasaki and the other directors.

- Company A: Pardon our bullish tone, but this is the best investment opportunity you are likely to see this year. As one of our board members recently said, we are already on track to out-Apple Apple and out-Google Google.

- Company B: Cooling the huge data centers that power the Internet costs millions of dollars and consumes massive amounts of energy. Our low-temperature server technology pays for itself in less than a year by reducing energy bills and extending the life of data center hardware.

- Company C: Our travel-search website has already proven so popular that last month we had 140,000 site visitors. By the way, we have interest from three other investment firms, so our advice would be to jump on this opportunity!

## Test Your Knowledge

To review chapter content related to each question, refer to the indicated Learning Objective.

⊛ 1. What writing choices can you make to adjust the formality of your reports? [LO-1]

2. What navigational elements can you use to help readers follow the structure and flow of information in a long report? [LO-1]

3. What are three supplementary parts often included in formal reports? [LO-2]

4. Why must the introduction of an unsolicited proposal include a statement of the problem or opportunity that the proposal addresses? [LO-3]

5. Why is the work plan a key component of a proposal? [LO-3]

6. How should you refer to the RFP in a solicited proposal? [LO-3]

7. What is the equivalent of a letter of authorization for a proposal? [LO-4]

⊛ 8. How does a synopsis differ from an executive summary? [LO-4]

9. Why does writing an RFP require such careful thought? [LO-5]

## Apply Your Knowledge

To review chapter content related to each question, refer to the indicated Learning Objective.

⊛ 1. How would you report on a confidential survey in which employees rated their managers' capabilities? Both employees and managers expect to see the results. Would you give

the same report to employees and managers? What components would you include or exclude for each audience? Explain your choices. [LO-1]

⊛ 2. What are the risks of not explaining the purpose of a proposal within the introduction? [LO-3]

⊛ 3. If a company receives a solicited formal proposal outlining the solution to a particular problem, is it ethical for the company to adopt the proposal's recommendations without hiring the firm that submitted the proposal? Why or why not? [LO-3]

4. Is an executive summary a persuasive message? Explain your answer. [LO-4]

## Practice Your Skills

**Message 15.A: Executive Summaries [LO-2]**

To access this document for his exercise, go to http://real-time-updates.com/bct12, click on Student Assignments, and select Chapter 15, Message 15.A. Download this PDF file, which is the executive summary of *Dietary Guidelines for Americans*, a publication from the U.S. Center for Nutrition Policy and Promotion. Using the information in this chapter, analyze the executive summary and offer specific suggestions for revising it.

### Exercises

Each activity is labeled according to the primary skill or skills you will need to use. To review relevant chapter content, you can refer to the indicated Learning Objective. In some instances, supporting information will be found in another chapter, as indicated.

1. **Message Strategies: Informational Reports [LO-1]** You and a classmate are helping Linda Moreno prepare her report on Electrovision's travel and entertainment costs (see the Report Writer's Notebook on pages 425–439). This time, however, the report is to be informational rather than analytical, so it will not include recommendations. Review the existing report and determine what changes would be needed to make it an informational report. Be as specific as possible. For example, if your team decides the report needs a new title, what title would you use? Draft a transmittal memo for Moreno to use in conveying this informational report to Dennis McWilliams, Electrovision's vice president of operations.

2. **Message Strategies: Informational Reports [LO-1]** Review a long business article in a journal or newspaper. Highlight examples of how the article uses headings, transitions, previews, and reviews to help the readers find their way.

3. **Message Strategies: Analytical Reports; Communication Ethics: Resolving Ethical Dilemmas [LO-1], Chapter 1** Your boss has asked you to prepare a feasibility report to determine whether the company should advertise its custom-crafted cabinetry in the weekly neighborhood newspaper. Based on your primary research, you think it should. As you draft the introduction to your report, however, you discover that the survey administered to the neighborhood newspaper subscribers was flawed. Several of the questions were poorly written and misleading. You used the survey results, among other findings, to justify your recommendation. The report is due in three days. What actions might you want to take, if any, before you complete your report?

4. **Completing: Producing Formal Reports [LO-4]** You are president of the Friends of the Library, a not-for-profit group that raises funds and provides volunteers to support your local library. Every February, you send a report of the previous year's activities and accomplishments to the County Arts Council, which provides an annual grant of $1,000 toward your group's summer reading festival. Now it's February 6, and you've completed your formal report. Here are the highlights:
   - Back-to-school book sale raised $2,000.
   - Holiday craft fair raised $1,100.
   - Promotion and prizes for summer reading festival cost $1,450.
   - Materials for children's program featuring local author cost $125.
   - New reference databases for library's career center cost $850.
   - Bookmarks promoting library's website cost $200.

   Write a letter of transmittal to Erica Maki, the council's director. Because she is expecting this report, you can use the direct approach. Be sure to express gratitude for the council's ongoing financial support.

5. **Distributing Reports; Communication Ethics: Resolving Ethical Dilemmas [LO-4], Chapter 1** You submitted what you thought was a masterful report to your boss over three weeks ago. The report analyzes current department productivity and recommends several steps you think will improve employee output without increasing individual workloads. Brilliant, you thought. But you haven't heard a word from your boss. Did you overstep your boundaries by making recommendations that might imply that she has not been doing a good job? Did you overwhelm her with your ideas? You'd like some feedback. In your last email to her, you asked if she had read your report. So far you've received no reply.

   Then yesterday, you overheard the company vice president talk about some productivity changes in your department—the same changes you recommended in your report. Now you're worried that your boss submitted your report to senior management and will take full credit for your terrific ideas. What, if anything, should you do? Should you confront your boss about this? Should you ask to meet with the company vice president? Discuss this situation with your teammates and develop a solution to this sticky situation. Present your solution to the class, explaining the rationale behind your decision.

6. **Revising for Clarity and Conciseness [LO-4]** The following sentence appears in your first draft of a report that analyzes perceived shortcomings in your company's employee health benefits:

   Among the many criticisms and concerns expressed by the workforce, at least among the 376 who responded to our online survey (out of 655 active employees), the issues of elder care, health insurance during retirement, and the increased amount that employees are being forced to pay every month as the company's contribution to health insurance coverage has declined over the past two years were identified as the most important.

   Revise this 69-word sentence to make it shorter, more direct, and more powerful.

7. **Producing Formal Reports [LO-4]** Government reports vary in purpose and structure. Read through the Department of Education's report "Helping Your Child Become a Reader," available at www.ed.gov. What is the purpose of this document? Does the title communicate this purpose? What type of report is this, and what is the report's structure? Which prefatory and supplementary parts are included? Now analyze the visuals. What types of visuals are included in this report? Are they all necessary? Are the titles and legends sufficiently informative? How does this report take advantage of the online medium to enhance readability?

## Expand Your Skills

### Critique the Professionals

Download the latest issue of the *International Trade Update* from http://trade.gov (look under Publications). What techniques does the report use to help readers find their way through the document or direct readers to other sources of information? What techniques are used to highlight key points in the document? Are these techniques effective? Using whatever medium your instructor requests, write a brief summary of your analysis.

**Sharpen Your Career Skills Online**
Bovée and Thill's Business Communication Web Search, at http://websearch.businesscommunicationnetwork.com, is a unique research tool designed specifically for business communication research. Use the Web Search function to find a website, video, PDF document, podcast, or presentation that offers advice on creating effective business reports. Write a brief email message to your instructor or a post for your class blog, describing the item that you found and summarizing the career skills information you learned from it.

# Cases

## Short Reports

**1. Message Strategies: Informational Reports [LO-1] [LO-2]**
Concern is growing in many youth sports about the negative consequences of existing approaches to player development and competition. The long-term athlete development (LTAD) approach aims to instill methods and mindsets that will make athlete development more successful in the long run while making sports more enjoyable for kids. The American Development Model (ADM) used by USA Hockey is one example of the LTAD approach in a specific sport.

**Your task:** Visit USA Hockey's ADM website at www.usahockey.com/ADM_Overview.aspx. Write a brief informational report (one to two pages) on the ADM concept, including the rationale behind it and the benefits it offers youth athletes.

**2. Message Strategies: Informational Reports [LO-1] [LO-2]**
Anyone contemplating stock market investing is likely to shudder at least a little bit at the market's penchant for taking a tumble now and again.

**Your task:** Write a brief informational report that contains a chart of one of the major stock market indices (such as the Dow Jones Industrial Average or the S&P 500) over the past 20 years. Pick out four significant drops in the index during this time period and investigate economic or political events that occurred immediately before or during these declines. Briefly describe the events and their likely effect on the stock market.

**3. Message Strategies: Informational Reports [LO-1] [LO-2]**
As you may know, the procedural requirements involved in getting a degree or certificate can be nearly as challenging as any course you could take.

**Your task:** Prepare an interim progress report that details the steps you've taken toward completing your graduation or certification requirements. After examining the requirements listed in your college catalog, indicate a realistic schedule for completing those that remain. In addition to course requirements, include steps such as completing the residency requirement, filing necessary papers, and paying necessary fees. Use a memo format for your report and address it to anyone who is helping or encouraging you through school.

**4. Message Strategies: Informational Reports [LO-1] [LO-2]**
Success in any endeavor doesn't happen all at once. For example, success in college is built one quarter or semester at a time, and the way to succeed in the long term is to make sure you succeed in the short term. After all, even a single quarter or semester of college involves a significant investment of time, money, and energy.

**Your task:** Imagine you work for a company that has agreed to send you to college full time, paying all your educational expenses. You are given complete freedom in choosing your courses, as long as you graduate by an agreed-upon date. All your employer asks in return is that you develop your business skills and insights as much as possible so that you can make a significant contribution to the company when you return to full-time work after graduation. To make sure that you are using your time—and your company's money—wisely, the company requires a brief personal activity report at the end of every quarter or semester (whichever your school uses). Write a brief informational report that you can email to your instructor, summarizing how you spent your quarter or semester. Itemize the classes you took, how much time you spent studying and working on class projects, whether you got involved in campus activities and organizations that help you develop leadership or communication skills, and what you learned that you can apply in a business career. (For the purposes of this assignment, your time estimates don't have to be precise.)

**5. Message Strategies: Informational Reports [LO-1] [LO-2]**
You've been in your new job as human resources director for only a week, and already you have a major personnel crisis on your hands. Some employees in the marketing department got their hands on a confidential salary report and learned that, on average, marketing employees earn less than engineering employees. In addition, several top performers in the engineering group make significantly more than anybody in marketing. The report was instantly passed around the company by email, and now everyone is discussing the situation. You'll deal with the data security issue later; for now, you need to address the dissatisfaction in the marketing group.

Case Table 15.1 lists the salary and employment data you were able to pull from the employee database. You also had the opportunity to interview the engineering and marketing directors to get their opinions on the pay situation; their answers are listed in Case Table 15.2.

**Your task:** The CEO has asked for a short report, summarizing whatever data and information you have on engineering and marketing salaries. Feel free to offer your own interpretation of the situation as well (make up any information you need), but keep in mind that because you are a new manager with almost no experience in the company, your opinion might not have a lot of influence.

**6. Message Strategies: Analytical Reports [LO-1] [LO-2]**
Your company develops a mobile phone app that helps people get detailed technical information about products while they are shopping. The original plan was to incorporate Quick Reference

**CASE TABLE 15.1** | **Selected Employment Data for Engineers and Marketing Staff**

| Employment Statistic | Engineering Department | Marketing Department |
| --- | --- | --- |
| Average number of years of work experience | 18.2 | 16.3 |
| Average number of years of experience in current profession | 17.8 | 8.6 |
| Average number of years with company | 12.4 | 7.9 |
| Average number of years of college education | 6.9 | 4.8 |
| Average number of years between promotions | 6.7 | 4.3 |
| Salary range | $58–165k | $45–85k |
| Median salary | $77k | $62k |

**CASE TABLE 15.2** | **Summary Statements from Department Director Interviews**

| Question | Engineering Director | Marketing Director |
| --- | --- | --- |
| 1. Should engineering and marketing professionals receive roughly similar pay? | In general, yes, but we need to make allowances for the special nature of the engineering profession. In some cases, it's entirely appropriate for an engineer to earn more than a marketing person. | Yes. |
| 2. Why or why not? | Several reasons: (1) Top engineers are extremely hard to find, and we need to offer competitive salaries; (2) the structure of the engineering department doesn't provide as many promotional opportunities, so we can't use promotions as a motivator the way marketing can; (3) many of our engineers have advanced degrees, and nearly all pursue continuous education to stay on top of the technology. | Without marketing, the products the engineers create wouldn't reach customers, and the company wouldn't have any revenue. The two teams make equal contributions to the company's success. |
| 3. If we decide to balance pay between the two departments, how should we do it? | If we do anything to cap or reduce engineering salaries, we'll lose key people to the competition. | If we can't increase payroll immediately to raise marketing salaries, the only fair thing to do is freeze raises in engineering and gradually raise marketing salaries over the next few years. |

(QR) codes into the app, so that people could scan QR stickers placed on product displays in retail stores. After decoding the QR code, the app would then pull up information about the product on display. However, you've recently learned about *near-field communication* (NFC), a short-range radio technology that might able to accomplish the same thing in a way that is simpler for consumers to use.

**Your task:** Research the prospects for QR codes and NFC technology, and write a short comparative report. Draw a conclusion about which technology you think will dominate in the coming years.

**7. Message Strategies: Analytical Reports [LO-1] [LO-2]** Mistakes can be wonderful learning opportunities if we're honest with ourselves and receptive to learning from the mistake.

**Your task:** Identify a mistake you've made—something significant enough to have cost you a lot of money, wasted a lot of time, harmed your health, damaged a relationship, created serious problems at work, prevented you from pursuing what could've been a rewarding opportunity, or otherwise had serious consequences. Now figure out why you made that mistake. Did you let emotions get in the way of clear thinking? Did you make a serious financial blunder because you didn't take the time to understand the consequences of a decision? Were you too cautious? Not cautious enough? Perhaps several factors led to a poor decision.

Write a brief analytical report to your instructor that describes the situation and outlines your analysis of why the failure occurred and how you can avoid making a similar mistake in the future. If you can't think of a significant mistake or failure you're comfortable sharing with your instructor, write about a mistake a friend or family member made (without revealing the person's identify or potentially causing him or her any embarrassment).

## EMAIL SKILLS

**8. Message Strategies: Analytical Reports [LO-1] [LO-2]** Think of a course you would love to see added to the core curriculum at your school. Conversely, if you would like to see a course offered as an elective rather than being required, write your email report accordingly.

**Your task:** Write a short email proposal, using the 2 + 2 = 4 approach. Prepare your proposal to be submitted to the academic dean by email. Be sure to include reasons supporting your idea.

**9. Message Strategies: Analytical Reports [LO-2]** Assume you will have time for only one course next term.

**Your task:** List the pros and cons of four or five courses that interest you and use the yardstick method to settle on the course that is best for you to take at this time. Write your report in memo format, addressing it to your academic adviser.

## PORTFOLIO BUILDER / TEAM SKILLS

**10. Message Strategies: Analytical Reports [LO-1] [LO-2]** Anyone looking at the fragmented 21st-century landscape of media and entertainment options might be surprised to learn that poetry was once a dominant medium for not only creative literary expression but also philosophical, political, and even scientific discourse. Alas, such is no longer the case.

**Your task:** With a team of fellow students, your challenge is to identify opportunities to increase sales of poetry—any kind of poetry, in any medium. The following suggestions may help you get started:

- Research recent bestsellers in the poetry field, and try to identify why they have been popular.
- Interview literature professors, professional poets, librarians, publishers, and bookstore personnel.
- Consider art forms and venues in which verse plays an essential role, including popular music and poetry slams.
- Conduct surveys and interviews to find out why consumers don't buy more poetry.
- Review professional journals that cover the field of poetry, including *Publishers Weekly* and *Poets & Writers*, from both business and creative standpoints.

Summarize your findings in a brief formal report; assume your target readers are executives in the publishing industry.

## PORTFOLIO BUILDER

**11. Message Strategies: Informational Reports [LO-1] [LO-2]** Health care costs are a pressing concern at every level in the economy, from individual households up through companies of all sizes on up to state and federal governments. Many companies that want to continue offering or to start offering some level of health insurance to their employees are struggling with a cost spiral that seems out of control.

**Your task:** Identify five ways that companies are reducing the cost of providing health care insurance for their employees (other than eliminating this benefit entirely). Compile your findings in a brief report that includes at least one real-life example for each of the five ways.

## PORTFOLIO BUILDER

**12. Message Strategies: Analytical Reports** Like any other endeavor that combines hard-nosed factual analysis and creative free thinking, the task of writing business plans generates a range of opinions.

**Your task:** Find at least six sources of advice on writing successful business plans (focus on start-up businesses that are likely to seek outside investors). Use at least two books, two magazine or journal articles, and two websites or blogs. Analyze the advice you find and identify points where most or all the experts agree and points where they don't agree. Wherever you find points of significant disagreement, identify which opinion you find most convincing and explain why. Summarize your findings in a brief formal report.

## PORTFOLIO BUILDER

**13. Message Strategies: Analytical Reports [LO-1] [LO-2]** After several false starts, tablet computers have finally caught on among business users. In addition to Apple's popular iPad, seemingly every computer company on the planet is looking to get a share of this market. Will they be a passing fad? A cool toy or a serious business tool?

**Your task:** Prepare a short analytical report that compares the advantages and disadvantages of tablet computers for traveling salespeople.

**14. Message Strategies: Analytical Reports** Spurred on in part by the success of numerous television shows and even entire cable networks devoted to remodeling, homeowners across the country are redecorating and rebuilding like never before. Many people are content with superficial changes, such as new paint or new accessories, but some are more ambitious. These homeowners want to move walls, add rooms, redesign kitchens, convert garages to home theaters—the big stuff.

With many consumer trends, publishers try to create magazines that appeal to carefully identified groups of potential readers and the advertisers who'd like to reach them. The do-it-yourself (DIY) market is already served by numerous magazines, but you see an opportunity in those homeowners who tackle the heavy-duty projects. Case Tables 15.3 through 15.5 summarize the results of some preliminary research you asked your company's research staff to conduct.

**Your task:** You think the data show a real opportunity for a "big projects" DIY magazine, although you'll need more extensive research to confirm the size of the market and refine the editorial direction of the magazine. Prepare a brief analytical report that presents the data you have, identifies the opportunity or opportunities you've found (suggest your own ideas based on the tables), and requests funding from the editorial board to pursue further research.

## Long Reports

**15. Message Strategies: Informational Reports [LO-1] [LO-2]** Your company is the largest private employer in your metropolitan area, and the 43,500 employees in your workforce have a tremendous impact on local traffic. A group of city and county transportation officials recently approached your CEO with a request to explore ways to reduce this impact. The CEO has assigned you the task of analyzing the workforce's transportation habits and attitudes as a first step toward identifying potential solutions. He's willing to consider anything from subsidized bus passes to company-owned shuttle buses to telecommuting, but the decision requires a thorough understanding of employee transportation needs. Case Tables 15.6 through 15.10 summarize data you collected in an employee survey.

## CASE TABLE 15.3 — Rooms Most Frequently Remodeled by DIYers

| Room | Percentage of Homeowners Surveyed Who Have Tackled or Plan to Tackle at Least a Partial Remodel |
|---|---|
| Kitchen | 60 |
| Bathroom | 48 |
| Home office/study | 44 |
| Bedroom | 38 |
| Media room/home theater | 31 |
| Den/recreation room | 28 |
| Living room | 27 |
| Dining room | 12 |
| Sun room/solarium | 8 |

## CASE TABLE 15.4 — Average Amount Spent on Remodeling Projects

| Estimated Amount | Percentage of Surveyed Homeowners |
|---|---|
| Under $5K | 5 |
| $5–10K | 21 |
| $10–20K | 39 |
| $20–50K | 22 |
| More than $50K | 13 |

## CASE TABLE 15.5 — Tasks Performed by Homeowner on a Typical Remodeling Project

| Task | Percentage of Surveyed Homeowners Who Perform or Plan to Perform Most or All of This Task Themselves |
|---|---|
| Conceptual design | 90 |
| Technical design/architecture | 34 |
| Demolition | 98 |
| Foundation work | 62 |
| Framing | 88 |
| Plumbing | 91 |
| Electrical | 55 |
| Heating/cooling | 22 |
| Finish carpentry | 85 |
| Tile work | 90 |
| Painting | 100 |
| Interior design | 52 |

## CASE TABLE 15.6 — Employee Carpool Habits

| Frequency of Use: Carpooling | Portion of Workforce |
|---|---|
| Every day, every week | 10,138 (23%) |
| Certain days, every week | 4,361 (10%) |
| Randomly | 983 (2%) |
| Never | 28,018 (64%) |

## CASE TABLE 15.7 — Use of Public Transportation

| Frequency of Use: Public Transportation | Portion of Workforce |
|---|---|
| Every day, every week | 23,556 (54%) |
| Certain days, every week | 2,029 (5%) |
| Randomly | 5,862 (13%) |
| Never | 12,053 (28%) |

## CASE TABLE 15.8 — Effect of Potential Improvements to Public Transportation

| Which of the Following Would Encourage You to Use Public Transportation More Frequently (check all that apply) | Portion of Respondents |
|---|---|
| Increased perception of safety | 4,932 (28%) |
| Improved cleanliness | 852 (5%) |
| Reduced commute times | 7,285 (41%) |
| Greater convenience: fewer transfers | 3,278 (18%) |
| Greater convenience: more stops | 1,155 (6%) |
| Lower (or subsidized) fares | 5,634 (31%) |
| Nothing could encourage me to take public transportation | 8,294 (46%) |

*Note:* This question was asked of respondents who use public transportation randomly or never, a subgroup that represents 17,915 employees, or 41 percent of the workforce.

## CASE TABLE 15.9 — Distance Traveled to/from Work

| Distance You Travel to Work (one way) | Portion of Workforce |
|---|---|
| Less than 1 mile | 531 (1%) |
| 1–3 miles | 6,874 (16%) |
| 4–10 miles | 22,951 (53%) |
| 11–20 miles | 10,605 (24%) |
| More than 20 miles | 2,539 (6%) |

|||||||||||||||||||||||||||||||||||||||||||||||||||||||||||||||||||||

CASE TABLE 15.10 | **Is Telecommuting an Option?**

| Does the Nature of Your Work Make Telecommuting a Realistic Option? | Portion of Workforce |
|---|---|
| Yes, every day | 3,460 (8%) |
| Yes, several days a week | 8,521 (20%) |
| Yes, random days | 12,918 (30%) |
| No | 18,601 (43%) |

**Your task:** Present the results of your survey in an informational report, using the data provided in the tables.

## TEAM SKILLS / PORTFOLIO BUILDER

**16. Message Strategies: Informational Reports [LO-1] [LO-2]**
As a researcher in your state's consumer protection agency, you're frequently called on to investigate consumer topics and write reports for the agency's website. Thousands of consumers have arranged the purchase of cars online, and millions more do at least some of their research online before heading to a dealership. Some want to save time and money, some want to be armed with as much information as possible before talking to a dealer, and others want to completely avoid the often-uncomfortable experience of negotiating prices with car salespeople. In response, a variety of online services have emerged to meet these consumer needs. Some let you compare information on various car models, some connect you to local dealers to complete the transaction, and some complete nearly all the transaction details for you, including negotiating the price. Some search the inventory of thousands of dealers, whereas others search only a single dealership or a network of affiliated dealers. In other words, a slew of new tools are available for car buyers, but it's not always easy to figure out where to go and what to expect. That's where your report will help.

By visiting a variety of car-related websites and reading magazine and newspaper articles on the car-buying process, you've compiled a variety of notes related to the subject:

- **Process overview.** The process is relatively straightforward and fairly similar to other online shopping experiences, with two key differences. In general, a consumer identifies the make and model of car he or she wants, and then the online car-buying service searches the inventories of car dealers nationwide and presents the available choices. The consumer chooses a particular car from that list, and then the service handles the communication and purchase details with the dealer. When the paperwork is finished, the consumer visits the dealership and picks up the car. The two biggest differences with online auto buying are that (1) you can't actually complete the purchase over the Internet (in most cases, you must visit a local dealer to pick up the car and sign the papers, although in some cities, a dealer or a local car-buying service will deliver it to your home) and (2) in most states, it's illegal to purchase a new car from anyone other than a franchise dealer (that is, you can't buy directly from the manufacturer, the way you can buy a Dell computer directly from Dell, for instance).

- **Information you can find online** (not all information is available at all sites). You can find information on makes, models, colors, options, option packages (often, specific options are available only as part of a package; you need to know these constraints before you select your options), photos, specifications (everything from engine size to interior space), mileage estimates, performance data, safety information, predicted resale value, reviews, comparable models, insurance costs, consumer ratings, repair and reliability histories, available buyer incentives and rebates, true ownership costs (including costs for fuel, maintenance, repair, and so on), warranty, loan and lease payments, and maintenance requirements.

- **Advantages of shopping online.** Advantages of shopping online include shopping from the comfort and convenience of home, none of the dreaded negotiating at the dealership (in many cases), the ability to search far and wide for a specific car (even nationwide, on many sites), rapid access to considerable amounts of data and information, and reviews from both professional automotive journalists and other consumers. In general, online auto shopping reduces a key advantage that auto dealers used to have, which was control of most of the information in the purchase transaction. Now consumers can find out how reliable each model is, how quickly it will depreciate, how often it is likely to need repairs, what other drivers think of it, how much the dealer paid the manufacturer for it, and so on.

- **Changing nature of the business.** The relationship between dealers and third-party websites (such as CarsDirect .com and Vehix.com) continues to evolve. At first, the relationship was more antagonistic, as some third-party sites and dealers frequently competed for the same customers, and each side made bold proclamations about driving the other out of business. However, the relationship is more collaborative in many cases now, with dealers realizing that some third-party sites already have wide brand awareness and nationwide audiences. As the percentage of new car sales that originate via the Internet continues to increase, dealers are more receptive to working with third-party sites.

- **Comparing information from multiple sources.** Consumers shouldn't rely solely on information from a single website. Each site has its own way of organizing information, and many sites have their own ways of evaluating car models and connecting buyers with sellers.

- **Understanding what each site is doing.** Some sites search thousands of dealers, regardless of ownership connections. Others, such as AutoNation, search only affiliated dealers. A search for a specific model might yield only a half dozen cars on one site but dozens of cars on another site. Find out who owns the site and what their business objectives are, if you can; this will help you assess the information you receive.

- **Leading websites.** Consumers can check out a wide variety of websites, some of which are full-service operations, offering everything from research to negotiation; others provide more specific and limited services. For instance, CarsDirect (www.carsdirect.com) provides a full range of services, whereas Carfax (www.carfax.com) specializes in uncovering the repair histories of individual used cars. Case Table 15.11 lists some of the leading car-related websites.

| CASE TABLE 15.11 | Leading Automotive Websites |
| --- | --- |
| **Site** | **URL** |
| AutoAdvice | www.autoadvice.com |
| Autobytel | www.autobytel.com |
| Autos.com | www.autos.com |
| AutoVantage | www.autovantage.com |
| Autoweb | www.autoweb.com |
| CarBargains | www.carbargains.com |
| Carfax | www.carfax.com |
| CarPrices.com | www.carprices.com |
| Cars.com | www.cars.com |
| CarsDirect | www.carsdirect.com |
| CarSmart | www.carsmart.com |
| Consumer Reports | www.consumerreports.org |
| eBay Motors | www.motors.ebay.com |
| Edmunds | www.edmunds.com |
| IMotors | www.imotors.com |
| IntelliChoice | www.intellichoice.com |
| InvoiceDealers | www.invoicedealers.com |
| JDPower | www.jdpower.com |
| Kelly Blue Book | www.kbb.com |
| MSN Autos | http://autos.msn.com |
| PickupTrucks.com | www.pickuptrucks.com |
| The Car Connection | www.thecarconnection.com |
| Vehix.com | www.vehix.com |
| Yahoo! Autos | http//autos.yahoo.com |

**Your task:** With a team assigned by your instructor, write an informational report based on your research notes. The purpose of the report is to introduce consumers to the basic concepts of integrating the Internet into their car-buying activities and to educate them about important issues.[12]

## PORTFOLIO BUILDER

**17. Message Strategies: Analytical Reports [LO-1] [LO-2]** As a college student and an active consumer, you may have considered one or more of the following questions at some point in the past few years:

a. What criteria distinguish the top-rated MBA programs in the country? How well do these criteria correspond to the needs and expectations of business? Are the criteria fair for students, employers, and business schools?

b. Which of three companies you might like to work for has the strongest corporate ethics policies?

c. What will the music industry look like in the future? What's next after online stores such as Apple's iTunes and digital players such as the iPod?

d. Which industries and job categories are forecast to experience the greatest growth—and therefore the greatest demand for workers—in the next 10 years?

e. What has been the impact of Starbucks's aggressive growth on small, independent coffee shops? On midsized chains or franchises? In the United States or in another country?

f. How large is the "industry" of major college sports? How much do the major football or basketball programs contribute—directly or indirectly—to other parts of a typical university?

g. How much have minor league sports—baseball, hockey, arena football—grown in small- and medium-market cities? What is the local economic impact when these municipalities build stadiums and arenas?

**Your task:** Answer one of the preceding questions using secondary research sources for information. Be sure to document your sources, using the format your instructor indicates. Give conclusions and offer recommendations where appropriate.

## PORTFOLIO BUILDER

**18. Message Strategies: Analytical Reports** An observer surveying the current consumer electronics landscape and seeing Apple products everywhere might be surprised to learn that during part of the company's history, it was regarded by some as a fairly minor player in the computer industry—and at times a few pundits even wondered whether the company would survive.

**Your task:** In a two- to three-page report, identify the reasons Apple has been successful and explain how other companies can apply Apple's strategies and tactics to improve their business results.

**19. Message Strategies: Analytical Reports** After 15 years in the corporate world, you're ready to strike out on your own. Rather than building a business from the ground up, however, you think that buying a franchise is a better idea. Unfortunately, some of the most lucrative franchise opportunities, such as the major fast-food chains, require significant start-up costs—some more than a half-million dollars. Fortunately, you've met several potential investors who seem willing to help you get started in exchange for a share of ownership. Between your own savings and money from these investors, you estimate that you can raise from $350,000 to $600,000, depending on how much ownership share you want to concede to the investors.

You've worked in several functional areas already, including sales and manufacturing, so you have a fairly well-rounded business résumé. You're open to just about any type of business, too, as long as it provides the opportunity to grow; you don't want to be so tied down to the first operation that you can't turn it over to a hired manager and expand into another market.

**Your task:** To convene a formal meeting with the investor group, you need to first draft a report that outlines the types of franchise opportunities you'd like to pursue. Write a brief report, identifying five franchises that you would like to explore further. (Choose five based on your own personal interests and the criteria already identified.) For each possibility, identify the nature of the business, the financial requirements, the level of support the company provides, and a brief statement of why you could run such a business successfully (make up any details you need). Be sure to carefully review the information you find about each franchise company to make sure you can qualify for it. For instance, McDonald's doesn't allow investment partnerships to buy franchises, so you won't be able to start up a McDonald's outlet until you have enough money to do it on your own.

For a quick introduction to franchising, see How Stuff Works (http://money.howstuffworks.com/franchising.htm). You can learn more about the business of franchising at Franchising.com (www.franchising.com) and search for specific franchise opportunities at Francorp Connect (www.francorpconnect.com). In addition, many companies that sell franchises, such as Subway, offer additional information on their websites.

# Proposals

**20. Message Strategies: Proposals [LO-3]** One of the banes of apartment living is those residents who don't care about the condition of their shared surroundings. They might leave trash all over the place, dent walls when they move furniture, spill food and beverages in common areas, destroy window screens, and otherwise degrade living conditions for everyone. Landlords obviously aren't thrilled about this behavior, either, because it raises the costs of cleaning and maintaining the facility.

**Your task:** Assume that you live in a fairly large apartment building some distance from campus. Write an email proposal that you could send to your landlord, suggesting that fostering a sense of stronger community among residents in your building might help reduce incidents of vandalism and neglect. Propose that the little-used storage area in the basement of the building be converted to a community room, complete with a simple kitchen and a large-screen television. By attending Super Bowl parties and other events there, residents could get to know one another and perhaps forge bonds that would raise the level of shared concern for their living environment. You can't offer any proof of this in advance, of course, but share your belief that a modest investment in this room could pay off long term in lower repair and maintenance costs. Moreover, it would be an attractive feature to entice new residents.

## PORTFOLIO BUILDER

**21. Message Strategies: Proposals [LO-1] [LO-3]** Presentations can make—or break—both careers and businesses. A good presentation can bring in millions of dollars in new sales or fresh investment capital. A bad presentation might cause any number of troubles, from turning away potential customers to upsetting fellow employees to derailing key projects. To help business professionals plan, create, and deliver more effective presentations, you offer a three-day workshop that covers the essentials of good presentations:

- Understanding your audience's needs and expectations
- Formulating your presentation objectives
- Choosing an organizational approach

- Writing openings that catch your audience's attention
- Creating effective graphics and slides
- Practicing and delivering your presentation
- Leaving a positive impression on your audience
- Avoiding common mistakes with electronic slides
- Making presentations online using webcasting tools
- Handling questions and arguments from the audience
- Overcoming the top 10 worries of public speaking (including *How can I overcome stage fright?* and *I'm not the performing type; can I still give an effective presentation?*)

**Workshop benefits:** Students will learn how to prepare better presentations in less time and deliver them more effectively.

**Who should attend:** Top executives, project managers, employment recruiters, sales professionals, and anyone else who gives important presentations to internal or external audiences.

**Your qualifications:** 18 years of business experience, including 14 years in sales and 12 years of public speaking. Experience speaking to audiences as large as 5,000 people. More than a dozen speech-related articles published in professional journals. Have conducted successful workshops for nearly 100 companies.

**Workshop details:** Three-day workshop (9 A.M. to 3:30 P.M.) that combines lectures, practice presentations, and both individual and group feedback. Minimum number of students: 6. Maximum number of students per workshop: 12.

**Pricing:** The cost is $3,500, plus $100 per student; 10 percent discount for additional workshops.

**Other information:** Each attendee will have the opportunity to give three practice presentations that will last from 3 to 5 minutes. Everyone is encouraged to bring PowerPoint files containing slides from actual business presentations. Each attendee will also receive a workbook and a digital video recording of his or her final class presentation on DVD. You'll also be available for phone or email coaching for six months after the workshop.

**Your task:** Identify a company in your local area that might be a good candidate for your services. Learn more about the company by visiting its website so you can personalize your proposal. Using the information listed above, prepare a sales proposal that explains the benefits of your training and what students can expect during the workshop.

## PORTFOLIO BUILDER

**22. Message Strategies: Proposals [LO-1] [LO-3]** For years, a controversy has been brewing over the amount of junk food and soft drinks being sold through vending machines in local schools. Schools benefit from revenue-sharing arrangements, but many parents and health experts are concerned about the negative effects of these snacks and beverages. You and your brother have almost a decade of experience running espresso and juice stands in malls and on street corners, and you'd love to find some way to expand your business into schools. After a quick brainstorming session, the two of you craft a plan that makes good business sense while meeting the financial concerns of school administrators and the nutritional concerns of parents and dietitians. Here are the notes from your brainstorming session:

- Set up portable juice bars on school campuses, offering healthy fruit and vegetable drinks along with simple, healthy snacks
- Offer schools 30 percent of profits in exchange for free space and long-term contracts
- Provide job-training opportunities for students (during athletic events, etc.)
- Provide detailed dietary analysis of all products sold
- Establish a nutritional advisory board composed of parents, students, and at least one certified health professional
- Assure schools and parents that all products are safe (e.g., no stimulant drinks, no dietary supplements)
- Support local farmers and specialty food preparers by buying locally and giving these vendors the opportunity to test-market new products at your stands

**Your task:** Based on the ideas listed, draft a formal proposal to the local school board, outlining your plan to offer healthier alternatives to soft drinks and prepackaged snack foods. Invent any details you need to complete your proposal.

## PORTFOLIO BUILDER / TEAM SKILLS

**23. Message Strategies: Proposals [LO-1] [LO-3]** It seems like everybody in your firm is frustrated. On the one hand, top executives complain about the number of lower-level employees who want promotions but just don't seem to "get it" when it comes to dealing with customers and the public, recognizing when to speak out and when to be quiet, knowing how to push new ideas through the appropriate channels, and performing other essential but difficult-to-teach tasks. On the other hand, ambitious employees who'd like to learn more feel that they have nowhere to turn for career advice from people who've been there. In between, a variety of managers and midlevel executives are overwhelmed by the growing number of mentoring requests they're getting, sometimes from employees they don't even know.

You've been assigned the challenge of proposing a formal mentoring program—and a considerable challenge it is:

- The number of employees who want mentoring relationships far exceeds the number of managers and executives willing and able to be mentors; how will you select people for the program?
- The people most in demand for mentoring also tend to be some of the busiest people in the organization.

- After several years of belt tightening and staff reductions, the entire company feels overworked; few people can imagine adding another recurring task to their seemingly endless to-do lists.
- What's in it for the mentors? Why would they be motivated to help lower-level employees?
- How will you measure the success or failure of the mentoring effort?

**Your task:** With a team assigned by your instructor, identify potential solutions to the issues (make up any information you need) and draft a proposal to the executive committee for a formal, companywide mentoring program that would match selected employees with successful managers and executives.

## LETTER WRITING SKILLS

**24. Message Strategies: Proposals [LO-3]** As a sales manager for Air-Trak, one of your responsibilities is writing sales proposals for potential buyers of your company's Air-Trak tracking system. The system uses the global positioning system (GPS) to track the location of vehicles and other assets. For example, the dispatcher for a trucking company can simply click a map display on a computer screen to find out where all the company's trucks are at that instant. Air-Trak lists the following as benefits of the system:

- Making sure vehicles follow prescribed routes with minimal loitering time
- "Geofencing," in which dispatchers are alerted if vehicles leave assigned routes or designated service areas
- Route optimization, in which fleet managers can analyze routes and destinations to find the most time- and fuel-efficient path for each vehicle
- Comparisons between scheduled and actual travel
- Enhanced security, protecting both drivers and cargo

**Your task:** Write a brief proposal in letter format to Doneta Zachs, fleet manager for Midwest Express, 338 S.W. 6th, Des Moines, Iowa 50321. Introduce your company, explain the benefits of the Air-Trak system, and propose a trial deployment in which you would equip five Midwest Express trucks. For the purposes of this assignment, you don't need to worry about the technical details of the system; focus on promoting the benefits and asking for a decision regarding the test project. (You can learn more about the Air-Trak system at www.air-trak.com.)[13]

## MyBCommLab

Go to **mybcommlab.com** for Auto-graded writing questions as well as the following Assisted-graded writing questions:

**15-1.** Why is the "you" attitude especially important with long, complex reports? [LO-1]

**15-2.** How do previews and reviews work in tandem to help readers? [LO-1]

**15-3.** Mybcommlab Only—comprehensive writing assignment for this chapter.

# Endnotes

**1.** Adapted from "Writing a Compelling Executive Summary," Garage Technology Ventures, accessed 5 February 2013, www.garage.com; "Crafting Your Wow! Statement," Garage Technology Ventures, accessed 5 February 2013, www.garage.com; Guy Kawasaki website, accessed 5 February 2013, www.guykawasaki.com.

**2.** A. S. C. Ehrenberg, "Report Writing—Six Simple Rules for Better Business Documents," *Admap*, June 1992, 39–42.

**3.** Michael Netzley and Craig Snow, *Guide to Report Writing* (Upper Saddle River, N.J.: Prentice Hall, 2001), 15.

**4.** "Tellabs Solutions and Applications," Tellabs 2005 Annual Report, accessed 11 November 2006, www.tellabs.com.

**5.** David A. Hayes, "Helping Students Grasp the Knack of Writing Summaries," *Journal of Reading* (November 1989): 96–101.

**6.** Philip C. Kolin, *Successful Writing at Work*, 6th ed. (Boston: Houghton Mifflin, 2001), 552–555.

**7.** Qvidian website, accessed 26 June 2012, www.qvidian.com.

**8.** John Morkes and Jakob Nielsen, "Concise, Scannable, and Objective: How to Write for the Web," UseIt.com, accessed 13 November 2006, www.useit.com.

**9.** Martin James, "PDF Virus Spreads Without Exploiting Any Flaw," *IT Pro*, 8 April 2010, www.itpro.co.uk.

**10.** Andrea Obana, "How to Write a Request for Proposal (RFP)," Fine Brand Media website, accessed 22 January 2004, www.finebrand.com;

Toby B. Gooley, "Ocean Shipping: RFPs That Get Results," *Logistics Management*, July 2003, 47–52.

**11.** Obana, "How to Write a Request for Proposal (RFP)"; Gooley, "Ocean Shipping: RFPs That Get Results," 47–52; "Writing a Good RFP," Infrastructure Issues, Mead & Hunt website, accessed 23 January 2004, www.meadhunt.com.

**12.** Adapted from Ieva M. Augstumes, "Buyers Take the Driver's Seat," *Dallas Morning News*, 20 February 2004, www.highbeam.com; Jill Amadio, "A Click Away: Automotive Web Sites Are Revved Up and Ready to Help You Buy," *Entrepreneur*, 1 August 2003, www.highbeam.com; Dawn C. Chmielewski, "Car Sites Lend Feel-Good Info for Haggling," *San Jose Mercury News*, 1 August 2003, www.highbeam.com; Cromwell Schubarth, "Autoheroes Handle Hassle of Haggling," *Boston Herald*, 24 July 2003, www.highbeam.com; Rick Popely, "Internet Doesn't Change Basic Shopping Rules," *Chicago Tribune*, 28 February 2004, www.highbeam.com; Matt Nauman, "Walnut Creek, Calif., Firm Prospers as Online Car Buying Becomes More Popular," *San Jose Mercury News*, 21 June 2004, www.highbeam.com; Cliff Banks, "e-Dealer 100," *Ward's Dealer Business*, 1 April 2004, www.highbeam.com; Cars.com website, accessed 30 June 2004, www.cars.com; CarsDirect.com website, accessed 30 June 2004, www.carsdirect.com.

**13.** Adapted from Air-Trak website, accessed 6 February 2013, www.air-trak.com.

Presentations give you the opportunity to put all your communication skills on display, from audience analysis and research to the design of presentation materials to public speaking. Learn how to plan effective presentations, overcome the anxieties that every speaker feels, respond to questions from the audience, and embrace the Twitter-enabled backchannel. Discover some tips and techniques for succeeding with online presentations, an increasingly common mode of communication in today's environment. Complement your talk with compelling visual materials and learn how to create presentation slides that engage and excite your audience.

wavebreakmedia ltd./Shutterstock

## LEARNING OBJECTIVES

After studying this chapter, you will be able to

**1** Describe the tasks involved in analyzing the situation for a presentation and organizing a presentation.

**2** Explain how to adapt to your audience and develop an effective opening, body, and close for a presentation.

**3** Discuss five steps for delivering a successful presentation.

**4** Explain the growing importance of the backchannel in presentations and list six steps for giving effective presentations online.

---

### MyBCommLab®

⭐ **Improve Your Grade!** Over 10 million students improved their results using the Pearson MyLabs. Visit **mybcommlab.com** for simulations, tutorials, and end-of-chapter problems.

---

### COMMUNICATION CLOSE-UP AT
## Principato-Young Entertainment

The business of being funny can be profoundly unfunny these days, particularly for comedians who want to break into movies and television shows. Fewer movies are being made, and the audience for television and online shows is so fragmented that trying to build a fan base is an uphill struggle. Making the situation even worse for comedians, many of whom are writers at heart, is the seemingly unstoppable growth of reality shows, which require neither writers nor actors in any conventional sense.

John Shearer/Wire Image/Getty Images

Talent agent Peter Principato (right, with actor Will Arnett) coaches his comedian clients to hone their presentations before pitching movie and TV show ideas to studio executives.

Talent agent Peter Principato knows this landscape as well as anyone, and as he puts it, "There's less and less real estate every year." Studios are increasingly reluctant to "green light" projects, particularly with the young and not-quite-top-of-the-marquee talent that is the specialty of Principato-Young Entertainment, the Beverly Hills company he cofounded with producer Paul Young. But comedy is in Principato's blood, so he works overtime to make his clients successful, even in this challenging environment.

In the entertainment industry, the road to success often starts with "the pitch," a brief presentation to one or more studio executives by an individual writer, actor, director, or producer or by a team of these people. If the executive is intrigued by the concept, it might be discussed further within the studio, and eventually a decision will be made about funding production.

With so much riding on this brief presentation, you can imagine that it's a high-anxiety event for the presenters, and making pitches is a vital communication skill. In fact, the ability to pitch effectively is so important that it has its own slang term: being "good in a room."

Pitches can fall flat for a number of reasons, whether the concept is not a good fit for a particular studio, the idea is so unusual that the executives are unwilling to risk investing in it, or the pitch is poorly presented. A presenter may fail by being unable to summarize what a new show or movie idea is all about, by smothering the executives in too many details, or by trying too hard to sell the concept.

The pointers Principato gives his clients constitute good advice for presentations in any industry, but they're vital in the entertainment industry. First, come up with a single compelling sentence that describes the show or movie. If presenters can't do this, chances are they haven't thought the idea out well enough, or the idea is so complicated that it would be too risky or too expensive to attempt. This one-line summary is essential for another reason, in that the first studio executive to hear the pitch will usually need to share it with other executives or potential financiers before a decision can be made. A catchy, succinct idea is a lot easier to repeat than a rambling, confused concept.

Second, expand on that one sentence with a single paragraph that builds interest by substantiating the concept and helping the listener envision what the show or movie would be like. Third, for a proposed series, explain how the concept would play out, week by week, by describing several episodes. Fourth, fill in the "big picture," such as by describing how the show would look on screen or by rounding out the main characters.

You've probably noticed how this advice follows the classic AIDA model of getting attention, building interest, increasing desire, and asking for a decision, which is what makes Principato's advice valuable for just about any profession.

The funny business is tough and getting tougher, but Principato is clearly doing something right. Principato-Young continues to expand and attract more of the young comedians who might be box office stars for the next several decades. And his love of comedy and comedians continues to motivate Principato himself. As he describes it, having his job "is like getting to hang out with your favorite band."[1]

# Planning a Presentation

You might not pitch the next Oscar winner to a studio executive as Peter Principato (profiled in the chapter-opening Communication Close-Up) hopes to do, but wherever your career takes you, oral presentations will offer important opportunities to put all your communication skills on display, including research, planning, writing, visual design, and interpersonal and nonverbal communication. Presentations also let you demonstrate your ability to think on your feet, grasp complex business issues, and handle challenging situations—all attributes that executives look for when searching for talented employees to promote.

If the thought of giving a speech or presentation makes you nervous, keep three points in mind. First, everybody gets nervous when speaking in front of groups. Second, being nervous is actually a good thing; it means you care about the topic, your audience, and your career success. Third, with practice, you can convert those nervous feelings into positive energy that helps you give more compelling presentations. You can take control of the situation by using the three-step writing process to prepare for successful presentations (see Figure 16.1 on the next page).

Planning oral presentations is much like planning any other business message: You analyze the situation, gather information, select the right medium, and organize the information. Gathering information for oral presentations is essentially the same as it is for written communication projects. The other three planning tasks have some special applications when it comes to oral presentations; they are covered in the following sections.

On the subject of planning, be aware that preparing a professional-quality business presentation takes time. Nancy Duarte, whose design firm has years of experience creating

**1 LEARNING OBJECTIVE**
Describe the tasks involved in analyzing the situation for a presentation and organizing a presentation.

Feeling nervous is perfectly normal when you're faced with an oral presentation; the good news is there are positive steps you can take to reduce your anxiety.

---

**REAL-TIME UPDATES**
LEARN MORE BY WATCHING THIS VIDEO

**Dealing with the difficult four**

Get advice on dealing with four difficult audience members: the Resister, the Expert, the Dominator, and the Rambler. Go to http://real-timeupdates.com/bct12 and click on Learn More. If you are using MyBCommLab, you can access Real-Time Updates within each chapter or under Student Study Tools.

| **1** Plan → | **2** Write → | **3** Complete |
|---|---|---|
| **Analyze the Situation**<br>Define your purpose and develop a profile of your audience, including their likely emotional states and language preferences. | **Adapt to Your Audience**<br>Adapt your content, presentation style, and room setup to the audience and the specific situation. Be sensitive to audience needs and expectations with a "you" attitude, politeness, positive emphasis, and bias-free language. Plan to establish your credibility as required. | **Revise the Message**<br>Evaluate your content and speaking notes. |
| **Gather Information**<br>Determine audience needs and obtain the information necessary to satisfy those needs. | | **Master Your Delivery**<br>Choose your delivery mode and practice your presentation. |
| **Select the Right Medium**<br>Choose the best medium or combination of media for delivering your presentation, including handouts and other support materials. | **Compose Your Presentation**<br>Outline an attention-getting introduction, body, and close. Prepare supporting visuals and speaking notes. | **Prepare to Speak**<br>Verify facilities and equipment, including online connections and software setups. Hire an interpreter if necessary. |
| **Organize the Information**<br>Define your main idea, limit your scope and verify timing, select the direct or indirect approach, and outline your content. | | **Overcome Anxiety**<br>Take steps to feel more confident and appear more confident on stage. |

**Figure 16.1  The Three-Step Process for Developing Oral and Online Presentations**
Although you rarely "write" a presentation or speech in the sense of composing every word ahead of time, the tasks in the three-step writing process adapt quite well to the challenge of planning, creating, and delivering both oral and online presentations.

Creating a high-quality presentation for an important event can take many days, so be sure to allow enough time.

presentations for corporations, offers this rule of thumb: for a one-hour presentation that uses 30 slides, allow 36 to 90 hours to research, conceive, create, and practice.[2] Not every one-hour presentation justifies a week or two of preparation, of course, but the important presentations that can make your career or your company certainly can.

## ANALYZING THE SITUATION

The purpose of most business presentations is to inform or persuade; you may also give presentations designed primarily to collaborate with others.

As with written communications, analyzing the situation for an oral presentation involves defining your purpose and developing an audience profile. The purpose of most of your presentations will be to inform or to persuade, although you may occasionally need to make a collaborative presentation, such as when you're leading a problem-solving or brainstorming session. Given the time limitations of most presentations and the live nature of the event, make sure your purpose is crystal clear so that you make the most of the opportunity and show respect for your listeners' time and attention.

Knowing your audience's state of mind will help you adjust both your message and your delivery.

When you develop your audience profile, try to anticipate the likely emotional state of your audience members. Figure 16.2 offers tips for dealing with a variety of audience mindsets.

You also need to determine whether your audience is comfortable listening to the language you speak. Listening to an unfamiliar language is much more difficult than reading that language, so an audience that might be able to read a written report might not be able to understand an oral presentation covering the same material (see "Communicating Across Cultures: Making Sure Your Message Doesn't Get Lost in Translation").

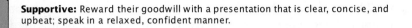

**Supportive:** Reward their goodwill with a presentation that is clear, concise, and upbeat; speak in a relaxed, confident manner.

**Interested but neutral:** Build your credibility as you present compelling reasons to accept your message; address potential objections as you move forward; show confidence in your message but a willingness to answer questions and concerns.

**Uninterested:** Use the techniques described in this chapter to get their attention and work hard to hold it throughout; find ways to connect your message with their personal or professional interests; be well organized and concise.

**Worried:** Don't dismiss their fears or tell them they are mistaken for feeling that way; if your message will calm their fears, use the direct approach; if your message will confirm their fears, consider the indirect approach to build acceptance.

**Hostile:** Recognize that angry audiences care deeply but might not be open to listening; consider the indirect approach to find common ground and to diffuse anger before sharing your message; work to keep your own emotions under control.

**Figure 16.2  Planning for Various Audience Mindsets**
Try to assess the emotional state of your audience ahead of time so you can plan your presentation approach accordingly.

## COMMUNICATING ACROSS CULTURES

# Making Sure Your Message Doesn't Get Lost in Translation

When speaking to an international audience, keep in mind that audience members' language fluency might vary widely. So take special care to ensure clear communication:

- **Speak slowly and distinctly.** The most common complaint of international audiences is that English speakers talk too fast. Articulate each word carefully, emphasize consonants for clarity, and pause frequently.
- **Repeat key words and phrases.** When audiences are not very familiar with your language, they need to hear important information more than once. Also, they may not be familiar with synonyms, so word key points in the same way throughout your presentation.
- **Aim for clarity.** Keep your message simple. Avoid complex sentence structures, abbreviations, acronyms, and metaphors. Replace two-word verbs with one-word alternatives (such as *review* instead of *look over*). Such verbs are confusing because the definition of each separate word differs from the meaning of the two words combined. Similarly, avoid slang and cultural idioms, such as *once in a blue moon*, which may be unfamiliar to an international audience. If you use words or phrases from the audience's native language, make sure you understand them fully.
- **Communicate with body language.** Emphasize and clarify verbal information with gestures and facial expressions. For instance, smile to emphasize positive points and use gestures to illustrate the meaning of words such as *up*, *down*, or *under*.

- **Support your spoken message with visuals.** Simple, clear visuals, from flip charts to electronic slides, can help you describe your key points. If possible, prepare captions in both English and your audience's native language.

### CAREER APPLICATIONS

1. One of the most important changes speakers need to make when addressing audiences in other cultures is to avoid colloquial figures of speech. Listen carefully to the next three course lectures you attend and identify phrases that could cause confusion (such as "hit one out of the park," "go for broke," or "get your ducks in a row"). Review your list and replace the problematic phrases with wording that is more likely to be understood by nonnative English speakers or audiences in other countries.

2. Make a list of 10 two-word verbs. How does the meaning of each separate word differ from the definition of the combined words? Replace each two-word verb with a single, specific word that will be clearer to an international audience.

*Sources:* Adapted from Ramez Naguib, "International Audiences," Toastmasters International, accessed 8 February 2013, www.toastmasters.org; Patricia L. Kurtz, *The Global Speaker* (New York: AMACOM, 1995), 35–47, 56–68, 75–82, 87–100; David A. Victor, *International Business Communication* (New York: HarperCollins Publishers, 1992), 39–45; Lalita Khosla, "You Say Tomato," *Forbes,* 21 May 2001, 36; Stephen Dolainski, "Are Expats Getting Lost in the Translation?" *Workforce,* February 1997, 32–39.

Learn as much as you can about the setting and circumstances of your presentation, from the size of the audience to seating arrangements to potential interruptions.

Also consider the specific circumstances in which you'll be making your presentation. Will you speak to five people in a conference room, where you can control everything from light to sound to temperature? Or will you be demonstrating a product on the floor of a trade show, where you might have from 1 to 100 listeners and little control over the environment? Will everyone be in the same room, or will some or all of your audience participate from remote locations via the Internet? What equipment will you have at your disposal?

For in-person presentations, pay close attention to seating arrangements. The four basic formats have distinct advantages and disadvantages:

- **Classroom or theater seating,** in which all chairs or desks face forward, helps keep attention focused on the speaker and is usually the best method for accommodating large audiences. However, this arrangement inhibits interaction among audience members, so it is not desirable for brainstorming or other collaborative activities.
- **Conference table seating,** in which people sit along both sides of a long table and the speaker stands at one end, is a common arrangement for smaller meetings. It promotes interaction among attendees, but it tends to isolate the speaker at one end of the room.
- **Horseshoe, or "U" shaped, seating,** in which tables are arranged in the shape of a "U," improves on conference table seating by allowing the speaker to walk between the tables to interact with individual audience members.
- **Café seating,** in which people sit in groups at individual tables, is best for breakout sessions and other small-group activities. However, this arrangement is less than ideal for anything more than short presentations because it places some in the audience with their backs to the speaker, making it awkward for both them and the presenter.

If you can't control the seating arrangement, at least be aware of what it is so you can adjust your plans if needed.

All these variables can influence not only the style of your presentation but the content. For instance, in a public environment full of distractions and uncertainties, you're probably better off keeping your content simple and short because chances are you won't be able to keep everyone's attention for the duration of your presentation.

Table 16.1 offers a summary of the key steps in analyzing an audience for oral presentations. For even more insight into audience evaluation (including emotional and cultural issues), consult a good public-speaking textbook.

**TABLE 16.1 | Analyzing an Audience for Oral Presentations**

| Task | Actions |
|---|---|
| To determine audience size and composition | • Estimate how many people will attend and whether they will all attend in person, online, or a mix of both.<br>• Find out if they share professional interests or other affiliations that can help you establish common ground with them.<br>• Analyze demographic and psychographic variables to see any significant differences or similarities should influence the content and style of your presentation. |
| To predict the audience's probable reaction | • Analyze why audience members are attending the presentation.<br>• Predict the mood that people will be in when you speak to them: supportive, interested but neutral, uninterested, apprehensive, or hostile.<br>• Find out what kind of backup information will impress and influence the audience: technical data, historical information, financial data, demonstrations, samples, and so on.<br>• Consider whether the audience has any biases that might work against you.<br>• Anticipate possible objections or questions. |
| To gauge the audience's level of understanding | • Analyze whether everybody has the same background and experience.<br>• Determine what the audience already knows about the subject.<br>• Decide what background information the audience will need to better understand the subject.<br>• Consider whether the audience is familiar with your vocabulary.<br>• Analyze what the audience expects from you.<br>• Think about the mix of general concepts and specific details you will need to present. |

## SELECTING THE BEST MEDIUM

The task of selecting the best medium might seem obvious. After all, you are speaking, so it's an oral medium. However, you have an array of choices these days, ranging from live, in-person presentations to *webcasts* or *webinars* (online presentations or seminars that people view live or download later from your website), *screencasts* (recordings of activity on computer displays with audio voiceover), or *twebinars* (online events that combine a webinar with the use of Twitter as a *backchannel*—see page 471—for real-time conversation[3]).

Explore these options early in your planning efforts so you can take full advantage of the ones at your disposal. For example, to reach an international audience, you might want to conduct a live presentation with a question-and-answer session for the on-site audience and post a video archive of the meeting on your website for audience members in other time zones.

Expect to give many online presentations in your career.

## ORGANIZING YOUR PRESENTATION

Organizing a presentation involves the same tasks as organizing a written message: Define your main idea, limit your scope, select the direct or indirect approach, and outline your content. As you work through these tasks, keep in mind that oral media have certain limitations. When reading written reports, audiences can skip back and forth, backing up if they miss a point or become confused and jumping ahead if they aren't interested in a particular part or are already familiar with the content. However, audiences for live presentations are more or less trapped in your time frame and sequence. Aside from interrupting you, they have no choice but to listen to your content in the exact order in which you present it.

### Defining Your Main Idea

If you've ever heard a speaker struggle to get his or her point across ("What I really mean to say is . . ."), you know how frustrating such an experience can be for an audience. To avoid that struggle, identify the most important message you want audience members to take away with them. Then compose a one-sentence summary that links this idea to your audience's frame of reference, much as an advertising slogan points out how a product can benefit consumers. Here are some examples:

If you can't express your main idea in a single sentence, you probably haven't defined it clearly enough.

> Convince management that reorganizing the technical support department will improve customer service and reduce employee turnover.
>
> Convince the board of directors that we should build a new plant in Texas to eliminate manufacturing bottlenecks and improve production quality.
>
> Address employee concerns regarding a new health-care plan by showing how the plan will reduce costs and improve the quality of their care.

Each of these statements puts a particular slant on the subject, one that directly relates to the audience's interests. Make sure your purpose is based on a clear understanding of audience needs so that you can deliver information your audience truly cares about.[4] For example, a group of new employees will be much more responsive to your discussion of plant safety procedures if you focus on how the procedures can save lives and prevent injuries rather than on how they will save the company money or conform to government regulations.

### Limiting Your Scope

Limiting your scope is important with any message, but it's particularly vital with presentations, for two reasons. First, for most presentations, you must work within strict time limits. Entrepreneurs pitching their business ideas to investors, for example, often have less than 10 minutes to introduce their companies and products. If you overestimate the amount of material you can cover within your allotted time, you're left with only unpleasant

Limiting your scope is important for two reasons: to ensure that your presentation fits the allotted time and to make sure you respect your audience members' time and attention.

alternatives: rushing through your presentation, skipping some of the information you've so carefully prepared, or trying to steal a few minutes from the next presenter.

Second, you can count on having audience attention for only a finite amount of time, and you'll lose the audience if you try to cover too much material. For example, audience attention levels and retention rates drop sharply after 20 minutes.[5] In other words, even if you are not given a time limit, keep your presentation as short as possible, taking only as much of the audience's time as you need to accomplish your purpose.

*The only sure way to measure the length of your presentation is to complete a practice run.*

The only sure way to know how much material you can cover in a given time is to practice your presentation after you complete it. As an alternative, if you're using conventional structured slides (see page 481), you can figure on 3 or 4 minutes per slide as a rough guide.[6] Of course, be sure to factor in time for introductions, coffee breaks, demonstrations, question-and-answer sessions, and anything else that takes away from your speaking time.

If you're having trouble meeting a time limit or just want to keep your presentation as short as possible, consider a hybrid approach in which you present your key points in summary form and give people printed handouts with additional detail.[7] By the way, whenever you're up against a time or space constraint, try to view it as a creative challenge. Such limitations can force you to focus on the most essential message points that are important to your audience.[8] (See Case 5 on page 501 for the special twist on time-constrained presentations known as *pecha-kucha*.)

## Choosing Your Approach

*Organize a short presentation the same way you would a brief written message; organize a longer presentation as you would a report.*

With a well-defined main idea to guide you and a clear idea about the scope of your presentation, you can begin to arrange your message. If you have 10 minutes or less to deliver your message, organize your presentation much as you would a brief written message: Use the direct approach if the subject involves routine information or good news; use the indirect approach if the subject involves negative news or persuasion. Plan to spend a minute or two during your introduction to arouse interest and to give a preview of what's to come. For the body of the presentation, be prepared to explain the who, what, when, where, why, and how of your subject. In the final few moments, review the points you've made, and close with a statement that will help your audience remember the subject of your speech (see Figure 16.3).

Longer presentations are organized like reports. If the purpose is to inform, use the direct approach and a structure imposed naturally by the subject: importance, sequence, chronology, spatial orientation, geography, or category. If your purpose is to analyze, persuade, or collaborate, organize your material around conclusions and recommendations or around a logical argument. Use the direct approach if the audience is receptive and the indirect approach if you expect resistance.

As you develop your presentation, keep in mind that presentations have one important advantage over written reports: You can adjust your outline on the fly if you need to. Identify the critical points in your presentation and ask yourself some "what if" questions to address possible audience reactions. For instance, if you're worried the audience might not agree with the financial assumptions you've made, you might prepare a detailed analysis that you can include in case you sense that a negative reaction is building or if someone openly questions you about it. Presentation software such as Microsoft PowerPoint makes it easy to adjust your presentation as you move along, allowing you to skip over any parts you decide not to use or to insert backup material at the last minute.

*Simplicity is critical in the organization of presentations.*

Regardless of the length of your presentation, remember to keep your organization clear and simple. If listeners lose the thread of your presentation, they'll have a hard time catching up and following your message in the remainder of your speech. Explain at the beginning how you've organized your material and try to limit the number of main points to three or four.

With every presentation, look for opportunities to integrate storytelling (see page 105) into the structure of your presentation. The dramatic tension (not knowing what will happen to the "hero") at the heart of effective storytelling is a great way to capture and keep the audience's attention.

**Progress Update: August 2013**

**Purpose:** To update the Executive Committee on our product development schedule.

I.   Review goals and progress.
    A. Mechanical design:
       1. Goal: 100%
       2. Actual: 80%
       3. Reason for delay: Unanticipated problems with case durability
    B. Software development:
       1. Goal: 50%
       2. Actual: 60%
    C. Material sourcing:
       1. Goal: 100%
       2. Actual: 45% (and materials identified are at 140% of anticipated costs)
       3. Reason for delay: Purchasing is understaffed and hasn't been able to research sources adequately.

II.  Discuss schedule options.
    A. Option 1: Reschedule product launch date.
    B. Option 2: Launch on schedule with more expensive materials.

III. Suggest goals for next month.

IV.  Q&A

*These elements of bad news are effectively supporting points for the main bad news to come.*

*Here is the key part of the message: the company has to choose between two unwelcome options.*

**Figure 16.3   Effective Outline for a 10-Minute Progress Report**
Here is an outline of a short presentation that updates management on the status of a key project. The presenter has some bad news to deliver (either the product launch will have to be delayed or the materials costs will be higher than anticipated), so she opted for an indirect approach to lay out the reasons for the delay before sharing the news.

## Preparing Your Outline

A presentation outline helps you organize your message, and it serves as the foundation for delivering your speech. Prepare your outline in several stages:[9]

- State your purpose and main idea and then use these to guide the rest of your planning.
- Organize your major points and subpoints in logical order, expressing each major point as a single, complete sentence.
- Identify major points in the body first and then outline the introduction and close.
- Identify transitions between major points or sections and then write these transitions in full-sentence form.
- Prepare your bibliography or source notes; highlight those sources you want to identify by name during your talk.
- Choose a compelling title. Make it brief, action oriented, and focused on what you can do for the audience.[10]

Many speakers like to prepare both a detailed *planning outline* (see Figure 16.4 on the next page) and a simpler *speaking outline* that provides all the cues and reminders they need to present their material. To prepare an effective speaking outline, follow these steps:[11]

- Start with the planning outline and then strip away anything you don't plan to say directly to your audience.
- Condense points and transitions to key words or phrases.
- Add delivery cues, such as places where you plan to pause for emphasis or use visuals.
- Arrange your notes on numbered cards or use the notes capability in your presentation software.

In addition to planning your speech, a presentation outline helps you plan your speaking notes as well.

You may find it helpful to create a simpler speaking outline from your planning outline.

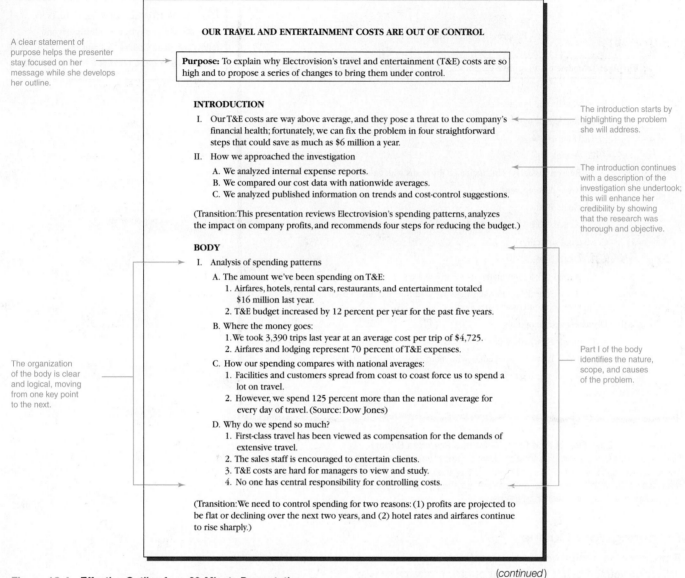

A clear statement of purpose helps the presenter stay focused on her message while she develops her outline.

**OUR TRAVEL AND ENTERTAINMENT COSTS ARE OUT OF CONTROL**

**Purpose:** To explain why Electrovision's travel and entertainment (T&E) costs are so high and to propose a series of changes to bring them under control.

**INTRODUCTION**

I. Our T&E costs are way above average, and they pose a threat to the company's financial health; fortunately, we can fix the problem in four straightforward steps that could save as much as $6 million a year.

II. How we approached the investigation
   A. We analyzed internal expense reports.
   B. We compared our cost data with nationwide averages.
   C. We analyzed published information on trends and cost-control suggestions.

(Transition: This presentation reviews Electrovision's spending patterns, analyzes the impact on company profits, and recommends four steps for reducing the budget.)

**BODY**

I. Analysis of spending patterns
   A. The amount we've been spending on T&E:
      1. Airfares, hotels, rental cars, restaurants, and entertainment totaled $16 million last year.
      2. T&E budget increased by 12 percent per year for the past five years.
   B. Where the money goes:
      1. We took 3,390 trips last year at an average cost per trip of $4,725.
      2. Airfares and lodging represent 70 percent of T&E expenses.
   C. How our spending compares with national averages:
      1. Facilities and customers spread from coast to coast force us to spend a lot on travel.
      2. However, we spend 125 percent more than the national average for every day of travel. (Source: Dow Jones)
   D. Why do we spend so much?
      1. First-class travel has been viewed as compensation for the demands of extensive travel.
      2. The sales staff is encouraged to entertain clients.
      3. T&E costs are hard for managers to view and study.
      4. No one has central responsibility for controlling costs.

(Transition: We need to control spending for two reasons: (1) profits are projected to be flat or declining over the next two years, and (2) hotel rates and airfares continue to rise sharply.)

The introduction starts by highlighting the problem she will address.

The introduction continues with a description of the investigation she undertook; this will enhance her credibility by showing that the research was thorough and objective.

The organization of the body is clear and logical, moving from one key point to the next.

Part I of the body identifies the nature, scope, and causes of the problem.

*(continued)*

**Figure 16.4** **Effective Outline for a 30-Minute Presentation**
This outline (based on Linda Moreno's report in Chapter 15) clearly identifies the purpose and the distinct points to be made in the introduction, body, and close. Notice also how the presenter wrote her major transitions in full sentence form to be sure she can clearly phrase these critical passages when it's time to speak.

MyBCommLab Apply Figure 16.4's key concepts. Go to **mybcommlab.com** and follow this path: Course Content → Chapter 16 → **DOCUMENT MAKEOVERS**

# Developing a Presentation

**2** **LEARNING OBJECTIVE**
Explain how to adapt to your audience and develop an effective opening, body, and close for a presentation.

Although you usually don't write out a presentation word for word, you still engage in the writing process—developing your ideas, structuring support points, phrasing your transitions, and so on. Depending on the situation and your personal style, the eventual presentation might follow your initial words closely, or you might express your thoughts in fresh, spontaneous language. This section covers the tasks of adapting to your audience and composing your presentation; Chapter 17 covers the task of creating slides to accompany your talk.

## ADAPTING TO YOUR AUDIENCE

Adapting to your audience addresses a number of issues, from speaking style to technology choices.

Your audience's size, the venue (in person or online), your subject, your purpose, your budget, the time available for preparation, and the time allotted for your talk all influence the style of your presentation. If you're speaking to a small group, particularly people you already

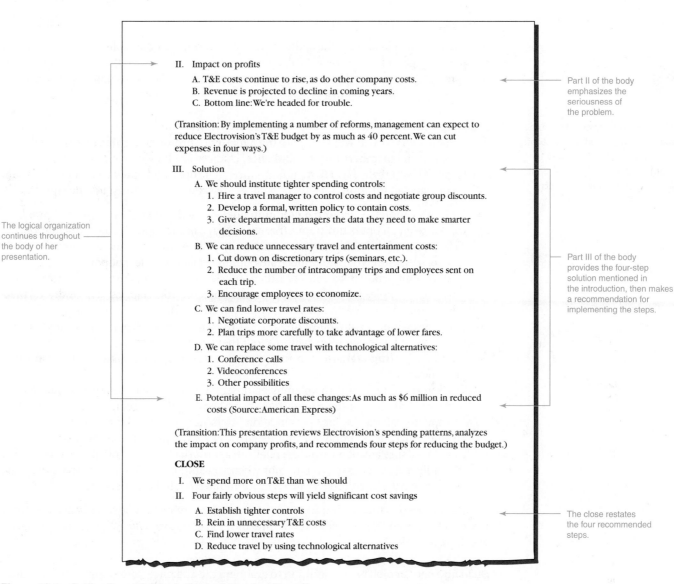

The logical organization continues throughout the body of her presentation.

II.  Impact on profits

    A.  T&E costs continue to rise, as do other company costs.
    B.  Revenue is projected to decline in coming years.
    C.  Bottom line: We're headed for trouble.

(Transition: By implementing a number of reforms, management can expect to reduce Electrovision's T&E budget by as much as 40 percent. We can cut expenses in four ways.)

III.  Solution

    A.  We should institute tighter spending controls:
        1.  Hire a travel manager to control costs and negotiate group discounts.
        2.  Develop a formal, written policy to contain costs.
        3.  Give departmental managers the data they need to make smarter decisions.
    B.  We can reduce unnecessary travel and entertainment costs:
        1.  Cut down on discretionary trips (seminars, etc.).
        2.  Reduce the number of intracompany trips and employees sent on each trip.
        3.  Encourage employees to economize.
    C.  We can find lower travel rates:
        1.  Negotiate corporate discounts.
        2.  Plan trips more carefully to take advantage of lower fares.
    D.  We can replace some travel with technological alternatives:
        1.  Conference calls
        2.  Videoconferences
        3.  Other possibilities
    E.  Potential impact of all these changes: As much as $6 million in reduced costs (Source: American Express)

(Transition: This presentation reviews Electrovision's spending patterns, analyzes the impact on company profits, and recommends four steps for reducing the budget.)

**CLOSE**

  I.  We spend more on T&E than we should
 II.  Four fairly obvious steps will yield significant cost savings

    A.  Establish tighter controls
    B.  Rein in unnecessary T&E costs
    C.  Find lower travel rates
    D.  Reduce travel by using technological alternatives

*Part II of the body emphasizes the seriousness of the problem.*

*Part III of the body provides the four-step solution mentioned in the introduction, then makes a recommendation for implementing the steps.*

*The close restates the four recommended steps.*

**Figure 16.4   Outline for a 30-Minute Presentation** *(continued)*

know, you can use a casual style that encourages audience participation. Use simple visuals and invite your audience to interject comments. Deliver your remarks in a conversational tone, using notes to jog your memory if necessary.

If you're addressing a large audience or if the event is important, establish a more formal atmosphere. During formal presentations, speakers are often on a stage or platform, standing behind a lectern and using a microphone so that their remarks can be heard throughout the room or captured for broadcasting or webcasting.

When you deliver an oral presentation to people from other cultures, you may need to adapt the content of your presentation. It is also important to take into account any cultural preferences for appearance, mannerisms, and other customs. An interpreter or event host can suggest appropriate changes for a specific audience or particular occasion.

**REAL-TIME UPDATES**

LEARN MORE BY WATCHING THIS VIDEO

**How to establish an emotional connection with any audience**

Entertainment executive Peter Guber talks about the art of purposeful storytelling. Go to http://real-timeupdates.com/ bct12 and click on Learn More. If you are using MyBCommLab, you can access Real-Time Updates within each chapter or under Student Study Tools.

## COMPOSING YOUR PRESENTATION

Like written documents, oral presentations are composed of distinct elements: the introduction, the body, and the close.

## Presentation Introduction

A good introduction arouses the audience's interest in your topic, establishes your credibility, and prepares the audience for what will follow. That's a lot to pack into the first few minutes of your presentation, so give yourself plenty of time to prepare the words and visuals you'll use to get your presentation off to a great start.

If your audience isn't likely to be naturally interested in your topic, your introduction will need to build interest by relating the subject to their personal concerns.

**Arousing Audience Interest**   Some subjects are naturally more interesting to some audiences than others. If you will be discussing a matter of profound significance that will personally affect the members of your audience, chances are they'll listen, regardless of how you begin. All you really have to do is announce your topic, and you'll have their attention. Other subjects call for more imagination. Here are six ways to arouse audience interest:[12]

- **Unite the audience around a common goal.** Invite listeners to help solve a problem, capitalize on an opportunity, or otherwise engage in the topic of your presentation.
- **Tell a story.** Well-told stories are naturally interesting and can be compelling. Of course, make sure your story illustrates an important and relevant point.
- **Pass around product samples or other objects.** If your company is in the textile business, for example, let the audience handle some of your fabrics. The more of their senses you can engage, the more likely people are to remember your message.
- **Ask a question.** Asking questions will get the audience actively involved in your presentation and give you information about them and their needs.
- **Share a startling statistic.** An intriguing, unexpected, or shocking detail can often grab the attention of your listeners.
- **Use humor.** Opening with an amusing observation about yourself, the subject matter of the presentation, or the circumstances surrounding the presentation can be an effective way to lighten the "pre-presentation jitters" for you and the audience or to make an emotional connection with your listeners. However, humor must be used with great care. Make sure any comments are relevant, appropriate, and not offensive to anyone in the audience. In general, avoid humor when you and the audience don't share the same native language or culture; it's too easy for humor to fall flat or backfire.

Regardless of which technique you choose, make sure you can give audience members a reason to care and to believe that the time they're about to spend listening to you will be worth their while.[13]

If someone else will be introducing you to the audience, you can ask this person to present your credentials.

**Building Your Credibility**   In addition to grabbing the audience's attention, your introduction needs to establish your credibility. If you're a well-known expert in the subject matter or have earned your audience's trust in other situations, you're already ahead of the game. However, if you have no working relationship with your audience or if you're speaking in an area outside your known expertise, you need to establish credibility and do so quickly; people tend to decide within a few minutes whether you're worth listening to.[14]

Techniques for building credibility vary, depending on whether you will be introducing yourself or having someone else introduce you. If another person will introduce you, he or she can present your credentials so that you won't appear boastful. If you will be introducing yourself, keep your comments simple, but don't be afraid to mention your relevant experience and accomplishments. Your listeners will be curious about your qualifications, so tell them briefly who you are and why you're the right person to be giving this presentation. Here's an example:

> I'm Karen Whitney, a market research analyst with Information Resources Corporation. For the past five years, I've specialized in studying high-technology markets. Your director of engineering, John LaBarre, has asked me to talk to you about recent trends in computer-aided design so that you'll have a better idea of how to direct your research efforts.

This speaker establishes credibility by tying her credentials to the purpose of her presentation, without boasting. By mentioning her company's name, her specialization and position, and the name of the audience's boss, she lets her listeners know immediately that she is qualified to tell them something they need to know. She connects her background to their concerns.

**Previewing Your Message**  In addition to arousing audience interest and establishing your credibility, a good introduction gives your audience members a preview of what's ahead, helping them understand the structure and content of your message. A report reader can learn these things by looking at the table of contents and scanning the headings, but in a presentation, you need to provide that framework with a preview.

Your preview should summarize the main idea of your presentation, identify major supporting points, and indicate the order in which you'll develop those points. Tell your listeners in so many words, "This is the subject, and these are the points I will cover." Once you've established the framework, you can be confident that the audience will understand how the individual facts and figures are related to your main idea as you move into the body of your presentation. If you are using an indirect approach, your preview can discuss the nature of your main idea without disclosing it.

*Use the preview to help your audience understand the importance, the structure, and the content of your message.*

## Presentation Body

The bulk of your speech or presentation is devoted to a discussion of the main supporting points from your outline. Whether you're using the direct or indirect approach, make sure the organization of your presentation is clear and your presentation holds the audience's attention.

**Connecting Your Ideas**  Help your listeners move from one key point to the next with generous use of transitions. Between sentences and paragraphs, use transitional words and phrases such as *therefore, because, in addition, in contrast, moreover, for example, consequently, nevertheless,* or *finally.* To link major sections of a presentation, use complete sentences or paragraphs, such as "Now that we've reviewed the problem, let's take a look at some solutions." Every time you shift topics, be sure to stress the connection between ideas. Summarize what's been said and then preview what's to come. You might also want to call attention to the transitions by using gestures, changing your tone of voice, or introducing a new slide or other visual.

*Use transitions to repeat key ideas and help the audience follow along, particularly in longer presentations.*

**Holding Your Audience's Attention**  After you've successfully captured your audience's attention in your introduction, you need to work to keep it throughout the body of your presentation. Here are a few helpful tips for keeping the audience tuned into your message:

*The most important way to hold an audience's attention is to show how your message relates to their individual needs and concerns.*

- **Relate your subject to your audience's needs.** People are naturally most interested in things that affect them personally.
- **Anticipate your audience's questions.** Try to anticipate as many questions as you can and address these questions in the body of your presentation. You'll also want to prepare and reserve additional material to use during the question-and-answer period, in case the audience asks for greater detail.
- **Use clear, vivid language.** If your presentation will involve abstract ideas, show how those abstractions connect with everyday life. Use familiar words, short sentences, and concrete examples. Be sure to use some variety as well; repeating the same words and phrases puts people to sleep.
- **Explain the relationship between your subject and familiar ideas.** Show how your subject is related to ideas that audience members already understand and give people a way to categorize and remember your points.[15] Be sure to make connections that your listeners are sure to get, too. For example, when Peter Principato and his team were brainstorming how to present one young writer/director to studio executives, Principato rejected the suggestion of comparing him to Charlie Kaufman. Kaufman is revered among comedy insiders, but Principato wasn't sure a mainstream television executive would understand the reference.[16]
- **Ask for opinions or pause occasionally for questions or comments.** Audience feedback helps you determine whether your listeners understand a key point before you launch into another section. Asking questions or providing comments also gives your audience members a chance to switch for a time from listening to participating, which helps them engage with your message and develop a sense of shared ownership.
- **Illustrate your ideas with visuals.** As Chapter 17 discusses, visuals enliven your message, help you connect with audience members, and help people remember your message more effectively.

## Presentation Close

Plan your close carefully so that your audience leaves with your main idea clear in their minds.

The close of a speech or presentation has two critical jobs to accomplish: making sure your listeners leave with the key points from your talk clear in their minds and putting your audience in the appropriate emotional state. For example, if the purpose of your presentation is to warn managers that their out-of-control spending threatens the company's survival, you want them to leave with that message ringing in their ears—and with enough concern for the problem to stimulate changes in their behavior.

**Restating Your Main Points**   Use the close to succinctly restate your main points, emphasizing what you want your listeners to do or to think. For example, to close a presentation on your company's executive compensation program, you could repeat your specific recommendations and then conclude with a memorable statement to motivate your audience to take action:

> We can all be proud of the way our company has grown. However, if we want to continue that growth, we need to take four steps to ensure that our best people don't start looking for opportunities elsewhere:
>
> - First, increase the overall level of compensation
> - Second, establish a cash bonus program
> - Third, offer a variety of stock-based incentives
> - Fourth, improve our health insurance and pension benefits
>
> By taking these steps, we can ensure that our company retains the management talent it needs to face our industry's largest competitors.

By summarizing the key ideas, you improves the chance that your audience will leave with your message clearly in mind.

Plan your final statement carefully so you can end on a strong, positive note.

**Ending with Clarity and Confidence**   If you've been successful with the introduction and body of your presentation, your listeners have the information they need and are in the right frame of mind to put that information to good use. Now you're ready to end on a strong note that confirms expectations about any actions or decisions that will follow the presentation—and to bolster the audience's confidence in you and your message one final time.

Some presentations require the audience to reach a decision or agree to take specific action, in which case the close provides a clear wrap-up. If the audience agrees on an issue covered in the presentation, briefly review the consensus. If they don't agree, make the lack of consensus clear by saying something like, "We seem to have some fundamental disagreement on this question." Then be ready to suggest a method of resolving the differences.

If you need to have the audience make a decision or agree to take action, make sure the responsibilities for doing so are clear.

If you expect any action to occur as a result of your speech, be sure to explain who is responsible for doing what. List the action items and, if possible within the time available, establish due dates and assign responsibility for each task.

Make your final remarks memorable and emotionally compatible with your message.

Make sure your final remarks are memorable and expressed in a tone that is appropriate to the situation. If your presentation is a persuasive request for project funding, you might emphasize the importance of this project and your team's ability to complete it on schedule and within budget. Expressing confident optimism will send the message that you believe in your ability to perform. Conversely, if your purpose is to alert the audience to a problem or risk, false optimism will undermine your message.

Whatever final message is appropriate, think through your closing remarks carefully before stepping in front of the audience. You don't want to wind up on stage with nothing to say but "Well, I guess that's it."

# Delivering a Presentation

With an outline, speaking notes, and any visual aids you plan to use (see Chapter 17 for those), you're almost ready to deliver your presentation. This section covers five essential topics that will help you prepare for and deliver engaging and effective presentations, starting with choosing your method.

**3** LEARNING OBJECTIVE
Discuss five steps for delivering a successful presentation.

## CHOOSING YOUR PRESENTATION METHOD

Depending on the circumstance of your presentation, you can choose from a variety of delivery methods:

- **Memorizing.** Except for extremely short speeches, trying to memorize an entire presentation is not a good idea. In the best of circumstances, you'll probably sound stilted; in the worst, you might forget your lines. Besides, you'll often need to address audience questions during your speech, so you need to be flexible enough to adjust your speech as you go. However, memorizing a quotation, an opening paragraph, and some strong finishing remarks can bolster your confidence and strengthen your delivery.

- **Reading.** In a few rare instances, you may need to read your speech from a prepared script. For instance, policy statements and legal documents are sometimes read in full because the wording can be critical. However, unless you're required or expected to read your presentation verbatim, reading is not a good choice. You won't talk as naturally as you would otherwise, and the result will be a monotonous, uninspiring presentation.[17] If you must read your speech for some reason, practice enough so that you can still make periodic eye contact with your audience and make sure the printout of your speech is easy to read.

- **Speaking from an outline or notes.** Speaking with the help of an outline or note cards is nearly always the easiest and most effective delivery mode. The outline or notes guide you through the flow of the speech while giving you the freedom to speak naturally and spontaneously, to maintain eye contact with your listeners, and to respond and improvise as circumstances warrant. If you print note cards, use heavy note cards instead of regular paper. They're quieter and easier to flip through as you talk.

- **Impromptu speaking.** From time to time, you may be called upon unexpectedly to give an *impromptu* or *extemporaneous* speech on the spot, without the benefit of any planning or practice. Take a few seconds to identify the one key idea you want to share with the audience. That idea alone may be enough to meet the audience's expectations, or it might be enough to get you started and allow you to piece together additional ideas on the fly. Then think about a structure that would help convey that idea. Telling a brief story can be particularly effective in these situations because the structure helps you organize what you want to say, even as you're speaking. If you are asked to speak on a topic and simply don't have the information at hand, don't try to fake it. Instead, offer to get the information to the audience after the meeting or ask if anyone else in the room can respond. Finally, before you even enter the meeting or other setting, if there is a chance you might be called on to say a few words, you can "prepare for the surprise" by thinking through what you might say in response to potential questions.[18]

Whichever delivery mode you use, be sure that you're thoroughly familiar with your subject. Knowing what you're talking about is the best way to build your self-confidence. If you stumble, get interrupted, or suffer equipment failures, your expertise will help you get back on track.

Speaking from carefully prepared notes is the best delivery mode for nearly all presentations.

## PRACTICING YOUR DELIVERY

Practicing your presentation is essential. Practice boosts your confidence, gives you a more professional demeanor, and lets you verify the operation of your visuals and equipment. A test audience can tell you if your slides are understandable and whether your delivery is effective.

The more you practice, the more confidence you'll have in yourself and your material.

A day or two before you're ready to step on stage for an important talk, make sure you and your presentation are ready:

- Can you present your material naturally, without reading your slides?
- Is the equipment working, and do you know how to use it?
- Could you still make a compelling and complete presentation if you experience an equipment failure and have to proceed without using your slides at all?
- Is your timing on track?
- Can you easily pronounce all the words you plan to use?
- Have you anticipated likely questions and objections?

With experience, you'll get a feel for how much practice is enough in any given situation. Practicing helps keep you on track, helps you maintain a conversational tone with your audience, and boosts your confidence and composure.

## PREPARING TO SPEAK

In addition to knowing your material thoroughly and practicing your delivery, make sure your location is ready, you have everything you'll need, and you're prepared to address audiences from other cultures, if that applies.

Whenever you can, scout the location for your presentation in advance. Check the seating arrangement to confirm it's appropriate for your needs and the audience's. Verify the availability and operation of all the equipment and supplies you're counting on, from the projection system to simple but vital necessities such as flip charts and marking pens. If you're using electronic slides, make sure you know how to get the file from your computer or other device to the projection system.

If you're addressing audience members who speak a different native language, consider using an interpreter. Working with an interpreter does constrain your presentation somewhat. For instance, you must speak slowly enough for the interpreter to keep up with you. Send your interpreter a copy of your speaking notes and your visuals as far in advance of your presentation as possible. If your audience is likely to include persons with hearing impairments, team up with a sign-language interpreter as well.

When you deliver an oral presentation to people from other cultures, take into account cultural differences in appearances, mannerisms, and other customs. Your interpreter or host will be able to suggest appropriate changes for a specific audience or occasion.

## OVERCOMING ANXIETY

Recognize that nervousness is an indication that you care about your audience, your topic, and the occasion. These techniques will help you convert anxiety into positive energy:[19]

- **Stop worrying about being perfect.** Successful speakers focus on making an authentic connection with their listeners, rather than on trying to deliver a note-perfect presentation.
- **Know your subject.** The more familiar you are with your material, the less panic you'll feel.
- **Practice, practice, practice.** The more you rehearse, the more confident you will feel.
- **Visualize success.** Visualize mental images of yourself in front of the audience, feeling confident, prepared, and able to handle any situation that might arise.[20] Remember that your audience wants you to succeed, too.
- **Remember to breathe.** Tension can lead people to breathe in a rapid and shallow fashion, which can create a lightheaded feeling. Breathe slowly and deeply to maintain a sense of calm and confidence.
- **Be ready with your opening line.** Have your first sentence memorized and on the tip of your tongue.
- **Be comfortable.** Dress appropriately but as comfortably as possible. Drink plenty of water ahead of time to hydrate your voice (bring water with you, too).
- **Take a three-second break.** If you sense that you're starting to race or ramble, pause and arrange your notes or perform some other small task while taking several deep breaths. Then start again at your normal pace.

Make sure you're comfortable with the equipment you'll be expected to use; you don't want to be fumbling with controls while the audience is watching and waiting.

You'll know you've practiced enough when you can present the material at a comfortable pace and in a natural, conversational tone.

If possible, visit the speaking venue ahead of time to familiarize yourself with the facilities and the equipment.

Preparation is the best antidote for anxiety; it gives you confidence that you know your material and that you can recover from any glitches you might encounter.

- **Concentrate on your message and your audience, not on yourself.** When you're busy thinking about your subject and observing your audience's response, you tend to forget your fears.
- **Maintain eye contact with friendly audience members.** Eye contact not only makes you appear sincere, confident, and trustworthy but can give you positive feedback as well.
- **Keep going.** Things usually get better as you move along, with each successful minute giving you more and more confidence.

No one enjoys mistakes, equipment failures, and other troubles, but they are survivable. To learn how several experienced presenters have overcome some serious glitches, see "Communication Miscues: Disasters Will Happen—Are You Ready?"

Confident delivery starts as soon as you become the focus of attention, before you even begin to speak, so don't rush. As you approach the front of the room, walk with confidence, breathe deeply, and stand up straight. Face your audience, adjust the microphone and other equipment as needed, count to three slowly, and then scan the audience. When you find a friendly face, make eye contact and smile. Look away, count to three again, and then begin your presentation.[21] If you are nervous, this slow, controlled beginning will help you establish rapport and appear more confident. Make sure your nonverbal signals send a message of confidence.

*Nonverbal signals tell the audience how you're feeling, so pay attention to the signals you send.*

Your posture is important in projecting more confidence. Stand tall, with your weight on both feet and your shoulders back. Avoid gripping the lectern or other physical structure. Use your hands to emphasize your remarks with appropriate gestures. Meanwhile, vary your facial expressions to make the message more dynamic.

---

**COMMUNICATION MISCUES**

## Disasters Will Happen—Are You Ready?

You've researched your topic, analyzed your audience, prepared a compelling message, crafted eye-catching visuals, and practiced until you're running like a smooth machine. You're ready to go.

Then you wake up with a sore throat and half a voice. You grab a few lozenges, hope for the best, and drive to the conference facility in plenty of time to set up your equipment. Oops, somebody forgot to tell you that your presentation has been moved up by an hour, and your audience is already in the room waiting for you. You scramble to turn on your laptop and get it connected to the projector, only to discover that you forgot the power cord and your battery is low. But that won't be a problem: Your laptop is dead anyway. Feeling smart, you pull out a CD-ROM with a backup copy of your PowerPoint slides and ask to use one of the several laptops you see scattered around the room. Nice idea, but they're equipped only with USB flash drives, so your CD is useless. The audience is getting restless; a few people get up to leave. You keep hoping you'll wake up from this bad dream so that your great day can really start. Sorry. This *is* your day.

Ask any business speaker with a few years of experience, and you'll hear all these horror stories and a few more. People who have driven to the wrong conference center, hit themselves in the head with a microphone, tripped over wires, started with a sure-fire joke that generated nothing but cold stares, or been rendered speechless by tough questions. Hoping you'll be spared isn't an effective response. You must be prepared for when—not if—something goes wrong.

If you assume that something *will* go wrong at some point, you can make peace with the possibility and focus on backup planning. Experts suggest that you make a list of every major problem you might encounter and imagine how you'll respond when these calamities strike you on the day of a big presentation. As much as possible, create a backup plan, such as calling ahead to reserve a second projector in the event that yours gets lost in transit. You won't be able to put backup resources in place for every possible glitch, but by at least thinking through the possibilities, you can decide how you'll respond. When disaster does strike, you'll look like a polished pro instead of a befuddled novice.

### CAREER APPLICATIONS

1. If you spy trouble ahead in your presentation, such as noticing that your laptop battery is about to go dead or that you somehow have an old copy of the presentation file, should you tell your audience what's wrong? Or should you try to "wing it"? Explain your answer.
2. What steps can you take to make absolutely sure that you have a usable backup copy of your electronic presentation slides outside your office? Why is this important?

*Sources:* Adapted in part from C. Peter Guiliano and Frank J. Currilo, "Going Blank in the Boardroom," *Public Relations Quarterly*, Winter 2003, 35+; Jennifer Rotondo and Mike Rotondo, Jr., *Presentation Skills for Managers* (New York: McGraw-Hill, 2002), 160–162; Mark Merritt, "No More Nightmares," *Presentations*, April 2001, 44+.

**REAL-TIME UPDATES**

LEARN MORE BY WATCHING THIS VIDEO

**The quiet person's guide to becoming a better public speaker**

Follow these tips to become an effective speaker, even if you don't feel like a "natural." Go to http://real-timeupdates.com/bct12 and click on Learn More. If you are using MyBCommLab, you can access Real-Time Updates within each chapter or under Student Study Tools.

Finally, think about the sound of your voice. Studies indicate that people who speak with lower pitches at a slightly faster-than-average rate are perceived as being more credible.[22] Try to sound poised and confident, varying your pitch and speaking rate to add emphasis. For instance, slow down slightly when you're making an important point.[23] Speak clearly and crisply, articulating all the syllables, and sound enthusiastic about what you're saying. Use silence instead of meaningless filler words such as *um, you know, okay,* and *like.* Silence adds dramatic punch and gives the audience time to think about your message.

## HANDLING QUESTIONS RESPONSIVELY

Don't leave the question-and-answer period to chance: anticipate likely questions and think through your answers.

Whether you take questions during a formal question-and-answer (Q&A) period or as they come up during your presentation, audience queries are often one of the most important parts of an presentation. They give you a chance to obtain important information, to emphasize your main idea and supporting points, and to build enthusiasm for your point of view. When you're speaking to high-ranking executives in your company, the Q&A period will often consume most of the time allotted for your presentation.[24]

Whether or not you can establish ground rules for Q&A depends on the audience and the situation. If you're presenting to a small group of upper managers or potential investors, for example, you will probably have no say in the matter: Audience members will likely ask as many questions as they want, whenever they want, to get the information they need. On the other hand, if you are presenting to your peers or a large public audience, establish some guidelines, such as the number of questions allowed per person and the overall time limit for questions.

Don't assume you can handle whatever comes up without some preparation.[25] Learn enough about your audience members to get an idea of their concerns and think through answers to potential questions.

When people ask questions, pay attention to nonverbal signals to help determine what each person really means. Repeat the question to confirm your understanding and to ensure that the entire audience has heard it. If the question is vague or confusing, ask for clarification; then give a simple, direct answer.

If you don't have the complete answer to an important question, offer to provide it after the presentation.

If you are asked a difficult or complex question, avoid the temptation to sidestep it. Offer to meet with the questioner afterward if the issue isn't relevant to the rest of the audience or if giving an adequate answer would take too long. If you don't know the answer, don't pretend you do. Instead, offer to get a complete answer as soon as possible or ask if someone else can offer information on the topic.

Be on guard for audience members who use questions to make impromptu speeches or to take control of your presentation. Without offending anyone, find a way to stay in control. You might admit that you and the questioner have differing opinions and, before calling on someone else, offer to get back to the questioner after you've done more research.[26]

If you ever face hostile questions, respond honestly and directly while keeping your cool.

If a question ever puts you on the hot seat, respond honestly but keep your cool. Look the person in the eye, answer the question as well as you can, and keep your emotions under control. Defuse hostility by paraphrasing the question and asking the questioner to confirm that you've understood it correctly. Maintain a businesslike tone of voice and a pleasant expression.[27]

No matter how the presentation has gone, conclude in a strong, confident manner.

When the time allotted for your presentation is almost up, prepare the audience for the end by saying something like, "We have time for one more question." After you reply to that last question, summarize the main idea of the presentation and thank people for their attention. Conclude with the same confident demeanor you've had from the beginning.

# Incorporating Technology in Your Presentation

**4** **LEARNING OBJECTIVE**
Explain the growing importance of the backchannel in presentations and list six steps for giving effective presentations online.

Like much of the rest of business communication, presentations have been high-tech affairs in many companies. Two aspects you will most likely encounter on the job are the backchannel and online presentations.

## EMBRACING THE BACKCHANNEL

Many business presentations these days involve more than just the spoken conversation between the speaker and his or her audience. Using Twitter and other electronic media, audience members often carry on their own parallel communication during a presentation via the **backchannel**, which presentation expert Cliff Atkinson defines as "a line of communication created by people in an audience to connect with others inside or outside the room, with or without the knowledge of the speaker."[28] Chances are you've participated in an informal backchannel already, such as when texting with your classmates or live-blogging during a lecture.

The backchannel presents both risks and rewards for business presenters. On the negative side, for example, listeners can research your claims the instant you make them and spread the word quickly if they think your information is shaky. The backchannel also gives contrary audience members more leverage, which can lead to presentations spinning out of control. On the plus side, listeners who are excited about your message can build support for it, expand on it, and spread it to a much larger audience in a matter of seconds. You can also get valuable feedback during and after presentations.[29]

By embracing the backchannel, rather than trying to fight it or ignore it, presenters can use this powerful force to their advantage. Follow these tips to make the backchannel work for you:[30]

- **Integrate social media into the presentation process.** For example, you can create a website for the presentation so that people can access relevant resources during or after the presentation, create a Twitter hashtag that everyone can use when sending tweets, or display the Twitterstream during Q&A so that everyone can see the questions and comments on the backchannel.

- **Monitor and ask for feedback.** Using a free service such as TweetDeck which organizes tweets by hashtag and other variables, you can monitor comments from the audience. To avoid trying to monitor the backchannel while speaking, you can schedule "Twitter breaks," during which you review comments and respond as needed.

- **Review comments to improve your presentation.** After a presentation is over, review comments on audience members' Twitter accounts and blogs to see which parts confused them, which parts excited them, and which parts seemed to have little effect (based on few or no comments).

- **Automatically tweet key points from your presentation while you speak.** Add-ons for presentation software can send out prewritten tweets as you show specific slides during a presentation. By making your key points readily available, you make it easy for listeners to retweet and comment on your presentation.

- **Establish expectations with the audience.** Explain that you welcome audience participation but that to ensure a positive experience for everyone, comments should be civil, relevant, and productive.

Twitter and other social media are dramatically changing business presentations by making it easy for all audience members to participate in the *backchannel*.

Resist the urge to ignore or fight the backchannel; instead, learn how to use it to your advantage.

**REAL-TIME UPDATES**

LEARN MORE BY WATCHING THIS VIDEO

**Maximize the rewards of the backchannel and minimize the risks**

This webinar hosted by author Cliff Atkinson outlines the principles of the social media backchannel and analyzes a real-life presentation where the backchannel spurred an audience revolt and what presenters can learn from this. Go to http://real-timeupdates.com/bct12 and click on Learn More. If you are using MyBCommLab, you can access Real-Time Updates within each chapter or under Student Study Tools.

## GIVING PRESENTATIONS ONLINE

Online presentations offer many benefits, including the opportunity to communicate with a geographically dispersed audience at a fraction of the cost of travel and the ability for a project team or an entire organization to meet at a moment's notice. However, this format also presents some challenges for the presenter, thanks to that layer of technology between you and your audience. Many of those "human moments" that guide and encourage you through an in-person presentation won't travel across the digital divide. For instance, it's often difficult to tell whether audience members are bored or confused, because your view of them is usually confined to small video images (and sometimes not even that). To ensure successful online presentations, keep the following advice in mind:

- **Consider sending preview study materials ahead of time.** Doing so allows audience members to familiarize themselves with any important background information. Also, by using

Online presentations give you a way to reach more people in less time, but they require special preparation and skills.

a free service such as SlideShare (www.slideshare.net), you can distribute your presentation slides to either public or private audiences, and you can record audio narrative to make your presentations function on their own.[31] Some presenters advise against giving out your slides ahead of time, however, because doing so gives away the ending of your presentation. If time allows, you can prepare preview materials that don't include your entire slide set.

- **Rehearse using the system live, if at all possible.** Presenting online has all the challenges of other presentations, with the additional burden of operating the presentation system while you are talking. Practice with at least one test viewer so you're comfortable using the system.[32]
- **Keep your presentation as simple as possible.** Break complicated slides down into multiple slides if necessary and keep the direction of your discussion clear so that no one gets lost.
- **Ask for feedback frequently.** Except on the most advanced telepresence systems, you won't have as much of the visual feedback that alerts you when audience members are confused, and many online viewers will be reluctant to call attention to themselves by interrupting you to ask for clarification. Setting up a backchannel via Twitter or as part of your online meeting system will help in this regard.
- **Consider the viewing experience from the audience members' point of view.** Will they be able to see what you think they can see? For instance, webcast video is often displayed in a small window on-screen, so viewers may miss important details.
- **Allow plenty of time for everyone to get connected and familiar with the screen they're viewing.** Build extra time into your schedule to ensure that everyone is connected and ready to start.

With online presentations, you often can't rely on nonverbal signals to sense audience confusion or disagreement, so check in with your listeners frequently to see if they have questions.

Last but not least, don't get lost in the technology. Use these tools whenever they'll help, but remember that the most important aspect of any presentation is getting the audience to receive, understand, and embrace your message.

For a reminder of the steps to take in developing an oral presentation, refer to "Checklist: Developing Oral and Online Presentations." For the latest advice on planning presentations, visit http://real-timeupdates.com/bct12 and click on Chapter 16.

---

**CHECKLIST ✔ Developing Oral and Online Presentations**

**A. Planning your presentation**
- Analyze the situation by defining your purpose and developing an audience profile.
- Select the best medium.
- Organize your presentation by defining the main idea, limiting the scope, choosing your approach, and preparing your outline.

**B. Developing your presentation**
- Adapt to your audience by tailoring your style and language.
- Compose your presentation by preparing an introduction, a body, and a close.
- Use your introduction to arouse audience interest, build your credibility, and preview your message.
- Use the body to connect your ideas and hold your audience's attention.
- Close with confidence and clarity, restating your main points and describing the next steps.

**C. Delivering your presentation**
- Choose a presentation method, which should be speaking from an outline or notes in nearly all situations.
- Practice until you can deliver your material naturally, without reading your slides.

- Prepare to speak by verifying the operation of all the equipment you'll need to use.
- Determine whether you should use an interpreter.
- Overcome anxiety by preparing thoroughly.
- Handle questions responsively.

**D. Embracing the backchannel**
- Integrate social media into the presentation process.
- Monitor and ask for feedback.
- Review comments to improve your presentation.
- Automatically tweet key points from your presentation while you speak.
- Establish expectations with the audience.

**E. Giving presentations online**
- Consider sending preview study materials ahead of time.
- Rehearse using the system live, if at all possible.
- Keep your presentation as simple as possible.
- Ask for feedback frequently.
- Consider the viewing experience from the audience members' point of view.
- Allow plenty of time for everyone to get connected and familiar with the screen they're viewing.

# Quick Learning Guide

## SUMMARY OF LEARNING OBJECTIVES

**1** Describe the tasks involved in analyzing the situation for a presentation and organizing a presentation. Although you rarely want to write out a presentation word for word, the three-step writing process is easy to adapt to presentations. The steps you take in planning presentations are generally the same as with any other business message: analyze the situation, gather information, select the right medium, and organize the information. The purpose of most business presentations is to inform or to persuade, although you may occasionally need to make a collaborative presentation. When you develop your audience profile, anticipate the likely emotional state of your audience members and plan to diffuse emotional situations if needed.

Organizing a presentation requires the same general tasks as organizing a written message (define your main idea, limit your scope, select the direct or indirect approach, and outline your content), but pay special attention to the demands a presentation puts on listeners. They are largely captive to your timing and sequence, so make doubly sure you have a clear purpose, and limit your scope to convey your main idea and necessary supporting points within your allotted time frame. At the same time, take advantage of the flexibility you have with speeches and presentations to adjust the flow and level of detail on the fly if you sense that the audience wants different information than you originally planned. After you complete your *planning outline*, consider simplifying it to create a *speaking outline* to guide you during your presentation.

**2** Explain how to adapt to your audience and develop an effective opening, body, and close for a presentation. To adapt to your audience, assess your audience's size and the venue (in person or online); your subject, purpose, and budget; and the time available for preparation and allotted for your presentation. Determine whether you need to adjust your presentation or engage an interpreter when addressing audiences from other cultures, and assess the specific circumstances in which you'll be making your presentation.

You rarely write out a presentation in full, but plan your word and phrase choices so you can speak in a way that delivers planned messages in a spontaneous way. This step also includes creating whatever visual support materials you plan to use.

An effective introduction arouses audience interest in your topic, builds your credibility, and gives your audience a preview of your message. If your topic doesn't naturally interest the audience, you need to work extra hard in your introduction (and throughout the presentation) to relate the material to the audience in as personal a manner as possible. If you can't demonstrate credibility in your subject area, you can "borrow" credibility from recognized experts by incorporating their insights and opinions into your presentation (giving proper credit, of course). Previewing your message in the introduction helps the audience members recognize the importance of your material and gives them a chance to prepare for it by understanding how you plan to present it.

The bulk of your speech or presentation is devoted to a discussion of the main supporting points from your outline. Throughout the body of your talk, take care to connect your supporting points so that listeners can follow your thinking. Also work to hold your audience's attention by relating your subject to their needs, anticipating their questions, using clear and vivid language, relating your subject to familiar ideas, asking for questions or comments, and illustrating your ideas with visuals.

The close of a speech or presentation has two critical jobs to accomplish: making sure your listeners leave with the key points from your talk clear in their minds and in the appropriate emotional state.

**3** Discuss five steps for delivering a successful presentation. First, choose the best delivery method, which is speaking naturally and spontaneously from notes or a speaking outline in nearly all instances. Second, practice until you can deliver your material naturally, without reading your slides. Third, prepare to speak by making sure that your location is ready, you have everything you'll need, and you're prepared to address audiences from other cultures, if that applies. Fourth, work to overcome anxiety before and during your presentation by letting go of worrying about being perfect, preparing more material than necessary, visualizing your success, remembering to breathe, being ready with your opening line, making yourself comfortable, taking a three-second break if you sense that you're starting to race, concentrating on your message and your audience rather than on yourself, maintaining eye contact with friendly audience members, and keeping going even if you stumble. Fifth, handle questions responsively by determining whether you can set boundaries for the Q&A period, prepare answers to potential questions, pay attention to nonverbal signals, be sure to respond to all questions, don't let questioners take control of the presentation, face hostile questions head-on without getting defensive, and alert the audience when the Q&A period is almost over.

**4** Explain the growing importance of the backchannel in presentations, and list six steps for giving effective presentations online. The backchannel is a parallel conversation taking place among audience members and other interested parties using Twitter and other media. To take advantage of the backchannel, you can integrate social media into your presentation, monitor and ask for feedback, review point by point comments to improve your presentation, automatically tweet key points from your presentation while you speak, and establish expectations with the audience.

To ensure a successful online presentation, consider sending preview materials ahead of time, keep your content and presentation as simple as possible, ask for feedback frequently, consider the viewing experience from the audience's side, and give participants time to get connected.

## KEY TERMS

**backchannel** A social media conversation that takes place during a presentation, in parallel with the speaker's presentation

CHECKLIST ✓
## Developing Oral and Online Presentations

**A. Planning your presentation**
- Analyze the situation by defining your purpose and developing an audience profile.
- Select the best medium.
- Organize your presentation by defining the main idea, limiting the scope, choosing your approach, and preparing your outline.

**B. Developing your presentation**
- Adapt to your audience by tailoring your style and language.
- Compose your presentation by preparing an introduction, a body, and a close.
- Use your introduction to arouse audience interest, build your credibility, and preview your message.
- Use the body to connect your ideas and hold your audience's attention.
- Close with confidence and clarity, restating your main points and describing the next steps.

**C. Delivering your presentation**
- Choose a presentation method, which should be speaking from an outline or notes in nearly all situations.
- Practice until you can deliver your material naturally, without reading your slides.
- Prepare to speak by verifying the operation of all the equipment you'll need to use.
- Determine whether you should use an interpreter.
- Overcome anxiety by preparing thoroughly.
- Handle questions responsively.

**D. Embracing the backchannel**
- Integrate social media into the presentation process.
- Monitor and ask for feedback.
- Review comments to improve your presentation.
- Automatically tweet key points from your presentation while you speak.
- Establish expectations with the audience.

**E. Giving presentations online**
- Consider sending preview study materials ahead of time.
- Rehearse using the system live, if at all possible.
- Keep your presentation as simple as possible.
- Ask for feedback frequently.
- Consider the viewing experience from the audience members' point of view.
- Allow plenty of time for everyone to get connected and familiar with the screen they're viewing.

## COMMUNICATION CHALLENGES AT **Principato-Young Entertainment**

You share Peter Principato's love of comedy, and now you get to learn from his decades of experience in the business. You've joined Principato-Young as his assistant, replacing the former assistant, who was just promoted to a talent manager with her own list of clients. That is the same career path you hope to pursue, so this opportunity seems perfect. Practice your presentation skills with these two challenges.

**INDIVIDUAL CHALLENGE:** Distilling something as complicated as a movie or a TV series down to a single sentence is a skill that will serve you well in any profession. Choose three of your all-time favorite movies and write a one-sentence "pitch" for each one, imagining yourself as the writer or director who is trying to convince a studio to spend millions of dollars to produce it.

**TEAM CHALLENGE:** In a team assigned by your instructor, pick a TV or web-based comedy program (something appropriate to discuss in class). Get a feel for the show, including its style, content, and characters—and what makes it distinct in the crowded marketplace. Now imagine you're turning back the clock to a year or so before this show started, and it's your job to pitch it to a studio executive who will make the decision to fund its production. Develop a five-minute pitch, following Principato's advice of leading with a memorable one-sentence introduction about what the show is, expanding on that with a one-paragraph introduction (be sure to identify the key characters), followed by ideas for a few episodes (you can use actual episodes for this). Be prepared to pitch your show to the class.

## Test Your Knowledge

To review chapter content related to each question, refer to the indicated Learning Objective.

1. What skills do business presentations give you the opportunity to practice and demonstrate? [LO-1]
2. What are the two most common purposes for giving presentations? [LO-1]
3. How can outlines help you with the writing and delivery of a presentation? [LO-1]
4. How can you get and keep the audience's attention? [LO-2]
5. How does the delivery method of impromptu speaking differ from the delivery method of speaking from notes? [LO-3]
6. As a speaker, what nonverbal signals can you send to appear more confident? [LO-3]
7. What can speakers do to maintain control during the question-and-answer period of a presentation? [LO-3]
8. What is the backchannel? [LO-4]

## Apply Your Knowledge

To review chapter content related to each question, refer to the indicated Learning Objective.

1. You just gave an in-depth presentation on the company's new marketing programs, intended for the specialists in the marketing department. The marketing manager then asked you to give a shorter version of the presentation to the company's top executives. Generally speaking, how should you modify the scope of your presentation for this new audience? [LO-1], [LO-2]
2. What role can entertainment play in an effective presentation? [LO-2]
3. If you're worried about forgetting your key message points, should you write them out and read them during your presentation? Why or why not? [LO-3]
4. Letting go of the idea that you have to be perfect can reduce your anxiety before a presentation. However, is it possible to

create ethical problems by being too relaxed about your message and your performance? Explain your answer. [LO-3]

5. What are the possible consequences of ignoring the backchannel during a presentation to a public audience (such as at a convention)? [LO-4]

## Practice Your Skills

### Messages for Analysis

Message 16.A: Analyzing the Structure of a Presentation [LO-1]

Find the transcript of a business-oriented speech or presentation by searching online for "speech transcription" or "presentation transcription." You can also browse www.americanrhetoric.com, which has thousands of transcriptions from speeches on a variety of subjects. Examine both the introduction and the close and analyze how these two sections work together to emphasize the main idea. Does the speaker want the audience to take any specific actions? To change any particular beliefs or feelings?

Next, identify the transitional sentences or phrases that clarify the speech's structure for the listener, especially those that help the speaker shift between supporting points. Using these transitions as clues, list the main message and supporting points; then indicate how each transitional phrase links the current supporting point to the succeeding one. Finally, prepare a brief (two- to three-minute) oral presentation summarizing your analysis for your class.

Message 16.B: Did the Introduction Get Your Attention? [LO-2]

To access this message, visit http://real-timeupdates.com/bct12, click on Student Assignments, and select Chapter 16, Message 16.B. Download and listen to this podcast, which is the introduction of a presentation to college seniors. Identify at least two techniques the speaker uses to try to grab your attention.

## Exercises

Each activity is labeled according to the primary skill or skills you will need to use. To review relevant chapter content, you can refer to the indicated Learning Objective. In some instances, supporting information will be found in another chapter, as indicated.

1. **Presentations: Planning and Developing [LO-1], [LO-2]** With a team of three other students, prepare a detailed outline (including descriptions of any visuals you would plan to use) for a 10-minute presentation on the advantages of attending your college or university. The presentation would be delivered by someone from the admissions office, and the audience would be visiting high school students and their family members. After completing the outline together, each team member should individually develop a 60-second introduction to the presentation. Meet again, have each team member give his or her introduction, and then discuss which was most effective and why. Be prepared to discuss your conclusion with the class.

2. **Presentations: Planning and Developing [LO-1], [LO-2]** Browse through the following topics to see which ones interest you:

   a. What I expect to learn in this course
   b. Past public speaking experiences: the good, the bad, and the ugly
   c. I would be good at teaching _____.
   d. I am afraid of _____.
   e. It's easy for me to _____.
   f. I get angry when _____.
   g. I am happiest when I _____.
   h. People would be surprised if they knew that I _____.
   i. My favorite older person
   j. My favorite charity
   k. My favorite place
   l. My favorite sport
   m. My favorite store
   n. My favorite television show
   o. The town you live in suffers from a great deal of juvenile vandalism. Explain to a group of community members why juvenile recreational facilities should be built instead of a juvenile detention complex.
   p. You are speaking to the Humane Society. Support or oppose the use of animals for medical research purposes.
   q. You are talking to civic leaders of your community. Try to convince them to build an art gallery.
   r. You are speaking to a first-grade class at an elementary school. Explain why they should brush their teeth after meals.
   s. You are speaking to a group of traveling salespeople. Convince them they should wear their seatbelts while driving.
   t. You are speaking to a group of elderly people. Convince them to adopt an exercise program.
   u. Energy issues (supply, conservation, alternative sources, national security, global warming, pollution, etc.)
   v. Financial issues (banking, investing, family finances, etc.)
   w. Government (domestic policy, foreign policy, social security taxes, welfare, etc.)
   x. Interesting new technologies (virtual reality, geographic information systems, nanotechnology, bioengineering, etc.)
   y. Politics (political parties, elections, legislative bodies and legislation, the presidency, etc.)
   z. Sports (amateur and professional, baseball, football, golf, hang gliding, hockey, rock climbing, tennis, etc.)

   Choose a topic and prepare a brief speech or presentation (5–10 minutes), with or without visuals, as your instructor indicates.

3. **Presentations: Planning, Developing, and Delivering [LO-1], [LO-2], [LO-3]** Identify a company whose prospects look bright over the next few years because of highly competitive products, strong leadership, fundamental changes in the market, or any other significant reason. Prepare a five-minute speech, without visuals, explaining why you think this company is going to do well in the near future.

4. **Presentations: Mastering Delivery [LO-3]** Watch any talk that interests you at the TED website, www.ted.com/talks, and compare the speaker's delivery with this chapter's "Checklist: Developing Oral and Online Presentations." Write a two-page report, analyzing the speaker's performance and suggesting improvements.

5. **Presentations: Mastering Delivery; Communication Ethics: Making Ethical Choices [LO-3], Chapter 1** Think again about the presentation you observed and analyzed in the previous exercise. How could the speaker have used nonverbal signals to unethically manipulate the audience's attitudes or actions?

6. **Presentations: Using the Backchannel; Collaboration: Team Projects [LO-4], Chapter 2** In a team of six students, develop a 15-minute slide presentation on any topic that interests you. Nominate one person to give the presentation; the other five will participate via a Twitter backchannel. Set up private Twitter accounts if your class doesn't already use them, and create a hashtag that everyone on the team can follow using TweetDeck or a similar tool. During the presentation, the five audience members should tweet comments and questions, and the presenter can take a Twitter break partway through to respond to backchannel messages. Be ready to discuss your experience with the entire class. For information on getting started on Twitter, visit http://real-timeupdates.com/bct12, click on Learn More, and then click on Twitter Screencast.

## Expand Your Skills

### Critique the Professionals

Find a product demonstration video on YouTube for any product that is appropriate to discuss in class. (Find a video that is at least 2 minutes long and was produced by the company that makes the product, not by a customer or other outside party.) Study the effectiveness of the demonstration, including the use of visuals, the presenter's speech and mannerisms. Did you find the demonstration compelling? Why or why not? If not, what would've made it more compelling? Using whatever medium your instructor requests, write a brief summary of your analysis. Be sure to include a link to the video.

### Sharpening Your Career Skills Online

Bovée and Thill's Business Communication Web Search, at http://businesscommunicationblog.com/websearch, is a unique research tool designed specifically for business communication research. Use the Web Search function to find a website, video, PDF document, podcast, or PowerPoint presentation that offers advice on public speaking or presentations in business. Write a brief email message to your instructor, describing the item that you found and summarizing the career skills information you learned from it.

---

## MyBCommLab

Go to **mybcommlab.com** for Auto-graded writing questions as well as the following Assisted-graded writing questions:

**16-1.** What three goals should you accomplish during the introduction of a presentation? [LO-2]

**16-2.** Why do you have to limit your scope when planning a presentation? [LO-1]

**16-3.** Mybcommlab Only—comprehensive writing assignment for this chapter.

---

## Endnotes

1. John Bowe, "Funny Money," *New York Times*, 30 December 2010, www.nytimes.com; Stephanie Palmer Taxy, Good in a Room website, accessed 13 March 2011, www.goodinaroom.com; Mike Fleming, "A Banner Day for Two Former Assistants," *Deadline Hollywood*, 20 January 2011, www.deadline.com.

2. Nancy Duarte, *Slide:ology: The Art and Science of Creating Great Presentations* (Sebastopol, Calif.: O'Reilly Media, 2008), 13.

3. Amber Naslund, "Twebinar: GE's Tweetsquad," 4 August 2009, www.radian6.com/blog.

4. Irwin Pollack, "Don't Just Give Presentations, Impact Your Audience," *Fort Worth Business Press*, 1 May 2006, 10.

5. Carmine Gallo, "Loaded for Bore," *BusinessWeek* online, 5 August 2005, www.businessweek.com.

6. Sarah Lary and Karen Pruente, "Powerless Point: Common Power-Point Mistakes to Avoid," *Public Relations Tactics*, February 2004, 28.

7. Garr Reynolds, *Presentation Zen* (Berkeley, Calif.: New Riders, 2008), 66.

8. Reynolds, *Presentation Zen*, 39–42.

9. Sherwyn P. Morreale and Courtland L. Bovée, *Excellence in Public Speaking* (Fort Worth, Tex.: Harcourt Brace College Publishers, 1998), 234–237.

10. John Windsor, "Presenting Smart: Keeping the Goal in Sight," *Presentations*, 6 March 2008, www.presentations.com.

11. Morreale and Bovée, *Excellence in Public Speaking*, 241–243.

12. Adapted from Eric J. Adams, "Management Focus: User-Friendly Presentation Software," *World Trade*, March 1995, 92.

13. Carmine Gallo, "Grab Your Audience Fast," *BusinessWeek*, 13 September 2006, 19.

14. Walter Kiechel III, "How to Give a Speech," *Fortune*, 8 June 1987, 180.

15. *Communication and Leadership Program* (Santa Ana, Calif.: Toastmasters International, 1980), 44, 45.

16. Bowe, "Funny 5 Money."

17. Steve Adubato, "Throw Away That Script, Use an Outline Instead," *NJBiz*, 23 October 2006, 17.

18. Cheryl Wiles, "Impromptu Speaking," *Harvard Management Communication Letter*, December 2001, 7–8.

19. Richard Zeoli, "The Seven Things You Must Know About Public Speaking," *Forbes*, 3 June 2009, www.forbes.com; Morreale and Bovée, *Excellence in Public Speaking*, 24–25.

20. Jennifer Rotondo and Mike Rotondo, Jr., *Presentation Skills for Managers* (New York: McGraw-Hill, 2002), 9.

21. Judy Linscott, "Getting On and Off the Podium," *Savvy*, October 1985, 44.

22. Iris R. Johnson, "Before You Approach the Podium," *MW*, January–February 1989, 7.

23. "Advice from a Voice Coach: Say It and Sell It," *Presentations*, 6 November 2006, www.presentations.com.

24. Rick Gilbert, "Presentation Advice for Boardroom Success," *Financial Executive*, September 2005, 12.

25. Rotondo and Rotondo, *Presentation Skills for Managers*, 151.

26. Teresa Brady, "Fielding Abrasive Questions During Presentations," *Supervisory Management*, February 1993, 6.

27. Robert L. Montgomery, "Listening on Your Feet," *The Toastmaster*, July 1987, 14–15.

28. Cliff Atkinson, *The Backchannel* (Berkeley, Calif.: New Riders, 2010), 17.

29. Atkinson, *The Backchannel*, 51, 68–73.

30. Olivia Mitchell, "10 Tools for Presenting with Twitter," Speaking About Presenting blog, 3 November 2009, www.speakingabout-presenting.com; Atkinson, *The Backchannel*, 51, 68–73, 99.

31. SlideShare website, accessed 3 August 2010, www.slideshare.net.

32. Geoffrey James, "How to Give an Online Presentation," BNET, 23 February 2011, www.bnet.com.

# 17 Enhancing Presentations with Slides and Other Visuals

## LEARNING OBJECTIVES

After studying this chapter, you will be able to

**1** Explain the role of visuals in business presentations and list the types of visuals commonly used.

**2** Explain the difference between structured and free-form slides and suggest when each design strategy is more appropriate.

**3** Outline the decisions involved in using a key visual and selecting color, artwork, and typefaces to create effective slide designs.

**4** Explain how to create effective slide content.

**5** Explain the role of navigation slides, support slides, and handouts.

## COMMUNICATION CLOSE-UP AT
## Presentation Zen
www.presentationzen.com

Nobody wants to give a boring presentation, and certainly nobody wants to sit through a boring presentation. Nevertheless, presentation expert Garr Reynolds claims that "most presentations remain mind-numbingly dull, something to be endured by presenter and audience alike." He aims to help improve this unfortunate situation by example and through his many books, blogs, and seminars.

Reynolds, an American who has lived, worked, and taught in Japan for many years, believes the solution to better presentations lies in adapting some of the principles of the Zen school of Buddhism. However, it isn't the spiritual practices of Zen he wants to infuse into presentations, but rather some of the overall approach and aesthetic sense of Zen—particularly the three principles of restraint, simplicity, and naturalness. His approach reflects these ideals through *restrained preparation*, *simple designs*, and *natural delivery*.

Most people can grasp the notions of restraint and naturalness, but simplicity is sometimes misunderstood. From a design and communication perspective, simplicity is not about "dumbing down" but rather about rising up—rising above the details and stripping away the distractions to focus on the essential elements of an idea or a problem. This approach to design leads to

© Li Ding/Alamy

Restraint, simplicity, and naturalness are some of the key elements of Zen-inspired design. Garr Reynolds, author of *Presentation Zen* and a popular blog of the same name, advises presenters to adopt these principles in the design and delivery of slide presentations.

slides that look dramatically different from conventional presentation slides.

Reynolds's advice for restrained preparation starts with walking away from your computer, to "plan analog" as he puts it, with just a notepad and a pen or pencil. This low-tech approach to planning offers several advantages. First, it helps you avoid falling into the trap of thinking that your *slides* are the presentation. The *message* is the heart of your presentation, and slides are simply one possible medium for expressing that message. Moreover, starting away from your computer is a good reminder that a presentation, even one with dazzling multimedia and special effects, is still a speech or a conversation that is supported by visuals. In other words, it involves primarily an oral medium, not an electronic medium.

Second, by figuring out your message before firing up your presentation software, you're not mentally locked into the single medium of electronic slides. With insight into audience needs and a well-defined message in place, you can then consider all your options and select whatever combination of media is best for the situation. You might discover, for example, that getting your listeners involved would help build consensus for your message. By incorporating another medium, such as flip charts or a whiteboard, you can record questions and suggestions from the audience during a few minutes of brainstorming.

Third, presentation software has so many features and functions that you can easily get caught up in these "bells and whistles" and thereby lose sight of your audience and lose track of your purpose. By having a clear, audience-focused message in mind before you start creating slides, you can focus on building effective slides to carry your message.

This restrained, audience-focused planning promotes Reynolds's next goal: simple, uncluttered slides. You will often find that the simplest way to convey a given message point is also the most effective. A few carefully chosen words, sometimes with a compelling image but sometimes without, are usually all you need to support the spoken message you will share at that moment in the presentation. To keep viewers focused on your message, avoid distracting them with anything that does not support that message. When it comes to editing and revising your slides, Reynolds says, "You must be ruthless."

In turn, simple slides with few words can encourage a more natural delivery by forcing you out from behind your slides, so to speak. If your slides are packed with every detail of your presentation, you can wind up being a bystander at your own presentation as both you and the audience read all that information. In contrast, if you know your material and you've practiced thoroughly, you will be able to speak much more fluidly and naturally, without relying on your slides. The result will be much more like a natural conversation, in which the connection is between you and your audience, not between your audience and your slides.[1]

(For a video summary of Reynolds's popular book *Presentation Zen*, see the Real-Time Updates "Learn More" link below.)

# Planning Your Presentation Visuals

By following the three-step development process in Chapter 16, you'll have a well-crafted, audience-focused message. The techniques in this chapter, which reflect the advice offered by experts such as Garr Reynolds (profiled in the chapter-opening Communication Close-Up), will help you enhance the delivery of that message with creative and effective visuals.

Visuals can improve the quality and impact of any presentation by creating interest, illustrating points that are difficult to explain with words alone, adding variety, and increasing the audience's ability to absorb and remember information. Behavioral research has shown that visuals can improve learning by up to 400 percent because humans can process visuals 60,000 times faster than text.[2]

For all the communication power of visuals, however, don't make the mistake of thinking that your visuals *are* your presentation. Particularly when using software such as Microsoft PowerPoint, Apple Keynote, or Google Presentations, communicators sometimes fall into the trap of letting the slides take center stage. Remember that your message is the presentation, not your visuals; your visuals are there to help support and clarify what you have to say.[3]

**1 LEARNING OBJECTIVE**
Explain the role of visuals in business presentations and list the types of visuals commonly used.

Remember that the purpose of visuals is to support your spoken message, not replace it.

## SELECTING THE TYPE OF VISUALS TO USE

You can select from a variety of visuals to enhance presentations, each with unique advantages and disadvantages:

- **Electronic slides.** Electronic slides created with PowerPoint or similar programs have a number of advantages: they are relatively easy to create and edit (at least for simple slides); slides can be made more engaging with images and various multimedia elements; slides are easy

**REAL-TIME UPDATES**
LEARN MORE BY WATCHING THIS VIDEO

**Get a quick video tour of Garr Reynolds's *Presentation Zen***

Fellow designer Matt Helmke offers a succinct overview of Reynolds's groundbreaking book. Go to http://real-timeupdates .com/bct12 and click on Learn More. If you are using MyBCommLab, you can access Real-Time Updates within each chapter or under Student Study Tools.

In most businesses, electronic presentations are now the presentation visual of choice, although they're certainly not the only option.

to incorporate into online meetings and webcasts; and you can record self-running presentations or screencasts for trade shows, websites, and other uses. The primary disadvantages are the amount of time that developing slides can consume, the equipment requirements, the potential complexity involved in creating more advanced presentations, and the risk that your hardware or software won't cooperate when it's show time.

- **Overhead transparencies.** Overhead transparencies are the very definition of old school, but they do have advantages. They can be created with nothing more than a marking pen, they don't require the latest computer or projection equipment, you can write on them during a presentation, and they never malfunction. On the downside, they're limited to static displays, they're virtually impossible to edit once you've printed them, and you or a partner are forced to stand next to the projector throughout your entire presentation.
- **Chalkboards and whiteboards.** Chalkboards and whiteboards are effective tools for recording points made during small-group sessions. With electronic whiteboards, you can print and email copies of whatever is written, too.
- **Flip charts.** Flip charts are another dependable low-tech tool for meetings and presentations. They are great for recording comments and questions during a presentation or for creating a "group memory" during brainstorming sessions, keeping track of all the ideas the team generates.
- **Other visuals.** Be creative when choosing visuals to support your presentation. A video of a focus group talking about your company can have a lot more impact than a series of slides that summarize what the group said. In technical or scientific presentations, a sample of a product or material lets your audience experience your subject directly. Designers and architects use mock-ups and models to help people envision what a final creation will look like. You might also want to incorporate other software in your presentation, such as a live spreadsheet to show financial data or a computer-aided design program to show a new product's design. If you're demonstrating the use of a software program, you can create a screencast that shows the software in action. Screencasting software also lets you add on-screen annotations and record an audio track to explain what is happening on-screen.

This chapter focuses on electronic presentations, the mainstay of business presentations today, although most of these design tips apply to other visuals as well.

## VERIFYING YOUR DESIGN PLANS

Think through your presentation outline carefully before designing your visuals.

After you have chosen the medium or media for your visuals, think through your presentation plan carefully before you start creating anything. Discerning audience members—the sort of people who can influence the direction of your career—are not easily fooled by visual razzle-dazzle. If your analysis is shaky or your conclusions are suspect, an over-the-top visual production won't help your presentation succeed. Review the plan for each visual and ask yourself how it will help your audience understand and appreciate your message.

Next, make sure your presentation style is appropriate for the subject matter, the audience, and the setting (see Figure 17.1). Take the time to double-check any cultural assumptions that might be inappropriate. Are you highlighting with a color that has negative emotional connotations in your audience's culture? Would your materials be too playful for a serious audience? Too serious for an audience that values creativity?

When it comes time to make design choices, from selecting fonts to deciding whether to include a photo, remember the advice from Chapter 16 and designers such as Garr Reynolds: Let simplicity be your guide. Doing so has several advantages. First, creating simple materials often takes less time, and time is the most precious commodity in today's business environment. Second, simple visuals reduce the chances of distraction and misinterpretation. Third, the more complex your presentation, the more likely something might go wrong.

Finally, use your time wisely. Presentation software seems to encourage experimentation and fiddling around with details and special effects, which can eat up hours of time

**Figure 17.1  Presentation Style**
Presentation software makes it easy to create an endless variety of visual styles. Compare the staid, "quiet" style on the left with the more dynamic style on the right.

you probably don't have. Based on your audience and situation, decide up front how much visual design is sufficient for your purpose and then stop when you get there. Use the time you'll save to rehearse your presentation—practice is far more important than minor design issues on your slides.

# Choosing Structured or Free-Form Slides

Perhaps the most important design choice you face when creating slides is whether to use conventional **structured slides** or the looser, **free-form slides** that many presentation specialists now advocate. Compare the two rows of slides in Figure 17.2 on the next page. The structured slides in the top row follow the same basic format throughout the presentation; in fact, they're based directly on the templates built into PowerPoint, which tend to feature lots of bullet points.

The free-form slides in the bottom row don't follow a rigid structure. However, choosing a free-form design strategy does not mean you should just randomly change the design from one slide to the next. Effectively designed slides should still be unified by design elements such as color and typeface selections, as Figure 17.2c and 17.2d show. Also, note how Figure 17.2d combines visual and textual messages to convey the point about listening without criticizing. This complementary approach of pictures and words is a highlight of free-form design.

Because the amount of content varies so dramatically between the two design approaches, the number of slides in a presentation can also vary dramatically. For instance, someone using structured slides might have 5 or 6 slides for a 20-minute presentation and spend 3 or 4 minutes on each one. In contrast, someone using free-form slides for the same presentation might have 60–80 slides or more and spend only 15 or 20 seconds on each one. Of course, this is only a general assessment. Don't feel that you need to create dozens of slides when using a free-form design; create only as many slides as you need to support your spoken message.

## Advantages and Disadvantages of Structured Slides

Structured slides have the advantage of being easy to create; you simply choose an overall design scheme for the presentation, select a template for a new slide, and start typing. If you're in a schedule crunch, going the structured route might save the day because at least you'll have *something* ready to show. Given the speed and ease of creating them, structured slides can be a more practical choice for routine presentations such as project status updates.

Also, because more information can usually be packed on each slide, carefully designed structured slides can be more effective at conveying complex ideas or sets of interrelated data to the right audiences. For example, if you are talking to a group of executives who

**2  LEARNING OBJECTIVE**
Explain the difference between structured and free-form slides and suggest when each design strategy is more appropriate.

Structured slides are usually based on templates that give all the slides in a presentation the same general look; free-form slides typically don't follow any set design plan.

Free-form slides often have far less content per slide than structured designs, which can require many more slides to cover a presentation of equal length.

Structured slides are usually the best choice for project updates and other routine information presentations, particularly if the slides are intended to be used only once.

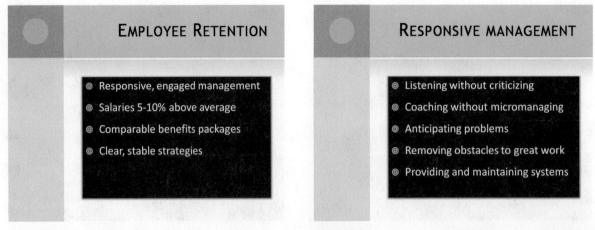

Figure 17.2a

Figure 17.2b

Figure 17.2c

Figure 17.2d

**Figure 17.2** **Structured Versus Free-Form Slide Design**
Compare the rigid, predictable design of the two slides in the top row with the free-form designs in the bottom row. Although the two free-form slides don't follow the same design structure, they are visually linked by color and font choices. As you compare these two styles, you can imagine how the free-form designs will require more slides to cover the same subject and require the speaker to convey more of the message. (Note that Figure 17.2d is a lighthearted but effective way of conveying the first bullet point in Figure 17.2b.)

must decide where to make budget cuts across the company's eight divisions, at some point in the presentation they probably will want to see summary data for all eight divisions on a single slide for easy comparison. Such a slide would be overcrowded by the usual definition, but this might be the only practical way to get a "big picture" view of the situation. (The best solution is probably some high-level, summary slides supported by a detailed handout, as "Creating Effective Handouts" on page 493 explains.)

The primary disadvantage of structured design is that mind-numbing effect Garr Reynolds describes, caused by text-heavy slides that all look alike. Slide after slide of dense, highly structured bullet points with no visual relief can put an audience to sleep.

Structured slide designs, which can lead to screen after screen of identical-looking bullet points, can be boring and overwhelming.

### Advantages and Disadvantages of Free-Form Slides

Well-designed free-form slides help viewers understand, process, and remember the speaker's message while keeping the focus on what the speaker is saying.

Free-form slide designs can overcome the drawbacks of text-heavy structured design. Such slides can fulfill three criteria researchers have identified as important for successful presentations: (1) providing complementary information through both textual and visual means, (2) limiting the amount of information delivered at any one time to prevent cognitive overload, and (3) helping viewers process information by identifying priorities and connections, such as by highlighting the most important data points in a graph.[4] (Of course, well-designed structured slides can also meet these criteria, but the constraints of prebuilt templates make doing so more of a challenge.)

With appropriate imagery, free-form designs can also create a more dynamic and engaging experience for the audience. Given their ability to excite and engage, free-form designs are particularly good for motivational, educational, and persuasive presentations—particularly when the slides will be used multiple times and therefore compensate for the extra time and effort required to create them.

Free-form slides have several potential disadvantages, however. First, effectively designing slides with both visual and textual elements is more creatively demanding and more time consuming than simply typing text into preformatted templates. The emphasis on visual content also requires more images, which take time to find.

Second, because far less textual information tends to be displayed on screen, the speaker is responsible for conveying more of the content. Ideally, of course, this is how a presentation *should* work, but presenters sometimes find themselves in less than ideal circumstances, such as being asked to fill in for a colleague on short notice.

Third, if not handled carefully, the division of information into smaller chunks can make it difficult to present complex subjects in a cohesive, integrated manner. For instance, if you're discussing a business problem that has five interrelated causes, it might be helpful to insert a conventional bullet-point slide as a summary and reminder after discussing each problem on its own.

*A key disadvantage of free-form slide designs is the time and effort often required to create them.*

# Designing Effective Slides

Despite complaints about "death by PowerPoint," the problem is not with that software itself (or with Apple Keynote or any other presentation program). The software is just a tool and, like other tools, can be used well or poorly. Unfortunately, lack of design awareness, inadequate training, schedule pressures, and the instinctive response of doing things the way they've always been done can lead to ineffective slides and lost opportunities to really connect with audiences.

Another reason for ineffective slides is the practice of treating slide sets as standalone documents that can be read on their own, without a presenter. (The emergence of websites such as SlideShare, www.slidehare.net, might be contributing to this problem, too, by making it so easy to share slide sets.) These "slideument" hybrids that try to function as both presentation visuals and printed documents don't work well as either: They often have too much information to be effective visuals and too little to be effective reports (in addition to being clumsy to read).

As "Creating Effective Handouts" on page 493 explains, the ideal solution is to create an effective slide set and a separate handout document that provides additional details and supporting information. This way, you can optimize each piece to do the job it is really meant to do. An alternative is to use the notes field in your presentation software to include your speaking notes for each slide. Anyone who gets a copy of your slides can at least follow along by reading your notes, although you will probably need to edit and embellish them to make them understandable by others.

However, if creating slideuments is your only option for some reason, be sure to emphasize clarity and simplicity. If you have to add more slides to avoid packing individual slides with too much text, by all means do so. Having a larger number of simpler slides is a better compromise all around than having a smaller number of jam-packed slides. Remember that the primary purpose of the slides is supporting your presentation, so make sure your slides work well for that purpose.

**3    LEARNING OBJECTIVE**
Outline the decisions involved in using a key visual and selecting color, artwork, and typefaces to create effective slide designs.

*"Death by PowerPoint" is a common complaint; however, the problem isn't with the tools but how they are used.*

*"Slideuments" are hybrids that try to function as both presentation slides and printed documents—and often fail at both tasks.*

*The ideal solution for many presentations is an effective set of slides and a complementary handout.*

*If you must create a slideument, make the slides as simple and clear as possible.*

## DESIGNING SLIDES AROUND A KEY VISUAL

With both structured and free-form design strategies, it is often helpful to structure specific slides around a key visual that helps organize and explain the points you are trying to make. For example, a pyramid suggests a hierarchical relationship, and a circular flow diagram emphasizes that the final stage in a process loops back to the beginning of the process. Figure 17.3 on the next page shows six of the many types of visual designs you can use to organize information on a slide.

*Organizing a slide around a key visual can help the audience quickly grasp how ideas are related.*

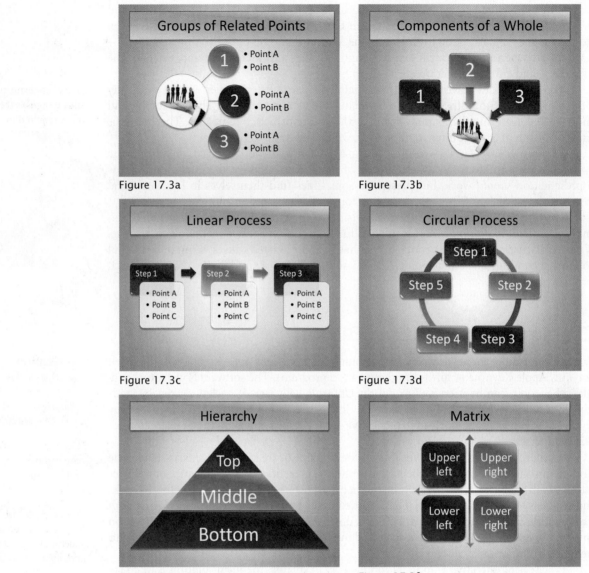

Figure 17.3a

Figure 17.3b

Figure 17.3c

Figure 17.3d

Figure 17.3e

Figure 17.3f

**Figure 17.3  Using a Key Visual to Organize Points on a Slide**
Simple graphical elements such as these "SmartArt" images in Microsoft PowerPoint make it easy to organize slide content using a key visual. Whether you're trying to convey the relationship of ideas in a hierarchy, a linear process, a circular process, or just about any other configuration, a key visual can work in tandem with your written and spoken messages to help audiences get your message.

## SELECTING DESIGN ELEMENTS

To design effective slides, remember the six principles of effective design: consistency, contrast, balance, emphasis, convention, and simplicity (review Chapter 9 for a refresher).

As you design and create slides, always keep the audience's experience in mind: What will it be like to view this slide while listening to a speaker? Chapter 9 highlights six principles of effective design: consistency, contrast, balance, emphasis, convention, and simplicity. Pay close attention to these principles as you select the design elements for your slides (covered in this section) and create content for each slide (covered in the following section).

### Color

Color is much more than mere decoration: It provides emphasis, isolation, and contrast; it increases readability and retention; it sends powerful nonverbal signals; and it can stimulate desired emotional responses.

Color is a critical design element, far more than mere decoration. It grabs the viewer's attention, emphasizes important ideas, creates contrast, and isolates slide elements. Color sends a powerful nonverbal message, too, whether it's elegance, technical sophistication, fiscal prudence, or hipster trendiness. You can study this effect as you view various websites or advertisements, for instance. A palette of cool grays and blues "says" something different than

## TABLE 17.1  Color and Emotion

| Color | Emotional Associations | Best Uses |
|---|---|---|
| Blue | Peaceful, soothing, tranquil, cool, trusting | Background for electronic business presentations (usually dark blue); safe and conservative |
| White | Neutral, innocent, pure, wise | Font color of choice for most electronic business presentations with a dark background |
| Yellow | Warm, bright, cheerful, enthusiastic | Text bullets and subheadings with a dark background |
| Red | Passionate, dangerous, active, painful | For promoting action or stimulating the audience; seldom used as a background ("in the red" specifically refers to financial losses) |
| Green | Assertive, prosperous, envious, relaxed | Highlight and accent color (green symbolizes money in the United States but not in other countries). |

*Source:* Adapted from Claudyne Wilder and David Fine, *Point,Click & Wow* (San Francisco: Jossey-Bass Pfeiffer, 1996), 63, 527.

a palette of warm oranges and browns, which says something different than a palette of hot pink and lime green.

Color can also play a key role in the overall acceptance of your message. Research shows that color visuals can account for 60 percent of an audience's acceptance or rejection of an idea. Color can increase willingness to read by up to 80 percent, and it can enhance learning and improve retention by more than 75 percent.[5]

Your color choices can also stimulate various emotions, as Table 17.1 suggests. For instance, if you want to excite your audience, add some warm colors, such as red and orange, to your slides. If you want to achieve a more relaxed and receptive environment, blue is a better choice.[6] Remember, color may have a different meaning in certain cultures, so if you are creating slides for international audiences, research those cultural differences.

When selecting color, limit your choices to a few compatible ones and keep in mind that some colors work better together than others. Contrasting colors, for example, increase readability, so when selecting colors for backgrounds, titles, and text, avoid choosing those that are close in hue, such as brown on green or blue on purple.[7] If you'll be presenting in a dark room, use dark colors such as blue for the background, a midrange of brightness for illustrations, and light colors for text. If you are presenting in well-lit rooms, reverse the colors: Use light colors for the background and dark colors for text. If you have some reason to change colors between slides, don't switch back and forth from very dark to very bright; the effect is jarring to the audience's eyes.[8]

### Artwork

Every slide has two layers or levels of visual elements: the background and foreground. The *background* is the equivalent of paper in a printed report and often stays the same from slide to slide, particularly with structured designs. The *foreground* contains the unique text and graphic elements that make up each individual slide.

Generally speaking, the less your background does, the better. As presentation designer Nancy Duarte explains, the background "should be open, spacious, and simple."[9] Cluttered or flashy backgrounds tend to distract from your message. The background needs to stay in the background; it shouldn't compete with the foreground elements. Be careful when using the design templates that come with your software. Many have backgrounds that are too busy, and some are too playful for business use. Bear in mind that you don't *need* to use a background at all, other than perhaps a solid color to set type and images against.

> The background should stay in the background, not compete with the foreground.

In the background, all artwork is essentially decorative. In the foreground, artwork can be either functional or decorative. *Functional artwork* includes photos, technical drawings, charts, and other visual elements containing information that is part of your message. In contrast, *decorative artwork* doesn't deliver textual or numerical information, and it may or may not be helpful. Decorative artwork can be helpful if it establishes an appropriate emotional tone or amplifies the message of a slide, partly because simple, high-impact images are easier to remember than text.[10] However, decorative artwork is unhelpful if it doesn't add value, is off topic, conveys an unprofessional image, or pulls viewer attention away from the essential elements on a slide (see Figure 17.4 on the next page). Decorative artwork is

> Artwork can be either decorative or functional; use decorative artwork only if it supports the message of the slide in question.

Figure 17.4a

Figure 17.4b

**Figure 17.4** **Effective and Ineffective Artwork**
Slide artwork can carry your message, support your message, or totally get in the way. Figure 17.4a could be an effective way to introduce a talk about teamwork, with one ant helping its "teammate" out of a tough spot. If this image were created using clip art, it would probably be too cartoony for a professional presentation. However, this image has a sophisticated, almost elegant, look in spite of the fact that it features ants. The slide in Figure 17.4b is a disaster. The visual confusion created by the clutter and mixed styles of artwork will distract the audience and obscure the message.

usually the least important element of any slide, but it often causes the most trouble. *Clip art*, collections of drawings you can insert in slides and other documents, is probably the biggest troublemaker of them all. You can find thousands of pieces of free clip art in presentation software or online, but few of them have any information value, and many give your slides an unprofessional, cartoony appearance.

### Typefaces and Type Styles

When selecting typefaces and type styles for slides, follow these guidelines:

Many of the typefaces available on your computer are difficult to read when projected, so they aren't good choices for presentation slides.

- Avoid script or decorative typefaces, except for limited, special uses.
- Use serif typefaces with care and only with larger text.
- Limit the number of typefaces to one or two per slide.
- When using thinner typefaces, use boldface so that letters won't look washed out.
- Avoid most italicized type; it is usually difficult to read when projected.
- Avoid all-capitalized words and phrases.
- Allow extra white space between lines of text.
- Be consistent with typefaces, type styles, colors, and sizes.

When selecting type sizes, consider the room(s) in which you'll be presenting. The farther the audience is from the screen, the larger your type must be in order to be readable from everywhere in the room. Venture capitalist and investor Guy Kawasaki (see page 409), who has sat through hundreds and hundreds of PowerPoint presentations, suggests using no type smaller than 30 points. Doing so not only ensures readable slides but forces you to distill every idea down to its essential core, simply because you won't have room to be wordy.[11] After you have selected your fonts and type styles, test them for readability by viewing sample slides from your audience's viewing location. If you don't have access to the conference room, a clever way to test readability at your computer is to stand back as many feet from the screen as your screen size in inches (17 feet for a 17-inch screen, for example). If the slides are readable at this distance, you're probably in good shape.[12]

Design inconsistencies confuse and annoy audiences; don't change colors and other design elements randomly throughout your presentation.

### MAINTAINING DESIGN CONSISTENCY

Audiences start to assign meaning to visual elements beginning with your first slide. For instance, if the first slide presents the most important information in dark red, 36-point, Gill Sans typeface, your audience will expect the same type treatment for the most important information on the remaining slides as well. Don't force viewers to repeatedly figure out the meaning of design elements by making arbitrary changes from slide to slide.

Fortunately, presentation software makes consistency easy to achieve, particularly for structured slide designs. You simply adjust the *slide master* using the colors, fonts, and other design elements you've chosen; these choices will then automatically show up on every slide in the presentation. In addition, you can maintain consistency by choosing a predefined layout from those available in your software—which helps ensure that bulleted lists, charts, graphics, and other elements show up in predictable places on each slide. Something as simple as switching from a single column of bullet points to two columns can cause problems for readers, as they try to figure out the meaning of the new arrangement. The less work readers have to do to interpret your slide designs, the more attention they can pay to your message.

# Creating Effective Slide Content

With some design fundamentals in mind, you're ready to create the textual and visual content for your slides. For every slide, remember to watch out for information overload. When slides have too much content—textual, visual, or both—particularly for several slides in a row, viewers can't process the incoming information fast enough to make sense of it and eventually tune out. In the words of Jim Confalone of New York's ProPoint Graphics, the presentation "becomes like wallpaper." Keep your slides clear and easy to grasp, and pace the flow of information at a speed that lets people connect your ideas from one slide to the next.[13]

**4** **LEARNING OBJECTIVE**
Explain how to create effective slide content.

No matter which design strategy you use, limit the amount of information on each slide to avoid overloading your viewers.

## WRITING READABLE CONTENT

One of the most common mistakes beginners make—and one of the chief criticisms leveled at structured slide designs in general—is stuffing slides with too much text. Doing so overloads the audience with too much information too fast, takes attention away from the speaker by forcing people to read more, and requires the presenter to use smaller type.

Effective text slides supplement your words and help the audience follow the flow of ideas. Use text to highlight key points, summarize and preview your message, signal major shifts in thought, illustrate concepts, or help create interest in your spoken message.

In a sense, slide text serves as the headings and subheadings for your presentation. Accordingly, choose words and short phrases that help your audience follow the flow of ideas, without forcing them to read in depth. You primarily want your audience to *listen*, not to *read*. Use your slides to highlight key points, summarize and preview your message, signal major shifts in thought, illustrate concepts, or help create interest in your spoken message. If the audience can benefit from additional information, provide those details in handouts (see page 493).

When writing content for text slides, keep your message short and simple (see Figure 17.5 on the next page):

Use slide text sparingly and only to emphasize key points, not to convey your entire message.

- Limit each slide to one thought, concept, or idea (without dividing things so far that the audience has trouble seeing the big picture).
- Limit text content to four or five lines with four or five words per line. For selected slides, it might make sense to exceed these limits, but do so infrequently.
- Don't show a large number of text-heavy slides in a row; give the audience some visual relief.
- Write short, bulleted phrases rather than long sentences.
- Use sentences only when you need to share a quotation or some other text item verbatim.[14]
- Phrase list items in parallel grammatical form to facilitate quick reading.
- Use the active voice.
- Include short, informative titles.
- When combining visuals with text, the more information the visual can convey, the less work your text needs to do.

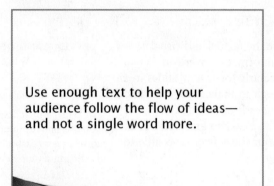

### Writing Readable Content

To choose effective words and phrases, think of the text on your slides as guides to the content, not the content itself. In a sense, slide text serves as the headings and subheadings for your presentation. Accordingly, choose words and short phrases that help your audience follow the flow of ideas, without forcing people to read in depth. You primarily want your audience to *listen*, not to *read*. Highlight key points, summarize and preview your message, signal major shifts in thought, illustrate concepts, or help create interest in your spoken message.

Figure 17.5a

### Writing Readable Content

- Text should be a guide to your content
- Use bullets like headings and subheadings
- Help audience follow the flow of ideas
- Encourage audience to *listen*, not *read*
- Highlight, summarize, preview, illustrate

Figure 17.5b

Use enough text to help your audience follow the flow of ideas— and not a single word more.

Figure 17.5c

Just enough

Figure 17.5d

MyBCommLab Apply Figure 17.5's key concepts. Go to **mybcommlab.com** and follow this path: Course Content → Chapter 17 → **DOCUMENT MAKEOVERS**

**Figure 17.5** **Writing Text for Slides**
Effective text slides are clear, simple guides that help the audience understand and remember the speaker's message. Notice the progression toward simplicity in these slides: Figure 17.5a is a paragraph that would distract the audience for an extended period of time. Figure 17.5b offers concise, readable bullets, although too many slides in a row in this structured design would become tedious. Figure 17.5c distills the message down to a single thought that is complete on its own but doesn't convey all the information from the original and would need embellishment from the speaker. Figure 17.5d pushes this to the extreme, with only the core piece of the message to serve as an "exclamation point" for the spoken message. Figure 17.5c and especially Figure 17.5d could be more even more powerful with a well-chosen visual that illustrates the idea of following the flow.

## CREATING CHARTS AND TABLES FOR SLIDES

Many graphics that work well in printed form need to be simplified for use in presentations because they are too dense and too complicated to be easily viewed on-screen.

Charts and tables for presentations need to be simpler than visuals for printed documents. Detailed images that look fine on the printed page can be too dense and too complicated for presentations. Remember that your audience will view your slides from across the room—not from a foot or two away, as you do while you create them. Don't force the audience study your charts and graphs in order to get the message. Follow these guidelines:

- **Reduce the detail.** Eliminate anything that is not absolutely essential to the message. If necessary, break information into more than one slide. If a deeper level of detail is helpful or necessary, hand out printed visuals that people can review during or after the presentation.
- **Simplify.** For example, if a bar chart is segmented by week, don't write "Week of 12/01," "Week of 12/08," and so on. Use the "Week of" label once and then just include the dates. Similarly, you might be able to remove the vertical scale from the left side of the chart and just show individual values above each bar.[15]
- **Shorten numbers.** If doing so doesn't hide essential details, you can round off numbers such as $12,500.72 to $12 or $12.5 and then label the axis to indicate thousands.

- **Limit the amount of data shown.** Line graphs look busy when they have more than two or three lines, bar charts look crowded with more than five or six bars, and tables are difficult to read if they have too many rows or columns.
- **Highlight key points.** Use arrows, boldface type, and color to direct your audience's eyes to the main point of a visual. Summarize the intent of the graphic in one clear title, such as "Earnings up by 15%."
- **Adjust the size and design.** Modify the size of a graphic to accommodate the size of a slide. Leave plenty of white space so that audience members can view and interpret content from a distance. Use colors that stand out from the slide's background and choose a typeface for labels that is clear and easy to read.

## ADDING ANIMATION AND MULTIMEDIA

Today's presentation software offers a wide array of options for livening up your slides, including sound, animation, video clips, transition effects from one slide to the next, and hyperlinks to websites and other resources. As with every other visual element, the key is to make sure any effects you use support your message. Always consider the impact that all these effects will have on your audience members and their desire to understand your message.[16]

Animation and special effects can be grouped into four categories: functional animation, transitions and builds, hyperlinks, and multimedia. These capabilities are briefly discussed in the following sections; to learn more about using them, consult the Help menu in your software.

### Functional Animation

PowerPoint and other presentation packages offer a mind-boggling set of tools for moving and changing things on screen. You can have a block of text cartwheel in from outer space, change colors, change font and font size, spin around in circles, blink on and off, wave back and forth, crawl around the screen following a predefined path, and then disappear one letter at a time, like some sort of erasing typewriter. You *can* do all this, but *should* you?

Just as static graphic elements can be either functional or decorative, so too can animated elements. For instance, having each bullet point fly in from the left side of the screen doesn't add any functional value to your communication effort. In contrast, a highlight arrow or color bar that moves around the screen to emphasize specific points in a technical diagram can be an effective use of animation and a welcome alternative to a laser pointer. You can control every aspect of the animation, so it's easy to coordinate the movement with the points you're making in your presentation. Using carefully controlled functional animation is also a great way to demonstrate sequences and procedures. For a training session on machinery repair, for example, you can show a schematic diagram of the machinery and walk your audience through each step of the troubleshooting process, highlighting each step on-screen as you address it verbally. Again, use animation in support of your message, not simply for animation's sake.

Although you can animate just about everything in an electronic presentation, resist the temptation to do so. Make sure each animation has a purpose.

### Transitions and Builds

In addition to animating specific elements on your slides, you can choose from various options for adding motion between slides. These **slide transitions** control how one slide replaces another on-screen. Subtle transitions can ease your viewers' gaze from one slide to the next—such as having the current slide gently fade out before the next one fades in. However, many of the transitions currently available (such as checkerboards, pinwheels, and spinning "newsflashes") are like miniature animated shows themselves and are therefore distracting. These pointless transition effects not only disrupt the flow of your presentation, they can make the whole thing seem amateurish. If you use a transition effect, use the same one throughout the presentation (so that audiences don't wonder if there is some significance to a new transition at some point during the presentation), and choose the effect carefully. Aim for a smooth,

Use subtle transition animations between slides to ease the viewer from one slide to the next; most transitions available in presentation software are too distracting.

subtle effect that is easy on the eye. And unless a sound effect is somehow integral to the message, there is no reason to add audio to a transition.

Using carefully designed builds can be a great way to reveal information in easy-to-process pieces.

**Builds** are much more useful than transitions, at least when used with care and thought. These effects control the release of text, graphics, and other elements on individual slides. For instance, with builds you can make a list of bullet points appear one at a time rather than having all of them appear at once, which makes it difficult to focus on a single point. This controlled release of information helps draw audience members' attention to the point being discussed and keeps them from reading ahead.

As with transitions, stick with the subtle, basic options for builds. The point of a build is to release information in a controlled fashion, not to distract or entertain the audience. Another useful option is to change the color of bullet points as you discuss each one. For instance, if your primary text color is a strong blue, you might have the text in each bullet point change to a light gray after you've finished talking about it. This subtle approach keeps the audience's attention focused on the bullet point you are currently discussing.

After you've assigned builds to your slides, you can control the build activity with a mouse or a remote control device. Experiment with the options in your software to find the most effective build scheme. In addition to building up text, you can build up graphical elements. For instance, to discuss monthly sales of three products over the past year, you can have a line graph of the first product appear by itself while you discuss it, and then you can click the mouse to display the second product's sales line, then the third.

## Hyperlinks

Hyperlinks and action buttons can be quite handy when you need flexibility in your presentations or want to share different kinds of files with the audience. A **hyperlink** instructs your computer to jump to another slide in your presentation, to a website, or to another program entirely. Depending on your presentation software, hyperlinks can be simple underlined text, invisible *hotspots* in graphical elements, or clearly labeled *action buttons*.

You can increase the flexibility of your presentation slides with hyperlinks that let you jump to different slides, websites, or other software screens with the click of a mouse.

Using hyperlinks is also a great way to customize your presentations. For instance, if you work in sales and call on a variety of customers, you can't be sure what sort of situation you'll encounter at each customer's site. You might be prepared to give an in-depth technical presentation to a group of engineers, only to have the company president walk in and request a brief financial overview instead. Or you might prepare a set of detailed technical slides but not show them unless the audience asks detailed questions.

Another challenging situation is finding out at the last minute that you have less time than you thought to make your presentation. If you've built in some flexibility, you won't need to rush through your entire presentation or scramble on the spot to find the most important slides. Instead, you can simply click an action button labeled "Five-minute

---

**THE ART OF PROFESSIONALISM**

# Being a Team Player

Professionals know that they are contributors to a larger cause, that it's not all about them. Just as in athletics and other team efforts, being a team player in business is something of a balancing act. On the one hand, you need to pay enough attention to your own efforts and skills to make sure you're pulling your own weight. On the other hand, you need to pay attention to the overall team effort to make sure the team succeeds. Remember that if the team fails, you fail, too.

Great team players know how to make those around them more effective, whether it's by lending a hand during crunch time, sharing resources, removing obstacles, making introductions, or offering expertise. In fact, the ability to help others improve their performance is one of the key attributes executives look for when they want to promote people into management.

Being a team player also means showing loyalty to your organization and protecting your employer's reputation—one of the most important assets any company has. Pros don't trash their employers in front of customers or in their personal blogs. When they have a problem, they solve it; they don't share it.

**CAREER APPLICATIONS**

1. If you prefer to work by yourself, should you take a job in a company that uses a team-based organization structure? Why or why not?

2. You can see plenty of examples of unprofessional business behavior in the news media and in your own consumer and employee experiences. Why should you bother being professional yourself?

overview" and jump right to the two or three most important slides in your presentation. With hyperlinks, you can even switch from the indirect approach to the direct approach or vice versa, based on the response you're getting from your audience. By building in links that accommodate these various scenarios, you can adjust your presentation at a moment's notice—and look polished and professional while you do it.

### Multimedia Elements

Multimedia elements offer the ultimate in active presentations. Using audio and video clips can be an effective way to complement your live message, such as including a recorded message from a company executive or scenes from a customer focus group. Just be sure to keep these elements brief and relevant, as supporting points for your presentation, not as replacements for it.

*Video clips can add memorable, engaging content to your presentations—as long as they are relevant, interesting, and brief.*

## Completing Slides and Support Materials

Just as you would review any message for content, style, tone, readability, clarity, and conciseness, you should apply the same quality control to your slides and other visuals. As you look over your presentation for the final time, make sure that all visuals are

**5** **LEARNING OBJECTIVE**
Explain the role of navigation slides, support slides, and handouts.

*Review each slide carefully to make sure it is clear and readable.*

- **Readable.** Can text be read from the back of the room? Does the text stand out from the background?
- **Consistent.** Are colors and design elements used consistently?
- **Simple.** Is each slide and the entire presentation as simple as possible? Can you eliminate any slides?
- **Audience centered.** Are the message and the design focused on the audience?
- **Clear.** Is the main point of a slide obvious? Easy to understand? Can the audience grasp the main point in just a few seconds?[17]
- **Concise and grammatical.** Is text written in concise phrases? Are bulleted phrases grammatically parallel?
- **Focused.** Does each slide cover only one thought, concept, or idea (or summarize a group of related ideas)? Does the slide grab the viewer's attention in the right place and support the key points of the message? Are arrows, symbols, or other techniques used to draw the audience's attention to the key sections of a chart or diagram?
- **Fully operational.** Have you verified every slide in your presentation? Do all the animations and other special effects work as you intended?

Keep in mind that you want the audience to listen to you, not study the slides, so make sure your slides are not distracting in any way.

For example, the *slide sorter* view (different programs have different names for this feature) lets you see some or all of the slides in your presentation on a single screen. Use this view to add and delete slides, reposition slides, check slides for design consistency, and verify the operation of any effects. Moreover, the slide sorter is a great way to review the flow of your story.[18]

*Use the slide sorter view to verify and modify the organization of your slides.*

With your slides working properly and in clear, logical order, you're just a few steps away from being ready. Now is a good time to think about a backup plan. What will you do if your laptop won't turn on or the projector dies? Can you get by without your slides? For important presentations, consider having backup equipment on standby, loaded with your presentation, and ready to go. At the very least, have enough printed handouts ready to give the audience so that, as a last resort, you can give your presentation "on paper."

### CREATING NAVIGATION AND SUPPORT SLIDES

Now that the content slides are ready, enhance your presentation with several slides that add "finish" to your presentation and provide additional information to benefit your audience:

- **Title slide(s).** Make a good first impression on your audience with one or two title slides, the equivalent of a report's cover and title page (see Figures 17.6a and 17.6b on the next page). A title slide should contain the title of your presentation (and subtitle, if appropriate), your name, your department affiliation (for internal audiences), and your

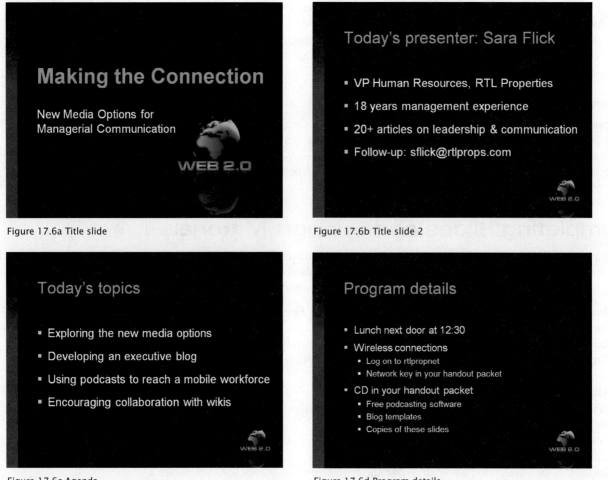

Figure 17.6a Title slide

Figure 17.6b Title slide 2

Figure 17.6c Agenda

Figure 17.6d Program details

**Figure 17.6   Navigation and Support Slides**
You can use a variety of navigation and support slides to introduce yourself and your presentation, to let the audience know what your presentation covers, and to provide essential details.

company affiliation (for external audiences). You may also include the presentation date and an appropriate graphic element. Depending on the amount of information you need to convey at this point, two title slides might be appropriate: one focusing on the topic of the presentation and a second with your affiliation and other information. This second slide can also be used to introduce the speaker and list his or her credentials.

- **Agenda and program details.** You can use these slides to communicate the agenda for your presentation and any additional information your audience might need. Because presentations pull your audience members away from their daily routines and work responsibilities, they can have questions about anything from break times or lunch plans to the password needed to log onto the facility's wireless network (see Figures 17.6c and 17.6d). By answering these questions at the beginning of your presentation, you'll minimize disruptions later and help the audience stay focused on your message.

Navigation slides help your audience keep track of what you've covered already and what you plan to cover next.

- **Navigation slides.** To tell your audience where you're going and where you've been, you can use a series of **navigation slides** based on your outline or agenda. This technique is most useful in longer presentations with several major sections. As you complete each section, repeat the slide but indicate which material has been covered and which section you are about to begin (see Figure 17.7). This sort of slide is sometimes referred to as a *moving blueprint*. You can then use the original slide again in the close of your presentation to review the points you've covered. As an alternative to the repeating agenda slide, you can insert a simple *bumper slide* at each major section break, announcing the title of the section you're about to begin.[19]

Figure 17.7a "Muting" topics already covered

Figure 17.7b Highlighting the next topic

**Figure 17.7** **Blueprint Slides**
Here are two of the ways you can use a *blueprint slide* as a navigational aid to help your audience
stay on track with the presentation. Figure 17.7a visually "mutes" and checks off the sections of the
presentation that have already been covered. In contrast, Figure 17.7b uses a sliding highlight box to
indicate the next section to be covered.

Figure 17.8 on the next page illustrates some of the many options you have for presenting various types of information. Note that although these slides don't follow a rigid structure of text-heavy bullet points, they are unified by the color scheme (silver background and
bold color accents) and typeface selections.

## CREATING EFFECTIVE HANDOUTS

*Handouts*, any printed materials you give the audience to supplement your talk, should be
considered an integral part of your presentation strategy. Plan them in tandem with your
presentation slides so that you use each medium as effectively as possible. Your presentation
should paint the big picture, convey and connect major ideas, set the emotional tone, and
rouse the audience to action (if that is relevant to your talk). Your handouts can then carry
the rest of the information load, providing the supporting details that audience members can
consume at their own speed, on their own time. You won't need to worry about stuffing every
detail into your slides, because you have the more appropriate medium of printed documents
to do that. As Garr Reynolds puts it, "Handouts can set you free."[20]

> View handouts as an integral part
> of your presentation strategy so
> that they work in harmony with
> your slides and spoken message.

Possibilities for good handout materials include the following:[21]

- **Complex charts and diagrams.** Charts and tables that are too unwieldy for the screen
  or that demand thorough analysis make good handouts.
- **Articles and technical papers.** Magazine articles that supplement the information in
  your presentation make good handout materials, as do technical papers that provide
  in-depth coverage of the material you've highlighted in your presentation.
- **Case studies.** Summaries of business case studies can make good supplemental reading
  material.
- **Recommended resources.** Lists of websites, bloggers, and other online resources
  related to your topic can be useful. For each source, provide a URL and a one- or two-
  sentence summary of its content.
- **Copies of presentation slides.** In many cases, audiences like to have print versions of
  the slides used by a speaker, containing the speaker's comments about each slide and
  blank lines for note taking. Use the page and print setup options in your software to
  choose the more useful arrangement.

> Use handout materials to support
> the points made in your presenta-
> tion and to offer the audience ad-
> ditional information on your topic.

Timing the distribution of handouts depends on their content, the nature of your presentation, and your personal preference. Some speakers like to distribute handout copies of their slides before the presentation begins so that the audience can take notes on

*Left*: This introductory slide is a blunt attention-getter, something that would have to be used with caution and only in special circumstances.

*Right*: This simple math equation gets the point across about how expensive high employee turnover is.

*Left*: This stylized bar graph sends a stark visual message about how bad the company's turnover really is.

*Right*: This slide is essentially a bullet list, with three groups of two bullets each. Repeating the photo element from the introductory slide emphasizes the message about employee turnover.

These two *navigation slides* show one way to introduce each of the four subtopics in this particular section. As the highlight moves around the central circle, the audience is reminded of which subtopics have been covered and which subtopic is going to be covered next. And each time it is shown, the message is repeated that all these problems are the "true cost of chaos" in the company's employment practices.

*Left*: This slide introduces three key points the speaker wants to emphasize in this particular section.

*Right*: This slide shows a linear flow of ideas, each with bulleted subpoints. This slide could be revealed one section at a time to help the speaker keep the audience's attention focused on a single topic.

*Left*: This flowchart packs a lot of information onto one slide, but seeing the sequence of events in one place is essential.

*Right*: This simple visual highlights the presenter's spoken message about being careful to choose the right tasks to focus on and then completing them quickly.

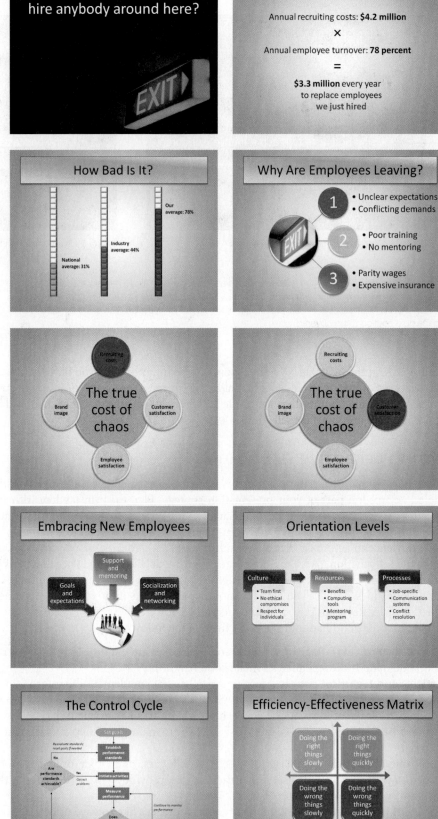

**Figure 17.8   Designing Effective Visuals: Selected Slides**
These slides, from a presentation that addresses a company's high employee turnover rate, illustrate the wide variety of design options you have for creating effective, appealing slides. (All the slides were created using features in PowerPoint.)

them. Doing so can be risky, however, particularly if you've organized your talk with the indirect approach, because the audience can read ahead and reach the conclusion and recommendations before you're able to build up to them yourself. Other speakers simply advise the audience of the types of information covered in handouts but delay distributing anything until they have finished speaking.

For a quick review of the key steps in creating effective visuals, see "Checklist: Enhancing Presentations with Visuals." For the latest information on presentation design, visit **http://real-timeupdates.com/bct12** and click on Chapter 17.

> **REAL-TIME UPDATES**
> LEARN MORE BY WATCHING THIS VIDEO
> **Turn your presentation into a video**
> Learn how to turn a PowerPoint presentation into a video anyone can watch, even without PowerPoint software. Go to http://real-timeupdates.com/bct12 and click on Learn More. If you are using MyBCommLab, you can access Real-Time Updates within each chapter or under Student Study Tools.

## CHECKLIST ✓ Enhancing Presentations with Visuals

**A. Plan your presentation visuals.**
- Make sure you and your message, not your visuals, remain the focus of your presentation.
- Select your visuals carefully to support your message; use a combination of visuals if needed.
- Review your plan for each visual to make sure it truly supports your message.
- Follow effective design principles, with an emphasis on accuracy and simplicity.
- Use your time wisely so that you have plenty of time to practice your presentation.

**B. Choose structured or free-form slides.**
- Structured slides using bullet-point templates are easy to create, require little design time or skill, and can be completed in a hurry. Best uses: routine, internal presentations.
- Primary disadvantages of structured slides are mind-numbing repetition of bullet-point format and the common tendency of stuffing too much information on them.
- Free-form slides make it easier to combine textual and visual information, to create a more dynamic and engaging experience, and to maintain a conversational connection with the audience. Best uses: motivational, educational, and persuasive presentations.
- Primary disadvantages of structured slides are the time, skill, and imagery required; added responsibilities for the speaker; and possibility of fragmenting complex topics.

**C. Design effective slides.**
- Avoid the temptation to create "slideuments," slides that are so packed with information that they can be read as standalone documents.
- Use color to emphasize important ideas, create contrast, isolate visual elements, and convey intended nonverbal signals.
- Limit color to a few compatible choices and use them consistently.
- Make sure your slide background doesn't compete with the foreground.

- Use decorative artwork sparingly and only to support your message.
- Emphasize functional artwork—photos, technical drawings, charts, and other visual elements containing information that is part of your message.
- Choose typefaces that are easy to read on-screen; limit the number of typefaces and use them consistently.
- Use slide masters to maintain consistency throughout your presentation.

**D. Create effective slide content.**
- Write content that will be readable from everywhere in the room.
- Write short, active, parallel phrases that support, not replace, your spoken message.
- Avoid complete sentences unless you need to quote verbatim.
- Limit the amount of text so that your audience can focus on listening, not reading.
- Simplify print graphics for use on slides but don't oversimplify.
- Use functional animation when it can support your message.
- Make sure slide transitions are subtle, if used at all.
- Use builds carefully to control the release of information.
- Use hyperlinks and action buttons to add flexibility to your presentation.
- Incorporate multimedia elements that can help engage your audience and deliver your message.

**E. Complete slides and support materials.**
- Review every slide carefully to ensure accuracy, consistency, and clarity.
- Make sure that all slides are fully operational.
- Use the slide sorter to verify and adjust the sequence of slides, if needed.
- Have a backup plan in case your electronic presentation plan fails.
- Create navigation and support slides.
- Create handouts to give the audience additional information and to minimize the amount of information you need to put on your slides.

# Quick Learning Guide

## SUMMARY OF LEARNING OBJECTIVES

**1** **Explain the role of visuals in business presentations, and list the types of visuals commonly used.** Visuals create interest, illustrate and clarify important points, add variety, and help the listener absorb the information you're presenting. In most businesses today, electronic slide presentations are the most common tool, but you might also use overhead transparencies, chalkboards and whiteboards (including electronic whiteboards), flip charts, product samples, models, video, and various software programs.

**2** **Explain the difference between structured and free-form slides, and suggest when each design strategy is more appropriate.** Structured slides follow the same design plan for most or all the slides in a presentation. They are often created by using the templates provided with PowerPoint and other electronic presentation programs. Structured slides tend to convey most of their information through bullet points. In contrast, free-form slides do not follow any set design scheme from slide to slide, although they can and should use color, font selection, and other design choices to create a unified feel across a presentation. Free-form slides often have just a single statement on each slide, requiring many more slides to cover the same amount of material as the typical structured design.

The ease and speed with which structured slides can be created make them most useful for routine presentations such as project update meetings, particularly for internal audiences and in situations in which the slide deck will be used only once. They can also be useful when the audience needs to see a number of information points on screen simultaneously in order to make comparisons. Given their ability to excite and engage, free-form designs are particularly good for motivational, educational, and persuasive presentations—particularly when the slides will be used multiple times and therefore compensate for the extra time and effort often required to create them.

**3** **Outline the decisions involved in using a key visual and selecting color, artwork, and typefaces to create effective slide designs.** Using a key visual involves selecting a single, simple visual element as a structure for the elements on a slide. For example, a circle can be used to identify the points in a repeating process, and a triangle can establish the interrelationship of three entities.

Color is a critical design element because it can grab the viewer's attention, emphasize important ideas, create contrast, isolate particular slide elements, stimulate emotions, and send powerful nonverbal messages such as elegance or technical sophistication. Color also affects the acceptance and retention of messages. When selecting color, limit your choices to a few compatible ones and use them consistently.

Slides have two layers of visual elements, the *background* (which should be as unobtrusive as possible) and the *foreground*, which carries the information content of the slide. Artwork on the background and foreground can be divided into *functional*, which conveys information directly, and *decorative*, which does not. Well-designed functional artwork is always useful and a great way to convey message points quickly. Decorative artwork can be useful if it supports the message point on a slide, but it can be distracting otherwise.

Typefaces and type styles need careful consideration to ensure that they are easily readable from every point in the presentation room. Clean, sans serif typefaces are usually the best choice, although serif typefaces can be useful when used in large sizes. In general, avoid decorative typefaces except for limited, special purposes.

**4** **Explain how to create effective slide content.** Slide content can be divided into three groups: text, tables and graphics, and animation and multimedia. To choose effective words and phrases, think of the text on your slides as a guide to the content, not the content itself. For all-text slides, try to limit the content to four or five lines, with four or five words per line, and use short phrases rather than full sentences.

To create effective tables and graphics, keep in mind that visuals for projection need to be simpler than those used for print documents. If necessary, create simplified versions for your slides and provide the full-detail versions in a printed handout.

Like artwork, animation can be functional or decorative. Functional animation can be a powerful way to demonstrate processes and procedures. Decorative animation is nearly always a distraction and should be avoided. Slide transitions, which control how one slide replaces another on screen, are a form of animation. Except for subtle transitions such as a gentle fade to black, avoid using most of the transitions that come with your software. Builds, on the other hand, can be extremely helpful by letting you control the release of individual text points or graphical elements on a slide.

Hyperlinks instruct your computer to jump to another slide in your presentation, to a website, or to another program entirely. They can be handy for designing flexibility into your presentations and for sharing other types of files with the audience.

Audio, video, and other multimedia files can complement your live message, but make sure they support your message rather than replace it.

**5 Explain the role of navigation slides, support slides, and handouts.** In addition to the slides that convey your content, you can create one or more *title slides* to introduce your presentation (and yourself, if necessary), *agenda and program detail slides* that tell viewers what to expect during the presentation and provide information to help them plan their time, and *navigation slides* that help you and your audience keep track of where you are in the presentation. Particularly for longer presentations, a *moving blueprint* slide is a great way to show the audience what has been covered so far and what is still to come.

Handouts should be considered an integral part of your presentation, working in conjunction with your slides and spoken message to provide audience members with additional details, supporting documents, and other material too detailed to include in the presentation itself.

## KEY TERMS

**builds** Effects that control the release of text, graphics, and other elements on individual slides

**free-form slides** Presentation slides that are not based on a template, often with each slide having a unique look but unified by typeface, color, and other design choices; tend to be much more visually oriented than structured slides

**hyperlink** Link embedded in a presentation that instructs your computer to jump to another slide in your presentation, to a website, or to another program

**navigation slides** Noncontent slides that tell your audience where you're going and where you've been

**slide transitions** Software effects that control how one slide replaces another on-screen

**structured slides** Presentation slides that follow the same design templates throughout and give all the slides in a presentation the same general look; they emphasize textual information in bullet-point form

## CHECKLIST ✓
## Enhancing Presentations with Visuals

A. **Plan your presentation visuals.**
- Make sure you and your message, not your visuals, remain the focus of your presentation.
- Select your visuals carefully to support your message; use a combination of visuals if needed.
- Review your plan for each visual to make sure it truly supports your message.
- Follow effective design principles, with an emphasis on accuracy and simplicity.
- Use your time wisely so that you have plenty of time to practice your presentation.

B. **Choose structured or free-form slides.**
- Structured slides using bullet-point templates are easy to create, require little design time or skill, and can be completed in a hurry. Best uses: routine, internal presentations.
- Primary disadvantages of structured slides are mind-numbing repetition of bullet-point format and the common tendency of stuffing too much information on them.
- Free-form slides make it easier to combine textual and visual information, to create a more dynamic and engaging experience, and to maintain a conversational connection with the audience. Best uses: motivational, educational, and persuasive presentations.

- Primary disadvantages of structured slides are the time, skill, and imagery required; added responsibilities for the speaker; and possibility of fragmenting complex topics.

C. **Design effective slides.**
- Avoid the temptation to create "slideuments," slides that are so packed with information that they can be read as standalone documents.
- Use color to emphasize important ideas, create contrast, isolate visual elements, and convey intended nonverbal signals.
- Limit color to a few compatible choices and use them consistently.
- Make sure your slide background doesn't compete with the foreground.
- Use decorative artwork sparingly and only to support your message.
- Emphasize functional artwork—photos, technical drawings, charts, and other visual elements containing information that is part of your message.
- Choose typefaces that are easy to read on-screen; limit the number of typefaces and use them consistently.
- Use slide masters to maintain consistency throughout your presentation.

D. **Create effective slide content.**
- Write content that will be readable from everywhere in the room.
- Write short, active, parallel phrases that support, not replace, your spoken message.

- Avoid complete sentences unless you need to quote verbatim.
- Limit the amount of text so that your audience can focus on listening, not reading.
- Simplify print graphics for use on slides but don't oversimplify.
- Use functional animation when it can support your message.
- Make sure slide transitions are subtle, if used at all.
- Use builds carefully to control the release of information.
- Use hyperlinks and action buttons to add flexibility to your presentation.
- Incorporate multimedia elements that can help engage your audience and deliver your message.

E. **Complete slides and support materials.**
- Review every slide carefully to ensure accuracy, consistency, and clarity.
- Make sure that all slides are fully operational.
- Use the slide sorter to verify and adjust the sequence of slides, if needed.
- Have a backup plan in case your electronic presentation plan fails.
- Create navigation and support slides.
- Create handouts to give the audience additional information and to minimize the amount of information you need to put on your slides.

## COMMUNICATION CHALLENGES AT Presentation Zen

Garr Reynolds was impressed enough with your student project portfolio and part-time work to hire you as a communication associate. You will work from your home in California, assisting him on various projects and eventually meeting with his U.S. clients.

**INDIVIDUAL CHALLENGE:** Reynolds gives you an intriguing assignment your first day on the job. He is developing some presentations, website content, and a printed brochure for an energy technology company doing some advanced research in wind and tidal power. He asks you to propose a color palette to use for all these materials. Using any software program you're comfortable with (you can use a word processor if you don't have access to a graphics program) choose five standard colors or mix your own. Reynolds wants one dark color to use for slide backgrounds, one contrasting color that could be used for type on the dark background, and three compatible accent colors to use for various purposes. One restriction: you can't use green. The client feels that green is becoming overused in the renewable energy industry and wants to stand out by using different colors. Create a couple of simple slides in PowerPoint, Keynote, or Google Docs showing how your color palette could be used.

**TEAM CHALLENGE:** With a team of classmates, search Creative Commons (http://creativecommons.org) for attractive photos that could be used on slides to help illustrate or emphasize the following message points in a presentation:

- Trends in health-care costs
- Competition
- High levels of employee engagement (the energy, enthusiasm, and effort employees put into their work)
- Consumer hyperchoice (situations in which shoppers have such an overwhelming array of choices in a given product category that making purchase decisions becomes difficult and stressful)
- Scalability (the ease with which a business process or an entire company can be expanded to handle a greater number of transactions)

For each message point, find three candidates and then decide as a team which one conveys the point most effectively and in the most appropriate style for a fairly formal business presentation. Create a slide show in which you show the photos and explain how each one conveys the concept in question. Make sure you follow the usage and attribution guidelines for any photos you find online.

## Test Your Knowledge

To review chapter content related to each question, refer to the indicated Learning Objective.

1. What is a screencast? [LO-1]
2. What are your options for supporting a presentation with visuals aids? [LO-1]
3. What should the role of the background be in a slide? [LO-3]
4. How does Guy Kawasaki's "30-point rule" for fonts help ensure readable and memorable slide content? [LO-3]
5. What is the recommended number of fonts to use per slide? [LO-4]
6. How do slide transitions differ from builds? [LO-4]
7. How is a moving blueprint slide used in a presentation? [LO-5]
8. How does the slide sorter view facilitate the editing process for an electronic presentation? [LO-5]

## Apply Your Knowledge

To review chapter content related to each question, refer to the indicated Learning Objective.

1. Would you choose a structured or free-form design plan for a presentation about upcoming changes in international accounting regulations? Why? [LO-2]

2. What is the fundamental problem with "slideuments"? [LO-2]
3. How can you use slide masters to enhance the effectiveness of your slides? [LO-3]
4. Is it ethical to use design elements and special effects to persuade an audience? Why or why not? [LO-3]
5. If you are giving a presentation to company management that uses the indirect approach to recommend that the company consolidate its manufacturing operations (a traumatic change that would result in the loss of hundreds of jobs, including a dozen management positions), would it be wise to hand out copies of your slides at the beginning of the presentation? Why or why not? [LO-5]

## Practice Your Skills

**Messages for Analysis**

**Message 17.A: Improving a Slide**

Examine the slide in Figure 17.9 and point out any problems you notice. How would you correct these problems?

**Message 17.B: Modifying for Presentation**

Examine the graph in Figure 17.10 and explain how to modify it for an electronic presentation, using the guidelines discussed in this chapter.

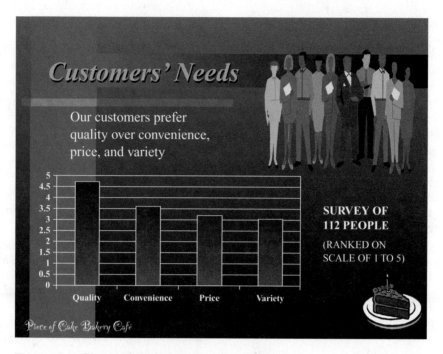

Figure 17.9 **Piece of Cake Bakery Customer Survey**

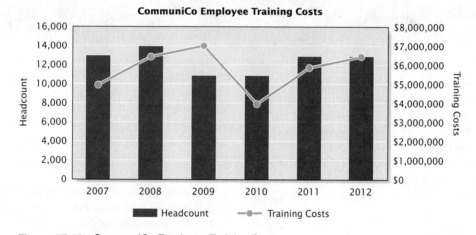

Figure 17.10 **CommuniCo Employee Training Costs**

**Message 17.C: Analyzing the Animation**

To access this PowerPoint presentation, visit http://real-time updates.com/bct12, click on Student Assignments, and select Chapter 17, Message 17.C. Download and watch the presentation in slide show mode (after you select Slide Show from the View menu, simply click your mouse to advance through the slides). After you've watched the presentation, identify at least three ways in which various animations, builds, and transitions either enhanced or impeded your understanding of the subject matter.

**Exercises**

Each activity is labeled according to the primary skill or skills you will need to use. To review relevant chapter content, you can refer to the indicated Learning Objective. In some instances, supporting information will be found in another chapter, as indicated.

1. **Designing Effective Slides [LO-2]** Find a business-related slide presentation on SlideShare (www.slideshare.net) and analyze the design. Do you consider it structured or free form? Does the design help the audience understand and remember the message? Why or why not? What improvements would you suggest to the design? Is the slide set understandable on its own?

2. **Designing Effective Slides [LO-3]** Think about a company you might like to start after graduation and imagine that you are giving a 20-minute presentation to potential investors. Review the design templates or themes available in whatever presentation software you have available, such as Microsoft PowerPoint, Apple Keynote, or Google Docs. Choose a template and color palette that best supports the message you want to convey to these financiers. Write a one-page report or brief blog post that includes a sample

slide using this theme and color palette and an explanation of how this design supports your message.

3. **Creating Effective Slide Content [LO-4]** Look through recent issues of several business periodicals for an article that discusses issues a specific company or industry is facing. Based on the information in the article and the guidelines discussed in this chapter, create three to five presentation slides summarizing these issues.

4. **Creating Effective Slide Content [LO-4]** Convert Table 2.2 on page 40 to presentation slides so that the content is easily readable in a large conference room. Choose whether to use free-form or structured slides, and decide how much content will be on the slides and how much will be spoken by the presenter. Provide speaker's notes along with your slides.

5. **Completing Slides and Support Materials [LO-5]** Find a business-oriented presentation on SlideShare (www.slideshare.net) that could use better navigation slides. Download the presentation and write at least three navigation slides that would help viewers follow the flow of the presentation.

## Expand Your Skills

### Critique the Professionals

Dave Paradi, author of *The Visual Slide Revolution*, specializes in helping presenters transform text-heavy slides into more readable and more effective visuals. Visit his YouTube channel at www.youtube.com/thinkoutsidetheslide, watch several of his "PowerPoint Slide Makeover" videos, and select the one that you find most helpful or enlightening. Using whatever medium your instructor requests, summarize the changes Paradi made to the slide in question and explain in your own words why these changes made the slide more effective.

### Sharpening Your Career Skills Online

Bovée and Thill's Business Communication Web Search, at http://businesscommunicationblog.com/websearch, is a unique research tool designed specifically for business communication research. Use the Web Search function to find a website, video, PDF document, podcast, or PowerPoint presentation that offers advice on creating slides and other presentation visuals. Write a brief email message to your instructor, describing the item that you found and summarizing the career skills information you learned from it.

# Cases

## PRESENTATION SKILLS

**1. Planning, Designing, and Creating Presentation Slides [LO-1], [LO-2], [LO-3], [LO-4]** Read the Communication Close-up at Southwest Airlines on page 198 in Chapter 8 and decide whether free-form or structured slides would be the most effective way to present this story to an audience of customer service agents to help them understand the power of social media.

**Your task:** Using whichever design approach you think is better, create a brief presentation (slides and speaking notes) to tell the story.

## PRESENTATION SKILLS

**2. Planning, Designing, and Creating Presentation Slides [LO-1], [LO-2], [LO-3], [LO-4]** Not long ago, snowboarding seemed to be on pace to pass skiing as the country's favorite way to zoom down snowy mountains, but the sport's growth has cooled off in recent years.[22]

**Your task:** Research and prepare a 10-minute presentation on participation trends in snowboarding and skiing, including explanations for the relative popularity of both sports. Include at least three quotations to emphasize key points in your presentation. Use either structured or free-form slides.

## PRESENTATION SKILLS

**3. Planning, Designing, and Creating Presentation Slides [LO-1], [LO-2], [LO-3], [LO-4]** Many companies publish stories of their founding and early years. The computer company Hewlett-Packard (HP), for example, tells the story of how founders Bill Hewlett and Dave Packard started the company in a garage in Palo Alto, California, in 1938, doing anything they could to "bring in a nickel." That garage is now preserved as "the birthplace of Silicon Valley," which helps maintain HP's image as a technology pioneer.[23]

**Your task:** Choose a company that has been in business for at least two decades and prepare a 10-minute presentation on its history.

## PRESENTATION SKILLS / TEAM SKILLS

**4. Planning, Designing, and Creating Presentation Slides [LO-1], [LO-2], [LO-3], [LO-4]** Changing a nation's eating habits is a Herculean task, but the physical and financial health of the United States depends on it. You work for the USDA Center for Nutrition Policy and Promotion (www.cnpp.usda.gov), and it's your job to educate people on the dangers of unhealthy eating and the changes they can make to eat more balanced and healthful diets.

**Your task:** Visit http://real-timeupdates.com/bct12, click on "Student Assignments," select Chapter 17, Case 2, and download the *Dietary Guidelines for Americans*. (If you worked on Message for Analysis 15.A on page 442, you've already seen the executive summary from this document.) With your team, develop a presentation no longer than 15 minutes, using free-form slides, that conveys the key points from Chapter 3 of the *Guidelines*, "Food and Food Components to Reduce." The objectives of your presentation are to alert people to the dangers of excessive consumption of the five components discussed in the chapter and to let them know what healthy levels of consumptions are. This chapter has a lot of information, but you don't need to pack it all into your slides; you can assume that the chapter will be available as a handout to anyone who attends your presentation. Create as many slides as you need, along with speaking notes that someone outside your team could use to give the presentation. You can use images from the *Guidelines* PDF, the websites of the U.S. Department of Agriculture and the U.S. Department of Health and Human Services, or a non-government source such as Creative Commons (http://creativecommons.org). Make sure you follow the usage and attribution guidelines for any photos you find on non-government sites.

## PRESENTATION SKILLS

**5. Planning, Designing, and Creating Presentation Slides [LO-1], [LO-2], [LO-3], [LO-4]** *Pecha-kucha* is a style of presentation that might be the ultimate in creative constraint: The speaker is limited to 20 slides, each of which is displayed for exactly 20 seconds before automatically advancing. Pecha-kucha Nights, which are open to the public, are now put on in cities all over the world. Visit www.pecha-kucha.org for more information on these events or to view some archived presentations.

**Your task:** Select one of the subjects from Exercise 2 on page 476 in Chapter 16 and develop a *pecha-kucha* style presentation with 20 slides, each designed to be displayed for 20 seconds. Use the slide timing capabilities in your presentation software to control the pace. Make sure you practice before presenting to your class so that you can hit the precise timing requirements.[24]

## PRESENTATION SKILLS / SOCIAL NETWORKING SKILLS

**6. Planning, Designing, and Creating Presentation Slides [LO-1], [LO-2], [LO-3], [LO-4]** You know those times when you're craving Thai food or the perfect fruit smoothie, but you don't know where to go? Or when you're out shopping or clubbing and want to let your friends know where you are? Foursquare's location-based services (https://foursquare.com/) connect you with friends and companies that offer products and services of interest.

**Your task:** Create a brief presentation explaining the Foursquare concept and its features and benefits. List two Foursquare competitors and give a brief assessment of which of the three you would recommend to your classmates.[25]

## PRESENTATION SKILLS / TEAM SKILLS / PORTFOLIO BUILDER

**7. Planning, Designing, and Creating Presentation Slides [LO-1], [LO-2], [LO-3], [LO-4]** In your job as a business development researcher for a major corporation, you're asked to gather and process information on a wide variety of subjects. Management has gained confidence in your research and analysis skills and would now like you to begin making regular presentations at management retreats and other functions. Topics are likely to include the following:

- Offshoring of U.S. jobs
- Foreign ownership of U.S. firms
- Employment issues involving workers from other countries
- Tax breaks offered by local and state governments to attract new businesses
- Economic impact of environmental regulations

**Your task:** With a team assigned by your instructor, choose one of the topics from the list and conduct enough research to familiarize yourself with the topic. Identify at least three important issues that anyone involved with this topic should know about. Prepare a 10-minute presentation that introduces the topic, comments on its importance to the U.S. economy, and discusses the issues you've identified. Assume that your audience is a cross-section of business managers who don't have any particular experience in the topic you've chosen.

## PRESENTATION SKILLS / PORTFOLIO BUILDER

**8. Planning, Designing, and Creating Presentation Slides [LO-1], [LO-2], [LO-3], [LO-4]** Depending on the sequence your instructor chose for this course, you've probably covered at least a dozen chapters at this point and learned or improved many valuable skills. Think through your progress and identify five business communication skills that you've either learned for the first time or developed during this course.

**Your task:** Create a six-slide presentation, with a title slide and five slides that describe each of the five skills you've identified. Be sure to explain how each skill could help you in your career. Use any visual style that you feel is appropriate for the assignment.

## PRESENTATION SKILLS / TEAM SKILLS

**9. Planning, Designing, and Creating Presentation Slides; Collaboration: Team Projects [LO-1], [LO-3], [LO-4], Chapter 2** Garr Reynolds offers an excellent brief introduction to effective slide design in his "Top Ten Slide Tips" at www.garrreynolds.com/presentation/slides.html.

**Your task:** With a team of two or three other students, create a free-form slide presentation that covers Reynolds's 10 tips. Be sure to give Reynolds credit for his information and ideas. You may include a few brief quotations from him, but for the most part, express his ideas in your own words. Illustrate his points as you see fit with visuals that you create yourselves or use with appropriate attribution from a source such as Creative Commons (http://creativecommons.org) or Morguefile (www.morguefile.com). Make sure you follow the usage and attribution terms for any photos you find online. (For these two sites, the terms should be listed for any photo you find.)

## PRESENTATION SKILLS / PORTFOLIO BUILDER

**10. Planning, Designing, and Creating Presentation Slides [LO-1], [LO-3], [LO-4]** In its competitive battles with AT&T and other telephone service providers, Verizon seeks to attract and keep not just customers but top employees. Engineers and technicians obviously play a vital role in a technology company such as Verizon, but the firm also needs specialists in everything from accounting to public relations to real estate.

**Your task:** Prepare a brief presentation Verizon recruiters could use at job fairs and other venues to entice both new graduates and experienced professionals to consider joining the company. Choose a structured or free-form design and then create an appropriate number of slides for a presentation that is at least 10 minutes but no longer than 15 (not including a question-and-answer period). Assume the audience members have heard of Verizon but don't have any in-depth knowledge about the company. You can learn more about the company and the benefits of working there by visiting www22.verizon.com/jobs.

# MyBCommLab

Go to **mybcommlab.com** for Auto-graded writing questions as well as the following Assisted-graded writing questions:

**17-1.** How do structured and free-form slide designs differ from one another? [LO-2]

**17-2.** What is the difference between decorative and functional artwork and animation? [LO-4]

**17-3.** Mybcommlab Only—comprehensive writing assignment for this chapter.

# Endnotes

1. Adapted from Garr Reynolds, *Presentation Zen* (Berkeley, Calif.: New Riders, 2008), 7, 10, 62–66, 103–104; Garr Reynolds, "Top Ten Slide Tips," Garr Reynolds website, accessed 7 February 2013, www .garrreynolds.com; Garr Reynolds, "Presentation Zen: The Video," accessed 19 March 2011, www.youtube.com.

2. "Polishing Your Presentation," 3M Meeting Network, accessed 8 June 2001, www.mmm.com/meetingnetwork/readingroom/ meetingguide_pres.html.

3. Michael Hyatt, "Five Rules to Better PowerPoint Presentations," 21 June 2005, Working Smart blog, www.michaelhyatt.com.

4. Cliff Atkinson, "The Cognitive Load of PowerPoint: Q&A with Richard E. Mayer," Sociable Media, accessed 15 August 2009, http:// www.sociablemedia.com/articles_mayer.htm.

5. Margo Halverson, "Choosing the Right Colors for Your Next Presentation," 3M Meeting Network, accessed 8 June 2001, www .mmm.com/meetingnetwork/readingroom/meetingguide_right_ color.html.

6. Carol Klinger and Joel G. Siegel, "Computer Multimedia Presenta-tions," *CPA Journal*, June 1996, 46.

7. Jon Hanke, "Five Tips for Better Visuals," 3M Meeting Network, accessed 25 May 2007, http://www.3m.com/meetingnetwork/ presentations/pmag_better_visuals.html.

8. Hanke, "Five Tips for Better Visuals."

9. Nancy Duarte, *Slide:ology: The Art and Science of Creating Great Presentations* (Sebastopol, Calif.: O'Reilly Media, 2008), 118.

10. Reynolds, *Presentation Zen*, 132.

11. Guy Kawasaki, "Rule of Thumb," *Entrepreneur*, May 2008, 44.

12. Duarte, *Slide:ology: The Art and Science of Creating Great Presentations*, 152.

13. Eric Markowitz, "How to Create a Great PowerPoint Presentation," *Inc.*, 7 February 2011, www.inc.com.

14. Jerry Weissman, *Presenting to Win: The Art of Telling Your Story* (Upper Saddle River, N.J.: Pearson Prentice Hall, 2006), 124.

15. Weissman, *Presenting to Win*, 144–147.

16. Sarah Lary and Karen Pruente, "Powerless Point: Common PowerPoint Mistakes to Avoid," *Public Relations Tactics*, February 2004, 28.

17. Nancy Duarte, "Avoiding the Road to PowerPoint Hell," *Wall Street Journal*, 22 January 2011, http://online.wsj.com.

18. Reynolds, *Presentation Zen*, 85.

19. Weissman, *Presenting to Win*, 162.

20. Reynolds, *Presentation Zen*, 66.

21. Ted Simons, "Handouts That Won't Get Trashed," *Presentations*, February 1999, 47–50.

22. Hugo Martin, "Snowboarding Craze Fades, Skiing Becomes Cool Again," *Seattle Times*, 7 February 2013, http://seattletimes.com.

23. HP website, accessed 11 February 2013, www.hp.com.

24. Adapted from PechaKucha20x20 website, accessed 4 August 2010, www.pecha-kucha.org; Reynolds, *Presentation Zen*, 41.

25. Adapted from Foursquare website, accessed 4 August 2010, http:// foursquare.com; Christina Warren, "Foursquare Reaches 100 Millions Checkins," Mashable, 20 July 2010, http://mashable.com.

## PART 7

# Writing Employment Messages and Interviewing for Jobs

The same techniques you use to succeed in your career can also help you launch and manage that career. Understand the employer's perspective on the hiring process so that you can adapt your approach and find the best job in the shortest possible time. Learn the best ways to craft a résumé and the other elements in your job search portfolio. Understand the interviewing process to make sure you're prepared for every stage and every type of interview.

## LEARNING OBJECTIVES

After studying this chapter, you will be able to

**1** List eight key steps to finding the ideal opportunity in today's job market.

**2** Explain the process of planning your résumé, including how to choose the best résumé organization.

**3** Describe the tasks involved in writing your résumé and list the major sections of a traditional résumé.

**4** Characterize the completing step for résumés, including the six most common formats in which you can produce a résumé.

## MyBCommLab®

⭐ **Improve Your Grade!** Over 10 million students improved their results using the Pearson MyLabs. Visit **mybcommlab.com** for simulations, tutorials, and end-of-chapter problems.

COMMUNICATION CLOSE-UP AT
**ATK** www.atk.com

One could say ATK is in the business of accuracy. Whether it's rocket motors for NASA, missiles and munitions for the U.S. Army, or ammunition for law enforcement and sporting uses, customers depend on ATK for accuracy and overall performance. Failure is not an option, because, as the company says, "Our customers' lives depend on the products we make."

Over the past few years, the multifaceted Minneapolis aerospace and defense company has been applying that obsession with accuracy and performance to one of the toughest problems any business faces: attracting, hiring, and keeping the quality employees who make business success possible. Along the way, ATK is one of a small but growing cadre of firms revolutionizing the practice of human resources (HR).

In the eyes of some professionals in finance, manufacturing, sales, and other data-driven functional areas, HR suffers from a

Courtesy of ATK

ATK's Carl Willis oversees the company's efforts to use advanced statistical analysis to predict workforce needs.

"reputational deficit," to put it politely. Most other functional areas have long since adopted information technology to improve decision making and demonstrate their contribution to the bottom line. However, HR is still viewed by some as a "soft" function that might do a fine job of processing employee paperwork but can't really prove how well it's doing the critical job of finding the right employees and making sure they stay on board. The information systems being used tend to focus on recordkeeping, compliance verification, and other important but not terribly strategic tasks.

Carl Willis, ATK's vice president of human resources, oversees the company's efforts in the emerging field of *predictive workforce analytics*, the use of statistical modeling to help a company keep its business needs and employee skill sets in alignment. Balancing this complex equation of supply and demand is particularly vital for a company such as ATK, where many jobs are highly specialized and the departure of a single employee can sometimes cause significant problems. ATK's system is so advanced that it can predict the "flight risk" of individual employees, and it was able to predict with remarkable accuracy the number of employees who would take early retirement before a particular retirement benefit was set to expire. By forecasting such events with accuracy, the company can ramp up hiring and focus on specific types of skills it will need to bring in.

At a broader level, the aerospace and defense sector is facing a shortage of key talent in the near future, as its aging workforce heads into retirement. ATK is counting on predictive analytics to help it characterize the skills required to perform those jobs and identify new employees who can provide them when the time comes.

With these tools in hand, a new generation of HR professionals is poised to make a more strategic contribution, armed with the data to prove it.[1]

# Finding the Ideal Opportunity in Today's Job Market

The efforts made by ATK (profiled in the chapter-opening Communication Close-Up) show the importance that top companies place on finding the right employees and the investments these companies are willing to make in both personnel and technology to attract and keep valuable talent. Whether you'll be looking for your first professional job on graduation or you're already in mid-career, you need to put as much thought and care into finding the right job as employers put into finding the right employees.

**1 LEARNING OBJECTIVE**
List eight key steps to finding the ideal opportunity in today's job market.

Identifying and landing the ideal job can be a long and difficult process, particularly in tough employment markets. Fortunately, the skills you're developing in this course will give you a competitive advantage. This section offers a general job-search strategy with advice that applies to just about any career path you might want to pursue. As you craft your personal strategy, keep these three guidelines in mind:

- **Get organized.** Your job search could last many months and involve multiple contacts with dozens of companies. You need to keep all the details straight to ensure that you don't miss opportunities or make mistakes such as losing someone's email address or forgetting an appointment.

If you haven't already, read the Prologue, "Building a Career with Your Communication Skills," before studying this chapter.

- **Start now and stick to it.** Even if you are a year or more away from graduation, now is not too early to get started with some of the essential research and planning tasks. If you wait until the last minute, you will miss opportunities and you won't be as prepared as other candidates.
- **Look for stepping-stone opportunities.** Particularly in today's tough job market, you might not find the opportunity you're looking for right away. You might need to take a job that doesn't meet your expectations while you keep looking to get on the right track. But view every job as an opportunity to learn workplace skills, observe effective and ineffective business practices, and fine-tune your sense of how you'd like to spend your career.

## WRITING THE STORY OF YOU

Whether you're about to begin your career or are already well into it, writing or updating your résumé is a great opportunity to step back and think about where you've been and where you'd like to go. Do you like the path you're on, or is it time for a change? Are you focused on a particular field, or do you need some time to explore?

What's your story? Thinking about where you've been and where you want to go will help focus your job search.

If you haven't yet, read the career-planning Prologue that starts on page xxxi, and particularly the "What Do You Want to Do?" section on page xxxiii, to help identify the nature of the work you'd like to do, if not a specific profession.

Next, using the advice on creating a personal brand on page xxxvi, begin writing the "story of you," the things you are passionate about, the skills you possess, your ability to help an organization reach its goals, the path you've been on so far, and the path you want to follow in the future (see Figure 18.1). Think in terms of an image or a theme you'd like to project. Are you academically gifted? An effective leader? A well-rounded professional with wide-ranging talents? A creative problem solver? A technical wizard? Writing your story is a valuable planning exercise that helps you think about where you want to go and how to present yourself to target employers.

## LEARNING TO THINK LIKE AN EMPLOYER

When you know your side of the hiring equation a little better, switch sides and look at it from an employer's perspective. To begin with, recognize that companies take risks with every hiring decision—the risk that the person hired doesn't meet expectations and the risk that

**My Story**

**Where I Have Been**

- Honor student and all around big shot in high school (but discovered that college is full of big shots!)
- Have worked several part-time jobs; only thing that really appealed to me in any of them was making improvements, making things work better

*What experiences from your past give you insight into where you would like to go in the future?*

**Where I Am Now**

- Junior; on track to graduate in 2014
- Enjoy designing creative solutions to challenging problems
- Not a high-end techie in an engineering sense, but I figure most things out eventually
- Not afraid to work hard, whatever it takes to get the job done
- I can tolerate some routine, as long as I have the opportunity to make improvements if needed
- Tend to lead quietly by example, rather than by visibly and vocally taking charge
- Knowing that I do good work is more important than getting approval from others
- I tend not to follow fads and crowds; sometimes I'm ahead of the curve, sometimes I'm behind the curve

*Where do you stand now in terms of your education and career, and what do you know about yourself?*

**Where I Want to Be**

- Get an advanced degree; not sure what subject area yet, though
- Haven't really settled on one industry or profession yet; working with systems of any kind is more appealing than any particular profession that I've learned about so far
- Develop my leadership and communication skills to become a more "obvious" leader
- Collaborate with others while still having the freedom to work independently (maybe become an independent contractor or consultant at some point?)
- Have the opportunity to work internationally, at least for a few years
- I like the big bucks that corporate executives earn, but I don't want to live in the public eye like that or have to "play the game" to get ahead
- Believe I would be good manager, but not sure I want to spend all my time just managing people
- What to be known as an independent thinker and creative problem solver, as somebody who can analyze tough situations and figure out solutions that others might not consider
- Are there jobs where I could focus on troubleshooting, improving processes, or designing new systems?

*What would you like your future to be? What do you like and dislike? What would you like to explore? If you haven't figured everything out yet, that's fine—as long as you've started to think about the future.*

**Figure 18.1  Writing the Story of You**
Writing the "story of you" is a helpful way to think through where you've been in your life and career so far, where you are now, and where you would like to go from here. Remember that this is a private document designed to help you clarify your thoughts and plans, although you probably will find ways to adapt some of what you've written to various job-search documents, including your résumé.

they let a better candidate slip through their fingers. Many companies judge the success of their recruiting efforts by *quality of hire*, a measure of how closely new employees meet the company's needs.[2] What steps can you take to present yourself as the low-risk, high-reward choice, as someone who can make a meaningful contribution to the organization?

Your perceived ability to perform the job is obviously an essential part of your potential quality as a new hire. However, hiring managers consider more than just your ability to handle the responsibilities you'll be given. They want to know if you'll be reliable and motivated and if you're somebody who "gets it" when it comes to being a professional in today's workplace. A great way to get inside the heads of corporate recruiters is to "eavesdrop" on their professional conversations by reading periodicals such as *Workforce Management* (www.workforce.com) and blogs such as Fistful of Talent (www.fistfuloftalent.com) and The HR Capitalist (www.hrcapitalist.com).

> Employers judge their recruiting success by *quality of hire*, and you can take steps to be—and look like—a high-quality hire.

> Follow the online conversations of professional recruiters to learn what their hot-button issues are.

## RESEARCHING INDUSTRIES AND COMPANIES OF INTEREST

Learning more about professions, industries, and individual companies is easy to do with the library and online resources available to you. Don't limit your research to readily available sources, however. Companies are likely to be impressed by creative research, such as interviewing their customers to learn more about how the firm does business. "Detailed research, including talking to our customers, is so rare it will almost guarantee you get hired," explains the recruiting manager at Alcon Laboratories.[3]

Table 18.1 lists some of the many websites where you can learn more about companies and find job openings. Start with The Riley Guide, www.rileyguide.com, which offers

> Employers expect you to be familiar with important developments in their industries, so stay on top of business news.

### TABLE 18.1  Selected Job-Search Websites

| Website* | URL | Highlights |
|---|---|---|
| Riley Guide | www.rileyguide.com | Vast collection of links to both general and specialized job sites for every career imaginable; don't miss this one—it could save you hours of searching |
| TweetMyJobs.com | http://tweetmyjobs.com | The largest Twitter job board, with thousands of channels segmented by geography, job type, and industry |
| CollegeRecruiter.com | www.collegerecruiter.com | Focused on opportunities for graduates with less than three years of work experience |
| Monster | http://home.monster.com | One of the most popular job sites, with hundreds of thousands of openings, many from hard-to-find small companies; extensive collection of advice on the job search process |
| MonsterCollege | http://college.monster.com | Focused on job searches for new college grads; your school's career center site probably links here |
| CareerBuilder | www.careerbuilder.com | One of the largest job boards; affiliated with more than 150 newspapers around the country |
| Jobster | www.jobster.com | Uses social networking to link employers with job seekers |
| USAJOBS | www.usajobs.opm.gov | The official job search site for the U.S. government, featuring everything from jobs for economists to astronauts to border patrol agents |
| IMDiversity | www.imdiversity.com | Good resource on diversity in the workplace, with job postings from companies that have made a special commitment to promoting diversity in their workforces |
| Dice.com | www.dice.com | One of the best sites for high-technology jobs |
| Net-Temps | www.net-temps.com | Popular site for contractors and freelancers looking for short-term assignments |
| Internship Programs.com | http://internshipprograms.com | Posts listings from companies looking for interns in a wide variety of professions |
| Simply Hired<br>Indeed | www.simplyhired.com<br>www.indeed.com | Specialized search engines that look for job postings on hundreds of websites worldwide; they find many postings that aren't listed on job board sites such as Monster |

*Note: This list represents only a small fraction of the hundreds of job-posting sites and other resources available online; be sure to check with your college's career center for the latest information.

Sources: TweetMyJobs.com, accessed 11 February 2013, http://tweetmyjobs.com; The Riley Guide, accessed 11 February 2013, www.rileyguide.com; SimplyHired website, accessed 11 February 2013, www.simplyhired.com; Indeed website, accessed 11 February 2013, www.indeed.com; CollegeRecruiter.com, accessed 11 February 2013, www.collegerecruiter.com; Jobster website, accessed 11 February 2013, www.jobster.com; InternshipPrograms.com, accessed 11 February 2013, http://internshipprograms.com.

advice for online job searches as well as links to hundreds of specialized websites that post openings in specific industries and professions. Your college's career center placement office probably maintains an up-to-date list as well.

To learn more about contemporary business topics, peruse some of these leading business periodicals and newspapers with significant business sections (in some cases, you may need to go through your library's online databases to gain full access):

- *Bloomberg Businessweek*: www.businessweek.com
- *Business 2.0*: http://money.cnn.com/magazines/business2
- *Fast Company*: www.fastcompany.com
- *Forbes*: www.forbes.com
- *Fortune*: http://money.cnn.com/magazines/fortune
- *Inc.*: http://www.inc.com/
- *New York Times*: www.nyt.com
- *USA Today*: www.usatoday.com
- *Wall Street Journal*: http://online.wsj.com

In addition, thousands of bloggers, microbloggers, and podcasters offer news and commentary on the business world. AllTop (http://alltop.com) is another good resource for finding people who write about topics that interest you. In addition to learning more about professions and opportunities, this research will help you get comfortable with the jargon and buzzwords currently in use in a particular field, including essential *keywords* to use in your résumé (see page 515).

## TRANSLATING YOUR GENERAL POTENTIAL INTO A SPECIFIC SOLUTION FOR EACH EMPLOYER

An essential task in your job search is presenting your skills and accomplishments in a way that is relevant to the employer's business challenges.

An important aspect of the quality-of-hire challenge is trying to determine how well a candidate's attributes and experience will translate into the challenges of a specific position. As Jim Schaper, CEO of the Alpharetta, Georgia, software company Infor Global Solutions, puts it, "We try to determine if newly minted graduates can apply knowledge they've already gained."[4] Customizing your résumé to each job opening is an important step in showing employers that you will be a good fit. As you can see from the sample résumés in Figures 18.3 through 18.5 on pages 519–521, customizing your résumé is not difficult if you have done your research. From your initial contact all the way through the interviewing process, in fact, you will have opportunities to impress recruiters by explaining how your general potential translates to the specific needs of the position.

## TAKING THE INITIATIVE TO FIND OPPORTUNITIES

When it comes to finding the right opportunities, the easiest ways are not always the most productive ones. The major job boards such as Monster and classified services such as Craigslist might have thousands of openings, but many thousands of job seekers are looking at and applying for these same openings. Moreover, posting job openings on these sites is often a company's last resort, after it has exhausted other possibilities.

Don't hesitate to contact interesting companies even if they haven't advertised job openings to the public yet—they might be looking for somebody just like you.

Instead of searching through the same job openings as everyone else, take the initiative and go find opportunities. Identify the companies you want to work for and focus your efforts on them. Get in touch with their human resources departments (or individual managers, if possible), describe what you can offer the company, and ask to be considered if any opportunities come up.[5] Your message might appear right when a company is busy looking for someone but hasn't yet advertised the opening to the outside world.

## BUILDING YOUR NETWORK

Start thinking like a networker now; your classmates could turn out to be some of your most important business contacts.

**Networking** is the process of making informal connections with mutually beneficial business contacts. Networking takes place wherever and whenever people communicate: at industry functions, at social gatherings, at alumni reunions—and all over the Internet, from LinkedIn to Facebook to Twitter. Networking is more essential than ever, because the vast majority of job openings are never advertised to the general public. To avoid the time and expense of sifting through thousands of applications and the risk of hiring complete strangers, most companies prefer to ask their employees for recommendations first.[6] The more people who know you, the better chance you have of being recommended for one of these hidden job openings.

Start building your network now, before you need it. Your classmates could end up being some of your most valuable contacts, if not right away then possibly later in your career. Then branch out by identifying people with similar interests in your target professions, industries, and companies. Read news sites, blogs, and other online sources. Follow industry leaders on Twitter. You can also follow individual executives at your target companies to learn about their interests and concerns.[7] Be on the lookout for career-oriented *Tweetups*, in which people who've connected on Twitter get together for in-person networking events. Connect with people on LinkedIn and Facebook, particularly in groups dedicated to particular career interests. Depending on the system and the settings on individual users' accounts, you may be able to introduce yourself via public or private messages. Just make sure you are respectful of people, and don't take up much of their time.[8]

*Put your network in place before you need it.*

Participate in student business organizations, especially those with ties to professional organizations. Visit *trade shows* to learn about various industries and rub shoulders with people who work in those industries.[9] Don't overlook volunteering; you not only meet people but also demonstrate your ability to solve problems, manage projects, and lead others. You can do some good while creating a network for yourself.

Remember that networking is about people helping each other, not just about other people helping you. Pay close attention to networking etiquette: Try to learn something about the people you want to connect with, don't overwhelm others with too many messages or requests, be succinct in all your communication efforts, don't give out other people's names and contact information without their permission to do so, never email your résumé to complete strangers, don't assume you can send your résumé to everyone you meet, and remember to say thank you every time someone helps you.[10]

*Networking is a mutually beneficial activity, so look for opportunities to help others in some way.*

To become a valued network member, you need to be able to help others in some way. You may not have any influential contacts yet, but because you're actively researching a number of industries and trends in your own job search, you probably have valuable information you can share via your social networks, blog, or Twitter account. Or you might simply be able to connect one person with another who can help. The more you network, the more valuable you become in your network—and the more valuable your network becomes to you.

Finally, be aware that your online network reflects on who you are in the eyes of potential employers, so exercise some judgment in making connections. Also, some employers are beginning to contact people in a candidate's network for background information, even if the candidate doesn't list those people as references.[11]

## SEEKING CAREER COUNSELING

Your college's career center probably offers a wide variety of services, including individual counseling, job fairs, on-campus interviews, and job listings. Counselors can give you advice on career planning and provide workshops in job search techniques, résumé preparation, job readiness training, interview techniques, self-marketing, and more.[12] You can also find career planning advice online. Many of the websites listed in Table 18.1 offer articles and online tests to help you choose a career path, identify essential skills, and prepare to enter the job market.

*Don't overlook the many resources available through your college's career center.*

## AVOIDING MISTAKES

While you're making all these positive moves to show employers you will be a quality hire, take care to avoid the simple blunders that can torpedo a job search, such as not catching mistakes in your résumé, misspelling the name of a manager you're writing to, showing up late for an interview, tweeting something unprofessional, failing to complete application forms correctly, asking for information you can easily find

**REAL-TIME UPDATES**
LEARN MORE BY VISITING THIS WEBSITE
**Follow these people to a new career**
Alison Doyle maintains a great list of career experts to follow on Twitter. Go to http://real-timeupdates.com/bct12 and click on Learn More. If you are using MyBCommLab, you can access Real-Time Updates within each chapter or under Student Study Tools.

Don't let a silly mistake knock you out of contention for a great job.

yourself on a company's website, or making any other error that could flag you as someone who is careless, clueless, or disrespectful. Assume that every employer will conduct an online search on you. Busy recruiters will seize on any of these errors as a way to narrow the list of candidates they need to spend time on, so don't give them a reason to toss out your résumé.

## Planning a Résumé

Although you will create many messages during your career search, your résumé will be the most important document in this process. You will be able to use it directly in many instances, adapt it to a variety of uses such an e-portfolio or a social media résumé, and reuse pieces of it in social networking profiles and online application forms. Even if you apply to a company that doesn't want to see résumés from applicants, the process of developing your résumé will prepare you for interviewing and preemployment testing.

Developing a résumé really benefits from multiple planning, writing, and completing sessions spread out over several days or weeks. You are trying to summarize a complex subject (yourself!) and present a compelling story to strangers in a brief document. Follow the three-step writing process (see Figure 18.2) and give yourself plenty of time.

Before you dive into your résumé, be aware that you will find a wide range of opinions about résumés, regarding everything from appropriate length, content, design, distribution methods, and acceptable degrees of creativity to whether it even makes sense to write a traditional résumé in this age of online applications. For example, you may encounter a company such as Union Square Ventures, which recently asked applicants to submit all the links that

**2** **LEARNING OBJECTIVE**
Explain the process of planning your résumé, including how to choose the best résumé organization.

Don't put your résumé off to the last minute or try to plan, write, and complete it in a single session.

---

**1 Plan** →   **2 Write** →   **3 Complete**

**Analyze the Situation**
Recognize that the purpose of your résumé is to get an interview, not to get a job.

**Gather Information**
Research target industries and companies so that you know what they're looking for in new hires; learn about various jobs and what to expect; learn about the hiring manager, if possible.

**Select the Right Medium**
Start with a traditional paper résumé and develop scannable, electronic plain-text, PDF, and online versions, as needed. Consider using PowerPoint and video for your e-portfolio.

**Organize the Information**
Choose an organizational model that highlights your strengths and downplays your shortcomings; use the chronological approach unless you have a strong reason not to.

**Adapt to Your Audience**
Plan your wording carefully so that you can catch a recruiter's eye within seconds; translate your education and experience into attributes that target employers find valuable.

**Compose the Message**
Write clearly and succinctly, using active, powerful language that is appropriate to the industries and companies you're targeting; use a professional tone in all communications.

**Revise the Message**
Evaluate content and review readability and then edit and rewrite for conciseness and clarity.

**Produce the Message**
Use effective design elements and suitable layout for a clean, professional appearance; seamlessly combine text and graphical elements. When printing, use quality paper and a good printer.

**Proofread the Message**
Review for errors in layout, spelling, and mechanics; mistakes can cost you interview opportunities.

**Distribute the Message**
Deliver your résumé, carefully following the specific instructions of each employer or job board website.

**Figure 18.2  Three-Step Writing Process for Résumés**
Following the three-step writing process will help you create a successful résumé in a short time. Remember to pay particular attention to the "you" attitude and presentation quality; your résumé will probably get tossed aside if it doesn't speak to audience needs or if it contains mistakes.

make up their online presence, rather than a résumé.[13] You may run across examples of effective résumés that were produced as infographics, interactive videos, simulated search engine results, puzzles, games, graphic novels—you name it, somebody has probably tried it.

When you hear conflicting advice or see trendy concepts that you might be tempted to try, remember the most important question in business communication: What is the most effective way to adapt your message to the individual needs of each member of your audience? An approach that is wildly successful with one company or in one industry could be a complete disaster in another industry. A design that says "clever and creative" to one recruiter can shout "amateurish gimmick!" to another. Your infographic résumé might look awesome but get rejected by an automated résumé scanner that can't make sense of it. To forge your own successful path through this maze of information, get inside the heads of the people you are trying to reach—try to think the way they think—and then apply the principles of effective communication you are learning in this course.

You will see lots of ideas and even some conflicting advice about résumés; use what you know about effective business communication to decide what is right for your résumés.

**REAL-TIME UPDATES**

LEARN MORE BY VISITING THIS WEBSITE

**See the cutting edge of creative résumé design**

These creatively unleashed résumés are definitely not a good fit for every industry or employer, but for the right audiences, they proved quite effective. Go to http://real-timeupdates.com/bct12 and click on Learn More. If you are using MyBCommLab, you can access Real-Time Updates within each chapter or under Student Study Tools.

## ANALYZING YOUR PURPOSE AND AUDIENCE

A **résumé** is a structured summary of a person's education, employment background, and job qualifications. Before you begin writing a résumé, make sure you understand its true function—as a brief, persuasive business message intended to stimulate an employer's interest in meeting you and learning more about you (see Table 18.2). In other words, the purpose of a résumé is not to get you a job but rather to get you an interview.[14]

As you conduct your research on various professions, industries, companies, and individual managers, you will have a better perspective on your target readers and their information needs. Learn as much as you can about the individuals who may be reading your résumé. Many professionals and managers are bloggers, Twitter users, and LinkedIn members, for example, so you can learn more about them online even if you've never met them. Any bit of information can help you craft a more effective message.

By the way, if employers ask to see your "CV," they're referring to your *curriculum vitae*, the term used instead of *résumé* in academic professions and in many countries outside the United States. Résumés and CVs are essentially the same, although CVs can be much more detailed and include personal information that is not included in a résumé.

Thanks to Twitter, LinkedIn, and other social media, you can often learn valuable details about individual managers in your target employers.

**REAL-TIME UPDATES**

LEARN MORE BY VISITING THIS WEBSITE

**Converting your résumé to a CV**

If you need to convert your U.S-style résumé to the *curriculum vitae* format used in many other countries (and in many academic positions in the United States), this website will tell you everything you need to know. Go to http://real-timeupdates.com/bct12 and click on Learn More. If you are using MyBCommLab, you can access Real-Time Updates within each chapter or under Student Study Tools.

| TABLE 18.2   **Fallacies and Facts about Résumés** | |
|---|---|
| **Fallacy** | **Fact** |
| The purpose of a résumé is to list all your skills and abilities. | The purpose of a résumé is to kindle employer interest and generate an interview. |
| A good résumé will get you the job you want. | All a résumé can do is get you in the door. |
| Your résumé will always be read carefully and thoroughly. | In most cases, your résumé needs to make a positive impression within 30 or 45 seconds; only then will someone read it in detail. Moreover, it will likely be screened by a computer looking for keywords first—and if it doesn't contain the right keywords, a human being may never see it. |
| The more good information you present about yourself in your résumé, the better, so stuff your résumé with every positive detail. | Recruiters don't need that much information about you at the initial screening stage, and they probably won't read it. |
| If you want a really good résumé, have it prepared by a résumé service. | You can certainly seek out formal or informal help, but if you have succeeded in this course, you have the skills needed to prepare an effective résumé. |

## GATHERING PERTINENT INFORMATION

If you haven't been building an employment portfolio thus far, you may need to do some research on yourself. Gather all the pertinent personal history you can think of, including the dates, duties, and accomplishments from any previous jobs you've held. Collect relevant educational experience that adds to your qualifications—formal degrees, skills certificates, academic awards, and scholarships. Also, gather any relevant information about school or volunteer activities that might be relevant to your job search, including offices you have held in any club or professional organization, presentations given, and online or print publications. You probably won't use every piece of information you come up with, but you'll want to have it at your fingertips before you begin composing your résumé.

## SELECTING THE BEST MEDIA

You should expect to produce your résumé in several media and formats. "Producing Your Résumé" on page 523 explores the various options.

## ORGANIZING YOUR RÉSUMÉ AROUND YOUR STRENGTHS

Although you will see a number of ways to organize a résumé, most are some variation of chronological, functional, or a combination of the two. The right choice depends on your background and your goals, as the following sections explain.

### The Chronological Résumé

The chronological résumé is the most common approach, but it might not be right for you at this stage in your career.

In a **chronological résumé**, the work experience section dominates and is placed immediately after your contact information and introductory statement (see Figure 18.5 on page 521 for an example). The chronological approach is the most common way to organize a résumé, and many employers prefer this format because it presents your professional history in a clear, easy-to-follow arrangement.[15] If you're just graduating from college and have limited professional experience, you can vary this chronological approach by putting your educational qualifications before your experience.

Develop your work experience section by listing your jobs in reverse chronological order, beginning with the most recent position and giving the most space to the most recent positions. For each job, start by listing the employer's name and location, your official job title, and the dates you held the position (write "to present" if you are still in your most recent position). Next, in a short block of text, highlight your accomplishments in a way that is relevant to your readers. This may require "translating" the terminology used in a particular industry or profession into terms that are more meaningful to your target readers. If the general responsibilities of the position are not obvious from the job title, provide a little background to help readers understand what you did.

### The Functional Résumé

The functional résumé is often considered by people with limited or spotty employment history, but many employers are suspicious of this format.

A **functional résumé**, sometimes called a *skills résumé*, emphasizes your skills and capabilities, identifying employers and academic experience in subordinate sections. This arrangement stresses individual areas of competence rather than job history. The functional approach also has three advantages: (1) Without having to read through job descriptions, employers can see what you can do for them; (2) you can emphasize earlier job experience; and (3) you can deemphasize any lengthy unemployment or lack of career progress. However, you should be aware that because the functional résumé can obscure your work history, many employment professionals are suspicious of it.[16] Moreover, it lacks the evidence of job experience that supports your skills claims. If you don't believe the chronological format will work for you, consider the combination résumé instead.

### The Combination Résumé

If you don't have a lot of work history to show, consider a combination résumé to highlight your skills while still providing a chronological history of your employment.

A **combination résumé** meshes the skills focus of the functional format with the job history focus of the chronological format. Figures 18.3 (page 519) and 18.4 (page 520) show examples of combination résumés. The chief advantage of this format is that it allows you to focus attention on your capabilities when you don't have a long or steady employment history, without raising concerns that you might be hiding something about your past.

As you look at a number of sample résumés, you'll probably notice many variations on the three basic formats presented here. Study these other options in light of the effective communication principles you've learned in this course and the unique circumstances of your job search. If you find one that seems like the best fit for your unique situation, by all means use it.

## ADDRESSING AREAS OF CONCERN

Many people have gaps in their careers or other issues that could be a concern for employers. Here are some common issues and suggestions for handling them in a résumé:[17]

- **Frequent job changes.** If you've had a number of short-term jobs of a similar type, such as independent contracting and temporary assignments, try to group them under a single heading. Also, if past job positions were eliminated as a result of layoffs or mergers, find a subtle way to convey that information (if not in your résumé, then in your cover letter). Reasonable employers understand that many professionals have been forced to job hop by circumstances beyond their control.

- **Gaps in work history.** Mention relevant experience and education you gained during employment gaps, such as volunteer or community work.

- **Inexperience.** Mention related volunteer work and membership in professional groups. List relevant course work and internships.

- **Overqualification.** Tone down your résumé, focusing exclusively on the experience and skills that relate to the position.

- **Long-term employment with one company.** Itemize each position held at the firm to show both professional growth and career growth within the organization and increasing responsibilities along the way.

- **Job termination for cause.** Be honest with interviewers and address their concerns with proof, such as recommendations and examples of completed projects.

- **Criminal record.** You don't necessarily need to disclose a criminal record or time spent incarcerated on your résumé, but you may be asked about it on job application forms. Laws regarding what employers may ask (and whether they can conduct a criminal background check) vary by state and profession, but if you are asked and the question applies to you, you are legally bound to answer truthfully. Use the interview process to explain any mitigating circumstances and to emphasize your rehabilitation and commitment to being a law-abiding, trustworthy employee.[18]

Frequent job changes and gaps in your work history are two of the more common issues employers may perceive as weaknesses.

# Writing a Résumé

As you follow the three-step process to develop your résumé, keep four points in mind. First, treat your résumé with the respect it deserves. A single mistake or oversight can cost you interview opportunities. Second, give yourself plenty of time. Don't put off preparing your résumé until the last minute and then try to write it in one sitting. Third, learn from good models. You can find sample résumés online at college websites and on job boards such as Monster and CareerBuilder. Fourth, don't get frustrated by the conflicting advice you'll read about résumés. Résumés are as much art as science, and there is more than one way to be successful with them. Consider the alternatives and choose the approach that makes the most sense to you, given everything you know about successful business communication.

If you feel uncomfortable writing about yourself, you're not alone. Many people, even accomplished writers, find it difficult to write their own résumés. If you get stuck, find a classmate or friend who is also writing a résumé and swap projects for a while. Working on each other's résumés might speed up the process for both of you.

**3** **LEARNING OBJECTIVE**
Describe the tasks involved in writing your résumé, and list the major sections of a traditional résumé.

If you're uncomfortable writing your own résumé, you might try to trade with a classmate and write each other's résumé.

**REAL-TIME UPDATES**
LEARN MORE BY WATCHING THIS VIDEO
**Learn to use LinkedIn's résumé builder**
See how to build and customize a résumé on LinkedIn and then use it on other social networking sites. Go to http://real-timeupdates.com/bct12 and click on Learn More. If you are using MyBCommLab, you can access Real-Time Updates within each chapter or under Student Study Tools.

## KEEPING YOUR RÉSUMÉ HONEST

Résumé fraud has reached epidemic proportions, but employers are fighting back with more rigorous screening techniques.

Estimates vary, but one comprehensive study uncovered lies about work history in more than 40 percent of the résumés tested.[19] And dishonest applicants are getting bolder all the time—going so far as to buy fake diplomas online, pay a computer hacker to insert their names into prestigious universities' graduation records, and sign up for services that offer phony employment verification.[20] "It's becoming common to cheat," observes professor George Gollin of the University of Illinois, Urbana, mentioning the 200,000 fake college degrees sold every year as one example.[21]

Applicants with integrity know they don't need to stoop to lying. If you are tempted to stretch the truth, bear in mind that professional recruiters have seen all sorts of fraud by job applicants, and frustrated employers are working aggressively to uncover the truth. Nearly all employers do some form of background checking, from contacting references and verifying employment to checking criminal records and sending résumés through verification services.[22] Employers are also beginning to craft certain interview questions specifically to uncover dishonest résumé entries.[23]

More than 90 percent of companies that find lies on résumés refuse to hire the offending applicants, even if that means withdrawing formal job offers.[24] And if you do sneak past these filters and get hired, you'll probably be exposed on the job when you can't live up to your own résumé. Given the networked nature of today's job market, lying on a résumé could haunt you for years—and could force you to keep lying throughout your career to hide the misrepresentations on your original résumé.[25]

## ADAPTING YOUR RÉSUMÉ TO YOUR AUDIENCE

The importance of adapting your résumé to your target readers' needs and interests cannot be overstated. In a competitive job market, the more you look like a good fit—a quality hire—the better your chances of securing interviews. Address your readers' business concerns by showing how your capabilities meet the demands and expectations of the position and the organization as a whole. For example, an in-house public relations (PR) department and an independent PR agency perform many of the same tasks, but the outside agency must also sell its services to multiple clients. Consequently, it needs employees who are skilled at attracting and keeping paying customers, in addition to being skilled at PR. If you are applying for both in-house and agency PR jobs, you need to adapt your résumé for each of these audiences.

Translate your past accomplishments into a compelling picture of what you can do for employers in the future.

Military service and other specialized experiences may need to be "translated" into terms more readily understandable by your target readers.

An essential step in adapting your résumé is using the same terminology as the employer uses to describe job responsibilities and professional accomplishments. In Figures 18.3 through 18.5, you can see how the sample résumés do this, echoing key terms and phrases from the job postings. With the rise of automated **applicant tracking systems** (databases that let managers sort through incoming applications to find the most promising candidates), matching your language to the employer's will help you get past the keyword filters these systems use to rank incoming résumés.

If you are applying for business positions after military service or moving from one industry to another, you may need to "translate" your experience into the language of your target employers. For instance, military experience can help you develop many skills that are valuable in business, but military terminology can sound like a foreign language to people who aren't familiar with it. Isolate the important general concepts and present them in the business language your target employers use.

**REAL-TIME UPDATES**

LEARN MORE BY READING THIS INFOGRAPHIC

### See how an applicant tracking system handles your résumé

Once you see how the system works, you'll understand why it's so crucial to customize the wording on your résumé for every job opening. Go to http://real-timeupdates.com/bct12 and click on Learn More. If you are using MyBCommLab, you can access Real-Time Updates within each chapter or under Student Study Tools.

## COMPOSING YOUR RÉSUMÉ

Draft your résumé using short, crisp phrases built around strong verbs and nouns.

Write your résumé using a simple and direct style. Use short, crisp phrases instead of whole sentences and focus on what your reader needs to know. Avoid using the word *I*, which can sound both self-involved and repetitious by the time you outline all your skills and accomplishments. Instead, start your phrases with strong action verbs such as these:[26]

| | | | | |
|---|---|---|---|---|
| accomplished | assumed | coordinated | explored | initiated |
| achieved | budgeted | created | forecasted | installed |
| administered | chaired | demonstrated | generated | introduced |
| approved | changed | developed | identified | investigated |
| arranged | compiled | directed | implemented | joined |
| assisted | completed | established | improved | launched |
| maintained | participated | recommended | set up | supervised |
| managed | performed | reduced | simplified | systematized |
| motivated | planned | reorganized | sparked | targeted |
| operated | presented | resolved | streamlined | trained |
| organized | proposed | saved | strengthened | transformed |
| oversaw | raised | served | succeeded | upgraded |

For instance, you might say, "Created a campus organization for students interested in entrepreneurship" or "Managed a fast-food restaurant and four employees." Whenever you can, quantify the results so that your claims don't come across as empty puffery. Don't just say you're a team player or detail oriented—show you are by offering concrete proof.[27] Here are some examples of phrasing accomplishments using active statements that show results:

| Avoid Weak Statements | Use Active Statements That Show Results |
|---|---|
| Responsible for developing a new filing system | Developed a new filing system that reduced paperwork by 50 percent |
| I was in charge of customer complaints and all ordering problems | Handled all customer complaints and resolved all product order discrepancies |
| I won a trip to Europe for opening the most new customer accounts in my department | Generated the highest number of new customer accounts in my department |
| Member of special campus task force to resolve student problems with existing cafeteria assignments | Assisted in implementing new campus dining program that balances student wishes with cafeteria capacity |

Providing specific supporting evidence is vital, but make sure you don't go overboard with small details.[28] Carefully select the most compelling evidence so that your message clear and immediate.

In addition to clear writing with specific examples, the particular words and phrases used throughout your résumé are critically important. The majority of résumés are now subjected to *keyword searches* in an applicant tracking system or other database, in which a recruiter searches for résumés most likely to match the requirements of a particular job. Résumés that don't match the requirements closely may never be seen by a human reader, so it is essential to use the words and phrases that a recruiter is most likely to search for. (Although most experts used to advise including a separate *keyword summary* as a stand-alone list, the trend nowadays is to incorporate your keywords into your introductory statement and other sections of your résumé.)[29]

Identifying these keywords requires some research, but you can uncover many of them while you are researching various industries and companies. In particular, study job descriptions carefully. In contrast to the action verbs that catch a human reader's attention, keywords that catch a computer's attention are usually nouns that describe the specific

Include relevant *keywords* in your introductory statement, work history, and education sections.

skills, attributes, and experiences an employer is looking for in a candidate. Keywords can include the business and technical terms associated with a specific profession, industry-specific jargon, names or types of products or systems used in a profession, job titles, and college degrees.[30]

Finally, beware of clichés that are used on so many résumés and social media profiles that they've probably lost most of their impact. For example, LinkedIn identified these 10 buzzwords and phrases as the most overused: *extensive experience, innovative, motivated, results-oriented, dynamic, proven track record, team player, fast-paced, problem solver,* and *entrepreneurial.*[31] Instead of *saying* you are all these things, *show* how you are, using solid evidence.

## Name and Contact Information

Your name and contact information constitute the heading of your résumé; include the following:

> Be sure to provide complete and accurate contact information; mistakes in this section of the résumé are surprisingly common.

- Name
- Physical address (both permanent and temporary, if you're likely to move during the job search process; however, if you're posting a résumé in an unsecured location online, leave off your physical address for security purposes)
- Phone number(s)
- Email address
- The URL of your personal webpage, e-portfolio, or social media résumé (if you have one)

> Use a professional-sounding email address for business correspondence, such as *firstname.lastname@something.com.*

If the only email address you have is through your current employer, get a free personal email address from one of the many services that offer them. It's not fair to your current employer to use company resources for a job search, and doing so sends a bad signal to potential employers. Also, if your personal email address is anything like precious.princess@something.com or PsychoDawg@something.com, get a new email address for your business correspondence.

## Introductory Statement

Of all the parts of a résumé, the brief introductory statement that follows your name and contact information probably generates the most disagreement. You can put one of three things here:[32]

> You can choose to open with a career objective, a qualifications summary, or a career summary.

- **Career objective.** A career objective identifies either a specific job you want to land or a general career track you would like to pursue. Some experts advise against including a career objective because it can categorize you so narrowly that you miss out on interesting opportunities, and it is essentially about fulfilling your desires, not about meeting the employer's needs. In the past, most résumés included a career objective, but in recent years more job seekers are using a qualifications summary or a career summary. However, if you have little or no work experience in your target profession, a career objective might be your best option. If you do opt for an objective, word it in a way that relates your qualifications to employer needs. Avoid such self-absorbed statements as "A fulfilling position that provides ample opportunity for career growth and personal satisfaction."

> If you have a reasonably focused skill set but don't yet have a long career history, a qualifications summary is probably the best type of introductory statement for you.

- **Qualifications summary.** A qualifications summary offers a brief view of your key qualifications. The goal is to let a reader know within a few seconds what you can deliver. You can title this section generically as "Qualifications Summary" or "Summary of Qualifications," or if you have one dominant qualification, you can use that as the title (see Figure 18.5 on page 521 for an example). Consider using a qualifications summary if you have one or more important qualifications but don't yet have a long career history. Also, if you haven't been working long but your college education has given you a dominant professional "theme," such as multimedia design or statistical analysis, you can craft a qualifications summary that highlights your educational preparedness.

- **Career summary.** A career summary offers a brief recap of your career, with the goal of presenting increasing levels of responsibility and performance. A career summary can be particularly useful for executives who have demonstrated the ability to manage increasingly larger and more complicated business operations—a key consideration when companies look to hire upper-level managers.

## Education

If you're still in college or have recently graduated, education is probably your strongest selling point. Present your educational background in depth, choosing facts that support your "theme." Give this section a heading such as "Education," "Technical Training," or "Academic Preparation," as appropriate. Then, starting with the most recent, list the name and location of each school you have attended, the month and year of your graduation (say "anticipated graduation in _____" if you haven't graduated yet), your major and minor fields of study, significant skills and abilities you've developed in your course work, and the degrees or certificates you've earned. If you're still working toward a degree, include in parentheses the expected date of completion. Showcase your qualifications by listing courses that have directly equipped you for the job you are seeking, and indicate any scholarships, awards, or academic honors you've received.

The education section should also include relevant training sponsored by business or government organizations. Mention high school or military training only if the associated achievements are pertinent to your career goals.

Whether you list your grade point average depends on the job you want and the quality of your grades. If you don't show your GPA on your résumé—and there's no rule saying you have to—be prepared to answer questions about it during the interview process because many employers will assume that your GPA is not spectacular if you didn't list it on your résumé. If you choose to show a grade point average, be sure to mention the scale, especially if it isn't a four-point scale. If your grades are better within your major than in other courses, you can also list your GPA as "Major GPA" and include only those courses within your major.

> If you are early in your career, your education is probably your strongest selling point.

## Work Experience, Skills, and Accomplishments

This section can be called "Work Experience," "Professional Experience," or "Work and Volunteer Experience," if you have limited work experience and want to bolster that with volunteer experience. Like the education section, the work experience section should focus on your overall theme in a way that shows how your past can contribute to an employer's future. Use keywords to call attention to the skills you've developed on the job and to your ability to handle responsibility. Emphasize what you accomplished in each position, not just the generic responsibilities of the job.

List your jobs in reverse chronological order, starting with the most recent. Include military service and any internships and part-time or temporary jobs related to your career objective. Include the name and location of the employer, and if readers are unlikely to recognize the organization, briefly describe what it does. When you want to keep the name of your current employer confidential, you can identify the firm by industry only ("a large video game developer"). If an organization's name or location has changed since you worked there, state the current name and location and include the old information preceded by "formerly . . ." Before or after each job listing, state your job title and give the years you worked in the job; use the phrase "to present" to denote current employment. Indicate whether a job was part time.

> When you describe past job responsibilities, identify the skills and knowledge you can apply to a future job.

Devote the most space to the jobs that are most recent or most closely related to your target position. If you were personally responsible for something significant, be sure to mention it. Facts about your skills and accomplishments are the most important information you can give a prospective employer, so quantify them whenever possible.

One helpful exercise is to write a 30-second "commercial" for each major skill you want to highlight. The commercial should offer proof that you really do possess the skill. For your résumé, distill the commercials down to brief phrases; you can use the more detailed proof statements in cover letters and as answers to interview questions.[33]

> Devote the most space to jobs that are related to your target position.

If you have a number of part-time, temporary, or entry-level jobs that don't relate to your career objective, you have to use your best judgment when it comes to including or excluding them. Too many minor and irrelevant work details can clutter your résumé, particularly if you've been in the professional workforce for a few years. However, if you don't have a long employment history, including these jobs shows your ability and willingness to keep working.

### Activities and Achievements

Include activities and achievements outside of a work context only if they make you a more attractive job candidate. For example, traveling, studying, or working abroad and fluency in multiple languages could weigh heavily in your favor with employers who do business internationally.

Because many employers are involved in their local communities, they tend to look positively on applicants who are active and concerned members of their communities as well. Consider including community service activities that suggest leadership, teamwork, communication skills, technical aptitude, or other valuable attributes.

You should generally avoid indicating membership or significant activity in religious or political organizations (unless, of course, you're applying to such an organization) because doing so might raise concerns for people with differing beliefs or affiliations. However, if you want to highlight skills you developed while involved with such a group, you can refer to it generically as a "not-for-profit organization" without mentioning its name.

Finally, if you have little or no job experience and not much to discuss outside of your education, indicating involvement in athletics or other organized student activities lets employers know that you don't spend all your free time hanging around your apartment playing video games. Also consider mentioning publications, projects, and other accomplishments that required relevant business skills.

*Include personal accomplishments only if they suggest special skills or qualities that are relevant to the jobs you're seeking.*

> **REAL-TIME UPDATES**
> LEARN MORE BY LISTENING TO THIS PODCAST
> **Résumé advice from a PR insider**
> Public relations executive Jessica Bernot offers her thoughts on how students can create effective résumés. Go to http://real-timeupdates.com/bct12 and click on Learn More. If you are using MyBCommLab, you can access Real-Time Updates within each chapter or under Student Study Tools.

### Personal Data and References

In nearly all instances, your résumé should not include any personal data beyond the information described in the previous sections. When applying to U.S. companies, never include any of the following: physical characteristics, age, gender, marital status, sexual orientation, religious or political affiliations, race, national origin, salary history, reasons for leaving jobs, names of previous supervisors, names of references, Social Security number, or student ID number.

Note that standards can vary in other countries. For example, you might be expected to include your citizenship, nationality, or marital status.[34] However, verify such requirements before including any personal data.

The availability of references is usually assumed, so you don't need to put "References available upon request" at the end of your résumé. However, be sure to have a list of several references ready when you begin applying for jobs. Prepare your reference sheet with your name and contact information at the top. For a finished look, use the same design and layout you use for your résumé. Then list three or four people who have agreed to serve as references. Include each person's name, job title, organization, address, telephone number, email address (if the reference prefers to be contacted by email), and the nature of your relationship.

Figures 18.3 through 18.5 show how a job applicant can put these guidelines to work in three job-search scenarios:

- **Scenario 1: Positioning Yourself for an Ideal Opportunity** (when you've found a job opening that aligns closely with your career goals and your academic and professional credentials)
- **Scenario 2: Positioning Yourself for an Available Opportunity** (when you can't find a job in your chosen field and need to adapt to whatever opportunities are available)
- **Scenario 3: Positioning Yourself for More Responsibility** (after you have some experience in your field and want to apply for positions of greater responsibility)

*When applying to U.S. companies, your résumé should not include any personal data such as age, marital status, physical description, or Social Security number.*

*Prepare a list of references but don't include them on your résumé.*

**The Scenario**

You are about to graduate and have found a job opening that is in your chosen field. You don't have any experience in this field, but the courses you've taken in pursuit of your degree have given you a solid academic foundation for this position.

**The Opportunity**

The job opening is for an associate market analyst with Living Social, the rapidly growing advertising and social commerce service that describes itself as "the online source for discovering valuable local experiences." (A market analyst researches markets to find potentially profitable business opportunities.)

**The Communication Challenge**

You don't have directly relevant experience as a market analyst, and you might be competing against people who do. Your education is your strongest selling point, so you need to show how your coursework relates to the position.

Don't let your lack of experience hold you back; the job posting makes it clear that this is an entry-level position. For example, the first bullet point in the job description says "Become an expert in market data . . .," and the required skills and experience section says that "Up to 2 years of experience with similar research and analysis is preferred." The important clues here are *become* (the company doesn't expect you to be an expert already) and *preferred* (experience would be great if you have it, but it's not required).

**Keywords and Key Phrases**

You study the job posting and highlight the following elements:

1. Working in a team environment
2. Research, including identifying trendy new businesses
3. Analyzing data using Microsoft Excel
4. Managing projects
5. Collaborating with technical experts and sales staff
6. Creating new tools to help maximize revenue and minimize risks
7. Bachelor's degree is required
8. Natural curiosity and desire to learn
9. Detail oriented
10. Hands-on experience with social media

---

### Emma Gomes
(847) 555-2153
emma.gomes@mailsystem.net
emmawrites.blogspot.com

**Address:**
860 North 8th Street, Terre Haute, IN 47809

**Permanent Address:**
993 Church Street, Barrington, IL 60010

#### Summary of Qualifications

- In-depth academic preparation in marketing analysis techniques
- Intermediate skills with a variety of analytical tools, including Microsoft Excel and Google Analytics
- Front-line experience with consumers and business owners
- Multiple research and communication projects involving the business applications of social media

#### Education

B.S. in Marketing (Marketing Management Track), Indiana State University, Terre Haute, IN, anticipated graduation: May 2014

*Program coursework*

- 45 credits of core business courses, including Business Information Tools, Business Statistics, Principles of Accounting, and Business Finance
- 27 credits of marketing and marketing management courses, including Buyer Behavior, Marketing Research, Product and Pricing Strategy, and seminars in e-commerce and social media

*Special projects*

- "Handcrafting a Global Marketplace: The Etsy Phenomenon," in-depth analysis of how Etsy transformed the market for handmade craft items by bringing e-commerce capabilities to individual craftspeople
- "Hybrid Communication Platforms for Small Businesses," team service project for five small businesses in Terre Haute, recommending best practices for combining traditional and social-media methods of customer engagement and providing a customized measurement spreadsheet for each company

#### Work and Volunteer Experience

**Independent math tutor, 2009–present.** Assist students with a variety of math courses at the elementary, junior high, and high school level; all clients have achieved combined test and homework score improvements of at least one full letter grade, with an average improvement of 38 percent

**Volunteer, LeafSpring Food Bank, Terre Haute, IN (weekends during college terms, 2012–present).** Stock food and supply pantries; prepare emergency baskets for new clients; assist director with public relations activities, including website updates and social media news releases.

**Customer care agent, Owings Ford, Barrington, IL (summers, 2011–2013).** Assisted the service and sales managers of this locally owned car dealership with a variety of customer-service tasks; scheduled service appointments; designed and implemented improvements to service-center waiting room to increase guest comfort; convinced dealership owners to begin using Twitter and Facebook to interact with current and potential customers.

#### Professional Engagement

- Collegiate member, American Marketing Association; helped establish the AMA Collegiate Chapter at Indiana State
- Participated in AMA International Collegiate Case Competition, 2011-2012

#### Awards

- Dean's List: 2012, 2013
- Forward Youth award, Barrington Chamber of Commerce, 2010

---

*Gomes includes phone and email contacts, along with a blog that features academic-oriented writing.*

*Using a summary of qualifications for her opening statement lets her target the résumé and highlight her most compelling attributes.*

*Her education is a much stronger selling point than her work experience, so she goes into some detail—carefully selecting course names and project descriptions to echo the language of the job description.*

*She adjusts the descriptions and accomplishments of each role to highlight the aspects of her work and volunteer experience that are relevant to the position.*

*The final sections highlight activities and awards that reflect her interest in marketing and her desire to improve her skills.*

---

**Notice how Gomes adapts her résumé to "mirror" the keywords and phrases from the job posting:**

1. Offers concrete evidence of teamwork (rather than just calling herself a "team player," for example)
2. Emphasizes research skills and experience in multiple instances
3. Calls out Microsoft Excel, as well as Google Analytics, a key online tool for measuring activity on websites
4. Indicates the ability to plan and carry out projects, even if she doesn't have formal project management experience
5. Indicates some experience working in a supportive or collaborative role with technical experts and sales specialists (the content of the work doesn't translate to the new job, but the concept does)
6. Suggests the ability to work with new analytical tools
7. Displays her B.S. degree prominently
8. Demonstrates a desire to learn and to expand her skills
9. Tracking the progress of her tutoring clients is strong evidence of a detail-oriented worker—not to mention someone who cares about results and the quality of her work
10. Lists business-oriented experience with Facebook, Twitter, and other social media

**Figure 18.3   Crafting Your Résumé, Scenario 1: Positioning Yourself for an Ideal Opportunity**
Even for an ideal job-search scenario, where your academic and professional experiences and interests closely match the parameters of the job opening, you still need to adapt your résumé content carefully to "echo" the specific language of the job description. (Job description keywords and key phrases quoted or adapted in part from "Associate Market Analyst" job opening posted on LivingSocial website, accessed 9 July 2012, http://corporate.livingsocial.com.)

**The Scenario**

You are about to graduate but can't find job openings in the field you'd like to enter. However, you have found an opening that is in a related field, and it would give you the chance to get some valuable work experience.

**The Opportunity**

The job opening is for a seller support associate with Amazon, the online retail giant. Employees in this position work with merchants that sell products through the Amazon e-commerce system to make sure merchants are successful. In essence, it is a customer service job, but directed at these merchants, not the consumers who buy on Amazon.

**The Communication Challenge**

This isn't the job you ultimately want, but it is a great opportunity with a well-known company.

You note that the position does not require a college degree, so in that sense you might be a bit overqualified. However, you also see a strong overlap between your education and the responsibilities and required skills of the job, so be sure to highlight those.

**Keywords and Key Phrases**

You study the job posting and highlight the following elements:

1. Be able to predict and respond to merchant needs; good business sense with the ability to appreciate the needs of a wide variety of companies
2. Strong written and oral communication skills
3. High degree of professionalism
4. Self-starter with good time management skills
5. Logically analyze problems and devise solutions
6. Comfortable with computer-based tools, including Microsoft Excel
7. Desire to expand business and technical skills
8. Customer service experience
9. Collaborate with fellow team members to resolve difficult situations
10. Record of high performance regarding quality of work and personal productivity

---

## Emma Gomes
(847) 555-2153
emma.gomes@mailsystem.net
emmawrites.blogspot.com

| **Address:** | **Permanent Address:** |
|---|---|
| 860 North 8th Street, Terre Haute, IN 47809 | 993 Church Street, Barrington, IL 60010 |

### Summary of Qualifications

- Front-line customer service experience with consumers and business owners
- Strong business sense based on work experience and academic preparation
- Intermediate skills with a variety of software tools, including Microsoft Excel and Google Analytics
- Record of quality work in both business and academic settings

*Gomes modified her summary of qualifications to increase emphasis on customer service.*

### Education

B.S. in Marketing (Marketing Management Track), Indiana State University, Terre Haute, IN, expected graduation May 2014

#### Program coursework

- 45 credits of core business courses, including Business Information Tools, Business Statistics, Principles of Accounting, and Business Finance
- 27 credits of marketing and marketing management courses, including Marketing Fundamentals, Buyer Behavior, Marketing Research, Retail Strategies and seminars in e-commerce and social media

*She adjusts the selection of highlighted courses to reflect the retail and e-commerce aspects of this particular job opening.*

#### Special projects

- "Handcrafting a Global Marketplace: The Etsy Phenomenon," in-depth analysis of how the Etsy e-commerce platform helps craftspeople and artisans become more successful merchants
- "Hybrid Communication Platforms for Small Businesses," team service project for five small businesses in Terre Haute, recommending best practices for combining traditional and social-media methods of customer engagement and providing a customized measurement spreadsheet for each company

*She adjusts the wording of this Etsy project description to closely mirror what Amazon is—an e-commerce platform serving a multitude of independent merchants.*

### Work and Volunteer Experience

**Independent math tutor, 2009-present.** Assist students with a variety of math courses at the elementary, junior high, and high school level; all clients have achieved combined test and homework score improvements of at least one full letter grade, with an average improvement of 38 percent

**Volunteer, LeafSpring Food Bank, Terre Haute, IN (weekends during college terms, 2012–present).** Stock food and supply pantries; prepare emergency baskets for new clients; assist director with public relations activities, including website updates and social media news releases

**Customer care agent, Owings Ford, Barrington, IL (summers, 2011–2013).** Assisted the service and sales managers of this locally owned car dealership with a variety of customer-service tasks; scheduled service appointments; designed and implemented improvements to service-center waiting room to increase guest comfort; convinced dealership owners to begin using Twitter and Facebook to interact with current and potential customers.

*She provides more detail regarding her customer support experience.*

### Professional Engagement

- Collegiate member, American Marketing Association; helped establish the AMA Collegiate Chapter at Indiana State
- Participated in AMA International Collegiate Case Competition, 2011-2012

*The final sections are still relevant to this job opening, so she leaves them unchanged.*

### Awards

- Dean's List: 2012, 2013
- Forward Youth award, Barrington Chamber of Commerce, 2010

---

**Notice how Gomes adapts her résumé to "mirror" the keywords and phrases from the job posting:**

1. Suggests strong awareness of the needs of various businesses
2. Examples of experience with written business communication; she can demonstrate oral communication skills during phone, video, or in-person interviews
3. Results-oriented approach to tutoring business suggests high degree of professionalism, as do the two awards
4. The ability to work successfully as an independent tutor while attending high school and college is strong evidence of self-motivation and good time management
5. Indicates ability to understand problems and design solutions
6. Suggests the ability to work with a variety of software tools
7. Demonstrates a desire to learn and to expand her skills
8. Highlights customer service experience
9. Offers concrete evidence of teamwork (rather than just calling herself a "team player," for example)
10. Tracking the progress of her tutoring clients is strong evidence of someone who cares about results and the quality of her work; Dean's List awards also suggest quality of work; record of working while attending high school and college suggests strong productivity

**Figure 18.4  Crafting Your Résumé, Scenario 2: Repositioning Yourself for Available Opportunities**
If you can't find an ideal job opening, you'll need to adjust your plans and adapt your résumé to the openings that are available. Look for opportunities that meet your near-term financial needs while giving you the chance to expand your skill set so that you'll be even more prepared when an ideal opportunity does come along. (Job description keywords and key phrases quoted or adapted in part from "Seller Support Associate" job opening posted on Amazon website, accessed 12 July 2012, https://us-amazon.icims.com/jobs).

## Emma Gomes

(847) 555-2153
emma.gomes@mailsystem.net
Twitter: www.twitter.com/emmagomes
1605 Queen Anne Avenue North, Seattle, WA 98109

### Market and Strategy Analyst

- Five years of experience in local and online retailing, with three years of focus on market opportunity analysis
- Strong business sense developed through more than 60 marketing programs across a range of retail sectors, including hospitality, entertainment, and fashion
- Recognized by senior management for ability to make sound judgment calls in situations with incomplete or conflicting data
- Adept at coordinating research projects and marketing initiatives across organizational boundaries and balancing the interests of multiple stakeholders
- Advanced skills with leading analysis and communication tools, including Excel, PowerPoint, and Google Analytics

### Professional Experience

**Associate Market Analyst, LivingSocial, Seattle, WA (July 2011-present).** Analyzed assigned markets for such factors as consumer demand, merchandising opportunities, and seller performance; designed, launched, and managed marketing initiatives in 27 retailing categories, including fashions and accessories; met or exceeded profit targets on 90 percent of all marketing initiatives; appointed team lead/trainer in recognition of strong quantitative and qualitative analysis skills; utilized both established and emerging social media tools and helped business partners use these communication platforms to increase consumer engagement in local markets.

**Seller support associate, Amazon, Seattle, WA (July 2009–June 2011).** Worked with more than 300 product vendors, including many in the fashion and accessories sectors, to assure profitable retailing activities on the Amazon e-commerce platform; resolved vendor issues related to e-commerce operations, pricing, and consumer communication; anticipated potential vendor challenges and assisted in the development of more than a dozen new selling tools that improved vendor profitability while reducing Amazon's vendor support costs by nearly 15 percent.

### Education

**Evening MBA program, University of Washington, Seattle, WA; anticipated graduation: May 2015.** Broad-based program combining financial reporting, marketing strategy, competitive strategy, and supply chain management with individual emphasis on quantitative methods, financial analysis, and marketing decision models.

**B.S. in Marketing (Marketing Management Track), Indiana State University, Terre Haute, IN, May 2009.** Comprehensive coursework in business fundamentals, accounting and finance, marketing fundamentals, retailing, and consumer communications.

### Professional Engagement

- Member, American Marketing Association
- Member, International Social Media Association
- Active in National Retail Federation and Retail Advertising & Marketing Association

### Awards

- Living Social Top Ten Deals (monthly employee achievement award for designing the most profitable couponing deals); awarded seven times, 2011—2013
- Social Commerce Network's Social Commerce Innovators: 30 Under 30; 2012

### Notice how Gomes adapts her résumé to "mirror" the keywords and phrases from the job posting:

1. Highlights her experience in market and business analysis and her continuing education in this area
2. Mentions skill at coordinating cross-functional projects
3. Lists experiences that relate to the collection and analysis of retail data
4. Emphasizes the work she has done with fashion-related retailing and retailing in general
5. Identifies experience and education that relates to quantitative and qualitative analysis (this point overlaps #1 and #3 to a degree)
6. Mentions project management experience
7. Lists areas that suggest effective communication skills
8. Lists education, with emphasis on coursework that relates most directly to the job posting
9. Mentions work experience and educational background related to these topics
10. Includes these programs in the list of software tools she uses

**Figure 18.5** **Crafting Your Résumé, Scenario 3: Positioning Yourself for More Responsibility**
When you have a few years of experience under your belt, your résumé strategy should shift to emphasize work history and accomplishments. Here is how Emma Gomes might reshape her résumé if she had held the two jobs described in Figures 18.3 and 18.4 and is now ready for a bigger challenge. (Job description keywords and key phrases quoted or adapted in part from "Senior Strategy Analyst" job opening posted on Nordstrom website, accessed 17 July 2012, http://careers.nordstrom.com).

# Completing a Résumé

**4** **LEARNING OBJECTIVE**
Characterize the completing step for résumés, including the six most common formats in which you can produce a résumé.

Completing your résumé involves revising it for optimum quality, producing it in the various forms and media you'll need, and proofreading it for any errors before distributing it or publishing it online. Producing and distributing a résumé used to be fairly straightforward: You printed it on quality paper and mailed or faxed it to employers. However, the advent of applicant tracking systems, social media, and other innovations has dramatically changed the nature of résumé production and distribution. Be prepared to produce several versions of your résumé, in multiple formats and multiple media.

Even if most or all of your application efforts take place online, starting with a traditional paper résumé is still useful, for several reasons. First, a traditional printed résumé is a great opportunity to organize your background information and identify your unique strengths. Second, the planning and writing tasks involved in creating a conventional résumé will help you generate blocks of text you can reuse in multiple ways throughout the job search process. Third, you'll never know when someone might ask for your résumé during a networking event or other in-person encounter, and you don't want to let that interest fade in the time it might take for the person to get to your information online.

## REVISING YOUR RÉSUMÉ

MyBCommLab Apply these key concepts. Go to **mybcommlab.com** and follow this path: Course Content → Chapter 6 → **DOCUMENT MAKEOVERS**

Avoid the common errors that will get your résumé excluded from consideration.

Ask professional recruiters to list the most common mistakes they see on résumés, and you'll hear the same things over and over again. Keep your résumé out of the recycling bin by avoiding these flaws:

- Too long or too wordy
- Too short or sketchy
- Difficult to read
- Poorly written
- Displaying weak understanding of the business world in general or of a particular industry or company

---

**COMMUNICATION MISCUES**

## Don't. Just Don't.

Even though employment recruiters might think they've seen it all by now, innovative job applicants still keep finding new ways to get their résumés tossed into the recycling bin. Here are a few examples for your amusement—and warning, if you're inclined to share a little too much information:

- The passing of a beloved pet is never easy, but should grief over a departed cat keep someone out of the workforce for three months? That's how one job applicant explained a three-month gap in his employment history.
- One applicant's résumé arrived in an envelope that had a picture of a car on it, along with an explanation saying it would be a gift for the hiring manager.
- A person's family medical history is obviously important to him or her, but it's not something to put on a résumé, as one job seeker did, for reasons unknown.
- In a valiant effort to cram as many mistakes as possible onto a single page, one creative candidate included a full body photo of herself—in thigh-high boots, no less—and used oversized, fluorescent pink paper. This résumé probably did look pretty as it fluttered off a recruiter's desk into the recycling bin.
- Expressing strong interest in a job is good, but not if that interest is expressed like this: "to keep my parole officer from putting me back in jail."

- One applicant's mother was proud of her, to be sure, but including a letter from her with a résumé made the applicant look like, well, a child.

These cringe-inducing blunders are worth more than a quick chuckle: They're a great reminder of why it is crucial to understand the purpose of a résumé and the effect a résumé has on hiring managers.

**CAREER APPLICATIONS**

1. Is it a good idea to "show some personality" in your résumé? Explain your answer.
2. How should you handle the employment section of your résumé if you really did take three months off work to grieve the loss of a pet?

*Sources:* Adapted from Rosemary Haefner, "Biggest Resume Mistakes," CNN.com, 21 May 2007, www.cnn.com; Sue Campbell, "Eight Worst Resume Mistakes," 1st-Writer.com, accessed 30 December 2008, www.1st-writer.com; "150 Funniest Resume Mistakes, Bloopers, and Blunders Ever," The Best Article Every Day blog, 2 June 2008, accessed 30 December 2008, www.bspcn.com; "Hiring Managers Share Top 12 Wackiest Resume Blunders in New CareerBuilder.com Survey," CareerBuilder.com, 25 April 2007, www.careerbuilder.com.

- Poor-quality printing or cheap paper
- Full of spelling and grammar errors
- Boastful
- Gimmicky design

The ideal length of your résumé depends on the depth of your experience and the level of the positions for which you are applying. As a general guideline, if you have fewer than 10 years of professional experience, try to keep a conventional printed résumé to one page. Recruiters appreciate brevity, and presenting yourself in a single page shows your ability to write concise, focused, audience-oriented messages.[35] For online résumé formats, you can always provide links to additional information. If you have more experience and are applying for a higher-level position, you may need to prepare a somewhat longer résumé.[36] For highly technical positions, longer résumés are often the norm as well because the qualifications for such jobs can require more description.

> If your employment history is brief, keep your résumé to one page.

## PRODUCING YOUR RÉSUMÉ

No matter how many media and formats you eventually choose for producing your résumé, a clean, professional-looking design is a must. Unless you have some experience in graphic design and you're applying in a field such as advertising or retail merchandising, where visual creativity is viewed as an asset, resist the urge to "get creative" with your résumé layout.[37] Recruiters and hiring managers want to skim your essential information in a matter of seconds, and anything that distracts or delays them will work against you. Moreover, complex layouts can confuse an applicant tracking system, which can result in your information getting garbled.

> "Clever" résumé designs can help you stand out from the crowd, but they can also get you rejected by applicant tracking systems and recruiters, so think carefully about using a nontraditional format.

Fortunately, good résumé design is not difficult to achieve. As you can see in Figures 18.3 through 18.5, good designs feature simplicity, order, effective use of white space, and clear typefaces. Make subheadings easy to find and easy to read, placing them either above each section or in the left margin. Use lists to itemize your most important qualifications. Color is not necessary by any means, but if you add color, make it subtle and sophisticated, such as a thin horizontal line under your name and address. The most common way to get into trouble with résumé design is going overboard.

Depending on the companies you apply to, you might want to produce your résumé in as many as six formats (all are explained in the following sections):

- Printed traditional résumé
- Printed scannable résumé
- Electronic plain-text file
- Microsoft Word file
- Online résumé, also called a multimedia résumé or social media résumé
- PDF file

> Be prepared to produce several versions of your résumé in multiple media.

Unfortunately, no single format or medium will work for all situations, and employer expectations continue to change as technology evolves. Find out what each employer or job posting website expects, and provide your résumé in that specific format.

### Considering Photos, Videos, Presentations, and Infographics

As you produce your résumé in various formats, you will encounter the question of whether to include a photograph of yourself on or with your résumé. For print or electronic documents you will be submitting to employers or job websites, the safest advice is to avoid photos. The reason is that seeing visual cues of the age, ethnicity, and gender of candidates early in the selection process exposes employers to complaints of discriminatory hiring practices. In fact, some employers won't even look at résumés that include photos, and some applicant tracking systems automatically discard résumés with any kind of extra files.[38] However, photographs are acceptable and expected for social media résumés and other online formats where you are not actively submitting a résumé to an employer.

> Do not include or enclose a photo in résumés you send to employers or post on job websites.

**REAL-TIME UPDATES**

LEARN MORE BY VISITING THIS WEBSITES

**Find inspiration in these creative résumés**

These eye-catching designs might give you a great idea for your résumé. Go to http://real-timeupdates.com/bct12 and click on Learn More. If you are using MyBCommLab, you can access Real-Time Updates within each chapter or under Student Study Tools.

In addition to these six main formats, some applicants create PowerPoint presentations, videos, or infographics to supplement a conventional résumé. Two key advantages of a PowerPoint supplement are flexibility and multimedia capabilities. For instance, you can present a menu of choices on the opening screen and allow viewers to click through to sections of interest. (Note that most of the things you can accomplish with PowerPoint can be done with an online résumé, which is probably more convenient for most readers.)

A video résumé can be a compelling supplement as well, but be aware that some employment law experts advise employers not to view videos, at least not until after candidates have been evaluated solely on their credentials. The reason for this caution is the same as with photographs. In addition, videos are more cumbersome to evaluate than paper or electronic résumés, and some recruiters refuse to watch them.[39] However, not all companies share this concern over videos, so you'll have to research their individual preferences. In fact, the online retailer Zappos encourages applicant videos and provides a way to upload videos on its job application webpage.[40]

An infographic résumé attempts to convey a person's career development and skill set graphically through a visual metaphor such as a timeline or subway map or as a poster with array of individual elements (see Figure 18.6). A well-designed infographic could be an intriguing element of the job-search package for candidates in certain situations and professions because it can definitely stand out from traditional résumés and can show a high level of skill in visual communication. However, infographics are likely to be incompatible with most applicant tracking systems and with the screening habits of most recruiters, so while you might stand out with an infographic, you might also get tossed out if you try to use an infographic in place of a conventional résumé. In virtually every situation, an infographic should complement a conventional résumé, not replace it. In addition, successful infographics require skills in graphical design, and if you lack those skills, you'll need to hire a designer.

*Videos, infographics, and other new approaches should complement your conventional résumé, not replace it.*

### Producing a Traditional Printed Résumé

Even though most of your application activity will take place online, having a copy of a conventional printed résumé is important for bringing to job fairs, interviews, and other events. Many interviewers expect you to bring a printed résumé to the interview, even if you applied online. The résumé can serve as a note-taking form or discussion guide, and it is tangible evidence of your attention to professionalism and detail.[41] When printing a résumé, choose a heavier, higher-quality paper designed specifically for résumés and other important documents. White or slightly off-white is the best color choice. Avoid papers with borders or backgrounds.

*Even though most of your application activity will take place online, having a copy of a conventional printed résumé is important.*

### Printing a Scannable Résumé

You might encounter a company that prefers *scannable résumés*, a type of printed résumé that is specially formatted to be compatible with optical scanning systems that convert printed documents to electronic text. These systems were quite common just a few years ago, but their use appears to be declining rapidly as more employers prefer email delivery or website application forms.[42] A scannable résumé differs from the traditional format in two major ways: it should always include a keyword summary, and it should be formatted in a simpler fashion that avoids underlining, special characters, and other elements that can confuse the scanning system. If you need to produce a scannable résumé, search online for "formatting a scannable résumé" to get detailed instructions.

*Some employers still prefer résumés in scannable format, but most now want electronic submissions.*

### Creating a Plain-Text File of Your Résumé

A *plain-text file* (sometimes known as an ASCII text file) is an electronic version of your résumé that has no font formatting, no bullet symbols, no colors, no lines or boxes, or other special formatting. The plain-text version can be used in two ways. First, you can include it in the body of an email message, for employers who want email delivery but don't want file attachments. Second, you can copy and paste the sections into the application forms on an employer's website.

*A plain-text version of your résumé is simply a computer file without any of the formatting you typically apply using word-processing software.*

# Bjorn Austraat
www.austraat.com

Business Results | Strategy Leadership | Talent Management

## Business Results

**Top Line Growth**
Multi-million dollar, long-term
customer relationships

$2.5M direct revenue
contribution and $10M+
pull-through value creation

**Bottom Line Impact**
45%-85% savings in customer
acquistion and service
operations costs

40%+ team productivity gains
through intelligent automation
and process redesign

## Skills

Expert Solution Selling

Executive Communication

Value Proposition Design

Sourcing Optimization

Service Transformation

In-depth Value Chain Analysis

Executive Needs Prioritization

Market Driver Assessment

Innovation Management

Go-to-Market Optimization

Team Building & Development

Expert Coaching & Mentoring

Performance Management

Thought Leadership

Intercultural Negotiations

## Strategy Leadership

**Enterprise Alignment**
Crucial 2011 planning
and budgeting clarity for
$165B global telecommunications
provider through revolutionary
data-backed framework
and tool set

**Strategy Innovation**
Successful business strategy
redesign for leading healthcare
information systems provider
with complete executive,
board and team buy-in

## Talent Management

**Award-Winning Leadership**
Top 5% performer and winner
of Founder's Award for
excellence in leadership
and team collaboration

**Scalable Solution Delivery**
18+ year successful track record of building, mentoring
and coaching diverse, scalable cross-functional teams in
consulting, high-technology and volunteer organizations

## Industry Expertise

Telecommunications / Mobility

Enterprise Software / SaaS

Internationalization / Globalization

Life Sciences

## Global Citizen

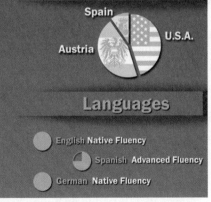

Spain

U.S.A.

Austria

## Advanced Degrees

**UC Berkeley,** MBA with Honors

**Monterey Institute,** MA

**University of Vienna,** MA

## Languages

English **Native Fluency**

Spanish **Advanced Fluency**

German **Native Fluency**

---

**Figure 18.6** **Infographic Résumé**
A well-designed infographic can be an intriguing part of a job-search package in some professions.
However, an infographic should always complement a conventional résumé, not try to replace it.
*Source:* Copyright © 2010 by Bjorn Austraat. Used by permission.

Make sure you verify the plain-text file you create with your word processor; it might need a few manual adjustments using a text editor such as NotePad.

A plain-text version is easy to create with your word processor. Start with the file you used to create your résumé, use the "Save As" choice to save it as "plain text" or whichever similarly labeled option your software has, and verify the result by using a basic text editor (such as Microsoft Notepad). If necessary, reformat the page manually, moving text and inserting space as needed. For simplicity's sake, left-justify all your headings rather than trying to center them manually.

### Creating a Word File of Your Résumé

Some employers and websites want your résumé in Microsoft Word format; make sure your computer is thoroughly scanned for viruses first, however.

In some cases, an employer or job-posting website will want you to upload a Microsoft Word file or attach it to an email message. (Although there are certainly other word processors on the market, Microsoft Word is the de facto standard in business these days.) This method of transferring information preserves the design and layout of your résumé and saves you the trouble of creating a plain-text version. However, before you submit a Word file to anyone, make sure your computer is free of viruses. Infecting a potential employer's computer will not make a good first impression.

### Creating a PDF Version of Your Résumé

Creating a PDF file is a simple procedure, but you need the right software. Adobe Acrobat (not the free Adobe Reader) is the best-known program, but many others are available, including some free versions. You can also use Adobe's online service, at www.acrobat.com/createpdf, to create PDFs without buying software. The advantages of creating PDFs are that you preserve the formatting of your résumé (unlike pasting plain text into an email message) and you create a file type that is less vulnerable to viruses than word-processer files. Both PDF and Word formats allow you to embed hyperlinks in the file as well, which gives your résumé some of the interactivity of an online/social media résumé.[43]

### Creating an Online or Social Media Résumé

You have many options for creating an online résumé, from college-hosted e-portfolios to multimedia résumés on commercial websites.

A variety of terms are used to describe online résumés, including *personal webpage*, *e-portfolio*, *social media résumé*, and *multimedia résumé*. Whatever the terminology used on a particular site, all these formats provide the opportunity to expand on the information contained in your basic résumé with links to projects, publications, screencasts, online videos, course lists, social networking profiles, and other elements that give employers a more complete picture of who you are and what you can offer (see Figure 18.7).

A good place to start is your college's career center. Ask whether the career center (or perhaps the information technology department) hosts online résumés or e-portfolios for students.

A commercial hosting service is another good possibility for an online résumé. For instance, the free service VisualCV (www.visualcv.com) lets you build an online résumé with video clips and other multimedia elements. This site is a good place to see numerous examples, from students just about to enter the workforce full-time all the way up to corporate CEOs.[44]

Regardless of the approach you take to creating an online résumé, keep these helpful tips in mind:

- **Remember that your online presence is a career-management tool.** The way you are portrayed online can work for you or against you, and it's up to you to create a positive impression. Most employers now conduct online searches to learn more about promising candidates, and 70 percent of those who do have rejected applicants because of information they dug up online.[45]
- **Take advantage of social networking.** Use whatever tools are available to direct people to your online résumé, such as including URL in your Twitter profile.
- **During the application process, don't expect or ask employers to retrieve a résumé from your website.** Submit your résumé using whatever method and medium each employer prefers. If employers then want to know more about you, they will likely do a web search on you and find your site, or you can refer them to your site in your résumé or application materials.

The site's social media sharing button makes it easy for viewers to copy his information to their networks.

He prominently links to his profile on the social network LinkedIn.

The career summary works effectively as an introductory statement to present a concise summary of his career so far and as an indication of the types of positions he is seeking.

His professional experience is his strongest selling point at this stage of his career, so it comes first after the summary.

The multimedia capabilities of the site allow him to embed professional videos that he has produced.

Farther down the screen, he includes professional affiliations, community service activities, education, awards and recognition, and links to news media articles in which his work was highlighted.

Farther down the screen, he links to other work projects, such as brochures and photos of promotional items he has produced.

**Figure 18.7 Social Media Résumé**
Reinaldo Llano, a corporate communications executive in the media industry, used the résumé hosting website VisualCV to create and present this multimedia/social media résumé.
*Source:* Visual CV Social Media Resume, by Reinaldo Llano. Copyright © 2012 by Reinaldo Llano. Reprinted with permission.

## PROOFREADING YOUR RÉSUMÉ

Employers view your résumé as a concrete example of your attention to quality and detail. Your résumé doesn't need to be good or pretty good—it needs to be *perfect*. Although it may not seem fair, just one or two errors in a job application package are enough to doom a candidate's chances.[46]

Your résumé is one of the most important documents you'll ever write, so don't rush or cut corners when it comes to proofreading. Check all headings and lists for clarity and parallelism and be sure your grammar, spelling, and punctuation are correct. Double-check all dates, phone numbers, email addresses, and other essential data. Ask at least three other people to read it, too. As the creator of the material, you could stare at a mistake for weeks and not see it.

Your résumé can't be "pretty good" or "almost perfect"—it needs to be *perfect*, so proofread it thoroughly and ask several other people to verify it, too.

## DISTRIBUTING YOUR RÉSUMÉ

How you distribute your résumé depends on the number of employers you target and their preferences for receiving résumés. Employers usually list their requirements on the career pages of their websites, so verify this information and follow it carefully. Beyond that, here are some general distribution tips:

- **Mailing printed résumés.** Take some care with the packaging. Spend a few extra cents to mail these documents in a flat 9 × 12 envelope, or better yet, use a Priority Mail flat-rate envelope, which gives you a sturdy cardboard mailer and faster delivery for just a few more dollars.

When distributing your résumé, pay close attention to the specific instructions provided by every employer, job website, or other recipient.

- **Emailing your résumé.** Some employers want applicants to include the text of their résumés in the body of an email message; others prefer an attached Microsoft Word or PDF file. If you have a reference number or a job ad number, include it in the subject line of your email message.

- **Submitting your résumé to an employer's website.** Many employers, including most large companies, now prefer or require applicants to submit their résumés online. In some instances, you will be asked to upload a complete file. In others, you will need to copy and paste sections of your résumé into individual boxes in an online application form.

Don't post a résumé on any public website unless you understand its privacy and security policies.

- **Posting your résumé on job websites.** You can post your résumé (or create one online, on some sites) on general-purpose job websites such as Monster (http://home.monster .com and http://college.monster.com) and CareerBuilder (www.careerbuilder.com), on more specialized websites such as Jobster (www.jobster.com) or Jobfox (www .jobfox.com), or with staffing services such as Volt (http://jobs.volt.com). Roughly 100,000 job boards are now online, so you'll need to spend some time looking for sites that specialize in your target industries, regions, or professions.[47] Before you upload your résumé to any site, however, learn about its confidentiality protection. Some sites allow you to specify levels of confidentiality, such as letting employers search your qualifications without seeing your personal contact information or preventing your current employer from seeing your résumé. Don't post your résumé to any website that doesn't give you the option of restricting the display of your contact information. Only employers that are registered clients of the service should be able to see your contact information.[48]

For a quick summary of the steps to take when planning, writing, and completing your résumé, refer to "Checklist: Writing an Effective Résumé." For the latest information on résumé writing, visit http://real-timeupdates.com/bct12 and click on Chapter 18.

---

**CHECKLIST** ✔ Writing an Effective Résumé

**A. Plan your résumé.**
- Analyze your purpose and audience carefully to make sure your message meets employers' needs.
- Gather pertinent information about your target companies.
- Select the required media types by researching the preferences of each employer.
- Organize your résumé around your strengths, choosing the chronological, functional, or combination structure. (Be careful about using the functional structure.)

**B. Write your résumé.**
- Keep your résumé honest.
- Adapt your résumé to your audience to highlight the qualifications each employer is looking for.

- Choose a career objective, qualifications summary, or career summary as your introductory statement—and make it concise, concrete, and reader-focused.
- Use powerful language to convey your name and contact information, introductory statement, education, work experience, skills, work or school accomplishments, and activities and achievements.

**C. Complete your résumé.**
- Revise your résumé until it is clear, concise, compelling—and perfect.
- Produce your résumé in all the formats you might need: traditional printed résumé, scannable, plain-text file, Microsoft Word file, PDF, or online.
- Proofread your résumé to make sure it is absolutely perfect.
- Distribute your résumé using the means that each employer prefers.

# Quick Learning Guide

## MyBCommLab

Go to **mybcommlab.com** to complete the problems marked with this icon ⭐.

## SUMMARY OF LEARNING OBJECTIVES

**1** List eight key steps to finding the ideal opportunity in today's job market. The eight steps discussed in the chapter are (1) writing the story of you, which involves describing where you have been in your career so far and where you would like to go in the future; (2) learning to think like an employer so you can present yourself as a quality hire; (3) researching industries and companies of interest to identify promising opportunities and to learn the language of the hiring managers; (4) translating your general potential into a specific solution for each employer so that you look like a good fit for each opening; (5) taking the initiative to approach interesting companies even if they haven't yet posted any job openings; (6) building your network so you and your connections can help each other in the job search process; (7) seeking career counseling if appropriate; and (8) avoiding the easily avoidable mistakes that can ruin your chances of getting a job.

**2** Explain the process of planning your résumé, including how to choose the best résumé organization. Planning a résumé starts with recognizing what it is: a persuasive message designed to get you job interviews. Gathering the necessary information involves learning about target industries, professions, companies, and specific positions, as well as gathering information about yourself. Choosing the best résumé organization depends on your background and your goals. A chronological résumé helps employers easily locate necessary information, highlights your professional growth and career progress, and emphasizes continuity and stability. If you can use the chronological format, you should because it is the approach employers tend to prefer. A functional résumé helps employers easily see what you can do for them, allows you to emphasize earlier job experience, and lets you downplay any lengthy periods of unemployment or a lack of career progress. However, many employers are suspicious of functional résumés for this very reason. The combination approach uses the best features of the other two and is often the best choice for recent graduates.

**3** Describe the tasks involved in writing your résumé, and list the major sections of a traditional résumé. Adapting to the audience is crucial, because readers are looking to see how well you understand their businesses and can present a solution to their talent needs. The major sections of a traditional résumé are (1) your name and contact information; (2) an introductory statement, which can be a career objective, a qualifications summary, or a career summary; (3) your education; (4) your work experience; and (5) activities and achievements that are professionally relevant. Most résumés do not need to include any personal data.

**4** Characterize the completing step for résumés, including the six most common formats in which you can produce a résumé. Quality is paramount with résumés, so the tasks of revising and proofing are particularly important. The six common résumé formats are traditional printed résumé, scannable résumé, electronic plain-text file, Microsoft Word file, PDF, and online résumé (which might be called a personal webpage, an e-portfolio, or a social media résumé).

## KEY TERMS

**applicant tracking systems** Computer systems that capture and store incoming résumés and help recruiters find good prospects for current openings

**chronological résumé** The most common résumé format; it emphasizes work experience, with past jobs shown in reverse chronological order

**combination résumé** Format that includes the best features of the chronological and functional approaches

**functional résumé** Format that emphasizes your skills and capabilities while identifying employers and academic experience in subordinate sections; many recruiters view this format with suspicion

**networking** The process of making connections with mutually beneficial business contacts

**résumé** A structured, written summary of a person's education, employment background, and job qualifications

---

## CHECKLIST ✓
### Writing an Effective Résumé

**A. Plan your résumé.**
- Analyze your purpose and audience carefully to make sure your message meets employers' needs.
- Gather pertinent information about your target companies.
- Select the required media types by researching the preferences of each employer.
- Organize your résumé around your strengths, choosing the chronological, functional, or combination structure. (Be careful about using the functional structure.)

**B. Write your résumé.**
- Keep your résumé honest.
- Adapt your résumé to your audience to highlight the qualifications each employer is looking for.
- Choose a career objective, qualifications summary, or career summary as your introductory statement—and make it concise, concrete, and reader-focused.
- Use powerful language to convey your name and contact information, introductory statement, education, work experience, skills, work or school accomplishments, and activities and achievements.

**C. Complete your résumé.**
- Revise your résumé until it is clear, concise, compelling—and perfect.
- Produce your résumé in all the formats you might need: traditional printed résumé, scannable, plain-text file, Microsoft Word file, PDF, or online.
- Proofread your résumé to make sure it is absolutely perfect.
- Distribute your résumé using the means that each employer prefers.

---

### TABLE 18.2 | Fallacies and Facts about Résumés

| Fallacy | Fact |
|---|---|
| The purpose of a résumé is to list all your skills and abilities. | The purpose of a résumé is to kindle employer interest and generate an interview. |
| A good résumé will get you the job you want. | All a résumé can do is get you in the door. |
| Your résumé will always be read carefully and thoroughly. | In most cases, your résumé needs to make a positive impression within 30 or 45 seconds; only then will someone read it in detail. Moreover, it will likely be screened by a computer looking for keywords first—and if it doesn't contain the right keywords, a human being may never see it. |
| The more good information you present about yourself in your résumé, the better, so stuff your résumé with every positive detail. | Recruiters don't need that much information about you at the initial screening stage, and they probably won't read it. |
| If you want a really good résumé, have it prepared by a résumé service. | You can certainly seek out formal or informal help, but if you have succeeded in this course, you have the skills needed to prepare an effective résumé. |

## COMMUNICATION CHALLENGES AT **ATK**

You work as a recruiter in the human resources department at ATK's Minneapolis headquarters, where part of your responsibility involves using the applicant tracking system to identify promising job candidates. Solve these challenges by using what you've learned about presenting oneself effectively on a résumé.

**INDIVIDUAL CHALLENGE:** One of today's tasks is selecting candidates to be interviewed for a management trainee position. This position involves significant interaction with other departments, so communication skills are vital. The applicant tracking system has turned up two candidates with almost identical qualifications. You have time to interview only one of them, however. Based on the way the two candidates described their education, which one would you invite in for an interview—and why?

a. Morehouse College, Atlanta, GA, 2003–2007. Received BA degree with a major in Business Administration and a minor in Finance. Graduated with a 3.65 grade-point average. Played varsity football and basketball. Worked 15 hours per week in the library. Coordinated the local student chapter of the American Management Association. Member of Alpha Phi Alpha social fraternity.

b. I attended Wayne State University in Detroit, Michigan, for two years and then transferred to the University of Michigan at Ann Arbor, where I completed my studies. My major was economics, but I also took many business management courses, including employee motivation, small business administration, history of business start-ups, and organizational behavior. I selected courses based on the professors' reputation for excellence, and I received mostly As and Bs. Unlike many other college students, I viewed the acquisition of knowledge—rather than career preparation—as my primary goal. I believe I have received a well-rounded education that has prepared me to approach management situations as problem-solving exercises.

**TEAM CHALLENGE:** To find candidates for an accounting associate position (a job typically filled by college graduates rather than more experienced professionals), you searched the application tracking system and found the following rather unconventional résumé. With one or two other students, decide whether you should (1) invite this candidate for an interview;

(2) reject the application without further analysis; (3) review the candidate's web-based e-portfolio, then make a decision about inviting him in for an interview; or (4) compare the candidate's qualifications relative to those of other applicants and invite him in for an interview only if you cannot find several qualified applicants. Explain your choice.

**Darius Jaidee**
809 N. Perkins Rd, Stillwater, OK 74075
Phone: (405) 369-0098
Email: dariusj@okstate.edu

**Career Objective:** To build a successful career in financial management

**Summary of Qualifications:** As a student at the University of Oklahoma, Stillwater, completed a wide variety of assignments that demonstrate skills related to accounting and management. For example:

**Planning Skills:** As president of the university's foreign affairs forum, organized six lectures and workshops featuring 36 speakers from 16 foreign countries within a nine-month period. Identified and recruited the speakers, handled their travel arrangements, and scheduled the facilities.

**Communication Skills:** Wrote more than 25 essays and term papers on various academic topics, including at least 10 dealing with business and finance. As a senior, wrote a 20-page analysis of financial trends in the petroleum industry, interviewing five high-ranking executives in accounting and finance positions at ConocoPhillip's refinery in Ponca City, Oklahoma, and company headquarters in Houston, Texas.

**Accounting and Computer Skills:** Competent in all areas of Microsoft Office, including Excel spreadsheets and Access databases. Assisted with bookkeeping activities in parents' small business, including the conversion from paper-based to computer-based accounting (Peachtree software). Have taken courses in accounting, financial planning, database design, web design, and computer networking.

For more information, including employment history, please access my e-portfolio at http://dariusjaidee.com.

## Test Your Knowledge

To review chapter content related to each question, refer to the indicated Learning Objective.

1. What does *quality of hire* mean? [LO-1]
2. Why is it important to have an organized approach to finding a new job? [LO-1]
3. Why is it important to contribute to any networks you belong to, in addition to looking for assistance for your own career? [LO-1]

4. What is the purpose of a résumé? [LO-2]
5. Why are some employers suspicious of the functional résumé? [LO-2]
6. What are keywords? [LO-3]
7. Should you include personal data on a résumé? Explain your answer. [LO-3]
8. What is a plain-text résumé? [LO-4]

# Apply Your Knowledge

To review chapter content related to each question, refer to the indicated Learning Objective.

⭐ 1. How can you "think like an employer" if you have no professional business experience? [LO-1]

2. If you were a team leader at a summer camp for children with special needs, should you include this in your employment history if you are applying for work that is unrelated? Explain your answer. [LO-3]

3. Can you use a qualifications summary if you don't yet have extensive professional experience in your desired career? Why or why not? [LO-3]

4. Some people don't have a clear career path when they enter the job market. If you're in this situation, how would your uncertainty affect the way you write your résumé? [LO-3]

5. Between your sophomore and junior years, you quit school for a year to earn the money to finish college. You worked as a loan-processing assistant in a finance company, checking references on loan applications, typing, and filing. Your manager made a lot of the fact that he had never attended college. He seemed to resent you for pursuing your education, but he never criticized your work, so you thought you were doing okay. After you'd been working there for six months, he fired you, saying that you'd failed to be thorough enough in your credit checks. You were actually glad to leave, and you found another job right away at a bank, doing similar duties. Now that you've graduated from college, you're writing your résumé. Will you include the finance company job in your work history? Explain. [LO-3]

# Practice Your Skills

## Message for Analysis

Read the following résumé information and then (1) analyze the strengths or weaknesses of the information and (2) revise the résumé so that it follows the guidelines presented in this chapter.

### Message 18.A: Writing a Résumé [LO-3]

Sylvia Manchester
765 Belle Fleur Blvd.
New Orleans, LA 70113
(504) 312-9504
smanchester@rcnmail.com

PERSONAL: Single, excellent health, 5'7", 136 lbs.; hobbies include cooking, dancing, and reading.

JOB OBJECTIVE: To obtain a responsible position in marketing or sales with a good company.

EDUCATION: BA degree in biology, University of Louisiana, 1998. Graduated with a 3.0 average. Member of the varsity cheerleading squad. President of Panhellenic League. Homecoming queen.

WORK EXPERIENCE

Fisher Scientific Instruments, 2004 to now, field sales representative. Responsible for calling on customers and explaining the features of Fisher's line of laboratory instruments. Also responsible for writing sales letters, attending trade shows, and preparing weekly sales reports.

Fisher Scientific Instruments, 2001–2003, customer service representative. Was responsible for handling incoming phone calls from customers who had questions about delivery, quality, or operation of Fisher's line of laboratory instruments. Also handled miscellaneous correspondence with customers.

Medical Electronics, Inc., 1998–2001, administrative assistant to the vice president of marketing. In addition to handling typical secretarial chores for the vice president of marketing, I was in charge of compiling the monthly sales reports, using figures provided by members of the field sales force. I also was given responsibility for doing various market research activities.

New Orleans Convention and Visitors Bureau, 1995–1998, summers, tour guide. During the summers of my college years, I led tours of New Orleans for tourists visiting the city. My duties included greeting conventioneers and their spouses at hotels, explaining the history and features of the city during an all-day sightseeing tour, and answering questions about New Orleans and its attractions. During my fourth summer with the bureau, I was asked to help train the new tour guides. I prepared a handbook that provided interesting facts about the various tourist attractions, as well as answers to the most commonly asked tourist questions. The Bureau was so impressed with the handbook they had it printed up so that it could be given as a gift to visitors.

University of Louisiana, 1995–1998, part-time clerk in admissions office. While I was a student in college, I worked 15 hours a week in the admissions office. My duties included filing, processing applications, and handling correspondence with high school students and administrators.

## Exercises

Each activity is labeled according to the primary skill or skills you will need to use. To review relevant chapter content, you can refer to the indicated Learning Objective. In some instances, supporting information will be found in another chapter, as indicated.

1. **Career Management: Researching Career Opportunities [LO-1]** Based on the preferences you identified in your career self-assessment (see page xxxiv in the Prologue) and the academic, professional, and personal qualities you have to offer, perform an online search for a career that matches your interests (starting with the websites listed in Table 18.1). Draft a brief report for your instructor, indicating how the career you select and the job openings you find match your strengths and preferences.

2. **Message Strategies: Writing a Résumé; Collaboration: Team Projects [LO-3], Chapter 2** Working with another student, change the following statements to make them more effective for a résumé by using action verbs.

   a. Have some experience with database design.

   b. Assigned to a project to analyze the cost accounting methods for a large manufacturer.

   c. I was part of a team that developed a new inventory control system.

   d. Am responsible for preparing the quarterly department budget.

e. Was a manager of a department with seven employees working for me.

f. Was responsible for developing a spreadsheet to analyze monthly sales by department.

g. Put in place a new program for ordering supplies.

3. **Message Strategies: Writing a Résumé [LO-3]** Using your team's answers to Exercise 2, make the statements stronger by quantifying them. (Make up any numbers you need.)

4. **Message Strategies: Writing a Résumé; Communication Ethics: Resolving Ethical Dilemmas [LO-3], Chapter 1** Assume that you achieved all the tasks shown in Exercise 2 not as an individual employee but as part of a work team. In your résumé, must you mention other team members? Explain your answer.

5. **Completing a Résumé [LO-4]** Using your revised version of the résumé in Message for Analysis 18.A , create a plain-text file that Sylvia Manchester could use to include in email messages.

6. **Completing a Résumé [LO-4]** Imagine you are applying for work in a field that involves speaking in front of an audience, such as sales, consulting, management, or training. Using material you created for any of the exercises or cases in Chapters 16 or 17, record a two- to three-minute video demonstration of your speaking and presentation skills. Record yourself speaking to an audience, if one can be arranged.

## Expand Your Skills

### Critique the Professionals

Locate an example of an online résumé (a sample or an actual résumé) from VisualCV (www.visualcv.com) or a similar website. Analyze the résumé using the guidelines presented in this chapter. Using whatever medium your instructor requests, write a brief analysis (no more than one page) of the résumé's strengths and weaknesses, citing specific elements from the résumé and support from the chapter. If you are analyzing a real résumé, do not include any personally identifiable data, such as the person's name, email address, or phone number, in your report.

### Sharpening Your Career Skills Online

Bovée and Thill's Business Communication Web Search, at http://businesscommunicationblog.com/websearch, is a unique research tool designed specifically for business communication research. Use the Web Search function to find a website, video, PDF document, podcast, or PowerPoint presentation that offers advice on creating an effective résumé. Write a brief email message to your instructor, describing the item you found and summarizing the career skills information you learned from it.

# Cases

## CAREER SKILLS / EMAIL SKILLS

**1. Career Planning: Researching Career Opportunities [LO-1]** Knowing the jargon and "hot button" issues in a particular profession or industry can give you a big advantage when it comes to writing your résumé and participating in job interviews. You can fine-tune your résumé for both human readers and applicant tracking systems, sound more confident and informed in interviews, and present yourself as a professional-class individual with an inquiring mind.

**Your task:** Imagine a specific job category in a company that has an informative, comprehensive website (to facilitate the research you'll need to do). This doesn't have to be a current job opening, but a position that you know exists or is likely to exist in this company, such as a business systems analyst at Apple or a brand manager at Unilever.

Explore the company's website and other online sources to find the following: (1) a brief description of what this job entails, with enough detail that you could describe it to a fellow student; (2) some of the terminology used in the profession or the industry, both formal terms that might serve as keywords on your résumé and informal terms and phrases that insiders are likely to use in publications and conversations; (3) an ongoing online conversation among people in this profession (for example, a LinkedIn Group, a popular industry or professional blog that seems to get quite a few comments, or an industry or professional publication that attracts a lot of comments); and (4) at least one significant issue

that will affect people in this profession or companies in this industry over the next few years (for example, if your chosen profession involves accounting in a publicly traded corporation, upcoming changes in international financial reporting standards would be a significant issue; similarly, for a company in the consumer electronics industry, the recycling and disposal of *e-waste* is an issue). Write a brief email message summarizing your findings and explaining how you could use this information on your résumé and during job interviews.

## CAREER SKILLS / EMAIL SKILLS

**2. Career Management: Researching Career Opportunities [LO-1]** Perhaps you won't be able to land your ultimate dream job right out of college, but that doesn't mean you shouldn't start planning right now to make that dream come true.

**Your task:** Using online job search tools, find a job that sounds just about perfect for you, even if you're not yet qualified for it. It might even be something that would take 10 or 20 years to reach. Don't settle for something that's not quite right—find a job that is so "you" and so exciting that you would jump out of bed every morning, eager to go to work (such jobs really do exist!). Start with the job description you found online and then supplement it with additional research so that you get a good picture of what this job and career path are all about. Compile a list of all the qualifications you would need in order to have a reasonable chance of landing such a job. Now compare this list with your current résumé. Write a brief email message to your instructor that identifies all the areas in which you would need to improve your skills, work experience, education, and other qualifications in order to land your dream job.

## CAREER SKILLS / TEAM SKILLS

**3. Planning a Résumé [LO-2]** If you haven't begun your professional career yet or you are pursuing a career change, the employment history section on your résumé can sometimes be a challenge to write. A brainstorming session with your wise and creative classmates could help.

**Your task:** In a team assigned by your instructor, you will help each other evaluate your employment histories and figure out the best way to present your work backgrounds on a résumé. First, each member of the team should compile his or her work history, including freelance projects and volunteer work if relevant, and share this information with the team. After allowing some time for everyone to review each other's information, meet as a team (in person if you can, or online otherwise). Discuss each person's history, pointing out strong spots and weak spots, and then brainstorm the best way to present each person's employment history.

Note: If there are aspects of your employment history you would rather not share with your teammates, substitute a reasonably similar experience of the same duration.

## CAREER SKILLS / TEAM SKILLS

**4. Writing a Résumé [LO-3]** The introductory statement of a résumé requires some careful thought, both in deciding which of the three types of introductory statement (see page 516) to use and what information to include in it. Getting another person's perspective on this communication challenge can be helpful. In this activity, in fact, someone else is going to write your introductory statement for you, and you will return the favor.

**Your task:** Pair off with a classmate. Provide each other with the basic facts about your qualifications, work history, education, and career objectives. Then meet in person or online for an informal interview, in which you ask each other questions to flesh out the information you have on each other. Assume that each of you has chosen to use a qualifications summary for your résumé. Now write each other's qualifications summary and then trade them for review. As you read what your partner wrote about you, ask yourself if this feels true to what you believe about yourself and your career aspirations. Do you think it introduces you effectively to potential employers? What might you change about it?

## PRESENTATION SKILLS / PORTFOLIO BUILDER

**5. Message Strategies: Completing a Résumé [LO-4]** Creating presentations and other multimedia supplements can be a great way to expand on the brief overview that a résumé provides.

**Your task:** Starting with any version of a résumé that you've created for yourself, create a PowerPoint presentation that expands on your résumé information to give potential employers a more complete picture of what you can contribute. Include samples of your work, testimonials from current or past employers and colleagues, videos of speeches you've made, and anything else that tells the story of the professional "you." If you have a specific job or type of job in mind, focus your presentation on that. Otherwise, present a more general picture that shows why you would be a great employee for any company to consider. Be sure to review the information from Chapter 17 about creating professional-quality presentations.

## CAREER SKILLS / VIDEO SKILLS

**6. Message Strategies: Completing a Résumé [LO-4], Chapter 9** In the right circumstances, brief videos can be an effective complement to a traditional job-search communication package.

**Your task:** Find a job opening that interests you (something you are at least partially qualified for at this stage of your career) and produce a two-minute video profile of yourself, highlighting the skills mentioned in the job description.

## MyBCommLab

Go to **mybcommlab.com** for Auto-graded writing questions as well as the following Assisted-graded writing questions:

18-1. How does a chronological résumé differ from a functional résumé, and when is each appropriate? [LO-2]

18-2. Explain the difference between a qualifications summary and a career summary. [LO-3]

18-3. Mybcommlab Only—comprehensive writing assignment for this chapter.

## Endnotes

**1.** Adapted from *ATK Corporate Profile,* accessed 10 February 2013, www.atk.com; Ed Frauenheim, "Weapons-Maker ATK Practices Personnel Precision," *Workforce Management,* March 2011, 22–23, 26; Ed Frauenheim, "Numbers Game: Companies Utilize Data to Predict Workforce Needs," *Workforce Management,* March 2011, 20–21; OrcaEyes website, accessed 23 March 2011, www.orcaeyes.com.
**2.** Courtland L. Bovée and John V. Thill, *Business in Action,* 5th ed. (Boston: Pearson Prentice Hall, 2011), 241–242.

3. Anne Fisher, "How to Get Hired by a 'Best' Company," *Fortune*, 4 February 2008, 96.

4. Jim Schaper, "Finding Your Future Talent Stars," *BusinessWeek*, 2 July 2010, www.businessweek.com.

5. Eve Tahmincioglu, "Revamping Your Job-Search Strategy," MSNBC .com, 28 February 2010, www.msnbc.com.

6. Jessica Dickler, "The Hidden Job Market," CNNMoney.com, 10 June 2009, http://money.cnn.com.

7. Tara Weiss, "Twitter to Find a Job," *Forbes*, 7 April 2009, www .forbes.com.

8. Miriam Saltpeter, "Using Facebook Groups for Job Hunting," Keppie Careers blog, 13 November 2008, www.keppiecareers.com.

9. Anne Fisher, "Greener Pastures in a New Field," *Fortune*, 26 January 2004, 48.

10. Liz Ryan, "Etiquette for Online Outreach," Yahoo! Hotjobs website, accessed 26 March 2008, http://hotjobs.yahoo.com.

11. Eve Tahmincioglu, "Employers Digging Deep on Prospective Workers," MSNBC.com, 26 October 2009, www.msnbc.com.

12. Career and Employment Services, Danville Area Community College website, accessed 23 March 2008, www.dacc.edu/career; Career Counseling, Sarah Lawrence College website, accessed 23 March 2008, www.slc.edu/occ/index.php; Cheryl L. Noll, "Collaborating with the Career Planning and Placement Center in the Job-Search Project," *Business Communication Quarterly* 58, no. 3 (1995): 53–55.

13. Rachel Emma Silverman, "No More Résumés, Say Some Firms," *Wall Street Journal*, 24 January 2012, http://online.wsj.com.

14. Randall S. Hansen and Katharine Hansen, "What Résumé Format Is Best for You?" QuintCareers.com, accessed 7 August 2010, www .quintcareers.com.

15. Hansen and Hansen, "What Résumé Format Is Best for You?"

16. Katharine Hansen, "Should You Consider a Functional Format for Your Resume?" QuintCareers.com, accessed 7 August 2010, www .quintcareers.com.

17. Kim Isaacs, "Resume Dilemma: Criminal Record," Monster.com, accessed 23 May 2006, www.monster.com; Kim Isaacs, "Resume Dilemma: Employment Gaps and Job-Hopping," Monster.com, accessed 23 May 2006, www.monster.com; Susan Vaughn, "Answer the Hard Questions Before Asked," *Los Angeles Times*, 29 July 2001, W1–W2.

18. John Steven Niznik, "Landing a Job with a Criminal Record," About .com, accessed 12 December 2006, http://jobsearchtech.about.com.

19. "How to Ferret Out Instances of Résumé Padding and Fraud," *Compensation & Benefits for Law Offices*, June 2006, 1+.

20. "Resume Fraud Gets Slicker and Easier," CNN.com, accessed 11 March 2004, www.cnn.com.

21. "Resume Fraud Still Major Problem HR Needs to Address," *HR Focus*, July 2012, 13–15.

22. Cari Tuna and Keith J. Winstein, "Economy Promises to Fuel Résumé Fraud," *Wall Street Journal*, 17 November 2008, http:// online.wsj.com; Lisa Takeuchi Cullen, "Getting Wise to Lies," *Time*, 1 May 2006, 59; "Resume Fraud Gets Slicker and Easier"; Employment Research Services website, accessed 18 March 2004, www.erscheck.com.

23. "How to Ferret Out Instances of Résumé Padding and Fraud."

24. Jacqueline Durett, "Redoing Your Résumé? Leave Off the Lies," *Training*, December 2006, 9; "Employers Turn Their Fire on Untruthful CVs," *Supply Management*, 23 June 2005, 13.

25. Cynthia E. Conn, "Integrating Writing Skills and Ethics Training in Business Communication Pedagogy: A Résumé Case Study Exemplar," *Business Communication Quarterly*, June 2008, 138–151; Marilyn Moats Kennedy, "Don't Get Burned by Résumé Inflation," *Marketing News*, 15 April 2007, 37–38.

26. Rockport Institute, "How to Write a Masterpiece of a Résumé," accessed 24 March 2008, www.rockportinstitute.com.

27. Lora Morsch, "25 Words That Hurt Your Resume," CNN.com, 20 January 2006, www.cnn.com.

28. Liz Ryan, "The Reengineered Résumé," *BusinessWeek*, 3 December 2007, SC12.

29. Vivian Giant, "Using the Right Keywords on Your Resume Will Be Very Important in 2013," Business Insider, 11 December 2012, www .businessinsider.com; Katharine Hansen, "Tapping the Power of Keywords to Enhance Your Resume's Effectiveness," QuintCareers .com, accessed 7 August 2010, www.quintcareers.com.

30. Hansen, "Tapping the Power of Keywords to Enhance Your Resume's Effectiveness."

31. Jolie O'Dell, "LinkedIn Reveals the 10 Most Overused Job-Hunter Buzzwords," Mashable, 14 December 2010, http://mashable.com.

32. Dave Johnson, "10 Resume Errors That Will Land You in the Trash," BNET, 22 February 2010, www.bnet.com; Anthony Balderrama, "Resume Blunders That Will Keep You from Getting Hired," CNN .com, 19 March 2008, www.cnn.com; Michelle Dumas, "5 Resume Writing Myths," Distinctive Documents blog, 17 July 2007, http://blog .distinctiveweb.com; Kim Isaacs, "Resume Dilemma: Recent Graduate," Monster.com, accessed 26 March 2008, http://career-advice.monster .com.

33. Karl L. Smart, "Articulating Skills in the Job Search," *Business Communication Quarterly* 67, no. 2 (June 2004): 198–205.

34. "When to Include Personal Data," ResumeEdge.com, accessed 25 March 2008, www.resumeedge.com.

35. Eve Tahmincioglu, "Looking for a Job in 2011? Here's How to Stand Out," MSNBC.com, 3 January 2011, http://today.msnbc.com.

36. "Résumé Length: What It Should Be and Why It Matters to Recruiters," *HR Focus*, June 2007, 9.

37. Rachel Zupek, "Seven Exceptions to Job Search Rules," CNN.com, 3 September 2008, www.cnn.com.

38. John Hazard, "Resume Tips: No Pictures, Please and No PDFs," Career-Line.com, 26 May 2009, www.career-line.com; "25 Things You Should Never Include on a Resume," HR World website, 18 December 2007, www.hrworld.com.

39. John Sullivan, "Résumés: Paper, Please," *Workforce Management*, 22 October 2007, 50; "Video Résumés Offer Both Pros and Cons During Recruiting," *HR Focus*, July 2007, 8.

40. Jobs page, Zappos website, accessed 24 March 2011, http://about .zappos.com/jobs.

41. Rachel Louise Ensign, "Is the Paper Résumé Dead?" *Wall Street Journal*, 24 January 2012, http://online.wsj.com.

42. Nancy M. Schullery, Linda Ickes, and Stephen E. Schullery, "Employer Preferences for Résumés and Cover Letters," *Business Communication Quarterly*, June 2009, 163–176.

43. Vivian Giang, "Now You Know Exactly What Recruiters Are Looking at on Your Resume," Business Insider, 12 December 2012, www.businessinsider.com.

44. VisualCV website, accessed 11 February 2013, www.visualcv.com.

45. Elizabeth Garone, "Five Mistakes Online Job Hunters Make," *Wall Street Journal*, 28 July 2010, http://online.wsj.com.

46. "10 Reasons Why You Are Not Getting Any Interviews," *Miami Times*, 7–13 November 2007, 6D.

47. Deborah Silver, "Niche Sites Gain Monster-Sized Following," *Workforce Management*, March 2011, 10–11.

48. "Protect Yourself From Identity Theft When Hunting for a Job Online," *Office Pro*, May 2007, 6.

## LEARNING OBJECTIVES

After studying this chapter, you will be able to

**1** Explain the purposes of application letters and describe how to apply the AIDA organizational approach to them.

**2** Describe the typical sequence of job interviews, the major types of interviews, and what employers look for during an interview.

**3** List six tasks you need to complete to prepare for a successful job interview.

**4** Explain how to succeed in all three stages of an interview.

**5** Identify the most common employment messages that follow an interview and explain when you would use each one.

### MyBCommLab®

⭐ **Improve Your Grade!** Over 10 million students improved their results using the Pearson MyLabs. Visit **mybcommlab.com** for simulations, tutorials, and end-of-chapter problems.

When a company communicates its core values with the help of a cartoon amphibian named Core Values Frog, you can guess the company doesn't quite fit the stuffy corporate stereotype. While it is passionately serious about customer satisfaction and employee engagement, the Las Vegas–based online shoe and clothing retailer Zappos doesn't take itself too seriously. In fact, one of the 10 values the frog promotes is "Create fun and a little weirdness."

Fun and a little weirdness can make a workplace more enjoyable, but CEO Tony Hsieh's commitment to employees runs much deeper than that. The company makes frequent reference to "the Zappos Family," and it embraces the ideals of taking care of one another and enjoying time spent together. These activities can range from parades in the workplace and other goofy events

Zappos CEO Tony Hsieh makes sure the company's interviewing process finds the candidates who are compatible with an offbeat customer- and colleague-focused culture.

Brad Swonetz/Redux.

to the Wishez program, in which employees can ask one another to fulfill personal wishes, from lighthearted desires such as getting backstage access at concerts to serious matters such as getting help during tough financial times.

To find employees who will thrive in and protect the unconventional Zappos culture, the company takes an unorthodox path when it comes to recruiting and interviewing. For example, in stark contrast to the companies that refuse to look at videos as part of job application packages, Zappos encourages applicants to send videos of themselves and even provides an upload facility on its website's application page.

The interviewing process is designed to find passionate, free-thinking candidates who fit the culture, from the offbeat antics to the serious commitment to customers and fellow employees. Some of the questions interviewees can expect to encounter include "What was the best mistake you made on the job?" and "On a scale of 1 to 10, how weird are you?"

Speaking of offbeat interviews, the company recently screened software engineering candidates using 30-minute coding challenges, in which the first programmer to solve the problem was "fast-tracked to Vegas" for the next round of interviews. Coding contests are not all that unusual for recruiting programmers, but it's unlikely that many feature an open bar, as the Zappos competition did.

A strong customer- and employee-focused culture, a strong commitment to maintaining that culture, and a recruiting strategy that finds the right people for that culture—this relentless focus on doing business the Zappos way keeps paying off. The company continues to grow and to be ranked as one of the best places to work in the United States.[1]

# Submitting Your Résumé

Whether you plan to apply to Zappos (profiled in the chapter-opening Communication Close-Up) or to any other company, your résumé in some form will usually be the centerpiece of your job-search package. However, it needs support from several other employment messages before, during, and after the interview process. These messages can include application letters, job-inquiry letters, application forms, and follow-up notes.

**1** LEARNING OBJECTIVE
Explain the purposes of application letters and describe how to apply the AIDA organizational approach to them.

## WRITING APPLICATION LETTERS

Whenever you mail, email, hand-deliver, or upload your résumé, you should include an **application letter**, also known as a *cover letter*, to let readers know what you're sending, why you're sending it, and how they can benefit from reading it. (Although this message is not usually a printed document anymore, many professionals still refer to it as a letter.) Take the same care with your application letter that you took with your résumé. A poorly written application letter can prompt employers to skip over your résumé, even if you are a good fit for a job.[2] Staffing specialist Abby Kohut calls the application letter "a writing-skills evaluation in disguise" and emphasizes that even a single error can get you bounced from contention.[3]

The best approach for an application letter depends on whether you are sending a **solicited application letter** to apply for an identified job opening or are *prospecting* with an **unsolicited application letter**—taking the initiative to write to companies even though they haven't announced a job opening that is right for you.[4] In many ways, the difference between the two is like the difference between solicited and unsolicited proposals (see page 397). Figure 19.1 on the next page shows an application message written in response to a posted job opening. The writer knows exactly what qualifications the organization is seeking and can "echo" those attributes back in his message.

Prospecting is more challenging because you don't have the clear target you have with a solicited message. You will need to do more research to identify the qualities the company would probably seek for the position you hope to occupy (see Figure 19.2 on page 539). Also, search for news items that involve the company, its customers, the profession, or the individual manager to whom you are writing. Using this information in your application letter helps you establish common ground with your reader—and it shows that you are tuned in to what is going on in the industry.

For either type of letter, follow these tips to be more effective:[5]

- Resist the temptation to stand out with gimmicky application letters; impress with knowledge and professionalism instead.
- If the name of an individual manager is at all findable, address your letter to that person, rather than something generic such as "Dear Hiring Manager." Search LinkedIn, the

Always accompany your résumé with an application letter (printed or email) that motivates the recipient to read the résumé.

As with proposals, the best approach for an application letter depends on whether your application is solicited or unsolicited.

| Position | | | Supply Chain Pricing Analyst | | Apply |
| --- | --- | --- | --- | --- | --- |
| Position code | T23-6678 | Location | Tacoma, WA | Status | Full-time |

Sea-Air Global Transport has an immediate opening for a supply chain pricing analyst in our Tacoma, WA, headquarters. This challenging position requires excellent communication skills in a variety of media, a polished customer service presence both in person and over the phone, and proven aptitude in statistical analysis and business mathematics.

The minimum educational requirement for this position is a bachelors degree or equivalent, preferably in business, statistical methods, or applied mathematics. Experience in customer service is highly desirable, and experience in transportation or logistics is a major plus.

Click here to learn more about Sea-Air or click here to explore the attractive compensation and benefits packages we offer all employees.

*Smith's application letter echoes the language of the job posting.*

27225 Eucalyptus Avenue
Long Beach, CA 90806
March 13, 2014

Sea-Air Global Transport
5467 Port of Tacoma Rd., Suite 230
Tacoma, WA 98421

Dear Hiring Manager:

Sea-Air Global Transport consistently appeared as a top transportation firm in the research I did for my senior project in global supply chain management, so imagine my delight when I discovered the opening for an export pricing analyst in your Tacoma headquarters (Position Code: T23-6678). With a major in business and a minor in statistical methods, my education has been ideal preparation for the challenges of this position.

In fact, my senior project demonstrates most of the skills listed in your job description, including written communication skills, analytical abilities, and math aptitude. I enjoyed the opportunity to put my math skills to the test as part of the statistical comparison of various freight modes.

As you can see from my résumé, I also have more than three years of part-time experience working with customers in both retail and commercial settings. This experience taught me the importance of customer service, and I want to start my professional career with a company that truly values the customer. In reviewing your website and reading several articles on Lloyd's List and other trade websites, I am impressed by Sea-Air's constant attention to customer service in this highly competitive industry.

My verbal communication skills would be best demonstrated in an interview, of course. I would be happy to meet with a representative of your company at their earliest convenience. I can be reached at dalton.k.smith@gmail.com or by phone at (562) 555-3737.

Sincerely,

Dalton Smith

*The first sentence grabs attention by indicating knowledge of the company and its industry.*

*The reference to his résumé emphasizes his customer service orientation and also shows he has done his homework by researching the company.*

*The letter doesn't include a handwritten signature because it was uploaded to a website along with his résumé.*

*The opening paragraph identifies the specific job for which he is applying.*

*In this discussion of his skills, he echoes the qualifications stated in the job posting.*

*In the close, he politely asks for an interview in a way that emphasizes yet another job-related skill.*

**Figure 19.1** **Solicited Application Message**
In this response to an online job posting, Dalton Smith highlights his qualifications while mirroring the requirements specified in the posting. Following the AIDA model, he grabs attention immediately by letting the reader know he is familiar with the company and the global transportation business.

company's website, industry directories, Twitter, and anything else you can think of to locate an appropriate name. Ask the people in your network if they know a name. If another applicant finds a name and you don't, you're at a disadvantage.
- Clearly identify the opportunity you are applying for or expressing interest in.
- Show that you understand the company and its marketplace.
- Never volunteer salary history or requirements unless an employer has asked for this information.

457 Mountain View Rd.
Clear Lake, IA 50428
June 16, 2014

Ms. Patricia Downing, Store Manager
Walmart
840 South Oak
Iowa Falls, IA 50126

Dear Ms. Downing:

Do you have any openings for people who want to move into store management? I am really looking for an opportunity to get a job like yours, even if it takes starting at a low level and working my way up.

Allow me to list some highlights from my enclosed résumé. First, I have a BA degree in retailing, which included such key courses as retailing, marketing, management, and business information systems. Second, I have worked as a clerk and as an assistant manager in a large department store. Third, I have experience in the customer-facing aspect of retailing, as well as operations, marketing, and personnel supervision.

Successful retailing is about more than systems and procedures. It is also about anticipating customer needs, fostering positive relationships with the community, and delivering the type of service that keeps customers coming back. Retailers that fail in any of these areas are doomed to decline in today's hypercompetitive sales environment. I am the sort of forward-thinking, customer-focused leader who can help you avoid this fate.

I will call you next Wednesday at 2:00 to explain why I would make a great addition to your team.

Sincerely,

Glenda Johns
Enclosure

The writer commits three major mistakes in the first paragraph: asking a question that she could answer herself by visiting the company's website, failing to demonstrate any knowledge of the company, and making the message all about her.

This paragraph merely repeats information from the enclosed résumé, which wastes the reader's time and wastes the opportunity for the writer to present a more complete picture of herself.

Johns attempts to show that she understands retailing, but this paragraph comes across as an arrogant lecture. The tone is particularly inappropriate, given that she is writing to the store's top manager.

The call to action is overly aggressive, and it presumes that the reader will be available and willing to take a phone call from a complete stranger about a job opening that might not even exist.

---

457 Mountain View Rd.
Clear Lake, IA 50428
June 16, 2014

Ms. Patricia Downing, Store Manager
Walmart
840 South Oak
Iowa Falls, IA 50126

Dear Ms. Downing:

Even with its world-class supply chain, admired brand name, and competitive prices, Walmart obviously would not be the success it is without enthusiastic, service-driven associates and managers. If you have or foresee an opening for such a professional, someone eager to learn the Walmart way and eventually move into a management position, please consider me for the opportunity.

As an associate or management trainee, I can bring a passion for retailing and the perspective I've gained through academic preparation and four years of experience. (Please refer to my enclosed résumé for more information.)

Working as a clerk and then as an assistant manager in a large department store taught me how to anticipate customer needs, create effective merchandising, and deliver service that keeps customers coming back. Moreover, my recent BA degree in retailing, which encompassed such courses as retailing concepts, marketing fundamentals, management, and business information systems, prepared me with in-depth awareness of contemporary retailing issues and strategies.

I understand Walmart prefers to promote its managers from within, and I would be pleased to start out with an entry-level position until I gain the necessary experience. Could we have a brief conversation about the possibilities of joining your team? I am available by phone at 641-747-2222 or email at glendajohns@mailnet.com.

Sincerely,

Glenda Johns

Glenda Johns
Enclosure

Johns gets the reader's attention by demonstrating good awareness of the company and the type of people it hires, presents herself as just such a professional, and then asks to be considered for any relevant job openings.

Johns uses the body of her letter to expand on the information presented in her résumé, rather than simply repeating that information.

The close builds the reader's interest by demonstrating knowledge of the company's policy regarding promotion.

The call to action is respectful, and it makes a response easy for the reader by providing both phone and email contact information.

---

**Figure 19.2  Unsolicited Application Letter**
Demonstrating knowledge of the employer's needs and presenting your qualifications accordingly are essential steps in an unsolicited application letter.

- Keep it short—no more than three paragraphs. Keep in mind that all you are trying to do at this point is move the conversation forward one step.
- Show some personality, while maintaining a business-appropriate tone. The letter gives you the opportunity to balance the facts-only tone of your résumé.
- Project confidence without being arrogant.

Because application letters are persuasive messages, the AIDA approach you learned in Chapter 12 is ideal, as the following sections explain.

### Getting Attention

*The opening paragraph of your application letter needs to clearly convey the reason you're writing and give the recipient a compelling reason to keep reading.*

The opening paragraph of your application letter must accomplish two important tasks: (1) clearly stating your reason for writing and (2) giving the recipient a reason to keep reading. Why would a recruiter want to keep reading your letter instead of the hundred others piling up on his or her desk? Because you show some immediate potential for meeting the company's needs. You've researched the company and the position, and you know something about the industry and its current challenges. Consider this opening:

> With the recent slowdown in corporate purchasing, I can certainly appreciate the challenge of new fleet sales in this business environment. With my high energy level and 16 months of new-car sales experience, I believe I can produce the results you listed as vital in the job posting on your website.

This applicant does a smooth job of mirroring the company's stated needs while highlighting his personal qualifications, along with evidence that he understands the broader market. He balances his relative lack of experience with enthusiasm and knowledge of the industry. Table 19.1 highlights some ways you can spark interest and grab attention in your opening paragraph. All these openings demonstrate the "you" attitude, and many indicate how the applicant can benefit the employer.

### TABLE 19.1 | Tips for Getting Attention in Application Letters

| Tip | Example |
| --- | --- |
| **Unsolicited Application Letters** | |
| Show how your strongest skills will benefit the organization. | If you need a regional sales specialist who consistently meets sales targets while fostering strong customer relationships, please consider my qualifications. |
| Describe your understanding of the job's requirements and show how well your qualifications fit them. | Your annual report stated that improving manufacturing efficiency is one of the company's top priorities for next year. Through my postgraduate research in systems engineering and consulting work for several companies in the industry, I've developed reliable methods for quickly identifying ways to cut production time while reducing resource use. |
| Mention the name of a person known to and highly regarded by the reader. | When Janice McHugh of your franchise sales division spoke to our business communication class last week, she said you often need promising new marketing graduates at this time of year. |
| Refer to publicized company activities, achievements, changes, or new procedures. | Today's issue of the *Detroit News* reports that you may need the expertise of computer programmers versed in robotics when your Lansing tire plant automates this spring. |
| Use a question to demonstrate your understanding of the organization's needs. | Can your fast-growing market research division use an interviewer with two years of field survey experience, a B.A. in public relations, and a real desire to succeed? If so, please consider me for the position. |
| Use a catchphrase opening if the job requires ingenuity and imagination. | *Haut monde*—whether referring to French, Italian, or Arab clients, it still means "high society." As an interior designer for your Beverly Hills showroom, not only could I serve and sell to your distinguished clientele, but I could do it in all these languages. I speak, read, and write them fluently. |
| **Solicited Application Letters** | |
| Identify where you discovered the job opening; describe what you have to offer. | Your job posting on Monster.com for a cruise-line social director caught my eye. My eight years of experience as a social director in the travel industry would allow me to serve your new Caribbean cruise division well. |

## Building Interest and Increasing Desire

The middle section of your application letter presents your strongest selling points in terms of their potential benefit to the organization, thereby building interest in you and creating a desire to interview you. As with the opening, the more specific you can be in the middle section, the better. And back up your assertions with some convincing evidence of your ability to perform:

Use the middle section of your application letter to expand on your opening and present a more complete picture of your strengths.

> **Poor:** I completed three college courses in business and managerial communication, earning an A in each course, and have worked for the past year at Imperial Construction.
> **Improved:** Using the skills gained from three semesters of college training in business and managerial communication, I developed a collection system for Imperial Construction that reduced annual bad-debt losses by 25 percent. By emphasizing a win–win scenario for the company and its clients with incentives for on-time payment, the system was also credited with improving customer satisfaction.

In a solicited letter, be sure to discuss each major requirement listed in the job posting. If you are deficient in any of these requirements, stress other solid selling points to help strengthen your overall presentation. Don't restrict your message to just core job duties, either. Also highlight personal characteristics that apply to the targeted position, such as your ability to work hard or handle responsibility:

> While attending college full time, I worked part-time during the school year and up to 60 hours a week each summer in order to be totally self-supporting while in college. I can offer your organization the same level of effort and perseverance.

Mention your salary requirements at this stage only if the organization has asked you to state them. If you don't know the salary that's appropriate for the position and someone with your qualifications, you can find typical salary ranges at the Bureau of Labor Statistics website, www.bls.gov, or a number of commercial websites. If you do state a target salary, tie it to the value you offer:

Don't bring up salary in your application letter unless the recipient has asked you to include your salary requirements.

> For the past two years, I have been helping a company similar to yours organize its database marketing efforts. I would therefore like to receive a salary in the same range (the mid-60s) for helping your company set up a more efficient customer database.

Toward the end of this section, refer the reader to your résumé by citing a specific fact or general point covered there:

> As you can see in the attached résumé, I've been working part time with a local publisher since my sophomore year. During that time, I've used client interactions as an opportunity to build strong customer service skills.

## Motivating Action

The final paragraph of your application letter has two important functions: to ask the reader for a specific action (usually an interview) and to facilitate a reply. Offer to come to the employer's office at a convenient time or, if the firm is some distance away, to meet with its

In the final paragraph of your application letter, respectfully ask for specific action and make it easy for the reader to respond.

nearest representative or arrange a telephone or Skype interview. Include your email address and phone number, as well as the best times to reach you:

> After you have reviewed my qualifications, could we discuss the possibility of putting my marketing skills to work for your company? I am available at (360) 555-7845 from 2 PM to 10 PM Monday to Friday or by email at john.wagner462@gmail.com.

**REAL-TIME UPDATES**

LEARN MORE BY VISITING THIS INTERACTIVE WEBSITE

**How much are you worth?**

Find real-life salary ranges for a wide range of jobs. Go to http://real-timeupdates.com/bct12 and click on Learn More. If you are using MyBCommLab, you can access Real-Time Updates within each chapter or under Student Study Tools.

After editing and proofreading your application letter, give it a final quality check by referring to "Checklist: Writing Application Letters." Then send it along with your résumé promptly, especially if you are responding to an advertisement or online job posting.

## FOLLOWING UP AFTER SUBMITTING A RÉSUMÉ

Deciding if, when, and how to follow up after submitting your résumé and application letter is one of the trickiest parts of a job search. First and foremost, keep in mind that employers continue to evaluate your communication efforts and professionalism during this phase, so don't say or do anything to leave a negative impression. Second, adhere to whatever instructions the employer has provided. If a job posting says "no calls," for example, don't call. Third, if the job posting lists a *close date*, don't call or write before then, because the company is still collecting applications and will not have made a decision about inviting people for interviews. Wait a week or so after the close date. If no close date is given and you have no other information to suggest a timeline, you can generally contact the company starting a week or two after submitting your résumé.[6] Keep in mind that a single instance of poor etiquette or clumsy communication can undo all your hard work in a job search, so maintain your professional behavior every step of the way.

Think creatively about a follow-up message; show that you've continued to add to your skills or that you've learned more about the company or the industry.

When you follow up by email or telephone, you can share an additional piece of information that links your qualifications to the position (keep an eye out for late-breaking news about the company, too) and ask a question about the hiring process as a way to gather some information about your status. Good questions to ask include:[7]

- Has a hiring decision been made yet?
- Can you tell me what to expect next in terms of the hiring process?
- What is the company's timeframe for filling this position?
- Could I follow up in another week if you haven't had the chance to contact me yet?
- Can I provide any additional information regarding my qualifications for the position?

---

**CHECKLIST** ✔ Writing Application Letters

- Take the same care with your application letter that you took with your résumé.
- If you are *prospecting* using an unsolicited message, do deep research to identify the qualities the company likely wants.
- For solicited messages in response to a posted job opening, word your message in a way that echoes the qualifications listed in the posting.
- Open the letter by capturing the reader's attention in a businesslike way.
- Use specific language to clearly state your interests and objectives.

- Build interest and desire in your potential contribution by presenting your key qualifications for the job.
- Link your education, experience, and personal qualities to the job requirements.
- Outline salary requirements only if the organization has requested that you provide them.
- Request an interview at a time and place that is convenient for the reader.
- Make it easy to comply with your request by providing your complete contact information and good times to reach you.
- Adapt your style for cultural variations, if required.

Whatever the circumstances, a follow-up message can demonstrate that you're sincerely interested in working for the organization, persistent in pursuing your goals, and committed to upgrading your skills.

If you don't land a job at your dream company on the first attempt, don't give up. You can apply again if a new opening appears, or you can send an updated résumé with a new unsolicited application letter that describes how you have gained additional experience, taken a relevant course, or otherwise improved your skill set. Many leading employers take note of applicants who came close but didn't quite make it and may extend offers when positions open up in the future.[8]

# Understanding the Interviewing Process

An **employment interview** is a meeting during which both you and the prospective employer ask questions and exchange information. The employer's objective is to find the best talent to fill available job openings, and your objective is to find the right match for your goals and capabilities.

As you get ready to begin interviewing, keep two vital points in mind. First, recognize that the process takes time. Start your preparation and research early; the best job offers usually go to the best-prepared candidates. Second, don't limit your options by looking at only a few companies. By exploring a wide range of firms and positions, you might uncover great opportunities you would not have found otherwise. You'll increase the odds of getting more job offers, too.

**2 LEARNING OBJECTIVE**
Describe the typical sequence of job interviews, the major types of interviews, and what employers look for during an interview.

Start preparing early for your interviews—and be sure to consider a wide range of options.

## THE TYPICAL SEQUENCE OF INTERVIEWS

Most employers interview an applicant multiple times before deciding to make a job offer. At the most selective companies, you might have a dozen or more individual interviews across several stages.[9] Depending on the company and the position, the process may stretch out over many weeks, or it may be completed in a matter of days.[10]

Employers start with the *screening stage*, in which they filter out applicants who are unqualified or otherwise not a good fit for the position. Screening can take place on your school's campus, at company offices, via telephone (including Skype or another Internet-based phone service), or through a computer-based screening system. Time is limited in screening interviews, so keep your answers short while providing a few key points that differentiate you from other candidates. If your screening interview will take place by phone, try to schedule it for a time when you can be focused and free from interruptions.[11]

The next stage of interviews, the *selection stage*, helps the organization identify the top candidates from all those who qualify. During these interviews, show keen interest in the job, relate your skills and experience to the organization's needs, listen attentively, and ask insightful questions that show you've done your research.

If the interviewers agree you're a good candidate, you may receive a job offer, either on the spot or a few days later by phone, mail, or email. In other instances, you may be invited back for a final evaluation, often by a higher-ranking executive. The objective of the *final stage* is often to sell you on the advantages of joining the organization.

During the screening stage of interviews, use the limited time available to confirm your fit for the position.

During the selection stage, continue to show how your skills and attributes can help the company.

During the final stage, the interviewer may try to sell you on working for the firm.

## COMMON TYPES OF INTERVIEWS

Employers can use a variety of interviewing methods throughout the interviewing process, and you need to recognize the different types and be prepared for each one. These methods can be distinguished by the way they are structured, the number of people involved, and the purpose of the interview.

### Structured versus Unstructured Interviews

In a **structured interview**, the interviewer (or a computer program) asks a series of questions in a predetermined order. Structured interviews help employers identify candidates who don't meet basic job criteria, and they make it easier for the interview team to compare answers from multiple candidates.[12]

A structured interview follows a set sequence of questions, allowing the interview team to compare answers from all candidates.

In an open-ended interview, the interviewer adapts the line of questioning based on your responses and questions.

In contrast, in an **open-ended interview**, the interviewer adapts his or her line of questioning based on the answers you give and any questions you ask. Even though it may feel like a conversation, remember that it's still an interview, so keep your answers focused and professional.

## Panel and Group Interviews

In a panel interview, you meet with several interviewers at once; in a group interview, you and several other candidates meet with one or more interviewers at once.

Although one-on-one interviews are the most common format, some employers use panel or group interviews as well. In a **panel interview**, you meet with several interviewers at once.[13] Try to make a connection with each person on the panel and keep in mind that each person has a different perspective, so tailor your responses accordingly.[14] For example, an upper-level manager is likely to be interested in your overall business sense and strategic perspective, whereas a potential colleague might be more interested in your technical skills and ability to work in a team.

In a **group interview**, one or more interviewers meet with several candidates simultaneously. A key purpose of a group interview is to observe how the candidates interact with potential peers.[15] Group interviews can be tricky, because you want to stand out while coming across as a supportive team player. Be sure to treat your fellow candidates with respect, while looking for opportunities to demonstrate the depth of knowledge you have about the company and its needs.

## Behavioral, Situational, Working, and Stress Interviews

In a behavioral interview, you are asked to describe how you handled situations from your past.

Interviewing techniques also vary based on the types of questions you are asked. Perhaps the most common type of interview these days is the **behavioral interview**, in which you are asked to relate specific incidents and experiences from your past.[16] Generic interview questions can often be answered with "canned" responses, but behavioral questions require candidates to use their own experiences and attributes to craft answers. Studies show that behavioral interviewing is a much better predictor of success on the job than traditional interview questions.[17] To prepare for a behavioral interview, review your work or college experiences to recall several instances in which you demonstrated an important job-related attribute or dealt with a challenge such as uncooperative team members or heavy workloads. Get ready with responses that quickly summarize the situation, the actions you took, and the outcome of those actions.[18]

In situational interviews, you're asked to explain how you would handle various hypothetical situations.

A **situational interview** is similar to a behavioral interview except that the questions focus on how you would handle various hypothetical situations on the job. The situations will likely relate to the job you're applying for, so the more you know about the position, the better prepared you'll be.

In a working interview, you perform actual work-related tasks.

A **working interview** is the most realistic type of interview: You actually perform a job-related activity during the interview. You may be asked to lead a brainstorming session, solve a business problem, engage in role playing, or even make a presentation.[19]

Stress interviews help recruiters see how you handle yourself under pressure.

The most unnerving type of interview is the **stress interview**, during which you might be asked questions designed to unsettle you, or you might be subjected to long periods of silence, criticism, interruptions, or even hostile reactions by the interviewer. The theory behind this approach is that you'll reveal how well you handle stressful situations, although some experts find the technique of dubious value.[20] If you find yourself in a stress interview, recognize what is happening and collect your thoughts for a few seconds before you respond.

You might encounter multiple types of interview questions within a single interview, so stay alert and try to understand the type of question you're facing before you answer each one.

## INTERVIEW MEDIA

Expect to use a variety of media when you interview, from in-person conversations to virtual meetings.

Expect to be interviewed through a variety of media. Employers trying to cut travel costs and the demands on staff time now interview candidates via telephone, email, instant messaging, virtual online systems, and videoconferencing, in addition to traditional face-to-face meetings.

Treat a telephone interview as seriously as you would an in-person interview.

To succeed at a telephone interview, make sure you treat it as seriously as an in-person interview. Be prepared with a copy of all the materials you have sent to the employer, including your résumé and any correspondence. In addition, prepare some note cards with key message points you'd like to make and questions you'd like to ask. If possible, arrange to speak on a landline so you don't have to worry about mobile phone reception problems. And remember that you won't be able to use a pleasant smile, a firm handshake, and other nonverbal signals to create a good impression. A positive, alert tone of voice is therefore vital.[21]

Email and IM are also sometimes used in the screening stage. Although you have almost no opportunity to send and receive nonverbal signals with these formats, you do have the major advantage of being able to review and edit each response before you send it. Maintain a professional style in your responses, and be sure to ask questions that demonstrate your knowledge of the company and the position.[22]

Many employers use video technology for both live and recorded interviews. For instance, Zappos often uses video interviews on Skype to select the top two or three finalists for each position and then invites those candidates for in-person interviews.[23] With recorded video interviews, an online system asks a set of questions and records the respondent's answers. Recruiters then watch the videos as part of the screening process.[24] Prepare for a video interview as you would for an in-person interview—including dressing and grooming—and take the extra steps needed to become familiar with the equipment and the process. If you're interviewing from home, arrange your space so that the webcam doesn't pick up anything distracting or embarrassing in the background. During any video interview, remember to sit up straight and focus on the camera.

Online interviews can range from simple structured questionnaires and tests to sophisticated job simulations that are similar to working interviews (see Figure 19.3). These simulations help identify good candidates, give applicants an idea of what the job is like, and reduce the risk of employment discrimination lawsuits because they closely mimic actual job skills.[25]

> **REAL-TIME UPDATES**
> **LEARN MORE BY WATCHING THIS VIDEO**
> **Video interviewing on Skype**
>
> Chances are you'll have at least one video interview using Skype or another Internet-based phone service. Watch this video for essential tips on preparing and participating in an online video interview. Go to http://real-timeupdates.com/bct12 and click on Learn More. If you are using MyBCommLab, you can access Real-Time Updates within each chapter or under Student Study Tools.

*When interviewing via email or IM, be sure to take a moment to review your responses before sending them.*

*In a video interview, speak to the camera as though you are addressing the interviewer in person.*

*Computer-based virtual interviews range from simple structured interviews to realistic job simulations to meetings in virtual worlds.*

## WHAT EMPLOYERS LOOK FOR IN AN INTERVIEW

Interviews give employers the chance to go beyond the basic data of your résumé to get to know you and to answer two essential questions. The first is whether you can handle the responsibilities of the position. Naturally, the more you know about the demands of the

*Suitability for a specific job is judged on the basis of such factors as*
- *Academic preparation*
- *Work experience*
- *Job-related personality traits*

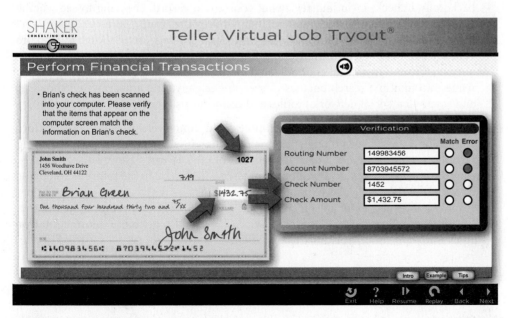

**Figure 19.3  Job Task Simulations**
Computer-based job simulations are an increasingly popular approach to testing job-related skills.
*Source:* Copyright © 2012 by Shaker Consulting Group. Reprinted with permission.

position, and the more you've thought about how your skills match those demands, the better you'll be able to respond.

The second essential question is whether you will be a good fit with the organization and the target position. All good employers want people who are confident, dedicated, positive, curious, courteous, ethical, and willing to commit to something larger than their own individual goals. Companies also look for fit with their individual cultures. Just like people, companies have different personalities. Some are intense; others are more laid back. Some emphasize teamwork; others expect employees to forge their own way and even to compete with one another. Expectations also vary from job to job within a company and from industry to industry. An outgoing personality is essential for sales but less so for research, for instance.

> Compatibility with an organizational culture and a position is judged on such factors as personal background, attitudes, and communication style.

## PREEMPLOYMENT TESTING AND BACKGROUND CHECKS

In an effort to improve the predictability of the selection process, many employers now conduct a variety of preemployment evaluations and investigations. Here are types of assessments you are likely to encounter during your job search:[26]

> Preemployment tests attempt to provide objective, quantitative information about a candidate's skills, attitudes, and habits.

- **Integrity tests.** Integrity tests attempt to measure how truthful and trustworthy a candidate is likely to be.
- **Personality tests.** Personality tests are designed to gauge such aspects as attitudes toward work, interests, managerial potential, dependability, commitment, and motivation.
- **Cognitive tests.** Cognitive tests measure a variety of attributes involved in acquiring, processing, analyzing, using, and remembering information. Typical tests involve reading comprehension, mathematics, problem solving, and decision making.
- **Language proficiency tests.** You may be asked to take a reading or writing test.
- **Job knowledge and job skills tests.** These assessments measure the knowledge and skills required to succeed in a particular position. An accounting candidate, for example, might be tested on accounting principles and legal matters (knowledge) and asked to create a simple balance sheet or income statement (skills).
- **Substance tests.** A majority of companies perform some level of drug and alcohol testing. Many employers believe such testing is necessary to maintain workplace safety, ensure productivity, and protect companies from lawsuits, but others view it as an invasion of employee privacy.
- **Background checks.** In addition to testing, most companies conduct some sort of background check, including reviewing your credit record, checking to see whether you have a criminal history, and verifying your education. Moreover, you should assume that every employer will conduct a general online search on you. To help prevent a background check from tripping you up, verify that your college transcripts are current, look for any mistakes or outdated information in your credit record, plug your name into multiple search engines to see whether anything embarrassing shows up, and scour your social network profiles and connections for potential problems.

Preemployment assessments are a complex and controversial aspect of workforce recruiting. For instance, even though personality testing is widely used, some research suggests that current tests are not a reliable predictor of job success.[27] However, expect to see more innovation in this area and greater use of testing in general in the future as companies try to reduce the risks and costs of poor hiring decisions.

If you're concerned about any preemployment test, ask the employer for more information or ask your college career center for advice. You can also get more information from the Equal Employment Opportunity Commission, at www.eeoc.gov.

# Preparing for a Job Interview

**3** **LEARNING OBJECTIVE**
List six tasks you need to complete to prepare for a successful job interview.

Now that you're armed with insights into the interviewing and assessment process, you're ready to begin preparing for your interviews. Preparation will help you feel more confident and perform better under pressure, and preparation starts with learning about the organization.

## LEARNING ABOUT THE ORGANIZATION AND YOUR INTERVIEWERS

Today's employers expect serious candidates to demonstrate an understanding of the company's operations, its markets, and its strategic and tactical challenges.[28] You've already done some initial research to identify companies of interest, but when you're invited to interview, it's time to dig a little deeper (see Table 19.2). Making this effort demonstrates your interest in the company, and it identifies you as a business professional who knows the importance of investigation and analysis.

Interviewers expect you to know some basic information about the company and its industry.

In addition to learning about the company and the job opening, learn as much as you can about the managers who will be interviewing you, if you can get their names. Search LinkedIn in particular; many professionals have profiles on the popular business networking site. Think about ways to use whatever information you find during your interview. For example, if an interviewer lists membership in a particular professional organization, you might ask whether the organization is a good forum for people to learn about vital issues in the profession or industry. This question gives the interviewer an opportunity to talk about his or her own interests and experiences for a moment, which builds rapport and might reveal vital insights into the career path you are considering. Just make sure your questions are sincere and not uncomfortably personal.

## THINKING AHEAD ABOUT QUESTIONS

Planning ahead for the interviewer's questions will help you handle them more confidently and successfully. In addition, you will want to prepare insightful questions of your own.

### TABLE 19.2  Investigating an Organization and a Job Opportunity

**Where to Look and What You Can Learn**

- *Company website, blogs, and social media accounts:* Overall information about the company, including key executives, products and services, locations and divisions, employee benefits, job descriptions
- *Competitors' websites, blogs, and social media accounts:* Similar information from competitors, including the strengths these companies claim to have
- *Industry-related websites and blogs:* Objective analysis and criticism of the company, its products, its reputation, and its management
- *Marketing materials (print and online):* The company's marketing strategy and customer communication style
- *Company publications (print and online):* Key events, stories about employees, new products
- *Your social network contacts:* Names and job titles of potential contacts within a company
- *Periodicals (newspapers and trade journals, both print and online):* In-depth stories about the company and its strategies, products, successes, and failures; you may find profiles of top executives
- *Career center at your college:* Often provides a wide array of information about companies that hire graduates
- *Current and former employees:* Insights into the work environment

**Points to Learn About the Organization**

- Full name
- Location (headquarters and divisions, branches, subsidiaries, or other units)
- Ownership (public or private; whether it is owned by another company)
- Brief history
- Products and services
- Industry position (whether the company is a leader or a minor player; whether it is an innovator or more of a follower)
- Key financial points (such as stock price and trends, if a public company)
- Growth prospects (whether the company is investing in its future through research and development; whether it is in a thriving industry)

**Points to Learn About the Position**

- Title
- Functions and responsibilities
- Qualifications and expectations
- Possible career paths
- Salary range
- Travel expectations and opportunities
- Relocation expectations and opportunities

## Planning for the Employer's Questions

Many general interview questions are "stock" queries you can expect to hear again and again during your interviews. Get ready to face these five at the very least:

You can expect to face a number of common questions in your interviews, so be sure to prepare for them.

- **What is the hardest decision you've ever had to make?** Be prepared with a good example (that isn't too personal), explaining why the decision was difficult, how you made the choice you made, and what you learned from the experience.
- **What is your greatest weakness?** This question seems to be a favorite of some interviewers, although it probably rarely yields useful information. One good strategy is to mention a skill or attribute you haven't had the opportunity to develop yet but would like to in your next position.[29] Another option is to discuss a past shortcoming you took steps to correct.
- **Where do you want to be five years from now?** This question tests (1) whether you're merely using this job as a stopover until something better comes along and (2) whether you've given thought to your long-term goals. Your answer should reflect your desire to contribute to the employer's long-term goals, not just your own goals. Whether this question often yields useful information is also a matter of debate, but be prepared to answer it.[30]
- **What didn't you like about previous jobs you've held?** Answer this one carefully: The interviewer is trying to predict whether you'll be an unhappy or difficult employee.[31] Describe something that you didn't like in a way that puts you in a positive light, such as having limited opportunities to apply your skills or education. Avoid making negative comments about former employers or colleagues.
- **Tell me something about yourself.** One good strategy is to *briefly* share the "story of you" (see page 505), quickly summarizing where you have been and where you would like to go—in a way that aligns your interests with the company's. Alternatively, you can focus on a specific skill you know is valuable to the company, share something business-relevant that you are passionate about, or offer a short summary of what colleagues or customers think about you.[32] Whatever tactic you choose, this is not the time to be shy or indecisive, so be ready with a confident, memorable answer.

Continue your preparation by planning a brief answer to each question in Table 19.3.

**TABLE 19.3    *Twenty-Five Common Interview Questions***

**Questions about College**

1. What courses in college did you like most? Least? Why?
2. Do you think your extracurricular activities in college were worth the time you spent on them? Why or why not?
3. When did you choose your college major? Did you ever change your major? If so, why?
4. Do you feel you did the best scholastic work you are capable of?
5. How has your college education prepared you for this position?

**Questions about Employers and Jobs**

6. Why did you leave your last job?
7. Why did you apply for this job opening?
8. Why did you choose your particular field of work?
9. What are the disadvantages of your chosen field?
10. What do you know about our company?
11. What do you think about how this industry operates today?
12. Why do you think you would like this particular type of job?

**Questions about Work Experiences and Expectations**

13. What was your biggest failure?
14. Describe an experience in which you learned from one of your mistakes.

15. What motivates you? Why?
16. What do you think determines a person's progress in a good organization?
17. Are you a leader or a follower?
18. What have you done that shows initiative and willingness to work?
19. Why should I hire you?

**Questions about Work Habits**

20. Do you prefer working with others or by yourself?
21. What type of boss do you prefer?
22. Have you ever had any difficulty getting along with colleagues or supervisors? With instructors? With other students?
23. What would you do if you were given an unrealistic deadline for a task or project?
24. How do you feel about overtime work?
25. How do you handle stress or pressure on the job?

*Sources:* Adapted from Alison Green, "The 10 Most Common Job Interview Questions," *U.S. News & World Report*, 24 January 2011, http://money.usnews.com; "Most Common Interview Questions," Glassdoor blog, 29 December 2011, www.glassdoor.com; *The Northwestern Endicott Report* (Evanston, Ill.: Northwestern University Placement Center).

As you prepare answers, look for ways to frame your responses as brief stories (again, 30 to 90 seconds) rather than simple declarative answers.[33] Cohesive stories tend to stick in the listener's mind more effectively than disconnected facts and statements.

> Look for ways to frame your responses as brief stories rather than as dry facts or statements.

## Planning Questions of Your Own

Remember that an interview is a two-way conversation: The questions you ask are just as important as the answers you provide. By asking insightful questions, you can demonstrate your understanding of the organization, steer the discussion into areas that allow you to present your qualifications to best advantage, and verify whether this is a good opportunity. Plus, interviewers expect you to ask questions and tend to look negatively on candidates who don't have any questions to ask. For a list of good questions you might use as a starting point, see Table 19.4.

> Preparing questions of your own helps you understand the company and the position, and it sends an important signal that you are truly interested.

## BOLSTERING YOUR CONFIDENCE

Interviewing is stressful for everyone, so some nervousness is natural. However, you can take steps to feel more confident. Start by reminding yourself that you have value to offer the employer, and the employer already thinks highly enough of you to invite you to an interview.

> The best way to build your confidence is to prepare thoroughly and address shortcomings as best you can. In other words, take action.

If some aspect of your appearance or background makes you uneasy, correct it if possible or offset it by emphasizing positive traits such as warmth, wit, intelligence, or charm. Instead of dwelling on your weaknesses, focus on your strengths. Instead of worrying about how you will perform in the interview, focus on how you can help the organization succeed. As with public speaking, the more prepared you are, the more confident you'll be.

### TABLE 19.4   Ten Questions to Consider Asking an Interviewer

| Question | Reason for Asking |
|---|---|
| 1. What are the job's major responsibilities? | A vague answer could mean that the responsibilities have not been clearly defined, which is almost guaranteed to cause frustration if you take the job. |
| 2. What qualities do you want in the person who fills this position? | This will help you go beyond the job description to understand what the company really wants. |
| 3. How do you measure success for someone in this position? | A vague or incomplete answer could mean that the expectations you will face are unrealistic or ill defined. |
| 4. What is the first problem that needs the attention of the person you hire? | Not only will this help you prepare, but it can signal whether you're about to jump into a problematic situation. |
| 5. Would relocation be required now or in the future? | If you're not willing to move often or at all, you need to know those expectations now. |
| 6. Why is this job now vacant? | If the previous employee got promoted, that's a good sign. If the person quit, that might not be such a good sign. |
| 7. What makes your organization different from others in the industry? | The answer will help you assess whether the company has a clear strategy to succeed in its industry and whether top managers communicate this to lower-level employees. |
| 8. How would you define your organization's managerial philosophy? | You want to know whether the managerial philosophy is consistent with your own working values. |
| 9. What is a typical workday like for you? | The interviewer's response can give you clues about daily life at the company. |
| 10. What are the next steps in the selection process? What's the best way to follow up with you? | Knowing where the company is in the hiring process will give you clues about following up after the interview and possibly give you hints about where you stand. |

*Sources:* Adapted from Heather Huhman, "5 Must-Ask Questions at Job Interviews," Glassdoor blog, 7 February 2012, www.glassdoor.com; Joe Conklin, "Turning the Tables: Six Questions to Ask Your Interviewer," *Quality Progress*, November 2007, 55; Andrea N. Browne, "Keeping the Momentum at the Interview; Ask Questions, Do Your Research, and Be a Team Player," *Washington Post*, 29 July 2007, K1.

## POLISHING YOUR INTERVIEW STYLE

Staging mock interviews with a friend is one good way to hone your style.

Competence and confidence are the foundation of your interviewing style, and you can enhance them by giving the interviewer an impression of poise, good manners, and good judgment. You can develop an adept style by staging mock interviews with a friend or using an interview simulator. Record these mock interviews so you can evaluate yourself. Your college's career center may have computer-based systems for practicing interviews as well (see Figure 19.4).

Evaluate the length and clarity of your answers, your nonverbal behavior, and the quality of your voice.

After each practice session, look for opportunities to improve. Have your mock interview partner critique your performance or critique yourself if you're able to record your practice interviews, using the list of warning signs shown in Table 19.5. Pay close attention to the length of your planned answers as well. Interviewers want you to give complete answers, but they don't want you to take up valuable time or test their patience by chatting about minor or irrelevant details.[34]

In addition to reviewing your answers, evaluate your nonverbal behavior, including your posture, eye contact, facial expressions, and hand gestures and movements. Do you come across as alert and upbeat or passive and withdrawn? Pay close attention to your speaking voice as well. If you tend to speak in a monotone, for instance, practice speaking in a livelier style, with more inflection and emphasis. And watch out for "filler words" such as *uh* and *um*. Many people start sentences with a filler without being conscious of doing so. Train yourself to pause silently for a moment instead as you gather your thoughts and plan what to say.

**REAL-TIME UPDATES**

LEARN MORE BY READING THIS INFOGRAPHIC

### Get a quick reminder of the key steps in preparing for an interview

Use these tips to refresh your memory before an interview. Go to http://real-timeupdates.com/bct12 and click on Learn More. If you are using MyBCommLab, you can access Real-Time Updates within each chapter or under Student Study Tools.

**Figure 19.4  Interview Simulators**
Experts advise you to practice your interview skills as much as possible. You can use a friend or classmate as a practice partner, or you might be able to use one of the interview simulators now available, such as this system from Perfect Interview. Ask at your career center, or search online for "practice interviews" or "interview simulators."
*Source:* Copyright © 2012 by Perfect Interview, LLC. Reprinted with permission.

## COMMUNICATING ACROSS CULTURES

# Successfully Interviewing Across Borders

Interviewing for a job in another country can be one of the most exciting steps in your career. To succeed, you need to pay close attention to the important elements of the interviewing process, including personal appearance, an awareness of what interviewers are really trying to learn about you, and what you should learn about the organization you're hoping to join.

Some countries and cultures place a much higher importance on dress and personal grooming than many employees in the United States are accustomed to; moreover, expectations of personal appearance can vary dramatically from country to country. Ask people who've been to the country before and observe local businesspeople when you arrive. Many people interpret inappropriate dress as more than a simple fashion mistake; they view it as an inability or unwillingness to understand another culture.

Whether or not these things should matter isn't the issue; they do matter, and successful job candidates learn how to respond to different expectations. For instance, business image consultant Ashley Rothschild points out that you could get away with wearing a boldly colored suit in Italy but probably not in Japan. Business professionals tend to dress formally in Italy, but as a worldwide fashion leader, the country has a broad definition of what is appropriate business attire.

Smart recruiters always analyze both nonverbal signals and verbal messages to judge whether an applicant truly has the qualities necessary for a job. In international employment situations, you'll probably be under even closer scrutiny.

Recruiters abroad will want to know if you really have what it takes to succeed in unfamiliar social settings, how your family will handle the transition, and whether you can adapt your personal work style and habits enough to blend in with the hiring organization.

Remember to ask plenty of questions and do your research, both before and after the interview. Some employees view overseas postings as grand adventures, only to collide headfirst with the reality of what it's like to live and work in a completely different culture. For instance, if you've grown accustomed to the independent work style you enjoy in your current job or in school, could you handle a more structured work environment with a hierarchical chain of command? Make sure to get a sense of the culture both within the company and within its social community before you commit to a job in another country.

### CAREER APPLICATIONS

1. Explain how you could find out what is appropriate dress for a job interview in South Africa.
2. Would it be appropriate to ask an interviewer to describe the culture in his or her country? Explain your answer.

*Sources:* Adapted from Jean-Marc Hachey, "Interviewing for an International Job," excerpt from *The Canadian Guide to Working and Living Overseas*, 3rd ed., accessed 23 February 2004, www.workingoverseas.com; Rebecca Falkoff, "Dress to Impress the World: International Business Fashion," Monster.com, accessed 23 February 2004, www.monster.com; Mary Ellen Slater, "Navigating the Details of Landing an Overseas Job," *Washington Post*, 11 November 2002, E4.

---

**TABLE 19.5 | Warning Signs: 25 Attributes Interviewers Don't Like to See**

1. Poor personal appearance
2. Overbearing, overaggressive, or conceited demeanor; a "superiority complex"; a know-it-all attitude
3. Inability to express ideas clearly; poor voice, diction, or grammar
4. Lack of knowledge or experience
5. Poor preparation for the interview
6. Lack of interest in the job
7. Lack of planning for career; lack of purpose or goals
8. Lack of enthusiasm; passive and indifferent demeanor
9. Lack of confidence and poise; appearance of being nervous and ill at ease
10. Insufficient evidence of achievement
11. Failure to participate in extracurricular activities
12. Overemphasis on money; interest only in the best offer
13. Poor scholastic record
14. Unwillingness to start at the bottom; expecting too much too soon
15. Tendency to make excuses
16. Evasive answers; hedging on unfavorable factors in record
17. Lack of tact
18. Lack of maturity
19. Lack of courtesy and common sense, including answering mobile phones, texting, or chewing gum during the interview
20. Being critical of past or present employers
21. Lack of social skills
22. Marked dislike for schoolwork
23. Lack of vitality
24. Failure to look interviewer in the eye
25. Limp, weak handshake

*Sources:* Adapted from Donna Fuscaldo, "Seven Deadly Interview Sins," Glassdoor blog, 4 April 2012, www.glassdoor.com; "Employers Reveal Outrageous and Common Mistakes Candidates Made in Job Interviews, According to New CareerBuilder Survey," CareerBuilder.com, 12 January 2011, www.careerbuilder.com; *The Northwestern Endicott Report* (Evanston, Ill.: Northwestern University Placement Center).

## PRESENTING A PROFESSIONAL IMAGE

Clothing and grooming are important elements of preparation because they reveal something about a candidate's personality, professionalism, and ability to sense the unspoken "rules" of a situation. Inappropriate dress is a common criticism leveled at interviewees, so stand out by looking professional.[35] Your research into various companies, industries, and professions should give you insight into expectations for business attire. If you're not sure what to wear and the company hasn't provided any guidance, refer to Table 2.4 on page 50 for tips on selecting appropriate business attire or ask someone who works in the same industry. And don't be afraid to call the company for advice.

You don't need to spend a fortune on interview clothes, but your clothes must be clean, pressed, and appropriate (see Figure 19.5). The following conservative look will serve you well in most business interview situations:[36]

- Neat, "adult" hairstyle
- For more formal environments, a conservative business suit (for women, that means no exposed midriffs, short skirts, or plunging necklines) in a dark solid color or a subtle pattern such as pinstripes
- For less formal environments, smart-looking "business casual," including a pressed shirt or blouse and nice slacks or a skirt.
- Limited jewelry (men, especially, should wear very little jewelry)
- No visible piercings other than one or two earrings (for women only)
- No visible tattoos
- Stylish but professional-looking shoes (no extreme high heels or casual shoes)
- Clean hands and nicely trimmed fingernails
- Little or no perfume or cologne (some people are allergic, and many people are put off by strong smells)
- Subtle makeup (for women)
- Exemplary personal hygiene

Remember, an interview is not the place to express your individuality or to let your inner rebel run wild. Send a clear

**Dress conservatively and be well groomed for every interview.**

**If you want to be taken seriously, dress and act seriously.**

**REAL-TIME UPDATES**

LEARN MORE BY VISITING THIS INTERACTIVE WEBSITE

**Prepare for your next interview with these Pinterest pins**

The Pinterest pinboard maintained by St. Edward's University offers dozens of helpful resources. Go to http://real-timeupdates.com/bct12 and click on Learn More. If you are using MyBCommLab, you can access Real-Time Updates within each chapter or under Student Study Tools.

**Figure 19.5  Professional Appearance for Job Interviews**
Make a positive first impression with careful grooming and attire. You don't need to spend a fortune on new clothes, but you do need to look clean, prepared, and professional.
*Source: Ariel Skelley/Alamy.*

signal that you understand the business world and know how to adapt to it. You won't be taken seriously otherwise.

## BEING READY WHEN YOU ARRIVE

When you go to your interview, take a small notebook, a pen, a list of the questions you want to ask, several copies of your résumé (protected in a folder), an outline of what you have learned about the organization, and any past correspondence about the position. You may also want to take a small calendar, a transcript of your college grades, a list of references, and a portfolio containing samples of your work, performance reviews, and certificates of achievement.[37] Think carefully if you plan to use a tablet computer or any other device for note taking or reference during an interview. You don't want to waste any of the interviewer's time fumbling with it. Also, turn off your mobile phone; in a recent survey of hiring professionals, answering calls or texting while in an interview was identified as the most common mistake job candidates make during their interviews.[38]

> Be ready to go the minute you arrive at the interviewing site; don't fumble around for your résumé or your list of questions.

Be sure you know when and where the interview will be held. The worst way to start an interview is to be late, and arriving in a stressed-out state isn't much better. Check the route you will take, but don't rely on time estimates from a bus or subway service or from an online mapping service. If you're not familiar with the route, the safest choice is to travel to the location a few days before the interview, if possible, to verify it for yourself. Leave yourself plenty of time for unforeseen problems.

If you have to wait for the interviewer, use this time to review the key messages about yourself you want to get across in the interview. Conduct yourself professionally while waiting. Show respect for everyone you encounter, and avoid chewing gum, eating, or drinking. Anything you do or say at this stage may get back to the interviewer, so make sure your best qualities show from the moment you enter the premises. To review the steps for planning a successful interview, see "Checklist: Planning for a Successful Job Interview."

# Interviewing for Success

At this point, you have a good sense of the overall process and know how to prepare for your interviews. The next step is to get familiar with the three stages that occur in some form in all interviews: the warm-up, the question-and-answer session, and the close.

> **4  LEARNING OBJECTIVE**
> Explain how to succeed in all three stages of an interview.

## THE WARM-UP

Of the three stages, the warm-up is the most important, even though it may account for only a small fraction of the time you spend in the interview. Studies suggest that many

> The first minute of the interview is crucial, so stay alert and be on your best business behavior.

---

### CHECKLIST ✔ Planning for a Successful Job Interview

- Learn about the organization, including its operations, markets, and challenges.
- Learn as much as you can about the people who will be interviewing you, if you can find their names.
- Plan for the employer's questions, including questions about tough decisions you've made, your perceived shortcomings, what you didn't like about previous jobs, and your career plans.
- Plan questions of your own to find out whether this is really the job and the organization for you and to show that you've done your research.
- Bolster your confidence by removing as many sources of apprehension as you can.

- Polish your interview style by staging mock interviews.
- Present a professional appearance with appropriate dress and grooming.
- Be ready when you arrive and bring along a pen, paper, a list of questions, copies of your résumé, an outline of your research on the company, and any correspondence you've had regarding the position.
- Double-check the location and time of the interview and map out the route beforehand.
- Relax and be flexible; the schedule and interview arrangements may change when you arrive.

**REAL-TIME UPDATES**
LEARN MORE BY LISTENING TO THIS PODCAST

**Expert tips for successful phone interviews**

Recruiting experts offer invaluable advice on nailing a phone interview. Go to http://real-timeupdates.com/bct12 and click on Learn More. If you are using MyBCommLab, you can access Real-Time Updates within each chapter or under Student Study Tools.

interviewers make up their minds within the first 20 seconds of contact with a candidate.[39] Don't let your guard down if it appears that the interviewer wants to engage in what feels like small talk; these exchanges are every bit as important as structured questions.

Body language is crucial at this point. Stand or sit up straight, maintain regular but natural eye contact, and don't fidget. When the interviewer extends a hand, respond with a firm but not overpowering handshake. Repeat the interviewer's name when you're introduced ("It's a pleasure to meet you, Ms. Litton"). Wait until you're asked to be seated or the interviewer has taken a seat. Let the interviewer start the discussion, and be ready to answer one or two substantial questions right away. The following are some common openers:[40]

- Why do you want to work here?
- What do you know about us?
- Tell me a little about yourself.

> Recognize that you could face substantial questions as soon as your interview starts, so make sure you are prepared and ready to go.

## THE QUESTION-AND-ANSWER STAGE

Questions and answers usually consume the greatest part of the interview. Depending on the type of interview, the interviewer will likely ask about your qualifications, discuss some of the points mentioned in your résumé, and ask about how you have handled particular situations in the past or would handle them in the future. You'll also be asking questions of your own.

### Dealing with Questions

> Listen carefully to questions before you answer.

Let the interviewer lead the conversation and never answer a question before he or she has finished asking it. Not only is this type of interruption rude, but the last few words of the question might alter how you respond. As much as possible, avoid one-word yes-or-no answers. Use the opportunity to expand on a positive response or explain a negative response. If you're asked a difficult or offbeat question, pause before responding. Think through the implications of the question. For instance, the recruiter may know you can't answer a question and only wants to know how you'll respond under pressure or whether you can construct a logical approach to solving a problem.

Whenever you're asked if you have any questions, or whenever doing so naturally fits the flow of the conversation, ask a question from the list you've prepared. Probe for what the company is looking for in its new employees so that you can show how you meet the firm's needs. Also try to zero in on any reservations the interviewer might have about you so that you can dispel them.

### Listening to the Interviewer

> Paying attention to both verbal and nonverbal messages can help you turn the question-and-answer stage to your advantage.

Paying attention when the interviewer speaks can be as important as giving good answers or asking good questions. Review the tips on listening offered in Chapter 2. The interviewer's facial expressions, eye movements, gestures, and posture may tell you the real meaning of what is being said. Be especially aware of how your answers are received. Does the interviewer nod in agreement or smile to show approval? If so, you're making progress. If not, you might want to introduce another topic or modify your approach.

### Handling Potentially Discriminatory Questions

> Federal, state, and local laws prohibit employment discrimination based on a variety of factors, and well-trained interviewers know to avoid questions that could be used to discriminate in the hiring process.

A variety of federal, state, and local laws prohibit employment discrimination on the basis of race, ethnicity, gender, age (at least if you're between 40 and 70), marital status, religion, national origin, or disability. Interview questions designed to elicit information on these topics are potentially illegal.[41] Table 19.6 compares some questions that are acceptable for employers to ask with questions that can land an employer in legal trouble if the questions are asked in order to gather information that can be used to discriminate in the hiring decision.[42]

If an interviewer asks a potentially unlawful question, consider your options carefully before you respond. You can answer the question as it was asked, you can ask tactfully

# Make Sure You Don't Talk Yourself Out of a Job

Even well-qualified applicants sometimes talk themselves right out of an opportunity by making avoidable blunders during a job interview. Take care to avoid these all-too-common mistakes:

- **Being defensive.** An interview isn't an interrogation, and the interviewer isn't out to get you. Treat interviews as business conversations, an exchange of information in which both sides have something of value to share. You'll give (and get) better information that way.

- **Failing to ask questions.** Interviewers expect you to ask questions, both during the interview and at its conclusion, when they ask if you have any questions. If you have nothing to ask, you come across as someone who isn't really interested in the job or the company. Prepare a list of questions before every interview.

- **Failing to answer questions—or trying to bluff your way through difficult questions.** If you can't answer a question, don't try to talk your way around it or fake your way through it. Remember that sometimes interviewers ask strange questions just to see how you'll respond. What kind of fish would you like to be? How would you go about nailing jelly to the ceiling? Why are manhole covers round? Some of these questions are designed to test your grace under pressure, whereas others are used to get you to think through a logical answer. (Manhole covers are round because a circle is the only shape that can't fall through an open hole of slightly smaller size, by the way.) Don't act like the question is stupid or refuse to answer it. As Lynne Sarikas, director of the MBA Career Center at Northeastern University, explains, these questions offer an opportunity to "demonstrate quick thinking, poise, creativity, and even a sense of humor."

- **Freezing up.** The human brain seems to have the capacity to just freeze up in stressful situations. An interviewer might have asked you a simple question, or perhaps you are halfway through an intelligent answer, and poof!—all your thoughts disappear and you can't organize words in any logical order. Try to quickly replay the last few seconds of the conversation in your mind to see if you can recapture the conversational thread. If that fails, you're probably better off explaining to the interviewer that your mind has gone blank and asking him or her to repeat the question. Doing so is embarrassing but not as embarrassing as chattering on and on with no idea of what you're saying, hoping you'll stumble back onto the topic.

- **Failing to understand your potential to contribute to the organization.** Interviewers care less about your history than about how you can help their organization in the future. Be sure to understand ahead of time how your skills can help the company meet its challenges.

## CAREER APPLICATIONS

1. What should you do if you suddenly realize that something you said earlier in the interview is incorrect or incomplete? Explain your answer.

2. How would you answer the following question: "How do you respond to colleagues who make you angry?" Explain your answer.

*Sources:* Adapted from "Because You Asked: Interviews Get a Little Strange," ManageSmarter, 25 September 2008, www.managesmarter.com; Thomas Pack, "Good Answers to Job Interview Questions," *Information Today,* January 2004, 35+; John Lees, "Make Them Believe You Are the Best," *The Times* (London), 21 January 2004, 3; "Six Interview Mistakes," Monster.com, accessed 23 February 2004, www.monster.com.

## TABLE 19.6 | Acceptable versus Potentially Discriminatory Interview Questions

| Interviewers May Ask This . . . | But Not This |
| --- | --- |
| What is your name? | What was your maiden name? |
| Are you over 18? | When were you born? |
| Did you graduate from high school? | When did you graduate from high school? |
| [No questions about race are allowed.] | What is your race? |
| Can you perform [specific tasks]? | Do you have physical or mental disabilities? Do you have a drug or alcohol problem? Are you taking any prescription drugs? |
| Would you be able to meet the job's requirement to frequently work weekends? | Would working on weekends conflict with your religion? |
| Do you have the legal right to work in the United States? | What country are you a citizen of? |
| Have you ever been convicted of a felony? | Have you ever been arrested? |
| This job requires that you speak Spanish. Do you? | What language did you speak in your home when you were growing up? |

*Sources:* Adapted from Dave Johnson, "Illegal Job Interview Questions," CBS Money Watch, 27 February 2012, www.cbsnew.com; "5 Illegal Interview Questions and How to Dodge Them," Forbes, 20 April 2012, www.forbes.com; Deanna G. Kucler, "Interview Questions: Legal or Illegal?" Workforce Management, accessed 28 September 2005, www.workforce.com.

Think about how you might respond if you were asked a potentially unlawful question.

whether the question might be prohibited, you can simply refuse to answer it, or you can try to answer "the question behind the question."[43] For example, if an interviewer inappropriately asks whether you are married or have strong family ties in the area, he or she might be trying to figure out if you're willing to travel or relocate—both of which are acceptable questions. Only you can decide which is the right choice based on the situation.

Even if you do answer the question as it was asked, think hard before accepting a job offer from this company if you have alternatives. Was the off-limits question possibly accidental (it happens) and therefore not really a major concern? If you think it was intentional, would you want to work for an organization that condones illegal or discriminatory questions or that doesn't train its employees to avoid them?

If you believe an interviewer's questions to be unreasonable, unrelated to the job, or an attempt to discriminate, you have the option of filing a complaint with the EEOC (www .eeoc.gov) or with the agency in your state that regulates fair employment practices.

**REAL-TIME UPDATES**

LEARN MORE BY WATCHING THIS VIDEO

**Stay calm by pressing your "panic reset button"**

Learn how to reset your emotions if you feel like you're starting to panic in a job interview. Go to http://real-timeupdates.com/bct12 and click on Learn More. If you are using MyBCommLab, you can access Real-Time Updates within each chapter or under Student Study Tools.

## THE CLOSE

Like the warm-up, the end of the interview is more important than its brief duration would indicate. These last few minutes are your final opportunity to emphasize your value to the organization and to correct any misconceptions the interviewer might have. Be aware that many interviews will ask whether you have any more questions at this point, so ask one or two from the list you brought or ask a question related to something that came up during the interview.

### Concluding Gracefully

Conclude an interview with courtesy and enthusiasm.

You can usually tell when the interviewer is trying to conclude the session. He or she may ask whether you have any more questions, check the time, summarize the discussion, or simply tell you that the allotted time for the interview is up. When you get the signal, be sure to thank the interviewer for the opportunity and express your interest in the organization. If you can do so comfortably, try to pin down what will happen next, but don't press for an immediate decision.

If this is your second or third visit to the organization, the interview may end with an offer of employment. If you have other offers or need time to think about this offer, it's perfectly acceptable to thank the interviewer for the offer and ask for some time to consider it. If no job offer is made, the interview team may not have reached a decision yet, but you may tactfully ask when you can expect to know the decision.

### Discussing Salary

Research salary ranges in your job, industry, and geographic region before you try to negotiate salary.

If you receive an offer during the interview, you'll naturally want to discuss salary. However, let the interviewer raise the subject. If asked your salary requirements during the interview or on a job application, you can say that your requirements are open or negotiable or that you would expect a competitive compensation package.[44]

How far you can negotiate depends on several factors, including market demand for your skills, the strength of the job market, the company's compensation policies, the company's financial health, and any other job offers you may be considering. Remember that you're negotiating a business deal, not asking for personal favors, so focus on the unique value you can bring to the job. The more information you have, the stronger your position will be.

Negotiating benefits may be one way to get more value from an employment package.

If salary isn't negotiable, look at the overall compensation and benefits package. You may find flexibility in a signing bonus, profit sharing, retirement benefits, health coverage, vacation time, and other valuable elements.[45]

To review the important tips for successful interviews, see "Checklist: Making a Positive Impression in Job Interviews."

---

**CHECKLIST** ✔ Making a Positive Impression in Job Interviews

**A. Be ready to make a positive impression in the warm-up stage.**
- Be alert from the moment you arrive; even initial small talk is part of the interviewing process.
- Greet the interviewer by name, with a smile and direct eye contact.
- Offer a firm (not crushing) handshake if the interviewer extends a hand.
- Take a seat only after the interviewer invites you to sit or has taken his or her own seat.
- Listen for clues about what the interviewer is trying to get you to reveal about yourself and your qualifications.
- Exhibit positive body language, including standing up straight, walking with purpose, and sitting up straight.

**B. Convey your value to the organization during the question-and-answer stage.**
- Let the interviewer lead the conversation.
- Never answer a question before the interviewer finishes asking it.
- Listen carefully to the interviewer and watch for nonverbal signals.
- Don't limit yourself to simple yes-or-no answers; expand on the answer to show your knowledge of the company (but don't ramble on).
- If you encounter a potentially discriminatory question, decide how you want to respond before you say anything.
- When you have the opportunity, ask questions from the list you've prepared; remember that interviewers expect you to ask questions.

**C. Close on a strong note.**
- Watch and listen for signs that the interview is about to end.
- Quickly evaluate how well you've done and correct any misperceptions the interviewer might have.
- If you receive an offer and aren't ready to decide, it's entirely appropriate to ask for time to think about it.
- Don't bring up salary but be prepared to discuss it if the interviewer raises the subject.
- End with a warm smile and a handshake and thank the interviewer for meeting with you.

## INTERVIEW NOTES

Maintain a notebook or simple database with information about each company, interviewers' answers to your questions, contact information for each interviewer, the status of thank-you notes and other follow-up communication, and upcoming interview appointments. Carefully organized notes will help you decide which company is the right fit for you when it comes time to choose from among the job offers you receive.

*Keeping a careful record of your job interviews is essential.*

For dozens of articles, videos, and other help on interviewing strategies, visit http://real-timeupdates.com/bct12 and click on Chapter 19.

# Following Up After the Interview

Staying in contact with a prospective employer after an interview shows that you really want the job and are determined to get it. Doing so also gives you another chance to demonstrate your communication skills and sense of business etiquette. Following up brings your name to the interviewer's attention once again and reminds him or her that you're actively looking and waiting for the decision.

**5 LEARNING OBJECTIVE** Identify the most common employment messages that follow an interview, and explain when you would use each one.

Any time you hear from a company during the application or interview process, be sure to respond quickly. Companies flooded with résumés may move on to another candidate if they don't hear back from you within 24 hours.[46]

## FOLLOW-UP MESSAGE

Send a follow-up message within two days of the interview, even if you feel you have little chance of getting the job. These messages are often referred to as "thank-you notes," but they give you an important opportunity to go beyond merely expressing your appreciation. You can use the message to reinforce the reasons you are a good choice for the position, modify any answers you gave during the interview if you realize you made a mistake or have

*A follow-up message after an interview is more than a professional courtesy; it's another chance to promote yourself to an employer.*

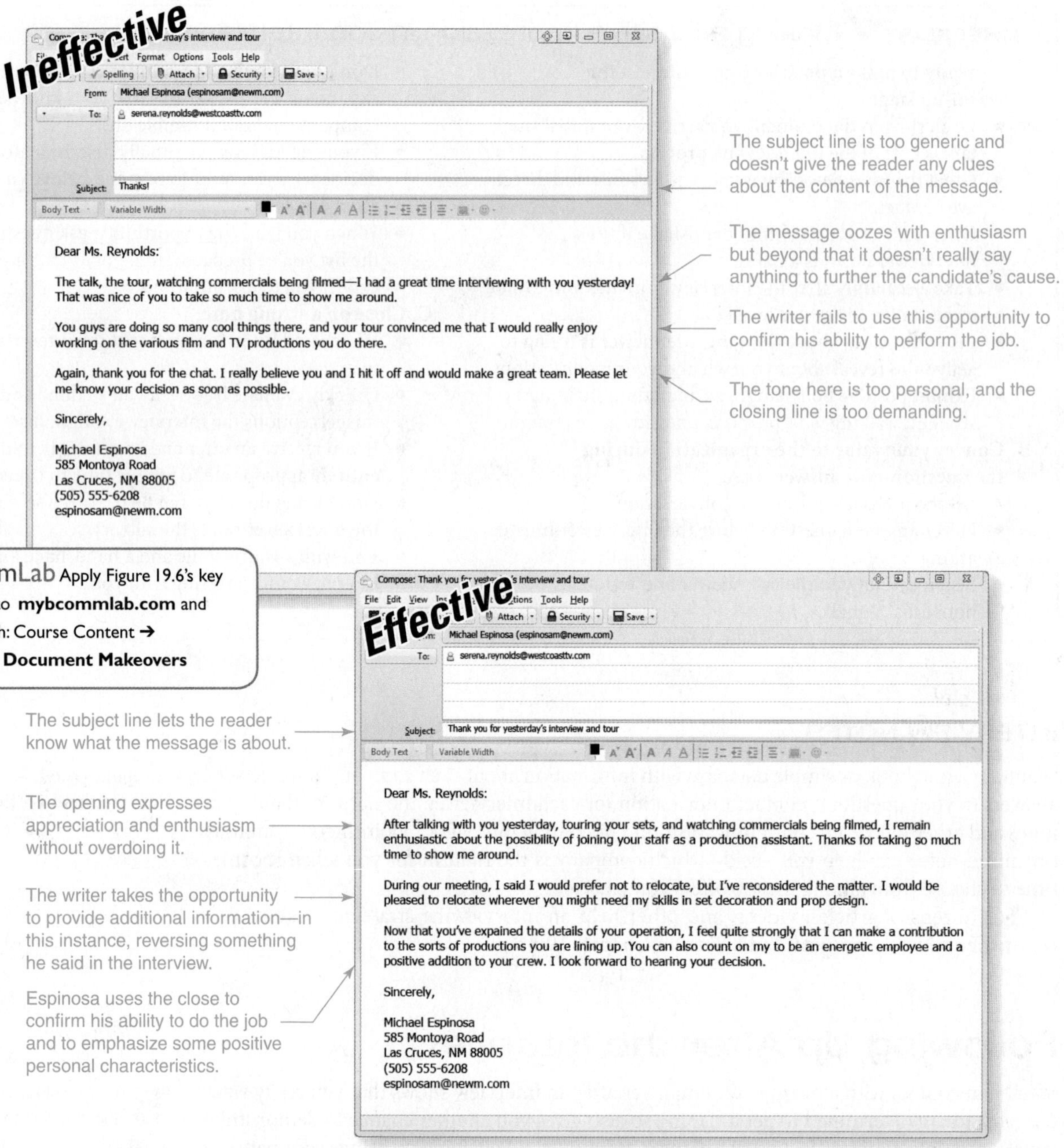

*Ineffective*

The subject line is too generic and doesn't give the reader any clues about the content of the message.

Dear Ms. Reynolds:

The talk, the tour, watching commercials being filmed—I had a great time interviewing with you yesterday! That was nice of you to take so much time to show me around.

The message oozes with enthusiasm but beyond that it doesn't really say anything to further the candidate's cause.

You guys are doing so many cool things there, and your tour convinced me that I would really enjoy working on the various film and TV productions you do there.

The writer fails to use this opportunity to confirm his ability to perform the job.

Again, thank you for the chat. I really believe you and I hit it off and would make a great team. Please let me know your decision as soon as possible.

The tone here is too personal, and the closing line is too demanding.

Sincerely,

Michael Espinosa
585 Montoya Road
Las Cruces, NM 88005
(505) 555-6206
espinosam@newm.com

MyBCommLab Apply Figure 19.6's key concepts. Go to **mybcommlab.com** and follow this path: Course Content → Chapter 19 → **Document Makeovers**

*Effective*

The subject line lets the reader know what the message is about.

Subject: Thank you for yesterday's interview and tour

Dear Ms. Reynolds:

The opening expresses appreciation and enthusiasm without overdoing it.

After talking with you yesterday, touring your sets, and watching commercials being filmed, I remain enthusiastic about the possibility of joining your staff as a production assistant. Thanks for taking so much time to show me around.

The writer takes the opportunity to provide additional information—in this instance, reversing something he said in the interview.

During our meeting, I said I would prefer not to relocate, but I've reconsidered the matter. I would be pleased to relocate wherever you might need my skills in set decoration and prop design.

Espinosa uses the close to confirm his ability to do the job and to emphasize some positive personal characteristics.

Now that you've expained the details of your operation, I feel quite strongly that I can make a contribution to the sorts of productions you are lining up. You can also count on my to be an energetic employee and a positive addition to your crew. I look forward to hearing your decision.

Sincerely,

Michael Espinosa
585 Montoya Road
Las Cruces, NM 88005
(505) 555-6206
espinosam@newm.com

**Figure 19.6** **Follow-Up Message: Ineffective and Effective**
Use the follow-up message after an interview to express continued interest in the opportunity, to correct or expand on any information you provided in the interview, and to thank the interviewer for his or her time.
*Source:* Used with permission from Microsoft.

changed your mind, and respond to any negatives that might have arisen in the interview (see Figure 19.6).[47] Email is usually acceptable for follow-up messages, unless the interviewer has asked you to use other media.

## MESSAGE OF INQUIRY

Use the model for a direct request when you write an inquiry about a hiring decision.

If you're not advised of the interviewer's decision by the promised date or within two weeks, you might make an inquiry. A message of inquiry (which can be handled by email if the interviewer has given you his or her email address) is particularly appropriate if you've received a job offer from a second firm and don't want to accept it before you have an answer from the first. The following message illustrates the general model for a direct request:

When we talked on April 7 about the fashion coordinator position in your Park Avenue showroom, you indicated that a decision would be made by May 1. I am still enthusiastic about the position and eager to know what conclusion you've reached.

→ Identifies the position and introduces the main idea

To complicate matters, another firm has now offered me a position and has asked that I reply within the next two weeks.

→ Places the reason for the request second

Because your company seems to offer a greater challenge, I would appreciate knowing about your decision by Thursday, May 12. If you need more information before then, please let me know.

→ Makes a courteous request for specific action last, while clearly stating a preference for this organization

## REQUEST FOR A TIME EXTENSION

If you receive a job offer while other interviews are still pending, you can ask the employer for a time extension. Open with a strong statement of your continued interest in the job, ask for more time to consider the offer, provide specific reasons for the request, and assure the reader that you will respond by a specific date (see Figure 19.7).

## LETTER OF ACCEPTANCE

When you receive a job offer you want to accept, reply within five days. Begin by accepting the position and expressing thanks. Identify the job you're accepting. In the next paragraph, cover any necessary details. Conclude by saying that you look forward to reporting for work. As always, a positive letter should convey your enthusiasm and eagerness to cooperate:

Use the model for positive messages when you write a letter of acceptance.

I'm delighted to accept the graphic design position in your advertising department at the salary of $2,875 per month.

→ Confirms the specific terms of the offer with a good-news statement at the beginning

Enclosed are the health insurance forms you asked me to complete and sign. I've already given notice to my current employer and will be able to start work on Monday, January 18.

→ Covers miscellaneous details in the body

The prospect of joining your firm is exciting. Thank you for giving me this opportunity, and I look forward to making a positive contribution.

→ Closes with another reference to the good news and a look toward the future

Be aware that a job offer and a written acceptance of that offer can constitute a legally binding contract, for both you and the employer. Before you send an acceptance letter, be sure you want the job.

Written acceptance of a job offer can be considered a legally binding contract.

## LETTER DECLINING A JOB OFFER

After all your interviews, you may find that you need to write a letter declining a job offer. Use the techniques for negative messages (see Chapter 11): Open warmly, state the reasons for refusing the offer, decline the offer explicitly, and close on a pleasant note, expressing gratitude. By taking the time to write a sincere, tactful letter, you leave the door open for future contact:

If you decide to decline a job offer, do so tactfully, using the model for negative messages.

Thank you for your hospitality during my interview at your Durham facility last month. I'm flattered that you would offer me the computer analyst position that we talked about.

→ Uses a buffer in the opening paragraph

I was fortunate to receive two job offers during my search. Because my desire to work abroad can more readily be satisfied by another company, I have accepted that job offer.

→ Precedes the bad news with tactfully phrased reasons for the applicant's unfavorable decision and leaves the door open

I deeply appreciate the time you spent talking with me. Thank you again for your consideration and kindness.

→ Lets the reader down gently with a sincere and cordial ending

**Figure 19.7 Ineffective version (email):**

From: Chang Li (changli46@gmail.com)
To: frank.lapuzo@lonestarfoods.com
Subject: Request for extension

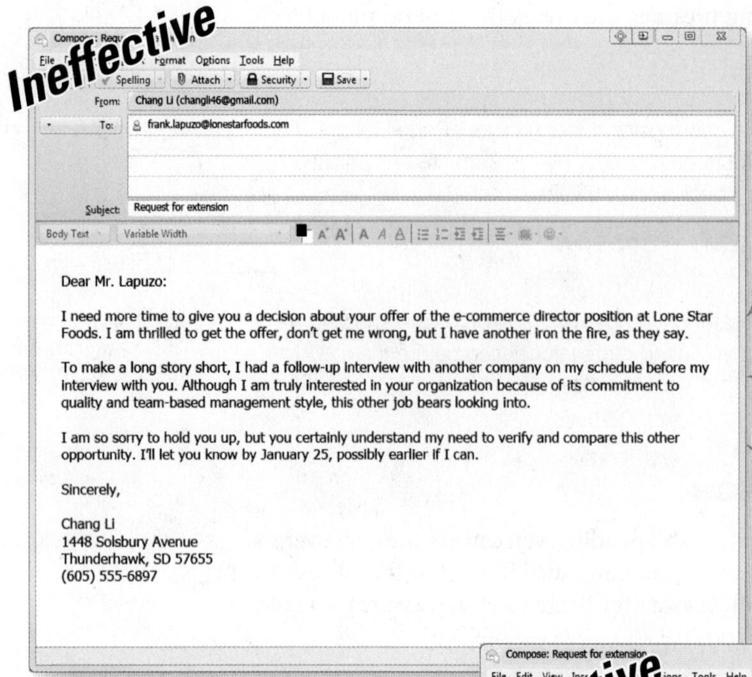

Dear Mr. Lapuzo:

I need more time to give you a decision about your offer of the e-commerce director position at Lone Star Foods. I am thrilled to get the offer, don't get me wrong, but I have another iron in the fire, as they say.

To make a long story short, I had a follow-up interview with another company on my schedule before my interview with you. Although I am truly interested in your organization because of its commitment to quality and team-based management style, this other job bears looking into.

I am so sorry to hold you up, but you certainly understand my need to verify and compare this other opportunity. I'll let you know by January 25, possibly earlier if I can.

Sincerely,

Chang Li
1448 Solsbury Avenue
Thunderhawk, SD 57655
(605) 555-6897

**Annotations (Ineffective):**

"I need" is a blunt and fairly offensive way to start any message, and particularly so when one is asking the reader to make an accommodation.

"To make a long story short" only makes the story longer, and saying "this other job bears looking into" sounds self-centered.

Apologizing isn't necessary under the circumstances, but the writer then commits a serious blunder by failing to ask for the extension to January 25.

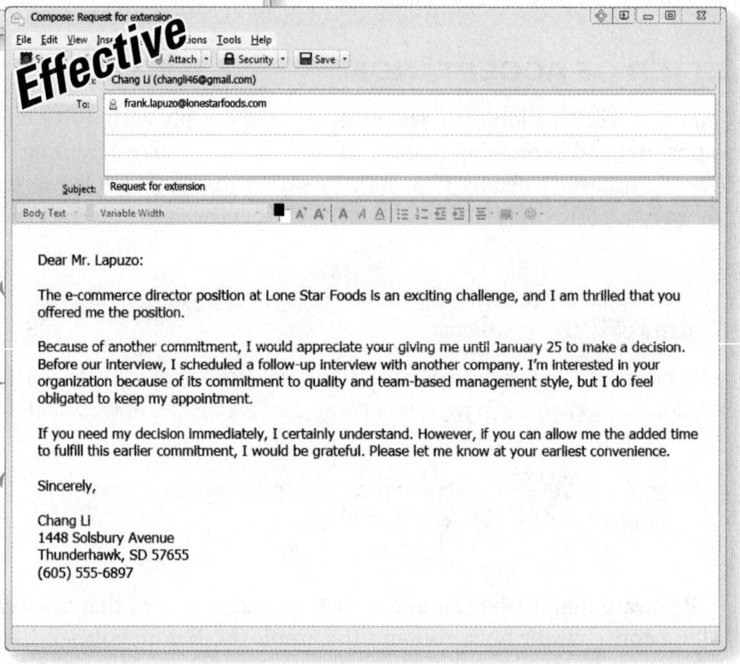

MyBCommLab Apply Figure 19.7's key concepts. Go to **mybcommlab.com** and follow this path: Course Content → Chapter 19 → **Document Makeovers**

**Figure 19.7 Effective version (email):**

Chang Li (changli46@gmail.com)
To: frank.lapuzo@lonestarfoods.com
Subject: Request for extension

Dear Mr. Lapuzo:

The e-commerce director position at Lone Star Foods is an exciting challenge, and I am thrilled that you offered me the position.

Because of another commitment, I would appreciate your giving me until January 25 to make a decision. Before our interview, I scheduled a follow-up interview with another company. I'm interested in your organization because of its commitment to quality and team-based management style, but I do feel obligated to keep my appointment.

If you need my decision immediately, I certainly understand. However, if you can allow me the added time to fulfill this earlier commitment, I would be grateful. Please let me know at your earliest convenience.

Sincerely,

Chang Li
1448 Solsbury Avenue
Thunderhawk, SD 57655
(605) 555-6897

**Annotations (Effective):**

This positive opener confirms the writer's interest in the job and serves as buffer before the upcoming request.

Phrasing this as the need to meet a prior commitment is a graceful way to communicate the idea of wanting to explore the other opportunity, without coming right out and saying so.

The respectful close acknowledges that it might not be possible for the reader to accommodate the request for an extension. The conditional phrasing ("if you can") is a good way to make the request without coming across as demanding.

**Figure 19.7 Request for a Time Extension: Ineffective and Effective**
Needing more time to decide on a job offer is not uncommon, particularly for candidates with desirable credentials. However, make the request in a respectful and subtle way. The reader understands you are comparing opportunities and looking for the best offer, so you don't need to belabor this point.
*Source:* Used with permission from Microsoft.

## LETTER OF RESIGNATION

Letters of resignation should always be written in a gracious and professional style that avoids criticism of your employer or your colleagues.

If you get a job offer and are employed, you can maintain good relations with your current employer by writing a letter of resignation to your immediate supervisor. Follow the approach for negative messages and make the letter sound as positive as possible, regardless of how you feel. Don't take this letter as an opportunity to vent any frustrations you may have. Say something favorable about the organization, the people you work with, or what you've learned on the job. Then state your intention to leave and give the date of your last day on the job. Be sure you give your current employer at least two weeks' notice:

My sincere thanks to you and to all the other Emblem Corporation employees for helping me learn so much about serving the public these past two years. You have given me untold help and encouragement.

You may recall that when you first interviewed me, my goal was to become a customer relations supervisor. Because that opportunity has been offered to me by another organization, I am submitting my resignation. I will miss my friends and colleagues at Emblem, but I want to take advantage of this opportunity.

I would like to terminate my work here two weeks from today (June 13) but can arrange to work an additional week if you want me to train a replacement.

My sincere thanks and best wishes to all of you.

*Uses an appreciative opening to serve as a buffer*

*States reasons before the bad news itself, using tactful phrasing to help keep the relationship friendly, should the writer later want letters of recommendation*

*Discusses necessary details in an extra paragraph*

*Tempers any disappointment with a cordial close*

To verify the content and style of your follow-up messages, consult the tips in "Checklist: Writing Follow-Up Messages."

---

## CHECKLIST ✔ Writing Follow-Up Messages

**A. Thank-you messages**
- Write a brief thank-you letter within two days of the interview.
- Acknowledge the interviewer's time and courtesy.
- Restate the specific job you're applying for.
- Express your enthusiasm about the organization and the job.
- Add any new facts that may help your chances.
- Politely ask for a decision.

**B. Messages of inquiry**
- If you haven't heard from the interviewer by the promised date, write a brief message of inquiry.
- Use the direct approach: main idea, necessary details, specific request.

**C. Requests for a time extension**
- Request an extension if you have pending interviews and need time to decide about an offer.
- Open on a friendly note.
- Explain why you need more time and express continued interest in the company.
- In the close, promise a quick decision if your request is denied and ask for a confirmation if your request is granted.

**D. Letters of acceptance**
- Send this message within five days of receiving the offer.
- State clearly that you accept the offer, identify the job you're accepting, and confirm vital details such as salary and start date.
- Make sure you want the job; an acceptance letter can be treated as a legally binding contract.

**E. Letters declining a job offer**
- Use the indirect approach for negative messages.
- Open on a warm and appreciative note and then explain why you are refusing the offer.
- End on a sincere, positive note.

**F. Letters of resignation**
- Send a letter of resignation to your current employer as soon as possible.
- Begin with an appreciative buffer.
- In the middle section, state your reasons for leaving and actually state that you are resigning.
- Close cordially.

---

## COMMUNICATION CHALLENGES AT **Zappos**

You recently joined the human resources department at Zappos headquarters in Las Vegas. Using what you know about interviewing, address these challenges. To learn more about working at Zappos, you can visit **http://about.zappos.com/jobs**.

**INDIVIDUAL CHALLENGE:** You're looking for experienced customer support specialists who remain calm when things get chaotic and stressful, who are flexible enough to interact with a wide range of personality types, and who are comfortable communicating over the phone, through IM, and on Twitter. With those requirements in mind, create a list of three or four

questions to use during the screening interviews (using Skype video calls) for these candidates.

**TEAM CHALLENGE:** Seven candidates survived the screening process, and now you're planning the on-site interviews. In a small group, discuss the types of people to include on the interview team (consult a management textbook if you're unfamiliar with positions in a typical corporation): Who should serve as host and handle the warm-up stage? Who should be involved in the question-and-answer stage? Who should handle the close? Justify your choices.

# Quick Learning Guide

## SUMMARY OF LEARNING OBJECTIVES

**1 Explain the purposes of application letters, and describe how to apply the AIDA organizational approach to them.** The purposes of an application letter are to introduce your résumé, persuade an employer to read it, and request an interview. With the AIDA model, get attention in the opening paragraph by showing how your work skills could benefit the organization, by explaining how your qualifications fit the job, or by demonstrating an understanding of the organization's needs. Build interest and desire by showing how you can meet the job requirements and, near the end of this section, be sure to refer your reader to your résumé. Finally, motivate action by making your request easy to fulfill and by including all necessary contact information.

**2 Describe the typical sequence of job interviews, the major types of interviews, and what employers look for during an interview.** The typical sequence of interviews involves three stages. During the screening stage, employers filter out unqualified applicants and identify promising candidates. During the selection stage, the pool of applicants is narrowed through a variety of structured and unstructured interviewing methods. In the final stage, employers select the candidates who will receive offers and, if necessary, promote the benefits of joining the company.

Interviews can be distinguished by the way they are structured (structured or unstructured interviews), the number of people involved (one-on-one, panel, or group interviews), and the purpose of the interview (behavioral, situational, working, or stress interviews). The behavioral interview, probably the most common in terms of purpose, requires candidates to use their own experiences and attributes to craft answers. The situational interview is similar, but instead of using incidents from the candidate's past, it explores how the candidate would respond to hypothetical situations in the future.

Employers look for two things during an employment interview. First, they seek evidence that an applicant is qualified for the position. Second, they seek reassurance that an applicant will be a good fit with the "personality" of the organization and the position.

**3 List six tasks you need to complete to prepare for a successful job interview.** To prepare for a successful job interview, (1) complete the research you started when planning your résumé, (2) think ahead about questions you'll need to answer and questions you'll want to ask, (3) bolster your confidence by focusing on your strengths and preparing thoroughly, (4) polish your interviewing style, (5) present a professional image with businesslike clothing and good grooming, and (6) arrive on time and ready to begin.

**4 Explain how to succeed in all three stages of an interview.** All employment interviews have three stages. The warm-up stage is the most important because first impressions greatly influence an interviewer's decision. The question-and-answer stage, during which you will answer and ask questions, is the longest. The close is your final opportunity to promote your value to the organization and counter any misconceptions the interviewer may have.

**5 Identify the most common employment messages that follow an interview, and explain when you would use each one.** Following an interview, send a thank-you message to show appreciation, emphasize your strengths, and politely ask for a decision. Send an inquiry if you haven't received the interviewer's decision by the date promised or within one or two weeks of the interview—especially if you've received a job offer from another firm. You can request a time extension if you need more time to consider an offer. Send a letter of acceptance after receiving a job offer that you want to take. Send a letter declining a job offer when you want to refuse an offer tactfully. Finally, if you are currently employed, send a letter of resignation after you have accepted the offer of another job.

## KEY TERMS

**application letter** Message that accompanies a résumé to let readers know what you're sending, why you're sending it, and how they can benefit from reading it

**behavioral interview** Interview in which you are asked to relate specific incidents and experiences from your past

**employment interview** Formal meeting during which you and an employer ask questions and exchange information

**group interview** Interview in which one or more interviewers meet with several candidates simultaneously

**open-ended interview** Interview in which the interviewer adapts his or her line of questioning based on the answers you give and any questions you ask

**panel interview** Interview in which you meet with several interviewers at once

**situational interview** Similar to a behavioral interview, except the questions focus on how you would handle various hypothetical situations on the job

**solicited application letter** Message sent in response to an announced job opening
**stress interview** Interview in which you might be asked questions designed to unsettle you or subject you to long periods

of silence, criticism, interruptions, and or hostile reactions by the interviewer
**structured interview** Interview in which the interviewer (or a computer) asks a series of prepared questions in a set order

**unsolicited application letter** Message sent to an organization that has not announced an opening
**working interview** Interview in which you perform a job-related activity

CHECKLIST ✓
## Writing Application Letters

- Take the same care with your application letter that you took with your résumé.
- If you are *prospecting* using an unsolicited message, do deep research to identify the qualities the company likely wants.
- For solicited messages in response to a posted job opening, word your message in a way that echoes back the qualifications listed in the posting.
- Open the letter by capturing the reader's attention in a businesslike way.
- Use specific language to clearly state your interests and objectives.
- Build interest and desire in your potential contribution by presenting your key qualifications for the job.
- Link your education, experience, and personal qualities to the job requirements.
- Outline salary requirements only if the organization has requested that you provide them.
- Request an interview at a time and place that is convenient for the reader.
- Make it easy to comply with your request by providing your complete contact information and good times to reach you.
- Adapt your style for cultural variations, if required.

CHECKLIST ✓
## Planning for a Successful Job Interview

- Learn about the organization, including its operations, markets, and challenges.
- Learn as much as you can about the people who will be interviewing you, if you can find their names.
- Plan for the employer's questions, including questions about tough decisions you've made, your perceived shortcomings, what

you didn't like about previous jobs, and your career plans.
- Plan questions of your own to find out whether this is really the job and the organization for you and to show that you've done your research.
- Bolster your confidence by removing as many sources of apprehension as you can.
- Polish your interview style by staging mock interviews.
- Present a professional appearance with appropriate dress and grooming.
- Be ready when you arrive and bring along a pen, paper, a list of questions, copies of your résumé, an outline of your research on the company, and any correspondence you've had regarding the position.
- Double-check the location and time of the interview and map out the route beforehand.
- Relax and be flexible; the schedule and interview arrangements may change when you arrive.

CHECKLIST ✓
## Making a Positive Impression in Job Interviews

A. **Be ready to make a positive impression in the warm-up stage.**
- Be alert from the moment you arrive; even initial small talk is part of the interviewing process.
- Greet the interviewer by name, with a smile and direct eye contact.
- Offer a firm (not crushing) handshake if the interviewer extends a hand.
- Take a seat only after the interviewer invites you to sit or has taken his or her own seat.
- Listen for clues about what the interviewer is trying to get you

to reveal about yourself and your qualifications.
- Exhibit positive body language, including standing up straight, walking with purpose, and sitting up straight.

B. **Convey your value to the organization during the question-and-answer stage.**
- Let the interviewer lead the conversation.
- Never answer a question before the interviewer finishes asking it.
- Listen carefully to the interviewer and watch for nonverbal signals.
- Don't limit yourself to simple yes-or-no answers; expand on the answer to show your knowledge of the company (but don't ramble on).
- If you encounter a potentially discriminatory question, decide how you want to respond before you say anything.
- When you have the opportunity, ask questions from the list you've prepared; remember that interviewers expect you to ask questions.

C. **Close on a strong note.**
- Watch and listen for signs that the interview is about to end.
- Quickly evaluate how well you've done and correct any misperceptions the interviewer might have.
- If you receive an offer and aren't ready to decide, it's entirely appropriate to ask for time to think about it.
- Don't bring up salary but be prepared to discuss it if the interviewer raises the subject.
- End with a warm smile and a handshake and thank the interviewer for meeting with you.

# Test Your Knowledge

To review chapter content related to each question, refer to the indicated Learning Objective.

1. What two message elements can you use when writing a follow-up message after submitting a résumé? [LO-1]
✪ 2. How can you apply the AIDA model to an application letter? [LO-1]
3. How does a structured interview differ from an open-ended interview? [LO-2]
4. Why do many employers now use situational or behavioral interviews? [LO-2]
5. Why are the questions you ask during an interview as important as the answers you give to the interviewer's questions? [LO-3]
✪ 6. How should you respond if an interviewer at a company where you want to work asks you a question that seems too personal or unethical? [LO-4]
✪ 7. What should you say in a thank-you message after an interview? [LO-5]
8. What is the potential legal significance of a letter of acceptance? [LO-5]

# Apply Your Knowledge

To review chapter content related to each question, refer to the indicated Learning Objective.

1. How can you distinguish yourself from other candidates in a screening interview and still keep your responses short and to the point? Explain. [LO-2]
2. How can you prepare for a situational or behavioral interview if you have no experience with the job for which you are interviewing? [LO-2]
3. If you lack one important qualification for a job but have made it past the initial screening stage, how should you prepare to handle this issue during the next round of interviews? Explain your answer. [LO-3]
4. What is an interviewer likely to conclude about you if you don't have any questions to ask during the interview? [LO-3]
✪ 5. What should you do if your mind goes blank after an interviewer asks you a question? [LO-4]

# Practice Your Skills

### Messages for Analysis

Read the following messages and then (1) analyze the strengths or weaknesses of each document and (2) revise each document so that it follows this chapter's guidelines.

### Message 19.A: Writing an Application Letter [LO-1]

I'm writing to let you know about my availability for the brand manager job you advertised. As you can see from my enclosed résumé, my background is perfect for the position. Even though I don't have any real job experience, my grades have been outstanding, considering that I went to a top-ranked business school.

I did many things during my undergraduate years to prepare me for this job:

- Earned a 3.4 out of a 4.0, with a 3.8 in my business courses
- Elected representative to the student governing association
- Selected to receive the Lamar Franklin Award
- Worked to earn a portion of my tuition

I am sending my résumé to all the top firms, but I like yours better than any of the rest. Your reputation is tops in the industry, and I want to be associated with a business that can pridefully say it's the best.

If you wish for me to come in for an interview, I can come on a Friday afternoon or anytime on weekends when I don't have classes. Again, thanks for considering me for your brand manager position.

### Message 19.B: Writing Application Follow-Up Messages [LO-1]

Did you receive my résumé? I sent it to you at least two months ago and haven't heard anything. I know you keep résumés on file, but I just want to be sure that you keep me in mind. I heard you are hiring health-care managers and certainly would like to be considered for one of those positions.

Since I last wrote you, I've worked in a variety of positions that have helped prepare me for management. To wit, I've become lunch manager at the restaurant where I work, which involved a raise in pay. I now manage a waitstaff of 12 girls and take the lunch receipts to the bank every day.

Of course, I'd much rather be working at a real job, and that's why I'm writing again. Is there anything else you would like to know about me or my background? I would really like to know more about your company. Is there any literature you could send me? If so, I would really appreciate it.

I think one reason I haven't been hired yet is that I don't want to leave Atlanta. So I hope when you think of me, it's for a position that wouldn't require moving. Thanks again for considering my application.

### Message 19.C: Thank-You Message [LO-5]

Thank you for the really marvelous opportunity to meet you and your colleagues at Starret Engine Company. I really enjoyed touring your facilities and talking with all the people there. You have quite a crew! Some of the other companies I have visited have been so rigid and uptight that I can't imagine how I would fit in. It's a relief to run into a group of people who seem to enjoy their work as much as all of you do.

I know that you must be looking at many other candidates for this job, and I know that some of them will probably be more experienced than I am. But I do want to emphasize that my two-year hitch in the Navy involved a good deal of engineering work. I don't think I mentioned all my shipboard responsibilities during the interview.

Please give me a call within the next week to let me know your decision. You can usually find me at my dormitory in the evening after dinner (phone: 877-9080).

## Message 19.D: Letter of Inquiry [LO-5]

I have recently received a very attractive job offer from the Warrington Company. But before I let them know one way or another, I would like to consider any offer that your firm may extend. I was quite impressed with your company during my recent interview, and I am still very interested in a career there.

I don't mean to pressure you, but Warrington has asked for my decision within 10 days. Could you let me know by Tuesday whether you plan to offer me a position? That would give me enough time to compare the two offers.

## Message 19.E: Letter Declining a Job Offer [LO-5]

I'm writing to say that I must decline your job offer. Another company has made me a more generous offer, and I have decided to accept. However, if things don't work out for me there, I will let you know. I sincerely appreciate your interest in me.

## Exercises

Each activity is labeled according to the primary skill or skills you will need to use. To review relevant chapter content, you can refer to the indicated Learning Objective. In some instances, supporting information will be found in another chapter, as indicated.

1. **Career Management: Preparing for Interviews [LO-3]** Google yourself, Bing yourself, scour your social networking profiles, review your Twitter messages, and explore every other possible online source you can think of that might have something about you. If you find anything potentially embarrassing, remove it if possible. Write a summary of your search-and-destroy mission (you can skip any embarrassing details in your report to your instructor!).

2. **Career Management: Researching Target Employers [LO-3]** Select a medium or large company (one that you can easily find information on) where you might like to work. Use Internet sources to gather some preliminary research on the company; don't limit your search to the company's own website.
   a. What did you learn about this organization that would help you during an interview there?
   b. What Internet sources did you use to obtain this information?
   c. Armed with this information, what aspects of your background do you think might appeal to this company's recruiters?
   d. Based on what you've learned about this company's culture, what aspects of your personality should you try to highlight during an interview?

3. **Career Management: Interviewing; Collaboration: Team Projects [LO-4], Chapter 2** Divide the class into two groups. Half the class will be recruiters for a large chain of national department stores, looking to fill manager trainee positions (there are 16 openings). The other half of the class will be candidates for the jobs. The company is specifically looking for candidates who demonstrate these three qualities: initiative, dependability, and willingness to assume responsibility.
   a. Have each recruiter select and interview an applicant for 10 minutes.
   b. Have all the recruiters discuss how they assessed the applicant in each of the three desired qualities. What questions did they ask or what did they use as an indicator to determine whether the candidate possessed the quality?
   c. Have all the applicants discuss what they said to convince the recruiters that they possessed each of these qualities.

4. **Career Management: Interviewing [LO-3]** Write a short email to your instructor, discussing what you believe are your greatest strengths and weaknesses from an employment perspective. Next, explain how these strengths and weaknesses would be viewed by interviewers evaluating your qualifications.

5. **Career Management: Interviewing [LO-3]** Prepare written answers to 10 of the questions listed in Table 19.3.

6. **Message Strategies: Employment Messages, Communication Ethics: Resolving Ethical Dilemmas [LO-5], Chapter 1** You have decided to accept a new position with a competitor of your company. Write a letter of resignation to your supervisor, announcing your decision.
   a. Will you notify your employer that you are joining a competing firm? Explain.
   b. Will you use the direct or the indirect approach? Explain.
   c. Will you send your letter by email, send it by regular mail, or place it on your supervisor's desk?

# Expand Your Skills

### Critique the Professionals

Visit LinkedIn Answers at www.linkedin.com/answers (open a free LinkedIn account if required). In the "Browse" panel, click on "Career and Education" and then "Job Search." Browse both "Open Questions" and "Closed Questions" to find three job-search insights you didn't know before. Using whatever medium your instructor requests, write a brief summary (no more than one page) of what you learned.

### Sharpening Your Career Skills Online

Bovée and Thill's Business Communication Web Search, at http://businesscommunicationblog.com/websearch, is a unique research tool designed specifically for business communication research. Use the Web Search function to find a website, video, PDF document, or PowerPoint presentation that offers advice on interviewing. Write a brief email message to your instructor, describing the item that you found and summarizing the career skills information you learned from it.

# Cases

## Writing Application Letters

### EMAIL SKILLS

**1. Message Strategies: Employment Messages (Application Letters) [LO-1]** Use one of the websites listed in Table 18.1 on page 507 to find a job opening in your target profession. If you haven't narrowed down to one career field yet, choose a business job for which you will have at least some qualifications at the time of your graduation.

**Your task:** Write an email message that would serve as your application letter if you were to apply for this job. Base your message on your actual qualifications for the position, and be sure to "echo" the requirements listed in the job description. Include the job description in your email message when you submit it to your instructor.

### MICROBLOGGING SKILLS

**2. Message Strategies: Employment Messages [LO-1]** If you want to know whether job candidates can express themselves clearly on Twitter, why not test them as part of the application process? That's exactly what the Minneapolis advertising agency Campbell Mithun does. Rather than having them using conventional application methods, the company asks intern candidates to tweet their applications in 13 messages.[48]

**Your task:** Find a job opening on Twitter by searching on any of the following hashtags: #hiring, #joblisting, or #nowhiring.[49] Next, write an "application letter" composed of 13 individual tweets (140 characters maximum). If your class is set up with private Twitter accounts, go ahead and send the tweets. Otherwise, email them to your instructor or post them on your class blog, as your instructor indicates.

### EMAIL SKILLS

**3. Message Strategies: Employment Messages [LO-1]** Finding job openings that align perfectly with your professional interests is wonderful, but it doesn't always happen. Sometimes you have to widen your search and go after whatever opportunities happen to be available. Even when the opportunity is not ideal, however, you still need to approach the employer with enthusiasm and a focused, audience-centric message.

**Your task:** Find a job opening for which you will be qualified when you graduate (or close to being qualified, for the purposes of this activity), but make it one that is outside your primary field of interest. Write an email application letter for this opening, making a compelling case that you are the right candidate for this job.

## Interviewing

### TEAM SKILLS / BLOGGING SKILLS

**4. Career Management: Researching Target Employers [LO-3]** Research is a critical element of the job-search process. With information in hand, you increase the chance of finding the right opportunity (and avoiding bad choices), and you impress interviewers in multiple ways by demonstrating initiative, curiosity, research and analysis skills, an appreciation for the complex challenges of running a business, and willingness to work to achieve results.

**Your task:** With a small team of classmates, use online job listings to identify an intriguing job opening that at least one member of the team would seriously consider pursuing as graduation approaches. (You'll find it helpful if the career is related to at least one team member's college major or on-the-job experience so that the team can benefit from some knowledge of the profession in question.) Next, research the company, its competitors, its markets, and this specific position to identify five questions that would (1) help the team member decide if this is a good opportunity and (2) show an interviewer that you've really done your homework. Go beyond the basic and obvious questions to identify current, specific, and complex issues that only deep research can uncover. For example, is the company facing significant technical, financial, legal, or regulatory challenges that threaten its ability to grow or perhaps even survive in the long term? Or is the market evolving in a way that positions this particular company for dramatic growth? In a post for your class blog, list your five questions, identify how you uncovered the issue, and explain why each question is significant.

### TEAM SKILLS

**5. Career Management: Interviewing [LO-4]** Interviewing is a skill that can be improved through practice and observation.

**Your task:** You and all other members of your class are to write letters of application for an entry-level or management-trainee position that requires an engaging personality and intelligence but a minimum of specialized education or experience. Sign your letter with a fictitious name that conceals your identity. Next, polish (or create) a résumé that accurately identifies you and your educational and professional accomplishments.

Now, three members of the class who volunteer as interviewers divide up all the anonymously written application letters. Then each interviewer selects a candidate who seems the most convincing in his or her letter. At this time, the selected candidates identify themselves and give the interviewers their résumés.

Each interviewer then interviews his or her chosen candidate in front of the class, seeking to understand how the items on the résumé qualify the candidate for the job. At the end of the interviews, the class decides who gets the job and discusses why this candidate was successful. Afterward, retrieve your letter, sign it with the right name, and submit it to the instructor for credit.

### TEAM SKILLS

**6. Career Management: Interviewing [LO-4]** Select a company in an industry in which you might like to work and then identify an interesting position within the company. Study the company and prepare for an interview with that company.

**Your task:** Working with a classmate, take turns interviewing each other for your chosen positions. Interviewers should take notes during the interview. When the interview is complete, critique each other's performance. (Interviewers should critique how well candidates prepared for the interview and answered the questions; interviewees should critique the quality of the questions asked.) Write a follow-up letter thanking your interviewer and submit the letter to your instructor.

# Following Up After an Interview

## LETTER WRITING SKILLS

### 7. Message Strategies: Employment Messages (Request for a Time Extension) [LO-5]
Because of a mix-up in your job application scheduling, you accidentally applied for your third-choice job before going after the one you really wanted. What you want to do is work in retail marketing with the upscale department store Neiman Marcus in Dallas; what you have been offered is a job with Longhorn Leather and Lumber, 65 miles away in the small town of Commerce, Texas.

You review your notes. Your Longhorn interview was three weeks ago with the human resources manager, R. P. Bronson, who has just written to offer you the position. The store's address is 27 Sam Rayburn Drive, Commerce, TX 75428. Mr. Bronson notes that he can hold the position open for 10 days. You have an interview scheduled with Neiman Marcus next week, but it is unlikely that you will know the store's decision within this 10-day period.

**Your task:** Write to Mr. Bronson, requesting a reasonable delay in your consideration of his job offer.

## LETTER WRITING SKILLS / EMAIL SKILLS

### 8. Message Strategies: Employment Messages (Letter Declining a Job Offer) [LO-5]
Fortunately for you, your interview with Neiman Marcus (see Case 7) went well, and you've just received a job offer from the company.

**Your task:** Write a letter to R. P. Bronson at Longhorn Leather and Lumber, declining his job offer, and write an email message to Clarissa Bartle at Neiman Marcus, accepting her job offer. Make up any information you need when accepting the Neiman Marcus offer.

## LETTER WRITING SKILLS

### 9. Message Strategies: Employment Messages (Letters of Resignation) [LO-5]
Leaving a job is rarely stress free, but it's particularly difficult when you are parting ways with a mentor who played an important role in advancing your career. A half-dozen years into your career, you have benefited greatly from the advice, encouragement, and professional connections offered by your mentor, who also happens to be your current boss. She seemed to believe in your potential from the very beginning and went out of her way on numerous occasions to help you. You returned the favor by becoming a stellar employee who has made important contributions to the success of the department your boss leads.

Unfortunately, you find yourself at a career impasse. You believe you are ready to move into a management position, but your company is not growing enough to create many opportunities. Worse yet, you joined the firm during a period of rapid expansion, so there are many eager and qualified internal candidates at your career level interested in the few managerial jobs that do become available. You fear it may be years before you get the chance to move up in the company. Through your online networking activities, you found an opportunity with a firm in another industry and have decided to pursue it.

**Your task:** You have a close relationship with your boss, so you will announce your intention to leave the company in a private, one-on-one conversation. However, you also recognize the need to write a formal letter of resignation, which you will hand to your boss during this meeting. This letter is addressed to your boss, but as formal business correspondence that will become part of your personnel file, it should not be a "personal" letter. Making up whatever details you need, write a brief letter of resignation.

---

# MyBCommLab

Go to **mybcommlab.com** for Auto-graded writing questions as well as the following Assisted-graded writing questions:

**19-1.** Why do employers conduct preemployment testing? [LO-2]

**19-2.** What are the three stages of every interview, and which is the most important? [LO-4]

**19-3.** Mybcommlab Only—comprehensive writing assignment for this chapter.

---

# Endnotes

**1.** Adapted from Zappos Jobs page, accessed 11 February 2013, http://about.zappos.com/jobs; "Wishez Is Live," Zappos Family blog, 17 November 2010, http://blogs.zappos.com; Tony Hsieh, "Amazon & Zappos, 1 Year Later," Zappos CEO & COO blog, 22 July 2010, http://blogs.zappos.com; Todd Raphael, "7 Interview Questions from Zappos," Todd Raphael's World of Talent blog, 22 July 2010, http://community.ere.net; Jeffrey M. O'Brien, "Zappos Knows How to Kick It,"

Fortune, 22 January 2009, http://about.zappos.com/ press-center; "Zappos Family Seattle Coding Challenge and Tech Tweet Up," Zappos Family blog, 22 March 2011, http://blogs.zappos.com.
**2.** Matthew Rothenberg, "Manuscript vs. Machine," The Ladders, 15 December 2009, www.theladders.com; Joann Lublin, "Cover Letters Get You in the Door, So Be Sure Not to Dash Them Off," *Wall Street Journal*, 6 April 2004, B1.

3. Lisa Vaas, "How to Write a Great Cover Letter," The Ladders, 20 November 2009, www.theladders.com.

4. Allison Doyle, "Introduction to Cover Letters," About.com, accessed 13 August 2010, http://jobsearch.about.com.

5. Doyle, "Introduction to Cover Letters"; Vaas, "How to Write a Great Cover Letter"; Toni Logan, "The Perfect Cover Story," *Kinko's Impress* 2 (2000): 32, 34.

6. Lisa Vaas, "How to Follow Up a Résumé Submission," The Ladders, 9 August 2010, www.theladders.com.

7. Alison Doyle, "How to Follow Up After Submitting a Resume," About.com, accessed 13 August 2010, http://jobsearch.about.com; Vaas, "How to Follow Up a Résumé Submission."

8. Anne Fisher, "How to Get Hired by a 'Best' Company," *Fortune*, 4 February 2008, 96.

9. Fisher, "How to Get Hired by a 'Best' Company."

10. Sarah E. Needleman, "Speed Interviewing Grows as Skills Shortage Looms; Strategy May Help Lock in Top Picks; Some Drawbacks," *Wall Street Journal*, 6 November 2007, B15.

11. Scott Beagrie, "How to Handle a Telephone Job Interview," *Personnel Today*, 26 June 2007, 29.

12. John Olmstead, "Predict Future Success with Structured Interviews," *Nursing Management*, March 2007, 52–53.

13. Fisher, "How to Get Hired by a 'Best' Company."

14. Erinn R. Johnson, "Pressure Sessions," *Black Enterprise*, October 2007, 72.

15. "What's a Group Interview?" About.com Tech Careers, accessed 5 April 2008, http://jobsearchtech.about.com.

16. Fisher, "How to Get Hired by a 'Best' Company."

17. Katherine Hansen, "Behavioral Job Interviewing Strategies for Job-Seekers," QuintCareers.com, accessed 13 August 2010, www.quintcareers.com.

18. Hansen, "Behavioral Job Interviewing Strategies for Job-Seekers."

19. Chris Pentilla, "Testing the Waters," *Entrepreneur*, January 2004, www.entrepreneur.com; Terry McKenna, "Behavior-Based Interviewing," *National Petroleum News*, January 2004, 16; Nancy K. Austin, "Goodbye Gimmicks," *Incentive*, May 1996, 241.

20. William Poundstone, "Beware the Interview Inquisition," *Harvard Business Review*, May 2003, 18+.

21. Peter Vogt, "Mastering the Phone Interview," Monster.com, accessed 13 December 2006, www.monster.com; Nina Segal, "The Global Interview: Tips for Successful, Unconventional Interview Techniques," Monster.com, accessed 13 December 2006, www.monster.com.

22. Segal, "The Global Interview: Tips for Successful, Unconventional Interview Techniques."

23. Barbara Kiviat, "How Skype Is Changing the Job Interview," *Time*, 20 October 2009, www.time.com.

24. HireVue website, accessed 4 April 2008, www.hirevue.com; in-2View website, accessed 4 April 2008, www.in2view.biz; Victoria Reitz, "Interview Without Leaving Home," *Machine Design*, 1 April 2004, 66.

25. Gina Ruiz, "Job Candidate Assessment Tests Go Virtual," *Workforce Management*, January 2008, www.workforce.com; Connie Winkler, "Job Tryouts Go Virtual," *HR Magazine*, September 2006, 131–134.

26. U.S. Equal Employment Opportunity Commission, "Employment Test and Selection Procedures," EEOC website, accessed 24 July 2012, www.eeoc.gov; Jonathan Katz, "Rethinking Drug Testing," *Industry Week*, March 2010, 16–18; Ashley Shadday, "Assessments 101: An Introduction to Candidate Testing," *Workforce Management*, January 2010, www.workforce.com; Dino di Mattia, "Testing Methods and Effectiveness of Tests," *Supervision*, August 2005, 4–5; David W. Arnold and John W. Jones, "Who the Devil's Applying Now?" *Security*

*Management*, March 2002, 85–88; Matthew J. Heller, "Digging Deeper," *Workforce Management*, 3 March 2008, 35–39.

27. Frederick P. Morgeson, Michael A. Campion, Robert L. Dipboye, John R. Hollenbeck, Kevin Murphy, and Neil Schmitt, "Are We Getting Fooled Again? Coming to Terms with Limitations in the Use of Personality Tests in Personnel Selection," *Personnel Psychology* 60, no. 4 (Winter 2007): 1029–1049.

28. Austin, "Goodbye Gimmicks."

29. Rachel Zupek, "How to Answer 10 Tough Interview Questions," CNN.com, 4 March 2009, www.cnn.com; Barbara Safani, "How to Answer Tough Interview Questions Authentically," The Ladders, 5 December 2009, www.theladders.com.

30. Nick Corcodilos, "How to Answer a Misguided Interview Question," *Seattle Times*, 30 March 2008, www.seattletimes.com.

31. Katherine Spencer Lee, "Tackling Tough Interview Questions," *Certification Magazine*, May 2005, 35.

32. Scott Ginsberg, "10 Good Ways to 'Tell Me About Yourself,'" The Ladders, 26 June 2010, www.theladders.com.

33. Joe Turner, "An Interview Strategy: Telling Stories," Yahoo! HotJobs, accessed 5 April 2008, http://hotjobs.yahoo.com.

34. "A Word of Caution for Chatty Job Candidates," *Public Relations Tactics*, January 2008, 4.

35. "Employers Reveal Outrageous and Common Mistakes Candidates Made in Job Interviews, According to New CareerBuilder Survey," CareerBuilder.com, 12 January 2011, www.careerbuilder.com.

36. Randall S. Hansen, "When Job-Hunting: Dress for Success," QuintCareers.com, accessed 5 April 2008, www.quintcareers.com; Alison Doyle, "Dressing for Success," About.com, accessed 5 April 2008, http://jobsearch.about.com.

37. William S. Frank, "Job Interview: Pre-Flight Checklist," *The Career Advisor*, accessed 28 September 2005, http://careerplanning.about.com.

38. "Employers Reveal Outrageous and Common Mistakes Candidates Made in Job Interviews, According to New CareerBuilder Survey."

39. T. Shawn Taylor, "Most Managers Have No Idea How to Hire the Right Person for the Job," *Chicago Tribune*, 23 July 2002, www.ebsco.com.

40. "10 Minutes to Impress," *Journal of Accountancy*, July 2007, 13.

41. Steven Mitchell Sack, "The Working Woman's Legal Survival Guide: Testing," FindLaw.com, accessed 22 February 2004, www.findlaw.com.

42. Mark Henricks, "3 Interview Questions That Could Cost Your Company $1 Million," BNET, 8 March 2011, www.bnet.com.

43. Todd Anten, "How to Handle Illegal Interview Questions," Yahoo! HotJobs, accessed 7 August 2009, http://hotjobs.yahoo.com.

44. "Negotiating Salary: An Introduction," *InformationWeek* online, accessed 22 February 2004, www.informationweek.com.

45. "Negotiating Salary: An Introduction."

46. Lisa Vaas, "Resume, Meet Technology: Making Your Resume Format Machine-Friendly," The Ladders, accessed 13 August 2010, www.theladders.com.

47. Alison Green, "How a Thank-You Note Can Boost Your Job Chances," *U.S. News & World Report*, 27 June 2012, http://money.usnews.com; Joan S. Lublin, "Notes to Interviewers Should Go Beyond a Simple Thank You," *Wall Street Journal*, 5 February 2008, B1.

48. Tiffany Hsu, "Extreme Interviewing; Odd Quizzes, Weird Mixers, Improv Pitches. Can You Get Past the Hiring Gatekeepers?" *Los Angeles Times*, 19 February 2012, B1.

49. From Ritika Trikha, "The Best Tips for Tweeting Your Way to a Job," *U.S. News & World Report*, 24 July 2012, http://money.usnews.com.

# A | Format and Layout of Business Documents

The format and layout of business documents vary from country to country. In addition, many organizations develop their own variations of standard styles, adapting documents to the types of messages they send and the kinds of audiences they communicate with. The formats described here are the most common approaches used in U.S. business correspondence, but be sure to follow whatever practices are expected at your company.

## First Impressions

Your documents tell readers a lot about you and about your company's professionalism. So all your documents must look neat, present a professional image, and be easy to read. Your audience's first impression of a document comes from the quality of its paper, the way it is customized, and its general appearance.

### PAPER

To give a quality impression, businesspeople consider carefully the paper they use. Several aspects of paper contribute to the overall impression:

- **Weight.** Paper quality is judged by the weight of four reams (each a 500-sheet package) of letter-size paper. The weight most commonly used by U.S. business organizations is 20-pound paper, but 16- and 24-pound versions are also used.
- **Cotton content.** Paper quality is also judged by the percentage of cotton in the paper. Cotton doesn't yellow over time the way wood pulp does, plus it's both strong and soft. For letters and outside reports, use paper with a 25 percent cotton content. For memos and other internal documents, you can use a lighter-weight paper with lower cotton content. Airmail-weight paper may save money for international correspondence, but make sure it isn't too flimsy.[1]
- **Size.** In the United States, the standard paper size for business documents is 8½ by 11 inches. Standard legal documents are 8½ by 14 inches. Executives sometimes have heavier 7-by-10-inch paper on hand (with matching envelopes) for personal messages such as congratulations.[2] They may also have a box of note cards imprinted with their initials and a box of plain folded notes for condolences or for acknowledging formal invitations.
- **Color.** White is the standard color for business purposes, although neutral colors such as gray and ivory are sometimes used. Memos can be produced on pastel-colored paper to distinguish them from external correspondence. In addition, memos are sometimes produced on various colors of paper for routing to separate departments. Light-colored papers are appropriate, but bright or dark colors make reading difficult and may appear too frivolous.

### CUSTOMIZATION

For letters to outsiders, U.S. businesses commonly use letterhead stationery, which may be either professionally printed or designed in-house using word processing templates and graphics. Letterhead typically contains the company name, logo, address, telephone and fax numbers, general email address, website URL, and possibly one or more social media URLs.

In the United States, businesses always use letterhead for the first page of a letter. Successive pages are usually plain sheets of paper that match the letterhead in color and quality. Some companies use a specially printed second-page letterhead that bears only the company's name.

### APPEARANCE

Nearly all business documents are produced using an ink-jet or laser printer; make sure to use a clean, high-quality printer. Certain documents, however, should be handwritten (such as a short informal memo or a note of condolence). Be sure to handwrite, print, or type the envelope to match the document. However, even a letter on the best-quality paper with the best-designed letterhead may look unprofessional if it's poorly produced. So pay close attention to all the factors affecting appearance, including the following:

- **Margins.** Business letters typically use 1-inch margins at the top, bottom, and sides of the page, although these parameters are sometimes adjusted to accommodate letterhead elements.
- **Line length.** Lines are rarely justified, because the resulting text looks too formal and can be difficult to read.
- **Character spacing.** Use proper spacing between characters and after punctuation. For example, U.S. conventions include leaving one space after commas, semicolons, colons, and sentence-ending periods. Each letter in a person's initials is followed by a period and a single space. However, abbreviations such as U.S.A. or MBA may or may not have periods, but they never have internal spaces.

- **Special symbols.** Take advantage of the many special symbols available with your computer's selection of fonts. In addition, see if your company has a style guide for documents, which may include particular symbols you are expected to use.
- **Corrections.** Messy corrections are unacceptable in business documents. If you notice an error after printing a document with your word processor, correct the mistake and reprint. (With informal memos to members of your own team or department, the occasional small correction in pen or pencil is acceptable, but never in formal documents.)

# Letters

All business letters have certain elements in common. Several of these elements appear in every letter; others appear only when desirable or appropriate. In addition, these letter parts are usually arranged in one of three basic formats.

## STANDARD LETTER PARTS

The letter in Figure A.1 shows the placement of standard letter parts. The writer of this business letter had no letterhead available but correctly included a heading. All business letters typically include these seven elements.

### Heading

The elements of the letterhead make up the heading of a letter in most cases. If letterhead stationery is not available, the heading includes a return address (but no name) and starts 13 lines from the top of the page, which leaves a 2-inch top margin.

### Date

If you're using letterhead, place the date at least one blank line beneath the lowest part of the letterhead. Without letterhead, place the date immediately below the return address. The standard method of writing the date in the United States uses the full name of the month (no abbreviations), followed

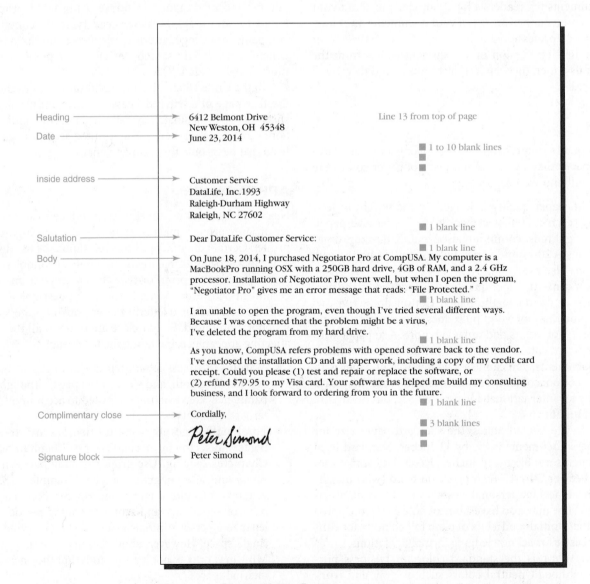

**Figure A.1** **Standard Letter Parts**

### TABLE A.1 | Common Date Forms

| Convention | Order | Examples |
|---|---|---|
| U.S. standard | Month day year | July 31, 2014<br>7/31/2014<br>7-31-2014 |
| Japan | Year month day | 14/07/31 |
| Europe (most countries) | Day month year | 31 July 2014<br>31/07/14<br>31.07.14 |
| International (ISO) format | Year month day | 2014-07-31 |

by the day (in numerals, without *st, nd, rd,* or *th*), a comma, and then the year: July 31, 2014 (7/31/2014). Many other countries use other formats (see Table A.1), which can create confusion in international correspondence. To avoid misinterpretation in such cases, spell out the month.[3]

### Inside Address

The inside address identifies the recipient of the letter. For U.S. correspondence, begin the inside address at least one line below the date. Precede the addressee's name with a courtesy title, such as *Dr., Mr.,* or *Ms.* The accepted courtesy title for women in business is *Ms.,* although a woman known to prefer the title *Miss* or *Mrs.* is always accommodated. If you don't know whether a person is a man or a woman (and you have no way of finding out), omit the courtesy title. For example, *Terry Smith* could be either a man or a woman. The first line of the inside address would be just *Terry Smith,* and the salutation would be *Dear Terry Smith.* The same is true if you know only a person's initials, as in *S. J. Adams.*

Spell out and capitalize titles that precede a person's name, such as *Professor* or *General* (see Table A.2 on the next page for the proper forms of address). The person's organizational title, such as *Director,* may be included on this first line (if it is short) or on the line below; the name of a department may follow. In addresses and signature lines, don't forget to capitalize any professional title that follows a person's name:

Mr. Ray Johnson, Dean
Ms. Patricia T. Higgins
Assistant Vice President

However, professional titles not appearing in an address or signature line are capitalized only when they directly precede the name:

President Kenneth Johanson will deliver the speech.
Maria Morales, president of ABC Enterprises, will deliver the speech.
The Honorable Helen Masters, senator from Arizona, will deliver the speech.

If the name of a specific person is unavailable, you may address the letter to the department or to a specific position within the department. Also, be sure to spell out company names in full, unless the company itself uses abbreviations in its official name.

Other address information includes the treatment of buildings, house numbers, and compass directions (see Table A.3 on page 573). The following example shows all the information that may be included in the inside address and its proper order for U.S. correspondence:

Ms. Linda Coolidge, Vice President
Corporate Planning Department
Midwest Airlines
Kowalski Building, Suite 21-A
7279 Bristol Ave.
Toledo, OH 43617

Canadian addresses are similar, except that the name of the province is usually spelled out:

Dr. H. C. Armstrong
Research and Development
Commonwealth Mining Consortium
The Chelton Building, Suite 301
585 Second St. SW
Calgary, Alberta T2P 2P5

The order and layout of address information vary from country to country. So when addressing correspondence for other countries, carefully follow the format and information that appear in the company's letterhead. However, when you're sending mail from the United States, be sure that the name of the destination country appears on the last line of the address in capital letters. Use the English version of the country name so that your mail is routed from the United States to the right country. Then, to be sure your mail is routed correctly within the destination country, use the foreign spelling of the city name (using the characters and diacritical marks

## TABLE A.2 | Forms of Address

| Person | In Address | In Salutation |
|---|---|---|
| **Personal Titles** | | |
| Man | Mr. [first & last name] | Dear Mr. [last name]: |
| Woman* | Ms. [first & last name] | Dear Ms. [last name]: |
| Two men (or more) | Mr. [first & last name] and Mr. [first & last name] | Dear Mr. [last name] and Mr. [last name] or Messrs. [last name] and [last name]: |
| Two women (or more) | Ms. [first & last name] and Ms. [first & last name] | Dear Ms. [last name] and Ms. [last name] or Mses. [last name] and [last name]: |
| One woman and one man | Ms. [first & last name] and Mr. [first & last name] | Dear Ms. [last name] and Mr. [last name]: |
| Couple (married with same last name) | Mr. [husband's first name] and Mrs. [wife's first name] [couple's last name] | Dear Mr. and Mrs. [last name]: |
| Couple (married with different last names) | Mr. [first & last name of husband] Ms. [first & last name of wife] | Dear Mr. [husband's last name] and Ms. [wife's last name]: |
| Couple (married professionals with same title and same last name) | [title in plural form] [husband's first name] and [wife's first name] [couple's last name] | Dear [title in plural form] [last name]: |
| Couple (married professionals with different titles and same last name) | [title] [first & last name of husband] and [title] [first & last name of wife] | Dear [title] and [title] [last name]: |
| **Professional Titles** | | |
| President of a college or university | [title] [first & last name], President | Dear [title] [last name]: |
| Dean of a school or college | Dean [first & last name] or Dr., Mr., or Ms. [first & last name], Dean of [title] | Dear Dean [last name]: or Dear Dr., Mr., or Ms. [last name]: |
| Professor | Professor or Dr. [first & last name] | Dear Professor or Dr. [last name]: |
| Physician | [first & last name], M.D. | Dear Dr. [last name]: |
| Lawyer | Mr. or Ms. [first & last name], Attorney at Law | Dear Mr. or Ms. [last name]: |
| Military personnel | [full rank, first & last name, abbreviation of service designation] (add Retired if applicable) | Dear [rank] [last name]: |
| Company or corporation | [name of organization] | Ladies and Gentlemen: or Gentlemen and Ladies: |
| **Governmental Titles** | | |
| President of the United States | The President | Dear Mr. or Madam President: |
| Senator of the United States | The Honorable [first & last name] | Dear Senator [last name]: |
| Cabinet member | The Honorable [first & last name] | Dear Mr. or Madam Secretary: |
| Attorney General | The Honorable [first & last name] | Dear Mr. or Madam Attorney General: |
| Mayor | The Honorable [first & last name], Mayor of [name of city] | Dear Mayor [last name]: |
| Judge | The Honorable [first & last name] | Dear Judge [last name]: |

*Use *Mrs.* or *Miss* only if the recipient has specifically requested that you use one of these titles; otherwise *always* use *Ms.* in business correspondence. Also, never refer to a married woman by her husband's name (e.g., Mrs. Robert Washington) unless she specifically requests that you do so.

that would be commonly used in the region). For example, the following address uses *Köln* instead of *Cologne*:

| | |
|---|---|
| H. R. Veith, Director | Addressee |
| Eisfieren Glaswerk | Company name |
| Blaubachstrasse 13 | Street address |
| Postfach 10 80 07 | Post office road |
| D-5000 Köln I | District, city |
| GERMANY | Country |

For additional examples of international addresses, see Table A.4 on pages 574–575.

Be sure to use organizational titles correctly when addressing international correspondence. Job designations vary around the world. In England, for example, a managing director is often what a U.S. company would call its chief executive officer or president, and a British deputy is the equivalent of a vice president. In France, responsibilities are assigned to individuals without regard to title or organizational structure, and in China the title

| TABLE A.3 | Inside Address Information | |
|---|---|
| **Description** | **Example** |
| Capitalize building names. | Empire State Building |
| Capitalize locations within buildings (apartments, suites, rooms). | Suite 1073 |
| Use numerals for all house or building numbers, except the number one. | One Trinity Lane; 637 Adams Ave., Apt. 7 |
| Spell out compass directions that fall within a street address. | 1074 West Connover St. |
| Abbreviate compass directions that follow the street address. | 783 Main St., N.E., Apt. 27 |

*project manager* has meaning, but the title *sales manager* may not.

To make matters worse, businesspeople in some countries sign correspondence without their names typed below.

In Germany, for example, the belief is that employees represent the company, so it's inappropriate to emphasize personal names.[4] Use the examples in Table A.4 as guidelines when addressing correspondence to countries outside the United States.

## Salutation

In the salutation of your letter, follow the style of the first line of the inside address. If the first line is a person's name, the salutation is *Dear Mr. or Ms. Name*. The formality of the salutation depends on your relationship with the addressee. If in conversation you would say "Mary," your letter's salutation should be *Dear Mary*, followed by a colon. Otherwise, include the courtesy title and last name, followed by a colon. Presuming to write *Dear Lewis* instead of *Dear Professor Chang* demonstrates a disrespectful familiarity that the recipient will probably resent.

If the first line of the inside address is a position title such as *Director of Personnel*, then use *Dear Director*. If the addressee is unknown, use a polite description, such as *Dear Alumnus, Dear SPCA Supporter*, or *Dear Voter*. If the first line is plural (a department or company), then use *Ladies and Gentlemen* (look again at Table A.2). When you do not know whether you're writing to an individual or a group (for example, when writing a reference or a letter of recommendation), use *To whom it may concern*.

In the United States some letter writers use a "salutopening" on the salutation line. A salutopening omits *Dear* but includes the first few words of the opening paragraph along with the recipient's name. After this line, the sentence continues a double space below as part of the body of the letter, as in these examples:

| | |
|---|---|
| Thank you, Mr. Brown, for your prompt payment of your bill. | Salutopening |
| Your payment of $88.13 was received on January 24, 2014. | Body |

Whether your salutation is informal or formal, be especially careful that names are spelled correctly. A misspelled name is glaring evidence of carelessness, and it belies the personal interest you're trying to express.

## Body

The body of the letter is your message. Almost all letters are single-spaced, with one blank line before and after the salutation or salutopening, between paragraphs, and before the complimentary close. The body may include indented lists, entire paragraphs indented for emphasis, and even subheadings. If it does, all similar elements should be treated in the same way. Your department or company may select a format to use for all letters.

## Complimentary Close

The complimentary close begins on the second line below the body of the letter. Alternatives for wording are available, but currently the trend seems to be toward using one-word closes, such as *Sincerely* and *Cordially*. In any case, the complimentary close reflects the relationship between you and the person you're writing to. Avoid cute closes, such as *Yours for bigger profits*. If your audience doesn't know you well, your sense of humor may be misunderstood.

## Signature Block

Leave three blank lines for a written signature below the complimentary close, and then include the sender's name (unless it appears in the letterhead). The person's title may appear on the same line as the name or on the line below:

Cordially,


Raymond Dunnigan
Director of Personnel

Your letterhead indicates that you're representing your company. However, if your letter is on plain paper or runs to a second page, you may want to emphasize that you're speaking legally for the company. The accepted way of doing that is to place the company's name in capital letters, a double space below the complimentary close, and then include the sender's name and title four lines below that:

Sincerely,
WENTWORTH INDUSTRIES



Helen B. Taylor
President

**TABLE A.4** | **International Addresses and Salutations**

| Country | Postal Address | Address Elements | Salutations |
|---|---|---|---|
| Argentina | Sr. Juan Pérez<br>Editorial Internacional S.A.<br>Av. Sarmiento 1337, 8° P.C.<br>C1035AAB BUENOS<br>AIRES–CF<br>ARGENTINA | S.A. = Sociedad Anónima (corporation)<br>Av. Sarmiento (name of street)<br>1337 (building number)<br>8° - 8th. P = Piso (floor)<br>C (room or suite)<br>C1035AAB (postcode + city)<br>CF = Capital Federal (federal capital) | Sr. = Señor (Mr.)<br>Sra. = Señora (Mrs.)<br>Srta. = Señorita (Miss)<br>Don't use given names except with people you know well. |
| Australia | Mr. Roger Lewis<br>International Publishing Pty. Ltd.<br>166 Kent Street, Level 9<br>GPO Box 3542<br>SYDNEY NSW 200<br>AUSTRALIA | Pty. Ltd. – Proprietory Limited<br>(corp.) 166 (building number)<br>Kent Street (name of street)<br>Level (floor)<br>GPO Box (P.O. box)<br>City + state (abbrev.) + postcode | Mr. and Mrs. used on first contact.<br>Ms. not common (avoid use).<br>Business is informal—use given name freely. |
| Austria | Herrn<br>Dipl.-Ing.J.Gerdenitsch<br>International Verlag Ges.m.b.H.<br>Glockengasse 159<br>1010 WIEN<br>AUSTRIA | Herrn – To Mr. (separate line)<br>Dipl.-Ing. (engineering degree)<br>Ges.m.b.H. (a corporation)<br>Glockengasse (street name)<br>159 (building number)<br>1010 (postcode + city)<br>WIEN (Vienna) | Herr (Mr.)<br>Frau (Mrs.)<br>Fräulein (Miss) obsolete in business, so do not use.<br>Given names are almost never used in business. |
| Brazil | Ilmo. Sr.<br>Gilberto Rabello Ribeiro<br>Editores Internacionais S.A.<br>Rua da Ajuda, 228–6° Andar<br>Caixa Postal 2574<br>20040–000<br>RIO DE JANEIRO–RJ<br>BRAZIL | Ilmo. = Ilustrissimo (honorific)<br>Ilma. = Ilustrissima (hon. female)<br>S.A. – Sociedade Anônima (corporation)<br>Rua = street, da Ajuda (street name)<br>228 (building number)<br>6° = 6th. Andar (floor)<br>Caixa Postal (P.O. box)<br>20040–000 (postcode + city)–RJ (state abbrev.) | Sr. = Senhor (Mr.)<br>Sra. = Senhora (Mrs.)<br>Srta. = Senhorita (Miss)<br>Family name at end, e.g., Senhor Ribeiro (Rabello is mother's family name)<br>Given names are readily used in business. |
| China | Xia Zhiyi<br>International Publishing Ltd.<br>14 Jianguolu<br>Chaoyangqu<br>BEIJING 100025<br>CHINA | Ltd. (limited liability corporation)<br>14 (building number)<br>Jianguolu (street name), lu (street)<br>Chaoyangqu (district name)<br>(city + postcode) | Family name (single syllable) first.<br>Given name (2 syllables) second, sometimes reversed.<br>Use Mr. or Ms. at all times (Mr. Xia). |
| France | Monsieur LEFÈVRE Alain<br>Éditions Internationales S.A.<br>Siège Social<br>Immeuble Le Bonaparte<br>64–68, av. Galliéni<br>B.P. 154<br>75942 PARIS CEDEX 19<br>FRANCE | S.A. = Société Anonyme (corporation)<br>Siège Social (head office)<br>Immeuble (building + name)<br>64–68 (building occupies 64, 66, 68)<br>av. = avenue (no initial capital)<br>B.P. = Boîte Postale (P.O. box)<br>75942 (postcode + city)<br>CEDEX (postcode for P.O. box) | Monsieur (Mr.)<br>Madame (Mrs.)<br>Mademoiselle (Miss)<br>Best not to abbreviate.<br>Family name is sometimes in all caps with given name following. |
| Germany | Herrn<br>Gerhardt Schneider<br>International Verlag GmbH<br>Schillerstraβe 159<br>44147 DORTMUND<br>GERMANY | Herrn = To Mr. (on a separate line)<br>GmbH (inc.—incorporated)<br>–straβe (street–'β' often written 'ss')<br>159 (building number)<br>44147 (postcode – city) | Herr (Mr.)<br>Frau (Mrs.)<br>Fräulein (Miss) obsolete in business.<br>Business is formal: (1) do not use given names unless invited, and (2) use academic titles precisely. |
| India | Sr. Shyam Lal Gupta<br>International Publishing (Pvt.) Ltd.<br>1820 Rehaja Centre<br>214, Darussalam Road<br>Andheri East<br>MUMBAI–400049<br>INDIA | (Pvt.) (privately owned)<br>Ltd. (limited liability corporation)<br>1820 (possibly office #20 on 18th floor)<br>Rehaja Centre (building name)<br>214 (building number)<br>Andheri East (suburb name)<br>(city + hyphen + postcode) | Shri (Mr.), Shrimati (Mrs.) but English is common business language, so use Mr., Mrs., Miss.<br>Given names are used only by family and close friends. |

**TABLE A.4 | International Addresses and Salutations (Continued)**

| Country | Postal Address | Address Elements | Salutations |
|---|---|---|---|
| Italy | Egr. Sig.<br>Giacomo Mariotti<br>Edizioni Internazionali S.p.A.<br>Via Terenzio, 2120138 MILANO<br>ITALY | Egr. = Egregio (honorific)<br>Sig. = Signor (not nec. a separate line)<br>S.p.A. = Società per Azioni (corp.)<br>Via (street)<br>21 (building number)<br>20138 (postcode + city) | Sig. = Signore (Mr.)<br>Sig.ra = Signora (Mrs.)<br>Sig.a (Ms.)<br>Women in business are addressed as Signora.<br>Use given name only when invited. |
| Japan | Mr. Taro Tanaka<br>Kokusai Shuppan K.K.<br>10–23, 5-chome, Minamiazabu<br>Minato-ku<br>TOKYO 106<br>JAPAN | K.K. = Kabushiki Kaisha (corporation)<br>10 (lot number)<br>23 (building number)<br>5-chome (area #5)<br>Minamiazabu (neighborhood name)<br>Minato-ku (city district)<br>(city + postcode) | Given names are not used in business.<br>Use family name + job title.<br>Or use family name + "-san" (Tanaka-san) or more respectfully, add "-sama" or "-dono." |
| Korea | Mr. Kim Chang-ik<br>International Publishers Ltd.<br>Room 206, Korea Building<br>33–4 Nonhyon-dong<br>Kangnam-ku<br>SEOUL 135–010<br>KOREA | English company names common Ltd. (a corporation)<br>206 (office number inside the building)<br>33–4 (area 4 of subdivision 33)<br>-dong (city neighborhood name)<br>-ku (subdivision of city)<br>(city + postcode) | Family name is normally first but sometimes placed after given name.<br>A two-part name is the given name. Use Mr. or Mrs. in letters, but use job title in speech. |
| Mexico | Sr. Francisco Pérez Martínez<br>Editores Internacionales S.A.<br>Independencia No. 322<br>Col. Juárez<br>06050 MEXICO D.F. | S.A. – Sociedad Anónima (corporation)<br>Independencia (street name)<br>No. = Número (number)<br>322 (building number)<br>Col. = Colonia (city district)<br>Juárez (locality name)<br>06050 (postcode + city)<br>D.F. = Distrito Federal (federal capital) | Sr. = Señor (Mr.)<br>Sra. = Señora (Mrs.)<br>Srta. = Señorita (Miss)<br>Family name in middle: e.g., Sr. Pérez (Martínez is mother's family).<br>Given names are used in business. |
| South Africa | Mr. Mandla Ntuli International<br>Publishing (Pty.) Ltd.<br>Private Bag X2581<br>JOHANNESBURG 2000<br>SOUTH AFRICA | Pty. = Proprietory (privately owned) Ltd. (a corporation)<br>Private Bag (P.O. Box)<br>(city + postcode) or (postcode + city) | Mnr. = Meneer (Mr.)<br>Mev. = Mevrou (Mrs.)<br>Mejuffrou (Miss) is not used in business.<br>Business is becoming less formal, so the use of given names is possible. |
| United Kingdom | Mr. N. J. Lancaster International<br>Publishing Ltd.<br>Kingsbury House<br>12 Kingsbury Road<br>EDGEWARE<br>Middlesex HA8 9XG<br>ENGLAND | N. J. (initials of given names)<br>Ltd. (limited liability corporation)<br>Kingsbury House (building name)<br>12 (building number)<br>Kingsbury Road (name of street/road)<br>EDGEWARE (city—all caps)<br>Middlesex (county—not all caps)<br>HA8 9XG | Mr. and Ms. used mostly.<br>Mrs. and Miss sometimes used in North and by older women.<br>Given names—called Christian names—are used in business after some time. Wait to be invited. |

If your name could be taken for either a man's or a woman's, a courtesy title indicating gender should be included, with or without parentheses. Also, women who prefer a particular courtesy title should include it:

> Mrs. Nancy Winters
> (Ms.) Juana Flores
> Ms. Pat Li
> (Mr.) Jamie Saunders

## ADDITIONAL LETTER PARTS

Letters vary greatly in subject matter and thus in the identifying information they need and the format they adopt. The letter in Figure A.2 on the next page shows how these additional parts should be arranged. The following elements may be used in any combination, depending on the requirements of the particular letter:

- **Addressee notation.** Letters that have a restricted readership or that must be handled in a special way should include such addressee notations as *PERSONAL, CONFIDENTIAL, or PLEASE FORWARD*. This sort of notation appears a double space above the inside address, in all-capital letters.
- **Attention line.** Although not commonly used today, an attention line can be used if you know only the last name of the person you're writing to. It can also direct a letter to a position title or department. Place the attention line on the first line of the inside address and put the company name on the second.[5] Match the address on the envelope

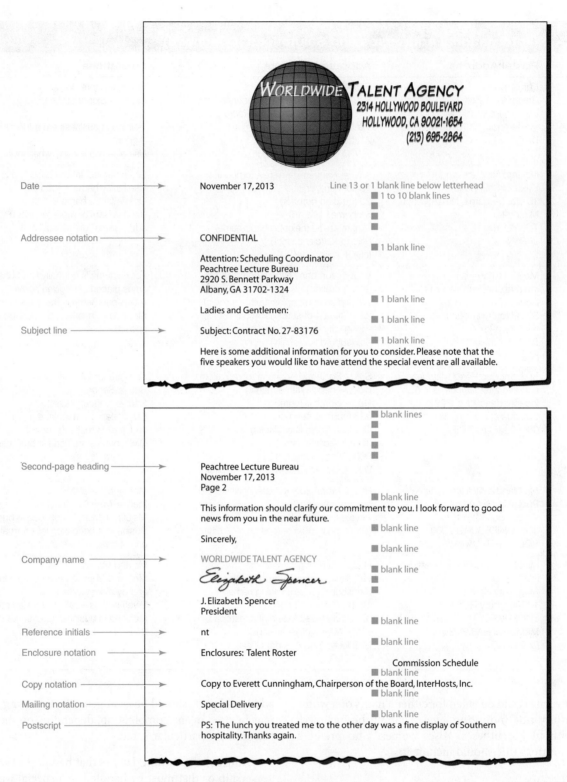

**WORLDWIDE TALENT AGENCY**
2314 HOLLYWOOD BOULEVARD
HOLLYWOOD, CA 90021-1654
(213) 695-2864

Date — November 17, 2013                    Line 13 or 1 blank line below letterhead
■ 1 to 10 blank lines
■
■
■

Addressee notation — CONFIDENTIAL
■ 1 blank line

Attention: Scheduling Coordinator
Peachtree Lecture Bureau
2920 S. Bennett Parkway
Albany, GA 31702-1324
■ 1 blank line

Ladies and Gentlemen:
■ 1 blank line

Subject line — Subject: Contract No. 27-83176
■ 1 blank line

Here is some additional information for you to consider. Please note that the five speakers you would like to have attend the special event are all available.

■ blank lines
■
■
■

Second-page heading — Peachtree Lecture Bureau
November 17, 2013
Page 2
■ blank line

This information should clarify our commitment to you. I look forward to good news from you in the near future.
■ blank line

Sincerely,
■ blank line

Company name — WORLDWIDE TALENT AGENCY
■ blank line

*Elizabeth Spencer*
■
J. Elizabeth Spencer
President
■ blank line

Reference initials — nt
■ blank line

Enclosure notation — Enclosures: Talent Roster
                              Commission Schedule
■ blank line

Copy notation — Copy to Everett Cunningham, Chairperson of the Board, InterHosts, Inc.
■ blank line

Mailing notation — Special Delivery
■ blank line

Postscript — PS: The lunch you treated me to the other day was a fine display of Southern hospitality. Thanks again.

**Figure A.2   Additional Letter Parts**

with the style of the inside address. An attention line may take any of the following forms or variants of them:

Attention Dr. McHenry

Attention Director of Marketing

Attention Marketing Department

- **Subject line.** The subject line tells recipients at a glance what the letter is about (and indicates where to file the letter for future reference). It usually appears below the salutation, either against the left margin, indented (as a paragraph in the body), or centered. It can be placed above the salutation or at the very top of the page, and it can be underscored. Some businesses omit the word

*Subject*, and some organizations replace it with *Re:* or *In re:* (meaning "concerning" or "in the matter of"). The subject line may take a variety of forms, including the following:

Subject: RainMaster Sprinklers
Re: About your February 2, 2014, order
In re: FALL 2012 SALES MEETING
Reference Order No. 27920

- **Second-page heading.** Use a second-page heading whenever an additional page is required. Some companies have second-page letterhead (with the company name and address on one line and in a smaller typeface). The heading bears the name (person or organization) from the first line of the inside address, the page number, the date, and perhaps a reference number. Leave two blank lines before the body. Make sure that at least two lines of a continued paragraph appear on the first and second pages. Never allow the closing lines to appear alone on a continued page. Precede the complimentary close or signature lines with at least two lines of the body. Also, don't hyphenate the last word on a page. All the following are acceptable forms for second-page headings:

Ms. Melissa Baker
May 10, 2014
Page 2
Ms. Melissa Baker, May 10, 2014, Page 2
Ms. Melissa Baker-2-May 10, 2014

- **Company name.** If you include the company's name in the signature block, put it a double space below the complimentary close. You usually include the company's name in the signature block only when the writer is serving as the company's official spokesperson or when letterhead has not been used.
- **Reference initials.** When businesspeople keyboard their own letters, reference initials are unnecessary, so they are becoming rare. When one person dictates a letter and another person produces it, reference initials show who helped prepare it. Place initials at the left margin, a double space below the signature block. When the signature block includes the writer's name, use only the preparer's initials. If the signature block includes only the department, use both sets of initials, usually in one of the following forms: *RSR/sm*, *RSR:sm*, or *RSR:SM* (writer/preparer). When the writer and the signer are different people, at least the file copy should bear both their initials as well as the typist's: *JFS/RSR/sm* (signer/writer/preparer).
- **Enclosure notation.** Enclosure notations appear at the bottom of a letter, one or two lines below the

reference initials. Some common forms include the following:

Enclosure
Enclosures (2)
Enclosures: Résumé
             Photograph
             Brochure

- **Copy notation.** Copy notations may follow reference initials or enclosure notations. They indicate who's receiving a *courtesy copy* (*cc*). Recipients are listed in order of rank or (rank being equal) in alphabetical order. Among the forms used are the following:

cc: David Wentworth, Vice President
Copy to Hans Vogel
748 Chesterton Road
Snohomish, WA 98290

- **Mailing notation.** You may place a mailing notation (such as *Special Delivery* or *Registered Mail*) at the bottom of the letter, after reference initials or enclosure notations (whichever is last) and before copy notations. Or you may place it at the top of the letter, either above the inside address on the left side or just below the date on the right side. For greater visibility, mailing notations may appear in capital letters.
- **Postscript.** A postscript is presented as an afterthought to the letter, a message that requires emphasis, or a personal note. It is usually the last thing on any letter and may be preceded by *P.S.*, *PS.*, *PS:*, or nothing at all. A second afterthought would be designated *P.P.S.* (post postscript).

## LETTER FORMATS

A letter format is the way of arranging all the basic letter parts. Sometimes a company adopts a certain format as its policy; sometimes the individual letter writer or preparer is allowed to choose the most appropriate format. In the United States, three major letter formats are commonly used:

- **Block format.** Each letter part begins at the left margin. The main advantage is quick and efficient preparation (see Figure A.3).
- **Modified block format.** Same as block format, except that the date, complimentary close, and signature block start near the center of the page (see Figure A.4 on page 579). The modified block format does permit indentions as an option. This format mixes preparation speed with traditional placement of some letter parts. It also looks more balanced on the page than the block format does. (Note: The address and contact information in the left margin of this letter is part of this company's particular stationery design; other designs put this information at the top or bottom of the page.)

Delauny Music
56 Commerce Circle • Davenport, IA 52806
(563) 555-4001 • delaunymusic.net

June 21, 2014                                     Line 13 or one line below letterhead
                                                 ■ 1 to 10 blank lines
                                                 ■

Ms. Claudia Banks
122 River Heights Drive
Bettendorf, IA 52722
                                                 ■ 1 blank line
Dear Ms. Banks:
                                                 ■ 1 blank line
Thank you for your recent purchase. We wish you many years of satisfaction with your
new Yamaha CG1 grand piano. The CG1 carries more than a century of Yamaha's heritage
in design and production of world-class musical instruments and will give you many years
of playing and listening pleasure.
                                                 ■ 1 blank line
Our commitment to your satisfaction doesn't stop with your purchase, however. As a vital
first step, please remember to call us sometime within three to eight months after your
piano was delivered to take advantage of the Yamaha Servicebond℠ Assurance Program.
This free service program includes a thorough evaluation and adjustment of the
instrument after you've had some time to play your piano and your piano has had time to
adapt to its environment.
                                                 ■ 1 blank line
In addition to this important service appointment, a regular program of tuning is essential
to ensure your piano's impeccable performance. Our piano specialists recommend four
tunings during the first year and two tunings every year thereafter. As your local Yamaha
dealer, we are ideally positioned to provide you with optimum service for both regular
tuning and any maintenance or repair needs you may have.

Sincerely,                                       ■ 1 blank line

                                                 ■ 3 blank lines
                                                 ■
                                                 ■
Madeline Delauny
Owner

tjr                                              ■ 1 blank line

                                                 ■ 1 blank line

**Figure A.3   Block Letter Format**

- **Simplified format.** Instead of using a salutation, this format often weaves the reader's name into the first line or two of the body and often includes a subject line in capital letters (see Figure A.5 on page 580). This format does not include a complimentary close, so your signature appears immediately below the body text. Because certain letter parts are eliminated, some line spacing is changed.

These three formats differ in the way paragraphs are indented, in the way letter parts are placed, and in some punctuation. However, the elements are always separated by at least one blank line, and the printed name is always separated from the line above by at least three blank lines to allow space for a signature. If paragraphs are indented, the indention is normally five spaces. The most common formats for intercultural business letters are the block style and the modified block style.

In addition to these three letter formats, letters may also be classified according to their style of punctuation. *Standard,* or *mixed, punctuation* uses a colon after the salutation (a comma if the letter is social or personal) and a comma after the complimentary close. *Open punctuation* uses no colon or comma after the salutation or the complimentary close. Although the most popular style in business communication is mixed punctuation, either style of punctuation may be used with block or modified block letter formats. Because the simplified letter format has no salutation or complimentary close, the style of punctuation is irrelevant.

# Envelopes

For a first impression, the quality of the envelope is just as important as the quality of the stationery. Letterhead and envelopes should be of the same paper stock, have the same color ink, and be imprinted with the same address and logo. Most envelopes used by U.S. businesses are No. 10 envelopes

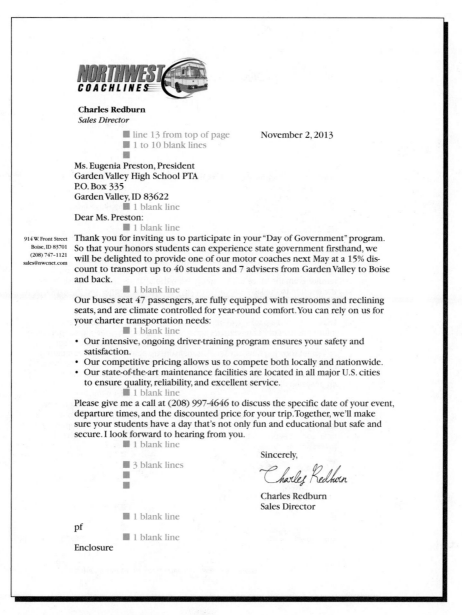

**Figure A.4**   **Modified Block Letter Format**

(9½ inches long), which are sized for an 8½-by-11-inch piece of paper folded in thirds. Some occasions call for a smaller, No. 6 ¾, envelope or for envelopes proportioned to fit special stationery. Figure A.6 on page 581 shows the two most common sizes.

## ADDRESSING THE ENVELOPE

No matter what size the envelope, the address is always single-spaced with all lines aligned on the left. The address on the envelope is in the same style as the inside address and presents the same information. The order to follow is from the smallest division to the largest:

1. Name and title of recipient
2. Name of department or subgroup
3. Name of organization
4. Name of building

5. Street address and suite number, or post office box number
6. City, state, or province, and zip code or postal code
7. Name of country (if the letter is being sent abroad)

Because the U.S. Postal Service uses optical scanners to sort mail, envelopes for quantity mailings, in particular, should be addressed in the prescribed format. Everything is in capital letters, no punctuation is included, and all mailing instructions of interest to the post office are placed above the address area (see Figure A.6). Canada Post requires a similar format, except that only the city is all in capitals, and the postal code is placed on the line below the name of the city. The post office scanners read addresses from the bottom up, so if a letter is to be sent to a post office box rather than to a street address, the street address should appear on the line above the box number. Figure A.6 also shows the proper spacing for addresses and return addresses.

**LJT** Workplace Solutions

May 5, 2013

Line 13 from top of page
■ 1 to 10 blank lines
■
■
■

Ms. Gillian Wiles, President
Scientific and Technical Contracts, Inc.
6348 Morehouse Dr.
San Diego, CA 92121

■ 2 blank lines
■

NEW SERVICES

■ 2 blank lines
■

Thank you, Ms. Wiles, for your recent inquiry about our services. Our complete line of staffing services offers high-level professionals with the skills you require. From the office to the factory, from the tech site to the trade show, from the law firm to the lab—we can provide you with the people and the expertise you need.

■ 1 blank line

I have enclosed a package of information for your review, including specific information on our engineers, designers/drafters, and engineering support personnel. The package also contains reprints of customer reviews and a comparison sheet showing how our services measure up against those of competing companies. We identify qualified candidates and recruit through a network of professional channels to reach candidates whose skills match the specific engineering disciplines you require.

■ 1 blank line

Please call me with any questions you may have. Whether you need a temporary employee for a day or an entire department staffed indefinitely, our staffing solutions give you the freedom you need to focus and the support you need to succeed. I will be glad to help you fill your staffing needs with Kelly professionals.

■ 3 blank lines
■

*Rudy Cohen*

RUDY COHEN
CUSTOMER SERVICE SPECIALIST

■ 1 blank line

jn

■ 1 blank line

Enclosures

999 WEST BIG BEAVER ROAD • TROY, MICHIGAN 48084-4782
TELEPHONE (248) 362-4444

**Figure A.5   Simplified Letter Format**

The U.S. Postal Service and the Canada Post Corporation have published lists of two-letter mailing abbreviations for states, provinces, and territories (see Table A.5 on page 582). Postal authorities prefer no punctuation with these abbreviations. Quantity mailings should always follow post office requirements. For other letters, a reasonable compromise is to use traditional punctuation, uppercase and lowercase letters for names and street addresses, but two-letter state or province abbreviations, as shown here:

Mr. Kevin Kennedy
2107 E. Packer Dr.
Amarillo, TX 79108

Canadian postal codes are alphanumeric, with a three-character "area code" and a three-character "local code" separated by a single space (K2P 5A5). Zip and postal codes should be separated from state and province names by one space. Canadian postal codes may be treated the same or may be put in the bottom line of the address all by itself.

## FOLDING TO FIT

The way a letter is folded also contributes to the recipient's overall impression of your organization's professionalism. When sending a standard-size piece of paper in a No. 10 envelope, fold it in thirds, with the bottom folded up first and the top folded down over it (see Figure A.7 on page 582); the open end should be at the top of the envelope and facing out. Fit smaller stationery neatly into the appropriate envelope simply by folding it in half or in thirds. When sending a standard-size letterhead in a No. 6 ¾ envelope,

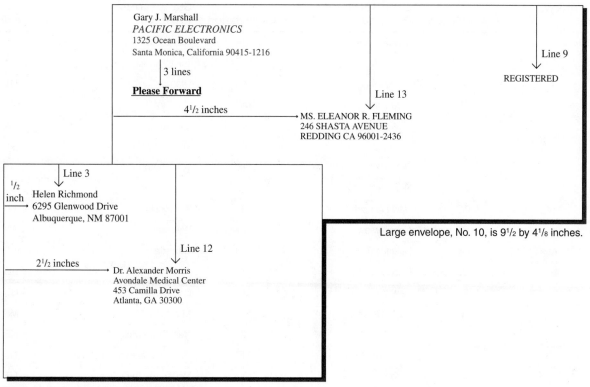

Figure A.6 **Prescribed Envelope Format**

fold it in half from top to bottom and then in thirds from side to side.

## INTERNATIONAL MAIL

Postal service differs from country to country, so it's always a good idea to investigate the quality and availability of various services before sending messages and packages internationally. Also, compare the services offered by delivery companies such as UPS and FedEx to find the best rates and options for each destination and type of shipment. No matter which service you choose, be aware that international mail requires more planning than domestic mail. For example, for anything beyond simple letters, you generally need to prepare *customs forms* and possibly other documents, depending on the country of destination and the type of shipment. You are responsible for following the laws of the United States and any countries to which you send mail and packages.

The U.S. Postal Service currently offers four classes of international delivery, listed here from the fastest (and most expensive) to the slowest (and least expensive):

- **Global Express Guaranteed** is the fastest option. This service, offered in conjunction with FedEx, provides delivery in one to three business days to more than 190 countries and territories.

- **Express Mail International** guarantees delivery in three to five business days to a limited number of countries, including Australia, China, Hong Kong, Japan, and South Korea.
- **Priority Mail International** offers delivery guarantees of 6 to 10 business days to more than 190 countries and territories.
- **First Class Mail International** is an economical way to send correspondence and packages weighing up to four pounds to virtually any destination worldwide.

To prepare your mail for international delivery, follow the instructions provided at **www.usps.com/international**. There you'll find complete information on the international services available through the U.S. Postal Service, along with advice on addressing and packaging mail, completing customs forms, and calculating postage rates and fees. The *International Mail Manual*, also available on this website, offers the latest information and regulations for both outbound and inbound international mail. For instance, you can click on individual country names to see current information about restricted or prohibited items and materials, required customs forms, and rates for various classes of service.[6] Various countries have specific and often extensive lists of items that may not be sent by mail at all or that must be sent using particular postal service options.

# TABLE A.5 | Two-Letter Mailing Abbreviations for the United States and Canada

| State/Territory/Province | Abbreviation | State/Territory/Province | Abbreviation | State/Territory/Province | Abbreviation |
|---|---|---|---|---|---|
| **United States** | | Massachusetts | MA | Tennessee | TN |
| Alabama | AL | Michigan | MI | Texas | TX |
| Alaska | AK | Minnesota | MN | Utah | UT |
| American Samoa | AS | Mississippi | MS | Vermont | VT |
| Arizona | AZ | Missouri | MO | Virginia | VA |
| Arkansas | AR | Montana | MT | Virgin Islands | VI |
| California | CA | Nebraska | NE | Washington | WA |
| Canal Zone | CZ | Nevada | NV | West Virginia | WV |
| Colorado | CO | New Hampshire | NH | Wisconsin | WI |
| Connecticut | CT | New Jersey | NJ | Wyoming | WY |
| Delaware | DE | New Mexico | NM | **Canada** | |
| District of Columbia | DC | Maryland | MD | Alberta | AB |
| Florida | FL | New York | NY | British Columbia | BC |
| Georgia | GA | North Carolina | NC | Manitoba | MB |
| Guam | GU | North Dakota | ND | New Brunswick | NB |
| Hawaii | HI | Northern Mariana | MP | Newfoundland and Labrador | NL |
| Idaho | ID | Ohio | OH | Northwest Territories | NT |
| Illinois | IL | Oklahoma | OK | Nova Scotia | NS |
| Indiana | IN | Oregon | OR | Nunavut | NU |
| Iowa | IA | Pennsylvania | PA | Ontario | ON |
| Kansas | KS | Puerto Rico | PR | Prince Edward Island | PE |
| Kentucky | KY | Rhode Island | RI | Quebec | QC |
| Louisiana | LA | South Carolina | SC | Saskatchewan | SK |
| Maine | ME | South Dakota | SD | Yukon Territory | YT |

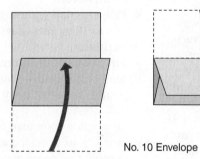
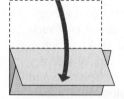
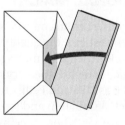

No. 10 Envelope

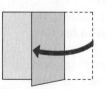

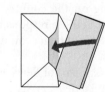

No. 6³/₄ Envelope

**Figure A.7** **Folding Standard-Size Letterhead**

# Memos

Electronic media have replaced most internal printed memos in many companies, but you may have occasion to send printed memos from time to time. These can be simple announcements or messages, or they can be short reports using the memo format.

On your document, include a title such as MEMO or INTEROFFICE CORRESPONDENCE (all in capitals) centered at the top of the page or aligned with the left margin. Also at the top, include the words *To, From, Date,* and *Subject*—followed by the appropriate information—with a blank line between as shown here:

MEMO

TO:
FROM:
DATE:
SUBJECT:

Sometimes the heading is organized like this:

MEMO

TO:                          FROM:
DATE:                       SUBJECT:

The following guidelines will help you effectively format specific memo elements:

- **Addressees.** When sending a memo to a long list of people, include the notation *See distribution list* or *See below* in the *To* position at the top; then list the names at the end of the memo. Arrange this list alphabetically, except when high-ranking officials deserve more prominent placement. You can also address memos to groups of people—*All Sales Representatives, Production Group, New Product Team.*
- **Courtesy titles.** You need not use courtesy titles anywhere in a memo; first initials and last names, first names, or even initials alone are often sufficient. However, use a courtesy title if you would use one in a face-to-face encounter with the person.
- **Subject line.** The subject line of a memo helps busy colleagues quickly find out what your memo is about, so take care to make it concise and compelling.
- **Body.** Start the body of the memo on the second or third line below the heading. Like the body of a letter, it's usually single-spaced with blank lines between paragraphs. Indenting paragraphs is optional. Handle lists, important passages, and subheadings as you do in letters.
- **Second page.** If the memo carries over to a second page, head the second page just as you head the second page of a letter.
- **Writer's initials.** Unlike a letter, a memo doesn't require a complimentary close or a signature, because your name is already prominent at the top. However, you may initial the memo—either beside the name appearing at the top of the memo or at the bottom of the memo.
- **Other elements.** Treat elements such as reference initials and copy notations just as you would in a letter. One difference between letters and memos is that while letters use the term *enclosure* to refer to other pieces included with the letter, memos usually use the word *attachment*.

Memos may be delivered by hand, by the post office (when the recipient works at a different location), or through interoffice mail. Interoffice mail may require the use of special reusable envelopes that have spaces for the recipient's name and department or room number; the name of the previous recipient is simply crossed out. If a regular envelope is used, the words *Interoffice Mail* appear where the stamp normally goes, so that it won't accidentally be stamped and mailed with the rest of the office correspondence.

Informal, routine, or brief reports for distribution within a company are often presented in memo form. Don't include report parts such as a table of contents and appendixes, but write the body of the memo report just as carefully as you'd write a formal report.

# Reports

Enhance the effectiveness of your reports by paying careful attention to their appearance and layout. Follow whatever guidelines your organization prefers, always being neat and consistent throughout. If it's up to you to decide formatting questions, the following conventions may help you decide how to handle margins, headings, and page numbers.

## MARGINS

All margins on a report page should be at least 1 inch wide. The top, left, and right margins are usually the same, but the bottom margins can be 1½ times deeper. Some special pages also have deeper top margins. Set top margins as deep as 2 inches for pages that contain major titles: prefatory parts (such as the table of contents or the executive summary), supplementary parts (such as the reference notes or bibliography), and textual parts (such as the first page of the text or the first page of each chapter).

If you're going to bind your report at the left or at the top, add half an inch to the margin on the bound edge (see Figure A.8): The space taken by the binding on left-bound reports makes the center point of the text a quarter inch to the right of the center of the paper. Be sure to center headings between the margins, not between the edges of the paper.

## HEADINGS

If you don't have a template supplied by your employer, choose a design for headings and subheadings that clearly distinguishes the various levels in the hierarchy. The first-level

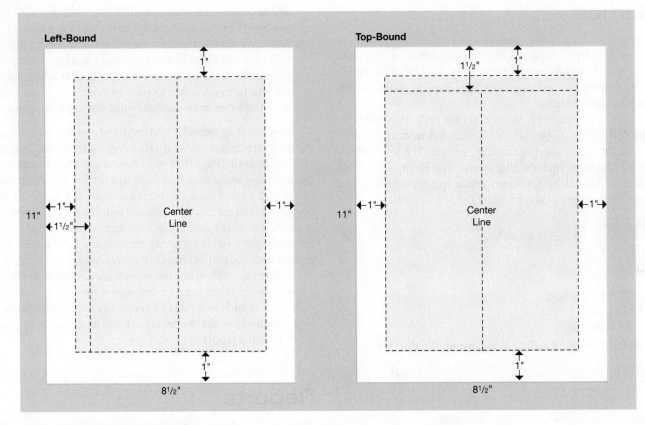

**Figure A.8** **Margins for Formal Reports**

headings should be the most prominent, on down to the lowest-level subheading.

## PAGE NUMBERS

Every page in a report is counted; however, not all pages show numbers. The first page of the report, normally the title page, is unnumbered. All other pages in the prefatory section are numbered with a lowercase roman numeral, beginning with *ii* and continuing with *iii, iv, v,* and so on. Start numbering again with arabic numerals (1, 2, and so on) starting at the first page of the body.

You have many options for placing and formatting the page numbers, although these choices are usually made for you in a template. If you're not using a standard company template, position the page number where it is easy to see as the reader flips through the report. If the report will be stapled or otherwise bound along the left side, for instance, the best place for the page number is the upper right or lower right corner.

## Endnotes

1. Mary A. De Vries, *Internationally Yours* (Boston: Houghton Mifflin, 1994), 9.
2. Patricia A. Dreyfus, "Paper That's Letter Perfect," *Money,* May 1985, 184.
3. Linda Driskill, *Business and Managerial Communication: New Perspectives* (Orlando, Fla.: Harcourt Brace Jovanovich, 1992), 470.

4. Lennie Copeland and Lewis Griggs, *Going International: How to Make Friends and Deal Effectively in the Global Marketplace,* 2nd ed. (New York: Random House, 1985), 24–27.
5. De Vries, *Internationally Yours,* 8. 6. U.S. Postal Service, *International Mail Manual,* Issue 34, 14 May 2007, www.usps.gov.

By providing information about your sources, you improve your own credibility as well as the credibility of the facts and opinions you present. Documentation gives readers the means for checking your findings and pursuing the subject further. Also, documenting your report is the accepted way to give credit to the people whose work you have drawn from.

What style should you use to document your report? Experts recommend various forms, depending on your field or discipline. Moreover, your employer or client may use a form different from those the experts suggest. Don't let this discrepancy confuse you. If your employer specifies a form, use it; the standardized form is easier for colleagues to understand. However, if the choice of form is left to you, adopt one of the styles described here. Whatever style you choose, be consistent within any given report, using the same order, punctuation, and format from one reference citation or bibliography entry to the next.

A wide variety of style manuals provide detailed information on documentation. These publications explain the three most commonly used styles:

- American Psychological Association, *Publication Manual of the American Psychological Association*, 6th ed. (Washington, D.C.: American Psychological Association, 2009). Details the author-date system, which is preferred in the social sciences and often in the natural sciences as well.
- *The Chicago Manual of Style*, 16th ed. (Chicago: University of Chicago Press, 2010). Often referred to only as "Chicago" and widely used in the publishing industry; provides detailed treatment of source documentation and many other aspects of document preparation.
- Joseph Gibaldi, *MLA Style Manual and Guide to Scholarly Publishing*, 3rd ed. (New York: Modern Language Association, 2008). Serves as the basis for the note and bibliography style used in much academic writing and is recommended in many college textbooks on writing term papers; provides a lot of examples in the humanities.

For more information on these three guides, visit http://real-timeupdates.com/bct12 and click on Appendix B. Although many schemes have been proposed for organizing the information in source notes, all of them break the information into parts: (1) information about the author (name), (2) information about the work (title, edition, volume num-ber), (3) information about the publication (place, publisher), (4) information about the date, and (5) information on relevant page ranges.

The following sections summarize the major conventions for documenting sources in three styles: *The Chicago Manual of Style* (Chicago), the *Publication Manual of the American Psychological Association* (APA), and the *MLA Style Manual* (MLA).

# *Chicago* Humanities Style

*The Chicago Manual of Style* recommends two types of documentation systems. The *documentary-note*, or *humanities*, style gives bibliographic citations in notes—either footnotes (when printed at the bottom of a page) or endnotes (when printed at the end of the report). The humanities system is often used in literature, history, and the arts. The other system recommended by *Chicago* is the *author-date* system, which cites the author's last name and the date of publication in the text, usually in parentheses, reserving full documentation for the reference list (or bibliography). For the purpose of comparing styles, this section concentrates on the humanities system, which is described in detail in *Chicago*.

## IN-TEXT CITATION—*CHICAGO* HUMANITIES STYLE

To document report sources in text, the humanities system relies on superscripts—arabic numerals placed just above the line of type at the end of the reference:

> Toward the end of his speech, Myers sounded a note of caution, saying that even though the economy is expected to grow, it could easily slow a bit.[10]

The superscript lets the reader know how to look for source information in either a footnote or an endnote (see Figure B.1 on the next page). Some readers prefer footnotes so that they can simply glance at the bottom of the page for information. Others prefer endnotes so that they can read the text without a clutter of notes on the page. Also, endnotes relieve the writer from worrying about how long each note will be and how much space it will take away from the page. Both footnotes and endnotes are handled automatically by today's word processing software.

For the reader's convenience, you can use footnotes for *content notes* (which may supplement your main text with asides about a particular issue or event, provide a cross-reference to another section of your report, or direct the reader to a related source). Then you can use endnotes for *source notes* (which document direct quotations, paraphrased passages, and visual aids). Consider which type of note is most common in your report, and then choose

NOTES

Journal article with volume and issue numbers

1. Jonathan Clifton, "Beyond Taxonomies of Influence," *Journal of Business Communication* 46, no. 1 (2009): 57–79.

Brochure

2. BestTemp Staffing Services, *An Employer's Guide to Staffing Services,* 2d ed. (Denver: BestTemp Information Center, 2013), 31.

Newspaper article, no author

3. "Might Be Harder Than It Looks," *Los Angeles Times,* 30 January 2013, sec. A, p. 22.

Annual report

4. The Walt Disney Company, *2012 Annual Report* (Burbank, Calif.: The Walt Disney Company, 2013), 48.

Magazine article

5. Kerry A. Dolan, "A Whole New Crop" *Forbes*, 2 June 2013, 72–75.

Television broadcast

6. Daniel Han, "Trade Wars Heating Up Around the Globe," *CNN Headline News* (Atlanta: CNN, 5 March 2013).

Internet, World Wide Web

7. "Intel—Company Capsule," Hoover's Online [cited 19 June 2011], 3 screens; available from www.hoovers.com/intel/-ID_13787-/free-co-factsheet.xhtml.

Book, component parts

8. Sonja Kuntz, "Moving Beyond Benefits," in *Our Changing Workforce,* ed. Randolf Jacobson (New York: Citadel Press, 2001), 213–27.

Unpublished dissertation or thesis

9. George H. Morales, "The Economic Pressures on Industrialized Nations in a Global Economy" (Ph.D. diss., University of San Diego, 2001), 32–47.

Paper presented at a meeting

10. Charles Myers, "HMOs in Today's Environment" (paper presented at the Conference on Medical Insurance Solutions, Chicago, Ill., August 2001), 16–17.

Online magazine article

11. Leo Babauta, "17 Tips to Be Productive with Instant Messaging," in *Web Worker Daily* [online] (San Francisco, 2011 [updated 14 November 2012; cited 14 February 2013]); available from http://webworkerdaily.com.

Interview

12. Georgia Stainer, general manager, Day Cable and Communications, interview by author, Topeka, Kan., 2 March 2011.

Newspaper article, one author

13. Evelyn Standish, "Global Market Crushes OPEC's Delicate Balance of Interests," *Wall Street Journal,* 19 January 2002, sec. A, p. 1.

Book, two authors

14. Miriam Toller and Jay Fielding, *Global Business for Smaller Companies* (Rocklin, Calif.: Prima Publishing, 2001), 102–3.

Government publication

15. U.S. Department of Defense, *Stretching Research Dollars: Survival Advice for Universities and Government Labs* (Washington, D.C.: GPO, 2002), 126.

**Figure B.1    Sample Endnotes—*Chicago* Humanities Style**

whether to present these notes all as endnotes or all as footnotes. Regardless of the method you choose for referencing textual information in your report, notes for visual aids (both content notes and source notes) are placed on the same page as the visual.

## BIBLIOGRAPHY—*CHICAGO* HUMANITIES STYLE

The humanities system may or may not be accompanied by a bibliography (because the notes give all the necessary bibliographic information). However, endnotes are arranged in order of appearance in the text, so an alphabetical bibliography can be valuable to your readers. The bibliography may be titled *Bibliography, Reference List, Sources, Works Cited* (if you include only those sources you actually cited in your report), or *Works Consulted* (if you include uncited sources as well). This list of sources may also serve as a reading list for those who want to pursue the subject of your report further, so you may want to annotate each entry—that is, comment on the subject matter and viewpoint of the source, as well as on its usefulness to readers. Annotations may be written in either complete or incomplete sentences. A bibliography may also be more manageable if you subdivide it into categories (a classified bibliography), either by type of reference (such as books, articles, and unpublished material) or by subject matter (such as government regulation, market forces, and so on). Following are the major

BIBLIOGRAPHY

| | |
|---|---|
| Online magazine article | Babauta, Leo. "17 Tips to Be Productive with Instant Messaging," In *Web Worker Daily* [online], San Francisco, 2011 [updated 14 November 2012, cited 14 February 2013]. Available from http://webworkerdaily.com. |
| Brochure | BestTemp Staffing Services. *An Employer's Guide to Staffing Services.* 2d ed. Denver: BestTemp Information Center, 2013. |
| Journal article with volume and issue numbers | Clifton, Jonathan. "Beyond Taxonomies of Influence." *Journal of Business Communication* 46, no. 1 (2009): 57–79. |
| Magazine article | Dolan, Kerry A. "A Whole New Crop," *Forbes,* 2 June 2013, 72–75. |
| Television broadcast | Han, Daniel. "Trade Wars Heating Up Around the Globe." *CNN Headline News.* Atlanta: CNN, 5 March 2013. |
| Internet, World Wide Web | "Intel—Company Capsule." *Hoover's Online* [cited 19 June 2011]. 3 screens; Available from www.hoovers.com/intel/-ID_13787-/free-co-factsheet.xhtml. |
| Book, component parts | Kuntz, Sonja. "Moving Beyond Benefits." In *Our Changing Workforce*, edited by Randolf Jacobson. New York: Citadel Press, 2001. |
| Newspaper article, no author | "Might Be Harder Than It Looks." *Los Angeles Times,* 30 January 2013, sec. A, p. 22. |
| Unpublished dissertation or thesis | Morales, George H. "The Economic Pressures on Industrialized Nations in a Global Economy." Ph.D. diss., University of San Diego, 2001. |
| Paper presented at a meeting | Myers, Charles. "HMOs in Today's Environment." Paper presented at the Conference on Medical Insurance Solutions, Chicago, Ill., August 2001. |
| Interview | Stainer, Georgia, general manager, Day Cable and Communications. Interview by author. Topeka, Kan., 2 March 2011. |
| Newspaper article, one author | Standish, Evelyn. "Global Market Crushes OPEC's Delicate Balance of Interests." *Wall Street Journal,* 19 January 2002, sec. A, p. 1. |
| Book, two authors | Toller, Miriam, and Jay Fielding. *Global Business for Smaller Companies.* Rocklin, Calif.: Prima Publishing, 2001. |
| Government publication | U.S. Department of Defense. *Stretching Research Dollars: Survival Advice for Universities and Government Labs.* Washington, D.C.: GPO, 2002. |
| Annual report | The Walt Disney Company, *2012 Annual Report,* Burbank, Calif.: The Walt Disney Company, 2013. |

**Figure B.2   Sample Bibliography—*Chicago* Humanities Style**

conventions for developing a bibliography according to *Chicago* style (see Figure B.2):

- Exclude any page numbers that may be cited in source notes, except for journals, periodicals, and newspapers.
- Alphabetize entries by the last name of the lead author (listing last name first). The names of second and succeeding authors are listed in normal order. Entries without an author name are alphabetized by the first important word in the title.
- Format entries as hanging indents (indent second and succeeding lines three to five spaces).
- Arrange entries in the following general order: (1) author name, (2) title information, (3) publication information, (4) date, (5) periodical page range.

- Use quotation marks around the titles of articles from magazines, newspapers, and journals. Capitalize the first and last words, as well as all other important words (except prepositions, articles, and coordinating conjunctions).
- Use italics to set off the names of books, newspapers, journals, and other complete publications. Capitalize the first and last words, as well as all other important words.
- For journal articles, include the volume number and the issue number (if necessary). Include the year of publication inside parentheses and follow with a colon and the page range of the article: *Journal of Business Communication* 46, no. 1 (2009): 57–79. (In this source, the volume is 46, the number is 1, and the page range is 57–79.)
- Use brackets to identify all electronic references: [Online database] or [CD-ROM].

- Explain how electronic references can be reached: Available from www.spaceless.com/WWWVL.
- Give the citation date for online references: Cited 23 August 2013.

# APA Style

The American Psychological Association (APA) recommends the author-date system of documentation, which is popular in the physical, natural, and social sciences. When using this system, you simply insert the author's last name and the year of publication within parentheses following the text discussion of the material cited. Include a page number if you use a direct quotation. This approach briefly identifies the source so that readers can locate complete information in the alphabetical reference list at the end of the report. The author-date system is both brief and clear, saving readers time and effort.

## IN-TEXT CITATION—APA STYLE

To document report sources in text using APA style, insert the author's surname and the date of publication at the end of a statement. Enclose this information in parentheses. If the author's name is referred to in the text itself, then the name can be omitted from parenthetical material.

> Some experts recommend both translation and back-translation when dealing with any non-English-speaking culture (Clifton, 2009).
> Toller and Fielding (2001) make a strong case for small companies succeeding in global business.

Personal communications and interviews conducted by the author would not be listed in the reference list at all. Such citations would appear in the text only.

> Increasing the role of cable companies is high on the list of Georgia Stainer, general manager at Day Cable and Communications (personal communication, March 2, 2011).

## LIST OF REFERENCES—APA STYLE

For APA style, list only those works actually cited in the text (so you would not include works for background or for further reading). Following are the major conventions for developing a reference list according to APA style (see Figure B.3):

- Format entries as hanging indents.
- List all author names in reversed order (last name first), and use only initials for the first and middle names.
- Arrange entries in the following general order: (1) author name, (2) date, (3) title information, (4) publication information, (5) periodical page range.
- Follow the author name with the date of publication in parentheses.
- List titles of articles from magazines, newspapers, and journals without underlines or quotation marks. Capitalize only the first word of the title, any proper nouns, and the first word to follow an internal colon.

- Italicize titles of books, capitalizing only the first word, any proper nouns, and the first word to follow a colon.
- Italicize titles of magazines, newspapers, journals, and other complete publications. Capitalize all the important words in the title.
- For journal articles, include the volume number (in italics) and, if necessary, the issue number (in parentheses). Finally, include the page range of the article: *Journal of Business Communication, 46*(1), 57–79. (In this example, the volume is 46, the number is 1, and the page range is 57–79.)
- Include personal communications (such as letters, memos, email, and conversations) only in text, not in reference lists.
- Electronic references include author, date of publication, title of article, name of publication (if one), volume, date of retrieval (month, day, year), and the source.
- For electronic references, indicate the actual year of publication.
- For webpages with extremely long URLs, use your best judgment to determine which URL from the site to use. For example, rather than giving the URL of a specific news release with a long URL, you can provide the URL of the "Media relations" webpage.
- APA citation guidelines for social media are still evolving. For the latest information, visit the APA Style Blog at http://blog.apastyle.org/apastyle.
- For online journals or periodicals that assign a digital object identifier (DOI), include that instead of a conventional URL. If no DOI is available, include the URL of the publication's home page (such as http://online.wsj.com for the *Wall Street Journal*).

# MLA Style

The style recommended by the Modern Language Association of America is used widely in the humanities, especially in the study of language and literature. Like APA style, MLA style uses brief parenthetical citations in the text. However, instead of including author name and year, MLA citations include author name and page reference.

## IN-TEXT CITATION—MLA STYLE

To document report sources in text using MLA style, insert the author's last name and a page reference inside parentheses following the cited material: (Matthews 63). If the author's name is mentioned in the text reference, the name can be omitted from the parenthetical citation: (63). The citation indicates that the reference came from page 63 of a work by Matthews. With the author's name, readers can find complete publication information in the alphabetically arranged list of works cited that comes at the end of the report.

> Some experts recommend both translation and back-translation when dealing with any non-English-speaking culture (Clifton 57).
> Toller and Fielding make a strong case for small companies succeeding in global business (102–03).

## REFERENCES

Online magazine article

Babauta, L. (2007, November 14). 17 tips to be productive with instant messaging. *Web Worker Daily*. Retrieved from http://webworkerdaily.com

Brochure

BestTemp Staffing Services. (2013). *An employer's guide to staffing services* (2nd ed.) [Brochure]. Denver, CO: BestTemp Information Center.

Journal article with volume and issue numbers

Clifton, J. (2009). Beyond taxonomies of influence. *Journal of Business Communication, 46*(1), 57.

Magazine article

Dolan, K. A. (2013, June 2). A whole new crop. *Forbes*, 72–75.

Television broadcast

Han, D. (2013, March 5). Trade wars heating up around the globe. *CNN Headline News*. [Television broadcast]. Atlanta, GA: CNN.

Internet, World Wide Web

Hoover's Online. (2011). *Intel—company capsule*. Retrieved from http://www.hoovers.com/intel/-ID_13787-/free-co-factsheet.xhtml

Book, component parts

Kuntz, S. (2001). Moving beyond benefits. In Randolph Jacobson (Ed.), *Our changing workforce* (pp. 213–227). New York, NY: Citadel Press.

Newspaper article, no author

Might be harder than it looks. (2013, January 30). *Los Angeles Times*, p. A22.

Unpublished dissertation or thesis

Morales, G. H. (2001). *The economic pressures on industrialized nations in a global economy*. Unpublished doctoral dissertation, University of San Diego.

Paper presented at a meeting

Myers, C. (2001, August). *HMOs in today's environment*. Paper presented at the Conference on Medical Insurance Solutions, Chicago, IL.

Interview

*Cited in text only, not in the list of references.*

Newspaper article, one author

Standish, E. (2002, January 19). Global market crushes OPEC's delicate balance of interests. *Wall Street Journal*, p. A1.

Book, two authors

Toller, M., & Fielding, J. (2001). *Global business for smaller companies*. Rocklin, CA: Prima Publishing.

Government publication

U.S. Department of Defense. (2002). *Stretching research dollars: Survival advice for universities and government labs*. Washington, DC: U.S. Government Printing Office.

Annual report

The Walt Disney Company. (2013). *2012 Annual report*, Burbank, CA: The Walt Disney Company.

**Figure B.3    Sample References—APA Style**

## LIST OF WORKS CITED—MLA STYLE

The *MLA Style Manual* recommends preparing the list of works cited first so that you will know what information to give in the parenthetical citation (for example, whether to add a short title if you're citing more than one work by the same author, or whether to give an initial or first name if you're citing two authors who have the same last name). The list of works cited appears at the end of your report, contains all the works that you cite in your text, and lists them in alphabetical order. Following are the major conventions for developing a reference list according to MLA style (see Figure B.4 on the next page):

- Format entries as hanging indents.
- Arrange entries in the following general order: (1) author name, (2) title information, (3) publication information, (4) date, (5) periodical page range.

- List the lead author's name in reverse order (last name first), using either full first names or initials. List second and succeeding author names in normal order.
- Use quotation marks around the titles of articles from magazines, newspapers, and journals. Capitalize all important words.
- Italicize the names of books, newspapers, journals, and other complete publications, capitalizing all main words in the title.
- For journal articles, include the volume number and the issue number (if necessary). Include the year of publication inside parentheses and follow with a colon and the page range of the article: *Journal of Business Communication* 46, 1 (2009): 57. (In this source, the volume is 46, the number is 1, and the page is 57.)
- Electronic sources are less fixed than print sources, and they may not be readily accessible to readers. So citations

## WORKS CITED

Online magazine article
Babauta, Leo. "17 Tips to Be Productive with Instant Messaging," *Web Worker Daily* 14 Nov. 2012. 14 Feb. 2013. http://webworkerdaily.com

Brochure
BestTemp Staffing Services. *An Employer's Guide to Staffing Services*. 2d ed. Denver: BestTemp Information Center, 2013.

Journal article with volume and issue numbers
Clifton, Jonathan. "Beyond Taxonomies of Influence." *Journal of Business Communication* 46, 1 (2009): 57–79.

Magazine article
Dolan, Kerry A. "A Whole New Crop" *Forbes*, 2 June 2013: 72–75.

Television broadcast
Han, Daniel. "Trade Wars Heating Up Around the Globe." *CNN Headline News*. CNN, Atlanta. 5 Mar. 2013.

Internet, World Wide Web
"Intel—Company Capsule." *Hoover's Online*. 2011. Hoover's Company Information. 19 June 2011 http://www.hoovers.com/intel/-ID_13787/free-co-factsheet.xhtml

Book, component parts
Kuntz, Sonja. "Moving Beyond Benefits." *Our Changing Workforce*. Ed. Randolf Jacobson. New York: Citadel Press, 2001. 213–27.

Newspaper article, no author
"Might Be Harder Than It Looks." *Los Angeles Times,* 30 Jan. 2013: A22.

Unpublished dissertation or thesis
Morales, George H. "The Economic Pressures on Industrialized Nations in a Global Economy." Diss. U of San Diego, 2001.

Paper presented at a meeting
Myers, Charles. "HMOs in Today's Environment." Conference on Medical Insurance Solutions. Chicago. 13 Aug. 2001.

Interview
Stainer, Georgia, general manager, Day Cable and Communications. Telephone interview. 2 Mar. 2011.

Newspaper article, one author
Standish, Evelyn. "Global Market Crushes OPEC's Delicate Balance of Interests." *Wall Street Journal,* 19 Jan. 2002: A1.

Book, two authors
Toller, Miriam, and Jay Fielding. *Global Business for Smaller Companies*. Rocklin, CA: Prima Publishing, 2001.

Government publication
United States. Department of Defense. *Stretching Research Dollars: Survival Advice for Universities and Government Labs*. Washington: GPO, 2002.

Annual report
The Walt Disney Company, *2012 Annual Report*. Burbank, Calif.: The Walt Disney Company, 2013.

**Figure B.4    Sample Works Cited—MLA Style**

for electronic sources must provide more information. Always try to be as comprehensive as possible, citing whatever information is available (however, see the note below about extremely long URLs).

- The date for electronic sources should contain both the date assigned in the source (if no date is shown, write "n.d." instead) and the date accessed by the researcher.
- The URL for electronic sources must be as accurate and complete as possible, from access-mode identifier (such as http or ftp) to all relevant directory and file names. If the URL is extremely long, however, use the URL of the website's home page or the URL of the site's search page if you used the site's search function to find the article. The *MLA Style Manual* no longer requires writers to include URLs for materials retrieved online. However, follow whatever guidelines your instructor gives you in this regard.
- MLA style requires you to indicate the medium of publication. For most sources, this will be "Web" or "Print," but you may also cite "CD-ROM" and other media, as appropriate.

# C | Correction Symbols

Instructors often use these short, easy-to-remember correction symbols and abbreviations when evaluating students' writing. You can use them too, to understand your instructor's suggestions and to revise and proofread your own letters, memos, and reports. Refer to the Handbook of Grammar, Mechanics, and Usage (pp. 594–620) for further information.

## Content and Style

| | |
|---|---|
| Acc | Accuracy. Check to be sure information is correct. |
| ACE | Avoid copying examples. |
| ACP | Avoid copying problems. |
| Adp | Adapt. Tailor message to reader. |
| App | Follow proper organization approach. (Refer to Chapter 4.) |
| Assign | Assignment. Review instructions for assignment. |
| AV | Active verb. Substitute active for passive. |
| Awk | Awkward phrasing. Rewrite. |
| BC | Be consistent. |
| BMS | Be more sincere. |
| Chop | Choppy sentences. Use longer sentences and more transitional phrases. |
| Con | Condense. Use fewer words. |
| CT | Conversational tone. Avoid using overly formal language. |
| Depers | Depersonalize. Avoid attributing credit or blame to any individual or group. |
| Dev | Develop. Provide greater detail. |
| Dir | Direct. Use direct approach; get to the point. |
| Emph | Emphasize. Develop this point more fully. |
| EW | Explanation weak. Check logic; provide more proof. |
| Fl | Flattery. Avoid compliments that are insincere. |
| FS | Figure of speech. Find a more accurate expression. |
| GNF | Good news first. Use direct order. |
| GRF | Give reasons first. Use indirect order. |
| GW | Goodwill. Put more emphasis on expressions of goodwill. |

| | |
|---|---|
| H/E | Honesty/ethics. Revise statement to reflect good business practices. |
| Imp | Imply. Avoid being direct. |
| Inc | Incomplete. Develop further. |
| Jar | Jargon. Use less specialized language. |
| Log | Logic. Check development of argument. |
| Neg | Negative. Use more positive approach or expression. |
| Obv | Obvious. Do not state point in such detail. |
| OC | Overconfident. Adopt humbler language. |
| OM | Omission. |
| Org | Organization. Strengthen outline. |
| OS | Off the subject. Close with point on main subject. |
| Par | Parallel. Use same structure. |
| Pom | Pompous. Rephrase in down-to-earth terms. |
| PV | Point of view. Make statement from reader's perspective rather than your own. |
| RB | Reader benefit. Explain what reader stands to gain. |
| Red | Redundant. Reduce number of times this point is made. |
| Ref | Reference. Cite source of information. |
| Rep | Repetitive. Provide different expression. |
| RS | Resale. Reassure reader that he or she has made a good choice. |
| SA | Service attitude. Put more emphasis on helping reader. |
| Sin | Sincerity. Avoid sounding glib or uncaring. |
| SL | Stereotyped language. Focus on individual's characteristics instead of on false generalizations. |
| Spec | Specific. Provide more specific statement. |
| SPM | Sales promotion material. Tell reader about related goods or services. |
| Stet | Let stand in original form. |
| Sub | Subordinate. Make this point less important. |
| SX | Sexist. Avoid language that contributes to gender stereotypes. |
| Tone | Tone needs improvement. |
| Trans | Transition. Show connection between points. |

| | | | |
|---|---|---|---|
| UAE | Use action ending. Close by stating what reader should do next. | USS | Use shorter sentences. |
| UAS | Use appropriate salutation. | V | Variety. Use different expression or sentence pattern. |
| UAV | Use active voice. | W | Wordy. Eliminate unnecessary words. |
| Unc | Unclear. Rewrite to clarify meaning. | WC | Word choice. Find a more appropriate word. |
| UPV | Use passive voice. | YA | "You" attitude. Rewrite to emphasize reader's needs. |

# Grammar, Mechanics, and Usage

| | | | |
|---|---|---|---|
| Ab | Abbreviation. Avoid abbreviations in most cases; use correct abbreviation. | lc | Lowercase. Do not use capital letter. |
| Adj | Adjective. Use adjective instead. | M | Margins. Improve frame around document. |
| Adv | Adverb. Use adverb instead. | MM | Misplaced modifier. Place modifier close to word it modifies. |
| Agr | Agreement. Make subject and verb or noun and pronoun agree. | NRC | Nonrestrictive clause (or phrase). Separate from rest of sentence with commas. |
| Ap | Appearance. Improve appearance. | P | Punctuation. Use correct punctuation. |
| Apos | Apostrophe. Check use of apostrophe. | Par | Parallel. Use same structure. |
| Art | Article. Use correct article. | PH | Place higher. Move document up on page. |
| BC | Be consistent. | PL | Place lower. Move document down on page. |
| Cap | Capitalize. | Prep | Preposition. Use correct preposition. |
| Case | Use cases correctly. | RC | Restrictive clause (or phrase). Remove commas that separate clause from rest of sentence. |
| CoAdj | Coordinate adjective. Insert comma between coordinate adjectives; delete comma between adjective and compound noun. | RO | Run-on sentence. Separate two sentences with comma and coordinating conjunction or with semicolon. |
| CS | Comma splice. Use period or semicolon to separate clauses. | SC | Series comma. Add comma before *and*. |
| DM | Dangling modifier. Rewrite so that modifier clearly relates to subject of sentence. | SI | Split infinitive. Do not separate *to* from rest of verb. |
| Exp | Expletive. Avoid expletive beginnings, such as it is, there are, there is, this is, and these are. | Sp | Spelling error. Consult dictionary. |
| | | S-V | Subject-verb pair. Do not separate with comma. |
| F | Format. Improve layout of document. | Syl | Syllabification. Divide word between syllables. |
| Frag | Fragment. Rewrite as complete sentence. | WD | Word division. Check dictionary for proper end-of-line hyphenation. |
| Gram | Grammar. Correct grammatical error. | | |
| HCA | Hyphenate compound adjective. | WW | Wrong word. Replace with another word. |

# Proofreading Marks

| Symbol | Meaning | Symbol Used in Context | Corrected Copy |
|---|---|---|---|
| ⚌ | Align horizontally | meaning<u>ful <sup>re</sup></u>sult | meaningful result |
| ‖ | Align vertically | 1. Power cable<br>2. Keyboard | 1. Power cable<br>2. Keyboard |
| bf | Boldface | Recommendations  bf | **Recommendations** |
| ≡ | Capitalize | Pepsico, Inc. | PepsiCo, Inc. |
| ]⊏ | Center | ]Awards Banquet⊏ | Awards Banquet |
| ◯ | Close up space | self- confidence | self-confidence |
| ℓ | Delete | harrassment and abuse ℓ | harassment |
| ds | Double-space | text in first line<br>text in second line  ds | text in first line<br><br>text in second line |
| ∧ | Insert | <sup>u</sup> and white<br>trquoise shirts | turquoise and white shirts |
| ⩔ | Insert apostrophe | our teams goals | our team's goals |
| ⩘ | Insert comma | a, b and c | a, b, and c |
| ⩱ | Insert hyphen | third quarter sales | third-quarter sales |
| ⊙ | Insert period | Harrigan et al | Harrigan et al. |
| �ᵛ ⩭ | Insert quotation marks | This team isn't cooperating. | This "team" isn't cooperating. |
| # | Insert space | real estate testcase | real estate test case |
| ital | Italics | Quarterly Report  ital | *Quarterly Report* |
| / | Lowercase | TULSA, South of here | Tulsa, south of here |
| ⌊⌋ | Move down | Sincerely, | Sincerely, |
| ⊏ | Move left | Attention: ⊏Security | Attention: Security |
| ⊐ | Move right | February 2, 2013 ⌐⌐ | February 2, 2013 |
| ⌈⌉ | Move up | THIRD-QUARTER SALES | THIRD-QUARTER SALES |
| STET | Restore | staff talked openly and frankly ℓ  STET | staff talked openly |
| ⌇ | Run lines together | Manager,<br>Distribution | Manager, Distribution |
| ss | Single space | text in first line<br>text in second line  ss | text in first line<br>text in second line |
| ◯ | Spell out | COD | cash on delivery |
| sp | Spell out | sp Assn. of Biochem. Engrs. | Association of Biochemical Engineers |
| ⌐⌐ | Start new line | Marla Fenton, Manager, Distribution | Marla Fenton,<br>Manager, Distribution |
| ¶ | Start new paragraph | ¶The solution is easy to determine but difficult to implement in a competitive environment like the one we now face. | The solution is easy to determine but difficult to implement in a competitive environment like the one we now face. |
| ∼ | Transpose | airy, light, casaul tone | light, airy, casual tone |

The rules of grammar, mechanics, and usage provide the guidance every professional needs in order to communicate successfully with colleagues, customers, and other audiences. Understanding and following these rules helps you in two important ways. First, the rules determine how meaning is encoded and decoded in the communication process. If you don't encode your messages using the same rules your readers or listeners use to decode them, chances are your audiences will not extract your intended meaning from your messages. Without a firm grasp of the basics of grammar, mechanics, and usage, you risk being misunderstood, damaging your company's image, losing money for your company, and possibly even losing your job. In other words, if you want to get your point across, you need to follow the rules of grammar, mechanics, and usage. Second, apart from transferring meaning successfully, following the rules tells your audience that you respect the conventions and expectations of the business community.

You can think of *grammar* as the agreed-upon structure of a language, the way that individual words are formed and the manner in which those words are then combined to form meaningful sentences. *Mechanics* are style and formatting issues such as capitalization, spelling, and the use of numbers and symbols. *Usage* involves the accepted and expected way in which specific words are used by a particular community of people—in this case, the community of businesspeople who use English. This handbook can help you improve your knowledge and awareness in all three areas. It is divided into the following sections:

- **Diagnostic Test of English Skills.** Testing your current knowledge of grammar, mechanics, and usage helps you find out where your strengths and weaknesses lie. This test offers 50 items taken from the topics included in this handbook.
- **Assessment of English Skills.** After completing the diagnostic test, use the assessment form to highlight the areas you most need to review.
- **Essentials of Grammar, Mechanics, and Usage.** This section helps you quickly review the basics. You can study the things you've probably already learned but may have forgotten about grammar, punctuation, mechanics (including capitalization, abbreviation, number style, and word division), and vocabulary (including frequently confused words, frequently misused words, frequently misspelled words, and transitional words and phrases). Use this essential review not only to study and improve your English skills but also as a reference for any questions you may have during this course.

## Diagnostic Test of English Skills

Use this test to determine whether you need more practice with grammar, punctuation, mechanics, or vocabulary. When you've answered all the questions, ask your instructor for an answer sheet so that you can score the test. On the Assessment of English Skills form (page 596), record the number of questions you answered incorrectly in each section.

The following choices apply to items 1–5. Write in each blank the letter of the choice that best describes the part of speech that is underlined.

A. noun
B. pronoun
C. verb
D. adjective
E. adverb
F. preposition
G. conjunction
H. article

_____ 1. The new branch location will be decided <u>by</u> next week.
_____ 2. We must hire only <u>qualified</u>, ambitious graduates.
_____ 3. After their <u>presentation</u>, I was still undecided.
_____ 4. See <u>me</u> after the meeting.
_____ 5. Margaret, pressed for time, turned in <u>unusually</u> sloppy work.

In the blanks for items 6–15, write the letter of the word or phrase that best completes each sentence.

_____ 6. (A. Russ's, B. Russ') laptop was stolen last week.
_____ 7. Speaking only for (A. me, B. myself), I think the new policy is discriminatory.
_____ 8. Of the five candidates we interviewed yesterday, (A. who, B. whom) do you believe is the best choice?
_____ 9. India has increased (A. it's, B. its) imports of corn and rice.
_____ 10. Anyone who wants to be (A. their, B. his or her) own boss should think about owning a franchise.
_____ 11. If the IT department can't (A. lie, B. lay) the fiber-optic cable by March 1, the plant will not open on schedule.
_____ 12. Starbucks (A. is, B. are) opening five new stores in San Diego in the next year.
_____ 13. The number of women-owned small businesses (A. has, B. have) increased sharply in the past two decades.

_____ 14. Greg and Bernyce worked (A. good, B. well) together.
_____ 15. They distributed the supplies (A. among, B. between) the six staff members.

The following choices apply to items 16–20. Write in each blank the letter of the choice that best describes the sentence structure problem with each item.

A. sentence fragment
B. comma splice
C. misplaced modifier
D. fused sentence
E. lack of parallelism
F. unclear antecedent

_____ 16. The number of employees who took the buyout offer was much higher than expected, now the entire company is understaffed.
_____ 17. The leader in Internet-only banking.
_____ 18. Diamond doesn't actually sell financial products rather it acts as an intermediary.
_____ 19. Helen's proposal is for not only the present but also for the future.
_____ 20. When purchasing luxury products, quality is more important than price for consumers.

For items 21–30, circle the letter of the preferred choice in each of the following groups of sentences.

21. A. What do you think of the ad slogan "Have it your way?"
    B. What do you think of the ad slogan "Have it your way"?
22. A. Send copies to Jackie Cross, Uniline, Brad Nardi, Peale & Associates, and Tom Griesbaum, MatchMakers.
    B. Send copies to Jackie Cross, Uniline; Brad Nardi, Peale & Associates; and Tom Griesbaum, MatchMakers.
23. A. They've recorded 22 complaints since yesterday, all of them from long-time employees.
    B. They've recorded 22 complaints since yesterday; all of them from long-time employees.
24. A. We are looking for two qualities in applicants: experience with computers and an interest in people.
    B. We are looking for two qualities in applicants; experience with computers and an interest in people.
25. A. At the Center for the Blind the clients we serve have lost vision, due to a wide variety of causes.
    B. At the Center for the Blind, the clients we serve have lost vision due to a wide variety of causes.
26. A. Replace your standard light bulbs with new, compact fluorescent bulbs.
    B. Replace your standard light bulbs with new, compact, fluorescent bulbs.
    C. Replace your standard light bulbs with new compact fluorescent bulbs.
27. A. Blue Cross of California may have changed its name to Anthem Blue Cross but the company still has the same commitment to California.
    B. Blue Cross of California may have changed its name to Anthem Blue Cross, but the company still has the same commitment to California.

28. A. Only eight banks in this country—maybe nine can handle transactions of this magnitude.
    B. Only eight banks in this country—maybe nine—can handle transactions of this magnitude.
29. A. Instead of focusing on high-growth companies, we targeted mature businesses with only one or two people handling the decision making.
    B. Instead of focusing on high growth companies, we targeted mature businesses with only one or two people handling the decision-making.
30. A. According to board president Damian Cabaza "having a crisis communication plan is a high priority."
    B. According to board president Damian Cabaza, "Having a crisis communication plan is a high priority."

For items 31–40, select the best choice from among those provided.

31. A. At her previous employer, Mary-Anne worked in Marketing Communications and Human Resources.
    B. At her previous employer, Mary-Anne worked in marketing communications and human resources.
32. A. By fall, we'll have a dozen locations between the Mississippi and Missouri rivers.
    B. By Fall, we'll have a dozen locations between the Mississippi and Missouri Rivers.
33. A. The Board applauded President Donlan upon her reelection for a fifth term.
    B. The board applauded president Donlan upon her reelection for a fifth term.
    C. The board applauded President Donlan upon her reelection for a fifth term.
34. A. If you want to travel to France, you need to be au courant with the business practices.
    B. If you want to travel to France, you need to be "au courant" with the business practices.
35. A. As the company's CEO, Thomas Spurgeon handles all dealings with the FDA.
    B. As the company's C.E.O., Thomas Spurgeon handles all dealings with the F.D.A.
36. A. The maximum speed limit in most states is 65 mph.
    B. The maximum speed limit in most states is 65 m.p.h.
37. A. Sales of graphic novels increased nine percent between 2008 and 2009.
    B. Sales of graphic novels increased 9 percent between 2008 and 2009.
38. A. Our store is open daily from nine a.m. to seven p.m.
    B. Our store is open daily from 9:00 a.m. to 7:00 p.m.
39. A. The organizing meeting is scheduled for July 27, and the event will be held in January 2014.
    B. The organizing meeting is scheduled for July 27th, and the event will be held in January, 2014.
40. A. We need six desks, eight file cabinets, and 12 trashcans.
    B. We need 6 desks, 8 file cabinets, and 12 trashcans.

For items 41–50, write in each blank the letter of the word that best completes each sentence.

_____ **41.** Will having a degree (A. affect, B. effect) my chances for promotion?

_____ **42.** Try not to (A. loose, B. lose) this key; we will charge you a fee to replace it.

_____ **43.** I don't want to discuss my (A. personal, B. personnel) problems in front of anyone.

_____ **44.** Let us help you choose the right tie to (A. complement, B. compliment) your look.

_____ **45.** The repairman's whistling (A. aggravated, B. irritated) all of us in accounting.

_____ **46.** The bank agreed to (A. loan, B. lend) the Smiths $20,000 for their start-up.

_____ **47.** The credit card company is (A. liable, B. likely) to increase your interest rate if you miss a payment.

_____ **48.** The airline tries to (A. accommodate, B. accomodate) disabled passengers.

_____ **49.** Every company needs a policy regarding sexual (A. harrassment, B. harassment).

_____ **50.** Use your best (A. judgment, B. judgement) in selecting a service provider.

## Assessment of English Skills

In the space provided, record the number of questions you answered incorrectly.

| Questions | Skills Area | Number of Incorrect Answers |
|---|---|---|
| 1–5 | Parts of speech | _____ |
| 6–15 | Usage | _____ |
| 16–20 | Sentence structure | _____ |
| 21–30 | Punctuation | _____ |
| 31–40 | Mechanics | _____ |
| 41–50 | Vocabulary | _____ |

If you had more than two incorrect answers in any of the skills areas, focus on those areas in the appropriate sections of this handbook.

## Essentials of Grammar, Mechanics, and Usage

The following sentence looks innocent, but is it really?

> We sell tuxedos as well as rent.

You sell tuxedos, but it's highly unlikely that you sell rent—which is what this sentence says. Whatever you're selling, some people will ignore your message because of a blunder like this. The following sentence has a similar problem:

> Vice President Eldon Neale told his chief engineer that he would no longer be with Avix, Inc., as of June 30.

Is Eldon or the engineer leaving? No matter which side the facts are on, the sentence can be read the other way. Now look at this sentence:

> The year before we budgeted more for advertising sales were up.

Confused? Perhaps this is what the writer meant:

> The year before, we budgeted more for advertising. Sales were up.

Or maybe the writer meant this:

> The year before we budgeted more for advertising, sales were up.

These examples show that even short, simple sentences can be misunderstood because of errors on the part of the writer. As you've learned in numerous courses over your schooling, an English sentence consists of the parts of speech being combined with punctuation, mechanics, and vocabulary to convey meaning. Making a point of brushing up on your grammar, punctuation, mechanics, and vocabulary skills will help ensure that you create clear, effective business messages.

## 1.0 Grammar

**Grammar** is the study of how words come together to form sentences. Categorized by meaning, form, and function, English words fall into various parts of speech: nouns, pronouns, verbs, adjectives, adverbs, prepositions, conjunctions, articles, and interjections. You will communicate more clearly if you understand how each of these parts of speech operates in a sentence.

### 1.1 NOUNS

A **noun** names a person, a place, a thing, or an idea. Anything you can see or detect with one of your senses has a noun to name it. Some things you can't see or sense are also nouns—ions, for example, or space. So are things that exist as ideas, such as accuracy and height. (You can see that something is accurate or that a building is tall, but you can't see the idea of accuracy or the idea of height.) These names for ideas are known as **abstract nouns**. The simplest nouns are the names of things you can see or touch: *car, building, cloud, brick*; these are termed **concrete nouns**. A few nouns, such as *algorithm, software,* and *code,* are difficult to categorize as either abstract or concrete but can reasonably be considered concrete even though they don't have a physical presence.

## 1.1.1 Proper Nouns and Common Nouns

So far, all the examples of nouns have been **common nouns**, referring to general classes of things. The word *building* refers to a whole class of structures. Common nouns such as *building* are not capitalized.

If you want to talk about one particular building, however, you might refer to the Glazier Building. The name is capitalized, indicating that *Glazier Building* is a **proper noun**.

Here are three sets of common and proper nouns for comparison:

| Common | Proper |
|--------|--------|
| city | Kansas City |
| company | Blaisden Company |
| store | Books Galore |

## 1.1.2 Nouns as Subject and Object

Nouns may be used in sentences as subjects or objects. That is, the person, place, thing, or idea that is being or doing (subject) is represented by a noun. So is the person, place, idea, or thing that is being acted on (object). In the following sentence, the nouns are underlined:

The <u>web designer</u> created the <u>homepage</u>.

The web designer (subject) is acting in a way that affects the home page (object). The following sentence is more complicated:

The <u>installer</u> delivered the <u>carpet</u> to the <u>customer</u>.

*Installer* is the subject. *Carpet* is the object of the main part of the sentence (acted on by the installer), and *customer* is the object of the phrase *to the customer*. Nevertheless, both *carpet* and *customer* are objects.

## 1.1.3 Plural Nouns

Nouns can be either singular or plural. The usual way to make a plural noun is to add *s* or *es* to the singular form of the word:

| Singular | Plural |
|----------|--------|
| file | files |
| tax | taxes |
| cargo | cargoes |

Many nouns have other ways of forming the plural. Some plurals involve a change in a vowel (*mouse/mice, goose/geese, woman/women*), the addition of *en* or *ren* (*ox/oxen, child/children*), the change from *y* to *ies* (*city/cities, specialty/specialties*), or the change from *f* to *v* (*knife/knives, half/halves;* some exceptions: *fifes, roofs*). Some words of Latin origin offer a choice of plurals (*phenomena/phenomenons, indexes/indices, appendixes/appendices*). It's always a good idea to consult a dictionary if you are unsure of the correct or preferred plural spelling of a word.

The plurals of compound nouns are usually formed by adding *s* or *es* to the main word of the compound (*fathers-in-law, editors-in-chief, attorneys-at-law*).

Some nouns are the same whether singular or plural (*sleep, deer, moose*). Some nouns are plural in form but singular in use (*ethics, measles*). Some nouns are used in the plural only (*scissors, trousers*).

Letters, numbers, and words used as words are sometimes made plural by adding an apostrophe and an *s* (*A's, Ph.D.'s, I's*). However, if no confusion would be created by leaving off the apostrophe, it is common practice to just add the *s* (*1990s, RFPs, DVDs*).

## 1.1.4 Possessive Nouns

A noun becomes possessive when it's used to show the ownership of something. Then you add *'s* to the word:

| | |
|--|--|
| the man's car | the woman's apartment |

However, ownership does not need to be legal:

| | |
|--|--|
| the secretary's desk | the company's assets |

Also, ownership may be nothing more than an automatic association:

| | |
|--|--|
| a day's work | the job's prestige |

An exception to the rule about adding *'s* to make a noun possessive occurs when the word is singular and already has two "s" sounds at the end. In cases like the following, an apostrophe is all that's needed:

| | |
|--|--|
| crisis' dimensions | Mr. Moses' application |

When the noun has only one "s" sound at the end, however, retain the *'s*:

| | |
|--|--|
| Chris's book | Carolyn Nuss's office |

With compound (hyphenated) nouns, add *'s* to the last word:

| Compound Noun | Possessive Noun |
|---------------|-----------------|
| mother-in-law | mother-in-law's |
| mayor-elect | mayor-elect's |

To form the possessive of plural nouns, just begin by following the same rule as with singular nouns: add *'s*. However, if the plural noun already ends in an *s* (as most do), drop the one you've added, leaving only the apostrophe:

| | |
|--|--|
| the clients' complaints | employees' benefits |

To denote joint possession by two or more proper nouns, add the *'s* to the last name only (*Moody, Nation, and Smith's* ad agency). To denote individual possession by two or more persons, add an *'s* to each proper noun (*Moody's, Nation's, and Smith's* ad agencies).

### 1.1.5 Collective Nouns

Collective nouns encompass a group of people or objects: *crowd, jury, committee, team, audience, family, couple, herd, class.* They are often treated as singular nouns. (For more on collective nouns, see Section 1.3.4, Subject–Verb Agreement.)

## 1.2 PRONOUNS

A **pronoun** is a word that stands for a noun; it saves repeating the noun:

> Employees have some choice of weeks for vacation, but *they* must notify the HR office of *their* preference by March 1.

The pronouns *they* and *their* stand in for the noun *employees.* The noun that a pronoun stands for is called the **antecedent** of the pronoun; *employees* is the antecedent of *they* and *their.*

When the antecedent is plural, the pronoun that stands in for it has to be plural; *they* and *their* are plural pronouns because *employees* is plural. Likewise, when the antecedent is singular, the pronoun has to be singular:

> We thought the contract had expired, but we soon learned that *it* had not.

### 1.2.1 Multiple Antecedents

Sometimes a pronoun has a double (or even a triple) antecedent:

> Kathryn Boettcher and Luis Gutierrez went beyond *their* sales quotas for January.

If taken alone, *Kathryn Boettcher* is a singular antecedent. So is *Luis Gutierrez.* However, when together they are the plural antecedent of a pronoun, so the pronoun has to be plural. Thus the pronoun is *their* instead of *her* or *his.*

### 1.2.2 Unclear Antecedents

In some sentences the pronoun's antecedent is unclear:

> Sandy Wright sent Jane Brougham *her* production figures for the previous year. *She* thought they were too low.

To which person does the pronoun *her* refer? Someone who knew Sandy and Jane and knew their business relationship might be able to figure out the antecedent for *her.* Even with such an advantage, however, a reader might receive the wrong meaning. Also, it would be nearly impossible for any reader to know which name is the antecedent of *she.*

The best way to clarify an ambiguous pronoun is usually to rewrite the sentence, repeating nouns when needed for clarity:

> Sandy Wright sent her production figures for the previous year to Jane Brougham. Jane thought they were too low.

The noun needs to be repeated only when the antecedent is unclear.

### 1.2.3 Pronoun Classes

**Personal pronouns** consist of *I, you, we/us, he/him, she/her, it,* and *they/them.*

**Compound personal pronouns** are created by adding *self* or *selves* to simple personal pronouns: *myself, ourselves, yourself, yourselves, himself, herself, itself, themselves.* Compound personal pronouns are used either *intensively,* to emphasize the identity of the noun or pronoun (I *myself* have seen the demonstration), or *reflexively,* to indicate that the subject is the receiver of his or her own action (I promised *myself* I'd finish by noon). Compound personal pronouns are used incorrectly if they appear in a sentence without their antecedent:

> Walter, Virginia, and *I* (not *myself*) are the top salespeople.
> You need to tell *her* (not *herself*) about the mixup.

**Relative pronouns** refer to nouns (or groups of words used as nouns) in the main clause and are used to introduce clauses:

> Purina is the brand *that* most dog owners purchase.

The relative pronouns are *which, who, whom, whose,* and *what.* Other words used as relative pronouns include *that, whoever, whomever, whatever,* and *whichever.*

**Interrogative pronouns** are those used for asking questions: *who, whom, whose, which,* and *what.*

**Demonstrative pronouns** point out particular persons, places, or things:

> *That* is my desk.          *This* can't be correct.

The demonstrative pronouns are *this, these, that,* and *those.*

**Indefinite pronouns** refer to persons or things not specifically identified. They include *anyone, someone, everyone, everybody, somebody, either, neither, one, none, all, both, each, another, any, many,* and similar words.

### 1.2.4 Case of Pronouns

The case of a pronoun tells whether it's acting or acted upon:

> *She* sells an average of five packages each week.

In this sentence, *she* is doing the selling. Because *she* is acting, *she* is said to be in the **nominative case.** Now consider what happens when the pronoun is acted upon:

> After six months, Ms. Browning promoted *her.*

In this sentence, the pronoun *her* is acted upon and is thus said to be in the **objective case.**

Contrast the nominative and objective pronouns in this list:

| Nominative | Objective |
|---|---|
| I | me |
| we | us |
| he | him |
| she | her |
| they | them |
| who | whom |
| whoever | whomever |

Objective pronouns may be used as either the object of a verb (such as *promoted*) or the object of a preposition (such as *with*):

Rob worked with *them* until the order was filled.

In this example, *them* is the object of the preposition *with* because Rob acted upon—worked with—them. Here's a sentence with three pronouns, the first one nominative, the second the object of a verb, and the third the object of a preposition:

*He* paid *us* as soon as the check came from *them*.

*He* is nominative; *us* is objective because it's the object of the verb *paid; them* is objective because it's the object of the preposition *from*.

Every writer sometimes wonders whether to use *who* or *whom*:

(*Who, Whom*) will you hire?

Because this sentence is a question, it's difficult to see that *whom* is the object of the verb *hire*. You can figure out which pronoun to use if you rearrange the question and temporarily try *she* and *her* in place of *who* and *whom*: "Will you hire *she*?" or "Will you hire *her*?" *Her* and *whom* are both objective, so the correct choice is "Whom will you hire?" Here's a different example:

(*Who, Whom*) logged so much travel time?

Turning the question into a statement, you get:

He logged so much travel time.

Therefore, the correct statement is:

Who logged so much travel time?

## 1.2.5 Possessive Pronouns

Possessive pronouns work like possessive nouns—they show ownership or automatic association:

| | |
|---|---|
| her job | their preferences |
| his account | its equipment |

However, possessive pronouns are different from possessive nouns in the way they are written. Possessive pronouns never have an apostrophe:

| Possessive Noun | Possessive Pronoun |
|---|---|
| the woman's estate | her estate |
| Roger Franklin's plans | his plans |
| the shareholders' feelings | their feelings |
| the vacuum cleaner's attachments | its attachments |

The word *its* is the possessive of *it*. Like all other possessive pronouns, *its* has no apostrophe. Some people confuse *its* with *it's*, the contraction of *it is*. (Contractions are discussed in Section 2.9, Apostrophes.)

## 1.2.6 Pronoun-Antecedent Agreement

Like nouns, pronouns can be singular or plural. Pronouns must agree in number with their antecedents—a singular antecedent requires a singular pronoun:

The president of the board tendered *his* resignation.

Multiple antecedents require a plural pronoun:

The members of the board tendered *their* resignations.

A pronoun referring to singular antecedents connected by *or* or *nor* should be singular:

Neither Sean nor Terry made his quota.

But a pronoun referring to a plural and a singular antecedent connected by *or* or *nor* should be plural:

Neither Sean nor the twins made *their* quotas.

Formal English prefers the nominative case after the linking verb *to be*:

| | |
|---|---|
| It is *I*. | That is *he*. |

However, for general usage it's perfectly acceptable to use the more natural "It's me" and "That's him."

## 1.3 VERBS

A **verb** describes an action or acts as a link between a subject and words that define or describe that subject:

They all *quit* in disgust.
Working conditions *were* substandard.

The English language is full of **action verbs**. Here are a few you'll often run across in the business world:

| | | |
|---|---|---|
| verify | perform | fulfill |
| hire | succeed | send |
| leave | improve | receive |
| accept | develop | pay |

You could undoubtedly list many more.

The most common **linking verbs** are all the forms of *to be*: I *am, was,* or *will be;* you *are, were,* or *will be.* Other words that can serve as linking verbs include *seem, become, appear, prove, look, remain, feel, taste, smell, sound, resemble, turn,* and *grow*:

> It *seemed* a good plan at the time.
> She *sounds* impressive at a meeting.
> The time *grows* near for us to make a decision.

These verbs link what comes before them in the sentence with what comes after; no action is involved. (See Section 1.7.5 for a fuller discussion of linking verbs.)

An **auxiliary verb** is one that helps another verb and is used for showing tense, voice, and so on. A verb with its helpers is called a **verb phrase**. Verbs used as auxiliaries include *do, did, have, may, can, must, shall, might, could, would,* and *should*.

### 1.3.1 Verb Tenses

English has three simple verb tenses: present, past, and future.

| | |
|---|---|
| **Present:** | Our branches in Hawaii *stock* other items. |
| **Past:** | We *stocked* Purquil pens for a short time. |
| **Future:** | Rotex Tire Stores *will stock* your line of tires when you begin a program of effective national advertising. |

With most verbs (the regular ones), the past tense ends in *ed*, and the future tense always has *will* or *shall* in front of it. But the present tense is more complex, depending on the subject:

| | First Person | Second Person | Third Person |
|---|---|---|---|
| **Singular** | I stock | you stock | he/she/it stocks |
| **Plural** | we stock | you stock | they stock |

The basic form, *stock*, takes an additional *s* when *he, she,* or *it* precedes it. (See Section 1.3.4 for more on subject–verb agreement.)

In addition to the three simple tenses, the three **perfect tenses** are created by adding forms of the auxiliary verb *have*. The present perfect tense uses the past participle (regularly the past tense) of the main verb, *stocked*, and adds the present-tense *have* or *has* to the front of it:

> (I, we, you, they) *have stocked*.
> (He, she, it) *has stocked*.

The past perfect tense uses the past participle of the main verb, *stocked*, and adds the past-tense *had* to the front of it:

> (I, you, he, she, it, we, they) *had stocked*.

The future perfect tense also uses the past participle of the main verb, *stocked*, but adds the future-tense *will have*:

> (I, you, he, she, it, we, they) *will have stocked*.

Verbs should be kept in the same tense when the actions occur at the same time:

> When the payroll checks *came in*, everyone *showed up* for work.
> We *have found* that everyone *has pitched* in to help.

When the actions occur at different times, you may change tense accordingly:

> The shipment *came* last Wednesday, so if another one *comes* in today, please return it.
> The new employee *had been* ill at ease, but now she *has become* a full-fledged member of the team.

### 1.3.2 Irregular Verbs

Many verbs don't follow some of the standard patterns for verb tenses. The most irregular of these verbs is *to be*:

| Tense | Singular | Plural |
|---|---|---|
| **Present:** | I *am* | we *are* |
| | you *are* | you *are* |
| | he, she, it *is* | they *are* |
| **Past:** | I *was* | we *were* |
| | you *were* | you *were* |
| | he, she, it *was* | they *were* |

The future tense of *to be* is formed in the same way that the future tense of a regular verb is formed.

The perfect tenses of *to be* are also formed as they would be for a regular verb, except that the past participle is a special form, *been*, instead of just the past tense:

| | |
|---|---|
| **Present perfect:** | you have been |
| **Past perfect:** | you had been |
| **Future perfect:** | you will have been |

Here's a sampling of other irregular verbs:

| Present | Past | Past Participle |
|---------|------|-----------------|
| begin | began | begun |
| shrink | shrank | shrunk |
| know | knew | known |
| rise | rose | risen |
| become | became | become |
| go | went | gone |
| do | did | done |

Dictionaries list the various forms of other irregular verbs.

### 1.3.3 Transitive and Intransitive Verbs

Many people are confused by three particular sets of verbs:

| lie/lay | sit/set | rise/raise |
|---------|---------|------------|

Using these verbs correctly is much easier when you learn the difference between transitive and intransitive verbs.

**Transitive verbs** require a receiver; they "transfer" their action to an object. **Intransitive verbs** do not have a receiver for their action. Some intransitive verbs are complete in themselves and need no help from other words (prices *dropped*; we *won*). Other intransitive words must be "completed" by a noun or adjective called a **complement**. Complements occur with linking verbs.

Here are some sample uses of transitive and intransitive verbs:

| Intransitive | Transitive |
|--------------|------------|
| We should include in our new offices a place to *lie* down for a nap. | The workers will be here on Monday to *lay* new carpeting. |
| Even the way an interviewee *sits* is important. | That crate is full of stemware, so *set* it down carefully. |
| Salaries at Compu-Link, Inc., *rise* swiftly. | They *raise* their level of production every year. |

The workers *lay* carpeting, you *set down* the crate, they *raise* production; each action is transferred to something. In the intransitive sentences, a person *lies down*, an interviewee *sits*, and salaries *rise* without affecting anything else. Intransitive sentences are complete with only a subject and a verb; transitive sentences are not complete unless they also include an object; or something to transfer the action to.

Tenses are a confusing element of the lie/lay problem:

| Present | Past | Past Participle |
|---------|------|-----------------|
| I *lie* | I *lay* | I *have lain* |
| I *lay* (something down) | I *laid* (something down) | I *have laid* (something down) |

The past tense of *lie* and the present tense of *lay* look and sound alike, even though they're different verbs.

### 1.3.4 Subject-Verb Agreement

Whether regular or irregular, every verb must agree with its subject, both in person (first, second, or third) and in number (single or plural).

| | First Person | Second Person | Third Person |
|-----------|--------------|---------------|--------------|
| **Singular** | I *am* | you *are* | he/she/it *is* |
| | I *write* | you *write* | he/she/it *writes* |
| **Plural** | we *are* | you *are* | they *are* |
| | we *write* | you *write* | they *write* |

In a simple sentence, making a verb agree with its subject is a straightforward task:

Hector Ruiz *is* a strong competitor. (third-person singular)
We *write* to you every month. (first-person plural)

Confusion sometimes arises when sentences are a bit more complicated. For example, be sure to avoid agreement problems when words come between the subject and verb. In the following examples, the verb appears in italics, and its subject is underlined:

The <u>analysis</u> of existing documents *takes* a full week.

Even though *documents* is a plural, the verb is in the singular form. That's because the subject of the sentence is *analysis*, a singular noun. The phrase *of existing documents* can be disregarded. Here is another example:

The <u>answers</u> for this exercise *are* in the study guide.

Take away the phrase *for this exercise* and you are left with the plural subject *answers*. Therefore, the verb takes the plural form.

Verb agreement is also complicated when the subject is a collective noun or pronoun or when the subject may be considered either singular or plural. In such cases, you often have to analyze the surrounding sentence to determine which verb form to use:

The <u>staff</u> *is* quartered in the warehouse.
The <u>staff</u> *are* at their desks in the warehouse.
The <u>computers</u> and the <u>staff</u> *are* in the warehouse.
Neither the staff nor the <u>computers</u> *are* in the warehouse.
<u>Every</u> computer *is* in the warehouse.
Many a <u>computer</u> *is* in the warehouse.

Did you notice that words such as *every* use the singular verb form? In addition, when an *either/or* or a *neither/nor* phrase combines singular and plural nouns, the verb takes the form that matches the noun closest to it.

In the business world, some subjects require extra attention. Company names, for example, are considered singular and therefore take a singular verb in most cases—even if they contain plural words:

> Stater Brothers *offers* convenient grocery shopping.

In addition, quantities are sometimes considered singular and sometimes plural. If a quantity refers to a total amount, it takes a singular verb; if a quantity refers to individual, countable units, it takes a plural verb:

> Three hours *is* a long time.
> The eight dollars we collected for the fund *are* tacked on the bulletin board.

Fractions may also be singular or plural, depending on the noun that accompanies them:

> One-third of the warehouse *is* devoted to this product line.
> One-third of the products *are* defective.

To decide whether to use a singular or plural verb with subjects such as *number* and *variety*, follow this simple rule: If the subject is preceded by *a*, use a plural verb:

> *A* number of products *are* being displayed at the trade show.

If the subject is preceded by *the*, use a singular verb:

> *The* variety of products on display *is* mind-boggling.

For a related discussion, see Section 1.7.1, Longer Sentences.

### 1.3.5 Voice of Verbs

Verbs have two voices, active and passive. When the subject comes first, the verb is in **active voice**; when the object comes first, the verb is in **passive voice**:

> **Active:**      The buyer *paid* a large amount.
> **Passive:**    A large amount *was paid* by the buyer.

The passive voice uses a form of the verb *to be*, which adds words to a sentence. In the example, the passive-voice sentence uses eight words, whereas the active-voice sentence uses only six to say the same thing. The words *was* and *by* are unnecessary to convey the meaning of the sentence. In fact, extra words usually clog meaning. So be sure to opt for the active voice when you have a choice.

At times, however, you have no choice:

> Several items *have been taken*, but so far we don't know who took them.

The passive voice becomes necessary when you don't know (or don't want to say) who performed the action; the active voice is bolder and more direct.

### 1.3.6 Mood of Verbs

Verbs can express one of three moods: indicative, imperative, or subjunctive. The **indicative mood** is used to make a statement or to ask a question:

> The secretary mailed a letter to each supplier.
> Did the secretary mail a letter to each supplier?

Use the **imperative mood** when you wish to command or request:

> Please mail a letter to each supplier.

With the imperative mood, the subject is the understood *you*.

The **subjunctive mood** is used to express doubt or a wish or a condition contrary to fact:

> If I *were* you, I wouldn't send that email.

The subjunctive is also used to express a suggestion or a request:

> I asked that Rosario *be* [not *is*] present at the meeting.

### 1.3.7 Verbals

**Verbals** are verbs that are modified to function as other parts of speech. They include infinitives, gerunds, and participles.

**Infinitives** are formed by placing a *to* in front of the verb (*to go, to purchase, to work*). They function as nouns. Although many of us were taught that it is "incorrect" to split an infinitive—that is, to place an adverb between the *to* and the verb—that rule is not a hard and fast one. In some cases, the adverb is best placed in the middle of the infinitive to avoid awkward constructions or ambiguous meaning:

> Production of steel is expected to *moderately exceed* domestic use.

**Gerunds** are verbals formed by adding *ing* to a verb (*going, having, working*). Like infinitives, they function as nouns. Gerunds and gerund phrases take a singular verb:

> *Borrowing* from banks *is* preferable to getting venture capital.

**Participles** are verb forms used as adjectives. The present participle ends in *ing* and generally describes action going on at the same time as other action:

> *Checking* the schedule, the contractor was pleased with progress on the project.

The **past participle** is usually the same form as the past tense and generally indicates completed action:

> When *completed*, the project will occupy six city blocks.

The **perfect participle** is formed by adding *having* to the past participle:

> *Having completed* the project, the contractor submitted his last invoice.

## 1.4 ADJECTIVES

An **adjective** modifies (tells something about) a noun or pronoun. Each of the following phrases says more about the noun or pronoun than the noun or pronoun would say alone:

> an *efficient* staff             a *heavy* price
> *brisk* trade                   *light* web traffic

Adjectives modify nouns more often than they modify pronouns. When adjectives do modify pronouns, however, the sentence usually has a linking verb:

> They were *attentive*.        It looked *appropriate*.
> He seems *interested*.       You are *skillful*.

### 1.4.1 Types of Adjectives

Adjectives serve a variety of purposes. **Descriptive adjectives** express some quality belonging to the modified item (*tall, successful, green*). **Limiting** or **definitive adjectives**, on the other hand, point out the modified item or limit its meaning without expressing a quality. Types include:

- Numeral adjectives (*one, fifty, second*)
- Articles (*a, an, the*)
- Pronominal adjectives: pronouns used as adjectives (*his desk, each employee*)
- Demonstrative adjectives: *this, these, that, those* (*these tires, that invoice*)

**Proper adjectives** are derived from proper nouns:

> *Chinese* customs              *Orwellian* overtones

**Predicate adjectives** complete the meaning of the predicate and are introduced by linking verbs:

> The location is *perfect*.        Prices are *high*.

### 1.4.2 Comparative Degree

Most adjectives can take three forms: simple, comparative, and superlative. The simple form modifies a single noun or pronoun. Use the comparative form when comparing two items. When comparing three or more items, use the superlative form:

| Simple | Comparative | Superlative |
|--------|-------------|-------------|
| hard | harder | hardest |
| safe | safer | safest |
| dry | drier | driest |

The comparative form adds *er* to the simple form, and the superlative form adds *est*. (The *y* at the end of a word changes to *i* before the *er* or *est* is added.)

A small number of adjectives are irregular, including these:

| Simple | Comparative | Superlative |
|--------|-------------|-------------|
| good | better | best |
| bad | worse | worst |
| little | less | least |

When the simple form of an adjective has two or more syllables, you usually add *more* to form the comparative and *most* to form the superlative:

| Simple | Comparative | Superlative |
|--------|-------------|-------------|
| useful | more useful | most useful |
| exhausting | more exhausting | most exhausting |
| expensive | more expensive | most expensive |

The most common exceptions are two-syllable adjectives that end in *y*:

| Simple | Comparative | Superlative |
|--------|-------------|-------------|
| happy | happier | happiest |
| costly | costlier | costliest |

If you choose this option, change the *y* to *i* and tack *er* or *est* onto the end.

Some adjectives cannot be used to make comparisons because they themselves indicate the extreme. For example, if something is perfect, nothing can be more perfect. If something is unique or ultimate, nothing can be more unique or more ultimate.

### 1.4.3 Hyphenated Adjectives

Many adjectives used in the business world are actually combinations of words: *up-to-date* report, *last-minute* effort, *fifth-floor* suite, *well-built* engine. As you can see, they are hyphenated when they come before the noun they modify. However, when such word combinations come after the noun they modify, they are not hyphenated. In the following example, the adjectives appear in italics and the nouns they modify are underlined:

> The <u>report</u> is *up to date* because of our team's *last-minute* <u>efforts</u>.

Hyphens are not used when part of the combination is a word ending in *ly* (because that word is usually not an adjective). Hyphens are also omitted from word combinations that are used so frequently that readers are used to seeing the words together:

> We live in a *rapidly shrinking* world.
> Our *highly motivated* employees will be well paid.
> Please consider renewing your *credit card* account.
> Send those figures to our *data processing* department.
> Our new intern is a *high school* student.

## 1.5 ADVERBS

An **adverb** modifies a verb, an adjective, or another adverb:

| | |
|---|---|
| **Modifying a verb:** | Our marketing department works *efficiently*. |
| **Modifying an adjective:** | She was not dependable, although she was *highly* intelligent. |
| **Modifying another adverb:** | When signing new clients, he moved *extremely* cautiously. |

An adverb can be a single word (*clearly*), a phrase (*very clearly*), or a clause (*because it was clear*).

### 1.5.1 Types of Adverbs

**Simple adverbs** are simple modifiers:

> The door opened *automatically*.
> The order arrived *yesterday*.
> Top companies were *there*.

**Interrogative adverbs** ask a question:

> *Where* have you been?

**Conjunctive adverbs** connect clauses:

> The boardroom isn't available for the meeting; *however*, the conference room should be clear.
> We met all our sales goals for April; *therefore*, all sales reps will get a bonus.

Words frequently used as conjunctive adverbs include *however*, *nevertheless*, *therefore*, *similarly*, *thus*, and *meanwhile*.

**Negative adverbs** include *not*, *never*, *seldom*, *rarely*, *scarcely*, *hardly*, and similar words. Negative adverbs are powerful words and therefore do not need any help in conveying a negative thought. Avoid using double negatives like these:

> I don't want no mistakes.
> (Correct: "I don't want any mistakes," or "I want no mistakes.")
> They couldn't hardly read the report.
> (Correct: "They could hardly read the report," or "They couldn't read the report.")
> They scarcely noticed neither one.
> (Correct: "They scarcely noticed either one," or "They noticed neither one.")

### 1.5.2 Adverb-Adjective Confusion

Many adverbs are adjectives turned into adverbs by adding *ly*: *highly*, *extremely*, *officially*, *closely*, *really*. In addition, many words can be adjectives or adverbs, depending on their usage in a particular sentence:

| | |
|---|---|
| The *early* bird gets the worm. [adjective] | We arrived *early*. [adverb] |
| It was a *hard* decision. [adjective] | He hit the wall *hard*. [adverb] |

Because of this situation, some adverbs are difficult to distinguish from adjectives. For example, in the following sentences, is the underlined word an adverb or an adjective?

> They worked <u>well</u>.
> The baby is <u>well</u>.

In the first sentence, *well* is an adverb modifying the verb *worked*. In the second sentence, *well* is an adjective modifying the noun *baby*. You may find it helpful to remember that a *linking verb* (such as *is* in "The baby is well") connects an adjective to the noun it modifies. In contrast, an *action verb* is modified by an adverb:

| Adjective | Adverb |
|---|---|
| He is a *good* worker. (What kind of worker is he?) | He works *well*. (How does he work?) |
| It is a *real* computer. (What kind of computer is it?) | It *really* is a computer. (To what extent is it a computer?) |
| The traffic is *slow*. (What quality does the have?) | The traffic moves *slowly*. (How does the traffic traffic move?) |
| This food tastes *bad* without salt. (What quality does the food have?) | This food *badly* needs salt. (How much is it needed?) |

### 1.5.3 Comparative Degree

Like adjectives, adverbs can be used to compare items. Generally, the basic adverb is combined with *more* or *most*, just as long adjectives are. However, some adverbs have one-word comparative forms:

| One Item | Two Items | Three Items |
|---|---|---|
| quickly | more quickly | most quickly |
| sincerely | less sincerely | least sincerely |
| fast | faster | fastest |
| well | better | best |

## 1.6 OTHER PARTS OF SPEECH

Nouns, pronouns, verbs, adjectives, and adverbs carry most of the meaning in a sentence. Four other parts of speech link them together in sentences: prepositions, conjunctions, articles, and interjections.

### 1.6.1 Prepositions

A **preposition** is a word or group of words that describes a relationship between other words in a sentence. A simple preposition is made up of one word: *of, in, by, above, below.* A *compound preposition* is made up of two prepositions: *out of, from among, except for, because of.*

A **prepositional phrase** is a group of words introduced by a preposition that functions as an adjective (an adjectival phrase) or as an adverb (adverbial phrase) by telling more about a pronoun, noun, or verb:

The shipment will be here *by next Friday.*
Put the mail *in the out-bin.*

Prepositional phrases should be placed as close as possible to the element they are modifying:

Shopping *on the Internet* can be confusing for the uninitiated. (*not* Shopping can be confusing for the uninitiated *on the Internet.*)

Some prepositions are closely linked with a verb. When using phrases such as *look up* and *wipe out,* keep them intact and do not insert anything between the verb and the preposition.

You may have been told that it is unacceptable to put a preposition at the end of a sentence. However, that is not a hard-and-fast rule, and trying to follow it can sometimes be a challenge. You can end a sentence with a preposition as along as the sentence sounds natural and as long as rewording the sentence would create awkward wording:

I couldn't tell what they were interested in.
What did she attribute it to?
What are you looking for?

Avoid using unnecessary prepositions. In the following examples, the prepositions in parentheses should be omitted:

All (of) the staff members were present.
I almost fell off (of) my chair with surprise.

Where was Mr. Steuben going (to)?
They couldn't help (from) wondering.

The opposite problem is failing to include a preposition when you should. Consider these two sentences:

Sales were over $100,000 for Linda and Bill.
Sales were over $100,000 for Linda and for Bill.

The first sentence indicates that Linda and Bill had combined sales over $100,000; the second, that Linda and Bill each had sales over $100,000, for a combined total in excess of $200,000. The preposition *for* is critical here.

When the same preposition can be used for two or more words in a sentence without affecting the meaning, only the last preposition is required:

We are familiar (with) and satisfied with your company's products.

But when different prepositions are normally used with the words, all the prepositions must be included:

We are familiar with and interested in your company's products.

Some prepositions have come to be used in a particular way with certain other parts of speech. Here is a partial list of some prepositions that have come to be used with certain words:

| | |
|---|---|
| according to | independent of |
| agree to (a proposal) | inferior to |
| agree with (a person) | plan to |
| buy from | prefer to |
| capable of | prior to |
| comply with | reason with |
| conform to | responsible for |
| differ from (things) | similar to |
| differ with (person) | talk to (without interaction) |
| different from | talk with (with interaction) |
| get from (receive) | wait for (person or thing) |
| get off (dismount) | wait on (like a waiter) |

If you are unsure of the correct idiomatic expression, check a dictionary.

Some verb-preposition idioms vary depending on the situation: You agree *to* a proposal but *with* a person, *on* a price, or *in* principle. You argue *about* something, *with* a person, and *for* or *against* a proposition. You compare one item *to* another to show their similarities; you compare one item *with* another to show differences.

Here are some other examples of preposition usage that have given writers trouble:

among/between: *Among* is used to refer to three or more (Circulate the memo *among* the staff); *between* is used to refer to two (Put the copy machine *between* Judy and Dan).

as if/like: *As if* is used before a clause (It seems *as if* we should be doing something); *like* is used before a noun or pronoun (He seems *like* a nice guy).

have/of: *Have* is a verb used in verb phrases (They should *have* checked first); *of* is a preposition and is never used in such cases.

in/into: *In* is used to refer to a static position (The file is *in* the cabinet); *into* is used to refer to movement toward a position (Put the file *into* the cabinet).

## 1.6.2 Conjunctions

**Conjunctions** connect the parts of a sentence: words, phrases, and clauses. A **coordinating conjunction** connects two words, phrases, or clauses of equal rank. The simple coordinating conjunctions include *and, but, or, nor, for, yet,* and *so.* **Correlative conjunctions** are coordinating conjunctions used in pairs: *both/and, either/or, neither/nor, not only/but also.* Constructions with correlative conjunctions should be parallel, with the same part of speech following each element of the conjunction:

> The purchase was *not only* expensive *but also* unnecessary.
> The purchase *not only was* expensive *but also was* unnecessary.

**Conjunctive adverbs** are adverbs used to connect or show relationships between clauses. They include *however, nevertheless, consequently, moreover,* and *as a result.*

A **subordinate conjunction** connects two clauses of unequal rank; it joins a dependent (subordinate) clause to the independent clause on which it depends (for more on dependent and independent clauses, see Section 1.7.1). Subordinate conjunctions include *as, if, because, although, while, before, since, that, until, unless, when, where,* and *whether.*

## 1.6.3 Articles and Interjections

Only three **articles** exist in English: *the, a,* and *an.* These words are used, like adjectives, to specify which item you are talking about. *The* is called the *definite article* because it indicates a specific noun; *a* and *an* are called the *indefinite articles* because they are less specific about what they are referring to.

If a word begins with a vowel (soft) sound, use *an;* otherwise, use *a.* It's *a history,* not *an history, a hypothesis,* not *an hypothesis.* Use *an* with an "h" word only if it is a soft "h," as in *honor* and *hour.* Use *an* with words that are pronounced with a soft vowel sound even if they are spelled beginning with a consonant (usually in the case of abbreviations): *an SEC application, an MP3 file.* Use *a* with words that begin with vowels if they are pronounced with a hard sound: *a university, a Usenet account.*

Repeat an article if adjectives modify different nouns: *The red house and the white house are mine.* Do not repeat an article if all adjectives modify the same noun: *The red and white house is mine.*

**Interjections** are words that express no solid information, only emotion:

| | |
|---|---|
| Wow! | Well, well! |
| Oh, no! | Good! |

Such purely emotional language has its place in private life and advertising copy, but it only weakens the effect of most business writing.

## 1.7 SENTENCES

Sentences are constructed with the major building blocks, the parts of speech. Take, for example, this simple two-word sentence:

> Money talks.

It consists of a noun (*money*) and a verb (*talks*). When used in this way, the noun works as the first requirement for a sentence, the **subject**, and the verb works as the second requirement, the **predicate**. Without a subject (who or what does something) and a predicate (the doing of it), you have merely a collection of words, not a sentence.

### 1.7.1 Longer Sentences

More complicated sentences have more complicated subjects and predicates, but they still have a simple subject and a predicate verb. In the following examples, the subject is underlined once, the predicate verb twice:

> Marex and Contron enjoy higher earnings each quarter.

*Marex* [and] *Contron* do something; *enjoy* is what they do.

> My interview, coming minutes after my freeway accident, did not impress or move anyone.

*Interview* is what did something. What did it do? It *did* [not] *impress* [or] *move.*

> In terms of usable space, a steel warehouse, with its extremely long span of roof unsupported by pillars, makes more sense.

*Warehouse* is what *makes.*

These three sentences demonstrate several things. First, in all three sentences, the simple subject and predicate verb are the "bare bones" of the sentence, the parts that carry the core idea of the sentence. When trying to find the subject and predicate verb, disregard all prepositional phrases, modifiers, conjunctions, and articles.

Second, in the third sentence, the verb is singular (*makes*) because the subject is singular (*warehouse*). Even though the plural noun *pillars* is closer to the verb, *warehouse* is the subject. So *warehouse* determines whether the verb is singular or plural. Subject and predicate must agree.

Third, the subject in the first sentence is compound (*Marex* [and] *Contron*). A compound subject, when connected by *and*, requires a plural verb (*enjoy*). Also, the second sentence shows how compound predicates can occur (*did* [not] *impress* [or] *move*).

Fourth, the second sentence incorporates a group of words—*coming minutes after my freeway accident*—containing a form of a verb (*coming*) and a noun (*accident*). Yet, this group of words is not a complete sentence for two reasons:

- **Not all nouns are subjects:** *Accident* is not the subject of *coming*.
- **Not all verbs are predicates:** A verb that ends in *ing* can never be the predicate of a sentence (unless preceded by a form of *to be*, as in *was coming*).

Because they don't contain a subject and a predicate, the words *coming minutes after my freeway accident* (called a **phrase**) can't be written as a sentence. That is, the phrase cannot stand alone; it cannot begin with a capital letter and end with a period. So a phrase must always be just one part of a sentence.

Sometimes a sentence incorporates two or more groups of words that do contain a subject and a predicate; these word groups are called **clauses**:

> My interview, because it came minutes after my freeway accident, did not impress or move anyone.

The **independent clause** is the portion of the sentence that could stand alone without revision:

> My *interview* did not impress or move anyone.

The other part of the sentence could stand alone only by removing *because*:

> (because) It came minutes after my freeway accident.

This part of the sentence is known as a **dependent clause**; although it has a subject and a predicate (just as an independent clause does), it's linked to the main part of the sentence by a word (*because*) showing its dependence.

In summary, the two types of clauses—dependent and independent—both have a subject and a predicate. Dependent clauses, however, do not bear the main meaning of the sentence and are therefore linked to an independent clause. Nor can phrases stand alone, because they lack both a subject and a predicate. Only independent clauses can be written as sentences without revision.

### 1.7.2 Types of Sentences

Sentences come in four main types, depending on the extent to which they contain clauses. A **simple sentence** has one subject and one predicate; in short, it has one main independent clause:

> Boeing is the world's largest aerospace company.

A **compound sentence** consists of two independent clauses connected by a coordinating conjunction (*and, or, but,* etc.) or a semicolon:

> Airbus outsold Boeing for several years, but Boeing has recently regained the lead.

A **complex sentence** consists of an independent clause and one or more dependent clauses:

> Boeing is betting [independent clause] that airlines will begin using moderately smaller planes to fly passengers between smaller cities [dependent clause introduced by *that*].

A **compound-complex sentence** has two main clauses, at least one of which contains a subordinate (dependent clause):

> Boeing is betting [independent clause] that airlines will begin using moderately smaller planes to fly passengers between smaller cities [dependent clause], and it anticipates that new airports will be developed to meet passenger needs [independent clause].

### 1.7.3 Sentence Fragments

An incomplete sentence (a phrase or a dependent clause) that is written as though it were a complete sentence is called a **fragment**. Consider the following sentence fragments:

> Marilyn Sanders, having had pilferage problems in her store for the past year. Refuses to accept the results of our investigation.

This serious error can easily be corrected by putting the two fragments together:

> Marilyn Sanders, having had pilferage problems in her store for the past year, refuses to accept the results of our investigation.

The actual details of a situation will determine the best way for you to remedy a fragment problem.

The ban on fragments has one exception. Some advertising copy contains sentence fragments, written knowingly to convey a certain rhythm. However, advertising is the only area of business in which fragments are acceptable.

### 1.7.4 Fused Sentences and Comma Splices

Just as there can be too little in a group of words to make it a sentence, there can also be too much:

> All our mail is run through a postage meter every afternoon someone picks it up.

This example contains two sentences, not one, but the two have been blended so that it's hard to tell where one ends and the next begins. Is the mail run through a meter every afternoon? If so, the sentences should read:

> All our mail is run through a postage meter every afternoon. Someone picks it up.

Perhaps the mail is run through a meter at some other time (morning, for example) and is picked up every afternoon:

> All our mail is run through a postage meter. Every afternoon someone picks it up.

The order of words is the same in all three cases; sentence division makes all the difference. Either of the last two cases is grammatically correct. The choice depends on the facts of the situation.

Sometimes these so-called **fused sentences** have a more obvious point of separation:

> Several large orders arrived within a few days of one another, too many came in for us to process by the end of the month.

Here, the comma has been put between two independent clauses in an attempt to link them. When a lowly comma separates two complete sentences, the result is called a **comma splice**. A comma splice can be remedied in one of three ways:

- **Replace the comma with a period and capitalize the next word:** " . . . one another. Too many . . ."
- **Replace the comma with a semicolon and do not capitalize the next word:** " . . . one another; too many . . ." This remedy works only when the two sentences have closely related meanings.
- **Change one of the sentences so that it becomes a phrase or a dependent clause.** This remedy often produces the best writing, but it takes more work.

The third alternative can be carried out in several ways. One is to begin the sentence with a subordinating conjunction:

> Whenever several large orders arrived within a few days of one another, too many came in for us to process by the end of the month.

Another way is to remove part of the subject or the predicate verb from one of the independent clauses, thereby creating a phrase:

> Several large orders arrived within a few days of one another, too many for us to process by the end of the month.

Finally, you can change one of the predicate verbs to its *ing* form:

> Several large orders arrived within a few days of one another, too many coming in for us to process by the end of the month.

In many cases, simply adding a coordinating conjunction can separate fused sentences or remedy a comma splice:

> You can fire them, or you can make better use of their abilities.
> Margaret drew up the designs, and Matt carried them out.
> We will have three strong months, but after that sales will taper off.

Be careful with coordinating conjunctions: Use them only to join simple sentences that express similar ideas.

Also, because they say relatively little about the relationship between the two clauses they join, avoid using coordinating conjunctions too often: *and* is merely an addition sign; *but* is just a turn signal; *or* only points to an alternative. Subordinating conjunctions such as *because* and *whenever* tell the reader a lot more.

### 1.7.5 Sentences with Linking Verbs

Linking verbs were discussed briefly in the section on verbs (Section 1.3). Here, you can see more fully the way they function in a sentence. The following is a model of any sentence with a linking verb:

> A *(verb)* B.

Although words such as *seems* and *feels* can also be linking verbs, let's assume that the verb is a form of *to be*:

> A *is* B.

In such a sentence, A and B are always nouns, pronouns, or adjectives. When one is a noun and the other is a pronoun, or when both are nouns, the sentence says that one is the same as the other:

> She is president.
> Rachel is president.
> She is forceful.

Recall from Section 1.3.3 that the noun or adjective that follows the linking verb is called a *complement*. When it is a noun or noun phrase, the complement is called a *predicate nominative*, when the complement is an adjective, it is referred to as a *predicate adjective*.

### 1.7.6 Misplaced Modifiers

The position of a modifier in a sentence is important. The movement of *only* changes the meaning in the following sentences:

> Only we are obliged to supply those items specified in your contract.
> We are obliged only to supply those items specified in your contract.
> We are obliged to supply only those items specified in your contract.
> We are obliged to supply those items specified only in your contract.

In any particular set of circumstances, only one of those sentences would be accurate. The others would very likely cause problems. To prevent misunderstanding, place such modifiers as close as possible to the noun or verb they modify.

For similar reasons, whole phrases that are modifiers must be placed near the right noun or verb. Mistakes in placement create ludicrous meanings:

> Antia Information Systems bought new computer chairs for the programmers with more comfortable seats.

The anatomy of programmers is not normally a concern of business writers. Obviously, the comfort of the chairs was the issue:

> Antia Information Systems bought programmers the new computer chairs with more comfortable seats.

Here is another example:

> I asked him to file all the letters in the cabinet that had been answered.

In this ridiculous sentence, the cabinet has been answered, even though no cabinet in history is known to have asked a question. *That had been answered* is too far from *letters* and too close to *cabinet*. Here's an improvement:

> I asked him to file in the cabinet all the letters that had been answered.

The term **dangling modifier** is often used to refer to a clause or phrase that because of its position in the sentence seems to modify a word that it is not meant to modify. For instance:

> Lying motionless, co-workers rushed to Barry's aid.

Readers expect an introductory phrase to modify the subject of the main clause. But in this case it wasn't the *co-workers* who were lying motionless but rather *Barry* who was in this situation. Like this example, most instances of dangling modifiers occur at the beginning of sentences. The source of some danglers is a passive construction:

> To find the needed information, the whole book had to be read.

In such cases, switching to the active voice can usually remedy the problem:

> To find the needed information, you will need to read the whole book.

### 1.7.7 Parallelism

Two or more sentence elements that have the same relation to another element should be in the same form. Otherwise, the reader is forced to work harder to understand the meaning of the sentence. When a series consists of phrases or clauses, the same part of speech (preposition, gerund, etc.) should introduce them. Do not mix infinitives with participles or adjectives with nouns. Here are some examples of nonparallel elements:

> Andersen is hiring managers, programmers, and people who work in accounting. [nouns not parallel]
> Andersen earns income by auditing, consulting, and by bookkeeping. [prepositional phrases not parallel]
> Andersen's goals are to win new clients, keeping old clients happy, and finding new enterprises. [infinitive mixed with gerunds]

# 2.0 Punctuation

On the highway, signs tell you when to slow down or stop, where to turn, and when to merge. In similar fashion, punctuation helps readers negotiate your prose. The proper use of punctuation keeps readers from losing track of your meaning.

### 2.1 PERIODS

Use a period (1) to end any sentence that is not a question, (2) with certain abbreviations, and (3) between dollars and cents in an amount of money.

### 2.2 QUESTION MARKS

Use a question mark after any direct question that requests an answer:

> Are you planning to enclose a check, or shall we bill you?

Don't use a question mark with commands phrased as questions for the sake of politeness:

> Will you send us a check today.

A question mark should precede quotation marks, parentheses, and brackets if it is part of the quoted or parenthetical material; otherwise, it should follow:

> This issue of *Inc.* has an article titled "What's Your Entrepreneurial IQ?"
> Have you read the article "Five Principles of Guerrilla Marketing"?

Do not use the question mark with indirect questions or with requests:

> Mr. Antonelli asked whether anyone had seen Nathalia lately.

Do not use a comma or a period with a question mark; the question mark takes the place of these punctuation marks.

## 2.3 EXCLAMATION POINTS

Use exclamation points after highly emotional language. Because business writing almost never calls for emotional language, you will seldom use exclamation points.

## 2.4 SEMICOLONS

Semicolons have three main uses. One is to separate two closely related independent clauses:

> The outline for the report is due within a week; the report itself is due at the end of the month.

A semicolon should also be used instead of a comma when the items in a series have commas within them:

> Our previous meetings were on November 11, 2011; February 20, 2012; and April 28, 2013.

Finally, a semicolon should be used to separate independent clauses when the second one begins with a conjunctive adverb such as *however, therefore,* or *nevertheless* or a phrase such as *for example* or *in that case:*

> Our supplier has been out of part D712 for 10 weeks; however, we have found another source that can ship the part right away.
> His test scores were quite low; on the other hand, he has a lot of relevant experience.

Section 4.4 provides more information on using transitional words and phrases.

Semicolons should always be placed outside parentheses:

> Events Northwest has the contract for this year's convention (August 23–28); we haven't awarded the contract for next year yet.

## 2.5 COLONS

Use a colon after the salutation in a business letter. You should also use a colon at the end of a sentence or phrase introducing a list or (sometimes) a quotation:

> Our study included the three most critical problems: insufficient capital, incompetent management, and inappropriate location.

A colon should not be used when the list, quotation, or idea is a direct object of the verb or preposition. This rule applies whether the list is set off or run in:

> We are able to supply
> staples
> wood screws
> nails
> toggle bolts
> This shipment includes 9 DVDs, 12 CDs, and 4 USB flash drives.

Another way you can use a colon is to separate the main clause and another sentence element when the second explains, illustrates, or amplifies the first:

> Management was unprepared for the union representatives' demands: this fact alone accounts for their arguing well into the night.

However, in contemporary usage, such clauses are frequently separated by a semicolon.

Like semicolons, colons should always be placed outside parentheses:

> He has an expensive list of new demands (none of which is covered in the purchase agreement): new carpeting, network cabling, and a new security system.

## 2.6 COMMAS

Commas have many uses; the most common is to separate items in a series:

> He took the job, learned it well, worked hard, and succeeded.
> Put paper, pencils, and paper clips on the requisition list.

Company style may dictate omitting the final comma in a series. However, if you have a choice, use the final comma; it's often necessary to prevent misunderstanding.

A second place to use a comma is between independent clauses that are joined by a coordinating conjunction (*and, but,* or *or*):

> She spoke to the sales staff, and he spoke to the production staff.
> I was advised to proceed, and I did.

A third use for the comma is to separate a dependent clause at the beginning of a sentence from an independent clause:

> Because of our lead in the market, we may be able to risk introducing a new product.

However, a dependent clause at the end of a sentence is separated from the independent clause by a comma only when the dependent clause is unnecessary to the main meaning of the sentence:

> We may be able to introduce a new product, although it may involve some risk.

A fourth use for the comma is after an introductory phrase or word:

> Starting with this amount of capital, we can survive in the red for one year.
>
> Through more careful planning, we may be able to serve more people.
>
> Yes, you may proceed as originally planned.

However, with short introductory prepositional phrases and some one-syllable words (such as *hence* and *thus*), the comma is often omitted:

> Before January 1 we must complete the inventory.
>
> Thus we may not need to hire anyone.
>
> In July we will complete the move to Tulsa.

Fifth, paired commas are used to set off nonrestrictive clauses and phrases. A **restrictive clause** is one that cannot be omitted without altering the meaning of the main clause, whereas a **nonrestrictive clause** can be:

> The *Time* magazine website, which is produced by Steve Conley, has won several design awards. [nonrestrictive: the material set off by commas could be omitted]
>
> The website that is produced by Steve Conley has won several design awards. [restrictive: no commas are used before and after *that is produced by Steve Conley* because this information is necessary to the meaning of the sentence—it specifies which website]

A sixth use for commas is to set off appositive words and phrases. (An **appositive** has the same meaning as the word it is in apposition to.) Like nonrestrictive clauses, appositives can be dropped without changing or obscuring the meaning of the sentence:

> Conley, a freelance designer, also produces the websites for several nonprofit corporations.

Seventh, commas are used between adjectives modifying the same noun (coordinate adjectives):

> She left Monday for a long, difficult recruiting trip.

To test the appropriateness of such a comma, try reversing the order of the adjectives: *a difficult, long recruiting trip.* If the order cannot be reversed, leave out the comma (a *good old friend* isn't the same as an *old good friend*). A comma should not be used when one of the adjectives is part of the noun. Compare these two phrases:

> a distinguished, well-known figure
>
> a distinguished public figure

The adjective-noun combination of *public* and *figure* has been used together so often that it has come to be considered a single thing: *public figure.* So no comma is required.

Eighth, commas are used both before and after the year in sentences that include month, day, and year:

> It will be sent by December 15, 2013, from our Cincinnati plant.

Some companies use the European style: 15 December 2013. No commas should be used in that case. Nor is a comma needed when only the month and year are present (December 2013).

Ninth, commas are used to set off a variety of parenthetical words and phrases within sentences, including state names, dates, abbreviations, transitional expressions, and contrasted elements:

> They were, in fact, prepared to submit a bid.
>
> Habermacher, Inc., went public in 1999.
>
> Our goal was increased profits, not increased market share.
>
> Service, then, is our main concern.
>
> The factory was completed in Chattanooga, Tennessee, just three weeks ago.
>
> Joanne Dubiik, M.D., has applied for a loan from First Savings.
>
> I started work here on March 1, 2003, and soon received my first promotion.

Tenth, a comma is used to separate a quotation from the rest of the sentence:

> Your warranty reads, "These conditions remain in effect for one year from date of purchase."

However, the comma is left out when the quotation as a whole is built into the structure of the sentence:

> He hurried off with an angry "Look where you're going."

Finally, a comma should be used whenever it's needed to avoid confusion or an unintended meaning. Compare the following:

> Ever since they have planned new ventures more carefully.
>
> Ever since, they have planned new ventures more carefully.

## 2.7 DASHES

Use dashes to surround a comment that is a sudden turn in thought:

> Membership in the IBSA—it's expensive but worth it—may be obtained by applying to our New York office.

A dash can also be used to emphasize a parenthetical word or phrase:

> Third-quarter profits—in excess of $2 million—are up sharply.

Finally, use dashes to set off a phrase that contains commas:

> All our offices—Milwaukee, New Orleans, and Phoenix—have sent representatives.

Don't confuse a dash with a hyphen. A dash separates and emphasizes words, phrases, and clauses more strongly than commas or parentheses can; a hyphen ties two words so tightly that they almost become one word.

When using a computer, use the em dash symbol. When typing a dash in email, type two hyphens with no space before, between, or after.

A second type of dash, the en dash, can be produced with computer word processing and page-layout programs. This kind of dash is shorter than the regular dash and longer than a hyphen. It is reserved almost exclusively for indicating "to" or "through" with numbers such as dates and pages: *2001–2002, pages 30–44.*

## 2.8 HYPHENS

Hyphens are mainly used in three ways. The first is to separate the parts of compound words beginning with such prefixes as *self-, ex-, quasi-,* and *all-*:

> self-assured        quasi-official
> ex-wife             all-important

However, do not use hyphens in words that have prefixes such as *pro, anti, non, re, pre, un, inter,* and *extra*:

> prolabor            nonunion
> antifascist         interdepartmental

Exceptions occur when (1) the prefix occurs before a proper noun or (2) the vowel at the end of the prefix is the same as the first letter of the root word:

> pro-Republican      anti-American
> anti-inflammatory   extra-atmospheric

When in doubt, consult your dictionary.

Hyphens are used in some types of spelled-out numbers. For instance, they are used to separate the parts of a spelled-out number from *twenty-one* to *ninety-nine* and for spelled-out fractions: *two-thirds, one-sixth* (although some style guides say not to hyphenate fractions used as nouns).

Certain compound nouns are formed by using hyphens: *secretary-treasurer, city-state.* Check your dictionary for compounds you're unsure about.

Hyphens are also used in some compound adjectives, which are adjectives made up of two or more words. Specifically, you should use hyphens in compound adjectives that come before the noun:

> an interest-bearing account        well-informed executives

However, you need not hyphenate when the adjective follows a linking verb:

> This account is interest bearing.
> Their executives are well informed.

You can shorten sentences that list similar hyphenated words by dropping the common part from all but the last word:

> Check the costs of first-, second-, and third-class postage.

Finally, hyphens may be used to divide words at the end of a typed line. Such hyphenation is best avoided, but when you have to divide words at the end of a line, do so correctly (see Section 3.5). Dictionaries show how words are divided into syllables.

## 2.9 APOSTROPHES

Use an apostrophe in the possessive form of noun (but not in a pronoun):

> On his desk was a reply to Bette *Ainsley's* application for the *manager's* position.

Apostrophes are also used in place of the missing letter(s) of a contraction:

| Whole Words | Contraction |
| --- | --- |
| we will | we'll |
| do not | don't |
| they are | they're |

## 2.10 QUOTATION MARKS

Use quotation marks to surround words that are repeated exactly as they were said or written:

> The collection letter ended by saying, "This is your third and final notice."

Remember: (1) When the quoted material is a complete sentence, the first word is capitalized. (2) The final comma or period goes inside the closing quotation marks.

Quotation marks are also used to set off the title of a newspaper story, magazine article, or book chapter:

> You should read "Legal Aspects of the Collection Letter" in *Today's Credit.*

Quotation marks may also be used to indicate special treatment for words or phrases, such as terms that you're using in an unusual or ironic way:

> Our management "team" spends more time squabbling than working to solve company problems.

When you are defining a word, put the definition in quotation marks:

> The abbreviation *etc.* means "and so forth."

When using quotation marks, take care to insert the closing marks as well as the opening ones.

Although periods and commas go inside any quotation marks, colons and semicolons generally go outside them. A question mark goes inside the quotation marks only if the quotation is a question:

> All that day we wondered, "Is he with us?"

If the quotation is not a question but the entire sentence is, the question mark goes outside:

> What did she mean by "You will hear from me"?

For quotes within quotes, use single quotation marks within double:

> Bonnie Schulman fired up the project team by saying, "We've all heard the doubts that this team can meet the goals outlined in '2015: The Strategic Imperative,' but I have total confidence in your ability and commitment."

Otherwise, do not use single quotation marks for anything, including titles of works—that's British style.

## 2.11 PARENTHESES AND BRACKETS

Use parentheses to surround comments that are entirely incidental or to supply additional information:

> Our figures do not match yours, although (if my calculations are correct) they are closer than we thought.
> Sally Wagner (no relation to our own John Wagner) was just promoted to general manager of the Detroit office.

Parentheses are used in legal documents to surround figures in arabic numerals that follow the same amount in words:

> Remittance will be One Thousand Two Hundred Dollars ($1,200).

Be careful to put punctuation marks (period, comma, and so on) outside the parentheses unless they are part of the statement in parentheses. And keep in mind that parentheses have both an opening and a closing mark; both should always be used, even when setting off listed items within text: *(1)*, not *1)*.

Brackets are used for notation, comment, explanation, or correction within quoted material:

> In the interview, multimillionaire Bob Buford said, "One of my major influences was Peter [Drucker], who encourages people and helps them believe in themselves."

Brackets are also used for parenthetical material that falls within parentheses:

> Drucker's magnum opus *(Management: Tasks, Responsibilities, Practices* [Harper & Row, 1979]) has influenced generations of entrepreneurs.

## 2.12 ELLIPSES

Use ellipsis points, or three evenly spaced periods, to indicate that material has been left out of a direct quotation. Use them only in direct quotations and only at the point where material was left out. In the following example, the first sentence is quoted in the second:

> The Dow Jones Industrial Average fell 276.39 points, or 2.6%, during the week to 10292.31.
> According to the *Wall Street Journal,* "The Dow Jones Industrial Average fell 276.39 points . . . to 10,292.31."

The number of dots in ellipses is not optional; always use three. Occasionally, the points of an ellipsis come at the end of a sentence, where they seem to grow a fourth dot. Don't be fooled: One of the dots is a period. Ellipsis points should always be preceded and followed by a space.

Avoid using ellipses to represent a pause in your writing; use a dash for that purpose:

> At first we had planned to leave for the conference on Wednesday—but then we changed our minds. [not *on Wednesday . . . but then*]

# 3.0 Mechanics

The most obvious and least tolerable mistakes that a business writer makes are probably those related to grammar and punctuation. However, a number of small details, known as writing mechanics, demonstrate the writer's polish and reflect on the company's professionalism.

When it comes to mechanics, also called *style,* many of the "rules" are not hard and fast. Publications and organizations vary in their preferred styles for capitalization, abbreviations, numbers, italics, and so on. Here, we'll try to differentiate between practices that are generally accepted and those that can vary. When you are writing materials for a specific company or organization, find out the preferred style (such as *The Chicago Manual of Style* or *Webster's Style Manual*). Otherwise, choose a respected style guide. The key to style is consistency: If you spell out the word *percent* in one part of a document, don't use the percent sign in a similar context elsewhere in the same document.

## 3.1 CAPITALIZATION

With capitalization, you can follow either an "up" style (when in doubt, capitalize: *Federal Government, Board of Directors*) or a "down" style (when in doubt, use lowercase: *federal government, board of directors*). The trend over the last few decades has been toward the down style. Your best bet is to get a good style manual and consult it when you have a capitalization question. Following are some rules that most style guides agree on.

Capital letters are used at the beginning of certain word groups:

- Complete sentence: Before hanging up, he said, "We'll meet here on Wednesday at noon."
- Formal statement following a colon: She has a favorite motto: Where there's a will, there's a way.
- Phrase used as sentence: Absolutely not!
- Quoted sentence embedded in another sentence: Scott said, "Nobody was here during lunch hour except me."
- List of items set off from text:

> Three preliminary steps are involved:
> Design review
> Budgeting
> Scheduling

Capitalize proper adjectives and proper nouns (the names of particular persons, places, and things):

> Darrell Greene lived in a Victorian mansion.
> We sent Ms. Larson an application form, informing her that not all applicants are interviewed.
> Let's consider opening a branch in the West, perhaps at the west end of Tucson, Arizona.
> As office buildings go, the Kinney Building is a pleasant setting for TDG Office Equipment.
> We are going to have to cancel our plans for hiring French and German sales reps.

Larson's name is capitalized because she is a particular applicant, whereas the general term *applicant* is left uncapitalized. Likewise, *West* is capitalized when it refers to a particular place but not when it means a direction. In the same way, *office* and *building* are not capitalized when they are general terms (common nouns), but they are capitalized when they are part of the title of a particular office or building (proper nouns). Some proper adjectives are lowercased when they are part of terms that have come into common use, such as *french fries* and *roman numerals*.

Titles within families or companies as well as professional titles may also be capitalized:

> I turned down Uncle David when he offered me a job.
> I wouldn't be comfortable working for one of my relatives.
> We've never had a president quite like President Sweeney.

People's titles are capitalized when they are used in addressing a person, especially in a formal context. They are not usually capitalized, however, when they are used merely to identify the person:

> Address the letter to Chairperson Anna Palmer.
> I wish to thank Chairperson Anna Palmer for her assistance.
> Anna Palmer, chairperson of the board, took the podium.

Also capitalize titles if they are used by themselves in addressing a person:

> Thank you, Doctor, for your donation.

Always capitalize the first word of the salutation and complimentary close of a letter:

> *Dear* Mr. Andrews:            *Yours* very truly,

The names of organizations are capitalized, of course; so are the official names of their departments and divisions. However, do not use capitals when referring in general terms to a department or division, especially one in another organization:

> Route this memo to Personnel.
> Larry Tien was transferred to the Microchip Division.
> Will you be enrolled in the Psychology Department?
> Someone from the personnel department at EnerTech stopped by the booth.

Capitalization is unnecessary when using a word like *company, corporation*, or *university* alone:

> The corporation plans to issue 50,000 shares of common stock.

Likewise, the names of specific products are capitalized, although the names of general product types are not:

> Apple Inc.            Xerox machine
> Tide laundry detergent

When it comes to government terminology, here are some guides to capitalization: (1) Lowercase *federal* unless it is part of an agency name; (2) capitalize names of courts, departments, bureaus, offices, and agencies but lowercase such references as *the bureau* and *the department* when the full name is not used; (3) lowercase the titles of government officers unless they precede a specific person's name: *the secretary of state, the senator, the ambassador, the governor, and the mayor* but *Mayor Gonzalez* (Note: style guides vary on whether to capitalize *president* when referring to the president of the United States without including the person's name); (4) capitalize the names of laws and acts: *the Sherman Antitrust Act, the Civil Rights Act*; (5) capitalize the names of political parties but lowercase the word *party: Democratic party, Libertarian party*.

When writing about two or more geographic features of the same type, it is now accepted practice to capitalize the common noun in addition to the proper nouns, regardless of word order:

> Lakes Ontario and Huron
> Allegheny and Monongahela Rivers
> Corson and Ravenna Avenues

The names of languages, races, and ethnic groups are capitalized: Japanese, Caucasian, Hispanic. But racial terms that denote only skin color are not capitalized: black, white.

When referring to the titles of books, articles, magazines, newspapers, reports, movies, and so on, you should capitalize the first and last words and all nouns, pronouns, adjectives, verbs, and adverbs, and capitalize prepositions and conjunctions with five letters or more. Except for the first and last words, do not capitalize articles:

> *Economics During the Great War*
> "An Investigation into the Market for Long-Distance Services"
> "What Successes Are Made Of"

When *the* is part of the official name of a newspaper or magazine, it should be treated this way too:

> *The Wall Street Journal*

Style guides vary in their recommendations regarding capitalization of hyphenated words in titles. A general guide is to capitalize the second word in a temporary compound (a compound that is hyphenated for grammatical reasons and not spelling reasons), such as *Law-Abiding Citizen*, but to lowercase the word if the term is always hyphenated, such as *Son-in-law*).

References to specific pages, paragraphs, lines, and the like are not capitalized: *page 73, line 3*. However, in most other numbered or lettered references, the identifying term is capitalized:

> Chapter 4      Serial No. 382-2203      Item B-11

Finally, the names of academic degrees are capitalized when they follow a person's name but are not capitalized when used in a general sense:

> I received a bachelor of science degree.
> Thomas Whitelaw, Doctor of Philosophy, will attend.

Similarly, general courses of study are not capitalized, but the names of specific classes are:

> She studied accounting as an undergraduate.
> She is enrolled in Accounting 201.

## 3.2 UNDERSCORES AND ITALICS

Usually a line typed underneath a word or phrase either provides emphasis or indicates the title of a book, magazine, or newspaper. If possible, use italics instead of an underscore. Italics (or underlining) should also be used for defining terms and for discussing words as words:

> In this report, *net sales* refers to after-tax sales dollars.

Also use italics to set off foreign words, unless the words have become a common part of English:

> Top Shelf is considered the *sine qua non* of comic book publishers.
> Chris uses a laissez-faire [no italic] management style.

## 3.3 ABBREVIATIONS

Abbreviations are used heavily in tables, charts, lists, and forms. They're used sparingly in prose. Here are some abbreviation situations to watch for:

- In most cases do not use periods with acronyms (words formed from the initial letter or letters of parts of a term): *CEO, CD-ROM, DOS, YWCA, FDA;* but *Ph.D., M.A., M. D.*
- Use periods with abbreviations such as *Mr., Ms., Sr., Jr., a.m., p.m., B.C.,* and *A.D.*
- The trend is away from using periods with such units of measure as *mph, mm,* and *lb.*
- Use periods with such Latin abbreviations as *e.g., i.e., et al.,* and *etc.* However, style guides recommend that you avoid using these Latin forms and instead use their English equivalents *(for example, that is, and others,* and *and so on,* respectively). If you must use these abbreviations, such as in parenthetical expressions or footnotes, do not put them in italics.
- Some companies have abbreviations as part of their names *(&, Co., Inc., Ltd.).* When you refer to such firms by name, be sure to double-check the preferred spelling, including spacing: *AT&T; Barnes & Noble; Carson Pirie Scott & Company; PepsiCo; Kate Spade, Inc.; National Data Corporation; Siemens Corp.; Glaxo Wellcome PLC; US Airways; U.S. Business Reporter.*
- Most style guides recommend that you spell out *United States* as a noun and reserve *U.S.* as an adjective preceding the noun modified.

One way to handle an abbreviation that you want to use throughout a document is to spell it out the first time you use it, follow it with the abbreviation in parentheses, and then use the abbreviation in the remainder of the document.

## 3.4 NUMBERS

Numbers may be correctly handled many ways in business writing, so follow company style. In the absence of a set style, however, generally spell out all numbers from one to nine and use arabic numerals for the rest.

There are some exceptions to this general rule. For example, never begin a sentence with a numeral:

> Twenty of us produced 641 units per week in the first 12 weeks of the year.

Use numerals for the numbers one through nine if they're in the same list as larger numbers:

> Our weekly quota rose from 9 to 15 to 27.

Use numerals for percentages, time of day (except with o'clock), dates, and (in general) dollar amounts:

> Our division is responsible for 7 percent of total sales.
> The meeting is scheduled for 8:30 a.m. on August 2.
> Add $3 for postage and handling.

When using numerals for time, be consistent: It should be *between 10:00 a.m. and 4:30 p.m.*, not *between 10 a.m. and 4:30 p.m.* Expressions such as *4:00 o'clock* and *7 a.m. in the morning* are redundant.

Use a comma in numbers expressing thousands (1,257), unless your company specifies another style. When dealing with numbers in the millions and billions, combine words and figures: 7.3 million, 2 billion.

When writing dollar amounts, use a decimal point only if cents are included. In lists of two or more dollar amounts, use the decimal point either for all or for none:

> He sent two checks, one for $67.92 and one for $90.00.

When two numbers fall next to each other in a sentence, use figures for the number that is largest, most difficult to spell, or part of a physical measurement; use words for the other:

> I have learned to manage a classroom of 30 twelve-year-olds.
> She won a bonus for selling 24 thirty-volume sets.
> You'll need twenty 3-inch bolts.

In addresses, all street numbers except One are in numerals. So are suite and room numbers and zip codes. For street names that are numbered, practice varies so widely that you should use the form specified on an organization's letterhead or in a reliable directory. All the following examples are correct:

| | |
|---|---|
| One Fifth Avenue | 297 Ninth Street |
| 1839 44th Street | 11026 West 78 Place |

Telephone numbers are always expressed in numerals. Parentheses may separate the area code from the rest of the number, but a slash or a hyphen may be used instead, especially if the entire phone number is enclosed in parentheses:

| | | |
|---|---|---|
| 382-8329 | (602/382-8329) | 602-382-8329 |

Percentages are always expressed in numerals. The word *percent* is used in most cases, but % may be used in tables, forms, and statistical writing.

Ages are usually expressed in words—except when a parenthetical reference to age follows someone's name:

> Mrs. Margaret Sanderson is seventy-two.
> Mrs. Margaret Sanderson, 72, swims daily.

Also, ages expressed in years and months are treated like physical measurements that combine two units of measure: *5 years, 6 months.*

Physical measurements such as distance, weight, and volume are also often expressed in numerals: *9 kilometers, 5 feet 3 inches, 7 pounds 10 ounces.*

Decimal numbers are always written in numerals. In most cases, add a zero to the left of the decimal point if the number is less than one and does not already start with a zero:

| | | |
|---|---|---|
| 1.38 | .07 | 0.2 |

In a series of related decimal numbers with at least one number greater than one, make sure that all numbers smaller than one have a zero to the left of the decimal point: 1.20, 0.21, 0.09.

Simple fractions are written in words, but more complicated fractions are expressed in figures or, if easier to read, in figures and words:

| | | |
|---|---|---|
| two-thirds | 9/32 | 2 hundredths |

When typing ordinal numbers, such as *3rd edition* or *21st century,* your word processing program may automatically make the letters *rd* (or *st, th,* or *nd*) into a superscript. Do yourself a favor and turn that formatting function off in your "Preferences," as superscripts should not be used in regular prose or even in bibliographies.

## 3.5 WORD DIVISION

In general, avoid dividing words at the end of lines. When you must do so, follow these rules:

- Don't divide one-syllable words (such as *since, walked,* and *thought*), abbreviations (*mgr.*), contractions (*isn't*), or numbers expressed in numerals (*117,500*).
- Divide words between syllables, as specified in a dictionary or word-division manual.
- Make sure that at least three letters of the divided words are moved to the second line: *sin-cerely* instead of *sincere-ly.*

- Do not end a page or more than three consecutive lines with hyphens.
- Leave syllables consisting of a single vowel at the end of the first line (*impedi-ment* instead of *imped-iment*), except when the single vowel is part of a suffix such as *-able, -ible, -ical,* or *-ity (re-spons-ible* instead of *re-sponsi-ble).*
- Divide between double letters (*tomor-row*), except when the root word ends in double letters (*call-ing* instead of *cal-ling*).
- Wherever possible, divide hyphenated words at the hyphen only: instead of *anti-inde-pendence,* use *anti-independence.*
- Whenever possible, do not break URLs or email addresses. If you have to break a long URL or email address, do not insert a hyphen at the end of the first line.

# 4.0 Vocabulary

Using the right word in the right place is a crucial skill in business communication. However, many pitfalls await the unwary.

## 4.1 FREQUENTLY CONFUSED WORDS

Because the following sets of words sound similar, be careful not to use one when you mean to use the other:

| Word | Meaning |
|---|---|
| accede | to comply with |
| exceed | to go beyond |
| accept | to take |
| except | to exclude |
| access | admittance |
| excess | too much |
| advice | suggestion |
| advise | to suggest |
| affect | to influence |
| effect | the result |
| allot | to distribute |
| a lot | much or many |
| all ready | completely prepared |
| already | completed earlier |
| born | given birth to |
| borne | carried |
| capital | money; chief city |
| capitol | a government building |
| cite | to quote |
| sight | a view |
| site | a location |

| Word | Meaning |
|---|---|
| complement | complete amount; to go well with |
| compliment | expression of esteem; to flatter |
| corespondent | party in a divorce suit |
| correspondent | letter writer |
| council | a panel of people |
| counsel | advice; a lawyer |
| defer | to put off until later |
| differ | to be different |
| device | a mechanism |
| devise | to plan |
| die | to stop living; a tool |
| dye | to color |
| discreet | careful |
| discrete | separate |
| envelop | to surround |
| envelope | a covering for a letter |
| forth | forward |
| fourth | number four |
| holey | full of holes |
| holy | sacred |
| wholly | completely |
| human | of people |
| humane | kindly |
| incidence | frequency |
| incidents | events |
| instance | example |
| instants | moments |
| interstate | between states |
| intrastate | within a state |
| its | indicates possession |
| it's | contracted form of *it is* |
| later | afterward |
| latter | the second of two |
| lead | a metal; to guide |
| led | guided |
| lean | to rest at an angle |
| lien | a claim |
| levee | embankment |
| levy | tax |
| loath | reluctant |
| loathe | to hate |
| loose | free; not tight |
| lose | to mislay |

| Word | Meaning |
|------|---------|
| material | substance |
| materiel | equipment |
| miner | mineworker |
| minor | underage person |
| moral | virtuous; a lesson |
| morale | sense of well-being |
| ordinance | law |
| ordnance | weapons |
| overdo | to do in excess |
| overdue | past due |
| peace | lack of conflict |
| piece | a fragment |
| pedal | a foot lever |
| peddle | to sell |
| persecute | to torment |
| prosecute | to sue |
| personal | private |
| personnel | employees |
| precedence | priority |
| precedents | previous events |
| principal | sum of money; chief; main |
| principle | general rule |
| rap | to knock |
| wrap | to cover |
| residence | home |
| residents | inhabitants |
| right | correct |
| rite | ceremony |
| write | to form words on a surface |
| role | a part to play |
| roll | to tumble; a list |
| root | part of a plant |
| rout | to defeat |
| route | a traveler's way |
| shear | to cut |
| sheer | thin, steep |
| stationary | immovable |
| stationery | paper |
| than | as compared with |
| then | at that time |
| their | belonging to them |
| there | in that place |
| they're | they are |
| to | a preposition |
| too | excessively; also |
| two | the number |

| Word | Meaning |
|------|---------|
| waive | to set aside |
| wave | a swell of water; a gesture |
| weather | atmospheric conditions |
| whether | if |
| who's | contraction of "who is" or "who has" |
| whose | possessive form of who |

In the preceding list, only enough of each word's meaning is given to help you distinguish between the words in each group. Several meanings are left out entirely. For more complete definitions, consult a dictionary.

## 4.2 FREQUENTLY MISUSED WORDS

The following words tend to be misused for reasons other than their sound. Reference books (including the *Random House College Dictionary*, revised edition; Follett's *Modern American Usage*; and Fowler's *Modern English Usage*) can help you with similar questions of usage:

**a lot:** When the writer means "many," *a lot* is always two separate words, never one.

**aggravate/irritate:** *Aggravate* means "to make things worse." Sitting in the smoke-filled room *aggravated* his sinus condition. *Irritate* means "to annoy." Her constant questions *irritated* [not *aggravated*] me.

**anticipate/expect:** *Anticipate* means "to prepare for": Macy's *anticipated* increased demand for athletic shoes in spring by ordering in November. In formal usage, it is incorrect to use *anticipate* for *expect*: I *expected* (not *anticipated*) a better response to our presentation than we actually got.

**compose/comprise:** The whole comprises the parts:

The company's distribution division *comprises* four departments.

The following usage is incorrect:

The company's distribution division *is comprised of* four departments.

In that construction, *is composed of* or *consists of* would be preferable. It might be helpful to think of *comprise* as meaning "encompasses" or "contains."

**continual/continuous:** *Continual* refers to ongoing actions that have breaks:

Her *continual* complaining will accomplish little in the long run.

*Continuous* refers to ongoing actions without interruptions or breaks:

A *continuous* stream of paper came out of the fax machine.

**convince/persuade:** One is *convinced* of a fact or that something is true; one is *persuaded* by someone else to do something. The use of *to* with *convince* is unidiomatic—you don't convince someone to do something, you persuade them to do it.

**correspond with:** Use this phrase when you are talking about exchanging letters. Use *correspond to* when you mean "similar to." Use either *correspond with* or *correspond to* when you mean "relate to."

**dilemma/problem:** Technically, a *dilemma* is a situation in which one must choose between two undesirable alternatives. It shouldn't be used when no choice is actually involved.

**disinterested:** This word means "fair, unbiased, having no favorites, impartial." If you mean "bored" or "not interested," use *uninterested.*

**etc.:** This abbreviated form of the Latin phrase *et cetera* means "and so on" or "and so forth," so it is never correct to write *and etc.* The current tendency among business writers is to use English rather than Latin.

**flaunt/flout:** To *flaunt* is to be ostentatious or boastful; to *flout* is to mock or scoff at.

**impact:** Avoid using *impact* as a verb when *influence* or *affect* is meant.

**imply/infer:** Both refer to hints. Their great difference lies in who is acting. The writer *implies,* the reader *infers,* sees between the lines.

**its/their:** Use *its* to indicate possession by a singular entity such as a company, not *their.* "HP released its quarterly results" is correct; "HP released their quarterly results" is not.

**lay:** This word is a transitive verb. Never use it for the intransitive *lie.* (See Section 1.3.3.)

**lend/loan:** *Lend* is a verb; *loan* is a noun. Usage such as "Can you loan me $5?" is therefore incorrect.

**less/fewer:** Use *less* for uncountable quantities (such as amounts of water, air, sugar, and oil). Use *fewer* for countable quantities (such as numbers of jars, saws, words, page, and humans). The same distinction applies to *much* and *little* (uncountable) versus *many* and *few* (countable).

**liable/likely:** *Liable* means "responsible for": I will hold you *liable* if this deal doesn't go through. It is incorrect to use *liable* for "possible": Anything is *likely* (not *liable*) to happen.

**literally:** *Literally* means "actually" or "precisely"; it is often misused to mean "almost" or "virtually." It is usually best left out entirely or replaced with *figuratively.*

**many/much:** See *less/fewer.*

**regardless:** The *less* suffix is the negative part. No word needs two negative parts, so don't add *ir* (a negative prefix) to the beginning. There is no such word as *irregardless.*

**try:** Always follow with *to,* never *and.*

**verbal:** People in the business community who are careful with language frown on those who use *verbal* to mean "spoken" or "oral." Many others do say "verbal agreement." Strictly speaking, *verbal* means "of words" and therefore includes both spoken and written words. Follow company usage in this matter.

## 4.3 FREQUENTLY MISSPELLED WORDS

All of us, even the world's best spellers, sometimes have to check a dictionary for the spelling of some words. People who have never memorized the spelling of commonly used words must look up so many that they grow exasperated and give up on spelling words correctly.

Don't expect perfection and don't surrender. If you can memorize the spelling of just the words listed here, you'll need the dictionary far less often and you'll write with more confidence:

| | |
|---|---|
| absence | convertible |
| absorption | corroborate |
| accessible | criticism |
| accommodate | |
| accumulate | definitely |
| achieve | description |
| advantageous | desirable |
| affiliated | dilemma |
| analyze | disappear |
| apparent | disappoint |
| appropriate | disbursement |
| argument | discrepancy |
| asphalt | dissatisfied |
| assistant | dissipate |
| asterisk | |
| auditor | eligible |
| | embarrassing |
| bankruptcy | endorsement |
| believable | exaggerate |
| brilliant | exceed |
| bulletin | exhaust |
| | existence |
| calendar | extraordinary |
| campaign | |
| category | fallacy |
| ceiling | familiar |
| changeable | flexible |
| clientele | fluctuation |
| collateral | forty |
| committee | |
| comparative | gesture |
| competitor | grievous |
| concede | |
| congratulations | haphazard |
| connoisseur | harassment |
| consensus | holiday |
| convenient | |

illegible
immigrant
incidentally
indelible
independent
indispensable
insistent
intermediary
irresistible

jewelry
judgment
judicial

labeling
legitimate
leisure
license
litigation

maintenance
mathematics
mediocre
minimum

necessary
negligence
negotiable
newsstand
noticeable

occurrence
omission

parallel
pastime
peaceable
permanent
perseverance
persistent
personnel
persuade
possesses

precede
predictable
preferred
privilege
procedure
proceed
pronunciation
psychology
pursue

questionnaire

receive
recommend
repetition
rescind
rhythmical
ridiculous

salable
secretary
seize
separate
sincerely
succeed
suddenness
superintendent
supersede
surprise

tangible
tariff
technique
tenant
truly

unanimous
until

vacillate
vacuum
vicious

## 4.4 TRANSITIONAL WORDS AND PHRASES

The following sentences don't communicate as well as they could because they lack a transitional word or phrase:

> Production delays are inevitable. Our current lag time in filling orders is one month.

A semicolon between the two sentences would signal a close relationship between their meanings, but it wouldn't even hint at what that relationship is. Here are the sentences again, now linked by means of a semicolon, with a space for a transitional word or phrase:

> Production delays are inevitable; _____, our current lag time in filling orders is one month.

Now read the sentence with *nevertheless* in the blank space. Then try *therefore, incidentally, in fact,* and *at any rate* in the blank. Each substitution changes the meaning of the sentence.

Here are some transitional words (conjunctive adverbs) that will help you write more clearly:

| | | |
|---|---|---|
| accordingly | furthermore | moreover |
| anyway | however | otherwise |
| consequently | incidentally | still |
| finally | likewise | therefore |
| | meanwhile | |

The following transitional phrases are used in the same way:

| | |
|---|---|
| as a result | in other words |
| for example | in the second place |
| in fact | on the other hand |
| | to the contrary |

When one of these words or phrases joins two independent clauses, it should be preceded by a semicolon and followed by a comma:

> The consultant recommended a complete reorganization; moreover, she suggested that we drop several products.

# Brand, Organization, Name, and Website Index

# Subject Index